MOON

BASEBALL

Road Trips

TIMOTHY MALCOLM

THE COMPLETE GUIDE TO ALL THE BALLPARKS, WITH BEER, BITES, AND SIGHTS NEARBY

CONTENTS

BASEBALL ROAD TRIPS

T-MOBILE PARK

WA

MT

ND

OR

ID

SD

WY

NE

The West Coast

ORACLE PARK

OAKLAND COLISEUM

NV

UT

CO

COORS FIELD

CA

KS

Arizona and the Rocky Mountains

DODGER STADIUM

ANGEL STADIUM

PETCO PARK

AZ

CHASE FIELD

NM

Pacific

Ocean

TX

MEXICO

CANADA

ME

MN

Target
Field

WI

MI

Rogers
Centre

VT

NH

Fenway
Park

ON

NY

MA

RI

American
Family Field

Comerica
Park

The Great
Lakes

Yankee
Stadium

Citi
Field

CT

IA

Wrigley
Field

Guaranteed
Rate Field

Chicago and
the Midwest

Progressive
Field

PNC
Park

PA

Citizens
Bank Park

The East
Coast

NJ

OH

Oriole Park at
Camden Yards

MD

DE

Kauffman
Stadium

IL

IN

Great
American
Ball Park

WV

Nationals
Park

MO

Busch
Stadium

KY

VA

The Heartland
and Texas

TN

NC

OK

AR

SC

Truist
Park

Atlantic

Ocean

Globe Life
Field

MS

AL

GA

Florida and the
Southeast

LA

FL

Minute Maid
Park

Tropicana
Field

Marlins
Park

Gulf of Mexico

0   200 mi

0   200 km

© MOON.COM

Play Ball!

Baseball was first coined "the national pastime" by the *New York Mercury* way back in 1856, 20 years before the founding of the National League. Amazingly, the term continues to be used today—although it doesn't hold quite the same water as it once did, with football and basketball also jockeying for attention from sports writers and television viewers.

Whether or not it lives up to its original nickname is a matter of opinion, but baseball remains as exciting as ever. Just watch the otherworldly Fernando Tatís Jr. connect with a pitch in the zone, the meteoric Mike Trout run down a curving fly ball, and the dazzling Gerrit Cole dial up an unhittable heater. You can lose yourself in the beauty of these phenomenal feats of athleticism.

Baseball fans will often tell you that with each game you watch, you're bound to see something you've never seen before. Hundreds of pitches are thrown, home runs are launched, outstanding defensive plays are made, and sometimes the ball moves in a way that baffles the batter, the umpire, the fans, and everyone watching at home. With every game we see, baseball offers us another reason to appreciate the uniqueness of human achievement.

Baseball is also a lens we can use to view America—to see its flaws as well as its ideals. The history of the game includes decades of segregation, systemic racism that lives on in everything from the way players are discussed to the stadium deals that take access away from underserved populations. Then there are the nicknames and chants that appropriate and offend Indigenous cultures. Even while we as fans acknowledge these problems and push owners, managers, players, and fellow fans to do better, we can still love baseball for the game itself. Even as we confront these realities, we can see that although baseball is messy and flawed, it can also instill sheer joy.

Hop in the car and chase that joy. It can be found in all of the parks, from jewel-box legends like Fenway and Wrigley to the most modern and corporatized venues like Truist Park and Globe Life Field. See the sport's landmarks along the way and learn its story from every angle. You'll also see the country at its rawest; history both frozen in time and unfolding before your eyes. Sit in a ballpark with the sunshine beaming down and a cold beer in your hand. You'll lose yourself in something incredible, something beautiful, something you've never seen before and may never see quite the same way again.

To appreciate baseball is to indulge in America. Enjoy the game.

10 TOP BALLPARKS

① SOAK IT ALL IN AT WRIGLEY FIELD IN CHICAGO

This quirky stadium and its defining features—the ivy-covered brick outfield wall, the old-school scoreboard, the W flag that proudly waves when the Cubs win—invite you to celebrate baseball at its most iconic (page 341).

2 GET GOOSEBUMPS AT FENWAY PARK IN BOSTON

Fenway is the most fascinating venue in baseball, with the Green Monster, the sharp angles of the outfield, Pesky's Pole in right field, and a block party on Jersey Street every game day (page 39).

3 EAT, DRINK, AND CELEBRATE GIANTS HISTORY AT ORACLE PARK IN SAN FRANCISCO

Indulge in the famed garlic fries and sip local craft beer at this ballpark that pays homage to a team with deep roots and larger-than-life legends (page 637).

4   CELEBRATE THE BEAUTY OF BASEBALL AT DODGER STADIUM IN LOS ANGELES

The stadium's architecture plays with angles and waves, both contrasting with and mimicking the rolling hills beyond the outfield. The bleachers are clean and cool, the blue fence pops just enough, and those uniforms are crisp as all get out. This ballpark is where baseball looks its best (page 587).

5 REVEL IN THE RETRO-CLASSIC FEEL OF ORIOLE PARK AT CAMDEN YARDS IN BALTIMORE

This stadium was the first to be designed in the retro-classic style, drawing inspiration from early-20th-century ballparks but with a sleek, modern twist (page 131).

6 GAWK AT THE VIEW AT PNC PARK IN PITTSBURGH

Walk across the Roberto Clemente Bridge to arrive at the stadium, then scope the view from home plate, and you'll get it right away: This is the best setting for a baseball game (page 250).

7 BASK IN THE SAN DIEGO SUN AT PETCO PARK

You're sure to have good weather, ideal for taking in a game, eating delicious local bites, and drinking a good craft beer or two (page 567).

8 WITNESS THE FUTURE OF BASEBALL AT T-MOBILE PARK IN SEATTLE

With a food program curated by a James Beard award winner, a beer selection that's brimming with unique brews, and multiple kid-friendly areas, this stadium offers one of the best modern game-day experiences (page 656).

9 JOIN IN THE FUN AT CITIZENS BANK PARK IN PHILADELPHIA

This deceptively small retro-classic venue has a whole lot going in its favor. The food and drink options highlight a wealth of local street foods, the outfield midway of Ashburn Alley is a great spot for pre-game fun, and the sightlines are among the best in baseball (page 111).

10 ENJOY A LITTLE BIT OF EVERYTHING AT TARGET FIELD IN MINNEAPOLIS

This ballpark lets you sample everything that baseball has to offer, all in one place—a field with kooky angles, fun nods to franchise history, open-air spaces for socializing, stellar food and drink, plentiful parking, and easy access via public transit (page 440).

BEST BASEBALL ATTRACTIONS AND EVENTS

NATIONAL BASEBALL HALL OF FAME AND MUSEUM

Cooperstown, NY

The **National Baseball Hall of Fame and Museum** is a dreamland offering days of excitement and enrichment. The climax is the Hall of Fame Gallery, where you can read the plaque of every single inductee. Nearby, **Doubleday Field** lures folks to sit in wonder in the grandstand. Add the magic of Main Street Cooperstown and some really good local beer, and you've got a perfect long weekend. It's little off the beaten path, but nonetheless essential. You may want to visit before or after going to Boston.

NEGRO LEAGUES BASEBALL MUSEUM

Kansas City, MO

At the must-visit **Negro Leagues Baseball Museum,** you'll learn all about gifted players like Satchel Paige, Buck Leonard, Josh Gibson, Cool Papa Bell, Jackie Robinson, and Hank Aaron. The highlight is a replica ballfield that's home to statues of the absolute greats.

FIELD OF DREAMS

Dyersville, IA

The **Field of Dreams** has become a show-place for exhibition and special regular season games, but it came to fame as the place where the beloved movie of the same name was shot. There seems to be some spirit in the sky out here, where a baseball field was cut into farmland. Experience it for yourself: walk or play on the field, or even watch a game.

BABE RUTH BIRTHPLACE & MUSEUM

Baltimore, MD

At the **Babe Ruth Birthplace & Museum,** you can visit the house where the mighty

entrance to the Negro Leagues Baseball Museum

BASEBALL ON A BUDGET

Attending a live baseball game these days is a pricey venture. You're bound to pay at least $40 for a seat close enough to the action, plus $15 or more for food, $10 or more for one drink, and about $20 for parking. Want that ice cream or maybe a t-shirt? Just one game could end up costing you more than $100. Here are some ways to save money and find the most affordable experiences, seats, and deals across the majors.

CHEAP SEATS

- Consider waiting until close to **first pitch** to grab a ticket to a game at **Coors Field** in Denver. Sometimes, two hours before the game starts, the Rockies sell **Rockpile** seats for **$4** ($1 for seniors and kids ages 12 and younger).
- **Tropicana Field** in St. Petersburg has some of the cheapest seats in baseball at **$10**, and best yet, they're not even in the upper-deck.
- Sure, it's high up there, but the **terrace level** at **American Family Field** in Milwaukee has seats for around **$10** at their cheapest. **Terrace reserved** seats are **$6** on Mondays.
- You can get a seat in the **400 level** for as low as **$11** at **Kauffman Stadium** in Kansas City.
- Tickets to a **Yankees game** may cost an arm and a leg, but **$15 grandstand seats** can be had for select games.
- At Cincinnati's **Great American Ball Park,** a ticket for the **rooftop Fioptics District** is around **$15** and includes a **concession credit.**
- Score a **Pirates Great Taste Ticket** at **PNC Park** in Pittsburgh for **$20.** This includes a **100-level** seat and a Miller Lite. Just know the seat doesn't offer that awesome view of the outfield backdrop.

INEXPENSIVE FOOD

- **Progressive Field** in Cleveland hosts **$1 hot dog nights** on Fridays. How many can you eat?
- Kid-sized hot dogs at **Oriole Park** in Baltimore cost just **$1.50.**
- At **Yankee Stadium,** Nathan's hot dogs cost **$3.**
- Want a good deal on food at **Marlins Park** in Miami? The **"$3 o $5" menu** (Miami's area code is 305) at **Obie's** and **Familia Fave's** offers **$5** pork tacos and **$3** hot dogs and popcorn, among other items.

BUDGET BEVERAGES

- With prices starting at **$4** per 12-ounce cup, **Chase Field** in Phoenix has some of the least expensive beer in baseball.
- At **Oriole Park,** small macro-brewed beers cost **$4,** while their large counterparts are **$8.**
- The beer emporium called **Power Alley** at **T-Mobile Park** in Seattle has relatively cheap macro-brewed beers. **$5** per beer isn't bad for a ballpark.

LOW-PRICED PARKING

- Parking at **PNC Park** in Pittsburgh is really cheap. It's just **$5,** with a short walk over the Roberto Clemente Bridge between you and the venue.
- Get to **Dodger Stadium** in Los Angeles early to secure a **$5 off-site parking space.** You will have to walk a little uphill to the stadium.
- Even in the **team-operated lots,** you should be able to park at **Oriole Park** for **$10-15.**

AFFORDABLE ACTIVITIES AND SOUVENIRS

- Entertain the kids at Atlanta's **Truist Park** by visiting **Hope & Will's Sandlot** and paying **$1** for each game and attraction.
- A tour of **Citizens Bank Park** in Philadelphia that visits the home dugout, multiple specialty seating areas, the press box, and media room costs **$10** ($6 for seniors and kids ages 3-14).
- For a great deal at **Kauffman Stadium,** check out the team's **20 Below Store,** where everything is **$20** or less.

THE OLD BALL GAME

Some baseball sites are no longer, but you can still pay tribute. Here are some spots to stop at when on your road trip.

- **Huntington Avenue Baseball Grounds** (Forsyth St. and World Series Way, Boston) is where the Red Sox played before Fenway. The stadium that was once here was a home for Tris Speaker and Cy Young, baseball's all-time-winningest pitcher. A statue of Young remains at the site, on the grounds of Northeastern University.
- **Nickerson Field** (Braves Field Way and Harry Agganis Way, Boston) was home to the Boston Braves from 1915 to 1952 and hosted the longest game in major league history, a 26-inning contest in 1920. Look for the plaque when walking Agganis to Braves Field Way.
- **Georgia State Stadium** (755 Hank Aaron Dr. SE, Atlanta), now the football home of Georgia State University, was the home of the Atlanta Braves from 1997 to 2016.
- **The Corner Ballpark** (Michigan Ave. and Trumbull Ave., Detroit) is one you'll know better as the former home of Tiger Stadium. Though the ballpark was torn down in 2009, the field was preserved. While you're here, you might even catch a game featuring local squads.
- **Municipal Stadium** (22nd St. and Brooklyn Ave., Kansas City) was home to the Kansas City Monarchs and Athletics. It was demolished in 1976, but today the site is a municipal garden where a plaque tells the stadium's story.

George Hermann Ruth was raised and take a tour through his life, learning more about his childhood, the famed "called shot" in the 1932 World Series, and his massive influence on baseball.

NATIONAL BALLPARK MUSEUM

Denver, CO

Just up the street from Coors Field, the under-the-radar **National Ballpark Museum** has artifacts from multiple jewel box parks, including a chunk of Fenway Park's Green Monster, chairs from former stadiums, and all sorts of game-worn jerseys.

OPENING DAY

late March or early April, Cincinnati

The Reds open each year at their home park. Accompanying that event is the pregame **Findlay Market Parade**, which has been

going on for more than 100 years. Typically, a former Red or other notable baseball figure serves as grand marshal.

JACKIE ROBINSON DAY

April 15, leaguewide

To commemorate the day Jackie Robinson made his major league debut and broke the color line, all of Major League Baseball honors him by having all on-field personnel wear Robinson's jersey number, 42.

PATRIOTS' DAY

third Monday in April, Boston

This day marks the earliest battles of the American Revolutionary War, so the Commonwealth of Massachusetts celebrates with fun, festivities, and high spirits. The storied Boston Marathon passes right by Fenway Park and the Red Sox always play at home at 11am.

OLD TIMER'S DAY

June, New York City

The Yankees bring back alumni to play a fun **pre-game exhibition.** If you ever wanted to see Wade Boggs get a crack at, say, Fritz Peterson, then this is the game for you.

CANADA DAY

July 1, Toronto

This day marks when Canada was effectively united as one country. Locals party and the Blue Jays usually play a home game.

MLB ALL-STAR GAME

mid-July, leaguewide

The **midsummer classic,** as it's known, actually happens just a couple weeks into summer, usually during the second week of July. The venue changes annually, with each team getting to host every 25-35 years. There are ancillary events held before the game, like the **Home Run Derby.**

HALL OF FAME WEEKEND

July, Cooperstown, NY

Usually in late July, baseball legends and as many as 75,000 fans visit Cooperstown for the induction of the new class of the **National Baseball Hall of Fame.** In addition to the induction ceremony, there are several other events over the weekend, including a parade.

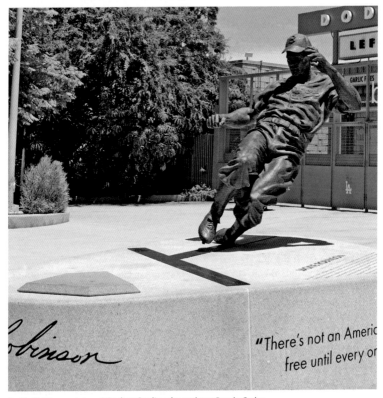

Jackie Robinson statue at Dodger Stadium by sculptor Branly Cadet

PLANNING YOUR ROAD TRIP

WHERE TO GO

THE EAST COAST

There's plenty of baseball to see in this **450-mile** trip along the East Coast. Which ballparks should you check off your wish list?

First is **Boston's Fenway Park,** home to the Red Sox and the Green Monster. **New York City** is where you'll find **Yankee Stadium, Citi Field,** and the Big Apple's two famous franchises, the Yankees and the Mets. Spend a few days taking in the sights, from the **Statue of Liberty** to **The High Line.** Just a few hours' drive from NYC is **Cooperstown** and the **National Baseball Hall of Fame and Museum,** a bucket-list item if ever there was one.

Heading south to **Philadelphia, Citizens Bank Park** is the quintessential retro-classic brick-and-steel park that hosts the Phillies. Be sure to eat a ton in Philly, home to some of the best **street food** and **sandwiches** in the USA.

Continuing to **Baltimore,** you have to see **Oriole Park at Camden Yards,** the 1992 ballpark that pays tribute to the past, embraces its locale, and influenced so many of the stadiums that followed. While in Baltimore, visit the **Babe Ruth Birthplace Museum,** the home of baseball's first world-changing talent. The last stop is just an hour away: **Washington DC** is where the Nationals play at **Nationals Park,** a stadium set against the quickly developing Navy Yard neighborhood. Give yourself another couple of days in Washington for the monuments and museums on the **National Mall.**

FLORIDA AND THE SOUTHEAST

Get lost in the sunshine while traveling between Georgia and Florida. This **750-mile** trip spans from **Atlanta** to **Tampa** and **St. Petersburg,** ending in **Miami.**

The new home of the Atlanta Braves, **Truist Park,** is inside a shopping and entertainment district. Atlanta has great little **neighborhoods,** mouth-watering **barbecue joints** and **gastropubs,** and cool **breweries** and **beer bars.**

Domed **Tropicana Field,** home to the Tampa Bay Rays in St. Petersburg, includes a live stingray tank. In Miami, **Marlins Park** oozes modernity and excitement. While you're in Florida, be sure to hit the **beach,** whether it be **Clearwater Beach** on the Gulf side or **Miami Beach** on the Atlantic shore.

Visit Florida in **March,** to see **Grapefruit League spring training.** Each year, half of the teams in baseball head here to get ready for the regular season. Spend a week and enjoy a whole bunch of games.

THE GREAT LAKES

Travel **530 miles** around Lake Erie and along the shore of Lake Ontario, visiting multiple ballparks along the way—you'll go international, crossing into Canada to finish things off.

The first and best park on the route is **PNC Park** in **Pittsburgh,** home to the Pirates and arguably the best view in baseball. While there, walk across the **Roberto Clemente Bridge** and chow down on a sandwich from **Primanti Bros.** Pay tribute to two local legends by visiting the **Roberto Clemente Museum** and the **Andy Warhol Museum.**

Next up is the retro-modern **Progressive Field,** where **Cleveland's** sporting nine play. Head west, then follow the lakeshore north to **Detroit,** where you'll find **Comerica Field,** home to the Tigers and a sweet carousel. There are **musical legacies** to explore in both Detroit and Cleveland.

The last stop is over the border in **Toronto** to watch the Blue Jays. At its opening, **Rogers**

Centre was a revolutionary venue, thanks to its retractable roof, but today it feels a bit creaky. Take time to enjoy **awesome food** in this **multicultural** city.

CHICAGO AND THE MIDWEST

Chicago anchors this **830-mile** trip that includes three smaller markets with devoted, passionate fans. First on the itinerary is **Wrigley Field**, Chicago's century-old ballpark that's laden with brick, ivy, and a lot of Cubs history. That's on the North Side of the city; on the South Side is **Guaranteed Rate Field,** the much newer home of the **White Sox**. Spend time in the Windy City hanging out in **Wrigleyville**, checking out the **world-class museums**, and eating **deep-dish pizza**.

At your next stop in **Milwaukee**, you'll see the Brewers at the retractable-roofed **American Family Field** before drinking local beer at any number of neighborhood **taprooms**.

Continue to **St. Louis**, where the Cardinals play at **Busch Stadium**. There's a lot to see right at **Ballpark Village**, but you'll

also want to head out to some of the city's **breweries**.

The last stop of this trip is **Cincinnati**, where the Reds play at the riverside **Great American Ball Park**. Couple your visit with a trip to **Findlay Market**—home to a famous opening day parade—and the **National Underground Railroad Freedom Center.**

THE HEARTLAND AND TEXAS

There's a little bit of everything on this long, **1,200-mile** trip that slices through the center of the country. Start in **Minneapolis** and **St. Paul** to watch the Minnesota Twins play at the superb **Target Field**, one of baseball's most picturesque retro-modern parks. Next, find a mid-century ballpark with a fabulous water fountain in Kansas City's **Kauffman Stadium**. Ending in Texas, you'll find two modern retractable-roof palaces in **Arlington's Globe Life Field**, home to the Texas Rangers, and **Houston's Minute Maid Park,** where the Astros play.

Stop a few times to see some history. First and foremost is the **Negro Leagues**

Baseball Hall of Fame and Museum in Cooperstown, New York

Baseball Museum in Kansas City, but there's also Mickey Mantle's Childhood Home in Commerce, Oklahoma. Iowa has two goodies for the baseball lover: the Bob Feller Exhibit inside Van Mater's City Hall and the Field of Dreams movie site in Dyersville.

Then there's the food. Bite into the stuffed burger known as a jucy lucy in Minneapolis, chow down on some legendary barbecue in Kansas City, and discover Tex-Mex fajitas as they were meant to be in Houston.

ARIZONA AND THE ROCKY MOUNTAINS

There are just two cities on this 800-mile trip, but it's all about the journey. In Denver, check out the Rockies at Coors Field, maybe while sitting in the Rockpile. Make a stop at the National Ballpark Museum, and whatever you do, grab a beer at a few of the top breweries in the country. Then in Phoenix, watch a Diamondbacks game at Chase Field, home to a swimming pool and one of the best kids' play areas in baseball. Climb Camelback Mountain while you're in town, then cool off with a beer from some solid Southwest breweries.

In between you have plenty of options for even more adventures. You can stop in Albuquerque, home to a minor league team that got its name from the long-running cartoon The Simpsons. Or take a side trip to Rocky Mountain National Park, where you can immerse yourself in epic views and gorgeous scenery.

Consider visiting Phoenix in March, too, as it's the home of Cactus League spring training. Half of Major League Baseball plays here, with all of the games in close proximity, so you can eat, sleep, and breathe baseball.

THE WEST COAST

There are a lot of reasons why you should tour 1,300 miles along the West Coast. Each ballpark has its charms and a few of them are among the best in baseball.

At Petco Park in San Diego, the Padres play against the cool backdrop of an old building while fans sip on some of the best craft beers in the game. Outside there's a whole world of bars and breweries, since San Diego is the epicenter of the craft beer movement.

Up the coast is Dodger Stadium in Los Angeles, an iconic mid-century structure. Eat a Dodger Dog while taking in a picture-perfect scene. Afterward see Hollywood and Venice Beach. Not far away is Angel Stadium in Anaheim. Just a home run away is Disneyland Park, a must-do even for adults.

San Francisco has one of baseball's most splendid venues in Oracle Park. Watch the Giants hit home runs into McCovey Cove while you eat garlic fries and drink stellar beer. Across the bay in Oakland is the Oakland Coliseum, where the Athletics play. This mid-century park isn't the most beautiful in the league, but the fans make the best of it—and have fun while they're at it. Stop for must-see spots like the Golden Gate Bridge and Fisherman's Wharf in San Francisco, and Jack London Square in Oakland.

At the end of your trip, way up north, is Seattle, a great city with a fun stadium in the Mariners' T-Mobile Park. The beer and food selection is some of the best in all of baseball. Head into the city for more mouth-watering finds courtesy of Pike Place Market, then sip on some coffee—it's Seattle, after all. The city is also home to must-stop pre- and post-game bars.

WHEN TO GO

BASEBALL SEASON

Major League Baseball's regular season begins anywhere between the last week of March and the first week of April. For the first month of play, games north of the 39th parallel (or north of Washington DC, Cincinnati, St. Louis, and the San Francisco Bay

Area) are prone to **cool** and **rainy weather** (and sometimes even **snow**), so think twice before booking early-season trips.

The season usually continues until the **second week of July,** when major league teams pause for about **four days** for the **all-star break.** Then the **second half** of the season begins with growing **playoff** implications and games becoming ever more important.

In **mid-summer,** it gets really **hot** in southern locations, especially **Phoenix, Dallas-Fort Worth-Arlington, Houston, Tampa,** and **Miami.** Other cities that are at times unbearably hot include **San Diego, Los Angeles, Atlanta, St. Louis, Kansas City,** and **Cincinnati.** East Coast cities like **Philadelphia** and **New York** have **high humidity** in the mid-summer months of **July** and **August,** while Great Lakes cities like **Cleveland** and **Chicago** can be afflicted with swarms of **insects.** For **mid-summer** games, pack **sunscreen** and a **DEET-free insect repellant,** stock up on **hats** and **sunglasses,** and wear **loose-fitting** and **light-colored clothing.**

The regular season ends anywhere between the **last week of September** and the **first week of October.** During the final few weeks of the regular season, the weather may get a little **brisk** back in those northern locations. The major league **postseason** begins in **early October** and lasts through the month, sometimes even into **November.** That means some games are played in temperatures under 60°F. Pack accordingly with **warmer clothing.**

The San Francisco Bay Area's **Mediterranean climate** makes it a wild card almost year-round. At any time of the **summer** it can feel **cold** and **damp.** Similarly, **Denver's** mountainous location makes for unpredictable weather. Be prepared with both **warm-** and **cool-weather gear.**

Minor league seasons for the highest levels (A to AAA) begin around **mid-April.** **Short-season A-ball** starts in **late July** because it's designed for players recently signed via the amateur draft that takes place in June. All minor league seasons end in **early- to mid-September** with **postseasons** taking place directly afterward, rarely going deep into October.

SPRING TRAINING

A rite of passage for passionate fans, **spring training** has been part of the game's fabric since the end of the 19th century. Exactly half of Major League Baseball's teams practice within the **Phoenix metropolitan area** in Arizona, while the other half train in the areas surrounding the **Gulf and Atlantic coasts of Florida.** In Arizona, most teams share a ballpark, while in Florida some teams have cities all to themselves.

Players begin reporting to spring training sites around **Valentine's Day.** More than a few hardcore fans show up in the first week or two to be around players in a **relatively lax setup** with fewer security measures in some places. Things start kicking into gear around the **end of February,** when **exhibition games** begin. By the **first week of March,** crowds really start showing up for games, peaking usually around or just after **St. Patrick's Day.** Spring training ends a few days before **opening day,** usually during the **last week of March.**

Because spring training runs alongside college spring break periods and takes place in classic vacation spots, **book your trip early,** right after the winter holidays. You'll be more likely to get your first choice of lodgings, and transportation prices won't be sky-high.

Plan at least **4-5 days** for a good spring training trip. Because some of these spring training cities are pretty close to one another, that's enough time to see a few parks. For example, in Florida, you could see the Yankees in Tampa, the Phillies in Clearwater, the Blue Jays in Dunedin, and the Pirates in Bradenton—all within four days.

BEFORE YOU GO

I've spent a lot of time at major league ballparks in my life, so I have some tips to share on planning the best trip possible.

READING THE SCHEDULE

The regular season starts in March or April and lasts until September or October. With very few exceptions, every team plays Tuesday and Wednesday and Friday to Sunday. The **traditional series** between two teams lasts **three days:** Monday to Wednesday or Tuesday to Thursday during the week, Friday to Sunday on weekends. **Two-game series** (typically Tuesday and Wednesday) and **four-game series** (Monday to Thursday, Thursday to Sunday, or Friday to Monday) are also common.

The most common **off days** are **Mondays** and **Thursdays.** When planning your road trip, consider these days as **driving** days or additional **sightseeing** days.

Teams may schedule a **day game** as the final contest of a **midweek series,** occurring on a Wednesday or Thursday. **Sunday** games are generally played in the **afternoon.** Teams may plan **Saturday** games for **late-afternoon,** either to accommodate television schedules or to better transition players to the Sunday early-afternoon contest.

A **homestand** is when a team plays **multiple series in a row** at its home park. A 10-game homestand could mean three games at home against team A, three games at home against team B, and four games at home against team C.

A **getaway day** refers to the last contest played in a location before at least one team has to **fly out** for a game in another location the next day. A getaway-day game is sometimes played in the **daytime,** and if both teams are flying out shortly after the contest, it's possible that you'll see players on both clubs **speed things up** by swinging early and making quick outs.

Want to see both the Mets and Yankees on a trip to **New York?** You'll need to plan a longer trip than you might think. Typically, **two teams** in the **same city or market** are never home at the same time, so your best bet is to plan a trip that **overlaps two series,** usually with a **long weekend** of Thursday to Saturday, Saturday to Monday, or Sunday to Tuesday. Other destinations that require a little schedule-finagling include **Chicago, Los Angeles,** and the **San Francisco Bay Area.**

BUYING TICKETS

You have several options for purchasing tickets. All major league teams sell their own tickets directly, which you can buy via their **website, phone,** or an in-person visit to the **ticket window** at the ballpark. Buying directly from the team ensures that you'll get your tickets quickly and securely (no fakes here). But this isn't always the most affordable outlet.

Major League Baseball partners with **StubHub,** a **ticket resale site,** to help sell leftover tickets. (It's also where people can upload and sell their previously purchased tickets to other users.) The best way to score a deal on StubHub is to check the website **close to first pitch,** when prices come down to their **lowest.** Once you get to the ballpark, you show your ticket's barcode on your phone and stroll on in.

You can also comparison shop at other ticket resale sites like **SeatGeek** and **TickPick.** Since these companies don't have an official relationship with MLB, ticket **prices can vary wildly.** Be on the lookout for scams: Always opt for the digital ticket so that it comes to you immediately after purchase.

TICKET PRICES

Over the last several years, teams have switched to a **dynamic pricing** system, charging more money for games that they predict will have **higher demand.** For example, you might pay $100 for a seat in the lower level at Fenway Park to watch the Red Sox play the Yankees. That same seat

PREPARING FOR A ROAD TRIP

Before embarking on a road trip, be sure your car is fit to enjoy the ride . The **Automobile Association of America** (www.aaa.com), better known as **AAA** (not the minor league baseball level, mind you), has a few recommendations:

- Make sure your **tires** are properly **inflated.** Check your **tire pressure** with a gauge before getting on the road. If you haven't **rotated** tires in more than two oil changes, consider visiting an auto repair shop for a quick rotation.
- Check that you have a **spare tire** in good condition. Keep a **jack** and **lug wrench** in your trunk with the spare. If you don't have a spare, be sure you have **roadside service,** so you can call for help if you get stranded on the road.
- Check your **fluid levels** and ensure that the motor oil, transmission fluid, brake fluid, coolant, air conditioning coolant, power steering, and wiper fluid are **topped off** or **freshly changed.** Schedule a service if you're not sure how to check or replace fluids on your own.
- Make sure your **radiator** and **cooling system** are working properly.
- Ensure that your car's **belts** and **hoses** are good to go. They don't need changing often, but if they're in bad shape, it's a good idea to swap them out.
- Double check that your **battery** is in good working order. Asking for a **battery test** from a repair shop or auto part store isn't a bad idea.
- Fill up your **gas tank** the night before you leave. There are few feelings better than turning on that engine and seeing a **full tank** as you head out on your epic adventure.

when the White Sox come to town will cost more like $60.

Some teams take this system really far, creating **pricing tiers,** charging higher amounts for contests against **major rivals** and **popular teams** than games featuring middling rivals and unpopular or poor-performing teams. Pricing changes depending on **game times,** too: A Sunday afternoon game in summer, when families are certain to buy seats, is usually more expensive than the Friday night game featuring the same teams.

PARKING AND TRANSPORTATION

You'll pay the most money to park in the **lots closest to the ballpark.** Generally, these spots, which offer both proximity and peace of mind, will cost **$20-25.** Consider this option if you're traveling with multiple people who can split the cost.

If a stadium is in a **central location** within its city, you may be able to park up to a half-mile away and pay more like **$10** for a spot. If the stadium is isolated in a **sports complex** or part of a larger **entertainment district,** you probably won't get much cheaper than the rate by the ballpark. In these cases, consider an **alternate method of transportation,** if it's available.

In a few cities, like Chicago and Boston, you can park in stadium-adjacent **neighborhoods** and **walk** to the ballpark. But be on the lookout for signs that prohibit parking in these areas. **Fines** for **illegal parking** can be steep.

To avoid the headache and wallet-pinching of parking altogether, consider taking **public transit** to the game. Most cities have a solid **light rail** or **train system** that has a station nearby or even right at a venue.

The East Coast

This relatively short trip takes you through the serious fandom of East Coast baseball, from Boston to Washington DC. Visit some of baseball's finest ballparks, learn about the most storied franchises, and meet the loudest fans. There's just something about the East Coast that translates to great baseball drama. Get cozy at a Red Sox game in baseball's oldest and smallest venue, Fenway Park. Listen to pinstriped fans yell for their favorite players in the new Yankee Stadium. Take in the history of baseball as you visit famous gravesites and the birthplace of Babe Ruth. This is the epic baseball road trip.

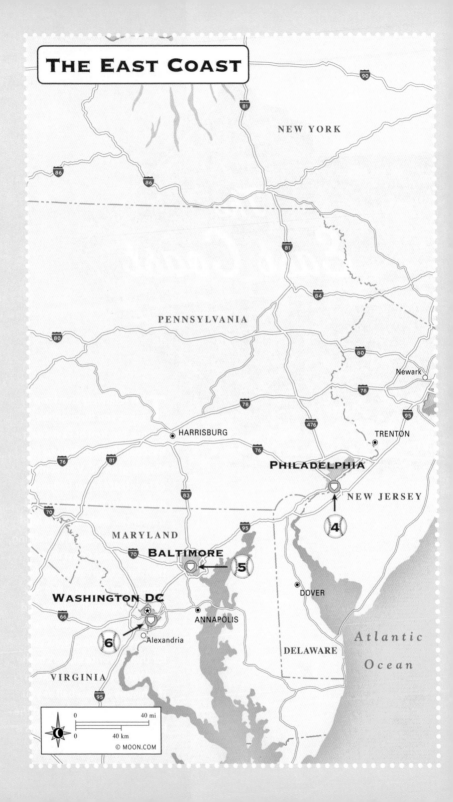

THE EAST COAST

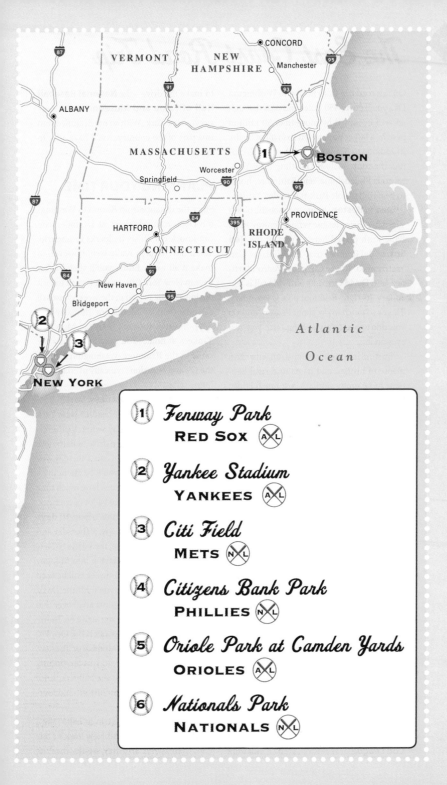

The East Coast Road Trip

On this road trip from Boston to Washington DC, you'll cover 450 miles and pass through an area occupied by more than 50 million people, a larger population than all of Spain. In addition to Beantown and the nation's capital, the route includes bustling New York, raucous Philadelphia, and Baltimore, home to beautiful Oriole Park at Camden Yards.

Start in **Boston,** home to baseball's oldest surviving major league venue, Fenway Park. Babe Ruth played here as part of the **Red Sox,** as did Jimmie Foxx, Ted Williams, Carl Yastrzemski, Roger Clemens, Pedro Martinez, and David Ortiz. Its outfield wall is legendary. Its right-field foul pole is legendary. There's so much to say about Fenway, and yet you don't have to say a thing once you cast eyes on it.

Boston is a tight, wound-up city with plenty of history, and its natural rival happens to be pretty similar—just much larger. **New York City,** your next stop, needs no introduction. The enormous metropolis is home to baseball's most famous team, the **Yankees,** and its forever little brother, the **Mets.** It's a short drive south to **Philadelphia,** where the **Phillies** set up shop. The fans here are tough but always passionate.

The last stretch of the trip includes stops in **Baltimore** and **Washington DC.** Baltimore is famous for being home to the **Orioles** since 1954, but it's also the **birthplace of Babe Ruth,** whose childhood home is a museum. Spend a gorgeous day at Oriole Park at Camden Yards, the venue that kicked off a love affair with the retro-classic ballpark, then drive another 45 minutes south to the District of Columbia. Catch a **Nationals** game here and be sure to walk around the National Mall.

For extra baseball excitement, the East Coast is home to baseball sites like the **Birthplace of Baseball Monument** in Hoboken, New Jersey, where the game is claimed to have begun; the ballparks of the storied **Cape Cod League** near Boston; and—if you want

to make the drive—the **National Baseball Hall of Fame and Museum** in Cooperstown, New York. With so much stuffed into this part of the country, you'll have a lot to appreciate.

PLANNING YOUR TIME

Since the distance from Boston to Washington DC is relatively short, at 450 miles, you can knock out all six ballparks in one trip. You'll have to plan really well, however, to make it all work. Either you'll spend a few days in New York City, or you'll need to visit during a swing period in the weekly baseball calendar (Sunday-Monday or Thursday-Friday), in order to catch both the Mets and Yankees at home. You may have to do the same in the Baltimore-Washington area, as the O's and Nats don't typically overlap their home series.

The **fast way** takes **six days.** Start in Boston on a Saturday, then head to New York for a Sunday and Monday swing. Visit Philadelphia on Tuesday, then drive to Baltimore on Wednesday and to DC on Thursday. For this version of the trip, you'll be attending a game every day, so you won't have much time to sightsee, and you'll need a lot of energy.

Want to breathe? Do this trip in **10 days to two weeks.** Start on, say, a Thursday and spend two days in Boston, then drive to New York for the weekend, staying into Monday or even Tuesday. Your midweek will be used up in Philadelphia, and you'll hit the DMV (DC, Maryland, and Virginia area) over that second weekend. Maybe you arrive on Thursday and that's when you catch the Orioles, or maybe you stay until Monday or Tuesday. Either way, you'll have no trouble finding things to do when not at the ballpark, since these are some of the most historic and touristed cities in America.

You can also split the trip in half. Take a **week** to visit Boston and New York in one trip, then spend **another week** traveling

Photos (top): National Baseball Hall of Fame and Museum in Cooperstown, New York; (middle left) birthplace of Babe Ruth; (middle right) the Mets' Home Run Apple outside Citi Field; (bottom) National Baseball Hall of Fame in Cooperstown.

from Philadelphia to Washington, with a **day trip** to Baltimore mixed in. If you can't find a time to visit both New York ballparks in one trip, consider Boston to one NYC venue, with a side trip to the National Baseball Hall of Fame in between. For this option, I suggest going in **spring,** as the turnpikes are swarmed in the summer, and Hall of Fame tourism spikes in the warmer months. On a second trip, visit the other NYC park, then head to Philly and the Baltimore-DC area. This can all be done in a **week** if you've already done the major sightseeing in the Big Apple.

The following is my recommendation for the fast way, preferably starting on a Saturday. Starting on a Wednesday is also a good option for this trip. I've tacked on an extra day at the end for sightseeing in DC. A word to the wise: If you plan on doing this version of the trip, factor in time for delays. The highways between Boston and Washington DC are notoriously busy, especially in the summer and during morning and evening rush hours. Be sure you've invested in an **E-Z Pass** for your vehicle, as you're bound to drive on **toll roads** sometime during this journey. (It's possible to take non-toll routes, but it takes far more time and is a headache to execute correctly.) Most every toll in this part of the world is read electronically. Look out for the parkways (Garden State, Taconic State), which may have old-fashioned booths with toll takers or baskets that only accept exact change. If you don't have an E-Z Pass, be sure to carry a bunch of loose bills and enough of each coin ($10 worth of quarters; $3 each worth of dimes and nickels will do).

Day 1

Arrive in **Boston.** Spend the afternoon sightseeing, maybe walking Newbury Street to Boston Common and a bit of the Freedom Trail, then catch a night game at **Fenway Park.**

Day 2

Wake up early in Boston and drive the 220 miles south to **New York City** (6am is a good target for leaving town). Get settled in and take the subway to **Yankee Stadium** for a day game. Afterward, get some rest and have a late dinner with a night in the Big Apple.

Day 3

Sleep in, then explore the city during the afternoon, whether you're checking out sights in Manhattan or walking around neighborhoods in Brooklyn or Queens. Take the subway to **Citi Field** for a night game.

Day 4

Again, get up early and drive the 100 miles south to **Philadelphia.** Spend much of your day in Center City and South Philadelphia, then enjoy a Phillies night game at **Citizens Bank Park.**

Day 5

Ideally, the Orioles will have a night game tonight, affording you some time to make the 100-mile drive south to **Baltimore.** If that's the case, spend the day around the Inner Harbor. After the game at **Oriole Park at Camden Yards,** consider a late-night drive to **Washington DC.** Knocking out those 40 miles now, instead of with all the morning traffic, is preferable.

Day 6

Hopefully, you're waking up in DC. If the Nationals have a day game, you're already here. If it's a night game, spend the day visiting the National Mall, then make your way to **Nationals Park.**

Day 7

If you have time, get in a little more sightseeing. In ideal circumstances, this is a Friday, meaning you still have a weekend ahead of you.

GETTING THERE

Air

If you're flying into Boston, you may choose to arrive at **Logan International Airport** (BOS, 1 Harborside Dr., Boston, 800/235-6426, www.massport.com), just northeast of Downtown in East Boston. From Logan, you can fly via **Air Canada** (888/247-2262, www.aircanada.com), **American Airlines** (800/433-7300, www.aa.com), **Delta** (800/221-1212, www.delta.com), **Frontier** (800/432-1359, www.flyfrontier.com), **jetBlue** (800/538-2583, www.jetblue.com), **Southwest** (800/435-9792, www.southwest.com), **Spirit** (801/401-2222, www.spirit.com), and **United** (800/864-8331, www.united.com), plus several international carriers. Just about every major American city is covered.

You have some options when flying home from DC. The largest airport in the area is **Washington Dulles International Airport** (IAD, 1 Saarinen Cir., Dulles, Virginia, 703/572-2700, www.flydulles.com). Airlines here include Air Canada, American Airlines, Delta, Frontier, Southwest, Spirit, and United, plus many international carriers.

There's also the smaller **Ronald Reagan Washington National Airport** (DCA, Smith Blvd., Arlington, Virginia, 703/417-8000, www.flyreagan.com). Making flights only within the 48 contiguous states, Reagan is serviced by Air Canada, American Airlines, Delta, Frontier, jetBlue, Southwest, and United.

Farther away from DC is **Baltimore/Washington International Thurgood Marshall Airport** (BWI, Hanover, Maryland, 410/859-7111, www.bwiairport.com). It facilitates service from Air Canada, Allegiant, American Airlines, Delta, Frontier, jetBlue, Southwest, Spirit, and United, plus several international carriers. Flights at BWI come from and go to most large cities in North America.

Train

If you don't want to drive the route from Boston to Washington DC, **Amtrak** (www.amtrak.com) is a worthwhile option and can be a real treat. You'll need to be savvy about scheduling four separate trips: Boston to New York, New York to Philadelphia, Philadelphia to Baltimore, and Baltimore to Washington DC. The **Acela** (express, more expensive) and **Northeast Regional** lines run from Boston to DC, stopping at every major city along the way. This line is the most frequented of any train line in America, so you'll never be alone.

In each city, you can get off at the main Amtrak hub and take public transit to the ballpark. Here are the Amtrak stops for the cities on the route:

- Boston: **Back Bay station** (Stuart St. and Dartmouth St.)
- New York City: **New York Pennsylvania Station** (31st St. and 8th Ave.)
- Philadelphia: **30th Street Station** (2955 Market St.)
- Baltimore: **Pennsylvania Station** (1500 N. Charles St.)
- Washington DC: **Union Station** (50 Massachusetts Ave. NE)

BOSTON
RED SOX

On the night of October 27, 2004, I stood outside, one mile west of Fenway Park. As Keith Foulke hugged Jason Varitek and the Red Sox clinched their first world championship in 86 years, a herd of humans ran past me. I poured these fans plastic cups of champagne as they cheered, cried, screamed, and became one with the moment. Soon, the area around Fenway Park was mobbed by thousands of people, most college students but plenty of them born-and-bred Sox fans from Boston, the suburbs, New Hampshire, Vermont, Maine, Connecticut, and elsewhere in New England. The city partied that evening like it had never before partied.

The Red Sox *are* Boston: scrappy, defiant, ever the underdog—even when they're the best in the world—and they'll tell you as much. When the Sox

are good, Boston is good; and when the Sox aren't good, you're gonna hear about it. Still, the fandom runs deep. The Celtics are one of basketball's two greatest franchises, the Bruins have lived a very full and profitable life in professional hockey, and the NFL's Patriots have redefined the idea of a sports dynasty. And yet, Boston remains a baseball town.

The franchise started in 1901 as the Boston Americans, the American League counterpart to the National League's Boston Braves. The team was renamed the Red Sox in 1908 as players began wearing red socks, and it would win championships in 1912, 1915, 1916, and 1918. Those last three titles came thanks in part to the exceptional pitching of young hurler George Herman Ruth. The kid could also hit a little, slamming a record 29 home runs in 1919, but owner Harry Frazee needed some dough and sold 24-year-old Ruth to the Yankees. That move was the beginning of decades of misfortune and bad play.

There were high points, though. Ted Williams, possibly the greatest natural hitter to ever play baseball, spent his entire career with the Sox. Carl Yastrzemski also played every one of his games in a Sox uniform, winning the Triple Crown (leading the league in batting average, home runs, and RBIs) in 1967, a season that nearly ended with a championship. And in 1975, one of baseball's greatest games—Game 6 of the World Series—ended with Carlton Fisk waving his fly ball fair and over the Green Monster to win the ball game.

There were also low points, like Bucky "Bleeping" Dent homering in a one-game playoff between the Yankees and Sox in 1978, Bill Buckner letting a critical grounder go through his legs in 1986, and—as bad as it gets—the Sox being the last team to integrate, calling up Black infielder Pumpsie Green to the majors in 1959, 12 years after Jackie Robinson debuted for the Brooklyn Dodgers.

In 2003, the Sox had another of those terrible finishes, as the Yankees beat them with a late comeback and game-winning home run in Game 7 of the American League Championship Series (ALCS). But 2004 changed everything—the Sox somehow came back from a 3-0 deficit at the hands of the Yankees, beating them in the ALCS before sweeping St. Louis to win that first World Series title in 86 years. Good times continued, with championships in 2007, 2013, and 2018, making this latest generation of Sox fans the richest in 100 years.

You'd think all that success would calm down a fan base and give them perspective. Nope. Red Sox fans will always claim that their team is up against the world, whether that world be baseball pundits, the Yankees, or something else entirely. You know what, though? It's pretty fun to be part of that. Because when the Sox do win, boy, is it a party—champagne and all.

PLANNING YOUR TIME

Boston is a great **long-weekend** city. Spend a day doing historic stuff, including walking the Freedom Trail and visiting the John F. Kennedy Presidential Library and Museum. Another day might include checking out college campuses and the areas around them, from Boston University to Northeastern to Harvard and the Massachusetts Institute of Technology (MIT). A third day could include checking out a neighborhood like the Back Bay or a nearby city like Somerville.

It's most convenient to stay in the center of Boston, anywhere from the **Back Bay** east to **Downtown** and the **North End,** but accommodations are priciest there. Staying in **Cambridge** or near **Logan International Airport** means saving money, but it also means having to spend more time getting to and from places. My suggestion is to budget for a higher-priced accommodation inside the city proper but keep a second option outside the city as a backup.

Important note: Boston has the most college students per capita of any U.S. city, which means the city is teeming with families around **Labor Day** (move-in time), in **mid-October** (homecoming, family weekend), and in **mid- to late May** (graduation and move-out time). During these periods, reserving hotel rooms and restaurant tables is all-out war, so lock down those reservations early.

If you want to see **Fenway** in all its glory, visiting in **midsummer** is the best option. The weather will probably be hot, but it could also be absolutely perfect. Choosing to visit in **April** means risking rain and undoubtedly being in cold weather (bring layers). **May** can also be pretty wet (and cold at night), so be warned.

You'll want to **avoid driving** in and around Boston. Public transportation is solid, and Boston is a perfect city for walking.

GETTING THERE

AIR

Flying into Boston? You'll undoubtedly be arriving at **Logan International Airport** (BOS, 1 Harborside Dr., 800/235-6426, www.massport.com), just northeast of Downtown in East Boston. The five-mile drive to Downtown takes 10 minutes when there's no traffic; with traffic, it's more like 20 minutes.

From Logan, you can fly via **Air Canada** (888/247-2262, www.aircanada.com), **American Airlines** (800/433-7300, www.aa.com), **Delta** (800/221-1212, www.delta.com), **Frontier** (800/432-1359, www.flyfrontier.com), **jetBlue** (800/538-2583, www.jetblue.com), **Southwest** (800/435-9792, www.southwest.com), **Spirit** (801/401-2222, www.spirit.com), and **United** (800/864-8331, www.united.com), plus several international carriers. Just about every major American city is covered.

Airport Transportation

The **MBTA** (Massachusetts Bay Transportation Authority, www.mbta.com), better known as the **T**, offers **bus** and **subway** service from the airport to the city. By bus ($1.70-2), take the Silver Line's route **SL1**, which connects the airport to the major train station South Station. By subway ($2.40-2.90), you'll want to board a **Massport shuttle bus** to the **Blue Line,** which starts at **Airport station** (Transportation Way and Service Rd.). If you're staying near Fenway Park, take a westbound train to **Government Center** (Tremont St. and Court St.), which offers a connection to the **Green Line** that stops near Fenway, at **Kenmore station.**

To **rent a car** after arriving at Logan, you should head to the lower level of the terminal and look for the blue-and-white **shuttle buses** at curbside. These buses will take you to the **Rental Car Center** (15 Transportation Way, East Boston). Located about two minutes from the terminals but on the other side of I-90, the RCC is home to kiosks of just about every major rental car company. There's also a Dunkin' Express here.

TRAIN

Amtrak (www.amtrak.com) serves Boston at two stations. The larger hub is **South Station** (700 Atlantic Ave., www.south-station.net), which opened in 1898 and is south of Downtown Boston. Both the T Silver Line bus and Red Line subway stop at South Station. The Silver Line heads toward Logan International Airport to the northeast, and to Chinatown to the west. The Red Line connects passengers going south to suburbs like Braintree and Ashmont, and passengers going north to **Park Street station** (Tremont St. and Winter St.), which is also home to the Green Line that runs to Fenway Park, and Cambridge farther up.

Closer to Fenway Park, near the Back Bay area of the city, is **Back Bay station** (Stuart St. and Dartmouth St.). The subway connection here is for the Orange Line, which runs through Downtown to the north and through Northeastern University to the south. You can walk from Back Bay station to Fenway Park; it's about 25 minutes west through the Back Bay neighborhood. It's a really nice walk, one I've done dozens of times, and it provides a nice introduction to a bustling area of the city.

Amtrak routes that serve Boston include the **Northeast Regional** and its express version, **Acela** (both of which run from Boston to Washington DC), the **Lake Shore Limited** (New York to Chicago), and the **Downeaster** (Boston to Brunswick, Maine).

BUS

Greyhound (800/231-2222, www.greyhound.com) stops at **South Station** (700 Atlantic Ave.). Rides to and from New York start at just over $10; the ride itself, depending on the time of day, could be as short as four hours and 20 minutes. You can also take **Megabus** (508/746-0378, http://us.megabus.com) from South Station. A ride to New York starts at about $14 and lasts at least 4.5 hours.

Fenway Park

There's a reason that the pivotal moment in *Field of Dreams,* a movie about baseball, family, and America, had to take place inside **Fenway Park** (4 Jersey St., www.mlb.com/redsox). It's because this is the epitome, the ballpark that screams baseball. A deep green, a left-field wall that looks like an impossible

giant to a little kid, kooky angles, steel posts in your face, narrow concourses, the smell of hot dogs, and the feeling that you and 30,000 other people are tucked in together to watch something special: Fenway Park is the gem of gems.

As baseball grew in popularity and clubs became stable at the turn of the 20th century, owners sought bigger ballparks—or renovated existing ones—so they could play host to a team and its 25,000 or more fans. These parks, built of steel and concrete, were called "jewel box" ballparks. They included Shibe Park in Philadelphia, the Polo Grounds and Ebbets Field in New York, and Tiger Stadium in Detroit. Just two jewel box parks remain today: Wrigley Field in Chicago and Fenway Park.

Fenway has its quirks, from the 37-foot-high wall known as the Green Monster to Pesky's Pole, the right-field foul pole that's closer to home plate than in any other park. There are plenty more quirks, like restricted-view seats and an oddly shaped outfield that includes an angled area called The Triangle, which makes playing center field a tricky proposition. All of this (and more) add up to make Fenway the most charming little park there is.

The Red Sox have renovated and added on to the ballpark numerous times, especially

Teammates by Toby Mendez depicts Ted Williams, Bobby Doerr, Johnny Pesky, and Dom DiMaggio.

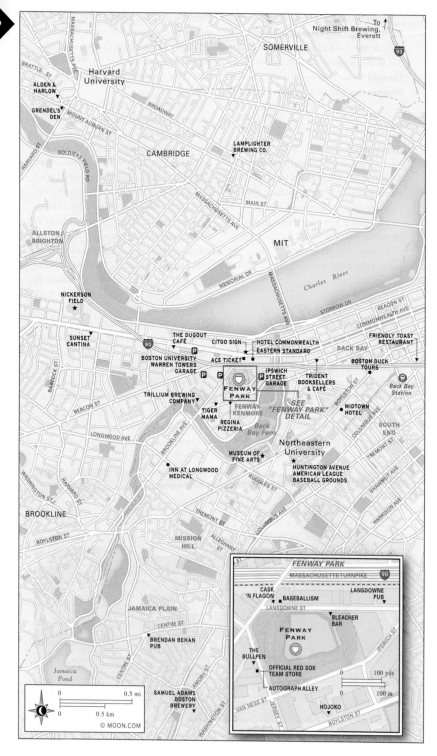

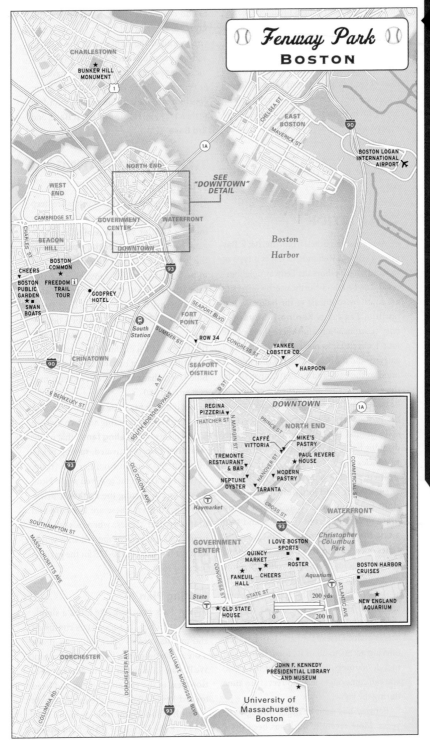

Fenway Park
BOSTON

CHARLESTOWN

★ BUNKER HILL
MONUMENT

1

1A

EAST
BOSTON

CHELSEA ST

MAVERICK ST

90

BOSTON LOGAN
INTERNATIONAL
AIRPORT ✈

NORTH END

SEE
"DOWNTOWN"
DETAIL

WEST
END

CAMBRIDGE ST

GOVERNMENT
CENTER

WATERFRONT

BEACON
HILL

CHARLES ST

DOWNTOWN

Boston

Harbor

CHEERS ★
BOSTON
COMMON ★

★ ■ BOSTON
PUBLIC
GARDEN

FREEDOM ⓘ
TRAIL
TOUR

★ ■ SWAN
BOATS

● GODFREY
HOTEL

93

FORT
POINT

SEAPORT BLVD

South
Station

SUMMER ST

▶ ROW 34

CONGRESS ST

YANKEE
LOBSTER CO. ▼

90

CHINATOWN

E BERKELEY ST

A ST

SEAPORT
DISTRICT

D ST

▼ HARPOON

93

SOUTH BOSTON BYPASS

OLD COLONY AVE

DOWNTOWN

1A

REGINA
PIZZERIA ★

THATCHER ST

N MARGIN ST

PRINCE ST

CAFFÉ
VITTORIA ▼

★ MIKE'S
PASTRY

NORTH END

HANOVER ST

TREMONTE
RESTAURANT
& BAR ▼

★ PAUL REVERE
HOUSE

NEPTUNE
OYSTER ▼

▼ MODERN
PASTRY

▼ TARANTA

COMMERCIAL ST

Ⓣ
Haymarket

CROSS ST

WATERFRONT

93

Christopher
Columbus
Park

GOVERNMENT
CENTER

CONGRESS ST

I LOVE BOSTON
SPORTS ■

QUINCY
MARKET
★
★
FANEUIL
HALL

■ ROSTER

★ CHEERS

Aquarium

Ⓣ

ATLANTIC AVE

BOSTON HARBOR
CRUISES

State
Ⓣ

Ⓣ ★ OLD STATE
HOUSE

STATE ST

0   200 yds

0   200 m

NEW ENGLAND ★
AQUARIUM

SOUTHAMPTON ST

MASSACHUSETTS AVE

93

DORCHESTER

DORCHESTER AVE

WILLIAM T. MORRISSEY BLVD

COLUMBIA RD

JOHN F. KENNEDY
PRESIDENTIAL LIBRARY
AND MUSEUM
★

University of
Massachusetts
Boston

since 2000. Major changes included creating a wider concourse area in the outfield, adding a right-field deck for group seating, installing a video board in deep center field, and, most intriguingly for fans, popping a couple rows of seats atop the Green Monster. Those chairs are hot tickets. Then again, sitting anywhere in Fenway makes for a pretty cool experience (well, maybe not in the obstructed-view seats).

All this is to say that Fenway Park is an experience. It's one every baseball fan must have.

ORIENTATION

Fenway's name comes from the Back Bay Fens, a park of wetlands (a fen is a type of wetland) that anchors the Fenway neighborhood. The Fens and Northeastern University are south by southeast of the ballpark. Just north of Fenway is **Kenmore Square,** a busy transportation hub where three of the four T Green Lines meet. Kenmore is also a gateway into the historic Back Bay neighborhood to the east, and Boston University to the west. On game days, expect Kenmore to be packed, both in the subway station and in the surrounding area. The game-day crowd spills around the ballpark, filling eateries, drinking holes, and shops while streets close to vehicles.

There are **five gates** at Fenway Park—one at the **left-field foul pole** (Gate A), the **right-field foul pole** (Gate B), and **home plate** or **Jersey Street** (Gate D), and **two along the Green Monster** (Gate C, Gate E). Gates open **90 minutes** before every game. (Now I'm going to reward you with some bonus knowledge: There's a secret sixth gate at Fenway. Check out the *Food and Drinks* section for more on that.)

Though it's outside Fenway, Jersey Street acts as a concourse of the park during games, offering access to all of its food, drink, and merch counters. Once you're in the park, you can come out to Jersey Street at any time during the game.

Fenway has seen changes through the years. More recently, work has been done

to add concourse space. Look for the **Big Concourse** (right field, grandstand), which wraps around the right end of the outfield and features numerous food vendors and picnic seating, something you couldn't have had at Fenway a couple decades ago. The other concourses in the park are named according to their location: **Home Plate, 1st Base,** and **3rd Base.**

TICKETS AND SEATING

Pricing

The Sox are popular, so ticket prices are steep most of the time. Tickets are priced according to a **six-tier structure.** For midweek games against **nonessential opponents,** the lowest price tier, or **tier five,** is likely to be activated, and it's possible that **tier four** (slightly more expensive) will be also. In real terms, a middle-of-the-road pavilion reserved seat will cost $50 for a tier five game and $65 for a tier four game. Next is **tier three,** which might signal a game from a **visiting rival** that isn't the Yankees (say, the Blue Jays). That pavilion reserved seat may cost around $80.

But if it's the first time in eight years that the Cardinals are coming to town (which means plenty of **traveling fans**), that might mean **tier two** is activated, raising prices by about 120 percent from tier five (think $110 for that pavilion reserved seat). Now, if the Sox are hosting the **Yankees,** prices soar even higher. These are **tier one** and **diamond tier** games, where a seat costs nearly 200-250 percent more than it would for a tier five game ($150-175 for the pavilion reserved seat).

Seating Plan

Fenway Park may look like it has a simple seating structure, but it's just as confusing and multifaceted as other ballparks, if not more so, because of its funny configuration. We'll start in right field, the **lowest section** next to the visitors' bullpen, and head toward Pesky's Pole and the infield. That's the **right-field lower box** (sections 1-8). About 15 rows up is the **right-field upper**

YOUR BEST DAY AT FENWAY PARK

Got tickets for a Red Sox game tonight? Heck yeah. Let me guide you through the best possible day you can have leading up to, during, and after the game.

10 HOURS BEFORE FIRST PITCH
Start the day with some breakfast at the **Friendly Toast Restaurant.** An eggs Benedict will fill you right up.

8 HOURS BEFORE FIRST PITCH
You're gonna want to walk off breakfast; what better way than getting in some history? Take the T's Orange Line from **Back Bay station** (Stuart St. and Dartmouth St.) to **State station** (Water St. and Devonshire St.), then walk along Water Street west to Washington Street to hook up with the **Freedom Trail.** You'll be close to the **Old State House.** Continue walking north to see sites like the **Paul Revere House** and the **Old North Church.** This walk is just 15 minutes; add in time to stop, learn, and relax, and that's a good hour and change.

6.5 HOURS BEFORE FIRST PITCH
While you're up in the **North End,** walk a few minutes to **Regina Pizzeria** for some iconic Boston pie. Then take in the rest of the North End on foot; get a cannoli from **Mike's Pastry** if you still have room.

5 HOURS BEFORE FIRST PITCH
Take Salem Street south to the Freedom Trail, picking it up where it intersects with Cross Street, and follow it to **Quincy Market** and **Faneuil Hall.** While here, look for a souvenir. Shop at **I Love Boston Sports** or **Roster.**

4 HOURS BEFORE FIRST PITCH
You're close to **Government Center**

The Bullpen

(Tremont St. and Court St.) and **State station** (Water St. and Devonshire St.), which means you're close to just about every T line. Use this time to stop by your hotel. Take a quick break and freshen up for the evening.

2.5 HOURS BEFORE FIRST PITCH
Get yourself to the T's Green Line, and look for a B, C, or D branch train. Head to **Kenmore station** (Kenmore St. and Commonwealth Ave.). Take a picture of the **Citgo Sign,** then walk toward Fenway. Get to Lansdowne Street: Have a drink at **Bleacher Bar** and buy a link from **The Sausage Guy.** Raise a toast at the **Cask 'n Flagon,** then take a nice walk around Fenway and onto Brookline Avenue.

Find the alley that leads to **The Bullpen.** Have one more pint, then leave the bar via Jersey Street, going through the **secret sixth gate** to get into Fenway.

30 MINUTES BEFORE FIRST PITCH
If you do just one thing on this itinerary, do this: Walk down one of those tunnels that lead to the seating area. Look at the field, the **Green Monster, Pesky's Pole.** It's just beautiful. Let your emotions do what they will.

DURING THE GAME
Buy a **Fenway Frank** and a beer. Sit in your seat. Don't get up.

AFTER THE GAME
If you're hungry or thirsty, take a Green Line B train out west to **Sunset Cantina.** Get the South of the Border nachos and a margarita. Or stay closer to the park and visit **Hojoko** for a late-night burger and Japanese whiskey.

Cask 'n Flagon

Fenway Park

box (sections 87-97), and the seats in the back of the first level here are the **outfield grandstand** (sections 1-10).

Starting in shallow right field and extending all the way around to the left-field foul pole, the lowest 13 rows are in the **field box** (sections 9-82). Behind those seats, for the next 14 rows, and also extending from shallow right field to the left-field foul pole, are seats in the **loge box** (sections 98-164). The seats way in the back, also starting in shallow right but extending to shallow left, are in the **infield grandstand** (sections 11-31). The final sections by the left-field foul pole, way in the back, are in the **outfield grandstand** (sections 32-33). In the outfield, you've got the **bleachers** (sections 34-43); the final five rows are the **upper bleachers.**

The **second level** of seating starts at home plate with the members-only **Dell Technologies Club.** Suites extend in either direction. The one area of non-suite seating here is the **right-field roof box** (sections 23-41), going from infield to outfield. Next to that, in right field, is the **Samuel Adams Deck** (referred to as the **Sam Deck**), which is typically a pre-reserved group-seating area—though there are **standing-room** tickets available for this section on a per-game basis.

Then there are the **obstructed-view seats,** known enemy of anyone who's ever set foot inside Fenway Park. All the obstructed-view seats are located in the **grandstand** between **sections 1-33.** If you don't sit in these sections, you're good as gold. (Read more about how to further avoid them in *Where to Buy Tickets.*)

Finally, the **third level** around home plate is the **home plate pavilion club** (sections 1-5). Going along the first-base line are the lower-level **pavilion club,** upper-level **pavilion box** (sections 1-13, odd numbers only), and **pavilion reserved** (section 15). Going along the third-base line are the lower-level **pavilion club,** upper-level **pavilion box** (sections 2-14, even numbers only), and **pavilion reserved** (sections 16, 18, 20).

Considered part of the third level, the **Monster Seats** (sections 1-10) sit atop the Green Monster and go from the left-field foul pole to center field. There are just three rows of seats and a **standing-room area.** The bleachers and Monster Seats are only accessible from behind their respective sections, though you can access the rest of the park with either ticket.

The Sox reserve **two seating areas for families:** grandstand sections 32 and 33. Alcohol is prohibited in these areas.

Where to Buy Tickets

Since Red Sox tickets are among the priciest in baseball, you may want to play the waiting game and hope a cheaper seat opens on StubHub or SeatGeek. That said, for a game with a rival opponent like the Yankees, you're going to pay a lot regardless.

Special to Boston is **Ace Ticket** (534 Commonwealth Ave., 617/783-3333, www.aceticket.com, 9am-8pm Mon.-Fri., 9am-7pm Sat., 9am-5pm Sun.), a reseller with a good reputation in town and a pickup booth right in Kenmore Square, just a three-minute walk from Fenway.

Before purchasing a ticket, visit **Precise**

Seating (www.preciseseating.com), a website that has detailed information on nearly every seat in the ballpark. In other words, check this website before buying a seat with an obstructed view; these seats exist thanks to the support poles holding up the upper deck. The first time I visited Fenway, I sat behind a support pole, and while I was super happy to be there, I just *hated* that seat. Another great resource is **Headspin Software** (www.headspinsoftware.com/red-sox-fenway-obstructed-view-seats.html), a website that lists exactly where all the obstructed-view seats are, plus what part of your view might be impacted.

If you do get an obstructed-view seat and you bought your ticket directly from the Red Sox, check into the **MLB Ballpark app.** The app gives users an opportunity to upgrade their seat during the game for a fee.

Best Seats

I've written about obstructed-view seats at Fenway, but I haven't yet mentioned that the seats themselves are, well, tight. This is an old ballpark that can't really spread out (only up), so fans have always been packed in here. Expect to be squeezed next to people, and don't look for a lot of legroom. For me, this is part of the charm. You'll feel like you're at the game with more than 35,000 of your closest friends. Plus, if you're sitting in the grandstand, you may be sitting in a navy-blue oak seat dating back to the 1930s.

If you want to be in the **shade,** sit in the grandstand, especially along the third-base line. If you're under the upper deck, you won't be in direct sunlight, though check before buying a ticket so you don't sit behind a support pole. Otherwise, the third-base line gets shade first during day games.

Although seats will be around $80 a pop, I like the **loge box area** from **sections 142 to 149.** Similarly, **pavilion box** sections 2, 4, 6, 8, 10, and 12 all offer **shade, great views,** and a slightly more **affordable** ticket price at $60 per person.

For **evening games,** sitting in the **right-field box area** (sections 1-7) can be a lot of fun since you're close to **foul ball** and/or **home-run ball territory,** depending on

which side of Pesky's Pole you're on. Also, you'll have a killer view of the Green Monster.

To sit atop the **Monster,** you'll have to shell out $200, and it's best to check the Red Sox website as soon as tickets go on sale for the season. The view from here is pretty cool, and it's popular. These are also among the newest seats in the park, so you'll actually have some **legroom** and space.

If you want to be in the wildest part of the park, head to the **bleachers.** I tend to look for a ticket in **section 41** or **42,** and the closer to row 20 (from above row 20), the better. The bleachers don't go up as much as they go back, so the view is easier on the eyes the closer you are to the fence.

Or if you're just looking to drink with folks while standing up, the Sox offer **standing-room** tickets for every game. Try the **Sam Deck** (right field, third level), where you'll get a decent selection of Sam Adams beer and a convivial atmosphere. Generally, Sam Deck tickets are among the **cheapest** in the park, averaging less than $40 for a tier three game.

KNOW BEFORE YOU GO

Like most other ballparks in the majors, Fenway allows **bags** that are up to 16 by 16 by 8 inches. **Soft coolers** are allowed, but no glass containers. One 16-ounce sealed plastic bottle of **water** is permitted. **Umbrellas** are also allowed but can only be opened during rain delays.

Accessibility

Every Fenway Park gate is **wheelchair-accessible,** with **elevators** at gates B, D, and E. (There are three elevators at Gate D and one each at Gates B and E.) If you use a wheelchair and are have tickets in the grandstand, visit either gate D or E to enter the park. Gate D has **wheelchair escorts** at the ready if you would like assistance getting to your seat via the use of one of the stadium's wheelchairs.

Service dogs are welcome at the ballpark. **Assisted listening devices** are also provided with a $20 cash deposit at either

Photos (top): Red Sox game at Fenway Park; (middle left) a classic bullpen cart; (middle right) vendor selling Fenway Franks; (bottom) a statue of Wally the Green Monster, the Red Sox mascot.

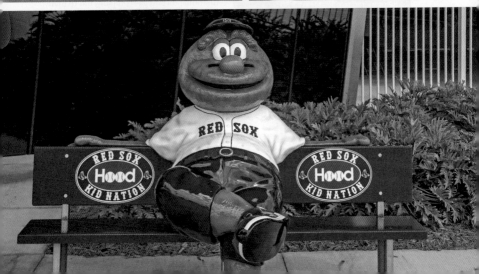

of the **fan service booths** (gates B and E). **Braille schedules** are available at the Red Sox ticket office.

There aren't a lot of **parking** options around Fenway, so finding a designated accessible spot could be tough. There are spots on **Jersey Street** between Van Ness and Boylston streets near Gate D. Considering that Gate D has the most accessibility options, this area might be the best bet. You may also find a general parking spot on **Ipswich Street,** which sidles up to the right field area of the park.

GETTING THERE

Take public transportation to Fenway if you can. Or if it's nice out, walk! Boston is the prototypical walking city; you'd be surprised how easily you can knock out two miles.

The T

For years, the mantra has been "Take the T to Fenway!" Boston has one of the more sophisticated subway systems in America, thanks to the **MBTA** (www.mbta.com, $1.70-2 bus, $2.40-2.90 subway). **The T,** as it's commonly known, is a great way to get to and from the ballpark. The **Green Line** goes to the park, so if you're not near it, get to either **Government Center** (Tremont St. and Court St.), **Park Street station** (Tremont St. and Winter St.) or **Downtown Crossing** (Washington St. and Summer St.), which all connect to the main Green Line. Downtown Crossing isn't a direct connection, but there's a walkway to Park Street, which is just two blocks away.

When grabbing a Green Line train, be sure to look for the **branch** you'll need, designated by a letter. You'll want a **B, C,** or **D train.** E trains branch out from Copley and head south (the walk from Northeastern station to the park isn't very long, but it's the least convenient). The B, C, and D lines all stop at **Kenmore station** (Kenmore St. and Commonwealth Ave.), located at **Kenmore Square,** which is where most Red Sox fans get out, as it's just a three-minute walk to the park. Kenmore Square is full of bars and restaurants.

While at Kenmore, look toward the westbound side of Commonwealth Avenue, then look up. Atop a six-story building on Beacon Street is the famous **Citgo Sign** (660 Beacon St.), an enormous beacon (pun intended) that has forever loomed over the Green Monster. Sure, it's just an advertisement for a multinational oil and gas company, but to many, it's an important piece of nostalgia.

If you're on the B or C lines, be sure to exit at Kenmore, as those trains continue west, farther away from the ballpark. If you're on the D line, you could continue one more stop to **Fenway station** (Park Dr. and Medfield St.), though the station is actually farther from the ballpark than Kenmore. Get off at Fenway station if you want to visit restaurants and bars either at the Landmark Center (such as Trillium Brewing) or on Boylston Street near the ballpark (such as Tiger Mama).

Note: **T service ends at 1am,** so if you're at the bars nearby and staying till last call, you'll need to hail a ride-share vehicle.

GAME COSTS

Tickets: Some of the priciest in baseball. At their least expensive, seats in the upper bleachers, the cheapest sit-down tickets in the park, cost **$22.** Be prepared to pay at least **$70** for a good seat.

Hot dog: A Fenway Frank will set you back about **$5.** That's average when compared to the rest of the league.

Beer: Anywhere between **$10** and **$14** for a pint of craft, which is about average among the different parks.

Parking: Forget it. Seriously, take the T or walk, if you can, because prices can hike **above $30** per car, easily. If you park far from Fenway, you can pay **less than $25,** but the T will get you closer.

BE A FAN

fans singing "Sweet Caroline"

Being a born-and-raised Philadelphian who lived in Boston and New York, I can talk for days about the psychology of the fans who live in these East Coast cities. Now, I'm not trying to be a homer, and I've watched sports in every major city in America, but I'm of the belief that by and large, fans in Boston, New York, and Philly are more serious about their sports (not just baseball) than fans anywhere else in the country (though Chicago, Oakland, and a few other cities come close). This road trip will feature, in my view, the **most intense fans** you'll find.

If you wear the **Yankee pinstripes** in Boston, prepare for a deluge of taunts ("Yankees suck!" is commonplace). Are there fights? Not often, but they do happen. Don't be an instigator (meaning, don't get drunk and start yelling at people); and if someone taunts you, smile, joke if you want, but never escalate.

Sox fans are pretty knowledgeable about baseball (they have a lot to say about the Celts, the Pats, and the Bruins, as well), and when they're not rowdy, being with them can be a great time. **Strike up a conversation** about baseball with the friendliest fan sitting near you or with the one wondering why you're wearing another team's cap at Fenway.

The Sox have a tradition that you may have heard of. As the game heads into the bottom of the eighth inning, you'll hear the first chords of Neil Diamond's iconic 1969 song **"Sweet Caroline."** The whole crowd joins in, emphasizing the trumpet hits in the chorus. I heard it for the first time in 1999, and I was right there with the crowd, singing and dancing. Back then, it was used only when the Sox were winning and the crowd was in good spirits, but since 2002 it's been used at **every home game.** There has been something of a backlash against the song from some parts of the fanbase, as its presence at Fenway became more frequent during a time when many non-die hard fans were jumping on the bandwagon. (Also, why is a New York songwriter being celebrated in Beantown?) Personally, I think the song is played out, but by now it's quintessentially Fenway Park, a harmless minute in between inning halves that usually gets the crowd going. It's a good time.

And when the team wins, you'll hear **three songs.** First is the Standells' 1966 hit **"Dirty Water,"** a self-deprecating track about Boston that registers as well as possible; then it's **"Tessie"** by local punk heroes the Dropkick Murphys (a song that's been with them since 2004); and finally, you'll hear **"Joy to the World"** by beloved, uh, Los Angeles band Three Dog Night. This song doesn't have a specific connection to the team or city—it's just a great song.

Driving

I don't recommend driving to the park, especially on weekdays, as **rush-hour traffic** in Boston spills throughout the city thanks to its small footprint. If you have to drive, how you get there is dependent on which parking garage or lot you'll use.

From the west, you might drive down Commonwealth Avenue or Beacon Street, so park in a garage or lot on those roads. I'd try the **Boston University Warren Towers garage** (700 Commonwealth Ave.), as it's only a 0.5-mile walk to the park from there, and you're removed from the bulk of game traffic.

From the south, you're probably taking Brookline Avenue up, so park anywhere north of the Back Bay Fens on Brookline. From the east (if you're coming from the inner city, especially), you should take Boylston Street west. Try parking in the garage at **16 Ipswich Street.** You'll then walk 0.4 mile west to the ballpark.

Finally, if you're coming from Downtown, Cambridge, or Logan airport, you might come in through Storrow Drive, which drops you off on Boylston Street past the Back Bay Fens. There are plenty of lots on Boylston just south of the park, but rates will be higher here.

The farther away from the park you are, the more likely you'll pay $15-20 for parking. If you park a block from Fenway, be prepared to pay $30 or more. You could also try for a spot on Beacon Street, but you'll pay the meter up to $22 for the full night.

PARK FEATURES AND SIGHTS

Jersey Street and Lansdowne Street

Get to Fenway Park well before the game begins, because you'll want to spend an hour or so on **Jersey Street.** Outside the ballpark, along the first-base line, Jersey Street (the former Yawkey Way, renamed because of former owner Tom Yawkey's legacy of racism) is like a pregame carnival, with food and merchandise vendors, and sometimes live music. It acts as part of the ballpark, so be sure to have your ticket ready for scanning. You can come back out of the park to Jersey Street at any time during the game.

Just around the corner, behind the Green Monster, is **Lansdowne Street,** home to bars and sidewalk vendors. This street is not part of the ballpark, so you should visit Lansdowne before going to Jersey.

Green Monster

Standing 37 feet tall in left field, the **Green Monster** (left-field fence) is one of the most iconic ballpark quirks. The wall is original to the ballpark and made of wood, though in the 1970s the Sox covered the wall in plastic to make it less harrowing for outfielders barreling toward it. It wasn't always known as the Green Monster: The wall wasn't painted green until 1947, and the name didn't really catch on until a few decades ago.

The **scoreboard** at the base of the wall has been there since 1934, always hand-operated, with workers inside the structure updating all the action from around the league during games. One worker comes out to the field to update National League scores, because that's the only way to access that part of the scoreboard. Look closely in the white

lines of the American League scoreboard, as you'll see dots and dashes—that's Morse code for the initials of former Sox owners Thomas and Jean Yawkey. (This may be the only reference left to Thomas Yawkey at Fenway.) Inside the wall are thousands of signatures from baseball players, celebrities, fans, and other notables. The area inside the Green Monster isn't open to the public, so the only way to see these signatures in person is if you have a connection at Fenway. Some premium tours may give you a quick peek.

At first, a slew of advertisements covered the Monster, but the green paint job cleaned it up, leaving nothing but the scoreboard. That changed in 1999 with the addition of a mural for the All-Star Game; in the 2000s came multiple advertisements.

Originally, there was nothing atop the Monster—just netting to catch home runs. But then came oversize Coca-Cola bottles, which were attached to the light fixtures towering over the wall. After that were the **Monster Seats,** opening in 2003 to much fanfare. They provide a stellar view and a chance to be one with baseball history.

Pesky's Pole

At Fenway Park, the outfield fence in right field makes a sharp turn toward the foul line. At the line, the fence makes another sharp turn to ride the line. At that corner stands **Pesky's Pole,** the right-field foul pole, anywhere from 295 to the officially recorded 302 feet from home plate. (The distance has been contested for a few reasons, most notably because the pole isn't directly on the first base/right field line. Measurements by other entities that aren't the Sox have put the distance at anywhere from 295 to 300 feet from the plate.) Its placement means balls that might normally be easy fly outs or fouls in other parks can slice past the pole (or hit it) for a comparatively easy home run. That is apparently how diminutive shortstop Johnny Pesky struck a handful of homers at Fenway; in time, the pole was named after him. When seeing it up close, you may find that fans have signed their name on it.

Wally's Clubhouse

For kids, there's **Wally's Clubhouse** (Kids Concourse, Champions Club), a play area for younger fans (around ages 12 and under) with crawling space, toys, a balloon artist, face painting, and an area for toddlers. It also has appearances by Wally the Green Monster, the Sox's giant, furry, green mascot—think somewhere between a Muppet and the Phillie Phanatic. Wally's Clubhouse is open from the third to seventh innings, and parental supervision is required.

The Red Chair

Cast your eyes to section 42, row 37, seat 21. Look at the far-right sign above the right-field bleacher seats, then start scanning the rows of seats below that sign. Eventually, you'll spot a **red chair** among a sea of navy blue. It marks the longest home run recorded at Fenway Park, an alleged 502-foot blast off the bat of Ted Williams in 1946. The ball is said to have hit the head of a fan sitting in what's now the red chair, tearing a hole through the man's straw hat.

FOOD AND DRINKS

While most major league ballparks constantly bring in new vendors, opt for local flavor, and try to one-up themselves with more outlandish concessions every year, the Red Sox are relatively subdued with their food offerings.

You can find the famous **Fenway Frank** (Home Plate Concourse, 1st Base Concourse, 3rd Base Concourse, Big Concourse, pavilion level, home plate deck, right-field roof deck, Twins '47 third-base deck) all over the place, at any standard concession stand at the park. A basic dog that's been around for about a century, it's the one must-eat at Fenway, and you should top it with mustard and relish.

Local pizza favorite **Regina Pizzeria** (Big Concourse, Gate E concourse, 1st Base

Photos (from top to bottom): ticket gate at Fenway Park; vendor selling popcorn; seating surrounding the home dugout.

Concourse, pavilion level, home plate deck, right field roof deck, Twins '47 third base deck), known for its crispy, brick-oven crust and inventive topping combinations, is at the park. If you fill up on other goodies at the park, you can visit its original location in the North End. (For more details, see the *Food* section.)

If you want lobster while at Fenway, you can get a lobster BLT or the trusty ol' lobster roll with mayonnaise and celery via **Yankee Lobster Co.** (Big Concourse). It may seem weird that "Yankee" is in the name, but Yankee Lobster is a New England institution, so the name stays. And if you want some **New England clam chowder** (the type with milk or cream), that's also at a few stands across the stadium (Big Concourse, Home Plate Concourse, right-field roof deck).

If America runs on Dunkin', Boston zooms on the stuff. **Dunkin' Donuts** (Big Concourse, Gate E concourse, Cumberland Deck) is the official coffee of Beantown, and it's available throughout the park.

Tully Tavern (right-field grandstand, $35-75 per game) doubles as a specialty bar and a ticketed seating area. Drink Tullamore D.E.W. Irish whiskey while sitting on barstools and watching the game. There are TVs and charging stations at the tavern, too.

Hit up any of the beer stands for rotating brews from **Sam Adams,** plus **26.2 Brew,** a lighter beer made with sea salt and coriander, from Marathon Brewing. You can also find local stalwart **Harpoon IPA.** But that's about it—Fenway keeps things light in the craft lane.

Over on Jersey Street, next to the team store, is **The Bullpen** (19-20 Jersey St., 617/247-3353, hours vary based on game days and times), which is open before, during, and after Sox games. You can enter via an alley off Brookline Avenue or via Jersey Street, then you'll head underground into a vast sports bar where you can throw down a couple Sam Adams beers with your buds. Tip: When you're ready to enter the park, go to the Bullpen's alley entrance on Brookline and have a beer, then head for the front door at Jersey Street. There, they'll scan your ticket

and get you into the game. No fuss, no muss, and a drink while you get ready. Another awesome point: You can come into the bar during the game, then return to your seat when you're done.

EVENTS

The Sox host a former player, coach, or personality at **Autograph Alley** (Jersey Street Team Store) before every home game, where John Hancocks are given for free.

For those thinking about taking a spring trip to Fenway, you may want to consider **Patriots' Day** (third Mon. in Apr.), a holiday in the Commonwealth of Massachusetts that commemorates the first battles of the American Revolution. On this day, the city of Boston shuts down and becomes a veritable playground. First, there's the annual running of the Boston Marathon, which proceeds through a good portion of the city, passing near Fenway Park at Kenmore Square. Then there's a Red Sox game at 11am. The early start time was scheduled in 1969 so that fans could see the finish of the marathon after the game, but today the men's winner crosses during the game. It's a pretty eventful fete throughout the city. Drinks flow, cookouts are encouraged, and spirits are certainly high. It's a pretty awesome day.

Tours

There are myriad **tours of Fenway Park** that fans can take. First is the **public tour** (9am-5pm daily non-game days Apr.-Oct., 9am-three hours before first pitch game days Apr.-Oct., 10am-5pm Nov.-Mar., $21, $15 ages 3-12). On it, a docent will tell you Sox history while showing you landmarks like Pesky's Pole and the Green Monster—you'll get to stand up there, too.

Fenway in Fifteen (noon-3pm daily non-game days May-Sept., noon-four hours before first pitch game days May-Sept., $15) takes fans on a whirlwind 15-minute tour that includes a visit to the Nation's Archives (as in Red Sox Nation, the team's fan club) at the Royal Rooters Club and Right-Field Roof Deck.

You can also take a **Pregame Tour** (three hours before first pitch game days only, $35-45), which includes a visit onto the warning track and stops in the grandstand and on top of the Green Monster.

SHOPPING

Like everything else at Fenway, the **Official Red Sox Team Store** (19 Jersey St., 617/421-8686, www.19jerseystreet.com, 9am-5pm Mon.-Sat., 10am-4pm Sun., and during games) has a lot of personality. The store is across the street from the park and was founded back in 1947 by Boston-raised brothers Henry and Arthur D'Angelo. Their knack for creating and selling Sox gear soon turned into the nationally known brand '47, so there's a lot of that merchandise here. Of course, you'll see the standard Sox T-shirts, jerseys, toys, bobbleheads, and plenty of hats here, and the stuff ain't cheap. Since the store is on Jersey Street, ticketholders can stop in during the game, but it gets packed then (and before games, too), so consider visiting during off hours.

BOSTON SIGHTS

HUNTINGTON AVENUE AMERICAN LEAGUE BASEBALL GROUNDS

The Red Sox have played at just two home ballparks since they began as a team in 1901: Fenway Park and the **Huntington Avenue American League Baseball Grounds** (Forsyth St. and World Series Way), which was built in two months in 1901. The latter closed after the 1911 season and was destroyed just a year later, but a few things happened there: The Americans (the original nickname of the Red Sox) won the 1903 World Series behind a 28-9 season from Cy Young, then took the 1904 AL pennant, and in 1907 debuted a 19-year-old outfielder named Tris Speaker, who'd go on to record 3,514 hits and enter the Hall of Fame as the greatest doubles hitter of all time. Today the grounds are in the middle of the Northeastern University campus, marked by a plaque and a statue of Young, who recorded 192 of his 511 career wins with the Sox.

Ballpark plaque completists will also want to visit **Nickerson Field** (Braves Field Way and Harry Agganis Way). Today it's home to Boston University track and field, lacrosse, and other sports, but between 1915 and 1952, it was Braves Field. Here, the Boston Braves played in the National League, winning one pennant in 1948. Also, the longest game in major league history, a 26-inning affair between the Braves and Dodgers in 1920, happened here ... ending in a tie. You'll find a plaque here by walking up Harry Agganis Way to Braves Field Way. All that exists of the old park are the concourses under the grandstand.

THE FREEDOM TRAIL

For an essential Boston experience, walk the **Freedom Trail** (www.thefreedomtrail.org), a host of monuments, historic sites, and markers that tell the story of Beantown's role in the American Revolution. You can do the trail via a **guided tour** (Boston Common Visitor Information Center, 139 Tremont St., 11am, noon, and 1pm daily, $12, $10 seniors and students, $6.50 ages 6-12, free ages 5 and under), which will last 90 minutes and hit all the important spots, or you can do it yourself by following the dark red line on the sidewalk and street. This line is the trail itself, connecting sites like the **Old North Church** (193 Salem St., 617/523-6676, www.oldnorth.com, 9am-6pm mid-Apr.-Oct., 10am-4pm Nov.-mid-Apr.); **Bunker Hill Monument** (43 Monument Sq., 617/242-7275, www.nps.gov, 10am-5pm daily); **Old State House** (206 Washington St., 617/720-1713, www.boston-history.org, 9am-5pm daily, $12, $10 seniors and students, free ages 18 and under), which served as the backdrop of the Boston Massacre; and **Paul Revere House** (19 North Sq., 617/523-2338, www.paulreverehouse. org, 9:30am-5:15pm daily mid-Apr.-Oct., 9:30am-4:15pm Tues.-Sun. Nov.-mid-Apr.,

$5, $4.50 seniors and students, $1 ages 5-17, free ages 4 and younger). Walking the Freedom Trail is a great way to get your historical fill of Boston in a few hours.

FANEUIL HALL MARKETPLACE

Beyond City Hall and just before the waterfront and North End is the historic **Faneuil Hall Marketplace,** popularly known by its two main attractions, Faneuil Hall and Quincy Market.

Faneuil Hall (4 S. Market St., 617/523-1300, www.faneuilhallmarketplace.com, 10am-9pm Mon.-Sat., 11am-7pm Sun.) opened in 1743 to be the centerpiece of Boston commerce and community. It's where Samuel Adams voiced concerns about the tyranny of the British monarchy, and where local politicians worked and gathered. It's also where enslaved people were bought and sold. The Hall is very much a symbol of the United States, and it's a highly popular tourist attraction, with folks in colonial garb leading tours and street musicians welcoming visitors. Walk in to see the Hall as it would have looked in the late 18th century—or just take some snaps of the iconic redbrick exterior.

Exit Faneuil Hall from the back and you'll be just in front of **Quincy Market** (4 S. Market St., 617/523-1300, www.quincy-market. com, 10am-9pm Mon.-Sat., 11am-7pm Sun.), an indoor food and gift marketplace built in 1823, and another major tourist attraction. Quincy Market is home to more than 100 shops, many of them food focused. If you have kids and need a pit stop with tables, chairs, and nearby bathrooms, head to the centrally located food court under a great dome. This attraction is first and foremost made for tourists to spend a few hours shopping in controlled chaos. Make a point to walk through it once.

While at the market, you may be drawn in by the sight of **Cheers** (1 Faneuil Hall Marketplace, 617/227-0150, www.cheersboston.

Photos (from top to bottom): Boston's Museum of Fine Arts; the Freedom Trail; Faneuil Hall.

com, 11am-10pm Sun.-Thurs., 11am-11pm Fri., 11am-midnight Sat., under $50). Yes, the bar area looks a bit like what you saw on the iconic TV show, and yes, there is a fair amount of memorabilia to be found (look for Sam Malone's Red Sox jacket). But lower those expectations—this is essentially a crowded tourist trap. It's better to head toward Beacon Hill to find the exterior of the location that you saw on TV. (See *Other Neighborhoods* in *Food* for more details.)

MUSEUM OF FINE ARTS

Not as grandiose as, say, the Metropolitan Museum of Art in New York, Boston's **Museum of Fine Arts** (MFA, 465 Huntington Ave., 617/267-9300, www.mfa.org, 10am-10pm Wed.-Fri., 10am-5pm Sat.-Tues., $25, $23 seniors and students, $10 ages 7-17, free ages 6 and under) nonetheless has a well-curated and wide collection of art from across the world. And it's quite close to Fenway Park—just a 10-minute walk south from the ballpark via the Back Bay Fens. The MFA splits its art by global region, with a small wing dedicated to contemporary art. The Americas collection is wonderful, including pieces of local interest, like John Singleton Copley's painting of Paul Revere, plus works by John Singer Sargent and Frida Kahlo. The museum hosts semi-regular events, including a cocktail party for ages 21 and older on the first Friday of each month.

JOHN F. KENNEDY PRESIDENTIAL LIBRARY AND MUSEUM

Looking for a fantastic half-day excursion? Learn about the life of America's 35th president at the **John F. Kennedy Presidential Library and Museum** (Columbia Point, 617/514-1600, www.jfklibrary.org, 9am-5pm daily, $14, $12 seniors and students, $10 ages 13-17), located south of Downtown on a peninsula shared by the Boston campus of the University of Massachusetts. The building is primarily concrete, highlighted by a sharp, angular tower, with a rectangular glass pavilion. The museum takes visitors through major phases and highlights of Kennedy's life, including his youth in the Boston area, his valor as a U.S. Navy lieutenant, his time as senator, the landmark 1960 presidential campaign, and his presidency. Special exhibits last six months or more. You'll also find paintings, gifts to and from the Kennedys, and some of Jacqueline Kennedy Onassis's clothing. The library holds Kennedy's original papers and correspondence, plus a large collection of papers by author Ernest Hemingway.

FOOD

NEAR FENWAY PARK

The most famous vendor around Fenway, parked on Lansdowne Street, is **The Sausage Guy** (49 Lansdowne St.). Dave Littlefield of South Shore suburb Hingham has been operating this stand since 1992, serving up sweet Italian, hot Italian (get that one), and other varieties of sausage before, during, and after Sox games. I'm especially fond of this spot, since Littlefield let me and a couple other folks huddle together and watch his TV during Game 4 of the 2004 ALCS, as Dave Roberts stole second base and the rest became history.

Let me tell you about the best plate of nachos I've ever eaten. They're the South of the Border nachos at **Sunset Cantina** (916 Commonwealth Ave., 617/731-8646, www.sunsetboston.com, 11am-1am Sun.-Thurs., 11am-2am Fri.-Sat., under $50), perfectly layered and covered with all the goods while maintaining that crispy base. Sunset is half sports bar, half drinking well for Boston University seniors and grad students, but it's always a good time, maintaining a decent beer list and better margarita list. When you order the nachos, be sure to add pulled pork.

Closer still to Fenway is the very fun **Hojoko** (1271 Boylston St., 617/670-0507, www.hojokoboston.com, 5pm-1am

Sun.-Wed., 5pm-2am Thurs.-Sat., under $40). This hotel-attached *izakaya*-style joint does small plates of Japanese pub grub in a funky setting with wood walls and an active bar. You can't go wrong with the cheeseburger.

For a wider variety of Asian fare, and a spot that expertly intersects tiki culture with art deco design, head to **Tiger Mama** (1363 Boylston St., 617/425-6262, www.tigermamaboston.com, 5pm-11pm Sun.-Thurs., 5pm-midnight Fri.-Sat., 11am-2:30pm Sun., under $50). Inside this neon space, you'll find cuisine from China as well as Southeast Asian locales like Thailand and Singapore, along with a menu of tiki drinks.

OTHER NEIGHBORHOODS

Wanna be a capital "T" tourist? Though the TV show *Cheers* was shot before a live studio audience in Los Angeles, the exterior shot of the pub showed a real bar in Boston. It happened to be the longtime Bull & Finch Pub, inside the very beautiful Hampshire House in the Beacon Hill neighborhood. In 2002, after years of being mobbed by tourists wanting to see the "location" of the famous series, the owner changed the name to **Cheers** (84 Beacon St., 617/227-9605, www.cheersboston.com, 11am-11pm daily, under $50). Go downstairs to sit at the bar, which is a replica of the famous TV set. That's right: You can grab that seat at the far end and be Cliff Clavin. The food here is pretty decent—burgers, sandwiches, pasta, and more, much of it named after the characters. Be warned, though. You're asking for a crowd if you're going on a weekend in the spring or summer.

You're in Boston: Get some oysters. Visit **Row 34** (383 Congress St., 617/553-5900, www.row34.com, 11:30am-10pm Sun.-Thurs., 11:30am-11pm Fri.-Sat., under $70) in the Seaport District for all the greatest oysters from New England, plus a stellar beer selection, great wine list, whole fish, burgers, and lobster rolls. It's a big place with high ceilings, and it's wicked fun.

For breakfast, hit up the **Friendly Toast Restaurant** (35 Stanhope St., 617/456-7849, www.thefriendlytoast.com, 7am-9pm Mon.-Thurs., 7am-10pm Fri., 8am-10pm Sat., 8am-8pm Sun., under $30) near the Back Bay neighborhood. You can also visit this all-day regional chain diner for lunch or dinner and take in the colorful seating and signage. The eggs Benedicts are a big hit.

For a more literary morning start, visit **Trident Booksellers & Café** (338 Newbury St., 617/267-8688, www.tridentbookscafe.com, 8am-midnight daily, under $30), which is part of bustling, shopper-friendly Newbury Street. Trident does big-time breakfasts all day, from sandwiches and waffles to its hearty egg plates and bowls. Even better: It's a bookstore, so find a bar seat or cozy table and eat while reading, taking notes, or conversing with a friend.

Cambridge

If you want to hop across the Charles River to check out well-educated Cambridge—home to both Harvard University and the Massachusetts Institute of Technology—my pick is the popular **Alden & Harlow** (40 Brattle St., 617/864-2100, www.aldenharlow.com, 5pm-1am Mon.-Wed., 5pm-2am Thurs.-Fri., 10:30am-2pm and 5pm-2am Sat., 10:30am-2pm and 5pm-1am Sun., under $50). This spot pulls off seemingly upscale plates of New England and American cuisine within a polished, urbane space, and all the food is very affordable. It's possible to have grilled fish for under $20.

For a cheap, collegial meal, try **Grendel's Den** (89 Winthrop St., 617/491-1160, www.grendelsden.com, 11:30am-midnight daily, under $25). It serves bigger plates like brisket with mashed potatoes, as well as sandwiches, salads, and burgers. The dimly lit eatery with brick walls is plenty inviting, and there are sure to be some *smaht* kids here to eavesdrop on.

North End

Boston's Little Italy, the North End is a must-visit for Beantown first-timers, if only to spend a night eating a fist-size breaded chicken dish and pasta before coffee and pastry. On warm nights, the narrow streets will fill up with performers and romancers, making for one of the more memorable and cozy areas in town. Because it's a high-tourism area, your best bet is to visit on a weeknight.

For many, a visit to **Regina Pizzeria** (11½ Thatcher St., 617/227-0765, www.pizzeriaregina.com, 11am-11:30pm Sun.-Thurs., 11am-12:30am Fri.-Sat., under $40) is mandatory. The 1926 shop making brick-oven pies is one of the best-known pizzerias in the United States. Snag a seat if you can inside the yellow-toned space, and order one of about 25 specialty pies, or make your own. The rest of the menu? That's it—just pizza and drinks (wine, beer, soda, water).

For a big dinner in the North End, you'll wrestle with tourist spots and overpriced pasta. My favorite experiences include the Peruvian and Italian combination at the upscale and cozy **Taranta** (210 Hanover St., 617/720-0052, www.tarantarist.com, 5pm-10pm daily, under $80), the first restaurant I ever made a reservation for. Around the block is **Neptune Oyster** (63 Salem St., 617/742-3474, www.neptuneoyster.com, 11:30am-9:30pm Sun.-Thurs., 11:30am-10:30pm Fri.-Sat., under $50), the very epitome of a New England raw bar with gorgeous white tile ceiling, subway tile walls, and all the oysters and wine you can handle. For a refined Italian pasta experience, try **TreMonte Restaurant & Bar** (76 Salem St., 617/530-1955, www.tremonterestaurant.com, 4pm-10pm Sun.-Tues., 4pm-10:30pm Wed.-Thurs., 4pm-11pm Fri.-Sat., under $50). The focus here is on the food, which is well priced compared to some of the more traditional, expensive fare on Hanover.

Since 1946, **Mike's Pastry** (300 Hanover St., 617/742-3050, www.mikespastry.com, 8am-10pm Sun.-Thurs., 8am-11pm Fri.-Sat., under $30) has been baking up some of the sweetest, most delectable Italian treats in the country. Most popular here are the cannoli (with more than 20 varieties), and boy, are they terrific. Come in and grab a peek at the colorful display cases, then get in line and prepare to order just about everything. Eat some there, and take the rest to go in the iconic white box with the white string. Try to visit early in the morning or late at night to avoid huge crowds.

But wait! There's another pastry spot just across the street from Mike's; people like it just as much, and its cannoli are also highly touted. This is **Modern Pastry** (257 Hanover St., 617/523-3783, www.modernpastry.com, 7am-11pm Sun.-Thurs., 7am-midnight Fri.-Sat., under $30), which has fancier digs thanks to its gorgeous green awning, a brick interior, and more dedicated seating space. You don't get as many types of cannoli, but the specialties (lobster tail pastry, anyone?) are fun. It's cash only here. Prepare for a line.

Before visiting Mike's or Modern for that end-of-night cannoli, opt for a cappuccino and tiramisu at **Caffé Vittoria** (290-296 Hanover St., 617/227-7606, 8am-midnight daily, under $20). The café opened in 1929 and hasn't lost any of its original charm. Admire the coffee machines at any of its three bars before grabbing a seat at a round-top. Like many North End haunts, the place can get crowded, so be choosy about when you visit (weekdays are always better).

BARS AND BREWERIES

NEAR FENWAY PARK

It's basically tradition that before a game (or after), you stop in for a drink at the **Cask 'n Flagon** (62 Brookline Ave., 617/536-4840, www.casknflagon.com, 11am-1am Sun.-Wed., 11am-2am Thurs.-Sat.). Perpetually packed on game days, the bar is nonetheless the perfect place to get a sense of the people, since the pub is right across the street from the park's Green Monster. There's good elevated bar food here, from pizzas to burgers (the Fenway is good), but if you're just going for a beer and to hang out on the patio, I'm with you.

Picture this: You grab a beer, then walk a couple steps and stand … in the outfield of the ballpark? **Bleacher Bar** (82A Lansdowne St., 617/262-2424, www.bleacherbarboston.com, 11am-1am Sun.-Wed., 11am-2am

Thurs.-Sat.) is accessible from Lansdowne and looks out onto Fenway at center field beneath the bleachers. If you're going anytime around a game, there will be a line and the place will be packed. But if you can, get in there and enjoy a beer while gazing out the large garage door at, well, the whole field. You're on ground level beyond the warning track in center field, so if you get in before a game, you'll be just feet from outfield practice. It's an incredible experience.

Not too long ago, a number of nightclubs lined Lansdowne Street behind Fenway Park. But in recent years, the area has been re-created with chain bars and music venues. The best spot on the new Lansdowne is the **Lansdowne Pub** (9 Lansdowne St., 617/247-1222, www.lansdownepubboston.com, 4pm-2am Mon.-Fri., 11am-2am Sat.-Sun.). This is a modern-day Irish pub, without all the dirt and rawness but with live music and drink specials.

So many fun memories have been made at **The Dugout Café** (722 Commonwealth Ave., 617/247-8656, noon-2am Mon.-Sat.), more familiarly known as "Le Duj-oh." This is a serious dive. Walk down the steps into this basement bar and revel in pitchers of beer, cheap pizza, and free popcorn while the games are on. The booths are comfy, the crowd can either be bumping or paltry, and it feels like home.

As much as it is a college bar town, Boston is known for breweries, too. **Trillium Brewing Company** (401 Park Dr., 857/449-0078, www.trilliumbrewing.com, 11am-11pm Sun.-Wed., 11am-midnight Thurs.-Sat.) remains a necessary stop for beer lovers. Go to its Fenway neighborhood location, inside shopping-and-entertainment spot Landmark Center, for a taproom experience. Despite the crowds here, it's worth it to try a couple New England IPAs.

Photos (from top to bottom): Cheers in Beacon Hill; Samuel Adams Boston Brewery; New England Aquarium.

OTHER NEIGHBORHOODS

A bespoke cocktail bar called **Drink** (348 Congress St., 617/695-1806, www.drinkfortpoint.com, 4pm-1am daily), accessible through a pseudo-secret door and down some stairs, where you give the bartender your flavor preferences instead of a specific drink order, has to be satire, right? Somehow, though, this spot in the Seaport District avoids being a punch line, probably because the drinks are so darn good and the vibe is so effortless. Give the mixologists an idea of what you want to drink and they'll go for it. It's a great place to go after (or before) a nice dinner. People love it here, so it's best to visit on a weeknight, when there isn't the possibility of a line. Food is served; I suggest the burger, with its perfect brioche bun.

For the authentic Irish pub experience—since you're in the land of *The Departed, Good Will Hunting,* and *Mystic River*—head to **Brendan Behan Pub** (378 Centre St., 617/522-5386, www.brendanbehanjp.com, noon-1am daily), named after the famous Irish novelist and playwright. There's a dark and cozy vibe here, live Irish music on Saturday evenings, and a draft list that includes Guinness (naturally), plus a whole lot of exceptional beers. Don't expect an onslaught of Irish culture; the atmosphere is more of a friendly dive. This Jamaica Plain spot is cash only.

My favorite brewery in the Boston area is **Night Shift Brewing** (87 Santilli Hwy., Everett, 617/294-4233, www.nightshiftfamily.com, 11am-11pm Mon.-Sat., 11am-8pm Sun.). With a pretty big taproom that has televisions, games, merchandise, and a long bar setup, Night Shift makes a perfect day-drinking destination. Plus, it does dark beers well. The brewery is in Everett, a city just north of Boston. You can get there by taking the T's Orange Line (get off at Wellington station, then walk 15 minutes, crossing the Malden River).

If you're a beer fan, you have to pay homage to the originator of the modern movement. The **Samuel Adams Boston Brewery** (30 Germania St., 617/368-5080, www.samueladams.com, 11am-5pm Mon.-Sat.) opened in 1988 and has since become the largest independent brewery in the United States, breaking ground for thousands more craft brewers along the way. Visit the brewery in Jamaica Plain for a tour that includes tastings, then hang out in the taproom (11am-8pm Mon.-Sat., noon-6pm Sun.), which showcases both tried-and-true styles and experimental varieties.

If you're up in Cambridge, get thee to **Lamplighter Brewing Co.** (284 Broadway, Cambridge, 617/945-0450, www.lamplighterbrewing.com, 11am-10pm Sun.-Mon., 11am-midnight Tues.-Sat.). The taproom looks right into the brewhouse, so you can watch the team work while you sip their product. Attention to detail is great here, and the bar with its honeycomb tile panel is quite cute. The front of the house includes a coffee shop with plenty to drink and morning grub like breakfast tacos.

RECREATION

NEW ENGLAND AQUARIUM

Boston's best kid hang is the **New England Aquarium** (1 Central Wharf, 617/973-5200, www.neaq.org, 9am-5pm Mon.-Fri., 9am-6pm Sat.-Sun., $32, $30 seniors, $23 children), home to the largest shark and ray touch tank on the East Coast, plus fur seals and Myrtle the Green Sea Turtle, an over 90-year-old reptile that weighs more than 500 pounds. You can take behind-the-scenes tours of the aquarium and experience animal encounters, during which you can get up close to harbor seals.

PARKS

Boston Common

Established in 1634, **Boston Common** (139 Tremont St., 5am-11pm daily) is the city's public green space, a 50-acre parkland for lounging, walking, skating, and cycling. Previously a cow pasture and a British camp before the American Revolution, it now has a little for everyone. The Frog Pond, in the middle of the park, has a spray pool that operates during the summer; elsewhere, softball fields host games when the weather is warm. Look for multiple monuments, including the Boston Massacre Monument, also known as the Crispus Attucks Monument, signifying the death of five men, including Attucks, at the hands of the British. Attucks's death marked the beginning of the events that would lead to the American Revolution. The Massachusetts State House faces the Common's northeastern end.

Boston Public Garden

Just across the street from the western end of Boston Common is the **Boston Public Garden** (4 Charles St.), one my absolute favorite places. This simply devised park is the first public botanical garden in America, with winding, interconnected pathways. A major feature of the park is the pond at its center, in which you can ride in **Swan Boats** (617/522-1966, www.swanboats.com, 10am-4pm daily Apr.-late June, 10am-5pm daily late June-Labor Day, $4, $3.50 seniors, $2.50 children). A driver will do all the work as you sit back and cruise around the pond for 15 minutes. While at the park, also look for the *Make Way for Ducklings* **installation,** celebrating the official children's book of Massachusetts, in which the Public Garden plays an important role.

TOURS

You can go whale-watching while in Boston. **Boston Harbor Cruises** (1 Long Wharf, 617/227-4321, www.bostonharborcruises.com, 7am-8pm daily, under $60) offers a tour that begins by the New England Aquarium and heads out to Stellwagen Bank National Marine Sanctuary to look for whales, dolphins, and other creatures. Other tours include a trip north toward Bunker Hill and the USS *Constitution,* and a trip on *Codzilla,* a 70-foot speedboat that can turn on a dime and is designed to get you wet.

One way to see the city in an unusual manner is by taking a trip via **Boston Duck Tours** (www.bostonducktours.com, Mar.-Oct., $46, $37 seniors and military, $31 ages 3-11, $10.50 ages 2 and under). These half-truck, half-boat transports drive on the streets past major attractions and head into the Charles River to give guests a different view of the city. The tours are pricey, and you're bound to have to "quack" at people when you pass them. Tours depart from three spots in the city, including the New England Aquarium.

SHOPPING

Around Fenway, but not affiliated with the Red Sox, are a couple baseball shops. There's a **Baseballism** (71 Landsdowne St., 857/315-5823, www.baseballism.com, 10am-6pm daily) across from the park. They sell what I call "baseball lifestyle" clothing and accessories, worn to show people you like the sport. They don't have a license to use MLB logos, so their hats, shirts, and other merch like small backpacks can't sport the official Red Sox logo or name, but they do present a vague idea of the team and city.

Inside Faneuil Hall Marketplace is **I Love Boston Sports** (1 N. Faneuil Hall Marketplace, #370, 617/531-3521, www.ilovebostonsports.com, 10am-8pm Mon.-Sat., 10am-7pm Sun.). This pro-Beantown store offers a few witty pieces of clothing and wall prints. They're not licensed, though, so don't expect official merch here.

Nearby is **Roster** (Marketplace Center, 200 State St., 617/737-1091, http://rosterstores.com, 10am-9pm Mon.-Sat., 11am-7pm Sun. spring-fall, 10am-7pm Mon.-Thurs., 10am-9pm Fri.-Sat., noon-6pm Sun. winter). This store is a good place to find licensed women's gear (that isn't just pink) from brands like '47, Mitchell & Ness, New Era, and more. There are plenty of jerseys here, too. Find V- or scoop-neck shirts, hats, and hoodies representing all Boston pro teams. Men's apparel is also available here, including tanks and baseball-style shirts.

ACCOMMODATIONS

Finding an affordable place to stay close to the action in Boston can be nearly impossible. From September to June, the city is crawling with college students, whose families visit on weekends. Add the usual tourism, and prices get jacked up quite a bit. In summer, it's no different: Between even more tourism, conventions, college visits, and out-of-town Sox fans, there are few cheap hotel rooms left. My advice is to get rooms well in advance, consider staying outside of the inner city, and don't scoff too much when you see a nightly rate higher than $300. It's typical.

A few other options: Stay close to Logan International Airport or even farther out in Winthrop Beach; for these areas, you're best off having a car. If you're steadfast on staying close to Downtown Boston, but you really don't want to pay much, there are a few chain hotels with cheaper rates.

NEAR FENWAY PARK

Hotel Commonwealth

Just around the corner at Kenmore Square is the **Hotel Commonwealth** (500 Commonwealth Ave., 617/933-5000, www.hotel-commonwealth.com, $200-300), which really leans into the Fenway experience. Some of the priciest rooms here include the Baseball Suite, with themed artwork, books, and in-room memorabilia; the Fenway King, which offers a view into the park from its balcony (though it's hard to see the field); and the Fenway Park Suite, which has a slightly better view from its balcony and also has chairs from the park, along with take-home gifts like dirt from Fenway. The ground floor of the hotel includes **Eastern Standard** (528 Commonwealth Ave., 617/532-9100, www.easternstandardboston.com, 7am-2am daily, under $70). Inside what once was legendary punk club the Rathskeller, Eastern Standard offers upscale food and environs for the everyday crowd, along with a heck of a cocktail list.

The hotel has a number of **Red Sox packages** that include game tickets, even Monster Seats. Get the **Bucket List package** that has two seats right above the dugout, a VIP tour, a visit to the top of the Green Monster, a signed baseball from a Sox legend, a scoreboard message during the game, a welcome basket, a $100 gift card to the team store, and accommodations in either the Fenway Park or Baseball Suite; the price starts at $2,500.

Then there's the **Knuckle Sandwiches package:** For a price starting at $10,000, get Monster Seats, autographed swag, a personalized scoreboard message, a VIP tour, accommodations in a Fenway-facing room, and the opportunity to have lunch with a Sox great, knuckleballer Tim Wakefield. This is for the lifelong Sox fan with money to burn.

OTHER NEIGHBORHOODS

There are plenty of upscale hotels in Boston, including the Omni Parker House, Copley Square, the Bostonian, and the Boston Park Plaza—just reserve a room well in advance and know that a lot of these accommodations will cost upward of $600 a night. For something slightly cheaper, try the **Godfrey Hotel** (505 Washington St., 617/804-2000, www.godfreyhotelboston.com, $300-500), just a block from Boston Common in the heart of the city. King and queen rooms are available.

If your budget isn't so high, opt for a less-expensive alternative like the **Midtown Hotel** (220 Huntington Ave., 617/262-1000, www.midtownhotel.com, $125-250). Don't expect four-star amenities here, but rooms are comfortable and service is friendly, and you're less than a mile walk from Fenway Park and the Boston Public Garden.

You could consider staying well outside Downtown Boston, yet still close to a T line. There's the **Inn at Longwood Medical** (342 Longwood Ave., 617/731-4700, www.innatlongwood.com, $150-350), just a four-block walk from the Longwood Green Line station (and only a mile walk to Fenway). The room decor is a bit dated, but everything is clean and comfy here.

GETTING AROUND

PUBLIC TRANSIT

I highly recommend getting around Boston via the **MBTA** (www.mbta.com, $1.70-2 bus, $2.40-2.90 subway), best known as **the T.** It's a good system that reaches all the necessary tourist spots, plus there are multiple stops near Fenway Park. Lines are color-coded and extend from the center of the city like tentacles. The Green Line is the main west-east route that offers a connection to hub stations like **Government Center** (Tremont St. and Court St.) and **Park Street** (Tremont St. and Winter St.). Farther west, it breaks into four routes that run through major college campuses and outlying neighborhoods like Allston-Brighton. The Orange Line runs southwest to north, connecting to the **Back Bay station** (Stuart St. and Dartmouth St.), which is used by Amtrak, and heading north through Downtown. The Red Line goes south to northwest; it's best for heading across the Charles River and venturing into Cambridge (Harvard University) and Somerville. The Blue Line starts in Downtown Boston and heads northeast, reaching notable stops like **Aquarium** (State St. and Atlantic Ave.) and **Airport** (Transportation Way and Service Rd.). Finally, the Silver Line is a system of bus routes that includes shuttle service inside Logan International Airport.

Stations to know include Government Center, Park Street, **State** (Water St. and Devonshire St.) and **Downtown Crossing** (Washington St. and Summer St.). At least two lines stop at each of these, and the stations are all walkable from one another, in case you need to change routes.

TAXI, UBER, AND LYFT

Lyft and Uber are generally cheaper than taxis in Boston by a couple dollars per ride. None of the taxi operators are strong enough for me to recommend. Lyft and Uber are similar in cost. I'd still take public transportation

if possible, but if you can't, either major ride-sharing service works.

CAR

So, you've decided to drive in Boston. This is an old city that has a little of just about everything. In Downtown and the historic areas, each neighborhood has its own unique street layout, and nothing is uniform. As the city expands into the Back Bay and South End, you'll find a more standard city-block layout, though some major boulevards and avenues run diagonally, dividing neighborhoods. As for highways, they're not to be found inside the heart of the city, thanks to a 15-year project completed in 2007 and known as the Big Dig, which moved the highways underground and created a system of tunnels into and through the North End and Downtown.

The major north-south artery **I-93** comes in from the north as the Northern Expressway, passing over the Charles River via the triangular, postmodern Leonard P. Zakim Bunker Hill Memorial Bridge. Then it goes underground, running along the harborside until coming back up past South Station in South Boston.

Major east-west artery **I-90** starts in Boston, coming off **MA-1A** in East Boston near Logan International Airport. I-90, which is also the **Massachusetts Turnpike,** or **Mass Pike,** immediately goes underground and becomes the Ted Williams Tunnel. I-90 continues under the Seaport District and Fort Point, comes up for air in Chinatown, then heads back underground and under street level through the Back Bay section of the city. It flies right past Fenway Park heading west, through Boston University and into Allston-Brighton, then through the rest of the state. The Mass Pike is a **toll road,** and the charges are collected electronically. If you're renting a car, be sure to ask how they process tolls.

Along the Charles River in Boston is **Storrow Drive,** which offers a direct route from western neighborhoods like Allston to Downtown, though traffic here is especially slow during rush hours.

THE CAPE COD LEAGUE

For many college baseball players, heading to southeastern Massachusetts offers a wealth of opportunity in the summer. **The Cape Cod League** (www.capecodbaseball.org, June-mid-Aug.) was established in 1885. It became NCAA-sanctioned in 1963, meaning enrolled college players in NCAA programs are permitted to participate, as long as they have at least one year of eligibility remaining and have attended at least one year of school. It's also a wood-bat league, helping big-league hopefuls get familiar with the stick after using metal bats for so long. Because of the Cape Cod League's strong reputation, the competition is pretty good—some fans will tell you that it's like watching double-A baseball. Each team in the league tends to have a couple players who become big-leaguers within a few years.

The 10 teams in the league each play a 44-game schedule. Games occur nearly every day, generally beginning between 4pm and 7pm. A three-round postseason finishes the season in August. All games are free, but donations are welcome; all you need to do is bring a lawn chair or a blanket and pull up at a designated seating spot. During the game, players may come by and ask for donations—and maybe even stop for a chat.

Here's a list of the 10 Cape Cod League parks:

- **Clem Spillane Field** (54 Marion Rd., Wareham), home to the Wareham Gatemen
- **Doran Park** (Upper Cape Cod Regional Technical School, 220 Sandwich Rd., Bourne), home to the Bourne Braves
- **Eldredge Park** (78 Eldredge Park Way, Orleans), home to the Orleans Firebirds
- **Guv Fuller Field** (790 Main St., Falmouth), home to the Falmouth Commodores
- **Lowell Park** (10 Lowell Ave., Cotuit), home to the Cotuit Kettleers
- **McKeon Field** (120 High School Rd., Hyannis), home to the Hyannis Harbor Hawks
- **Red Wilson Field** (Dennis-Yarmouth Regional High School, 210 Station Ave., South Yarmouth), home to the Yarmouth-Dennis Red Sox
- **Stony Brook School** (384 Underpass Rd., Brewster), home to the Brewster Whitecaps
- **Veterans Field** (702 Main St., Chatham), home to the Chatham Anglers
- **Whitehouse Field** (75 Oak St., Harwich), home to the Harwich Mariners

In Downtown Boston and in the North End, streets take circuitous routes. From this area going west, street layouts are easier to follow. **Beacon Street** spans from Boston Common and the Massachusetts State House in the east to the city of Newton, west of Beantown. This major street is just north of Fenway Park and provides a boundary for Kenmore Square. Other major east-west streets include **Commonwealth Avenue, Boylston Street,** and **Huntington Avenue.** Major north-south arteries include **Massachusetts Avenue,** which separates the Back Bay from the Kenmore and Fenway areas; **Charles Street,** which provides the western boundary of the Boston Common; and the combination of **Cambridge Street** and **Tremont Street,** the former coming off the Longfellow Bridge into Downtown Boston from the north, and the latter extending from it and heading south, snaking the Boston Common and providing a boundary for the South End.

NEW YORK CITY
YANKEES AND METS

New York City's reputation precedes it. It's the largest city in America and the world's fifth-largest urban area. Broken into five boroughs and home to more than 8 million people, New York is an important tourist destination, a center of finance and commerce, and a transportation hub. It's also home to two Major League Baseball franchises, whose reputations also precede them.

Moving from Baltimore in 1903 and originally named the Highlanders, New York's American League baseball team was first called the Yankees in 1904. The name stuck, and ever since, the franchise has been baseball's most successful and storied, winning a record 27 world championships and giving us a host of first-name figures: Babe, Lou, Joe, Mickey, Yogi, Mariano, and Derek.

Babe Ruth is the biggest of those names.

Purchased from the Red Sox in 1919, Ruth was already baseball's premier slugger, but with the Yankees he became a legend clad in navy pinstripes. Superb hitter Lou Gehrig came next, ushering in the first Yankee dynasty. That bled right into the years of Joe DiMaggio, America's sweetheart hitter, who kept the titles coming through the 1940s. Mickey Mantle and Yogi Berra were next. Between 1923 and 1962—40 seasons—the Yankees won exactly half the championships.

While the Yankees won it all in 1962, new neighbors the Mets lost nearly all the time. Their history starts with attorney William Shea, who wanted to get more baseball in New York after the National League's Dodgers and Giants both left for the West Coast in 1957. Shea began forming the Continental League, which would be separate from the American and National Leagues. Eventually, the National League agreed to add two teams for '62, and Shea took the reserved New York spot meant to replace the void created by the Dodgers' and Giants' exits. At first, the Mets stank, losing a record 120 games in their inaugural season. But just seven years later, the Mets made an incredible run. The 1969 Miracle Mets, as they were known, captured a world championship off the backs of star pitchers Tom Seaver and Jerry Koosman.

The Mets would get back to the World Series in 1973. That was also the year the Yankees' fortunes began to turn again. Between the '65 and '73 seasons, the Yanks failed to reach the postseason, but a group of investors led by George Steinbrenner bought the Yankees in January '73. "The Boss," as he was called, pushed out the other members of the group by the end of the season. Steinbrenner promised a return to glory; that came just four years later, as the 1977 Yanks won their 21st title, thanks in part to the heroics of slugger Reggie Jackson. They'd repeat in 1978 before falling into an era of big spending and small returns.

Neither New York team would see success again until 1986, when the Mets' mix of veteran excellence and young athleticism

carried them to their second championship. The Yanks returned to the promised land after building a stellar core of players in the 1990s, most notably shortstop Derek Jeter and relief pitcher Mariano Rivera. Between 1996 and 2000, the pinstripes would hoist the trophy four out of five times. While the Mets had some solid seasons in the late 2000s, they were more known for choking than winning big games, becoming something of a punchline. The Yanks would get one more championship in 2009, and the Mets returned to the World Series in 2015 but failed to beat the Royals.

Through history, the Yankees have been the straitlaced, machinelike success with their navy and gray, no-nonsense look, their sparkling stadiums, and their legendary talent. The Mets, meanwhile, play the role of a lovable clown that, once in a while, surprises the heck out of everyone. While Yankees fans expect their team to always be competitive, Mets fans just hope they can hold their heads high by the end of the season. And yet both teams have rich histories, multifaceted characters, and a special quality that makes them absolutely perfect for their massive city. The Yankees are the city's bold swagger, and the Mets are all the anxieties screaming beneath the surface. What a city.

Allow yourself to embrace New York just as many embrace its teams. Walking up and down the streets of this city can be one of the most exhilarating and lively experiences you'll have. You're among millions of people moving to a special rhythm. Download some high-energy and uber-positive songs. Sing and dance while you walk, if you feel the urge. Let that rhythm take you over.

PLANNING YOUR TIME

You could stay in New York for two weeks and not even scratch the surface of what the city has to offer, but that may be too much time away. Although a **week** is ideal, you can pack in a mix of major sights and under-the-radar hangouts over **4-5 days.** Spend one

Previous: Yankee Stadium

day hitting the big tourist attractions (Times Square and Broadway, Central Park, Brooklyn Bridge), one day visiting a neighborhood or two in Manhattan, another day focused in Queens, and a fourth day focused in Brooklyn. You can easily add more days—a second day in any borough, more time in the Bronx, a day out to the Statue of Liberty and back, a day at Coney Island—but whatever you do, don't try to see all of New York in a day or two. You'll wear yourself out.

If you plan to visit the **Statue of Liberty,** block off a full day for it and don't plan anything else. It takes a while to get there and back (including lines for the ferry), and you'll want to rest and play it simple afterward. If you don't get a **Broadway** ticket in advance, plan on spending some time waiting for a ticket, either at the box office or a TKTS booth.

New York is great between **May and September,** with evenings especially great for baseball. Beware of day games deep in the summer (June-August), as temperatures can and will climb into the 90s with high humidity. If you're planning on visiting in **March** or **April,** or **late in the season** (or **postseason**), bring layers. Temperatures for those night games early and late in the season can sink into the 40s. Also, it'll rain in April and May.

If you're hoping to catch both the Yankees and Mets at their respective ballparks in one trip, you should keep in mind that they're **almost never home at the same time.** It's best to book a trip where you catch one of the teams on a Saturday or Sunday, and the other on a Monday or Tuesday.

So where should you stay? **Manhattan** is pricey, but it's the best bet for getting around and seeing the most sights. Just be ready to pay up. **Midtown** and **Lower Manhattan** have plenty of hotels, and the **Upper West Side** is a pretty great place to score a deal. **Downtown Brooklyn** and **Williamsburg** are obvious hot spots, and **Long Island City** in Queens is getting more and more tourism. For something out of the way, consider the **South Bronx** or even **Hoboken, New Jersey,** as long as you're close enough to the train station.

Many bars close at 4am in New York, so taking a 10pm nap before going out can be a good idea.

GETTING THERE

AIR

John F. Kennedy International Airport

The largest and most-trafficked airport in the area is **John F. Kennedy International Airport** (JFK, JFK Expressway and I-678, Queens, 718/244-4444, www.jkfairport.com), resting at the edge of Jamaica Bay in Queens. Nearly every major international carrier flies in and out of JFK. Domestically, JFK is home to **American Airlines** (800/433-7300, www.aa.com), **Delta** (800/221-1212, www.delta.com), and **jetBlue** (800/538-2583, www.jetblue.com).

AIRPORT TRANSPORTATION

To get out of JFK and into the city, you have some options.

Option one: Take the **subway.** Hop on the **AirTrain** ($7.75) to connect to **Jamaica station** (E, J, and Z lines) or **Howard Beach station** (A line), which are operated by the **MTA** (Metropolitan Transportation Authority, http://new.mta.info, $2.75 base per ride). From there, you'll be able to connect to locations in Manhattan, Queens, and Brooklyn. This process will take some time (anywhere from 25 minutes to an hour), so be patient. However, it's the best option, especially if you're packing light and you're not in a hurry.

Option two: You can grab a **rental car** by visiting counters at each terminal (every major rental agency is represented), then taking the **AirTrain** (free) to **Federal Circle station** to pick up the car. This, as you can tell, is a process. Moreover, driving in New York City is not for the faint of heart, so consider an alternative.

Option three: You can hail a **taxi** or **ride-sharing vehicle.** Both are plentiful, but be ready to pay. Cabs will cost at least $52 to Manhattan (flat fare), and $24 to parts of Queens. Ride-sharing services charge more than $50 per ride from JFK to Manhattan.

LaGuardia Airport

LaGuardia Airport (LGA, I-278 and LaGuardia Rd., Queens, 718/533-3400, www.laguardiaairport.com) is on the other side of Queens from JFK, closer to Manhattan. Serving LaGuardia are **Air Canada** (888/247-2262, www.aircanada.com), **American Airlines** (800/433-7300, www.aa.com), **Delta** (800/221-1212, www.delta.com), **Frontier** (800/432-1359, www.flyfrontier.com), **jetBlue** (800/538-2583, www.jetblue.com), **Southwest** (800/435-9792, www.southwest.com), **Spirit** (801/401-2222, www.spirit.com), and **United** (800/864-8331, www.united.com). Unless you're going to or coming from Canada or the Caribbean, you're flying domestic here. LaGuardia is the Southwest hub in New York.

AIRPORT TRANSPORTATION

The problem with LaGuardia is that the only connection to the **subway** is a **bus** operated by the **MTA** (http://new.mta.info, $2.75 base per ride). Your best bet is to take the **M60 bus** to the **31st St./Astoria Blvd. subway station** (31st St. and Astoria Blvd., Queens). It's cheaper than the alternatives, which include picking up a **rental car** via shuttle or hopping in a **taxi** or **ride-share vehicle.** Taxi rides start at $3. From 8am-6pm daily, a $0.50 surcharge is added, and from 4pm-8pm weekdays, a $1 surcharge is added.

Newark Liberty International Airport

Newark Liberty International Airport (EWR, 3 Brewster Rd., Newark, NJ, 973/961-6000, www.newarkairport.com) is across the Hudson River in New Jersey and offers flights from **Air Canada** (888/247-2262, www.aircanada.com), **Allegiant (**702/505-8888, www.allegiantair.com), **American Airlines** (800/433-7300, www.aa.com), **Delta** (800/221-1212, www.delta.com), **Frontier** (800/432-1359, www.flyfrontier.com), **jetBlue** (800/538-2583, www.jetblue.

com), **Spirit** (801/401-2222, www.spirit.com), **United** (800/864-8331, www.united.com), and **Virgin Atlantic** (800/862-8621, www.virginatlantic.com). Newark is a major United hub and is also served by many international carriers.

AIRPORT TRANSPORTATION

To take public transportation, you'll have to grab the **AirTrain** ($7.75) to **Newark Liberty Airport station.** From there, it's a ride on **New Jersey Transit** ($15.25, www.njtransit.com) to **New York Pennsylvania Station** (31st St. and 8th Ave.), one of the city's major rail hubs smack in the middle of Manhattan. The train ride to Penn Station is about 25 minutes.

Rental cars are available by taking the AirTrain to the rental car center, home to all major companies. Or you can take a **taxi** or **ride-share vehicle,** but be ready to pay at least $50 to get into Manhattan. Staying in Jersey? You're probably paying $25-35.

CAR

The drive from **Boston** to New York can take **3.5-4.5 hours,** and that's if traffic is moving at a relatively steady pace. There are a handful of routes you can take. The fastest, usually, is **I-90 West** to **I-84 West** to **I-91 South** to **CT-15,** also called the **Merritt Parkway,** a scenic road that cuts through Connecticut and doesn't allow trucks. This route is **220 miles.** Another way is via I-90 West to I-84 West to **I-684 South,** for a total of **230 miles.**

As you enter the greater New York metropolitan area, the highway layout is confusing. To stick to major highways, head to **I-87,** which runs south right into New York City. If you want a more scenic route that won't include trucks, there's the **Hutchinson River Parkway** (later **I-678**); that'll get you into Queens (near Citi Field) via the Whitestone Bridge. If you want to head into Manhattan from there, keep on I-678 and follow signs for the **Grand Central Parkway,** because that'll get you over the East River via the Robert F. Kennedy Bridge (also called the Triborough Bridge).

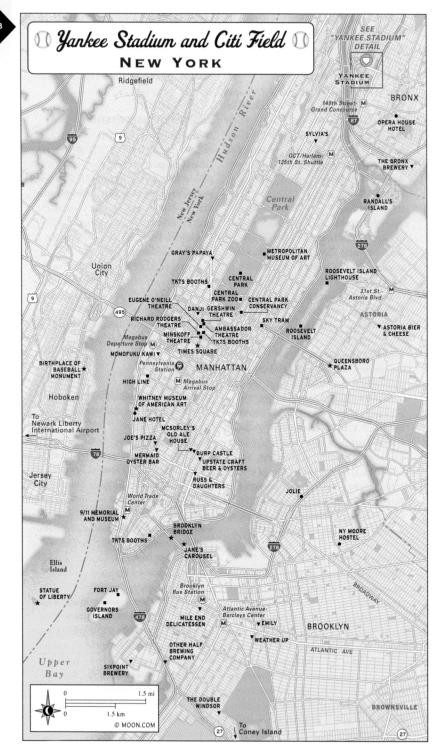

🔘 *Yankee Stadium and Citi Field* 🔘
NEW YORK

SEE
"YANKEE STADIUM
DETAIL"

YANKEE
STADIUM

Ridgefield

BRONX

Hudson River

149th Street-
Grand Concourse

OPERA HOUSE
HOTEL

SYLVIA'S

GCT/Harlem-
125th St. Shuttle

THE BRONX
BREWERY

New Jersey
New York

Central
Park

RANDALL'S
ISLAND

Union
City

GRAY'S PAPAYA

METROPOLITAN
MUSEUM OF ART

ROOSEVELT ISLAND
LIGHTHOUSE

TKTS BOOTHS

CENTRAL
PARK

31st St.-
Astoria Blvd.

EUGENE O'NEILL
THEATRE

CENTRAL
PARK ZOO

CENTRAL PARK
CONSERVANCY

ASTORIA

DANJI

GERSHWIN
THEATRE

ASTORIA BIER
& CHEESE

RICHARD RODGERS
THEATRE

SKY TRAM

MINSKOFF
THEATRE

AMBASSADOR
THEATRE

ROOSEVELT
ISLAND

Megabus
Departure Stop

TKTS BOOTHS

MOMOFUKU KAWI

TIMES SQUARE

QUEENSBORO
PLAZA

BIRTHPLACE OF
BASEBALL
MONUMENT

Pennsylvania
Station

MANHATTAN

HIGH LINE

Megabus
Arrival Stop

Hoboken

WHITNEY MUSEUM
OF AMERICAN ART

To
Newark Liberty
International Airport

JANE HOTEL

MCSORLEY'S
OLD ALE
HOUSE

JOE'S PIZZA

BURP CASTLE

MERMAID
OYSTER BAR

UPSTATE CRAFT
BEER & OYSTERS

Jersey
City

RUSS &
DAUGHTERS

JOLIE

World Trade
Center

9/11 MEMORIAL
AND MUSEUM

NY MOORE
HOSTEL

TKTS BOOTHS

BROOKLYN
BRIDGE

Ellis
Island

JANE'S
CAROUSEL

STATUE
OF LIBERTY

FORT JAY

Brooklyn
Bus Station

BROADWAY

GOVERNORS
ISLAND

Atlantic Avenue-
Barclays Center

MILE END
DELICATESSEN

EMILY

BROOKLYN

OTHER HALF
BREWING
COMPANY

WEATHER UP

ATLANTIC AVE

Upper
Bay

SIXPOINT
BREWERY

0   1.5 mi

0   1.5 km

THE DOUBLE
WINDSOR

BROWNSVILLE

© MOON.COM

To
Coney Island

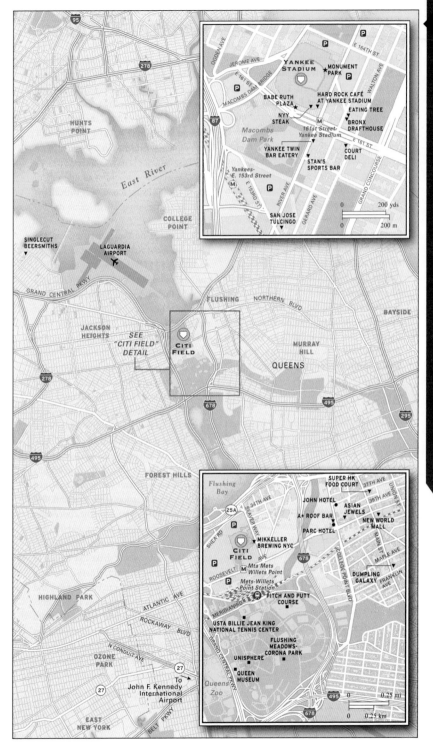

Inset — Yankee Stadium area:

OGDEN AVE
E 164TH ST
JEROME AVE
P
YANKEE STADIUM
MONUMENT PARK
P
WALTON AVE
E 161ST ST
MACOMBS DAM BRIDGE
P
BABE RUTH PLAZA
HARD ROCK CAFÉ AT YANKEE STADIUM
EATING TREE
87
NYY STEAK
BRONX DRAFTHOUSE
Macombs Dam Park
M
161st Street-Yankee Stadium
COURT DELI
E 161 ST
YANKEE TWIN BAR EATERY
RIVER AVE
GERARD AVE
GRAND CONCOURSE
STAN'S SPORTS BAR
Yankees-E. 153rd Street
M
E 153RD ST
0   200 yds
SAN JOSE TULCINGO
0   200 m

Main map:

95
278
HUNTS POINT
East River
COLLEGE POINT
SINGLECUT BEERSMITHS
LAGUARDIA AIRPORT
GRAND CENTRAL PKWY
FLUSHING
NORTHERN BLVD
BAYSIDE
JACKSON HEIGHTS
SEE "CITI FIELD" DETAIL
CITI FIELD
MURRAY HILL
QUEENS
278
678
495
295
FOREST HILLS
495
HIGHLAND PARK
ATLANTIC AVE
ROCKAWAY BLVD
OZONE PARK
N CONDUIT AVE
27
27
To ▶
John F. Kennedy International Airport
Queens Zoo
EAST NEW YORK
BELT PKWY

Inset — Citi Field detail:

Flushing Bay
SUPER HK FOOD COURT
37TH AVE
25A
34TH AVE
SEAVER WAY
JOHN HOTEL
39TH AVE
UNION ST
ASIAN JEWELS
A+ ROOF BAR
NEW WORLD MALL
PARC HOTEL
CITI FIELD
MIKKELLER BREWING NYC
678
COLLEGE POINT BLVD
MAIN ST
MAPLE AVE
P
ROOSEVELT AVE
M
Mta Mets Willets Point
Mets-Willets Point Station
DUMPLING GALAXY
FRANKLIN AVE
MERIDIAN RD
PITCH AND PUTT COURSE
USTA BILLIE JEAN KING NATIONAL TENNIS CENTER
GRAND CENTRAL PKWY
FLUSHING MEADOWS-CORONA PARK
UNISPHERE
QUEEN MUSEUM
495
678
0   0.25 mi
0   0.25 km

TRAIN

There are plenty of ways to get to New York via **Amtrak** (www.amtrak.com), which stops at **New York Pennsylvania Station** (31st St. and 8th Ave., Manhattan). The always-busy **Acela** and **Northeast Regional** ride the same rail, but the Acela is faster and more expensive. With multiple trips a day, these trains offer an easy option to get from Boston to New York. Rides start at about $70 and take up to 4.5 hours.

Additional routes that stop at Penn Station include the **Carolinian** (New York to Charlotte), **Crescent** (New York to New Orleans), **Empire Service** (New York to Niagara Falls), **Lake Shore Limited** (New York to Chicago), **Pennsylvanian** (New York to Pittsburgh), **Adirondack** (New York to Montreal), **Ethan Allen Express** (New York to Rutland, VT), **Maple Leaf** (New York to Toronto), **Vermonter** (St. Albans, VT, to Washington DC), **Cardinal** (New York to Chicago), **Keystone Service** (New York to Harrisburg, PA), and **Silver Service** (New York to Miami).

BUS

Traveling by bus is an affordable way to get to New York. If you're taking **Greyhound** (www.greyhound.com), a ride starts at $15 from Boston, and you'll arrive at the **Port Authority Bus Terminal** (625 8th Ave., Manhattan). If you're staying in Brooklyn (especially near Park Slope, Prospect Heights, Red Hook, Fort Greene, or Clinton Hill), consider taking a Greyhound to the **Brooklyn bus station** (206 Livingston St., Brooklyn).

You can also take **Megabus** (http://us.megabus.com) from Boston. The ride starts at $30 and drops you off at the **Megabus arrival stop** (27th St. and 7th Ave., Manhattan). If taking Megabus out of New York, board at the **Megabus departure stop** (34th St. between 11th Ave. and 12th Ave.).

Yankee Stadium

The Cathedral. The Bronx Zoo. The House That Ruth Built. Wait… that was the previous incarnation. Yankee fans may tell you that this is the House That Jeter Built, but whatever they call it, it has the same name: **Yankee Stadium** (1 E. 161st St., www.mlb.com/yankees). It opened in 2009 just a block from the famous old one. Compared with its predecessor, the stadium is an upgrade in importance, a living monument with all the amenities—including a hefty game-day bill for fans.

Yankee Stadium is a crucial component of the character of New York City. Outside, the stadium is all Indiana limestone and arched cutouts, calling to mind a modernized version of a Roman temple. Inside, it looks conspicuously like the old Yankee Stadium, but straightened out a bit. Two decks rise from the right-field foul pole and wind around to the left-field pole, while the outfield backdrop is gray stone, big advertisements, and a stark scoreboard some 500 feet from home plate. The key outfield dimensions take after its older, late sibling. Similarly, the fence in right field (referred to as "the short porch in right") is pushed in so that a 315-foot fly ball out there can get over. A gorgeous white frieze (broadly known as "the facade") juts out from the roof over the upper deck, just like at the first version of the stadium. But the hallways are wider here, the concession choices are robust (and pricey), and the construction is so sound and flawless that the upper deck just doesn't shake like it used to on a chilly October night. (That's a shame.)

Still, if any ballpark can be expensive and boastful, this is the one. This palace suits baseball's crown franchise. Even though it's a little cold, unlike the squeezed-in environs of the House That Ruth Built, you still feel an aura when walking about this ballpark. It's proof there's nothing in sports like Yankee Stadium.

YOUR BEST DAY AT YANKEE STADIUM

Tonight it's you and Yankee Stadium. Awesome, right? You have a full day in the city ahead of you—let's make it count.

11 HOURS BEFORE FIRST PITCH
Today you'll have an iconic New York experience, including major tourist attractions and popular spots. Take the subway to **Brooklyn Bridge-City Hall station** (Centre St. and Park Row, Manhattan) so you can walk the length of the **Brooklyn Bridge.** This is great early morning exercise, too!

9 HOURS BEFORE FIRST PITCH
Hop on the F train and head back into Manhattan, destination **Russ & Daughters.** You gotta get a bagel. With lox, naturally.

8 HOURS BEFORE FIRST PITCH
Walk west toward Lafayette Street, then head up to Bleecker Street to get on a northbound 4, 5, or 6 train. Your next stop is a few hours at the **Metropolitan Museum of Art** in Central Park. Spend some time checking out the European paintings, but don't forget the rare armor and African art.

5 HOURS BEFORE FIRST PITCH
Now that you've walked off that bagel, grab a late lunch at **Sylvia's.** Fill up on fried chicken or shrimp and catfish.

3 HOURS BEFORE FIRST PITCH
Walk west to the 125th Street station for the A/C and B/D lines. Take a B or D train north to **161st Street-Yankee Stadium station** (161st St. and River Ave.). Once you've arrived, grab a beer at the **Bronx Drafthouse.** If you want more of a sports-

Russ & Daughters

bar experience, head to **Stan's Sports Bar.**

1.5 HOURS BEFORE FIRST PITCH
Head inside Yankee Stadium and make a beeline for **Monument Park.** After spending some time paying respects to the greats, take a walk to the **Great Hall.**

DURING THE GAME
Grab dinner at **Lobel's.** See if you can sneak into the bleachers, even for a few minutes. Meet new folks at the **MasterCard Batter's Eye Deck.**

AFTER THE GAME
Head back into Manhattan for beers at **McSorley's Old Ale House** and nearby **Burp Castle.** Later at night, when it's not so crowded, check out the bright lights of **Times Square** (42nd St. and Broadway).

Need one last bite? Get thee to **Gray's Papaya** for a late-night hot dog. If that isn't close enough, any spot with "papaya" in the name will do.

ORIENTATION

Yankee Stadium lives at the intersection of River Avenue and 161st Street, just like the former version, a few blocks from the Harlem River and the Metro-North train tracks. It's on an island of sorts, though it's within screaming distance from lower- and middle-class homes, elementary schools, and the regular rhythms of the Boogie Down Bronx.

There are four entry gates at Yankee Stadium—2, 4, 6, and 8. They are located at the north, south, east, and west ends of the park. Gates open 90 minutes before first pitch for 6:35pm games. For all other games, Gates 6 and 8, and both the Babe Ruth Plaza and Suite Entrance, will open two hours before first pitch.

Yankee Stadium

TICKETS AND SEATING

Pricing

Unlike essentially every other ballpark in baseball, the Yankees don't go overboard with dividing their seating into sections with various pricing levels. That said, some games will definitely have **higher ticket prices** than others. For instance, if you're trying to go to a Yankees versus **Red Sox** duel, deemed a **premium game,** be ready to pay up to 150 percent more than what you'd pay for, say, an Orioles game. An average seat for an O's contest might be around $40, while that same seat for a Red Sox game might be more like $100. Other teams that cause the Yankees to push the "premium game" button include the **Mets** and sometimes the **Cubs, Dodgers,** and **Phillies.**

Seating Plan

The stadium's lowest level has two specific areas: the **champions suites** (sections 11-13, 27B-29) are on the farthest ends of the first- and third-base lines, approximately at mid-outfield distance. Around home plate are the **legends suites** (sections 14A-27A). These are seriously expensive, cushioned seats with full wait service, a private entrance, and inclusive food and nonalcoholic drinks. They seem to be filled only for the most important games.

Just above that is the **100 level.** From the lower right-field seats all the way around the foul area to the lower left-field seats, you have the **field seats** (sections 103-136).

The lowest area of the second deck is part of the **200 level** and called **main** (sections

205-217 and 223-234); in the outfield, the 200 level is the **bleachers** (sections 201-204 and 235-239). In center field, groups can sit in the **batter's eye seats** as part of the **MasterCard Batter's Eye Deck.**

Between the 200 and 300 level are the **luxury suites** (1-67) and, in the left-field corner, the **Audi Yankees Club.** The home plate area of the 200 level is where you'll find the **Delta Sky 360 suites** (sections 218A-222).

The highest level of the second deck is the **300 level,** broken up into the **terrace** (sections 305-316 and 324-334) and, around home plate, the **Jim Beam suites** (sections 317-323), which offer cushioned seats.

The top deck at the stadium is the **400 level,** and from the right-field foul pole around the foul area to the left-field pole, it's called the **grandstand** (sections 405-434B).

The Yankees reserve **sections 407A and 433** in the grandstand level for those who'd like to enjoy the game **alcohol-free.**

Where to Buy Tickets

Despite the high price of Yankee tickets, you can still find deals on third-party reseller websites like **SeatGeek,** at least for nonessential games. A 200-level seat can be had for about $20, which is a terrific price. **StubHub** is the Yankees' official reseller, so prices will generally be higher, but you can also have full trust that your ticket is legitimate. It's worth it to try the indirect seller route before buying a ticket through the team itself. A deal can be had.

If you do buy a ticket through the Yankees (or Ticketmaster), you can upgrade your seat at the **Yankee Stadium Ticket Office** (Gate 4) up to two hours before first pitch of the game.

Best Seats

If you're trying to save money on your ticket, you can find a seat in the **bleachers** or the **grandstand** for a decent price. If you're a big-time fan and want a true Yankee Stadium experience, the bleachers really bring it home. There, you'll be among the loudest and proudest of pinstripe fans, called the **bleacher creatures.** I've done both the left- and right-field bleachers (as not a Yankees fan), and it's a trip. (The right side is the rowdiest.)

That said, the bleachers will cook you during an afternoon game, as the stadium's open layout makes it akin to a grill top. If you're looking for any **shade** whatsoever, the back rows of the first-base and right-field line of the 100 level (**sections 107-116**) can provide relief. Otherwise, bear with it, or just go to a night game.

Other fun fan spots include standing at a rail at the **MasterCard Batter's Eye Deck** (center field, 200 level), where craft beer and cocktails flow and everyone is having a good time. It's open to all ticketholders.

If you want a **stellar view** and don't mind paying just a little for it, look for seats in the main section, preferably between **sections 223 and 232B,** or if you're hoping for shade, between **sections 208 and 217.**

If you're at Yankee Stadium for the first and possibly only time in your life, you could splash out and get that seat in the **Delta Sky 360 suites.** Just make sure you have enough friends to fill the suite.

KNOW BEFORE YOU GO

The Yankees allow **bags** if they're at most 16 by 16 by 8 inches, plus one smaller, soft **personal item.** You can bring in a single-serve unopened container of a **nonalcoholic beverage** if it's in a carton or plastic bottle. Empty plastic **water bottles** are also allowed.

Strollers are allowed in, but the big ones have to be checked in and stored at **Guest Relations and Ticket Sales** (Gate 6, Great Hall).

Finally, the Yankees are one of the only teams I know with a clearly stated **dress code:** Clothing deemed to be obscene is not allowed.

Accessibility

The Yankees are ahead of the curve when it comes to making the stadium more accessible for fans. You can contact **Disabled Services** (Yankee Stadium Lobby at Gate 2, 718/579-4510) for assistance either before heading to the park or speak to someone in person once you arrive.

For help with hearing, seeing, and experiencing the game in the best way possible, the Yankees offer a few options. These include **induction loops** at places like concession stands, ticket windows, and other areas; a few different types of **assistive listening devices** (Guest Relations, free if you leave ID); **Braille** and **large print schedules** (Disabled Services, Guest Relations); **sensory kits** (free if you leave ID or a credit

GAME COSTS

Tickets: Among the most expensive in baseball. Sure, you can sit in the grandstand for **$15** or the high outfield for **$35,** but if you want a decent seat in the 200 level, you'll pay more than **$60.** Want a 100 level seat? Be prepared to pay **$100** or more.

Hot dog: These are pricey. It's possible to find a **$3** hot dog at a Nathan's stand, but most dogs at the stadium will start at around **$6.**

Beer: You can find **$6** beers, but they're not craft. Those are more like **$12** (and there aren't many of them).

Parking: What do you think? Expensive, with rates usually hitting **$30** to park near the stadium.

BE A FAN

jubilant Yankees fans

Yankees fans can be boisterous and brash. I've sat in the bleachers at Yankee Stadium twice as a non-Yankee fan: In 2009 I was wearing head-to-toe Phillies gear for a tilt against Philadelphia, and in 2015 I attended the American League wild card game with my brother-in-law, who was decked out in opposing Astros gear. On both occasions there was playful banter, but it was otherwise all good. The trick is to laugh things off, play along, and try not to argue with the hundreds of Yankees fans around you. (If you do happen to witness or be part of anything unseemly, find a security guard immediately.)

When you go to Yankee Stadium, pay attention to the **bleachers** in the top of the first inning. It's tradition at the stadium to do **"roll call."** Everyone in section 203, in unison, yells out whatever they're calling each Yankee player, starting in the outfield, then going around the diamond from first to third. The fans continue chanting at a player until he turns and acknowledges the bleacher creatures. It's very cool. I got chills being among the couple thousand fans chanting "DER-EK JE-TER" as the Captain lifted his glove, causing a round of cheers.

Finally, Red Sox fans know that they and Yankees fans are like oil and water. If you wear **Sox gear** at Yankee Stadium, just be ready for the insults and vitriol, and try to keep your cool. **Mets fans** get a more tempered reaction, while fans of nearby kind-of-rivals like the **Orioles, Blue Jays,** and **Phillies** may get more patronizing smiles than glares.

The Yankees are the only team in baseball that plays **"God Bless America"** at every game, doing so before "Take Me Out to the Ballgame" during the seventh-inning stretch. And if the Yankees win, you'll undoubtedly hear Frank Sinatra's classic 1980 version of **"Theme from *New York, New York."*** No matter where you land on the fandom spectrum (except Sox fans), you can't help but sing along.

---

card) for both kids and adults, containing fidget toys, noise-canceling headphones, and sunglasses; and **wheelchair** and **scooter storage** (Guest Relations, or contact nearest security personnel).

If you want to secure a **wheelchair taxi** before and/or after the game, call the **Accessible Dispatch Program** (646/599-9999, www.accessibledispatch.org). There's also a **smartphone app** called Accessible Dispatch NYC.

Elevators are located at **Gate 2** (for access to the main and terrace/grandstand levels, visitors with disabilities only), **Gate 4** (access to Great Hall Landing, visitors with disabilities only), the **Great Hall** (access to main and terrace/grandstand levels, all visitors), **Gate 6** (access to New York Yankees Museum, visitors with disabilities only), and **Gate 8** (access to field level and bleachers, all visitors).

Parking is another story. Try for one of the limited **designated accessible** spots in any of the parking lots around the stadium. A **New York City-issued accessible parking permit** must be visible in the car. If you'll be **renting a car,** contact the agency in advance to inquire about getting a permit. If you have your own car, you'll need to **apply by mail** for a visitor/tourist version of the permit. (See www1.nyc.gov for more information.)

GETTING THERE

Subway

The best way to reach Yankee Stadium is via the **subway** (http://new.mta.info, $2.75 base per ride). The trains that take you there include the **B** (orange), **D** (orange), and **4** (green). The B line is a rush-hour, weekday-only train that runs between Brighton Beach in Brooklyn to the Bronx. The D line travels from Coney Island in Brooklyn up to 205th Street in the Bronx. The 4 train starts in Crown Heights, Brooklyn, then runs along Lexington Avenue on the east side of Manhattan, up to Woodlawn in the Bronx. From any of these trains, exit at the **161st Street-Yankee Stadium station** (161st St. and River Ave.).

Metro-North

A surefire way to get to the park quickly is by using **Metro-North Railroad** (http://new.mta.info), the MTA's aboveground train system. Join legions of fans wearing pinstripes on Metro-North's **GCT/Harlem-125th Street Shuttle** (from $14) to **Yankees-East 153rd Street station** (153rd St. near River Ave. and 157th St.) in the Bronx. This train starts at **Grand Central Terminal** (42nd St. and Park Ave., Manhattan), then heads north, arriving at the stop for Yankee Stadium about 15 minutes later. It's a 10-minute walk to the stadium from there. Service begins about three hours before first pitch; the return route ends about two hours after the likely final out time. Metro-North allows its riders to drink beer on the train, so don't be surprised if your fellow fans are indulging on the ride.

If you're staying north of the city, Metro-North's **Hudson Line** stops at Yankees-East 153rd Street station starting about three hours before first pitch. After weekday afternoon games, Metro-North employs a train called the **Yankee Clipper,** which leaves three hours and change after the final out and zips up the line, making few stops. There's no direct route to Yankee Stadium for folks riding Metro-North's Harlem and New Haven Lines. These riders should disembark at **Harlem-125th Street station** (125th St. and Park Ave., Manhattan) and then hop on a Hudson Line train north to Yankees-East 153rd Street (for no extra fee).

Driving

If you want to drive to Yankee Stadium, well, good luck. The closest highway is **I-87,** or the **Major Deegan Expressway,** which will be backed up at any time of day. You could take the **Harlem River Drive** to 135th Street, then take that over to Adam Clayton Powell Jr. Boulevard up to the Macombs Dam Bridge, which will drop you right in front of the stadium; but again, you're in for loads of traffic. An alternate route is to take I-87 to the **Grand Concourse,** then drive that north to 161st Street, but there will be traffic on that route, too.

Want to park near the stadium? You're in the hands of **City Parking** (718/588-7817, www.cityparking.nyc), which operates the many parking lots and garages around the venue. Costs start at $25. For bigger games, expect those prices to rise dramatically. If you park farther away from the stadium, you'll be able to save $10 or so. Consider lots like the **380 East 162nd Street Garage** and **AD Parking** (Elton Ave. and 163rd St.). You'll have to walk up to a mile to the ballpark from these spots, however.

PARK FEATURES AND SIGHTS

Outside the stadium, you can check out **Babe Ruth Plaza** (between Gates 4 and 6), but it's essentially a brick and concrete walk marked with a plaque and a very small detailing of the Great Bambino's career. Baltimore does him much more justice with its museum.

Take the kids to the **Plymouth Rock Kids Clubhouse** (right field, 300 level). It has a miniature baseball field, plus oversize baseball-themed playground equipment. There's also a 6-foot-tall replica of a World Series trophy. (What, they couldn't lend the kids one of their 27 real ones?) A shaded area keeps the sun away, while nursing mothers have a private space to feed and rest.

Great Hall

Gate 6 is the most popular entrance into the stadium. It'll drop you in around right field at the foot of the **Great Hall** (100 level, right field to home plate), which is essentially a 31,000-square-foot postmodern shopping mall that's meant to simulate a wide Manhattan avenue. In the crowded hour before first pitch, it will certainly feel like one. The hall also features high ceilings, enormous banners showing Yankee stars past and present, and a 24- by 36-foot high-definition video board.

Monument Park

There's nothing like **Monument Park** (center field, open with gates and closed 45 minutes before first pitch). Back in the old Yankee Stadium, the team put up heavy red granite blocks studded with bronze plaques to honor great coaches and players like Miller Huggins, Lou Gehrig, and Babe Ruth. The blocks surrounded a flagpole in deep center field (in play) until the 1970s, when renovation moved the monuments behind the outfield fence. In the current Yankee Stadium, Monument Park includes six of those red granite blocks—reserved for Huggins, Gehrig, Ruth, Joe DiMaggio, Mickey Mantle, and George Steinbrenner—plus retired numbers and plaques for 19 more folks, and plaques for another 11 people. An additional plaque is dedicated to the remembrance of the September 11, 2001, terrorist attacks. If you want to visit Monument Park, get there as the gates open, as the line can get long.

New York Yankees Museum

You should definitely visit the **New York Yankees Museum** (main level, section 210, open 90 minutes before first pitch and closes after eighth inning, free). Permanent exhibits include all the Yankees' world championship trophies since 1977 (that would be six) and the locker used by Thurman Munson, the leader of the mid-1970s Yankee teams who died in a plane crash during the 1979 season. Specialty exhibits rotate through every few years.

FOOD AND DRINKS

Yankee Stadium has a steak house! It's called **NYY Steak** (1 E. 161 St., Gate 6, 646/977-8325, www.nyysteak.com, generally opens

Photos (from top to bottom): Great Hall at Yankee Stadium; Monument Park; Yankees team store.

one hour before gates on game days, 11am-11pm Mon.-Sat., 11am-10pm Sun. non-game days, under $150), and it's open year-round. While most ballpark restaurants go overboard with team colors and logos, NYY Steak has wood walls and bronze mirrors on the ceilings. Of course, there are televisions, too, and quite a bit of Yankee memorabilia upon which to gaze. As a traditional steak house, it serves USDA prime New York strip, bone-in strip, and rib eye, plus mashed potatoes, creamed spinach, and lobster macaroni and cheese. Lobster tail, Canadian salmon, and lump crab cakes are also on offer. A decent selection of wines from France and Napa Valley round out the menu. There are better steak houses, and more affordable ones; but if you're a Yankee fan or just want the experience of a ballpark steak house, check it out. Get a reservation ahead of time (up to 15 days before), and don't worry about a dress code: T-shirt and jeans is just fine.

A bit more casual, and still a thing after all these years, is the **Hard Rock Café at Yankee Stadium** (1 E. 161 St., Gate 6, 646/977-8888, www.hardrock.com, 10am-one hour after end of night games, 10am-7pm Mon.-Thurs., 10am-8pm Fri.-Sat., 10am-6pm Sun. day games during season; 11am-7pm Fri., 11am-5pm Sat.-Thurs. off-season). You probably already know what you're getting at the Hard Rock: big portions of elevated bar food like burgers and sandwiches, plus USDA choice steaks. There are rock and roll artifacts to be seen, like one of outfielder/musician Bernie Williams's guitars, plus a giant guitar signed by musicians and players.

The top concession at Yankee Stadium is **Lobel's** (section 133, 321), the only place to get food from one of New York's most revered butcher shops, whose location on Madison Avenue in Manhattan is a destination for those wanting top-quality meat. At the stadium, Lobel's produces a USDA prime steak sandwich and burger, plus a meat-loaf burger that's seriously tasty. Head to the location on the first level to watch butchers cut the meat used throughout the stadium. That'll get you hungry.

The fried masterpiece of the stadium is found at **Big Mozz** (section 127). The Big Mozz is, well, a big mozzarella stick with garlic, parsley, and pecorino romano cheese on the outside. Inside is salty, creamy Wisconsin mozzarella.

Those wanting some wine (and grub to go with it) should check out **City Winery** (sections 105, 112), the ballpark outpost of this popular New York-based concert venue and restaurant chain. They pour bottles primarily from Napa Valley and pair them with burgers and fries.

If you're at the **MasterCard Batter's Eye Deck** (center field, 200 level), you may want to grab a maple chicken sandwich or roast beef po'boy. When in doubt at Yankee Stadium, get beef.

If you need something quick, head to the **Pepsi Food Court** (sections 125-127B). With plenty of seating and televisions showing the game, you won't miss much. If you're going to get one thing here, go for the Celebration Shake, a milkshake topped with miniature cupcakes. Sugar rush!

Yankee Stadium carries a ton of Anheuser-Busch InBev beers, which means Budweiser and its sister brands. You may see Pinstripe Pils from Blue Point Brewing Company and think it's a craft brew, but Blue Point is also owned by AB InBev. The point is this: Yankee Stadium is not good for craft beer. You can find an option from Brooklyn Brewery, Bronx Brewery, and Catskill Brewery in sections 110, 217, and 320, but that's it for local craft.

EVENTS

Fans can watch **batting practice** from just about any seat in the park until 45 minutes after the gates open or until guests arrive with tickets for the seat you're occupying. The Yankees have no official policy on **autographs,** so try to get down to field level in the **100 level** at least an hour before the game starts. You might get lucky.

For those wanting a big ol' dose of Yankees history, the team has been celebrating **Old-Timers' Day** (typically June) consistently since 1947. On this day, a host of former Yanks are introduced and then split into two teams for a fun exhibition game. In the early years of the event, players who made their bones with other franchises were honored along with Yankee greats, but since the 1980s it's been a Yankee-only affair. The game starts about three hours ahead of the regularly scheduled Yankees contest that day.

Tours

Want a closer look at the stadium? The Yankees conduct **tours** of varying sizes. The **classic tour** (Hard Rock Café, Gate 6, 161st St. and River Ave., 646/977-8687, every 20 minutes 11am-1:40pm daily, except days with 1:10pm and 4:05pm home games, $20-25, $20-23 seniors and ages 14 and under, free ages 3 and under) may take folks to the New York Yankees Museum, Monument Park, the press box, and, sometimes, the dugout.

The **pregame tour** (Gate 6, 646/977-8687, $40) is a guided look at the museum and Monument Park, with a finale that includes watching batting practice from section 105 (in the short porch in right field). There are several tour departure times; these vary based on when the game starts.

You can experience **Hands on History** (Gate 6, 646/977-8400, 90 minutes before gates open, $125), a chance to get as close as it gets to iconic Yankees memories. You're taken to the New York Yankees Museum, where the curator gives you a historical rundown. Then you put on some latex gloves and get the opportunity to touch artifacts like Mickey Mantle's 1963 contract, Babe Ruth's 1922 bat, a home plate from the original Yankee Stadium, Lou Gehrig's 1938 jersey, and the jersey Derek Jeter wore when striking his 3,000th career hit. This experience does not include a game ticket, which must be purchased separately. You have to go to the game to do Hands on History.

SHOPPING

The main **Yankee Stadium Team Store** (1 E. 161st St., Gate 6, 646/977-8777, 10am-5pm Mon.-Sat., 10am-4pm Sun.) is set inside the Great Hall and has the usual fare of shirts, jerseys, hats, and memorabilia. Prices here are a bit higher, and the crowds will pack it in before a game. Go later in the game if you can. Also in the Great Hall is the **Home Plate Store** (home plate, 100 level), which has a similar collection of items. It should be less crowded than the main store.

Citi Field

When it was finally time to get the Mets out of Shea Stadium, they decided to stay right where they were, at the edge of Flushing Meadows Corona Park and close enough to LaGuardia Airport that the sound of jets taking off and landing could still be a regular occurrence during a ball game.

But since the Mets were created in part to fill the void left by the Dodgers and Giants, and memories of those teams remained strong for some New Yorkers (including the Mets' ownership), **Citi Field** (41 Seaver Way, www.mlb.com/mets) was designed with those teams in mind. The facade is reminiscent of the one at the Dodgers' old Ebbets Field, while the seats are Polo Grounds green, nodding to the massive Manhattan ballpark that hosted the Giants. At first, this met criticism: Isn't this the Mets' park, after all? Sure, the old iconic Home Run Apple came over from Shea, but why make room for teams that left town back in 1957?

Here's the thing, though: With Citi Field embracing the entire New York baseball experience (not counting that other team in town), it positions the Mets as the every-fan's team. While the Yankees have all that pride and honor, the Mets are goofy, sometimes a confusing mess; but they're always New York's team. Citi Field's many features and quirks—the design, the seats, the apple, the Jackie Robinson Rotunda—it all represents New York.

Citi Field has aged very well. At first I scoffed at the wider concourses of the park, but in time I've appreciated them as New Yorkers zig and zag through like it's a busy

YOUR BEST DAY AT CITI FIELD

Today is about exploring Brooklyn and Queens—and indulging in the neighborhoods' copious food and drink options.

10 HOURS BEFORE FIRST PITCH
Either take the subway or walk the length of the **Brooklyn Bridge** by starting at **Brooklyn Bridge-City Hall station** (Centre St. and Park Row, Manhattan). Afterward, check out the waterfront and visit **Jane's Carousel.**

8 HOURS BEFORE FIRST PITCH
Grab an F train from the nearby York Street station and head to the Bergen Street station, then walk a couple blocks to **Mile End Delicatessen,** where you can enjoy a Montreal-style bagel or a smoked meat sandwich.

7 HOURS BEFORE FIRST PITCH
Continue on the F train outbound to Smith-9th Street, just a block from **Sixpoint Brewery.** It's beer o'clock, so try the double IPA.

5 HOURS BEFORE FIRST PITCH
Grab the G train toward Queens, stopping at Court Square to change over to the 7 to Queensboro Plaza. Take that to **Mets-Willets Point station** (Roosevelt Ave. and Seaver Way, Queens), but you're not going to Citi Field just yet. Instead, go into the heart of **Flushing Meadows Corona Park.** While you're there, learn a little something at the **Queens Museum** and re-create your favorite movie scene at the **Unisphere.**

3 HOURS BEFORE FIRST PITCH
Now it's time for **Citi Field.** Upon arriving,

Jackie Robinson Rotunda at Citi Field

visit **Mikkeller Brewing NYC** before taking a photo with the **Home Run Apple** and entering the park via the **Jackie Robinson Rotunda.**

1.5 HOURS BEFORE FIRST PITCH
Visit the **Mets Hall of Fame & Museum,** then get just about any food you could possibly want. If you're a first-timer, it's gotta be **Shake Shack.**

DURING THE GAME
Shop for some gear at the **Mets Team Store** and **The 7 Line.** Visit the **Jim Beam Highball Club** if you have a hankering for dumplings, then stop at **La Newyorkina** for a *paleta* (fruit-based popsicle).

AFTER THE GAME
Looking for some fancy cheese and upscale brews? Hop in a cab or ride-share vehicle and head to **Astoria Bier & Cheese** in Queens.

avenue. Moreover, the food and beer selections are outstanding, the fan experience is more intimate than at Yankee Stadium, and it's extremely accessible for city residents, as it's located just steps from the MTA's 7 line. While Shea Stadium will always have a place in New Yorkers' hearts for its no-frills, old-school charm, Citi Field shines as one of the better parks in baseball.

ORIENTATION

There are six entry gates at Citi Field, with three located along the left field line closest to the parking lots. You'll want to enter at the home-plate entrance, the **Jackie Robinson Rotunda,** as it truly is the best way to experience a Mets game from the start.

Gates at Citi Field open two hours before first pitch on Saturdays and Sundays; only the

Jackie Robinson Rotunda, Hodges Entrance, and ticket windows open two hours beforehand from Monday to Friday.

TICKETS AND SEATING
Pricing and Seating Plan

The Mets are among the many clubs that employ **dynamic ticket pricing** whenever they feel it's appropriate. That means for some games, seat costs will be a lot higher than for others. Pricey games include **special events** (home opener, holidays) and any time a **major rival** comes to town. When the Yankees play the **Mets** at Citi Field, tickets are 200 percent more expensive than a standard, non-rival game. Other major rivals that typically mean higher ticket prices include the **Phillies, Nationals,** and popular teams with traveling fanbases like the **Dodgers** and **Cubs.**

At Citi Field, you can't expect to pay a set price to sit in any one level. Here, seating levels are split into **subregions** with slightly different names and price points. For example, the **100 level** at Citi Field—starting from right center field and working in toward home plate—includes **field reserved** (sections 101-103); **baseline box** (sections 104-106); **baseline gold** (section 107) and **baseline silver** (sections 107-108); **field gold, silver,** and **box** (sections 109-110); **metropolitan platinum, gold, silver, bronze,** and **box** (sections 111-114); and **Delta platinum, gold,** and **silver,** and the **Hyundai Club** (sections 11-19 and 115-120). Then it goes back the other way toward left field, starting with **metropolitan platinum, gold, silver, bronze,** and **box** (sections 121-124); **field gold, silver,** and **box** (sections 125-126); **baseline silver** (section 127-129); **baseline gold** (section 128); **baseline box** (sections 130-132); and **field reserved** (sections 133-139). Finally, out in center field near the Home Run Apple, is **Big Apple reserved** (sections 140-142). Next to those seats is the **Citi Pavilion** (section 143).

This is a lot to digest, so let me break it down a bit for you. Take section 113: Metropolitan platinum is rows 1-2, the most expensive seats in the section. Just behind that is metropolitan gold, rows 3-6. Slightly lower in cost still is metropolitan silver, seats in rows 7-12. Seats in rows 13-22 are a little less, and they're part of metropolitan bronze. Finally, the seats in the back of the section (rows 23-31) are in metropolitan box and cost the least of any seats in the section.

Why so many sub-regions? It's because the Mets feel that if you're sitting in row six of section 113, you should have to spend more than the person sitting in the row right behind you. In short, the closer you are to the action, the more you'll pay, and sometimes it's by a matter of inches.

Let's continue. The **200 level** is reserved for **suites,** winding from the right-field line around to the left-field line. The **300 level** starts with the stand-alone **Coca-Cola Corner** (sections 301-305) in right field. Then, in foul territory working toward home plate, are **excelsior box** (sections 306-312) and **excelsior gold** (sections 313-325), which winds around the home-plate area. **Excelsior box** (sections 326-333) comes back along the third-base line and left-field line, and the left-field seats are the **Bud Light Landing** (sections 334-339).

The **400 level** and **500 level** together are the **promenade level.** (Citi Field, like many ballparks, splits up the top and bottom rows of the nosebleed seats, charging a different price for the two halves.) The 400 level, starting in foul right field, is **promenade box** (sections 401-410). Around home plate is **promenade gold** (sections 411-418); then the third-base line to left field and out toward center field is all **promenade box** (sections 419-437). In the 500 level, the seats along the right-field line are **promenade outfield** (sections 501-505); then we go in with **promenade reserved** (sections 506-509) and around home plate with **promenade infield** (sections 510-518). Along the third-base and left-field line is **promenade reserved** (sections 519-531), and **promenade outfield** comes back at the very top of left field (sections 532-538). I don't recommend sitting in the 500 level—it's too far up.

Citi Field

Where to Buy Tickets

StubHub is the Mets' official reseller, and it's a good way to grab a quick ticket. In fact, you can wait until just a few hours before first pitch to get your seat from StubHub. Generally, tickets will cost a little less here.

You can also use the **MLB Ballpark app** to get Mets tickets and to upgrade your seat when you enter the park.

Best Seats

Citi Field gets a lot of sun, but you're in better shape sitting along the **third-base line,** especially in the back rows of the **100** and **300 levels.** This area will be in the sun for the early part of afternoon games, but by **late afternoon** it's in the **shade.** Try for tickets in **metropolitan box** (sections 121-124) and **field box** (sections 125-126) down low,

and the **excelsior box** (sections 326-333) up high. I highly recommend excelsior box, as seats are typically less than $30 and the **views** are quite good.

Another solid idea is to grab a cheap promenade outfield seat, then hang out by the two-top tables near the **Big Apple reserved** (sections 140-142) area. If there are plenty of available seats, chances are good that an usher will let you take a seat at the top rows of the section. Here, the views are pretty nice, and you're close to food and drink options.

I also enjoy sitting in the **field reserved area** (sections 130-139), especially in the sweet spot between sections 135 and 138. These seats are best during a night game (no sun) and provide awesome views of the game and access to the best beer in the park.

KNOW BEFORE YOU GO

The Mets don't allow **backpacks** into the park. Other **bags,** including **purses** and **diaper bags,** are allowed inside, as long as they're no larger than 16 by 16 by 8 inches. Empty reusable **water bottles** are allowed, too. No other food or beverage is allowed into Citi Field.

Tailgating is allowed in the parking lots surrounding Citi Field, though the Mets prohibit the consumption of alcohol.

Accessibility

If you need an **elevator** to your seating level, enter through the **Hodges, Seaver, or Stengel VIP entrances** (whether or not you're VIP). There are **11 elevators** at the park, including two at the Hodges entrance, two at section 109, one at section 121, two at section 125, one at section 133, one at section 142, and one at the Jackie Robinson Rotunda.

For general assistance, visit one of the **fan assistance stations** (behind section 142, behind section 306, behind section 412). **Wheelchairs** can be stored at any of the stations. Visit the **Ticket Services Office** (Jackie Robinson Rotunda) and turn in either a photo ID or valid credit card to get an **assistive listening device.**

Service animals are permitted at the ballpark. Fans needing a **quiet space** can head to the **Hodges, Seaver,** or **Stengel elevator lobbies.** The Mets offer **sensory bags,** light-sensitivity **sunglasses,** noise-reducing **headphones,** and **weighted lap pads** at the **Ticket Services Office** (Jackie

GAME COSTS

Tickets: Ticket prices are about average, maybe slightly more expensive, than the rest of the league. The cheapest seats are about **$13,** while 300 level tickets go for about **$30.** Seats in the 100 level start at about **$50.**

Hot dog: Expect to pay **$6.50** for a Nathan's. Ouch!

Beer: Prices start at **$10**—the most expensive beer in baseball if we're talking about macro brews. Craft beer is more like **$15.**

Parking: On the higher end of the league, at **$25** around the park.

Robinson Rotunda). Have an ID or credit card ready as a deposit.

For **accessible parking,** head to **lots A, B, F,** or **G** to nab one of the 350 designated spots. Be sure to display a valid state-issued **disabled parking placard.**

GETTING THERE

Subway

The best way to reach Citi Field is via the **subway** (http://new.mta.info, $2.75 base per ride). Take the **7 line** to the **Mets-Willets Point station** (Roosevelt Ave. and Seaver Way, Queens), then follow the walkway to Citi Field. (If you go the opposite way out of the station, you'll reach the Billie Jean King National Tennis Center.) The 7 line runs between Flushing-Main Street and 34th Street-Hudson Yards in Manhattan. Times Square and Grand Central Terminal are both on the line, so if you're coming from somewhere else, you can likely transfer to a 7 train at either of those stations. Another good place to transfer onto a 7 is **Queensboro Plaza** (27th St. and Queens Plaza, Queens). Both the local and express (denoted

by a diamond shape) 7 trains are good for Mets games.

Finally, a tip: If you're getting a **MetroCard,** be sure it has more than $6 available before taking your trip to Citi Field. You don't want to be in line refilling the card after the game.

For some people traveling from Long Island and outer neighborhoods in Queens, the **Long Island Railroad** (http://new.mta. info, up to $19) is an option. You'll have to take the **Port Washington** branch of the railroad, which stops at Mets-Willets Point.

Driving

You might want to drive to Citi Field, and I wouldn't blame you. Driving to the park isn't too bad—just be prepared for traffic. From Manhattan, you're likely taking **I-278 West** via the Robert F. Kennedy (Triborough) Bridge into Queens, then hopping on the **Grand Central Parkway.** That'll take you right to the park.

From Brooklyn, you'll take **I-278 East,** then either meet up with the Grand Central Parkway or turn east onto **I-495** to Flushing Meadows Corona Park. Taking **I-495 East** from Long Island City in Queens (or Midtown Manhattan via the Queens Midtown Tunnel) is another option, though on weekdays it can be a snarling mess.

If you're coming from the north (the Bronx, Westchester County), you're likely to take **I-678 South** over the Whitestone Bridge. That'll dump you right near the park. (Follow signs for LaGuardia/Grand Central Parkway; don't continue onto the Van Wyck Expressway.)

Whenever I've driven to Citi Field, I've parked in a **Mets lot** (E Lot or F Lot, $25) around the ballpark. There are five other lots outside of the general ballpark area, but those are also controlled by the Mets—best to park at the ballpark. Or you can pay just $5 if you park at the reserved **Southfield Commuter Lot** (Roosevelt Ave. and Seaver Way) before noon for weekday night games, before 9am for weekday games starting at 1:10pm, and before 8am for weekday games starting at noon.

I don't recommend parking in the Willets

BE A FAN

Mets fans embrace the anxiety of rooting for their team. The fans are smart, relatable, and ultimately lovable. But if you get belligerent and nasty while wearing your team colors (especially if you're a Phillies or Yankees fan), well, don't say I didn't warn you. I'm a Phillies fan, and that means I'm not supposed to get along with Mets fans. Years ago, I went to Shea Stadium and received a barrage of insults before watching some other Phillies fans get into a drunken fight. But during my time at Shea and at every game I've attended at Citi Field while wearing Phils gear, I've never started anything, and guess what? I haven't had any problems.

The Mets have a unique tradition. After "Take Me Out to the Ballgame" plays during the seventh-inning stretch, you'll hear the beginning strains of **"Lazy Mary,"** a 1958 remake of a famous Italian song, by Lou Monte. The festive song was picked by fans in the 1990s as the tune the team should play during the stretch, and it has since become an ironclad tradition. If the Mets win, you'll hear **"Meet the Mets,"** the iconic rallying cry written by Ruth Roberts and Bill Katz in 1963, one year after the team's debut.

Point neighborhood abutting Citi Field. It's essentially a haven of auto repair and auto body shops, and parking spots simply don't exist.

PARK FEATURES AND SIGHTS

The home-plate entrance is the best way to first see Citi Field. Just outside the stadium, you'll find thousands of **bricks** set into the ground in an area called the **Fanwalk.** The bricks were purchased by Mets fans so that they could have their own part of the ballpark lot.

In **parking Lot B,** you can find plaques that indicate the location of the infield bases of old **Shea Stadium.**

From the home-plate entrance, step into the **Jackie Robinson Rotunda**. The rotunda was inspired by the design of Ebbets Field in Brooklyn, where Robinson broke into the majors and broke the color barrier, and includes an oversize sculpture of the number 42 that's great for photo ops. Look around the archways to see pictures of Robinson and information about his nine values: courage, excellence, persistence, justice, teamwork, commitment, citizenship, determination, integrity. From the rotunda, you can take the giant escalator or staircases up to the field-level concourse.

Next to the rotunda is the **Mets Hall of Fame & Museum** (home-plate entrance, open from gate opening until gate closing). Enter via the rotunda for this 3,700-square-foot experience featuring interactive kiosks and exhibits filled with items from the franchise's history, including baseball bats, Dwight Gooden's cleats from the championship 1986 season, jerseys worn by everyone from Gary Carter to Pedro Martinez, and even luggage tags used by the players. Look for the team's two **World Series trophies** (1969, 1986) and for the **Mets Hall of Fame wall** with plaques of those voted into the exclusive group—names include Mike Piazza, Darryl Strawberry, Jerry Koosman, and Ralph Kiner, who for years was the voice of the team.

Home Run Apple

My first favorite video game was *R.B.I. Baseball '93* for the Sega Genesis, because I could spend hours in the "stadium view" mode, examining the unique ballparks the game made for each team. While the game versions weren't copycats, they were modeled after the real things and had some of those real-life quirks. I loved checking out R.B.I.'s version of Shea Stadium, zooming to center field to see the iconic **Home Run Apple.**

In 1980, the Mets installed a nine-foot-tall motorized, fiberboard apple resting inside a top hat in Shea Stadium's center field. The apple was designed to rise out of the hat like a magic trick, after every home run. To hammer it home, the hat even read "Mets Magic." (The slogan would be changed to "Home Run" within a few years.) Of course, the Mets between 1980 and 1984 were putrid, so there was little magic to celebrate. Sadly, the apple would get stuck a lot and was damaged in bad weather, so it started looking pretty rotten. (Mets fans may tell you this is on brand for the team.)

Regardless of all that, the apple is awesome. It was the one thing I loved about the Mets when watching them on TV back in the early 1990s.

When the Mets left Shea, the apple was originally set to be destroyed, but fans wouldn't have it, petitioning the club to save the quirky fruit sculpture that had become so symbolic of the franchise. The Mets put the **old apple** in a plaza outside Citi Field (near the Jackie Robinson Rotunda entrance), which is great for photo ops. The team then built a new, 18-foot-tall apple that now rests comfortably in **center field**, but without a top hat. Despite new technology, the Citi Field apple has had complications, sometimes rising when it's not supposed to, and other times just not coming up at all.

Mr. Met

Be on the lookout for **Mr. Met,** one of the better mascots in baseball simply because he's funny to look at (it's a man with a baseball for a head). Mr. Met greets fans at **Fan Fest** (center field) 85 minutes before first pitch, 50 minutes before first pitch, and in the second inning of every game. At Fan Fest, there's also a dunk tank and a child-friendly food vendor.

FOOD AND DRINKS

Citi Field has one of the best food and beverage experiences in baseball, offering the kind of diversity one might expect from a major New York tourist attraction. If you can dream up the cuisine, there's a pretty good chance you'll find it here.

For food, a good first stop is the center-field arcade **Taste of the City,** which includes the most highly trafficked vendors. A part of the ballpark since its 2009 opening, **Shake Shack** (center field) is the famous burger and milkshake concept that started in New York City. While it's rather ubiquitous today, with locations across the globe, few things remain as good as a Shackburger, fries, and vanilla shake. Lines get long here immediately, so visit as soon as the gates open. Also in Taste of the City and from the same owner are **Blue Smoke** (center field), known for its barbecue and chopped pork sandwich; **El Verano Taqueria** (center field) with tacos and nachos; and **Box Frites** (center field), which offers garlic fries, bacon and cheese fries, and other fun and messy ballpark bites. Finally, there's a David Chang concept: **Fuku** (center field), dishing out fried chicken and related goodies.

Other great finds are **Arancini Bros.** (sections 102, 411) with its risotto balls, buffalo balls, and a cheesecake; **Bash Burger** (section 136) with its gourmet burgers, salt and vinegar fries, and gelato offerings; **Catch of the Day** (section 102), serving up lobster rolls and Nathan's hot dogs steamed in beer; **Dan & John's Wings** (section 335), home to wings from Buffalo, New York, natives; **Emmy Squared** (section 105), a Citi Field location of Brooklyn pizza darling Emmy (see the *Food* section for more on the original location); and **Pat LaFrieda Meat Purveyors** (section 139, promenade food court), where you can grab a filet mignon sandwich from a revered New York meat-packer.

At the **World's Fare Market** (section 105), **Daruma of Tokyo** serves sushi, and **Mama's of Corona** offers Italian sandwiches.

A sit-down experience can be had at the **Metropolitan Grille** (excelsior level, left-field corner, under $100), though it can get pricey and it's not for everyone. The restaurant, which offers views of the field, is open only to those with tickets for the promenade gold, excelsior gold and box, field reserved, baseline gold and silver, field gold, silver, and box; metropolitan platinum, gold, silver, and box; and various suites and clubs. Entrées include New York strip, ribs, and house-made gnocchi, along with market table selections (read: buffet) for a prix fixe of $44. Offerings there include assorted meats and cheeses, hot dogs and other smoked meats, and antipasti.

Also not for everyone is the **Foxwoods Club** (excelsior level, home plate, under $50). This is open to all the folks who can visit in the Porsche Grille, plus people in Bud Light Landing and Coca-Cola Corner. Essentially a giant cafeteria with a long bar and independent food vendors around the perimeter, this spot is best for grabbing some grub on a rainy night, up to an hour before first pitch.

Almost every fan in the ballpark (except for folks sitting in the outfield) can visit the **Jim Beam Highball Club** (promenade level, home plate). Here, get cocktails made with Jim Beam and associated products, along with food from a small selection of vendors. In the past, hot chicken, Flushing-style Chinese dumplings, and doughnuts were among the grub you could get. There's also a cool view overlooking the field here, making it a decent indoor spot for upper-level fans during cold or rainy games.

For something sweet, head to **La Newyorkina** (Jim Beam Highball Club, Foxwoods Club). This *paletería* sells Mexican-style popsicles (*paletas*) in vivid, wondrous flavors (white sangria, anyone?). Other locations of La Newyorkina can be found throughout the city, including on the High Line.

Kosher stands (sections 115, 130, 408, Sun.-Thurs.) can be found in Citi Field, offering certified hot dogs, knishes, pretzels, and more kosher foods.

And then there's beer. Early on, the place to be for suds was **Big Apple Brews** (center field), home to dozens of taps, bottles, and cans. That stand has grown more and more

Photos (from top to bottom): Mr. Met, the team mascot; the Home Run Apple; beer booth at Citi Field.

mediocre with each year, with Anheuser-Busch InBev offerings (Blue Point, Goose Island, Shock Top) dominating the list. Luckily, however, Citi Field has craft beer in other places.

First, go to **Mikkeller Brewing NYC** (126th St. and 37th Ave., right-field gate, 718/766-2717, www.mikkellernyc.com, 4pm-10pm Wed.-Thurs., noon-midnight Fri.-Sat., noon-10pm Sun., open two hours before first pitch game days Mon.-Tues.). The acclaimed and artful Danish brewery with satellite locations across the world opened its New York outpost at the ballpark in 2018. Mikkeller is a brewery that happens to be inside a ballpark, with just a few Mets-centric tweaks in its otherwise Ikea-ish taproom. Find 60 taps including plenty of Mikkeller brews, along with collaborations made with the Mets and New York in mind. It's only accessible from outside the park, so head here before going to the Jackie Robinson Rotunda. Best of all, it's open year-round.

My favorite spot for a quick local beer is the **Empire State Craft stand** (section 132). You'll find some of those Mikkeller project beers plus offerings from breweries like Queens, LIC Beer Project, Brooklyn, Five Boroughs, Interboro, Sixpoint, and Newburgh. The line is usually nonexistent here, and some breweries produce tallboy cans that are great for a few innings of imbibing.

EVENTS

If you're hoping to acquire some **autographs,** fans are permitted to head down toward the field in the **100 level** any time until an hour before first pitch. As for **batting practice,** you'll see the visitors get to work about 90 minutes before first pitch.

After Sunday afternoon games, the Mets host a kids-run-the-bases event called the **Mr. Met Dash.** Kids ages 12 and under can participate by lining up outside the Bullpen Gate at 126th Street after the end of the game.

Tours

The Mets offer a handful of **Citi Field tours.** The **non-game day tours** (Jackie Robinson Rotunda, 11am Wed. and Fri., $20, $15 ages 12 and under) take guests to the press box, dugout, bullpens, and Mets clubhouse.

The **15 Minutes of Fame: Selfie Tour** (Hodges VIP entrance, east of home-plate entrance, 100-160 minutes before first pitch, $65) takes fans onto the warning track behind home plate and into a special area to watch the end of batting practice.

The **Take Me Out to Citi Field Tour** (Hodges VIP entrance, east of home-plate entrance, 160-220 minutes before first pitch, $45) is for the early birds, and it covers plenty of ground, from club areas to the press conference space downstairs, to the bullpens.

Finally, a special **All-Star Tour** (Hodges VIP entrance, east of home-plate entrance, 160 minutes before first pitch, $200) includes watching batting practice from the field, plus going on the standard tour of the ballpark.

SHOPPING

The main outlet is the **Mets Team Store** (Jackie Robinson Rotunda and section 415, 718/672-0077, 10am-5pm Mon.-Fri., 11am-4pm Sat.-Sun non-game days, opens with gates on game days). Here you'll find the usual shirts, jerseys, hats, and memorabilia, plus fun Mr. Met and Mrs. Met gear.

Also in the park, find the kiosk for **The 7 Line** (section 140, center field), a small business that started with a website and sells fan-centric T-shirts and other apparel. Various other kiosks selling hats, nostalgia gear, and other clothes and items are sprinkled throughout Citi Field.

NEW YORK CITY SIGHTS

Welcome to a city with no shortage of sights. If it's your first time in New York, there are a few bucket-list items to check off.

CENTRAL PARK

You know that verdant rectangle smack in the center of Manhattan as **Central Park** (southern entrances at 59th St. and 8th Ave., or 59th St. and 5th Ave., Manhattan), an 843-acre oasis inside the city that doesn't sleep. The **Central Park Conservancy** (www.centralparknyc.org) maintains the park, which pulls in visitors for its sights, trails, and nearby museums.

On your visit here, start from the southern end: First is **Central Park Zoo** (64th St. and 5th Ave., Manhattan, 212/439-6500, www.centralparkzoo.com, 10am-4:30pm daily, $14-20, $11-17 seniors, $9-15 ages 3-12, free ages 2 and under). See grizzly bears, snow monkeys, red pandas, sea lions, penguins, and rainforest animals like lemurs. The zoo schedules **daily penguin feedings** (10am, 2:30pm) for the public to watch.

Hop over to 65th Street and you'll find the **Balto statue** (67th St. near East Dr., Manhattan), which immortalizes a sled dog that in 1925 completed a harrowing journey to deliver medicine from Anchorage, Alaska, to Nome, where children were near death from diphtheria. West of that is **The Mall,** home to **SummerStage in Central Park** (71st St. near East Dr., Manhattan), which hosts free concerts and performances by jazz legends, the Metropolitan Opera, and solid under-the-radar bands and artists throughout the warm season. At the north end of The Mall is **Bethesda Fountain** (73rd St., Manhattan), an iconic spot for photos. The fountain also has a sculpture of an angel dating to 1873.

Head west on nearby Terrace Drive, then meet up with West Drive south; you'll find Frisbee Hill and the grounds for the **New York Lawn Bowling Club** (www.nybowls.com), where folks dress formally to play a game not unlike boccie. If you take Terrace Drive past West, you'll reach **Strawberry Fields** (72nd St. and Terrace Dr., Manhattan), the mosaic dedicated in 1985 to honor John Lennon. It's a meeting place for fans of the artist, who was shot and died in 1980 just across the street from his apartment at The Dakota.

On East Drive north toward 79th Street, look for the striped awnings marking the **Loeb Boathouse** (75th St. and East Dr., Manhattan, 212/517-2233, www.thecentralparkboathouse.com). You can **rent a rowboat** ($15 per hour) or take a **gondola tour** on the abutting lake. Just to the east is the bronze sculpture *Alice in Wonderland* (75th St. near East Dr.), featuring Alice, the Mad Hatter, and the White Rabbit.

The eastern edge of the center of Central Park is where you'll find the **Metropolitan Museum of Art** (1000 5th Ave., Manhattan, 212/535-7710, www.metmuseum.org, 10am-5:30pm Sun.-Thurs., 10am-9pm Fri.-Sat., $25, $17 seniors, $12 students, free ages 12 and under; New York State residents pay what they wish). The Met really is as good as it gets. A sprawling museum with multiple levels, it's home to a serious collection of modern art from Matisse, Picasso, Balthus, and others. There's an impressive American Wing with furniture from the 17th-19th centuries; rare armor from the 16th century; the awesome Africa, Oceania, and Americas collection with ceremonial objects, gold, and more; a gorgeous Asian Art section; and the labyrinthine European Paintings area that includes America's foremost grouping of works by Monet, Cézanne, and Van Gogh, among many others. Plus, there's a rooftop hang (in season), plenty of special exhibits, and regular events. Your ticket is good for three days, so you can visit multiple times if you want to see everything.

North of 86th Street is the **Jacqueline Kennedy Onassis Reservoir**—you'll see plenty of people running and walking around that. Farther up, just past 97th Street, is the **North Meadow,** home to the park's many baseball fields, which are active during the spring and summer. Baseball fans of all ages should swing by to check out the semi-pro-quality talent as they play.

TIMES SQUARE

When assembling your New York City bucket list, **Times Square** (42nd St. and Broadway, Manhattan, www.timessquarenyc.org)

should be atop the list. Decades ago, it was an area rife with prostitution, panhandlers, and small-time crime, but these days Times Square is a major tourist destination. What once was a menagerie of pornography theaters, cheap burger joints, and electronics stores is now a pop culture overload: headlines scrolling across oversized news tickers, street performers busking for money, tourists packing into overpriced chain restaurants like the Hard Rock Café. Still, it's exhilarating to walk around this neon-lit wonderland, especially past midnight because it's still well populated and brighter than ever.

Look around for iconic signage: the Coca-Cola sign, studios for ABC's *Good Morning America*, and the TKTS booth, where Broadway show seats can be had. When it's warmer, you're bound to see women wearing (seemingly) nothing but body paint and the (nearly) Naked Cowboy, strumming a guitar.

The best way to get here is to take the subway, arriving at **Times Square-42nd Street** (42nd St. and 7th Ave.); once there, head to the pedestrian plaza. A note: Watch for the people dressed as children's cartoon characters. They have been known to harass passersby and touch people without their consent.

STATUE OF LIBERTY

You probably know the story: In the mid-1860s, after the Civil War, the United States' old friend France decided to gift the country a 305-foot neoclassical statue of the Roman goddess Libertas, free of the shackles of slavery, raising a torch, and casting a stoic and defiant gaze into the future. The **Statue of Liberty** (Liberty Island, 877/523-9849, www.statuecruises.com, 8am-6:20pm daily Memorial Day-Labor Day, sunrise-sunset daily Labor Day-Memorial Day, $21.50, $17 seniors, $12 ages 4-12, free ages 3 and under) was dedicated in 1886 and stands on Liberty Island in the middle of New York Harbor. Whether viewed by incoming immigrants to Ellis Island, by tourists for the first time, or by locals simply catching a glimpse, it's an awesome sight.

It's a good idea to devote a full day to your visit to the statue. Ensure you have enough time to hop on a ferry to Liberty Island, go through security, get to the top of the statue, peruse the scene, come down, and get back on the ferry. It may take more than an hour just to board the ferry.

You can just visit the statue's pedestal, which includes a museum; but if you want to get to the crown, reserve tickets well in advance. The climb to the top is not for everyone (people with existing heart conditions, people with a fear of heights, those younger than 4). You'll ascend 377 steps up a spiral staircase from the main lobby to the crown platform (you can take an elevator from lobby to pedestal, but then you have to walk to the tippy top), and there's no air-conditioning here. Be aware of the people around you, and try not to hold up the line as you go. The park has lockers ($0.25 per usage) available for cameras, medication, keys, and other items that are prohibited at the top. All the work is worthwhile: It's incredible to see all of New York City, Jersey City, Staten Island, and more from atop Lady Liberty.

9/11 MEMORIAL AND MUSEUM

The **9/11 Memorial and Museum** (180 Greenwich St., Manhattan, 212/312-8800, www.911memorial.org, 9am-8pm daily, $26, $20 seniors and students, $15 ages 7-12, $12 FDNY, NYPD, and PAPD) is located on the grounds where the deadliest terrorist attack in history took place. The memorial itself consists of the two largest constructed waterfalls in North America, set at the location of the North and South Towers of the World Trade Center. Ledges lining the perimeter of the pool at the base of each waterfall display the names of the 2,977 victims who died on September 11, 2001, in the attacks in New York, at the Pentagon in Washington DC, and near Shanksville, Pennsylvania. Nearby are the **Memorial Glade,** which honors the recovery and rescue workers who have either died or are sick from exposure to toxins at the site, and the **Survivor Tree,** a pear tree that endured the attacks and still stands today.

The museum is seven stories below the memorial, carved in the bedrock of the World Trade Center site. Through artifacts, stories, and technology, it tells the story of that clear September morning; the museum also gives historical context to the Al Qaeda attacks and addresses the aftermath of the attacks. There's a heart-wrenching memorial wall showing photographs of those killed in the attacks, along with regularly changing exhibits.

WHITNEY MUSEUM OF AMERICAN ART

The **Whitney Museum of American Art** (99 Gansevoort St., Manhattan, www.whitney.org, 10:30am-6pm Wed.-Thurs. and Sat.-Mon., 10:30am-10pm Fri., $25, $18 seniors and students, free ages 18 and under) is one of my favorite museums. Given a dramatic, new concrete-and-glass home that opened in 2015, it stands at the end of the High Line pedestrian park, has multiple roof decks, and showcases some downright exciting and sometimes challenging modern pieces.

BROOKLYN BRIDGE

One bucket-list activity in New York is walking the length of the **Brooklyn Bridge.** Built between 1870 and 1883, the bridge is a marvel of human ingenuity and engineering. It's a beautiful structure, with Gothic Revival towers that demand your full attention, and a network of cables and stays that gives the bridge a commanding look. You can see it all from 18 feet above the automobile lanes, where the pedestrian walkway rests. It's a nice 1.1-mile walk from one end to the other, with the endpoint at Cadman Plaza in Brooklyn. Walk to the riverfront and visit **Jane's Carousel** (Old Dock St., Brooklyn, www.janescarousel.org, 11am-7pm Wed.-Mon. mid-May-mid-Sept.,

Photos (from top to bottom): Statue of Liberty; Brooklyn Bridge; Coney Island.

11am-6pm Thurs.-Sun. mid-Sept.-mid-May, $2), a 1922 Philadelphia Toboggan merry-go-round that rests between the Brooklyn and Manhattan Bridges in the neighborhood known as DUMBO (Down Under the Manhattan Bridge Overpass). To start your walk, take the subway (4, 5, or 6 line) to **Brooklyn Bridge-City Hall station** (Centre St. and Park Row, Manhattan). It's a short walk from the station to the pedestrian walkway. From Cadman Plaza, an A or C train can take you back to Manhattan.

CONEY ISLAND

If you want some sand and surf, New York has that, too. Head to historic **Coney Island** (Neptune Ave. and Ocean Pkwy., Brooklyn), a neighborhood serving as the city's very own beach getaway. Coney Island is best known for two things: amusement rides and hot dogs. The former are at **Luna Park** (1000 Surf Ave., Brooklyn, 718/373-5862, www.lunaparknyc.com, daily June-Aug., Sat.-Sun. Apr.-May and Sept.-Oct., hours vary by day, $29-42), which is home to the legendary Coney Island Cyclone, the 1927 wooden roller coaster whose cars can get up to speeds of 60 miles per hour. For hot dogs, you'll have to get in line at **Nathan's Famous** (1310 Surf Ave., Brooklyn, 718/333-2202, www.nathans-famous.com, 10am-midnight Mon.-Thurs., 10am-2am Fri.-Sat., 10am-1am Sun., under $20), a green shack with plenty of outdoor seating and those famous franks. Order two or three, along with some fries, and keep an eye out for a free picnic table.

FOOD

NEAR YANKEE STADIUM

The area around Yankee Stadium has an international flair. For classic home-style Jamaican cuisine, check out **Eating Tree** (892 Gerard Ave., Bronx, 718/293-5025, 9am-9pm daily, under $30). With a small dining room with a splash of green, this is a no-frills spot where dishes like oxtail and brown stew chicken are best served in a take-out tin, either to-go or at a spot in the small dining area.

Find Mexican food at **San Jose Tulcingo** (109 E. 153rd St., Bronx, 917/631-9253, 7am-11pm Mon.-Sat., 8am-11pm Sun., under $30), which serves up tacos and enchiladas, and breakfast fare like chilaquiles. The space is unfussy and just fine for families.

If it's a Jewish deli you're looking for, check out **Court Deli** (96 E. 161st St., Bronx, 718/993-1380, www.courtdelinyc.com, 6am-9pm Mon.-Sat., 7am-7pm Sun., under $20). Here you can get an overstuffed sandwich with corned beef, pastrami, and tongue (or chopped liver, or brisket, or bologna). The deli has several tables and booths, but takeout is also available.

NEAR CITI FIELD

The Queens neighborhood of Flushing has a large Chinese immigrant population, which means it has a deep roster of regional and specialty Chinese restaurants, from eateries focusing on *xiao long bao* (soup dumplings) to Szechuan houses (this is where to go for spicy food). You can also find great Thai, Japanese, and other Asian restaurants in the community. If you have some time before a ball game, you could walk around Main Street in Flushing and stop at whichever place looks good (it's hard to go wrong). Still, I have suggestions. You pretty much need to start your Flushing food experience at the **New World Mall** (136-20 Roosevelt Ave., Queens, 718/353-0551, www.newworld-mallny.com, 10am-10pm daily), a compendium of shops and eateries that serves as a hub of sorts in this bustling neighborhood. At the mall's food court, choices include **Lanzhou Handmade Noodle,** with its hearty, rustic noodle soups, and **Conway Bistro,** with a combination of classic Chinese street food and sour-sweet Thai-influenced soups.

Another favorite of mine is in the **Super HK Food Court** (37-11 Main St., Queens). There, you'll find the stall **Dumpling Galaxy** (212/518-3265, 10am-9pm daily, under

$30). The owners of this stall operated Tian Jin Dumpling House at another mall nearby, but that closed for a while, moving here with a new name. Order a dozen or so dumplings—pork, beef, fish. They're supple, filled perfectly, and just plain awesome.

If one morning you want to try traditional dim sum (small plates of dumplings, buns, and cakes served with tea), head to **Asian Jewels** (133-30 39th Ave., Queens, 718/359-8600, www.asianjewelsny.com, 9am-11:30pm Mon.-Fri., 8:30am-11:30pm Sat.-Sun., under $70). It may look like a temple from the outside, but the red-toned Asian Jewels is much more informal; it's also typically busy. Try to sit by the kitchen door so you can intercept the servers as they come out with fresh treats. When asking for an item, give your ordering card to the server so he or she can mark it off. Dim sum is lots of fun with a group, and munching on treats like steamed rice rolls and Dungeness crab served with Japanese eggplant is a great way to experience this fun and friendly neighborhood.

OTHER NEIGHBORHOODS

Picking just a few restaurants and eateries to visit in New York is nearly impossible. You could spend months trying to sample every style of cuisine the city has to offer. Have an open mind and don't despair if your first choice is booked up. Don't resort to eating near Times Square—most restaurants in that area exist to get tourist money. If you want the local experience, stick to the neighborhoods.

Manhattan

If you need to eat something around the Theater District, go to **Danji** (346 W. 52nd St., Manhattan, 212/586-2880, www.danjinyc.com, noon-2:30pm and 5pm-midnight Mon.-Fri., 11am-3pm and 5pm-midnight Sat., 11am-3pm and 4pm-11pm Sun., under $60). In a cute minimalist space, you can get Korean street food and other mash-ups, like kimchi poutine and spicy Korean fried chicken wings.

Now, if you want authentic New York-style pizza (thin crust, greasy, tangy cheese), go for **Joe's Pizza** (7 Carmine St., Manhattan, 212/366-1182, www.joespizzanyc.com, 10am-4am Sun.-Wed., 10am-5am Thurs.-Sat., under $20). For the classic experience, walk to the counter, order a slice (and a soda), and grab a seat to enjoy it. This place is small.

If you want a true New York bagel, you can cross it off the bucket list at **Russ & Daughters** (179 E. Houston St., Manhattan, 212/475-4880, www.russanddaughters.com, 8am-6pm Fri.-Wed., under $20), the landmark Jewish appetizing shop (essentially, a place that sells bagels and their accompaniments, but no meat). They sell great bagels (pillowy and chewy, with the right crispness) and plenty of fresh lox to put on top. They also offer sandwiches and other items. The line may be long (especially on weekends), but service is swift. You should take your food to go.

If you're looking for a real New York hot dog (cheap, with kraut and onions, available whenever), you gotta hit **Gray's Papaya** (2090 Broadway, Manhattan, 212/799-0243, www.grayspapaya.nyc, 24 hours daily, under $10). Started by former co-owners of the hot dog chain Papaya King, Gray's sells a frank for less than $2, and it's perfect, especially at 4:15 a.m., right after the bars close. Why the papaya? Gray's (and every other papaya-named place in town) sells papaya juice, along with other fruity concoctions. The marriage is perfect and best enjoyed quickly while standing inside the confines of the bright yellow space.

I'll tell you what's good before or after a ball game: oysters. Head to **Mermaid Oyster Bar** (79 Macdougal St., Manhattan, 212/260-0100, www.themermaidinn.com, 5pm-10pm Mon.-Thurs., 5pm-10:30pm Fri., 4pm-10:30pm Sat., 4pm-10pm Sun., under $70). While it's a more upscale experience, there's a nice informal vibe. You can stand by the bar, sip a gin cocktail, and even get a half-dozen oysters while waiting for your table. The oysters are sourced from all over, including New Brunswick (Canada), Long Island, Virginia, and Washington State.

For the epitome of Harlem soul, head to the always-busy **Sylvia's** (328 Malcolm X Blvd., Manhattan, 212/996-0660, www.sylviasrestaurant.com, 11am-10:30pm Mon.-Tues., 9am-10:30pm Wed.-Sat., 11am-8pm Sun., under $50). Founded by Sylvia Woods in 1962, this Harlem landmark serves up plates like chicken livers and fried chicken with sides such as buttered corn (weekdays), okra and tomato gumbo, and garlic mashed potatoes. Other options include barbecue ribs, catfish, and salmon cakes ... come and get it. Sylvia's does a white-tablecloth experience in a packed space with a friendly ambience. This is the kind of place you have to visit at least once.

New York is home to hundreds of restaurants run by some of the biggest names in the culinary world. It's hard to pick one that stands out, you can't go wrong with a David Chang restaurant. **Momofuku Kawi** (20 Hudson Yards, Manhattan, 646/517-2699, https://kawi.momofuku.com, 11:30am-3pm and 5:30pm-11:30pm Sun.-Thurs., 11:30am-3pm and 5pm-12:30am Fri.-Sat., under $150) reimagines Korean cuisine through executive chef Eunjo Parj. Every seat in this warm wood-toned space is good, so sit back and dive into sweet and sour ribs, pork belly, rice cake dumplings, and oxtail and brisket *jjim*.

Brooklyn

In Brooklyn, I love the Montreal homage **Mile End Delicatessen** (97 Hoyt St., Brooklyn, 8am-10pm Mon.-Fri., 10am-10pm Sat.-Sun., under $30). Go here for lunchtime staples like high-stacked smoked meat sandwiches, plus pierogis, chopped liver, and wood-fired bagels. The chic, contemporary space blends deli style with modern elements like subway tile, handcrafted wood tables, and exposed piping.

It's easy to find good burgers in New York, but the best might just be at **Emily** (919 Fulton St., Brooklyn, 347/844-9588, www.pizzalovesemily.com, 5:30pm-10:30pm

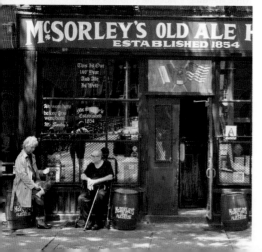

Photos (from top to bottom): the original Nathan's Famous at Coney Island; bagel from Russ & Daughters; McSorley's Old Ale House.

Mon.-Thurs., 5:30pm-11:30pm Fri., noon-3pm and 5pm-11:30pm Sat., noon-3pm and 5pm-10:30pm Sun., under $50). This homey neighborhood restaurant has an expensive but terrific burger, plus great pizzas and killer snacks like hot wings.

BARS AND BREWERIES

NEAR YANKEE STADIUM

The best bar near the stadium is the **Bronx Drafthouse** (884 Gerard Ave., Bronx, 929/265-9759, www.bronxdrafthouse.com, 11:30am-2am Mon.-Thurs., 11am-3am Fri.-Sat., noon-2am Sun.). A relatively new place, it is nicely appointed with subway tile and wood finishes, and has a good drink selection with both popular mainstream fare and local craft.

For a louder experience, you can head to **Stan's Sports Bar** (836 River Ave., Bronx, 718/993-5548, www.stanssportsbar.com, open before, during, after Yankees games), which is only in operation when the Yankees are playing. It'll get pretty crowded, the prices are higher than what you'd expect for "cheap" beer, and the boozy, testosterone-filled culture of the bar might be a turnoff to some. If you're looking for a couple beers and an opportunity to be around some die-hard Yankees fans, well, this is definitely the place. I'll also steer you to **Yankee Twin Bar Eatery** (844 River Ave., Bronx, 718/665-5508, www.yankeetwineaterybar.com, 5:30am-8:30pm daily), which doubles as a breakfast spot (get fried egg and cheese on a roll, naturally). Yankee Twin serves cheapish beer and doesn't have nearly the crowds of the other bars along River Avenue and on 161st Street.

NEAR CITI FIELD

There really isn't a lot around Citi Field in the way of alcohol. Since you're close enough to Downtown Flushing, you've got a cool hotel

hang in **A+ Roof Bar** (39-16 College Point Blvd., Queens, 929/204-7875, 6pm-2am daily), atop the Parc Hotel and offering views of Citi Field and the skyline. The bar carries several varieties of Japanese whiskey, along with the regular American spirit brands. This is a good place to go if you're wanting to stay near the ballpark after the game.

OTHER NEIGHBORHOODS

Manhattan

One of my favorite bars in the world is the quiet Belgian beer hangout **Burp Castle** (41 E. 7th St., Manhattan, 212/982-4576, 5pm-midnight Mon.-Thurs., 5pm-2am Fri., 4pm-2am Sat., 4pm-11pm Sun.). Tucked in the East Village, Burp Castle is like a monastery, but devoted to exalting beer. The walls are dressed in beer-themed murals, and the bar carries Belgians (naturally)—about a dozen on tap and 40 in bottles. It's a cozy place with a few candle-lit tables and barstools. If the space gets a little too loud, the lone bartender will shush the room. The idea is to enjoy your beer, maybe with quiet reflection, a good book, a crossword, or a notebook. I've done all of these things at Burp Castle, and I wouldn't trade those experiences for the world.

Not too far away from Burp Castle is another icon, but of a very different style. As aged as the sawdust on the floor, **McSorley's Old Ale House** (15 E. 7th St., Manhattan, 212/473-9148, www.mcsorleysoldalehouse.nyc, 11am-1am Mon.-Sat., 1pm-1am Sun.) is a true throwback dating to 1854 (it allowed only men until 1970). Walk in and sit at a round table, maybe among new friends. At some point, an employee (an Irish gentleman, perhaps) will ask for your order. You have two options: light (an amber-colored ale) or dark (a stout-colored ale). Both are good and made for drinking three to four in a sitting. McSorley's sells food, including cheese plates (American is included) with raw onions. Enjoy the loud vibe.

On the Lower East Side is another favorite of mine, **Upstate Craft Beer & Oysters** (95 1st Ave., Manhattan, 646/791-5400, www.

upstatenyc.com, 5pm-10:30pm Mon.-Wed., 5pm-11pm Thurs.-Sat., 5pm-10pm Sun.). Upstate has an exceptional oyster selection with a finely curated and heavily local beer list. It's cozy inside and very New York in style. This place is my heart. Make a reservation or get here as close to when they open as possible, because there aren't many seats, and they fill up quickly.

Queens

Over in Astoria, Queens, is one of my favorite breweries in America, **SingleCut Beersmiths** (19-33 37th St., Queens, 718/606-0788, www.singlecut.com, 5pm-10pm Wed., 4pm-11pm Thurs., 1pm-midnight Fri., 11am-midnight Sat., 11am-10pm Sun.). Open since 2012, it pays homage to rock and roll (single cut is a style of guitar body) with vinyl records played on the regular and bands performing at a loft above the brewhouse. The beers are outstanding, and it never gets too crazy here. This spot gets my highest recommendation.

And hey, while you're in Astoria, hightail it to **Astoria Bier & Cheese** (3414 Broadway, Queens, 718/545-5588, www.astoriabierandcheese.com, noon-11pm Mon.-Thurs., noon-midnight Fri.-Sat., noon-10pm Sun.), which sells, well, beer and cheese. Get yourself a cheese board and order a few beers (Alewife, Newburgh, and Ommegang are among the options), then pick up something from their store to bring back to the hotel. The back patio is small but cute, perfect for a summer afternoon.

Brooklyn

For craft beer enthusiasts, a trip to **Other Half Brewing Company** (195 Centre St., Brooklyn, 917/765-6107, www.otherhalfbrewing.com, noon-10pm Mon.-Wed., noon-midnight Thurs.-Fri., 10am-midnight Sat., 11am-10pm Sun.) is something of a necessity. They make a lot of juicy New England IPAs, with the tap list changing all the time, so head to this modern industrial space with bespoke picnic tables and neon lights to sample a bunch. There's a lot of hype around this spot, but the beer justifies it.

Brooklyn is also home to **Sixpoint Brewery** (9th St. and 2nd Ave., Brooklyn, www.sixpoint.com), which opened its magnificent warehouse-like taproom in 2020. It was a long time coming: Sixpoint started as a small-time brewery in Red Hook, Brooklyn, but has since come to epitomize New York City beer. Its brews are available throughout the country—Resin just might be the best everyday double IPA in America.

Want something strong? I really enjoy the cocktails at **Weather Up** (589 Vanderbilt Ave., Brooklyn, www.weatherupnyc.com, 5:30pm-2am daily). The white subway tile sets the tone for an understated but serious journey through the cocktail experience, presented in a seemingly effortless manner by the mixologists. Its verdant patio is quite the place to enjoy a drink late at night, or just pull up to a leather barstool and let the time go.

For a more relaxed pub atmosphere, I dig **The Double Windsor** (210 Prospect Park West, Brooklyn, 347/725-3479, www.doublewindsorbrooklyn.com, 3pm-2am Mon.-Thurs., 3pm-4am Fri., noon-4am Sat., noon-2am Sun.). This is your classic, no-frills neighborhood bar, a refreshing scene in Brooklyn, with good beers on tap made by local folks. The space is active and cozy, with exposed brick and chalkboards. The Double Windsor is down-to-earth and great for throwing back a few beers.

The Bronx

If you're staying in the Bronx, you might want to visit **The Bronx Brewery** (856 E. 136th St., Bronx, 718/402-1000, www.thebronxbrewery.com, 3pm-7pm Mon.-Wed., 3pm-8pm Thurs.-Fri., noon-8pm Sat., noon-7pm Sun.). With a large backyard area with games and plenty of seating, this is a perfect summer drinking spot. They make beers for all palates, from IPAs to sours to pilsners.

BROADWAY THEATERS

Whether or not you're a theater maven, going to a Broadway show while in New York is something of a rite of passage. You have to do it! While there are myriad shows open at any one time, a handful of productions have been on stage for years. These recommendations list some of the tried-and-true experiences, musicals that are guaranteed to make you smile.

Broadway productions usually run eight shows each week—generally Tuesday to Sunday, and with matinees twice a week (Saturday is a given, and either Wednesday or Sunday is typical). Tickets tend to be cheaper for shows and matinees early in the week.

Buy tickets in advance at www.broadway.com or www.playbill.com, or call Telecharge (212/239-6200). For the best deal on tickets, try the **TKTS booths** (open daily from 10am for matinees, 3pm for evening shows), which offer same-day, marked-down tickets for up to 50 percent off. Get to TKTS when it opens, and know that you probably won't get tickets for the hottest show of the moment here. There are locations at Times Square (47th St. and Broadway, Manhattan), South Street Seaport (Front St. and John St., Manhattan), and Lincoln Center (62nd St. and Columbus Ave., Manhattan).

Your best bet for comedy is **The Book of Mormon,** the Trey Parker and Matt Stone (creators of *South Park*) show about missionaries getting in over their heads in Africa. It lives at the **Eugene O'Neill Theatre** (230 W. 49th St., Manhattan, $70-400).

The Lion King reigns as Broadway's brightest and most exciting family show (recommended for ages 8 and older), showing at the **Minskoff Theatre** (1515 Broadway, Manhattan, $100-250). You've heard this one: It's the story of earning one's way into power, of defending family honor, and of the bond between a father and son in the circle of life, all set to delicious music by Elton John and Tim Rice, and with gorgeous, colorful visuals.

Another favorite for the younger audience is **Wicked.** This is the story of how two rivals become friends in the Land of Oz. Since 2004 (when the opening cast featured the one-two punch of Idina Menzel and Kristin Chenoweth, plus Broadway legends Joel Grey, Carole Shelley, and Norbert Leo Butz), *Wicked* has set up shop at the **Gershwin Theatre** (222 W. 51st St., Manhattan, $100-150).

For a fancy, sexy night out, go see **Chicago.** The story of nightclub dancer Roxie Hart has been going strong since 1996, with the starring role featuring everyone from original player Ann Reinking to Brooke Shields, Melanie Griffith, Bebe Neuwirth, and Rita Wilson. The show is at the **Ambassador Theatre** (219 W. 49th St., Manhattan, $50-170).

Then there's **Hamilton.** The acclaimed hip-hop musical from Lin-Manuel Miranda about founding father Alexander Hamilton broke new ground on Broadway. It sells out quickly, so get your tickets far in advance. It plays at the **Richard Rodgers Theatre** (226 W. 46th St., Manhattan, $200-500).

RECREATION

PARKS AND ISLANDS

The High Line

Sort of a park but also sort of an opportunity to just be among people and watch people, **The High Line** (34th St. at 11th Ave., Manhattan, or Gansevoort St. at Washington St., Manhattan, 7am-11pm daily summer, 7am-10pm daily spring and fall, 7am-7pm daily winter) is an old elevated freight line turned into an attractively landscaped, aboveground walkway. At 1.45 miles long, it makes for a nice two-hour jaunt with a few stops built in. Small carts and stalls on the High Line sell popsicles, drinks, and other goodies, while plenty of platforms and seating areas allow folks to relax. Chances are that on a warm day you'll spot plenty of people just lying about. It's wheelchair accessible, there are numerous entrances (every few blocks, essentially), and there are restrooms at 30th Street, 16th Street, and Gansevoort Street. Weekends can get very crowded.

Flushing Meadows Corona Park

At **Flushing Meadows Corona Park** (Meridian Rd. and United Nations Ave., Queens, www.nycgovparks.org), you'll find a vast green space of 897 acres that serves as a community gathering place for Queens residents.

Flushing Meadows is just a hop over the 7 track from Citi Field (the ballpark is technically inside the park), serving as the site of the 1939 New York World's Fair and 1964 New York World's Fair. At the latter event, officials unveiled the **Unisphere** (Avenue of the Americas, Queens), a stainless steel globe surrounded by thrusting fountains, symbolizing the hope of humankind. Today it's a photo-op spot that's been in countless TV shows and films.

The park is also home to the **Queens Museum** (Meridian Rd. and New York Ave., Queens, 718/592-9700, www.queensmuseum.org, 11am-5pm Wed.-Sun., $8, $4 seniors, free ages 18 and under), whose collection includes Tiffany glass items and a pretty amazing architectural model of the city. Exhibits change every six months or so at this nice two-hour diversion and rainy-day spot.

If you'd rather stay outdoors, the park has a fun **pitch and putt course** (100 Flushing Meadows Pedestrian Bridge, Queens, 718/271-8182, www.golfnyc.com, 9am-1am daily Memorial Day-Labor Day, 9am-4pm Mon.-Sat., 9am-3pm Sun. Labor Day-Memorial Day, $18.75-21 per 18 holes), a tidy 18-hole course where holes play up to 80 yards. (It's a lot like golf, but it's not quite the same thing.) Bring just a 9 iron, wedge, and putter. Bonus: You can play late at night, even after a Mets game.

Flushing Meadows is home to the **USTA Billie Jean King National Tennis Center** (Queens, 718/760-6200, www.usta.com), accessible from the subway at Mets-Willets Point station. This is where the tennis world

gathers every August and September for the U.S. Open. If you're driving to a Mets game during U.S. Open time, be prepared for some traffic. If you're taking the subway, be on the lookout for athletic people holding large Wilson bags—they just might be tennis stars.

Randall's Island

One Memorial Day weekend, I walked the Robert F. Kennedy (Triborough) Bridge and spotted some white-clad folks playing cricket down on an island below. So I took the walkway down to **Randall's Island** (20 Randall's Island Park, www.randallsisland.org, 5am-midnight daily). There are more than 60 ball fields at Randall's Island, many of them reserved for baseball and softball, so pack a picnic and go to check out some adult-league ball games.

Roosevelt Island

Accessible via a 418-foot vertical lift bridge in Queens (Vernon Blvd. and 36th Ave., Queens) or **sky tram** (60th St. and 2nd Ave., Manhattan, $2.25 one-way, $4 round-trip, free students), **Roosevelt Island** is a narrow strip of land in the middle of the East River that's home to 11,000 New York City residents. It's part of the borough of Manhattan. Head north to the **Roosevelt Island Lighthouse** (900 Main St., Manhattan) to check out a 50-foot-tall stone lighthouse built in 1872.

Governors Island

Governors Island (www.govisland.com) has for a few decades been one of the finest play spaces for New Yorkers. An all-park, 172-acre island south of Manhattan's Battery Park and just across the Buttermilk Channel from Brooklyn, it offers awesome views of the Manhattan skyline and Statue of Liberty. Head to **The Hills** (870-898 Gresham Rd.), which rise 70 feet up and allow for those views. Also look for **Fort Jay** (Andes Rd.), which was first built after the American Revolution and stood finished in preparation for the War of 1812, though it never saw combat. Each year, the island hosts the visual art festival **Portal** (www.4heads.org, weekends in Sept.), formerly the Governors Island Art Fair.

DETOUR: GATE OF HEAVEN CEMETERY

Babe Ruth's grave at Gate of Heaven Cemetery

About 25 miles north of New York City in the hamlet of Hawthorne is one of the most famous cemeteries in America. **Gate of Heaven Cemetery** (10 W. Stevens Ave., Hawthorne, NY, 914/769-3672, http://gateofheavenny.com, 9am-4:30pm daily) is the final resting place of some interesting names in American history, including James Cagney, steel magnate Charles Schwab, publisher Condé Nast, and CBS co-founder Arthur Judson.

Most interesting for Yankees fans might be the gravesite of the Great Bambino himself, **Babe Ruth.** Located at Section 25, Plot 1115, Graves 3 and 4, Ruth lies alongside his second wife, Claire. The large tombstone shows Jesus Christ standing by a representation of Ruth as a stout young boy dressed in baseball clothing. Fans, baseball lovers, and historians routinely leave baseballs and other items at the gravesite.

Babe isn't the only baseball name interred at Gate of Heaven. Also look for **Billy Martin,** longtime infielder and manager who was eternally at odds with Yankees owner George Steinbrenner in the 1970s and 1980s; **Ralph Branca,** the Dodgers pitcher who surrendered Bobby Thomson's "shot heard 'round the world" to end a three-game playoff for the National League pennant in 1951; **John McSherry,** a longtime umpire; **Sal Yvars,** a career backup catcher in the 1940s and 1950s; and **Bill Froats,** a pitcher who played in just one major league game in 1955 for the Tigers.

GETTING THERE

Without traffic, it's about **45 minutes** from Midtown Manhattan to Gate of Heaven Cemetery, a drive of about **30 miles.** You'll travel north on Madison Avenue to the Madison Avenue Bridge, then hop onto I-87 and go north for 9.5 miles until exiting for NY-100/Central Park Avenue. When exiting, look for the merge to the Sprain Brook Parkway North and take it (it happens quickly). You'll stay on the Sprain Brook until the exit for Hawthorne. Then turn right, then left, and you'll see a roadside altar to the Virgin Mary. Turn onto that road, turn right at the end of the street, then make your first left and take that down to the cemetery entrance.

ACCOMMODATIONS

When selecting accommodations in New York, think most about location and affordability. First, is it close enough to the subway? And second, can you spend less than $200 per night? If both answers are yes, and the place has a good reputation, you should book your room immediately. Manhattan stays will start around $200 per night, especially if you're booking close to your visit. In the other boroughs, you could get away with a place for less, often around $150-200 per night.

NEAR YANKEE STADIUM

You'll only find budget-level chain hotels within a mile of Yankee Stadium, but go a bit farther out into the South Bronx and find **Opera House Hotel** (436 E. 149th St., Bronx, 718/407-2800, www.operahousehotel.com, $130-250). This hotel, set inside the former Bronx Opera House, takes on the modern boutique look with king and queen rooms. It also has a Yankees special: Book your room 60 days in advance, and they'll cut 20 percent off the rate.

NEAR CITI FIELD

With LaGuardia Airport just down the river and Downtown Flushing across the street, there are more than a few places to stay near Citi Field. If you're looking to avoid chains, try the **John Hotel** (133-12 37th Ave., Queens, 718/886-8556, www.johnhotel.com, $130-200), which offers relatively affordable full and queen rooms in a modern space.

Boasting a rooftop bar with views of Citi Field, the **Parc Hotel** (3916 College Point Blvd., Queens, 718/358-8897, www.theparchotel.com, $200-300) is a little expensive, but it has clean rooms with floor-to-ceiling windows, plenty of pillows on the bed, and artisan bath products.

OTHER NEIGHBORHOODS

In Manhattan, consider the **Jane Hotel** (113 Jane St., Manhattan, 212/924-6700, www. thejanenyc.com, $100-300), a quirky place that was designed to resemble quarters on a luxury liner. Beds are in cabins, and some rooms have bunks with communal bathrooms. This is great for the solo traveler, and it's just a few blocks from the 1, 2, and 3 trains.

In Brooklyn, there are plenty of hostels for solo travelers, like the **NY Moore Hostel** (179 Moore St., Brooklyn, 347/227-8634, www.nymoorehostel.com, $100-200), which has spacious and pleasant private and dorm rooms, no curfew, 24-hour reception, a courtyard, and a location close to the L train.

For those just wanting a private hotel experience, there's **Hotel Le Jolie** (235 Meeker Ave., Brooklyn, 718/625-2100, www. hotellejolie.com, $200-300). This spot has twin, queen, and king rooms decorated with millennial touches (bold-patterned wallpaper, charging docks), and it's just a six-minute walk to the L train.

GETTING AROUND

Much of New York City (except Lower Manhattan), is a grid, so it's easy to navigate. North-south streets in Manhattan are avenues. **1st Avenue** is east and **11th Avenue** is west. In between, from 1st to 11th, are **2nd, 3rd, Lexington, Park, Madison, 5th, 6th, 7th, 8th, 9th** (or **Columbus**), **10th** (or **Amsterdam**), then **11th** (or **West End**). West-east streets in Manhattan are streets, and they're mostly numbered. So, 220th Street is to the north, and the numbers go all the way down to 1st in the Bowery area.

Just south of 1st Street is **Houston Street** (HOW-ston), and then the rest of Lower Manhattan, Tribeca, and the Financial District. Major west-east streets to know include **125th Street** (Harlem), **86th Street** (Upper West Side and Upper East Side), **66th Street** (Lincoln Center and lower Central Park area), **42nd Street** (Midtown, Times Square, Broadway), **34th Street** (Garment District and Empire State Building), **14th Street** (Union Square), **Canal Street** (Lower

Manhattan, Chinatown), **Chambers Street** (Tribeca, World Trade Center), and **Wall Street** (New York Stock Exchange).

Broadway is a sometimes-diagonal road that runs north to south. At the foot of Central Park, Broadway is **Columbus Circle,** and a few blocks south, it becomes the Great White Way as the center of the great American theater district, also known as Broadway. **Times Square** is at 42nd Street and Broadway. After Union Square Park, Broadway runs parallel to other north-south streets and heads into the Financial District, with major landmarks including the World Trade Center, City Hall, and the New York Stock Exchange.

When traveling around the city, always give yourself ample time to navigate the subways, and be patient once you're on a train, as delays may occur. Don't walk more than two people abreast on sidewalks, and if you need to stop, move all the way to the inside (toward a building) of the sidewalk.

PUBLIC TRANSIT

New York has the most robust public transit system in America. The **MTA** (http://new. mta.info, $2.75 base per ride) runs the buses and trains, including the New York City subway.

If you're using MTA, you'll want to get a **MetroCard,** which is available by visiting a machine at any underground station landing. If you're staying in NYC for at least two days, purchase a $20 card right away (whether at the airport or at the first station you visit in the city) and refill after using it six times. Swiping the card through the reader at subway stations is an art form—one smooth motion, not too fast. If you can't get it right the first couple times, don't despair—everyone has been there.

Subway

The subway system can look confusing, but here's a general primer.

Know your major stations. **Grand Central Terminal-42nd Street** (42nd St. and Park Ave., Manhattan) and **Times Square-42nd Street** (42nd St. and 7th Ave.) are just a few blocks from each other, but the former connects with the 4-5-6 lines, which run along the east side of Manhattan, while the latter connects with the 1-2-3 lines, which run along the west side of Manhattan. You might also want to get to Times Square for the N-Q-R lines, which head into Queens. And if you happen to go to the wrong station, there's a **shuttle** (called Shuttle) that connects the two stations.

A bit farther south in Manhattan is **14th Street-Union Square** (14th St. and Broadway, Manhattan), which is where the N-Q-R hits the 4-5-6. The L is also here, and that line runs straight into Brooklyn (specifically, into ultra-gentrified hipster neighborhood Williamsburg). Going west, the L runs into both the 1-2-3 and A-C-E lines, which run along the west side of Manhattan, and the B-D-F-M lines, which connect the Bronx and Queens to Brooklyn via Manhattan.

In Brooklyn, **Atlantic Avenue-Barclays Center** (Flatbush Ave. and Atlantic Ave., Brooklyn) is where the 2-3, 4-5, B-D, and N-Q-R lines all meet. For Brooklynites, this is a good way to find your way into Manhattan or Queens.

In Queens, **Queensboro Plaza** (Queens Blvd. and 27th St., Queens) connects the N to the 7, which heads to Citi Field.

In the Bronx, **149th Street-Grand Concourse** (149th St. and Grand Concourse, Bronx) connects the 2 with the 4-5, or west side of Manhattan trains to east side of Manhattan trains. Go one more stop north on the 4 for Yankee Stadium.

Bus

New York's **bus system** ($2.75-3 per ride, $6.75 express bus ride) is also run by the MTA. It's vast. There's a bus route for every Manhattan avenue and for every main west-to-east artery. There are approximately 80 bus routes in Brooklyn, 100 routes in Queens, and about 60 routes in the Bronx, plus about 30-40 routes in Staten Island. To ride the bus, simply dip your MetroCard in the reader by the driver. Once it's detected, take your card. That's it!

Commuter Rail

Staying outside of the city? From Newark and Hoboken, you can take **New Jersey Transit** ($4.25-5.25, www.njtransit.com) into **New York Pennsylvania Station** (31st St. and 8th Ave.). Or, from Newark, Hoboken, and Jersey City, you can take **PATH** (www.panynj.gov/path), a limited rail that connects major Jersey cities to **World Trade Center** (Barclay St. and Church St.). The closest subway line to the World Trade Center is the E, though the R-W and 1-2-3 are just blocks away.

If you're up north in Westchester County or Dutchess County, you may want to take **Metro-North Railroad** ($7-35, www.mta.info/mnr), also part of the MTA. Trains generally run multiple times each day and are quiet (postgame cars leaving Yankee Stadium may be louder). Metro-North allows passengers to drink alcohol on board. (Pro tip: **Beer Table** (www.beertable.com) at Grand Central sells outstanding beer for your train ride.)

These trains travel to and from **Grand Central Terminal** (42nd St. and Park Ave., Manhattan), a gorgeous 1913 station with 60 shops and 35 eating destinations. If you've never been to Grand Central, I suggest going just to experience it. One of the coolest New York experiences is to find yourself in the middle of the main concourse, where passengers from a host of train and subway lines, all walking purposefully with tunnel vision, converge. You'll be immersed in a human pinball machine, or what can be best described as the center of anyone's universe at any moment. Look up and you'll see the stunning barrel-vaulted ceiling showing a mural of constellations. For decades, this mural couldn't be seen. Roof leakage in the 1940s led to officials covering up the original mural with boards, and though a second mural was painted on the boards, decades of cigarette smoke from passengers obscured it. Today the original mural has been recovered and restored.

TAXI, UBER, AND LYFT

If any American city is synonymous with the yellow taxicab, it's New York. Because of Lyft and Uber, there aren't as many taxis on the roads as there used to be, but it's still a fine choice for getting around, especially if you're going somewhere that isn't easily accessible via the subway. Taxis have a minimum fare of $2.50 and charge $0.50 per one-fifth of a mile. After 8pm, rides are surcharged $0.50. **Yellow Cab** (800/609-8731) is the big operator in town.

To hail a taxi, stand on the sidewalk along a relatively busy street (in Manhattan, that's basically every street). Look for the light panel atop the cab: If the center alone is lit, that means it's available. Raise one arm close to the street to let the cab know you're looking, and it should pull over as close to you as possible. Once it's stopped, get into the back seat and close the door, then tell the driver your destination. When the driver has reached the destination, you can pay. These days, cabs accept credit cards, and there's an electronic panel in the back seat that handles transactions and supplies entertainment while the cab is en route.

Yellow taxis in Manhattan can and should drive outside of Manhattan, even if drivers protest about having to leave the borough. Outside Manhattan, you may see green cabs: These go everywhere within the five boroughs.

As for Lyft and Uber, they're all over the place in the New York area. It's generally the same cost between taxis, Lyft, and Uber. For shorter distances, taxis are better, but for longer trips, you'll get more bang for your buck with the ride-share services.

CAR

I do not recommend driving in New York City, especially if it's your first time here. Traffic patterns can be challenging and signage confusing, but more than anything, the speed and rhythm of New York driving is unlike driving anywhere else in America. Take it from someone who has logged

COOPERSTOWN AND THE NATIONAL BASEBALL HALL OF FAME

National Baseball Hall of Fame and Museum in Cooperstown

If you have the time, find a way to visit the **National Baseball Hall of Fame and Museum** (25 Main St., Cooperstown, NY, www.baseballhall.org, 9am-9pm daily Memorial Day weekend-Labor Day, 9am-5pm daily Labor Day-Memorial Day weekend, $25, $20 seniors, $15 ages 7-12, free ages 6 and under). This is a bucket-list trip for any baseball fan, and trust me, the museum is worth it.

Plan to spend 2-3 days going back to the museum, as you'll want to take your time studying its vast collection. You'll find gloves and bats used before 1900; jerseys, hats, and photographs of the Dead Ball Era; world championship rings; a ball from just about every no-hitter ever thrown; team-specific exhibits; special exhibits that change each year; a Phillie Phanatic outfit; and, of course, the beautiful Hall of Fame itself, showing the plaques of each inductee. You could easily spend 3-4 hours just in the hall itself.

Nearby is **Doubleday Field** (1 Doubleday Ct., 607/547-2270), first used in 1920; the venue can hold nearly 10,000 people. It regularly hosts games but is otherwise just cool to look at for a few minutes.

To get to the museum, I suggest driving, then taking the **trolley** (8:30am-9pm daily Memorial Day-Labor Day, 9:30am-7:15pm Sat.-Sun. Labor Day-mid-Oct., $2). Park off NY-28 in the blue or red lot, and the trolley will pick you up there, taking you directly to Doubleday Field and the museum.

Don't just confine your stay to the hall and museum; Cooperstown is a fun small town beside Otsego Lake that's oozing with charm. Walk Main Street to visit a bat manufacturer, bookstore, wax museum, and numerous cafés. And don't miss a visit to **Brewery Ommegang** (656 County Highway 33, 607/544-1800, www.ommegang.com, noon-5pm Wed.-Thurs., noon-7pm Fri.-Sat., 11am-4pm Sun.). A 10-minute drive south from Downtown Cooperstown, this revered brewery known for its exceptional Belgian-style beers offers a fun and spacious place to hang, with outdoor seating, plenty of merchandise, and tours. It's well worth a few hours in between visits to the Hall of Fame.

GETTING THERE

From Midtown Manhattan, the drive to Cooperstown is about **190 miles** and takes around **four hours.** To get there, the best route starts by going over the George Washington Bridge to NJ-17 North. That'll turn into NY-17 North. Continue up NY-206 West, NY-10 North, and NY-28 North to reach Cooperstown. The road may meander a bit, but it's no more time than the major highway route off to the east. This route gives you a quieter ride with more local flavor.

thousands of hours driving into, out of, and through the city: People here are smart and tough, and they're usually focused on getting to their destination quickly. To drive here means being defensively aggressive—keeping a watch on everyone and everything around you while maximizing your speed and efficiency at every opportunity.

Parking

If you want to give driving a go, know that you will hit traffic somewhere, no matter what time of day you're driving. Avoid **peak rush hour** (8am-9:30am and 4:30pm-6pm weekdays). **Parking** can be a nice slice of hell: If you can find street parking that isn't attached to a meter, get that spot, but you'll need to know how to parallel park. Also, read the signs: In New York, most of the streets are cleaned at least once each week, and when that happens, cars have to vacate their parking spots (the alternate side of the street opens up for parking). This could be for three to four hours a week. If you fail to move your car when street cleaning occurs, you will be ticketed. Want to park in a lot? You'll pay $20-50 a day, depending on where you park and when you arrive.

Toll Roads and Bridges

You'll have to pay a **toll** on some roads and bridges, like the **Robert F. Kennedy (Triborough), George Washington,** and **Verrazzano-Narrows,** while others are free. The Queensboro Bridge (also known as the 59th Street Bridge), Brooklyn Bridge, Manhattan Bridge, and Williamsburg Bridge are all free. Smaller bridges that connect the Bronx to Manhattan farther north are free (my favorites are the Third Avenue Bridge, which goes into Manhattan, and the Willis Avenue Bridge, which goes into the Bronx). Consider taking them if you're trying to avoid paying the toll.

Major Roads and Highways

I-87 slashes through the west side of Westchester County to the north, then runs along the Harlem River in the Bronx before connecting to I-278. **I-95** comes in from Connecticut and the east side of Westchester County, hugging the east side of the Bronx before cutting across toward the Hudson River. The George Washington Bridge carries I-95 into New Jersey, where it continues toward Newark.

I-278 continues from I-87 in the Bronx onto the Robert F. Kennedy (Triborough) Bridge, and into Queens as the **Grand Central Parkway** before quickly veering south toward Brooklyn. Here, it's called the **Brooklyn-Queens Expressway,** and it connects to major Brooklyn neighborhoods and, for a moment, the (near JFK airport) **Belt Parkway,** before going to the Verrazzano-Narrows Bridge into Staten Island. I-278 cuts through Staten Island into Elizabeth, New Jersey, where it meets up with I-95 (at this point the New Jersey Turnpike).

Back in Queens and staying on the Grand Central Parkway, you can get to LaGuardia Airport and Citi Field. **I-678** comes off the Hutchinson River Parkway north of Queens, then heads into Queens, running past Citi Field en route south to John F. Kennedy International Airport. Also in Queens is **I-495,** also known as the **Long Island Expressway.** This, as you might expect, goes to Long Island.

There are no major highways in Manhattan (which is why the subway is so necessary). The only slight exceptions are **FDR Drive,** which runs along the Harlem River and East River as the easternmost route in Manhattan, and the **West River Drive** and **Henry Hudson Parkway,** or **NY-9A,** which runs along the Hudson River as the westernmost route in Manhattan (well, most of the time at least). Since these are the most "express" routes up and down the borough, they are usually pretty packed.

SIDE TRIP: BIRTHPLACE OF BASEBALL MONUMENT

Believed to be the site of the first baseball game, played in approximately 1846, **Elysian Fields** in Hoboken, New Jersey, is marked by the **Birthplace of Baseball Monument** (11th St. and Washington St.). A stone with a plaque notes that the first game may have been played there between the Knickerbockers and the New Yorks.

GETTING THERE

You can take **New Jersey Transit** ($4.25-5.25, www.njtransit.com) to Hoboken (1 Hudson Pl., Hoboken). Alternately, you can take **PATH** (www.panynj.gov/path), a limited rail service that connects major Jersey cities to the **World Trade Center** (Barclay St. and Church St., Manhattan). From the Hoboken train station, you may have to hail a cab for a minute, or you can walk north up Washington Street, through the heart of the city. The ride from Manhattan takes about **30 minutes.**

From **Midtown Manhattan,** the quickest way to Hoboken should be a trip across 42nd Street west to the Lincoln Tunnel, which rests deep down in the Hudson River, to NJ-495 West for just one exit. Get off at Park Avenue and merge onto Willow Avenue going south. Turn left onto 14th Street, then turn right onto Washington Street to reach 11th. It's a **four-mile** drive that takes about **15 minutes** without traffic.

TRENTON, NEW JERSEY

Trenton offers a relaxing respite between big-city baseball games in New York and Philadelphia. Across the Delaware River and about 30 miles northeast of Philadelphia, New Jersey's capital city is home to the Yankees' double-A minor league affiliate, and it also has a robust history in the game.

Baseball in Trenton goes back to 1867, when the Philadelphia Athletics (not those Athletics) beat the Trenton Atlantic 66-8. In time, the sport would grow, and baseball would continue to be played in Trenton. Starting in the 1930s, the city was home to minor league teams like the Senators (Fall of Famer Goose Goslin played for them) and the Giants. Willie Mays made his minor league debut with the Trenton Giants in 1950; he was in New York by 1951.

GETTING THERE

Train

Grab a Northeast Corridor train on **New Jersey Transit** (www.njtransit.com, under $20) from **New York Pennsylvania Station** (31st St. and 8th Ave., Manhattan) to the **Trenton Transit Center** (72 S. Clinton Ave.). This is a 90-minute trip, give or take. To get to Arm & Hammer Park from the train station, you can walk 1.5 miles south on NJ-129 to Cass Street West, or you can hop in a ride-sharing vehicle.

Car

From **New York,** the fastest way to Trenton is via **I-95** to **I-195.** For this route, you'll drive out of Manhattan via the Lincoln Tunnel, taking NJ-495 from there straight to I-95 South. That's the **New Jersey Turnpike,** a toll road that zips straight through New Jersey. Exit I-95 at I-195 West, then continue on NJ-29 into Trenton. Arm & Hammer Park is off NJ-29 at Cass Street/Thunder Road. The **70-mile** drive should take no more than **90 minutes** without traffic.

For a more **scenic route,** take I-95 from the Lincoln Tunnel to I-280 West through the Newark/East Orange area. Hop onto I-287 South from there, and drive for 22 miles until exiting onto US-202 South/US-206 South. This nice finish will take you through rural areas of Central and South Jersey, including

Princeton University, until coming into Trenton. This **two-hour** drive is an **85-mile** trip.

ARM & HAMMER PARK

Also known as Mercer County Waterfront Park, **Arm & Hammer Park** (1 Thunder Rd.) is home for the Trenton Thunder, the double-A affiliate of the **Yankees** since 2003. The team was born in 1994, soon becoming a Red Sox affiliate before switching over to their rivals. Quite a few great players have spent some time in Trenton, including Nomar Garciaparra (whose number is retired), Aaron Judge, CC Sabathia, Alex Rodriguez, Derek Jeter, and Roger Clemens. If you want to get a taste of Yankee baseball without paying a lot of money, and see a game in between New York and Philadelphia, watching the Thunder play makes a heck of a lot of sense.

Resting beside the Delaware River, Arm & Hammer seats 6,150 fans in a classic minor league-style configuration with a split level of **seating around the infield** (sections 101-122 and sections 201-216 with a picnic area), an extended **picnic area** along the left-field line, a **family fun area** along the right-field line, and a bombardment of advertisements on a tall outfield fence. There's also a **suite level** (suites 1-15) extending from first base around home plate to third base.

Arm & Hammer is affordable; seats are no more than $15. The food includes both traditional ballpark fare and some specialty items. Look for a sandwich featuring Trenton's most famous food product, **pork roll** (like Canadian bacon). Other offerings include crab fries from famous Philadelphia-area restaurant **Chickie's & Pete's,** and desserts like soft-serve ice cream, Philadelphia water ice (essentially Italian ice), and gelati (a mix of ice cream and water ice).

PHILADELPHIA
PHILLIES

The best way to describe Philadelphia's sports scene is with this quote: "Philadelphia is the only city where you can experience the thrill of victory and the agony of reading about it the next day." Who said it? Only the greatest baseball player in Philadelphia Phillies history, Hall of Famer Mike Schmidt. He knew what so many have found out over time: Philadelphia fans expect a lot out of their sports teams, and a poor effort won't be ignored. Phillies fans in particular hold their team to a high standard.

The Phillies have lost more games than any other American sports franchise. They were futile for decades, long the second fiddle to the more strapping Athletics. But then the A's moved to Kansas City (and later Oakland), leaving the Phils alone to languish in the basement of the hearts of all

Philly sports fans (and of the National League standings). Things changed after the team moved to Veterans Stadium in 1971, and Mike Schmidt joined the team with future Hall of Fame pitcher Steve Carlton. After 97 years, the Phillies won their first world championship in 1980. Twenty-eight years later, during another run of success, the Phils took their second title. During those years, fans packed their new home of Citizens Bank Park with an impressive three-year sellout streak. When the Phils are good, the fans come out, but don't be fooled: Even when the team is terrible, the fans are always watching, just with half an eye open while grumbling at the television.

Today the Phils continue to rock CBP, fueled by the presence of megastar Bryce Harper. He plays hard and doesn't mind showing his emotions, making him a perfect athlete for the sometimes-fickle Philly fan base. Then again, he absolutely will have to experience the agony of reading about his performance once in a while.

PLANNING YOUR TIME

Most visitors can handle Philadelphia in a **weekend.** One day includes the ball game, plus maybe noodling around South Philadelphia and unearthing its charms. Another day includes the nickel tour of the historic landmarks and other sites in the downtown area, called Center City. If you want a more adventurous trip, tack on **another two days,** get a little deeper into the Old City area, check out the Philadelphia Museum of Art, and spend an evening in the hipster havens of Northern Liberties and Fishtown. The longer you stay, the more neighborhoods you can visit, and there's a lot to discover.

Regardless of how long you visit, you probably won't be staying near the ballpark because there's barely any lodging around there, and you'd spend too much time on public transportation. The right move is to get a hotel room in the heart of **Center City,** within walking distance of landmarks and one train ride to Citizens Bank Park.

CBP can be unbearably **humid** for **midsummer day games** (July and August), and if you're sitting along the uncovered lower level along the first-base line, expect the sun on top of you in the afternoon and in your eyes in the early evening. Thinking about visiting in **April**? Be prepared to bundle up and stay dry, because temperatures will dip into the 40s and 50s at night, with **rain** possible. The best conditions for a Phils game tend to be between **May** and **July** (**September** isn't bad, either), with **June and July night games** often gorgeous and relatively comfortable.

GETTING THERE

AIR

The major airport in Philadelphia, and the one you would be flying into, is **Philadelphia International Airport** (PHL, 8000 Essington Ave., www.phl.org). Located at the very southern end of the city, the airport is at minimum a 5-minute drive from Citizens Bank Park and a 15- to 20-minute drive from Center City Philadelphia. The easiest route into Center City is I-95 North to I-676 West, though that can get backed up quickly.

The airport is home to **Air Canada** (888/247-2262, www.aircanada.com), **American Airlines** (800/433-7300, www.aa.com), **Delta** (800/221-1212, www.delta.com), **Frontier** (800/432-1359, www.flyfrontier.com), **jetBlue** (800/538-2583, www.jetblue.com), **Southwest** (800/435-9792, www.southwest.com), **Spirit** (801/401-2222, www.spirit.com), and **United** (800/864-8331, www.united.com), plus several international carriers. You can fly to basically every major American city from Philly.

Airport Transportation

You can reach Center City from the airport via **SEPTA** (Southeastern Pennsylvania Transit Authority, www.septa.org, $2.50 single ride) on the **R1** regional rail line. The Center

Citizens Bank Park
PHILADELPHIA

To Fairmount Park

To Evil Genius Beer Company, Martha, and Memphis Taproom

PHILADELPHIA ZOO

KELLY DR

N 34TH ST

76

OLDE KENSINGTON

W GIRARD AVE

PAESANO'S

PHILADELPHIA MUSEUM OF ART

ROCKY STEPS

SPRING GARDEN ST

N BROAD ST

RIDGE AVE

95

LANCASTER AVE

LOGAN SQUARE

YARDS BREWING COMPANY

30th Street Station

MARKET ST

Megabus M

M

UNIVERSITY CITY

CHESTNUT ST

676

LOGAN SQUARE

JFK PLAZA

READING TERMINAL MARKET

FRANKLIN SQUARE

NATIONAL CONSTITUTION CENTER

WALNUT ST

SPRUCE ST

HIDDEN RIVER OUTFITTERS

VERNICK FOOD & DRINK

Suburban M

Jefferson

Greyhound Station

CENTER CITY

M

Jefferson

INDEPENDENCE NATIONAL HISTORICAL PARK

University of Pennsylvania

River

Schuylkill

LOEWS PHILADELPHIA HOTEL

RITTENHOUSE SQUARE

Walnut-Locust

LIBERTY BELL

MITCHELL & NESS NOSTALGIA CO.

MUSEUM OF THE AMERICAN REVOLUTION

676

River

Delaware

805

MONK'S CAFÉ

SHIBE VINTAGE SPORTS

MIDDLE CHILD

INDEPENDENCE HALL

WASHINGTON SQUARE

PADDLE PENN'S LANDING

RITA'S ITALIAN ICE

Lombard South M

S BROAD ST

LOMBARD ST

SOUTH ST

BOB AND BARBARA'S LOUNGE

CHRISTIAN ST

PHILADELPHIA HOTEL BELLA VISTA

To Bartram's Garden

GRAYS FERRY AVE

WASHINGTON AVE

POINT BREEZE

ITALIAN MARKET

SOUTHWARK

LITTLE SAIGON

95

Delaware River

76

GRAYS FERRY

Ellsworth-Federal

PHO 75

SOUTH PHILLY BARBACOA

PAT'S KING OF STEAKS

S CHRISTOPHER COLUMBUS BLVD

S 3RD ST

S 17TH ST

E PASSYUNK AVE

PASSYUNK SQUARE

To Bartram's Garden

SOUTH PHILADELPHIA

BREWERY ARS

SNYDER AVE

W PASSYUNK AVE

JOHN'S ROAST PORK

WHITMAN

To Philadelphia International Airport

W OREGON AVE

291

TONY LUKE'S

FDR Park

CHICKIE'S & PETE'S

PACKER AVE

76

PACKER PARK

SEE DETAIL

PATTISON AVE

NRG M

CITIZENS BANK PARK

To Philadelphia International Airport

Wells Fargo Center

Lincoln Financial Stadium

95

LEAGUE ISLAND BLVD

0   0.5 mi
0   0.5 km

© MOON.COM

COURTYARD BY MARRIOTT PHILADELPHIA SOUTH AT THE NAVY YARD

Detail map

P   P   P

HARTRANT ST

ASHBURN ALLEY

FEDERAL DONUTS

CITIZENS BANK WAY

CITIZENS BANK PARK

NEW ERA PHILLIES TEAM STORE

S DARIEN ST

VETERANS STADIUM LIBERTY BELL

XFINITY LIVE!

PATTISON AVE

S 11TH ST

P

0   200 yds
0   200 m

City stops are **Suburban Station** (16th St. and John F. Kennedy Blvd.) and **Jefferson Station** (12th St. and Filbert St.).

For a rental car, walk outside from the baggage claim to Zone 9 on South Commercial Road to catch a five-minute shuttle to the agency you've chosen. The big ones are all here.

CAR

From **New York City,** Philadelphia is merely a **95-mile** shot west on **I-78** and south on **I-95,** which for much of the drive is the **New Jersey Turnpike.** This can be a swift, **90-minute** drive or a painful **2.5-hour** drive, depending on when you make it. The best times to go are 10am-1pm and after 8pm.

If you're driving in from **Trenton,** New Jersey, it's a quicker **35 miles** and **40 minutes,** starting with **US-1 South** to **I-295 South** to **I-95 South.** Taking US-1 the whole way down (to **I-76 East**) will add on another 20 minutes, sometimes much more, as the road stays on street level for quite a while (as **Roosevelt Boulevard**).

TRAIN

Amtrak (www.amtrak.com) buzzes into Philadelphia at landmark **30th Street Station** (2955 Market St.). A beautiful Depression-era station with high ceilings and art deco touches, 30th Street is walking distance from the heart of Center City but also provides transit connections via **SEPTA** (www.septa.org, $2.50 single ride). The **Market-Frankford Line** is the best way through Center City, though there's also **trolley service** to Jefferson Station.

Amtrak routes that connect New York to Philadelphia include the highly trafficked **Northeast Regional** and **Acela Express,** connecting the major East Coast cities; the **Pennsylvanian,** which starts in New York City and pushes west toward Pittsburgh; the **Cardinal,** starting in New York and heading west toward Chicago; the **Carolinian,** also starting in New York and ending in Charlotte; the **Crescent,** connecting New York to New Orleans; the **Keystone,** going from New York to Harrisburg, Pennsylvania; and the **Silver Service/Palmetto,** running from New York to Tampa and Miami. The Amtrak routes going south from New York City stop in **Trenton** before reaching Philadelphia. Depending on the train, the ride takes 1-1.5 hours; tickets start around $30.

BUS

Greyhound (www.greyhound.com) isn't a bad option from **New York City.** There are

statue of Phillies pitcher Steve Carlton by sculptor Zenos Frudakis

multiple daily trips, lasting 2-3 hours, that start at $10. The **Greyhound station** (1001 Filbert St.) is accessible to Center City destinations and the Broad Street Line subway, which takes you to Citizens Bank Park.

For an alternative, **Megabus** (http://us.megabus.com) has several daily routes from New York City, which start at $15. Megabus drops passengers off at **30th Street Station** (2955 Market St.); it'll take an additional rail ride to reach Center City, and two of them to reach Citizens Bank Park.

Citizens Bank Park

For three decades, the Phillies played in one of baseball's largest venues, the nearly 67,000-seat Veterans Stadium, which was round, concrete, and devoid of character. In 2004, they flipped the script, opening the intimate-feeling **Citizens Bank Park** (1 Citizens Bank Way, www.mlb.com/phillies); when the Phillies are good, it has the ability to catch fire like few other stadiums.

Every one of Philly's professional sports teams plays in the same small area, called the sports complex. On the rare Sunday afternoon in September or October when the Phillies and the NFL's Eagles are both at home, the area can be a madhouse. Whether or not anyone else is playing at the same time, Phillies games generally take on a spirited tone, with tailgating permitted in the parking lots surrounding the stadium, and fans clad in red, white, and blue.

Citizens Bank Park is like a stock image of a retro-classic ballpark. Made of red brick and steel, CBP looks and feels like a venue that has been around forever. The small left- and right-field corners make home runs possible at all times, and the park's architecture, allowing for a few wind tunnels, can lead to absolute crush jobs to center and right-center field from power hitters. The result: Citizens Bank Park is one of baseball's friendliest parks for home runs. With seating

constructed on top of the field, and plenty of angles with standing-room areas dotting the concourses (especially in the outfield concourse called Ashburn Alley), there's no shortage of places to watch those dingers fly.

ORIENTATION

The ballpark is in South Philly, three miles from the Center City district, where you're probably staying. It's part of the area known as the sports complex. There are three entry gates at Citizens Bank Park: **first base, third base,** and the popular **left field** entrance.

Gates open at **Ashburn Alley** two hours before first pitch. For a good way to enter, opt for the left-field gate. Upon walking in, you'll see the Phillies Wall of Fame and a courtyard with installations signifying the Phillies' retired numbers.

TICKETS AND SEATING

Pricing and Seating Plan

The Phils use **dynamic pricing.** Expect more expensive tickets when the **Yankees, Red Sox,** and **division rivals** come to town. The cheap games are typically reserved for games against teams that aren't performing well. So, for example, a seat in the field level outfield area (an average seat) would cost something like $30 for a game against the Marlins or Rockies, while that same seat might be more like $60 for a Yankees game.

CBP has **four levels,** but there's nuance in the pricing structure and naming conventions. The **100 level** is the lower level: The **outfield Field seats** (sections 101-107 in right field and sections 140-148 in left field) are moderately priced, while **infield Field seats** (sections 108-139) are more expensive and specially priced according to their proximity to the infield (right behind the plate and between the dugouts is the high roller-friendly **Diamond Club,** with personal service and cushy seating).

In the **200 level,** sections 201-205 are the **Pavilion,** a short deck in right field, while sections 241-245 are the **Scoreboard Porch** in left field, and these two areas are similarly

Citizens Bank Park

priced. Sections 206-211 are also called the **Pavilion,** but they're located in foul territory; sections 233-237 are the **Arcade,** and these sections are priced like the lower-level seats in the outfield. Sections 212-232 are the **Hall of Fame suites area** (sections 215-229 are the **Hall of Fame Club,** which includes a separate, large food-and-drink area for patrons).

The **300 level** starts the upper deck: Sections 301-310 are the **Pavilion Deck,** the big section out at the top of right field in fair and foul territories. Sections 312-329 are the **Terrace,** priced at the same level as the **Arcade** and **Pavilion** seats. Sections 330-333 are also called **Terrace,** but these left-field seats are lower priced.

The **400 level** includes sections 412-434, and this **Terrace Deck** area is the nosebleed. The Phils also sell **Rooftop Bleacher** seats, which are way out atop the buildings in center field and are the cheapest seats in the park. Finally, there typically are **standing-room-only** tickets. If you want this option, you'll have to ask in person at the box office. Sometimes these tickets are real bargains when high-profile teams come to town.

Where to Buy Tickets

You can get Phillies tickets through the **MLB Ballpark app,** which also offers rewards and exclusive content. Typically, you can get discounted seats through **StubHub** just before a game, but if the Phils are drawing fans, be ready to pay a little more than you'd like regardless of your method.

Best Seats

All of the chairs at Citizens Bank Park are angled toward the infield, which means no craning your neck to see the action at home plate. Plus, the chairs are aligned so that nobody is directly in front of anyone else.

I've enjoyed games from just about everywhere at Citizens Bank Park, and my favorite place is **row 1 of section 330 in the Terrace.** The sightline is perfect, giving you a complete view of the action while not too far from the infield. Plus, the shade should be your friend much of the day, and the cost is affordable for solo travelers and families alike.

For night games, you can't go wrong with the front rows of the Pavilion in **sections 201-205** or in the **left-field lower level, sections 142-145.** The fans here are pretty rowdy, even when the place isn't packed, giving you the true Philly game-day experience. For day games, if you want to pay more for your ticket, lower-level seats are great, but opt for **sections 125-132.** The sun will be behind you, and the sightlines rule.

If you just want to hang out and enjoy the action, snag a cheap ticket and just walk around, because the concourses are full of railings where you can place your beer and food and just watch the game. If you're alone or with a friend, you can often nudge into one of the primo standing areas in **Ashburn Alley,** the ballpark's outfield concourse. These include a large patio area in left-center field and the absolutely awesome railing above the visitors' bullpen in right-center field. If you can grab a spot

YOUR BEST DAY AT CITIZENS BANK PARK

Let's imagine you're spending the evening at Citizens Bank Park for a Phillies game. Here's how to maximize your Philly experience before, during, and after the game.

8 HOURS BEFORE FIRST PITCH
Head over to **Reading Terminal Market** for an early lunch. I suggest **DiNic's** for a roast pork sandwich, but you can just as easily buy slices of Lebanon bologna and eat them off your hand. Who am I to judge?

7 HOURS BEFORE FIRST PITCH
Walk off that full belly by looking for a T-shirt or throwback jersey, because it's better to fit in than to be an enemy here. You have two options: a T-shirt at **Shibe Vintage Sports** or a jersey at **Mitchell & Ness Nostalgia Co.** If you don't buy something, at least you'll get a history lesson through clothing.

6 HOURS BEFORE FIRST PITCH
Next, walk 15 minutes southwest through Center City and have a beer or two at **Monk's Café.**

4 HOURS BEFORE FIRST PITCH
Walk over to Broad Street and catch the Orange Line at the **Walnut-Locust SEPTA station** (200 S. Broad St.). Hop off at the **Ellsworth-Federal SEPTA station** (Broad St. and Ellsworth St.) and walk east on Ellsworth about 10 minutes to **South Philly Barbacoa.** Yes, you're here for more food, but it's essential. Take this opportunity to walk around the famed **Italian Market.**

2 HOURS BEFORE FIRST PITCH
Head back to the Ellsworth-Federal station

Philles fans enjoying a game

and go south. Your next stop is **NRG station** (3600 S. Broad St.). From there, walk along Pattison Avenue toward Citizens Bank Park, then head in through the left-field gate.

DURING THE GAME
Check out the **Phillies Wall of Fame** and get in line for **Chickie's & Pete's** famous crab fries. Catch some of the contest while standing around **Ashburn Alley.**

AFTER THE GAME
Make some new friends by heading to one of the bars at **Xfinity Live!** If you crave a slightly more insider's experience, take the Broad Street Line north to the **Lombard-South SEPTA station** (Broad St. and South St.) and visit **Bob and Barbara's Lounge.**

No matter where you start the post-game activity, end it by taking a car to **Pat's King of Steaks** for a cheesesteak. If you've never been, you have to go, and no better time than 3:38am.

there, and the game is wild, you'll just love listening to Philly fans (hopefully playfully) give it to an opposing pitcher. (Trivia: When the ballpark was constructed, the Phillies put the home bullpen over the visitors' bullpen, exposing their own pitchers to the fans. It didn't go very well. Later during that first season, the Phils swapped the placement of the bullpens.)

KNOW BEFORE YOU GO

You can bring in a 16- by 16- by 8-inch **bag,** but glass containers are a no-no. If attending in April or even late September, check weather conditions and maybe bring a **sweatshirt, jacket,** or **coat.** Going to a day game at any time of the year? Wear some **sunscreen.**

The Phillies allow **tailgating** in parking lots A-H, K, and M-N. Lots M and N are where you'll find the rowdy crowd.

Accessibility

Guests with disabilities can enter Citizens Bank Park at any gate. **Elevators** are located at sections 103, 112, 119, 123, 133, 137, and 141. If needing assistance, fans can visit **guest services** (sections 122, 318). This is also where to go if you need a **wheelchair.** A photo ID or valid credit card is necessary as a deposit, but wheelchairs are otherwise free. **Service animals** are welcome at Citizens Bank Park.

Fans with disabilities can get a **complimentary ticket** for their government-funded **attendant** by calling 215/463-1000. **Wheelchair seats** have up to three seats next to them that can be used for companions; these spaces are typically at the top of the section.

Accessible parking is available in the stadium's **preferred lots** (P, Q, R, S, and V, $18). Be sure to display your state-issued disabled **parking placard.**

GETTING THERE

Subway

The best method for traveling to Citizens Bank Park, especially if you're staying in Center City, is by taking the subway via SEPTA. The **Broad Street Line,** or the **Orange Line,** runs underneath Broad Street, connecting City Hall and points south to the sports complex. The stop you want for Citizens Bank Park is **NRG station** (3600 S. Broad St.). A one-way fare is $2.50, but buy your return trip before starting your journey.

Driving

Because the sports complex is full of parking lots, and because both **I-76** and **I-95** thread near the venues, driving to the game isn't a bad idea. **Official sports complex lots** (named A-H, K, M-N, T-X) go for $18, while **preferred parking lots** closer to the stadium (P-S) are typically reserved for

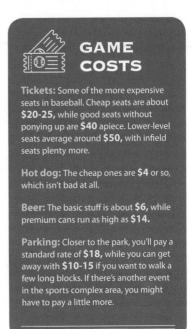

GAME COSTS

Tickets: Some of the more expensive seats in baseball. Cheap seats are about **$20-25,** while good seats without ponying up are **$40** apiece. Lower-level seats average around **$50,** with infield seats plenty more.

Hot dog: The cheap ones are **$4** or so, which isn't bad at all.

Beer: The basic stuff is about **$6,** while premium cans run as high as **$14.**

Parking: Closer to the park, you'll pay a standard rate of **$18,** while you can get away with **$10-15** if you want to walk a few long blocks. If there's another event in the sports complex area, you might have to pay a little more.

fans with parking passes. **Private vendors** around the official lots charge fluctuating rates that depend on the expected attendance at the sports complex; usually their rates are low, but you'll have to walk a bit.

Tailgating is permitted in lots A-H, K, and M-N. The M and N lots surround a warehouse called Jetro; this area is known for its rowdier crowd.

PARK FEATURES AND SIGHTS

Before heading into the park, check out the **Veterans Stadium Liberty Bell** (third-base gate) that welcomes fans. The bell was rescued from the now-imploded stadium that hosted the Phils from 1971 to 2003, then refurbished for the new park. At the Vet, it first rested in center field, about halfway up the grandstand, where it was struck by a home-run ball hit by slugger Greg Luzinski. Later the bell moved to the very top of the stadium, where nobody could touch it. But now you can!

BE A FAN

You've probably heard some stories about Philadelphia sports fans. Maybe you're a little nervous heading into the belly of the beast. Here's my tip: If you wear the logo of the Mets, Braves, Nationals, Red Sox, or Yankees, or if you're rooting for your favorite team as it plays the Phils, prepare to hear something from Philly fans. Your best response is to playfully go along with it; if you attempt to retaliate or talk back, it may get worse, and nobody wants a situation to escalate. Truthfully, while they're very passionate, most Philly sports fans are gentle.

the neon Liberty Bell

Pay attention after the Phillies hit a home run: The **Liberty Bell** out in right-center field will light up and ring, then you'll hear a **recording of a vintage homer call** from Harry Kalas, the late Phils play-by-play voice. "That ball's outta here!" he may scream. After a Phils win, the bell will ring once more, then you'll hear Kalas's beloved version of the classic 1959 tune **"High Hopes."** Stay for that, as the fans may sing along with Harry.

Ashburn Alley

Modeled after the outfield concourse at Oriole Park at Camden Yards, **Ashburn Alley** (outfield, 100 level) is the hub of activity at Citizens Bank Park. Home to most of the popular food vendors, it's a place where folks can stand and watch the game against a railing, and even learn the history of one of baseball's oldest franchises.

Look for the **Ashburn Alley sign,** modeled after an iconic green Philadelphia street sign. Nearby is a **statue of Richie Ashburn,** the man for whom the alley was named. Ashburn was a speedy Phillies Hall of Fame outfielder during the 1940s and 1950s, and later its super-casual, tell-it-like-it-is broadcaster for more than 30 years. The statue (which depicts Ashburn running, naturally) is right in the middle of the alley in center field. Surrounding him are **placards** on the ground signifying franchise all-stars. (A **statue of Harry Kalas** can be found just west of the scoreboard on the concourse in left field.)

Ashburn Alley is also home to some of the best **standing-room** spots in the park, including the railing above the opposing team's bullpen and a patio overlooking

left-center field that also has a few high-top tables.

Over in the right-field area of the alley, look for **The Yard** (section 104), a 13,000-square-foot children's experience highlighted by a Wiffle ball field resembling the ballpark. Here, kids can play speed pitch, try their hand at launching hot dogs using the same toy used by the Phillie Phanatic when the team mascot shoots wieners into the stands, and go up a climbing wall. The Yard opens with ballpark gates, then closes in the seventh inning.

Phillies Wall of Fame

Located at the left-field gate is the **Phillies Wall of Fame,** a collection of plaques honoring notable names in Philadelphia baseball history, including former Athletics (1901-1954). It's an impressive group of names in the Wall of Fame, including Mike Schmidt, Steve Carlton, Dick Allen, Jim Thome, Roy Halladay, Connie Mack, Jimmie Foxx, and Harry Kalas.

Art installations in front of the Wall of Fame depict the Phillies' retired numbers—1 for Richie Ashburn, 14 for Jim Bunning, 20 for Mike Schmidt, 32 for Steve Carlton, and

36 for Robin Roberts—and look for two world championship trophy replicas (in honor of the wins in 1980 and 2008).

Phillie Phanatic

Born in 1978, the **Phillie Phanatic** is without question baseball's best mascot. Tall, green, furry, and stout, the Phanatic is the template for just about every modern-day sports mascot, strutting about with a kid-size wit and a devil-may-care attitude. He's known for polishing bald men's heads, bumping his rear end against fans, pumping up the crowd by cheering atop the Phils' dugout, and dancing on that same location sometime around the sixth inning of each game. Before contests, he'll ride onto the field in his custom ATV, then often go on to tease the opposing team's players. Each year, typically in late April, the Phils will throw him a big Sunday afternoon birthday party, and a couple dozen mascots across the sporting world will attend, as will his mother, Phoebe. Whether or not you're bringing kids to the game, you have to watch the Phanatic at work.

FOOD AND DRINKS

How does fried chicken and doughnuts sound? **Federal Donuts** (section 140) is a mega-popular Philadelphia-based eatery that serves up those two things, and they do them well. A fried chicken sandwich is $10, while a two-pack of warm doughnuts is $5 (try the cookies and cream option). Get in line early for this vendor.

Other popular options are **Tony Luke's** (Ashburn Alley), the famous Philly cheesesteak and roast pork sandwich purveyor (the roast pork with broccoli rabe is a favorite of many), and **Chickie's & Pete's** (Ashburn Alley), where people will wait an hour just to get their hands on a cup of the famous crab fries (crispy fries seasoned with a special Old Bay-style blend and served with a tangy, queso-like condiment). If you want

Photos (from top to bottom): Ashburn Alley at Citizens Bank Park; Phillie Phanatic; Phillies fans on the first base line.

a cheesesteak, opt against Tony Luke's (no offense) and visit **Campo's Steaks** (Ashburn Alley), which has shorter lines but equally delicious fare. Outside of a cheesesteak, the Heater is the sandwich to get.

With **Bull's BBQ** (left-field plaza, 100 level), Citizens Bank Park has given a 1970s-era slugger the opportunity to run his own barbecue stand. Bull's serves up ribs and grilled turkey legs and is overseen by Greg Luzinski, famed slugger who swatted 223 homers for the Phils between 1970 and 1980.

If you want to sit down or hang out with a couple beers, check out **Pass and Stow** (third-base gate). This beer garden has a variety of local brews and also offers pizza. Next to it is a **Shake Shack,** which has seating for 120 and serves burgers, crinkle-cut fries, shakes, and thick desserts called concretes. Whatever you do, your dessert should be a water (pronounced WOOD-er) ice from **Rita's Italian Ice** (kiosks throughout). The national chain was born in Philly, so pay homage.

The main restaurant at the ballpark is **Harry the K's** (left field at the Scoreboard Porch), a two-level bar and grill named after Harry Kalas that serves summertime fare like burgers, hot dogs, and chicken fingers. Since it's the main sit-down option at the park, lines get long. Note that you're not assured a view of the game if you're here.

The best beer selection is at **The Backyard Bar at The Yard** (Ashburn Alley, section 104). There's a full bar here with plenty of cans. Otherwise, you'll come across local beer at kiosks on the concourses. Typical beers at the park include offerings by Flying Fish (from New Jersey), Yards (from Philly), and Troegs (from Hershey, Pennsylvania). Troegs's Sunshine Pils is a great summer beer.

EVENTS

Batting practice is viewable, but you have to get to the park early. Gates open at Ashburn Alley two hours before first pitch, giving fans about 20 minutes of Phillies batting practice to catch. Visitor batting practice takes place afterward, lasting until about 40 minutes before the game begins. **Autograph** hounds should beeline to the first- and third-base lines during batting practice—kids will typically get the OK to stand around for a bit with a pen and ball.

The Phils host a few popular **theme games** each year. Look for the **Phillie Phanatic's birthday celebration** (mid-to-late Apr.), exciting fireworks displays for **Independence Day** (early July), and an **alumni weekend** (Aug.) that brings back former players and personalities, culminating in the induction of that year's Wall of Fame recipient. The Phils also offer **Dollar Dog Night,** of which there are a dozen or so each season, typically falling on a midweek evening.

Tours

The Phillies offer a 90-minute **ballpark tour** (10:30am Mon.-Sat. Apr.-Sept. non-game days, 10:30am and 12:30pm Mon.-Sat. Apr.-Sept. game days, 10:30am Mon., Wed., Fri. Oct.-Mar., $10, $6 seniors and ages 3-14) that includes visits to the Phillies dugout, Diamond Club, Hall of Fame Club, broadcast booth, and media room. For the price, it's a pretty good deal, though it's not as thorough as tours at other parks.

SHOPPING

The Phillies have one of the better team stores in baseball. The **New Era Phillies Team Store** (One Citizens Bank Way, section 134, 267/570-2333, 10am-6pm Mon.-Sat., closes to public and opens just for ticketholders when gates open on game days) is open year-round and offers a slew of merchandise over two levels. You'll find the usual T-shirts and jerseys, including throwbacks and iconic player tops, plus myriad hats and outerwear. But the coolest stuff has to do with the Phillie Phanatic. From plush dolls to children's books to novelty gifts, the store has plenty of mascot-related material.

For more throwbacks, visit the **Mitchell & Ness Alley Store** (Ashburn Alley), which offers flannel jerseys, including a wide selection of 1970s- and 1980s-era outfits. You can find pennants and banners here, too.

PHILADELPHIA SIGHTS

INDEPENDENCE NATIONAL HISTORICAL PARK

No first-time trip to Philadelphia is complete without spending time at **Independence National Historical Park.** It's home to several important landmarks, among them **Independence Hall** (Chestnut St. between 5th St. and 6th St., www.nps.gov/inde, 9am-7pm daily Memorial Day-Labor Day, 9am-5pm daily Labor Day-Memorial Day, free), the 1732 building where the Declaration of Independence and U.S. Constitution were signed. Peer into the Assembly Room, where the signings took place; the Courtroom of the Pennsylvania Supreme Court, home to a colonial act of rebellion in 1776; and the Governor's Council Chamber, which includes the very tool used to draw the boundary between Pennsylvania and Maryland. You must have a ticket to enter via a tour, and lines get long for them, so your best bet is to reserve one in advance for $1 per person. Note: Tickets are unnecessary in January and February.

Just across the street from Independence Hall is the **Liberty Bell** (Market St. at 6th St., 9am-7pm daily Memorial Day-Labor Day, 9am-5pm daily Labor Day-Memorial Day, free), which requires no tickets—just walk into the Liberty Bell Center, go through a security screening, and you're good. Be sure to spend time walking through the exhibition that explains the history of the bell, which was first installed at the Pennsylvania State House before it became a symbol of national unity after the Civil War, plus a symbol of the women's suffrage and civil rights movements. The bell ends the tour, and it's a sight.

Be sure to visit the **National Constitution Center** (525 Arch St., 215/409-6700, www.constitutioncenter.org, 9:30am-5pm Mon.-Sat., noon-5pm Sun., $14.50, $13 seniors and students, $11 ages 6-11). Along with special exhibits, the museum tells the story of freedom and democracy, from a 360-degree theatrical presentation called "Freedom Rising" to the exhibit "The Story of We the People," which includes a copy of the Emancipation Proclamation and interactive features like a virtual presidential oath of office. If you also want to visit the **Museum of the American Revolution** (101 S. 3rd St., www.amrevmuseum.org, 9:30am-6pm daily Memorial Day-Labor Day, 10am-5pm daily Labor Day-Memorial Day, $21, $18 seniors and students, $13 ages 6-17), featuring artifacts from the war, plus interactive documents and re-creations of important moments in colonial history, you can get a joint ticket ($29, $19 ages 6-18) that includes admission to the National Constitution Center.

PHILADELPHIA MUSEUM OF ART

Even its placement in the city is artistic: Set at the end of a diagonal parkway lined by the flags of the world, the **Philadelphia Museum of Art** (2600 Benjamin Franklin Pkwy., 215/763-8100, www.philamuseum.org, 10am-5pm Sun., Tues., Thurs., and Sat., 10am-8:45pm Wed. and Fri., $20, $18 seniors, $14 students and ages 13-18, pay-what-you-wish Wed. nights and first Sun. of month) is an iconic beige-and-white stone building with Greek columns and a massive front courtyard. Inside is an outstanding volume of art spanning centuries, with works from artists like Paul Cezanne, Henri Matisse, Pablo Picasso, Rembrandt, Cy Twombly, and Philly native Thomas Eakins. It also specializes in Asian art. Typically, the museum has a major featured exhibit that draws tourists to the city all on its own.

Check out the impressionist works (Monet, Manet, Degas, and Renoir are here), and take pictures of the golden Diana statue at the Great Stair Hall. Oh, and speaking of stairs, the best way to enter the museum is by galloping up the front steps like Rocky Balboa. Yup, these are the **Rocky Steps.** When you leave, pay homage to Rocky by taking a photo in front of his statue at street level.

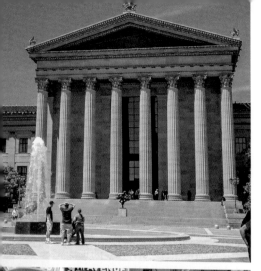

READING TERMINAL MARKET

A staple of the Philadelphia experience since the late 1800s, **Reading Terminal Market** (51 N. 12th St., www.readingterminalmarket.org, 8am-6pm daily) is the heart of this blue-collar city. It's also a paradise for foodies, a place to indulge in Amish and Pennsylvania Dutch specialties like apple butter; Lebanon bologna, and scrapple (the bologna must be enjoyed with yellow mustard, and the scrapple is a great accompaniment for eggs); soft pretzels; rich, milky ice cream from **Bassett's,** a long-standing icon; fresh fish and produce; and roast pork sandwiches from **DiNic's,** which will have a line but is worth the wait. Put it this way: The sandwich has been named the best in America. Yeah, it's that good. Block out two hours to really enjoy the market, but be ready to walk in tight crowds.

ITALIAN MARKET

Philadelphia's famous **Italian Market** (9th St. between Fitzwater St. and Passyunk Ave., 215/278-2903, www.italianmarketphilly.org, market open daily, food stalls 8am-5pm Tues.-Sat., 8am-3pm Sun.) is worth a meander during your trip. Dotted with produce vendors, butchers, cheesemongers, fishmongers, and stands of hot and cold food, the street market bustles from morning to evening under a collection of worn awnings. It used to be a very Italian place, but in recent decades Korean, Vietnamese, and Mexican vendors have become just as important, and the market is all the better for it.

Photos (from top to bottom): the Philadelphia Museum of Art; Reading Terminal Market; Pat's King of Steaks.

FOOD

NEAR CITIZENS BANK PARK

You can get the famous crab fries from **Chickie's & Pete's** (1526 Packer Ave., 215/218-0500, www.chickiesandpetes.com, 11am-2am daily, under $40), a mile north of Citizens Bank Park. This spot is also known for its crab legs and convivial bar scene. There are plenty of televisions, all tuned into Philly sports when the games are on. Chickie's also makes a good spot to grab a bite before the game, though you should expect crowds. Fun fact: After resigning from being a major league umpire, and up until his death in 2006, Philly native Eric Gregg worked the door and took IDs. Imagine being thrown out by him!

OTHER NEIGHBORHOODS

Philly is a great food city, and it sort of happened overnight. Take, for example, **South Philly Barbacoa** (1140 S. 9th St., 215/360-5282, www.southphillybarbacoa.com, 9am-4pm Mon. and Fri., 5am-5pm Sat.-Sun., under $20), a cash-only spot at the Italian Market in South Philly known for its barbacoa and lamb tacos. With lines out the door, Cristina Martinez's little Mexican wonder seriously lives up to the hype, garnering her TV spots and recognition in the form of a James Beard Award nomination.

A veteran in the Philly scene, **Pho 75** (1122 Washington Ave., #F, 215-271-5866, www.phoseventyfive.com, 9am-8pm daily, under $10) is the place to go for soul-warming bowls of Vietnamese noodle soup. Get a bowl with well-done brisket, flank, soft tendon, and tripe, and a drink of iced salty pickled lemon juice, and your hangover from the night before will magically disappear. The seating is cafeteria-style, so prepare to make a couple friends. This small chain is cash only. It's a few blocks from the Italian Market.

For a good dinner, you have your pick from the entire city. I'll give you two ideas, though. First: **Southwark** (701 S. 4th St., 267/930-8538, www.southwarkrestaurant.com, 5pm-2am Wed.-Mon., under $60), in the Queen Village neighborhood, has a tidy menu of fresh entrées and pasta dishes, plus great meat, cheese, and pâté, inside a sleek, upscale tavern setup with white tablecloths. Second is **Vernick Food & Drink** (2031 Walnut St., 267/639-6644, www.vernickphilly.com, 5pm-11pm Tues.-Sun., under $80), which wants you to indulge in new American classics done with local ingredients. The space, which is close to Rittenhouse Square, feels special; sit at the pass, where you can watch the cooks at work, or in a dimly lit dining area.

Philly is the sandwich capital of America, home to workhorse delis and corner spots that pile meat and cheese into crusty hoagie rolls like it's nobody's business. If you want an all-in-one, modernized sandwich experience, try **Middle Child** (248 S. 11th St., 267/930-8344, www.middlechildphilly.com, 7am-3pm Tues.-Fri., 8am-3pm Sat.-Sun., under $20) in Center City. For breakfast, there's a sandwich, bagels, and toast, and for lunch a bunch of fun sandos that turn the standard deli experience up to 11. For a really good hoagie, head up to Northern Liberties and visit **Paesano's** (148 W. Girard Ave., 267/886-9556, www.paesanosphillystyle.com, 11am-11pm daily, under $20), a homey, cash-only spot that does hot and cold sandwiches. Opt for a cold choice like the Daddy Wad, an Italian hoagie with capicola, soppressata, mortadella, salami, prosciutto, hot peppers, provolone, and oregano vinaigrette.

John's Roast Pork (14 Snyder Ave., 215/463-1951, www.johnsroastpork.com, 9am-7pm Tues.-Sat., under $15) falls just short of DiNic's at Reading Terminal Market when it comes to roast pork sandwiches, but you might be shocked to learn that its cheesesteak is outstanding. Find it in South Philly.

If it's your first time in the city, you have to visit the Passyunk Square area that's home to both Geno's and my choice, **Pat's King of Steaks** (1237 E. Passyunk Ave., 215/468-1546, www.patskingofsteaks.com, 24 hours daily, under $20). Here's the thing: Pat's never closes. Go late at night or early in the morning, preferably after a couple stiff drinks, and wait in line. Get to the window and say just this: "Whiz wit." You'll get a cheesesteak with Cheez Whiz and onions, and it'll be your indoctrination into this crazy, meaty, cheesy world. (Pro tip: Ketchup makes it even better.)

The Original Tony Luke's (39 E. Oregon Ave., 215/551-5725, www.tonylukes.com, 6am-midnight Mon.-Thurs., 6am-2am Fri.-Sat., 10am-8pm Sun., under $15) is worth the visit. The flagship location in South Philly has all the good stuff, from good cheesesteaks to a killer roast pork sandwich with broccoli rabe to Philly specialties like the chicken cheesesteak, old-fashioned pizza steak, and my favorite, the cheesesteak hoagie, combining two perfect sandwiches.

Most of these sandwich places are no more than a 10-minute drive from Citizens Bank Park, so they're good options for your pregame or postgame needs. One last tip: Most neighborhood pizza and sandwich spots make a pretty good cheesesteak, so it's actually hard to go wrong.

BARS AND BREWERIES

NEAR CITIZENS BANK PARK

If you want to make a day of your visit to Citizens Bank Park, and you've decided not to drive, you could visit **Xfinity Live!** (1100 Pattison Ave., 267/534-4264, www.xfinitylive.com, opens 9am-11am daily, specific times vary by day). This is one of those monstrous multi-concept bar and entertainment venues. Located across the street from both the ballpark and the other major stadiums and arenas in Philly, it gets a lot of business. The main bar, called the **NBC Sports Arena,** is the centerpiece hangout with big-screen televisions, including an arena-sized screen. The smaller bars are themed: There's a country bar with a mechanical bull, and another bar

has a deep craft beer selection. Not going to the game? An hour after the last event of the day begins, parking for Xfinity Live! is free. If you come earlier, be prepared to pay $20 to park nearby.

OTHER NEIGHBORHOODS

In addition to being a good food city, Philadelphia is also a hell of a drinking city. You'll need to hit up **Bob and Barbara's Lounge** (1509 South St., 215/545-4511, www.bobandbarbaras.com, noon-2am Tues.-Fri., 3pm-2am Sat.-Mon.), on the border between Center City and South Philly, if only to order the Citywide Special, which is a Pabst Blue Ribbon and shot of Jim Beam for $4. It's also just a fun bar, hosting a Thursday night drag show (10:15pm Thurs., $8). Just note: Everyone knows about Bob and Barbara's, so chances are it'll be packed at night.

In the 1980s and '90s, Fishtown and Kensington were neglected neighborhoods. These days, all the kids play in this gentrified area, where rents are soaring and you're bound to hear the word "hipster" more than thrice a day. If a mini-Brooklyn is your thing, head to **Memphis Taproom** (2331 E. Cumberland St., 215/425-4460, 11:30am-2am Mon.-Fri., 11am-2am Sat.-Sun.), which retains much of the charm of a throwback taproom. It has a great beer list, good pub grub and burgers, and an outdoor beer garden. Nearby, **Martha** (2113 E. York St., 215/867-8881, www.marthakensington.com, 4:30pm-2am Mon. and Wed.-Fri., 2pm-2am Sat., noon-2am Sun.) has a living room feel and a long bar. Beer, wine, cheese, and hoagies are all on offer here.

For a long time, Philly was a brewing hub, specifically in an area known as Brewerytown in North Philadelphia. While the old breweries are long gone, there are a few new ones there, headlined by **Crime and Punishment Brewing Co.** (2711 W. Girard Ave., 215/235-2739, www.crimeandpunishmentbrewingco.com, 4pm-midnight Mon.-Wed., 4pm-1am Thurs.-Fri., 11am-1am Sat., 11am-midnight Sun.). They're not afraid to try anything, but they can really knock a European-style beer out of the park. As its name hints, it's a very literary place, and it's also pretty chill. Be sure to read the history of Brewerytown when you're there.

Also in North Philadelphia, **Evil Genius Beer Company** (1727 N. Front St., 215/425-6820, www.evilgeniusbeer.com, 4pm-10pm Wed., 4pm-midnight Thurs., 2pm-midnight Fri., noon-midnight Sat., noon-9pm Sun.) is a fun brewery where all the beers have catchy names, the games are plentiful, and you can play Nintendo.

Head south to the small but very solid **Brewery ARS** (1927 W. Passyunk Ave., 215/960-5173, www.breweryars.com, 5pm-10pm Wed.-Thurs., 5pm-11pm Fri., noon-11pm Sat., 1pm-8pm Sun.), a garage brewery with super-flavorful farmhouse beers and IPAs. It's southwest of Passyunk Square.

In Northern Liberties is **Yards Brewing Company** (500 Spring Garden St., 215/525-0175, www.yardsbrewing.com, 11:30am-10pm Mon.-Tues., 11:30am-4pm Wed., 11:30am-11pm Thurs.-Fri., 11am-11pm Sat., 11am-10pm Sun.). Born in 1994 and committed to serving styles popular during colonial times, Yards is known for its Philadelphia Pale Ale, Brawler, and Washington's Porter. Its large taproom and brewery offers tours and a full food menu.

Monk's Café (264 S. 16th St., 215/545-7005, www.monkscafe.com, 11:30am-2am daily) in the heart of Center City is a must-visit for every passionate American beer drinker (and my absolute favorite bar in the United States). This is the country's preeminent Belgian beer emporium and home to a staggering inventory that includes its own Flemish sour ale, all listed in its well-known beer bible. On tap are some of the finest beers in the world, including IPAs like Pliny the Elder. It'll get crowded, so get there pre-happy hour if you can. The back bar typically has more room than the front bar, but either place feels like a worn-in cellar perfect for hanging with friends. Order some pommes frites (that's french fries to you) and mussels and enjoy a couple strong brews. By the time you leave, you'll feel a little tipsy and a lot happy.

RECREATION

BOATING, KAYAKING, AND PADDLEBOARDING

Two relatively wide rivers run either past or through Philadelphia—the Schuylkill and the Delaware—so you have more than a few opportunities to take a boat, kayak, or paddleboard out and have a good time. Start with **Hidden River Outfitters** (Walnut St. at Schuylkill River, 267/588-3512, www.hiddenriveroutfitters.com, June-Sept., $40-60), which offers kayak tours on the Schuylkill River (the one with the iconic Boathouse Row) and hour-long paddleboard lessons. Tours and lessons are not recommended for those younger than 13.

Just five miles west of Citizens Bank Park is **Bartram's Garden** (5400 Lindbergh Blvd., www.bartramsgarden.org, 10am-4pm Mon.-Fri., 10am-6pm Sat.-Sun., free), a 45-acre botanical garden offering native species, as well as the oldest male *Ginkgo biloba* tree in North America, plus medicinal plants whose roots are in a 1751 work published by Benjamin Franklin. There are also free kayak and rowboat programs (11am-3pm Sat. May-Oct., conditions permitting) on the Schuylkill River.

Over on the Delaware River, there's **Paddle Penn's Landing** (301 S. Columbus Blvd., 215/928-8803, www.delawareriverwaterfront.com, 3pm-sunset Fri., noon-sunset Sat.-Sun. early-late May and early-late Sept., 3pm-sunset Mon.-Thurs., noon-sunset Fri.-Sun. Memorial Day-Labor Day, $8 per half hour). You can rent a single or tandem kayak, a rowboat, or a pedal boat (either a dragon, pirate ship, or swan). The swans are fun for couples.

PARKS

When William Penn planned the layout of Center City hundreds of years ago, he wanted to ensure people were never too far from a park. Those parks remain today in each corner of Center City. Up northwest is **Logan Square** (Benjamin Franklin Pkwy. and 19th

Philadelphia Zoo

St.), home to a fountain that gets a workout in the summer. Note: Not too far from here is **JFK Plaza** (Arch St. and 15th St.), location of arguably the most famous reproduction of Robert Indiana's famous *LOVE* sculpture. In the northeast corner of Center City is **Franklin Square** (Vine St. and 6th St.). In the southeast corner, there's **Washington Square** (Locust St. and 6th St.), and over in the southwest end is **Rittenhouse Square** (Locust St. and 19th St.), which has multiple walking paths, plenty of grassy space, and probably the best people-watching in the city.

Fairmount Park

Remember when Will Smith (as the Fresh Prince in the song "Summertime") rapped "back in Philly, we'd be out in the park"? He was talking about **Fairmount Park** (www. phila.gov), which spans 2,052 acres and includes historic homes, cool statues, ballfields, and plenty of picnic space. Essential sights in the park include the **Please Touch Museum** (4231 Ave. of the Republic, 215/581-3181, www.pleasetouchmuseum. org, 9am-5pm Mon.-Tues. and Thurs.-Sat., 10am-5pm Wed., 11am-5pm Sun., $19 ages 1 and older), a completely hands-on venue for children ages 3-12; the **Shofuso Japanese House and Garden** (Lansdowne Dr. and Horticultural Dr., 215/878-5097,

www.japanphilly.org, 10am-4pm Wed.-Fri., 11am-5pm Sat.-Sun., $12, $8 seniors, students, and ages 5-17), a house built in 1953 with a tea garden and teahouse; and the **Philadelphia Zoo** (3400 W. Girard Ave., 215/243-1100, www.philadelphiazoo.org, 9:30am-5pm daily, $24, $19 ages 2-11), the country's first zoo and a good place to spot all the popular animals. Most interesting are the (appropriately named) catwalks made for lions and tigers, who pass over visitors on the zoo's main promenade.

SHOPPING

Happy to see that throwback jersey available at your favorite team's store? Thank **Mitchell & Ness Nostalgia Co.** (1201 Chestnut St., 267/273-7622, www.mitchellandness.com, 10am-7pm Mon.-Sat., 11am-5pm Sun.), the clothier that made old-school sports uniforms popular again. The flagship store of this Philly-born company sells those beautiful powder-blue Phillies jerseys from the 1970s and early 1980s, but there's also a good selection of tops from across the league. Maybe you'll find that vaunted Seattle Pilots hat here. Check out the display of authentic Jackie Robinson jerseys, too.

Just down the block and competing with Mitchell & Ness for local fans is **Shibe Vintage Sports** (137 S. 13th St., 215/566-2511, www.shibevintagesports.com, 11am-8pm Mon.-Sat., 11am-6pm Sun.). It has a great selection of the kinds of clothes clued-in Philly fans will wear, from shirts celebrating old Veterans Stadium to 1940s logo caps. Want to rep the old Philadelphia Athletics? They have that merchandise, too, including caps and tops showing the team's old elephant logo. Some of the goods are officially licensed, and other stuff is made by local artists and screen-printers.

ACCOMMODATIONS

NEAR CITIZENS BANK PARK

The only accommodation close to the ballpark is the **Courtyard by Marriott Philadelphia South at the Navy Yard** (1001 Intrepid Ave., 215/644-9200, www.marriott.com, $150-300), a 1.3-mile drive south from home plate in the ultramodern, refurbished Navy Yard area. The hotel has a small café with lunch and dinner options, plus a small bar open in the evening, and stylish sitting areas on the ground floor.

OTHER NEIGHBORHOODS

You have options in Center City and close to the Broad Street subway line that runs to the sports complex. Two blocks east of City Hall and the Broad Street Line, and inside an iconic structure on the city skyline, the **Loews Philadelphia Hotel** (1200 Market St., 215/627-1200, www.loewshotels.com, $140-300) is a fine option with plenty of history. The building, once called the PSFS Building (built for the Philadelphia Saving Fund Society), was constructed in 1932 and is considered the United States' first modern skyscraper. Some of the hotel's 581 guest rooms and 12 suites have awesome views of

the city, with their color scheme designed to match the tone of the city skyline. The hotel has an in-hotel restaurant and the 31st-floor Concierge Club and Library, and the ground floor includes a studio for the local NBC affiliate.

If you want to stay closer to the Italian Market in South Philadelphia, check out **Philadelphia Hotel Bella Vista** (752 S. 10th St., 800/680-1270, www.philadelphiahotelbellavista.com, $150-225). With 21 guest rooms running the bed-and-breakfast gamut, from the airy and modern Summer Breeze to the old-fashioned Victorian, there's a choice for every traveler.

GETTING AROUND

PUBLIC TRANSIT

In Philadelphia, it's **SEPTA** (www.septa.org, $2.50 single ride) that gets you around. The most important subway lines for Center City visitors are the **Broad Street Line,** or **Orange Line,** which runs north to south along Broad Street; and the **Market-Frankford Line,** sometimes called **the El** (it's an elevated line outside of Center City), which runs west to east along Market Street (and then Frankford Ave.) and is colored blue on the transit map. Major stations in Center City include **City Hall** (City Hall Courtyard at Broad St. and Market St.), **Walnut-Locust** (200 S. Broad St.), and **Lombard-South** (Broad St. and South St.), which are all on the Broad Street Line; and **Jefferson Station** (11th St. and Market St.), **Suburban Station** (16th St. and John F. Kennedy Blvd.), and **30th Street Station** (2955 Market St.), which are all on the Market-Frankford Line.

SEPTA also maintains a large **bus network,** along with **trolley cars.** From Center City, there's a trolley line along Market Street. It starts at 13th Street and stretches west to 30th Street, then outward toward points in West Philadelphia and the suburbs.

TAXI, UBER, AND LYFT

Philly is a Lyft and Uber city. Lyft tends to offer more affordable prices from Philadelphia International Airport to Center City (about $20 per ride). If you're looking to visit a neighborhood outside Center City (South Philadelphia or Fishtown, let's say), you can easily ride-share that trip. Basically, between ride-sharing and the subway options in Center City, you probably don't need a rental car in the city.

CAR

If you do want a car, it's because you're trying to visit a lot of things in a short amount of time, and your destinations are spread across the city. You can easily rent a car at the airport. If you need a car while in Center City, the major rental car companies are here, including **Avis** (www.avis.com) and **Budget** (www.budget.com) at Broad and Arch Streets, and **Hertz** (www.hertz.com), a few blocks away at 13th and Filbert Streets.

If you're driving around Philly, know that its city plan is an iconic **grid system** developed by William Penn. That means driving around Center City (the downtown area) isn't so terrible. In this area, major north-south streets start with the easternmost Columbus Boulevard and Front Street, and then are numbered—2nd, 3rd, etc.—with 14th Street named Broad Street (the main north-south street in the city). Major east-west streets are named for trees, like Chestnut, Walnut, Pine, Filbert, etc., with an exception for Market Street (the main east-west street in the city). At the intersection of Broad and Market is City Hall. Once you leave Center City, the grid begins to fall apart, and street names change considerably.

I-95 is the main north-south highway, straddling the Delaware River on the eastern end of the city, connecting Philadelphians to New York City up north and Baltimore down south. **I-76** sneaks in from the northwestern suburbs (farther west it's the Pennsylvania Turnpike) along the city's other major river, the Schuylkill (SCHOOL-kill), before heading east in South Philadelphia, passing Citizens Bank Park and stretching into New Jersey (take it farther east to the Jersey Shore). **I-676** connects I-95 to I-76 via a spur through Center City. Otherwise, remember **Broad Street,** or **PA-611,** which starts down near Citizens Bank Park and runs north, straight through the city; and **Market Street,** which cuts through the heart of Center City heading west to east.

Because of a lack of highways in Center City, you're likely to encounter **traffic** in that area much of the time. Just keep an eye out for **one-way streets** and maybe brush up on your **parallel parking.** Also, be wary of the **Philadelphia Parking Authority** (www.philapark.org); much of Center City's street parking is metered, and if you don't put enough time in yours, you'll have to pay the piper later.

BALTIMORE
ORIOLES

Even knowledgeable baseball fans may think the Baltimore Orioles have been in the major leagues since, oh, the very early 1900s. Surely they were in the American League with the New York Yankees and Boston Red Sox, right? Well… no, but sort of.

In 1901, Ban Johnson of the newly formed American League settled on starting a team in Charm City because he couldn't get one in New York. The Baltimore Orioles were formed in 1901, led by future Hall of Fame manager John McGraw and pitcher Joe McGinnity; however, McGinnity and others, including top hitter Dan McGann, left to play for the New York Giants. Desperate for a solution to his team's woes, Johnson negotiated an agreement to get an AL team in New York, so he moved the club to the Big Apple. The Orioles

became the Highlanders, and a few years later, they were the Yankees. We know what happened from there.

The Orioles as we know them began playing in 1954. Before that, they were the American League's Milwaukee Brewers (in 1901) and, more famously, the St. Louis Browns (1902-1953), a third-division franchise that won just one pennant. After moving to Charm City, though, the organization began building quite a resume: three world championships, seven American League pennants, and some of the game's greatest players, like Frank Robinson, Brooks Robinson, Eddie Murray, Jim Palmer, and Cal Ripken Jr. Also drawing attention were killer home and road uniforms, a cool as all get-out logo, and arguably the most influential ballpark in the game's history. The O's are an easy-to-love team that seems to always be punching up against its division rivals, especially the Yankees.

There's a little more to B'more baseball. The Baltimore Black Sox represented the city in the Eastern Colored League in the 1920s, and the Elite Giants played between 1938 and 1948 in the Negro National League. Roy Campanella was part of the latter team.

The city is also the birthplace of arguably the greatest player in baseball history: Babe Ruth. Of course, he left Baltimore to define the early success of the Yankees.

Baseball gets its fair share of love in Baltimore, but it's a lot of work. Because of a lower payroll and suspect team-building strategies, the Orioles always seem to be trying to catch up with the all-powerful Yankees and, in recent decades, the Red Sox. That second-division lifestyle can turn off some fans, but if baseball is good in Charm City, the fans show up and pray for some "Orioles magic."

PLANNING YOUR TIME

It's possible to boil down Baltimore to a **day trip,** but I suggest a **weekend** sojourn to better experience the city's diversity and points of interest. If you want to visit the Inner Harbor, try to buy tickets in advance

for museums and sights, and make yourself a plan for getting there and getting out.

If you're opting for **3-4 days** in Charm City, a day trip to Patapsco Valley State Park is a good idea. Another suggestion: Plan a long weekend that includes both Baltimore and Washington DC. Making this extra convenient is the MARC Train, which travels from DC to B'more.

Baltimore is in the mid-Atlantic region of the country and so has a similar climate to nearby Philadelphia. In **March** and **April,** and sometimes **October,** it can get cold, especially at night, and it's often **rainy. May** and **late September** are great times to visit. You're bound to feel some **heat** if you come between **June** and **mid-September,** when temperatures will climb past 75°F. If you're visiting in spring or fall, bring a jacket and possibly an umbrella.

GETTING THERE

AIR

The closest airport to Baltimore is **Baltimore/Washington International Thurgood Marshall Airport** (BWI, I-195 and MD-170, Hanover, MD, 410/859-7111, www.bwiairport.com). It offers flights with **Air Canada** (888/247-2262, www.aircanada.com), **Allegiant** (702/505-8888, www.allegiantair.com), **American Airlines** (800/433-7300, www.aa.com), **Delta** (800/221-1212, www.delta.com), **Frontier** (800/432-1359, www.flyfrontier.com), **jetBlue** (800/538-2583, www.jetblue.com), **Southwest** (800/435-9792, www.southwest.com), **Spirit** (801/401-2222, www.spirit.com), and **United** (800/864-8331, www.united.com), plus several international carriers. Flights at BWI come from and go to most large cities in North America.

Airport Transportation
It takes about 15 minutes to get from BWI to

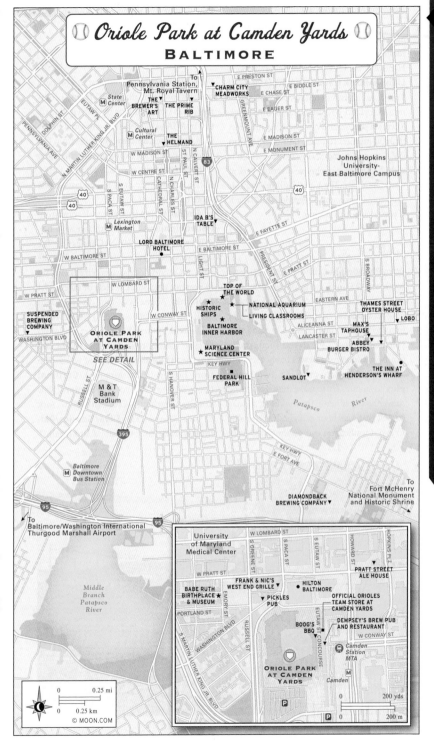

Oriole Park at Camden Yards
BALTIMORE

To Pennsylvania Station, Mt. Royal Tavern

State Center

E PRESTON ST

CHARM CITY MEADWORKS

E CHASE ST

E BIDDLE ST

THE BREWER'S ART

THE PRIME RIB

E EAGER ST

Cultural Center

THE HELMAND

E MADISON ST

W MADISON ST

E MONUMENT ST

W CENTRE ST

Johns Hopkins University- East Baltimore Campus

PENNSYLVANIA AVE

DOLPHIN ST

EUTAW PL

N MARTIN LUTHER KING JR BLVD

S PACA ST

S EUTAW ST

CATHEDRAL ST

N CHARLES ST

N CALVERT ST

ST PAUL ST

LIGHT ST

GREENMOUNT AVE

PRESIDENT ST

S BROADWAY

Lexington Market

IDA B'S TABLE

E FAYETTE ST

LORD BALTIMORE HOTEL

W BALTIMORE ST

E BALTIMORE ST

E PRATT ST

EASTERN AVE

W LOMBARD ST

TOP OF THE WORLD

THAMES STREET OYSTER HOUSE

W PRATT ST

HISTORIC SHIPS

NATIONAL AQUARIUM

LIVING CLASSROOMS

LOBO

SUSPENDED BREWING COMPANY

W CONWAY ST

BALTIMORE INNER HARBOR

ALICEANNA ST

LANCASTER ST

MAX'S TAPHOUSE

ABBEY BURGER BISTRO

WASHINGTON BLVD

ORIOLE PARK AT CAMDEN YARDS

MARYLAND SCIENCE CENTER

SEE DETAIL

KEY HWY

THE INN AT HENDERSON'S WHARF

RUSSELL ST

S HANOVER ST

FEDERAL HILL PARK

SANDLOT

M & T Bank Stadium

Patapsco River

KEY HWY

E FORT AVE

Baltimore Downtown Bus Station

To Fort McHenry National Monument and Historic Shrine

DIAMONDBACK BREWING COMPANY

To Baltimore/Washington International Thurgood Marshall Airport

Middle Branch Patapsco River

University of Maryland Medical Center

W LOMBARD ST

W PRATT ST

PRATT STREET ALE HOUSE

FRANK & NIC'S WEST END GRILLE

HILTON BALTIMORE

BABE RUTH BIRTHPLACE & MUSEUM

PICKLES PUB

OFFICIAL ORIOLES TEAM STORE AT CAMDEN YARDS

PORTLAND ST

BOOG'S BBQ

DEMPSEY'S BREW PUB AND RESTAURANT

W CONWAY ST

Camden Station MTA

ORIOLE PARK AT CAMDEN YARDS

Camden

S GREENE ST

EMORY ST

S PACA ST

RUSSELL ST

S EUTAW ST

EUTAW ST CONCOURSE

HOWARD ST

HOPKINS PLZ

WASHINGTON BLVD

S MARTIN LUTHER KING JR BLVD

0   0.25 mi

0   0.25 km

0   200 yds

0   200 m

© MOON.COM

Downtown Baltimore, though your driving time may vary. To hop in a rental car, you'll have to take the free shuttle to the **rental car facility** (Stoney Run Rd. and New Ridge Rd., Hanover). For an alternative, you can take a **Light RailLink train** from **MTA** (Maryland Transit Administration, 410/539-5000, www. mta.maryland.gov, $0.90-2.10 one-way). There's a station at BWI, and it's a little less than 30 minutes to reach **Camden station** (W. Conway St. and S. Howard St.), which is right behind the warehouse at Oriole Park at Camden Yards. The Light RailLink train is very convenient, and I recommend using it if you're close to a station.

CAR

From **Philadelphia,** drive about 90 minutes south on **I-95,** then merge onto **I-895,** staying on that highway for one exit before hopping off at **US-40.** Drive US-40 West straight into the heart of the city. Keep in mind that you'll be on busy I-95, so rush-hour traffic can be maddening and will likely turn this **100-mile** drive into more of a **two-hour-plus** adventure. Try to make the drive during slower hours, either in the middle of the day or well past rush hour at night. If you're able to avoid traffic, you can do the drive from

Philadelphia to Baltimore in about an **hour and 40 minutes.**

TRAIN

From **Washington DC,** the best way to travel to Baltimore is via the **MARC Train,** a commuter rail system linking the two cities that's run by **MTA** (410/539-5000, www.mta.maryland.gov). The **Camden Line** runs from DC south to Baltimore, exiting at the ballpark at **Camden station** (Conway St. and Eutaw St.). A one-way trip costs $8 and lasts a little more than an hour.

Amtrak trains (www.amtrak.com) from **Philadelphia** pull into Baltimore at **Pennsylvania Station** (1500 N. Charles St.). The station is about two miles north of Oriole Park at Camden Yards, so you'll either want to hop in a ride-share vehicle or take **Light RailLink.** A one-way trip on the Light RailLink costs between $0.90 and $2.10.

Amtrak routes that connect Philadelphia to Baltimore include the **Acela** and **Northeast Regional** (both of which run from Boston to Washington), **Cardinal** (New York to Chicago), **Carolinian** (New York to Charlotte), **Crescent** (New York to New Orleans), and **Silver Service/Palmetto** (New York to Tampa and Miami).

one entrance to Oriole Park at Camden Yards

The ride takes around one hour; tickets start at $20.

BUS

The main bus station in town is the **Baltimore Downtown Bus Station** (2110 Haines St., 410/752-7682). It's served by **Greyhound** (www.greyhound.com). Rides from **Philadelphia** are cheap on Greyhound, starting at $15 or so, and will last about two hours.

On **Megabus** (http://us.megabus.com), you'll also be riding for about two hours from Philadelphia, but prices are roughly double that of Greyhound, and your drop-off is at the **White Marsh Mall** (8200 Perry Hall Blvd.), about 18 miles northeast of Downtown Baltimore.

Oriole Park at Camden Yards

On April 6, 1992, under a clear blue sky in Baltimore, Maryland, baseball changed forever. As the Orioles prepared to play the Cleveland Indians on opening day, 44,568 people packed into the first of a new kind of baseball venue. This new home, called **Oriole Park at Camden Yards** (333 W. Camden St., www.mlb.com/orioles), sparkled with a forest-green outfield fence and seats; unusual angles that could lead to doubles and triples; a sleek out-of-town scoreboard; a majestic clock over the main video board, sponsored by the local newspaper; and the pièce de résistance: a glorious, historic warehouse set behind right and center field, providing the perfect setting of Americana. Best of all, people could travel between the warehouse and the ballpark during a game, whether to shop or grab a quick bite. Once the park debuted, nearly every other major league team decided it was time to open its own version of Oriole Park.

The park takes numerous cues from golden-age ballparks like Shibe Park, Ebbets Field, and Forbes Field, but it was envisioned with the modern fan in mind. Architects considered sight lines for those both in the seats and walking about the concourses. They created a midway-like area fit for making a day at the ballpark a full experience. They did it all smack in the middle of an urban center, transforming a nine-to-five part of Baltimore into a nearly year-round destination. And finally, they made sure no football team could take the park for half the year, setting a trend away from multipurpose stadiums. This was a baseball venue from start to finish.

I first visited Oriole Park in its first few years, awestruck by its beauty. Compare it to multipurpose, doughnut-shaped stadiums of the 1960s and 1970s, and it's no contest. The natural green grass and sandy-brown warning track run against the deep-green fence, while the golden-brown brick of the warehouse soars above. For a kid who was used to nothing but cold Veterans Stadium in Philadelphia, Oriole Park was a revelation.

Even now, Oriole Park remains a revelation to many. You could easily think it's been around for a hundred years, and you'll wonder why half the league played in enclosed, concrete caverns for so long. While a number of parks have opened since 1992 with many bells and whistles, it's so hard to compare them to this original. This place is as good as it gets.

ORIENTATION

Oriole Park at Camden Yards is centrally located in Downtown Baltimore, just a few minutes' walk from the Inner Harbor and a 10-minute drive east of popular Fells Point. There are seven entry gates at the stadium. When arriving, try to enter via **Gate A,** the Eutaw Street concourse entrance that puts you right between the ballpark and the B&O Warehouse. Just be ready to stand in a crowd for a few minutes. **Gate H,** on the opposite side of Eutaw, is another good choice and is typically less crowded. Both of these gates open two hours before first pitch, while the others open 90 minutes beforehand.

Oriole Park at Camden Yards

TICKETS AND SEATING

Pricing

The O's maintain a **dynamic pricing** model. Contests against the **Red Sox, Yankees, Nationals,** and **Phillies** will sport the highest prices since demand is greatest. For an average seat at Oriole Park, you'll pay around $60 for a game against a **top rival.** To save some money, look for games against **non-rivals** or teams that don't travel well (meaning they don't draw big crowds as the visiting team). Those games will cost you about $30 for an average seat.

During lean years, the Orioles introduced a fantastic promotion that makes it much more affordable for families to attend a game: **Kids Cheer Free.** Per the deal, two children ages nine and under get a free ticket with the purchase of a regularly priced upper-deck ticket.

Students with valid school identification can get $10 left-field upper reserve (300 level) seats for Friday games.

Seating Plan

Interestingly, the sections of Oriole Park's **lower level** are numbered not 101 and onward, but 1 and onward. Even-numbered sections are the lower rows, called the **field level.** Sections 4-86 wind around from the right-field foul pole toward home plate, then out to left field. Sections 90-98 are the **Eutaw Bleachers,** out in center field beneath the scoreboard. Odd-numbered sections are higher up, called the **terrace level.** Sections 1-87 wind around, again from the right-field foul pole to home plate and around to left field.

The **200 level** is the **club level.** These even-numbered sections, 204-288, wind from near the right-field foul pole around to home plate and out to left field. One level above that is the **upper boxes,** which are the lower rows of the **300 level;** these are all even-numbered, 306-388. The higher rows of the 300 level are the **upper reserved.** They, too, are even-numbered, 306-388, and follow the same path.

There are **standing-room-only** areas out in left center field and right center field, plus there's the **Budweiser Roof Deck** in deep center field. For some games, **groups** rent it out completely, but usually anyone can hang out here, whether standing at a **rail** or sitting at a **picnic table.** You can also find a **drink rail** between sections 268 and 280 in the club level; you can get **standing-room** tickets for

this area, which will cost less than most seats.

Group seating areas include the **Miller Lite Flight Deck** (200 level, right field), which is good for at least 24 people and includes a $15 food and beverage voucher. Over in the **Left Field All-Inclusive Picnic Perch** (200 level, left field), ticket holders can get all-you-can-eat hog dogs, nachos, soda, and other goodies.

For fans with peanut allergies, the Orioles have a **Peanut Allergy Suite** on the club level that's available during select dates each season. This is a good option for those who are very sensitive to peanuts; call the Orioles at 888/848-2473 for more information.

Where to Buy Tickets

If you're just looking for quick tickets, the best bet is to peruse the secondary market, à

YOUR BEST DAY AT ORIOLE PARK AT CAMDEN YARDS

You're going to Birdland tonight for an Orioles game. Here's how to spend your time in Charm City beforehand and afterward.

9 HOURS BEFORE FIRST PITCH
If you're just here for the day, pay a quick visit to the **Baltimore Inner Harbor.** If I had to pick just one attraction, I'd go with a tour of the USS *Constellation* via **Historic Ships** (301 E. Pratt St.). When you've finished, hop on the **Baltimore Water Taxi** (Memorial Day-Labor Day, free) toward Fells Point.

7 HOURS BEFORE FIRST PITCH
You have to visit **Max's Taphouse,** a Fells Point icon with a heck of a tap list. Consider this a prelunch drink.

6 HOURS BEFORE FIRST PITCH
For lunch, may I suggest oysters? My favorite spot is **Thames Street Oyster House.** Load up on shellfish or go big with a lobster roll.

4 HOURS BEFORE FIRST PITCH
For the remainder of the day, you'll be near the ballpark, so if you're driving, find a parking spot for the night. If not, your best bet right now is to take Lyft or Uber.

Head to the **Babe Ruth Birthplace & Museum,** but be sure to get here before 5pm, when it closes. Read up on the story of the Great Bambino, including a retelling of his famous "called shot."

3 HOURS BEFORE FIRST PITCH
It's not very far to the ballpark (about three blocks), but before heading in, mix it up with some O's fans at the famous **Pickles Pub.** Enjoy your cheap beer and converse about the history of the song "Orioles Magic (Feel It Happen)."

the USS *Constellation* in Baltimore's Inner Harbor

2 HOURS BEFORE FIRST PITCH
Arrive at Gate A to walk into the **Eutaw Street** concourse. You'll be right beside the **B&O Warehouse** here, so take your time admiring the place.

DURING THE GAME
Visit the **Official Orioles Team Store at Camden Yards** and order a sandwich from **Boog's BBQ.** Say hi to Boog Powell if he's there. Spend some time hanging out at the Eutaw Street concourse, looking for all the **baseballs** that note warehouse hits, and take a selfie or two at **Legends Park.** Snap a few other photos from **section 40** to take in the whole view. Get some Chesapeake fries from **Baseline Burgers.**

AFTER THE GAME
Hail a Lyft or Uber and finish your night at **Mt. Royal Tavern** for cheap Natty Bohs, a shot or two, and the best company you can keep after midnight.

la **StubHub,** for inexpensive deals, especially closer to first pitch. With the **MLB Ballpark app,** it's possible to upgrade your seats after getting into Oriole Park.

Best Seats
If you're visiting Oriole Park at Camden Yards for the first time, you really should get seats along the **third-base line,** whether you're low (back rows of **sections 55-65**) or up in the 300 level (**sections 352-368**). Club seats are good, too (**sections 250-262**). This location allows for the best views of the park: Looking straight out at the warehouse is one of the prettiest sights in the game. Another spot to try for is behind home plate, up high (**sections 328-336**); these seats are quite affordable, and the views are also spectacular.

It's fun in the **Eutaw Bleachers** (sections 90-98), but during afternoon games the sun will be shining on you. Plus, some seats in **section 92** are **obstructed.**

Good seats for **avoiding the sun** are in the back rows of the **third-base side** of the **terrace level.** During afternoon games, the sun can really get you if you're a little lower in the field level or in the right-field corner.

KNOW BEFORE YOU GO

The Orioles allow **nonalcoholic drinks** in **plastic bottles,** as long as they're **unopened** at the gate and fit inside a 16- by 16- by 8-inch **soft cooler** or container. Nothing hard-sided is allowed inside the park. Cowbells, air horns, and noisemakers of any kind are not permitted.

Accessibility

Elevators are available near section 36 and behind section 78. Visit one of three **fan assistance centers** (behind home plate on lower- and upper-level concourses, first floor B&O Warehouse) for an **assistive listening device.** At the same place, you can rent a **wheelchair** for free. A photo ID or valid credit card is required as a deposit.

Looking for **accessible parking**? Visit **Lot A** or **Lot B,** which have spots open on a first-come, first-served basis. You'll need to display your state-issued disabled **parking placard.**

GETTING THERE

Public Transit

Baltimore doesn't have a very robust public transit system, but if you're staying close to a train line, you can get to the ballpark easily. The **Light RailLink** ($0.90-2.10 one-way) operated by **MTA** (410/539-5000, www.mta. maryland.gov) runs between the northern suburbs and Baltimore/Washington International Thurgood Marshall Airport. You'll exit at **Camden station** (Conway St. and Howard St.).

The MTA also operates the **MARC Train,** a commuter rail system linking Washington

GAME COSTS

Tickets: It really depends on whether the Orioles are in playoff contention or not. If they are, you'll pay **$40-50** for a decent seat in the back of the field level. If they're not contending, you should be able to find a field-level seat for about **$20-30.** Of course, if the Yankees, Red Sox, Nationals, or Phillies are in town, expect to pay more than average.

Hot dog: You'll pay about **$5,** but a kid-size frank is just **$1.50,** the lowest price in baseball for a hot dog.

Beer: A small macro beer is about **$4.** Large macros are **$8,** while premium canned beer and craft will start at around **$7.**

Parking: Cheaper than at most other stadiums. You should be able to snag a spot for **$10-15,** even at team-operated parking areas.

DC to Baltimore. The **Camden Line** runs from DC south to Baltimore, exiting at the ballpark.

When hopping off the light rail or MARC Train, you'll walk through the **Breezeway** to reach the ballpark's busy **Gate A.**

Finally, the MTA's **Metro SubwayLink** can get you from Downtown to Midtown, though there are few stops. It starts at Johns Hopkins University School of Medicine before continuing east toward Oriole Park. The closest stop to the ballpark is **Charles Center** (Baltimore St. and Charles St.). It's about a 12-minute walk to the park from here.

Driving

Main arteries on the way to Oriole Park include **I-395,** an extension of I-95 that exits right at the ballpark, and **Martin Luther King Jr. Boulevard,** which weaves between the ballpark and M&T Bank Stadium, connecting with all the stadium-area parking lots.

BE A FAN

Orioles fans are a cheerful sort, welcoming to all, even if they have to bite their tongues when Red Sox and Yankees fans invade from the north. They believe in **"Orioles magic,"** a term coined in a song called **"Orioles Magic (Feel It Happen),"** written and performed by jingle composer Walter Woodward back in 1980, a few months after the club won the American League pennant. The song was written to capture the spirit of the Orioles and old Memorial Stadium during a 1979 season filled with comeback wins. You're unlikely to hear the song these days, but at the very least, you now know something about Baltimore Orioles history.

You will, however, hear **"Thank God I'm a Country Boy"** by John Denver. The song extolling country living has been played during the seventh-inning stretch of every Orioles home game since 1975. Does it make sense that you're hearing this song at a ballpark inside Baltimore, Maryland? Not really, but the tradition lives on.

Maybe the best little tradition in all of baseball—nay, sports writ large—exists at this ballpark. As you know, **"The Star-Spangled Banner"** is performed before every professional sporting event in America. Well, at Oriole Park, there's an enhancement: When the performer approaches the line "O say does that star-spangled banner yet wave," instead of keeping quiet, just about every single person in the ballpark, in unison, yells **"O!"** as a shout-out to their team.

Off Martin Luther King Jr. Boulevard are **Lot F, Lot G,** and **Lot H,** the three lots used for general parking. You can pay for spots here in advance, and prices aren't very expensive, so it's a good option.

Otherwise, you can park in a number of lots and garages in Downtown Baltimore. Consider **Baltimore Street** and **Fayette Street** for spots, as you might be able to pay around $10, and the walk to the ballpark is just five minutes or so.

PARK FEATURES AND SIGHTS

Eutaw Street and the B&O Warehouse

The first thing you should do upon visiting Oriole Park at Camden Yards is to walk **Eutaw Street** (outfield, open two hours before first pitch), the ground-level concourse between the ballpark and the B&O Warehouse. This midway dressed up with festoon lighting includes eateries and carnival attractions. Look for the **baseballs** embedded in the sidewalk; they show the location of home runs hit over the right-field fence and past the seats.

Let me talk a little more about the **B&O Warehouse** (Eutaw Street concourse, right field) because it's the structure that practically drew a blueprint for an entire generation of ballparks. Built from 1899 to 1905, used as storage for the Baltimore & Ohio Railroad, and spanning 1,116 feet in length and rising eight stories high, it's an imposing and commanding brick structure that was converted into Orioles team offices as the club recognized its utility. The O's built Oriole Park with the warehouse in mind, letting it define the outfield backdrop in such a way that it not only recalled venues of baseball's golden age of ballparks. The presence of the warehouse also reinvented the template for the modern ballpark. Nearly every baseball venue built after Oriole Park uses a defining visual cue on the order of the warehouse.

While on Eutaw Street, you'll walk alongside the warehouse. Look for a **plaque** marking a spot on the building's exterior that was hit by a shot from Hall of Famer Ken Griffey Jr. during the 1993 MLB Home Run Derby. Next, stand for a moment and imagine the people at the windows of the warehouse cheering after Cal Ripken Jr. broke Lou Gehrig's consecutive games record in 1995. This building is a special part of modern baseball history.

Legends Park

Way out in center field, by the end of the Eutaw Street concourse, is **Legends Park.** This tree-filled area includes nearly eight-foot-tall **bronze statues** of legendary Orioles—Frank Robinson, Brooks Robinson, Cal Ripken Jr., Eddie Murray, Jim Palmer, and manager Earl Weaver—made by sculptor Antonio Tobias Mendez. This is a nice place to take a few photos or just take a breather from the fan-centric Eutaw Street area.

Kids' Corner

Got kids? Look for the **Kids' Corner** (Gate C, right field), whose main attraction is a treehouse and play set made from a 400-year-old redwood and called the **Bird House.** It's not very large, so be prepared to be packed in with scores of children. Also here are Skee-Ball and giant bobbleheads, plus kids can munch on chicken nuggets and corn dogs.

FOOD AND DRINKS

When Oriole Park opened, it did so with the scent of smoke emanating from a barbecue pit, launching a trend that continues today at ballparks across the country. **Boog's BBQ** (Eutaw Street concourse, center field) is the first of the country's ballpark eateries run by a former star player. Here, ex-Orioles slugger Boog Powell watches over pit beef, pork, and turkey. Sides include baked beans, Old Bay-seasoned coleslaw, and chips. It's a popular stop, so get there first thing. While the food won't come near the kind of 'cue you'd get in Texas or the Carolinas, and the prices are higher, it's worth it to say you've had it. It's a nice-looking spot, with a vintage truck outside, a general store that sells Orioles and Boog's merchandise, and cool signage. If Powell is there (which

Photos (from top to bottom): the team mascot, Oriole Bird; B&O Warehouse at Camden Yards; statue of Babe Ruth by sculptor Susan Luery.

he is for most games), you can even get a photo with him.

While on Eutaw Street, look for craft cocktails at **Bar 478** (Eutaw Street concourse, center field), a vintage Airstream trailer sitting exactly 478 feet beyond home plate. They also serve beer and wine.

For some delicious Baltimore-specific grub, look for **Harris Creek Oyster & Seafood** (Eutaw Street concourse, right field). Try the jumbo lump crab cake and oyster po'boy sandwich with fresh Chesapeake Bay oysters. Harris Creek also shucks oysters on the half shell, a Baltimore tradition.

The Baltimore neighborhood of Washington Village is also known as Pigtown, since during the 1800s it was home to butcher shops where pigs being carried on B&O Railroad cars were slaughtered and processed. At Oriole Park, that tradition is noted with **Pigtown Stack** (section 68). Get the sandwich shop's namesake sandwich of barbecue pork, mustard slaw, tobacco onions, and pickle. It's like an elevated McRib.

If you want more stuff bathed in Old Bay seasoning, try the Old Bay *elote* (Mexican-style street corn) at **Corona Street Taco** (section 70). Order the gravy fry chipper, essentially a poutine of kettle chips topped with mozzarella and gravy, at **Harbor Crisps** (section 68).

Orioles fans love **Chesapeake fries,** which are waffle fries tossed in Old Bay and then topped with warm crab dip. Find them at any of the **Baseline Burgers** stands.

There's plenty of good local beer at the **Free State Pub** (section 53), including selections from Flying Dog, Heavy Seas, Key Brewing Co., and Monument City Brewing. Portable stands for Maryland-area breweries include **Flying Dog** (section 23) and **Heavy Seas** (Eutaw Street concourse, center field; section 334).

On Eutaw Street and inside the B&O Warehouse is **Dempsey's Brew Pub and Restaurant** (Eutaw Street concourse, right field, 410/843-7901, open during game days, 11am-9pm daily non-game days, under $40). This is one of those basic ballpark restaurants that does elevated bar grub, burgers, and

sandwiches in a sit-down atmosphere. It's good if your party needs seating and air-conditioning with lunch or dinner. Look for the sausage roll and the crab cake sandwich, plus the Pigtown stack you can also find in the infield concourse. The place is named after an Orioles legend, catcher Rick Dempsey, whose jersey and bobbleheads can be found throughout.

For a sit-down bite, but only if you have a club level ticket, you can visit the **All-Star Café** (home plate, 200 level, open until fifth inning). It's basically a food court with grub from around the stadium, but in air-conditioned comfort inside the club area.

EVENTS

Kids looking for **autographs** should go down toward the home and away dugouts starting when the gates open. While nothing is promised, players and coaches may sign a bit up until 45 minutes before first pitch. The Orioles invite **former players** and **coaches** to sign autographs on Eutaw Street during Monday and Thursday games. After Sunday home games, kids ages 4-14 can **run the bases.**

Themed games at the park include a Father's Day catch on the field, an annual LGBTQ+ pride celebration, yoga at the Yard, and multiple bark-at-the-park events where good boys and girls are invited, maybe even to parade on the warning track. And if you're into that sort of thing, there's also an annual Margaritaville night. Parrotheads, unite!

Tours

The Orioles run regular, 90-minute **tours** (410/574-6234, 10am, 11am, noon, 1pm Mon.-Sat., noon, 1pm, 2pm, 3pm Sun. mid-Feb.-Nov., no tours before afternoon games, $9, $6 seniors and ages 4-14, free ages 3 and under) that visit the home dugout, the scoreboard control room, the press levels, Legends Park, and Eutaw Street.

SHOPPING

The **Official Orioles Team Store at**

PRESIDENTIAL FIRST PITCHES

The tradition of a "first pitch," in which a dignitary throws a baseball ceremoniously before a game begins, may have started in 1890, per the earliest known documentation of such an event, found in the *Pittsburgh Dispatch* newspaper. Whether or not it was the first, we've been watching first pitches for more than a century. These days, before every game at every minor- and major-league ballpark, someone walks out to the mound and performs the ritual.

Sitting American presidents have thrown first pitches since 1910. Most of them have happened either in Washington DC or in Baltimore. Here's a look at a few of my favorite presidential first pitches:

- 1910: In what is regarded as the first ceremonial first pitch by a president at a major league contest, **President William H. Taft,** an avid baseball fan, throws the ball before a game between the Washington Nationals (future Senators) and Philadelphia Athletics at National Park.
- 1932: After being booed while appearing at the 1931 World Series in Philadelphia during the darkest days of the Great Depression, **President Herbert Hoover** throws out the first pitch at Griffith Stadium before an opening day contest between the Nationals/Senators and Boston Red Sox. He has the home field advantage and is cheered.
- 1940: One of many first pitches thrown by **President Franklin D. Roosevelt,** this doozy, coming before a Nationals/Senators versus Red Sox game, hits and breaks the camera of *Washington Post* photographer Irving Schlossenberg.
- 1976: At the All-Star Game in Philadelphia, **President Gerald Ford** pulls off a neat trick, throwing two first pitches—one with his left hand, one with his right hand.
- 1992: For the very first game at Oriole Park at Camden Yards, **President George H. W. Bush** tosses the first pitch. The O's beat the Cleveland Indians, 2-0.
- 2001: Arguably the most famous presidential first pitch comes from **President George W. Bush.** Before Game 3 of the World Series and a little more than a month after the September 11 terrorist attacks, Bush takes the mound at Yankee Stadium and throws an absolute strike.

Camden Yards (333 W. Camden St., Eutaw Street concourse, right field near Gate H, 410/843-7880, open during games, 10am-5pm daily non-game days) is inside the B&O Warehouse and includes all the fun stuff you'd find at any other official team store in a major league ballpark.

BALTIMORE SIGHTS

BABE RUTH BIRTHPLACE & MUSEUM

For any baseball fan, paying a visit to the **Babe Ruth Birthplace & Museum** (216 Emory St., 410/727-1539, www. baberuthmuseum.org, 10am-5pm Tues.-Sun., $10, $8 seniors, $5 ages 5-16, free ages 4 and under) is essential, though be prepared for a relatively quaint place.

The museum is the span of four row homes, one of them being Ruth's birthplace. You can see the upstairs bedroom where Ruth was born, decorated with furniture that sets it at the turn of the 20th century. Exhibits at the museum, which comprises most of the property, include a look at Ruth's childhood in Baltimore and a detailing of the Great Bambino's famed "called shot" in the 1932 World Series. You can also check out some old jerseys and plenty of Ruthian ephemera.

It's easy to get here: While at the Babe Ruth statue at Oriole Park, you'll see a painted baseball on the sidewalk, then another. Follow them, one to the next, until you end up at the museum, which is just three blocks from the ballpark.

BALTIMORE INNER HARBOR

A major tourist attraction, the **Baltimore Inner Harbor** (E. Pratt St. and Light St.) is constantly packed, especially during the summer. Be sure to avoid tourist trap venues that you'd find anywhere in the country, and eat before you go because the chain-centric restaurant scene here is mediocre.

The Inner Harbor is worth visiting at least once, considering some of the most important sights in the city are here, including the USS *Constellation*. Part of **Historic Ships** (301 E. Pratt St., 410/539-1797, www.historicships.org, 10am-4:30pm daily, $15-18, $13-16 seniors and students, $7-9 ages 6-14, free ages 5 and under), a grouping of four historic military ships, the *Constellation* is the one to prioritize, as it was the last sail-only warship built by the U.S. Navy, back in 1854. It was used to capture slave ships in an effort to end the Atlantic slave trade in the 1850s. You can go on all four ships, though two might be just fine, given the crowds. You can walk about the decks of the *Constellation* and the other historic ships while chatting with docents about how and why they were commissioned.

At the southwest corner of the harbor is the **Maryland Science Center** (601 Light St., 410/685-2370, www.mdsci.org, 10am-5pm Tues.-Fri., 10am-6pm Sat., 11am-5pm Sun., $26, $25 seniors, $20 ages 3-12, free ages 2 and under). Like many science centers in America, it's interactive, with larger-than-life playscapes taking on an educational tone. Exhibits cover topics like dinosaurs and fossils, local ecology, and physics, all with a hands-on bent.

To get a view of the whole harbor and city, head to the top of the World Trade Center, called **Top of the World** (401 E. Pratt St., 410/837-8439, www.viewbaltimore.org, 10am-6pm Sun.-Thurs., 10am-9pm Fri.-Sat.

Memorial Day-Labor Day, 10am-6pm Wed.-Thurs., 10am-7pm Fri.-Sat., 11am-6pm Sun. Labor Day-Memorial Day, $6, $5 seniors, $4 ages 3-12, free ages 2 and under). The vista is on the 27th floor of the tallest hexagonal building in the world.

NATIONAL AQUARIUM

A top attraction in Baltimore and the East Coast, the **National Aquarium** (501 E. Pratt St., www.aqua.org, 10am-4pm Mon.-Thurs., 10am-8 pm Fri., 10am-5pm Sat.-Sun., $40, $35 seniors, $30 ages 3-11) can fill an entire day, especially since it has 17,000 animals and more than two million gallons of tanks. Exhibits include Dolphin Discovery, home to six Atlantic bottlenose dolphins; Upland Tropical Rain Forest, an incredible and immersive environment with tamarins, a blue poison-dart frog, sloths, and a yellow-footed tortoise; and Shark Alley, where you can see sharks swimming around you in a ring-shaped tank. Look for the sand tiger shark, sandbar shark, and nurse shark, which lurks down low. The aquarium is located at the Inner Harbor.

FOOD

NEAR ORIOLE PARK AT CAMDEN YARDS

Around Oriole Park, the food scene is either fast food, mediocre chain fare, or crowded bars and pubs with extensive food menus that are decent.

One of my recommendations for this area is **Pratt Street Ale House** (206 W. Pratt St., 410/244-8900, www.prattstreetalehouse.com, 11am-midnight Sun.-Thurs., 11am-1am Fri.-Sat., under $40), which is a bar and restaurant that masks itself as British, although very little of the fare is such. You'll get nachos, wings, and a sandwich here, but it's more about the patio setting and beers.

My other recommendation is **Frank & Nic's West End Grille** (511 W. Pratt St.,

Valid through 9/30/2021

Buy Any 2
Freshly Baked
Cookies,
Brownies, or Scones
Get 1 FREE

Mix or Match Select Items

To redeem: Present this coupon in the cafe.

X3C7W8B

**Buy any 2 Freshly baked Cookies,
Brownies, or Scones, Get 1 FREE:**
*Promotion excludes individually wrapped ite

1 redemption per coupon.
Items included are subject to change.
Ask Cafe cashier for more details.

purchased as part of the offer are returned, in which case such items are available for a refund (in 30 days). Exchanges of the items sold at no cost are available only for items of equal or lesser value than the original cost of such item.

Opened music CDs, DVDs, vinyl records, electronics, toys/games and audio books may not be returned, and can be exchanged only for the same product and only if defective. NOOKs purchased from other retailers or sellers are returnable only to the retailer or seller from which they were purchased pursuant to such retailer's or seller's return policy. Magazines, newspapers, eBooks, digital downloads, and used books are not returnable or exchangeable. Defective NOOKs may be exchanged at the store in accordance with the applicable warranty.

Returns or exchanges will not be permitted (i) after 30 days or without receipt or (ii) for product not carried by Barnes & Noble.com, (iii) for purchases made with a check less than 7 days prior to the date of return.

Policy on receipt may appear in two sections.

Return Policy

With a sales receipt or Barnes & Noble.com packing slip, a full refund in the original form of payment will be issued from any Barnes & Noble Booksellers store for returns of new and unread books, and unopened and undamaged music CDs, DVDs, vinyl records, electronics, toys/games and audio books made within 30 days of purchase from a Barnes & Noble Booksellers store or Barnes & Noble.com with the below exceptions:

Undamaged NOOKs purchased from any Barnes & Noble Booksellers store or from Barnes & Noble.com may be returned within 14 days when accompanied with a sales receipt or with a Barnes & Noble.com packing slip or may be exchanged within 30 days with a gift receipt.

A store credit for the purchase price will be issued (i) when a gift receipt is presented within 60 days of purchase, (ii) for all textbook returns and exchanges, or (iii) when the original tender is PayPal.

410/685-6800, www.frankandnics.com, 11:30am-10pm daily, under $40), which knows exactly what it does: basic appetizers, salads, burgers, sandwiches. It carries a few beers even a craft lover can appreciate, as well as 16-ounce cans of Natty Boh (a locally born beer known more formally as National Bohemian).

OTHER NEIGHBORHOODS

Downtown and Midtown

In Downtown, visit **Ida B's Table** (235 Holliday St., 410/844-0444, www.idabstable.com, 11:30am-2pm and 4pm-8pm Tues.-Thurs., 11:30am-2pm and 5pm-9pm Fri., 10am-3pm and 5pm-9pm Sat., 10am-3pm and 5pm-8pm Sun., under $50) for some serious soul food that reaches into the history of the Atlantic slave trade for some of its culinary sources. Named after anti-lynching activist and journalist Ida B. Wells, this spacious and pretty industrial-modern spot does jambalaya, the West African peanut stew *maafe,* the beautiful Ethiopian stew *sega wat,* and hot chicken livers.

Up in Midtown, there's a nice variety of cuisines, with most restaurants having a white tablecloth philosophy. Two options here are the Afghan spot **The Helmand** (806 N. Charles St., 410/752-0311, www.helmand.com, 5pm-10pm Sun.-Thurs., 5pm-11pm Fri.-Sat., under $70) and the renowned, jacket-and-tie steak house **The Prime Rib** (1101 N. Calvert St., 410/539-1804, www.theprimerib.com, 5pm-10pm Mon.-Thurs., 5pm-11pm Fri.-Sat., 4pm-9pm Sun., under $125).

I recommend dining at **The Brewer's Art** (1106 N. Charles St., 410/547-6925, www.thebrewersart.com, 4pm-2am daily, under $70), inside a townhouse. The folks here serve a food menu that's meant to work in tandem with their home-brewed, mostly Belgian-style beers. It's a step up from casual but not too formal, so consider this a nice night out, and maybe a prelude before hitting up the best breweries in town.

Photos (from top to bottom): a tall ship in Baltimore's Inner Harbor; the National Aquarium in Baltimore; Pickles Pub.

Fells Point

It's worth visiting the Fells Point neighborhood for the seafood alone. Here you'll find a guy on the street shucking dollar oysters, or you can eat a little more formally at **Thames Street Oyster House** (1728 Thames St., 443/449-7726, www.thamesstreetoysterhouse.com, 5pm-9:30pm Mon.-Tues., 11:30am-2:30pm and 5pm-9:30pm Wed.-Thurs. and Sun., 11:30am-2:30pm and 5pm-10:30pm Fri.-Sat., under $60). The strategy here is to get some oysters and clams from the raw bar. Then, if it's lunch, try a lobster roll or crab cake. For dinner, big dishes like lobster polenta rule the day. The well-lit, seaboard-cool, narrow dining space can fill up, but stay calm and stick it out. The food is worth it.

For an alternative to Thames Street, try the **Abbey Burger Bistro** (811 S. Broadway, 410/522-1428, www.abbeyburgerbistro.com, 5pm-1am Mon., 11am-1am Tues.-Wed., 11am-2am Thurs.-Fri., 10am-2am Sat., 10am-1am Sun., under $30), also in Fells Point. This is a small chain in Baltimore that features a whole range of burgers, including one with peanut butter. It's good for both the sports bar crowd and families.

The casual and familiar **Lobo** (1900 Aliceanna St., 410/327-0303, www.lobofellspoint.com, 5pm-10pm Mon.-Thurs., 5pm-11pm Fri.-Sat., under $40) is the rare restaurant that rises to the top while retaining a sense of character and neighborhood friendliness. You'll find sandwiches and a raw bar, plus big home-style entrées and nods to Thai and Vietnamese fare.

BARS AND BREWERIES

NEAR ORIOLE PARK AT CAMDEN YARDS

Over in the Pigtown neighborhood, and a walkable distance (0.7 mile) west of Oriole Park, is **Suspended Brewing Company** (912 Washington Blvd., 410/926-8847, www.suspendedbrewing.com, 4pm-9pm Fri., 1pm-8pm Sat.-Sun.). A fun and fancy-free place with some nice wood walls and tables, a friendly bar, and high ceilings, it feels like a perfect weekend hangout with friends. The beers are tasty, with a preference toward sours.

Before a game (or right after it), pay a visit to **Pickles Pub** (520 Washington Blvd., 410/752-1784, www.picklespub.com, 11am-2am daily). Around since 1988, Pickles is an orange sea on game days, a sea that floods outside and into the streets. It's always a fun scene, but be prepared to be among many people. Pickles offers cheap Natty Bohs and other macro fare, and it sells moderately priced hot dogs for fans. Its regular menu is all pub fare and crab sandwiches. Come here for the vibe and hopefully to catch some of that Orioles magic.

OTHER NEIGHBORHOODS

Down in Latrobe Park, there's **Diamondback Brewing Company** (1215 E. Fort Ave., #008, 443/388-9626, www.diamondbackbeer.com, 4pm-9pm Tues.-Thurs., noon-11pm Fri.-Sat., noon-8pm Sun.), a smart brewery that has a robust lager program as well as some tasty IPAs and easy-drinking fare. Pizzas are available through its kitchen. This is a nice place to hang for a few hours sipping some beers.

Mead is plentiful at **Charm City Meadworks** (400 E. Biddle St., 443/961-1072, www.charmcitymeadworks.com, 5pm-10pm Wed.-Fri., noon-10pm Sat., noon-5pm Sun.). Producing a deep line of this honey-based alcoholic beverage, this Midtown spot has an industrial space with some seating and an easygoing vibe. They also provide board games to play, and there's a small outdoor area.

Want a fun, no-frills watering hole? Also in Midtown is **Mt. Royal Tavern** (1204 W. Mt. Royal Ave., 410/669-6686, 10am-2am daily). Here, the beer-and-shot game is on point (Natty Bohs are cheap here), the vibe is low-key and friendly, and the jukebox has good stuff in it. Look up to see a bar patron's re-creation of the Sistine Chapel ceiling. Mt. Royal is cash only.

Over in Fells Point, pay a visit to **Max's Taphouse** (737 S. Broadway, 410/675-6297, www.maxs.com, 11am-2am daily). Its beer list is outstanding, featuring local, national, and international names. The space is thoughtful and fun: Look for the repurposed beer-bottle candles, and the vibe is buzzy and exciting, though the place can get packed and loud. The food menu of elevated pub fare is quite nice. Note: Max's is cigar-friendly.

On the other side of the Inner Harbor is a playground for adults that's also kid-friendly. At **Sandlot** (1000 Wills St., 410/568-4916, www.sandlotbaltimore.com, 4pm-11pm Mon.-Fri., 11am-11pm Sat.-Sun. Apr.-Oct.), you won't find Benny the Jet or Squints here, but you will get a beachy outdoor bar with a good selection of beer, original cocktails and slushies, and a baseball-themed menu of nachos and sandwiches. This is a very popular outdoor bar with plenty of sand and Instagram vibes. For the best experience, think about taking the Baltimore Water Taxi across the Inner Harbor. (Parking is a real problem.) If you have kids, let them just play in the sand. Don't get upset if the service is slow; just relax and enjoy the views.

RECREATION

Before you get out into the Inner Harbor, here's a story: In 1936, a military helicopter reportedly spotted something resembling an unusual reptile in Bush River, some 25 miles northeast of Baltimore near the Chesapeake Bay. As the years progressed, more sightings of an odd reptilian creature were reported; then, in the mid-1970s, a rash of sightings emerged. Ever since, folks by the Chesapeake have been on the lookout for Chessie, a snakelike creature that could be anywhere from 12 to 30 feet long.

Starting in the 1970s, in tribute to all these Chessie sightings, **dragon boats** hit the Inner Harbor. These days, they continue to take tourists and locals alike on the water for a quick, self-guided trip. To get in one, try **Living Classrooms** (301 E. Pratt St., 410/528-1060, www.livingclassrooms.org, 11am-6pm daily Apr.-Memorial Day, 11am-10pm daily Memorial Day-Labor Day, afternoons Fri.-Sun. Labor Day-Nov., $20 for a half hour for up to four people). This organization is known for giving young Baltimoreans their first work experience, and it also leads job training programs, so the money is going to a good cause.

Noticeable from the Inner Harbor because it's 80 feet up, **Federal Hill Park** (300 Warren Ave.) has played an important role in Baltimore's history. It was used by the military during the War of 1812, and the Union army fortified the hill during the Civil War. A display cannon stands at the hill today, by the best overlook, to mark its military history. The park also has a basketball court and playground, and is accessible by taking 100 steps up from ground level. You can also drive up the hill and park on Warren Avenue.

Looking to spend some time with some taller hills? Visit **Patapsco Valley State Park** (8020 Baltimore National Pike, Ellicott City, 9am-sunset daily). About 10 miles southwest of Downtown Baltimore via I-95, this 16,000-plus-acre park is sprawling and wild, with quite a few good trails. My pick is the **Cascade Trail** (trailhead on River Rd., two miles north of Gun Rd., Elkridge), a very easy walk. From the trailhead, head up the Cascade Trail for less than a half-mile, staying to the left when there are intersections. You'll soon come to a picturesque waterfall after climbing just a few hundred feet in elevation. Continue on the trail to cross some creeks and catch additional falls. The entire Cascade Trail network is just a few miles in total. To do all of it, go up to the intersection with the Morning Choice Trail, then turn back. Opt to stay to the right to follow the same route back, or make a left to do a small loop.

ACCOMMODATIONS

NEAR ORIOLE PARK AT CAMDEN YARDS

There are more than a few chain hotels near the ballpark. If you want something independent, try the **Lord Baltimore Hotel** (20 W. Baltimore St., 410/539-8400, www.lordbaltimorehotel.com, $100-250), just a 10-minute walk northeast of the grounds. Lord Baltimore has plenty of affordable rooms, allows pets weighing up to 80 pounds, and has an on-site tavern, bakery, and rooftop bar and lounge with beautiful city views.

A number of hotels near the park offer Orioles packages, though none of them include game-day tickets. Opt for the Triple Play Package at the **Hilton Baltimore** (401 W. Pratt St., 443/573-8700, www.hilton.com, $150-400), which includes parking, breakfast, and a $20 gift card to the ballpark. Also, many rooms at the hotel overlook Oriole Park, as it's just across the street.

OTHER NEIGHBORHOODS

If you want to stay in Fells Point and not spend an arm and a leg, choose **The Inn at Henderson's Wharf** (1000 Fell St.,

410/522-7777, www.choicehotels.com, $200-350). It's an Ascend property from the Choice Hotels corporation, so it's not independent, but it's also not $500 a night (which is typical for this area). Rooms are clean and well-appointed, and you might be able to score a view of the Inner Harbor.

GETTING AROUND

PUBLIC TRANSIT

As a smaller city, Baltimore doesn't have the most sophisticated transit system; however, there are train lines that go to and from Oriole Park at Camden Yards, and to and from Downtown. The **Light RailLink** ($0.90-2.10 one-way), operated by **MTA** (410/539-5000, www.mta.maryland.gov), runs between the northern suburbs and Baltimore/Washington International Thurgood Marshall Airport. It threads north to south, primarily along Howard Street. Main stations include **Camden station** (Conway St. and Howard St.) at the ballpark; **Lexington Market** (Lexington St. and Howard St.) in Downtown Baltimore; and **Cultural Center** (Preston St. and Howard St.) in Midtown.

The MTA's **Metro SubwayLink** can get

Lord Baltimore Hotel

you from Downtown to Midtown, though there are few stops. It starts at Johns Hopkins University School of Medicine before continuing east toward Oriole Park. The closest stop to the ballpark is **Charles Center** (Baltimore St. and Charles St.), and the Midtown station is **State Center** (Preston St. and Eutaw St.). From there, it continues northwest into the suburbs.

The **Baltimore Water Taxi** (Memorial Day-Labor Day, free) traverses the Inner Harbor area with five main routes. These ferries can seat a few dozen passengers at a time, shepherding them to established stops on the route. The green and yellow routes stop at most of the piers, though you'll want yellow or blue for going to Fells Point. Try embarking at **Harborplace** (201 E. Pratt St.) to avoid the crowds at **Aquarium** (501 E. Pratt St.).

TAXI, UBER, AND LYFT

Uber and Lyft charge about the same for a typical ride in Baltimore, though with surge pricing, you'll find better success with Lyft. Taxis are more expensive during down times, but when surge rates are in effect, the difference between cabs and ride-sharing services is negligible. Either way, considering Baltimore's weaker transit system and high traffic, you might rather rely on ride-sharing with local drivers to get around.

CAR

Baltimore will test your patience as a driver. The big problem is on the Beltway, where traffic is generally bad, especially during rush hour. You'll likely hit some traffic while you're inside the Beltway, too.

Baltimore is inside a circular loop, **I-695,** called the **Beltway,** which offers connections to **I-83** (north to Harrisburg), **I-95** (northeast to Philadelphia and southwest to Washington), and **I-97** (south to Annapolis), plus **I-195** (ending at Baltimore/Washington International Thurgood Marshall Airport), **I-795** (northwest to Owings Mill), and **I-895** (an alternate route to I-95 through the city).

Chances are you won't deal with the Beltway once you're in the city; it's more likely you'll be living by I-95 and inner-city routes like **US-40,** which runs right along the northern boundary of the inner city, and **US-1,** which also skirts the boundary of the inner city.

When driving in the city, know that there's also **I-395,** which is accessible via I-95 south of Downtown and comes right into town at Oriole Park. Some other important thoroughfares are **Baltimore Street, Fayette Street,** and **Lombard Street** (west to east), and **Light Street** and **Calvert Street** (north to south).

WASHINGTON DC
NATIONALS

You know Washington DC as our nation's capital, a destination for politics, society, tourism, and commerce. It's possible to visit each of the major landmarks in a day, as the U.S. Capitol building, Washington Monument, White House, and Lincoln Memorial are all within walking distance of one another. Beyond them are unique-to-Washington sites like the National Archives and U.S. Treasury, and of course the Smithsonian, a massive collection of museums and educational centers that offers a glimpse into American history.

Washington DC is also a bustling city on the Eastern Seaboard with its own distinct culture and flavor. The city's baseball team has played an important part in this, starting in 1901 with the introduction of the Senators, an American

League franchise that for a while battled at the top of the standings with the New York Yankees and Philadelphia Athletics. The Senators won their only World Series championship in 1924, then drifted into the second and third division for a long time. During the 1950s, ownership brokered a deal to take the existing Senators to Minneapolis-St. Paul, becoming the Minnesota Twins. In response, the American League immediately added a new Washington franchise, also called the Senators. They'd last 11 seasons before once again departing, this time for Dallas-Fort Worth to become the Texas Rangers.

In 1969, the Montreal Expos entered Major League Baseball, specifically the National League East division. Outfitted in powder blue, red, and white, Les Expos were a minor hit at first but really took off later in the 1970s and early 1980s, when Hall of Famers Gary Carter, Andre Dawson, and Tim Raines propelled the team toward the top of the standings. The Expos won a division title in 1981 and often seemed on the verge of greatness, but they failed to return to the postseason. They seemed primed to make the playoffs in 1994, but a labor dispute prematurely ended that season, along with any hopes of an Expos championship run. Worse, it portended the end days for Montreal baseball. Major League Baseball soon took over the hemorrhaging franchise, eyeing a move down the line.

That move came in 2004, when the Expos trekked south to Washington. The franchise was renamed the Nationals, and a few years later, it lucked into serious young talent: Stephen Strasburg and Bryce Harper. Savvy front office changes complemented that core, and Washington was quickly back to being a top squad. With fresh young talent like the brilliant Juan Soto and dynamic Victor Robles, and led in part by Strasburg, the Nationals in 2019 won the city's first baseball championship in 95 years.

Maybe that title will help create a generation of dedicated Washington baseball fans. Since the Nationals are still new, the club is accumulating its fan base. So while groups from Philadelphia and New York may still loudly invade Nationals Park, and the team has had trouble drawing crowds in contention years, there's a youthful energy about the scene. Keep in mind the team's 2019 rallying song, "Baby Shark"—it's a tune meant for toddlers.

PLANNING YOUR TIME

There's so much to see in Washington DC that you can easily spend a **week** (or two!) here without ever getting bored. Between the national landmarks and museums, the buzzy neighborhoods like Adams Morgan and Logan Circle, the Navy Yard and baseball games, and the nearby destinations like Mount Vernon and the Arlington National Cemetery, you'll be busy.

But if you only have a **long weekend,** spend a full day hitting all the important spots around the National Mall, then spend another day neighborhood hopping. The rest of your time should be baseball time.

If you want to be centrally located, staying in or near the **Navy Yard** works well, but you can also stay north of the National Mall near Metro's Red or Green/Yellow Lines. You could also stay around **Logan Circle** for a hipster experience. Whatever you do, try to take Metro as much as possible.

Expect a **humid summer** and **temperate spring** and **fall** seasons in Washington. The city also has some of that southern swamp heat, and it'll get pretty unbearable in the middle of summer. Bring sunblock for just about any day game. In **April** and **September,** a jacket may be needed for night games.

GETTING THERE

AIR

Washington Dulles International Airport

The biggest of the area's airports is **Washington Dulles International Airport** (IAD, 1 Saarinen Cir., Dulles, VA, 703/572-2700, www.flydulles.com). Airlines here include **Air Canada** (888/247-2262, www.aircanada. com), **American Airlines** (800/433-7300, www.aa.com), **Delta** (800/221-1212, www. delta.com), **Frontier** (800/432-1359, www. flyfrontier.com), **Southwest** (800/435-9792, www.southwest.com), **Spirit** (801/401-2222, www.spirit.com), and **United** (800/864-8331, www.united.com), plus a whole lot of international carriers.

AIRPORT TRANSPORTATION

For public transit from Dulles, take the **Silver Line Express** (703/572-7661, every 15-20 minutes, $5) to the **Wiehle Avenue Memorial station** (1908 Reston Station Blvd., Reston, VA), which will connect you to the rest of the Metro light rail system.

Rental cars are available at a separate facility from the airport, accessible by shuttle bus. If traffic is good, the 30-mile drive from the airport east to Nationals Park takes about 30 minutes. To get there, take VA-267 and I-66. Note: VA-267 is a **toll road,** and driving it from end to end costs $3.25.

Ronald Regan Washington National Airport

A smaller airport, **Ronald Reagan Washington National Airport** (DCA, Smith Blvd., Arlington, VA, 703/417-8000, www.flyreagan.com) makes flights only within the 48 contiguous states. Reagan is serviced by **Air Canada** (888/247-2262, www.aircanada.com), **American Airlines** (800/433-7300, www.aa.com), **Delta** (800/221-1212, www.delta.com), **Frontier** (800/432-1359, www.flyfrontier. com), **jetBlue** (800/538-2583, www.jetblue. com), **Southwest** (800/435-9792, www.

southwest.com), and **United** (800/864-8331, www.united.com).

AIRPORT TRANSPORTATION

Reagan has a **Metrorail station,** operated by DC's public transit authority, known as **Metro** (Washington Metropolitan Area Transit Authority, www.wmata.com, $2-6 per ride). The station, which is on the **Blue Line,** is accessible via terminals B and C. (If you're at Terminal A, take the airport shuttle to Terminals B and C to catch the train.) The Blue Line heads right into Downtown Washington; to connect to the ballpark, change to the **Green Line** at **L'Enfant Plaza** (429 L'Enfant Plaza SW).

There's a **rental car shuttle** at the airport, but it's also possible to walk to the rental car area, **Terminal Garage A,** which is accessible from Terminal A. Reagan is just five miles west of Washington via I-395 and I-695. Without traffic, it's a 10-minute drive.

Baltimore/Washington International Thurgood Marshall Airport

Farthest away from the city is **Baltimore/ Washington International Thurgood Marshall Airport** (BWI, Hanover, MD, 410/859-7111, www.bwiairport.com). It has flights with **Air Canada** (888/247-2262, www.aircanada.com), **Allegiant** (702/505-8888, www.allegiantair.com), **American Airlines** (800/433-7300, www.aa.com), **Delta** (800/221-1212, www.delta.com), **Frontier** (800/432-1359, www.flyfrontier.com), **jetBlue** (800/538-2583, www.jetblue.com), **Southwest** (800/435-9792, www.southwest. com), **Spirit** (801/401-2222, www.spirit. com), and **United** (800/864-8331, www. united.com), plus several international carriers.

AIRPORT TRANSPORTATION

To take public transportation into DC, hop on a **BWI Express Metro bus** (hourly, 6:30am-9:30pm Mon.-Fri.), operated by DC's public transit authority, known as **Metro** (www.wmata.com, $2-6 per ride). The bus takes riders to the **Greenbelt Metrorail**

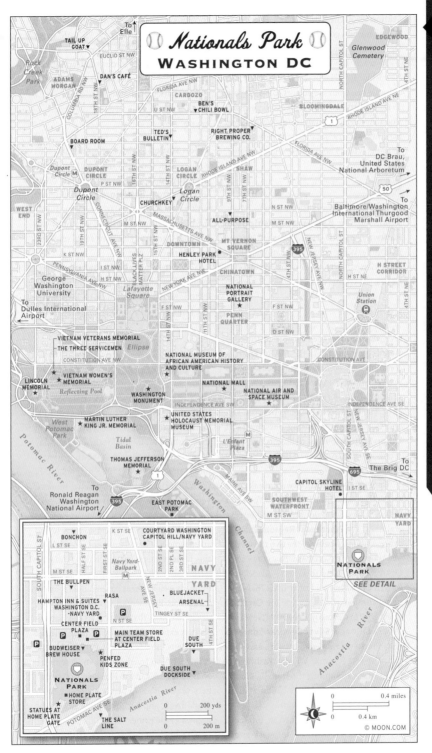

Nationals Park
WASHINGTON DC

To Elle

TAIL UP GOAT ▼

EUCLID ST NW

Glenwood Cemetery

EDGEWOOD

DAN'S CAFÉ

Rock Creek Park

ADAMS MORGAN

COLUMBIA RD NW

18TH ST NW

FLORIDA AVE NW

CARDOZO

BLOOMINGDALE

NORTH CAPITOL ST

4TH ST NE

BEN'S ▼ CHILI BOWL

U ST NW

BOARD ROOM

TED'S ▼ BULLETIN

RIGHT PROPER BREWING CO.

RHODE ISLAND AVE NE

To DC Brau, United States National Arboretum

FLORIDA AVE NW

Dupont Circle M

DUPONT CIRCLE

16TH ST NW

14TH ST NW

LOGAN CIRCLE

RHODE ISLAND AVE NW

SHAW

9TH ST NW

7TH ST NW

50

To Baltimore/Washington International Thurgood Marshall Airport

P ST NW

Dupont Circle

Logan Circle

CHURCHKEY

N ST NW

M ST NW

WEST END

23RD ST NW

19TH ST NW

CONNECTICUT AVE NW

M ST NW

MASSACHUSETTS AVE NW

ALL-PURPOSE

M ST NW

H STREET CORRIDOR

H ST NE

4TH ST NE

K ST NW

I ST NW

H ST NW

DOWNTOWN

HENLEY PARK HOTEL

MT VERNON SQUARE

395

NEW JERSEY AVE NW

NORTH CAPITOL ST

Union Station 🚇

George Washington University

PENNSYLVANIA AVE NW

Lafayette Square

BLACK LIVES MATTER PLZ

NEW YORK AVE NW

CHINATOWN

NATIONAL PORTRAIT GALLERY ★

F ST NW

PENN QUARTER

F ST NW

D ST NW

To Dulles International Airport

VIETNAM VETERANS MEMORIAL
THE THREE SERVICEMEN

Ellipse

14TH ST NW

17TH ST NW

NATIONAL MUSEUM OF AFRICAN AMERICAN HISTORY AND CULTURE

CONSTITUTION AVE NW

CONSTITUTION AVE

LINCOLN MEMORIAL ★

VIETNAM WOMEN'S ★ MEMORIAL

Reflecting Pool

WASHINGTON MONUMENT ★

NATIONAL MALL

NATIONAL AIR AND SPACE MUSEUM ★

INDEPENDENCE AVE SW

INDEPENDENCE AVE SE

West Potomac Park

MARTIN LUTHER KING JR. MEMORIAL ★

Tidal Basin

UNITED STATES HOLOCAUST MEMORIAL MUSEUM ★

L'Enfant Plaza M

SOUTH CAPITOL ST

NEW JERSEY AVE SE

4TH ST SE

THOMAS JEFFERSON MEMORIAL ★

Potomac River

To Ronald Reagan Washington National Airport

395

1

EAST POTOMAC PARK

395

Washington Channel

CAPITOL SKYLINE HOTEL ●

SOUTHWEST WATERFRONT

M ST SW

I ST SE

695

To The Brig DC

NAVY YARD

NATIONALS PARK 🏟

SEE DETAIL

Anacostia River

Detail inset:

SOUTH CAPITOL ST

BONCHON ▼

L ST SE

HALF ST SE

FIRST ST SE

K ST SE

COURTYARD WASHINGTON CAPITOL HILL/NAVY YARD ●

2ND ST SE

2ND PL SE

3RD ST SE

M ST SE

Navy Yard-Ballpark M

NEW JERSEY AVE SE

NAVY

YARD

THE BULLPEN ▼

RASA ▼

BLUEJACKET ▼

HAMPTON INN & SUITES WASHINGTON D.C. -NAVY YARD ▼

ARSENAL ▼

P

TINGEY ST SE

N ST SE

CENTER FIELD PLAZA

P

P

MAIN TEAM STORE AT CENTER FIELD PLAZA

4TH ST SE

DUE SOUTH ▼

P

BUDWEISER ▼ BREW HOUSE

PENFED KIDS ZONE ▼

DUE SOUTH ▼ DOCKSIDE

NATIONALS PARK 🏟

■ HOME PLATE STORE

STATUES AT HOME PLATE GATE ★

POTOMAC AVE SE

Anacostia River

THE SALT ▼ LINE

0   200 yds

0   200 m

0   0.4 miles

0   0.4 km

© MOON.COM

Station (5550 Greenbelt, College Park, MD). To find the bus, go to the lower level and look for Public Transit signs.

To reach the **rental car center** (7432 New Ridge Rd., Hanover, MD), you can take a shuttle bus from the airport. BWI is about 35 miles northeast of DC and Nationals Park. The drive, via the Baltimore-Washington Parkway (MD-295), can take anywhere from 45 minutes to 1.5 hours, depending on traffic.

CAR

It's just **40 miles** from **Baltimore** to Washington on the **Baltimore-Washington Parkway,** or **MD-295.** The road passes Baltimore/Washington International Thurgood Marshall Airport. The drive takes **1-1.5 hours,** depending on traffic.

TRAIN

From **Baltimore,** the best way to travel to Washington DC is via the **MARC Train,** a commuter rail system linking the two cities that's run by **MTA** (Maryland Transit Administration, 410/539-5000, www.mta.maryland. gov). The **Camden Line** runs between DC and Baltimore, depositing passengers at **Union Station** (50 Massachusetts Ave. NE). A one-way trip costs $8 and lasts a little more than an hour.

Want to take **Amtrak** (www.amtrak.com) to Washington from Baltimore? You're in luck: The city is a major hub, served by several lines. The **Northeast Regional** and its express sibling **Acela** are the two most popular train lines in North America, connecting DC to Boston, New York, and Philadelphia, as well as Baltimore. Other lines that connect Baltimore to DC include the **Cardinal** (New York to Chicago), **Crescent** (New York to New Orleans), **Silver Service/Palmetto** (New York to Tampa and Miami), and **Vermonter** (St. Albans, VT, to Washington DC). After the hourlong trip from Baltimore, Amtrak trains stop at DC's Union Station. Tickets start from $8.

Union Station was opened in 1908 and serves as both a historic landmark and a gorgeous and sunny gateway to the nation's capital. Union Station is a 3.5-mile drive north of Nationals Park, essentially taking you from the Navy Yard up to Capitol Hill (through the National Mall) and into the Stanton Park neighborhood.

BUS

Union Station (50 Massachusetts Ave. NE) is the site of the city's main bus terminal. **Greyhound** (www.greyhound.com) operates daily from **Baltimore** to Washington, with rides starting at around $10. Buses leave about twice each hour, and rides will last anywhere from an hour to 90 minutes, depending on traffic.

You can also take **Megabus** (http://us.megabus.com) from Baltimore to Washington, with prices around $10-15 per trip. The bus will drop you off at Union Station.

Nationals Park

For their first four years of existence, the Nationals played their home games at RFK Stadium, the cookie-cutter former home of the Washington football team and later-day Senators squads. But in 2008, they moved into **Nationals Park** (1500 S. Capitol St. SE, www.mlb.com/nationals), a retro-modern venue that's less brick and more steel. Like many ballparks of its era, Nationals Park has a walkable open-air outfield concourse and an enormous scoreboard over center field. In this respect, there isn't much differentiating it from New York's Citi Field and Yankee Stadium, as well as Great American Ballpark in Cincinnati. But there's no single landmark or design element that epitomizes the Nationals Park experience—no home-run apple like in Queens, no Monument Park like in the Bronx, and no riverboat like in Cincinnati. Nationals Park can feel like a paint-by-numbers venue. It's also pretty expensive, with food, drink, and parking prices among the highest in the game.

The best qualities of the park are its

YOUR BEST DAY AT NATIONALS PARK

Let's imagine you're spending the evening at Nationals Park. Here's how to maximize your DC experience before, during, and after the game.

10 HOURS BEFORE FIRST PITCH
Start the day with a brisk walk on the **Mount Vernon Trail.** Do the three-mile up and back that starts at the north trailhead in Arlington, Virginia, and turns around at Arlington National Cemetery.

8 HOURS BEFORE FIRST PITCH
After that nice start, drive up to the Mount Pleasant neighborhood to grab a late breakfast (or early lunch) at **Elle.** Chicken liver mousse toast, anyone?

6 HOURS BEFORE FIRST PITCH
If you have a car, park it at your hotel, then make it a Metro day the rest of the way. Take Metro to the **Federal Triangle** (302 12th St. NW) or **Smithsonian** (12th St. at National Mall) station, then head to the **National Museum of African American History and Culture.** Spend at least two hours here to take in the experience.

4 HOURS BEFORE FIRST PITCH
Hop back on Metro and head down to the **Navy Yard-Ballpark station** (200 M St. SE). Walk the couple blocks east and one south to **Bluejacket** brewery. Get yourself a few beers here, and if you're hungry, order some mussels at in-house restaurant **Arsenal.**

National Museum of African American History and Culture

2 HOURS BEFORE FIRST PITCH
Make an appearance at **The Bullpen.** Take some selfies with the **statues** at the **Home Plate Gate,** then wind back around to the **Center Field Gate,** where you'll want to enter. When inside, head to **Center Field Plaza,** where you can lounge at a high-top table. Chat up some Nationals fans—they're friendly folks.

DURING THE GAME
Hit up one of the **District Drafts stands** for a local brew, then grab a bite from **Chiko,** which serves Korean-Chinese fusion dishes.

AFTER THE GAME
Take an Uber or Lyft to Adams Morgan, where you can pay a visit to **Dan's Café.** Have a couple strong drinks before finishing the night at the famous **Ben's Chili Bowl.** Eat two half-smokes for the true DC experience.

---

cleanliness and its location by the Anacostia River in the Navy Yard neighborhood of Washington DC. In the years since the venue opened, the Navy Yard has seen a tremendous amount of commercial growth. These days, bars, restaurants, and shops make it a full-day experience. Fans come early to hang out before attending a game, making the ballpark and its surroundings a destination for those visiting the city.

ORIENTATION

Part of the Navy Yard area of the city, the ballpark is about a 25-minute walk south of the U.S. Capitol, bordering the Anacostia River. Just across the river from the park is Anacostia Park and I-295/MD-295, also known for long stretches as the Baltimore-Washington Parkway. There are five entry gates at Nationals Park, including the popular **center field** entrance.

Nationals Park

TICKETS AND SEATING

Pricing

The Nationals use a **dynamic pricing** model, so you're bound to see higher ticket costs for a game against, say, the **Phillies, Mets, and Yankees** than for a game against, say, the Diamondbacks. A seat in the outfield reserved level (essentially an average spot across all of the stadium's options) will cost something like $30 for a lesser opponent like Arizona, while it may cost more like $50 for those top teams like the Phillies and Yankees.

Seating Plan

Nationals Park has segmented its seating sections quite a bit. Let's start with the **field level (100 level).** Starting in left center field is **outfield reserved** (sections 100-107); then moving into foul territory is **left-field corner** (sections 108-110); then **left-field baseline box** and **baseline reserved** (sections 111-113), with box representing the first 24 rows; next are **visitor dugout box** and **infield box** (sections 114-118), again with box closer to the field; then **home-plate box,** the **Delta Sky360 Club, infield box,** and **PNC Diamond Club** (sections 119-126). On the other side of home plate are the **home dugout box** and **infield box** (sections 127-131); **right-field baseline box** and **baseline reserved** (sections 132-134); **right-field corner** (sections 135-137);

and **outfield reserved** (sections 138-143).

Up one to the **club/mezzanine level (200 level)**, sections start by the left-field foul pole with **left-field mezzanine** (sections 201-205), then around the infield are **club level** (sections 206-211 and 216-221) and **club level MVP** (sections 212-215), and in right field are **right mezzanine** (sections 223-235) and **scoreboard pavilion** (sections 237-243). The deck above the right-field mezzanine is called the **right-field terrace** (sections 222-236) and is split between upper and lower rows.

On the **300 level** is the **gallery** (sections 301-321). The **400 level** includes the **grandstand** (sections 401-402) in the right-field

foul area and the **upper gallery** (sections 403-420) around the infield.

Where to Buy Tickets

You'd be wise to check third-party sites like **StubHub** and **SeatGeek** before the game, as there should be pretty good seats available for less than what you'd pay through the Nationals website. The Nationals are also on the **MLB Ballpark app,** which offers seat upgrades for those at the park.

Best Seats

The third-base line is almost always a good choice. Since most ballparks are aligned such that the sun sets over that area, you'll get shade there most of the time (although for 1pm starts, you may have to sit in sun for a bit). At Nationals Park, you'll want seats between **sections 109 and 117,** in the back rows starting around KK. Club seats between **sections 201 and 209** (rows E and back) are great, and you'll get an air-conditioned concourse with food and drink options. The back rows (row J and back) of **sections 401-409** in the upper gallery will have shade.

For an affordable and rowdy experience, the **outfield reserved seats** (sections 101-103) are fun and offer fine views of the field, plus you're just steps away from the Center Field Plaza and other dining options. If a rival comes into town (like the Phillies or Mets), the right-field part of **outfield reserved** (sections 140-143) might get filled up with those opposing fans. That makes for a fun time.

Left-field corner (sections 108-110) is a diamond in the rough. You might think your view would be compromised here; but you're close enough to the field, the shade should still be in your general area, and prices are cheaper than for the infield field-level seats.

GAME COSTS

Tickets: You can grab seats at less than **$20** in the 300 and 400 levels. On average, you'll pay around **$45-60,** which is around the league average, maybe a bit higher..

Hot dog: You'll pay a league-high price for dogs here (**$7** or more), while the gourmet options will run you close to **$10.**

Beer: Expect to pay at least **$9** for a beer, which is also pricey compared with the rest of the league.

Parking: You'll pay **$20-50** per spot if you're going with a team-controlled lot or garage. Outside those places, with more walking, you'll pay closer to **$15.**

KNOW BEFORE YOU GO

You can bring in a **bag** of up to 16 by 16 by 8 inches with **soft containers** for food. Clear, empty plastic **water bottles** are allowed in the park, as are juice boxes and baby food. Filled water bottles are not permitted.

There are about 250 **bike racks** positioned around the exterior of the ballpark, and there's also a bicycle valet near Garage C (1st St. SE and N St. SE). Drop your bike off two hours before the game and retrieve it up to one hour after the end of the game.

Nursing mothers should note there is a **nursing lounge** (section 223) in the park. This air-conditioned space has televisions, comfortable chairs, diaper-changing stations, and a toddler play area.

Accessibility

Nationals Park has three sets of **elevators** (sections 113, 120, 134). The one at section 120 visits only the Delta Sky360 Club and club level. **Ramps** are located behind sections 107 and 131. Guests with mobility issues may use a **Segway,** though the park doesn't have any to rent.

Assistive listening devices are available at Main Guest Services (center field gate), as are **wheelchairs** for fans who need them. You'll need to turn in a photo ID as a deposit for either.

Some **accessible parking spots** are available in the **GEICO Garage** and **Garage C.** You must purchase a spot in advance online. Be sure to display your state-issued disabled **parking placard.**

GETTING THERE

Metro

The best way to get to Nationals Park is to take **Metro** (www.wmata.com, $2-6 per ride). You'll want to hop on the **Green Line** and get off at **Navy Yard-Ballpark** (200 M St. SE), which is just a three-minute walk to the park. To connect to the Green Line, your best bet is to travel to **L'Enfant Plaza** (600 Maryland Ave. SW), which offers transfers to other Metro lines.

BE A FAN

Nationals fans are welcoming and wonderful folks. They're not as welcoming and wonderful if you happen to be wearing a Mets jersey or, worse, a Phillies jersey. But that's the extent of it, and you won't even face jeers or insults.

When the Nationals hit a home run or win a game, a loud **air horn** sounds, reminiscent of what you might hear on a naval submarine.

During the 2019 world championship run, the team adopted the fanciful children's song **"Baby Shark"** as its theme after hitter Gerardo Parra started using it as walkup music to break a slump. Since it's connected to so many positive moments in the team's recent history, don't be surprised to hear it when visiting Nationals Park.

Nationals fans

Driving

I don't recommend driving anywhere in Washington, if you can help it. But if you need to drive to Nationals Park, you'll likely rely on either **I-695** or **I-295** to get there. Both highways let cars off at **South Capitol Street SW,** which edges right past the ballpark. **M Street** is the main thoroughfare going west to east in the Navy Yard neighborhood.

The Nationals operate several **parking lots** and **garages** in this area, with the bulk of them on M Street SE. **Lot W** is at M Street SE and 7th Street SE, and if you don't mind the 15-minute walk to the park, it's a good option. The closest garages are the **GEICO Garage** and **Garage C,** which are on N Street by the ballpark. Just know that you're bound to pay as much as $40-50 if you want to park in a team lot.

You can also park in the **Southwest Waterfront** area (by M St. SW and 4th St. SW), as lots there may charge less than $20. But keep in mind that this entire Downtown area, from Capitol Hill to the Navy Yard over to the national monuments, is made for tourism and people coming and going.

PARK FEATURES AND SIGHTS

Before heading into the park, be sure to check out the **statues** at the **Home Plate Gate** (S. Capitol St. and Potomac Ave. SE). Those immortalized include **Walter Johnson,** the first great star of the Washington Senators franchise and one of the greatest pitchers ever; **Frank Howard,** a brutish slugger for the Senators who was among American League home-run leaders in the 1960s and 1970s; and **Josh Gibson,** arguably the greatest offensive player in Negro Leagues history, who during his peak played for the Homestead Grays, primarily in Washington.

Take your kids to the **PenFed Kids Zone** (Right Field Gate) if you want to get all that energy out of their system. While this isn't the most extensive child play area at a ballpark, there's a jungle gym with slides and climbing areas that's made for kids ages 3-8. Be sure that your children are wearing socks if they're going to play; if the temperature is too high, ballpark staff may close it down because the plastic gym set can get pretty hot.

Look above section 105 in left field to check out a **rooftop garden,** built in 2016, which grows vegetables, fruits, and herbs that are all used by food service vendors at Nationals Park.

FOOD AND DRINKS

You can and should get the **half-smoke** (sausage smoked and grilled, then plopped in a bun with onions, chili, and cheese), a noted Washington specialty, at the famous **Ben's Chili Bowl** (sections 109, 140, 315). Be sure to order it "all the way" for the chili and cheese experience.

Other locals to look for include **Chiko** (section 238), purveyor of Korean-Chinese fun bites. They do bulgogi hoagies with a special kimchi Cheese Whiz. Next, pupusas! The Salvadoran treats of flour dough stuffed with cheese and heated up on the skillet are available at **La Casita Pupuseria** (section 140). They do pork, chicken, or bean; be sure to top yours with pickled veggies. There's also **Hank's Oyster Bar** (section 108), where you can snag oyster po'boys and fries doused in Old Bay seasoning.

For a good hot dog, head to **Haute Dogs & Fries** (section 106), whose array of franks includes the banh mi, the three-piece suit (essentially the half-smoke with a frankfurter), and the DC Dog: mustard, barbecue sauce, blue cheese, chopped onions, and pickles.

The park's restaurant is the **Red Porch Restaurant,** part of the **Budweiser Brew House** (100 level, center field, seating until seventh inning, under $40), which is right near the Center Field Gate and is like a lot of other ballpark sit-down spots. Get in early if you want a good view. Your menu will include loaded versions of American favorites like pulled pork tots, nachos, pizzas, burgers, and shrimp tacos. Also, you'll have about an hour to enjoy the experience, as they like to keep things moving.

When walking about the park, you might be tempted to have beers and socialize at the **Center Field Plaza** (100 level, center field). This area is essentially a clearinghouse for Anheuser-Busch InBev brands, so the bars here are going to have Budweiser, Bud Light, and its "craft" portfolio beverages like **Goose**

Photos (from top to bottom): Screech, the Nationals' mascot; Ben's Chili Bowl in Adams Morgan; the Presidents Race.

Island, **Shock Top,** and Virginia-based **Devil's Backbone.** There's plenty of space for hanging out, though, so maybe grab one beer. Plus, for those who can't have foods with gluten, there's the **Gluten Free Grill** (Center Field Plaza), offering specialized ballpark fare.

The best beer in the park is probably at the **District Drafts stands** (sections 110, 128, 138, 222, 303, 310), which generally has offerings from DC Brau, Mad Fox, Heavy Seas, Port City, Right Proper, and Atlas.

EVENTS

One of the most anticipated during-commercial events in baseball is the **Presidents Race,** which began in 2005 and takes place in the middle of the 4th inning at every home game (if a game extends to a 13th inning, the race is run in the middle of that frame, as well). The race has historically featured oversize, comical versions of the four presidents of Mount Rushmore: George Washington, Thomas Jefferson, Abraham Lincoln, and Theodore "Teddy" Roosevelt. The four trek along the warning track from the center-field area to the first-base area. For the first several seasons, Roosevelt was shut out entirely, but he won his first race on the final day of the 2012 season, the first playoff year in Nationals history. You should bet on Abraham Lincoln to take it, though Washington is pretty stout, as well.

Your best best for **autographs** is to attend a **Sunday game,** when two Nationals players will sign from the top of the home dugout, starting 70 minutes before first pitch. To get an autograph, head to section 103 to get a voucher as soon as the gates open.

If you want to visit DC in January, you can check out **Winterfest** (Jan., www.mlb.com/nationals), a weekend-long event at the ballpark where players and coaches make themselves available to fans, and the team throws a small wintry party for fans.

Tours

The Nationals offer two kinds of game-day **tours:** the **Senator's Tour** (10:30am, 1 pm, $15, $10 seniors and ages 12 and under),

which shows off primarily club and suite areas, and the **Pregame Tour** (three hours before first pitch, free), which is more or less a standard concourse tour. On non-game days, you can get the Senator's Tour and the **Governor's Tour** (dates vary, $25, $20 seniors and ages 12 and under), which is the best experience. It runs through clubs, suites, the visiting team's clubhouse, and the Nats' dugout, and sometimes includes a trip to the bullpen to throw a pitch.

SHOPPING

The big one is the cleverly named **Main Team Store at Center Field Plaza** (Center Field Plaza, N St. SE and 1st St. SE, 202/640-7777, open for game days, 10am-5pm Mon.-Fri., 10am-4pm Sat. non-game days). Besides the regular swag like jerseys, hats, outerwear, bobbleheads, and team-licensed clothing, there's a selection of authentic game-used baseballs and apparel for sale. On game days, store hours differ depending on the time of first pitch. It opens two hours before first pitch for games earlier than 4:05pm. On days when games start later, the store is open from 10am until three hours before first pitch; it then reopens two hours before first pitch.

Other stores include the **Home Plate Store** (S. Capitol St. SE and Potomac Ave. SE, 90 minutes before first pitch game days), a smaller version of the main store, and the usual fare, like the **New Era Store** (sections 107, 114, 131), **47 Brand merchandise** (section 138), and a stand-alone **authentic items stand** (section 113).

WASHINGTON DC SIGHTS

THE NATIONAL MALL

At 146 acres, from the U.S. Capitol to the Lincoln Memorial, and bounded on the north by the White House and on the south by the Tidal Basin and Potomac River, the **National Mall** is the centerpiece of

American democracy, an open area for public gathering and education. Whether you're a kid or an adult, the National Mall can be a playground. If you can spend a week in Washington DC, make sure half the time is in and around the Mall—you'll only scratch the surface of what's here.

Be sure to visit the **Thomas Jefferson Memorial** (16 E. Basin Dr. SW, free), an architectural wonder that is across the Tidal Basin. Opening in 1943, this absolutely gorgeous building references both Rome's Pantheon and the rotunda of the University of Virginia, which Jefferson designed.

Head to the **National Air and Space Museum** (600 Independence Ave. SW, 202/633-2214, www.airandspace.si.edu, 10am-5:30pm daily, free) for a little something for everyone. You'll see the vintage planes flown by the Wright Brothers and other pioneering pilots, plus craft and artifacts from NASA history, including LM-2, an Apollo lunar module.

The **Vietnam Veterans Memorial** (5 Henry Bacon Dr., free), designed by Maya Lin, remains a striking installation that demands full attention. More than 58,000 names of the dead and missing soldiers of the Vietnam War are chiseled onto the walls. Also nearby are two other necessary sights: the statue **The Three Servicemen** and another statue, the **Vietnam Women's Memorial.**

Lincoln Memorial

The indisputable symbol of strength in peace known as the **Lincoln Memorial** (National Mall, west end, free) stands as an achievement. Every American should visit once, and it's a good place to take a moment to reflect. Dedicated in 1922, the memorial that honors the 16th president never closes. An impressive 19-foot-tall statue of a seated Lincoln is the main draw here, but be sure to read both the Gettysburg Address and the president's second inaugural address, which are inscribed on the interior walls. Look for the names of each state in the Union at both the time of Lincoln's death and the time of the memorial's dedication.

The Lincoln Memorial, of course, was the site of Martin Luther King Jr.'s iconic "I Have a Dream" speech on August 28, 1963, during the March on Washington. The **reflecting pool** begins beneath the memorial and extends 2,029 feet toward the Washington Monument.

Washington Monument

Standing 555 feet tall, the mighty obelisk the **Washington Monument** (National Mall, west-center end, www.nps.gov/wamo, 9am-5pm daily, $1, free under age 2) is the world's tallest of its kind, and in the late 1880s was the world's tallest structure, period. Purchase a ticket to ascend via elevator to the top (the pyramidion) to view from the **observation deck.** Note that strollers and bulky items are not permitted inside the Monument. There are eight windows looking out to Washington—be sure to look through them all for the complete 360-degree view. After finishing, go downstairs to the museum, then back to the elevator to head down. On the way, the elevator will stop for views of specially inscribed commemorative stones that are more than 130 years old.

Martin Luther King Jr. Memorial

Carved from granite is a depiction of one of America's greatest leaders and advocates for equality. The **Martin Luther King Jr. Memorial** (1964 Independence Ave. SW, free) is by the Tidal Basin, just southeast of the Lincoln Memorial. The statue of Dr. King is unusual—a bit blocky and stern—but the space surrounding it is powerful. The many quotes inscribed on the wall along the perimeter of the memorial are worth the visit alone. The memorial is in line with the Lincoln Memorial, creating a connection between Dr. King's permanent monument and the place where he made his greatest stand for equality.

National Museum of African American History and Culture

Between the Washington Monument and U.S. Capitol are some of the most outstanding museums in the country. My favorite here is the **National Museum of African**

American History and Culture (1400 Constitution Ave. NW, 844/750-3012, www. nmaahc.si.edu, 10am-5:30pm daily, free, timed entry passes required on weekends and for groups of 10 or more). Come on a weekday and walk right in for a close and moving examination of African American history and culture. Artifacts on display include some of the most incredible pieces of Americana, from Nat Turner's bible to the boombox carried by Radio Raheem in the Spike Lee joint *Do the Right Thing*.

Regular exhibits include A Changing America, which documents Black movements for equity, like Black Power, as well as the regressive systemic policies that hurt disadvantaged and underrepresented people; and Cultural Expressions, which offers an overview of the many cultures of the African diaspora through displays of clothing, appliances, crafts, and more. The museum hosts daily events, from film screenings and author events to workshops that help children understand race, ethnicity, and culture.

UNITED STATES HOLOCAUST MEMORIAL MUSEUM

Just outside the National Mall, toward the south, is the **United States Holocaust Memorial Museum** (100 Raoul Wallenberg Pl. SW, 202/488-0400, www.ushmm. org, 10am-5:30pm daily, free, tickets required for permanent exhibition Mar.-Aug.), one of the most powerful places to visit in America. Be sure to get to the permanent exhibition, which tells the story of the Holocaust with video footage, stories, and pull-no-punches details of Nazi behavior and actions during one of the ugliest moments in human history. Because of the subject matter, it's recommended for children ages 11 and older.

Smaller exhibits focus on specific aspects of the Holocaust and its impact, from photographs of the blue sky above concentration camps to assessments of modern-day genocides and atrocities. Events at the museum include author talks and film screenings. Be sure to set aside at least two hours to experience the museum; more time is recommended in order to absorb and emotionally register what you see and hear.

NATIONAL PORTRAIT GALLERY

There's really no art museum quite like the **National Portrait Gallery** (8th St. NW and F St. NW, www.si.edu, 11:30am-7pm daily, free). Part of the Smithsonian Institution, the museum displays portraits of famous Americans. Here you'll find the highly regarded portraits of President Barack Obama and First Lady Michelle Obama, plus regular exhibits that change out every once in a while. Be sure to visit the Kogod Courtyard, home to a floating glass canopy, one of the coolest ceilings you'll ever encounter.

UNITED STATES NATIONAL ARBORETUM

The largest arboretum in America is the **United States National Arboretum** (3501 New York Ave. NE, 202/245-2726, www. usna.usda.gov, 8am-5pm daily, free). When walking the 412 acres, be sure to visit the National Capitol Columns, 22 columns that were once part of the U.S. Capitol as support for the East Portico, and the National Grove of State Trees, where each state is represented by its flora. A special on-site treat is the **National Bonsai and Penjing Museum** (202/396-3510, www.bonsai-nbf. org, 10am-4pm daily, free), home to bonsai trees from Japan, China, and North America. Look for the Japanese white pine that survived the bombing in Hiroshima, as well as an exhibit of intricate viewing stones.

FOOD

NEAR NATIONALS PARK

Since you're in the Navy Yard part of the city, you should enjoy some seafood down by the water. Your best option is **The Salt Line** (79

Photos (top): National Mall; (middle left) the National Portrait Gallery; (middle right) the Martin Luther King Jr. Memorial by sculptor Lei Yixin; (bottom) United States National Arboretum.

OUT OF THE MOUNTAIN OF DESPAIR,
A STONE OF HOPE

Potomac Ave. SE, 202/506-2368, www.the-saltline.com, 3pm-midnight Mon.-Thurs., 3pm-1am Fri., 11am-1am Sat., 11am-midnight Sun., under $50), which has a classic Eastern Seaboard feel, oysters, clams, and a trendy seafood charcuterie board. It's right on the dock with patio seating, too.

Set back from the water is **Due South** (301 Water St., 202/479-4616, www.due-southdc.com, 11am-10pm Sun.-Thurs., 11am-11pm Fri.-Sat., under $40). This is your basic, decent southern fare place, good for a beer or cocktail with some grub before a game. Smoked wings, fried green tomatoes, and fried chicken are hits here. Due South has an outdoor satellite spot called **Due South Dockside** (Anacostia Riverwalk Trail, Yards Park, opens 11am daily) that serves mostly as a hangout for those coming and going to Nationals Park. Get frozen cocktails and small bites like sliders and pizza.

It's a chain, but there's a reason people love **Bonchon** (1015 Half St. SE, 202/488-4000, www.bonchon.com, 11:30am-9:30pm Sun.-Thurs., 11:30am-11pm Fri.-Sat., under $20). This is a major outlet for Korean fried chicken, that awesomely crispy, double-fried treat that comes in a few special flavors. Soy garlic is always great, and the spicy version can be numbingly delicious for heat lovers.

For Indian, you should hit up **RASA** (1247 1st St. SE, 202/804-5678, www.rasagrill.com, 11am-9pm Sun.-Thurs., 11am-10pm Fri.-Sat., under $30). This colorful, cute space with basket chairs and funky art specializes in bowls chock-full of Indian ingredients and named after popular songs. They also have a spiked version of lassi, a popular yogurt-based drink.

OTHER NEIGHBORHOODS

In Adams Morgan, you'll pay a little bit more, but everything is worth it at **Tail Up Goat** (1827 Adams Mill Rd. NW, 202/986-9600, www.tailupgoat.com, 5:30pm-10pm daily, under $60). The menu at this smartly designed space that always seems to be buzzing constantly changes, but you'll always get fun takes on Mediterranean cuisine plus a drink menu filled with Caribbean flavors. Who knew ragù and rum could work so well together?

One of my favorite Logan Circle spots is **Ted's Bulletin** (1818 14th St. NW, 202/265-8337, www.tedsbulletin.com, 7am-10pm Sun.-Thurs., 7am-11pm Fri.-Sat., under $40). Ted's has a few locations around the area, but this one has been designed with items taken from the old Philadelphia Civic Center (where Wilt Chamberlain ruled the hardwood in the 1950s and 1960s). The menu is American and has plenty of kid favorites, along with all-day breakfast.

The brick-walled and mid-century-designed **Elle** (3221 Mt. Pleasant St. NW, 202/652-0040, www.eatatelle.com, 7am-4pm and 5:30pm-11:30pm Mon. and Wed.-Fri., 7am-4pm Tues., 8am-4pm and 5:30pm-11:30pm Sat.-Sun., under $20 breakfast and lunch, under $40 dinner), a relaxed spot in Mount Pleasant, is pronounced "Ellie." Get a breakfast sandwich in the morning, chicken liver mousse toast or a ham butter sandwich in the afternoon, and well-thought-out dinners in the evening. The bar is splendid, too.

In the Shaw neighborhood, get great pizza at **All-Purpose** (1250 9th St. NW, 202/849-6174, www.allpurposedc.com, 5pm-10pm Mon.-Thurs., 11am-2:30pm and 5pm-11pm Fri.-Sat., 11am-9pm Sun., under $40), specializing in "Jersey-style" pizza, which is basically New York-style but with a higher sauce-to-cheese ratio and a crispier crust. You can also have good cured meats here. Brunch features more pizza and eggs.

Up in the U Street area is **Ben's Chili Bowl** (1213 U St. NW, 202/667-0909, www.benschilibowl.com, 6am-2am Mon.-Thurs., 6am-4am Fri., 7am-4am Sat., 11am-midnight Sun., under $20), the famous purveyor of the half-smoke (sausage in a bun with cheese, chili, and onions). Burgers, chili bowls, and thick milkshakes round out this awesome little attraction that's a must for anyone visiting DC. Don't miss the beautiful mural on the side wall that depicts images of important Americans.

BARS AND BREWERIES

NEAR NATIONALS PARK

The brewery for famed DC beer bar Church-Key, **Bluejacket** (300 Tingey St. SE, 202/524-4862, www.bluejacketdc.com, 11am-1am Sun.-Thurs., 11am-2am Fri.-Sat.) is set inside the Boilermaker Shops, a 1919 warehouse. The brewery occupies an impressive open space with high ceilings and an industrial feel. The beer here covers a full range, from ambitiously hopped IPAs to basic pilsners and bocks to sweet stouts. Part of the brewery is a restaurant, **Arsenal** (under $40), which has the same hours. You'll find elevated American from burgers to diver scallops to ingredient-packed sandwiches. Mussels and oysters are also on offer. This spot is a perfect pregame hang—just get here early, because it gets crowded with fans.

One of the best bars around Nationals Park is in a hotel. **Top of the Yard Rooftop Bar** (1265 1st St. SE, 202/800-1000, www.hamptoninn3.hilton.com, 5pm-11pm Mon.-Thurs., 3pm-midnight Fri., 1pm-midnight Sat., 1pm-11pm Sun.) is on the roof of the Hampton Inn. Go here for pregame or postgame drinks, or if you want to watch the game from a fun vantage point, get here a little early and scope out a spot overlooking the ballpark. Standing beyond center field, Top of the Yard offers a clean view of the field.

For a big beer garden experience, visit **The Brig DC** (1007 8th St. SE, 202/675-1000, www.thebrigdc.com, 3pm-2am Mon.-Fri., 11am-2am Sat.-Sun.), which focuses on German fare like bratwurst, Bavarian pretzels, Schöfferhoffer, and Paulaner. Local and national beers are also available. There are plenty of televisions, and it's dog-friendly. If you're feeling up for it, order one of those giant beer mugs.

For an outdoor party, hit up **The Bullpen** (1201 Half St. SE, opens two hours before every home game begins, closes two hours after every home game ends). Owned by the same folks that own Due South, The Bullpen

is the place you visit before the game to get a beer, meet some people, and get yourself worked up for the game. In lieu of tailgating, this place works well.

OTHER NEIGHBORHOODS

Up by Logan Circle is well-known DC beer bar **ChurchKey** (1337 14th St. NW, 202/567-2576, www.churchkeydc.com, 4pm-1am Mon.-Thurs., 4pm-2am Fri., 11:30am-2am Sat., 11:30am-1am Sun.). The dark space with a casual vibe prides itself on having five casks, 50 taps, and 500 bottles of beer, which come from all over—making this spot a big draw for beer lovers. Attached restaurant **Birch & Barley** (5:30pm-10pm Tues.-Thurs., 5:30pm-11pm Fri., 11am-3pm and 5:30pm-11pm Sat., 11am-3pm and 5pm-8pm Sun., under $40) has contemporary takes on American cuisine—oysters, charcuterie boards, duck, pork belly, and the like.

In the Dupont Circle area, there's **Board Room** (1737 Connecticut Ave. NW, 202/518-7666, www.boardroomdc.com, 4pm-2am Mon.-Thurs., 4pm-3am Fri., noon-3am Sat., noon-2am Sun.), a big bar with a lot of board games. Pay a flat fee of $2 to play as many as you'd like. The beer list is decent, but they don't serve food (get it delivered or bring it from somewhere else).

If you want to spend time in Adams Morgan, stop at the infamous **Dan's Café** (2315 18th St. NW, 202/265-0299, 7pm-2am Thurs., 7pm-3am Fri.-Sat.), a very unusual bar in that you pour everything yourself. You pick the spirit (in pocket-size bottles) and mixers, then you do the work, pouring the mixture in a plastic squeeze bottle. Cheap beer is also available, as well as a great jukebox, a friendly owner, and a truly cool dive vibe.

I'm a big fan of **Right Proper Brewing Co.** (624 T St. NW, 202/607-2337, www.rightproperbrewing.com, 11:30am-11pm Mon.-Thurs., 11:30am-1am Fri., 11:30am-11pm Sat., 11:30am-10pm Sun.), which has a smallish taproom and kitchen in the Shaw neighborhood with a fun mural and plenty of good beer.

Open since 2011, **DC Brau** (3178

Bladensburg Rd. NE #B, 202/621-8890, www. dcbrau.com, 4pm-9pm Thurs., 3pm-11pm Fri., noon-8pm Sat., noon-6pm Sun.) is the O.G. brewery in town and still makes a damn good drink. DC Brau keeps things light and simple. The brewery and taproom is just some cafeteria tables and a lot of concrete. This spot is about five miles from the National Mall. To get there, take US-50 to Bladensburg Road.

RECREATION

PARKS AND TRAILS

Craving a picturesque walk or run past monuments? Set out on the **Mount Vernon Trail** (N. Lynn St. and Lee Hwy., Arlington, VA), an 18-mile multiuse trail that starts by Theodore Roosevelt Island and continues south past Arlington National Cemetery, the Pentagon, Ronald Reagan Washington National Airport, and Alexandria en route to Mount Vernon, George Washington's plantation, where he lived before and after his presidency with wife Martha, children, indentured servants, and enslaved people. The up-and-back trail runs parallel to the Potomac River. For a good three-mile trip, head south on the trail from the north trailhead to Arlington National Cemetery, then turn back.

A small, forested playground in the middle of the Potomac River, **Theodore Roosevelt Island and Little Island** (George Washington Memorial Pkwy., between Roosevelt Bridge and Key Bridge, Arlington, VA, 6am-10pm daily) are protected and managed by the National Park Service, offering trails and kayaking opportunities. Spend time on the **swamp trail,** which rises on a boardwalk above marshland, and connect to the **woods trail** that slashes through much of the islands' interior. Be sure to keep your eyes and ears open for birds—you could find anything from turkey vultures to a variety of warblers and vireos. More than 200 species call the island home. To reach the islands, take the footbridge from the Mount Vernon Trail. Parking is available in the lot on the landlocked side of the footbridge.

Speaking of parks on the Potomac, **East Potomac Park** (Ohio Dr. SW) is 395 acres of family-friendly greenery that's also home to the 36-hole **East Potomac Golf Course** (972 Ohio Dr. SW, 202/554-7660, www.golfdc. com, sunrise-sunset daily, $13-31 Mon.-Thurs., $14-35 Fri.-Sun., $11-20 seniors

Theodore Roosevelt Island

Mon.-Fri., $5-17 ages 5-18 daily) and, at its very northern tip, the **Thomas Jefferson Memorial** (16 E. Basin Dr. SW), the marble structure echoing Jefferson's home, Monticello. If visiting the park for the playground or picnic ground, drive south on Ohio Drive past the golf course. Park in one of the spots along the road. Up at the golf course entrance is **East Potomac Mini Golf** (970 Ohio Dr. SW, 202/554-7660, www.golfdc.com, 10am-sunset daily, $7, $6 seniors and ages 18 and under). While at the park in March or April, be sure to look for the famous cherry blossoms that signify spring's arrival.

ACCOMMODATIONS

NEAR NATIONALS PARK

Just a 10-minute walk from Nationals Park, the contemporary **Capitol Skyline Hotel** (10 I St. SW, 202/488-7500, www.capitolskyline.com, $100-250) is an affordable stay with a popular pool, plus a wide variety of room sizes (double beds, king beds, suites). Some rooms have a view of Nationals Park, too.

Consider staying at the **Hampton Inn & Suites Washington DC-Navy Yard** (1265 1st St. SE, 202/800-1000, www.hilton.com, $200-400). It's pricey, but you're across the street from Nationals Park; and if you head to the rooftop bar, Top of the Yard, you'll get to watch the game from a long-distance seat. Some rooms also have that view.

Check in advance to see if the **Courtyard Washington Capitol Hill/Navy Yard** (140 L St. SE, 202/479-0027, www.marriott.com, $100-250) is offering a special baseball package. A package the hotel offered previously includes overnight self-parking, two Nationals hats, and a discount on game tickets.

OTHER NEIGHBORHOODS

Looking for a hotel on the other side of the National Mall, closer to places like the National Portrait Gallery and Ford's Theatre? I suggest the **Henley Park Hotel** (926 Massachusetts Ave. NW, 202/638-5200, www.henleypark.com, $100-250), a mile north of the National Mall but close to multiple Metro stops and, best of all, affordable. The rooms are charming, with just enough floral patterns.

GETTING AROUND

PUBLIC TRANSIT

Most of the time, the best way around the city is via **Metro** (www.wmata.com, $2-6 per ride). Rides can be expensive, but Metro offers accessibility and convenience. The Green and Yellow Lines run north and south, hitting multiple landmarks including Nationals Park at **Navy Yard-Ballpark** (200 M St. SE). The Blue, Orange, and Silver Lines thread across Capitol Hill and through the National Mall before heading up to Chinatown and the heart of Downtown.

It's likely your main station will be **L'Enfant Plaza** (429 L'Enfant Plaza SW), though if you're spending time in Dupont Circle, Logan Circle, and Adams Morgan, you'll get to know the Red Line and the station for **Dupont Circle** (1525 20th St. NW).

TAXI, UBER, AND LYFT

Washington DC has a robust taxi system—expect to pay $3.50 for the first eighth of a mile, then $2.16 each additional mile. Uber and Lyft also have a huge presence. You're bound to pay a little more with Uber than with Lyft, and both will narrowly beat taxi prices.

CAR

I've driven through every major American city, and I'm telling you: Washington DC is atop my list of the worst places to drive, thanks to the tourists and daily commuters all trying to get in and out of this small district with limited highway access. If you plan on driving, you'll probably rely on the **grid**. You'll notice that every address and street is

Washington DC Metro station

labeled with a two-letter ordinal direction (for northwest, northeast, southwest, southeast). Essentially, this directional tells you in which part of the city you're hanging in relation to the U.S. Capitol, which acts as an imaginary midpoint. So, anything southeast of the U.S. Capitol (like Nationals Park) has an address with SE.

Nationals Park is on **South Capitol Street**; it's the imaginary north-south line dividing the east and west halves of the city from each other. **North** and **South Capitol** is a major artery that connects with **I-395**, the highway that goes under the National Mall and Downtown Washington. There's also **East Capitol,** which begins behind the U.S. Capitol building. (There's no West Capitol, because that would run right through the length of the National Mall. Just think of the Reflecting Pool as that line.)

Down in the Navy Yard, get acquainted with **M Street,** which is the major west-east road. A bit north of there is the diagonal **Pennsylvania Avenue,** which stops at the U.S. Capitol, picks up on the other side, then stops at the White House before picking up on the other side and continuing onward.

Major interstates in the DC area include **I-395** and **I-695,** which spur through the District (395 runs north to south and 695 is a connector north of the Navy Yard); **I-295,** which runs along the east side of the Anacostia River before connecting with the Baltimore-Washington Parkway; **I-495,** which loops around the District and is known as the Beltway; and **I-95,** which is the main highway along the East Coast but runs in tandem with the Beltway before continuing north to Baltimore.

Florida
and the
Southeast

Though the Southeast may lack deep baseball history, it more than makes up for it in summertime fun. Between visits to the three parks on this road trip, which stretches from Atlanta to Miami, you'll romp on beaches, sip rum drinks, and eat fried seafood. You'll probably never even have to wear a jacket. This region is also notable for hosting Grapefruit League spring training near Tampa. Loyal fans come to Florida every year to watch their favorite players prepare for the long regular season.

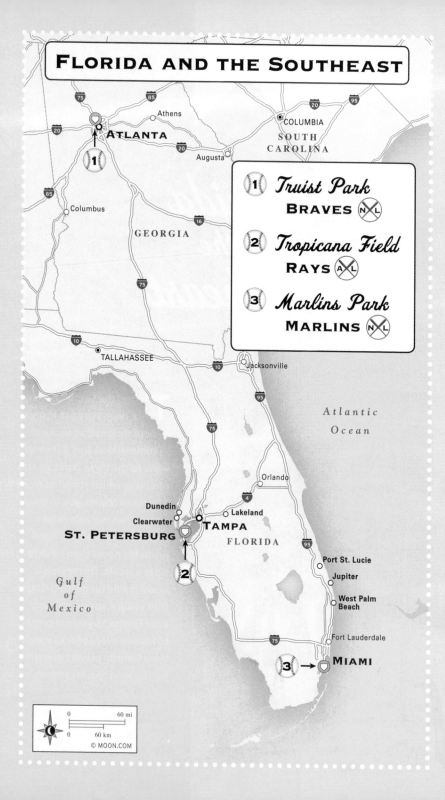

Florida and the Southeast Road Trip

For the first 75 years of big-league baseball, the southeastern United States was just a happy getaway. Teams started hopping trains to Hot Springs, Arkansas, to prepare for the regular season in the late 1800s. The Phillies were the first club to train in Florida, setting up shop in Jacksonville in 1889. Nearly two decades later, full-fledged spring training began in Florida, with multiple teams making cities throughout the Sunshine State their temporary March home. But regular season baseball would take a little longer to establish itself here.

In 1966, the Milwaukee Braves moved to Atlanta. It took another 27 years for the Southeast to get a second baseball team in the Florida (now Miami) Marlins. The Tampa Bay Rays came five years later, in 1998.

This is to say the atmosphere in Atlanta, St. Petersburg, and Miami isn't quite the East Coast. And that's fine! There are plenty of perks to this area, including warm weather, pleasant evenings with few (if any) rain-outs, and good food, shopping, and family-friendly experiences designed to keep kids happy and busy (like, say, the chance to touch a sting ray).

This road trip starts in transportation hub Atlanta, stops in St. Petersburg, then ends in Miami, spanning nearly 750 miles of Georgia and Florida.

Land in **Atlanta** and explore the city's diverse neighborhoods. Then drive up to the suburbs, where mega malls and entertainment surround a night with the **Braves,** a storied franchise with notable Hall of Fame talent like Hank Aaron, Greg Maddux, Chipper Jones, John Smoltz, and Tom Glavine. After Atlanta, make the 6.5-hour drive down to **Tampa** and **St. Petersburg.** You may want to hit this area on a weekend, checking out white-sand beaches while seeking the best Cuban sandwich in town. The **Tampa Bay Rays** are a quirky team with a short history and a domed stadium that belies a fantastic fan experience.

Finally, drive four hours across the state to **Miami,** one of America's most colorful, vibrant cities and also home to a severely underrated ballpark. The **Marlins,** now playing in the ultracontemporary Marlins Park, boast two world championships in a history that began in 1993. Stay out late when you're here.

PLANNING YOUR TIME

You have a few options for doing this trip. If you want to knock all three cities out in one go, I recommend doing the trip over a full **week.** Plan on spending two days in Atlanta, two days in Tampa and St. Petersburg, and three days in Miami. Get into Atlanta early on a Saturday and see a game that night. Use Sunday and part of Monday to explore, then drive down I-75 to Tampa Bay, where you'll spend the next **two days.** Go to the game Tuesday, then spend half of Wednesday in Tampa or St. Petersburg before trekking east to Miami. Relax Wednesday night and save up your energy for the next three days. Hit the beach and tourist spots Thursday before catching the Friday night game at Marlins Park. End your trip Saturday and fly home. The pace of this trip is very doable.

If you want to spend more than a couple days in Miami or the Tampa Bay area, you might want to break the trip into **two parts.** You can visit Atlanta and Tampa together, allotting a **long weekend** to both cities. Then, maybe later in the season when it's not as steaming hot, fly into Miami for another **long weekend.**

Keep weather in the back of your mind if visiting either Florida city in **August or September.** This is peak **hurricane season,** and a locality may not know about an incoming storm until about three days before it hits the shore. If you're traveling to the Sunshine State during this time, loosely sketch an **evacuation plan** (have cash ready, consider your rental car insurance, and research inland airports and lodging options in case you have to leave quickly).

The following is my recommended itinerary for the three-city, one-week version of this road trip.

Day 1

Fly into **Atlanta** in the morning, then get to the hotel, nap, and clean up. About four hours before first pitch, consider driving up to Cumberland to spend the rest of the evening in and around **Truist Park.** You may want to hop in a ride-share vehicle if you're planning on drinking, but I recommend saving your partying for later in the trip.

Day 2

Spend the day in Atlanta, maybe checking out a tourist attraction early in the day, such as Martin Luther King Jr. National Historical Park. Afterward, visit some of the city's cooler neighborhoods like Little Five Points and Cabbagetown.

Day 3

Maybe you'll want to see another sight before heading south on I-75 to **Tampa.** Consider an early afternoon drive to avoid the worst of the traffic in both big cities. Leaving at 1pm means getting into Tampa around 8pm or 9pm. Take your time driving and stop for an early dinner. Rest when you get to your accommodation.

Day 4

Consider hopping in a ride-share vehicle to spend the day in **St. Petersburg** and Clearwater. Hit the beach, eat some grouper, then hang out in Downtown St. Pete before a Rays game at **Tropicana Field.**

Day 5

You have options today. You can hit the road early or hang around Tampa for a couple hours to check out the sights. Either way, you'll end the day in **Miami** after a four-hour drive southeast. I recommend getting into Miami before dinner to give yourself the option of engaging in some nightlife.

Day 6

Start the day at Miami Beach, taking photos and soaking up some sun. Visit Wynwood for a beer or two, then hit up **Marlins Park** for a night game. End the evening either back in Wynwood or in Little Havana.

Day 7

You may want an extra day in Miami. If so, enjoy more beaches, more drinks, and more fun in the sun. If not, you can catch a flight back home. Either way, you've done all three areas justice.

GETTING THERE

Air

Hartsfield-Jackson Atlanta International Airport (ATL, 800/897-1910, www.atl.com) is 10 miles south of Atlanta and the world's busiest airport by passenger traffic. It's a hub for **Delta** (800/221-1212, www.delta.com) and a focus city for **Frontier** (800/432-1359, www.flyfrontier.com), **Southwest** (800/435-9792, www.southwest.com), and **Spirit** (801/401-2222, www.spirit.com). It also services **American Airlines** (800/433-7300, www.aa.com), **jetBlue** (800/538-2583, www.jetblue.com), and **United** (800/864-8331, www.united.com), plus several international carriers.

You have a number of airport choices in Florida. The major airport in the Tampa-St. Pete area is **Tampa International Airport** (TPA, 4100 George J. Bean Pkwy., Tampa, 813/870-8700, www.tampaairport.com). To and from here, you can fly **Air Canada** (888/247-2262, www.aircanada.com), American Airlines, Delta, Frontier, jetBlue, Southwest, Spirit, and United.

You can also fly into **St. Pete-Clearwater International Airport** (PIE, 14700 Terminal Blvd. #221, St. Petersburg, 727/453-7800, www.fly2pie.com), primarily served by

Photos (top): spring training game in Florida; (middle left) Martin Luther King Jr.'s childhood home in Atlanta; (middle right) Billy the Marlin at Miami's Bobblehead Museum; (bottom) World of Coca-Cola in Atlanta.

Allegiant (702/505-8888, www.allegiantair. com). You can get here from Cleveland, Cincinnati, Indianapolis, Pittsburgh, and smaller cities across the East and Midwest. Most major rental car companies are at the baggage claim area, while a few more are off-site, accessible via individual shuttles. The airport is just 15 minutes north of Tropicana Field via I-275 and FL-686/688.

Another option, about an hour south of Tampa, is **Sarasota-Bradenton International Airport** (SRQ, 6000 Airport Cir., Sarasota, 941/359-2770, www.srq-airport. com). Airlines that fly in and out of here include Air Canada, Allegiant, American Airlines, Delta, Frontier, jetBlue, and United. Among the destinations served are East Coast cities like Boston, New York, Philadelphia, Washington DC, Charlotte, and Atlanta, plus midwestern points like Chicago, Minneapolis-St. Paul, and St. Louis.

For Miami, you're likely to fly into or out of **Miami International Airport** (MIA, 2100 NW 42nd Ave., 305/876-7000, www. miami-airport.com). Major North American airlines that serve Miami include Air Canada, American Airlines, Delta, Frontier, Spirit, and United. Miami is also home to a number of carriers that fly to and from the Caribbean islands.

Another option is to use **Fort Lauderdale-Hollywood International Airport** (FLL, 100 Terminal Dr., Fort Lauderdale, 954/359-1200, www.broward.org). It's home to Air Canada, Allegiant, American Airlines, Delta, Frontier, jetBlue, Southwest, Spirit, and United. A few Caribbean carriers fly out of here.

About 70 miles north of Miami via I-95 is **Palm Beach International Airport** (PBI, 1000 James L. Turnage Blvd., West Palm Beach, 561/471-7400, www.pbia.org). Airlines that fly into and out of here include Air Canada, American Airlines, Delta, Frontier, jetBlue, Southwest, Spirit, and United. A smaller number of Caribbean carriers also come in and out of the airport.

Train

I don't recommend using **Amtrak** (www. amtrak.com) to do this trip, as the three areas just don't connect very well, especially when you're factoring in the location of the ballparks. But you could take a train into Atlanta at **Peachtree Station** (1688 Peachtree Rd. NW, 800/872-7245), a bit north of Downtown Atlanta and well south (by about 10 miles) of Truist Park. No matter what, you should get a rental car once you're in Atlanta, and then drive the rest of the route.

Other train stations on the route include Tampa's **Union Station** (601 N. Nebraska Ave.). Its location necessitates renting a car or hailing a cab or ride-share to reach Tropicana Field in St. Petersburg. **Miami Station** (8303 NW 37th Ave.) is well north of Downtown Miami and Marlins Park, so this is another time that you'll want to hail a cab or rent a car.

ATLANTA
BRAVES

If you were watching baseball in the 1990s, you'll remember that the Atlanta Braves were unavoidable. Once owned by media magnate Ted Turner, the Braves were christened "America's Team" and had their very own national cable TV spotlight. The fact that the team was outstanding—led by Hall of Famers Greg Maddux, Tom Glavine, John Smoltz, and Chipper Jones—didn't hurt, either. For a while there, the Braves were as synonymous with baseball as the Yankees, peanuts, and Cracker Jacks.

That run of success serves as the apex for a city long associated with second-class baseball. From 1884 to 1965, the main team in town was the minor league Crackers. That club was successful, winning 21 pennants, but no matter what the city did to boost its profile, Atlanta remained a minor

league city until 1966. During the same period, the Atlanta Black Crackers played in the Negro Leagues but saw little success.

In 1966, the major league Braves arrived from Milwaukee (before that, they'd been in Boston) and within a couple years took a division crown, but that success was fleeting. Aside from a surprise division title in 1982, the Braves regularly finished near or at last place through 1990. At that point, they turned a corner, and how: Between 1991 and 2005, the Braves were in the postseason every year and were on national cable television just about every night, though they only won one championship during that period (in 1995). After that incredible run, the Braves retooled a bit, had a few decent seasons, then retooled again. Recently, though, they've reemerged with a successful, playoff-contending team led by young talent like Ronald Acuna and Ozzie Albies (though without Turner's money and heft, not quite America's Team).

The great play doesn't always translate to full houses, though; historically, the Braves have had trouble drawing crowds, even when the team is good. Is it because fans got tired of solid teams that almost never won the World Series? Or maybe Atlanta isn't a big-time baseball city to begin with (I'd argue that college and pro football are more important here). Whatever the case, the team's 2017 move from the city of Atlanta to an entertainment district in the northern suburbs means that if you want to catch a Braves game, you have to be all in. And despite a couple playoff berths in recent years, the fan reaction has been as lukewarm as always.

With their name and iconography, the Braves reflect a history of cultural appropriation. Even worse, though, is the racist "tomahawk chop" that's affiliated with the team. This "war chant" plays all the time at Truist Park, making a gross caricature of Native American history and culture. Talking about the Braves means facing these crucial aspects of the team's past and present.

PLANNING YOUR TIME

You can spend just a **weekend** in Atlanta, or you can spread your time out over a **week** by visiting neighborhoods like Cabbagetown and Little Five Points. If you're in town just for baseball, you may want to stay in The Battery itself. But if you're craving a tour of the city, stay Downtown and hop in an Uber to see a Braves game.

Atlanta can be a fun and accessible city if you opt to engage with its eclectic neighborhoods, so try to mix some independent discovery time in with the booked visits to major sites like the Martin Luther King Jr. National Historical Park and Jimmy Carter Presidential Library and Museum.

Atlanta can get pretty hot in **midsummer,** but it's not the kind of sweaty, swampy heat that you'll find in other southern cities like Houston and Dallas. If you can, aim for an evening game in May.

GETTING THERE

AIR

Hartsfield-Jackson Atlanta International Airport (ATL, 800/897-1910, www.atl.com) is 10 miles south of Atlanta and the world's busiest airport by passenger traffic. It's a hub for **Delta** (800/221-1212, www.delta.com) and a focus city for **Frontier** (800/432-1359, www.flyfrontier.com), **Southwest** (800/435-9792, www.southwest.com), and **Spirit** (801/401-2222, www.spirit.com). It also services **American Airlines** (800/433-7300, www.aa.com), **jetBlue** (800/538-2583, www.jetblue.com), and **United** (800/864-8331, www.united.com), plus several international carriers.

Airport Transportation

Hartsfield-Jackson connects to Atlanta's public transit system, **MARTA** (Metro Atlanta

a showcase of bats used by Braves players through the years

Regional Transportation Authority, www. itsmarta.com, $2.50 one-way), with trains leaving every 10-15 minutes. You can take the **Gold** or **Red Line** to Five Points, the central station of the MARTA train system and one of the most exciting neighborhoods in the city. If you want to get from the airport to Truist Park, you'll need to find another mode of transportation, since the Braves play 17 miles northwest of Downtown Atlanta in the suburbs.

TRAIN

Just one **Amtrak** (www.amtrak.com) line stops at **Peachtree Station** (1688 Peachtree Rd. NW, 800/872-7245). The **Crescent** route begins in New York City and runs south by southwest through Philadelphia, Washington DC, and Charlotte before reaching Atlanta. It continues southwest through Birmingham en route to its end in New Orleans.

Peachtree Station is north of Downtown Atlanta, by the intersection of I-75 and I-85. There is no easy way to get to the park from the train station. The only public transportation option includes a bus ride and rapid transit trip, clocking in at more than two hours.

BUS

In Atlanta, **Greyhound** (www.greyhound. com) has a station at the **airport** (6000 N. Terminal Pkwy., 404/765-9598) and another **Downtown** (232 Forsyth St. SW, 404/584-1728).

Truist Park

In 1997, the Braves began playing at the converted Centennial Olympic Stadium, renamed Turner Field. Just 20 years into their stay at this decent city ballpark, the team moved northwest into the suburbs. Now the Braves anchor their own mixed-use entertainment district called The Battery, playing ball at **Truist Park** (755 Battery Ave. SE, www.mlb.com/braves) in the unincorporated community of Cumberland.

Truist Park and The Battery symbolize a new way of thinking about the ballpark experience. It used to be that you could park maybe a block or two from the stadium, walk over, turn in your ticket, and watch a game for a couple bucks. Then teams got wiser and

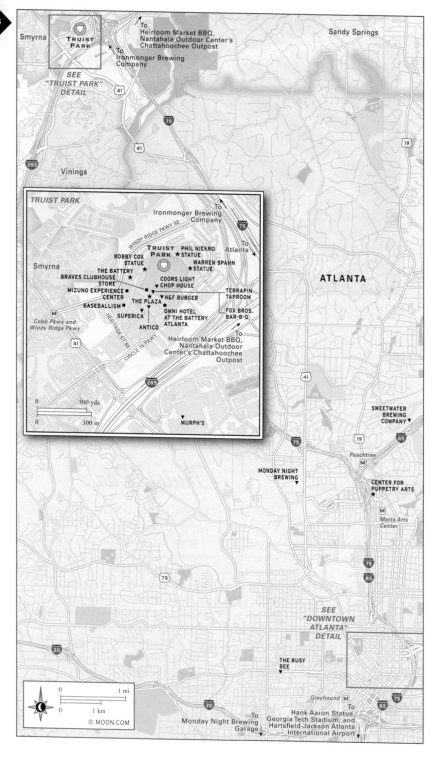

Smyrna

To Heirloom Market BBQ, Nantahala Outdoor Center's Chattahoochee Outpost

Sandy Springs

To Ironmonger Brewing Company

SEE "TRUIST PARK" DETAIL

Vinings

TRUIST PARK

Ironmonger Brewing Company

WINDY RIDGE PKWY SE

To Atlanta

Smyrna

TRUIST PARK

PHIL NIEKRO STATUE

BOBBY COX STATUE

WARREN SPAHN STATUE

THE BATTERY

BRAVES CLUBHOUSE STORE

COORS LIGHT CHOP HOUSE

ATLANTA

MIZUNO EXPERIENCE CENTER

TERRAPIN TAPROOM

THE PLAZA

H&F BURGER

BASEBALLISM

FOX BROS. BAR-B-Q

SUPERICA

OMNI HOTEL AT THE BATTERY ATLANTA

Cobb Pkwy and Windy Ridge Pkwy

HERITAGE CT SE

ANTICO

To

CIRCLE 75 PKWY

Heirloom Market BBQ, Nantahala Outdoor Center's Chattahoochee Outpost

0   300 yds
0   300 m

MURPH'S

SWEETWATER BREWING COMPANY

Peachtree

MONDAY NIGHT BREWING

CENTER FOR PUPPETRY ARTS

Marta Arts Center

SEE "DOWNTOWN ATLANTA" DETAIL

THE BUSY BEE

0   1 mi
0   1 km

© MOON.COM

Greyhound

To Monday Night Brewing Garage

To Hank Aaron Statue, Georgia Tech Stadium, and Hartsfield-Jackson Atlanta International Airport

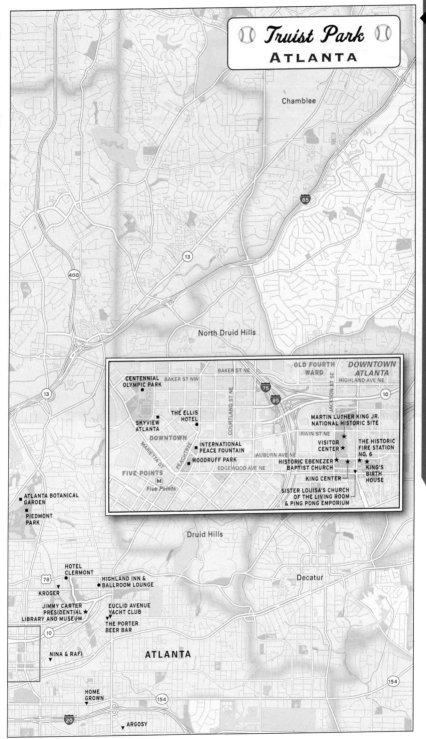

Truist Park
ATLANTA

Chamblee

North Druid Hills

OLD FOURTH WARD

DOWNTOWN ATLANTA

CENTENNIAL OLYMPIC PARK

BAKER ST NW

BAKER ST NE

HIGHLAND AVE NE

THE ELLIS HOTEL

MARTIN LUTHER KING JR. NATIONAL HISTORIC SITE

SKYVIEW ATLANTA

DOWNTOWN

IRWIN ST NE

VISITOR CENTER ★

THE HISTORIC FIRE STATION NO. 6 ★

INTERNATIONAL PEACE FOUNTAIN

WOODRUFF PARK

AUBURN AVE NE

HISTORIC EBENEZER BAPTIST CHURCH ★

KING'S BIRTH HOUSE

FIVE POINTS

EDGEWOOD AVE NE

KING CENTER

Five Points

SISTER LOUISA'S CHURCH OF THE LIVING ROOM & PING PONG EMPORIUM

ATLANTA BOTANICAL GARDEN

PIEDMONT PARK

Druid Hills

Decatur

HOTEL CLERMONT

HIGHLAND INN & BALLROOM LOUNGE

KROGER

JIMMY CARTER PRESIDENTIAL ★ LIBRARY AND MUSEUM

EUCLID AVENUE YACHT CLUB

THE PORTER BEER BAR

NINA & RAFI

ATLANTA

HOME GROWN

ARGOSY

Truist Park

charged for parking and for food and drink, and increased ticket prices. Now you have Truist (and another new park, Globe Life Field in Arlington, Texas), which anchors a whole district designed to get you shopping, eating, drinking, and hanging out—it's baseball as a lifestyle, and the game isn't the only thing that matters. In fact, almost everything but the game matters now.

This is likely how many of us will be experiencing live baseball in the future. Not every team will do this, but most will probably try to sell a trip to the ballpark as a half-day hang at an all-encompassing tourist spot. Whether that's a good thing or a bad one is for you to decide, but there's no doubt that this is an unabashedly American enterprise.

What's most curious about Truist is its location up in the suburbs. The Braves moved from an area that was relatively accessible for a huge swath of the city's population to an area that isn't very accessible at all. If you don't drive or own a car, you'll need to take a bus from Atlanta at least 35 minutes to the ballpark. When you get there, you'll be in a place where everything is priced higher because those are the only options. In short, it's hard to believe that this ballpark was devised with everyone in mind.

Truist Park is a good-looking ballpark that was executed well. There are many shopping and dining options around it, and the sight lines are all great. It's a big park that doesn't look very big, which is a positive. But it is also inconvenient for many, feels cold and opportunistic at times, and doesn't seem to have the abundant character you'll find at, say, Wrigley

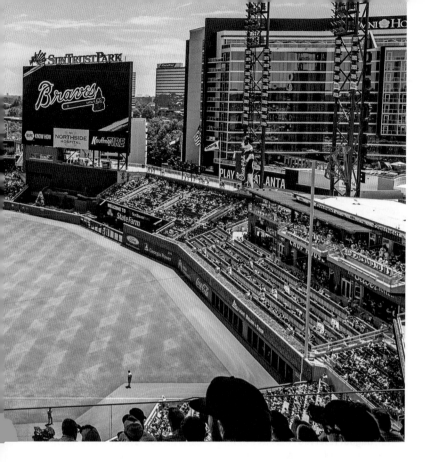

Field or even Citi Field. Truist is a long way from the jewel-box parks of the past.

ORIENTATION

Truist Park is located in Cumberland, a city that's part of unincorporated Atlanta and located 12 miles north by northwest of Downtown Atlanta. The stadium is part of a shopping and entertainment center called The District.

Truist Park has five entry gates. The **Chop House Gate** is the most dramatic, with its connection to the rest of the Battery. Fans typically flock to this gate, so it'll also have the longest lines.

TICKETS AND SEATING

Pricing

The Braves follow a **dynamic pricing** model, so you'll want to compare prices for whatever game you want to see. Most of the time, you can get in for pretty cheap. Ticket prices are generally higher for **weekend games** and contests against **rival opponents.** For instance, a seat in the vista infield section for a Pirates game may cost $30, while that same seat for a Mets game may cost $50-60.

Seating Plan

The ultramodern Truist Park naturally has a variety of seating options that might make your head spin. On the **100 level,** we'll start down by the field. Around home plate is the **Truist Club** (sections 1-9), then we head

THE TROUBLE WITH THE TOMAHAWK CHOP

Let's start right at the top: The Braves have a history of race-related controversies. The team name itself has been a point of contention, but there are even more problematic elements that the team has embraced in the past. In 1986, the team retired a mascot named Chief Noc-a-Homa ("knock a homer"); he was last played by a Native American person and would perform a fictitious "war dance" whenever the team scored a run. It wasn't until 1990 that the team got rid of their longstanding logo of a screaming (some say laughing) Native American.

While the Braves have finally done away with these troubling historical traditions, the continued existence of the "tomahawk chop" today indicates that the team still needs to reconcile with its racist depictions of Indigenous Americans. The chop happens periodically during games—typically during a rally. It's spurred by a music cue that accompanies the chop, during which time fans also yell out a pseudo "war chant."

The tradition likely began at Florida State University, where fans would raise and lower their wrists and hands repeatedly in a chopping motion while engaging in a "war chant" in support of their team, the Seminoles. FSU star Deion Sanders brought the chop to Atlanta when he joined the Braves in 1991, and with the team beginning a run of outstanding play, the act caught on. For many Braves fans, the chop is a strongly nostalgic tradition, evoking memories of great moments and winning teams.

Ultimately, the chop is a racist act that depicts Native Americans as cartoonish savages. In 2019, Ryan Helsley, a member of Cherokee Nation who was pitching for the Cardinals during a game at Truist Park, spoke out against the chop, calling it disrespectful to Indigenous Americans. In response, the Braves said they would discuss the future of the chop. As of the 2020 season, the result of that discussion was inconclusive.

If you're going to Truist Park, you'll have to grapple with hearing it and seeing it repeatedly, knowing the team has done little to discourage fans from participating.

to the right-field foul pole, coming toward home plate, with **dugout corner** (sections 10-12), **dugout reserved** (sections 13-15), and **dugout infield** (sections 16-21). Wrapping around home plate behind the Truist Club are the **chairman seats** (sections 22-30), and then going toward the left-field foul pole are **dugout infield** (sections 31-35), **dugout reserved** (sections 36-39), and **dugout corner** (sections 40-42).

Now, the back rows of the 100 level: Starting from the right-field foul pole and heading toward home plate are **diamond corner** (sections 107-112), **diamond reserved** (sections 113-114), and **diamond infield** (sections 116-120). The **executive seats** (sections 122-130) wrap around home plate with the **champions suites** (1-10) hanging above. Heading toward left field are **diamond infield** (sections 131-135), **diamond reserved** (sections 137-138), and **diamond corner** (sections 140-143). In the outfield, you'll find the **home run porch** in **left field** (sections 144-151) and **right field** (sections

152-155), then the **Chop House Terrace** (sections 156-160).

On to the **200 level:** It starts at the right-field foul pole, heading toward home plate, with **terrace corner** (sections 210-212), **terrace reserved** (sections 213-215), and **terrace infield** (sections 216-218). The **Infiniti Club** (sections 220-231) is next, wrapping around home plate. Going toward left field are **terrace infield** (sections 233-238), **terrace reserved** (sections 239-241), **terrace corner** (sections 242-243), and the indoor-outdoor **Hank Aaron Terrace** (sections 244-246). That isn't all: The **Home Depot Clubhouse** (section 250) is in left center field, the **Harrah's Cherokee Casinos Back Porch** (section 252) is in dead center field, and the **Coors Light Chop House** (sections 257-259) is in deep right field. **Suites** line the right-field corner, then the first-base line around to the third-base infield area.

Next, the **300 level:** Starting in deep right field and moving toward home plate,

YOUR BEST DAY AT TRUIST PARK

You're going to spend some time in Atlanta and catch a Braves game? Cool: Here's what you should do.

10 HOURS BEFORE FIRST PITCH
SBreakfast is the most important meal of the day, and it's best served at **Home Grown.**

8 HOURS BEFORE FIRST PITCH
Walk off your big meal at **Piedmont Park.** You can also wander through the **Atlanta Botanical Garden** while you're there.

6 HOURS BEFORE FIRST PITCH
Visit the **Martin Luther King Jr. National Historical Park.** Check in at the **visitors center,** then take the tour of **King's Birth Home.**

4 HOURS BEFORE FIRST PITCH
Get in a ride-share vehicle and head north just a bit to **Monday Night Brewing.** Have yourself a pint or two before hailing another ride. Destination: **Truist Park.**

Monument Garden

2 HOURS BEFORE FIRST PITCH
Arrive at **The Battery.** Order a drink at **Terrapin Taproom** and grab a taco from the bar at **Superica.** Before heading into the park, check out the **statues** paying tribute to Hank Aaron, Warren Spahn, Phil Niekro, and manager Bobby Cox.

DURING THE GAME
Spend some time scoping out **Monument Garden** and reading up on Greg Maddux's pinpoint control. Get a sugary treat at **Waffle House** and visit the **Hank Aaron Terrace** to glimpse some home run history.

AFTER THE GAME
Give yourself some time to cruise around The Battery before getting into a ride-share vehicle (preferably with others to save some cash) back to the city. If you want to finish the night with a drink, I suggest **The Porter Beer Bar,** one of my favorite bars in the United States.

the Atlanta Botanical Garden

the park has **vista corner** (sections 312-314), **vista reserved** (sections 315-317), and **vista infield** (sections 318-333), which wraps around home plate to third base. Then there's **vista reserved** (sections 335-339), **vista corner** (sections 340-344), and the **Coca-Cola Corner** (sections 345-347) at the left-field foul pole.

Finally, the **400 level:** Near the right-field foul pole and going toward home plate are **grandstand reserved** (sections 410-417) and then **grandstand infield** (sections 418-433), which wraps around home plate to third base. **Grandstand reserved** (sections 434-439) and **grandstand corner** (sections 440-444) finish the level.

Where to Buy Tickets

Check **StubHub** and **SeatGeek** to see if you can score tickets for less than the box office rate, which is usually pretty cheap. For weekend games, when ticket prices are generally higher, consider waiting closer to first pitch to nab tickets. For weekday games, however, don't worry too much—you can probably get a good seat for little cost, even well in advance.

The Braves participate in the **MLB Ballpark app's** seat upgrade function. Download the app, and you might be able to get a better seat after entering the ballpark.

Best Seats

If you want to be **out of the sun,** get seats along the **first-base line** toward the **right-field corner.** The best options include the back rows of **sections 110-120,** the back rows of **sections 315-328,** and nearly the entirety of **sections 414-431.** Unlike the seating in most parks, the third-base line here is the hot spot.

If you're looking for the food and drink experience with some socialization, the **Chop House Terrace** (sections 156-160) is a big draw. It comes with in-seat service and access to the Chop House restaurant. Note that season ticket holders get first dibs, so you may not be able to score tickets here.

GAME COSTS

Tickets: Prices are just about average, but it depends on the opponent since the team follows a dynamic pricing model. The cheap seats will cost about **$15,** while 200 level tickets will run you closer to **$60.**

Hot dog: On average, dogs cost **$4-5,** though you may be able to find a **$3** option. These prices are good compared with the rest of the league.

Beer: The cheaper beers are about **$6,** and you can find premium ales for closer to **$9.** That's not too bad, all things considered.

Parking: This is expensive. You'll probably pay **$30-40** depending on how long you're staying in The Battery.

The best value is in the **terrace level.** Opt for **terrace infield** (sections 216-218 and 233-238) for good views at an affordable price.

KNOW BEFORE YOU GO

MLB's 16- by 16- by 8-inch **bag** rule is in effect here; anything bigger is banned. **Radios** and **televisions** with **headphones** are allowed into the park, but bullhorns, noisemakers, and beach balls are prohibited. Also not allowed are cigarettes and selfie sticks.

Tailgating is permitted at Truist Park but only at **Lot N29,** which is located on Circle 75 Parkway northwest of the home-plate entrance. Grills can be set up only on the provided grassy area, and tents are prohibited.

Nursing mothers should note there's a **nursing room** (section 141) that's air-conditioned and has rocking chairs and diaper-changing areas. **Sunscreen stations** throughout the park have free dispensers of sunscreen. They're mostly near the **family restrooms** (sections 112, 138, 148, 216, 240, 329).

Accessibility

As a new ballpark, Truist Park was constructed with accessibility in mind. For families, the Braves offer the **Exceptional Fans Program** (www.braves.com/exceptionalfans), which includes a welcome kit containing credentials that can get you past the concessions lines if necessary, a **sensory map,** and **fidget toys.** The Braves also have a **social storybook** that details what fans should expect when visiting Truist Park. For more information, contact the team's **Accessible Seating Department** (404/577-9100, opt. 5).

If you need assistance in reaching your seat, **complimentary wheelchairs** are available. This service is offered on a first-come, first-served basis. **Elevators** at Truist Park are at the first base gate, third base gate, left field gate, Terrapin Taproom, and Hope and Will's Sandlot. **Service animals** are welcome at Truist Park.

The park has a number of **accessible seating** sections. Your best bet for booking tickets is to call or email the **Accessible Seating Department** (404/577-9100, opt. 5, accessibleservices@braves.com).

Head to one of the **guest services booths** (sections 111, 218, 233, 314) to pick up an **assistive listening device.** You'll need to hand in a valid photo ID as a deposit. If you need an **interpreter** or **translator,** visit the guest services booth at section 111. **Noise-cancelling headphones** are available at the 111 booth, as well.

If you need a **quiet space,** head to specific **elevator lobbies** (sections 120, 137), guest services at sections 218 and 233, and the "kid's area" of the **nursing lounge** (section 141).

Accessible parking is available in **Lot N29** or the **Red Deck,** but be sure that a valid **accessible parking placard** is visible. If you park in N29, an accessible **shuttle** will take you to Battery Avenue near the third-base gate. Consider reserving your parking spot in advance, to ensure you get one.

GETTING THERE

Public Transit

There is no train that gets you to Truist Park. The only public transit that reaches the venue is **bus 10** from **CobbLinc** (www.cobbcounty.org, $2.50 one-way), Cobb County's transit service. The bus, whose destination is the **Marietta Transfer Station,** departs from the **MARTA Arts Center station** (Arts Center Way NE and 15th St. NE) and reaches the closest stop to the ballpark, **Cobb Parkway and Windy Ridge Parkway** in Cumberland, in about 35 minutes. It's an eight-minute walk east on Windy Ridge Parkway to The Battery.

Driving

You'll most likely need to drive or take a ride-share vehicle to the ballpark. For **ride-share vehicle drop-off** and **pickup,** head to the

Photos (from top to bottom): Truist Park; gloves of the greats at Truist Park; former Braves pitcher Tom Glavine.

intersection of Windy Ridge Parkway SE and Heritage Court SE, two blocks south and one block west of right field. This is an official Rideshare Zone; look for the signs.

Naturally, the Braves and The Battery won't mind if you drive, because there are a host of **parking lots** surrounding the venue, and multiple lots in and around The Battery. Your best bet is to **pay in advance** online (www.mlb.com/braves); otherwise, most lots accept only credit cards. There's shuttle service at some of the lots (south of Akers Mill Rd.) that are especially far from the park.

You're bound to pay at least $30 for a space on game day, because the Braves charge $20 if you're there for up to three hours; and as we know, games usually last longer than that. If you stay more than four hours, it's a $40 charge. My recommendation is to take a ride-share vehicle and aim to spend a little postgame time at The Battery, if only to stay out of the crush of people trying to get home.

PARK FEATURES AND SIGHTS

The Battery

Truist Park is symbolic of a new era of ballparks constructed to be anchors of massive entertainment districts. **The Battery** (800 Battery Ave. SE) might be the ultimate example. The Braves are behind the creation of this district, which surrounds the ballpark and combines shopping, dining, drinking, and playing, with all paths leading to Truist Park and the experience of big-league baseball. It's capitalistic, it's commercialistic, and it excludes a large swath of fans who can't afford the high prices or don't have a way to get to the suburbs of Atlanta; but it's impressive in its singular vision.

The Battery was designed to encourage people to spend many hours before, during, and after baseball within its boundaries. For shoppers, it has a record store, a sweet shop, a Baseballism, and a high-end gift shop. For diners, options include pizza, burgers, a steak house, a very good Tex-Mex spot, and plenty more. There are two hotels, plenty of walking space, and a Vegas-like feel-good

atmosphere. Before each game, there's plenty of activity at **The Plaza** (between Power Alley and Truist Park), which includes a turf space with activity booths. On Sundays, there are autograph opportunities with former Braves. A stage at the plaza's Georgia Power Pavilion has live music, too.

If you spend no money and just decide to walk around here, you may just be enchanted by how much work went into getting people into the mood to watch a ball game. At the very least, The Battery is an interesting showplace hinting at the future of the baseball-watching experience.

The Battery and Truist Park are located just north of **The Perimeter,** the I-285 loop that circles the Atlanta metropolitan area. The commercial and entertainment area that includes The Battery includes properties just across The Perimeter; you can get to the other side by walking the pedestrian bridge that originates at the Circle 75 Parkway near Heritage Court SE. That walkway takes you to the Galleria, a shopping mall with more Braves parking, Murph's, and the Renaissance Atlanta Waverly Hotel & Convention Center.

In the Park

Once in the park, you'll need to get to the **Hank Aaron Terrace** (sections 244-246), which is home to the very bat Aaron used, and the ball he hit, for that then-record-breaking 715th home run in 1974. The area also includes a display of 715 bat knobs inscribed with the date of every homer Aaron hit.

The Braves did a nice job decorating Truist Park with **artwork by local and global artists.** Many of the pieces are in the club areas of the park, but be on the lookout for paintings by Richard Sullivan depicting great moments in the team's history. Local artist Jason Williams creates detailed LEGO brick pieces; there's one at the main entrance corridor. **Statues** around the park include tributes to **Hank Aaron** (Monument Garden, section 125), **Warren Spahn** (left-field gate), **Phil Niekro** (third-base gate), and manager **Bobby Cox** (first-base gate).

Kids can hang out at **Hope & Will's**

BE A FAN

There are more than a few modern-day mascots at Truist Field that make the experience worthwhile. Look for **life-size bobblehead mascots** of Braves legends like Hank Aaron, Chipper Jones, Greg Maddux, and Dale Murphy. The Braves' official mascot **Blooper**—a very Muppety fellow with funny ears and a furry body—roams around the park, so keep an eye out for him.

The Freeze

But nothing, and I mean nothing, tops The Freeze. Not a mascot as much as a phenomenon, **The Freeze,** debuting in 2017, is Nigel Talton, a competitive track sprinter in a full-body spandex suit who challenges a lucky (or unlucky) fan to a race. Between innings during the middle of every game, The Freeze gives his opponent a five-second head start to race from the left-field foul pole to the right-field foul pole, and nearly every time, the bodysuited sprinter passes the fan en route to a victory. The Freeze has lost only a few times, making each race appointment viewing.

Sandlot (sections 152-155), where they'll find games and attractions costing $1.

MONUMENT GARDEN

A must-visit at Truist is **Monument Garden** (section 125), which is essentially the history of the Braves wrapped up in a tidy space. Highlights include the Braves Hall of Fame, where plaques acknowledge the more than 30 players and personalities honored by the team; an interactive exhibit devoted to the folks whose numbers have been retired; a display showing the history of the team's uniforms (including that sweet baby-blue road jersey from the early 1980s); and audio calls of historic moments in franchise history, including Sid Bream's NLCS-winning slide. There are also two cool nods to the great Hank Aaron: a statue capturing his 715th home run, and a sculpture made of 755 of Aaron's bats, commemorating his final homer count.

FOOD AND DRINKS

A lot of the attention at Truist is focused on

right field and the Chophouse Gate, which is also part of The Battery. Here you'll find a few major dining options. For one, there's **Terrapin Taproom** (section 156, 755 Battery Ave. SE #100, 404/494-1202, www.terrapin-taproom.com, 11am-9pm daily and during games, under $50), a large restaurant and bar area. It's home to beer from the local Terrapin Brewery (now owned by Anheuser-Busch InBev). You can find some beers here that were brewed specifically for the ballpark, like the Baseball Saison. It's worth it to sample some of these creations. Terrapin serves meat plates, sandwiches, and starters from local barbecue favorite **Fox Bros. Bar-B-Q.**

Also at the Chophouse Gate is **H&F Burger** (section 153), home to the popular original burger with two beef patties, American cheese, and pain de mie (a soft bread) buns. In the same area is the sit-down **Coors Light Chop House** (section 156), open to the public before and during the game. It's first come, first served, and the menu includes burgers and sandwiches, salads, and bar-style starters. Prices aren't too bad, especially for a ballpark restaurant, but you're better off visiting the many vendors at The Battery. Even better, check out the rest of the park's food offerings instead of what's attached to The Battery.

Good news: There's a **Waffle House** (section 311) in Truist Park. Yup, the famous late-night haunt and morning necessity with the blinding yellow sign has a stand selling waffles, hash browns, and a Texas Philly melt (chopped steak with cheese on Texas toast).

The park's most gargantuan items can be found at **Braves Big Bites** (section 113). Standouts include the Blooper Burger, an enormous concoction of four burger patties, a hot dog, chicken tenders, and all the fixings in Texas toast; and a ridiculous vessel of spicy chicken in a waffle boat with pecans and honey.

The beer selection at Truist is Terrapin-heavy. The Coors Light Chop House has a more robust selection, including selections from Atlanta-area stalwart **Sweetwater.** The **Dugout Lounge** locations on the first- and third-base side of the 100 level carry some Sam Adams and Yuengling options.

EVENTS

The gates will open 90 minutes before game time (two hours beforehand on Fridays and on Sunday nights, and for premium gates at nearly every game), allowing you to catch some of **batting practice** (the visiting team, mostly); on Saturdays, they open three hours early. That gives you the opportunity to see all of batting practice. The Braves start hitting at 4:40pm for a 7:20pm game.

If you're planning on getting player autographs, you can head down near the dugouts up to an hour before first pitch. There is no guarantee, but players tend to approach the crowd of kids by the dugouts.

On Sunday afternoons, the Braves host **Alumni Sundays** (Georgia Power Pavilion at The Plaza, 11:30am Sun.), during which at least one former player will sit for autographs for about an hour. And after those Sunday home games, children ages 4-14 are invited to **run the bases** (section 135, meet at bottom of eighth inning).

After every Friday-night game, the Braves host a **fireworks display.** Once the game ends, you'll want to get into foul territory, close to home plate, for the best viewing experience.

The Braves have a couple **entertainment teams** that perform throughout the park, nodding to various musical styles that make Atlanta a multicultural hub. The **ATL Breakers,** a hip-hop and trick-dance troupe, excite crowds at the Fan Plaza before each game. A really cool touch are performances by the **Heavy Hitters,** a drumline that nods to the rhythmically proficient sounds found at high schools and historically Black colleges and universities across the Southeast. The Hitters perform at the Fan Plaza before and after games, and you may just hear them around the park during the game.

Tours

Want to see Truist Park from behind the scenes? The Braves host **tours** (9am, 10:30am, noon, 1:30pm, and 3pm Mon.-Sat., 1pm and 2:30pm Sun. Apr.-Sept., 9:30am, 11am, 12:30pm, and 2pm Mon.-Sat. Oct.-Mar., $20, $12 ages 12 and under), except when there's an afternoon game. The tour may take you to a dugout, the press box, and Monument Garden.

SHOPPING

The main store at Truist Park is the **Braves Clubhouse Store** (75 Circle Pkwy., Right Field Gate, 404/614-3300, 10am-6pm Mon.-Sat., noon-6pm Sun., also open during games). The 5,000-square-foot space has the usual finds for a ballpark team store: plenty of jerseys, hats, men's and women's clothing, kids' clothes, and toys and novelty items. The store is at the right-field gate and connected to The Battery.

ATLANTA SIGHTS

GEORGIA STATE STADIUM (TURNER FIELD)

Looking down at **Georgia State Stadium** (755 Hank Aaron Dr. SE), you may not realize it immediately, but yes, that's old **Turner Field.** Built in 1996 for the Summer Olympics as Centennial Stadium, then reconfigured into a ballpark in 1997, it was a pretty darn decent place for baseball for about 20 years. Then the Braves decided to up and move to the suburbs. At the stadium, you'll see plenty of things that remind you of Turner Field. You can spot the **Hank Aaron statue** (Georgia Ave. at Victory Plaza) that was built for Turner Field and remained in its original place instead of moving with the team (because the Braves commissioned a new statue of Aaron at Truist Park). Both the Braves' original video board and outfield upper deck also remain.

MARTIN LUTHER KING JR. NATIONAL HISTORICAL PARK

A must-visit if you're in Atlanta, the **Martin Luther King Jr. National Historical Park** (www.nps.gov/malu) spreads itself out over numerous city blocks, mirroring the enormous impact of Dr. Martin Luther King Jr. as an agent of global change. Here are King's birthplace and final resting place, plus structures and exhibits that reveal his many accomplishments.

The site encompasses an L-shaped area of the historically Black Sweet Auburn neighborhood. Start at the **visitors center** (450 Auburn Ave., 404/331-5190, ext. 5046, 9am-5pm daily), where folks can take free tours (10am daily, every 30 minutes) that include a visit to King's childhood home. Exhibits at the visitors center include Courage To Lead, which details King's journey from Atlanta to national prominence, along with the evolution of the American civil rights movement.

Across the street from the visitors center is the **King Center** (449 Auburn Ave., 404/526-8900, www.thekingcenter.org, 9am-6pm daily summer, 9am-5pm daily fall-spring, free), which serves as a living memorial to King, holding nearly one million documents associated with King. It's also the site of King's Tomb, where both King and Coretta Scott King are buried. An eternal flame burns at the site. Neighboring the King Center is **Historic Ebenezer Baptist Church** (407-413 Auburn Ave., 770/435-2535), which was built between 1914 and 1922 and was King's childhood parish.

Also on-site is **King's Birth Home** (501 Auburn Ave.), which is where King spent the first 12 years of his life. The **Historic Fire Station No. 6** (39 Boulevard NE), which served Sweet Auburn and illustrates King's impact on the desegregation of public institutions throughout Atlanta, is here as well. Visitors can take self-guided tours of the fire station.

JIMMY CARTER PRESIDENTIAL LIBRARY AND MUSEUM

On 35 acres of a spot that's relatively isolated from Atlanta's busy streets, the **Jimmy Carter Presidential Library and Museum** (441 Freedom Pkwy. NE, 404/865-7100, www.jimmycarterlibrary.gov, 9am-4:45pm Mon.-Sat., noon-4:45pm Sun., $8, $6 seniors and students, free ages 16 and under) profiles the 39th president, who attempted to bring calm to a weary nation, got involved in the Palestinian-Israeli conflict, and has devoted his post-political career to human rights across the world.

Visitors can enter a replica of Carter's Oval Office that includes artifacts from his days in office, and follow Carter through a day of his presidency. The center's archive contains more than 27 million pages of presidential papers; plus, you can view Carter's 2002 Nobel Peace Prize. Surrounding the center are landscaped gardens open to the public. The center also hosts concerts, workshops, and special author events.

Photos (top): the former Turner Field; (middle left) the legendary Hank Aaron of the Braves; (middle right) kids playing in a fountain at Truist Park; (bottom) Jimmy Carter Presidential Library and Museum.

CENTER FOR PUPPETRY ARTS

After just three minutes in the Jim Henson Collection Gallery at the **Center for Puppetry Arts** (1404 Spring St. NW, 404/873-3391, www.puppet.org, 9am-5pm Tues.-Fri., 10am-5pm Sat., noon-5pm Sun., $12.50), I had to stop and clear my eyes. If you've ever been affected by puppetry—whether through *Sesame Street* and Henson's Muppets or through puppets of all kinds around the world—you should put this under-the-radar museum, theater, and workshop center on your list.

The center, devised by Atlanta businessman and puppeteer Vincent Anthony, runs educational programming where toddlers and older kids can learn puppetry and be wowed by the art form. It also hosts screenings of puppet-centric films and theatrical performances for all ages. It's home to the **Worlds of Puppetry Museum,** which features the largest collection anywhere of Henson's puppets. The Henson exhibit takes visitors through his career, from his early days producing commercials to his single-handedly changing the future of children's entertainment. You can see real Muppets here, including Miss Piggy, Gonzo, Big Bird, and Kermit the Frog. View Henson's early ideas scribbled on paper, and sing along with videos presented as part of the exhibit.

The **Global Collection** exhibit showcases puppets from across the world, some dating back several centuries. A special exhibit space changes annually, alternating focus between Henson and international puppetry.

FOOD

NEAR TRUIST PARK

Surprisingly, there is a great Tex-Mex restaurant near Truist Park. Head across The Perimeter and into The Battery for enchiladas, taco plates, and fantastic margaritas at **Superica** (455 Legends Pl. #800, The Battery, 770/675-6318, www.superica.com, 11am-10pm Mon.-Fri., 10am-11pm Sat., 10am-10pm Sun., under $50). Chef and restaurateur Ford Fry created this concept with a couple locations across the country, based on the food he enjoyed as a kid on the Gulf Coast of Texas, and it's some of the best Tex-Mex I've ever had. The crunchy tacos are stellar.

The Battery also has an outpost of local pizza favorite **Antico** (2605 Circle 75 Pkwy., The Battery, 678/890-2222, www.little-italia.com, 11am-10:30pm Mon.-Thurs., 11am-11pm Fri.-Sat., 11am-10pm Sun., under $40). Try the lasagna pizza, or go with a white-sauce option (Verdura is my pick). Sister concept Caffe Antico, which specializes in gelato and pastries, is also located here, and both are open late on game nights.

Instead of settling for a chain restaurant in the area surrounding the ballpark, drive two miles east to **Heirloom Market BBQ** (2243 Akers Mill Rd. SE, 770/612-2502, www.heirloommarketbbq.com, 11am-8pm Tues.-Sat., under $40) for a super experience that combines southern barbecue and Korean cuisine. You can get brisket and Korean pork, plus sides ranging from beans and mac and cheese to kimchi slaw and Korean sweet potatoes. As with many good barbecue spots, there should be a line, and the space is tiny, so give yourself some time.

OTHER NEIGHBORHOODS

The best barbecue in Atlanta may be inside a supermarket. Visit the **Kroger** (725 Ponce de Leon Ave. NE, 470/351-4222, 11am-8pm daily, under $30) just north of the Old Fourth Ward, where you'll find **B's Cracklin' Barbecue.** Here, pitmaster Bryan Furman serves up brisket, ribs, and sides like beans, fried okra, and corn bread.

Not too far away, in the southern end of the Old Fourth Ward, grab slices of authentic Jersey-style pie and crispy, cheesy Detroit pizza at **Nina & Rafi** (661 Auburn Ave. NE #220, 404/549-8997, www.ninaandrafi.com, 11am-midnight daily, under $40). The bright and well-windowed space has a cool, long bar and beautiful tile floors, plus outdoor seating.

Over the past few years, the East Atlanta Village neighborhood has become a hot spot for foodies. Chief among the reasons is **Argosy** (470 Flat Shoals Ave. SE, 404/577-0407, www.argosy-east.com, 5pm-2:30am Mon.-Fri., noon-2:30am Sat., 12:30pm-midnight Sun., under $50). This casual gastropub is set in a funky spot with two levels of seating, industrial touches, and leather couches for those who'd rather lounge a bit. The beer list here is impressive, including more than 40 taps and lots of bottles, and the food is well-executed American fare like burgers, sandwiches, and wood-fired pizza. Brunch is both popular and good.

A stalwart with big-time history, **The Busy Bee** (810 Martin Luther King Jr. Dr. SW, 404/525-9212, www.thebusybeecafe.com, 11am-7pm daily, under $40), located west of Downtown, is a must if it's your first time in town. Founded in 1947 by "Momma Lucy" Jackson, Busy Bee quickly became one of the places to be, especially for the African American community. Martin Luther King Jr. dined here, as have many civil rights leaders. You'll find top-notch soul food like fried chicken, candied yams, fried fish, ham hock (May-Oct. only), oxtail, and barbecue ribs. Busy Bee is typically packed, so reserve some time for the trip. Once you're inside, be sure to admire the photos of all the famous people who've eaten here.

At **Home Grown** (968 Memorial Dr. SE, 404/222-0455, www.homegrownga.com, 7am-3pm Mon.-Fri., 7am-2pm Sat.-Sun., under $20 breakfast and brunch, under $25 lunch) in the Reynoldstown neighborhood, chef and owner Kevin Clark's mission is to serve people who want good food. One of the best dining experiences you can have, the community-centric Home Grown serves up casual southern comfort food in a sunny diner. Breakfast is served all day, highlighted by the Comfy Chicken Biscuit (served open-faced in sausage gravy), while lunch includes homemade pimento cheese and fried green tomatoes (the Grant Stack), and a killer fried bologna sandwich on Texas toast. Music here darts from trap to Todd Rundgren, and the employees all seem to absolutely love the place.

BARS AND BREWERIES

NEAR TRUIST PARK

Close to Truist Park, inside The Battery, you'll find bland chain bars and restaurants. There is an exception in **Murph's** (2 Galleria Pkwy. #1C-27, 770/612-3356, www.eatatmurphs.com, 11am-9pm Sun.-Thurs., 11am-10pm Fri.-Sat.). Yes, it's in a mall, but it's co-owned

Antico pizzeria

by Braves legend Dale Murphy, possibly the nicest man in baseball history. You'll get the usual grub and drinks here, from burgers and wings to golden ales and bronze ales. On the wall are plenty of framed jerseys, donated by Murphy, who won the National League MVP award in 1982 and 1983.

Other than Murph's, you'll have to go four miles from the park before you find the next worthwhile option. **Ironmonger Brewing Company** (2129 Northwest Pkwy. SE #105, Marietta, 678/742-8551, www.ironmongerbrewing.com, 4pm-8pm Tues.-Sat.) is a reasonably fun brewery and taproom that's extra fun if you're into axe throwing. Yes, these folks have a designated space for this trendy activity—just make sure you're wearing closed-toe shoes. The beer runs the gamut in style and quality, making for a nice stop an hour or two before the game.

OTHER NEIGHBORHOODS

Monday Night Brewing (670 Trabert Ave. NW, 404/352-7703, www.mondaynightbrewing.com, 1pm-6pm Sun.-Thurs., 1pm-7pm Fri., noon-6pm Sat.) is named for the owners' original brew nights. You'll find indoor and outdoor space plus a variety of beers, with a decent share of IPAs. Food trucks stop by regularly. They also own the **Monday Night Brewing Garage** (933 Lee St. SW, 4pm-8pm Mon.-Fri., noon-8pm Sat., noon-6pm Sun.), which features barrel-aged and sour beers. This is a clean space with high ceilings and a relaxed vibe.

Beer lovers in town should visit **SweetWater Brewing Company** (195 Ottley Dr. NE, 770/876-0251, www.sweetwaterbrew.com, 3pm-8pm Wed.-Fri., noon-7pm Sat.-Sun.) for the history alone, as it's been brewing and serving ales since 1997. The taproom is outfitted with a spectacular rectangular bar, and outdoor seating options make this a great place to visit on a cooler afternoon or evening.

Scour a book to find your beer of choice at **The Porter Beer Bar** (1156 Euclid Ave. NE, 404/223-0393, www.theporterbeerbar.com, 11:30am-midnight Mon.-Thurs., 11:30am-2:30am Fri., 11am-midnight Sun.) in Little Five Points. In a cool, dimly lit bar with accommodating servers and bartenders, you'll get lost trying to find the perfect beer to accompany your buffalo shrimp po'boy or, if you're up for it, mussels and salt-and-vinegar popcorn.

The fun **Euclid Avenue Yacht Club** (1136 Euclid Ave. NE, 404/688-2582, www.theeayc.com, 3pm-2am Mon., noon-2:30am Tues.-Sat., noon-midnight Sun.) has been around since 1987 and never disappoints. Though it's not actually a yacht club, it has the air of one, with wood finishing and pastoral pictures. It's a fun bar with tons of cheap and wacky drinks, a relaxed vibe, and fun events like a burlesque trivia night. Food offerings include boiled peanuts and corn dogs. It's on the same block as The Porter Beer Bar.

People have had the greatest nights of their lives at **Sister Louisa's Church of the Living Room & Ping Pong Emporium** (466 Edgewood Ave. SE, 404/522-8276, www.sisterlouisaschurch.com, 5pm-3am Mon.-Sat., 5pm-midnight Sun.) in Downtown. This art gallery, bar, and table tennis hangout has plenty of artwork and other goodies that range from slightly blasphemous to code red. It's worth a trip if you want to spend a cheap beer or two taking in neon-tinged, sarcastic spirituality.

RECREATION

PARKS

At 189 acres, **Piedmont Park** (1320 Monroe Dr. NE, www.piedmontpark.org, 6am-11pm daily) provides a refreshing wealth of green space to the city, where residents and visitors enjoy picnic areas, ball fields, Lake Clara Meer, and a variety of annual festivals. Piedmont is home to the **Atlanta Botanical Garden** (1345 Piedmont Ave. NE, 404/876-5859, www.atlantabg.org, 9am-5pm Tues.-Sun., $22, $16 ages 3-12), where you can take a peaceful walk through an orchid house, an edible garden, a children's garden, and a popular Japanese garden with maples and rare bamboo.

Numerous city parks are sprinkled throughout Downtown Atlanta. The big one is **Centennial Olympic Park** (265 Park Ave. West NW), which was created as a gathering place for visitors during the 1996 Summer Olympics. It was also the site of the bombing on July 27, 1996, during the Olympics. These days, it serves as a sweeping stretch of green space that provides separation between the Midtown skyline and the landmarks that dot the park's west end. Check out the Fountain of Rings, an interactive water feature that synchronizes with music, or take a ride on **SkyView Atlanta** (168 Luckie St. NW, no phone, noon-11pm Sun.-Thurs., noon-midnight Fri., 10am-midnight Sat., $14, $13 seniors and students, $10 ages 3-11), a 20-story Ferris wheel that provides some high-quality views of the city.

Woodruff Park (91 Peachtree St. NW), previously Central City Park, is fully outfitted for the modern park lover. Amenities include a bocce ball court, table tennis, children's play area, and plenty of green space on which to stretch out. At the north end of the park is the **International Peace Fountain** (Auburn Ave. and Peachtree St.), an impressive water display built before the 1996 Olympics to honor Atlanta's place in the civil rights movement. It's a good place for a photo-op. The park hosts meditation and yoga sessions, plus a few Atlanta festivals.

Up in the northwest in Sandy Springs, you'll find the Chattahoochee River and its designated public-use site, the **Chattahoochee National Recreation Area.** For those wanting a quiet experience, I recommend going to **Powers Island** (5450 Interstate North Pkwy., Sandy Springs, 678/538-1200, sunrise-sunset daily, $5 parking). This area at the southern end of the park includes land east of the river and the small Powers Island, accessible by footbridge. You'll find plentiful parking, a 2.5-mile hiking trail—with one slight elevation spike—that loops and runs beside the river, and a kayak launch site accessible on the island. If you want to rent a kayak or tube, check out the **Nantahala Outdoor Center's Chattahoochee Outpost** (5450 Interstate North Pkwy., Sandy Springs, 404/596-7517, www.noc.com, $25-130). The NOC also hosts kayaking courses and a tube-and-brew experience in partnership with SweetWater Brewing Company.

SHOPPING

Atlanta is home to Mizuno, the sporting goods manufacturer that makes bats, gloves, and other equipment and apparel used in the majors. In 2017, it opened the **Mizuno**

Woodruff Park

Experience Center (875 Battery Ave. SE #740, The Battery, 770/675-6590, www.mizunousa.com, 11am-10pm daily), aimed at telling the story of the company and selling some merch along the way. Engage your talents in a bat swing simulator where you'll get a reading to determine your optimum bat weight and length, then buy a bat.

It wouldn't be a modern, mixed-use development district near a major league ballpark without a **Baseballism** (900 Battery Ave. SE #1015, 678/903-5437, www.baseballism.com, 10am-6pm Tues.-Sun.). This clothing store with locations across the country sells baseball-themed apparel that doesn't use official major league logos. So you can get a shirt that says "Win the BATL" in Braves red, but it's not a Braves shirt.

ACCOMMODATIONS

NEAR TRUIST PARK

If you want to stay up near the park and The Battery, you have a wealth of chain hotel options at your fingertips. All budgets are served, too.

Right next to the park, the **Omni Hotel at the Battery Atlanta** (2625 Circle 75 Pkwy., The Battery, 678/567-7327, www.omnihotels.com, $120-300) is the perfect stay if you want to be on top of the action. Walk outside and you'll be steps from Truist Park. Not only that, but some premium rooms and suites have views of the field. The elevated pool deck also offers a look into the park. Through the Omni, big spenders can get a helicopter tour of The Battery and the ballpark.

OTHER NEIGHBORHOODS

The **Highland Inn & Ballroom Lounge** (644 N. Highland Ave. NE, 404/874-5756, www.thehighlandinn.com, $60-120) is a fine option if you're on a budget. The 1920s-era building in the Poncey-Highland neighborhood is within walking distance of Ponce City Market and other Midtown destinations.

Although the rooms are on the smaller side, they're comfortable and manageable.

You may opt to stay at the **Hotel Clermont** (789 Ponce de Leon Ave., 470/485-0485, www.hotelclermont.com, $210-250), which has more than 90 rooms and suites, plus a rooftop bar and restaurant. All rooms have king or queen beds, plus tiled bathrooms and lounge chairs. For entertainment, you can simply go to the basement and visit the iconic **Clermont Lounge** (404/874-4783, 5pm-3am Mon.-Sat., under $20). The Clermont is a dive bar and strip club that's a combination of campy, dingy, and fantastical. It's a blast. My suggestion is to go late at night, order a beer and a shot, chat up some folks, and enjoy the show.

Downtown, **The Ellis Hotel** (176 Peachtree St. NW, 404/523-5155, www.ellishotel.com, $140-200) is a high-rise boutique with 127 rooms and suites. Accommodations are simple and clean, and the hotel has a women-only floor, a dog-friendly floor, and a fresh-air floor, where each room has a 24-hour air-filtering machine plus sealed mattresses and pillows.

GETTING AROUND

PUBLIC TRANSIT

Take public transportation via **MARTA** (404/848-5000, www.itsmarta.com), which has four rapid transit lines primarily inside the city's loop. All lines intersect at **Five Points** (30 Alabama St. SW). The north-south Red and Gold Lines head to the airport and, going north, break off into the suburbs. The Green and Blue Lines run west to east and provide connections to tourist attractions like the King Center, CNN Center, and Phillips Arena. The system operates 5am-2am on weekdays and 6am-2am on weekends; generally, trains arrive every 12-20 minutes.

You need to purchase a **Breeze Card** at a MARTA station vending machine. The cards are $2, and it's an additional $2.50 for each fare. Inside the city, MARTA has many bus

STRETCH YOUR LEGS

It's a 6.5-hour drive from Atlanta to Tampa, Florida, so you might want to stop and take a few quick breaks. Here are two interesting places where you can do just that.

VALDOSTA, GEORGIA
About four hours south of Atlanta, this small city has a few art galleries and museums. Check out the Annette Howell Turner Center for the Arts (527 N. Patterson St., 229/247-2787, www.turnercenter.org), with public exhibit galleries including an East African collection. For a bite to eat, there's Steel Magnolias (132 N. Patterson St., 229/259-0010, www.steelmagnoliasvaldosta.com, 11am-2pm and 5pm-9pm Tues.-Sat., 11am-2:30pm Sun., under $40), serving cozy southern cooking at affordable prices.

GAINESVILLE, FLORIDA
Home to the University of Florida, this city about 1.5 hours north of Tampa has a true college vibe. You'll be glad to stop by Cypress & Grove Brewing Company (1001 NW 4th St., 352/376-4993, www.cypressandgrove.com, 3pm-9pm Mon.-Fri., noon-9pm Sat.-Sun.), which has indoor and outdoor seating plus pretty good brews. It's in an old ice factory.

routes. Breeze Cards are recommended if you're riding the bus, but you can also insert coins or cash (up to $5) in the fare box.

TAXI, UBER, AND LYFT

You're going to want to take Uber. Prices are much cheaper for Uber than for Lyft and cabs—we're talking up to 40 percent cheaper.

CAR

Because attractions are spread out a bit in Atlanta, you're likely going to need a car. Be aware that Atlanta has a lot of traffic, so factor in extra driving time.

I-285 loops around the city, connecting with every major highway that branches out from the city, starting with the north-south I-75, which continues northwest to Chattanooga, Tennessee, before straddling the western edge of the Blue Ridge Mountains toward Lexington, Kentucky, and Cincinnati, Ohio. I-75 leaves the city to the southeast, heading toward Tampa and Miami. Its mirror image is I-85, which heads northeast to Charlotte, North Carolina, and Richmond, Virginia. It leaves the city southwest to Montgomery, Alabama. I-75 and I-85 cut through the center of the city. The major west-east arterial is I-20, which goes west to Birmingham, Alabama, and all the way to Dallas, Texas, and east into South Carolina.

TAMPA AND
St. PETERSBURG
TAMPA BAY RAYS

By the 1910s, it was customary for major league baseball teams to pack up and head to a warmer, quieter part of the country to prepare for the upcoming season. At first, locations included Hot Springs, Arkansas, and cities like Tulsa, Oklahoma, and Phoenix, Arizona. But in 1913, the Chicago Cubs decided to spend the spring before the season in Tampa, and that was the beginning of a fruitful relationship. For more than 100 years, teams have chosen the Florida Gulf Coast as a second home, making it an area stuffed with baseball history.

For two months every year, this chunk of Florida is chock-full of baseball fans. There are Yankees fans in Tampa and Phillies fans in Clearwater, plus Blue Jays backers in Dunedin and Tigers followers in Lakeland. When the weather warms up

view from the concourse at Tropicana Field

and teams head back to their homes for the regular season, the Tampa and St. Pete area turns its attention to the Tampa Bay Rays.

The Rays started play in 1998 as the Devil Rays, playing in a nondescript dome called Tropicana Field. The Devil Rays weren't good, losing more than 90 games in each of their first 10 seasons. Then, in 2008, after changing their name to the succinct Rays (like a ray of sun rather than the sea creature), they turned it around and won the American League pennant, losing the World Series in five games to the Phillies. The change was due to a maverick front office that mastered the art of drafting and developing new talent while surrounding that youth with fine role players.

The philosophy stuck and has carried on in Tampa ever since. No team is better at identifying good young hitters and pitchers en route to playoff appearances. The Rays have made the playoffs multiple times since that charmed 2008 season.

The Rays' skill at finding talent is a happy result of its low position in baseball's economic hierarchy. Because the team makes less money than others, it usually gets an additional draft pick most years, and it typically trades its top talent (who are nearing big raises) for promising prospects. The team

doesn't make much money, and Tropicana Field's location is convenient only for St. Petersburg residents; it's less so for folks living across the bay in Tampa. The lack of revenue has always been a problem, and it could at some point lead to the team moving out of the area. Another proposed option would have the Rays playing half of their games in the area and playing the other half in Montreal. Yes, one day, the Tampa Bay Rays may become the Transcontinental Rays.

PLANNING YOUR TIME

You can spend a **weekend** in the Tampa-St. Petersburg area and cover good ground, but if you've never seen any of the Florida State League parks nearby, you might want to reserve **another 2-4 days** for **side trips** to cities like Clearwater, Dunedin, and Bradenton. Just be sure to get all your tickets ahead of time.

You can get an inexpensive or moderately priced room in **Downtown St. Petersburg** and be close to nightlife options and Tropicana Field. Plus, the Salvador Dalí Museum is within walking distance. I prefer staying in St. Pete, but there are more rooms in Tampa.

You don't have to worry about the weather when visiting the Trop, since it's an enclosed dome. But do be mindful of visiting in

August or September, as that's **hurricane season,** and it's not out of the question that storms could wreak real havoc on the area and even postpone a game.

Outside of the stadium, the region's weather in the **spring** is just dandy, with temperatures in the 70s and 80s with plenty of sunshine. **Mid-summer** means **humidity** with the mercury climbing well into the 90s, and evening **sun-showers** (when light rain falls while the sun is shining) are common.

GETTING THERE

AIR

Tampa International Airport

The major airport in the area is **Tampa International Airport** (TPA, 4100 George J. Bean Pkwy., Tampa, 813/870-8700, www.tampaairport.com). To and from here, you can fly **Air Canada** (888/247-2262, www.aircanada.com), **American Airlines** (800/433-7300, www.aa.com), **Delta** (800/221-1212, www.delta.com), **Frontier** (800/432-1359, www.flyfrontier.com), **jetBlue** (800/538-2583, www.jetblue.com), **Southwest** (800/435-9792, www.southwest.com), **Spirit** (801/401-2222, www.spirit.com), and **United** (800/864-8331, www.united.com).

AIRPORT TRANSPORTATION

For rental cars, hop on the **SkyConnect train** at the main terminal. That'll take you to the **rental car center,** where all major companies have desks.

As for public transit, the only option is to take a **bus** operated by **HART** (Hillsborough Area Regional Transit, 813/254-4278, www.gohart.org, $1-3) or **PSTA** (Pinellas Suncoast Transit Authority, 727/540-1900, www.psta.net, $1.10-2.25). Buses leave from the rental car center. HART serves Tampa with a network of buses; PSTA travels around St. Petersburg and Clearwater.

St. Pete-Clearwater International Airport

You can also fly nonstop into **St. Pete-Clearwater International Airport** (PIE, 14700 Terminal Blvd. #221, St. Petersburg, 727/453-7800, www.fly2pie.com), which is served primarily by **Allegiant** (702/505-8888, www.allegiantair.com). You can get here from Cleveland, Cincinnati, Indianapolis, Pittsburgh, and smaller cities across the East and Midwest. Most major rental car companies are at the baggage claim area, and a few more are off-site, accessible via individual shuttles. The airport is just 15 minutes north of Tropicana Field via I-275 and FL-686/688.

Sarasota-Bradenton International Airport

Another option, about an hour south of Tampa, is **Sarasota-Bradenton International Airport** (SRQ, 6000 Airport Cir., Sarasota, 941/359-2770, www.srq-airport.com). Airlines that fly in and out of here include Air Canada, Allegiant, American Airlines, Delta, Frontier, jetBlue, and United. Among the destinations served are East Coast cities like Boston, New York, Philadelphia, Washington DC, Charlotte, and Atlanta, plus midwestern points like Chicago, Minneapolis-St. Paul, and St. Louis. Head to baggage claim to **rent a car,** as all the major companies have desks there. No public transit connection exists here.

CAR

The fastest way to Tampa-St. Pete from **Atlanta** is a **6.5-hour** drive south on **I-75.** This **460-mile** jaunt passes through many small towns and cities throughout Georgia and Florida.

An alternate, slower route that doesn't include interstates leaves Atlanta south on **US-41.** That turns into **US-19,** which you'll take south into Florida. It merges with US-98, but stay on US-19 as it hugs the Gulf of Mexico and enters the Tampa-St. Petersburg-Clearwater area. This option is an **8.5-hour, 480-mile** drive.

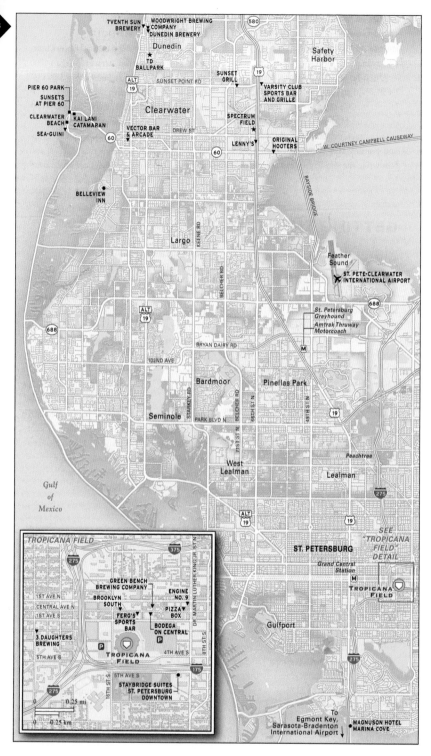

7VENTH SUN BREWERY
WOODWRIGHT BREWING COMPANY
DUNEDIN BREWERY
Dunedin
TD BALLPARK
SUNSET POINT RD
SUNSET GRILL
VARSITY CLUB SPORTS BAR AND GRILLE
Safety Harbor
ALT 19
PIER 60 PARK
SUNSETS AT PIER 60
CLEARWATER BEACH
KAI LANI CATAMARAN
SEA-GUINI
Clearwater
VECTOR BAR & ARCADE
DREW ST
SPECTRUM FIELD
LENNY'S
ORIGINAL HOOTERS
W. COURTNEY CAMPBELL CAUSEWAY
BELLEVIEW INN
Largo
KEENE RD
BELCHER RD
BAYSIDE BRIDGE
Feather Sound
ST. PETE-CLEARWATER INTERNATIONAL AIRPORT
ALT 19
688
St. Petersburg Greyhound
Amtrak Thruway Motorcoach
M
BRYAN DAIRY RD
102ND AVE
STARKEY RD
Bardmoor
Pinellas Park
PARK BLVD N
BELCHER RD
66TH ST N
49TH ST N
19
Seminole
71ST ST N
Peachtree
West Lealman
Lealman
Gulf of Mexico
ALT 19
275
19
ST. PETERSBURG
SEE "TROPICANA FIELD" DETAIL
Grand Central Station
M
TROPICANA FIELD
Gulfport
275
To Egmont Key, Sarasota-Bradenton International Airport
MAGNUSON HOTEL MARINA COVE

TROPICANA FIELD
275
375
1ST AVE N
CENTRAL AVE N
1ST AVE S
GREEN BENCH BREWING COMPANY
BROOKLYN SOUTH
FERG'S SPORTS BAR
ENGINE NO. 9
PIZZA BOX
BODEGA ON CENTRAL
DR. MARTIN LUTHER KING JR. ST N
8TH ST S
3 DAUGHTERS BREWING
5TH AVE S
P
TROPICANA FIELD
P
4TH AVE S
16TH ST S
275
5TH AVE S
175
STAYBRIDGE SUITES ST. PETERSBURG DOWNTOWN
0   0.25 mi
0   0.25 km

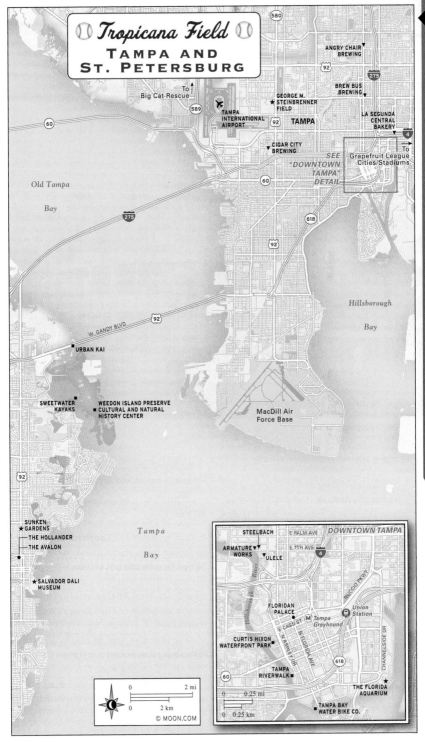

🏀 *Tropicana Field* ⚾
TAMPA AND
ST. PETERSBURG

580

ANGRY CHAIR
BREWING

92

275

BREW BUS
BREWING

To
Big Cat Rescue

589

GEORGE M.
★ STEINBRENNER
FIELD

60

TAMPA
INTERNATIONAL
AIRPORT

92

TAMPA

LA SEGUNDA
CENTRAL
BAKERY

4
To

CIGAR CITY
BREWING

SEE
"DOWNTOWN
TAMPA"
DETAIL

Grapefruit League
Cities/Stadiums

Old Tampa

Bay

275

60

618

92

Hillsborough

Bay

W. GANDY BLVD.

92

URBAN KAI

SWEETWATER
KAYAKS

WEEDON ISLAND PRESERVE
CULTURAL AND NATURAL
HISTORY CENTER

MacDill Air
Force Base

92

SUNKEN
★ GARDENS

THE HOLLANDER

THE AVALON

Tampa

Bay

★ SALVADOR DALI
MUSEUM

STEELBACH

E PALM AVE

DOWNTOWN TAMPA

ARMATURE ▼▼
WORKS ▼ULELE

E 7TH AVE

4

FLORIDAN
PALACE

M Tampa
Greyhound

Union
Station

CURTIS HIXON
WATERFRONT PARK

618

TAMPA
RIVERWALK ■

60

THE FLORIDA
AQUARIUM

0   2 mi

0   2 km

© MOON.COM

0   0.25 mi

0   0.25 km

TAMPA BAY
WATER BIKE CO.

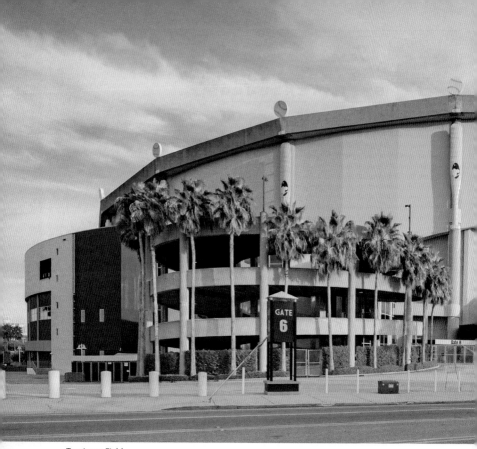

Tropicana Field

TRAIN

You can travel along the East Coast and into Tampa via **Amtrak** (800/872-7245, www.amtrak.com). It drops you off at **Union Station** (601 N. Nebraska Ave., Tampa), which opened in 1912 and was restored in 1998. The only Amtrak route that stops here is the **Silver Star,** part of the Silver Service route. The Silver Star starts in New York City, but as it reaches Lakeland in Central Florida, it makes a detour to Tampa before heading back to Lakeland and running south to Miami. There's no direct connection from Atlanta to Tampa on Amtrak.

From Tampa, you can hop on an **Amtrak Thruway motorcoach,** which carries passengers across the bay to a **bus stop** (5251 110th Ave. N., Clearwater) a few miles north of St. Petersburg. This route also reaches Orlando, Sarasota, and Fort Myers.

BUS

You can get a ride with **Greyhound** (www.greyhound.com), which will drop you at the **Tampa Greyhound bus station** (601 Polk St., Tampa, 813/229-2174), located in Downtown Tampa. From **Atlanta,** a trip to Tampa starts at around $35 and lasts about 12 hours, with multiple stops (including Orlando).

As an alternative, you can head to the **St. Petersburg Greyhound bus station** (3801 70th Ave. N., Pinellas Park, 727/520-1951). The trip here from Atlanta is also about 12 hours, sometimes longer, and will cost about $50. This station is a 15-minute drive north from Tropicana Field.

Tropicana Field

Aesthetically speaking, **Tropicana Field** (1 Tropicana Dr., St. Petersburg, www.mlb.com/rays) is the most unattractive ballpark in baseball. It's a funny-looking dome, a large indoor arena that feels better suited for Wrestlemania or a Paul McCartney concert. The dome is made of concrete. There's Astroturf on the field. Balls often hit the catwalks spanning the ceiling. Beyond its looks, this is a disorienting place: Sitting down low in the stands, you feel like you can touch center field. Tropicana is unlike anything baseball has taught us a stadium is supposed to be.

And yet, no major league franchise gets the fan experience better than the Tampa Bay Rays. Come alone, come with a buddy,

come with your family; no matter who you're with, you're bound to have fun here. The Rays clearly thought hard about vendors, concessions, and what sorts of ancillary experiences people want. Tropicana features a hidden museum, publicly accessible outdoor party areas, and even a ray touch tank like the kind you'll find in an aquarium. Sometimes a home run ball actually splashes into the tank.

The grounds crew dances here. Fans play weird instruments, scream, cheer, and are generally excited about baseball. You might find that you really start to love watching baseball here.

Then you walk out of the building, on the west end of Downtown St. Petersburg, and walk a couple blocks up to Central Avenue where all the bars and breweries reside. You have a beer or two, you talk to passionate

Rays fans, and you'll probably start to understand the appeal.

Yes, Tropicana Field is unquestionably the biggest eyesore in baseball. But just as you shouldn't underestimate the smart front office here, you also can't judge the book by its cover.

ORIENTATION

There are six entry gates at Tropicana Field, most of which are located along 16th Street South and 5th Avenue South. Gates open 90 minutes before first pitch, but **The Outfielder Bar & Grill** (Gate 7) lets folks inside three hours before the game starts, unless it's a day game. Also open three hours early is **Ballpark & Rec** (center field). Much of the parking at the Trop is behind the stadium, facing the outfield.

TICKETS AND SEATING

Pricing

Tickets are pretty darn cheap for Rays games. That is, unless the **Yankees, Red Sox,** or another team that travels well (draws crowds) and doesn't regularly visit, like the **Cardinals, Cubs, Dodgers,** or **Phillies,** is in town. Expect ticket prices to be more than 130 percent higher when the Rays play the Yankees, who have plenty of fans in the Tampa area since the Bronx Bombers spend spring training here. For bouts against the Red Sox and Phillies (those teams also have their spring training site nearby, and Philadelphians love retiring to the Tampa area), ticket prices might be close to 100 percent more expensive than a normal game. If the Rays are hosting the Athletics on a weekday, a 100-level seat could cost you just $30. If the Yankees are in town, and it's a weekend, that same seat may be priced at around $80. For a typical game, you can usually get a seat in the 200 or 300 level for less than $20.

Seating Plan

The Trop is unusual in its section numbering: The even-numbered sections are on the right side of home plate, and the odd-numbered

sections are left of the plate. At home plate are sections 101 and 102, and the sections fan out in opposite directions, increasing in number by two with each section.

In the **100 level,** the lowest rows of seats by the field make up the **fieldside box** (sections 101-126). Just above those rows is **lower box preferred** (sections 101-122). The highest part of the lower level around the infield is split between the **lower box** (sections 107-128) and the **Rays Club** (sections 104-126). In the corners, you'll find **Loge 105** (sections 129-138), and in left and right field is the area called **outfield** (sections 139-150).

Upstairs in the **200 level,** you'll find the **press level** (sections 203-224), which is not the press box, and **club boxes,** which stop short of the foul poles.

In left field, you'll find a **third level (300 level)** that holds the **GTE Financial Party Deck** (sections 341-355). There's also a third level of seats around the infield, but the Rays don't sell tickets for that area because they haven't been able to fill the park enough to justify doing so.

Where to Buy Tickets

Considering the Rays don't typically sell out, you should be fine grabbing tickets through the team's own **box office,** especially just before the game. If you want to try your luck at third-party sellers, there's **StubHub** and **SeatGeek,** where you often can find cheap tickets very close to first pitch.

You can also use the **MLB Ballpark app** to try to upgrade your seats, but only if you purchase tickets via the Rays.

Best Seats

Since the Rays play exclusively **indoors,** you won't have to battle the sun when attending a game at the Trop. And since seats are usually inexpensive and are never too far away from the action, it's hard to go wrong in terms of getting a solid view of the game.

Don't pay for the expensive seats closer to the field. If you want to sit around the infield in the 100 level, just grab seats in the **middle to back rows of any section.**

YOUR BEST DAY AT TROPICANA FIELD

Before going to that Rays game tonight, make this imagined schedule your plan.

10 HOURS BEFORE FIRST PITCH
Visit the iconic Tampa bakery and sandwich shop **La Segunda Central Bakery** for your morning pastry and *café cubano,* and order a Cuban sandwich to go. The sandwich can be for later—if you're able to contain your excitement.

9.5 HOURS BEFORE FIRST PITCH
Get familiar with the ecology of the Tampa-St. Pete area by visiting the **Florida Aquarium.** If you have some money to spare, go diving with sharks.

6.5 HOURS BEFORE FIRST PITCH
For lunch, trek over to **Curtis Hixon Waterfront Park** and have a picnic with that Cuban sandwich. Afterward, do an easy half-mile stroll on the **Tampa Riverwalk.**

5.5 HOURS BEFORE FIRST PITCH
If you're going to visit one brewery in the area, make it **Cigar City Brewing.** Be sure to sip some of their trademark Jai Alai beer.

4 HOURS BEFORE FIRST PITCH
Whether you're staying in Tampa or St. Petersburg, use this time to freshen up. From this point on, I recommend using ride-sharing for transportation.

Florida Aquarium

2.5 HOURS BEFORE FIRST PITCH
Before going to the stadium, grab yourself a stool at **Green Bench Brewing Company.** Enjoy the good beer and lively atmosphere.

1 HOUR BEFORE FIRST PITCH
Head to Tropicana Field and start by pregaming at **Ballpark & Rec.** Take some time to stroll around at the **Ted Williams Museum and Hitters Hall of Fame.**

If you're with the kids, get some energy out at **Raymond's Tree House** and pose for a cardboard memento at the **Topps Make Your Own Baseball Card booth.**

DURING THE GAME
Grab some firecracker shrimp at **RumFish,** and experience one of the most unique 15 minutes of any baseball game by visiting the **Rays Touch Experience.**

AFTER THE GAME
Head back to Central Avenue. You'll want to get some inexpensive beer at **Ferg's Sports Bar.** End the evening with a quick bite at **Bodega on Central.** Be sure to look down at the sidewalk for plaques signifying the **Jim Healey & Jack Lake Baseball Boulevard.**

Tampa Riverwalk

For example: If you sit in **row R** of a 100-level section, you'll pay about half as much as what you'd pay for a seat one row closer in Q (so start at row R and work your way back). Or you can simply buy a ticket for a **seat up high** (anywhere in the 200 or 300 level) for cheap, then make your way to the 100 level later in the game (this works best if the crowd is light and you find a nice usher).

If you're looking to party, you can grab a seat in the **GTE Financial Party Deck**

GAME COSTS

Tickets: Tickets: You're in luck. The most inexpensive seats here cost **$10,** while the average good seat is more like **$30.**

Hot dog: A **$6** wiener is a touch pricier than you might want. The loaded and fried ones are more like **$8** and represent a better bang for the buck.

Beer: The cheaper domestic stuff is **$9.50** per can, while the premium options are more like **$11.50.** That's about average across the league.

Parking: If you're paying more than **$15,** something is wrong. Parking prices here are decent relative to the rest of the league.

(sections 341-355) for really cheap—even the first-row seats are affordable. These do have the worst view in the park, though, as they're pushed back way out in left field.

KNOW BEFORE YOU GO

Tailgating is allowed at Tropicana Field, but you must keep your party to your parking spot (you can purchase additional spots for more room). Grills must be gas-only. The tailgating scene at the Trop is pretty light, but it's nonetheless a fun option.

Tropicana Field allows only **diaper bags** and **medically necessary bags,** and those have to adhere to the size guidelines of 16 by 16 by 8 inches. No backpacks whatsoever are allowed. **Soft-sided coolers** no more than 16 by 16 by 8 inches and containing food are permitted. Food must be wrapped as individual servings. Plain plastic **water bottles** no larger than one liter and single-serving children's **juice boxes** are the only drinks allowed in.

Surprisingly, **bats** and **brooms** (for series "sweeps") are allowed. So are **TVs** and **radios** (smaller than 16 by 16 by 8 inches). You can bring a **stroller** inside; it's best if it folds up and can be parked under a seat, away from

aisles and walkways. If not, check the stroller with guest services at Gate 1. **Umbrellas** are also allowed inside, but they must be placed under your seat.

The Rays have a program called **Tag-a-Kid.** Visit guest services at Gate 3 to get your kid a wristband that details the child's ticketed seat location (just in case they get separated from you).

The Trop is completely **cashless,** so bring your credit and/or debit card, or plan to use Apple Pay or Google Pay.

Accessibility

If you need **wheelchair access** to the stadium, head to **gate 5.** Assistance is provided from gate to seat, and from seat to gate when the game ends. This service is offered on a first-come, first-served basis only.

There are five **elevators** (gates 1, 2, 3, 5, 6) that stop at both the 100 and 200 levels.

Guests needing **accessible parking** will find the most options in **Lots 1 and 7,** though there are no guarantees.

GETTING THERE

Public Transit

It's possible to take public transit to Tropicana Field. With **PSTA** (www.psta.net, $2.25), you should take the **Route 15 bus,** which connects to **Grand Central Station** (Central Ave. and 32nd St., St. Petersburg). On the opposite end, it heads into Downtown St. Pete for a quick loop.

Driving

The best mode of transportation for getting to the Trop is to drive (or opt for ride-sharing). There are multiple **parking lots** around the ballpark, and no space is more than $15, making this one of the more affordable and accessible options in the majors. If you're among the first 100 cars to park at the Trop with at least four people in your car, parking is free.

You could try to find a parking spot in Downtown St. Petersburg, but be wary of meters and parking limitations. It can be tough to find a spot, and you may end

BE A FAN

The fan experience at Tropicana Field is top-notch, helped along by the fact that the fans themselves are good folks. They may be rooting for a small-market team that doesn't get tons of love, but they have a lot of fun with it.

I have one word for you: **cowbells.** Back in 2006, the Rays started giving out cowbells to fans. Why? Because of that *Saturday Night Live* sketch making fun of super serious 1970s studio musicianship by way of the classic Blue Öyster Cult song "Don't Fear the Reaper." Owner Stuart Sternberg was so amused by the sketch that he decided the Rays also needed more cowbell. Some years ago, the Rays instituted a set of guidelines for when to ring the cowbells, so that they're not just blasting throughout the game. Fans are instructed to ring their bells when a Rays pitcher has two strikes against a batter, when a Rays player gets on base, or when the Rays score a run.

Watch when the **grounds crew** comes out in the middle of each game. Sometimes one of those crew members will just spontaneously break out in a dance. That's the **dancing grounds crew member,** an entertainment fixture at the Trop.

up walking quite a distance to reach the stadium.

PARK FEATURES AND SIGHTS

Out in left field in an area the Rays call Grand Slam Alley, find an area of arcade games and simulators sponsored by **GameTime** (section 133), a southeastern U.S.-based chain of arcades. The area here is made for adolescents and tweens, though of course, older "kids" can try their hand at some games, too.

In right field, smaller kids can have some fun at **Raymond's Tree House** (section 148), the hangout of Raymond, the Rays mascot (who is a furry blue creature labeled a "sea dog"). There's a chalkboard here, plus workstations with creative activities. Nearby is the **Topps Make Your Own Baseball Card booth** (section 148, $5). You'll get a picture taken against an "outfield" backdrop, and the staff there will turn it into your very own trading card.

Ray Touch Tank

The Tampa Bay Rays take their name seriously, giving fans a chance to visit the

35-foot-long, 10,000-gallon ray tank in the **Rays Touch Experience** (section 150, right center field) and get close up to one of the cownose rays swimming about. Walk up a staircase to the second level to enter the room (if the room is filled to capacity, you'll have to wait a moment), wash your hands at the designated station, then find an open space at the tank to peer in and potentially graze a ray while it swims past. When finished, be sure to wash your hands again.

The tank is in the open in right center field, and there have been a few occasions of a hitter pulverizing a pitch into the tank for a home run. The most famous: A walk-off blast by Jose Lobaton in Game 3 of the 2013 American League Division Series against the Red Sox—one of the biggest home runs in Rays' history.

Ted Williams Museum and Hitters Hall of Fame

You may be surprised that at Tropicana Field, home to one of the Boston Red Sox's biggest rivals, you can find the **Ted Williams Museum** (Gate 1, www.tedwilliamsmuseum.com, free). The original Ted Williams Museum was located about 85 miles north of the Tampa-St. Pete area in Hernando, Florida, one of Williams's former homes. It lasted a dozen years before having to shutter, but all the exhibits were moved to the Trop, where they remain today. The museum offers a retrospective of Williams's life from his youth to his early baseball career, and from his service in the military to his later years. See autographed jerseys, memorabilia, and plenty of photographs. Climb stairs near the rotunda at Gate 1 to find this semi-hidden gem.

Continue with the **Hitters Hall of Fame,** an interesting collection of exhibits featuring some of the game's greatest hitters ... and some who were just pretty good. For example, there's Hank Aaron and Jim Thome, then Lou Piniella, who before becoming a manager had an 18-year career that was, well, pretty good. Nonetheless, it's a worthy, fun, and free jaunt through baseball history with plenty of jerseys, photos, and other pieces of memorabilia in cases.

162 Landing

Tropicana is home to a group party seating area called **162 Landing** (section 139). Any and every baseball fan should walk by here when visiting. The seating area is named for game 162, specifically the night of September 28, 2011, and its entrance includes a timeline of that night. This was one of the most thrilling regular season nights in baseball history, full of playoff implications, insane plays, and shocking finishes. In order to sneak into the postseason that night, the Rays had to defeat the Yankees—and they needed the Orioles to win against the Red Sox. With the Yankees leading 7-0 in the eighth inning, the Rays rallied. They scored six runs in the eighth, then one in the ninth to tie. Soon after that, the Sox blew a one-run lead in the ninth inning of their game; Baltimore ended the game with a walk-off. Just after that, Evan Longoria's home run in the 12th won the Rays' game and put them in the postseason. At 162 Landing, you can relive the magic of one of the coolest nights in baseball history.

FOOD AND DRINKS

If you enter through Gate 7 in left center field, you can get right into **The Outfielder Bar & Grill** (Gate 7). It's called a full-service restaurant, but think of it more like a beer bar with food service. They serve burgers, pulled pork nachos, hot dogs, wings, and other ballpark staples. Don't eat here if you want variety. The beer list is decent, however. You're likely to find brews from locals like Cigar City and Crooked Thumb, plus Pennsylvania favorite Yuengling.

For a little more fun, head upstairs to **Ballpark & Rec** (center field). This bright space of light blues and yellows has Skee-Ball machines and other arcade games, plenty of seating, and an expansive outdoor patio with yard games and picnic tables. This is the spot to visit before the game; it opens three hours ahead of first pitch.

The Trop has a few dedicated food-and-drink areas that act as miniature food halls. Grab a bite at one of the vendors in the area, and either pull up a chair or stool at a nearby table or take the grub back to your ticketed seat. In the deepest part of the park is the **Budweiser Porch** (center field), home to a number of stands that will change from time to time but offer street foods, loaded hot dogs, meaty goodness, and more. Also here is **RumFish,** which serves up mahi-mahi tacos and my favorite, firecracker shrimp in boom boom sauce. You can order food at one of the touch screens in the area, or you can go to the specific vendor.

You can also grab grub at the **First Base Food Hall** (100 level) or the **Third Base Food Hall** (100 level). You'll find **Bird & Batter** at both locations, serving up chicken-based goodies like sandwiches and tenders. Also at both are **Central Burger,** which is, of course, a burger joint; **Whoa Doggy's,** a hot dog and corn dog spot; and **Kahwa,** which brews up espresso and bakes cinnamon rolls and other pastries. Look for **Pacific Counter** (First Base Food Hall) for sushi bowls, spam musubi, and seaweed salad. I also recommend the barbecue pulled pork nachos at **Sizzle** (Third Base Food Hall, GTE Deck).

For a good Cuban sandwich at the park, try **Cubanos** (section 121), which also sells a Reubano and a *medianoche* sandwich (pork, ham, swiss cheese, pickles, and mustard on soft bread). Try **Walk Off Tacos** (section 107) for good tacos and street corn—more specifically, a giant ear of corn with Tajín (a chili-lime seasoning) and *queso blanco* (a crumbly white cheese).

If you're getting a soft drink, buy the **all-you-can-drink** option and go back as often as you please to a **Coca-Cola Refresh Station** (sections 142, 149, 212, GTE Deck).

For more booze, the Trop has **Vinfielder** (section 208) for wine drinkers and **Cooperstown Cocktails** (section 128) for the spirited ones. A decent selection of local craft beer can be found at **Craft Beer Corner** (section 136). Tampa-based brewery **Coppertail Brewing** (sections 113 and 122) has two stands.

EVENTS

Fans are permitted to seek **autographs** either until **batting practice** ends or until 40 minutes before first pitch when there is no batting practice. The Rays request that fans wait at field level on the outfield side of each dugout.

Sundays at the Trop are **Family Fun Days.** All kids ages 14 and under can **run**

the bases, as long as they get to the First Base Food Hall at the end of the game. The Rays also put out some games on the field with live music playing, to keep families on the field a little longer after the game ends. That live music is played by **DJ Kitty,** a full-size mascot version of a viral video cat who hyped up fans in 2010.

Each year the Hitters Hall of Fame hosts an **induction ceremony** (Feb.) at the ballpark. There, the hall welcomes a new player, and a number of other awards are given out, including a pitching prize named for late Hall of Famer Roy Halladay, and a lifetime achievement award.

Tours

The Rays conduct behind-the-scenes **tours** (727/825-3448, dates vary) of Tropicana Field. Highlights include a run through the Ted Williams Hitters' Hall of Fame and the ray touch tank.

SHOPPING

The **Rays Republic Main Team Store** (Gate 1, open during all games, closes one hour after final out, 10am-6pm Mon.-Fri., 10am-4pm Sat. non-game days) is a two-story shop with all the usual stuff: T-shirts, jerseys, hats, and

firecracker shrimp in boom boom sauce at RumFish

clothing for all ages. There are also some fun finds: leather chairs, anyone?

The Rays Republic stores include the **First Base Team Store** (section 128) and the **Third Base Team Stor**e (section 127), which offer a smaller inventory of the most popular merch. The **New Era Hat Shop** (section 115) has all the caps you might want. **The Rays 'Em Right Kids Store** (right field, section 150) has fun stuff for children. The **Tervis Store** (Budweiser Porch, center field) sells drinkware. There are also two **kiosks** (sections 105, 205) that feature new stuff. Finally, there's an **authentics store** (Gate 1) that has game-used items.

TAMPA AND ST. PETERSBURG SIGHTS

When in Downtown St. Pete, look closely where you walk. You may come across one of the plaques of the **Jim Healey & Jack Lake Baseball Boulevard** (throughout St. Petersburg). Healey and Lake were instrumental in getting the Rays to the Tampa Bay area, and in 1998, a series of historical markers were laid on sidewalks across the city. You can try to document the whole set by starting at longtime baseball field **Al Lang Stadium** (230 1st St., St. Petersburg) and heading up to Central Avenue to the Trop. The information on the plaques is sometimes interesting, like on the one that details the origins of the Rays. Others are less so, but the walk is entertaining anyway.

STEINBRENNER FIELD

Tampa is home to **Yankees spring training,** and the Bronx Bombers take the field every February at what's now called **George M. Steinbrenner Field** (1 Steinbrenner

Photos (from top to bottom): Steinbrenner Field in Tampa; Salvador Dalí Museum; the Sunken Gardens.

Dr., Tampa). Since this is the home of the Yankees, you'd better believe there are some luxuries that other fans do not get during spring training.

Seating Plan

At Steinbrenner Field, the **100 level** spans from shallow right field in foul territory to shallow left field in foul territory. There are higher-priced box seats down low. A second level of seating, the **200 level,** is behind the 100 level, but there's just one concourse. The **3rd Base Club** on the third-base line and the **Bullpen Club** on the first-base line are **standing areas** perfect for enjoying a beer and casually watching the game. Access to their **rooftops** is sold as a premium package. **Loge boxes** at the top of the seating area offer a more spacious and all-inclusive experience with a buffet, best for groups.

In right center field, you'll find the **Seminole Hard Rock Cabanas,** a premium option where guests (usually groups) can sit back in comfortable chairs at a covered area overlooking the whole field. Cabanas get a catered buffet of stadium favorites, plus cocktail service. If you're a die-hard Yankees fan who's going to Tampa with a group, this is the best option for you.

Food

Most of the food at the ballpark is of the basic baseball variety—burgers, loaded fries, and hot dogs. You can get a family meal (probably better for two people) of eight chicken tenders and a pound of fries in a souvenir bucket, and there's Central Texas-style barbecue of brisket and pork at the park, thanks to a 500-pound on-site smoker.

SALVADOR DALÍ MUSEUM

Experience the wild world of the acclaimed Spanish surrealist artist at the **Salvador Dalí Museum** (1 Dali Blvd., St. Petersburg, 727/823-3767, www.thedali.org, 10am-5:30pm Fri.-Wed., 10am-8pm Thurs., $25, $18 ages 13-17 and college students, $10 ages 6-12, free ages 5 and under). Here, inside this fantastical building with a glass

bubble called "The Enigma," are more than 2,400 Dalí works—photographs and paintings like the famous *The Disintegration of the Persistence of Memory*, plus sketches, illustrations, objects, and more. The museum also has a few long-running exhibits, including Dreams of Dalí in Virtual Reality, in which you'll find yourself inside some of the artist's works. Kids can go on a **Little Surrealist tour** of the museum with family members; it's free with your ticket on Saturday mornings. The museum was designed by architectural firm HOK, whose former HOK Sport offshoot designed half of the existing major league ballparks.

SUNKEN GARDENS

Sunken Gardens (1825 4th St. N., St. Petersburg, 727/551-3102, www.stpete.org, 10am-4:30pm Mon.-Sat., noon-4:30pm Sun., $12, $10 seniors, $6 ages 2-17, free under age 2) is a treasure, a wild world tucked within the confines of St. Pete. Dating to the early 20th century, the gardens are full of precious exotic plants like bougainvillea, fruit trees, and shrimp plants. There's a butterfly garden here, plus a Japanese garden and a cactus garden. You'll find a flock of flamingos as well as old structures commissioned by original garden owner George Turner Sr. Don't touch anything in the garden, but do get lost in this four-acre wonderland.

FLORIDA AQUARIUM

Over in Tampa, right against the Ybor Channel, is the **Florida Aquarium** (701 Channelside Dr., Tampa, 813/273-4000, www.flaquarium.com, 9:30am-5pm daily, $27-30, $24-27 seniors, $23-26 children), home to more than 20,000 animals and plants. Find rays, lobsters, sea turtles, sharks, and all kinds of seahorses. Bring your swimsuit and a towel so you can dive into aquatic habitats to **swim with animals** ($85 nonmembers), even **sharks** ($110 nonmembers). Got kids? Be sure to stop by the Splash Pad for water fun that doesn't cost extra.

BIG CAT RESCUE

Remember *Tiger King*, the Netflix docuseries about zookeeper Joe Exotic? While in Tampa, you can visit **Big Cat Rescue** (12802 Easy St., Tampa, 813/920-4130, www.bigcatrescue. org, 9am-5pm Fri.-Tues., $49, $34 ages 9 and under), which has a connection to the show. It calls itself a sanctuary for lions, tigers, jaguars, cougars, leopards, and other big cats that were previously abused in captivity. (You may want to watch the documentary for a refresher.) The day tour, which lasts 90 minutes, doesn't allow children younger than 10. Those kids have their own tour, available noon Saturdays and Sundays, where they must be accompanied by an adult.

FOOD

NEAR TROPICANA FIELD

Hang out on Central Avenue before a game and afterward for the best scene in the Tampa-St. Pete area. Stop at the outdoor hangout **Bodega on Central** (1120 Central Ave., St. Petersburg, 727/623-0942, www.eatatbodega. com, 11am-9pm Sun.-Wed., 11am-11pm Thurs.-Sat., under $20). This walk-up counter with some indoor bar seating and a nice little outdoor seating area has some righteous sandwiches, like *fritas* (burgers made with beef and pork, topped with French fries) and Cubans. The origins of the Cuban sandwich are tied to Tampa, and Tampa residents will gladly remind you of that.

For the New York sandwich experience, check out **Brooklyn South** (1437 Central Ave., St. Petersburg, 727/914-4967, www. brooklynsouthcheese.com, under $30). In this dainty deli, you can get yourself a good sandwich with quality meat and cheese or order a cheese board or charcuterie board, sit back with a beer or craft soda, and just enjoy.

Try **Pizza Box** (923 Central Ave., St. Petersburg, 727/623-0444, www.pizza-box727.com, noon-10pm Tues.-Thurs., noon-midnight Fri.-Sat., under $30), where

the intense aromas of cheese, oregano, and tomato sauce will pull you into this narrow space. Sit back and enjoy a wood-fired pizza, and pair it with some Griffy Sticks (parmesan breadsticks).

OTHER NEIGHBORHOODS

The Cuban sandwich is said to have been created sometime around 1900. Open since 1915, **La Segunda Central Bakery** (2512 N. 15th St., Tampa, 813/248-1531, www.lasegundabakery.com, 6:30am-3pm daily, under $20) was likely one of the first places to sell Cubans—and they still make a great one. You can also get an array of delicious pastries and desserts, from cheese turnovers to miniature cups of flan.

Near the Hillsborough River, a couple blocks from Water Works Park, is **Armature Works** (1910 N. Ola Ave., Tampa, 813/250-3725, www.armatureworks. com, 7am-10pm Mon.-Thurs., 7am-11pm Fri., 8am-11pm Sat., 9am-9pm Sun.), a renovated warehouse that's home to the **Heights Public Market,** a squeaky-clean food hall. For a good brunch (or lunch, or dinner) here, head to **Steelbach** (813/693-5478, www.steelbach.com, 11:30am-11pm Mon.-Thurs., 11:30am-midnight Fri., 9:30am-midnight Sat., 9:30am-10pm Sun., under $50). A large space with exposed piping, lots of lighting, shiny tables, and just a touch of wood, Steelbach looks like a paint-by-numbers modern restaurant, but the southern grub is on point.

Up the river a bit is **Ulele** (1810 N. Highland Ave., Tampa, 813/999-4952, www.ulele. com, 11am-10pm Sun.-Thurs., 11am-9pm Fri.-Sat., under $50). Pronounced "you-lay-lee," this restaurant is inspired by the cuisine of Indigenous Floridians; its food is all locally sourced. The large dining room with high windows screams Florida, while its menu packed with grilled meats, chili dishes, fresh Gulf fish, and southern comfort flourishes hits the mark.

BARS AND BREWERIES

NEAR TROPICANA FIELD

Up the block from the ballpark and worth your time, **Green Bench Brewing Company** (1133 Baum Ave. N., St. Petersburg, 727/800-9836, www.greenbenchbrewing.com, noon-10pm Sun. and Tues.-Thurs., noon-midnight Fri.-Sat.) has a bright, inviting, and very busy spot that's always packed and happening before and after Rays games. Come for the IPAs, but stay for the lagers. They have a pretty outdoor seating area with games and shade, plus mead and cider on tap for those who don't want beer. This is a phenomenal brewery in all respects.

Want a pure sports bar experience? **Ferg's Sports Bar** (1320 Central Ave., St. Petersburg, 727/822-4562, www.fergssportsbar.com, 11am-9pm daily) is that place. Ferg's is like the grown-up version of a homemade fort. Multiple bars, tables of all shapes and sizes, and TVs are everywhere. Get to Ferg's after a game, especially if you want to turn up the party. There's a full kitchen with bar grub, so you can grab some cheese fries if you need 'em.

Down the block is **Engine No. 9** (56 Dr. Martin Luther King Jr. St. N., St. Petersburg, 727/623-0938, www.no9burgers.com, 11:30am-midnight daily), a burger spot with a very good craft beer list. There's a nice combination of local and popular national fare. If you're a Cubs fan, come here; it's very much a Chicago bar favoring the Cubbies.

A walkable half mile or so west of the stadium is **3 Daughters Brewing** (222 22nd St. S., St. Petersburg, 727/495-6002, www.3dbrewing.com, 2pm-10pm Mon.-Thurs., 2pm-midnight Fri., noon-midnight Sat., noon-8pm Sun.). With plenty of outdoor seating, a large indoor area with lots of games (tables have laminated game boards on them, like Clue, Sorry, and Scrabble), a vast beer selection, and a huge stage area for concerts, this could be a daylong hangout.

OTHER NEIGHBORHOODS

The great Florida brewery for years, **Cigar City Brewing** (3924 W. Spruce St., Tampa, 813/348-6363, www.cigarcitybrewing.com, noon-8pm daily) is a must for any beer drinker heading into the Tampa-St. Pete area. Though Cigar City is known nationwide, its taproom is pretty relaxed. You can sit up at the front bar or at the more expansive back bar, where you can score familiar fare and more inventive stuff made only for the taproom. There's also a full kitchen, serving up sandwiches like Cubanos and burgers, plus bar fare like wings and pretzels. You can take some beer to go, as well.

The other major brewery to know about in Tampa is **Angry Chair Brewing** (6401 N. Florida Ave., Tampa, 813/238-1122, www.angrychairbrewing.com, 4pm-10pm Mon.-Wed., 3pm-11pm Thurs., noon-midnight Fri.-Sat., noon-9pm Sun.). Known for its impressive imperial stouts and its love of heavy metal music, Angry Chair is an essential stop for hardcore beer lovers. The no-frills taproom has fun artwork and wacky

Green Bench Brewing Company

bar stools. It's a good place to hang for a few hours and drink liberally. It also anchors the Seminole Heights area, home to a couple other breweries and beer bars. One is **Brew Bus Brewing** (4101 N. Florida Ave., Tampa, 813/990-7310, www.brewbususa.com, 4pm-10pm Mon.-Thurs., noon-midnight Fri., 11am-midnight Sat., 11am-8pm Sun.), which has a bright and cheery taproom. As a bonus, it also conducts bus tours to nearby breweries—and they serve their own beer on the buses.

RECREATION

WATER SPORTS

Hoping to get out onto Tampa Bay? There's the **Tampa Bay Water Bike Co.** (333 S. Franklin St., boat slip #15, Tampa, 813/465-8025, www.tampawaterbikes.com, 10am-sunset daily, $30-45, $25-40 ages 15 and under), which puts you on a contraption that's like a bicycle but with water skis. You'll be pedaling and floating at the same time.

Across the bay in St. Petersburg, you can hang out with **Urban Kai** (13090 Gandy Blvd. N., St. Petersburg, 813/598-1634, www.urbankai.com, from $25). They run stand-up paddleboard and kayak tours through the mangrove area at Gandy Beach, as well as sunset happy hours. They also rent paddleboards and kayaks.

PARKS

With its tidy eight acres against the Hillsborough River in Tampa, **Curtis Hixon Waterfront Park** (600 N. Ashley Dr., Tampa) is a fine meeting spot and a lovely way to pass time on a sunny (but not too warm) day. Stretch out on the great lawn or stroll the nearby **Tampa Riverwalk,** which runs right alongside the river.

A wildlife refuge that can also be a day-tripping vacation spot, **Egmont Key** (727/644-6325, www.floridastateparks.org, 8am-sunset daily) is great if you want to soak in the sunshine and adventure on a quiet beach. You can only get there by private boat, so take the **Tampa Bay Ferry** (Anderson Blvd., St. Petersburg, 727/398-6577, www.tampabayferry.com, 1-2 departures daily Mar.-Labor Day, 1 departure Tues.-Sun. Labor Day-Nov., 1 departure Wed.-Sun. Dec.-Feb., $25, $12.50 ages 11 and under). It'll take no more than 30 minutes to get to Egmont Key, so you can maximize your time looking for gopher tortoises and collecting shells. Get some photos of 150-year-old

Curtis Hixon Waterfront Park

Egmont Key Lighthouse (closed to the public) and visit the ruins of Fort Dade, constructed during the Spanish-American War. You can still find the mine storehouse, various batteries, and the dining hall, among other structures.

Weedon Island, which stretches out into Tampa Bay north of Downtown St. Pete, is a fine destination if you want to paddle or kayak. Check in with Weedon Island Preserve (www.weedonislandpreserve.org, 7am-sunset daily, free), which operates 3,190 acres of the island, home to alligators, armadillos, turtles, snakes, and a host of birds. Visit the Weedon Island Preserve Cultural and Natural History Center (1800 Weedon Dr. NE, St. Petersburg, 727/453-6500) to learn more about the ecosystems of the preserve, then head into the water. You can rent canoes and kayaks through Sweetwater Kayaks (1800 Weedon Dr. NE, St. Petersburg, 727/570-4844, www.sweetwaterkayaks.com, 9am-5pm daily, $17-30 per hour).

ACCOMMODATIONS

NEAR TROPICANA FIELD

The only accommodation I recommend within walking distance of the ballpark is the Staybridge Suites St. Petersburg Downtown (940 5th Ave. S., St. Petersburg, 727/821-0777, www.ihg.com, $100-250). Expect a nice mid-price hotel made for those wanting an extended stay or homier amenities. Each room and suite has a full kitchen. It's just five blocks from Tropicana Field and has an outdoor pool.

OTHER NEIGHBORHOODS

In Downtown St. Petersburg you'll find The Hollander (421 4th Ave. N., St. Petersburg, 727/873-7900, www.hollanderhotel.com, $100-250) and The Avalon (443 4th Ave. N., St. Petersburg, 727/317-5508, www.avalonstpetersburg.com, $100-250), sibling hotels

that target younger travelers. The former has an outdoor pool with cocktails (and a party atmosphere), while the latter has a more vibrant aesthetic, though both have an art deco sensibility. Rooms at both are a touch smaller than what you're probably used to, but they're clean and well-appointed.

Get game tickets and put in promo code TBSPORTS with the Magnuson Hotel Marina Cove (6800 Sunshine Skyway Ln. S., St. Petersburg, 727/867-1151, www.marinacoveresort.com, $120-200) to get up to 20 percent off your stay. This kid-friendly stay on a beach has 144 rooms and 11 town houses, plus two swimming pools. Rooms are a bit dated, with loud colors and older furniture, but some have bay views, and all are pretty clean.

In Tampa, you can stay in the heart of the city near Union Station at the historic Floridan Palace (905 N. Florida Ave., Tampa, 813/225-1700, www.floridanpalace.com, $120-250). This is an old-school spot, a 1926 hotel of 19 stories that towers above everything around it. Back in the day, celebrities would drop by constantly, and when the Cincinnati Reds had spring training in Tampa, they stayed here. Be sure to check out the gorgeous Crystal Dining Room, which serves an upscale menu with a robust wine list, and the Sapphire Lounge, where you can sip a martini while watching a game. Rooms are outfitted with Beaux-Arts-style furniture.

GETTING AROUND

PUBLIC TRANSIT

If you're going to be in Downtown Tampa, you can take the TECO Line Streetcar (www.tecolinestreetcar.org, 7am-11pm Mon.-Thurs., 7am-2am Fri., 8:30am-2am Sat., 8:30am-11pm Sun., free) operated by HART (www.gohart.org). The streetcar makes 11 stops on a single route, connecting Ybor City to the Channel District (home to the Florida Aquarium) and Downtown, with trains making stops every

15 minutes. HART also runs a **bus service** that covers the Tampa municipal area, but it doesn't connect with St. Petersburg or Clearwater.

In St. Petersburg and Clearwater, there's the **PSTA bus network** (www.psta.net, $2.25). It covers a huge area and connects multiple locations. If you want to get from Tampa to Clearwater on PSTA, take **Route 52,** which starts at **Grand Central Station** (Central Ave. and 32nd St., St. Petersburg). The ride will take about two hours with all the stops.

PSTA runs a trolley, the **St. Petersburg Downtown Looper** (7am-10pm Mon.-Thurs., 7am-midnight Fri., 8am-midnight Sat., 8am-10pm Sun., free), which connects to points of interest like the Dalí Museum and the Museum of Fine Arts. It does not, however, connect to Tropicana Field. If you're in Clearwater, opt to take the **Jolley Trolley** (www.clearwaterjolleytrolley.com, $5 unlimited rides, cash and exact change only). This cheerful yellow transporter runs back and forth from Clearwater Beach to Clearwater, and also picks up folks heading to **Phillies spring training** (727/445-1200, $14 round-trip) from their hotels.

TAXI, UBER, AND LYFT

This is the quintessential location for ride-sharing: The Tampa-St. Pete area is sprawling, you'll want to visit attractions across the whole Tampa Bay area, and there's no single option for getting everywhere via public transportation. A single ride from Tampa International Airport to Tropicana Field isn't very expensive (less than $40); it's only about 20 miles from point to point.

CAR

While I recommend ride-sharing here, you can certainly drive yourself around. In Tampa, the major highway is **I-4,** whose western terminus is just north of Downtown Tampa. It extends northeast to Orlando and Daytona Beach. **I-75** stays east of Tampa, but extension **I-275** heads into the city, crossing

Old Tampa Bay and running through St. Petersburg before crossing Tampa Bay to the south and joining back up with I-75, making a half-loop of sorts.

US-19 cuts down the center of the Clearwater and St. Petersburg peninsula, while **US-41** hugs the coastline on the Tampa side, heading into the city and paralleling I-275 before separating and continuing north toward Gainesville.

Central Avenue runs west to east and is the main street in St. Petersburg. In Downtown, it serves as the cultural hub of the city. The north-south streets are numbered, though 9th Street is **Dr. Martin Luther King Jr. Street** in Tampa. In Downtown Tampa, west-to-east **Kennedy Boulevard** and **Jackson Street** run in opposite directions next to each other, and the main north-south streets include **Florida Avenue** and **Nebraska Avenue.**

GRAPEFRUIT LEAGUE SPRING TRAINING

Not very long ago, you could have plunked down $15 for a decent seat at a Florida ballpark for spring training, but as more fans have traveled to the Sunshine State for spring baseball, the teams have raised ticket prices, with some even instituting **dynamic pricing** models.

So how much will it cost you to attend a Grapefruit League spring training game? For a seat facing the infield, you're likely to pay around $30-40 on average, while a lawn seat in the berm will usually cost you around $10-15.

CLEARWATER

Northwest of St. Petersburg and just across Old Tampa Bay from the Big Guava, Clearwater has plenty of beaches. The white-sand beaches of Clearwater are renowned, making it a major tourist destination. Plus, there's baseball here. I'd argue that the relationship between this city and the Phillies is the richest and most successful among spring flings in all of baseball.

Getting There

From **Tampa,** it's a simple **23-mile, 30-minute** drive west on FL-60, primarily on the Courtney Campbell Causeway. The nearly 10-mile road over Old Tampa Bay provides a splendid view all the way. It's as if you're smack in the middle of the bay, without a care in the world.

Spectrum Field

The Phillies can claim the longest ongoing spring-training relationship with its base city of any team in baseball, having resided in Clearwater since 1948. In 2004, the team opened **Spectrum Field** (601 Old Coachman Rd.), a comfortable venue with plenty of options for eating and drinking.

The **100 level** stretches around foul territory from right to left field. You'll find a **picnic pavilion** close to the left-field foul pole, then the popular **Frenchy's Tiki Pavilion** in straightaway left field, run by a popular seafood shack in town. Come early for first-come, first-served seating at the bar (get the grouper), or grab a chair next door at the **Local Craft Shack** for Tampa-area beer. Across the outfield and behind the fence is an expansive **grass berm** where folks can spread out on blankets. A small line of **club seats** takes up space in the **200 level** behind home plate and along the first-base line.

Spectrum Field has a **kids' zone** (left-field corner by the picnic pavilion) with a playground and concession stand made for children. Hungry? Look for the **build-your-own hot dog cart,** delicious pies from local favorite **Westshore Pizza,** and the **Strike Out Café** (right field), which offers barbecue sandwiches and cheesesteaks, among other meaty delights.

Food

One spring training tradition for many a Phillies fan is to precede a ball game with a trip to **Lenny's** (21220 US-19, 727/799-0402,

www.lennysfood.com, 6am-3pm daily, under $30). You may have to wait a few minutes for a seat, but when you get one, look around at the license plates, posters, and baseball photos all over the walls. Then settle in for a great breakfast starring eggs Benedict, fresh-baked bagels, and hearty specialty plates. For lunch, there's a host of sandwiches and burgers. During spring training, Phillies fans will be all over the place; they even sell Phils-themed Lenny's merchandise here.

All-day dining in comfy surroundings? It's down at the **Sunset Grill** (2328 Sunset Point Rd., 727/723-2346, www.sunsetgrill-clearwater.com, 7:30am-9pm Mon.-Sat., 7:30am-8pm Sun., under $40). You'll get a mix of traditional surf-and-turf fare (prime rib, salmon) and Greek street food like gyros and spanakopita, plus Italian fare. Make sure to get some pie for dessert—the key lime is a winner.

For a more upscale experience requiring you to put on your best Hawaiian shirt, there's **Sea-Guini** (430 S. Gulfview Blvd. #100, Clearwater Beach, 727/450-6236, www.opalsands.com/restaurant, 7am-10pm daily, under $80). The name says it all: There's seafood and gourmet Italian here amid environs in coral and electric-gold tones. Go big with grouper or the cioppino, or order a personal pizza while tending to a glass of wine from the restaurant's deep list.

Nightlife and Entertainment

You're bound to want to check out the bars by the beach, but those mammoth multiroom beachside spots will eat up your wallet and give you a splitting headache (unless you crave that kind of scene, in which case be my guest). Instead, give yourself a sensory overload of bleeps, bloops, and blinking lights by way of **Vector Bar & Arcade** (629 Cleveland St., 727/754-9933, www.vectorarcadeclearwater.com, 5pm-midnight Mon.-Thurs., 5pm-2am Fri., noon-2am Sat., 4pm-midnight Sun.). It has several pinball machines and arcade games, plus bubble hockey, a 1987 Double Dragon machine, and a bunch of console systems. There's also a whole lot of good beer on the list here.

The area is home to a bunch of bars employing scantily clad women, including the **original Hooters** (2800 Gulf to Bay Blvd., 727/797-4008, www.originalhooters. com, 11am-11pm Sun.-Thurs., 11am-midnight Fri.-Sat.). For a sports bar, I'd rather step into **Varsity Club Sports Bar and Grille** (24091 US-19, 727/726-6551, www. varsityclubsportsbarclearwater.com, 11am-midnight Sun.-Thurs., 11am-2am Fri.-Sat.). With its cozy bar, plenty of space for seating, lively atmosphere, and burgers named after baseball teams, it's a great spot to sit back and watch the games.

Recreation

When in Clearwater, drive the three miles or so west over FL-60, or the Clearwater Memorial Causeway, to **Clearwater Beach.** This is a splendid beach destination where the sand is a cool, soft white. It'll be packed most every summer day, and especially on weekends. Families may take a break from the beach at **Pier 60 Park** (Causeway Blvd. and Mandalay Ave., Clearwater Beach). The park has a playground for little ones and a concession stand. In the evening, the park throws a little party called **Sunsets at Pier 60** (www.sunsetpier60.com). You'll see buskers, craft tents, and on weekend evenings, outdoor movie screenings.

If you want to head out in the water, get on a boat through **Kai Lani Catamaran** (Clearwater Beach Marina, Slip 49, 25 Causeway Blvd., 727/446-6778, www.kailanicat. com, 10am-7pm daily, $60, $30 ages 12 and under). This highly rated business runs catamaran tours in Clearwater Bay and beyond, including a dolphin sightseeing adventure and a sunset cruise. Both trips offer alcohol for purchase.

Accommodations

Right by Clearwater Bay, a two-minute drive south of Downtown Clearwater, is the **Belleview Inn** (25 Belleview Blvd., Belleair, 727/441-1774, www.thebelleviewinn.com, $180-450). This Gilded Age hotel built at the turn of the 20th century has seen its share of guests, from Presidents Jimmy Carter and Gerald Ford to musician Bob Dylan. It's a splendid restored building with 35 original guest rooms still intact. You can upgrade your stay by adding a tee time for the nearby 18-hole country club course.

DUNEDIN

Just north of Clearwater, the neighboring city of Dunedin is home to Toronto Blue Jays spring training—and some great beer.

Getting There

From **Tampa,** it's a **25-mile, 35-minute** drive on FL-60 West to US-19 North to FL-580 West to Dunedin. From **St. Petersburg,** hop on US-19 and go north about **20 miles** to FL-580 West, for a **30-minute** drive time.

TD Ballpark

Parked in the middle of a residential neighborhood, the longtime home of **Blue Jays** spring training **TD Ballpark** (373 Douglas Ave.) is as basic as it gets in the Grapefruit League. Its sparsity and lack of frills can be refreshing.

Built in 1990, TD has two seating levels. The **100 level** runs from mid right field in foul territory around to deep left field in foul territory. The **200 level** starts above the 100 level in foul right field, then comes around to just behind the third-base bag. That's it—no fancy suites, no grass berm, just two levels of seating.

That said, there are some amenities. There's a **bar** on the concourse at the third-base line, and another out in right field with drink rails. A **boardwalk** wraps around the outfield behind the fence, giving fans more viewing areas. The most unique quality about TD is a **food vendor** near the first-base dugout, a hyper-energetic sort who riles up the crowd and has a heck of a time out there. His name is Chad—enjoy him.

A word to the wise: Wear **sunscreen** when at TD, as shade is hard to find. One of the top five sunburns of my life came after watching a game here.

Bars and Breweries

What Dunedin has over most of Florida is its wealth of beer-drinking options, plus a brewing community that's hard to beat anywhere in America.

A few of my favorite breweries in town include **7venth Sun Brewery** (1012 Broadway, 727/733-3013, www.7venthsun. com, 3pm-8pm Wed.-Sun.), which has a small taproom with a covered patio outside and friendly bartenders; **Dunedin Brewery** (937 Douglas Ave., 727/736-0606, www.dunedinbrewery.com, noon-7pm daily), the original local spot that has a charming roadhouse taproom and an affinity for late native son and famous pitchman Billy Mays; and must-visit **Woodwright Brewing Company** (985 Douglas Ave., 727/238-8717, www.woodwrightbrewing. com, 5pm-midnight Thurs., noon-midnight Fri.-Sat., noon-8pm Sun.), which has a great origin story. Essentially, a bunch of woodworkers bought a beautiful old building and used it as a shop. One of the woodworkers and his wife got really into home brewing, and the shop soon flipped to a brewery and taproom specializing in German brews. There's a lot of care (and beautiful woodwork) in this place.

LAKELAND

East of Tampa, about 35 miles away, is Lakeland. It's been the spring home of the Detroit Tigers for decades, and its history means that Grapefruit League fans should make a point to visit it at least once.

Getting There

From **Tampa,** take a 35-mile (40-minute) drive east on I-4 to Lakeland. You'll jump off I-4 at FL-539 South.

Publix Field at Joker Marchant Stadium

Publix Field at Joker Marchant Stadium (2301 Lakeland Hills Blvd.) is a classic ballpark that opened in 1966 as the spring training home of the **Detroit Tigers.** There have been a few renovations, most recently in

2017, but one thing remains: those Tigers. They've been here since the beginning.

The stadium's **100 and 200 levels** both wrap around the infield in foul territory. You'll pay more if you sit down low and closer to the plate; your best bet may be seats in **sections 114-116** and **214-216,** which are moderately priced. There are **five suites** above the 200 level near home plate, as well as the **Miller Lite 34 Club,** with covered seats, an indoor bar, and all-inclusive buffet. Finally, there's a grass berm in left field where blankets are encouraged.

At the berm, there's a **bar** with 360-degree seating and, during spring training, servers who will deliver your drink. Other bars include a **Margaritaville** (right-field line) with a deck. During spring training, it's typically used as a group ticket section. Down the first-base line, find the **Hooters Dugout,** which also features private servers. Parents can find a **playground** next to the berm.

The grub here is ballpark-friendly—plenty of hot dogs and fries. But you can also get Detroit favorite **Little Caesars Pizza** here, either in slice or pie form.

Sights

If it's raining or you need a respite from the sun, opt to visit the **Polk Museum of Art** (800 Palmetto St., 863/688-7743, www. polkmuseumofart.org, 10am-5pm Tues.- Sat. June-Labor Day, 10am-5pm Tues.-Sat., 1pm-5pm Sun. Labor Day-May, free). This Smithsonian affiliate at Florida Southern College houses more than 2,800 pieces from artists who span the mostly contemporary spectrum. You'll find Pablo Picasso, Marc Chagall, Andy Warhol, and Hung Liu. Florida-made art is well represented, as is African art coming from multiple cultures, including the Zulu, Swazi, and Batonka.

PORT ST. LUCIE

About 90 minutes north of Miami and a straight shot east of Tampa and St. Petersburg, Port St. Lucie is one of the last remaining Grapefruit League locations on the Atlantic coast. The Mets have the run of things here, and you'll see plenty of halfway optimistic New Yorkers hanging out on the beaches nearby in the spring.

Getting There

From **Tampa,** you'll have to drive about 2.5 hours across Florida via I-4 East, FL-60 East, and Florida's Turnpike to reach Port St. Lucie. It's a 160-mile trip.

Clover Park

The **Mets** play their spring training games at **Clover Park** (31 Piazza Dr.). The **field-level seats** at Clover, called **lower reserve,** span from deep right field in foul territory around to deep left field in foul territory, and number 1-22. Above those seats and covering the infield area are the **upper reserve** and covered seating areas, numbered sections 104-116. There's also a grassy hill in right field, called **The Hill,** which is meant for fans who want to lounge. The **Left Field Party Terrace** (left field) is the place to grab a drink while hanging out in the outfield or before heading back to your seat.

Don't go looking for crazy food creations at Clover Park, as most of the fare is standard ballpark grub.

Food and Breweries

If you're looking for a type of food in Port St. Lucie, the answer is Italian; there are a number of spots serving up red sauce on white tablecloths. Check out **Corleone Ristorante Italiano** (8621 S. Federal Hwy., 772/323-0355, www.corleonesrestaurant. com, 4pm-9:30pm Tues. and Sat.-Sun., noon-9:30pm Wed.-Fri., under $70). While this restaurant isn't too frilly, its rich plates will hit the spot, especially when you want pasta in fra diavolo sauce or a hearty dish of veal marsala.

Only a couple minutes' drive north of Clover Park is **Hop Life Brewing Company** (679 Enterprise Dr. #101, 772/249-5055, www.hop-life.com, noon-8pm Mon.-Thurs., noon-9pm Fri.-Sat., noon-6pm Sun.), where a bunch of local folks brew a bunch of IPAs. Hop Life has a big taproom that fills up on weekends with live music. There's some outdoor space, too,

and the whole place is pet-friendly. This is a nice place to spend a couple hours.

Recreation

Right along the coastline, you'll have endless outdoor fun at **Savannas Preserve State Park** (772/398-2779, www.floridastateparks. org, 8am-sunset daily, $3 per vehicle). The 6,800-acre park sits mostly on marshland, and you'll find all kinds of flora, from Florida pine scrub to apple cactus. There's plenty of fishing to do here—just bring a pole—and it's not unusual to spot a bald eagle. A canoe and kayak launch area is located 0.75 mile north of the **education center** (2541 SE Walton Rd.). From the center, you can hook up with a trail system that winds about 8.5 miles through the narrow park area.

Accommodations

Most of the hotels in the Port St. Lucie area are chains peppered along I-95 to the west or US-1 to the east. Even farther to the east in Jensen Beach is the **Jensen Beach Inn** (1899 NE Jensen Beach Blvd., Jensen Beach, 772/334-1466, www.jensen-beach-inn.com, $150-250). The six rooms here, all named after animals you may find in the area, combine rusticity with a somewhat dated aesthetic. Most importantly, they're clean and charming. The hotel offers continental breakfast daily, and there's a bistro on-site for those who want a little more protein.

JUPITER

Just south of Port St. Lucie on the east coast of Florida, Jupiter is worth visiting to see two baseball teams in one place.

Getting There

The **190-mile drive** from **Tampa** to Jupiter takes you along I-4 East, FL-60 East, and Florida's Turnpike before you exit for FL-706 East and Jupiter. That's a nearly **three-hour** drive. From **Miami,** it's a straight **90-mile, 1.5-hour** drive up I-95 North to Jupiter.

Roger Dean Chevrolet Stadium

Roger Dean Stadium (4751 Main St.) hosts

two teams every spring: the **St. Louis Cardinals** and **Miami Marlins**. But that isn't all: During the regular season, it hosts both the Cardinals' and Marlins' rookie league and class-A Florida State League teams. I don't envy the person who has to keep all those schedules organized, but I do appreciate how versatile this ballpark can be. Contrary to what you might think, Roger Dean Chevrolet Stadium isn't named after a baseball guy with a car company sponsorship tacked on later. In fact, Roger Dean ran a Chevrolet dealership in the area starting in the 1960s.

The park has two seating levels: The **100 level** starts near the right-field foul pole with the **Corona Beach House**—a seating area with drink railings, four-top tables, and all-you-can-eat bar-style food options—and wraps around the infield to a thin area near the left-field foul pole. The **200 level** starts in shallow right field in foul territory, wrapping around to shallow left field in foul territory. Note: On the first-base and right-field side of the ballpark, seat numbers start at 1 on the left side of the row, but on the third-base and left-field side, seat numbers start at 1 on the right side of the row. There's also a **party tent area** in deep left field in foul territory, along with four seated sections known as **301-304**. Opposite that is the **Cassidy Cool Zone** (right field), a group area with buffet-style food service.

Food at the ballpark is kept simple: hot dogs, nachos, chicken tenders, burgers, and the like. There's a **kids' area** on the third-base side of the park that includes speed pitch, an inflatable slide, and other inflatables. Unfortunately, the kids' area is only open for Florida State League games, not for spring training.

Bars and Breweries

For good beer, check out **Civil Society Brewing Co.** (1200 Town Center Dr. #101, 561/855-6680, www.civilsocietybrewing.com, 3pm-11pm Tues.-Thurs., noon-midnight Fri.-Sat., noon-9pm Sun.). They do hops better than anyone else in the state. Come by and sit at the long bar to sample a bunch of brews while admiring the hand-painted murals on the walls. It's a laid-back hangout.

WEST PALM BEACH

Something of a northern suburb of Miami, West Palm Beach is a spot known for its art museums and a bustling downtown. The best places to focus on, though, are its beaches and parks, as well as the two highly successfully franchises that play their spring training games at the same ballpark here.

Getting There

From **Miami,** West Palm Beach is a quick **75-mile** jaunt north, lasting about **75 minutes.** Drive I-95 North and you'll get there. From Tampa, take I-4 East to FL-60 to Florida's Turnpike. Merge onto I-95 South and continue until exit 70. Take FL-704 East into the city. This route is just over **200 miles** and takes nearly **3.5 hours.**

FITTEAM Ballpark of the Palm Beaches

FITTEAM Ballpark of the Palm Beaches (5444 Haverhill Rd. N.) entertains fans of two teams every spring: the **Astros** and **Nationals.** The **first level** of seating wraps around the foul area from left field to right field. Special **field box** and **home-plate box seats** down near the warning track are pricier than regular seats. A **picnic area** is in left field close to the foul pole. There are a few **suites** and **party deck seats,** sold to groups, on a **second level.** In the outfield is the **Banana Boat Lawn,** which covers much of the outfield area and represents the cheapest tickets.

Ticket prices are standard, with regular infield seats going for between $25 and $31 for less important opponents. There is a **dynamic pricing** structure, though, with marquee games (the Red Sox and their fans are visiting, let's say) costing about 50 percent more than the cheapest game.

Food offerings include standard fare like hot dogs, fries, chicken, and ice cream. There's also a **stand-alone bar** (home plate) here.

After each Sunday game, children ages

4-12 can **run the bases** by lining up between sections 121 and 122 in the ninth inning.

Sights

Covering 600 acres in Loxahatchee, about 30 minutes west of West Palm Beach, Lion Country Safari (2003 **Lion Country Safari Rd.**, Loxahatchee, 561/793-1084, www.lioncountrysafari.com, $39, $35 seniors, $30 ages 3-9, free ages 2 and under, $8 parking) is a zoo with hundreds of animals, including lions, giraffes, rhinoceroses, and water buffaloes. You can drive through to see animals from your vehicle, or you can walk through and see smaller animals like tortoises, sloths, and porcupines, and hop on rides like a water slide, or even play miniature golf. If you walk, you can also feed some of the animals: giraffes, specific birds, and koi.

Food

It's really bright at **Galley** (600 Okeechobee Blvd., 561/231-6100, www3.hilton.com, 4pm-midnight daily, under $50), a light-filled restaurant attached to the Hilton West Palm Beach. The ultimate in feel-good American bistro fare, it serves up tidy burgers and personal pizzas in a living room-like space with whimsy-filled shelves and plenty of greenery.

Plenty of cultural touches and great food can be found at the no-frills **Queen of Sheeba** (716 N. Sapodilla Ave.,

561/514-0615, www.queenofsheebawpb.com, 11:30am-2:30pm and 5:30pm-9:30pm Tues.-Sat., under $50). Order some injera and a vegetable sampler to get a nice taste of Ethiopian food, and add some lentils along the way. While gazing at the straw baskets that decorate the space, finish your meal with some strong coffee.

Recreation

About 12 miles south of FITTEAM Ballpark of the Palm Beaches is **Okeeheelee Park** (7115 Forest Hill Blvd., 561/966-6600, www.okeeheeleepark.com). The 1,700-acre park with multiple lakes also has a 27-hole championship **golf course** (561/964-4653, greens fees under $70) with plenty of water hazards to avoid, plus a disc golf course and a BMX track for those looking to improve their riding.

Accommodations

For an affordable stay, consider **Tideline Ocean Resort & Spa** (2842 S. Ocean Blvd., Palm Beach, 561/540-6440, www.marriott.com, $150-300). This Marriott hotel has spacious and comfortable rooms with the basic amenities like cable and/or satellite TV, high-speed internet, and complimentary on-site parking. Best of all, though, it's right on the beach. It's just a hop, skip, and a jump to the Atlantic Ocean.

MIAMI
MARLINS

Not to disparage any Marlins fans

out there, but let's be serious: Miami is not a base-ball city. It's a tourism city, a nightlife hot spot, a splashy paradise of beautiful architecture, beauti-ful people, and beautiful beaches. Other than jai alai, the "U" (the late '80s to early '90s University of Miami football program), Dan Marino (and his Isotoners), and the Dwyane Wade-era Miami Heat, sports take a back seat here, and that's okay!

The major league Marlins (named after minor league teams that played in Miami for decades) opened play in 1993 as one of two expansion teams (the other being the Colorado Rockies). Wearing teal green and pinstripes and featuring a 45-year-old opening day starter, knuckleballer Charlie Hough, the then-Florida Marlins were quickly a league-wide punchline. Then owner

Wayne Huizenga spent a bunch of money to bring in some stars, and they, along with some upstart players, went and won a world championship in the franchise's fifth year of existence. Huizenga got rid of all the good players, making the team a laughingstock again. No matter: Six years later, in 2003, new owner Jeffrey Loria's upstart players went and won another world championship.

Until 2020, those two titles were the only times the Fish reached the postseason. Blame that on the owners, who historically have sold off big-time talent, including some of the greatest and most exciting players of the past three decades: Gary Sheffield, Miguel Cabrera, Mike Piazza, Giancarlo Stanton, Hanley Ramirez, Christian Yelich, and JT Realmuto. The response to this has been low fan support, which means thinner profit margins, which lead to lower payrolls and more trades.

What can stop the cycle? Maybe a ballpark. In 2012, the Marlins unveiled Marlins Park and a new look for the franchise, naming the team the Miami Marlins and debuting a new color scheme. Things have moved slowly since the opening of Marlins Park, but a new ownership group, led by Hall of Famer Derek Jeter, is aiming to bring great baseball to South Florida for good.

PLANNING YOUR TIME

Sure, Miami can be done in a **weekend.** Spend some time on the beach, catch a ball game, and hang out in Wynwood for a spell. A miniature vacation of **4-5 days** is even better. You'll get in more beach time, a chance to get into the city's active club scene, and the opportunity to visit more neighborhoods. You can even take a side trip to a nearby city like Fort Lauderdale or Palm Beach.

Be sure to get your tickets for **Vizcaya Museum & Gardens** ahead of time to ensure you can get a tour. Don't forget to pack a swimsuit, no matter the time of year. Summer weekends mean lots of tourists, so consider a trip that includes some weekdays,

and make those your beach days to help avoid crowds.

Miami is a hot place, but if it's too hot, the Marlins will close the roof and blast the air-conditioning, so the chances of your sitting in unbearable heat are slim. Still, it's always a good idea to bring sunscreen at all times of the year. An umbrella isn't a bad idea either, because South Florida in the summer means rain for about an hour every evening.

GETTING THERE

AIR

Miami International Airport

You're likely to fly into **Miami International Airport** (MIA, 2100 NW 42nd Ave., Miami, 305/876-7000, www.miami-airport.com). Major North American airlines that fly into and out of Miami include **Air Canada** (888/247-2262, www.aircanada.com), **American Airlines** (800/433-7300, www.aa.com), **Delta** (800/221-1212, www.delta.com), **Frontier** (800/432-1359, www.flyfrontier.com), **Spirit** (801/401-2222, www.spirit.com), and **United** (800/864-8331, www.united.com). Miami is also home to a number of carriers that fly to and from the Caribbean islands, as well as other international carriers.

AIRPORT TRANSPORTATION

To get a rental car from the airport, head to the third floor to find the **MIA Mover,** in between the Flamingo and Dolphin garages. This monorail service takes people to the rental car center. All major car rental businesses have a spot here.

The airport is part of the **Miami Metrorail** (www.miamidade.gov, $2.25 per ride) system. You can hop on the **Orange Line,** which heads into Downtown Miami. You'll first stop at **Earlington Heights** (2100 NW 41st St.), where you can change to the **Green Line,** which runs on the same rail as the Orange Line until Earlington, when it heads north and west toward Hialeah. The closest stop to Marlins Park is **Culmer** (NW 11th St. and NW 7th Ave.) on both the Green and Orange Lines. It's a 0.8-mile, nearly 20-minute walk southwest from Culmer to the ballpark.

Fort Lauderdale-Hollywood International Airport

Another option is to fly into **Fort Lauderdale-Hollywood International Airport** (FLL, 100 Terminal Dr., Fort Lauderdale, 954/359-1200, www.broward.org). It's home to Air Canada, **Allegiant** (702/505-8888, www.allegiantair.com), American Airlines, Delta, Frontier, **jetBlue** (800/538-2583, www.jetblue.com), **Southwest** (800/435-9792, www.southwest.com), Spirit, and United. A few Caribbean carriers also serve this airport.

AIRPORT TRANSPORTATION

If arriving at Terminal 1, you can walk to the **rental car center** here, while those coming in at Terminals 2-4 should head outside to grab a **shuttle bus** to the center. All major rental companies are here. You'll want to rent a car, as it's a 30-minute drive south to Downtown Miami.

The only rail connected to this airport is the **Tri-Rail** (www.tri-rail.com, up to $8.75 weekdays, $5 weekends), which runs from Palm Beach International Airport to the north down to Miami International Airport, with several stops in between.

Palm Beach International Airport

About 70 miles north of Miami via I-95 is **Palm Beach International Airport** (PBI, 1000 James L. Turnage Blvd., West Palm Beach, 561/471-7400, www.pbia.org). Airlines that fly into and out of here include Air Canada, American Airlines, Delta, Frontier, jetBlue, Southwest, Spirit, and United. A small number of Caribbean carriers also come in and out of this airport.

AIRPORT TRANSPORTATION

You'll want to **rent a car** and drive closer to Miami. All the major companies are here, and they're conveniently located near the baggage claim.

The **Tri-Rail** (www.tri-rail.com, up to $8.75 weekdays, $5 weekends) is accessible from PBI, offering connections to points south like Boca Raton, Fort Lauderdale, Hollywood, and the Miami Metrorail.

CAR

There are two primary ways to get across Florida from Tampa or St. Petersburg to Miami, each offering something different.

Florida's Turnpike

You can take **Florida's Turnpike:** Head east on **I-4** until a junction with **FL-570 East.** Hop on that for a spell until you reach US-98 South. That'll lead you to FL-60 East, which will take you to Florida's Turnpike. Take that into Miami. This **270-mile drive,** lasting a little more than **four hours** in good traffic, runs through Central Florida communities south of Orlando, including the Lake Kissimmee area.

Everglades Parkway

The other option is to drive through the **Everglades.** This **280-mile, four-hour** drive takes place primarily on **I-75 South.** Grab it from Tampa or St. Pete, and take it past Fort Myers as it turns east toward the other side of the state. At this point, the highway is the **Everglades Parkway,** rolling through the Everglades and Francis S. Taylor Wildlife Management Area.

This route is also known as **Alligator Alley** because you're surrounded by 'em. If you spot wildlife on the road, take care—either pass safely, if you can, or stop well ahead of the animal and wait for it to move, flashing your blinkers and sounding your horn. Fuel up your car before this part of the trip, as there's no cheap gas along this 80-mile stretch. It's also a toll road, so invest in a **SunPass** (www.sunpass.com) for your vehicle.

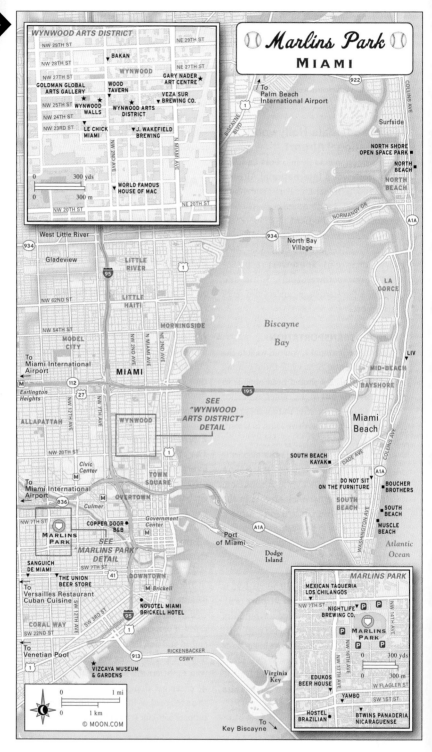

Marlins Park
MIAMI

WYNWOOD ARTS DISTRICT

NW 29TH ST

NE 29TH ST

NW 28TH ST

▼ BAKAN

NW 27TH ST

WYNWOOD

NE 27TH ST

GOLDMAN GLOBAL
ARTS GALLERY

WOOD
TAVERN ▼

GARY NADER
ART CENTRE ★

NW 25TH ST ★

VEZA SUR
BREWING CO. ▼

★ WYNWOOD
WALLS

NW 24TH ST

WYNWOOD ARTS
DISTRICT

NW 23RD ST

▼ LE CHICK
MIAMI

★ J. WAKEFIELD
BREWING

0   300 yds

0   300 m

▼ WORLD FAMOUS
HOUSE OF MAC

NW 20TH ST

NE 20TH ST

To Palm Beach
International Airport

Surfside

NORTH SHORE
OPEN SPACE PARK ■

NORTH
BEACH ■

NORTH
BEACH

West Little River

North Bay
Village

Gladeview

LITTLE
RIVER

LITTLE
HAITI

NW 62ND ST

MORNINGSIDE

NW 54TH ST

MODEL
CITY

Biscayne
Bay

LA
GORCE

To
Miami International
Airport

MIAMI

LIV ■

MID-BEACH

Earlington
Heights

BAYSHORE

ALLAPATTAH

WYNWOOD

Miami
Beach

SEE
"WYNWOOD
ARTS DISTRICT"
DETAIL

NW 20TH ST

Civic
Center

SOUTH BEACH
KAYAK ■

To
Miami International
Airport

TOWN
SQUARE

DO NOT SIT
ON THE FURNITURE

BOUCHER
BROTHERS ■

OVERTOWN

Culmer

SOUTH
BEACH ■

COPPER DOOR
B&B ●

Government
Center

MUSCLE
BEACH ■

NW 7TH ST

MARLINS
PARK

SEE
MARLINS PARK
DETAIL

Port
of Miami

Atlantic
Ocean

SANGUICH
DE MIAMI ▼

SW 7TH ST

Dodge
Island

THE UNION
BEER STORE ▼

To
Versailles Restaurant
Cuban Cuisine

DOWNTOWN

Brickell

MARLINS PARK

MEXICAN TAQUERIA
LOS CHILANGOS ▼

CORAL WAY

NOVOTEL MIAMI
BRICKELL HOTEL ●

NIGHTLIFE
BREWING CO. ▼

MARLINS
PARK

SW 22ND ST

To
Venetian Pool

RICKENBACKER

CSWY

Virginia
Key

0   300 yds

0   300 m

★ VIZCAYA MUSEUM
& GARDENS

EDUKOS
BEER HOUSE ▼

W FLAGLER ST

YAMBO ▼

SW 1ST ST

0   1 mi

0   1 km

© MOON.COM

To
Key Biscayne

HOSTEL
BRAZILIAN ▼

BTWINS PANADERIA
NICARAGUENSE ▼

Once out of the Everglades, I-75 turns south once again and goes into the Miami metropolitan area. I-75 becomes **FL-826.** Take that into **FL-836 East** (the **Dolphin Expressway**), a toll road that runs past the airport and toward Downtown.

TRAIN

Amtrak (800/872-7245, www.amtrak.com) rolls into Miami at **Miami Station** (8303 NW 37th Ave.). The only Amtrak route that stops here is the **Silver Service/Silver Meteor/Palmetto,** which comes from Orlando and Jacksonville; it has service all the way north from New York. There is one daily train from **Tampa.**

BUS

Via **Greyhound** (www.greyhound.com), a ride from **Tampa** to Miami's **Greyhound bus station** (3801 NW 21st St., 305/871-1810) will cost around $22, but prepare for an eight- to nine-hour trip with multiple stops. The station is just outside Miami International Airport.

Megabus (http://us.megabus.us) also travels from Tampa to Miami. It pulls in at the Greyhound station, and rides are about $25. It'll take close to six hours or so for this trip.

Marlins Park

The Marlins spent their first 20 seasons at the ballpark formerly known as the multipurpose Joe Robbie Stadium, a venue that lacked character. In 2012, they moved into **Marlins Park** (501 Marlins Way, www.mlb.com/marlins) for a complete 180.

Taking some cues from retractable-roof venues built in the past few decades and influenced by neo-modernism and abstract art, Marlins Park is a unique, potentially groundbreaking facility. With its sleek, angular lines, white exterior, and massive glass facade, Marlins Park rejects the nostalgic baseball aesthetics of brick and steel. Its wide main concourse has a space-age vibe with very few bells and whistles. Locally commissioned art provides pops of vivid color throughout. The deep-blue seats look like an ocean. The geometric body of the park's roof is hypnotizing and smart. And when the day is clear (but the weather is warm), the glass facade that spans the entirety of the outfield shows off a heck of a skyline view.

Miami skyline from Marlins Park

Marlins Park has a retractable roof.

While the park hasn't been a regular sell-out (the Marlins have to be good for a while first), it should be a rockin' place when the Fish get to that point.

Wrigley's old-style coziness. Fenway's cramped and stubborn charm. Oracle's foggy liveliness. Few ballparks personify their locations as well as these, but Marlins Park makes the list. It's the most underrated ballpark there is.

ORIENTATION

Marlins Park is located at the former Orange Bowl site in the Little Havana neighborhood of the city. It's a little away from mass transit but accessible enough for city dwellers.

There are four entry gates at Marlins Park, located at **home plate, first base, third base,** and **center field.** There are also two plazas. The **West Plaza** is where you'll find the home plate and first base entrances, while the **East Plaza** is home to the third base and center field entrances. Both plazas host outdoor events including concerts, and the West Plaza is where you'll find shopping like the New Era Team Store.

TICKETS AND SEATING

Pricing

The Marlins will hike up ticket prices for games they deem "**marquee,**" which essentially means events like **opening weekend** and games against teams that'll draw opposing fans, like the **Yankees** and **Red Sox** (and maybe the Phillies, Braves, and Mets). The average seat will cost about $20-25 for

non-marquee opponents like, say, the Brewers, while rivals will push that seat price to about $50-60.

Seating Plan

Let's go around the ballpark. The **field level** and **promenade level** comprise the **lower bowl** at Marlins Park, accessible from the promenade concourse. Starting at the right-field foul pole and moving toward home plate are **baseline reserved** (sections 1-6) in the lower rows and **The Social: Estrella Jalisco** (sections 1-3), a standing-room area with drink rails, in the higher rows. Next, near the first-base area, are **base reserved** (sections 7-8) plus, way down low, **first-base dugout** club (sections FL1-FL3). Wrapping around home plate are the promenade-level **home plate box** (sections 9-20) and, down low, **The**

Club: Dex Imaging (sections FL4-FL8). By third base are **base reserved** (sections 21-22) and the field level **Humana Cabana** (sections FL9-FL11). Then, in the left-field foul area toward the pole is **baseline reserved** (sections 23-27). At the foul pole and curving around into left field behind the outfield fence is **Marlins Crew** (sections 28-32), which is above the **left-field social area.** In center field are the standing-room **Budweiser Bar** and ticket-only standing-and-seating area **AutoNation Alley.** Seating continues in right field with **bullpen reserved** (sections 34-36) and, over the visitors' bullpen, the fun, fan-friendly area **Comunidad 305** (sections 38-40). Out in right field, there's a single deck of **elevated seating** called the **home run porch** (sections 134-141).

The next tier (**200 level**) of seats is

YOUR BEST DAY AT MARLINS PARK

You've got a full day in Miami plus a Marlins game tonight. You can do plenty; here's an itinerary.

10 HOURS BEFORE FIRST PITCH
Start the day right by heading to the beach. Specifically, plan a trip to **South Beach.** Get there early enough to snag a street parking spot a couple blocks away, then lounge out in the sand while taking in the view. Consult **Boucher Brothers** to rent a beach chair, and maybe a kayak if you're up for it.

7.5 HOURS BEFORE FIRST PITCH
Dust off that sand and drive back into town, then south to **Vizcaya Museum & Gardens.** Walk around the gardens and take in some American Gilded Age indulgences. Be sure to book your tickets in advance.

5 HOURS BEFORE FIRST PITCH
Time for a big lunch. Nothing is better than a Cuban at **Sanguich de Miami.** Enjoy every bite of crispy bread, salty meat, and gooey cheese.

3.5 HOURS BEFORE FIRST PITCH
Head over to **J. Wakefield Brewing**

a Cuban from Sanguich de Miami

Bobblehead Museum

and grab a beer or two. Be sure to sample a fruited sour.

1.5 HOURS BEFORE FIRST PITCH
Head toward **Marlins Park,** first visiting the **New Era Team Store.** Next, check out the **Marlins Home Run Sculpture,** then head into the ballpark and spend a little time scoping out the **Bobblehead Museum.** Pregame before first pitch with a trip to the **Biscayne Bay Brew Hall.**

DURING THE GAME
Settle in with a *fritanga* burger from **Pincho.** If you'd rather have some seafood, grab ceviche or sushi from **SuViche.** Get that second wind late in the game by sipping a *café cubano* from **Café La Rica.**

AFTER THE GAME
Wait out the traffic by walking next door to **Nightlife Brewing Co.** If you're still feeling up for some fun, hop in a rideshare vehicle and make a beeline to **Wood Tavern.**

After all that, you may need a late-night snack. The best spot to go is **Versailles Restaurant Cuban Cuisine.**

split between the **founders** and **legends levels.** Starting at the right-field foul pole, there are **legends** (sections 201-206) and, on top of that, the **fiesta suites** (sections 202-204). Then come seats in **legends platinum** (sections 207-211), with the **championship suites** (section S15) and

MVP suites (sections S16-S22) right on top of them. Around home plate are the **hall of fame club** (sections S1-S14) and, atop that, **legends suites** (sections S23-S34). Then along the third-base line are **legends platinum** (sections 219-222) and, atop that, **MVP suites** (sections S37-S41) and championship suites (section S42). Finally, in deep left field, you'll find **legends** (sections 223-228).

The upstairs (**300 level**) is all **vista box** (sections 302-327). In sections 306-310 and 320-322, the rows are split into lower and upper halves with stairs in between. Opt for lower rows (generally A-J). Depending on the game (say a midweek game against a team that won't draw many opposing fans), the Marlins may not sell tickets for this section.

Where to Buy Tickets

You're typically in good shape buying tickets straight from the **Marlins box office,** but if you're close to game day, comparison shop via **StubHub** and other **third-party ticket resellers.**

If you do purchase seats via the Marlins, you might be able to upgrade your seats through the **MLB Ballpark app.**

Best Seats

Most of the time, the roof will be over Marlins Park, so there won't be much reason to worry about where the sun is during a game. If the roof is open, however, eye the seats in the **back of the first-base line,** as in **sections 5-9.**

Aim to get a seat with a great view of the field (**sections 207-211, sections 9-11** and **18-20**), or opt for **standing-room** tickets and just spot up in the outfield by the Budweiser Bar. Maybe spend an inning or two at the left-field social area to check out that scene.

Want more party time? Get an **Estrella Jalisco Party Pass,** a cheap, **standing-room** ticket that will give you access to **The Social: Estrella Jalisco** (sections 1-3) and the upper level of **AutoNation Alley** (center field). Or, if you want to be immersed in Miami culture, there's **Comunidad 305** (sections 38-40), an area where banners are encouraged, and musical instruments like bongo drums, guiros, maracas, and trumpets are suggested. The area is inspired by the fan experience at soccer matches and during the World Baseball Classic, where supporters

GAME COSTS

Tickets: These are usually pretty inexpensive. You can score infield field-level seats for as little as **$25.** The cheap seats are typically less than **$10.**

Hot dog: The regular hot dog is **$5.25.** This is about average, maybe a tick higher. At some stands, it's possible to get a **$3** dog.

Beer: You can get beer for **$5** at certain stands, but that's macro-brewed stuff. A larger-size macro beer will be **$12,** while craft can cost between **$10.50** and **$14.50.**

Parking: If you park at a Marlins-designated garage or lot by the ballpark, be prepared to pay at least **$15.** It'll be **$10** or less if you park farther away in non-team lots.

chant and play noisemakers and instruments. Those with instruments are asked to enter the park at the **center field entrance.**

If you're with kids and trying not to break the bank, opt for **lower-level vista box seats** along the **first-base line** (sections 306-310).

KNOW BEFORE YOU GO

A **soft-sided bag** no larger than 16 by 16 by 8 inches is permitted at Marlins Park, as is a clear, soft-sided **empty bottle** or a bottle of **water.** Food (like sandwiches, snacks, and fruit) is also allowed, as long as it's stored in a clear plastic bag. You can bring in a **laptop.**

Miami is a hot place, but if it's too hot, the Marlins will close the **roof** and blast the **air conditioning,** so the chances of sitting in unbearable heat are slim. Still, it's always a good idea to bring **sunscreen** at all times of the year. An **umbrella** also isn't a bad idea, because South Florida in the summer means rain for about an hour every evening.

BE A FAN

The Marlins haven't always been known for a large fan base. But Fish fans I've met are pretty knowledgeable about the team and its history, and they're welcoming of other fans.

You'll get a nice dose of Miami culture by hanging out in or near **Comunidad 305** (sections 38-40), where fans are encouraged to bring **musical instruments** and treat the game more like a soccer match.

You may hear a song called **"Just Gettin' Started"** by Poo Bear, featuring DJ Khaled, Nicky Jam, and Kent Jones. The song was commissioned by Marlins ownership in 2018 to be the team's rally song.

fans on the outfield walkway at Marlins Park

Accessibility

Wheelchair-accessible seating is available throughout the ballpark; call the Marlins **ticket office** (305/480-2524) for details. At all seating areas, a maximum of three companions are permitted.

Speak with any guest services team member to retrieve an **assistive listening device.** (A photo ID is required as a deposit.) **Braille** and **tactile signs** are located throughout the park. You can borrow a **wheelchair** by contacting a guest services team member or by texting MARLINS with your name and location to 69050. **Strollers** for children with disabilities are also available; for assistance, ask for an entrance supervisor upon getting to Marlins Park.

There are eight **elevators** spread out over **five locations** (sections 1, 7, 18, 28, 34) at Marlins Park. Two **ramps** (first base entrance, third base entrance) head to the promenade level.

All four of the **parking garages** surrounding Marlins Park and all **surface lots** except West 3 and East 2 have accessible parking spaces. A disabled parking placard or license plate is required to park in these spots.

GETTING THERE

Public Transit

It's not a bad idea to take public transit to Marlins Park via the **Miami Metrorail** (www.miamidade.gov, $2.25 per ride). Both the **Green Line** and **Orange Line** stop at the closest station to the park, **Culmer** (NW 11th St. and NW 7th Ave.). It's a 0.8-mile, nearly 20-minute walk southwest from Culmer to the ballpark. Another option is to hop off at **Civic Center** (NW 15th St. and NW 12th Ave.), then walk nearly a mile south on NW 12th Avenue, turning west on NW 7th Street to reach Marlins Park.

Driving

To get to the park from the west or east, you may take the **Dolphin Expressway, a toll road.** If you don't have a **SunPass** (www.sunpass.com), Florida's toll-reading tag, cameras will record your license plate and you'll be charged twice as much as what you'd pay with a SunPass. My suggestion is to take main avenues and streets to reach the ballpark. From the east, you'll drive **West Flagler Street** into the area. From the west, follow West Flagler to **SW 1st Street.** From the north and south, **NW 17th Avenue** is the closest main drag. As an alternative, you can take **NW 12th Avenue.**

If you park in one of the ballpark's four **reserved garages** or four **reserved lots,** book a spot online (www.mlb.com/marlins) at least **two hours before first pitch.** You'll pay $15 for most games in advance, or $20 for marquee games (if the Yankees or Red Sox are in town, or it's opening day). If you don't pay in advance, prepare to pay $20 for weekend games and $25 for marquee matchups.

You can also park east of the ballpark in the **Overtown neighborhood,** or south of Marlins Park in **Little Havana.** Street parking may be hard to come by, but parking lots in these areas will generally cost you $10 or less. Or park across the Miami River near the **Civic Center** (NW 15th St. and NW 12th Ave.), where you'll pay $10; some lots offer **free shuttles** to Marlins Park.

PARK FEATURES AND SIGHTS

Until the end of the seventh inning, kids and parents can stop by **Billy's Kids Zone** (section 34), a small play area for those shorter than 42 inches. The main attraction here is Billy's Boathouse, where team mascot Billy the Marlin entertains children, usually at the top of the fifth inning. Parents are encouraged to line up with their children around the bottom of the fourth. Near the Boathouse is a virtual home-run derby area, where guests ages 12 and older can take a crack at hitting a big-league homer while wearing a VR headset.

To see one of the park's several unusual features, look behind home plate: You'll see two **450-gallon saltwater fish tanks** there. Don't worry about balls hitting the tanks—the Marlins installed a layer of polycarbonate to protect them.

The roof isn't the only thing that opens at Marlins Park: The glass wall behind left field is an **"operable" facade,** meaning it can open and shut depending on weather conditions. Either way, the wall out there offers a clear view of the Miami skyline.

Marlins Home Run Sculpture

Over the years, the Marlins have made major changes to the ballpark experience. When it opened, the park featured one of the most ridiculous and amazing sights baseball has ever seen: the **Marlins Home Run Sculpture.** Famous pop artist Red Grooms created this unusual and wildly colorful piece displaying a Miami scene: palm trees, pink flamingos, the beach, and the ocean down below, and four arches, each taller than the one in front of it. When the Marlins hit a home run, the sculpture lit up, showing a brilliant orange sun, seahorses, and shells, while marlins "swam" along the arches. Another marlin popped up from the top of the sculpture and spun around, as waterfalls blasted from either side. You'd have to see it to believe it.

The Home Run Sculpture was something of a divisive piece, so after a few years the Marlins took it down from its very visible center-field perch. In 2020, they re-erected it at the ballpark's East Plaza. There, you can see it in all its outrageous glory—it still lights up any time the Fish homer inside the park.

If you want to see more sculptures and art, there's plenty of it sprinkled around the park, both inside and outside, bringing a big dose of color to the park. Look for, among other pieces, the fun **alphabetic tribute to the Miami Orange Bowl** (East Plaza), the enormous mural *Play Ball* (section 11) by Kenny Scharf, and the postmodern, three-dimensional *Baseball in Motion* (section 1, above the concession stand) by Dominic Pangborn.

Bobblehead Museum

If there's one sight at Marlins Park you'll have to catch, it's the **Bobblehead Museum** (section 34), full of interesting and kooky baseball-themed bobbleheads collected over the years by former Marlins owner Jeffrey Loria. When it opened with the park, the museum held more than 1,000 of those toys; but when Loria sold the Marlins in 2017, he decided to donate about 900 of them to the National Baseball Hall of Fame and Museum. Still, about 400 stayed in Miami. It's essentially a big display case with shelves, but it's still a joy to scour. Every team is represented here, with some fun oddballs sprinkled in.

FOOD AND DRINKS

Marlins Park has one of the finest food selections of any park in America. First, it's well curated: There are about 15 individual vendors on the promenade concourse, each showing up once, each selling a distinct type of food. You'll find cheap hot dogs, popcorn, and other stadium favorites at just two places. Empanadas, barbecue beef, and sweets can each be found at their own single stand.

If you think this means lines are terrible, think again. The second great thing about Marlins Park's food selection is that it's diverse as all get-out. This is the one park where you really don't need to get a hot dog. Some popular Miami restaurants and eateries have stands here, serving up abbreviated menus of their greatest hits. You can get Cuban sandwiches, tacos, ceviche, and Latin-inspired fare, plus chicken sandwiches, salads, and pizza. People usually fan out pretty well with all of these options.

If you must, get hot dogs and the like at **Obie's** (section 13) and **Familia Faves** (section 37). Both these concessions have a special **$3 o $5 menu** The $3 selections include hot dogs, popcorn, pretzels, nachos, water, and soda, while for $5, you can get domestic beer or pork tacos.

The famous and altruistic chef José Andrés has a vendor stand at the park: Visit **Butterfly Tacos y Tortas y La Pepa** (section 8) for pork, beef, and mushroom tacos, plus a chicken torta, mole fries, and the pollo frito bocata, a chicken sandwich stuffed with French fries, the Cuban way.

Close to the right-field foul pole, naturally, is **Fowl Pole** (section 5), a chicken paradise with one of those chicken and waffle cones, plus a hot chicken sandwich. **Pincho** (section 19) does burgers with a Latin American spin. Try the *fritanga* burger, which joins a big beef patty with a fried mound of cheese. This stand also serves up sweet potato tots. Nearby is

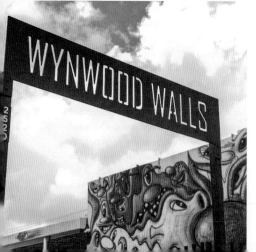

Photos (from top to bottom): Marlins Home Run Sculpture by sculptor Red Grooms; *fritanga* burger from Pincho; the Wynwood Arts District.

SuViche (section 23), specializing in—what else—sushi and ceviche. Next to that is **Novecento** (section 24), where you can grab an empanada or steak sandwich.

Ever try a *café cubano*? The notoriously strong, four-ounce espresso drink will pep you right up, and it's available at **Café La Rica** (section 39).

Those wanting a quick snack should head to **El Mercadito** (section 1), which offers grab-and-go sandwiches, salads, and other healthy options, plus drinks and chips. Near El Mercadito is **The Change Up** (section 2), where the park's chefs feature a rotating specialty concept such as Creole cuisine, which would feature shrimp po'boys, gumbo, and more. Finally, **Goya La Cocina** (section 40) features Latin American-inspired grub with a Goya touch—this is where you can get a Cuban sandwich, plus a rice and bean bowl and Goya chicken nachos.

Upstairs on the 200 and 300 levels, you'll find a more standardized concession layout, though look for **Rincon Habana** (sections 223, 315), which serves the same fare as Goya La Cocina.

Visit **Biscayne Bay Brew Hall** (section 15), a 3,000-square-foot bar and taproom featuring beer from this popular local craft brewery. Other than this spot, you won't find a lot of craft beer. The **Budweiser Bar** in center field is all Anheuser-Busch InBev products, including Miami's own **Veza Sur,** as well as **Goose Island** and **Estrella Jalisco.** You'll also find plenty of these latter two labels elsewhere in the park.

If you want frozen drinks and cocktails, head to **Fat Tuesdays** (section 2) or the aptly named **Frozen Drinks** (section 18).

EVENTS

You can attempt to score **autographs** next to the dugouts up to 45 minutes before first pitch, though there's no guarantee that players and coaches will sign.

Sunday home games are called **Family Sunday Fundays.** Pregame festivities take place at section 15, and children ages 14 and younger can **run the bases** after the game. After the game has ended, head to the bottom of the first-base helix ramp, accessible from section 6 of the promenade concourse.

Tours

The Marlins run a single **tour** (877/627-5467, 10am, noon, and 2pm Mon., Wed., and Fri.-Sat., $10) that isn't available when the team is playing. The tour may take folks into a clubhouse, through a dugout, and past interesting sights like the Bobblehead Museum and the home-plate fish tanks.

SHOPPING

The Marlins are an oddity in that their team store is not only outside the ballpark but also outside the gate and metal detectors. Because of that, it may be best to visit the **New Era Team Store** (501 Marlins Way, 305/480-1300, 10am-one hour after game ends on game days, 10am-4pm Mon.-Fri., 10am-3pm Sat. non-game days) before heading into Marlins Park. You can still go to the store during the game, but to do so, you'll need to head to the first-base entrance and get your hand stamped for reentry. If you don't mind missing some of the action, this actually isn't a bad way to shop, since most people will be watching the game. The team store is worth the potential inconvenience. Stylish and modern, with leather chairs and a minimalist aesthetic, it's an environment actually conducive to hanging around for a few minutes. All the usual stuff is here, like shirts, hats, jerseys, and memorabilia, but keep an eye out for World Baseball Classic merchandise, which is hard to find elsewhere.

There's also an **in-ballpark team store** (section 12), and a few smaller **kiosks** sell **hats** (sections 6 and 25), **custom jerseys** (section 15), and **game-used memorabilia** (section 6).

MIAMI SIGHTS

WYNWOOD ARTS DISTRICT

If you want to start somewhere for arts and culture, head straight to the **Wynwood Arts District** (NW 26th St. and NW 2nd Ave., www.wynwoodmiami.com). Full of art galleries, bars, and boutiques, with walls painted with murals and graffiti, and with the constant chatter of young people filling the air, it's the place to be in Miami if you're not into the whole beach-and-club scene. Of special note are those walls, actually an initiative called **Wynwood Walls** (www.thewynwoodwalls.com). A number of local and global artists have participated in this by turning the ordinary fronts, sides, and backs of buildings into beautiful works of art. Check out more works by those artists at the **Goldman Global Arts Gallery** (266 NW 26th St., 786/615-4233, www.ggagallery.com, 11am-9pm daily, free). Then, pay a visit to the modern and Latin American art collections at **Gary Nader Art Centre** (62 NE 27th St., 305/576-0256, www.garynader.com, 10am-6pm Mon.-Fri., noon-10pm Sat., free).

VENETIAN POOL

Whether or not you have kids, you might want to pay a visit to the **Venetian Pool** (2701 De Soto Blvd., Coral Gables, 305/460-5306, 11am-6:30pm Mon.-Fri., 10am-4pm Sat.-Sun. Memorial Day-Aug., $15 ages 13 and older, $10 ages 3-12). This famous 820,000-gallon pool created from a coral rock quarry in 1923 is fed with spring water and has two waterfalls, plus grottoes and a bridge. It's an incredible pool, perfect for that steamy Miami morning or afternoon. Note: Children younger than three are not permitted, and parents must show proof of children's age if they are at or near age three.

VIZCAYA MUSEUM & GARDENS

On the Deering Channel south of Downtown is **Vizcaya Museum & Gardens** (3251 S. Miami Ave., 305/250-9133, www.vizcaya.org, 9:30am-4:30pm Wed.-Mon., $22, $15 ages 13-17, $10 ages 6-12, free ages 5 and under), a historic home that symbolizes early 20th century wealth in South Florida. The centerpiece is the Mediterranean Revival-style mansion where business executive James Deering lived from its 1916

the Venetian Pool

opening until his death in 1925. In 1994, the estate was deemed a National Historic Landmark, and a few years later, it opened as a museum. Tour the house and gardens to view the objects and art that remain, from Napoleonic-era furniture to outdoor statues dating to the 18th century. While visits to Vizcaya are generally self-guided, you can get a **private tour** (305/860-8442) if you're with a group.

FOOD

NEAR MARLINS PARK

Don't bet on great food within walking distance of Marlins Park: For the closest stuff, you'll really want to drive a few minutes west into Little Havana. Still, there are a few worthwhile spots for those spilling out of the park. **Mexican Taqueria Los Chilangos** (1801 NW 7th St., 786/230-0124, www.mexicantaquerialoschilangos.com, 6pm-12:30am Sun.-Mon. and Wed.-Thurs., 6pm-1:30am Fri.-Sat., under $20) is a food truck operating only in the evenings. The usual taco fare is available (carne asada, al pastor, chorizo), along with burritos, quesadillas, tostadas, and Mexican drinks.

For a quick pregame bite of empanadas and sweet breads (called mantecadas), visit **Btwins Panadería Nicaraguense** (1550 SW 1st St. #15, 305/649-4130, under $20), a mom-and-pop Nicaraguan spot just south of the ballpark across West Flagler Street. Bring cash and be ready to order.

For something a little more relaxed, try **Yambo** (1643 SW 1st St., 305/649-0203, under $30), which looks like a restaurant sprouted inside a dusty antiques store. A couple horse statues greet you out front. Go inside to peruse paintings, old signs, and masks, then nab a bite of some Nicaraguan food. Get the carne asada, served with plenty of rice and beans. You can't go wrong with traditional nacatamal (similar to a tamale).

OTHER NEIGHBORHOODS

Wynwood

Wynwood is home to quite a few top draws. **Le Chick Miami** (310 NW 24th St., 786/216-7086, www.lechickrotisserie.com, noon-10:30pm Sun.-Wed., noon-11:30pm Thurs.-Sat., under $50) does some super casual dishes like fried chicken (in and out of sandwiches), burgers, and street corn, but also more upscale items like New York strip steak, inside a cozy and modern eatery with brick walls and good lighting. This is a solid neighborhood restaurant.

Bakan (2801 NW 2nd Ave., 305/396-7080, www.bakanwynwood.com, noon-11pm Sun.-Wed., noon-2am Thurs.-Sat., under $50) elevates the traditional Mexican experience of tacos, meaty dishes, and margaritas inside a cool spot with a beautiful outdoor patio. Get tacos, enchiladas, sopas (soups), and mole dishes here, along with a nice collection of margaritas and agave-based cocktails.

If you're searching for good soul food, look no further than **World Famous House of Mac** (2055 NW 2nd Ave., 786/636-6967, www.houseofmac.com, noon-11pm Mon.-Thurs., noon-2am Fri.-Sat., noon-midnight Sun., under $40). Here, owner Derrick Turton (also known as Chef Teach) cooks up several varieties of mac and cheese, plus comfort staples like fried chicken and waffles and jerk pasta. Turton was once rapper Pitbull's manager, so celebrities roll through from time to time—keep your eyes open.

Little Havana

While Tampa claims to be the birthplace of the Cuban sandwich, my favorite version is in Miami at **Sanguich de Miami** (2057 SW 8th St., 305/539-0969, www.sanguich.com, 10am-9pm Mon.-Thurs., 10am-10pm Fri.-Sat., 10am-8pm Sun., under $20). Tuck into this 25-seat café and nab a counter seat, if you can. Take in everything: the Spanish tile, the perfectly organized shelves, the brass embellishments, the speedy cooks making crispy, cheesy, meaty, wholly satisfying Cuban sandwiches. Aside from

Cubans, a few sandwiches and snacks are offered, along with coffee drinks and other beverages.

West of Marlins Park in the Little Havana neighborhood is a true Miami tradition. **Versailles Restaurant Cuban Cuisine** (3555 SW 8th St., 305/444-0240, www.versailles-restaurant.com, 8am-1am Mon.-Thurs., 8am-2:30am Fri.-Sat., 9am-1am Sun., under $40) is as popular as it gets in town. It opened in 1971 as a hub of Cuban activity, and today it's the place to be at nearly any hour. Go late, preferably after a night at the bar or club, and dive into some chicharróns with rice and beans, a sandwich, or a whole fish. Be sure to sit back and watch everyone in the space have a blast.

BARS AND BREWERIES

NEAR MARLINS PARK

The one bar I recommend near the park is **Edukos Beer House** (1701 W. Flagler St. #101, 786/452-0488, www.edukosmiami.com, 4pm-11pm Mon.-Thurs., 4pm-midnight Fri.,

Sat.). A funky place with stone walls and a tiny, circular bar, Edukos feels like a hidden gem. The bar has a unique and terrific beer list that includes some local favorites and great, harder-to-find fare from across the country. Pair your beer with Latin American bites like empanadas and arepas (stuffed grilled cornmeal cakes), plus burgers and well-executed sandwiches.

As for breweries, there's one right next to the park inside the home-plate parking garage. **Nightlife Brewing Co.** (1588 NW 7th St., 786/787-2337, www.nightlifebrewingco.com, noon-9pm Mon., 4pm-11pm Tues.-Thurs., 4pm-midnight Fri., 1pm-midnight Sat., noon-10pm Sun.) has a laid-back, stylish taproom with blown-up vintage photographs of Miami, a cool wood backdrop at the bar, and plenty of seating.

OTHER NEIGHBORHOODS

Wynwood

Miami is still growing as a beer city, but my favorite place so far is **J. Wakefield Brewing** (120 NW 24th St., 786/254-7779, www.jwakefieldbrewing.com, noon-11pm Mon.-Thurs., noon-1am Fri.-Sat., noon-10pm Sun.). This small but thoughtful brewery and taproom has hip graffiti murals on the walls,

South Beach

a sleek L-shaped bar, friendly bartenders, and an adventurous collection of beers. Try any of the fruited sour offerings.

Visit **Wood Tavern** (2531 NW 2nd Ave., 305/748-2828, www.woodtavern.com, 5pm-2am Mon., 5pm-3am Tues.-Fri., noon-3am Sat., 3pm-midnight Sun.), a laid-back bar with both indoor and outdoor seating. The wood patio outside gets packed when the weather is good. There's artsy graffiti on just about everything here, including the trash cans. Come when you want to chill among tons of people without getting all dressed up for the club.

I have to applaud Anheuser-Busch InBev for launching a craft brewery that maintains a strong Latin vibe throughout. **Veza Sur Brewing Co.** (55 NW 25th St., 786/362-6300, www.vezasur.com, noon-midnight Sun. and Tues.-Thurs., noon-2am Fri.-Sat.) makes beers of all styles that often include ingredients from Mexican, Central American, South American, and Caribbean cuisines. Both the indoor bar and outdoor patio seating areas will usually be crowded, and soccer watch parties are common occurrences, too. This place is a blast.

Little Havana

Looking for hard-to-find beers, the most chill environs in Miami, and plenty of throwback pro wrestling on TV? **The Union Beer Store** (1547 SW 8th St., 786/313-3919, www.unionbeerstore.com, 5pm-11pm Mon., 1pm-midnight Tues.-Wed., 1pm-1am Thurs., 1pm-2am Fri., noon-2am Sat., noon-10pm Sun.) is the place for you. Order a beer, watch some vintage WWE action, grab a taco from **El Punto Tacos & Tattoos** in the back-room kitchen. On your way out, you can buy some beer to go from the storage fridges.

Miami Beach

Distill Miami into two or three things, and one is bound to be nightlife. The city's club scene is massive, so you have to sample at least a few spots here. One of the better clubs for newbies to the scene is the cheeky and adventurous **Do Not Sit on the Furniture** (423 16th St., 510/551-5067, www.donotsitonthefurniture.com, 11pm-5am

Wed.-Thurs., 10pm-5am Fri.-Sat., cover $15-20), which specializes in live house music as well as house and techno DJ sets. You won't blow a ton of money here, as both cover and drink prices are quite reasonable. Plus, it's lit so that it's just dark enough inside, and it doesn't take itself too seriously: The main room is highlighted by an enormous disco ball and a disco shark.

Also on Miami Beach is the mega-popular **LIV** (4441 Collins Ave., 305/674-4680, www.livnightclub.com, 11pm-5am Wed.-Sun., cover $30-40, special performances up to $200), part of the five-star Fontainebleau Miami Beach hotel. In a space that once played host to legends like Frank Sinatra and Tony Bennett, LIV is a fully immersive modern-day club experience with four full-service bars. This a see-and-be-seen club where all action focuses on the space's centerpiece dome and steel trusses, known as the "spider." Some of the biggest hit-makers of the day might perform at LIV, and if you're lucky, you might happen to see a celebrity.

RECREATION

BEACHES AND PARKS

South Beach

First and foremost is **South Beach** (Ocean Dr. and 10th St., Miami Beach), the southern end of Miami Beach that faces the Atlantic Ocean. A greenbelt separates the street from the sand—here you can find volleyball courts, art installations, and the famous **Muscle Beach,** a workout area where the buffest folks flex and lift. It's a quick walk to the ocean, and the best time to go is morning or just before sunset on a weekday.

If you're not staying at a hotel with beach service, visit a **Boucher Brothers kiosk** for beach chairs, umbrellas, kayak rentals, and parasail boat tours. Boucher Brothers operates eight kiosks in Miami: one bayside at the **Mondrian South Beach Hotel** (1100 West Ave.) and seven on Miami Beach. There are three kiosks between 44th and 48th Streets

Bill Baggs Cape Florida State Park

on Miami Beach, while the primary South Beach location is at 22nd Street on the beach.

For another kayak option, try **South Beach Kayak** (1771 Purdy Ave., Miami Beach, 305/975-5087, www.southbeach-kayak.com, 10:30am-6pm Mon.-Fri., 9am-6pm Sat.-Sun., $20-30 per hour). They also host a **sunset kayak tour** ($65-120) out on Biscayne Bay.

North Beach

Just seven miles or so north of South Beach is, unsurprisingly, **North Beach** (Collins Ave. and 79th St., Miami Beach). Not as flashy as its sister to the south, North Beach is quieter, laid-back, and family-friendly. A long boardwalk spans the length of the beach, passing through **North Shore Open Space Park** (Collins Ave. and 85th St., Miami Beach), which has a dog run and playground.

Bill Baggs Cape Florida State Park

For a superb beach, go 15 minutes southeast of Miami via FL-913 to **Bill Baggs Cape Florida State Park** (1200 Crandon Blvd., Key Biscayne, 8am-sunset daily, $4-8 per vehicle, $2 pedestrians and bicyclists). You can launch a kayak or paddleboat at the park, but there are no rentals. **Bicycle rentals** ($9-20 per hour) are available, though.

Also here is the **Cape Florida Lighthouse** (305/361-5811, 9am-4pm Thurs.-Mon.). Take a tour at 10am and 1pm on days it's open, or ascend the 109 steps yourself. At the top is a balcony with great views of Biscayne Bay and Miami Beach.

ACCOMMODATIONS

NEAR MARLINS PARK

Don't expect posh lodging near the ballpark. The closest thing to standard accommodations within walking distance is the **Hostel Brazilian** (133 SW 17th Ct., 866/925-8676, $50-100). As this is a hostel, expect the most basic amenities. You'll stay in a shared dormitory with other folks, and you'll also share a bathroom with people. This is fine if you're looking to save some money, but there are good options for just a little more cash that are just a bit farther from Marlins Park.

OTHER NEIGHBORHOODS

About 1.2 miles east of Marlins Park, the **Copper Door B&B** (439 NW 4th Ave., 305/454-9065, www.copperdoorbnb.com, $80-200) has 22 guest rooms and three suites in a circa 1940s building. The modern, clean rooms wouldn't be out of place in a hipster boutique hotel. Guests can't get enough of the married couple that owns the place. Breakfast is served daily. It's hard to find a better deal in the city.

Closer to Downtown and along the shoreline, you'll find plenty of chain boutique hotels. One of the more affordable and pleasant is **Novotel Miami Brickell Hotel** (1500 SW 1st Ave., 786/600-2600, http://all.accor. com, $100-250). The hotel has 275 rooms with queen and king beds, plus a Peruvian restaurant and a rooftop bar and swimming pool.

GETTING AROUND

PUBLIC TRANSIT

Miami doesn't have a very sophisticated public transit system. The **Miami Metrorail** (www.miamidade.gov, $2.25 per ride) is the primary method of rail travel in the city, offering a limited system of transportation. The Metrorail **Green Line** starts up in suburban cities like Hialeah and comes into town before connecting to Downtown stops like **Government Center** (NW 1st Ave. and NW 2nd St.) and **Brickell** (SW 1st Ave. and SW 12th St.). The line then heads south toward the commercial district of Dadeland.

When Downtown, you can hop on the **Metromover** (www.miamidade.gov, free), a daily service that takes riders around the neighborhood, connecting them to key locations. The Metromover has three routes: The **Omni Loop** starts north of Downtown and heads in toward Government Center, then around toward Bayfront Park and back up

to Museum Park; the **Brickell Loop** does the same Downtown loop that includes Government Center and Bayfront Park, but it goes south of there and hits locations like Brickell City Centre and the Tenth Street Promenade; and the **Inner Loop** just does the Downtown circle including Government Center, Bayfront Park, and a few other stops. It's a fine way to get around Downtown, but it's most convenient if you're spending more than a couple hours there.

The city also has a vast network of **buses,** including **trolleys.** Major routes include the **A,** which connects Downtown passengers to Miami Beach, and the **8,** which travels along Calle Ocho, or SW 8th Street.

TAXI, UBER, AND LYFT

Generally, Uber and Lyft will be cheaper and, on the whole, a friendlier experience than taking taxis in Miami. Uber and Lyft are similar in cost in Miami.

CAR

The main highway into Miami is **I-95,** which starts way up in Maine and travels the entire East Coast to get here. I-95 threads just west of Downtown Miami before ending, merging into **US-1.** You can drive US-1 through Miami, too, as it is known as **Biscayne Boulevard** in the main city limits.

Two offshoots of I-95 also cut into the city: **I-595** comes off **I-75** and hooks up with Fort Lauderdale, while **I-195** offers a direct connection to Miami Beach from Downtown Miami. I-75 enters the Miami area from the northwest, then turns south before cutting through Hialeah, then loops back north.

Heavily trafficked thoroughfares include **Calle Ocho,** the famous Latin artery also known as **SW 8th Street.** Look for **West Flagler Street,** which connects Downtown to outer areas, including the airport. The main north-south streets include **NW 12th Avenue** and **NW 27th Avenue.**

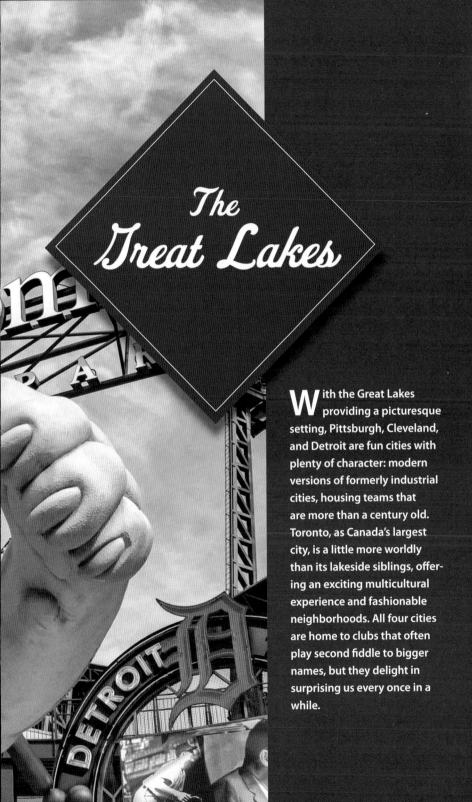

The Great Lakes

With the Great Lakes providing a picturesque setting, Pittsburgh, Cleveland, and Detroit are fun cities with plenty of character: modern versions of formerly industrial cities, housing teams that are more than a century old. Toronto, as Canada's largest city, is a little more worldly than its lakeside siblings, offering an exciting multicultural experience and fashionable neighborhoods. All four cities are home to clubs that often play second fiddle to bigger names, but they delight in surprising us every once in a while.

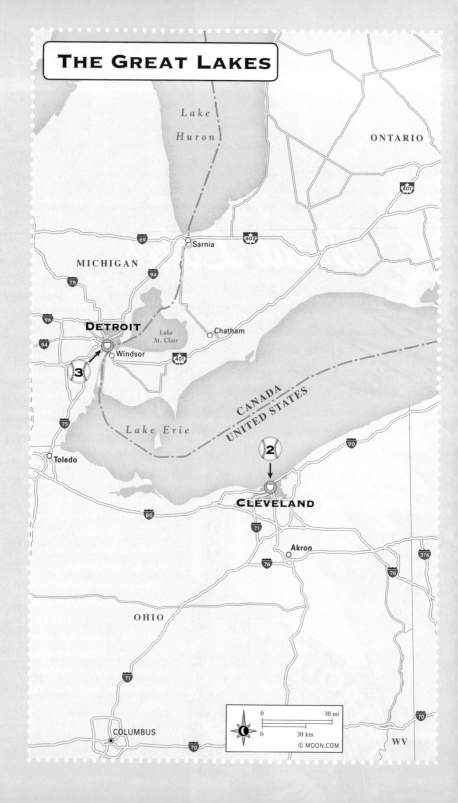

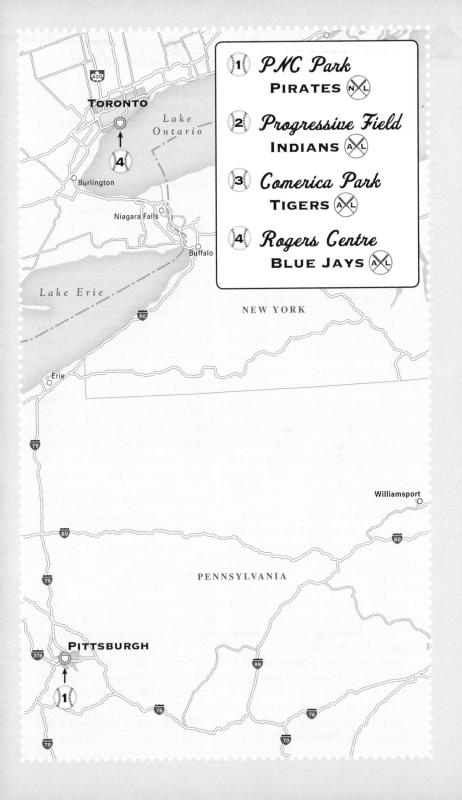

① **PNC Park**
PIRATES Ⓝ ⊗ Ⓛ

② **Progressive Field**
INDIANS Ⓐ ⊗ Ⓛ

③ **Comerica Park**
TIGERS Ⓐ ⊗ Ⓛ

④ **Rogers Centre**
BLUE JAYS Ⓐ ⊗ Ⓛ

TORONTO
Lake Ontario
Burlington
Niagara Falls
Buffalo

Lake Erie

NEW YORK

Erie

Williamsport

PENNSYLVANIA

PITTSBURGH

The Great Lakes Road Trip

Pittsburgh, Cleveland, and Detroit are large metropolises that came to prominence in the early 20th century. Each has been impacted greatly by changing times but has still evolved with its people, even as the cities' populations have decreased over the past seven decades. And while their teams don't have the might of the Yankees, Dodgers, or Cubs, their fans are steadfast.

Set along Lake Ontario and located about four hours northeast of Detroit, Toronto is also a city of the early 20th century, but one that has continued to grow. Baseball came to town in 1977; about a decade later, the Blue Jays moved into the enormous, contemporary SkyDome (today known as Rogers Centre). In contrast, the Pirates, Indians, and Tigers played in older parks up until the 1990s, when they moved slowly into retro-classic and retro-modern parks that harkened to their home cities' most prosperous days.

There are a lot of good things about the Great Lakes region. Lakeside beaches offer fun and relaxation in the summer. The beer is young and old, from craft darlings like Great Lakes and Bells to old-school stalwarts like Iron City and Stroh's. Foodies will find upscale delights just as often as comforts like sausages and greasy fries.

This road trip begins in Pittsburgh and ends 530 miles later in Toronto, Ontario, spanning much of Lake Erie's shores and cozying up to Lake Ontario. The middle section of the route takes you from Cleveland to Detroit, on a drive that can feel a bit repetitive: lots of gray highway, green trees and fields, and perennially cloudy skies.

Start in **Pittsburgh.** Taking in a **Pirates** game at PNC Park will grant you the best view in baseball. Next is **Cleveland,** a baseball hotbed that's home to the **Indians** and some of the sport's most dedicated fans. You'll carry on to **Detroit,** which is seeing its way out of tough times and has its own great park. The **Tigers** personify the city's

fighting spirit. The trip ends with a final leg up to **Toronto,** an inventive city with exceptional dining options. See the **Blue Jays** play at the Rogers Centre, a ballpark with a hotel built right into the outfield backdrop.

PLANNING YOUR TIME

Can you tackle this trip in **one week**? Absolutely. Spend two days in Pittsburgh, a day in Cleveland, two days in Detroit, and two days in Toronto.

That's not enough time to really appreciate these locations, though, so I recommend taking **10 days.** This will give you up to four days in Toronto, which has plenty of neighborhoods and spaces to discover, as well as an extra day to check out a smaller city with a minor league team like Toledo, Ohio, or the home of the Little League World Series, **Williamsport,** Pennsylvania.

You can also divide the trip into **two parts.** Combine Pittsburgh and Cleveland, which are separated by about two hours. Add Williamsport or maybe Akron, Ohio, to the route if you want to stretch it to a **week.** Then start a second trip with three days in Toronto, followed by a drive southwest to Detroit for a two-day stay. End the trip with a sojourn in Toledo, if you want to tack on a day or two, for another full **week.**

It's only eight hours total from Pittsburgh to Toronto if you were to drive it all in one shot. Be wary of the major highways (especially I-90 and I-75) that might have some backups around rush hour (7:30am-9:30am and 4:30pm-6:30pm weekdays). In Michigan, the speed limit can be up to 75 mph, which is different from surrounding states. Of course, Canada uses the metric system, which means you'll be reading kilometers per hour (kph). Urban highway speeds typically get up to 100 kph, or 62 mph.

The following is my recommended itinerary for the 10-day version of this road trip.

Photos (top): one of Comerica Park's decorative tigers; (middle left) sculpture of Roberto Clemente at PNC Park by sculptor Susan Wagner; (middle right) Progressive Field, home to the Cleveland Indians; (bottom) Toronto's Left Field Brewery.

Day 1

Arrive in **Pittsburgh,** preferably on a Friday, and spend the day and evening seeing neighborhoods like Shadyside, the Strip District, and Lawrenceville.

Day 2

Take time in the morning to visit the Cultural District and Point State Park. Before an afternoon game at **PNC Park,** be sure to walk across the Roberto Clemente Bridge. Get to bed early so you can wake up and hit the road to Cleveland.

Day 3

Begin your drive to **Cleveland** by 9am. You should arrive a couple hours before first pitch for an afternoon game, giving you ample time to scope out **Progressive Field** and the Gateway District. After the game, hang out Downtown a bit more.

Day 4

I recommend using this as a rest and transition day. Options include a hike or two at Cuyahoga Valley National Park, or a day trip to **Akron** or **Toledo** for a minor league game.

Day 5

Arrive in **Detroit** around mid-morning, so you'll have a full day in front of you. Have a Coney dog, see the Detroit Riverwalk, and visit Hitsville U.S.A. (now the Motown Museum) before the Tigers game at **Comerica Park.**

Day 6

Spend more than half the day in Detroit before driving northeast to **Toronto.** I recommend starting the drive before rush hour so you won't hit major traffic in either city. Be sure to have your passport as you enter Canada.

Day 7

Wake up in Toronto and plan on a fun day exploring neighborhoods like Kensington Market, Queen West, and the Danforth.

Day 8

Hang out around Old Toronto and the Entertainment District. Catch a Blue Jays game tonight at the **Rogers Centre.**

Day 9

Spend today on the beach at Centre Island.

Toronto Blue Jays art

Day 10

Depending on when you're planning to leave, you may have a little more time to explore another Toronto neighborhood. After that, it's time to say good-bye to Canada's largest city and your Great Lakes baseball road trip.

GETTING THERE

Air

Fly into **Pittsburgh International Airport** (PIT, 1000 Airport Blvd., 412/472-3525, www.flypittsburgh.com), 20 miles west of Downtown Pittsburgh via I-376 West. Airlines here include **Air Canada** (888/247-2262, www.aircanada.com), **Allegiant** (702/505-8888, www.allegiantair.com), **American Airlines** (800/433-7300, www.aa.com), **Delta** (800/221-1212, www.delta.com), **Frontier** (800/401-9000, www.flyfrontier.com), **jetBlue** (800/538-2583, www.jetblue.com), **Southwest** (800/435-9792, www.southwest.com), **Spirit** (801/401-2222, www.spirit.com), and **United** (800/864-8331, www.united.com).

You'll fly out of **Toronto Pearson International Airport** (YYZ, 6301 Silver Dart Dr., Mississauga, www.torontopearson.com), located 15 miles northwest of the city. Airlines include Air Canada, American Airlines, Delta, and United, plus several other international carriers. There are two terminals (Terminal 1 and Terminal 3), and you can get to most major American cities from here.

Train

Doing this trip via train is too convoluted and would delay you more than you'd like. But if you're arriving via rail, you'll be heading into **Pittsburgh Union Station** (1100 Liberty Ave.). **Amtrak** (www.amtrak.com) operates two lines that stop in Pittsburgh: the **Capitol Limited,** which starts in Washington DC and continues west to Chicago, and the **Pennsylvanian,** which connects New York City and Philadelphia to the Steel City.

To continue to Cleveland from Pittsburgh, you'll go via the Capitol Limited. It's close to a three-hour trip that'll cost a minimum of about $20. There's no direct train from Cleveland to Detroit or from Detroit to Toronto.

If taking the train out of Toronto, it'll be from **Toronto Union Station** (65 Front St. W., 888/842-7245, www.torontounion.ca). You can hop on Amtrak's **Maple Leaf** line here, which heads toward Buffalo and other New York cities (Rochester, Syracuse, Albany) before turning south to New York City.

PITTSBURGH
PIRATES

Dressed in black and yellow, often called the Bucs and Buccos, and raising the "Jolly Roger" after victories, the Pittsburgh Pirates are a classic National League franchise that's been playing baseball near the confluence of the Allegheny, Monongahela, and Ohio Rivers for more than a century.

The Pirates were formed in the 1880s and joined the young National League in 1887, an organization that at the time also included the teams known today as the Atlanta Braves, Chicago Cubs, Philadelphia Phillies, and San Francisco Giants. One of the early success stories of the league, the Buccos won pennants in 1901, '02, '03, and '09, with a World Series championship coming in that last season. The Pirates, while at majestic Forbes Field, also employed Dead Ball Era

legend Honus Wagner, who hit for a career .328 average and finished with 3,420 hits. The Pirates hit a low period between 1927 and 1960, failing to win the pennant during that time and having to watch every other NL team (even the Phillies, their archrival) take the league at some point.

Luck changed in 1960, as an upstart Pittsburgh team led by famed hitter Roberto Clemente took the pennant. In the World Series, the Pirates took the far stronger Yankees to seven games, winning it all with arguably the most memorable hit in championship history: a ninth-inning, game- and series-winning home run from future Hall of Famer Bill Mazeroski.

For the next decade, the Pirates became a force that routinely won their division, taking home another title in 1971. A year later, Clemente, in his late 30s, recorded his 3,000th career hit on the season's final day. On December 31 of that year, while Clemente was on a trip to aid earthquake victims in Nicaragua, the plane he was in crashed in the Atlantic Ocean, killing him and everyone else on board. The Hall of Famer was and still is the face of Pirates baseball, an inspiring and giving man who possessed stunning athleticism and hitting ability.

The Pirates won another title in 1979, backed by slugger Willie "Pops" Stargell and the Sister Sledge song "We Are Family," and reigned atop the NL East division for a spell in the early 1990s before enduring a disastrous stretch of mostly last-place finishes that ended in 2013. That year, the team nearly returned to the National League Championship Series, and the next two years did lead to playoff appearances. But in 2016, the Buccos returned to the bottom half of their division, where they've since remained.

Though the Buccos have been one of baseball's worst-performing organizations, their robust history of great players and championship teams have kept Pirates fans coming to the gorgeous PNC Park. Optimism is always in the air in April, and though things don't usually turn out well for Pittsburgh, pride in the team has always been strong.

PLANNING YOUR TIME

A smaller city, Pittsburgh can be tackled in **two days** or a **long weekend.** A visit to PNC Park will highlight one day, and it can be coupled with a trip to the nearby Andy Warhol Museum and a visit to one of the local inclines, which have a gorgeous view of the skyline. On the second day, head into neighborhoods like the **Strip District** and **Shadyside.**

When staying in Pittsburgh, **Downtown** (known as the **Golden Triangle**) is a good option because you can walk to the ballpark and a few of the major sights, and then use ride-sharing for neighborhood visits. You could also room in the **Shadyside** area if you plan on spending more time in the neighborhoods outside the Golden Triangle.

Pittsburgh is in western Pennsylvania, east of what we'd consider the Midwest, and west of what we'd consider the mid-Atlantic region. All this is to say Pittsburgh has a little midwestern climate and a little mid-Atlantic climate. It gets **hot** in **midsummer,** but it's typically **less humid** than Philly and Baltimore. During the **winter,** it'll get **cold** and **snowy,** but it won't usually be as bad as lake cities like Cleveland and Chicago. It'll be **chilly** in **April, May,** and **September.** The best time to visit is **midsummer** between **June and August.** The first couple weeks of June are perfect, and **summer night games** are awesome.

GETTING THERE

AIR

The main airport in the area is **Pittsburgh International Airport** (PIT, 1000 Airport Blvd., 412/472-3525, www.flypittsburgh.

com), 20 miles west of Downtown Pittsburgh via I-376 West. Airlines servicing travelers here include **Air Canada** (888/247-2262, www.aircanada.com), **Allegiant** (702/505-8888, www.allegiantair.com), **American Airlines** (800/433-7300, www.aa.com), **Delta** (800/221-1212, www.delta.com), **Frontier** (800/401-9000, www.flyfrontier.com), **jetBlue** (800/538-2583, www.jetblue.com), **Southwest** (800/435-9792, www.southwest.com), **Spirit** (801/401-2222, www.spirit.com), and **United** (800/864-8331, www.united.com). The airport has one terminal with four concourses.

Airport Transportation

There's no connection to mass transit from the airport. You could grab the **28X Airport Flyer bus** from the **Port Authority** (412/442-2000, www.portauthority.org, $2.50) that connects passengers to Downtown. Otherwise, you can order a ride-sharing vehicle, hail a taxi, or **rent a car** via one of the major players. The rental counters are downstairs by baggage claim, and the cars are just a quick walk from there.

TRAIN

The turn-of-the-20th-century landmark **Pittsburgh Union Station** (1100 Liberty Ave.), built in the Beaux-Arts style, is where **Amtrak** (800/872-7245, www.amtrak.com) pulls into town. Amtrak operates two lines that stop in Pittsburgh: the **Capitol Limited,** which starts in Washington DC and continues west to Chicago, and the **Pennsylvanian,** which connects New York City and Philadelphia to the Steel City. To get to Pittsburgh from Cleveland by rail, you'll take the Capitol Limited for a three-hour trip that'll cost a minimum of about $20.

Union Station is on the eastern end of Downtown Pittsburgh, a mile from the ballpark. You can walk west on Penn Avenue to 6th Street, then turn right to head onto the Roberto Clemente Bridge toward PNC Park. The walk will take about 20 minutes.

BUS

Pittsburgh's **Greyhound Station** (55 11th St., 412/392-6514, www.greyhound.com) is just across the street from Union Station. Greyhound buses run regularly to and from **Cleveland** (the three-hour ride starts at $10-15). Buses also arrive from **Philadelphia** (a six-to nine-hour ride that'll cost around $30-40).

If you're taking **Megabus** (128 10th St., 877/462-6342, http://us.megabus.com) to Pittsburgh, the terminal is just two blocks northwest of the Greyhound station. The ride from Philadelphia takes around eight hours and costs $30. Megabus doesn't serve Cleveland.

PNC Park

When **PNC Park** (115 Federal St., www.mlb.com/pirates) opened in 2001, it resembled other retro-classic parks built before it, like Oriole Park at Camden Yards in Baltimore and Oracle Park in San Francisco. Made of limestone and steel fabricated in Pennsylvania, PNC fits into the landscape of the city around it. There's an impressive, two-deck seating area around the infield. Its lines are sharp and clean, evoking parks of the past, like Forbes Field, former home of the Pirates. Though its primary feature is the water just beyond the right-field stands, there's even more to see beyond the outfield. A triumph of ballpark design and location, PNC carries one of the coolest views of any ballpark in the world: the Pittsburgh skyline just across the Monongahela River, along with a few bridges that cross that body of water. For the pleasing visual experience alone, PNC Park is a must-visit.

With its riverside trail and a limestone-and-steel exterior that blends in with the rest of the city's architecture, PNC fits like a glove in the Pittsburgh cityscape. Best of all, the park is easy to reach on foot, thanks to the nearby Roberto Clemente Bridge, which closes to vehicles on game days. From the moment you begin your journey to PNC Park, you know you're in for a fantastic experience.

The ballpark oozes comfort and charm. With an in-game presentation that feels like a fun minor league experience, and relatively affordable parking and food, it's one of the better MLB venues for a group or family outing.

ORIENTATION

PNC is located on the shore of the North Side neighborhood, beside the site of the now-demolished Three Rivers Stadium. The ballpark is part of a miniature sports complex that garners plenty of tourism year-round—it's just a few minutes' walk to the Steelers' football stadium, Heinz Field.

There are five gates at PNC Park. Most of the gates open 90 minutes before first pitch. However, the **Clemente Gate,** which is the closest to the Roberto Clemente Bridge, opens 2 hours before first pitch on day games, and 2.5 hours before first pitch for games that start at 7:05pm or later. Other gates are at left field, right field, and home plate.

TICKETS AND SEATING

Pricing

At PNC Park, tickets are priced differently and **dynamically** by **location** and **opponent.**

The closer you are to home plate, the more expensive the seat in relation to other seats in your level. A seat in the PBC Baseline section may cost $35-40 for a game against the Marlins, who won't draw many fans to the park. But if the popular Cardinals are facing the Buccos, that seat's price may increase to about $50-60. For a weekend contest against the Yankees, whose fans are everywhere, that seat may even be more like $70-80.

You can get a 100 level seat and a Miller Lite at the Miller Lite Skull Bar with a $20 **Pirates Great Taste Ticket.** Just note that your seat will be in a section that doesn't have that primo view (and may have direct sunshine).

Seating Plan

PNC Park has a ton of seating in foul territory with a few bleacher-like areas in the outfield. There are three levels at the park: the **100 level** (all sections called "box"), the **200 level,** also called the **PBC Level** (short for Pittsburgh Baseball Club) or the **club level,** and the **300 level** (all sections called "grandstand"). The 100-300 level seats in the outfield have additional designations, from "bleachers" to "rooftop" to "reserved."

Let's start in the **100 level** by the right-field foul pole. Here, you'll find the **corner box** (section 101), **outfield box** (sections

game at PNC Park

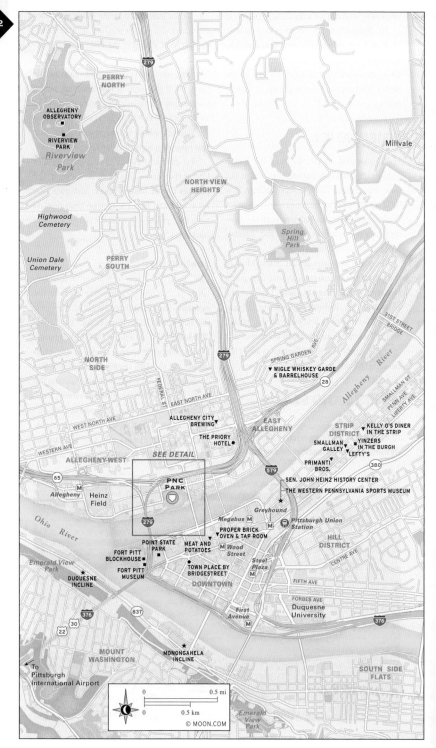

PERRY
NORTH

ALLEGHENY
OBSERVATORY

RIVERVIEW
PARK

*Riverview
Park*

NORTH VIEW
HEIGHTS

*Highwood
Cemetery*

*Spring
Hill
Park*

*Union Dale
Cemetery*

PERRY
SOUTH

31ST
STREET
BRIDGE

NORTH
SIDE

279

Allegheny River

SPRING GARDEN AVE

WIGLE WHISKEY GARDE
& BARRELHOUSE

28

SMALLMAN ST

PENN AVE

LIBERTY AVE

FEDERAL ST

EAST NORTH AVE

WEST NORTH AVE

ALLEGHENY CITY
BREWING

THE PRIORY
HOTEL

EAST
ALLEGHENY

STRIP
DISTRICT

KELLY O'S DINER
IN THE STRIP

SMALLMAN
GALLEY

YINZERS
IN THE BURGH

LEFTY'S

380

WESTERN AVE

ALLEGHENY-WEST

SEE DETAIL

575

PRIMANTI
BROS.

SEN. JOHN HEINZ HISTORY CENTER
THE WESTERN PENNSYLVANIA SPORTS MUSEUM

65

M

Allegheny

Heinz
Field

PNC
Park

M

Greyhound

M

Ohio River

279

Magabus

M

Pittsburgh Union
Station

HILL
DISTRICT

PROPER BRICK
OVEN & TAP ROOM

*Emerald View
Park*

POINT STATE
PARK

FORT PITT
BLOCKHOUSE

FORT PITT
MUSEUM

MEAT AND
POTATOES

M

Wood
Street

TOWN PLACE BY
BRIDGESTREET

Steel
Plaza

M

CENTRE AVE

FIFTH AVE

DUQUESNE
INCLINE

DOWNTOWN

FORBES AVE

Duquesne
University

376

376

30

22

837

*First
Avenue*

M

MOUNT
WASHINGTON

MONONGAHELA
INCLINE

SOUTH SIDE
FLATS

To
Pittsburgh
International Airport

*Emerald
View
Park*

0   0.5 mi

0   0.5 km

© MOON.COM

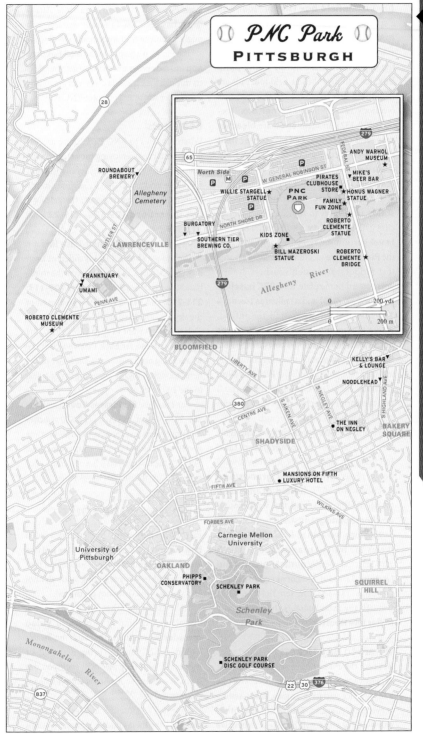

THE GREAT LAKES ✹ PITTSBURGH ✹ PIRATES

103-107), **infield box** (section 108), and a split area (sections 109-124) that wraps around the infield. In the split area, the lower rows make up the **lower infield box,** and the upper rows make up the **home plate box.** Back toward the left-field foul pole are the **infield box** (section 125), **outfield box** (sections 127-129), and **corner box** (sections 130-132). In the outfield are **bleacher reserved** (sections 133-138), **center field reserved** (sections 139-141), **right field reserved** (sections 142-145), and **corner reserved** (sections 146-147).

Dividing the 100 and PBC levels are **suites** and, closer to right field in foul territory, the **Iron City Skull Bar.** The **PBC Level** starts in the right-field foul area with the **Pirates Cove** (sections 201-205), an area that includes concession vouchers. It then goes toward home plate with **PBC baseline** (sections 207-210) and a split area (sections 211-221) that wraps around the infield, where the lower rows are the **PBC lower home plate,** and the upper rows are the **PBC upper home plate.** Continuing toward the left-field foul pole, there's the **PBC baseline** (sections 222-228). Out in left field, you'll find the **upper bleacher reserved** (sections 235-238) beneath the scoreboard.

Finally, the **300 level** starts by the right-field foul pole with the **corner grandstand** (sections 301-302), then continues toward home plate with **outfield grandstand** (sections 303-307), **infield grandstand** (sections 308-312), and the wraparound area **home plate grandstand** (sections 313-319). Going toward the left-field foul pole, there's the **infield grandstand** (sections 320-325), followed by **outfield grandstand** (sections 327-330) and **corner grandstand** (sections 331-333). In left field and just beneath the scoreboard is the group-only **Miller Lite Rooftop** (sections 335-339).

Where to Buy Tickets

Because the Pirates have some of the least expensive tickets in baseball, there won't be a lot of price variation among ticket-selling services. Generally, **StubHub** and other **third-party sites** will have less expensive rates, especially closer to game time. Attendance has been low in recent years, so you might be able to find some really sweet seats.

The Pirates participate in the **MLB Ballpark app** upgrade program, so if you get your tickets through their box office, you can potentially get a better seat after you enter PNC Park.

Best Seats

When it comes to PNC Park, there are few things better than enjoying the action on the field with the commanding yellow Roberto Clemente Bridge and the city skyline directly beyond. For the **best views,** try getting a seat in **sections 109-124, 211-221,** or **313-319.**

At PNC, seats on the **first-base line** are the first to get **shade.** (This is different from most parks, where the shade covers the third-base side first). Seats in **sections 109-113, 211-213,** and **310-313** offer a great view of the skyline but also provide shade.

If you don't want to spend too much, the 300 level isn't so far back that you can't see what's going on. Considering the lower prices here, though, I highly suggest getting a seat in the 100 level.

For families, the **Pirates Cove** (sections 201-205) is great, as you'll get a $10 voucher for concessions and merchandise. Plus, some goodies, like popcorn and soda, come free. But with these seats, you'll have to crane your neck a bit for the view of the skyline.

KNOW BEFORE YOU GO

PNC allows a 16- by 16- by 8-inch soft-sided **bag** or **cooler,** and unopened **water bottles** are allowed as long as they fit inside that bag. Carbonated beverages (along with alcohol and sports drinks) are not permitted.

PNC is one of the few parks where just about any kind of **camera** or **video recorder** is permitted. That said, the Pirates would rather you not bring a tripod or monopod, and they also will seek you out if you try to use your photos and videos for commercial use.

Parents can procure an **identification bracelet** for their child at a guest relations

YOUR BEST DAY AT PNC PARK

Are you heading to PNC Park for a game? Here's how to plan your day before arriving at the ballpark in the evening.

10 HOURS BEFORE FIRST PITCH

Breakfast is the most important meal of the day. Get it at **Kelly O's Diner in the Strip.**

9 HOURS BEFORE FIRST PITCH

Take a little walk around the Strip District, and head into **Yinzers in the Burgh** to pick up that T-shirt all the locals will understand.

8 HOURS BEFORE FIRST PITCH

Bone up on Pittsburgh history by visiting the **Senator John Heinz History Center.** While you're there, get an understanding of sports culture in the Steel City at the on-site **Western Pennsylvania Sports Museum.**

5 HOURS BEFORE FIRST PITCH

Head back into the Strip District and grab a bite at **Primanti Bros.** if it's your first time in town. Another option is to chow down on a hot dog at **Franktuary.**

4 HOURS BEFORE FIRST PITCH

Reserve a tour of the **Clemente Museum** and get an up-close glimpse of Roberto Clemente's career and the history of the Pirates.

2.5 HOURS BEFORE FIRST PITCH

Start heading toward Downtown, either by driving or hopping in a ride-share vehicle. If you want to change into game gear, this is a good time to head back to your hotel.

entrance to PNC Park

2 HOURS BEFORE FIRST PITCH

Walk to the park. Be sure to take the **Roberto Clemente Bridge** so you can get the full experience of walking into Buccos territory. Then stop at **Mike's Beer Bar** to grab a beer.

When you've had your fill, get to **PNC Park.** Check out the **statues** dotting the perimeter, which depict figures like Willie Stargell and Roberto Clemente.

1 HOUR BEFORE FIRST PITCH

If you're early enough, I recommend taking a **pregame tour.** Then swing by **Manny's BBQ** and say hello to Manny Sanguillen, if he's there.

DURING THE GAME

Take a look at the **Pirates Hall of Fame.** If you're hungry, grab yourself a Pittsburgh Cone from **Familee BBQ.** Or, if you just need dessert, opt for the Shipwreck Sundae at **Sweet Spot.**

AFTER THE GAME

Celebrate a win (or mourn a loss) with the locals by visiting **Kelly's Bar & Lounge.** Call a ride-share vehicle to get there.

Manny's BBQ

Entering PNC Park from the Roberto Clemente Bridge is a truly unique experience. Bronze sculpture by Susan Wagner.

booth. The personalized bracelet will include the child's seat location in case parents and children become separated. **Nursing mothers** can go to a private location by checking in with guest relations on the lowest level of the **Peoples Home Plate Rotunda** (home plate). There's also a **quiet room** for those needing it.

Accessibility

Accessible seating is available throughout the park; call the Pirates **ticket office** (412/323-5000) for details. PNC Park has **elevators** (sections 101, 113, 117, 125, left field lounge) in five locations.

Assistive listening devices and **noise-cancelling headphones** are available at guest services at the **home plate rotunda.** (Turn in a photo ID or valid

credit card as a deposit.) Other **guest services kiosks** are at sections 117 and 317, plus near the Legacy Square gate and right field gate. **Service animals** are welcome at PNC Park.

Guests who need help immediately can text SECURITY with their seat location to 61592. For a **quiet space,** visit the guest relations office at the home plate rotunda or a private room at Legacy Square. There's also a **sensory room** at Suite 65 containing bubble walls, touch panels, and bean bags. You can spend 15 minutes in the room. For more information, head to guest relations and be sure to have a photo ID or valid credit card ready as a deposit.

All of the parking lots around PNC Park are set up with accessibility in mind, but accessible spaces are first come, first served.

GETTING THERE

Light Rail

It's not a bad idea to take public transit to PNC Park. The best option is **light rail,** operated by **Port Authority of Allegheny County** (www.portauthority.org, $2.75 per ride). The **Blue** and **Red Lines** both stop at **Allegheny Station** (Reedsdale St. and North Shore Dr.) and **North Side Station** (Reedsdale St. and Tony Dorsett Dr.), both within easy walking distance of PNC Park.

Light rail makes sense for those staying Downtown, closer to the Monongahela River. The closest station here is **1st Avenue** (1st Ave. and Crosstown Blvd.).

Driving

Most people drive to PNC Park, but this can be a frustrating experience close to game time. Major highways near the park include **I-579,** which cuts across Downtown and comes over the Allegheny River before hooking up with **I-279.** I-279 slices along the Allegheny riverside, passing PNC Park in the North Side; it will be backed up with game traffic, so avoid it if possible. As an alternative, go up to Lawrenceville and cross the **31st Street Bridge** into the North Side, then take **PA-28 South** to Ohio Street to find parking northeast of the ballpark.

Consider parking in Downtown Pittsburgh (the Golden Triangle) and walking the **Roberto Clemente Bridge** to the stadium. You can find parking for $5-10 in this area, especially near Liberty Avenue and 7th Street. An alternative is to drive south on Wood Street to 3rd Avenue, then up

Smithfield Street. There are plenty of garages here. If you want to park in the North Side, there are a number of lots just north of the ballpark and between PNC and Heinz Field. You'll probably pay $15-20 for a spot here.

PARK FEATURES AND SIGHTS

The Pirates have a **Family Fun Zone** (Federal St., open 2.5 hours before Sunday afternoon games, free), that often features inflatables and a moon bounce. Look for the **Kids Zone** (right field gate), which includes miniature replicas of the ballpark where kids can take swings and run the bases, as well as a playset. The Kids Zone is only for children ages 5-10.

Roberto Clemente Bridge

The absolute best way to get to PNC Park is by walking across the **Roberto Clemente Bridge** (6th St. and Fort Duquesne Blvd.) from Downtown. Also known as the 6th Street Bridge, the Clemente is the gorgeous yellow span that rises above the park's outfield backdrop, connecting the North Side to Downtown Pittsburgh. The bridge is one of the Three Sisters bridges. Just east of the Clemente is the Andy Warhol Bridge, and to the right of that is the Rachel Carson Bridge, named for the marine biologist who wrote the influential environmentalist tome *Silent Spring*. Start at 6th Street and Fort Duquesne and walk the span, which is closed to vehicles on game days. You'll see right into the park as you cross—one of the coolest views in baseball.

As you approach the park, look for some **statues** around its exterior. There's legendary turn-of-the-20th-century hitter **Honus Wagner** (home plate); 1960s defensive ace **Bill Mazeroski** (right field), celebrating his iconic World Series-winning walk-off home run in 1960; slugging leader of the 1970s Pirates **Willie Stargell** (left field); and of course, **Roberto Clemente** (center field by the bridge).

FOOD AND DRINKS

If it's your first time at the ballpark or in Pittsburgh, you might want to get yourself a sandwich at **Primanti Bros.** (section 110). The Pittsburgh institution serves sandwiches stuffed with fries and slaw. There are multiple Primanti Bros. locations throughout the city, including its original spot in the Strip District. (For more details on the original location, see the *Food* section.)

If there's one item that might distract you from stopping at Primanti Bros., it's the Pittsburgh Cone at **Familee BBQ** (section 132). This is a waffle cone filled with kielbasa, pierogi, swiss cheese, sauerkraut, and Russian dressing.

Pittsburgh has a barbecue joint named after a former star player. **Manny's BBQ** (center field) is named for Manny Sanguillen, the Pirates' catcher throughout much of the 1970s. Sanguillen hangs out here, so shake his hand before diving into some pulled pork nachos.

Don't be put off by the name **Quaker Steak & Lube** (sections 109, 322). This favorite among Western Pennsylvanians, which started in Sharon, Pennsylvania, and has since spread to other parts of the country, dishes out buckets of chicken wings, perfect for a few friends. Half-buckets and single orders are also available. Get the Louisiana Lickers sauce for the full experience.

After a big, meaty meal, nothing sounds better than ice cream. Head to **Sweet Spot** (section 107) for a cool treat via local dairy Islay's. Sweet Spot has waffle cones and cake cones, but I suggest getting the Shipwreck Sundae. It's like a s'mores sundae: ice cream in a plastic baseball helmet, served with marshmallows that have been covered in chocolate and graham cracker crumbs. For beer, hit up **Beers of the Burgh** (section 107) or **Allegheny Beverage** (sections 116, 125, 309, 321). PNC Park is a little behind on featuring local breweries, but you can find Pennsylvania-based **Troegs** and **Victory** here, plus Pottsville favorite **Yuengling.** If I were you, I'd get Victory's Prima Pils or an Iron City brew from the **Miller Lite Skull Bar** (section 101).

Photos (top): inside PNC Park; (middle left) PNC Park at sunset; (middle right) the team mascot, Pirate Parrot; (bottom) a beautiful day at the park.

EVENTS

For **autographs,** you should try to get close to the dugouts as soon as the gates open. The Pirates don't promise you'll get a John Hancock, but they also don't discourage your giving it a go.

Kids ages 14 and under are welcome to **run the bases** after select Sunday games. Kids should line up with guardians by the right field Riverwalk starting in the eighth inning.

Tours

The Pirates conduct both daily and pregame **tours** (412/325-4700, $10, $8 seniors and ages 6-14, free ages 5 and under). The **daily tours** (10am and noon Mon., noon and 2pm Fri. and first Sat. of each month) last about 90 minutes. **Pregame tours** occur before first pitch (check the website for availability) and last 60-100 minutes. At a tour, you may visit the Pirates' clubhouse and dugout, plus the batting cages, press box, and PBC level.

SHOPPING

You can purchase those Bucco wares at the **Pirates Clubhouse Store** (115 Federal St., left field gate, 412/325-4465, 10am-6pm Mon.-Fri., 11am-5pm Sat. non-game days, 10am-end of game Mon.-Fri., 11am-end of game Sat., start of game to end of game Sun. game days). You'll find all kinds of stuff here, from a whole lot of hats to T-shirts and jerseys to novelty items like mugs, bobbleheads, pins, and bats. Look for the very cool pillbox hats that the Pirates wore in the late 1970s and early 1980s. The store also includes a neat look at the evolution of the Pirates logo and colors.

If you're a memorabilia hunter, you may want to check out **Hunt Auctions** (section 125). On game days, the auction company facilitates opportunities to purchase Pirates memorabilia. Items up for auction change by the game.

GAME COSTS

Tickets: You can find tickets between **$20** and **$30** at PNC, especially if the Pirates aren't so hot. Even lower-level tickets can be inexpensive (**$40-50,** and sometimes less).

Hot dog: The cheapest hot dogs here are **$3.50.**

Beer: Prices are about average, as **$10** gets you a large, macro-brewed domestic beer. You'll pay closer to **$15** for good craft.

Parking: This is really good value. You can park Downtown for as little as **$5** and walk over to the park. Closer to PNC in the North Side, prepare to pay more like **$15.**

PITTSBURGH SIGHTS

CLEMENTE MUSEUM

In the hip, gentrified Lawrenceville neighborhood is a tribute to one of baseball's greatest talents. The **Clemente Museum** (3339 Penn Ave., 412/621-1268, www.clementemuseum. com, guided tour only, $20) is all about Pittsburgh's favorite son, Hall of Famer Roberto Clemente. The museum isn't open to the public; however, you can take a guided tour by calling well ahead of time. Tours last 90 minutes and detail Clemente's life; the museums shows off artifacts and memorabilia like game-worn jerseys and hats, contracts, and trophies like his Gold Glove awards. If you're a little thirsty, there happens to be a wine cellar on location (the folks who own the place also make their own wine). For any baseball fan, this is a must-visit.

BE A FAN

Pirates fans are generally easygoing. Rivals include division opponents the Reds, Cubs, Brewers, and Cardinals, though meetings rarely ever see flare ups. The Pirates' biggest rival used to be the Phillies, thanks to their shared statehood and tendency toward being good and bad at nearly the same times throughout much of their histories. Since the Buccos moved from the NL East to the NL Central, however, tensions haven't really been that high. All this is to say that you're safe wearing other teams' clothing here.

Maybe you've heard broadcaster Greg Brown's call to **"raise the Jolly Roger"** after the Pirates win a game. If the Buccos emerge victorious At home, the Pirates raise a flag depicting an angry pirate; it has been part of the team's identity for decades. The term "Jolly Roger" has long been used to describe the flag a pirate ship raises when it's ready to attack.

Part of the Pirates' lighthearted and fun in-game entertainment is the team's **Great Pierogi Race.** Typically between the fifth and sixth innings of every game, up to seven of the **Pirates Pierogies** mascots—Bacon Burt, Cheese Chester, Jalapeno Hannah, Oliver Onion, Pizza Penny, Potato Pete, and Sauerkraut Saul—run the warning track from the left-field foul area around to right field. If anything, maybe it'll make you hungry for delicious pierogis.

ANDY WARHOL MUSEUM

The **Andy Warhol Museum** (117 Sandusky St., 412/237-8300, www.warhol.org, 10am-5pm Tues.-Thurs. and Sat.-Sun., 10am-10pm Fri., $20, $10 seniors, students, and ages 3-18, free ages 2 and younger) is an essential attraction in Pittsburgh, and it's just two blocks east of PNC Park. This museum in the famed pop artist's hometown features about 350 of his films and more than 4,000 videotapes. Plus, there's everything from his student work to portraits of Elizabeth Taylor and Elvis Presley. For children, there are interactive installations like *Silver Clouds,* a room filled with floating silver balloons. You can also visit The Factory hands-on studio to make Warhol-style art.

SENATOR JOHN HEINZ HISTORY CENTER

Want a complete run-through of everything Pittsburgh? Spend a few hours at the **Senator John Heinz History Center** (1212 Smallman St., 412/454-6000, www.heinzhistorycenter.org, 10am-5pm daily, $18, $15 seniors, $9 students and ages 6-17, free ages 5 and younger). With a name like Heinz, you can bet there's plenty of ketchup here, with a permanent exhibit detailing the history of the famous condiment company. This impressive history center has much more, including a tear-jerking ode to Fred Rogers, an exhibit featuring products and companies from Pittsburgh, and a smaller museum inside: The **Western Pennsylvania Sports Museum.** There, get a deeper look at Pirates history (and view exhibits about the Steelers, Penguins, and high school and college sports).

DUQUESNE AND MONONGAHELA INCLINES

The unique geography and history of Pittsburgh are such that something like the **Duquesne Incline** (1197 W. Carson St., 412/381-1665, www.duquesneincline.org, 5:30am-12:30am Mon.-Sat., 7am-12:30am Sun., round-trip $5, $2.50 ages 6-11, free ages 5 and under) and **Monongahela Incline** (125 W. Station Square Dr., www.monongahelaincline.com, 5:30am-12:45am Mon.-Sat., 8:45am-midnight Sun., round-trip $3.50, $2.50 ages 6-11, free ages 5 and under) can exist and remain alive and well today. These funiculars climb 600 feet up **Mount Washington,** historically taking cargo and residents from the industrial plants by the Monongahela River up to the rest of

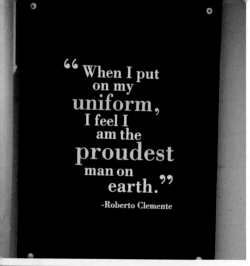

> " When I put on my **uniform**, I feel I am the **proudest** man on earth. "
>
> -Roberto Clemente

the city. These days, the inclines are primarily tourist attractions, though some folks do take them as part of their daily commutes. The prize awaits at the top, where you can get an awesome view of Downtown. The Duquesne Incline is farther west toward the tip of the Golden Triangle (and allows a view of PNC Park), while the Monongahela Incline provides a view above the Smithfield Street Bridge and points farther east.

FOOD

NEAR PNC PARK

Grab a big ol' burger at **Burgatory** (342 North Shore Dr., 412/586-5846, www.burgatorybar.com, 11am-10pm Sun.-Thurs., 11am-11pm Fri.-Sat., under $40), at the near-the-ballpark location of this popular Pittsburgh chain. You can get bison, elk, or Wagyu beef, plus thick milkshakes, floats, and other sweet treats. The industrial space with plenty of televisions, a full bar, and a rustic color palette means you don't have to dress up to enjoy the goods here.

If you're craving meat and potatoes, go to **Meat and Potatoes** (649 Penn Ave., 412/325-7007, www.meatandpotatoespgh.com, 5pm-1am Mon., 5pm-10pm Tues.-Thurs., 5pm-midnight Fri., 10:30am-2pm and 5pm-midnight Sat., 10:30am-2pm and 5pm-10pm Sun., under $40). Here, you have plenty of options for both meat (chops, sandwiches, and burgers) and potatoes (mashed, fried, poutine). Just across the Roberto Clemente Bridge from PNC Park, this Downtown establishment has a mid-century feel. It's upscale-looking and -tasting, but it's quite affordable.

Some of the best pizza outside of the East Coast is at **Proper Brick Oven & Tap Room** (139 7th St., 412/281-5700, www.properpittsburgh.com, under $40). They do

Photos (from top to bottom): Roberto Clemente quote; memorabilia at the Clemente Museum; the Duquesne Incline.

Neapolitan-style pies, including the local homage Black and Gold, which features crispy potato slices. Pastas, Italian appetizers, and original cocktails make this a fun place to go for a semi-casual dinner. It's also across the Clemente from PNC Park.

OTHER NEIGHBORHOODS

If you've never been to Pittsburgh, you're going to need a sandwich from **Primanti Bros.** (46 18th St., 412/263-2142, www.primantibros.com, 24 hours daily, under $20). Open all the time, this famous shop has been in its Strip District space since 1933; it has other locations across the area. You may encounter some Pittsburghers who say the shop isn't worth the time, but I think it's a bucket-list item. Every sandwich is topped with french fries (that's their thing), along with coleslaw and tomatoes, so you just need to decide what kind of protein you want. Counter seating is available.

Enjoy some eggs at any number of the never-serious diners in the Strip District. My pick is **Kelly O's Diner in the Strip** (100 24th St., 412/232-3447, www.kellyos.com, 5am-3pm Mon.-Sat., 7am-3pm Sun., under $30), which has a deep breakfast menu and does omelets and eggs Benedict quite well. Outside, it looks like a giant metal box, but inside it's cozy.

Also in the Strip District is **Smallman Galley** (54 21st St., 412/517-6100, www.smallmangalley.org, 11am-10pm Tues.-Thurs., 11am-midnight Fri., 10am-midnight Sat., 10am-3pm Sun., under $30), a really fun miniature food hall. There are four rotating-chef incubator concepts here. Expect decent take-out lunch options, from sandwiches to barbecue. You can sit by the brick walls right across from the counters, so the smell and atmosphere get to be pretty charming.

Lawrenceville hot-dog haunt **Franktuary** (3810 Butler St., 412/586-7224, www.franktuary.com, 11:30am-9:30pm Tues.-Thurs., 11:30am-10:30pm Fri.-Sat., 11:30am-8pm Sun., under $30) features a whole bunch of fun combinations. I enjoy the PA Duchess, which is topped with apple compote, grilled onions, and white cheddar. You can also create your own wiener at this buzzy place that's not at all formal. It's a good stop for a midday or post-game snack.

Up Butler on the way to Lawrenceville, have a blast at **Umami** (202 38th St., 412/224-2354, www.umamipgh.com, 4:30pm-midnight Tues.-Thurs., 4:30pm-2am Fri.-Sat., under $40). This is a Japanese *izakaya*-style restaurant, meaning the focus is on drinking while having a steady dose of small plates. Sit at the bar if you can to down a few beers or some sake; at the same time, let the smoke from the *robatayaki* cooking hit your senses and drive you to order a whole bunch off the menu.

If you want to spend some time in the Shadyside neighborhood, visit **Noodlehead** (242 S. Highland Ave., www.noodleheadpgh.com, noon-10pm daily, under $30), a Thai mom-and-pop spot that's added some modern magic. Street-food noodle bowls and dishes are served up here, along with Thai fried chicken and steamed pork belly buns. The plants and picnic-style tables give it a casual vibe. This spot is BYOB and cash only.

BARS AND BREWERIES

NEAR PNC PARK

About a 15-minute walk from PNC Park and on the same side of the Allegheny River is **Allegheny City Brewing** (507 Foreland St., 412/904-3732, www.alleghenycitybrewing.com, 5pm-10pm Wed.-Thurs., 4pm-midnight Fri., 2pm-midnight Sat., noon-7pm Sun.). The small brewery does a little of everything but primarily IPAs, with some really tasty dark offerings. The cozy taproom is a little rustic and has a few games to play. Outdoor seating is available.

Established in far western New York in the early 2000s, **Southern Tier Brewing Co.** (316 North Shore Dr., 412/301-2337, www.stbcbeer.com) opened its first satellite taproom in Pittsburgh in 2017. The location has both tried-and-true Southern Tier beers (like 2XIPA and 2XSMASH) and local-only creations. There's plenty of room, along with a clear view into the brewhouse, big garage doors that can be raised when the weather is nice, and an outdoor area with turf. Lots of merchandise is for sale, too.

If you're near PNC Park and you want a beer, the selection at **Mike's Beer Bar** (110 Federal St., 412/322-2337, www.mikesbeerbar.com, 11am-12:30am Mon.-Thurs., 11am-2am Fri.-Sat., 9am-12:30am Sun.) really can't be beat. They've got hundreds of beers on hand. One thing to keep in mind: If you're coming just before or after a Buccos game, patience will be a virtue. Things get busy and service can be slow.

OTHER NEIGHBORHOODS

I'm a big fan of Lawrenceville's **Roundabout Brewery** (4901 Butler St., 412/621-0540, www.roundaboutbeer.com, 4pm-10pm Wed.-Fri., noon-10pm Sat., noon-7pm Sun.), which constantly changes its taps, so you'll never know what's coming. Roundabout invites food trucks to serve, but it also offers New Zealand-style meat pies (the owner worked down there for a spell) and pretzels daily. It's a small place, but there's plenty of light, and beer flights come on a round platter.

My favorite boozy experience in Pittsburgh is an absolute treasure. **Wigle Whiskey Garden & Barrelhouse** (1055 Spring Garden Ave., 412/235-7796, www.wiglewhiskey.com, 5pm-10pm Wed.-Fri., 3pm-10pm Sat., 2pm-7pm Sun. Apr.-Oct.) is one of a few locations run by the renowned Wigle Whiskey, which has been nominated for a James Beard Award and makes seriously awesome whiskey (you'll be amazed that Pittsburgh has whiskey this good). The barrelhouse is the best experience, as it combines the education of a boozy tour with the fun of a beer garden. Its operating schedule is essentially the same as baseball season. Find it in the East Allegheny neighborhood.

Despite the Strip District's reputation for being hipper than it used to be, the bars here still carry a bit of divey charm. **Lefty's** (2021 Penn Ave., 412/281-1033, 1pm-midnight Mon., 1pm-1am Tues.-Thurs., 1pm-2am Fri., 11am-2am Sat., 11:30am-midnight Sun.) fits the bill with boozy drinks, an eclectic crowd of locals, and plenty of Iron City beer available. They're known for a cheap Long Island iced tea variation. This is a good place to visit at the end of the night.

Over near Shadyside is **Kelly's Bar & Lounge** (6012 Centre Ave., 412/363-6012, noon-2am Mon.-Sat., 5pm-midnight Sun.), which Pittsburghers call a dive bar, but I think of it as a nice art-deco lounge with a good beer list. It's pretty chill. There's food, too.

RECREATION

Established in 1889, the 456-acre **Schenley Park** (Schenley Dr. and Panther Hollow Rd.) is Pittsburgh's quintessential large municipal green space, abutting Carnegie Mellon University and the Carnegie Museum of Natural History, and with I-376 on its opposite end. The park is known for its clear views of Downtown Pittsburgh and is home to **Phipps Conservatory** (www.phipps.conservatory.org, 9:30am-11pm daily, $18-20, $17-18 seniors and students, $12 ages 2-18, free under age 2), whose lovely orchids bloom year-round and whose desert plants are fun finds inside a climate-adjusted greenhouse. Also here are the **Schenley Park Disc Golf Course** (Overlook Dr. by the ice-skating rink) and multiple playgrounds. Easy and moderate trails, like the 2.3-mile up-and-back Lower Panther Hollow Trail, thread through the interior of the park.

A great spot for hiking and running is **Riverview Park** (Mairdale Ave. and Riverview Dr.), up in Perry North. On a hill, the park is topped by **Allegheny Observatory** (412/321-2400, www.pitt.edu, by guided tour only, Apr.-Oct., free), which was built in 1900. The observatory is operated by the University of Pittsburgh and can be visited only on a tour. You can get there, with a workout, by taking the woodsy Observatory Trail from the visitors center to the paved Cherry Blossom Trail. Together it's about 0.7 mile.

If you want to be right at the very tip of the Golden Triangle, visit **Point State Park** (601 Commonwealth Plaza), a 36-acre green space at the confluence of Pittsburgh's three rivers. It's home to the **Fort Pitt Museum** (601 Commonwealth Plaza, 412/281-9284, www.heinzhistorycenter.org, 10am-5pm daily, $8, $7 seniors, $4.50 students and ages 6-17, free ages 5 and under), which re-creates a fort that was built by the British and used during the French and Indian War, then again during the American Revolution. The museum, operated by the Heinz History Center, tells the story of the fort and of life during the 18th century. Also on-site is the actual **Fort Pitt Blockhouse** from 1764, plus a fountain and beautiful views of the three rivers and the cityscape.

SHOPPING

If you're in the Strip District, you can grab some Pirates T-shirts and hats at **Yinzers in the Burgh** (2127 Penn Ave., 412/434-0113, www.yinzersintheburgh.com, 9am-5pm daily). There's more Steelers merch than anything here, but you'll find Pirates jerseys, bobbleheads, and much more by perusing this heaven on earth for Yinzers (a local term for Pittsburgh residents).

Photos (from top to bottom): downtown Pittsburgh, Phipps Conservatory; Fort Pitt Museum.

ACCOMMODATIONS

NEAR PNC PARK

A 15-minute walk from PNC Park, **The Priory Hotel** (614 Pressley St., 412/231-3338, www.thepriory.com, $100-250) was built in 1888 with 25 rooms. A major 2017 renovation added a wing, and the 42-room hotel now has a pub, fitness center, and a ballroom. The nicely appointed rooms are affordable, though be warned that the lowest-priced single rooms have twin beds. I recommend the Priory for its history, accessibility, and affordability alone, but there's more: It also has a Pirates package that includes game tickets, an in-room basket of baseball treats, and two Pirates hats. This is a good deal.

Downtown, but just a 15-minute walk to the park via the Roberto Clemente Bridge, is **Town Place by BridgeStreet** (424 Stanwix St., 412/646-8696, www.townplace.bridgestreet.com, $150-300), a more expensive accommodation, but for good reason. The rooms here are like ultramodern, sleek apartments with washers and dryers in the units, plus hardwood floors and kitchens with stainless-steel appliances. Some of the rooms have awesome views of the skyline, too.

OTHER NEIGHBORHOODS

If you want to stay in the heart of Shadyside, drop your bags at **The Inn on Negley** (703 S. Negley Ave., 412/661-0631, www.innonnegley.com, $190-300). This is a quintessential bed-and-breakfast with comfortable Victorian-inspired rooms named after types of apples, such as Granny Smith, Braeburn, and Macintosh. Breakfast is included in the rate (the inn has three chefs on staff), and there's high tea in the afternoon. Looking for something cozy and romantic? This is it. On the edges of Shadyside is the **Mansions on Fifth Luxury Hotel** (5105 5th Ave., 412/381-5105, www.mansionsonfifth.com, $100-250). Owned by the same folks who run the Priory, the Mansions was a Gilded Age estate that later served as dorm space for folks like Andy Warhol and actor George Peppard. The beautiful property now has 13 guest rooms and suites, some with fireplaces and jetted tubs, and all with queen or king beds. A pub serves up scotches and cocktails, and there's also a wine cellar on-site.

GETTING AROUND

PUBLIC TRANSIT

The **Port Authority of Allegheny County** (www.portauthority.org, $2.75 per ride) runs public transit in Pittsburgh. There's a **bus system** with dozens of lines, as well as a **light rail** system with multiple routes that connect the outer city and suburbs.

Tourists will be interested primarily in the light rail's **Blue** and **Red Lines,** which start at **Allegheny Station** (Reedsdale St. and North Shore Dr.) and head to **North Side Station** (Reedsdale St. and Tony Dorsett Dr.), both within easy walking distance of PNC Park. Golden Triangle stops include **Wood Street Station** (6th Ave. and Wood St.), **Steel Plaza Station** (5th Ave. and Ross St.), and **First Avenue** (1st Ave. and Crosstown Blvd.).

TAXI, UBER, AND LYFT

Consider using a ride-sharing service while in Pittsburgh. **Uber** generally offers less expensive rates than **Lyft.** The taxi system in the city isn't so robust.

CAR

The major west-east highways are **I-376,** which meets up with **I-80** northwest of the city, passes by Pittsburgh International Airport, rides right along the Monongahela River, then connects to **I-76** (the **Pennsylvania Turnpike**) to the east. **I-279** starts near the tip of the Golden Triangle as an extension of I-376, then runs north into East Allegheny as **Parkway North.** It connects to **I-79** up north. Also starting in

WILLIAMSPORT AND THE LITTLE LEAGUE WORLD SERIES

About 3.5 hours east of Pittsburgh is the small city of **Williamsport,** Pennsylvania. Most famously, it's the place where, every August, the most talented young baseball players in the world convene for the **Little League World Series.**

Little League Baseball actually started in Williamsport in 1939, and it remains headquartered in the city to this day. The first LLWS was played here in 1947. Games today are played at **Volunteer Stadium** (182 Borderline Rd.) and **Howard J. Lamade Stadium** (100 Borderline Rd.) in South Williamsport. In the annual tournament, 10 U.S. teams and 10 international teams play against each other, with the U.S. winner facing the international winner in a one-game showdown. A U.S. team has won 36 times, and an international squad has won 37 times, led by Taiwan (17 titles). Plenty of major leaguers have played in the tournament, from Gary Sheffield to Todd Frazier, who homered and won as a pitcher in the championship game for his Toms River, New Jersey, team in 1998.

Parking and admission to LLWS games are free, though you'll pay for concessions and merchandise. Seats are first come, first served. While you're in town, you should also visit the **World of Little League Museum** (525 Montgomery Pike, South Williamsport, www.littleleague.org, 9am-5pm daily, $5, $3 seniors, $2 ages 5-12, free ages 4 and under). The museum includes images and artifacts from Little League's history, plus interactive exhibits, and offers a tour.

GETTING THERE

It's a 200-mile, 3.5-hour drive from Pittsburgh to Williamsport. To get there, follow US-22 East, I-99 North, and I-80 East.

the Golden Triangle is **I-579,** which runs through the outer edge of Downtown and connects with I-279 up in East Allegheny. **PA-28** comes into East Allegheny from the north, then meets I-279. When I-279 leaves for the Golden Triangle, **PA-65** continues along the Ohio River, providing a more local route toward Cleveland.

If all of that sounds confusing, well, it is. Pittsburgh's unique geography means highways and major arteries blitz in and out of the Golden Triangle, causing regular traffic tie-ups. You might be better off staying on the city streets. Major roads include **Centre Avenue,** which comes in from the Shadyside area toward the University of Pittsburgh before weaving into Downtown; and **Penn Avenue** and **Liberty Avenue,** which each straddle the Allegheny River and become main roadways in the Strip District and Lawrenceville.

Another thing to note: There are a lot of **bridges** in Pittsburgh. If you find yourself unexpectedly getting on a bridge, don't panic. Just turn around at the next intersection, or drive until you reach another bridge and can cross back the way you came.

CLEVELAND
INDIANS

There was a time when the opening minutes of the 1989 baseball movie *Major League* were an accurate depiction of professional baseball in Cleveland. As Randy Newman's "Burn On" plays, shots of the industrial city are interspersed with newspaper headlines detailing the decades-long history of the Indians—one that was rife with disappointment and failure.

The Cleveland baseball franchise began in 1894 in the Western League as the Grand Rapids Rustlers, and in 1900 it moved to Cleveland and became the Lake Shores. The team's presence filled a void left by the former National League franchise in town, the Cleveland Spiders, a team that won a few league titles behind talents like pitcher Cy Young and hitter Jesse Burkett. By 1900 the Western League was renamed the American League,

and in 1901 the Cleveland franchise set up shop at League Park, northeast of Downtown Cleveland. In 1915, after a few more name changes—including the Naps, after top hitter Nap Lajoie—the team settled on Indians, after some newspaper writers suggested it.

The Indians played in League Park until 1946, but fans didn't see much good baseball there. They only reached the World Series once from 1915 to 1946, winning it in 1920. Real success came after a move to Municipal Stadium by Lake Erie. There, the Indians won the 1948 World Series behind pitchers Bob Feller and Bob Lemon and hitters Lou Boudreau, Joe Gordon, and Larry Doby, the first Black player in the American League. They'd stay competitive for several years after that win but would fail to hoist a championship trophy; by the late 1950s, the glory days had faded away. A long, cold run of pitiful play followed, with the Indians failing to get to second place in their league and division for 34 straight seasons.

In 1994, five years after the release of *Major League,* things changed. The Indians moved from their homely digs, Municipal Stadium, to Jacobs Field (now Progressive Field), a modern steel structure with a retro vibe—a house built for pennant contenders. The Indians instantly lived up to that promise, led by a potent offense of future Hall of Famers (Jim Thome, Eddie Murray, and, later, Roberto Alomar) and supported by a stacked farm system. From then on, only a few poor seasons kept the Indians from being an automatic annual threat for the American League crown.

Not surprisingly, the fans responded. From 1995 to 2001, the Indians kept the most impressive sellout streak in baseball history: 455 games. While game attendance hasn't since reached those exhilarating highs, you can bet the team is no longer a punching bag or befitting of Newman's *Major League* theme song about a fire on the Cuyahoga River.

There's just one issue: The Indians haven't won the World Series in more than 70 years. They have come close, with heartbreaking Game 7 losses in 1997 and 2016. This is a city thirsty for victory, with a devoted fan base that keeps the faith all year long. It's a classic baseball town.

PLANNING YOUR TIME

There was a time you could swing in and out of Cleveland in a day, but that's no longer the case. I suggest at least a **weekend** (or better yet, two days in the middle of the week) to absorb all the big attractions in the city. If you've got more time, you can pack a lot into **three or four days.** Spend a day at the ballpark and other nearby sites, including **East 4th Street.** Take at least a half day, if not a full day, to check out the **Rock & Roll Hall of Fame** (buy your ticket ahead of time and try to go in the middle of the week for smaller crowds). On your third day, you can squeeze in a trip to the Ohio City and Tremont neighborhoods. Staying Downtown is the best way to explore Cleveland, as you'll frequently be in this neighborhood, but it will be easy to take trips elsewhere in the city from here. Expanding the trip another day gives you some breathing room, and you can explore nearby **Cuyahoga Valley National Park.**

When booking your trip to Cleveland, keep in mind that **Progressive Field** is just one mile from **Lake Erie,** so when it's cold at the lake, it can be really cold in the ballpark. Same goes for the **wind,** which can whip up unpredictably. Your best bet is to avoid attending games in **March and April,** when the temperature typically doesn't get above 60°F. Cleveland baseball in **May and late June** is outstanding, with the best weather conditions and temperatures. The city can be quite pleasant in **midsummer,** with average temperatures in the low 80s, but **humidity** and **mosquitoes** can make **July and August** day games unbearable. Oh, and don't forget about the **midges,** which come off Lake Erie in **early June** and **early October,** pestering people for a few days at a time.

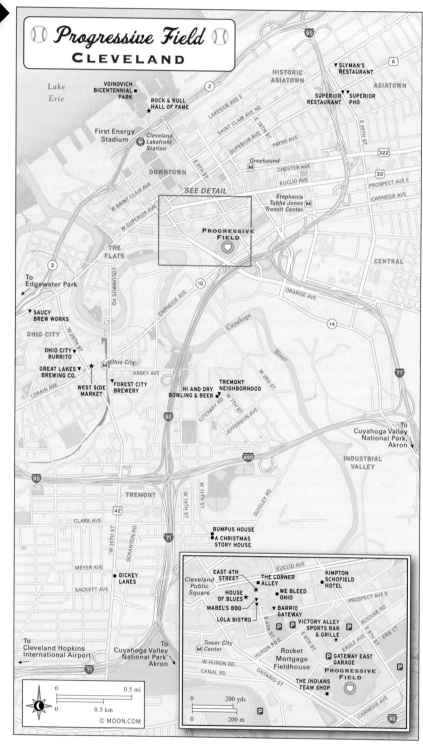

GETTING THERE

AIR

The major passenger airport in town is **Cleveland Hopkins International Airport** (CLE, 5300 Riverside Dr., 216/265-6000, www.clevelandairport.com), which is served by **Air Canada** (888/247-2262, www.aircanada.com), **Allegiant** (702/505-8888, www.allegiantair.com), **American Airlines** (800/433-7300, www.aa.com), **Delta** (800/221-1212, www.delta.com), **Frontier** (800/401-9000, www.flyfrontier.com), **jetBlue** (800/538-2583, www.jetblue.com), **Southwest** (800/435-9792, www.southwest.com), **Spirit** (801/401-2222, www.spirit.com), and **United** (800/864-8331, www.united.com). The airport provides nonstop flights to just about every major American city, and with just one terminal and three gates, it's an easy place to navigate.

Airport Transportation

To **rent a car,** you'll need to hop on a **shuttle** from baggage claim 7 to the **consolidated rental car center** (19601 Maplewood Ave.). There, you can find most major rental car companies. From Cleveland Hopkins International, it's a 12-minute drive, primarily on **I-71,** to Progressive Field and the Gateway District.

Cleveland's public transit authority, **RTA** (Greater Cleveland Regional Transit Authority, 216/566-5100, www.riderta.com), provides service from the airport to Downtown, with trains departing every 15 minutes or so. You'll take the **Red Line** to Tower City Center (if you're staying Downtown) or West 25th Street (if you're staying in Ohio City). Folks staying Downtown can also take the **Waterfront Line** to the stop nearest to their accommodations.

CAR

The drive from Pittsburgh to Cleveland is just **two hours** and **130 miles** when you take I-76 West, I-80 West, and I-480 into the city. A more scenic route includes a ride on **PA-51 North,** along the Ohio River and its old factories, until it hits **OH-14 West,** which you can take into Cleveland. Depending on traffic, this **140-mile** drive could take up to **four hours.**

TRAIN

Amtrak (www.amtrak.com) serves the city at **Cleveland Lakefront Station** (200 Cleveland Memorial Shoreway, 216/696-5115). Lines served from Cleveland include the **Capitol Limited** (west to Chicago, east to Pittsburgh and Washington DC) and the **Lake Shore Limited** (west to Chicago, east to Buffalo and Boston or New York City). If taking the Capitol Limited from Pittsburgh, expect a three-hour ride departing midday; tickets start at $29.

Staying in the Downtown area isn't a bad idea if you're taking the train. It's a doable one-mile, 20- to 25-minute walk from the train station through the Gateway District to Progressive Field.

BUS

It's a short 0.6-mile walk to Progressive Field from Cleveland's **Greyhound bus station** (1465 Chester Ave., 216/781-0520, www.greyhound.com). Greyhound offers a daily trip from Pittsburgh that starts at $14; typically, the trip is 3-4 hours, but some trips include a stop in Erie, Pennsylvania, prolonging the fun by another 2-3 hours.

You can take Megabus from New York City to Cleveland; the bus will drop you off at the **Stephanie Tubbs Jones Transit Center** (2115 E. 22nd St., 877/462-6342, http://us.megabus.com). This nearly nine-hour ride is only available Thursday-Sunday, but the cost, starting at $40, can't be beat. Megabus does not offer a route from Pittsburgh to Cleveland.

Progressive Field

Progressive Field

Opening in 1994, **Progressive Field** (2401 Ontario St., www.mlb.com/indians), previously called Jacobs Field, was one of the first of a new wave of retro-inspired ballparks across America. With its tall light fixtures, asymmetrical outfield dimensions, and grandstand seating above a high left-field fence, "The Jake" (as it's lovingly called even to this day) resembled some of the magical parks of the 1940s and 1950s. Plus, its placement in the Downtown area gives it one of the finer backdrops in baseball, with the Cleveland skyline towering over left center field.

Considering all the ballparks that have opened since The Jake, it's now a relative veteran among major league venues (only 10 parks are older), but it's been updated a bit to reflect changing times. The concourses now have plenty of openings with solid sight lines for standing-room patrons, and the right-field area has received a substantial makeover to include more eating and entertainment areas. Progressive Field has aged pretty well from its early days as the scene of explosive Indians teams with Hall of Fame talent like Jim Thome, Eddie Murray, and Roberto Alomar Jr., to recent squads that regularly contend for the postseason.

ORIENTATION

Progressive Field is in Downtown Cleveland, in a neighborhood known as the Gateway

District. Being Downtown means it's a cinch to find something to do before and after the game.

The ballpark has four entry gates. Three of the gates are in the outfield along Eagle Avenue, closer to the main parking garage and Gateway Plaza, which connects the ballpark to the Rocket Mortgage Fieldhouse sports arena.

TICKETS AND SEATING

Pricing

The Indians use **dynamic pricing,** which means games against certain opponents, and on certain days, will have higher ticket prices. At Progressive Field, a middle-of-the-road seat (say in section 450) may cost around $25-30 for a game against a team that doesn't draw many fans (such as the Rays), while a team with a big following (like the Yankees or Red Sox) means that same seat would cost more like $40-50.

The cheapest tickets in the park are for standing room in the **Right Field District** ($15). This ticket includes a free first drink. Come up to two hours early on select Friday and Saturday nights for pregame drink specials, DJs, and live bands. You'll also find a variety of local vendors in this area, plus a two-story bar called The Corner that has close to 40 beers on tap and a roof deck with an open-air firepit.

If you have children ages 12 and under, you can get them a **KeyBank Kids ticket** ($10-15, with purchase of adult ticket). The ticket is good for a seat in the **family deck** (sections 303-316).

YOUR BEST DAY AT PROGRESSIVE FIELD

Let's say you're heading to Progressive Field for a night game. Here's how to pack in a Cleveland experience centered around an evening with the Indians.

7 HOURS BEFORE FIRST PITCH
If you're staying Downtown, I suggest taking the Red Line RTA train to the **Ohio City Rapid Station**—that way you can enjoy the day without the stress of driving.

Now you can start your day with a cup of coffee at **West Side Market.** The smell of fresh fish and butchered pork should get you going, too.

5 HOURS BEFORE FIRST PITCH
Time for lunch. While you're in Ohio City, do as the citizens do and visit **Ohio City Burrito.**

4 HOURS BEFORE FIRST PITCH
Make a pilgrimage to **Great Lakes Brewing Company.** It's just a couple blocks from Ohio City Burrito. Have a Rally Drum Red Ale, which pays homage to Indians superfan John Adams.

2 HOURS BEFORE FIRST PITCH
Grab the Red Line at the Ohio City Rapid Station and take it Downtown to **Tower City Center.** From here, it's about a half-mile walk to **Progressive Field.**

Progressive Field

1.5 HOURS BEFORE FIRST PITCH
Check out the brews and grub in the ballpark's **Right Field District.** Grab a beer with a couple hundred of your newest friends at **The Corner.** Just before first pitch, check out Indians Hall of Famers and other greats honored at **Heritage Park.**

DURING THE GAME
Order a hot dog and spread on that **Bertman Original Ball Park Mustard.** Maybe sneak over to say hello to **John Adams and his drum.**

AFTER THE GAME
Since you took the train, plan on hanging out around East 4th Street tonight. Go bowling and aim for that 300 (okay, 150) score at **The Corner Alley.**

Seating Plan
Progressive Field has **four levels** in three **"districts."** Let's start with the districts. The **Left Field District** covers the foul area along the left-field line and the fair area left of the 410-foot angle in center field; it includes the **Home Run Porch** (a standing-room spot) and **left field bleachers.** The **Right Field District** covers the foul area along the right-field line and the fair area right of the 410-foot angle in center field; it includes Heritage Park, the Kids Clubhouse, and a bar called The Corner. This district also has **standing-room-only** spots targeted to millennial fans. Finally, the **Infield District** includes the **Home Plate Club** (an area accessible to box-seat ticket holders) and the **club seats.**

Now for the levels. The lower bowl consists of the **100 level,** with sections 103-113 in right field; sections 117-179 in foul territory from right to left field; and the **bleachers,** which occupy sections 180-185 in left field, located above the fence and beneath the scoreboard.

There is **no 200 level.** It was eliminated in the 2019 renovation that opened up the concourses and added the entertainment areas. The **300 level** includes the **family deck** in right field and **club seats** along the first-base line. The club seats include free food and non-alcoholic drinks from the **Discount Drug Mart Club** (sections 326-348), a collection of vendors anchored by a large bar and grill.

The **400 and 500 levels** are in the upper deck; the 400 level, known as the **box seats,** stretches from right field in fair territory (section 403) around to the third-base line (section 478). The 500 level, or **reserved seats,** starts at section 528, along the first-base line, and stretches to section 577, along the third-base line.

Where to Buy Tickets
Generally, Indians tickets are inexpensive through **StubHub,** which the team has partnered with as its third-party vendor. Try your hand there before purchasing through the **official team website,** as those prices tend to be higher.

Best Seats
If you're attending a day game, look for seats along the **third-base line,** particularly in the **lower bowl** (sections 162-174), as this is the area that gets **shade.** Go for seats in the **Field Box Back** or **Lower Box** rows, as they're pushed back and a little easier on the wallet. If you're looking to spend even less, seats along the third-base side of the **view box** (sections 460-468) are pretty solid, providing a great view of the whole field.

Want a unique experience for little dough? Go for a seat in the **upper bleachers** (sections 180-185), where you'll be among rowdier fans. One tip for those seats: Opt for a night game because the metal bleachers can get pretty warm if the sun is beating on them.

KNOW BEFORE YOU GO

Progressive Field is fine with you bringing in **small packs** (16 by 16 by 8 inches or smaller), plus soft-sided **cooler bags** and personal-sized food and beverage items (but sealed in containers and original bottles, respectively). No outside alcohol is allowed. No glass, noisemakers, pepper spray, or pets are allowed in, either. You can't bring in any

GAME COSTS

Tickets: The cheapest tickets are in the Right Field District and will run you **$15.** If you want a lower-level seat, be ready to pay at least **$40** per ticket.

Hot dog: A straight-up wiener will run you about **$5** (don't forget to add some Ball Park Mustard). Gourmet options will run up to **$10.**

Beer: Progressive Field is one of the more affordable major league sites for a beer. You can get a can of beer for as little as **$5,** though local brews can cost up to **$12.**

Parking: If you want to park a block from the stadium, you'll have to pay **$20** or so. A couple lots charge as little as **$5.** Spots costing **$10-15** are common.

food or drinks if you're in the premium seating areas (such as suites).

If you're coming between June and August, bring some sunscreen for day games. I advise against bringing bug spray for the midges, as they're actually attracted to it.

Accessibility
Head to **Window 1** at the left field gate or to any window at the right field gate or **infield gate** for an **accessible ticket window.**

There are plenty of **accessible seating** sections at Progressive Field. Call the Indians **ticket office** (216/420-4487) for more details. **Wheelchairs** are available on a first-come, first-served basis. Check with an employee at Progressive Field for assistance.

Assistive listening devices and **noise-cancelling headphones** are available at the **Fan Service Center** (section 153). **Sensory bags** are available at the fan service center with the deposit of a valid driver's license.

Elevators (sections 117, 149, 159) are in three locations across the stadium. **Service animals** are welcome at Progressive Field.

BE A FAN

If you visited Progressive Field between 2011 and 2014, mentioning LeBron James meant hearing for 20 minutes how he ripped out the heart of a city, leaving fans angry and bereft. A decade and an NBA title later, things aren't so hostile anymore, but have sympathy for the Indians fan who hasn't seen a World Series winner since 1948.

Keep an ear out for two songs. In the middle of the eighth inning, there's **"Hang On Sloopy"** by the McCoys. It's the official song of Ohio, so you'll hear fans chanting **"O-H-I-O"** in between the chorus. And if the Indians win, you'll get Ian Hunter's original version of **"Cleveland Rocks."** For bonus points, stay till the end and scream **"Ohio!"** with the rest of the diehards.

Accessible parking is offered at **The Gateway East Garage** (650 Huron Rd.). Be sure to keep a disabled parking placard visible.

GETTING THERE

Public Transit

If you're staying in the heart of the city, you can take **RTA** (216/566-5100, www.riderta. com, $2.50 per ride) to the park. The **Blue, Green,** and **Red Lines** stop at **Tower City Center** (50 Public Sq.); from here, a walkway will lead you to Progressive Field. Taking the train is much cheaper than parking. Just know that you have an hour after the final out to get onto the train.

Driving

I-90 borders the southeastern edge of Progressive Field. To the north of the stadium is **US-20.** There are a wealth of **parking lots** surrounding the ballpark. The cheapest lots are near **Tower City Center** (between W. Prospect Ave. and W. Huron Rd. at W. 2nd St. and W. 3rd St.), where you'll pay $5-10. Closer lots, along **Prospect Avenue** heading east, will cost $10-15. If you don't want to walk much at all, park between Bolivar Road and Erie Court at **East 9th Street,** but be prepared to pay up to $20. The **Gateway East Garage** (650 Huron Rd. E.) is right by the ballpark and will cost $10-15; get there early to secure a spot.

PARK FEATURES AND SIGHTS

John Adams's Drum

Listen carefully, especially if the Indians get a rally going, and you might hear a single, rhythmic drumbeat. You may wonder where the heck it's coming from. Well, head to the very top row of the bleachers, underneath the left-field scoreboard. There, you'll find **John Adams** (section 183), a solitary fan with an enormous **bass drum** propped in the seat next to him.

Adams wanted to mimic the seat-banging noise he and other kids growing up as Indians fans generated, but without a wooden seat to strike, he opted for bringing his drum to a game in 1973. After a newspaper report said he'd be at the next game, Adams returned, and the tradition has continued for nearly 50 years. He used to pay for two seats (one for him, one for the drum), but the Indians decided years ago that he and his percussion instrument could come for free. (Unlike the team itself, Adams has not been accused of appropriating Native American culture through his drumming.) Adams rarely misses a game, hitting the drum to pump up the crowd and get the stadium rocking.

The best part is that Adams is a genuinely kind person. If you visit him and say hello, there's a chance he'll let you bang on the drum. (He let me do it once. That was a thrill.)

Heritage Park

Before heading to your seat, visit **Heritage Park** (center field, 100 level), the Indians Hall of Fame area. It's paved with **bricks** purchased by fans and has **plaques** honoring notables like Larry Doby, Bob Feller, Tris Speaker, and Cy Young. The park is also home to a **statue** of Frank Robinson, who was with the Indians in 1975 when he became the first Black manager in major league baseball history. Just beyond the center-field gates are statues of Indians Hall of Famers Larry Doby, Bob Feller, Jim Thome, and Lou Boudreau.

Home Run Porch

You might want to check out the view from the **Home Run Porch** (left-field foul pole, 100 level). Stake out a spot against the railing and hope some right-handed slugger will pop one your way. (In Game 7 of the 2016 World Series, non-slugger Rajai Davis hit one of the biggest home runs in Indians history to the Porch.)

Kids Clubhouse

For some stimulation for the kids, the place to be is the **Kids Clubhouse** (behind section 125), a two-level wonderland of activities and playground equipment. Baseball-themed fun includes a timed race from home plate to first base, a pitching simulator, an interactive batting-stance simulator, and a small-scale baseball field where youngsters can step up to the plate. Also here are an interactive locker room; a huge, two-story slide shaped like a baseball bat; family concession stands (serving cotton candy, ice-cream sundaes, burgers, and popcorn); lactation rooms for mothers; and a parents lounge.

FOOD AND DRINKS

Progressive Field has several food and drink spots where fans can enjoy local fare while

Photos (from top to bottom): John Adams and his drum; Cleveland's mascot, Slider; Indians game at Progressive Field.

standing around and watching some of the game. They're popular places, headlined by the **Right Field District** (right field around the foul line), home to **The Corner** (open to all ticketed patrons), a two-level super bar with close to 40 beers on tap, a "pour-your-own" beer option—which allows you to control how much you want—and a roof deck with an open-air firepit. The Corner is popular, especially among fans in the 21-45 age bracket. Fans hightail it here once the gates open to get the primo spots along the railings at both levels and in the cushy seating around the firepit. If you can't nab one of those spots, it'll be hard to get a view of the game from here.

In addition to The Corner, the District (as the Right Field District is called) houses a host of vendors familiar to denizens of Northeast Ohio. They can be found in the District's different sections, named after some of Cleveland's **neighborhoods.** In **Ohio City,** you'll find **Great Lakes Brewing Company** (section 107), a famous Cleveland brewery that serves beer with carb-heavy bites. In **Cleveland Heights,** there's **Melt Bar and Grilled** (section 113), doling out grilled cheese creations like the Chorizo & Potato, which has sausage, potato hash, and sharp cheddar. Local Cal-Mex standby **Barrio** (section 109), in **Tremont,** offers build-your-own tacos plus a small but potent selection of tequila and margaritas.

The **Infield District** (surrounding home plate) has another dozen or so local vendors. Want an enormous sandwich? **Fat Head's Brewery** (section 158) has the South-side Slopes—kielbasa topped with sautéed pierogi, cheese, and horseradish sauce. Grab a quesadilla or nachos with *queso fundido* (melted cheese) at **Momocho** (section 139), and sit under twinkle lights at the beer garden of the Infield District location of **Great Lakes Brewing Company** (section 164).

The only true restaurant at Progressive Field is the **Terrace Club** (left-field foul line, open two hours before first pitch for night games, open one hour before first pitch for day games, under $50). The club has one seating before the game when it opens, then a second seating once the game begins. To score a table before the game, make a **reservation** through the team website; during the game, you'll have to chance it with a walk-up. The view through the restaurant's glass windows is pretty cool (though you may not be able to see center field). The food is standard "elevated" American fare with a burger, pulled pork, salads, and a few desserts. It's not a bad way to pregame.

You're going to need a **hot dog,** available at numerous stands in the ballpark. After getting one, spread on some **Bertman Original Ball Park Mustard,** a special brown mustard originally made for visitors to the old Indians stadium, League Park. Smooth but with just enough of a bite, it's the perfect condiment. Everyone swears by it.

EVENTS

Fans can get **autographs** by moving to the front rows in **sections 125-134** and **169-175** up to 45 minutes before first pitch. Nothing is guaranteed, however. If you want to catch **batting practice,** enter through the right field gate, which always opens two hours before first pitch.

Friday nights are a blast at the ballpark, as the Indians typically host **dollar dog night** and a **fireworks display** after each game. On Fridays and Saturdays, the team throws a **block party** in the Right Field District. Around mid-season, they throw a **birthday party** for their **mascot Slider,** a fuchsia-colored creature inspired in part by Jim Henson's Muppets.

Tours

Progressive Field tours (216/420-4487, Mon.-Sat. May-Aug., $15, $12 seniors and ages 14 and under) last an hour and include visits to the visitors' clubhouse (on select days), a dugout (also on select days), and private and ticketed areas of the ballpark, such as the press box, party suites, and Home Plate Club. Public tours are not available on days there are home games, during select stretches of summer, and on July 4.

A TROUBLING NAME AND LOGO

You may recall the old logo of Cleveland's baseball team, a smiling, red-skinned Native American character named Chief Wahoo. The team adopted the racially insensitive logo in 1947, but the original image goes back to 1932, when a local newspaper published a caricature of a smiling Native American to mark a baseball victory for Cleveland.

For another 70 years, the team was represented by variations of this racist image. After years of protesting by Indigenous communities, the team finally dropped Chief Wahoo in 2019. At Progressive Field, you won't see Chief Wahoo on the players' uniforms, but you will see fans wearing gear with the old logo—and the team still sells merchandise with it.

But there's more progress in the works: In December 2020 the team announced that it would change its name after lengthy conversations with Indigenous communities. At the time of publication, Cleveland planned to announce its new name before the 2022 season.

SHOPPING

The **Indians Team Shop** (2401 Ontario St., section 167, 216/420-4327, 10am-5pm Mon.-Sat., noon-5pm Sun.) has a modest collection of jerseys, caps, memorabilia, and more. Merchandise focuses on the franchise's classic "C" logo. Other shops include the **New Era Hat Stand** (sections 102, 151) and the **game-used memorabilia stand** (section 167).

CLEVELAND SIGHTS

ROCK & ROLL HALL OF FAME

Hello Cleveland! Don't you dare think you'll be the first person to scream this upon entering the **Rock & Roll Hall of Fame** (1100 E. 9th St., www.rockhall.com, 10am-5:30pm Sun.-Tues. and Thurs.-Fri., 10am-9pm Wed. and Sat. late May-June, 10am-5:30pm Sun.-Tues., 10am-9pm Wed.-Sat. July-Aug., 10am-9pm Wed., 10am-5:30pm Thurs.-Tues. Sept.-late May, $26, $24 seniors, $16 ages 6-12, free ages 5 and under). Since 1995, the iconic museum with the triangular entryway has offered visitors a detailed look at the history of popular Western music—with a focus on rock, naturally.

The best things in here? Good golly, Miss Molly, there's a whole lotta stuff goin' on: instruments played by the Beatles, Alice Cooper's boots, Tupac Shakur's handwritten rhymes, Jimi Hendrix's jackets and guitars, Michael Jackson's outfits from the Grammy Awards, ZZ Top's neon-green axes. It goes on and on. Exhibits include deep dives into the British Invasion, hip-hop's evolution, and the roots of rock. Level 3 is where you can view all the inductees. Also check out *The Power of Rock Experience*, a 25-minute interactive presentation with a film by Academy Award winner Jonathan Demme. A note: The presentation uses strobe and haze effects.

Throughout the year, the museum hosts concerts and live events. On Wednesday nights, when the museum has extended hours, there are special talks, movie screenings, and themed events. Wednesday is a good time to visit because of the extended hours, but the museum also remains open later during other select days in the summer. Either way, you'll want to block out at least three hours for a visit, and likely more. Your ticket is good only for the day you paid for. Plan ahead and prepare, and then enjoy this absolute must-visit.

WEST SIDE MARKET

Part of Cleveland's Ohio City neighborhood, the big public **West Side Market** (1979 W. 25th St., 216/664-3387, www.westsidemarket.org, 7am-4pm Mon. and Wed., 7am-6pm

BOB FELLER
1936-'41, '45-'56 - RHP
Inducted 1957

GREATEST PITCHER IN CLUB HISTORY. TRIBE ALL-TIME LEADER IN WINS (266), STRIKEOUTS (2581), STARTS, COMPLETE GAMES AND INNINGS. "RAPID ROBERT" LED AMERICAN LEAGUE IN WINS SIX TIMES AND STRIKEOUTS SEVEN TIMES. SET CLUB SINGLE-SEASON RECORDS FOR STRIKEOUTS (348), INNINGS (371), SHUTOUTS (10) AND COMPLETE GAMES (36) IN 1946. PITCHED CLUB RECORD

Fri.-Sat., 10am-4pm Sun.) has been open since 1912. It's packed with tourists and locals walking around and perusing hundreds of food vendors. Here, as at Philadelphia's Reading Terminal Market and Seattle's Pike Place Market, you'll find butchers and deli-meat purveyors, pasta makers, fishmongers, produce stands, bakers, cheesemongers, and the occasional specialty food seller and florist.

It'll get crowded on the weekends, so aim to visit on a weekday. The market is also a great place to visit in the early morning, when the coffee is hot and the smell of fresh fish lingers. The bathrooms are downstairs, and there's an ATM on-site (not all vendors here accept credit and debit cards, and some require a minimum payment to take cards).

EAST 4TH STREET

A 10-minute walk (or four-minute drive) northwest from Progressive Field is **East 4th Street** (between Euclid Ave. and Huron Rd.). This area began as a theater district in the early 20th century before falling into an era of dilapidation. Then, starting in 2002, it began morphing into a popular dining and entertainment sector resembling a busy Brooklyn neighborhood. It's home to the **House of Blues** (308 Euclid Ave., 216/523-2583, www. houseofblues.com, 11:30am-10pm Tues.-Fri., 4pm-11pm Sat.), various restaurants, and a popular bowling alley.

FOOD

NEAR PROGRESSIVE FIELD

Want to splurge on food in Cleveland? There's no better option than **Lola Bistro** (2058 E. 4th St., 216/621-5652, www.lolabistro.com, 5pm-10pm Sun.-Thurs., 5pm-11pm Fri.-Sat., under $60), the acclaimed restaurant from

Photos (from top to bottom): Bob Feller plaque at Heritage Park; Rock & Roll Hall of Fame; Edgewater Park.

celebrity chef Michael Symon that sets the upscale culinary tone in the city. In its warm digs, you'll want to settle in with a glass of wine and a pricey piece of steak. Lola helps anchor the popular East 4th Street district.

Also on East 4th Street and a part of Michael Symon's empire is **Mabel's BBQ** (2050 E. 4th St., 216/417-8823, www.mabelsbbq, 11:30am-10pm Sun.-Thurs., 11:30am-midnight Fri.-Sat., under $40), which makes Cleveland-style barbecue, where the meat is coated in a sauce made with Bertman's Original Ball Park Mustard. The meats and spices have an Eastern European influence; we're talking kielbasa with a snappy zip, and rubs with mustard seed and coriander. Mabel's has an impressive bourbon list, as well.

Part of the 5th Street Arcades shopping mall, **Barrio Gateway** (503 Prospect Ave. #E, 216/862-4652, www.barrio-tacos.com, 4pm-2am Mon.-Thurs., 11am-2am Fri.-Sun., under $20) offers a vast taco selection, including a make-your-own option. There's also a respectable margarita and local beer menu. The space is eclectic and fun, headlined by wall art inspired by Día de los Muertos. Barrio has multiple locations in town, including one in the **Tremont neighborhood** (806 Literary Rd., 216/999-7714, www.barrio-tacos.com, 4pm-2am Mon.-Thurs., 11am-2am Fri.-Sun., under $20).

OTHER NEIGHBORHOODS

Barrio Gateway isn't the only essential stop for Mexican American street fare. Go to **Ohio City Burrito** (1844 W. 25th St., 216/664-0908, www.ohiocityburrito.com, 10:30am-10pm Mon.-Sat., under $15) for burritos, tacos, quesadillas, and nachos. Hang in the orange-colored, easygoing dining room at this original location. Ohio City Burrito also has a stand at Progressive Field as well as another location in town.

Get some corned beef at **Slyman's Restaurant** (3106 St. Clair Ave., 216/621-3760, www.slymans.com, 6am-2:30pm Mon.-Fri., 9am-1pm Sat., under $25), a famed sandwich stop in the AsiaTown neighborhood.

In addition to corned beef, Slyman's does all the classics, including pastrami, Reubens, and egg salad. The no-frills dining room is a place to sit down for a few moments and just savor the meat. Nearby and doing the same thing, along with a top-notch breakfast, is **Superior Restaurant** (3000 Superior Ave., 216/621-5899, www.thesuperiorrestaurant.com, 5:30am-3pm Mon.-Fri., 5:30am-2pm Sat., under $25), another no-nonsense place where the sandwiches sing.

And while you're in AsiaTown, be sure to visit a couple nearby places specializing in Vietnamese and Chinese cuisine. I recommend **Superior Pho** (3030 Superior Ave. #105, 216/781-7462, www.superiorpho.com, 10:30am-8pm Tues.-Sat., 10:30am-7pm Sun., under $20), where the pho is perfect on a cooler day. (Don't confuse this spot with Superior Restaurant around the corner.)

BARS AND BREWERIES

NEAR PROGRESSIVE FIELD

You can grab a quick drink or two at **Victory Alley Sports Bar & Grille** (721 Bolivar Rd., 216/860-4988, www.victorycleveland.com, open two hours before every event at Progressive Field and Rocket Mortgage FieldHouse, under $25), which is worthy primarily because it's literally a few feet from the ballpark. They have the standard national beers on tap, along with a couple locals from places like Great Lakes Brewing Company, plus plenty of televisions for watching games.

OTHER NEIGHBORHOODS

Beer drinkers should flock to the Ohio City neighborhood, home to some of the city's best craft breweries. **Great Lakes Brewing Company** (2516 Market Ave., 216/771-4404, www.greatlakesbrewing.com, 11:30am-midnight Mon.-Thurs., 11:30am-1am Fri., 11am-1am Sat., under $30) is a must-visit for completists. Born back in the 1980s, Great Lakes has plenty of history; its old-school bar was once occupied by Prohibition agent Eliot Ness. Enjoy an amber lager named for Ness or the Dortmunder Gold Lager, and order a bite from the restaurant menu.

A few blocks away, **Forest City Brewery** (2135 Columbus Rd., 216/228-9116, www.forestcitybrewery.com, 4pm-11pm Tues.-Thurs., 4pm-midnight Fri., noon-midnight Sat., noon-10pm Sun., under $25) is a fun hang. On cooler days, the warm, cozy taproom works, but it's at its best when the weather is nice: Forest City claims the oldest beer garden in the city. The garden is also home to "Big Red," Ohio's tallest red mulberry tree. A varied tap list, plus craft sodas, means everyone should be happy here.

Just a bit north from those joints is **Saucy Brew Works** (2885 Detroit Ave., 216/666-2568, www.saucybrewworks.com, 11am-10pm Sun.-Wed., 11am-midnight Thurs.-Sat., under $25), which serves a solid variety of beer and leans on IPAs and sours. The two-story taproom makes it easy to find a spot to drink, and if you're hungry, order one of the brewery's thin-crust pizzas.

RECREATION

PARKS

Get in some beach time at **Edgewater Park** (W. 73rd St. at US-6), a 174-acre recreation area that hugs Lake Erie and has boat launches, pavilions, picnic areas, swimming spots, and some sand. On a hot summer day, you're bound to find sunbathers, kids splashing about, and folks just itching to steal a few minutes on the shore. Complementing the experience is the **Edgewater Beach House** (7600 Cleveland Memorial Shoreway, 216/954-3408, Memorial Day-Labor Day), which offers made-to-order snacks and drinks, including beer and craft cocktails. On Thursday evenings in the summer, the beach hosts a concert series. Photo op alert: Be sure to get a selfie in front of one of five versions

of the **Cleveland script sign** (Upper Edgewater Dr., off Cliff Dr.), which rests on the shoreline. The signs display the city's name in a distinctive script.

You can also find a Cleveland script sign at **Voinovich Bicentennial Park** (800 E. 9th St. Pier), a lakeside square that offers views of the skyline, the Rock & Roll Hall of Fame, and FirstEnergy Stadium, home of the Cleveland Browns football team. The park hosts summer festivals and yoga classes.

Cuyahoga Valley National Park

Just a half hour from Downtown Cleveland is **Cuyahoga Valley National Park** (Boston Store Visitor Center, 1550 Boston Mills Rd., Peninsula, 330/657-2752, 9:30am-5pm daily, park 24 hours daily, www.nps.gov/cuva, free), with more than 32,000 acres of forests, hills, and waterways. Block out time to check out **Brandywine Falls** (Stanford Rd. at Brandywine Rd., Sagamore Hills), an 86-foot cascade accessible via a short hike on a wooden walkway. For a longer hike, trek part of the 20-mile **Ohio and Erie Canal Towpath Trail** (accessible from Boston Store Visitor Center). Along this former pathway for boat towing, find the 19th-century Stanford House, owned by one of the first white settlers of northeastern Ohio, back when it was annexed by the Colony of Connecticut. To get here, hop on I-77 South for 11 miles, exit at Pleasant Valley Road, and take that east to Brookside Road. Turn right, then make a quick left onto Riverview Road. The drive from Downtown Cleveland is a little over 20 miles.

BOWLING

Because the American Bowling Congress set up shop in the Midwest in the early 20th century, Cleveland has always been seen as something of a notable bowling hub. If you can spare some time for a game or two, the city has plenty of options. Just a few blocks from Progressive Field in the East 4th Street area, **The Corner Alley** (402 Euclid Ave., 216/298-4070, www.thecorneralley.com, 11:30am-midnight Sun.-Thurs.,

11:30am-2am Fri.-Sat., $25-35 per hour Fri.-Sun., $15-30 per hour Mon.-Thurs., food and drink extra) pairs bowling with booze and bar bites for a fun, modern, and slightly expensive experience.

Not too far south from Ohio City is **Dickey Lanes** (3275 W. 25th St., 216/741-9774, 4pm-midnight Mon.-Sat., 1pm-5pm Sun., under $40) in the Clark-Fulton neighborhood. This is your classic old-school spot with vintage, mid-century modern seating and manual scoring, plus cold beer.

Want a different experience? Check out **Hi and Dry Bowling & Beer** (2221 Professor Ave., 216/566-9463, www.hianddrycleveland.com, 3pm-2am Mon.-Thurs., 11:30am-2am Fri., 11am-2am Sat.-Sun., under $30), which has beer, cocktails, and bar grub, along with duckpin bowling, popular in some midwestern and mid-Atlantic areas. You roll a small ball down a shorter lane in an attempt to knock down short, chubby pins.

SHOPPING

For fun, third-party Cleveland baseball apparel like, say, a *Major League* Rick Vaughn "Wild Thing" T-shirt, visit **We Bleed Ohio** (530 Euclid Ave. #43, 440/941-1178, www.webleedohio.com). The shop also sells clothing promoting the city's football and basketball teams, along with civic pride gear.

ACCOMMODATIONS

NEAR PROGRESSIVE FIELD

A cool hotel just a four-minute walk from the ballpark, the **Kimpton Schofield Hotel** (2000 E. 9th St., 216/357-3250, www.theschofieldhotel.com, $120-250) is set in a circa-1902 building and offers hip amenities like a yoga mat in each room, discounted rates at a boutique fitness studio, a daily wine hour, and a complimentary guitar you can rent for

in-room jam sessions (hey, you're near the Rock & Roll Hall of Fame). Rooms are tastefully modern, done in beiges and blues with wood and marble accents.

OTHER NEIGHBORHOODS

Are you one of those people who can't wait to binge 24 hours of *A Christmas Story* each year? You can spend a night at the actual Parker family residence shown in the film, called **A Christmas Story House** (3159 W. 11th St., 216/298-4919, www.achristmasstoryhouse.com, $445-745, $995-4,000 Christmas season), which has been lovingly re-created to look exactly as it did in the movie. Yes, a leg lamp is here, too. Up to six people can stay at the house, which is—during the day—a museum with **public tours** (starting at 10:15am daily, $10-15).

You could also stay at the house next to the Parker residence, or as it calls itself, the **Bumpus House** (3153 W. 11th St., 216/298-4919, www.bumpushouse.com, $250-345, $395-995 Christmas season). Known as the home of the rowdy dogs that bother the Parker family, this house has been re-created to look like a circa-1940s Cleveland house with a few "hillbilly" accents thrown in.

GETTING AROUND

PUBLIC TRANSIT

Get around via **RTA** (216/566-5100, www.riderta.com, $2.50 per ride). RTA has a **rapid-transit light rail system** that connects Downtown to neighborhoods like Ohio City and Tremont. The **Blue Line** and **Green Line** both run along the lakefront as the **Waterfront Line,** then head toward Progressive Field and eastward. The **Red Line** moves north to south, connecting with the Blue and Green Lines at **Tower City Center** (50 Public Sq.), the stop for Progressive Field, before heading across the Cuyahoga River toward Ohio City and Cleveland Hopkins International Airport. If you're hanging out in Ohio City, you'll want to use the **Ohio City Rapid Station** (Pearl Rd. and W. 25th St.). The Red Line stops here, taking folks to Tower City Center.

RTA also operates a robust **bus system** that stretches into just about every neighborhood, and a **Downtown trolley** (B and E Lines 7am-7pm Mon.-Fri., C Line 7am-11pm Mon.-Fri., 11am-11pm Sat.-Sun.). If you're staying Downtown, you may be interested in the trolley's C Line, which stops at Public Square, Prospect Avenue and 9th Street (one block from Progressive Field), and along St. Clair Avenue, providing a connection to West 3rd Street and the Warehouse District. This is a good option if your feet are particularly tired.

TAXI, UBER, AND LYFT

A taxi from Cleveland Hopkins International Airport to Downtown will run about $20, as will a Lyft, but an Uber will cost more like $30, thanks to surge pricing. Typically, taxis are the cheapest of the three in Cleveland, but the operators in town are known for unreliable service.

CAR

All the rental companies have lots at Cleveland Hopkins International Airport, and multiple companies have locations Downtown, including **Budget** (www.budget.com), **Enterprise** (www.enterprise.com), and **Hertz** (www.hertz.com). If you're hoping to spend a few days in the area, and especially if you're eyeing a trip to Cuyahoga Falls National Park, renting a car or driving isn't a bad idea. Otherwise, you can spend your time in the general area and do just fine with ride-sharing, light rail, and walking.

To navigate the highways in Cleveland, know that **I-90** comes from the west, paralleling the Lake Erie shoreline. Then it wraps around the Downtown area, where it becomes known as the **Innerbelt Freeway,** before heading east along the lakeside. You can access neighborhoods like Tremont, Ohio City, the Gateway District, Downtown, and AsiaTown via I-90.

Two important interstates start at I-90: **I-71,** which begins in Tremont and heads southwest past Cleveland Hopkins International Airport and toward Columbus and Cincinnati; and **I-77,** which begins beside Progressive Field and continues south toward Canton and, much later, Charlotte, North Carolina. **I-480** is an outer-city belt connecting suburbs west to east, and **I-80** is another 15 minutes outside the city, running alongside Cuyahoga Valley National Park.

A more local road is **US-6/OH-2,** which is known as the **Cleveland Memorial Shoreway** as it glides along the Lake Erie shoreline in Downtown. It provides access to the Rock & Roll Hall of Fame, FirstEnergy Stadium (home of the Cleveland Browns football team), and other lakeside attractions.

AKRON, OHIO

If you're spending closer to a week in the Cleveland area, or if you want to see Canal Park Stadium, one of the more impressive minor league ballparks in America, visit Akron, home of the RubberDucks. The double-A affiliate of the Indians plays in the Eastern League.

GETTING THERE

Car
The fastest way to Akron from **Cleveland** is a **40-mile, 45-minute** drive south on I-77 to OH-59 East, or Dart Avenue, which straddles the city's downtown. Exit off Dart Avenue at Cedar Street, then turn left onto Main Street. Canal Park Stadium is in the center of town.

Bus
You can hop on a **Greyhound bus** (631 S. Broadway St., www.greyhound.com, $5) to reach Akron from Cleveland, a journey of about an hour. The Akron station is an 0.8-mile jaunt from Canal Park Stadium. Walk north on Rosa Parks Drive to South Main Street and continue heading north toward the ballpark.

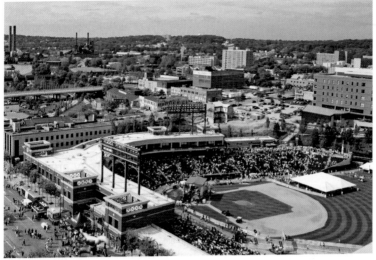

Canal Park Stadium

CANAL PARK STADIUM

Canal Park Stadium (300 S. Main St., 330/253-5151, www.milb.com/akron), home to Indians affiliate the **Akron RubberDucks,** was built in 1997 by noted ballpark developer HOK, the team behind Oriole Park at Camden Yards and many of the other retro-style baseball stadiums across the country. You can see it in the brick facade, the outfield fence—which has asymmetrical dimensions and unconventional heights—the tiered bullpens, and the skyline views.

There are **two levels** of seating in foul territory: Seats in the **main level** (sections 1/2-20) typically run $5-11; **upper-level suites** are available for groups. Tickets for an area called **Homerville** in right field include swivel chairs at a railing and up to two complimentary drinks at the tiki bar. There's also

a **picnic area** in left field, and in right field is a **tiki terrace** and separate restaurant called **The Game Grill & Bar** (300 S. Main St., 330/252-0804, 5pm-9pm Mon.-Fri., noon-4pm Sat.-Sun., under $30). While the food is your standard American grill fare (burgers, sandwiches, and salads), the outdoor tables make it a nice place to kick back before or during the game.

The park is also home to the **Greater Akron Baseball Hall of Fame** (330/867-6004, www.gabhof.org), which honors individuals from the greater Akron area, as well as former Akron baseball players and personalities, who have made a significant contribution to baseball, from Little League and youth coaches to former major leaguers. The Hall of Fame is open to the public when the gates are open for a RubberDucks game.

DETROIT
TIGERS

Detroit is a special city, armed with the toughness of an East Coast metropolis but nailed down in the Midwest with all its manufacturing might. Detroit means business, and no symbol in the city—neither the bold letters of the GM logo, nor the pure Americana of the name "Ford" in a blue oval—screams Detroit more than the elegant, commanding "D" that the Detroit Tigers baseball club has been rocking since nearly the beginning of its existence.

The Tigers were born in 1894 as part of the Western League, jumping to the American League as a founding franchise in 1901. By that time, as Henry Ford was rolling his very first automobiles through the city, the Tigers were already playing home games at Bennett Park, at the intersection of Michigan and Trumbull Avenues in the Corktown

section of the city. In 1912, Bennett Park was demolished, and Navin Field was built in its place. Navin was later expanded and renamed Briggs Stadium. In 1961, that park was renamed Tiger Stadium, a field synonymous with Tigers baseball—big, brash, bold, and without any pretense.

Early on, the club had success, thanks primarily to Ty Cobb, an all-time great hitter who'd stop at nothing to get his. Cobb would set the major league record for career base hits, among other things, and the Tigers would win American League pennants from 1907 to 1909. They won their first World Series championship in 1935, boasting a team that starred Hall of Famers Hank Greenberg, Mickey Cochrane, Goose Goslin, and Charlie Gehringer. They won another title in 1945, toward the end of Greenberg's career, then fell into a period of mediocrity. This was a time of huge gains in Detroit's manufacturing industry, as plants built military tanks and bombers during World War II, then saw a heyday of auto construction.

Then came 1968. Just a year before that, the Uprising of 1967 (also called the 12th Street Riot) brought into full view the city's long-brewing racial tensions. During the civil unrest that lasted several days, Detroit's Black residents clashed with the city's majority-white police department. Forty-three people died, and more than 7,000 people were arrested. As the city reeled from the aftermath of the riot, the Tigers spent their 1968 season winning a franchise record of 103 games behind pitchers Denny McLain and Mickey Lolich, and future Hall of Fame hitter Al Kaline. They capped the season with a World Series win, which some people credit with bringing a feeling of unity back to Detroit.

Much like Detroit's auto industry, the modern-day Tigers have seen peaks and valleys. Through much of the 1970s, the team was mediocre, but in 1984 they stormed through the American League and won the World Series easily. Then they missed the playoffs throughout much of the '80s and the

entirety of the '90s. They moved to Comerica Park in 2000, as Tiger Stadium had proven too old and beyond repair. Comerica quickly became a cozy home. After losing an unfathomable 119 games in 2003, they reached the World Series just three years later, in 2006. Playoff success returned from 2011 to 2014, but then the luck died. Lately, the Tigers have been terrible. But make no mistake, this city loves its baseball. When the Tigers are going, they really go—and the fans respond in kind.

Some of baseball's greatest players have donned the "D," from all-time double-play tandem "Sweet" Lou Whitaker and Alan Trammell to the great Miguel Cabrera. In the future, more great talents will wear that uniform. The Motor City may change, and its character may evolve by necessity, but one thing is sure to remain: the "D."

PLANNING YOUR TIME

Detroit can be done in a **weekend,** no problem. Reserve some time to visit one of the major **museums** in town, whether you're more into music (Motown Museum), cars (Henry Ford Museum), or art (Detroit Institute of Arts). Spend the rest of that day exploring the neighborhoods just outside Downtown, like **Midtown, Corktown,** and **Eastern Market.** A second day is all about **Downtown** and **Comerica Park.** If you extend your trip to three or four days, opt to hang out in **Belle Isle** for at least a half day. Maybe spend some time on the **Detroit River** itself.

Your best bet for accommodations is to stay in **Downtown** Detroit, since you'll be closer to the ballpark and won't have to rely on driving or ride-sharing too much. But if you'd rather be outside the major tourism district, staying in a nearby city like **Dearborn** or **St. Clair Shores** isn't a bad idea. It's only a 20-minute drive at most into Downtown from either location.

If you're coming to Comerica Park in **March, April, May, September,** or **October,** you should prepare for **colder weather.**

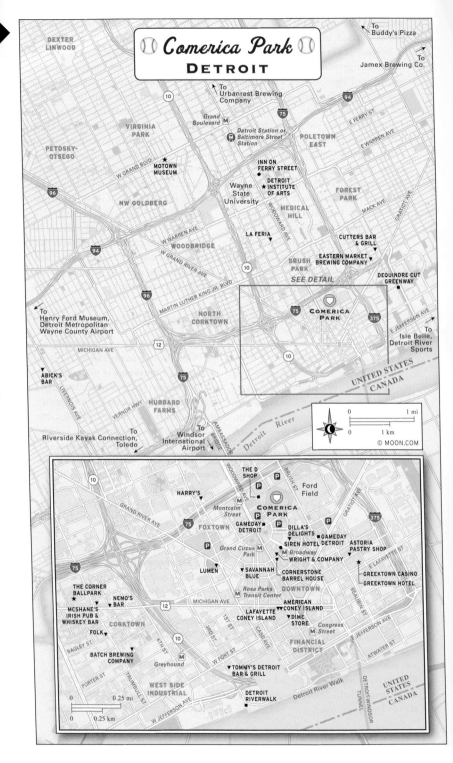

Comerica Park
DETROIT

To Buddy's Pizza

To Jamex Brewing Co.

DEXTER LINWOOD

To Urbanrest Brewing Company

Grand Boulevard

Detroit Station of Baltimore Street Station

VIRGINIA PARK

POLETOWN EAST

E FERRY ST

E WARREN AVE

PETOSKY-OTSEGO

W GRAND BLVD

★ MOTOWN MUSEUM

INN ON FERRY STREET

DETROIT INSTITUTE OF ARTS

Wayne State University

FOREST PARK

MACK AVE

GRATIOT AVE

NW GOLDBERG

MEDICAL HILL

WOODWARD AVE

W WARREN AVE

LA FERIA

CUTTERS BAR & GRILL

WOODBRIDGE

EASTERN MARKET BREWING COMPANY

W GRAND RIVER AVE

BRUSH PARK

DEQUINDRE CUT GREENWAY

SEE DETAIL

MARTIN LUTHER KING JR. BLVD

COMERICA PARK

To Henry Ford Museum, Detroit Metropolitan Wayne County Airport

NORTH CORKTOWN

To Isle Belle, Detroit River Sports

MICHIGAN AVE

E JEFFERSON AVE

UNITED STATES
CANADA

ABICK'S BAR

HUBBARD FARMS

LIVERNOIS AVE

VERNOR HWY

AMBASSADOR BRIDGE

Detroit River

Riverside Kayak Connection, Toledo

To Windsor International Airport

0   1 mi
0   1 km

© MOON.COM

THE D SHOP

Ford Field

HARRY'S

Montcalm Street

COMERICA PARK

BRUSH ST

WOODWARD AVE

GRATIOT AVE

FOXTOWN

GAMEDAY DETROIT

DILLA'S DELIGHTS

GAMEDAY DETROIT

ASTORIA PASTRY SHOP

Grand Circus Park

Broadway

SIREN HOTEL

WRIGHT & COMPANY

E LAFAYETTE ST

LUMEN

SAVANNAH BLUE

CORNERSTONE BARREL HOUSE

GREEKTOWN CASINO
GREEKTOWN HOTEL

Rosa Parks Transit Center

DOWNTOWN

THE CORNER BALLPARK

NEMO'S BAR

MICHIGAN AVE

AMERICAN CONEY ISLAND

BEAUBIEN ST

MCSHANE'S IRISH PUB & WHISKEY BAR

CORKTOWN

LAFAYETTE CONEY ISLAND

DIME STORE

Congress Street

E JEFFERSON AVE

FOLK

1ST ST

3RD ST

CASS AVE

FINANCIAL DISTRICT

BAGLEY ST

BATCH BREWING COMPANY

8TH ST

Greyhound

W FORT ST

ATWATER ST

PORTER ST

TRUMBULL ST

TOMMY'S DETROIT BAR & GRILL

DETROIT-WINDSOR TUNNEL

WEST SIDE INDUSTRIAL

DETROIT RIVERWALK

Detroit River Walk

UNITED STATES
CANADA

W JEFFERSON AVE

0   0.25 mi
0   0.25 km

It's pretty cold early in the season with spring daytime temperatures hanging out in the 40s and 50s. Night-game temps are in the 20s and 30s. Things don't really warm up until around **Memorial Day,** so just remember those coats, gloves, and hats. The best time to visit is **mid-season. July** temperatures tend to be around 75-85°F, on average. It rains about a quarter of the time in Detroit, spread out equally across the year, so always bring an **umbrella.** And since the city is close to **Lake Erie** (and Lake St. Clair), swirling **winds** are always a possibility.

GETTING THERE

AIR

Detroit Metropolitan Wayne County Airport

Detroit Metropolitan Wayne County Airport (DTW, W. G. Rogell Dr. and Goddard Rd., Romulus, 734/247-7678, www.metroairport.com) is the major facility for air travel in the Detroit area. Located in the southwest suburb of Romulus, the airport is a 25- to 45-minute drive from Downtown Detroit.

The airport is served by **Air Canada** (888/247-2262, www.aircanada.com), **American Airlines** (800/433-7300, www.aa.com), **Delta** (800/221-1212, www.delta.com), **Frontier** (800/432-1359, www.flyfrontier.com), **jetBlue** (800/538-2583, www.jetblue.com), **Southwest** (800/435-9792, www.southwest.com), **Spirit** (801/401-2222, www.spirit.com), and **United** (800/864-8331, www.united.com).

AIRPORT TRANSPORTATION

If you're hoping to **rent a car,** you'll follow signs for ground transportation and then hop on a **shuttle** to the rental car center. Most of the major companies have desks here. Depending on traffic, it can take anywhere from 25 to 45 minutes to reach Downtown from the airport. The drive is primarily on I-94 East; then you head south on I-75 for two exits to reach Downtown.

Thinking about taking public transportation? Detroit's public transit authority, **SMART** (Suburban Mobility Authority for Regional Transportation, www.smartbus.org, $2-2.50), operates a large network of **buses.** The **FAST Michigan line,** or **261 bus,** takes folks into Downtown Detroit in the most direct manner.

Windsor International Airport

Closer to Downtown Detroit but located in Canada is **Windsor International Airport** (YQG, 3200 County Rd. 42, Windsor, Ontario, 519/969-2430, www.yqg.ca). Just across the Detroit River from Detroit, this airport offers flights to other Canadian cities like Toronto and Calgary. **Air Canada** flies into here, along with a couple smaller Canadian airlines. From the airport, it's a 20- to 25-minute drive into Downtown Detroit via McDougal Street. You'll cross into the Motor City via the Detroit-Windsor Tunnel. Note that you'll also have to stop at the border crossing. Have a passport ready.

AIRPORT TRANSPORTATION

The **rental car** desks are just across from the baggage claim. Three agencies are here: **Avis** (519/966-2782, www.avis.ca), **Budget** (519/969-5611, www.budget.ca), and **Enterprise** (519/966-7923, www.enterprise.ca).

CAR

The quickest way from **Cleveland** to Detroit is to snake along Lake Erie on **I-90 West, I-280 North** (to get around Toledo, Ohio), and then **I-75 North.** This **170-mile** ride should take **2.5-3 hours.**

For something much more scenic (but with a longer drive time), hop on **US-20 West.** When it merges with **US-6 West,** stay on the **Great Army of the Republic Highway** until it hits **OH-2,** west of Sandusky, Ohio. You'll take OH-2 until it connects to **I-280 North.** From I-280, continue onto **I-75 North** into Detroit. It's the same distance, but this route will take more like **3.5 hours.** Drive it early on a summer evening—you'll watch the sun setting over Lake

YOUR BEST DAY AT COMERICA PARK

It's a Motor City day, and you have tickets for tonight's Tigers game. What are you going to do before, during, and after? Here's your itinerary.

10 HOURS BEFORE FIRST PITCH
Today is a day to pay tribute to some of Detroit's legends. Start the day at **Dilla's Delights** to tip a cap to legendary hip-hop producer J. Dilla. Grab a vegan doughnut or two, plus a coffee.

9 HOURS BEFORE FIRST PITCH
You can take the QLine light rail to **Grand Boulevard** or drive, but either way, spend the next couple of hours at the **Motown Museum.** Learn the history of Hitsville U.S.A., a machine of a record company that produced the sweetest sounds of the 1960s and 1970s.

6 HOURS BEFORE FIRST PITCH
It's a 10-minute drive to **Buddy's Pizza,** the birthplace of the Detroit pie. Make the pilgrimage to stuff yourself silly on this cheesy and bready square meal.

4.5 HOURS BEFORE FIRST PITCH
Get back on the road and head southwest to **The Corner Ballpark** to honor the legacy of old Tiger Stadium. Take some photos, maybe catch one of the club ball games that play there, and do your best impression of Cecil Fielder or Reggie Jackson hitting one onto the roof.

3 HOURS BEFORE FIRST PITCH
You have to drink a beer at **Nemo's Bar,** a long-standing Detroit sports bar. If you're

Motown Museum

driving, park here and take the shuttle to Comerica Park.

1.5 HOURS BEFORE FIRST PITCH
Make a quick pregame stop at **Harry's** for one more beer. It'll be crowded with fans, but try to make your way up to the roof deck to take in the views. Now it's time to enter **Comerica Park.**

DURING THE GAME
Visit **The D Shop** for some Tigers swag. Spend time admiring the **statues** and catching up on franchise history at the **Detroit Tigers Hall of Fame.** Got kids with you? Visit the **carousel.** Maybe grab a bite of a pizza place gone big at **Little Caesars.**

AFTER THE GAME
Get a Coney dog at **Lafayette Coney Island,** then down one more pint at **Tommy's Detroit Bar & Grill.**

Erie for a nice portion of the way, and it's a really sweet sight.

TRAIN

Amtrak (800/872-7245, www.amtrak.com) has just one route connecting to Detroit. The **Wolverine** is part of the **Michigan Services** route, and it takes folks from Detroit west to Ann Arbor and over to Chicago, where

plenty of other routes can be picked up. If you're looking for a train that goes from **Cleveland** to Detroit, you can get halfway there, to **Toledo,** via Amtrak's **Capitol Limited.** Then you'll have to transfer to a bus—part of Amtrak's Thruway connecting service—that can take you to Detroit.

The Amtrak station is **Detroit Station,** also known as the **Baltimore Station** (11 W. Baltimore Ave.). The station is a straight shot, 2.5 miles north from Comerica Park.

BUS

You could get from **Cleveland** to Detroit via **Greyhound** (1001 Howard St., 313/961-8011, www.greyhound.com). A nonstop trip runs about 3-4 hours; some routes stop in Toledo for a transfer, adding an hour to the trip time. The ride will cost around $20-25.

Comerica Park

It was hard to replace Tiger Stadium. We're talking about one of America's quintessential ballparks, a palace that screamed "jewel box" with its deep blue tones, its delicious overhang, and its concrete-and-steel profile. That place was made for baseball.

But give the Tigers credit. In 2000, they opened **Comerica Park** (2100 Woodward Ave., www.mlb.com/tigers) in Downtown Detroit, a stadium that has retro-classic architectural flourishes but also its own character. It doesn't look anything like Tiger Stadium, but it certainly is the Tigers' stadium.

You may notice all the tigers strewn about the park, from the large statues to the sculpted heads adorning the building's exterior. You also may notice the park's wild dimensions—the center-field fence is 420 feet from home plate, the longest distance in all of baseball. And out there in center field is one heck of a view: a fountain with an ivy backdrop, statues of some of the franchise's biggest names, and above all of that, a bit of the Detroit cityscape punctuated by the Detroit Athletic Club, a 1915 building that absolutely shines at all times. In left field is a mammoth scoreboard topped by two stalking tigers. Down at field level, you'll see a strip of dirt connecting the pitcher's mound to home plate—this is a keyhole, one of two still in existence in the majors and a pretty throwback to baseball's past.

From the keyhole to the giant scoreboard to the statues, the nods to the mid-century

game are subtle and perfect. Plus, the seating is thoughtfully positioned, and concessions are quite decent here. Add it all up, and Comerica is one of baseball's most underrated parks.

ORIENTATION

There are four entry gates at Comerica Park, one in center field, one at the corner of Adams Avenue and Brush Street, another at the corner of Brush and Montcalm Streets, and a fourth at the corner of Witherell and Montcalm Streets. Gates open 90 minutes before first pitch.

TICKETS AND SEATING

Pricing

The Tigers employ **dynamic pricing,** so prices will rise for select games, including the home opener and contests against popular teams like the **Yankees** and **Red Sox.** For example, a seat in the pavilion out in left field, for a midweek game against the Rangers, may go for around $20. That same seat for a weekend contest against the Red Sox may cost more like $35-40.

Seating Plan

Comerica Park has **two main levels** of seating, split between lower and upper. Within each section are a whole lot of subsections.

LOWER LEVEL

Right field is split in half: The seats in the lower rows are the **grandstand** (sections 101-106), and the upper rows are the **bleachers** (sections 101-106). Next is the foul pole area known as **Kaline's Corner** (sections 107-111), which has five sections crammed into it. In foul territory, going right to left, you'll find the **lower baseline box** (sections 112-114); then there's a **split area** where most of the rows are the **outfield box** (sections 115-117), and the back rows are the **terrace** (sections 116-118). Next is another **split area** where the lower rows are **lower infield box** (sections 118-119) and the upper rows are **infield box** (sections 118-119).

Comerica Park

The infield from first base around to third base is broken into four areas: from front to back, the front rows are **on-deck circle** (sections 120-135); the first batch of middle rows is **lower infield box** (sections 120-135); the second batch of middle rows is **infield box** (sections 120-135); and the back rows are the **Tiger Den** (sections 120-135), a premium area.

By third base, the lower rows of the next area are **lower infield box** (sections 136-137), and the upper rows are **infield box** (sections 136-137). Shallow left field, in foul territory, is the **outfield box** (sections 138-140), and behind that is the **terrace** (sections 136-141). Deep left field is **left field baseline box** (sections 141-143), and, finally, the left field area spanning the outfield is **pavilion** (sections 144-151).

UPPER LEVEL

The upper level has its own deck and concourse. First, there's the **right field balcony** (sections 1-3) atop the bleachers. Then, starting at the foul pole, the lower rows are **upper box right field** (sections 210-219), and the upper rows are **mezzanine** (sections 210-219).

Coming around to the infield is the **upper deck:** A lower area of seats is **upper box infield** (sections 321-337), and the upper area of seats is **upper reserved infield** (sections 321-337). **Club seats** are in the lowest part of this deck around the infield. Then in shallow left field, the lower rows are **upper box left field** (sections 338-346), and the upper rows are **upper grandstand** (sections 338-343) and **skyline** (sections 344-345), whose views of the skyline could, ironically, be better.

SUITES

Between the lower and upper levels are the **suites**. The **lower suites** are numbered from 101 to 118 along the first-base line, then 122 to 138 along the third-base line, and 148 to 153 in the left-field corner. The **upper suites** are numbered from 201 to 216 along the first-base line, then 217 to 253 from home plate all the way out to the left-field corner.

Where to Buy Tickets

In recent years, the Tigers haven't been good, but that hasn't shown in the ticket prices, which are about average compared with the league (and high for a team that hasn't been doing well). Your best bet is to wait until game day and see what's available at the **ticket windows.** Compare prices with

StubHub and other third-party websites, as they should have inexpensive **last-minute** options.

The Tigers also participate in the **MLB Ballpark app**'s upgrade option, so you could buy grandstand or skyline tickets and upgrade when you're in the park—you might get some sweet seats.

Best Seats

Comerica Park is one of only two stadiums (Truist Park in Atlanta is the other) where home plate faces south by southeast, which means the sun will shade the **first-base line** before the third-base line. To avoid the sun, consider seats in the **lower baseline box** (sections 112-114). These seats also tend to be in the sweet spot of offering lower-level views at affordable prices.

GAME COSTS

Tickets: The Tigers are either one of the priciest seats in baseball (when they're good) or just average (when they're bad). Recently, infield lower-level seats have been going for **$50-80.** Seats closer to the outfield run more like **$30** in the lower level, **$20** in the upper level. Not too bad.

Hot dog: A regular hot dog is about **$5,** which is about the average price.

Beer: You can get a cheap beer for around **$7.** The premium stuff, at 24 ounces, is going to be more like **$12-14.**

Parking: A **$15** parking spot can be had with just a little walk through Downtown or Foxtown. You'll pay **$25** or so closer to the park.

For another way to avoid the sun, consider sitting in the **bleachers** (sections 103-106). These seats are cheaper, the back rows are under an overhang, and you have easy access to the outfield concessions and walkway.

On the upper level, try sitting along the first-base line in the **upper box right field** (sections 216-219) area, offering lower-row seats with a decent chance of **shade** at an affordable price.

The **Tiger Den** (sections 120-135) is a highly coveted area with cushioned wooden chairs and solid views of the whole game. If you're going to a **weekday game** that doesn't seem too popular, think about grabbing last-second third-party tickets for this section. Or give the MLB Ballpark app a shot for an upgrade here.

KNOW BEFORE YOU GO

Soft-sided coolers are allowed in the ballpark if they're smaller than 16 by 16 by 8 inches. Guests can also bring in individual portions of food, as long as they fit into those 16- by 16- by 8-inch bags, as well as sealed bottles of unflavored **water.** Juice boxes are usually cool to bring in, provided they're for kids or folks with medical needs.

Mothers who are nursing are welcome to use the **nursing lounge** (Guest Services, section 210), which is open throughout the game.

Hey, it's the Motor City: Got a **car problem** while parked in a lot operated by Olympia Development? Let them know, because the attendants can help with jumps and keys locked in the car. (For more information, see *Driving* in the *Getting There* section.) The lot can also call **AAA** on your behalf, if you're a member.

Since Detroit is just across the river from Canada, **Canadian currency** is accepted at both the box office and the team store. The current exchange rate will be applied.

Accessibility

Look for **ramps** at sections 119 and 141, with additional ramps for higher levels available at sections 109, 125, and 140. For **accessible seating** options, call the Tigers **ticket office** (866/668-4437). For **wheelchair assistance,** ask at the entry gate or head to guest services at section 130. You may have to wait for a wheelchair because there are a limited number available. **Elevators** are located at sections 109 and 130.

For help throughout your time at Comerica, look for **guest services** (sections 130, 210, 330). **Service animals** are welcome at Comerica Park.

There are **accessible parking spaces** in the **Tiger Garage** and **D Garage,** and in **Lots 1, 2, 4,** and **5.** Be sure that you have a **reserved-area parking permit** and a state-issued disabled parking placard or license plate.

GETTING THERE

QLine

The **QLine** (www.qlinedetroit.com, $2 per four-hour pass) is one way to get to the ballpark, at least if you're near where it runs. This single-line **light rail** runs along Woodward

BE A FAN

You'll have no trouble being a fan of any team at Comerica Park. Tigers fans are pretty chill, especially for a four-sport city.

After most Tigers wins, you'll hear **"Go Get 'Em Tigers,"** a very kitschy song with a jingle-esque quality that was written by Arthur "Artie" Fields, an orchestra leader based in Detroit who also wrote songs for the MC5 and Parliament-Funkadelic. Fields wrote "Go Get 'Em Tigers" in 1968 for the eventual World Series champions. You may also hear **"Eye of the Tiger"** by Survivor.

Whenever the Tigers hit a home run, or if they win, look up at the **scoreboard:** The eyes of the **giant tigers** out there will light up, and you'll hear some growls.

Avenue from Grand Boulevard in the city's New Center section to Congress Street in Downtown. The closest ballpark stop is **Montcalm Street** (Montcalm St. and Woodward Ave.). From there, it's just a couple of blocks to the park.

Detroit People Mover

If you're staying Downtown or you're anywhere in the Downtown area before the game, you may opt to take the **Detroit People Mover** (www.thepeoplemover.com, 6:30am-midnight Mon.-Thurs., 6:30am-2am Fri., 9am-2am Sat., noon-midnight Sun., $0.75 per ride), an **elevated train** that opened in 1987 to modernize Downtown transportation by getting people around a little quicker. The closest stations to Comerica Park are **Grand Circus Park station** (Park Ave. and Woodward Ave.) and **Broadway station** (Broadway St. and John R. St.), about a five-minute walk. The entire ride around Downtown on the People Mover lasts about 15 minutes.

SMART

Detroit's **bus** network, **SMART** (www.smartbus.org, $2-2.50), covers most parts of the city. The closest lines to the ballpark are the **610,** which connects north to Wayne State University near the city's Amtrak station, then continues along the Detroit River northeast; and 461/462 (also called the **Fast Woodward**), which runs straight up Woodward Avenue, heading northwest to the city

of Pontiac. Both routes stop just a few blocks from the ballpark.

Shuttle

The best idea for getting to the park is to visit a bar that operates a shuttle before the game. Those establishments include **Nemo's Bar** (1384 Michigan Ave., 313/965-3180) and **Tommy's Detroit Bar & Grill** (624 3rd Ave., 313/965-2269), along with a handful of others. The shuttles are generally free to ride, but each bar has its own parking policy (some charge, some don't). Call ahead to confirm details.

Driving

It's not the worst idea to drive to Comerica Park. **I-75** and **I-375** intersect just northeast of the ballpark. On I-75 (also called the **Fisher Freeway**), the most used exit is **Grand River Avenue.** You may want to avoid driving in Foxtown (the neighborhood adjacent to Comerica) near game time; instead, try to stay around the West Side or in Corktown, exiting I-75 at **Rosa Parks Boulevard.**

Look for the parking lots operated by **Olympia Development,** which are typically marked by signs featuring the company's logo. These are the Tigers' **official parking lots.** The closest to the park are at **850 Witherell Street, 200 Madison Street,** and **61 East Elizabeth Street.** Parking here will cost you around $25, so I suggest scoping out the ones along **Cass Avenue** near Grand

River Avenue, which normally cost about $15. These lots are not more than a half mile from the park by foot. The closer you get, the more you'll pay; prices go up to $25. Whatever you do, don't try to park on a **QLine rail,** because you'll be levied a hefty fine.

PARK FEATURES AND SIGHTS

Comerica Park has a **carousel** (section 119, $2) in the Big Cat Food Court. Just wait in line to put your tyke onto one of the merry-go-round's hand-painted tigers for a ride. On Sundays, kids ages 14 and under ride free. (The lines will be longer, though.)

Another amusement ride in the park is the **Fly Ball Ferris wheel** (section 132, $2). The 50-foot-high, purple-and-green structure includes cute cars shaped like baseballs. It's free on Sundays for kids ages 14 and under, but prepare for lines.

Detroit Tigers Hall of Fame

Head to left center field to check out the **Detroit Tigers Hall of Fame** (center field, 100 level). Here, you'll find **statues** of all-time Tigers. There's 1960s and 1970s stalwart Willie Horton, former hit king Ty Cobb, slugger Hank Greenberg, dynamic 1920s and 1930s hitter Charlie Gehringer, 1940s pitching ace Hal Newhouser, and 3,000-hit club member Al Kaline. Each statue is between 11 and 14 feet tall, portraying these legends in action, with protrusions of jagged metal acting as a stand-in for movement. They're my favorite statues in baseball. Bonus: In between the statues, there are rails to lean against that have views of the game.

Tiger Statues

You can't miss the **15-foot-high tiger statue** at Gate A. Elsewhere around the park, you'll find eight more tiger statues at up to 12 feet tall. Be sure to also look for the **tiger heads** that decorate the ballpark's facade.

Photos (from top to bottom): Detroit Tigers mosaic; tiger statue at Comerica Park; Tigers hat.

The baseballs in the tigers' mouths light up in the evening.

Chevrolet Fountain

The team pays tribute to the city's auto industry with the **Chevrolet Fountain** (center field). Way out in center field, beyond the fence, is an oversize Chevy logo. When the Tigers do something good, water shoots out from behind it. At both ends of the fountain, you'll see vehicles propped up on platforms—don't worry, they're not going anywhere.

FOOD AND DRINKS

Start your eating adventure at **Big Cat Court** (Gate A), home to a large cross-section of vendors. For a snack with a Detroit twist, head to the **Midtown** area of Big Cat Court for the **Coney dog egg roll,** a take on the American Chinese food where the filling is made of hot dog, chili, mustard, and onions. There's also **313 Burger Co.,** which carries not just the traditional beef burger, but also French onion and meatless options. My suggestion is the Late Night Burger, which is breakfast on a burger bun—bacon, egg, cheese, and a beef patty. The stand called **Mexican** has gluttonously loaded brisket nachos.

There are numerous spots to grab a Detroit-area original: **Little Caesars pizza** (sections 115, 137, 217, 323, 334, Big Cat Court). Little Caesars was founded by Mike Ilitch, who went on to own the Tigers, as well as the NHL's Detroit Red Wings. (These days, his family trust owns the club.)

Comerica is known for a pretty awesome beer selection. For the best beer in the park, get in line at **Michigan Craft** (section 104), home to solid selections from American super-brewery **Bell's Brewery, Founders Brewing Co.,** and **Atwater Brewery** (owned by Molson Coors), which also has a stand in section 136.

You can also grab a brewski at the **Beer Hall** (Fox Sports Detroit Brushfire Grill, section 133). The **Blue Moon Brewhouse** (section 330) unsurprisingly has a bunch of Blue Moon options, as well as other Molson Coors beers on tap, along with lounge seating.

Want a harder drink? Head to **Coppercraft Distillery** (section 104), which serves up mixed drinks and cocktails that include spirits from this Holland, Michigan, spot.

There's also a cigar bar in the ballpark. **The Cigar Bar** (section 112) is reserved for guests in the premium seating areas like the Tiger Den.

EVENTS

You're permitted to try for **autographs** once the gates open (90 minutes before game time) and up to 45 minutes before first pitch by just going down to the front rows of the field level.

If this is your first time at Comerica Park, you can head to **Guest Services** (sections 130, 210, 330) to pick up a certificate that commemorates your inaugural visit.

On most Friday nights, the Tigers host a **fireworks display** after the game. On Sundays, weather permitting, kids ages 4-14 can **run the bases.** Kids and their guardians should line up under the scoreboard in left field (100 level) when the game ends.

Tours

The Tigers host **tours** (313/471-2074), which are offered on **game days** (11am and 1pm Tues. and Fri., $5, free ages 3 and under) and **non-game days** (11am, 1pm, and 3pm Tues. and Fri., $6, $4 ages 4-14, free ages 3 and under) from June through September. The tour includes visits to the home dugout; visitors' clubhouse; press box (also called the Ernie Harwell Media Center after the legendary Tigers broadcaster); and the Walk of Fame (main lower-level concourse), which marks important moments in Tigers history with "decade bats" and informational displays. The number of tour spots is restricted, so call ahead to check availability.

SHOPPING

The main team store is **The D Shop** (Witherell St. and Montcalm St., Gate A, section 119, 313/471-2673, 10am-4pm Mon.-Fri., also open when gates open on game days)—and it's a big place. It has T-shirts and player shirts, jerseys, and specialty wear like jackets, gloves, and a robust selection of hats.

DETROIT SIGHTS

THE CORNER BALLPARK

Smack in the heart of Corktown, just 1.5 miles west of Comerica Park, is **The Corner Ballpark** (Michigan Ave. and Trumbull Ave., www.detroitpal.org), the former site of Tiger Stadium. Built in 1912 as Navin Field, the steel-and-concrete structure was known for being the quintessential ballpark. With its regal second deck and faraway scoreboard, Tiger Stadium was majestic. The Tigers stopped playing there in 1999, and the stadium was torn down by 2009, though the field itself would be saved. A decade later, the Detroit Police Athletic League took over the site. Now, the Corner Ballpark exists as a place for club baseball teams to play, and it still preserves the memory of old Tiger Stadium. You can visit for pictures, and you'll often be able to catch games featuring some local squads.

MOTOWN MUSEUM

"Tears of a Clown." "Ain't Too Proud to Beg." "What's Going On." Some of the biggest songs of all time were recorded at what's known as **Hitsville U.S.A.,** now the **Motown Museum** (2648 W. Grand Blvd., 313/875-2264, www.motownmuseum.org, 10am-6pm Tues.-Sat., $15, $10 seniors and ages 5-17, free ages 4 and under). Go to check out music history, from original outfits worn by Motown stars (like the Supremes, Temptations, Four Tops, and Miracles) to record sleeves showing the robust history of this incredible music style. The most important part of a visit here is seeing the studios that were responsible for some of the most unforgettable recordings of the 1960s and 1970s. It's well worth your time. This is awesome history.

HENRY FORD MUSEUM

If you're interested in some of Detroit's history, check out the **Henry Ford Museum** (20900 Oakwood Blvd., Dearborn, 313/982-6001, www.thehenryford.org, 9:30am-5pm daily, $25, $22.50 seniors, $18.75 ages 5-11, free ages 4 and under). The museum is all about American ingenuity, with exhibits that showcase everything from lighting to musical instruments to telephones to, of course, vehicles. The museum regularly hosts events where people can build their own Model T. The most incredible item here: the very bus that Rosa Parks stepped onto in 1955, taking that front-section seat and helping to spur the civil rights movement.

DETROIT INSTITUTE OF ARTS

One of the most impressive art museums in America, the **Detroit Institute of Arts** (5200 Woodward Ave., www.dia.org, 9am-4pm Tues.-Thurs., 9am-10pm Fri., 10am-5pm Sat.-Sun., $14, $9 seniors, $8 students, $6 ages 6-17, free ages 5 and under) has a vast collection of art spanning media, centuries, and world regions. A particular focus is the **General Motors Center for African American Art,** with about 600 pieces detailing the work of African American artists in painting, photography, printing, and more. In the Rivera Court are the stunning floor-to-ceiling Detroit Industry Murals by Diego Rivera, which occupy all four walls and depict the artist's take on modern industry. Also, check out the **Josephine F. Ford Sculpture Garden,** featuring a dozen 20th-century sculptures from renowned artists like Etienne Martin, Alexander Calder, and Richard Serra. The museum also hosts concerts and performances, and has a robust collection of puppets from the early 20th century.

GREEKTOWN CASINO

Just a couple blocks south of Comerica Park, and close to Downtown, is the city's early-20th-century Greek immigrant neighborhood, known as Greektown. Over the years, the community has changed; tourism drives the area these days, led by **Greektown Casino** (660 Macomb St., 313/223-2999, www.greektowncasino.com), which draws those who like to play slots (about 3,000 on-site), poker, and table games like craps and blackjack. You must be 21 or older to be on the floor.

The casino has two levels: On street level, find slots as well as a large bar and a few stand-alone eating establishments. Upstairs are more slots, plus table games, the high-limit room, a food court, and smaller bars. The poker room is accessible from the second floor, as is a stop for the Detroit People Mover. Greektown is a fine spot for a rainy-day activity if you enjoy gambling. Otherwise, only casino lovers need apply.

FOOD

NEAR COMERICA PARK

Let's talk about Detroit's **Coney dog,** a local specialty that consists of a cheap hot dog topped with onions and chili. It purportedly takes its name from Coney Island, the famed beach and amusement park area in New York. It's thought that as Greek immigrants moved away from New York and into the Midwest, they named their variation after the hot dogs found at Coney Island (the addition of onions and chili is unique to the midwestern version). No matter its origins, it's perfect when you're craving a fatty snack, especially late at night.

Two Detroit spots argue that they started the whole Coney craze. Just a 0.5-mile walk from Comerica Park in Downtown Detroit is one: the famous **Lafayette Coney Island** (118 W. Lafayette Blvd., 313/964-8198, 8:30am-3am Mon.-Thurs., 8:30am-4am Fri.-Sat., 8:30am-2am Sun., under $20). Open late and looking like a diner that has

Photos (from top to bottom): Henry Ford Museum; Detroit Institute of Arts; Greektown Casino.

barely changed since the mid-20th century, Lafayette is an absolute must. Also on the menu are a loose hamburger (think the consistency of a sloppy joe), bean soup, Greek fare, doughnuts, and craft beer. It's cash only.

Right next to Lafayette is the second of the Coney originators, **American Coney Island** (114 W. Lafayette Blvd., 313/961-7758, www.americanconeyisland.com, 24 hours daily, under $20). American is open all day and its digs are flashier, with merchandise and tile floors. The menu is similar to what you'll get at Lafayette. I like Lafayette by a hair more, but you ought to try both to decide for yourself.

One of Downtown's better restaurants is **Lumen** (1903 Grand River Ave., 313/626-5005, www.lumendetroit.com, 3pm-11pm Tues.-Thurs., 11:30am-11:30pm Fri.-Sat., 11:30am-9pm Sun., under $50), serving chef-driven North American plates like poutine, trout, seared tuna, and mussels, all of which are a little pricier than you might expect. It's a fashionable place with floor-to-ceiling windows and a patio. When the weather gets cold, it has igloos (transparent dome tents) for larger parties that want to dine outdoors. (In winter, a few restaurants and bars in Detroit offer igloo tables.)

Downtown Detroit has seen a resurgence in American restaurants over the past several years, including **Wright & Company** (1500 Woodward Ave., 2nd floor, 313/962-7711, www.wrightdetroit.com, 4pm-midnight Tues.-Thurs., 4pm-2am Fri.-Sat., under $50). This bustling gastropub is set in a 19th-century building and offers duck, pork, shrimp, and pasta, along with plenty of alcohol at a swanky bar. For a similar feel but a menu of soul food, check out **Savannah Blue** (1431 Times Sq., 313/926-0783, www.savannahbluedetroit.com, 4pm-11pm Mon.-Thurs., 4pm-midnight Fri.-Sat., noon-8pm Sun., under $50).

For brunch, there's **Dime Store** (719 Griswold St. #180, 313/962-9106, www.eatdimestore.com, 8am-3pm daily, under $40), a friendly and airy, popular place, especially on the weekends. They have plenty of eggs Benedicts and inventive hash dishes, plus sandwiches, salads, and snacks. They have a full bar and coffee, of course.

For just a straight-up quick breakfast Downtown, pay homage to the late Detroit-born hip-hop producer J. Dilla at **Dilla's Delights** (242 John R. St., 313/346-3771, www.dillasdelights.com, 7am-5pm Wed.-Sat., under $20). This corner shop run by his uncle has both traditionally made yeast and cake doughnuts, as well as vegan varieties. They also have coffee and an on-site turntable. Maybe you'll hear *Donuts*, the last album Dilla made before he died in 2006—seriously, the man loved doughnuts.

Get yourself some Greek desserts at Downtown's **Astoria Pastry Shop** (541 Monroe St., 313/963-9603, www.astoriapastryshop.com, 8am-midnight Sun.-Thurs., 8am-1am Fri.-Sat., under $30). Established in 1971, this spot is a must for baklava, walnut rolls, and macaroons. On weekends, you may have to wait in a line, but it goes quickly.

OTHER NEIGHBORHOODS

The Coney dog isn't the only foodstuff for which Detroit is known. You need to try **Detroit pizza**—a sturdy and crusty pie cut in squares, with cheese on top that goes all the way to the crust for a salty explosion. The originator is **Buddy's Pizza** (17125 Conant St., 313/892-9001, www.buddyspizza.com, 11am-9pm Sun.-Thurs., 11am-10pm Fri.-Sat., under $30). Buddy's has been around since 1946 at this location in the Conant Gardens neighborhood, and the checkered tablecloths and wood paneling date it quite a bit. But the pizza is sublime. Get the Original Pepperoni and the Detroit Zoo (cheese, roasted tomatoes, and basil) for maximum deliciousness.

For breakfast or brunch, head to the West Side darling **Folk** (1701 Trumbull Ave., 313/290-5849, www.folkdetroit.com, 9am-3pm Thurs.-Mon., under $40). A buzzy and visually appealing bistro-style space with subway tiles and greenery, Folk has a small but powerful menu of eggy dishes, salads, and sandwiches. They offer coffee, beer, and cocktails, too. It's a great weekend morning spot, but it'll be packed.

Just beyond Gratiot Avenue and on the other side of I-75 in Eastern Market is **Cutters Bar & Grill** (2638 Orleans St., 313/393-0960, www.cuttersdetroit.com, 10am-10pm Mon.-Thurs., 10am-2am Fri., 10am-midnight Sat.). This is a divey place that looks more bar than grill, but the burgers here kick butt (including the specialty cheese- and bacon-stuffed burgers). It's a good local spot in the heart of one of Detroit's cooler neighborhoods.

In Midtown, try **La Feria** (4130 Cass Ave., 313/285-9081, www.laferiadetroit.com, 11:30am-10pm Mon.-Thurs., 11:30am-midnight Fri.-Sat., under $40) for Spanish tapas that rotate on and off the menu. The brick-walled, modest digs are casual and comfortable. It's great anytime, but best with a group.

BARS AND BREWERIES

NEAR COMERICA PARK

Beloved by many, **Harry's** (2482 Clifford St., 313/964-1575, www.harrysdetroit.com, 11am-2am daily) is a crucial stop before a Tigers game. The first floor is a bit worn, but it's perfect for a whole bunch of people to pregame with beers and shots (there's food here, too; think wings). Upstairs, a roof deck offers nice views of the skyline. It's great in warmer weather, but get here early because it'll get crowded.

Looking for something strong? **Cornerstone Barrel House** (1456 Woodward Ave., 313/338-3238, www.cornerstonedetroit.com, 4pm-11pm Mon., 11:30am-midnight Tues.-Thurs., 11:30am-2am Fri.-Sat., 11am-10pm Sun.) has a whiskey list that's deeper than most, with everything from budget selections to high-priced, celebration bourbons. You can also get a sandwich or elevated pub fare here. Try Cornerstone out as a lunch spot or stop in after a game.

On the edge of Downtown is one of Detroit's most historic bars. **Tommy's Detroit Bar & Grill** (624 3rd Ave.,

313/965-2269, www.tommysdetroit.com, 11am-2am Sun.-Fri., 4pm-2am Sat.) was once a stop on the Underground Railroad; later, it served as a notorious speakeasy during Prohibition. These days, it's a lively tavern with an average beer list, though there are some good Michigan beers available. But you're really here for the good company, the old bar feel, and the incredible history. Bonus: The bar runs **shuttles** that go to and from Comerica Park for every game.

OTHER NEIGHBORHOODS

The one bar you have to hit before or after the game is Corktown's long-standing **Nemo's Bar** (1384 Michigan Ave., 313/965-3180, http://nemosdetroit.com, 11am-2am daily), open since 1965. A fantastic sports bar with tin ceilings, plenty of Detroit sports photos and ephemera, and an always buzzing atmosphere, it's a great place to meet folks or to soak in the Motor City's sports scene. Nemo's runs **shuttles** to and from Comerica on game days, so make this your pregame stop before heading to the park.

Corktown's **Batch Brewing Company** (1400 Porter St., 313/338-8008, www.batch-brewingcompany.com, 11am-10pm Mon.-Thurs., 11am-midnight Fri.-Sat., 10am-8pm Sun.) is a quintessential 21st-century brewery with industrial flourishes like an exposed ceiling and hardwood tables, subway tiles, twinkle lights, and a menu of about 15 or so beers at any one time. This family-friendly spot has some food options and has board games for patrons to play.

Over in Eastern Market, there's **Eastern Market Brewing Company** (2515 Riopelle St., 313/502-5165, www.easternmarket.beer, 4pm-10pm Mon.-Wed., noon-midnight Fri.-Sat., noon-8pm Sun.). They use hops from the Midwest in some of their beers, a welcome change from nearly every other brewery in existence that sources hops from either the Pacific Northwest or Oceania. It's a cute place with brick walls, plants, and windows that look out onto a beautiful mural across the street.

Want a famous neighborhood bar? Try

Abick's Bar (3500 Gilbert St., 313/894-9329, 9am-2am Mon.-Sat., noon-2am Sun.), a corner spot that's steeped in Detroit history. Family-owned since it opened in 1919, Abick's has walls of artifacts, an original tin ceiling, a cozy and welcoming bar, and plenty of regulars. There's also a small cigar lounge, but you can have a fine enough time just coming in for a beer and a shot. It's cash only. Find it about halfway between Downtown and Dearborn, a few blocks south of US-12.

Some of the best breweries in the Detroit area are outside the city itself. Try **Urbanrest Brewing Company** (2615 Wolcott St., Ferndale, 586/945-5121, www.urbanrest.com, 4pm-10pm Mon.-Wed., 4pm-11pm Thurs., 4pm-midnight Fri., noon-midnight Sat., noon-9pm Sun.), about 12 miles north of Downtown Detroit. The spacious and artful taproom has a tasty menu of beers that run the gamut of styles, plus charcuterie boards. Urbanrest also hosts food trucks.

Jamex Brewing Co. (21721 Harper Ave., St. Clair Shores, 586/944-2030, www.jamexbrewing.com, 4pm-midnight Wed.-Thurs., 4pm-1am Fri., noon-1am Sat., noon-10pm Sun.), about 13 miles northeast of Downtown, is a quieter taproom with some bar seats, outdoor space, and friendly folks at work. They produce a variety of styles, from straight lagers and IPAs to milkshake beers and hard seltzers.

RECREATION

PARKS

Belle Isle

Sitting on the Detroit River, on the border between Detroit and Windsor, Ontario, is **Belle Isle** (access via E. Grand Blvd. and Jefferson Ave., www.belleisleconservancy.org, 5am-10pm daily, free for pedestrians and bicyclists), a longtime getaway for city residents, especially families. There's just one way to get on this 962-acre park by car, and that's by driving on the MacArthur Bridge.

You'll need to purchase a **Recreation Passport** (available at the park, www.michigan.gov/dnr, daily pass $9) to bring your vehicle on the island.

On the island, visit the **Belle Isle Aquarium** (3 Inselruhe Ave., 313/402-0466, 10am-4pm Fri.-Sun., free), which opened in 1904 and has a unique collection of fish, including all seven North American species of gar, ray-finned fish that look like darts. Check out the **Anna Scripps Whitcomb Conservatory** (900 Inselruhe Ave., 313/821-5428, 10am-5pm Wed.-Sun., free), home to tropical trees, cacti, and a Japanese *tohro* (lantern) made of white granite.

You can also spend some time on the **Belle Isle Beach** (5am-10pm daily mid-June-Labor Day). Take a carriage ride, enjoy a playground, and get ice cream at a park stand.

Detroit Riverwalk

Stretch those legs by traveling the 3.5-mile **Detroit Riverwalk** (Steve Yzerman Dr. at Jefferson Ave.), which starts at the site of the former Joe Louis Arena and continues along the Detroit River until it reaches Gabriel Richard Park. While on the walk, you'll pass major landmarks like the GM Renaissance Center and the E. Horace Dodge Fountain. When the walk reaches Atwater Street, you can continue into the city via the **Dequindre Cut Greenway** (Atwater St. near Orleans St.), a two-mile greenway on a former railroad. You'll pass murals and street art while walking this quiet path that threads right into the Eastern Market neighborhood and up to Forest Park.

WATER SPORTS

Detroit River Sports (14601 Riverside Blvd., 313/908-0484, www.detroitriversports.com, Thurs.-Sun. May-Oct., $20-120) offers guided tours of the Detroit River by **kayak.** Choose a morning tour to and around Belle Isle, or opt for an evening sunset or full-moon trip.

To rent a kayak and go it alone, go with **Riverside Kayak Connection** (4016 Biddle Ave., Wyandotte, 734/285-2925, www.

riversidekayak.com, May-Oct., $7-30), located about 25 minutes south of Downtown Detroit. They rent kayaks as well as canoes, stand-up paddleboards, pontoon paddle boats, and even bicycles, if you want to stay on land. Riverside also leads tours of the Detroit River.

SHOPPING

Across the street from Comerica Park is **Gameday Detroit** (41 E. Adams Ave., 313/285-8104, www.gamedaydet.com, open during Tigers home games). It sells T-shirts, jerseys, hats, bobbleheads, autographed memorabilia, and more sporting the Tigers logo—as well as merch representing Detroit's other sports teams. Everything is just a little bit overpriced, so compare with the team store across the street when shopping. They also have a location a few blocks east on Brush Street (1436 Brush St., 313/962-5151, www.gamedaydet.com, open during Tigers home games).

ACCOMMODATIONS
NEAR COMERICA PARK

There are a few hotels within walking distance of Comerica Park. Of these, one of the more moderately priced is the **Siren Hotel** (1509 Broadway St., 313/277-4736, www.thesirenhotel.com, $180-350). It's home to nine well-thought-out, tidy rooms with modern design touches and amenities (flat-screen TVs, Italian linens, terrazzo tiles in the bathrooms). More impressive are the other areas in the hotel, including two high-quality restaurants, a coffee bar, and a barbershop.

If you want to hang out in the heart of Greektown, there's the **Greektown Hotel** (1200 St. Antoine, 313/223-2999, www.greektowncasino.com, $120-300). With 400 rooms, this tower right in Downtown makes for an accessible, albeit tourist-laden, stay.

Greektown guest rooms have king or queen beds, and most rooms have sweet views of Downtown. The only downside here is the late check-in: 4pm.

OTHER NEIGHBORHOODS

If you're not staying around Downtown, there's not much else to choose from in the rest of Detroit. One solid option, with quite a bit of history, is the **Inn on Ferry Street** (84 E. Ferry St., 313/871-6000, www.innonferrystreet.com, $150-300). Located in Midtown and comprising six buildings built in the late 19th century, the inn has 40 rooms with king or queen beds. Complimentary breakfast is served daily, and the hotel operates a shuttle that takes folks anywhere within a five-mile radius.

GETTING AROUND
PUBLIC TRANSIT

Detroit has slowly increased its public transportation offerings over the decades. One of its latest moves, launched in 2017, the **QLine light rail** (www.qlinedetroit.com, $2 per four-hour pass) runs along Woodward Avenue from **Grand Boulevard** (Woodward Ave. and Grand Blvd.) in the New Center section of the city to **Congress Street** (Woodward Ave. and Congress St.) in Downtown. The closest ballpark stop is **Montcalm Street** (Montcalm St. and Woodward Ave.).

One thing Detroit has in droves: buses! **SMART** (www.smartbus.org, $2-2.50) is a network of buses covering most parts of the city. The closest lines to Comerica Park are the **610** and **461/462.**

For those touring Downtown or looking to get from one place to another pretty quickly, there's the monorail-like **Detroit People Mover** (www.thepeoplemover.com, 6:30am-midnight Mon.-Thurs., 6:30am-2am Fri., 9am-2am Sat., noon-midnight Sun., $0.75 per ride). The closest stations to Comerica Park are **Grand Circus Park**

station (Park Ave. and Woodward Ave.) and **Broadway station** (Broadway St. and John R. St.). The entire ride around Downtown on the People Mover lasts about 15 minutes.

TAXI, UBER, AND LYFT

Uber and Lyft are good options for getting around. On average, Uber may be slightly more affordable, though always be mindful of surge pricing.

For a ride to and from the airport, you could also call up **Detroit Metro Airport Taxi & Transportation Service** (734/717-7737, www.detroitairport-taxi.com). Compared with ride-sharing services, the ride to and from Downtown may cost 50 percent more, at least during low traffic periods.

CAR

They don't call it the Motor City for nothing. Detroit is a car city that's routinely ranked among the worst driving cities in America. Some of that is due to traffic, which can be bad on major highways at any time of day. Other elements that factor in include break-ins, high insurance penalties, and expensive parking. If you're renting a car, think about adding on extra insurance, just in case.

The maximum speed in Michigan is **75 mph.** In the city, the limit goes down to **55 mph** on highways, but it soon changes to **70 mph** once you start venturing farther out. Be mindful of your and other people's speeds.

To navigate Detroit, think of the city limits as a **triangle,** whose long edge is the river. The other edges are **I-696,** which creates a northern outer boundary, and **I-275,** which is the western outer boundary. Anything inside these highways is part of the Detroit metro area.

Major highways that thread through the triangle include **I-75,** which comes in from the north, running through Foxtown just past Comerica Park, then continuing along the Detroit River and Lake Erie toward Toledo. An offshoot of that is **I-375,** a spur that turns into Downtown and puts a border around that part of the city.

There's also **I-94,** running from the northeast down through Midtown and then out to the west. **I-96** starts in Detroit as part of I-75 near the Ambassador Bridge, then continues west by northwest as the **Jeffries Freeway,** heading toward Lansing.

Downtown Detroit is where two diagonal thoroughfares nearly converge: **Michigan Avenue,** or **US-12** (which runs west), and **Gratiot Avenue** (which runs northeast). Also near this area is another big-time road, **Grand River Avenue,** which shoots northwest. At the center of Downtown is **MI-1,** or **Woodward Avenue,** a major north-south artery. Primary west-east streets include **Mack Avenue** in Midtown and **Lafayette Street** in Downtown and closer to the river. **Fort Street** in the West Side is well trafficked and is an easy way to get into the city if you're not taking I-75.

TOLEDO, OHIO

The blue-collar, manufacturing city of Toledo, Ohio, has a rich baseball history. The game has been played here since the late 19th century, with an early team being named the Mud Hens after the area's American coots, a duck-like bird. Ever since, Toledo has almost always had a baseball team named the Mud Hens. In 1965, a minor league franchise came to Toledo from Richmond, Virginia, and adopted the moniker for themselves.

While the Toledo Mud Hens have been an affiliate of a few major league clubs, its longest (and current) relationship is with the Tigers (1967-1973 and 1987-present). The Mud Hens are a classic triple-A baseball team, and their ballpark, Fifth Third Field, is one of the minor league's most splendid venues.

I recommend visiting Toledo for a **day** if you need a stop in between Cleveland and Detroit. It can also be a **side trip** while you're staying in Detroit, since the two cities are just an hour apart. Toledo and Fifth Third Field will give you a relaxing dose of good old-fashioned baseball fun, and you won't need to pay too much to enjoy the game.

GETTING THERE

Train and Bus

Amtrak (www.amtrak.com) serves Toledo via the **Martin Luther King Jr. Plaza station** (415 Emerald Ave.). The **Lake Shore Limited** route offers connections from **Cleveland** to the east and **Chicago** to the west. There's no rail connection to **Detroit,** but Amtrak offers a **connecting bus service** to the Motor City from the Toledo station.

You can take **Greyhound** (www.greyhound.com) from **Cleveland** to Toledo for about $15 and then go onward to **Detroit,** also for about $15. Pick up the bus from the Martin Luther King Jr. Plaza station.

Car

From **Cleveland,** you can either drive the straight shot west on I-90 to Toledo, a nearly **two-hour, 115-mile** drive; or you can take the scenic route of OH-2, which will **add about 45 minutes** but includes more time along Lake Erie.

When driving from Toledo to **Detroit,** the easiest way is straight up I-75 North, an **hour's drive** of about **60 miles.** Another option is to head up US-24 North to US-12 East. You'll **add a half hour** or more taking this route.

When looking to **park** for a Mud Hens game, find a spot on the street in Downtown Toledo. Parking is free after 5pm on weekdays and during weekends. If you can't find street parking, lots nearby shouldn't be too expensive—never pay more than $5.

FIFTH THIRD FIELD

You might be confused if you do an Internet search for the name of the Mud Hens' ballpark. There was a park in nearby Dayton once called Fifth Third Field, but it's now Day Air Park. You're looking for Toledo's **Fifth Third Field** (406 Washington St.), home of the Toledo Mud Hens since 2002. The park is in the heart of Toledo's Warehouse District as part of an entertainment center called **Hensville,** and it offers impressive views of the city's Downtown and, just beyond center

field, the Maumee River. Undoubtedly, it's one of the best ballparks in all of minor league baseball.

Tickets and Seating

The park has two general seating levels, including the **100 level** (sections 101-119) that wraps from the left-field foul pole around to the right-field pole. A **picnic terrace** (sections 120-122) is in the outfield on this level, and the **Kiwanis Club Kids Play Area** in center field is made for ages 3-12 and features playground equipment.

The **200 level** (sections 201-219) starts shy of the left-field foul pole and wraps around to deep right field. Above the 200 level is the **club level** (sections 1-32), which wraps around the foul area. At home plate up here is the **Lexus Birdcage Club** (home plate, club level, $36, $26 children), which offers club-level ticket holders an all-you-can-eat buffet. The price reflects both the buffet and a club seat—it's a good deal for those who want creature comforts.

Then there's **The Roost** (right field, sections 220-221), an air-conditioned, indoor party area with outdoor seats that overlook the right-field corner (with some actually in fair territory above right field). This could easily be one of the best party areas in major league baseball, and yet it's in a minor league park. It's rented out by groups during games, so to sit here you might need to know the right people.

Tickets get scooped up for most games, so you may need to peruse third-party websites like **SeatGeek** for seats. Still, try to pay no more than $25 for a standard seat anywhere. First-level seats regularly go for no more than $20. Luckily, there's no bad seat here.

Food

There's one main **concourse** in the foul area above the 100 level. Top concessions include **Mudzarella's** (section 104), home to chicken parmesan sandwiches and pizza; **Gilhooley's Grill** (section 108), with hot items like brisket mac and cheese and pot roast poutine; and **Glass City Cheesesteaks** (section 113), a cart that does a whole bunch of sandwiches with a Philly cheesesteak twist. Keeping with the Pennsylvania theme, there's plenty of **Yuengling beer** (sections 103, 107, 112, 117) on tap here. Get a boozy, icy treat or a spiked coffee at **Frozhen Cocktails** (section 118). There are party and patio areas at either end of the concourse.

Shopping

To stock up on Mud Hens gear, head to the **Swamp Shop** (406 Washington St., 419/725-4367, 11am-5pm Mon.-Fri., 10am-2pm Sat., also open on game days). For a minor league shop, there's an impressive selection of hats, T-shirts, and accessories. Plus, with its modern-industrial look of brick walls and hardwood floors, it's one of the better-looking team shops in baseball, period.

SIGHTS

Toledo is known as Ohio's "Glass City" since it has a history of glass manufacturing. Fittingly, the **Toledo Museum of Art** (2445 Monroe St., 419/255-8000, www. toledomuseum.org, 10am-4pm Tues.-Wed., 10am-9pm Thurs.-Fri., 10am-5pm Sat., noon-5pm Sun., free) has a beautiful, award-winning glass pavilion, plus a studio for glassmaking. Also here is an art collection with 25,000 works by artists including Cézanne, Van Gogh, Monet, Picasso, and Rembrandt.

Take the kids to the **Toledo Zoo** (2 Hippo Way, 419/385-4040, www.toledozoo.org, 10am-4pm daily, $22, $19 seniors and ages 2-11, free under age 2). You'll find tigers, grizzly bears, polar bears, koalas, crocodiles, elephants, and a red panda, along with other animals. There's also an aquarium on-site, home to sharks and green sea turtles. The zoo hosts regular events including a big kids' party in the summer, adult wine tastings, and Christmas in July.

FOOD

Very down to earth, **Manhattan's Pub 'n Cheer** (1516 Adams St., 419/243-6675, www. manhattanstoledo.com, 11am-11pm Mon., 11am-midnight Tues.-Thurs., 11am-2:30am Fri.-Sat., 10am-2pm Sun., under $40) satisfies every hunger with burgers, steak, pasta dishes, pizzas, and small sandwiches. But you'll want to get the Toledo-style chili mac: spaghetti and chili topped with cheese and served with garlic toast (it's similar to Cincinnati chili).

No stop in Toledo is complete without paying a visit to **Tony Packo's Café** (1902 Front St., 419/691-6054, www.tonypacko. com, 10:30am-10pm Mon.-Thurs.,

Fifth Third Field

10:30am-11pm Fri.-Sat., 11:30am-9pm Sun., under $20). This haunt for Hungarian grub, open since the 1930s, makes one of the city's most beloved chili dogs, along with chicken paprikash (boneless chicken over dumplings), stuffed cabbage, and a good ol' roast beef sandwich. While here, pay special attention to all the autographed hot dog buns lining the wall (a tradition started by Burt Reynolds). Cleveland Indians pitcher Bob Feller signed one!

BARS AND BREWERIES

I don't recommend sticking around the entertainment district known as Hensville. Sure, the party pops off here before and after Mud Hens games, but prices are expensive and complaints about service and food quality are common. Instead, head to **Wesley's Bar & Grill** (1201 Adams St., 419/255-3333, www.wesleysbar.com, 3pm-2am Mon.-Sat., 3pm-midnight Sun.), a funky little place that carries good beer and is never serious. There are plenty of televisions and a little bit of outdoor seating, too.

Ye Olde Durty Bird (2 S. St. Clair St., 419/243-2473, 11am-11pm Tues.-Thurs., 11am-midnight Fri.-Sat., 11am-10pm Sun.-Mon.) is a cool pub in an 1867 building with stone walls, burgers, and a stage for occasional live music.

For some craft beer, try **Patron Saints Brewery** (4730 W. Bancroft St. #8, 419/720-2337, www.patronsaintbrewery.com, 5pm-10pm Wed.-Thurs., 4pm-11pm Fri.-Sat.), where you'll find a relaxed vibe and a great spot for kids and pets. There's no food, but you can bring some in.

RECREATION

About 15 minutes west of Downtown Toledo is **Wildwood Preserve MetroPark** (5100 Central Ave., 419/270-7500, 7am-8pm daily), a 493-acre park with a network of hiking and biking trails, plus a playground and the Manor House, a Georgian Revival colonial-style home that was constructed for the founders of a spark plug company that helped Toledo thrive in the early 20th century. The house hosts cultural events and can be rented out for private celebrations.

ACCOMMODATIONS

There are just a few places to stay in Downtown Toledo. Think about heading to the city's oldest neighborhood, the Vistula Historic District, for an overnight at the **Casey-Pomeroy House** (802 N. Huron St., 419/243-1440, www.caseypomeroy.com, $125-200), a bed-and-breakfast in a restored 1870 building. Quaint rooms with light Victorian touches await here.

GETTING AROUND

The main **public transit** service in Toledo is **TARTA** (Toledo Area Regional Transit Authority, www.tarta.com, $1.50), a **bus network** that stops running in the early to mid-evening hours.

Driving is a good idea in this city. Major highways include **I-75,** which comes in from the south over the Maumee River and then goes around the inner city's western and northern borders before continuing north toward Detroit; and **I-280,** which comes off from I-90 to the south and runs up the eastern end of the city, then across the river and into I-75.

In the city, major Downtown roads include the west-east **Monroe Street** and **OH-25,** a north-south road known in parts of the city as the **Greenbelt Parkway, Michigan Street,** and **Anthony Wayne Trail.** There's also **Cherry Street,** or **OH-120,** a diagonal thoroughfare that connects I-75 to Downtown and the Vistula Historic District before crossing the Maumee River into East Toledo.

TORONTO
BLUE JAYS

With nearly three million people living here, Toronto is the fourth-largest city in North America. And this metropolis isn't just cheese curds and Labatt Blue (they have those things, of course); Toronto is a multicultural wonderland, a hub of young energy, and a hungry city just waiting to be explored. With fashionable and hot neighborhoods like Queen West, the Danforth, and Parkdale, some old-school spirit (Old Toronto, Distillery District), and even some green space and Lake Ontario beaches, there's so much to experience here.

Moreover, multiple professional sports thrive here. Yes, ice hockey is still king, but baseball has been part of the city's DNA for decades, long before the 1977 Major League Baseball expansion that birthed the Blue Jays. Go back to the late 19th

century, when the game was played at local parks, and the Toronto Baseball Club handily defeated opponents. During this era, the Toronto Maple Leafs baseball club was established; by the 1930s, the team was affiliated with major league clubs as a minor league feeder. Babe Ruth's first professional home run was said to have been hit in Toronto, naturally splashing into Lake Ontario.

Businesspeople in Toronto lobbied hard to get a major league team in the city, coming close in 1976 with the near move of the San Francisco Giants. Finally, in 1977, Major League Baseball expanded into Seattle and Toronto. The Blue Jays played their first 10 seasons in the open-air Exhibition Stadium, which had been reconfigured from a football stadium. It wasn't ideal, but the Jays stuck it out, even winning an AL East title in 1985.

In 1989, the Jays got their current home, the enormous and then-state-of-the-art SkyDome (renamed Rogers Centre in 2005). The Jays have made more than a few memories there, including back-to-back world championships (1992 and 1993) and countless blasts from the likes of José Bautista, Edwin Encarnación, and Josh Donaldson during a successful period in the 2010s. Today, baseball continues to thrive in Toronto, especially when the Jays are contending. During that run in the 2010s, the Jays had the highest home attendance in the American League.

Note: Most prices listed in this chapter are given in **Canadian dollars (C$).** When visiting, it's helpful to know the **exchange rate** of the U.S. dollar against the Canadian dollar (also known as the **loonie**). Most businesses in Toronto accept U.S. dollars, but the exchange rate may not be in your favor. Consider exchanging a modest amount of money (say, 50 percent of your food and entertainment budget) ahead of time, which ensures a fair exchange rate. If you're planning to primarily pay with plastic, check with your credit card company to see if you'll be charged a **foreign transaction fee** (typically 3 percent) on purchases.

PLANNING YOUR TIME

Considering the city's size, you can spend a **week** in Toronto and not scratch the surface of its neighborhoods. If you're pressed for time or want to budget a shorter trip, a **weekend** tour of the city will suffice. Opt to spend a day in **Old Toronto** and the **Entertainment District,** the areas closest to Rogers Centre, and another day exploring one of the closer neighborhoods, preferably **Kensington Market**—if it's your first time in the city—or the hip and restaurant-packed **Queen West.** For longer stays, be sure to fit in a tour of the Danforth (Greektown), Parkdale, and the Ossington Avenue area, plus a quick stop at The Distillery District. Other ideas include hitting Crothers Woods and the Don River area, and Centre Island for a beach day.

How long you stay will factor into where you stay. If you're on the weekend itinerary, opt for an accommodation in **Downtown** Toronto (**Old Toronto** or **Harbourfront,** the latter the busy tourist area with hotels along Lake Ontario). Taking public transportation works for this kind of trip, too. If you plan on spending four days or more in the city, a **boutique hotel** somewhere in **Queen West** or **Parkdale** would be just fine. You could rent a car for a longer adventure, but public transportation and ride-sharing work well enough that you probably won't need it.

Since the Jays play in a **retractable-roof stadium,** you can visit any time during the season, but considering Toronto can be **chilly** in the **spring** and **fall, midsummer** is really the best option. Temperatures tend to top out in the 80s in **July** and **August** with lows in the 60s. There may be some **rainy** days in July and August, but not a whole lot more than you'd encounter at other times of the year.

Previous: Rogers Centre and the CN Tower

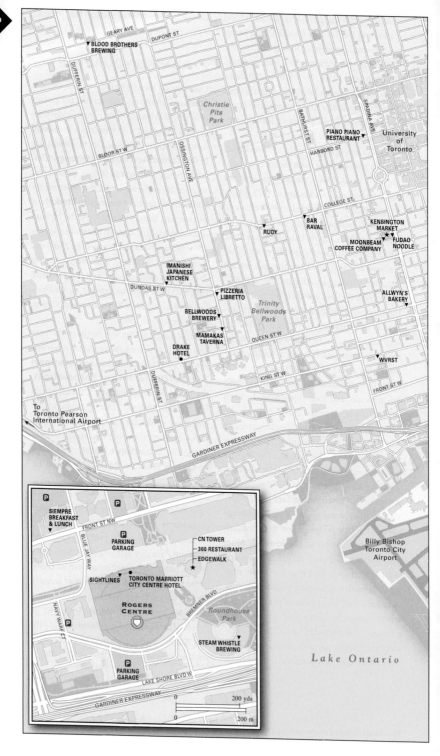

BLOOD BROTHERS BREWING

GEARY AVE

DUPONT ST

DUFFERIN ST

Christie
Pits
Park

BLOOR ST W

OSSINGTON AVE

BATHURST ST

SPADINA AVE

PIANO PIANO
RESTAURANT

HARBORD ST

University
of
Toronto

COLLEGE ST

RUDY

BAR
RAVAL

KENSINGTON
MARKET

MOONBEAM
COFFEE COMPANY

FUDAO
NOODLE

IMANISHI
JAPANESE
KITCHEN

DUNDAS ST W

PIZZERIA
LIBRETTO

Trinity
Bellwoods
Park

ALLWYN'S
BAKERY

BELLWOODS
BREWERY

MAMAKAS
TAVERNA

QUEEN ST W

DRAKE
HOTEL

WVRST

KING ST W

DUFFERIN ST

FRONT ST W

To
Toronto Pearson
International Airport

GARDINER EXPRESSWAY

Billy Bishop
Toronto City
Airport

P

SIEMPRE
BREAKFAST
& LUNCH

FRONT ST NW

P

BLUE JAY WAY

P

PARKING
GARAGE

CN TOWER

360 RESTAURANT

EDGEWALK

SIGHTLINES

TORONTO MARRIOTT
CITY CENTRE HOTEL

NAVY WARF CT

ROGERS
CENTRE

BREMNER BLVD

Roundhouse
Park

STEAM WHISTLE
BREWING

Lake Ontario

P

PARKING
GARAGE

LAKE SHORE BLVD W

GARDINER EXPRESSWAY

0   200 yds

0   200 m

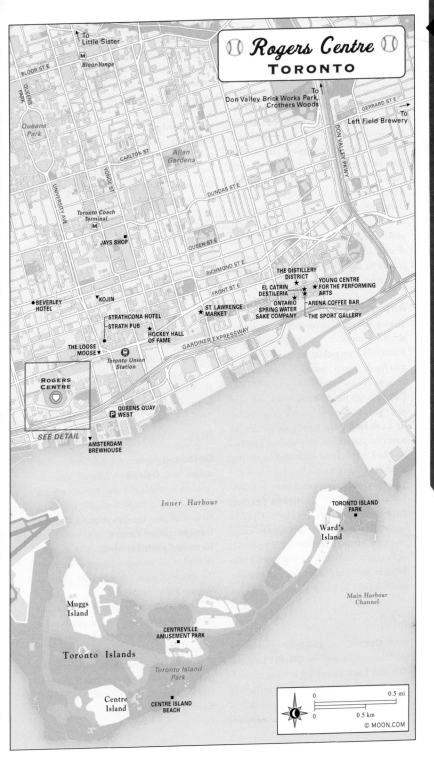

Rogers Centre
TORONTO

To Little Sister

BLOOR ST E

Bloor-Yonge

Don Valley Brick Works Park, Crothers Woods

To

GERRARD ST E

To Left Field Brewery

QUEENS PARK

Queens Park

DON VALLEY PKWY

CARLTON ST

Allan Gardens

YONGE ST

DUNDAS ST E

Toronto Coach Terminal

UNIVERSITY AVE

JAYS SHOP

QUEEN ST E

RICHMOND ST E

THE DISTILLERY DISTRICT

YOUNG CENTRE FOR THE PERFORMING ARTS

FRONT ST E

EL CATRIN DESTILERIA

BEVERLEY HOTEL

KOJIN

ONTARIO SPRING WATER SAKE COMPANY

ARENA COFFEE BAR

ST. LAWRENCE MARKET

THE SPORT GALLERY

STRATHCONA HOTEL

STRATH PUB

HOCKEY HALL OF FAME

THE LOOSE MOOSE

GARDINER EXPRESSWAY

Toronto Union Station

ROGERS CENTRE

QUEENS QUAY WEST

SEE DETAIL

AMSTERDAM BREWHOUSE

Inner Harbour

TORONTO ISLAND PARK

Ward's Island

Muggs Island

Main Harbour Channel

CENTREVILLE AMUSEMENT PARK

Toronto Islands

Toronto Island Park

Centre Island

CENTRE ISLAND BEACH

0   0.5 mi

0   0.5 km

© MOON.COM

GETTING THERE

AIR

The major airport in Toronto is the busiest in Canada: **Toronto Pearson International Airport** (YYZ, 6301 Silver Dart Dr., Mississauga, www.torontopearson.com), located 15 miles northwest of the city. Airlines serving Pearson include **Air Canada** (888/247-2262, www.aircanada.com), **American Airlines** (800/433-7300, www.aa.com), **Delta** (800/221-1212, www.delta.com), and **United** (800/864-8331, www.united.com), plus international carriers. There are two terminals (Terminal 1 and Terminal 3), and you can fly to and from most major American cities from here.

Airport Transportation

The top car-rental businesses have counters at both terminals in the airport, making for a relatively easy pickup experience. Getting into the city from Pearson can be a struggle because of traffic; you'll likely take ON-401 East to Allen Road South, which will send you right into the city, but that drive can last up to an **hour.** The same goes for driving south on ON-427 to the Gardiner Expressway East, which is the more scenic route that straddles Lake Ontario.

Airport passengers can connect to Downtown Toronto with the **Union Pearson Express** (www.upexpress.com, C$12.35 one-way), also called the **UP Express.** Trains from the **airport station** (at Terminal 1, across from the Link Train that shuttles folks between terminals) leave every 15 minutes, and rides last 25 minutes.

CAR

From **Detroit,** it's a **230-mile** drive east by northeast to Toronto via **ON-401 East** and **ON-403 East.** How long it takes depends on a number of factors, particularly the time it takes to cross the border into Canada. Typically, getting into Canada is relatively

painless, compared to coming back into the United States (which can sometimes last an hour or more). Getting from Detroit to Toronto could take anywhere from **4-4.5 hours.** The return trip might take closer to five hours, if not slightly more. On this drive, you'll cross the border at either the **Ambassador Bridge** or the **Detroit-Windsor Tunnel;** remember to bring passports for all travelers. After crossing, you'll go through the Ontario cities of Windsor, London, Hamilton, and Mississauga (the sixth-largest city in Canada).

TRAIN

In Old Toronto, **Union Station** (65 Front St. W., 888/842-7245, www.torontounion.ca) has been in service since 1927 and is home to **Amtrak** (www.amtrak.com). The **Maple Leaf** line provides service between Toronto and **New York City,** stopping at cities in Upstate New York (Albany, Syracuse, Rochester, Buffalo) along the way. There's no train service from Detroit to Toronto. The station is a little over a half mile from Rogers Centre.

BUS

Greyhound (www.greyhound.com) offers service from **Detroit** to Toronto. Multiple rides are available per day, starting around US$40. The trip length is usually 4-5 hours. Buses pull into the **Greyhound Canada Transportation Centre,** also called the **Toronto Coach Terminal** (610 Bay St., 800/661-8747, www.greyhound.com). From the terminal, it's a 1.3-mile walk south to Rogers Centre.

If you're coming from the east, you can take **Megabus** (https://us.megabus.com) to Toronto. Cities serviced include Baltimore, Buffalo, New York, Philadelphia, and Washington DC. From **New York,** expect a half-day journey at a decent cost (starting at US$50). Megabus also pulls into the Toronto Coach Terminal.

CROSSING THE BORDER

From **Detroit,** there are two ways into Canada, which also happen to be the two busiest border crossings between the United States and Canada. For newbies, I suggest taking the **Ambassador Bridge (I-75),** which has more lanes (19 passenger-car lanes total) and connects to the major freeways.

The **Detroit-Windsor Tunnel (Randolph St. and Jefferson Ave.)** has 10 passenger-car lanes total and, for those who don't mind a quick drive through Windsor to reach the highway, can be faster since it's not as heavily trafficked.

Don't cross the border around **rush hours** (7:30am-9am, 4:30pm-6pm). During the summer, especially on long holiday weekends, you'll wait a little longer than usual (up to an hour isn't out of the question), but most of the time, it'll take no more than 15 minutes to get across. Everyone in the vehicle must have a valid passport. In order to help your time at the crossing go more quickly, be courteous and speak clearly to officials.

If taking a **train** from the United States into Canada, you'll be asked to supply proof of identification while making your reservation. For adults, a **passport** is the most commonly accepted form of ID. For children age 15 and younger, a certified copy of a **birth certificate** is accepted, though a passport is also welcome. When taking the trip, be sure to have that ID ready. Customs and Immigrations officers will check your information ahead of your trip to clear you across the border. You'll receive a **declaration form** ahead of time. Inspectors may come through the train at the border crossing, so be prepared to show ID and answer questions.

For **bus** travel, bring a valid **passport** (children younger than 15 can use a **birth certificate**) and the address of where you're staying in Canada. At the border you'll disembark the bus and be interviewed by immigration officials. **Baggage inspection** is possible, and you'll be asked to declare items.

Customs

The Canadian government requires all travelers to **declare** all **plant, food, animal,** and **food** items they're bringing in. That includes, but is not limited to, fresh fruits and vegetables, baked goods and candies, fish and seafood, dairy products, infant formula, meat and poultry, tea and coffee, condiments, and even seashells and sand. Permits are required for meat and dairy products, nuts, plants, fruits, and live animals; request yours at least one month in advance through the **Centre of Administration for Permissions** (www.inspection.gc.ca).

Most weapons, including some hunting and fishing knives, are prohibited; you'll need documentation that allows you to bring a firearm into the country. If you're bringing **camping gear,** make sure it's clean and that soil isn't lingering in your car.

Rogers Centre

For their first 13 seasons, the Toronto Blue Jays played in the cold, uncomfortable confines of Exhibition Stadium, home to some poor seat locations (thanks to Canadian football's oversize field) and an outfield grandstand that seemed to extend to infinity. But in 1989, the Jays moved two miles east, closer to Old Toronto and into the magnificent SkyDome. It was the first stadium in the world with a fully retractable motorized roof, meaning games could be played both under the sky and indoors. It was also home to a hotel with rooms peering out onto the field. When it opened, there was much fanfare, with an event featuring Canadian celebrities like Andrea Martin of *SCTV* and Alan Thicke of *Growing Pains.*

In 2005, the ballpark became the **Rogers Centre** (1 Blue Jays Way, www.mlb.com/bluejays). (The Blue Jays are owned by Rogers Communications, a telecommunications company that also operates television networks.) While a few things changed to help modernize the facility, the hotel is still there, as is the cold concrete shell that fits the park right in with other venues built before the retro-classic craze of the 1990s.

Rogers Centre

Rogers does end up feeling a little too much like the cookie-cutter multipurpose parks of the 1970s and 1980s, including Veterans Stadium in Philadelphia, Riverfront Stadium in Cincinnati, and Three Rivers Stadium in Pittsburgh. But the outfield offers so much more, including the hotel (the Toronto Marriott City Centre, with 70 of its 348 rooms offering field views), a huge Daktronics video board (33 feet high by 110 feet wide), and cool banners for the Blue Jays' division and world championships. Plus, when the roof is open, the view of the outfield and the CN Tower from behind the infield foul area is pretty neat. If Rogers is full (when the Jays are good), the stadium can really rock. All told, Rogers needs serious renovations to be considered a top major league park (and those renovations could happen, per team reports), but it does

its job well enough and can look great in the right light.

ORIENTATION

Rogers Centre's Downtown location—a quick two blocks north from the waterfront's hotels, restaurants, and parks; another block south of Old Toronto; and accessible to public transportation—is enviable. If you're staying anywhere near or in Downtown Toronto, you can get to Rogers pretty easily.

There are an astounding 15 gates at Rogers Centre, which open two hours before first pitch on Saturday and Sunday, and 90 minutes early on weekdays. The gates are positioned every 150 feet or so around nearly the entire circumference of the venue (but there are none in center field).

TICKETS AND SEATING

Pricing

Ticket prices can fluctuate depending on the Jays' performance that season and who the team is playing that day. Generally, tickets to see the Jays play the **Red Sox** and **Yankees** will cost a bit more, and yes, those fans will travel to Rogers Centre for weekends. A game against the Rangers on a Wednesday may cost you C$25 for a middle-of-the-road seat, while a game against the Red Sox on a Saturday may cost you C$40-50 for that same seat.

Seating Plan

It's important to know that sections at Rogers Centre are often **split** down the middle into two aisles, with the left side of the section designated with an **L** and the right side designated with an **R.** On the left side of the field, R seats are closer to home plate, while on the right side of the field, L seats are closer to home plate.

There are **three levels** of general seating at Rogers Centre. The **100 level** wraps around the entirety of the field (save for the hitters' eye, a blank wall in center field that allows the batter to see the ball coming). Sections 101L and 101R are to the right of center field, and sections continue clockwise, around foul territory, until getting to section 142 in left center. The same goes for the **200 level,** which starts at section 204R to the right of the video board area, then runs clockwise around the park until reaching section 244L in left center.

The **300 level** and **400 level** are **luxury**

YOUR BEST DAY AT ROGERS CENTRE

Tonight, you have tickets to Rogers Centre for a Blue Jays game. Here's how to spend your day, evening, and night in Toronto.

10 HOURS BEFORE FIRST PITCH
Start the day with the most important meal: breakfast. Head to **St. Lawrence Market,** specifically **Carousel Bakery,** for a peameal bacon sandwich. Pro tip: Order two. Take a little time to walk around the market.

8 HOURS BEFORE FIRST PITCH
Head east, through David Crombie Park on the Esplanade, to **The Distillery District.** You might need to recharge, so visit **Arena Coffee Bar** and be sure to peruse the awesome sports photography while you're there at **The SPORT Gallery.**

7 HOURS BEFORE FIRST PITCH
Ride-share or cab it to the **Hockey Hall of Fame** to get in the right mood to watch Toronto sports. Sure, it's hockey, but think of it this way: You'll have something more to talk to Jays fans about. Pose for a photo with the Stanley Cup.

4 HOURS BEFORE FIRST PITCH
Hungry? Enjoy a late lunch at **WVRST,** where you'll have your pick of everything from kangaroo to pheasant. Pair your meats with a pretzel (with raclette and gouda cheese sauce, naturally), then roll yourself out the door.

Hockey Hall of Fame

3 HOURS BEFORE FIRST PITCH
It's time for a beer. Walk around the corner to **The Loose Moose,** order a pint, and befriend a Jays fan or three.

2 HOURS BEFORE FIRST PITCH
If it's a weekend, head to the park and be among the first through the gates. Post up at the **WestJet Flight Deck** with your new friends.

DURING THE GAME
If you don't mind leaving the Flight Deck, be sure to order some poutine at **Four One Six.**

AFTER THE GAME
Call a car to take you west to **Bellwoods Brewery** to enjoy one of the more iconic brewery experiences north of the border. As an alternative, head east to **Left Field Brewery** for a nightcap while wearing a rally cap.

---

suite levels that stop in the outfield; out there are the **WestJet Flight Deck** (300 level) and **Sightlines Restaurant** (400 level). The Flight Deck is a choice, standing-room-only hangout that simply requires a ticket for the game. It's typically populated with fans in their twenties and thirties who want to party with diehards. Sightlines is a buffet-style experience with seats overlooking the field; a ticket for this section is required upon entry, and it's about C$30-45 plus a buffet charge of about C$65.

The **500 level** starts at section 504L, right

of the video board and hotel, and wraps around the park until reaching section 544R, left of the video board and hotel.

For families not wanting to be around those consuming alcohol, there are **alcohol-free family seating** sections at **237L, 238R, 517R,** and **516L.**

The Jays have several **peanut- and nut-reduced games** each season. This means that if you're allergic to nuts, the Jays reserve a bunch of seats for people with nut allergies during those select games. Ask the Blue Jays in advance about this seating option.

Where to Buy Tickets

Generally, you can find pretty inexpensive tickets on a third-party site like **StubHub** or **SeatGeek,** with prices 30-40 percent cheaper in some instances, especially if you wait closer to game day. (Note that all prices on U.S.-based sites like StubHub and Seat-Geek are in U.S. dollars.) The Jays are also on the **MLB Ballpark app,** with which you can purchase tickets on mobile devices.

Best Seats

If you want to hang with some fun folks, your best bet to is to buy a 500 level seat, then get to the **WestJet Flight Deck** (300 level, out-field) after the gates open. You'll essentially be paying C$30 for a standing spot with an awesome view of the whole field, plus a par-ty-like atmosphere.

Or you could just stay in the 500 level. If so, I suggest sitting between **sections 522** and **526,** which are around home plate. These seats may be up high, but they pro-vide a perfect view of the game. Plus, when the roof is open, you get a great view of the skyline.

The seats with the best bang for your buck are between **sections 234** and **236.** Sit in the back of these sections for **shade** and a more affordable ticket—you'll still get a great view. Try the 200 level seats in left field—**sections 241-243**—which are less expensive but not too far away from the action.

If the roof is open, know that much of the outfield will be in the **shade** (as the roof rests above the outfield). Generally, the **last few rows** of the foul-side **100 and 200 levels** will also be shaded during day games, as they're covered by overhangs. That said, I once attended a game at Rogers during Memorial Day weekend and really felt the sun on me while sitting along the first-base line. If you're attending a day game between Memorial Day and Labor Day, bring **sunscreen.**

KNOW BEFORE YOU GO

Rogers Centre is a bit more lax than other ballparks on what you can bring inside. For

GAME COSTS

Tickets: Depending on the opponent, nosebleed seats aren't too bad. For less popular games, those tickets start at **C$18,** while for top teams, you might pay closer to **C$25.** Better seats in the lower bowl will cost at least **C$50** apiece, and for better opponents nearly **C$65** per seat.

Hot dog: Expect to pay about **C$6** for a hot dog, making it somewhere in the middle of the pack among major league ballparks.

Beer: Not too bad after conversion. Macro beers are about **C$5** a pop, while the better stuff is more like **C$10.** Want a tall can? That'll run you **C$12.**

Parking: At the stadium (underground), you'll pay about **C$35.** Around the ballpark, you can find a lot where you'll pay closer to **C$20.**

instance, **outside food and drinks** are allowed as long as the item is wrapped or left in a container; in addition, the bag the items are in can't go over the size limit of 16 by 16 by 8 inches. (No glass containers are allowed, however.) You can technically carry up to 30 grams of dried **cannabis** into Rogers Centre, but anything more and you will be subject to prosecution. There's absolutely **no smoking** at Rogers Centre—that goes for cannabis and tobacco alike.

There's a large **Sikh community** in Toronto, and a baptized Khalsa Sikh wear-ing all five articles of faith is permitted to discreetly carry his or her symbolic **kirpan** (a small dagger).

Tailgating is not permitted at Rogers Centre; you're best off having a drink before heading to the game and taking public transportation.

Rogers Centre's **retractable roof** means you'll never have to worry about shivering or getting wet. The roof will be closed if the

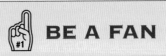

BE A FAN

You can guarantee that, no matter your colors, Jays fans will be hospitable (well, maybe not as much if you're a Red Sox or Yankees fan). Seriously, though, these fans are great.

At the seventh-inning stretch, before "Take Me Out to the Ball Game," Rogers Centre blares a song called **"OK Blue Jays."** It was written by Jack Lenz and Tony Kosinec in 1983 and has been part of every Jays home game since then. Because of that, the full version (which you probably won't hear at the park) references two folks that date back to that era: ace pitcher Dave Stieb and then-Oakland Athletics manager Billy Martin. The song's lyrics demand "Bring on the Brewers," which made sense in 1983 because, back then, the Milwaukee nine was in the American League. But hey, it's a really catchy tune.

temperature is forecast to be below 50°F, if the risk of rain is better than 75 percent, or if the wind is anywhere near or above 40 mph. The roof can close at any time during a game, but it will only open before the seventh inning.

Rogers Centre accepts **U.S. currency,** so there's no need to exchange money for the game. However, the prices are listed only in Canadian dollars, so you'll need to know the **current exchange rate.** The Blue Jays tend to keep the exchange rate relatively fair.

Accessibility

For **accessible seating** options call the Jays **ticket office** (855/682-6736). The best entrance for those needing assistance is **Gate 7** (Bremner Bouelvard, right side of home plate). **Wheelchairs** are available by calling the **fan services team** (416/341-1000). Your wheelchair can be stored at guest services during the game.

Sensory bags that include noise-cancelling headphones, fidget tools, verbal cue cards, and **weighted lap pads** are available at all fan services locations. You can find **fan services** at sections 120, 135, 212, 236, 508, and 532. Look for **elevators** (sections 108, 119, 124, 135) in four locations across the stadium.

Quiet spaces are located at the Gate 3 elevator lobby and Gate 13 elevator lobby. Medically necessary **oxygen tanks** are permitted inside the stadium. **Service animals**

are welcome at Rogers Centre.

Call 416/341-1540 to secure an **accessible parking spot** in advance of your game. Have your disabled parking permit number ready when you call. Any remaining available spots are sold on a first-come, first-served basis on the day of the game.

GETTING THERE

Public Transit

Public transportation is the best way to get to Rogers Centre. If you hop on a **subway** car courtesy of the **TTC** (Toronto Transit Commission, www.ttc.ca, C$3.25 one-way), you'll exit at **Union Station** (65 Front St. W.) and walk to the ballpark via **SkyWalk,** a 0.3-mile aboveground walkway that connects Union Station to the CN Tower and Rogers Centre.

Driving

If you're driving to the ballpark, there's a **parking garage underneath the stadium** (305 Brenner Blvd., up to C$35). The lot is divided into four color-coded zones (red, green, blue, and yellow). It may be closed to single-game ticket holders depending on the game (say, if the Jays have a full house that night). You can find cheaper places to park that aren't far away, like garages **Queens Quay West** (208 Queens Quay W., about C$15), and **315 Front Street** (315 Front St., about C$20).

PARK FEATURES AND SIGHTS

Toronto Marriott City Centre Hotel

By far the quirkiest thing about Rogers Centre, and the feature that has been talked about the most since the park's 1989 opening, is the hotel. These days, it's called the **Toronto Marriott City Centre Hotel** (1 Blue Jays Way, 516/341-7100, www.marriott.com, C$200-300 city and field views when Blue Jays on road; C$400-800 city view, C$500-1,000 when Blue Jays at home during regular season). In the hotel's **field-view rooms,** large windows look out at the playing field. Make no mistake, watching a live Jays game happen from the comfort of your hotel room is a bucket-list item for devoted baseball fans. (Just a note: The park and hotel have a zero-tolerance policy for inappropriate behavior in the field-view rooms. Violators will be ejected from the park and their room.)

Blue Jays Level of Excellence

Look for the **Blue Jays Level of Excellence** (on the facing of the ledge underneath the 500 level), which honors the greatest players and personalities in franchise history, including Hall of Famers Roberto Alomar, Roy Halladay, and executive Pat Gillick, plus beloved stars like Carlos Delgado, Tony Fernandez, and Joe Carter, who is one of two players to hit a walk-off home run to win the World Series (Game 6, 1993). The space lists the names and uniform numbers of each member. You may have to squint to catch them all.

FOOD AND DRINKS

Sightlines (1 Blue Jays Way, 416/341-2600, opens one hour before first pitch, C$25-35 plus C$63 buffet ticket, C$37 buffet ticket for ages 2-14) is one of the better restaurant experiences at a major league ballpark, though it's slightly too expensive for what amounts to a buffet dinner (drinks are extra). Still, the options are good, including sirloin, barbecue chicken, ballpark food like smoked meat sliders and hot dogs, and a Tex-Mex area with build-your-own fajitas. For Sunday games, Sightlines does brunch with pastries, eggs, sausage, and bacon. If you're looking to avoid the crowds, want a good seat, and don't mind paying a little extra, Sightlines is a nice option.

That Rogers Centre allows outside food and drink is a clue that the in-house options may not be the most robust. There are a few wild options, including **Log Cabin Topped Tots** (All-Star Chicken Counter, section 134). These are tater tots drenched with maple beans, pulled pork, bacon, and cheese. Also at the All-Star Chicken Counter, look for **funnel cake poutine,** which is the carnival treat topped with vanilla ice cream, chocolate sauce, caramel drizzle, and marshmallows.

If you want the most typically Toronto-style junk food, head to **Four One Six** (500 level), which has poutine and hot dogs with toppings like smoked meat, cheese curds, chorizo and habanero cheese gravy, and chili-lime sour cream. There are plenty of fulfilling combinations here.

In 2019, the Jays instituted **Dugout Deals** (sections 137, 239, 536), which are essentially a variety of items you can purchase for less than C$5. Those items include a hot dog, an ice-cream cone, nachos with cheese, and a 12-ounce Bud or Bud Light.

Want better beer? Well, you'll need to look hard. Rogers Centre has yet to make available much in the way of local craft beer. Look for offerings from **Hockley Valley Brewing** (Beverage Wall, section 118; King Club, section 121; Tallcan/Draught, section 234). Otherwise, you can get a **Mill Street** (available around the ballpark), which is owned by the same folks who make Budweiser.

EVENTS

Gates open two hours before first pitch on Saturday and Sunday, and 90 minutes on weekdays. To get player **autographs** before the game, head to the end of the 100 level aisles (on the far side of each dugout) and hang there until up to 45 minutes before first pitch. If you bring a bat to be autographed, check it with **Fan Services** (sections 120,

135, 212, 236, 508, 532) before heading to your seat.

On most Sundays each season, the Jays mark **Jr. Jays Sundays,** during which kids can participate in games set up on the concourses. After each of these games, kids have the opportunity to **run the bases** (assemble at sections 105, 205, 505 beginning in the eighth inning). Through September, during these Sunday games the Jays host a kid-friendly **block party** with inflatables, games, and other activities.

About once every month, the ballpark hosts **Loonie Dogs Night,** which means Schneiders hot dogs (the official wiener of Ontario) are C$1. If the exchange rate is good, that's a heck of a deal.

Last but not least, July 1 is **Canada Day,** which marks the anniversary of the Constitution Act of 1867, the document that united New Brunswick and Nova Scotia with the Province of Canada (parts of modern-day Ontario and Quebec). Typically, the Jays will celebrate Canada Day with a series of themed events during the home series closest to the holiday.

Tours

The Blue Jays host a **tour** (416/341-2770, 11am, 1pm, and 3pm daily, C$15) of Rogers Centre. Purchase tickets online or on the day of the tour at the Jays Shop (Gate 5). You'll probably want to call ahead to ensure the tour will run on the day you're planning to visit. The one-hour-minimum tour often includes stops like a clubhouse, the media center, and a luxury suite. Sometimes the tour will visit the field, too.

SHOPPING

The main store is called **Jays Shop Stadium Edition** (Gate 5, 416/341-2904, 10am-5pm daily, open only to ticket holders during games). Look for the wall of caps, plus plenty of jerseys, including sweet throwbacks.

Photos (from top to bottom): beer from Left Field Brewery; Rogers Centre; Ace, the Toronto Blue Jays' mascot.

(Thankfully, the Jays now wear the same style of jersey they wore back in the 1980s and early 1990s.) More unusual offerings include a miniature batting cage made from toy blocks and a PopSocket to attach to the back of your smartphone.

TORONTO SIGHTS

CN TOWER

At 1,815 feet tall, the slender and commanding **CN Tower** (301 Front St. W., 416/868-6937, www.cntower.ca, 9am-10:30pm daily) is possibly Canada's most iconic landmark. Built in 1976—and the world's tallest free-standing structure at its completion—the tower offers a restaurant experience, incredible views of Toronto, and an adventure for tourists seeking a thrill.

360 Restaurant (301 Front St. W., 416/362-5411, www.cntower.ca, under C$120) is all about the view. The food includes a **prix-fixe meal** (three courses for C$79) or an à la carte option, which costs a touch more. The revolving restaurant, which completes a circuit every 70 minutes, boasts Canadian dishes like fresh fish, steak from Prince Edward Island, and lobster caught in the Atlantic Ocean. For those who want to tell their friends they dined more than 1,150 feet up in the air, with incredible views of the city, then this is certainly the place to be.

If you're just hoping to catch the view, visit the tower's two **observation decks** (C$38-53, C$34-49 seniors, C$28-43 ages 4-12). One, at 1,122 feet high, has a glass floor. You won't know how to deal with it until you get there. The other, at 1,136 feet up, is called LookOut Level, with floor-to-ceiling glass windows. This may not be a fun experience for those afraid of heights.

Finally, for those wanting a real thrill, there's **EdgeWalk** (416/601-3833, 9am-8pm daily, C$195). This 1.5-hour experience includes a 30-minute walk outside around the edge of CN Tower, 1,168 feet above the ground. From the safety of a very strong harness system, you'll lean backward from a platform and feel the entirety of Toronto beneath you.

KENSINGTON MARKET

Kensington Market (Spadina Ave. and Dundas St., www.kensington-market.ca) is the hip part of Toronto. As such, it's regularly packed with hipsters, tourists, cool folks, and just everyday Torontonians living their lives. The market itself is the neighborhood. Dating back to the 1800s and coming of age as a wave of immigrants entered the city in the 1950s and 1960s, it's full of small shops, bakeries, and other popular hangouts. Don't drive to Kensington Market on Sundays, as the streets close down for pedestrians and performers.

While in the neighborhood, check out **Fudao Noodle** (358 Spadina Ave., 647/346-8588, www.fudaonoodlehouse.com, 11am-11pm daily, under C$20), which specializes in noodle dishes with robust broths, and Chinese hot-pot dishes sure to make you happy. Also visit **Moonbeam Coffee Company** (30 St. Andrew St., 866/595-0327, www.moonbeamcoffee.com, under C$10), the prototypical independent coffee shop with small tables, quiet vibes, and strong coffee.

ST. LAWRENCE MARKET

The packed **St. Lawrence Market** (93 Front St. E., 416/392-7219, www.stlawrencemarket.com, 8am-6pm Tues.-Thurs., 8am-7pm Fri., 5am-5pm Sat.) started back in 1803 and continues to stand as a hub for municipal commerce. The two-level market has vendors selling everything from jams and cheese to meaty breakfast sandwiches. And for that meaty sandwich, visit **Carousel Bakery** (Upper Level, 416/363-4247). This famous Downtown spot is home to the peameal bacon sandwich, featuring pork loin slices rolled in cornmeal. It's a simple sandwich—meat and mustard in a small kaiser roll—but it's the perfect morning pick-me-up. Check out **Olympic Cheese Mart** (Upper Level, 416/363-7602), the market's first cheese shop, and a home for Canadian and European varieties. You're in good hands here.

HOCKEY HALL OF FAME

Sure, it's not baseball, but this sport is important to Canadians. Visit the **Hockey Hall of Fame** (30 Yonge St., 416/360-7765, www.hhof.com, 10am-5pm Mon.-Fri., 9:30am-6pm Sat., 10:30am-5pm Sun. Sept.-June, 9:30am-6pm Mon.-Sat., 10am-6pm Sun. July-Aug., C$20, C$16 seniors, C$14 ages 4-13, free ages 3 and under) to really soak in the history and pageantry of the greatest game on ice. Right in the middle of Downtown Toronto, the museum is filled with treasured finds, from game-worn jerseys to trophies to walls with logo-stamped hockey pucks. Look for the "locker room" exhibit, the display showing the evolution of goaltender masks, and the Grand Hall, where you can read up on all the inductees to the Hall of Fame and pose with the Stanley Cup (one of three in existence).

THE DISTILLERY DISTRICT

If it's your first time in Toronto, you should pay a visit to **The Distillery District** (Parliament St. and Mill St., www.thedistillerydistrict.com). The area was founded in 1832 as the Gooderham and Worts Distillery, which made more than two million gallons of whiskey per year at one point. In the 1990s, the distillery ceased operations, and it was soon designated a National Historic Site. Investors eventually redeveloped the area into a gentrified pedestrian dining and entertainment area. Home to the **Young Centre for the Performing Arts** (50 Tank House Ln., 416/866-8666, www1.youngcentre.ca, 1pm-8pm Tues.-Sat.), plus a bit of retail, the District is a happening place and should be on your list.

Of note here is **El Catrin Destileria** (18 Tank House Ln., 416/203-2121, www.elcatrin.ca, noon-11pm Mon.-Wed., noon-midnight Thurs., 11:30am-1am Fri., 10:30am-1am Sat., 10:30am-11pm Sun., under C$70), a Mexican tapas restaurant.

It's a boisterous hangout with a firepit and colorful tables.

There is still a "distillery" here, in the form of the **Ontario Spring Water Sake Company** (51 Gristmill Ln., 416/365-7253, www.ontariosake.com, noon-6pm Sun.-Thurs., noon-7pm Fri., 11am-7pm Sat.), which offers tastings and a tour of the brewery operations. The sake, made from fresh spring water, is quite delicious.

Have a cup of Joe (Thornton) at **Arena Coffee Bar** (15 Tank House Ln., 416/861-8514, www.thesportgallery.ca, 9am-7pm Mon.-Wed., 9am-8pm Thurs., 9am-9pm Fri., 10am-9pm Sat., 11am-7pm Sun., under C$10), a sports-themed café that's inside **The SPORT Gallery** (www.thesportgallery.ca), a gallery with beautiful sports photography and art, plus the photo archives of *SPORT* magazine, the publication that was created in the mid-20th century to celebrate the games we play. Check out their line of apparel, including some sweet Blue Jays gear plus awesome minor league jerseys for the Vancouver Mounties, Montreal Royals, and Toronto Maple Leafs.

FOOD

Toronto isn't kidding when it comes to food. Because of the city's diverse makeup, you're bound to encounter some of the finest Chinese, Vietnamese, Japanese, Greek, Cambodian, and Italian grub you've ever tasted. And that's just the tip of the iceberg. Below are my suggestions in a few styles of cuisine, but I also suggest chatting up a bartender or Jays fan—whoever looks friendly. Torontonians are eager to share their favorite places, and they typically won't steer you wrong.

NEAR ROGERS CENTRE

Need some bacon and eggs before first pitch? Visit **Siempre Breakfast & Lunch** (348 Front St. W., 647/346-8222, www.siemprerestaurant.com, 7am-3:30pm Mon.-Fri., 7am-4pm Sat.-Sun., under C$20). Simple breakfasts are elevated beautifully inside an artsy, high-ceiling space, with specials like Canadian eggs Benedict with peameal bacon, a ham and cheese sandwich, and a Montreal-style bagel with lox. For lunch, there are burgers, salads, sandwiches, and more. Plenty of coffee, too.

For a couple pints and plates of the local fare, pick **The Loose Moose** (146 Front St. W., 416/977-8840, www.theloosemoose.ca, 11am-1am Mon.-Wed., 11am-2am Thurs.-Sat., 11am-midnight Sun., under C$25). Essentially, if you seek decent elevated pub grub like fries, nachos, and burgers, plus an inviting scene with plenty of Blue Jays fans hanging around before and after games, this is a good choice.

Want to get your hands on some sausage? The place to be is **WVRST** (609 King St. W., 416/703-7775, www.wvrst.com, 11:30am-11pm Mon.-Wed., 11:30am-midnight Thurs., 11:30am-1am Fri.-Sat., 11:30am-10pm Sun., under C$25), which offers an array of meats, from game (hen, elk, crocodile) to the traditional stuff (Italian, brats, chorizo) to vegan and vegetarian links. Also here: a killer beer list. You'll get a little dizzy figuring out what you want.

OTHER NEIGHBORHOODS

If you're in the Trinity-Bellwoods and Queen West areas, consider **Imanishi Japanese Kitchen** (1330 Dundas St. W., 416/706-4225, www.imanishi.ca, 5:30pm-11pm Sun.-Thurs., 5:30pm-midnight Fri.-Sat., under C$50), a snapshot of inventive, ultramodern home-style Japanese cooking. We're not talking sushi; inside a space that resembles a cozy, warm living room, you'll get comfort food. If it's offered, get the corn *kakiage,* a type of tempura. You can also get udon, perfectly crispy fried chicken, and grilled squid. It's a really fun place.

Nearby is one of five locations of **Pizzeria Libretto** (221 Ossington Ave., 416/532-8000, www.pizzerialibretto.com, 11:30am-11pm daily, under C$30), which specializes in Neapolitan-style pies. For lunch, you can order a three-course meal starting with salad, then a pizza or the linguine pomodoro (a tomato-based sauce), and finally a dessert. (How about a scoop of gelato?) Well-known and to this day a popular haunt, it's a good hang.

For legendary pizza, hit up **Piano Piano Restaurant** (88 Harbord St., 416/929-7788, www.pianopianotherestaurant.com, noon-3pm and 5pm-10pm Sun.-Wed., noon-3pm and 5pm-11pm Thurs., 11:30am-3pm and 5pm-11pm Fri.-Sat., under C$50) in Harbord Village. Inside this pretty pink building are wood-fired pizza and high-quality appetizers, as well as pasta and meat and fish dishes like veal parmesan and seabass. It's a date-night place, a quick stop, and a family-friendly experience, all in one.

Near Old Toronto is one of David Chang's newer spots, **Kojin** (190 University Ave., 3rd Fl., 647/253-6227, http://kojin.momofuku.com, 11:30am-2pm and 4pm-10pm Mon.-Thurs., 11:30am-2pm and 4pm-11pm Fri., 5pm-11pm Sat., 5pm-10pm Sun., under C$100) is a bit pricey, but hey, you pay for the name (and the food is damn good, too). Look for steak from local cattle and, if you have a friend or two, get a whole chicken in a pot. A bit bistro-style but extremely modern, with sexy woods and leather benches, it's a hot place.

Want a quick-and-dirty bucket list of Toronto eating? There are famous beef patties, jerk chicken, and oxtail at **Allwyn's Bakery** (404 Queen St. W., 11am-10pm Mon.-Fri., noon-11pm Sat., 11:30am-9pm Sun., under C$30) in the Alexandra Park section of Downtown. For burgers and poutine, go to **Rudy** (619 College St., 647/748-7839, www.rudyresto.com, noon-9pm Sun.-Wed., noon-10pm Thurs. and Sat., 11:30am-10pm Fri., under C$20) in Trinity-Bellwoods. The burger selection is limited (get the Rude Dude, a double cheeseburger with their house sauce), but the offerings are perfect. Milkshakes are available, too. Also in Trinity-Bellwoods, go Greek at **Mamakas Taverna** (80 Ossington Ave., 416/519-5996, www.mamakas.ca, 5:30pm-10:30pm daily, under C$50), which serves up lamb, grilled fish with Santorini capers, village salads, and absolutely no gyros. It's a cute, modern spot with white subway tile, an L-shaped bar, and leather seating, too. Find Indonesian snacks and local craft beer at the cozy **Little Sister** (2031 Yonge St., 416/488-2031, www.little-sisterto.com, 4:45pm-9:30pm Sun.-Mon., 4:45pm-10pm Tues.-Wed., 4:45pm-11pm Thurs.-Sat., under C$40) in Midtown's Mount Pleasant West section. Order a few skewers and *babi kecap* (braised pork with a sweet soy sauce), add a brew, and you're good to go.

BARS AND BREWERIES

NEAR ROGERS CENTRE

You can walk from Rogers Centre to **Steam Whistle Brewing** (255 Bremner Blvd., 416/362-2337, www.steamwhistle.ca, 11am-6pm daily), a brewery that only does a pilsner. That's it, as the brewery adheres to the Bavarian Purity Act of 1516. One of Toronto's early craft breweries, it's located in a brick roundhouse. You can come for a tour, pose for pictures by the old train car outside, and gulp down a pint of the crisp, golden stuff.

For a pregame pint or three, head to **Amsterdam BrewHouse** (245 Queens Quay W., 416/504-1020, www.amster-dambeer.com, 11am-midnight Sun.-Wed., 11am-11pm Thurs., 11am-2am Fri.-Sat.). Though there's a food menu, you're well off just ordering the beer here, which is primarily their own. They also sell beer from other local breweries. When the weather is cooperating, the move here is to sit out on the upstairs patio that overlooks Lake Ontario.

OTHER NEIGHBORHOODS

Just gorgeous, with its twinkle lights overhead, its indoor-outdoor drinking area, and its convivial atmosphere, **Bellwoods Brewery** (124 Ossington Ave., www.bellwoodsbrewery.com, 2pm-midnight Mon.-Wed., 2pm-1am Thurs.-Fri., noon-1am Sat., noon-midnight Sun.) in Beaconsfield is the Toronto brewery you have to hit. They make good beers across the spectrum, always leaping on hot styles, and they sell bottles to take home. (Note: breweries in Ontario can have bottle shops along with taprooms; the former are just a way to take home the beer.)

Check out the small, rustic, and outstanding **Blood Brothers Brewing** (165 Geary Ave., 647/628-6062, www.bloodbrothersbrewing.com, noon-11pm Sun.-Thurs., noon-midnight Fri.-Sat.) in Davenport. Newbies should try Blood Light, a sessionable pale ale with some juicy, fruity hops.

Baseball fans need to visit **Left Field Brewery** (36 Wagstaff Dr., 647/346-5001, www.leftfieldbrewery.ca, 11am-9pm daily), near the Danforth. The brewery features a range of selections named for baseball terms (Southpaw, Eephus, and my favorite, A Very Pleasant Good) and is home to a very good boy named Wrigley, who will meet you when you walk in.

The most gorgeous bar you've ever seen is at **Bar Raval** (505 College St., 647/344-8001, www.thisisbarraval.com, 11am-2am Mon.-Fri., 10am-2am Sat.-Sun) in Little Italy. Just stand back and gaze at the wood that frames the drink selection, sprouting tentacles around the interior and crossing the copper-tile ceiling. Pull up to the bar and enjoy classic cocktails with a tapa or two. Romantic and light during the day, a bit more exciting at night, it's the class act of Toronto.

RECREATION

PARKS AND BEACHES
Toronto Islands
If you're in Toronto during the summer, you might want to spend a little time relaxing along Lake Ontario. A good place to do it is at the **Toronto Islands,** which

are accessible via a ferry. You can catch it at the **Jack Layton Ferry Terminal** (Bay St. and Queens Quay, typically 8am-10pm daily, under C$10, under C$6 seniors and students, under C$4 ages 13 and under, free ages 0-1).

The popular place to visit is **Centre Island** (www.centreisland.ca), home to the **Centreville Amusement Park** (416/203-0405, 10:30am-6pm daily, under C$40 per person). There are several dozen rides, including a Ferris wheel, bumper cars, a log flume, and a small roller coaster. There are also ponies, miniature golf, and a train ride. It's a perfect place for families with smaller children. **Centre Island Beach** is available to island-hoppers, too. It has changing rooms and lockers, bike rentals, and picnic areas. It gets crowded here, and the beach is more for sunbathing and kid-play than swimming. If you want to swim, head west on the shore to get better waves.

Crothers Woods

About a mile north of Lake Ontario, not too far east of Downtown, is a stretch of parkland running along the Don River. It's highlighted by **Crothers Woods** (27 Redway Rd.), which has six miles of trails plus great skyline views. It's also home to plenty of species of native flora, including eastern hemlock and sugar maple trees. Walk Redway Road to a trailhead that leads to a narrow dirt trail. Stay on it, to the left, to find the gravel Sun Valley Trail. You can also walk the Lower Don River Trail, which straddles the water, or do the easy Cottonwood Flats trail, coming in at just under a half mile.

Don Valley Brick Works Park

Also part of the Don River Valley is **Don Valley Brick Works Park** (550 Bayview Ave.), or Evergreen Brick Works. Home for nearly 100 years to a brick manufacturer with a quarry, the park today is a

Photos (from top to bottom): sandwich from Carousel Bakery in St. Lawrence Market; Steam Whistle Brewing; Amsterdam BrewHouse.

Centre Island Beach

restoration site with ponds, trails, and a cultural center. You can visit the **Young Welcome Centre & Centre for Green Cities** (550 Bayview Ave., 416/596-7670, www.evergreen.ca, 9am-5pm Mon.-Fri., 8am-5pm Sat., 10am-5pm Sun.), which can provide additional information about the park and brickworks. It also has a market and café. As for the park itself, you can walk the mile-long Don Valley Brick Works Trail, which includes boardwalks over marshes, vistas looking out to the city skyline, and old, disused railroad crossings.

SHOPPING

A secondary location of the **Jays Shop** (Eaton Centre, 220 Yonge St. #125A, 416/792-5254, 10am-9:30pm Mon.-Fri., 9:30am-9:30pm Sat., 10am-7pm Sun.) is quite similar to the one at Rogers Centre. Though the selection is smaller, the shop won't be as crowded. Plenty of hooded sweatshirts, a wall of hats, copious jerseys, and children's and women's clothes are available.

ACCOMMODATIONS

NEAR ROGERS CENTRE

Of course, the closest hotel to the ballpark is Rogers Centre's **Toronto Marriott City Centre Hotel** (1 Blue Jays Way, 516/341-7100, www.marriott.com, C$200-300 city and field view when Blue Jays on road; C$400-800 city view, C$500-1,000 when Blue Jays at home during regular season). The hotel has standard queen and king rooms, plus two-level suites that can sleep up to four (with a rollaway bed). The best option is a field-view room, where the large windows look out at the playing field. Watching a live Jays game happen from the comfort of your hotel room is a bucket-list item for dedicated baseball fans.

Want the luxury experience close to Rogers Centre and CN Tower without spending an arm and a leg? Head to the **Strathcona Hotel** (60 York St., 416/363-3321, www.thestrathconahotel.com, C$150-300). This smart hotel has clean, minimalist rooms of different sizes; one option is a "micro" space of 80 square feet with a twin bed—perfect for the on-the-go solo traveler. Part of the hotel is the **Strath Pub** (416/840-4010, www.thestrathpub.ca, 11am-11:30pm Mon.-Fri.,

4pm-11:30pm Sat., 5pm-10:30pm Sun.), a spacious and sports-friendly tavern with televisions, grub, and plenty of beer.

A little more than a half mile north of the ballpark is the **Beverley Hotel** (335 Queen St. W., 416/493-2786, www.thebeverleyhotel.ca, C$150-250), smack in the middle of Downtown Toronto. The Beverley has both large rooms with queen beds and studios for solo visitors. Its on-site bar has Mexican street food and a lounge area that's open late. A rooftop patio is available when it's warm out.

OTHER NEIGHBORHOODS

The longtime **Drake Hotel** (1150 Queen St. W., 416/531-5042, www.thedrakehotel.ca, C$150-300) in Queen West is a higher-priced but vibrant property. With a lounge and café, regular music performances and DJ sets, and an art gallery featuring local creators, it's got its finger on the pulse of the city. The hotel's rooftop patio can mean sound reaches even the rooms farthest from the rooftop, so consider bringing ear plugs. The Drake has studios, medium-size rooms, and larger suites. I recommend the cute crash-pad rooms, which are structured like tiny houses and are perfect for one or two people. Guests at the hotel can also get complimentary yoga sessions and spinning classes nearby.

GETTING AROUND

PUBLIC TRANSIT

Toronto is a decent city for public transportation, though the network is a bit outdated for the always-growing metropolis. You can see many of the key neighborhoods by taking the **subway** (www.ttc.ca, C$3.25 one-way), operated by TTC. The main station is **Union Station** (65 Front St. W.), which anchors the **1 (Yellow Line)** that connects to most essential Downtown areas. The **2 (Green Line)** goes west to east; a key station to access is

Bloor-Yonge (2 Bloor St. E.). **Streetcars** ride along the main streets Downtown, filling in the gaps the subways can't reach.

TAXI, UBER, AND LYFT

There's a large ride-sharing presence in Toronto. Say you're going from Pearson International Airport to Rogers Centre—Lyft and Uber will cost about the same (C$35-40 per ride). The city also has plenty of taxis, which have a base of C$3.25 and charge C$0.25 for every 0.143 kilometer (0.08 mile). A cab ride from the airport to the ballpark costs about C$48.

CAR

Toronto isn't a city with many wide highways; instead, there are plenty of wide streets. Far north of the city is the west-east **ON-401,** which connects the large Toronto districts of North York and Scarborough; it's also the main highway passing Pearson International Airport. Going north-south is **ON-427,** which connects with **Queen Elizabeth Way** closer to Lake Ontario. That major road becomes the **Gardiner Expressway,** the major west-east thoroughfare within Downtown Toronto. It's a heavily trafficked road. East of Downtown, the Gardiner Expressway turns into the north-moving **Don Valley Parkway,** which travels along the Don River as it heads to Lake Simcoe.

Within Downtown, get to know **Queen Street,** which runs west to east through the city's most popular neighborhoods (Parkdale, Queen West, Downtown). The major north-south street is **University Road,** which heads into the University of Toronto. As it passes Queen's Park, it becomes **Avenue Road,** running through the popular Yorkville neighborhood, home to the Bloor-Yonge subway station. **Bloor Street** runs west to east up here and has plenty of restaurants and shops, especially at the Mink Mile, the city's popular upscale district. Back near Lake Ontario, **Front Street** threads west to east past Old Toronto and near Rogers Centre.

Chicago and the Midwest

This trip checks up on some of baseball's oldest franchises. Chicago's Wrigley Field is the star, surrounded by the bustling bars of Wrigleyville, but don't forget about the South Siders, the White Sox. Jog north to see the beer-centric Milwaukee Brewers before heading down the Mississippi River valley to surprisingly hip St. Louis. You'll end your trip in Cincinnati, but not before stopping to visit the Louisville Slugger Museum in Kentucky.

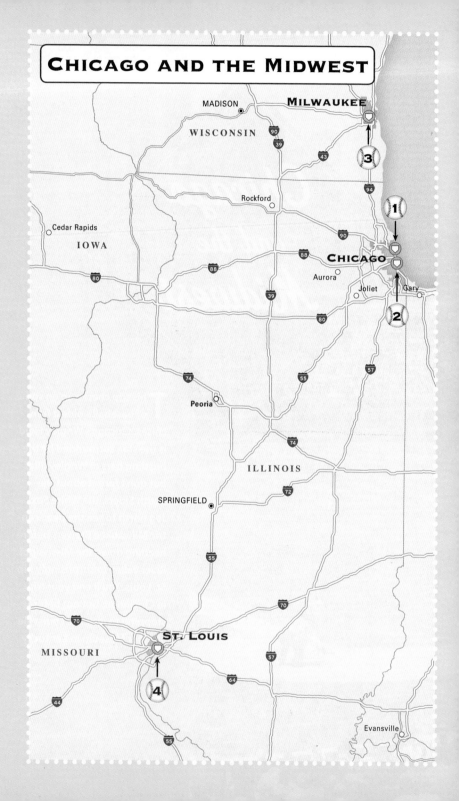

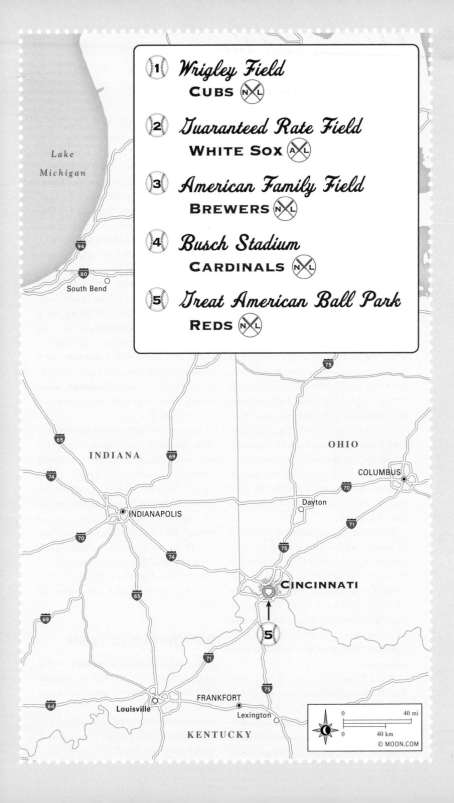

1. **Wrigley Field**
   CUBS Ⓝ Ⓛ

2. **Guaranteed Rate Field**
   WHITE SOX Ⓐ Ⓛ

3. **American Family Field**
   BREWERS Ⓝ Ⓛ

4. **Busch Stadium**
   CARDINALS Ⓝ Ⓛ

5. **Great American Ball Park**
   REDS Ⓝ Ⓛ

Lake Michigan

South Bend

INDIANA

OHIO

COLUMBUS

Dayton

INDIANAPOLIS

CINCINNATI

Louisville

FRANKFORT

Lexington

KENTUCKY

0   40 mi
0   40 km

© MOON.COM

Chicago and the Midwest Road Trip

If there's a thread that connects baseball cities like Chicago, Milwaukee, St. Louis, and Cincinnati, it might just be the radio. While the world connects over streaming audio and video, radio is the classic broadcasting format that links these locations to one another and to their rich baseball histories.

Ever wonder why the Cubs, a franchise that saw 17 U.S. presidents come and go between championships, have such a huge fan base? The answer is radio. Early on, the Cubs bet big on radio, buying up airtime on signals across the Midwest and ensuring people deep in Indiana, Iowa, Nebraska, and South Dakota could hear the game from Wrigley. The Cubs' rival, the St. Louis Cardinals, did the same, growing a fandom that stretched to parts of Oklahoma, Arkansas, and Kentucky, and even southern and central Illinois. Not to be outdone, the Cincinnati Reds expanded their radio reach into both Cubs' and Cards' territory. The White Sox battled hard against the Cubs for popularity in Chicago and carved out a decent market, but the National League club had already flexed its muscle so much that the Pale Hose became, and continue to be, an extremely local phenomenon.

Milwaukee has long had its own pull. Just 90 minutes north of Chicago, the city once was part of Cubs country, but the arrival of the Braves in 1953 began to push out the Windy City's influence. Though the Braves left a little more than a decade later, the city never turned back to Chicago. Baseball came back via a move by the Seattle Pilots in 1970, and since then, all of Wisconsin has been Brewerville.

Radio doesn't hold as much sway these days, but the original territories are forever strong in the Midwest. The Cubs, Brewers, Cardinals, and Reds all jockey for position in the National League Central division, while the White Sox just keep fighting for relevance, not merely in the American League but also in their own city.

This 830-mile trip starts in Chicago and ends in Cincinnati. The middle section stops in Milwaukee and St. Louis, and you'll have the opportunity for a side trip to the Louisville Slugger Museum. You'll start in **Chicago,** where you'll witness the crosstown clash of the **Cubs** and **White Sox.** Spend a few days in the Windy City before heading north to **Milwaukee,** home to beer, brats, and the **Brewers.** Hang with some of the game's finest fans at a tailgate before making the drive southwest to **St. Louis.** You'll encounter a devoted **Cardinals** fan base and a beautiful Downtown area. Finish your trip with a drive east, first to **Louisville** and a bucket-list destination, the Louisville Slugger Museum; then head to **Cincinnati,** where a small market begets incredibly passionate fans of the **Reds.**

Turn on the radio when driving this route. On a pitch-black night in May 2011, I was passing through Iowa on my way from Milwaukee. At some point, I began fidgeting with the radio. Much to my surprise, the voice of Marty Brennaman boomed into my car, and for the next three hours, I cruised through the Hawkeye State while listening to a 19-inning Reds versus Phillies game being played in Philadelphia. Even way out in Iowa, I could hear the Reds' radio broadcast. Out here in the open fields, radio still matters.

PLANNING YOUR TIME

I recommend budgeting **nine days** for this trip. It's easiest to start in Chicago because of its status as a primary transportation hub. With two airports facilitating every major airline between them and a train station that offers travelers more than a dozen Amtrak routes daily, the Windy City is the most

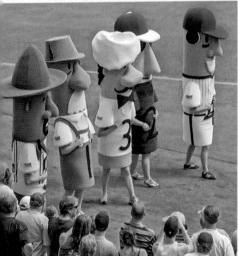

Photos (top): Chicago's *Cloud Gate*; (middle left) Milwaukee Brewers Famous Racing Sausages; (middle right) deep-dish pizza; (bottom) Louisville Slugger Museum.

accessible city for starting a trip like this. By starting in Chicago, you'll drive for a total of 12-13 hours, which is quite doable over nine days.

You can easily start in Milwaukee (continuing to Chicago, then St. Louis and Cincinnati) and cut down the driving time by about 90 minutes, but you'll have fewer options in terms of flights and trains. Another option is to begin in Cincinnati and head west to St. Louis, then north to Chicago and finally to Milwaukee. Both of these alternate routes can be tackled in **nine days,** with two full days in Chicago and St. Louis.

The Cubs and White Sox almost never play at home at the same time, so booking a Chicago trip means considering a multiday stay of Thursday to Saturday, Saturday to Monday, or Sunday to Tuesday. Budget at least **three days** in Chicago (you can easily spend a week in the Windy City), then spread the rest of your trip across the other cities. Spend **a day and a half** each in St. Louis, Milwaukee, and Cincinnati, and you'll have some time left over to visit the Louisville Slugger Museum.

If you can't get to five games in nine days, think about splitting the trip into **two parts.** Plan on **4-5 days** in Chicago and Milwaukee over two series (say Friday for a Brewers game, Sunday at the Cubs, and Monday at the White Sox), then do **4-5 days** for St. Louis and Cincinnati, visiting Louisville in between.

While Chicago, Milwaukee, and St. Louis are in the Central time zone, Cincinnati is in the Eastern time zone. When traveling from St. Louis to Cincinnati, you'll have to jump ahead an hour.

Here is how I'd do a nine-day trip that includes five baseball games in four cities.

Day 1

Fly into **Chicago,** preferably on a Saturday. If you get in early, spend the day seeing sights and taking it relatively easy.

Day 2

You're visiting either **Wrigley Field** or **Guaranteed Rate Field** today. If you're going to a Cubs game, spend abundant time in Wrigleyville.

Day 3

Today means more fun in Chicago, capped off by either a White Sox or Cubs game. Get to bed early tonight, as you'll want to get on the road early tomorrow.

Day 4

Drive to **Milwaukee** in the morning and give yourself plenty of time to visit a few sights. You'll also be seeing a Brewers game at **American Family Field** tonight. If you're feeling it, have a beer or two afterward.

Day 5

Spend the morning seeing a little more of Milwaukee before departing in the early afternoon. Leave around noon, drive for three hours on I-55 South, and stop in Bloomington, Illinois, to stretch your legs and enjoy a late lunch. Drive for another three hours on I-55 South to **St. Louis.** Have dinner, relax, and rest up for a full day tomorrow.

Day 6

Dart around St. Louis today before checking out a Cardinals game at **Busch Stadium.** You'll be pooped after this day.

Day 7

Get up early today as you're about to embark on a four-hour drive to **Louisville.** During the drive, you'll cross into the Eastern time zone and leap ahead an hour. Spend a couple hours in the afternoon at the **Louisville Slugger Museum,** and if the Bats are in town, go to Louisville Slugger Field. You'll end the night in town.

Day 8

Wake up and drive the 90 minutes or so on I-71 North to **Cincinnati.** See the sights, take in the Queen City, then check out the Reds at **Great American Ball Park.**

Day 9

Your final day will be spent in Cincinnati before flying home.

GETTING THERE

Air

If you're flying into Chicago, chances are better than 50 percent that it'll be into **Chicago O'Hare International Airport** (ORD, 10000 W. O'Hare Ave., 800/832-6352, www.flychicago.com). Airlines that fly in and out of O'Hare include **Air Canada** (888/247-2262, www.aircanada.com), **American Airlines** (800/433-7300, www.aa.com), **Delta** (800/221-1212, www.delta.com), **Frontier** (800/401-9000, www.flyfrontier.com), **jetBlue** (800/538-2583, www.jetblue.com), **Spirit** (801/401-2222, www.spirit.com), and **United** (800/864-8331, www.united.com). American, Frontier, and Spirit call O'Hare a hub airport, so those airlines have a larger presence here. Flight delays are common both arriving into and departing from O'Hare.

The other major airport in the city is **Chicago Midway International Airport** (MDW, 5700 S. Cicero Ave., 773/838-0600, www.flychicago.com, MDW). Airlines that call Midway home include Delta, **Allegiant** (702/505-8888, www.allegiantair.com), and **Southwest** (800/435-9792, www.southwest.com), which considers Midway its largest base airport.

For flying out of Cincinnati, the major airport is **Cincinnati/Northern Kentucky International Airport** (CVG, 3087 Terminal Dr., Hebron, KY, www.cvgairport.com) in the Kentucky suburb of Hebron, 15-20 minutes southwest of Cincinnati. The airport is served by Air Canada, Allegiant, American Airlines, Delta, Frontier, Southwest, and United.

Train

If you're taking **Amtrak** (www.amtrak.com) into Chicago, you'll be arriving at **Union Station** (225 S. Canal St.). Amtrak lines that stop in Chicago include **Hiawatha** (Milwaukee to Chicago), **Lake Shore Limited** (Boston and New York to Chicago), **Southwest Chief** (Los Angeles to Chicago), **Capitol Limited** (Washington DC to Chicago), **City of New Orleans** (New Orleans to Chicago), **Illinois Service** (St. Louis area to Chicago), **California Zephyr** (San Francisco to Chicago), **Cardinal** (New York to Chicago via West Virginia), **Empire Builder** (Seattle and Portland to Chicago via Montana), **Michigan Services** (Detroit and Grand Rapids to Chicago), and **Texas Eagle** (San Antonio to Chicago).

You can connect to Milwaukee from Chicago via the Hiawatha line. There are no direct routes from Milwaukee to St. Louis, so you'll have to get a train back to Chicago, then continue to St. Louis via Illinois Service or Texas Eagle. There's also no direct train route from St. Louis to Cincinnati (the only option is going back to Chicago once again to connect to the Cardinal line), so your best bet is to rent a car.

In Milwaukee, you'll arrive at **Milwaukee Intermodal Station** (433 W. St. Paul Ave.), which is three miles east of American Family Field. In St. Louis, the main train station is **St. Louis Station** (430 S. 15th St., 800/872-7245), a 20-minute, 0.8-mile walk west from Busch Stadium.

CHICAGO
CUBS AND WHITE SOX

With two outs in the bottom of the ninth inning on October 26, 2005, Juan Uribe corralled an Orlando Palmeiro ground ball and quickly sniped it to first baseman Paul Konerko to end the World Series and hand the Chicago White Sox their first championship in 88 years. One half of the Windy City went nuts.

Eleven years later, in the bottom of the ninth inning on November 2, 2016, Kris Bryant corralled a Michael Martinez ground ball and quickly sniped it to first baseman Anthony Rizzo to end the World Series and hand the Chicago Cubs their first championship in 108 years.

This is Chicago baseball: two teams that were wildly successful in the earliest days, only to suffer tremendously for generations before finally achieving glory.

The White Sox rarely made the postseason, floundering in the second and third division while an eccentric, gifted, and mostly good-natured owner, Bill Veeck, turned the team into a sideshow. He'd dress the players in shorts (for one game in 1976), install a shower in the outfield to combat Chicago summers, hire oddball fans to be comic relief, let the stadium's organist play rock and pop hits of the day, and, and, at least under his watch, fans destroyed disco records one fateful night in 1979 that nearly burned down the stadium.

The Sox have had colorful broadcasters like Harry Caray, the ultimate man of the people, and the extremely divisive Hawk Harrelson, who was endearing to many Sox fans but the worst part of catchphrase culture to outsiders. All this is to say that the Sox, South Side residents since their inception, have always been fun to follow. And somehow, they're the team that nobody considers.

Up on the North Side are the Cubs, winners of back-to-back championships in 1907 and 1908 and then … nothing. Their history is one of torture. They won a couple pennants in the 1920s and 1930s, led by prodigious slugger Hack Wilson and exceptional hitter Gabby Hartnett, but lost the World Series each time.

Then came the 1945 World Series, during which William Sianis, owner of the Billy Goat Tavern, was said to have placed a curse on the team because someone insulted his goat (which Sianis had brought with him to Game 4 of the series). In 1969, when the Cubs were leading a series against the Mets, a black cat walked onto the field during a game. The Cubs lost the series; the Mets went on to win the World Series that year. In 1984, while the Cubs were playing in their first postseason since '45, a player flubbed a ground ball and the Padres took the NLCS. In 2003, multiple fans interfered with a foul pop that outfielder Moises Alou probably would have caught during Game 6 of the NLCS, helping turn the tide in favor of the Florida Marlins. Whether or not the curse was a factor for all those years, things changed completely in 2016 when the Cubbies beat Cleveland in Game 7 of the World Series.

That's Chicago baseball. It comes with generations of failure, stress, anger, and sadness. But it also boasts some of the most indelible images in baseball history. It's gorgeous stuff.

PLANNING YOUR TIME

You should spend a **long weekend,** at least, in Chicago. I recommend closer to a **week** if you'd like to get the full flavor of the Windy City. Spend a day hitting the most obvious tourist attractions (consider getting tickets ahead of time for Willis Tower), then plan on a full day around **Wrigleyville** and another full day in **Bridgeport** and near Guaranteed Rate Field. If you want to catch **both clubs in one trip,** you'll have to consider a **wrap-around weekend** (a Friday to a Monday or Tuesday), as the Sox and Cubs never play at home at the same time.

Chicago has plenty of hotels spread across its metro area. Staying in **the Loop** means you'll have easy access to the CTA and L train, though you can also stay out near one of the airports and still have train access and not be too far away from the action.

Midsummer is definitely an option for baseball in Chicago, though temperatures will soar into the 90s. **Late May** and **early June** can be good, too, though **rain** can be a problem, and at night temperatures can dip into the 40s and 50s. Whatever you do, try to get tickets to a **day game** for the **optimal Wrigley experience,** as for its first several decades the park only hosted afternoon games. With **Guaranteed Rate Field,** you'll be just fine with either a **day or night game.**

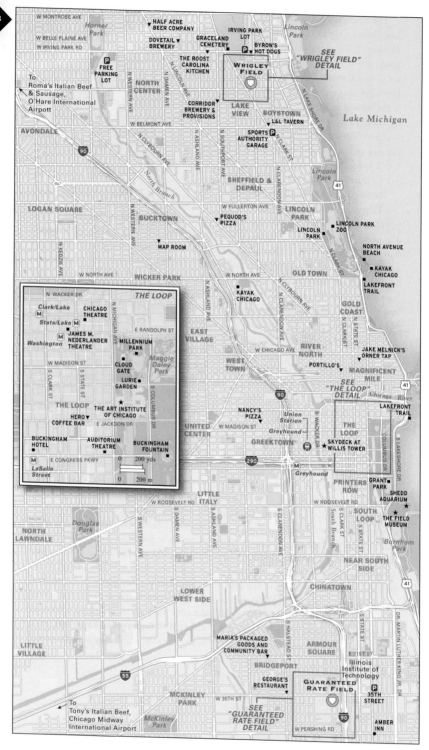

Wrigley and Guaranteed Rate Fields
CHICAGO

WRIGLEY FIELD

0   200 yds
0   200 m

- N CLARK ST
- N SEMINARY AVE
- N SHEFFIELD AVE
- CAMRY LOT P
- COROLLA LOT P
- W GRACE ST
- WRIGLEYVILLE
- THE GMAN TAVERN ▾
- BIG G'S PIZZA ▾
- PRIUS LOT P
- HIGHLANDER LOT P
- MURPHY'S BLEACHERS
- W WAVELAND AVE
- BUDWEISER BRICKTOWN TAVERN
- GALLAGHER WAY
- WRIGLEY FIELD
- HARRY CARAY STATUE
- LUCKY DORR
- CUBS STORE
- BANKS STATUE
- THE INN AT WRIGLEYVILLE
- W ADDISON ST
- CUBBY BEAR ▾
- SANTO AND WILLIAMS STATUES
- W EDDY ST
- RAV4 LOT P
- MERKLE'S BAR & GRILL ▾
- STRETCH BAR & GRILL
- W CORNELIA AVE
- CLARK STREET SPORTS

Outter Harbor

0   1 mi
0   1 km
© MOON.COM

Northerly Island Park

Lake Michigan

GUARANTEED RATE FIELD

- W 33RD ST
- TURTLE'S BAR AND GRILL
- Illinois Institute of Technology
- LOT G P
- Armour Square Park
- CHICAGO SPORTS DEPOT
- CHISOX BAR & GRILL
- Sox-35th M M
- 35TH STREET RED HOTS
- W 35TH ST
- GRANDSTAND LTD.
- SOX WORLD CHAMPIONS
- 35th Street "Lou" Jones/ Bronzeville
- S WENTWORTH AVE
- S LA SALLE ST
- GUARANTEED RATE FIELD
- KATHY DE'S DELI
- W 37TH ST
- S LOWE AVE
- S PARNELL AVE
- S NORMAL AVE
- LOT F P
- W 38TH ST
- 90
- LOT L P
- BALLPARK PUB
- W PERSHING RD
- 0   200 yds
- 0   200 m

LAKEFRONT TRAIL
S LAKE SHORE DR
Burnham Park
OAKLAND

GETTING THERE

AIR

Chicago O'Hare International Airport

If you're flying into Chicago, chances are better than 50 percent that it'll be into **Chicago O'Hare International Airport** (ORD, 10000 W. O'Hare Ave., 800/832-6352, www.flychicago.com). Once the busiest airport in the world, it's still pretty dang packed, with nonstop flights to more than 200 destinations. Airlines that fly in and out of O'Hare include **Air Canada** (888/247-2262, www.aircanada.com), **American Airlines** (800/433-7300, www.aa.com), **Delta** (800/221-1212, www.delta.com), **Frontier** (800/401-9000, www.flyfrontier.com), **jetBlue** (800/538-2583, www.jetblue.com), **Spirit** (801/401-2222, www.spirit.com), and **United** (800/864-8331, www.united.com). American, Frontier, and Spirit call O'Hare a hub airport, so those airlines have a larger presence. Delays are commonplace, so don't be surprised if your departure time gets pushed out.

AIRPORT TRANSPORTATION

From the airport, you can hop on the **Blue Line** via **CTA** (Chicago Transit Authority, www.transitchicago.com, $0.75-2.50 per ride, $5 from O'Hare), part of the rapid transit system affectionately known as the **"L"** (short for elevated train). Follow signage for the trains to the city; the CTA station is in the lower level of the airport parking garage. Purchase a **Ventra card** ($5 initial fee), then add to it as needed. The Blue Line connects O'Hare, in the northwestern end of the city, to Downtown and the Loop. The main Downtown station is **Clark/Lake** (100/124 W. Lake St.), which has elevated, ground-level, and subway platforms. From the **State/Lake station** (200 N. State St.), you can transfer (free with Ventra card) to the **Red Line,** which has stops for both ballparks (head north for Wrigley and south for Guaranteed Rate Field). You can also connect to the ballparks by transferring to the Red Line from the Blue

Line's **Washington station** (W. Washington St. and N. Dearborn St.).

You could also take a **Metra train** (www.metrarail.com, $6.25) from the airport. To board, take the **Metra shuttle bus** to the **O'Hare Transfer Station** (Zemke Blvd. and Mannheim Rd.). From the transfer station, take the **North Central service** east into the city. The last stop is **Union Station** (210 S. Canal St., 312/322-4269), Chicago's main train station, in the West Loop Gate neighborhood.

If you're **renting a car,** take the shuttle from the lower-level baggage claim to the **Multi-Modal Facility** (10255 W. Zemke Blvd.). Every major car rental agency is here. To get out of O'Hare by car, take I-190 to I-90 East, or the Kennedy Expressway. That will take you the rest of the 15 miles into the city. The drive takes 30-40 minutes, depending on traffic.

Chicago Midway International Airport

The other major airport in the city is the South Side's **Chicago Midway International Airport** (MDW, 5700 S. Cicero Ave., 773/838-0600, www.flychicago.com), which is eight miles closer to Downtown and the Loop than O'Hare. Airports that call Midway home include Delta, **Allegiant** (702/505-8888, www.allegiantair.com), and **Southwest** (800/435-9792, www.southwest.com), which considers Midway its largest base airport.

AIRPORT TRANSPORTATION

The **Orange Line** of the **L** (www.transitchicago.com, $0.75-2.50 per ride) comes to Midway. Take that inbound to the city. Major stops in the Loop include the **Clark/Lake station** (100/124 W. Lake St.) and **State/Lake station** (200 N. State St.). For either ballpark, you'll exit at State/Lake, then walk a half block south on State to transfer to the **Red Line** (free with Ventra card). Head north for Wrigley Field or south for Guaranteed Rate Field.

To **rent a car** from Midway, head down to Lower Level Door 2 and get onto a **shuttle** bus that takes you to the **Rental Car Facility** (5150 W. 55th St.). Most major car rental companies are here. To get to Downtown and the Loop from Midway, take I-55 North and I-90 West. This 10-mile drive takes 30-40 minutes, depending on traffic.

TRAIN

You can certainly get to Chicago by train via **Amtrak** (www.amtrak.com). Trains stop at **Union Station** (225 S. Canal St.). In the West Loop Gate neighborhood, the station has been around since 1925; its Corinthian columns and beaux arts-style exterior symbolize the city's early 20th-century might as a hub of commerce and manufacturing.

Amtrak lines that serve the city include **Hiawatha** (Milwaukee to Chicago), **Lake Shore Limited** (Boston and New York to Chicago), **Southwest Chief** (Los Angeles to Chicago), **Capitol Limited** (Washington DC to Chicago), **City of New Orleans** (New Orleans to Chicago), **Illinois Service** (St. Louis area to Chicago), **California Zephyr** (San Francisco to Chicago), **Cardinal** (New York to Chicago via West Virginia), **Empire Builder** (Seattle and Portland to Chicago via Montana), **Michigan Services** (Detroit and Grand Rapids to Chicago), and **Texas Eagle** (San Antonio to Chicago).

BUS

There are three main **Greyhound stations** (www.greyhound.com) in Chicago. The more heavily trafficked stations are close together. The first is in **Greektown** (630 W. Harrison St.), near the intersection of I-90 and I-290. The second is a few blocks northeast, just across from **Union Station** (225 S. Canal St.). Be sure that you carefully compare the price of a trip to both stations, as there's often a wide discrepancy. If you arrive at the Greektown station, it's a half-mile walk north to Union Station.

The third Greyhound station is on the **South Side** (14 W. 95th St.). This station offers a connection to the CTA Red Line via **95th/Dan Ryan** (S. State St. and W. 95th St.,

at I-94/Dan Ryan Expy.). Continue north on the Red Line to either Guaranteed Rate Field or Wrigley Field.

Wrigley Field

No ballpark in baseball carries as much mythology as **Wrigley Field** (1060 W. Addison St., www.mlb.com/cubs). Constructed during World War I and opened in April 1914, Wrigley is a baseball paradise.

The first time I visited Wrigley was on a press trip. Within minutes of entering, I was standing on the brilliant bluegrass. With caution, I crept toward the outfield, and before I knew it, I was touching the Boston ivy covering the brick outfield fence, a distinctive feature of the park since 1937.

The ivy might be the most noticeable thing about this quirky, pocket-size venue tucked into a formerly working-class North Side neighborhood. In the old days, folks would mosey from their front steps right to the ballpark's bleachers. Other fans living across the street would park beach chairs on their roofs for a perfect view of the field below. This was back when the Cubs played only day games, since those very neighbors also didn't want bright lights distracting their evenings. The lights came on in August 1988, and since then, the neighborhood has changed—more bars and restaurants have sprouted up around the stadium, and those houses across the street now rent out their rooftops to those ready to plunk down a couple thousand bucks for the view.

Wrigley's story follows the evolution of baseball. For decades, it was simply the ballpark down the street, a place that never quite filled up (partly because the Cubs weren't very good) but was full of happily frustrated fans who didn't mind paying $3 to shout at the players while drinking some beers. Now you have to spend a paycheck for good seats, good food, and good drinks, as the Cubs have learned how to monetize their jewel-box park.

Looking to party before the game? You

could head over to the team's new entertainment district, part of its 1060 Project, a nearly decade-long development effort aimed at updating Wrigley for the modern age of experiences. This is just a little different from wandering over to the bleachers from your front stoop.

As much as the Cubs have added to their celebrated ballpark, the original spark remains. You can see it in the tight seating across the entire venue, and in the joy that overcomes a crowd upon seeing the marquee outside home plate scream "Cubs Win." Despite the many changes the old place has seen, Wrigley remains the every-fan's ballpark—always has been, always will be.

ORIENTATION

Wrigley Field was built in the early 20th century in a North Side neighborhood now called **Wrigleyville.** It's surrounded by homes, restaurants, bars, and other small businesses. The streets can be narrow and don't necessarily follow a grid pattern. The bigger roads include North Clark Street, a diagonal that runs past the park entrance; West Addison Street, which intersects with Clark at the home plate entrance; and North Sheffield Avenue, a major north-south thoroughfare that creates the right field boundary. Because of the park's unique placement and parking options, consider getting to Wrigleyville early to orient yourself with the area.

There are six gates at Wrigley Field. All gates open two hours before first pitch, giving you ample time to scope out the park. The **Marquee Gate** at home plate is the main entrance under the iconic Wrigley marquee; I suggest going in this way for your first visit.

TICKETS AND SEATING

Pricing

There's a lot of demand for tickets at Wrigley Field. Not only are prices high, but the closer you want to sit to home plate, the more money you'll be shelling out. The Cubs use a **dynamic pricing** model, which means

games against some opponents will cost more. The culprits are always the rival **Cardinals** and **Brewers.** Additionally, any time the **Yankees, Red Sox,** and **Dodgers** come to town, expect even higher prices. The average seat for a midweek game against a lesser draw like Miami might run about $50. When the Cardinals come to town, that seat can be more like $70, and if the Yankees are visiting (which happens once every six years), expect ticket prices closer to $100.

Seating Plan

Something to remember about Wrigley's configuration: The **Cubs dugout** is on the **third-base line** and not the first-base line, which is standard practice.

The **club level** at Wrigley starts at the left-field foul pole. The lower seating area is the premier **W Club** (sections 3-5), which has a view of the Cubs' batting tunnel and third base. A few rows back and down the left-field line a bit is **club box outfield** (sections 3-7). The lower part of mid left field is **bullpen box** (sections 6-7). Next, along the third-base line, is **club box infield** (sections 8-12). Then, around home plate and over to around first base, the sections are split: The upper rows are **club box home plate** (sections 13-22), and the lower rows make up the **American Airlines 1914 Club** (sections 13-22). Next, above the visitors' dugout, is **club box infield** (sections 23-27), and the rest of the right-field line is **club box outfield** (sections 28-32). The lower rows of shallow right field make up the **Maker's Mark Barrel Room** (sections 27-29), a brick-walled premium bar area with TVs and seating right at first base. The seats in **bullpen box** (sections 30-31) are in the first few rows of the sections close to the right-field line.

Next is the **field level.** We start at the left-field foul pole, in toward third base, with **field box outfield** (sections 101-108). Beside third base, you'll find **field box infield** (sections 109-111), and around home plate to the first-base line is **field box home plate** (sections 112-122). Along the first-base line, find **field box infield**

YOUR BEST DAY AT WRIGLEY FIELD

While you may not be able to get yourself on an episode of "Bill Swerski's Super Fans," you can certainly have a 10-Ditka day while catching a Cubs game. Let's assume the game is at night, so you've got a full day in the Windy City ahead of you.

10 HOURS BEFORE FIRST PITCH
Start the day by taking a brisk walk, run, or bike ride on the **Lakefront Trail.**

8 HOURS BEFORE FIRST PITCH
Late breakfast? Early lunch? Whatever you want to call it, get a Chicago dog at **Portillo's.** If you want killer Italian beef, visit **Roma's Italian Beef & Sausage.** Either way, you're winning.

6.5 HOURS BEFORE FIRST PITCH
Indulge your inner art critic at the **Art Institute of Chicago.** Check in with some of the greatest works from around the world.

4 HOURS FIRST PITCH
This would be a good time to head back to your hotel, relax, then change for the game.

3 HOURS BEFORE FIRST PITCH
Get thee to **Wrigleyville.** Stop at **The GMan Tavern** for a beer. Then walk to **Cubby Bear** for a shot and an Old Style before finishing up at **Murphy's Bleachers.** Have one more beer while you make small talk with the fun fans. Then it's time to head to **Wrigley Field.**

statue of Billy Williams by sculptor Lou Cella

1 HOUR BEFORE FIRST PITCH
You could hang out at **Gallagher Way,** but you've had enough to drink. Instead, just walk around. Take photos. Be sure to get close to the **outfield ivy.**

Take photos of the **statues** of **Ernie Banks, Billy Williams,** and **Ron Santo.** Maybe not the Harry Caray statue, though.

DURING THE GAME
Buy an Old Style at **Beer & Wine** and pair it with a North Side Twist Giant Pretzel from the **pizza stand.** Journey out to the **bleachers** and have a good time with the rowdy and friendly fans there.

AFTER THE GAME
Stay in Wrigleyville. I recommend heading down Clark to **L&L Tavern.** If you need a quick postgame bite, make it a slice from **Big G's Pizza.**

(sections 123-126); the last several sections to the right-field foul pole are **field box outfield** (sections 127-134).

The **terrace level (200 level)** starts at the left-field foul pole. The lower rows make up **terrace box corner** (sections 202-205) and **terrace box outfield** (sections 206-208), while the middle rows comprise **terrace reserved outfield** (sections 202-208). Some of the back rows in this area are part of **terrace reserved outfield corner** (sections 203-205). Along the left-field line, the first couple rows are **terrace box infield**

(sections 209-212). The middle rows all the way to the first-base line are part of **terrace reserved preferred** (sections 209-226), and the back rows all the way around are part of **terrace reserved infield** (sections 209-226). The front rows around home plate are **terrace box home plate** (sections 213-222). The rest of the seating area to the right-field foul pole is split: The front rows are in **terrace box outfield** (sections 227-229) and **terrace box corner** (sections 230-233); the middle rows are **terrace reserved outfield** (sections 227-233); and the back rows of a

Wrigley Field

few sections are **terrace reserved outfield corner** (sections 230-232).

The **upper box level (300 level)** is a little simpler. Starting at the left-field foul pole, the first few sections are **upper box outfield** (sections 303L-304L). Next, along mid-outfield, is **upper box midfield** (sections 305L-307L). Down the rest of the third-base line is **upper box infield** (sections 308L-314L), and around home plate is the **Catalina Club** (sections 315L-318R). Along the first-base line is **upper box infield** (sections 319R-326R), while in mid-outfield is **upper box midfield** (sections 327R-329R), and out along right field is **upper box outfield** (sections 330R-331R).

The **reserved level (400 level)** starts at the left-field foul pole. Along the left-field line is **upper reserved outfield** (sections 403L-408L). Around the infield is **upper reserved infield** (sections 409L-415L and 418R-426R), and back along the right-field line is **upper reserved outfield** (sections 427R-431R).

The main seating area of the **outfield** is the **Budweiser Bleachers** (sections 501-515), which are in left and right field. A deep seating section over **center field** (sections 536-538) is also available for fans. Sections designated only for groups include the **LG Porch,** over the bleachers in left field, which has a private bar and drink rail, plus unlimited beer, wine, and snacks; the **Hornito's Hacienda** in the first few rows of seats against the left field fence, which has unlimited beer, wine, and snacks, a drink rail, and standing room space for group members; and the **Budweiser Patio** (sections

516-518), which is tucked near the right field foul pole with unlimited ballpark food, beer, wine, and snacks, plus a cocktail option and some standing room ticket spots for group members only.

Finally, there are the **rooftop seats** (773/248-7663, www.wrigleyrooftops.com). Eleven distinct structures with ticketed rooftops are spread around the outfield area on Waveland and Sheffield Avenues, across the street from the park. They're available for each game, offer all-inclusive food and drink, and typically host groups. If you're interested, call as soon as you know what game you want to see, but know that you're bound to socialize more than focus on the game, you can't actually go into the ballpark with a rooftop ticket, and you almost certainly will be pretty far from the action. I recommend the rooftops only if you're hosting or part of a party, and if it's not your first time at Wrigley.

Where to Buy Tickets

There's no clear-cut best way to get Cubs tickets, since the service selling the cheapest options can vary by the day. Try the **team's website** first, but be sure to cross-check with **StubHub** and **SeatGeek.** If the game you want has potential to sell out (it's on the weekend, and the Cardinals or Brewers are in town), prepare to nab any ticket you find. Otherwise, you can consider waiting closer to first pitch to see if you can get a cheaper price on a last-minute ticket. You can buy Cubs tickets via the **MLB Ballpark app,** but there's no upgrade capability.

You may want to try to snag tickets via the **10/Sixty promotion.** For this, the Cubs release **60 lower-level terrace seats** for every game at just $10 each. These seats are released online as soon as the new season's schedule is announced, and they go quickly.

Best Seats

I say, especially if it's your first time, spring for the more expensive seats. Go for the classic **field box home-plate view** (sections 112-122) that puts the whole playing area in front of you. As an alternative, try the **front rows of the upper deck** (sections 308L-314L and 319R-326R).

You should avoid **upper reserved** (sections 403L-431R) if possible, unless you're in the first few rows and you've scoped out your seats ahead of time on a website that shows the view. Because of its age, Wrigley still has a number of **poles** that hold up the overhang, so there's a chance your view of the field will be **obstructed.**

GAME COSTS

Tickets: High as high can be. Attending a game at Wrigley Field is far pricier than attending a game at any other park in the majors. There are cheap seats to be had ($15 or so), but you'll have to sit way up high for a weekday game. Otherwise, be prepared to pay at least $30 for nosebleed seats, and somewhere around $100 for field box seats toward the back of the baselines.

Hot dog: Higher than average at around $6.50. You're better off getting a giant pretzel.

Beer: More expensive than at most parks, with the average macro costing you close to $10.

Parking: Excruciatingly expensive. You might pay close to $40 for a space close to the park. There is a free lot, and if you're early and patient, you might be able to snag a spot in Wrigleyville, the neighborhood around the park.

You're also risking it buying **terrace seats,** especially if they're not terrace box corner, terrace box outfield, terrace box infield, or terrace box home plate. This level also has an overhang held up by posts, so if you're back **past row six** (where the columns are installed), you might have an **obstruction** to battle. If you're in the front rows of the terrace level, especially on the **third-base side,** you'll be in **shade.** So consider getting seats in the **terrace infield** or **terrace home plate** (sections 209-213).

If you want to chug Old Style beers and chat it up with rowdy and friendly fans, the **bleachers** are great fun. Just remember that for day games, you're going to bake. Bring sunscreen and wear a hat.

KNOW BEFORE YOU GO

Bringing in a **bag**? It must be no larger than 16 by 16 by 8 inches. Factory-sealed **plastic bottles** are allowed at Wrigley, but hard-sided coolers and thermoses are a no-go. The same goes for glass bottles, cans, and alcoholic beverages. Wrigley allows fans to wear **costumes,** as long as they're deemed appropriate.

Nursing mothers can visit the **nursing station** inside Gallagher Way Gate from the moment gates open until the end of the game. You can check a **stroller** at bike valet (alley east of the CTA Red Line stop on Addison St.).

Accessibility

For **accessible seating,** call the Cubs **ticket office** (800/843-2827). Up to three companions can sit in the same area. Personal care attendants must have paid tickets. **Service animals** are welcome at Wrigley Field.

For assistance while at Wrigley, visit one of the **fan services booths** (main concourse behind home plate, left field inside Budweiser Bleachers gate). **Assistive listening devices** and **noise-cancelling headphones** are available at the home plate booth. **Sensory kits** are available both from the home plate booth and the kiosk at the Budweiser Bleachers gate.

BE A FAN

Wrigley Field has forever been called "The Friendly Confines," and the team has forever been labeled the lovable losers of baseball, though both monikers are said with tongue firmly planted in cheek. The truth is, Chicagoans throughout history have desperately wanted their Cubbies to win, and that has led to a fandom teetering between happily absent and extremely frustrated.

"Fly the W" signage in a window near Wrigley Field

In some years, Wrigley has been terribly empty; in others, the park has been packed. The fans are midwestern nice with a big-city streak, meaning they certainly can charm you and make you feel at home, but at the same time, they can be extremely bitter and resentful about their team's fate (you'll hear the worst of it in the outfield, home to the **Bleacher Bums**). Fans aren't as aggressive as folks in New York, Boston, or Philadelphia, but they certainly have something to say. Cardinals fans and Cubs fans don't get along. This rivalry doesn't raise red flags in the way the Yankees versus Red Sox or Phillies versus Mets tilts do, but if you're a Redbirds fan in Chicago, be courteous and don't get into trouble.

The long-suffering Cubs have some wonderful traditions. Legend goes that in 1970, a disgruntled Cubs fan in the bleachers tossed a home run ball hit by Hank Aaron back onto the field. The act soon became tradition, and to this day, fans at Wrigley are known to throw an **opposing player's home run ball** back into play. Some fans bring a **spare baseball** just in case they get lucky enough to snag a homer. So instead of tossing the valuable item, they send back a cheap imitation but still get to participate in the tradition.

When the Cubs win, you'll see the raising of a white flag showing a blue "W" over the scoreboard. That's **The W**, and since 1937, when the scoreboard was built, it flies any time the Cubbies come out on top. Next, you'll hear the Steve Goodman song **"Go, Cubs, Go,"** written before the 1984 season as a new kind of rally song for the club. That year, the Cubs shockingly won the National League East division title. (Sadly, Goodman died of leukemia at age 36, just days before the team clinched that crown.) There's both heartbreak and blind joy in the song. You can't help but feel for the fans of the National League's most snakebitten and deserving franchise.

Elevators can be found at **seven locations:** the Marquee Gate, left field gate, Wintrust right field gate, left field corner near Budweiser Bleachers, right field corner near Budweiser Bleachers, Budweiser Bleachers gate, and the Budweiser Bleachers concourse.

Accessible parking can be found at the **Camry Lot** (1126 W. Grace St.), 2.5 miles north of Wrigley Field. That means hopping on a **shuttle** (in this case, a golf cart) to the ballpark. Parking is also available at **3900 North Rockwell Street,** but only for night and weekend games. The shuttle service from this lot is a school bus.

GETTING THERE

Public Transit

To get to Wrigley by public transit from the Loop/Downtown, hop on the CTA's **Red Line train** (www.transitchicago.com, $0.75-2.50 per ride) and go north. You can transfer to the Red Line's Lake station from **State/Lake station** (200 N. State St.), which is on the Brown, Orange, Green, and Pink Lines. The transfer is free with a Ventra card; it's about a half-block walk between stations. You can also transfer to Lake station from the Blue Line's **Washington station** (W. Washington St. and N. Dearborn St.). Exit at **Addison** (W. Addison St. and N. Sheffield Ave.), which is just a block from the stadium.

Driving

If you're driving to Wrigley, you could take **US-41,** or **Lake Shore Drive,** north to **IL-19,** or **West Irving Park Road.** Drive that just a few blocks west to **North Sheffield Avenue,** then turn left (south) to reach the park. You can also head up **North Clark Street** into **Wrigleyville.**

You may want to arrive earlier than you might expect. On the narrow, one-way streets of Wrigleyville, traffic can back up. Plan ahead for where you want to park, as the lots are spread out quite a bit. The main lots, most of which are sponsored by Toyota, are just north of the park. At Waveland, between Seminary and Clifton Avenues, are the **Prius** and **Highlander Lots.** A block north, on Grace Street at Clifton, is the **Camry Lot.** Next to that, closer to Clark Street, is the **Corolla Lot.** Up Seminary, at Irving Park Road, is the **Irving Park Lot;** south of the park, at Eddy Street near Racine Avenue, is the **Rav4 Lot.** Some of these lots are for season ticket holders. The Camry Lot and Irving Park Lot are both **cash** lots. Expect to pay as much as $40.

The Cubs do have a **free parking lot** (3900 N. Rockwell St.), but it's 2.2 miles from the park and available only for night and weekend games. From the lot, the team operates a **shuttle** that starts running 2.5 hours before first pitch and ends operation about an hour after the game ends. The cheapest lots not operated by the Cubs are close to $20 (try the **Sports Authority Garage** at N. Clark St. and Fletcher St.), but they're few and far between. Most lots in the area will charge you closer to $40.

You can try to park in and around **Wrigleyville,** but you'll see plenty of permit-only spots on the streets (you will be ticketed if you park here). The best bet for a free, non-permit spot is to circle Graceland Cemetery. Go up North Kenmore Avenue to West Montrose Avenue, turn left, then head to North Clark Street and drive south to West Irving Park Road, where you'll turn right. Just be mindful of any signage.

PARK FEATURES AND SIGHTS

The Cubs have featured an **organist** at Wrigley Field since 1941, so listen for little musical interludes and songs throughout the game. The organist is Gary Pressy; he has been behind the keys for more than 30 years.

Why do the foul poles say **"Hey Hey"?** That was the catchphrase uttered by longtime Cubs broadcaster Jack Brickhouse, who called games from 1948 to 1981; he died in 1998. **Retired numbers** adorn the tops of the foul poles. The left field pole has Ernie Banks (14), Ron Santo (5), and Ferguson Jenkins (31), while the right field pole has Billy Williams (26), Ryne Sandberg (23), Greg Maddux (31), and Jackie Robinson, whose 42 is retired league-wide.

Gallagher Way

Opened in 2018 to bring an experience-driven element to Wrigley, **Gallagher Way** (N. Clark St. and Waveland Ave.) is a big, open space of green turf that's adjacent to the park and surrounded by restaurants and bars. It's a cool spot to visit before the gates open, if only to snag a beer and get to know some fans. There's often live music on game days, along with kids' activities and tailgate games.

All of the bars and restaurants are accessible to the public up to two hours before first pitch and starting one hour after the final out, but when gates are open some of the area is open only to ticketholders. That said, some shops and restaurants allow the non-ticket-holding public during games.

Outfield Ivy

For more than 80 years, the **outfield ivy** has been a gorgeous feature of Wrigley Field. Back in the 1930s, a young Bill Veeck—who took over some responsibilities with helping run the Cubs after the death of his father, William Veeck Sr., team president at the time—looked for ways to enhance the fan experience in the ballpark, selling it as a respite for urban families. One idea that he came up with was to plant beautiful greenery.

In 1937, Veeck planned on planting Boston ivy to adorn the brick outfield wall for the '38 season. Head groundskeeper Charlie Dorr had other ideas and started planting the ivy right away. On October 1, 1937, Wrigley Field's iconic ivy was first seen by the public.

Scoreboard and Flags

The beautiful forest green **scoreboard** was built in 1937 and has changed only slightly since. Scores and pitcher information are changed constantly by veteran operator Darryl Wilson and a team of at least two others who hang out inside the board throughout the game. They keep up with league happenings via a laptop, then get to work, which means replacing seven-pound plates round the clock. The scoreboard doesn't have the space to show the score of every major league game on some days, but that's the price you pay for having a timeless piece of baseball history watching over the proceedings.

A good way of keeping track of National League standings is by reading the **flags** over the scoreboard. From left to right are the NL West, NL Central, and NL East standings; when they change, the flags, each one festooned with a team's logo, are repositioned accordingly. When the Cubs win, the famous **white W flag** is hoisted up as well.

Statues

Closer to the third-base side of home plate is a statue of **Ernie Banks** (N. Clark St. and W. Addison St.) at the plate. The base of his statue reads "Let's Play Two!" The most famous quote from Mr. Cub signified his desire to play baseball as much as possible. Exciting and powerful, Banks played all 19 of his seasons with Chicago, finishing his career with 512 home runs and easy election to the National Baseball Hall of Fame.

At right field are statues of **Billy Williams** and **Ron Santo** (N. Sheffield Ave. and W.

Photos (from top to bottom): Wrigley Field's famous scoreboard; Budweiser Bleachers entrance; Wrigley Field bleachers and ivy wall.

Addison St.). Both played alongside Banks. Williams collected 2,711 career hits plus 426 home runs en route to a Hall of Fame induction. Santo was a consistent offensive force who also played a pretty good third base. Santo also reached the Hall of Fame, but not until two years after his death.

In center field at the entrance to the Budweiser Bleachers is a statue of **Harry Caray** (N. Sheffield Ave. and W. Waveland Ave.) that some might describe as unusual (I admit I think it's creepy). It depicts a boisterous Caray, the longtime Cubs (and before that White Sox) broadcaster, wearing a very wrinkled jacket while faces (representing fans) and the Wrigley grandstand protrude from his lower legs. Enjoy the nightmares!

FOOD AND DRINKS

Opened in Chicago in 1949, **Garrett Popcorn Shops** is one of the Windy City's favorite snacks. You can find the company's products throughout Wrigley Field, but my suggestion is to stop by **Marquee Classics** (section 116). There, you can get Garrett's famous **Garrett Mix,** a combination of caramel and cheddar popcorn, plus food from **Buona,** the popular chain that specializes in meaty sandwiches with gravy and hot and sweet peppers. Marquee also sells hot chocolate early and late in the season. You may need it—it can get cold out here.

Another Chi-Town stalwart that you can find at the park is sausage king **Hot Doug's** (Bleachers Platform 14). While Hot Doug's brick-and-mortar spot has been closed since 2014, the brand lives on, serving up hot sausages to hungry fans.

You know what goes great with an Old Style beer? A pretzel. And boy, does Wrigley have a knot for you: The **North Side Twist Giant Pretzel** is only available at one **pizza stand** (section 103), and it is large. This two-pound pretzel—nicely salted and served with sides of beer cheese, chipotle honey mustard, and cinnamon frosting—is a perfect accompaniment for a day of drinking beers under the summer sun.

As for beer, you can find offerings from midwestern craft favorites **Bell's** and **3 Floyd's,** along with goodies from local favorites **Half Acre** and **Revolution,** at **Beer & Wine** (sections 106, 119, 121). There's a large selection of **Goose Island** beverages at Beer & Wine and a number of food vendors. The Chicago-based brewery, owned by Anheuser-Busch InBev, makes pretty good beer. But when you're in Wrigley, you need to drink some **Old Style,** brewed by Pabst Brewing Company but, previously, by the G. Heileman Brewing Company. Old Style Lager is the official swill of Chicago, easy going down and cheap at the bar. You need one, two, or even three when watching the Cubbies, and it's available at most tap stations including at Beer & Wine.

Wrigley has a few unique branded bars and hangouts; you'll need special tickets to access these areas. Among these bars is the **Maker's Mark Barrel Room** (behind visitors' dugout near section 29), which serves whiskey drinks against a brick backdrop and neon lighting. The **Catalina Club** (sections 315L-318R), in the upper box level, is spacious and inviting, serving summery food (grilled items, small snacks).

EVENTS

The chances of getting a player **autograph** while hanging out next to a dugout are slim; the Cubs seem to discourage that practice. Instead, children ages 13 and under can visit the **Magellan Kids Corral** (section 12) from gate opening to 45 minutes before first pitch, and they can also hang out near the **players' parking lot** (Waveland Ave. near Caretakers Way) in a designated Kids Corral area. Players will start coming out about 30 minutes after the game ends, and some may sign their John Hancocks.

Tours

The Cubs offer only **off-season tours** (773/388-8270, dates vary, $30, free ages 1 and under) of Wrigley Field. Tours meet at the Cubs Store at Gallagher Way then head into the park for a 60-minute adventure. You'll visit the Cubs' dugout, the visitors' clubhouse, the field, and new venues like the Maker's Mark Barrel Room.

SHOPPING

Because Wrigley Field was built more than 100 years ago, the Cubs couldn't wedge a team store into the existing structure. Instead, the **Cubs Store** (3637 N. Clark St., 10am-9pm Mon.-Sat., 10am-7pm Sun.) is out in Gallagher Way, worthy of 8,400 square feet of retail space. You can find plenty of hats, shirts, jerseys, jackets, and LCD screens on which you can watch games. Plus, there's a photo booth where you can take a photo at virtual Wrigley Field and get it on your smartphone. The store is open to the public during games. Ticketholders can visit the store—and Gallagher Way—at any point during the game.

There are plenty other kiosks and stores around the park, so you can get your fill of merch without heading to Gallagher Way. The **Cubs Team Store** (Marquee Gate) is a smaller version of the main Cubs Store, while **Cubs Gear** (sections 120, 133, Budweiser Bleachers lower level) also has a small but solid selection of merchandise. There are also the **New Era kiosks** (section 104, Budweiser Bleachers upper level). You can find plenty of T-shirts, hats, and novelty items at these stands.

Guaranteed Rate Field

The White Sox have been anchoring the South Side of Chicago for more than 100 years. For many of those years, their home was the beautiful and hefty Comiskey Park. That concrete-and-steel behemoth could seat nearly 32,000 at the time of its opening. It lasted from 1910 to 1990.

In its wake came a new Comiskey—a park known today as **Guaranteed Rate Field** (333 W. 35th St., www.mlb.com/whitesox). Opening in 1991, it had more pizzazz and modern touches than its predecessor, but it

connected to the past in some really great ways. The outfield grandstand was framed by a gorgeous row of signage (à la Yankee Stadium), centered by a showstopping scoreboard topped by pinwheels, a nod to former owner Bill Veeck, who first installed them at the original Comiskey. The upper deck extended at a steep angle, also reminiscent of Yankee Stadium. Finally, the iconic light towers of the first Comiskey Park were reproduced for the updated version. This new Comiskey felt like an organic update of White Sox history.

But the Sox had bad timing. Just a year after the opening of the new Comiskey, the Baltimore Orioles welcomed fans into Oriole Park at Camden Yards. That yard, plus Progressive Field in Cleveland and the former Globe Life Park in Arlington, Texas, changed the game for baseball venues. Comiskey II immediately felt antiquated, thanks to its too-high upper deck and basic layout.

The Sox have updated the park several times, however, maintaining a semblance of freshness. Today, Guaranteed Rate Field isn't the most awe-inspiring and jaw-dropping venue, but it has good bones, looks really good on television, and can really rock when the Pale Hose are playing well.

ORIENTATION

Guaranteed Rate Field is in a residential area of the South Side, technically bordering the Bridgeport neighborhood of Chicago. I-90 runs right beyond left field, while 35th Street, a major thoroughfare, hurdles over the highway then dips below rail lines just west of the ballpark.

There are five gates at Guaranteed Rate Field. Gates 3 and 5 are attached to ticket windows; Gate 5 is also attached to the Chicago Sports Depot team store. Gates open 90 minutes before first pitch.

TICKETS AND SEATING
Pricing

The White Sox are one of the many teams in major league baseball with a **dynamic ticket**

YOUR BEST DAY AT GUARANTEED RATE FIELD

This is your day to celebrate all things White Sox, which means embracing the underrated parts of Chicago. So, before you head to the park, consider this itinerary.

10 HOURS BEFORE FIRST PITCH
All you'll need at **Hero Coffee Bar** is coffee and a pastry. Tucked just enough away, this cute place is worth a big, bold drink with a bready bagel.

8 HOURS BEFORE FIRST PITCH
Spend some time at the outstanding **Field Museum,** home to the largest fossilized skeleton of a T. rex ever found. What are you waiting for?

5 HOURS BEFORE FIRST PITCH
Make a beeline for Bridgeport, taking CTA if you can. Visit **Maria's Packaged Goods and Community Bar** for a drink and some Korean-Polish fusion fare.

3.5 HOURS BEFORE FIRST PITCH
You're on the South Side now. Head to **Ballpark Pub** for a beer and a Pale Hose history lesson.

2 HOURS BEFORE FIRST PITCH
Walk to **Guaranteed Rate Field** and try to finagle your way into someone's tailgate. If you score an Italian dog, you get bonus points. Afterward, take selfies at the **Champions Monument Plaza.** It's as if you were at the 2005 World Series!

Field Museum

1.5 HOURS BEFORE FIRST PITCH
Walk down the third-base line toward the **Chicago Sports Depot.** As the gates open, stop in and buy some shorts, like the ones the Sox wore that time in the 1976 season, along with some vintage Bulls gear. Once inside the park, visit the **statues.**

DURING THE GAME
You need to have a beer or two at **Craft Kave.** Be sure to visit the **Mexican street food vendor** in section 104. Order the *elote,* a grilled corn treat.

AFTER THE GAME
Finish the night nearby at **Turtle's Bar and Grill.** Have a beer and enjoy the tasty offerings. Maybe have Italian beef because it—like the Sox—just doesn't get the love it so richly deserves.

---

pricing model. Ticket prices depend on the day of the game (weekend tilts are usually more expensive), whether big giveaways or special events are attached to the game (fireworks, opening day, a concert), and the opponent taking on the Sox (teams with big followings, like the Yankees and Red Sox, will typically mean more money, as will games against the Cubs, naturally). And the closer you want to be to home plate, the more your ticket will cost.

Seating Plan
Guaranteed Rate Field has a relatively simple seating plan. There are essentially **two levels**—a **lower** and an **upper**—with club boxes in between. The upper level (500 level) is only in foul territory. Section numbers are lowest in right field, growing higher around foul territory to left field.

The **100 level** starts in right center field with **outfield reserved** (sections 100-105). **The Patio,** a specialty group section, takes up the area just in front of these seats between sections 101 and 103. **The Goose Island,** a specialty section with a bar mostly for groups and season ticket holders, is in the right field corner. On the other side of the right-field foul pole, heading toward home plate, are **lower corners** (sections 108-110), **lower box corners** (sections 111-113) in deep foul territory, **lower box** (sections 114-118) in mid and shallow right field, and then **gold box** (sections 119-145), which wraps around the infield. **Diamond box** takes up the first 10 rows around the infield (but not at home plate), while **platinum box** encompasses rows 11-25. At home plate are the premium **Wintrust Scout Seats.**

Heading toward the left-field foul pole, you'll find **lower box** (sections 146-150) in shallow to moderate left field, then **lower box corners** (sections 151-153) in deep foul territory, and **lower corners** (sections 154-156) to the left-field foul pole. In the outfield are **outfield reserved** (sections 157-159) and, in left center field, the **bleachers** (sections 160-164).

The **300 level** is the **club level,** resting below the deck. In right field by the foul pole are the suite-style **Huntington Bank Stadium Club,** then **club box** (sections 311-318), **premium club box** (sections 320-330), the premium **Guaranteed Rate Club** behind home plate, the **premium club box** (sections 334-344), and **club box** (sections 346-357) on the left-field side.

Finally, the **500 level** starts at the right-field foul pole with **upper corners** (sections 506-509), then **upper reserved** (sections 510-520) along the right-field line. **Upper box** (sections 522-542) wraps around the infield, and the first six rows of this section are part of **premium upper box.** The rest of the level is **upper reserved** (sections 544-558).

Where to Buy Tickets

The best bet for Sox tickets is to try third-party sites like **SeatGeek** and Chicago-based **Vivid Seats** (www.vividseats.com). Watch out for companies who can resell on these sites, as they'll tend to have higher **processing fees;** instead, look for individual sellers.

If you buy Sox tickets through the team, you should download the **MLB Ballpark app,** as you may be able to upgrade your seats when you enter the park.

GAME COSTS

Tickets: Not too bad, especially relative to the Cubs. Expect to pay **$40-50** for a seat toward the back of the 100 level; this is better than average compared with other parks. Weekday games against low-draw teams can mean a ticket 50 percent cheaper than one for normal weekend affairs.

Hot dog: Just about average, maybe a touch less, at **$4.50-5.** That's decent.

Beer: Just about average, maybe a touch more. Start at **$7** for the macro brews and go from there. The selection is so good that you might not care too much.

Parking: For the team lots, you'll pay either **$20** or **$25,** depending on when you get your space secured. Is that a couple bucks more expensive than you'd like? There's a convenient train option if you'd like to save some cash.

Best Seats

If you want **shade,** the best place to sit is the back of the **100 level** along the right-field line, so consider the back 10-15 rows of **lower box** (sections 114-118) and the back 10-15 rows of a portion of **gold box** (sections 119-126). The back rows of the right-field line in the **500 level** are under an overhang and can be shaded. Look for seats in the back rows of **upper reserved** (sections 510-520) and **upper box** (sections 522-526).

The **500 level** is a decent **value,** with seats typically costing close to $20 ($30 in upper box), and **good views** abound. For **night games** especially, you can't go wrong in the first couple rows of **upper box** or in the first row or two of **upper reserved.** Just be careful not to get the seat closest to home plate in the first two rows of your section, as the **high fence** may block your view. Note: The Sox try to enforce a rule that if you have

Guaranteed Rate Field

upper-level tickets and there's a big crowd (at least 25,000 people), you should stay in the upper level.

The **bleachers** (sections 160-164) are just that—long rows of hard metal. In the sun, they can get pretty **hot,** but during a night game, they're not too shabby. It's a fun spot for hanging with a **rowdier** contingent of fans. I recommend sitting here if you've been to the park before. If not, get a regular seat in **foul territory** so you can be closer to home plate and get a good view of the outfield.

KNOW BEFORE YOU GO

The White Sox permit **tailgating** in all **team-owned parking lots** around Guaranteed Rate Field. Lot gates open two hours before first pitch; **small grills** are allowed, but kegs are not.

You can bring **outside food** into the park as long as it fits in a clear plastic bag that can be put under your seat. Plastic bottles of **water** under one liter are permitted. Soft-sided bags no larger than 16 by 16 by 8 inches are allowed in, but no soda, alcohol, glass bottles, or cans.

If you've been told you have to **check an item,** head to the trailer at West 35th Street and South Shields Avenue, where you can keep your item safe for the duration of the game; you'll have to pay a fee, however.

Parents or guardians can visit any guest relations booth to get a free **identification bracelet** for their child that includes their seat location.

Nursing mothers can get access to the

ballpark's **nursing room** (section 352) by visiting any guest relations booth.

Here's something new, different, and seasonally cool: The Sox have **rain rooms** (sections 107 and 537). These are sheltered areas with misting devices hanging from the ceiling. If it's too hot outside, get to a rain room and let the water cool you down.

Speaking of getting wet: The Sox kept one of the old Comiskey Park showers and rebranded it the **Plumbers 911.com Shower** (section 161). Just hop into the open-sided stall on a particularly hot day (but don't totally disrobe, please). Some folks go in barefoot, but you might want to have a pair of flip-flops at the ready.

Finally, the Sox have a **shoeshine stand** (section 155). How cool is that?

Accessibility

To purchase tickets for **accessible seats,** call 312/674-5246, or visit the Gate 4 ticket window at the stadium. **Gate 5** is the best entrance for accessibility. **Elevators** are located at Gates 3 and 5.

The White Sox offer **assistive listening devices, large-print** versions of the schedule, **noise-cancelling headphones,** and **interpreter services** at the **guest relations booths** (100 level, club level, 500 level). There's a **quiet space** available at suite 460. **Service animals** are welcome at Guaranteed Rate Field.

The best parking lot for accessibility is **Lot B** (S. Shields Ave. and W. 34th St.), which is close to Gate 5.

BE A FAN

You may not have met a Sox fan in the wild, but that's how they want it. White Sox fans keep things local and close to the vest, living and dying with their club without raising their voices too loud. Chat with a Pale Hose fan and you're bound to be impressed by their institutional knowledge.

The Sox have one of the best **home run celebrations** in baseball. Whenever the home team swats a dinger, the **scoreboard** lights up, the seven **pinwheels** atop it go round (and then spell out H-O-M-E-R-U-N), and **20 fireworks** are shot into the air. It's really fun.

GETTING THERE

Public Transit

Undoubtedly the best way to Guaranteed Rate Field is via the Red Line of the **CTA** (www.transitchicago.com, $0.75-2.50 per ride). Disembark at **Sox-35th station** (W. 35th St. and S. Wentworth St.), which is just a half block east of the ballpark.

From the Loop/Downtown, you can transfer to the Red Line's Lake station from **State/Lake station** (200 N. State St.), which is on the Brown, Orange, Green, and Pink Lines. The transfer is free with a Ventra card; it's about a half-block walk between stations. You can also transfer to Lake station from the Blue Line's **Washington station** (W. Washington St. and N. Dearborn St.).

You can also take the **Rock Island District line** of the commuter rail **Metra** (www.metrarail.com, $4) from the Loop to **35th Street "Lou" Jones/Bronzeville station** (W. 35th St. and S. LaSalle St.), just 1.5 blocks east of the park. You can access Metra Downtown from **LaSalle Street station** (414 S. LaSalle St.).

Driving

If you opt to drive to the park, the most direct way is via **I-94 South,** exiting at **35th Street** (Illinois College of Optometry). You can also drive south on **South State Street** from the Loop to 35th Street.

The easy way to **park** for a game is to enter one of the **team-owned lots** around the stadium. Spots will cost $20 ahead of time and $25 at the gate. The Sox would prefer you pay with a credit or debit card, but if you want to use **cash,** go to **Lot F** (37th St. and Princeton Ave.), **Lot L** (38th St. and Princeton Ave.), or **Lot G** (33rd St. and Normal Ave.).

If you want to pay a little less, scope out the **commercial lots** around the park in the **Armour Square** and **Bridgeport** neighborhoods. Chances are, businesses will be selling game-time parking for closer to $10. For a free spot, you can try parking in the **residential area** around the ballpark, but most streets are **restricted** or **permit-only.**

PARK FEATURES AND SIGHTS

Take the kids to the **Xfinity Kids Zone** (left-field corner, all levels), an expansive area that isn't just a playground with a baseball diamond. You'll find batting cages, practice areas, and the usual playscapes in this totally immersive space that's good for a couple innings of busy time. Athletic shoes are required in the Kids Zone.

Look for a number of **statues** (on either side of Fan Deck in center field) featuring some of the greatest White Sox personalities and players: founding owner Charles Comiskey, Minnie Minoso, Carlton Fisk, Billy Pierce, Harold Baines, Luis Aparicio, Nellie Fox, Frank Thomas, and Paul Konerko.

Champions Monument Plaza

It took the White Sox 88 years to win their third world championship, so they honor it prominently. Outside the park at home plate is **Champions Monument Plaza** (Gate 4), home to a granite-and-bronze monument with two **statues,** plus images from the 2005 world championship season. The monument rests on a diamond of bricks inscribed with personalized messages from fans, and half the perimeter of that diamond is lined with markers dedicated to the team's greatest players. It makes for a fine introduction to the ballpark and Pale Hose history.

Organ

For 41 years, Nancy Faust delighted Sox fans as the team organist. She retired in 2010, leaving behind a wildly influential career. For one, she gave birth to Harry Caray's tradition of singing "Take Me Out to the Ball Game" because the announcer just loved her version of the song. She revived the Steam song "Na Na Hey Hey Kiss Him Goodbye" by playing it in the 1970s, turning it into a stadium staple. The Sox continue the tradition of spotlighting an **organ** (section 132), and these days it's played by Lori Moreland. You'll hear Moreland's magic fingers starting an hour before first pitch and then throughout every game. Of course, when an opposing pitcher is removed after being battered, Moreland will play "Na Na Hey Hey Kiss Him Goodbye."

Blue Seats

Amid the sea of green at Guaranteed Rate Field, you'll find two very **blue seats** (sections 159 and 101). The one in section 159 is the destination of a **Paul Konerko grand slam** in Game 2 of the 2005 World Series, which turned a 4-2 deficit to a 6-4 lead. The one in section 101 marks where **Scott Posednik's ninth-inning home run** landed, to win that same game 7-6.

FOOD AND DRINKS

For some authentic Chicago fare, visit **Beggar's Pizza Pub** (section 163). Beggar's is a South Side pizza chain, so you'll find

Photos (from top to bottom): Southpaw, the White Sox mascot; Goose Island Brewing; White Sox in the dugout.

its deep-dish here, but there are also some sandwiches like Italian beef and meatball on offer, along with the Comiskey burger, a double-patty extravaganza with salty cheddar spread and a relish-dominant version of pico de gallo.

You can find **Garrett Popcorn** and **hot chocolate** (also the chocolaty, frozen concoction known as a **malt cup**) at Guaranteed Rate; just head to section 101. Want hot chocolate with some Jim Beam and Patron? Head to sections 144 and 538 for **boozy hot cocoa.**

My pick for the best food at the park is at section 104: a **Mexican street food stand** selling chicharróns, churros, tamales, and a ballpark favorite: *elote* (corn on the cob topped with cheese and spices).

If you can get to the **club level** (sections 328, 346), get your hands on the **Southside horseshoe:** french fries with Italian sausage, giardiniera peppers (a pickled condiment), and a cheddar sauce made with Modelo beer. That's a heart-hitting Chicago monstrosity—and oh boy, it's good.

Sit down at a counter or table at the **Xfinity Zone** (section 109). Here you can order food like hot dogs, sausages, and popcorn, plus both local and macro-brewed beer, and your order will come to you.

The park's stand-alone restaurant is **Chi-Sox Bar & Grill** (320 W. 35th St., Gate 5, 312/674-5860, 11am-midnight Thurs.-Mon. non-game days, 11am-2am game days, under $40), a packed, boisterous sports bar connected to the ballpark but open to the public. The food is subpar, the service can take too long, but at least you can find some cans and draft pours of Revolution and Bell's, both solid craft breweries. If you're in a big group, come after the game if you want a couple drinks among Sox fans; otherwise, there are better choices for boozing near the park.

Craft Kave (right-field corner underneath The Goose Island, around section 108) is the obvious spot to find a craft beer. This is the best beer bar in baseball. You'll find hundreds of beers from local and regional spots, plus a rotating tap list and multiple coolers filled with harder-to-find fare. In short, anyone who likes trying new beer should visit Craft Kave. To get a full idea of the beers available at Craft Kave, visit the White Sox website for an A-to-Z beer list. It's seriously impressive.

The Sox have a strong relationship with two breweries. The Anheuser-Busch InBev-owned **Goose Island** has a seating area with food and drink service and a bar out in the right-field corner. It's called **The Goose Island** and features a 10-foot-tall goose sculpture. But there's also **Revolution Brewing #SoxSocial Tap Room** (section 159). This bar features beer from the popular **Revolution Brewing,** a Chicago spot, in an indoor-outdoor space with a pinball machine, crane game, and patio hangout.

EVENTS

You can seek **autographs** before the game, but only if your ticket is for the 100 level. Until about 25 minutes before first pitch, fans with 100 level seats can head to the far side of each dugout with pen and hat (or shirt or poster or scorecard). Because the gates open 90 minutes before first pitch, you should be able to catch some of **batting practice,** but most likely the away team.

The White Sox don't operate regular **tours;** if you're interested in getting a behind-the-scenes look at Guaranteed Rate Field, call 312/674-1000, ext. 7182.

SHOPPING

The main team store is the **Chicago Sports Depot** (35th St. near Shields Ave., Gate 5, noon-5pm non-game days, 11am-one hour after final out game days), arguably the best team store in the majors. For one, the two-level emporium has everything you want for the home team, like Sox jerseys, shirts, vintage wear, hats, and novelty items. You'll also get a sense of the team's history through the murals and photos dotting the store, and extras like jersey customization and virtual reality games round out the experience. But it's not just a Sox store: You can find gear from all the other teams in the city, even the Cubs. There's a decent selection of merchandise for Big 10 colleges, too. Since the store is attached to the ballpark, it's only open to ticketed fans when the gates are open.

Other gift shops in the park include the **Home Plate Shop** (section 132), the **Hall of Fame Shop** (section 531), and the **Scoreboard Gift Shop** (lower level, center field). These have a more minimal selection of merchandise.

CHICAGO SIGHTS

WILLIS TOWER

Want to stand (or sit) near the very top of the third-tallest building in the Western Hemisphere? You should visit the **Skydeck at Willis Tower** (233 S. Wacker Dr., www.theskydeck.com, 9am-10pm daily Mar.-Sept., 10am-8pm daily Oct.-Feb., $26, $18 ages 3-11, free ages 2 and under). For 24 years after it was built in 1973, the then-Sears Tower was the tallest in the world. Here on the 103rd floor, you can inch out onto The Ledge, enclosed glass boxes 1,353 feet up that allow you to look down at the city elow. The rest of the Skydeck offers views out of its floor-to-ceiling windows, where you can see four states (Illinois, Michigan, Indiana, and Wisconsin). You'll get a half hour to enjoy yourself up here. Make sure you get your ticket well in advance. If you're uncomfortable with heights, you may want to sit this one out.

ART INSTITUTE OF CHICAGO

You may remember the scene from *Ferris Bueller's Day Off* in which Cameron stared at a painting in the **Art Institute of Chicago** (111 S. Michigan Ave., 312/443-3600, www.artic.edu, 10:30am-8pm Wed.-Fri., 10:30am-5pm Sat.-Tues., $25, $19 seniors, students, and ages 14-17, free ages 13 and under). That work is Georges Seurat's "A Sunday on La Grande Jatte-1884," the iconic pointillist painting that shows Parisians relaxing on a weekend afternoon. You'll obviously want to see that original (preferably while humming the Dream Academy's cover of the Smiths' "Please, Please, Please Let Me Get What I Want"), but there are plenty of other amazing works on display, including world-renowned galleries of impressionist art, a wonderful African art gallery, and some awesome armor from the Renaissance era. The painting "Nighthawks" by Edward Hopper is also here.

SHEDD AQUARIUM

Open since 1930, the **Shedd Aquarium** (1200 S. Lake Shore Dr., www.sheddaquarium.org, 11am-5pm Thurs., 9am-5pm Fri.-Wed., $40, $30 ages 3-11, free ages 2 and under) packs in quite a few animals—more than 30,000 of them, in fact. You'll find the giant Pacific octopus, multiple species of sharks, and beluga whales. The whales hang out in the Abbott Oceanarium, a huge tank where you can have encounters with some of the aquarium's most notable animals. Tip for families with children ages 5-12: The aquarium's **Family First Saturdays** ($50 per person, admission included) occurs the first Saturday of each month, offering hands-on activities and a behind-the-scenes look at the aquarium.

FIELD MUSEUM

Home to the largest fossilized *Tyrannosaurus rex* skeleton ever found, the **Field Museum** (1400 S. Lake Shore Dr., 312/922-9410, www.fieldmuseum.org, 9am-5pm Thurs.-Mon., $26, $23 seniors and students, $19 ages 3-11, free ages 2 and under) is Chicago's museum of natural history. Walking through here is like going through a giant interactive textbook, with exhibits devoted to early Egyptian culture, Africa, the Ancient Americas, birds, the Pacific, and the story of evolution. The museum also hosts regular lectures and has child-friendly exhibits with hands-on play opportunities.

FOOD

NEAR WRIGLEY FIELD

Outside Wrigley in **Gallagher Way,** you'll find a number of restaurants and bars. Chief among them is the **Budweiser Bricktown Tavern** (3647 N. Clark St., 773/377-4770, www.brickhousetavernchi.com, 11am-2am Mon.-Fri., 10am-3am Sat., 10am-2am Sun., under $50). A sports bar with a polished look—marble bar, finished wood ceiling—and an inviting outdoor patio with Wrigleyville views, Bricktown boasts a menu of modern American favorites. Opt for the hot chicken sandwich, fish tacos, or the Chicago dog as you peruse the beer list of mostly Anheuser-Busch InBev brands, though there is a little room for local craft spots on the taps.

Look for the building with the yellow signage. That's **Byron's Hot Dogs** (1017 W. Irving Park Rd., 773/281-7474, www.byronschicago.com, 10:30am-10pm daily, under $20), your place for all kinds of hot dogs and sausage sandwiches, plus big burgers like the Punisher, a double patty topped with gyro meat. Open on the North Side since 1975, Byron's has frequently been named a favorite for their wieners, and folks line up to grab theirs, asking for whatever toppings they desire from the small counter. The traditional Chicago hot dog has yellow mustard, sweet relish, a dill pickle, chopped onions, tomatoes, pickled sport peppers, and celery salt. You don't put ketchup on this one.

For New York-style pizza, there's **Big G's Pizza** (3716 N. Clark St., 773/281-2444, www.big-gspizza.com, 11am-midnight Mon.-Wed., 11am-2am Thurs., 11am-4am Fri., noon-5am Sat., noon-3am Sun., under $30). Open extremely late for your nightlife needs, Big G's offers pizza by the slice and three pie sizes. Since it's right up the block from Wrigley, the menu uses baseball terms: The Grand Slam pies have five toppings, and the toppings are wild (like macaroni and cheese or s'mores).

Southern-style food ... in Chicago?

Yes, and it's good at **The Roost Carolina Kitchen** (1467 W. Irving Park Rd., 312/261-5564, www.theroostcarolinakitchen.com, 11am-9pm Mon.-Sat., 11am-7pm Sun., under $50). Get fried chicken, hot chicken sandwiches, and breakfast items like egg sandwiches and biscuits and gravy. The cozy dining room has some stools and tables, plus a bar area with a subway tile backdrop.

NEAR GUARANTED RATE FIELD

Sometimes the only thing you need is a killer deli sandwich, and that's what you'll find at **Kathy De's Deli** (3642 S. Parnell Ave., 773/373-2688, 7am-4pm Mon.-Fri., 10am-4pm Sat., under $30). Just a half-mile walk southwest of Guaranteed Rate is this little shop known for a bunch of sandwiches—meatball, beef, and double cheeseburgers—plus cold subs, salads, and pasta. There might be a line for lunch, but it's a great stop before a day game.

Or maybe you need a Chicago dog. You can get yours a block or so west of the ballpark at **35th Street Red Hots** (500 W. 35th St., 773/624-9866, 10am-8pm Mon.-Fri., 10am-6pm Sat., under $20). Grab yourself a cheap hot dog and fries, a Polish sausage and fries, or maybe fried shrimp; then settle into the narrow surroundings that have a counter and some barstools (a couple benches are outside, too).

About a half mile west of the ballpark is the very direct **George's Restaurant** (3445 S. Halsted St., 773/247-4770, 9am-9pm Mon.-Fri., 9am-8pm Sat., under $30). A casual spot in a dimly lit, very '90s space, George's serves up an array of classic Greek diner food: gyros, sandwiches, hot dogs, and chili (try the Mother-in-Law, a tamale topped with chili). This stop is good anytime.

OTHER NEIGHBORHOODS

If you need your Chicago dog elsewhere, there's always **Portillo's** (100 W. Ontario St., 312/587-8910, www.portillos.com, 10am-11pm daily, under $20), a popular

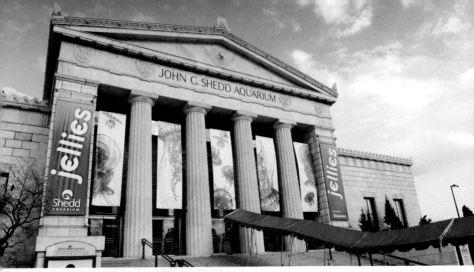

Photos (top): Shedd Aquarium; (middle left) lion outside the Art Institute of Chicago during the 2016 World Series; (middle right) Willis Tower; (bottom) Portillo's.

local chain. You can get hot dogs, beef and sausage, burgers, fries, and more inside what resembles part of a re-created 1940s town. Be sure you look around to catch tableaux of gangsters trying to get away with crimes; nearby are framed Michael Jordan jerseys. Find it a few blocks west of the Magnificent Mile district.

Really good Chicago-style pizza (also known as deep-dish or pan pizza) is, well, really good. **Pequod's Pizza** (2207 N. Clybourn Ave., 773/327-1512, www.pequodspizza.com, 11am-2am Mon.-Sat., 11am-midnight Sun., under $40) in Lincoln Park is a pizza pub, so grab some drinks, chill against the brick wall with TVs showing whatever game is going on, and enjoy the depths of temptation.

Another pizza option that's like deep-dish is stuffed pizza. **Nancy's Pizza** (1000 W. Washington Blvd., 312/733-9920, www.nancyspizza.com, 3pm-11pm Mon.-Thurs., 11:30am-midnight Fri., 3pm-midnight Sat., 3pm-10pm Sun., under $30) in the West Loop area claims to have started the whole thing. Nancy's was started by Rocco and Nancy Palese, Italian immigrants who wanted to try their own take on pan pizza. Enjoy your thick pie in a clean and comfortable dining room with a colorful retro look.

A good distance southwest of the Loop is where you'll find some of Chi-Town's best Italian beef. That's at **Tony's Italian Beef** (7007 S. Pulaski Rd., 773/284-6787, www.tonysbeef.com, 7:30am-10pm Mon.-Fri., 8am-10pm Sat.-Sun., under $40), which since 1975 has been a South Side staple for the city's quintessential sandwich. Italian beef is a hoagie roll filled with shaved beef sirloin, au jus (better known around these parts as gravy), and a combination of hot (giardiniera) and sweet peppers. It's best early in the afternoon or late at night. (Tip: The neighborhood spots always do it better than the tourist traps.) For a great North Side neighborhood spot, try **Roma's Italian Beef & Sausage** (4237 N. Cicero Ave., 773/725-5715, www.romaschicago.com, 10am-10pm daily, under $30). This very chill place has a few barstools against a window, quick service, and juicy beef in big rolls.

Just north of the Loop are the best Buffalo wings I've ever eaten. They're at **Jake Melnick's Corner Tap** (41 E. Superior St., 312/266-0400, www.jakemelnicks.com, noon-9pm Sun.-Thurs., noon-11pm Fri.-Sat., under $40). These are substantial wings with perfect texture, well coated with the hot stuff and served in a basket with the dressing of your choice. Along with a host of wing flavors and styles, there are pizzas, burgers, and fries. This is some of the best pub food in the country. You'll also find a good selection of beer on tap, a sporty vibe, and friendly people.

Need some coffee? I dig **Hero Coffee Bar** (22 E. Jackson Blvd., 312/285-2434, www.herocoffeebars.com, 8am-2pm Tues.-Sat., under $20), a European-looking, brick-walled Loop spot hidden from the bustle of the central business district. There are a couple outdoor tables and chairs and, best of all, some decent bagels.

BARS AND BREWERIES

NEAR WRIGLEY FIELD

Your Wrigley Field experience isn't complete without hopping around the numerous bars that dot the Wrigleyville area surrounding the park. Before, during, and after every game, doors are swung open as fans throw back shots and clutch cans of Old Style. Most of these bars are along **Clark Street,** the diagonal thoroughfare that passes the home plate entrance of the park, but a few more choice bars are in the general vicinity.

There are two insanely popular bars to hit in Wrigleyville. First is **Cubby Bear** (1059 W. Addison St., 773/327-1662, www.cubbybear.com, 11am-2am daily), which faces the home plate entrance and is swamped every game day. Be ready for loud patrons, sticky floors, and potential frustration that your order isn't being heard.

The other biggie is **Murphy's Bleachers** (3655 N. Sheffield Ave., 773/281-5356, www.murphysbleachers.com, 11am-2am Sun.-Fri., 11am-3am Sat.), just beyond center field and arguably the most popular of all Wrigleyville bars. This has been a Chicago institution since Prohibition, when it was a hot dog stand. Cubs players and countless celebrities (Eddie Vedder, for one) have been known to stop in for a drink, and the rooftop is legendary. You can watch a game from up there, but you have to reserve well in advance. Your best bet is to watch the bar's social media feeds around January. If you can't get rooftop spots, at least visit for a drink. This is a bucket-list spot.

For drinks at **Gallagher Way,** I recommend **Lucky Dorr** (1101 W. Waveland Ave., 773/388-8249, www.luckydorr.com, 4pm-11pm Mon.-Thurs., 4pm-midnight Fri.-Sat., 4pm-10pm Sun.). There's plenty of seating, whether you're inside the dining room with its brick walls and subway tiles, or on the outdoor patio. You can munch on a pretzel (the only food offering here) while sipping a Chicago-area craft beer.

A little more polished than the other spots in Wrigleyville, **Stretch Bar & Grill** (3485 N. Clark St., 773/755-3980, www.thestretchchicago.com, 5pm-2am Wed.-Fri., 11am-2am Sat., 11am-midnight Sun.) is best for those who want a craft cocktail with their beer. Across the street, **Merkle's Bar & Grill** (3516 N. Clark St., 773/244-1025, www.merkleschicago.com, 5pm-2am Wed.-Fri., 11am-3am Sat., 11am-2am Sun.) is named for Fred Merkle, the player who committed one of the worst baserunning errors in history back in 1908 against the Cubs, helping push Chicago to the World Series. The place gets nicely packed for games, but there should be room to navigate. I approve of the beer list, and the staff is super helpful.

I'm a big fan of **L&L Tavern** (3207 N. Clark St., 773/528-1303, 5pm-2am Mon.-Thurs., 1pm-2am Fri., 2pm-3am Sat., 3pm-2am Sun.), which is down Clark a bit. Your everyday dive that's been around for decades, L&L has a decent beer list, but you're here to have some cheap drinks and laugh with a bartender. According to legend, some famous serial killers have stopped by L&L for drinks; whether or not those stories are true, plenty of interesting people have come in through the doors under the Budweiser sign.

Just a block or so north of the park is **GMan Tavern** (3740 N. Clark St.,

Murphy's Bleachers

773/549-2050, www.gmantavern.com, 3pm-2am Mon.-Fri., noon-3am Sat.-Sun.). Short for Gingerman, GMan is open late, attracts a good crowd, and has pool tables (it was turned into a pool hall for scenes of the 1987 movie *The Color of Money*). It also keeps a good selection of both cheap and more adventurous beers, and has regular live music. One caveat: It's cash only.

A few blocks west of the hubbub is the closest true brewery to Wrigley. **Corridor Brewery & Provisions** (3446 N. Southport Ave., 773/270-4272, www.corridorchicago. com, 11am-9pm Mon.-Thurs., 11am-10pm Fri.-Sat., 11am-8pm Sun.) is a modern hipster restaurant and taproom that has plenty of brewing tanks, industrial lighting, and rough wood booths. The beer, mostly hazy ales, is pretty good, and the food, Neapolitan pizzas and pub grub, is also solid.

NEAR GUARANTEED RATE FIELD

Your pre- or post-Sox haunt might just be **Ballpark Pub** (514 W. Pershing Rd., 773/675-4687, www.theballparkpub.com, 11am-midnight daily). The batter's box at the entrance might be a tip-off that this is a baseball bar. Beyond that, there are Sox logos, old Sox photos, and a general white, gray, and black aesthetic. Beer ranges from the obvious to the slightly adventurous, and there are decent burgers and barbecue.

The classic **Turtle's Bar and Grill** (238 W. 33rd St., 312/225-7333, 11am-2am Sun.-Fri., 11am-3am Sat.) is small but packs a punch with a solid beer list, friendly staff, and a killer food menu. Look for the Italian burger, topped with prosciutto, provolone, and marinara, and the Italian beef. The garlic parmesan fries are also well worth your order.

OTHER NEIGHBORHOODS

A solid taproom not too far from Wrigley is **Dovetail Brewery** (1800 W. Belle Plaine Ave., 773/683-1414, www.dovetailbrewery.com, 4pm-10pm Mon., noon-10pm Tues.-Wed., noon-11pm Thurs., noon-midnight Fri., 11am-midnight Sat., 11am-8pm Sun.). Instead of chasing fads and trends, Dovetail brews quality tried-and-true styles in more of a European tradition. They have snacks like pretzels and cheese boards that you can enjoy in a clean and simple taproom. I highly recommend this place, which is about a dozen blocks west of Graceland Cemetery.

Arguably the big beer name in town is **Half Acre Beer Company** (4257 N. Lincoln Ave., 773/248-4038, www.halfacrebeer. com, 3pm-9pm Mon.-Wed., noon-9pm Thurs.-Sun.). The taproom is tiny, though there's ample seating, lots of exposed timber, and loads of natural light. There are tours, as well. Beer runs the gamut from traditional to very wild, and the food menu is full of snacks. Find it north of Irving Park Road, a few blocks northwest of Dovetail Brewery.

I have to recommend **Map Room** (1949 N. Hoyne Ave., 773/252-7636, www. maproom.com, 6:30am-2am Mon.-Fri., 7:30am-3am Sat., 11am-2am Sun.) in Bucktown for a few reasons. One, the beer selection includes beers both from across the world and from the Windy City. Two, it's a cool place with flags hanging from the tin ceiling and a generally casual vibe (there are pastries and coffee in the morning). Three, the bar sports a travelers' theme and has more than 200 travel guides for patrons to peruse.

Not quite within walking distance of Guaranteed Rate Field, as it's on the other side of Bridgeport, **Maria's Packaged Goods and Community Bar** (960 W. 31st St., 773/890-0588, www.community-bar. com, noon-9pm daily) is made for sitting back and chilling out. An effortless neighborhood bar, it's where you can order up a Chicago Handshake (a shot of bitter Jeppson's Malört with a can of Old Style). But it's also where you can drink a heck of a craft beer, get a good cocktail, and satisfy your hunger at Kimski, the attached eatery serving Korean and Polish fusion.

PERFORMING ARTS

Chicago boasts one of the best theater scenes in the world. The city is home to about 200 theater companies that perform in everything from black-box spaces to big houses, the most iconic of which is the **Chicago Theatre** (175 N. State St., www.msg.com/the-chicago-theatre). Known for its stunning marquee, the theater hosts regular shows—everything from touring productions to comedy sets to national music acts.

Other important venues include the **Auditorium Theatre** (50 Ida B. Wells Dr., www.auditoriumtheatre.org), an 1889 structure that hosts more than 200 events per year, and the **James M. Nederlander Theatre** (23 W. Randolph St., www.broadwayinchicago.com). The Nederlander opened in 1926 but closed in 1981 to make way for a shopping mall. It was preserved, however, and these days it presents multiple touring shows per year. The majestic gold and deep red **CIBC Theatre** (18 W. Monroe St., www.broadwayinchicago.com) has been around since 1906 and was a major spot for vaudeville in its first few decades. From 2016 to early 2020, it was where Chicagoans could see *Hamilton*.

RECREATION

PARKS

Grant Park

A nearly 313-acre green gate to Chicago, **Grant Park** (E. Balbo Dr. at S. Columbus Dr., 6am-11pm daily) is in front of the heart of the Loop, extending to the shores of Lake Michigan. First named Lake Park, then renamed in 1901 to honor President Ulysses S. Grant, the park hosts concerts and live events, is home to gardens and

Photos (from top to bottom): Chicago Theatre; *Cloud Gate* by sculptor Anish Kapoor; kayakers on the Chicago River.

tourist attractions, and has a few ballfields, as well.

You may want to see **Buckingham Fountain** (301 S. Columbus Dr., operating May-Oct.), referred to as the park's centerpiece and dedicated in 1927. The fountain looks a bit like a wedding cake with water squirting from it in all directions. Come for the hourly **water display** (9am-dusk daily) during the day, or visit around sunset when the water display adds lights and music (10:30pm nightly).

For nearly 150 years, the northwestern end of the park was a yard owned by the Illinois Central Railroad, but in 2004 it was unveiled as **Millennium Park** (201 E. Randolph St.), designed by renowned architect Frank Gehry. Walk through the **Lurie Garden** (www.luriegarden.org), home to lilies, peonies, goldenrods, and cranesbills. Head to the **Jay Pritzker Pavilion,** where folks watch live music performances under a network of metal tubes. Be sure to take photos with *Cloud Gate* (N. Michigan Ave. near W. Washington St.), the highly polished, bean-shaped, stainless-steel sculpture created by Sir Anish Kapoor. It offers clear-as-day reflections of the surroundings.

Lincoln Park

The largest park in Chicago, up in the Lincoln Park neighborhood about 1.5 miles south of Wrigley Field, is also called **Lincoln Park** (2045 N. Lincoln Park W., 6am-11pm daily). A narrow strip of parkland along Lake Michigan, Lincoln Park is the site of the **Lincoln Park Zoo** (2001 N. Clark St., 312/742-2000, www.lpzoo.org, 7am-6pm Mon.-Fri., 7am-7pm Sat.-Sun., free), where guests can see all kinds of animals—giraffes, bears, elephants, rattlesnakes, rhinoceroses, seals, and lots of birds, including flamingos—for free. Lincoln Park also has walking trails through gardens; a pond and nature sanctuary; playgrounds; and the **North Avenue Beach** (1601 N. Lake Shore Dr.). Swimming is only permitted here when lifeguards are on duty (11am-7pm daily summer). There is access to Lake Michigan for kayakers and canoeists; head to the southern end of the beach. Chicagoans pack the beach on weekends in summer.

Lakefront Trail

The **Lakefront Trail** (Lake Shore Dr., www.chicagoparkdistrict.com) is an 18-mile route that's perfect for a morning run, a walk with the kids, or an opportunity to stretch your legs and see the Chicago skyline. There are separate paths for pedestrians and bicyclists, which helps limit potential accidents. The trail stretches north to south from Ardmore Avenue to 71st Street. Some of the main access points include North Avenue, East Randolph Street, and 31st Street.

WATER SPORTS

You can head out onto Lake Michigan or the Chicago River via **Kayak Chicago** (312/852-9258, www.kayakchicago.com, $30 per hour, $120 per day). The outfitter rents single and double kayaks and stand-up paddleboards from several locations, including **North Avenue Beach** (1603 N. Lake Shore Dr., 10am-7pm daily) and the **Chicago River** (1220 W. Le Moyne St., 10am-7pm daily). Children younger than 12 must be accompanied by an adult.

SHOPPING

You can get licensed baseball and city-specific gear at **Clark Street Sports** (3465 N. Clark St., 773/661-0703, www.clarkstreetsports.com, 10am-6pm Tues.-Sat., 10am-4pm Sun.). The store has a decent selection of Cubs and White Sox gear, though the former outmatches the latter, considering the store is in Wrigleyville.

Down on the South Side, check out **Grandstand Ltd.** (600 W. 35th St., 773/927-1984, 10am-7pm Mon.-Fri., 10am-6pm Sat., 10am-5pm Sun.) for an overwhelming selection of White Sox gear. You'll find jerseys from all eras (including the early 20th century), plus some Cubs merchandise and even Blackhawks, Bears, and Bulls items.

ACCOMMODATIONS

NEAR WRIGLEY FIELD

To stay a stone's throw from Wrigley Field, book at room at **The Inn at Wrigleyville** (3617-3619 N. Sheffield Ave., 312/239-6079, www.wrigleyfieldinn.com, $500-1,000), which is across the street from the left-field bleachers. Some rooms, like the four-bedroom Legends Suite, have views of the park, but mostly of seats along the third-base line. The inn's six suites are outfitted like gussied-up apartments—dark furniture contrasts against light gray walls and hardwood floors. The inn doesn't provide parking, so you'll have to find a spot on the street like everyone else.

NEAR GUARANTEED RATE FIELD

If you want to stay less than a mile from Guaranteed Rate Field, consider the **Amber Inn** (3901 S. Michigan Ave., 773/285-1000, www.theamberinn.com, $80-200). While it's a very basic motor inn with standard rooms, it's inexpensive, close to the ballpark, and not lacking for good service.

OTHER NEIGHBORHOODS

Stay in the Loop at the **Buckingham Hotel** (425 S. Financial Pl., 312/663-8910, www.thebuckinghamclub.com, $150-400), just a few blocks west of Grant Park and close to the CTA Blue Line. All the rooms are queens and kings, and there's a hotel bar and on-site tavern.

GETTING AROUND

PUBLIC TRANSIT

Chicago has one of America's most extensive public transit systems in the **CTA** (www.transitchicago.com, $0.75-2.50 per ride). The quickest method of getting around is the **"L"** (short for elevated train), a system of eight color-coded lines that spread out around the city. In the late-19th century, the various rapid transit lines were serviced by different operators, and a rail financier was able to build an elevated track that looped around the central business district and connected all the routes. The track was coined "the Loop," and in time the Downtown area was also given that moniker.

Today, five lines run around the Loop, while two more rapid transit lines thread into the area. You'll occasionally have to transfer to a different line by leaving a station and heading to another.

The **Green Line** starts near Oak Park to the west, goes around the Loop, and then heads into the South Side. The **Pink Line** also starts west of the Loop, but farther south, near Cicero, before it meets up with the Green Line at Ashland Avenue and ends in the Loop. The **Orange Line** starts at Midway International Airport and ends in the Loop. The **Purple Line** begins way up north near Evanston before running alongside the Red Line en route to the Loop, where it ends. The **Brown Line** starts on the North Side near North Park University, passing Montrose Avenue and Irving Park Road before joining the Red and Purple Lines and going through the Loop.

The **Blue Line** launches at O'Hare International Airport and comes into the Loop from the northwest, then leaves shortly after, cutting through the Theatre District and Federal Center before turning sharply west, ending out in Forest Park. The **Red Line** is the major north-south line, starting at Howard station at the edge of the city and running down into the Loop, then quickly out and toward the South Side. The Red Line is the major route for both Wrigley Field and Guaranteed Rate Field. Finally, the **Yellow Line** is a small suburban line that extends off the Red and Purple Lines from Howard station.

Major stations for the L in the Loop include **Clark/Lake station** (100/124 W. Lake St.), which offers a Loop connection to

SIDE TRIP: LITTLE CUBS FIELD

Little Cubs Field

In case you need a tiny reminder of why Wrigley Field is so great, get to **Little Cubs Field** (1160 W. Empire St., Freeport, 800/369-2955, www.littlecubsfield.com, sunrise-sunset daily). This pseudo field of dreams has brick walls covered in ivy like Wrigley, plus an exterior marquee and bleachers in left field. Its scoreboard is also a replica of the one at Wrigley. Make a visit here if you didn't get enough of Wrigley during the game. You can take photos of all the cool details, watch a Little League game (6pm most weeknights late-Apr.-early July, free), or even reserve time on the field ($45, two hours maximum) to play a ball game of your own.

GETTING THERE
Little Cubs Field is in Freeport, west of Chicago. The drive to Freeport from Downtown Chicago is about **120 miles** and takes around **two hours.** The most direct route takes you west on I-90 and US-20.

the Blue Line, and **State/Lake station** (200 N. State St.), from where you can transfer to the Red Line after a short walk.

You'll want to invest in a **Ventra card** ($5) upon arriving in Chicago. This card is the easy way to use rapid transit; just touch it to the reader when entering a station or bus and refill it at a vending machine at any station.

CTA also has a sophisticated **bus network.** Many bus routes cut through and around the Loop. Consult the CTA website for the bus you want.

TAXI, UBER, AND LYFT

In 2020, Chicago levied a tax increase on ride-share services like Lyft and Uber to battle traffic congestion in the busiest parts of town. Consequently, if you're traveling in the Loop, the Near North Side, Near South Side, or Near West Side, your ride will be a little pricier than you might otherwise expect. It's even more expensive if you travel to or from the central business district via ride-share on a weekday.

The tax increase means that getting around in a taxi may be cheaper than a ride-share trip by a couple bucks. You might want to check out **Yellow Cab** (312/829-4222) or simply hail a taxi on the street. To do so, stand safely on the sidewalk and raise your arm when you see a cab approaching that has its top light on, indicating the driver is looking for fares.

CAR

Chicago has the **grid** pattern of New York, but it's nowhere near as chaotic, so you can certainly drive in the Windy City. But with the city's good public transit and affordable taxis, it's not my preferred method of transportation. If you do drive, there will be traffic, especially if you travel during rush hours (8am-9:30am, 5pm-6:30pm Mon.-Fri.).

I-90 is the major highway going through the city, entering from the south as the **toll Chicago Skyway** before meeting with **I-94.** It then parallels the Loop's western boundary before continuing northwest to O'Hare International Airport. Here, I-90 once again becomes a toll road; it continues to Rockford, Illinois, and Madison, Wisconsin. The west-east I-94 snakes around Lake Michigan's southern border before joining with I-90 through the city as the **Kennedy Expressway.** I-94 then breaks off near Irving Park and continues north as the **Edens Expressway,** heading to Milwaukee.

I-55 comes in from the southwest and cuts through Chinatown en route to **US-41** at Lake Michigan. **I-290** spurs off I-90 northwest of the city, then crawls into the city from the west, meeting up with I-90 and I-94 and fizzling out as it crosses the South Branch of the Chicago River and enters the Loop. **Lake Shore Drive** is **US-41,** riding right along Lake Michigan and offering a picturesque introduction to Chicago (from the south, get off I-90 at S. Ewing Ave. and travel north on that road to US-41).

The highways are good for getting in and out of the Chicago area; otherwise, stick to the city roads. In the Loop, major thoroughfares include the north-south **Michigan Avenue, State Street,** and **Clark Street,** and the west-east **Madison Street, Monroe Street,** and **Adams Street.** South of the Loop, west-east streets may be numbered, going from low to high as you head south, into the 200s.

A section of Michigan Avenue from the Chicago River north to Oak Street is an upscale shopping district known as the **Magnificent Mile. Madison Street** is the dividing line between north and south, and **State Street** is the dividing line between west and east. Heading into the North Side, **Clark Street** and **Lincoln Avenue** are important diagonals (Clark runs right against Wrigley Field).

MILWAUKEE
BREWERS

Some cities are major metropolises, bustling and noisy. Some cities are devoid of character and a challenge to define. But Milwaukee is neither: It's a smaller city (though a half-million people is nothing to sneeze at) teeming with personality. And what does that personality consist of? Beer, bratwurst, and Brewers baseball.

Resting on the western shore of Lake Michigan, Wisconsin's largest city took its name from the Algonquian word meaning "the good land." It was later called home by French Canadians, Germans, Poles, and other European immigrants. Starting in the mid-19th century, the contributions of these immigrants have helped define the city to this day. Prime among those contributions: beer. Milwaukee is home to the Milwaukee Brewery (the oldest functioning brewery in America), the Miller

Brewing Company, and Leinenkugel. It's also where Pabst, Schlitz, and Blatz began. These days, along with Miller's presence, the city has more than a few craft breweries, German food and beer halls, and scores of bars—large and small—that are well worth your time.

Milwaukee has always had some baseball. From 1902 to 1952, the Brewers of the American Association (a minor league team) played in town. Other teams included a Negro Leagues club (the Milwaukee Bears) and a squad in the All-American Girls Professional Baseball League (the Milwaukee Chicks). In 1953, the city went big league when the Boston Braves moved to the new Milwaukee County Stadium. For 13 treasured seasons, the Braves thrilled the city, winning the World Series in 1957 behind stars Hank Aaron, Eddie Mathews, and Warren Spahn. In 1966, they left for Atlanta, but a few years later, Allan "Bud" Selig bought the Seattle Pilots and moved them to Milwaukee. Since starting play in 1970, the Brewers have been the city's beloved team of almost-haves. Although the Brewers have never won a World Series, they've put some real talent on display, from Robin Yount, Paul Molitor, and Cecil Cooper of the Harvey's Wall-bangers days of the early 1980s (named after former manager Harvey Kuenn) to the stars of a quite-recent run of good play: Lorenzo Cain, Christian Yelich, and Ryan Braun.

Milwaukee is a tidy city with a big heart for its ball club. Fans are known to tailgate early for games, then take it to the bars around the ballpark after the final out. Copious beers are imbibed, plenty of smoked meat is consumed, and good times are almost always had, regardless of the final score. This is a true blue (and yellow) baseball town.

PLANNING YOUR TIME

Milwaukee is small enough to visit in one **weekend,** as long as you devote two full days to the city. The first day should include the ball game, as you'll undoubtedly want to soak in the fun of the tailgating scene. Give yourself a full second day to recover while checking out some history and art. Visiting Milwaukee over **4-5 days** in the middle of summer is ideal, as you'll have plenty of time to bounce around the bars, take in a show or two (maybe during Summerfest; just be sure to get tickets when they go on sale around March or April), and enjoy the city's parks and museums.

When staying in Milwaukee, basing yourself in **East Town,** the heart of the city, is a good way to go, as there are plenty of hotels and easy access to highways and public transit.

In the **spring,** high temperatures will typically top off at 65°F and low temps can get into the 30s, so you'll want to bring not only a **jacket** but a **heavier coat,** plus other warm clothing. **Summer** means upper temps in the high 70s and low 80s. This time of year is really wonderful and not very rainy. As the calendar hits **September,** the mercury starts to fall below 70°F again. Generally, you won't have to worry about weather conditions at American Family Field since it has a **retractable roof.** When it's **cold** (and it will be **early in the season**), the roof will be closed; if the weather is nice (and it typically is in the summer), you'll get the sky.

GETTING THERE

AIR

Fly into Milwaukee via **General Mitchell International Airport** (MKE, 5300 S. Howell Ave., www.mitchellairport.com), which is served by **Air Canada** (888/247-2262, www.aircanada.com), **American Airlines** (800/433-7300, www.aa.com), **Allegiant** (702/505-8888, www.allegiantair.com), **Delta** (800/221-1212, www.delta.com), **Frontier** (800/401-9000, www.flyfrontier.com), **Southwest** (800/435-9792, www.southwest.com), and **United** (800/864-8331, www.united.com). You can fly nonstop to

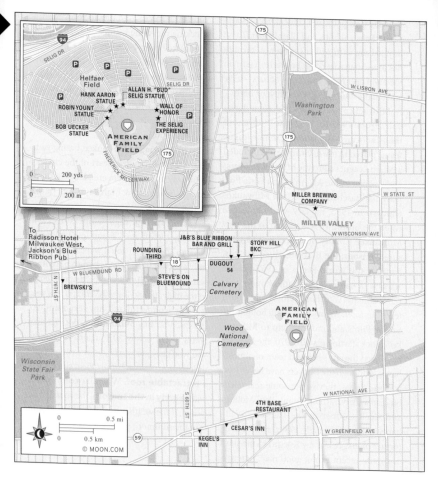

and from Chicago, Detroit, New York, Philadelphia, Boston, Washington DC, Los Angeles, San Francisco, Seattle, Dallas, Houston, Miami, Tampa, and Atlanta, among other locations.

Airport Transportation

The airport's **rental cars** are accessible from the baggage claim area. To reach Downtown from the airport, it's a 15-minute drive of about 10 miles on I-94 West and I-794 East. To get to American Family Field, the drive is about the same duration and distance via I-94.

You can take a **bus** from the airport to Downtown through **Milwaukee County Transit** (www.ridemcts.com, $2.25). The

Green Line and **80** are the two routes that connect Downtown to the airport.

CAR

It's a straight shot up **I-90 West** to **I-94 West** from **Chicago** to Milwaukee. The **95-mile** drive takes about **1.5 hours** without traffic, but be ready for some slowdowns during rush hours.

TRAIN

Milwaukee Intermodal Station (433 W. St. Paul Ave.) is the rail hub in town, located near the hotels of West Town but just a mile west of East Town landmarks, hotels,

and restaurants, and about three miles east of American Family Field. The station is served by **Amtrak** (www.amtrak.com) via the **Hiawatha** (Chicago to Milwaukee) and the **Empire Builder** (Chicago to Portland and Seattle). There are 14 trains daily between the cities (12 on Sundays). The trip is just 90 minutes and starts at only $25, an honest-to-goodness steal. The Hiawatha stops at the airport en route to Milwaukee Intermodal Station.

BUS

You can take a bus via **Greyhound** (www.greyhound.com) from Chicago to Milwaukee. Greyhound's hub is also the **Milwaukee Intermodal Station** (433 W. St. Paul Ave.). Multiple buses from Chicago are offered per day, with prices starting at $15. The ride to Milwaukee from Chicago takes about two hours.

American Family Field

From its opening in 2001 to 2020, the Brewers' stadium was called Miller Park, synonymous with the city's beer-drinking culture and brewing muscle. These days, it's **American Family Field** (1 Brewers Way, www.

American Family Field

mlb.com/brewers), as the Madison-based American Family Insurance company took on naming rights starting in 2021, but nothing has really changed about the ballpark. Sitting about two miles west of Downtown Milwaukee, surrounded by parking lots aplenty, American Family Field looks like an enormous brick warehouse that sprouted a spaceship. With a retractable roof (good for those cold and rainy Wisconsin springs), the ballpark is efficient, clean, and spacious.

To the purist, though, the stadium isn't very pleasing to the eye, and it's a far cry from the city's former ballpark, the ramshackle and character-driven Milwaukee County Stadium. Indoors, especially when the roof is over the field, the park can look and sound as cold as an airport hangar. Plus, the huge signs that serve as an outfield backdrop aren't the prettiest things in the world (though the bright yellow slide in left field is a cute curveball).

That said, when the Brewers are hot, this place rocks hard. There are a lot of group seating areas, party spots, and good standing-room areas, and tickets are among the most affordable in baseball. In addition, the Brewers never seem to take themselves too seriously, from the great sausage race to the ever-present influence of native son and broadcaster Bob Uecker. If Yankee Stadium is a buttoned-up, serious politico, American Family Field is the scrappy little cousin who's just trying to have a good time.

ORIENTATION

Miller Park is located west of Downtown Milwaukee beside I-94. North of the park,

along US-18 (Bluemound Rd.), and south of the park, along WI-15 (National Ave.), you'll find all the bars that fans visit before and after the game.

There are five entry gates at American Family Field, including the **Clock Tower entrance.** This is a brick structure with a traditional analog clock.

TICKETS AND SEATING

Pricing

The Brewers use **dynamic pricing** for their tickets. Cubs games are always high priced because it's a short drive north for opposing fans, with costs generally increasing by 5-10 percent. (Yankees and Red Sox games also tend to be higher priced, due to their popularity.) For a less notable opponent, terrace seats range $10-30, while the loge runs $15-55. Field seats range $15-125.

On Mondays, terrace reserved seats are just $6, and on Fridays, guests in the Miller Lite Beerpen get a free T-shirt. In addition, high school and college students can get discounted tickets on Fridays for the terrace reserved or loge sections.

Seating Plan

The **field level (100 level)** wraps around the foul area from right field to left field, starting with **outfield box** (sections 106-109). **Infield box** (sections 110-125) stretches from mid right field, behind home plate, and over to mid left field. Continuing to left field is **outfield box** (sections 126-131). There are field-level **bleachers** (sections 101-104) that start close to center field and end at far right

YOUR BEST DAY AT AMERICAN FAMILY FIELD

Let's say you're heading to American Family Field for a night game. Here's how to party like a Milwaukeean.

8 HOURS BEFORE FIRST PITCH
Start your day with some art. Visit the awesome **Milwaukee Art Museum** and be sure to check out the Burke Brise Soleil. Plan to spend several hours here to soak it all in.

4 HOURS BEFORE FIRST PITCH
Ride-share it to **J&B's Blue Ribbon Bar and Grill.** You'll need a little food, so split an order of garbage fries with a friend. After an hour, hop on the bar's **shuttle** and head for the stadium.

3 HOURS BEFORE FIRST PITCH
The parking lots of **American Family Field** open three hours before the game for **tailgating.** If you haven't already been invited to a local's tailgate, bring some money and see if you can play the "I'm here for the first time" card with some die-hard Brewers fans. Chances are they'll be glad to offer you a brat and a beer (or three).

1 HOUR BEFORE FIRST PITCH
Outside the stadium, take in the **Brewers**

Milwaukee Art Museum

Walk of Fame. Once you're inside, visit the **Bob Uecker seat** at section 422.

DURING THE GAME
Make a beeline to **Local Brews** for some Third Space beer. Then walk over to section 210 for **bratchos.** Be sure to visit the **Brewers Team Store on the Field Level** mid-game.

AFTER THE GAME
Take the shuttle back to J&B's Blue Ribbon Bar and Grill, then take a self-guided pub crawl of the neighborhood. I suggest **Steve's on Bluemound.**

field. The all-inclusive **Aurora Health Care Bullpen** is a galley up against the right-field fence that's reserved for groups. The dining area called **Restaurant To Be Named Later** is in left field.

Unlike most ballparks, the **loge level (200 level)** is its own stand-alone space with a separate concourse. **Outfield box** (sections 206-209) starts in far right field, followed by **infield box** (sections 210-227), which stretches from mid right field around to mid left field. Next is **outfield box** (sections 228-232), this time on the left-field side. There are **bleachers** (sections 201-205, 233-236) on either end of this level. The **Associated Bank Check Deck** (left center field) is reserved for groups of 42.

The **club level (300 level)** is accessible only to fans with designated tickets. There are **suites** and **private clubs** here, plus four sections in right field called the **Johnsonville Party Deck** (302-305) that are designated for group seating. The **Johnson Controls Stadium Club** (left-field line) is an eatery with a bar that requires a special pass; it's a ticketed section. The **Northwestern Mutual Legends Club** (left-field line) is a large **group suite** with party space and a separate bar. The Legends Club is all-inclusive; your ticket comes with food and beverages.

The vast **terrace level (400 level)** stretches from the right-field foul pole to just beyond the pole in left field. Most of this is **terrace reserved** (404-440), though the first 3-7 rows are **boxes,** depending on the section. The farthest two sections in left field are in **Bernie's Terrace** (sections 441-442), which is where mascot Bernie Brewer lives. The terrace level has its own concourse.

Alcohol is not permitted in the **family sections** (sections 217, 238, 417).

Where to Buy Tickets

You'd be wise to wait until late to buy those Brewers tickets because a third-party vendor like **SeatGeek** or **StubHub** will generally have inexpensive seats, especially if you don't mind sitting up high. If you want a better seat after you've gotten into the park, download the **MLB Ballpark app,** which offers seat upgrades from time to time.

Best Seats

The **first-base line** is the best spot for your baseball-viewing needs. You'll get **shade** if the sun is overhead, and you'll have a pretty keen view of the sausage race as it hits the home stretch. Try **section 109** for inexpensive field seats along the shallow part of the right-field line. **Sections 208-209** are also solid, as are the **boxes** between **sections 409** and **416.** For an inexpensive seat with a fun group of fans, go for the **field bleachers,** primarily **sections 103** and **104.** If you crave a seat by home plate, look at **section 218** or **219.** These tickets run around $40-50 apiece, but you'll be rewarded with an awesome view.

One thing to keep in mind is the **sun** during day games and the early innings of summer night games; to best avoid the sun's rays, sit along the first-base line, which is in the shadow of the roof's start position. The sun will beat down on the third-base line and will be in the view of folks sitting in left field during sunset. If the sun is out, be prepared for **shadows** on the field, simply because of the roof's construction and foul-line glass windows.

KNOW BEFORE YOU GO

The Brewers permit small **bags, purses,** or **fanny packs** (measuring 16 by 16 by 8

GAME COSTS

Tickets: You can get good terrace seats for **$30** for nonessential opponents, or you can pay closer to **$55** for a lower-level seat. When the Cubs are in town (and maybe the Yankees or Red Sox), prices will increase to about **$40** for the best terrace seats.

Hot dog: A regular dog starts at about **$5.50,** with premium dogs and brats going for a couple bucks more.

Beer: Beer is pricier here than you might expect. It's about **$7** for Miller products, **$10** for local labels, and more like **$12** for the expensive craft stuff.

Parking: Not too bad, starting at about **$15** for general lots if you pay when you get there. It's a little cheaper if you pay ahead. The most expensive spots are about **$30.**

inches or smaller), plus soft-sided **cooler bags** and personal servings of food and beverages that are sealed in containers and original bottles. No outside alcohol is allowed inside the stadium. Glass containers, noisemakers, pepper spray, and pets are also prohibited. In midsummer, bring some **sunscreen,** and in April and May, bring a **sweatshirt** or **jacket.**

American Family Field's parking lots open three hours before the game for **tailgating.** You can tailgate at any fan lot, but you must keep it to one vehicle per space. **Grills** with gas or propane tanks, and self-contained charcoal grills are allowed at your tailgate, but open fires are not permitted. Charcoal must be dumped in coal bins provided at each lot. Tailgates must be finished 30 minutes after first pitch.

Accessibility

Accessible seating is available throughout the park. At the entry gate, you can ask for **wheelchair assistance** to your seat. For

BE A FAN

The biggest thing to know about Brewers fans is that they love to party. Tailgating is a popular pregame activity in the lots at American Family Field.

The other big thing to know: Don't be a Cubs fan. Okay, just kidding. While there's rarely any heated behavior between Brewers and Cubs fans, a lot of Cubs fans invade the ballpark when their team visits Milwaukee, since Chicago is a quick drive away. Brewers fans don't especially love this phenomenon. If you're a Cubs fan, be nice and try to have fun with the home fans.

Brewers fans

Get ready for **"The Beer Barrel Polka,"** written by Czech musician Jaromir Vejvoda in 1927 and popularized during World War II, when Allied soldiers celebrated victories by singing the song. The Brewers play it after "Take Me Out to the Ballgame" during the seventh inning stretch. More than a few fans sing along, and some may even dance to it (by essentially hopping about).

more assistance, call the Brewers **ticket office** (414/902-4000) or **guest relations** (414/902-4900) ahead of your game. Once you're at the stadium, you can contact guest relations in person at sections 116, 221, and 419. At the section 116 location, you can get **assistive listening devices.**

Elevators are located in the left field corner and at the clock tower. **Wheelchair lifts** are at sections 221 and 236, and also at the Associated Bank Check Deck, Johnson Controls Stadium Club, Leinie Lodge, and Northwestern Mutual Legends Club. **Service animals** are welcome at American Family Field.

There is **accessible parking** at most lots close to the ballpark, including Brewers 2, Thomas, Aaron, and Miller. A regular parking pass and valid disabled parking placard must be visible in your car.

GETTING THERE

Public Transit

You could take a bus to the game via **Milwaukee County Transit** (www.ridemcts.com, $2.25), which operates a **Brewers Line** starting two hours before first pitch. Service ends a half hour after the final out. The bus stops a few times in the Water Street restaurant district before progressing along

Wisconsin Avenue west, through Marquette University, until it reaches the park.

Another option is to take the **Blue Line,** which you can access at Wisconsin and North 2nd Street. This bus stops at the Milwaukee VA Medical Center, necessitating a 0.7-mile walk north to the park. It's not the most efficient option.

Driving

Driving to the park isn't a terrible option, considering parking is less expensive here than at most stadiums. To get to the park from Downtown, take I-94 West for about **three miles.** Take the Mitchell Boulevard/VA Medical Center exit, turn left, then follow the road to the stadium parking lots.

The **general parking lots** ($12-13 in advance, $15-20 day-of) are **Molitor, Uecker,** and **Yount.** These aren't too far from the ballpark. The **preferred parking lots** ($17-19 in advance, $25-30 day-of) are **Braves, Brewers, Cooper, Fingers, Kuenn, Mathews, Miller,** and **Money.** These are just a hop, skip, and a jump from the park. Your best bet is to get **advance passes** when buying your game ticket. The Miller lot is right off I-94, which heads east to Downtown, so you won't get lost arriving or departing (but you will be in traffic).

The pro move is to grab a beer before the game at a nearby bar that runs **shuttles** to and from American Family Field. Some of the bars that offer game-day shuttles include **Brewski's** (304 N. 76th St., 414/475-0500), **City Lights Brewing Co.** (2200 W. Mount Vernon Ave., 414/436-1011), **Dugout 54** (5328 W. Bluemound Rd., 414/259-1200), **J&B's Blue Ribbon Bar and Grill** (5230 W. Bluemound Rd., 414/443-1844), **Jackson's Blue Ribbon Pub** (11302 W. Bluemound Rd., 414/988-4485), **Rounding Third** (6317 W. Bluemound Rd., 414/475-1982), **Steve's on Bluemound** (5841 W. Bluemound Rd., 414/527-3210), and **Who's on Third** (1007 N. Old World 3rd St., 414/897-8373).

If you're taking a ride-share to the ballpark, you'll be dropped off at the designated **pickup and drop-off zone** next to the **Gantner Lot.** From there, you can take the pedestrian pathway and bridge to enter the park.

PARK FEATURES AND SIGHTS

When the Brewers hit a home run, look at the big **yellow slide** in left field. Above it, note the **"Get Up, Get Up, Get Outta Here, Gone!"** signs. That's Bob Uecker's home run catchphrase, which lights up once the ball leaves the yard. Below the signs and atop the slide is the treehouse called **Bernie's Dugout.** Mascot Bernie Brewer travels down the slide, then grabs a Brewers flag and waves it about. This has been a tradition since 1980, when, at old Milwaukee County Stadium, Bernie (then a person dressed in lederhosen) slid from a chalet into a giant beer mug after each home run. Tip: You can find the old chalet at **Lakefront Brewery** (1872 N. Commerce St., 414/372-8800, www.lakefrontbrewery.com, 11am-8pm Mon.-Thurs., 11am-9pm Fri., 9am-9pm Sat., 10am-5pm Sun.).

Want to go down Bernie Brewer's slide yourself? **Bernie's Slide Experience** (before select home games, 2-8 people, $150-175 per person) gives fans the opportunity to head down the big yellow slide. Guests will get a tour of American Family Field plus up to five slide rides and photo ops.

Be on the lookout for a bichon frise mixed-breed dog. Named **Hank** (after former Milwaukee Brave and Brewer Hank Aaron), the then-stray wandered into the Brewers' spring training facility in 2014. Ever since, he's been an unofficial mascot of the team. Chances are you won't see Hank at the ballpark (he only attends some home games), but you never know.

Sausage Race

Possibly no in-game tradition is as perfectly aligned with its ballpark and home city than the Brewers' **sausage race,** in which oversize cartoon versions of tube-shaped grilled meat run around the foul area of American Family Field, from the left-field foul pole to the right-field line, in hopes of achieving a glorious victory—until the next game day, that is.

The ritual, which began in the early 1990s, is performed by five characters known as the **Famous Racing Sausages:** Brett Wurst (a lederhosen-clad bratwurst), Stosh Jonjak (a fly, upstart Polish kielbasa), Guido (an Italian sausage dressed as a stereotype of a chef), Frankie Furter (your good ol' all-American hot dog), and Cinco (an outdated stereotype, like Guido, but this time a chorizo under a sombrero). On Sunday afternoons, the sausages participate with miniature versions of themselves (called **Little Weenies**) in a relay race, and twice a year the sausages team up to face the Pittsburgh Pirates' Racing Pierogies in a showdown.

Bob Uecker Seat

At the very top of **section 422** at home plate, there looks to be a lonely gentleman hanging out in one of two green seats. But head up there, and you'll realize it's Mr. Baseball himself, longtime Brewers announcer and Milwaukee native and beloved goofball **Bob Uecker,** immortalized as a neat **statue** that was unveiled in 2014. The statue's location is a callback to his infamous Miller Lite commercial quote: "I must be in the front row!" Fans can sit in the chair beside Uecker but, for once, he won't talk back.

Photos (top): Bernie's Dugout; (middle left) the Famous Racing Sausages; (middle right) team mascot Bernie Brewer; (bottom) the Wall of Honor at the Hot Corner.

Hot Corner

There's a lot to check out at the **Hot Corner** (left field corner, field level). First, there's the **Wall of Honor,** which celebrates notable names in franchise history including Prince Fielder, Pat Listach, and Corey Hart. The Milwaukee Braves Wall of Honor commemorates famous names from the Braves' residency in Milwaukee, such as Hank Aaron, Eddie Mathews, and Warren Spahn. Nearby is the All-American Girls Professional Baseball League Wall of Honor, an exhibit showcasing artifacts from the women's baseball league based in the Midwest between 1943 and 1954, immortalized in the 1992 film *A League of Their Own.*

Statues

Look for a bronzed version of **Bob Uecker** outside the stadium, along with statues of **Hank Aaron, Robin Yount,** and former Brewers owner and baseball commissioner **Allan H. "Bud" Selig.** Around the exterior of the stadium is the **Brewers Walk of Fame,** which honors famous Brewers players and personalities, including **Paul Molitor, Gorman Thomas, Warren Spahn,** and **Geoff Jenkins.** Honorees are indicated by granite slabs set in the ground and shaped like home plate.

The Selig Experience

The Brewers honor Allan H. "Bud" Selig, the man who brought baseball back to Milwaukee in 1970, with an exhibit called **The Selig Experience** (left field, loge level). A documentary showing here tells the story of Selig and the Brewers, along with a look into the former owner's office. It may seem odd to see a former owner exalted in a way typically reserved for American presidents, but keep in mind that Selig single-handedly created the Brewers and reigned over a busy period of baseball history. This exhibit is a one-of-a-kind experience.

FOOD AND DRINKS

If you're not full after tailgating, American Family Field has more than a few solid options for grub. Be sure to put **bratchos** (sections 106, 117, 124, 210, 221, 228) on your bucket list. Essentially nachos with a Wisconsin twist, these are kettle chips doused in nacho cheese, *pico de gallo* (a type of salsa), jalapeños, sour cream, and ground Klement's sausage. If there's one food to have at a Brewers game, this is the one. Of course, you might also need to get a **bratwurst,** available at stands throughout the stadium. Order one with Secret Stadium Sauce, a condiment that tastes like a cross between barbecue sauce and ketchup with some added heat.

AJ Bombers (section 124) is a Milwaukee-based burger joint that serves up their grub with concretes (thick-as-a-brick milkshakes), tater tots, and buffalo chicken egg rolls. During the season, AJ Bombers will change up their concrete specials; flavors like malted whoopie pie are perfect for coming off that late-game energy dip.

For a great selection of Wisconsin beer, patronize **Local Brews** (section 207). You'll find selections from breweries like **Lakefront** and **Third Space** here, along with Miller varieties. You can also find local beer in sections 108, 123, 214, and 225. A good choice is Third Space's Happy Place Pale Ale; it's the best bang-for-your-buck brew at the ballpark. The line will be long at Local Brews, so prepare accordingly.

Need a seat with your meal? Out in left field, on the field level, is **Restaurant To Be Named Later** (414/902-4000, opens with gates on game days, also open non-game days, under $60). Though the name seems like a mistake, it's real, inspired by the phenomenon where teams can't immediately agree to the terms of a trade, so the phrase "player to be named later" is employed. You can purchase tables on either the Home Run Porch or Bullpen Porch, and that's your spot for the game with a $30 food-and-beverage credit. People can also eat at the restaurant during the game, but you'll have to get there early to snag a seat.

EVENTS

Fans can watch **batting practice** once the

gates open, but there's no guarantee the Brewers will be out there. If you want **autographs,** try to get to the front rows around the first base and third base dugouts; players may come by, though again, nothing is guaranteed.

Along with the usual theme nights, the Brewers celebrate **Cabin Fever** (early season), when fans purchasing a theme-night ticket receive a Brewers flannel shirt, and **Bark at the Park** (mid-season), where dogs are welcome to attend a game with their owners.

Look for the annual **Negro Leagues Tribute Game** (mid-season), in which the Brewers don uniforms of the old Milwaukee Bears. In 2019, the team marked its first **Kickoff to Summer concert** (Memorial Day weekend), a free show after the game.

Tours

The Brewers have one of the more affordable **ballpark tours** (414/902-4635, various days, $15 adults, $10 seniors and youth), though dates and times are limited. You'll get to hang in the dugout and the visiting clubhouse, plus you'll get a view of Bob Uecker's broadcast booth, the press box, and the luxury suites.

SHOPPING

The **Brewers Team Store at Home Plate Gate** (home plate gate, open when parking lots open until a half hour after game ends, game days only) is notable for its wall of more than 200 hats. You can buy a cap featuring the team's old mitt logo, arguably the best in the game's history. Much larger and a better experience overall, the **Brewers Team Store on the Field Level** (third-base line, field level, 10am-7pm Mon.-Fri., 10am-6pm Sat., 11am-4pm Sun. during season, 10am-6pm Mon.-Sat. Oct.-Feb.) will get packed before games, but there's plenty to check out here. Look for the inexpensive four-pack Brewers button set and postcards featuring the Famous Racing Sausages.

MILWAUKEE SIGHTS

MILWAUKEE ART MUSEUM

A stunning building with magnificent structural wings on the shore of Lake Michigan, the **Milwaukee Art Museum** (700 N. Art Museum Dr., 414/224-3200, www.mam.org, 10am-5pm Tues.-Sun., $19, $17 seniors and students, free ages 12 and under) is worth at least a few hours of your visit, if only for the architecture. Be sure to visit after 10am so you can get up on the **Burke Brise Soleil,** those Boeing 747-like wings with a 217-foot span that unfold and fold twice daily. The Brise Soleil is part of the **Quadracci Pavilion,** designed by noted Spanish architect Santiago Calatrava. Other treats in this architectural marvel include Windhover Hall's 90-foot-high glass ceiling and the Reiman Bridge, which you can walk across to access the Downtown area.

Inside the museum, more than 40 galleries display some of the 30,000 pieces in the museum's collection. The European and American art here includes a massive haul of works by Wisconsin native Georgia O'Keeffe. Look for items from the museum's American decorative arts inventory, such as furniture dating to the 18th century.

HARLEY-DAVIDSON MUSEUM

Follow the evolution of the American motorcycle at the **Harley-Davidson Museum** (400 W. Canal St., 877/436-8738, www.harley-davidson.com, 9am-6pm daily May-Sept., 10am-6pm daily Oct.-Apr., $20, $14 seniors and students, $10 ages 5-17, free ages 4 and under). The museum is set on 20 acres in the middle of the city and has 450 motorcycles, including the earliest-known Harley-Davidson, Serial Number One. Sit on bikes at the Experience Gallery, and view 100 tank graphics in the Tank Gallery. In the Custom Culture gallery, the 13-foot

"King Kong" motorcycle reigns supreme. The museum also has a shop and café on-site. On Thursdays from October to April, admission is just $10 for adults.

MILLER BREWING COMPANY

Whether or not you drink their beers, you should pay homage to the **Miller Brewing Company** (4251 W. State St., 414/931-2337, www.millercoors.com, 10am-6pm Mon.-Fri., 10am-6:30pm Sat., 10am-3:30pm Sun. Memorial Day-Labor Day; 10am-5pm Mon.-Fri., 10am-5:30pm Sat. Labor Day-Memorial Day, visitors center free). While at the brewery's visitors center, take a **tour** (every 30 minutes, 10am-3:30pm daily, $10, free ages 20 and under) of its main facility. The tour includes a history of the company, a trip through some underground caves and a Bavarian-style inn, visits to the brewhouse and packaging center, and, naturally, some complimentary suds (for visitors 21 and older). A gift shop is on-site at the visitors center.

FOOD

NEAR AMERICAN FAMILY FIELD

If you're going to visit Milwaukee for a Brewers game, you've got to hit up a German hall that serves traditional fare. **Kegel's Inn** (5901 W. National Ave., West Allis, 414/257-9999, www.kegelsinn.com, 11am-2pm and 4:30pm-9pm Mon.-Thurs., 11am-2pm and 4pm-10pm Fri., 4:30pm-9pm Sat., under $40) is a swift four-minute drive west of American Family Field and has roots stretching back to the 1920s. The beautiful, cozy dining room and bar has old-world charm with original wood decor, including some pretty bar seats. On Fridays, Kegel's hosts a popular fish fry in the German tradition. Reserve a few days in advance or you may have to wait in line a bit; either way, it's worth it.

Want a spot with dynamite service and new American food? **Story Hill BKC** (5100 W. Bluemound Rd., 414/539-4424, www.storyhillbkc.com, 11am-9pm Tues.-Fri., 9am-9pm Sat., 9am-2pm Sun., under $50) is the place, featuring midwestern-grown ingredients in well-prepared classics. Sample the Wisconsin cheese plate to experience the finest of the region's terroir. Bonus: Story Hill has an attached bottle shop, so you can bring back some local beer after sampling it at the restaurant.

OTHER NEIGHBORHOODS

Situated in West Town, the **Milwaukee Brat House** (1013 N. Old World 3rd St., 414/273-8709, www.milwaukeebrathouse.com, 11am-2am Sun.-Thurs., 11am-2:30am Fri.-Sat., under $30) feels like it's been here forever, despite its 2008 founding. Under tin ceilings, this bar serves up plenty of local beer, but the highlight is the sausages, from classic Usinger's bratwurst (cheddar jalapeño is always a hit) to smoked chicken, hot Hungarian, and vegan options. The Brat House runs a **shuttle** to and from Miller Park on game days.

For the traditional German experience, check out **Mader's Restaurant** (1041 N. Old World 3rd St., 414/271-3377, www.madersrestaurant.com, 11:30am-9pm Mon.-Thurs., 11:30am-10pm Fri.-Sat., 11am-9pm Sun., under $30 lunch, under $60 dinner), also in West Town. For many locals, it's a special-occasion restaurant, but at lunchtime, the vibe is much more casual. View the stained-glass windows and order the Reuben rolls. The wiener schnitzel is a meal and a half.

You're in for a pleasant surprise at **Odd Duck** (2352 S. Kinnickinnic Ave., 414/763-5881, www.oddduckrestaurant.com, 5pm-10pm daily, bar 3pm-midnight daily, under $50), which isn't afraid to mix Vietnamese, Chinese, Italian, Portuguese, West African, and vegan dishes on a nightly basis. The brown- and beige-toned dining room is airy and hip, a fun place to down a couple cocktails while munching on charcuterie.

Everything is served as a small plate here, making for an exciting evening of sharing among friends. Find it in the Bay View neighborhood a bit south of Downtown.

BARS AND BREWERIES

NEAR AMERICAN FAMILY FIELD

If you're looking to drink beer, you've come to the right city. Milwaukee loves its suds, as evidenced by the number of corner and neighborhood taprooms, many of them identifiable by Pabst Blue Ribbon signs swaying above the door. Go on a pub crawl before or after a game: Visit **Bluemound Road** between North 64th Street and North 51st Street, or **National Avenue** between 60th and 34th Streets. The best part: Both of these areas are mighty close to American Family Field, and most of the bars near the park offer **shuttles** that take patrons to and from the game. Some of those bars include **Brewski's** (304 N. 76th St., 414/475-0500), **City Lights Brewing Co.** (2200 W. Mount Vernon Ave., 414/436-1011), **Dugout 54** (5328 W. Bluemound Rd., 414/259-1200), **Jackson's Blue Ribbon Pub** (11302 W. Bluemound Rd., 414/988-4485), **Rounding Third** (6317 W. Bluemound Rd., 414/475-1982), **Steve's on Bluemound** (5841 W. Bluemound Rd., 414/527-3210), and **Who's on Third** (1007 N. Old World 3rd St., 414/897-8373).

Allow me to recommend a few of the more iconic and infamous bars in these areas. First is **J&B's Blue Ribbon Bar and Grill** (5230 W. Bluemound Rd., 414/443-1844, www.jbblueribbon.com, 3pm-2am Mon.-Thurs., 11am-2:30am Fri.-Sun.), which has a friendly atmosphere, a large selection of beer (from PBR to New Glarus), and **shuttle service**

Photos (from top to bottom): Harley-Davidson Museum; display of beer inside the stadium; Pfister Hotel.

to and from the ballpark. J&B's makes for the perfect hangout before and after the game.

With its blue and yellow stools, its astounding collection of baseball photos and memorabilia, and its many televisions, **4th Base Restaurant** (5117 W. National Ave., 414/647-8509, www.the4thbase.com, 10am-midnight Sun.-Thurs., 10am-12:30am Fri.-Sat.) is perfect for a postgame drink. If you're looking to dine, be open-minded: There's no fixed menu, just a lot of surf, turf, and pub appetizers. The chef is open to making whatever he might have, and because of that, you may pay more than you anticipated. But 4th Base is fun, thanks to the warm customers and staff telling good Brewers stories.

Just a few blocks west of 4th Base is a place with more good Brewers stories. Visit **Cesar's Inn** (5527 W. National Ave., 414/383-7388, www.cesarsinn.net), an old-school taproom below some well-kept boarding rooms. It's likely Amanda will take your order, which should be a cold beer and a whiskey shot. Don't overthink it. As for the history: The bar was once owned by former Brewers manager Harvey Kuenn and his wife. Now that's a baseball bar.

OTHER NEIGHBORHOODS

Halfway between American Family Field and Downtown is **Third Space Brewing** (1505 W. St. Paul Ave., 414/909-2337, www.thirdspacebrewing.org, 4pm-9pm Wed.-Thurs., 2pm-10pm Fri., noon-10pm Sat., noon-7pm Sun.), a brick-walled hangout spot with outdoor space, food trucks, brewery tours, and a vast collection of good beer. The brewery isn't afraid to try big, bold IPAs, but it's just as comfortable with lighter, summer-friendly fare.

There's even a baseball-themed brewery in Milwaukee. Check out the Third Ward's **Broken Bat Brewery** (231 E. Buffalo St., 414/316-9197, www.brokenbatbrewery.com, 4pm-10pm Tues.-Thurs., 3pm-11pm Fri., noon-11pm Sat., noon-6pm Sun.), which has offerings like Crooked Number, Mr. Oktoberfest, Golden Sombrero, and 755, which is named for hammerin' Hank Aaron's career

home-run total. Hilariously, the brewery added some "juice" to that beer and called it 762*, in honor of Barry Bonds. The brewery is in a basement, and part of its cool decor is a wall of baseball cards inside the bathroom.

RECREATION

PARKS

Milwaukee RiverWalk

Spanning more than 20 city blocks, the 3.1-mile **Milwaukee RiverWalk** (N. Weil St. at N. Riverboat Rd.) also known as RiverWalk Way, straddles either side of the Milwaukee River, connecting the Lower East Side to the Third Ward. The path, which can vary from boardwalk to concrete, cruises past condominiums, local street art, and busy cafés.

Lake Park

Milwaukee has some neat parks, but few have the options of **Lake Park** (2975 N. Lake Park Rd.), which is home to the circa-1888 **North Point Lighthouse** (2650 N. Wahl Ave., 414/332-6754, 1pm-4pm Sat.-Sun., $8, $5 seniors, students, and ages 5-11, free ages 4 and under). The lighthouse is no longer in operation but is maintained by a nonprofit that oversees tours and a museum inside.

The rest of the park includes a par-3 golf course, a stage for summer concerts, and a field for lawn bowling. Starting Memorial Day, the **Milwaukee Lake Park Lawn Bowling Association** (www.milwaukeelawnbowls.com, May-Oct.) hosts an event nearly every day until October, with learn-to-play classes for those interested.

ACCOMMODATIONS

Milwaukee lacks much in the way of hotels near the ballpark. However, if you're willing to stay on the western edge of the city and want to tie your stay into the game-day experience, the **Radisson Hotel Milwaukee**

West (2303 N. Mayfair Rd., 414/257-3400, www.radisson.com, $150-300) offers a baseball package that starts at $150 per night. With your room, you'll get a baseball-themed welcome gift, a $25 gift card to a nearby restaurant, and prescheduled shuttle service to and from the ballpark.

Smack in the middle of Downtown Milwaukee is one of its finest landmarks, the **Pfister Hotel** (424 E. Wisconsin Ave., 414/273-8222, www.thepfisterhotel.com, $200-600). Opened in 1893 and coined the "Grand Hotel of the West," the Pfister has almost always been the peak of luxury in town. The hotel's Victorian lavishness, from balcony embellishments to staircase banisters, paintings, and rugs, is impressive. It's also home to **Blu** (414/298-3196, www.blumilwaukee.com, 5pm-1am Mon.-Thurs., 4pm-2am Fri.-Sat., under $50), a cocktail bar on the 23rd floor, where a view of the city awaits. All the Pfister's rooms have feather bed toppers, tall windows, and high-speed Internet. It's pricey, but worth the splurge.

At a lower price point and emphasizing a slightly more modern approach, the **Plaza Hotel** (1007 N. Cass St., 414/276-2101, www.plazahotelmilwaukee.com, $150-300) promises art deco rooms with a modern, personal touch (think bright walls, chic art prints, and equipped kitchens). There's a café with an ivy-covered courtyard, perfect for light breakfasts before sampling the city.

For a quintessential Milwaukee lodging experience, stay at the **Brewhouse Inn & Suites** (1215 N. 10th St., 414/810-3350, www.brewhousesuites.com, $100-250). This hotel is the former Pabst Brewery, meaning you'll be staying where they used to make Pabst Blue Ribbon. Cool sights include copper brewing kettles in the atrium, as well as a stained-glass depiction of King Gambrinus, a legendary European beer icon. Rooms reflect the look of a renovated brewery: plenty of exposed brick walls and high ceilings.

GETTING AROUND

PUBLIC TRANSIT

Milwaukee County Transit (www.ridemcts.com, $2.25) operates an extensive **bus network.** If you're staying Downtown or in the area near Marquette University, you'll want to know the color-coded lines. The **Green Line** runs north to south, paralleling Lake Michigan and connecting Downtown to General Mitchell International Airport. The **Blue Line** runs past landmarks like the Milwaukee Public Museum and the Harley-Davidson Museum.

You'll also want to know about **The Hop** (www.thehopmke.com, 5am-midnight Mon.-Fri., 7am-midnight Sat., 7am-10pm Sun., $1), a **streetcar** that slashes through Downtown, starting in the north at Burns Commons and ending in the south at Milwaukee Intermodal Station. Considering its affordability and convenience, The Hop is a decent choice if you're traveling around Downtown.

TAXI, UBER, AND LYFT

Both Lyft and Uber have robust presences in Milwaukee. You can also download the **TAXIMKE app,** which utilizes ride-sharing technology to hail you a cab to the airport.

Bar-hopping Downtown? **WaterTaxiMKE** (414/563-7025) operates boats that cross and ride along the Milwaukee River, Lake Michigan, and other waterways. Text the number with your location, and WaterTaxiMKE will respond with more information about your potential trip.

CAR

Considering the walkability of Downtown, the shuttles to and from ball games, and the presence of Lyft and Uber, you can get around Milwaukee without a car, and I recommend it. If you need to rent one, the airport is home to all the major car rental companies.

Downtown Milwaukee is wide, encompassing both sides of the Milwaukee River. The east side of the river, toward Lake Michigan, is called **East Town;** it is full of modern structures and has a more bustling profile. **West Town** is home to museums and chain hotels, plus **BMO Harris Bradley Center** (1001 Vel R. Phillips Ave.), home to basketball's Bucks, and **Milwaukee Intermodal Station** (433 W. St. Paul Ave., 800/872-7245, www.amtrak.com), the city's main train station.

I-94 is the major highway in the city, running north until it crosses the Menomonee River at the Marquette Interchange, where it sharply turns west toward Madison. **I-43,** which comes in from the southwest before meeting with I-94, continues north toward Sheboygan and Green Bay. Then there's **I-794,** a spur that cuts through Downtown before hooking up with I-94 at the Marquette Interchange.

The highways can be confusing to navigate. It's helpful to know that I-94 abuts American Family Field, and if you take it east, you can get Downtown. Milwaukee drivers are known for being a bit aggressive (watch for folks driving quickly in the right lane of multilane streets to pass you). For these reasons, driving in the city isn't the best option.

BELOIT, WISCONSIN

Looking for the opposite of American Family Field? Head southwest of Milwaukee to visit Beloit, Wisconsin, where quaint Harry Pohlman Field plays host to the Beloit Snappers.

GETTING THERE

You can reach Beloit with a **75-mile** drive southwest on I-43 from Milwaukee. The drive takes around **75 minutes** in good traffic conditions.

For a slightly more scenic route of about **95 miles,** take I-94 West 45 miles to WI-26 South. Take that another 31 miles to I-90 East. After 14 miles, you'll reach WI-81; take that west into Beloit. This drive takes a little over **1.5 hours.**

HARRY POHLMAN FIELD

A small-time throwback with a cool bleacher feel, **Harry Pohlman Field** (2301 Skyline Dr., 608/362-2272, www.snappersbaseball.com), home to the **Beloit Snappers,** is pretty much the same park it was when it was built in 1982. Once the Brewers' class-A team, the Snappers are now part of the Oakland Athletics' system. They play in the Midwest League, a far cry from the majors, and where mostly 19- to 21-year-olds begin their big-league dreams. Play begins in April with the season ending in early September.

You can sit behind home plate in a newer seat or hang out in metal **bleachers,** which fill the outer areas in foul territory. You can also hang out in the **Coors Cow Pasture,** a picnic area closer to left field, or the **Miller on Deck** party area closer to right field. Tickets are cheap (under $15), food and drink are relatively cheap (hot dogs, burgers, brats, and beer go for under $6 each), and the vibe is ultracasual.

ST. LOUIS
CARDINALS

Perhaps no city is more of a baseball city than St. Louis. Sitting on the Mississippi River, positioned as the "Gateway to the West," this smaller city is home to blues music, great barbecue, and the Cardinals. St. Louis has loved its top baseball team since its beginnings in 1882 in the long-defunct American Association.

The team started in the National League in 1892 as the first version of the St. Louis Browns but became the Cardinals in 1900. After some early scuffling, the Cards really took off in the 1920s with Rogers Hornsby. Between 1926 and 1934, the team won five league pennants and took three world championships.

The Cardinals saw more success in the 1940s, with three additional World Series wins, thanks to groundbreaking general manager Branch

Rickey, who created the modern-day minor league system for the team. Ever since growing talent like Stan Musial and Ducky Medwick, the Cardinals have always seemed to find and develop outstanding talent. Over many decades, the Cards' skill at development has led to numerous pennants and championships—like in 1964 and 1967, thanks in part to stars like Bob Gibson and Orlando Cepeda, then again in 1983, 2006, and 2011.

It may be the homegrown aspect of Cardinals baseball that most connects with fans, who live anywhere from Oklahoma to Alabama, and from Indiana to Colorado (thanks to the strength of the team's radio broadcasts, dating back to the early 20th century). Cardinals ballplayers seem to stay Cardinals ballplayers, and those who aren't grown here usually become perfect fits for the franchise once they arrive. Go to a game and find a slew of names on fans' backs: Pujols, Goldschmidt, Carpenter, Edmonds, Rolen, Smith (Ozzie), McGee, Gibson, and Musial—those are just a few of the Cardinals that fans will always revere.

PLANNING YOUR TIME

You can handle St. Louis in a **weekend,** though a long, **four-day weekend** is ideal. Plan on spending one day at **Busch Stadium** and Downtown, checking off the **Gateway Arch.** A second day is best spent at **Forest Park** and in the **Central West End** neighborhood. Beyond that, you might want to spend a half day checking out the **Soulard** neighborhood—home to blues clubs and party bars—and maybe a little time at **The Hill** for Italian grub.

You can do much of St. Louis using public transportation, so plan on staying near a stop that facilitates both MetroLink lines. **Downtown** works well as a base (plus you're close to the ballpark), as does **Central West End.**

If you've never been to St. Louis, be prepared for the **heat.** It routinely gets into the 80s starting in **May,** with 90°F days

somewhat frequent between **July** and **August** (and 100°F days are very possible).

April, May, and **June** are the wettest months of the year, with occasional wild **storms.** Especially during this time of year, the area is prone to **tornadoes.** Busch Stadium has multiple shelter-in-place areas for this reason. When there isn't rain in the forecast, April, May, and late in the season can be simply gorgeous here.

GETTING THERE

AIR

You'll be flying into **St. Louis Lambert International Airport** (STL, 10701 Lambert International Blvd., 314/890-1333, www.fly-stl.com), which is about 15 miles northwest of Busch Stadium. Lambert offers flights via **Air Canada** (888/247-2262, www.aircanada.com), **American Airlines** (800/433-7300, www.aa.com), **Delta** (800/221-1212, www.delta.com), **Frontier** (800/401-9000, www.flyfrontier.com), **Southwest** (800/435-9792, www.southwest.com), and **United** (800/864-8331, www.united.com). Flights head to most major American airports, plus Toronto, and to smaller regional airports throughout the Midwest.

Airport Transportation

Most major **car rental agencies** have offices in the area around the airport, accessible via **shuttle bus.** The quickest way into the city is usually to hop onto I-70 East from the airport. After about 14 miles, you'll merge onto I-44 South, which will take you right into the heart of the city. Without traffic, this **15-mile** drive takes about **20 minutes.**

CAR

From **Milwaukee,** you'll drive about **375 miles** south to St. Louis, a nearly **six-hour** trip. The ride starts on **I-94 South,** turning

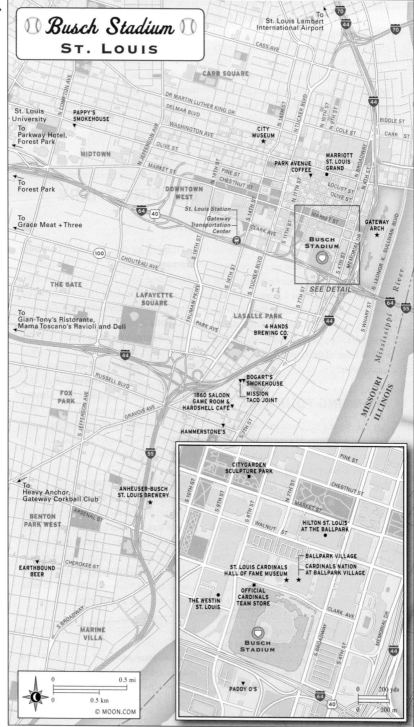

into **I-294 South** in Des Plaines, just west of Chicago. At a split with I-55, take **I-55 South** another 275 miles, through Springfield, Illinois, until you come into St. Louis over the Mississippi River. Merge onto **I-64 West** and exit for Downtown.

To get here directly from **Chicago,** take **I-55** all the way south, a **300-mile** drive of about **4.5 hours.**

TRAIN

Amtrak (www.amtrak.com) runs through St. Louis, with trains stopping at **Gateway Station** (430 S. 15th St.), a 20-minute, 0.8-mile walk west of Busch Stadium. Located in Downtown St. Louis, the train station is within walking distance of most accommodations in the city.

Amtrak lines serving St. Louis include the **Illinois Service,** connecting Mound City to Chicago; the **Missouri River Runner,** running twice daily between St. Louis and Kansas City (paralleling the Missouri River); and the **Texas Eagle,** running from Chicago south to San Antonio. You can connect to the **Sunset Limited** in San Antonio, which takes riders west to Los Angeles.

BUS

Take **Greyhound** (www.greyhound.com) to St. Louis from **Milwaukee,** with fares starting at about $35, or from **Chicago,** starting at about $18. Buses will drop off passengers at the **Gateway Transportation Center** (430 S. 15th St., 314/231-4485), part of the St. Louis Station, about 0.8 mile west of Busch Stadium.

You can also hop on a **Megabus** (https://us.megabus.com) from **Chicago** to St. Louis. This ride can be as cheap as $5. The bus will drop you off at the **Gateway Transportation Center** (430 S. 15th St.).

Busch Stadium

If your team is the St. Louis Cardinals, then you want an authoritative, well-proportioned home befitting a franchise that has won 11 world championships and 19 National League pennants. **Busch Stadium** (700 Clark St., www.mlb.com/cardinals), which opened in 2006 in Downtown St. Louis, just blocks from the Mississippi River and Gateway Arch, definitely fits the bill. It's not cozy, but you never feel like you're inside an echo chamber. And it's rich in deep Cardinals red and old American brick and steel; when you're inside, you feel like you're at the right place for this franchise.

This is the third ballpark in St. Louis to be named Busch Stadium. The first was a latter-day name for Sportsman's Park, the Cards' home from 1920-1966. Busch Memorial Stadium, a cookie-cutter park with a little more character than its cousins Three Rivers, Riverfront, and Veterans Stadiums, survived from 1966 to 2005. This newest iteration of Busch is a retro-classic park with one level of outfield bleachers, allowing for a clear view of the St. Louis skyline, highlighted by the Gateway Arch. A big scoreboard screams "Budweiser," the first name in St. Louis industry. A walkable outfield midway, plus the Ballpark Village (and the neighboring Cardinals Hall of Fame and Museum) just beyond the gates, make Busch a destination for baseball fans hours before the game begins.

For these reasons, you can see why folks across the Midwest will travel hundreds of miles to catch a Cardinals game. The team has done a fine job preserving its robust history and incorporating its story into the ballpark and surrounding area. And, once you're inside for the contest, it's hard not to focus just on the game itself. Busch has few distractions for a newer venue, which is refreshing. When you go to Busch Stadium, you'll want to watch some baseball.

ORIENTATION

Centrally located, Busch Stadium is smack in the middle of the Downtown area and is accessible by the city's major thoroughfares. The stadium is bordered to the south by I-64 and is just two blocks west of I-44.

There are six entry gates at Busch Stadium,

Busch Stadium

including two in the outfield. Gates 1, 5, and 6 are closer to Broadway, while Gates 2, 3, and 4 are near 8th Street. Gates open 1.5 hours before first pitch Monday through Thursday and 2 hours beforehand Friday through Sunday.

TICKETS AND SEATING

Pricing

The Cardinals use **dynamic pricing** for games, altering the cost of a ticket depending on the opponent, the giveaway, and the day and time of the game. Generally, Friday and Saturday night games tend to be higher priced than weekday games. Sunday games tend to sit in the middle, price-wise. If you want the lowest possible cost, plan a trip that gets you to a Cardinals game on a **Monday.**

You'll probably have to pony up for **Cubs** games, no matter the day. An average seat at Busch Stadium will cost somewhere around $35 for a weekday game against an opponent like Miami or Arizona, but that same seat will cost more like $60-70 if the Cubs are in town over a weekend night.

Want a good deal on tickets? Get to the **8th Street ticket windows** (left-field line at 8th St.) between 9am and two hours before first pitch on any game day to purchase a **voucher for two tickets** priced at $11.20. The deal is sponsored by radio station KMOX 1120 AM, which broadcasts Cardinals games. Then, 15 minutes before the game begins, head to **Gate 1** (right-field corner at Broadway and I-64) to redeem your voucher. (The line gets long, so get there earlier to avoid missing first pitch.) Your tickets

will be sealed in an envelope, so it's like a lottery. These could be great seats. At worst, you'll get standing-room-only tickets. If you don't mind the risk of SRO tickets and don't plan on seeing the park before the game, this could be a good option for you.

Seating Plan

More than most major league parks, Busch Stadium seems to believe no two seats are alike. The stadium is laid out like any other multilevel retro-modern ballpark. It's just that here, there's greater variation of price depending on where you want to sit.

The **Field Level (100 level)** fans out from home plate to the edges. It includes a bunch of seating areas, all differently priced, including the **Cardinals Club** (behind home plate), **diamond box** (behind the dugouts), **home**

field box (sections 145-155), **infield field box** (sections 141-144 and 156-160), the **dugout box** (sections 132-139 and 161-166 lower rows), the **first** and **third base field box** (sections 135-140 and 160-165 upper rows), the **lower left and right field box** (sections 127-134 and 166-172 lower rows), the **left field and right field box** (sections 128-135 and 163-167 upper rows), the **lower left and right field bleachers** (sections 101-109 lower rows and 189-197), and the **right field bleachers** (sections 107-111 upper rows).

It continues in the **Loge Level (200 level)**. From right field around the foul area to left field, there's the **right field loge** (sections 228-235), the **first base loge** (sections 237-240), the **infield Redbird club** (sections 241-246 and 254-257), the **home Redbird**

YOUR BEST DAY AT BUSCH STADIUM

Ballpark Village

First pitch is tonight at Busch Stadium, but you have a whole day in St. Louis ahead of you. Here's what to do to get in the spirit.

10.5 HOURS BEFORE FIRST PITCH
Wherever you're staying, get some coffee and some food to tide you over. If you're Downtown, visit **Park Avenue Coffee** for its gooey butter cake.

10 HOURS BEFORE FIRST PITCH
Start with an early visit to the **Gateway Arch.** Take the tram to the top, hang around for a half hour, take some photos, and come back down to earth. Budget 2-3 hours minimum for getting into and visiting the Arch.

7 HOURS BEFORE FIRST PITCH
Walk south toward Soulard, the great party neighborhood that's home to some cool blues clubs. Since it's about noon, grab a midday drink at **1860 Saloon, Game Room & Hardshell Café.**

6 HOURS BEFORE FIRST PITCH
Stand in line at **Bogart's Smokehouse,** then chow down on St. Louis barbecue. Savor the flavor of the ribs and be sure get some fire-and-ice pickles with your order. If you eat well, you won't need anything for

a while. When you're done, prepare to walk north toward the ballpark.

4 HOURS BEFORE FIRST PITCH
Grab a beer at **4 Hands Brewing Co.** since it's on the way. Drink a City Wide and revel in the pregame atmosphere.

2.5 HOURS BEFORE FIRST PITCH
Pay a visit to the **St. Louis Cardinals Hall of Fame Museum.** You'll want to spend at least an hour here to soak in Cardinals history.

1.5 HOURS BEFORE FIRST PITCH
Mill around **Ballpark Village,** the entertainment district surrounding the ballpark, and grab a memento from the **Majestic Athletic Store.** Now it's time to make your way into **Busch Stadium.**

DURING THE GAME
Grab a beer at **1764 Craft Pub.** A little later in the game, treat yourself to **Dinger's Donuts.** Mostly, though, you'll want to pay attention to the game.

AFTER THE GAME
Skip across the street to **Paddy O's** to hang with fans and have a drink. If you're still up for it, head back into Soulard and take in any one of the crazy bars there.

club (sections 247-253 behind home plate), the **National Car Rental Club** (sections 258-260), the **3rd base loge** (sections 261-263), the **left field loge** (sections 265-271), the **Budweiser Bowtie Bar's left field porch** (left-field corner), and **Big Mac Land** (section 272). There are also various **suite areas** between the first and second decks and second and third decks.

In the **Pavilion Level (300 level),** from right field around foul territory to left field, are the **right field pavilion** (sections 331-335), the **first base pavilion** (sections 337-340), the **infield pavilion** (sections 341-346 and 354-357), the **home pavilion** (sections 347-353, behind home plate), the **third base pavilion** (sections 358-360), and the **left field pavilion** (sections 361-372).

The **Terrace Level (400 level)** goes from right field around foul territory to left. It includes the **right field terrace** (sections 431-435), the **first base terrace** (sections 437-440), the **infield terrace** (sections 441-448 and 452-454), and the **home terrace** (sections 449-451, behind home plate).

Specialty sections include the **MVP Deck, Coca-Cola Rooftop Deck,** and **Coca-Cola Scoreboard Patio,** as well as **Left Field Landing** and **Homer's Landing.** These areas, located across the outfield, are all-inclusive seats you can buy individually or in groups. Typically, they come with a full game-day buffet, plus soda and beer.

Beyond the stadium, technically inside **Ballpark Village,** are the **Cardinals Nation Rooftop** and **Budweiser Brew House Deck.** Cardinals Nation offers a buffet meal (from $60), while the Brew House Deck (from $10) requires you to pay for grub. At both sites, drinks are extra. You'll have a field view, but you're pretty far away, so you'll likely need to squint to see who's playing the outfield. If you want to go to the game but don't care too much about watching the game, these are solid options.

Where to Buy Tickets

The **Cardinals website** does ticket buyers a favor by listing prices for every kind of seat for every Cardinals game. Use this to

GAME COSTS

Tickets: It depends on the day of the week, opponent, and if there's a special program before or after the game. Generally, be prepared to pay at least **$20** for a seat on a weekend and more like **$10** for a seat during the week. Want a good seat, say in the Field Level closer to the infield? It'll be about **$80-100** for the most coveted weekend and rivalry games, closer to **$50-70** for weekday and nonessential contests.

Hot dog: It's **$5** here, right in the middle compared with other parks, and **$7-12** for larger, more meal-worthy options (brats are **$6.75** and up).

Beer: A 20-ounce macro-brewed beer is **$10.** Cans are a touch cheaper at **$9.50.** Craft beer, which is scattered about this very Bud-centric park, is **$13** for a 20-ouncer and **$22.50** for a 32-ouncer. This is an expensive place for suds.

Parking: The closer to the ballpark you are, the more money you'll pay (think **$15-25**). If you park a few blocks away in a garage, you could pay more like **$5-10.**

compare ticket prices with those at **StubHub.** More often than not, you'll get a much cheaper ticket via StubHub.

Best Seats

To find a spot in the **shade,** look for the **overhang** that shields the seats in the back rows of the 100 level. These are along the **third-base line** in the **left field box** (sections 163-167). Higher up, the **infield Redbird club** (sections 241-246) has shaded seats.

For a midday game, for the best **sun protection** and comfort, you'll be in great shape in the middle to back rows of the **left field box** (sections 163-167). Prices tend to be less than $30 for midweek day games. On the weekends, prepare to pay twice as much, if not more.

Looking for a **good deal** on the weekends? Opt for sections 361-365 of the **left field pavilion** (300 level). Yes, these are higher up, but seats here should cost less than $35. The **right field bleachers** (sections 107-111) are typically around the same price. There's one problem, though: The sun will set in your eyes if you're sitting out in the bleachers.

If you want the **best view** of the park, grab seats in the **first** or **third base pavilion areas,** specifically **section 358,** which offers a view of the Gateway Arch and shows the whole field. On a weekend evening, these seats go for about $50 a pop.

For the best possible seat, regardless of price, you can't go wrong in **sections 145-148,** part of the **home field box.** For games early or in the middle of the week, you might be able to snag these seats for less than $70. On big-ticket days and weekends, you'll pay about $100 per seat.

KNOW BEFORE YOU GO

Busch Stadium is one of the parks where **outside food and drink** are allowed, as long as they fit inside a 16- by 16- by 8-inch **bag.** Alcohol, bottles, cans, thermoses, and hard-sided coolers are prohibited. If it's rainy or really sunny and hot, you may bring an **umbrella** into the stadium.

The Cardinals have a free Wi-Fi network called **Cardinals WiFi.**

Accessibility

The stadium offers transportation via **carts** or **wheelchairs** to help fans to and from their seats. **Braille signage** is found throughout Busch Stadium, especially outside restrooms and stairwells. **Service animals** are welcome at Busch Stadium.

Head to **guest relations** (section 148, 314/345-5331) for **assistive listening devices.** A second guest relations booth is at section 340.

You can find **elevators** (family pavilion, between Gate 6 and east ramp, Gate 2, Gate 3) in four locations.

Accessible parking is available at **SP+ Parking near gate 2** (Cerre St. near Historic Route 66), the **Stadium West Parking Garage,** and the **Stadium East Parking Garage.**

GETTING THERE

Public Transit

If you can, take a **MetroLink train** (www.metrostlouis.org, $2.50) to Busch Stadium. Both the **Red Line** and **Blue Line** stop at **Stadium station,** which is outside the **Westin St. Louis** (811 Spruce St.). Taking MetroLink works best if you're staying in the Central West End or if you don't want to walk from the stadium to hotels near the **Convention Center** (6th St. and Washington Ave.).

Driving

Busch Stadium is right against I-64, with an exit dumping traffic onto the ballpark-straddling Clark Avenue. There's also an exit from I-44 that's just two blocks from the venue, so getting here by car isn't a problem. (Note: Clark Avenue is closed to vehicles between South Broadway and 8th Street when the gates are open on game days, so you may have to drive around a bit in traffic to find parking.)

Parking can be pretty inexpensive, with some garages just blocks away charging $5-10. My suggestion: Get to the park early, then drive up 4th Street, going north toward Kiener Plaza Park. There are lots off of **Locust Street, Pine Street, Chestnut Street,** and **Market Street.** There's also affordable parking off **Cerre Street.** Whenever possible, try to **reserve** a spot ahead of time via www.stlouisparking.com.

You can also **ride-share** to the park. A Lyft from the Central West End to Ballpark Village costs $12-15. Surge pricing will likely be in effect, which means a ride to and from the park will be quite a bit more than a parking fee and gas mileage.

BE A FAN

You may have heard that Cardinals fans are "baseball's best fans." I can neither confirm nor deny this, but I can say that folks at Busch Stadium are pretty easy to get along with. Wearing another team's logo around the park, I did get a few "Who are you?" looks, but everyone was quite chatty. Now, that logo wasn't a Cubs emblem, which is another story. Cubs fans and Cardinals fans don't get along too well, though generally the rivalry stays within the confines of the ballpark and doesn't get violent. Still, heated words may be exchanged.

You're bound to hear the song **"Here Comes the King"** at the end of the seventh inning of each game. This song, otherwise known as the **Budweiser theme song,** written in 1971 for the beer company, is played by the Cardinals' organist. On the day of the **home opener,** baseball season begins with a parade of **Budweiser Clydesdales** along the warning track as "Here Comes the King" plays in the background.

PARK FEATURES AND SIGHTS

St. Louis Cardinals Hall of Fame Museum

The Cardinals are one of the most decorated franchises in baseball history, making the club's history museum a must-see. A visit to the **St. Louis Cardinals Hall of Fame Museum** (700 Clark Ave., 314/345-9600, www.mlb.com/cardinals, 10am-6pm daily, open through seventh inning on game nights, $12, $10 seniors, $8 children) means walking through a seven-room gallery that shows off some of the team's 11 World Series trophies and models of every Cardinals ballpark from Sportsman's Park to the current Busch Stadium. Be sure to view all of the Cardinals' Hall of Famers in a special room of plaques, and give yourself the opportunity to wear a World Series ring and hold a real baseball bat. Part of Ballpark Village, the museum is directly across the street from the stadium. If you have a ticket to the game, visit before you walk into the stadium, as you can't just go back and forth between the Busch Stadium and Ballpark Village. Carve out a half-hour for your visit.

Ballpark Village

Since St. Louis is a baseball city, it makes perfect sense that there's a massive entertainment district devoted to the Cardinals right beside Busch Stadium. **Ballpark Village** (601 Clark Ave., 314/797-7530, www.stlballparkvillage.com) combines Cardinals baseball with food, drink, music, shopping, and even apartments. It generally opens at 11am daily, and the bars within may remain open until 2am or 3am. Most retail shops close by 10pm.

There's a standard group of bars here, including one with a mechanical bull (PBR St. Louis) and one that's a giant sports bar with a 40-foot television (Fox Sports Midwest Live!). If you're trying to stay as close to the park as possible before or after the game while drinking some Budweiser products, this is the place for you. The **Budweiser Brew House** (314/241-5575, 11am-10pm Sun.-Thurs., 11am-11pm Fri.-Sat.) is the biggest bar here, boasting more than 200 taps—it's impressive seeing just how many breweries Anheuser-Busch InBev owns or operates. If you visit, think about heading up to the **Rooftop Bud Deck** that offers a clear view of the field.

Also in the Village is **Majestic Athletic Store** (314/345-9700), selling plenty of Cardinals T-shirts, hats, jerseys both modern and vintage, and toys. The **Bud Shop** (341/241-5575) features kitschy T-shirts with local jokes and points of interest.

Family Pavilion

Open about 1.5 hours before first pitch, the

Family Pavilion (Field Level, sections 101-105) gives parents an opportunity to wear out the little ones. The pavilion includes a toddler play area inside "Fredbird Field," plus a speed pitch game, virtual reality game, and nursing station. This area is under cover, so it's a good hideout for those rainy or really hot days; of course, that also means it gets pretty busy during those times.

FOOD AND DRINKS

The sit-down restaurant at Busch Stadium is **Cardinals Nation Restaurant and Bar** (601 Clark Ave., 314/345-9880, www.stlballparkvillage.com, 11am-9pm Mon.-Wed., 11am-10pm Thurs.-Sat., 11am-8pm Sun., under $30), technically across the street from the park. This sports bar and grill is covered in red and decorated with authentic jerseys and baseball bats (look for the ceiling fans). There are plenty of burgers, sandwiches, and salads, and your typical run of mainstream wine and beer options, plus some house cocktails.

Try the beef brisket at **Broadway BBQ** (section 109), which comes in a sandwich with chips or on a platter with coleslaw and potato salad. It's a bit expensive, as are Country Bob's BBQ nachos at the same vendor. Topped with pulled pork, barbecue sauce, cheese sauce, two kinds of peppers, and a third, spicy sauce, these nachos are pretty remarkable.

One of the better pound-for-pound options is the **Asian stir-fry** (sections 136, 242), a typical Americanized Chinese noodle dish that's made fresh to order. You can add a protein for a bit more money, and overall, it's a higher price than you'd want to pay; but if you're hungry, it's a solid deal.

The local option is **Kohn's** (sections 147, 446), a purveyor of Jewish-style deli items that is based in St. Louis. You'll want the killer pastrami sandwich with salad (the salad is actually sauerkraut), served on sturdy

Photos (from top to bottom): Ballpark Village; Fredbird, the Cardinals' mascot; seats at Busch Stadium.

bread. Corned beef sandwiches and knishes are also available.

The gluttonous option is **grilled chicken bats** (section 429), which are smoked chicken legs topped with barbecue or hot honey sauce and served with chips and charred jalapeños.

You could just skip to dessert and reach for **Dinger's Donuts** (sections 145, 454), the best food purchase you can make at Busch Stadium. These are warm, fried mini-doughnuts drizzled with a chocolate or vanilla glaze and covered in sprinkles and cinnamon sugar. Best yet? They're served in a plastic Cardinals helmet.

As for beer, you're going to find a whole lot of Budweiser, plus Anheuser-Busch InBev brands and products (**Goose Island, Shock Top, Redbridge**). You'll also see a lot of brands owned by other macro breweries (**Boulevard, Blue Moon**). Don't despair—you can find local craft beer here; it's just expensive. Head to **1764 Craft Pub** (section 141), which has more than 20 beers available. Look for offerings from **Perennial Artisan Ales, Mother's Brewing Co.** of Springfield, Missouri, and **4 Hands Brewing Co.** There's more than a little **Schlafly** served here; look for it at sections 142, 198 (center field), 245, 254, and 265.

EVENTS

Looking for pregame, pre-gate entertainment? Head to **Ford Plaza** (between Gates 5 and 6, center field), home to concerts, prize booths, and visits from Cardinals mascot Fredbird. On some mornings, the Cardinals will host yoga sessions at the plaza.

You can get down close to the dugouts during **batting practice,** which starts just before gates open (the Cardinals hit then) but continues with the road team for another 45 minutes or so. The team doesn't guarantee that players will make themselves available for **autographs.**

A great thing about the Cardinals: Just about every game includes a **giveaway** or special theme. If you want collectibles, get to the gate early on your game day.

Tours

The Cardinals host year-round **tours** (314/345-9565, 11am and 12:30pm Nov.-opening day, 9:30am, 11am, 12:30pm, and 2pm during season, no tours on home game days, $18, $16 seniors, $14 ages 4-15, free ages 3 and under) that include a stop at the radio broadcast booth; inside the Cardinals Club, where world championship trophies are displayed; and typically, the Cardinals dugout. The tours also include admission to the St. Louis Cardinals Hall of Fame Museum, so if you're spending a day in St. Louis when the Cards aren't playing at Busch Stadium, this makes for a good deal.

SHOPPING

The **Official Cardinals Team Store** (8th St. and Clark Ave., sections 166-169, 10am-6pm daily, open to the public until one hour after final out on game days) has the same kind of stuff you'll find at other team stores in ballparks across the country. Keep your eyes peeled for beautiful throwback jerseys, purses and wallets, kids' apparel, and Pride-themed memorabilia.

Satellite locations of the team store are called **Fan's Nest.** Head to the **Fan's Nest on the Field Level** (section 134), which has a custom jersey-lettering service. Busch Stadium also has a **Build-a-Bear Store at Ford Plaza.**

In Ballpark Village, **Majestic Athletic Store** (601 Clark Ave., 314/345-9700) sells Cardinals T-shirts, hats, jerseys, and toys.

ST. LOUIS SIGHTS

GATEWAY ARCH

It's one of America's greatest landmarks, a sight to behold since 1965: The **Gateway Arch** (11 N. 4th St., 877/982-1410, www.gatewayarch.com, 8am-10pm daily summer, 9am-6pm daily winter, $12-32, $8-18 ages 3-15) rises 630 feet above St. Louis at the Mississippi riverfront.

Inside the arch is a **tram** that rides all the way up the arch. The tram's cars are more like small Ferris wheel compartments that seat five, traveling at about 3 mph during a four-minute ride. They stop near the top of the arch, at which point you then walk up a few steps to reach the **observation deck.** Here, you can see about 30 miles east, into Illinois, and west, across St. Louis. On average, the experience lasts about 45-60 minutes, but you can stay at the top for as long as you like. One of the options for visiting the arch includes a one-hour St. Louis riverfront cruise, which offers a history lesson on steamboat travel. There's also a **museum** at the Gateway Arch site. Be ready to go through security upon arrival.

ANHEUSER-BUSCH BREWERY

Love beer? Even if you're a craft fan, you should pay a visit to the **Anheuser-Busch St. Louis Brewery** (1200 Lynch St., 314/577-2626, www.budweisertours.com, 9am-5pm Mon.-Sat., 11am-5pm Sun., 9:30am-5pm daily, free or $5 in advance). Founded in 1852, the brewery offers 45-minute **tours** that show off the seven-step brewing process and pay a visit to the famous Budweiser Clydesdales. While here, have a brewski at the on-site **biergarten** (11am-8pm daily May-Aug., 11am-7pm daily Mar.-Apr. and Sept.-Oct., 11am-6:30pm daily Jan.-Feb., 11am-6pm daily Nov.-Dec.), which offers outdoor seating under twinkle lights.

CITY MUSEUM

The coolest place in St. Louis is **City Museum** (750 N. 16th St., 314/231-2489, www.citymuseum.org, 9am-5pm Mon.-Thurs., 9am-midnight Fri.-Sat., 11am-5pm Sun., $16-21, free ages 2 and younger), a 10-story wonderland for kids and adults that was created to be an ever-changing city inside the city. On a visit here, you and your kids will be climbing all the time. Wear closed-toe shoes and rent a pair of knee pads. You'll need them, because you'll be on your hands and knees traveling up caged bridges, through airplanes, in caves (bring a flashlight or headlamp), and across buildings. Kids have the run of the place during the day, and it gets crowded. On Friday and Saturday nights, though, it's an adult affair, with two bars open and plenty of fun to be had. The museum's rooftop has a huge slide, a Ferris wheel, a school bus hanging from the edge of the building, and gardens, along with more things to climb.

FOOD

NEAR BUSCH STADIUM

It's a mile from Busch Stadium to **Bogart's Smokehouse** (1627 S. 9th St., 314/621-3107, www.bogartssmokehouse.com, 10:30am-4pm Mon.-Tues., 10:30am-8pm Wed.-Sat., under $40), but I recommend walking—at least on the way back when you're fighting off a food coma. This is serious St. Louis barbecue, and the meats are juicy, from pulled pork to wings to burnt ends to ribs. You'll also want to try a little of every sauce available (Mad Maddie's Vinegar is a beautiful thing), but these meats stand up on their own. Be sure to pair your plate with a side of peppery, garlicky fire-and-ice pickles and baked beans, and get ready to stand in line, especially on nice weekend days.

Hey, as long as you're down here, visit the nearby location of small Missouri chain **Mission Taco Joint** (908 Lafayette Ave., 314/858-8226, www.missiontacojoint.com, 11am-1:30am Mon.-Sat., 11am-midnight Sun., under $20). Offering the kind of authentic tacos you might find in the Mission District in San Francisco, this spot has a slew of options, along with burritos, *tortas* (sandwiches), and cocktails (including a margarita). They make their own corn tortillas, too.

OTHER NEIGHBORHOODS

If you want to be a St. Louis barbecue completist, you have to visit **Pappy's Smokehouse** (3106 Olive St., 314/535-4340, www.pappyssmokehouse.com, 11am-8pm Mon.-Sat., 11am-4pm Sun., under $40) in Midtown. Snag a checkered-tablecloth picnic table if you can, or just sit in the large dining room. Either way, you're going to get the legendary ribs, smoked over applewood and cherrywood. Sides include potato salad and applesauce. The brisket isn't bad, either.

You've got to eat fried chicken when you're in town. Visit **Grace Meat + Three** (4270 Manchester Ave., 314/533-2700, www.stl-grace.com, 11am-9pm Wed.-Fri., 10am-9pm Sat., 10am-8pm Sun., under $30) for the good stuff, including a $10 half bird, a hot chicken salad sandwich, or fried bologna. With a main, you get three sides (thus the name). This clean, inviting bistro space has plenty of seating. Find it southeast of Forest Park.

If you have time, head out to The Hill and go on a miniature food crawl in St. Louis's version of Little Italy. For red sauce and wine, head to **Gian-Tony's Ristorante** (5356 Daggett Ave., 314/772-4893, www.giantonys. com, 5pm-9:30pm Mon.-Thurs., 5pm-10pm Fri.-Sat., 4:30pm-8:30pm Sun., under $60). This spot is classic Sicilian, serving dishes like *linguine con pesce, farfallini salmone,* and a selection of succulent veal plates.

Don't leave The Hill (or St. Louis) without trying the local delicacy of fried ravioli, breaded and dropped in oil; it's downright addictive. Get it at **Mama Toscano's Ravioli and Deli** (2201 Macklind Ave., 314/776-2926, www.mamatoscano.com, 8am-5:30pm Tues.-Fri., 8am-5pm Sat., under $20). Beyond the ravioli (served in batches of 10), you can get sandwiches at Mama Toscano's. There are only a few tables.

If you want a morning coffee, visit **Park Avenue Coffee** (417 N. 10th St., 314/231-5282, www.parkavenuecoffee.com, 7am-6pm Mon.-Sat., 7:30am-6pm Sun., under $15). It's open early for the Downtown visitor. The

Photos (from top to bottom): St. Louis Gateway Arch; Citygarden Sculpture Park; St. Louis Art Museum in Forest Park.

thing to get here is the gooey butter cake, also known as chess pie, another St. Louis specialty. This indulgent treat is made of butter, sugar, eggs, cream cheese, and flour.

BARS AND BREWERIES

NEAR BUSCH STADIUM

The Cardinals bar is **Paddy O's** (618 S. 7th St., 314/588-7313, www.stlpaddyos.com, 10am-3am daily), just across the interstate (you can walk underneath it) from the ballpark. This is a large bar with a whole lot of space for you and your friends before or after the game. It's a red sea here on game days. The usual macro-brewed beers are available, and there's also a rooftop bar. The food is affordable (under $15) and includes barbecue dishes.

Give yourself 15 minutes to walk south from Busch Stadium to **4 Hands Brewing Co.** (1220 S. 8th St., 314/436-1559, www.4handsbrewery.com, noon-10pm Mon.-Thurs., noon-midnight Fri.-Sat., 11am-9pm Sun). Makers of City Wide, a popular American pale ale, 4 Hands has a two-level taproom with plenty of seating upstairs. Some of the proceeds from City Wide sales go to local organizations.

OTHER NEIGHBORHOODS

My favorite brewery in St. Louis, **Perennial Artisan Ales** (8125 Michigan Ave., 314/631-7300, www.perennialbeer.com, 4pm-10pm Wed.-Thurs., 4pm-11pm Fri., noon-11pm Sat., noon-5pm Sun.), is down in the Patch neighborhood. With a deep roster of Belgian beers, plus boozy stouts and experimental ales, Perennial makes for a fun few hours of tap and bottle hunting. Plenty of games are available in the taproom, and small bites are available for snacking.

Closer to Downtown but still south in the Gravois Park neighborhood is **Earthbound Beer** (2724 Cherokee St., 314/769-9576, www.earthboundbeer.com, 4pm-midnight Tues.-Fri., noon-midnight Sat., noon-10pm Sun.). Earthbound isn't afraid to put some spice in its beer, from sea salt sours to a Thai basil IPA to a core blonde beer with black pepper and cardamom. This is one of the coolest breweries you'll step foot in, simply for its custom-made wood tables and an upstairs seating area with a terrace walkway.

Nearby, in Bevo Mill, is the **Heavy Anchor** (5226 Gravois Ave., 314/352-5226, www.theheavyanchor.com, 5pm-1am Mon.-Sat.), a top neighborhood bar that serves an eclectic list of beers and hosts comedy shows, live music, and trivia and open mic nights. There are a couple arcade games, too. This is a fun hangout.

If you have time, spend a few hours in Soulard, the iconic neighborhood filled with blues music and a party atmosphere. Some of the establishments to hit include **Hammerstone's** (2028 S. 9th St., 314/773-5565, www.hammerstones.net, 6:30am-1:30am Mon.-Fri., 8am-1:30am Sat., 9am-midnight Sun.), with live blues daily; and the Cajunspiced **1860 Saloon, Game Room & Hardshell Café** (1860 S. 9th St., 314/231-1860, www.1860saloon.com, 11am-1:30am Mon.-Sat., 11am-midnight Sun.), which also has regular live shows plus arcade games, shuffleboard, and more. The 1860 Saloon also offers a free **shuttle** to Cardinals games on all game days.

RECREATION

PARKS

Forest Park

Established in 1876 next to Central West End, **Forest Park** (5595 Grand Dr., 6am-10pm daily) is the great green space that serves as a unifying hub of the city. Comprising 1,371 acres, the park played host to the 1904 Summer Olympics and also includes some of the city's most important attractions. The park has a 22.5-acre lake with a picnic area on an island, plus a greenhouse, and a skating rink.

One of the top draws in Forest Park is the **St. Louis Zoo** (Government Dr., 314/781-0900, www.stlzoo.org, 8am-5pm Mon.-Thurs., 8am-7pm Fri.-Sun. Memorial Day-Labor Day, 9am-5pm daily Labor Day-Memorial Day, free but some attractions cost $3.95-7.95 per person), home to lions and tigers (and other big cats), sea lions, elephants, hippopotamuses, alpacas, primates, and more.

The **Missouri History Museum** (5700 Lindell Blvd., 314/746-4599, www.mohistory.org, 10am-5pm Wed.-Mon., 10am-8pm Tues., free) is headlined by an exhibit displaying the history of St. Louis, including stories of the travelers and explorers who traveled to and through the Gateway to the West.

The **St. Louis Art Museum** (1 Fine Arts Dr., 314/721-0072, www.slam.org, 10am-5pm Tues.-Thurs. and Sat.-Sun., 10am-9pm Fri., free) has a collection spanning 5,000 years and featuring works by artists such as Henri Matisse, Vincent van Gogh, and Horace Pippin. The museum also displays contemporary art, photography and new media, and handmade items.

Citygarden Sculpture Park

In the middle of Downtown St. Louis, just four blocks west of the Gateway Arch, is **Citygarden Sculpture Park** (801 Market St., www.citygardenstl.org, sunrise-10pm daily, free). It features 24 sculptures including the devastating *Eros Bendato*, where the detached head of the Greek god of love rests on its side. This is one of many cool public art installations dotting the St. Louis landscape. The park is a good respite for families as it has a children's splash plaza and 180-foot-long pool.

CORKBALL

Sure, this is a baseball city, but you can't forget about **corkball.** Established in St. Louis around the 1890s, corkball is a miniature version of baseball that uses a 1.6-ounce ball; the types of hits are determined by how far the ball is struck. Want to play or watch?

The **Gateway Corkball Club** (3871 Walsh St., 314/832-7473, www.gatewaycorkballclub.com) has been stoking the fire for city residents since 1929. They follow a traditional baseball schedule (Apr.-Oct.).

ACCOMMODATIONS

NEAR BUSCH STADIUM

A five-minute, 0.2-mile walk to Busch Stadium, **Hilton St. Louis at the Ballpark** (1 S. Broadway, 314/421-1776, www.hilton.com, $120-250) is a good-value stay if you want to be close to the action and not have to worry about driving to the stadium or parking. It also offers a Grand Slam package that includes two or four tickets in outfield box seats plus a baseball-themed souvenir.

The **Marriott St. Louis Grand** (800 Washington Ave., 314/621-9600, www.marriott.com, $140-250) is a 10-minute, 0.5-mile walk from the ballpark and offers a Grand Slam Ticket Package. The deal features two box seat tickets, a $20 food and drink voucher for the hotel bar and restaurant, and complimentary valet parking for one vehicle.

OTHER NEIGHBORHOODS

If you're hoping to stay in Central West End or close to the Grove district, the **Parkway Hotel** (4550 Forest Park Ave., 314/256-7777, www.theparkwayhotel.com, $150-250) is a great option. The rooms are no-fuss but comfortable, and service is quite good. Parking is available in a garage next to the hotel.

GETTING AROUND

PUBLIC TRANSIT

The public transit system in St. Louis is known as **Metro** (www.metrostlouis.org). It includes **MetroBus** ($2) and **MetroLink** ($2.50). The MetroBus network is vast, whereas MetroLink has two lines that begin in Illinois and cross into Downtown St. Louis. They run on the same tracks until the **Forest Park-DeBaliviere station** (250 DeBaliviere Ave.), then split. The **Red Line** connects Lambert International Airport to Downtown; the **Blue Line** visits suburbs like Maplewood.

TAXI, UBER, AND LYFT

In St. Louis, prices are similar among taxicabs, Uber rides, and Lyft rides. From the airport to Busch Stadium, a ride is $35 (give or take a dollar or two each way), regardless of which service you use. If you want a good taxi company, opt for **County Taxi** (314/991-5300, www.countycab.com), also known as **Yellow Taxi**, which boasts good service.

CAR

Downtown St. Louis has a grid pattern. **Market Street** is the main west to east thoroughfare, and tree-named streets surround it (Chestnut, Walnut, Pine, Olive, Locust). Numbered streets run north to south; **14th Street** is more trafficked than those surrounding it.

Thanks to the city's robust, well-planned highway system, St. Louis doesn't have terrible traffic. A loop of sorts travels around the city (**I-255 to I-270**), but various highways stream toward Downtown St. Louis from all directions. **I-64** runs west to east from the suburb of Wentzville, Missouri, through Downtown, right past Busch Stadium, and on toward Louisville. I-64 is joined with **US-40** in the Downtown area. As it approaches the Mississippi River, it hooks up with **I-55,** which goes north to south from Chicago toward Memphis. From I-255 south of the city, I-55 is a good way into the city.

I-70 is the other major highway that cuts through the city, coming from the west and Kansas City, entering Downtown from the north with **I-44,** then crossing the Mississippi River on the Stan Musial Veterans Memorial Bridge, and heading east toward Indianapolis. I-44 comes in from the southwest and

Springfield, Missouri; it terminates at I-70 after entering Downtown.

MO-100 connects the southwestern suburbs to Downtown. It is called **Manchester Avenue** as it passes through the Grove district. At Vandeventer Avenue, it becomes **Choteau Avenue,** a major thoroughfare in Downtown St. Louis. From the south is **MO-30,** which is also **Historic Route 66** and **Gravois Avenue.** Once it crosses I-44/I-55, it becomes **Tucker Boulevard,** a road that runs south to north through Downtown before becoming the on-ramp to I-70.

PEORIA, ILLINOIS

Peoria may be a small city between Chicago and St. Louis, but it also has a solid professional baseball history. Clubs played in Peoria as early as the 1870s, and through the decades they had some fun names (Distillers, Hoosiers, Tractors). During World War II, Peoria was home to the Redwings, a team in the All-American Girls Professional Baseball League remembered in the film *A League of Their Own.* But by 1957, there was no professional baseball at all in Peoria, men's or women's.

That changed in 1983 when the Peoria Suns were established as a minor league team (later becoming the Chiefs). Aside from one season, the Chiefs have always been an affiliate of the Cubs or Cardinals. Notable alumni include Greg Maddux, Albert Pujols, Wally Joyner, and Rafael Palmeiro.

If you have time when driving between Milwaukee (or Chicago) and St. Louis, Peoria makes the perfect midway stop, with an affordable baseball experience awaiting you.

GETTING THERE

Car

From **Milwaukee,** the more scenic route to Peoria is a **230-mile, four-hour** drive. Take I-43 South, I-90 East, then I-39 South. Exit at IL-18 West and take that to IL-26 South. Merge with IL-116 and cross the Illinois

River at US-150 West. Then turn onto IL-29 South and take that into town.

Want to stick to highways? Take I-94 East toward Chicago and merge onto I-294 as it stays on the outskirts of the Windy City. At I-55, head south toward Bloomington. There, you'll change to I-74 West, which brings you right to Peoria. This route is also **230 miles** and takes around **four hours.**

Bus

Greyhound (www.greyhound.com) services Peoria from **Milwaukee.** You'll pay between $50 and $80 for a nearly 10-hour ride that stops in Chicago and Champaign, Illinois. In Chicago, you'll transfer to a Greyhound partner company's bus, then finish the trip to Peoria. The bus deposits passengers at the **City Link Building** (407 SW Adams St.).

DOZER PARK

Opening in 2002 as O'Brien Field and now named **Dozer Park** (730 SW Jefferson Ave., 309/680-4000, www.milb.com/peoria), the venue that plays host to the class-A **Peoria Chiefs** is a classic, small-city minor league park with a substantial number of amenities for baseball fans.

There's limited seating, mostly concentrated around the infield in foul territory. **Dugout seats** (sections 103-112) are affordable, costing less than $20. **Field seats** (sections 113-114) provide views of third base and are also under $20. **Reserved seats** (sections 101-102) offer first-base views and can be had for about $11. **Lawn seating** is available near the foul poles and in left field for about $9 a ticket. The **suites** are upstairs; tickets include a buffet meal. You're better off doing general admission, though.

A number of concession stands and mobile food and drink stands are concentrated around the infield. **Hook and Ladder** (section 104) has loaded nachos and tacos; **Burgertopia** (section 108) offers a couple decent burgers; and **Engine House** (section 113) serves up pulled pork and brats. Good craft beer can be found at **3 Up 3 Down** (section 109).

A play area for kids called the **RLI Play Zone** (center field) includes inflatables. Look for the **speed pitch cage** (section 114), where a particularly impressive fastball can win you a prize. Visitors of all ages can try their hand here.

FOOD

A few blocks northeast of Dozer Park is the **Blue Duck Barbecue Tavern** (212 SW Water St., 309/981-5801, www.blueduck-barbecue.com, 11am-2pm and 5pm-10pm Tues.-Thurs., 11am-2pm and 4pm-10pm Fri., 11am-10pm Sat., under $40), a smokehouse in an old rail depot. They've got ribs plus brisket, a whole bunch of shareable plates and appetizers, and a good beer list with mostly domestic offerings.

For a beer in a classic Irish pub setting, there are two solid options in Peoria. Check out **Ulrich's Rebellion Room** (631 Main St., 309/676-1423, www.ulrichsrebellionroom.com, 5pm-4am Mon.-Wed. and Sat., 11am-2pm and 5pm-4am Thurs.-Fri., 9pm-4am Sun., under $30), which is open late, has a comfortable, friendly vibe, and packs its menu with no-frills bar grub. There's also **Kelleher's Irish Pub & Eatery** (619 SW Water St., 309/673-6000, www.kellehersirishpub.com, 11am-midnight Mon.-Thurs., 11am-2am Fri.-Sat., under $40). This pretty space has all the trappings—a wood bar, brick walls, and a menu of Irish pub favorites.

RECREATION

The major city park is **Glen Oak Park** (2218 N. Prospect Rd., http://peoriaparks.org, 5am-11pm daily). A 117-acre public park, it's home to the **Peoria Zoo** (2320 N. Prospect Rd., 309/686-3365, www.peoriazoo.org, 10am-5pm daily, $9.75, $8.75 seniors, $6.75 ages 2-12, free age 1 and under), which is small but packed. Look for an African lion, giraffes, zebras, rhinoceroses, Siberian tigers, and a number of Australian animals. Also here is **Luthy Botanical Garden** (2520 N. Prospect Rd., 309/681-3506, 10am-5pm daily, free), a serene getaway that's home to tropical plants and a number of theme gardens: a rose garden, crabapple area, herb garden, and otheres.

ACCOMMODATIONS

Hotels are affordable in Peoria. The independent **Mark Twain Hotel** (225 NE Adams St., 309/676-3600, www.marktwainhotel. com, $100-175) is one of the higher-priced options. The comfortable rooms include 260-square-foot studios. Free parking is available, and there's a fitness center on-site.

Budget hotels dot the area where I-74 runs into US-150, near the Northwoods Mall in the western end of the city. The best among these is the **Comfort Suites** (1812 W. War Memorial Dr., 309/688-3800, $60-150), which rates solidly for service and cleanliness.

GETTING AROUND

There is public transportation in Peoria. **City Link** (www.ridecitylink.org, $1) is a **bus service** with 21 routes, including several that run through the Downtown area. Buses run every half hour or so on weekdays and every hour or so on Saturdays. There's less service on Sundays.

Driving around the city is a cinch. From the southeast, **I-74** slices through Downtown Peoria and heads northwest. Parallel to the Illinois River is **IL-29,** also known as **Adams Street** (west to east) and **Jefferson Avenue** (east to west). Both roads intersect with **Main Street,** which runs north and south before doglegging west at Bradley University. **Glen Oak Avenue** becomes **Prospect Road** at another dogleg near Glen Oak Park. If you stay in the area bounded by Adams, Jefferson, and Glen Oak, and you don't go too far in either direction from Main Street, you'll never get lost.

CINCINNATI
REDS

Founded in 1882, the Cincinnati
Reds are baseball's oldest franchise, and that's a big deal to Cincinnatians. The city stops everything on opening day to celebrate the occasion with the Findlay Market Parade, which crawls right through Downtown toward Great American Ball Park.

The Reds were originally the Resolute Base Ball Club on Cincinnati, but later changed their name to the Red Stockings—due to their rather edgy (for the time) red knee socks with short pants. That team folded quickly, but a new version of the Red Stockings emerged in 1876 as a charter member of the National League. They were expelled from the league for serving beer at their games. Another iteration of the Red Stockings started up in 1882 in the American Association,

but because there was already an established Boston team with the same name, writers shortened Cincinnati's nickname to "Reds." That name—and that team—stuck, with the Reds joining the National League in 1890.

The Reds, who played in tiny Crosley Field from 1912 to 1970, weren't a very strong team from the outset, failing to finish in even second place in the National League until 1919, when they broke through for their first world championship. Another drought followed, lasting until 1939, when the team, led by hitter Ernie Lombardi and pitcher Bucky Walters took the NL pennant—and, a year later, the world title. Yet another slide followed, highlighted by a phase between 1953 and 1958 when the team changed its nickname to the Redlegs (since "Red" was, at the time, a pejorative term for a member of the Communist Party).

But once the team went back to calling itself the Reds, its fortunes began to change. Young hitter Frank Robinson helped lead the club to a 1961 NL pennant, and he soon had backup in the form of Pete Rose, a mousy man who could flat-out hit the baseball. Robinson would be traded to Baltimore after 1965; after a few more years, Rose and a new core that included catcher Johnny Bench, slugger Tony Perez, and slick-fielding shortstop Dave Concepcion took the league by storm. Between 1970-1979, and especially after moving into the multipurpose Riverfront Stadium in 1971, the Reds dominated the game. They reached the postseason six times during the decade, won the National League pennant four times, and took home two championships (in 1975 and 1976). At the height of their powers, they were the Big Red Machine, managed by Sparky Anderson and capable of scoring countless runs. More talent in the form of Joe Morgan, George Foster, and Ken Griffey Sr. made the team nearly unstoppable.

During the 1980s, the Reds retooled, emerging once again in 1990 with a championship, thanks in part to star players Barry Larkin and Eric Davis. But that was the last major push from the Reds. They've had only a few playoff appearances since that year, failing to win a single game in the NLCS since that season. Their small-market position is a challenge, as they don't typically keep players for long and have trouble buying premium talent in the form of free agents.

There have been a few recent bright spots, chief among them the supremely talented hitter Joey Votto, who has spent his entire career in Cincinnati. The team also opened Great American Ball Park in 2003, a venue that befits the club's history. And of course, there's always that opening day parade. One thing you can definitely say about Cincinnati: These folks love their team.

PLANNING YOUR TIME

Cincinnati may be the perfect **long week-end** city. There's enough here to fill up **2-3 days,** and when you leave, you'll feel as if you experienced quite a bit of the area. Plan on spending part of one day in the **Over-the-Rhine neighborhood,** but also visit at least one of the city's best museums, such as the **National Underground Railroad Freedom Center** or the **Cincinnati Art Museum.** Factor in food and drink, and a **Reds game,** and you got yourself a good long weekend.

You can stay anywhere within the Cincinnati area, including close to Cincinnati/ Northern Kentucky International Airport. The preferred mode of travel here is by car, whether you're driving or catching a rideshare. If you want to concentrate your time in the Downtown and Over-the-Rhine areas, then opt to stay **Downtown.** As an alternative, there are chain hotels worth looking into over the Ohio River in **Newport, Kentucky.** You can take a boat from there to Great American Ball Park or just walk across a pedestrian bridge.

Great American Ball Park
CINCINNATI

CAMP WASHINGTON
CAMP WASHINGTON CHILI ▼

CENTRAL PKWY

SPRING GROVE AVE

75

CORRYVILLE

To Listermann Brewing Company →

University of Cincinnati

Megabus M

71

GILBERT AVE

EAST WALNUT HILLS

CUF

MT AUBURN

VINE ST

CENTRAL PKWY

To Four Seasons Marina, Scenic River Canoe Excursions →

COLUMBIA PKWY

FINDLAY MARKET ★

WEST END

W LIBERTY ST

TUCKER'S RESTAURANT ▼

CINCINNATI ART MUSEUM ★

EDEN PARK

QUEEN CITY RIVERBOAT & YACHT CHARTERS

Union Terminal

OVER-THE-RHINE

SYMPHONY HOTEL & RESTAURANT

LOW SPARK

GRAETER'S ICE CREAM
PANINO ▼
HOMAGE ■

3 POINTS URBAN BREWERY ▼

CINCINNATI PLAYHOUSE IN THE PARK ▼

QUEEN CITY RADIO

WASHINGTON PARK

VINE ST

Greyhound

M

MT ADAMS

OHIO
KENTUCKY

FAIRFIELD AVE

75

Bellevue

To Riverside Boat Launch Ramp ←

50

HARU ▼

MITA'S RESTAURANT & BAR ▼

SEE DETAIL

471

QUEENSGATE

71

GREAT AMERICAN BALL PARK

TAYLOR-SOUTHGATE BRIDGE

PURPLE PEOPLE BRIDGE

AQUA ON THE LEVEE GARAGE P

E 6TH ST

WASHINGTON AVE

Paul Brown Stadium

JOHN A. ROEBLING BRIDGE

BB RIVERBOATS ▼

COACH'S CORNER ▼

PROHIBITION BOURBON BAR ▼

GATEWAY BED & BREAKFAST

Ohio River

Newport

Covington

71

Park Hills

To Cincinnati/Northern Kentucky International Airport →

DETAIL

E 5TH ST
VINE ST
WALNUT ST
MAIN ST

SKYLINE CHILI ▼

E 4TH ST

SYCAMORE ST
BROADWAY ST

O'MALLEY'S IN THE ALLEY ▼

E 3RD ST

71

NATIONAL UNDERGROUND RAILROAD FREEDOM CENTER ▼

JOHNNY BENCH WAY

M

The Banks

SECOND ST E

CENTRAL RIVERFRONT GARAGE P ★

GUILD CINCINNATI ●

JOE NUXHALL WAY

REDS TEAM SHOP ▼

GREAT AMERICAN BALL PARK

TASTE OF BELGIUM ▼

E FREEDOM WAY

THE STRETCH ▼

P

MOERLEIN LAGER HOUSE ▼

OHIO RIVER SCENIC BYWAY

Ohio River

0   0.5 mi

0   0.5 km

0   100 yds

0   100 m

© MOON.COM

Cincinnati is curious geographically and has a climate that's one foot in the Midwest and another very much in the South. The **summer** can be sweltering, with temperatures regularly hitting the mid- to upper 80s, sometimes the 90s. Summer **rain** and occasional **thunderstorms** are typical. The most pleasing time to visit Great American Ball Park is early in the season. **April nights** can be cool, but you can generally expect first-pitch temperatures around 65-70°F. **May** and **June** are pretty perfect, with first-pitch highs in the mid-70s.

GETTING THERE

AIR

The major airport in the area is **Cincinnati/ Northern Kentucky International Airport** (CVG, 3087 Terminal Dr., Hebron, KY, www. cvgairport.com), in the Kentucky suburb of Hebron, 15-20 minutes southwest of Cincinnati. The airport is served by **Air Canada** (888/247-2262, www.aircanada.com), **Allegiant** (702/505-8888, www.allegiantair. com), **American Airlines** (800/433-7300, www.aa.com), **Delta** (800/221-1212, www. delta.com), **Frontier** (800/401-9000, www. flyfrontier.com), **Southwest** (800/435-9792, www.southwest.com), and **United** (800/864-8331, www.united.com). There's one terminal with two concourses.

Airport Transportation

Rental cars are available via a five-minute **shuttle** ride from the baggage claim area. To reach Downtown, take I-275 East and I-71 North, then exit at 2nd Street. This drive is less than 15 miles and takes around 20 minutes.

You can also head into Downtown Cincinnati via **TANK** (Transit Authority of Northern Kentucky, www.tankbus.org, $3.50 one-day pass), the regional **bus system.** From the airport, you can board the **2X Airporter** and reach Downtown in about a half hour.

CAR

There are two major highway options from **St. Louis** to Cincinnati. The northern route, which includes driving through Indianapolis, is a **350-mile, 5.5-hour** drive on **I-70 East** to **I-74 East.**

The southern route goes through Louisville and is a **360-mile, 5.5-hour** drive on **I-64 East** to **I-71 North.** A third route, far more scenic, is in between the two: a **350-mile, seven-hour** jaunt along **US-50 East,** cutting through Hoosier National Forest in Indiana.

When driving from St. Louis to Cincinnati, prepare to lose an hour. Set your clock ahead an hour once you cross into Indiana.

TRAIN

Cincinnati's Queensgate neighborhood has a beautiful art deco **Amtrak station** (www. amtrak.com) in **Union Terminal** (1301 Western Ave.). Designed by Paul Philippe Cret and built between 1929 and 1933, it features a luminous golden dome inside. The station services Amtrak's **Cardinal line,** which runs between Chicago and New York City. There's no direct connection from **St. Louis** to Cincinnati, but riders can take the **Lincoln Service** or **Texas Eagle** lines from St. Louis to Chicago and then connect to the Cardinal line. The trip costs about $100-150, and it will take nearly a full day of travel.

Union Terminal is about two miles northwest of Great American Ball Park and Downtown Cincinnati. To get there, you can arrange a ride-share vehicle.

BUS

If you're taking **Greyhound** (www.greyhound.com) from **St. Louis,** you'll arrive at the **Cincinnati Bus Station** (1005 Gilbert Ave.). The trip from St. Louis takes 7-10 hours, including a transfer in Indianapolis. You'll pay around $85 for the ride. The Greyhound station is just over a mile northeast of Downtown.

YOUR BEST DAY AT GREAT AMERICAN BALL PARK

You have a day in Cincinnati before taking in a Reds game at Great American later that evening. Here's how you should indulge.

10 HOURS BEFORE FIRST PITCH
Up and at 'em! Grab breakfast at **Tucker's Restaurant.** You're in Cincinnati, so make sure there's *goetta* (a kind of sausage) on your plate.

8.5 HOURS BEFORE FIRST PITCH
Take a quick walk north to **Findlay Market.** Sure, you just ate, but you can buy some provisions for a picnic lunch later on. This is a must-see Cincinnati landmark, so take pictures and walk off your big breakfast.

7 HOURS BEFORE FIRST PITCH
Continue your day in the Over-the-Rhine district by paying a visit to **Homage.** Pick up a cool Reds-themed T-shirt, along with any other gifts that strike your fancy.

6.5 HOURS BEFORE FIRST PITCH
Just two blocks west of Homage is **Washington Park.** If it's sunny, enjoy a picnic lunch and have yourself a beverage from **The Porch.**

4 HOURS BEFORE FIRST PITCH
Head down toward the ballpark. Grab a ride down to **O'Malley's in the Alley** for a cold drink and good conversation. If you're alone, here's where you chat up some Reds fans and make a few new friends.

Washington Park

2 HOURS BEFORE FIRST PITCH
Walk the few blocks southeast to **Great American Ball Park** and visit the **Cincinnati Reds Hall of Fame & Museum.** Spend some time here absorbing Reds history.

When you're finished, head to the park's **Fioptics District** and visit its **Cincinnati Bell GigaBar** for a game of boccie with a beer.

DURING THE GAME
You must have a Coney dog from **Skyline Chili.** If you want more beer, hit up **section 118** for the local goods.

AFTER THE GAME
Hop a ride north and finish the night at **Queen City Radio.** If you'd prefer something sweet, end the night with two scoops of black raspberry chocolate chip from **Graeter's Ice Cream.**

Megabus (https://us.megabus.com) also serves Cincinnati, depositing passengers at the **University of Cincinnati campus** (Commons Way at W. University Ave.). You'll have to change buses in Chicago during a ride that lasts 12-13 hours in all, but you'll pay more like $60-70. The campus is three miles north of Downtown, so you'll need to take a ride-share to get to the ballpark or your hotel.

Great American Ball Park

Opening in 2003 along the banks of the Ohio River, **Great American Ball Park** (100 Joe Nuxhall Way, www.mlb.com/reds) replaced the multipurpose doughnut-shaped Cinergy Field—formerly Riverfront Stadium—as the home of the Reds. It isn't as loud as Yankee Stadium or even Busch Stadium, parks that seem to reflect the decorated histories of

The Great American Ball Park is on the Ohio River.

their teams; instead, Great American feels quiet and quirky. Considering that the Reds have been around forever yet haven't had quite the success of, say, the Cardinals, this place feels just right for Cincinnati.

You might think a ballpark sitting beside a body of water would get more attention, but Great American feels more like a retread of the retro-classic and retro-modern ballpark movements than it does something new and exciting. There are elements of the jewel-box, throwback feel here, including a mammoth video board and enormous light towers in the outfield, and then there's a little bit of quirk in the outfield, with the riverboat party deck in center field. And, of course, the water is just beyond the right field seats.

Great American does a decent job connecting to the history of the team, with its exceptional Hall of Fame and museum and the replica of the infamous Crosley Terrace, a sloped part of the playing field at the Reds' old stadium, Crosley Field. These elements are welcome and help tie together the experience, but ultimately Great American never quite feels unique and doesn't fully take advantage of its waterside location.

ORIENTATION

Great American Ball Park sits close to the Ohio River, with US-27 (the Ohio River Scenic Byway) running between the park and the river. On the other side of the park is I-71. Joe Nuxhall Way, on the west side of the park, along the first base line, is the main road that's home to restaurants, bars, and other businesses.

The park has eight entry gates that typically open 90 minutes before first pitch, but there are exceptions: For Monday-Friday evening games in April, May, and September, gates open one hour ahead of time. On opening day, gates open two hours prior to first pitch.

The gate you'll want is **Gapper's Alley** (left of home plate, section 119), which isn't as crowded as the nearby main gate at Crosley Terrace. It's called Gapper's Alley because it's a gap in the ballpark that allows for a view straight to the field from the wide concourse.

TICKETS AND SEATING

Pricing

The Reds use a **dynamic pricing** model for tickets. Games against **rivals** like the **Cardinals, Cubs,** and **Indians** will generally cost more than games against teams not considered draws, like the Marlins and Diamondbacks. For a weekend game against the Cardinals, a ticket for a middle-of-the-road seat at the park may cost around $60, while for a game against the Marlins that same seat may cost around $30.

Seating Plan

There are **five levels** of seating at Great American Ball Park. The **100 level** includes the **diamond seats** (sections 1-5) behind home plate; the **scout box** (sections 22-25) just behind those seats; the **terrace outfield** (101-106) in left field; the **terrace line** in distant left field (sections 107-110) and right field (sections 136-139); the **field box** (sections 107-112, 134-139) along the foul

GAME COSTS

Tickets: Great American Ball Park is on the moderate to high end of the ticket spectrum. You'll pay **$50-60** for good lower-level seats, around **$40** for mid-tier seats, and closer to **$20** for upper-level choices. The cheapest seats can come in as low as **$5.**

Hot dog: Expect to pay around **$5** for a hot dog, about in line with league averages. Signature hot dogs and local fare like the Big Red Smokey sausage will cost a few bucks more.

Beer: It's **$5** for Bud, but expect to pay the usual **$12-15** for really good stuff in larger sizes.

Parking: It's cheap! Closer to the ballpark, you might pay **$10-20,** but a few blocks away, you can score spots for as low as **$5.**

lines; the **infield box** (sections 113-121, 127-133) that wraps around the infield; the **scout seats** (sections 122-126); and the **sun deck/moon deck** (sections 140-146).

In between the lower and upper concourses, on the **200** and **300 levels,** are the **FOX Sports Club,** which includes the **premium club home area** (sections 220-228), and **regular club seating** (sections 301-307). All of the sections here include access to a buffet and unlimited nonalcoholic drinks.

On the upper concourse, the **400 level** includes the **bleachers** (sections 401-406); the **Fioptics District rooftop patio** (sections 408-410); the **outer mezzanine** (sections 411-414) along the left-field line; the **mezzanine** (sections 415-419) along the third-base line; and the **view level box** (sections 420-437), which wraps around the rest of the infield.

The **500 level** starts with section 509 in the left field corner by the foul pole, then wraps around the infield area (with **The Gap**

between sections 519 and 520 at the third base side of home plate) and continues to deep right field in foul territory where you'll find section 537 and the **TriHealth Family Zone.** Section 509 is the **value view,** home to the cheapest seats in the park; in sections 510-537, prices are determined by how far up in the section you sit.

The ballpark has a number of **group seating areas,** including the **TriHealth Riverboat Deck** (center field, accessible from lower concourse), **Laura's Lean Bullpen Decks** (center field, above visitors' bullpen), the **Budweiser Bullpen Decks** (right field, above home bullpen), **Redlegs Landing** (sections 436-437), **Ole Smoky Party Barn** (section 137), and the **Handlebar at the Riverfront Club** (right-field line, 300 level). Standing room is available at the Handlebar, and it'll cost you about $100, and only for select games.

Where to Buy Tickets

You can find slightly less expensive tickets at **StubHub,** but more seats will generally be available via the **Reds website** and **ticket office.** You can also get your tickets via the **MLB Ballpark app,** which offers seat upgrade options. Savvy fans tend to get cheap tickets through the app and then use the upgrade function immediately upon entering the park to score a sweet deal on an up-close seat.

Best Seats

Thanks to its riverside location, Great American Ball Park looks stunning from just a few levels up, and near home plate. For that reason, I recommend **sections 420-424** in the **view level box.** The closer to the rail the better, but these seats are best for **night games,** as the sun can be bad here. Seats in the **mezzanine section** (sections 415-419) are slightly less expensive and also supply a heck of a view. The sun is a concern here, too.

If you're looking for an all-in-one experience, try the **Fioptics District** (sections 408-410), a rooftop patio with a bar that comes at a cheap ticket price (usually around $15) and includes a concession credit. For something

BE A FAN

Reds fans are pretty genial, unless you're a Cardinals, Cubs, or Indians fan, of course. Then they'll just be slightly less friendly. When the Reds play the Indians, the teams vie for the **Ohio Cup**. At the end of the annual series of interleague games, the team with the most wins against the other takes home a trophy proving Buckeye State superiority. If the teams each win the same number of games against each other, the previous trophy holder retains it. Fun fact: From 1989 to 1996, before interleague play was baked into their regular season, the teams met for a one-game playoff in the state capital of Columbus just before the season started.

Cincinnati Reds mascots

The Reds have more mascots than the typical team, trotting out four specific figures during the course of a game. In the vein of Philadelphia's Phillie Phanatic is **Gapper**, a furry, red creature who's named after the alley (or gap) in the park. **Mr. Red** is the original mascot, a jovial human with a giant baseball head (he was the logo during the Big Red Machine days of the 1970s). Then there's **Mr. Redlegs**—a second baseball head—who was the Reds logo in the 1950s but looks like he's straight out of 1882 with his handlebar mustache and pillbox hat. He debuted as the mascot in 2007 to replace Mr. Red (who returned in 2012). Finally, there's **Rosie Red**—a third baseball head—sporting lipstick and a bob haircut. She is dressed like a player from the All-American Girls Professional Baseball League of the 1940s and 1950s. She came aboard in 2008 and honors the Rosie Reds, a group of women Reds fans that formed in 1964.

Over the last few years, the Reds have played **"Unstoppable"** by Cincinnati-based band Foxy Shazam after every win.

a bit more premium, there's the **FOX Sports Club** (200 and 300 levels), where your ticket includes a full buffet and nonalcoholic drinks in an air-conditioned space.

If you're looking to **avoid the sun,** sit in the back rows of the **100 level** along the **first-base line.** Or you can head to the last few rows of the **500 level** around the infield, as those seats are underneath an **extended awning.**

KNOW BEFORE YOU GO

Great American Ball Park is one of the best venues in sports for bringing in **food and drink.** You can bring in your own grub, provided it's packed in the usual 16- by 16- by 8-inch soft-sided **cooler** (or a smaller size). Even better: Unopened **water bottles, soft drinks,** and **sports drink** bottles are also allowed inside.

The park offers automatic **digital** check-in and real-time information transmission via MLB's Ballpark app for those who own devices equipped with Apple iOS 7 or higher.

The **Pampers Nursing Suite** is available to breastfeeding mothers and includes gliders, a private restroom, changing stations, lockers, a sink, ice, refrigeration, and rocking chairs. Only nursing mothers and their infants are allowed inside. To get here, take the elevator for the FOX Sports Club that features the Rosie Red mascot.

Accessibility

For **wheelchair assistance** during the game, find the nearest Reds event staff employee or head to one of the **TriHealth Fan Accommodation Stations** (sections 119, 420). Those stations are also where you can get **assisted listening devices.** There are seven **elevators** at Great American, located at sections 101, 110, 121, 127, and

135. **Service animals** are welcome at Great American Ball Park.

The best place for **accessible parking** is in the east section of the **Central Riverfront Garage** (171 Joe Nuxhall Way, $20) or in the **East Garage** (435 E. Pete Rose Way, $12). For the Central Riverfront Garage, call 513/765-7400, option 3, to obtain passes ahead of time.

GETTING THERE

Public Transit

The **Bell Connector** (www.cincinnatibellconnector.com, 6:30am-midnight Mon.-Thurs., 6:30am-1am Fri., 8am-1am Sat., 9am-11pm Sun. and holidays, $1 for two-hour pass, $2 for day pass) is a **streetcar service** that stops at **The Banks station** (2nd St. and Main St.) near the ballpark and continues on a loop through Downtown and Over-the-Rhine. This is a great option for fans staying Downtown.

You can also take a **METRO bus** (www.go-metro.com, $1.75 within city), operated by the Southwest Ohio Regional Transit Authority, which has the hilarious acronym of **SORTA**. Bus routes that stop near the ballpark include the **11, 17, 23X, 42X,** and **100.** The closest station is **The Banks station.**

For those staying in Kentucky, **TANK** (www.tankbus.org, $3.50 one-day pass) is a **bus service** that heads across the border into Cincinnati. The **9, 16, 25,** and **33** routes stop near the park.

Driving

Great American Ball Park is near multiple highways, including I-75, I-71, I-471, and US-50. Be prepared for traffic on any of these highways, especially for weekday evening games, as you'll be fighting rush-hour traffic to and from the city.

There are a variety of **parking** options around Great American Ball Park. Naturally, the closer you are, the more you're going to pay. You can park at the **Central Riverfront Garage** (99 2nd St., www.parking.com/cincinnati), which will charge up to $20 for spots that are just a half-block walk east to the ballpark. **Prepay** for the Central Riverfront Garage online. Alternatively, there are plenty of lots along **4th Street** that will cost $5-15.

You can also park over the river in **Newport, Kentucky.** Try the **Aqua on the Levee Garage** (217 Washington Ave., Newport, $5 for 24 hours), then walk across the Ohio River on the pedestrian-only **Purple People Bridge** (3rd St. at Saratoga St.). From the bridge, turn left onto the Ohio River Trail and take the trail to the ballpark. The whole walk from the garage is 20 minutes. Just one tip: Get to the Aqua lot early to ensure you get a spot.

PARK FEATURES AND SIGHTS

For young fans, the **Kroger Fan Zone** (outside section 107, lower concourse) is the place to be. The outdoor venue has a large Wiffle ball field where, on Sundays, kids can get baseball lessons. Look for a play set, carnival games, a mobile clubhouse that sells merchandise and offers information on the team's kids club, and Wally's Outpost Bar, where parents can pull up a stool or just stand around and have a drink. Kid-friendly concerts are held out here, too.

Cincinnati Reds Hall of Fame & Museum

Great American Ball Park is home to the best in-ballpark museum experience, the **Cincinnati Reds Hall of Fame & Museum** (lower concourse by section 127, 10am-8pm night games, 10am-two hours after game ends day games, 10am-5pm non-game days Apr.-Sept., 10am-5pm Tues.-Sun. Oct.-Mar., $12, $8 seniors and students, free ages 12 and under). The museum, spread across two levels, includes several exhibits, including a timeline of Reds history, an exhibit honoring legendary local broadcasting team Marty Brennaman and Joe Nuxhall, a champions gallery with World Series trophies on display, and a baseball card archive. The hall itself is a dynamic room showing the plaques of every player and notable awarded with the franchise's highest honor. Among those names are Johnny Bench, Barry Larkin, Joe Morgan, Eppa Rixey, and Frank Robinson.

Crosley Terrace

The Reds honor their past with **Crosley Terrace** (Gate A, home plate). This area outside the ballpark replicates a sloped part of the outfield at the Reds' longtime stadium, Crosley Field (1912-1970). Crosley Terrace pays tribute to great players and managers of the past with **statues** of Frank Robinson, Ernie Lombardi, and Joe Nuxhall.

Riverboat

Maybe the most iconic sight at Great American Ball Park is the **replica riverboat** beyond center field. That's the **TriHealth Riverboat Deck** (center field, accessible from lower concourse), a group seating area where tickets include a full buffet and two beers. The boat offers picturesque views of the Ohio River into Kentucky. Just to the right of the deck are the **PNC Power Stacks** (right center field), riverboat-style smokestacks that emit fire when a Reds pitcher throws a strikeout. The stacks launch fireworks when the Reds win a game.

FOOD AND DRINKS

To check off a bucket-list item, visit **Skyline Chili** (sections 103, 116, 130, 518, 535), but don't expect what most Americans call chili. **Cincinnati-style chili** is actually more like spaghetti sauce. At the park, it's put on a hot dog (called a **Coney**), along with shredded cheese and chopped onions. If you want to try Cincinnati chili over spaghetti, you'll need to visit one of Skyline's locations in town. (See the *Food* section for more details.)

For another local specialty, visit **Goetta Gravy Fries** (sections 138, 432) or **Hot Fry Box** (section 110) for the wonders of *goetta* (pronounced "get-ta"), a Cincinnati-area staple of sausage ground with oats. At the ballpark, *goetta* is mixed with gravy and is

Photos (from top to bottom): PNC Power Stacks; Cincinnati Reds merchandise; young fans at a Reds game.

poured onto fries or tater tots topped with cheese and bacon.

Look for the **Big Red Smokey** stands throughout the park. This concession sells Kahn's Big Red Smokey, a favorite sausage of Cincinnati.

The closest thing to a restaurant at the ballpark is the **Machine Room Grille** (upper concourse, left field, 513/765-7606, opens when gates open), a brick-and-steel sports bar and grill with the usual American bar fare, plus various seating options including a patio. Plenty of televisions show the game and other ball games and sporting events.

For the best beer at the ballpark, head to **section 118** for local labels like **Fifty West Brewing Company, Braxton Brewing Company,** and **Fretboard Brewing Company.** Over in **section 134** is a beer and liquor stand that sells **frosé** (frozen rosé), best on those severely hot days.

All ticketed fans can hang out at the standing-room **Budweiser Bowtie Bar** (right field, staircase available in lower concourse). If you're into Bud and want to socialize during the game, this is the place. But if you want to socialize and wouldn't mind some **craft beer,** visit the **Cincinnati Bell GigaBar,** which is open to everyone and not ticketed. This rooftop patio area and full bar offers beer and liquor, plus lounge furniture and boccie and cornhole courts. Come here with a friend or three.

Before the game starts, check out **Garden Bar** (Crosley Terrace, Gate A), which serves beer ($5 happy hour), wine, and soda in a mostly standing-room space among trees.

Want to go all in on the food experience? There are two **all-you-can-eat stands** (lower concourse, section 144; upper concourse, section 428, $20). For $20, you'll get five hot dogs plus unlimited popcorn, peanuts, chips, and soft drinks. To enjoy these spoils, you have to buy a separate **all-you-can-eat pass** (which you can do when buying your ticket), then redeem it at the stands for a wristband.

If you don't wish to wait in line for a concession, the Reds' MLB Ballpark app includes the **Ballpark Express Concessions Pickup** option. Use it to order your food, then pick it up when it's ready.

EVENTS

Batting practice begins two hours before the game. Fans can also get **autographs** (sections 111-113 and 133-135) up to 10 minutes before first pitch, though nothing is guaranteed.

The Reds host multiple **postgame fireworks displays** throughout the season. Check the schedule before the season begins to find out exact dates.

Tours

You can take a **tour** (513/765-7923, daily Apr.-Sept., two hours before first pitch during day games, Sat. during off-season, $22, $17 seniors and students, free ages 4 and under) of Great American Ball Park, which includes admission to the Reds Hall of Fame & Museum. Tours include stops at the press box, the Reds' dugout, and behind home plate.

SHOPPING

The **Reds Team Shop** (100 Joe Nuxhall Way, 513/765-7950, 10am-5pm daily non-game days Apr.-Sept., 10am-one hour after game on game days Apr.-Sept., 10am-5pm Tues.-Sat. Oct.-Mar.) is accessible from Crosley Terrace. The store occupies two levels and has a large selection of merchandise with plenty of apparel. There's also a customization area for jerseys and bats. Prices here can be a bit expensive.

CINCINNATI SIGHTS

FINDLAY MARKET

Since 1852, Cincinnatians have visited **Findlay Market** (1801 Race St., 513/665-4839, www.findlaymarket.org, 9am-6pm Tues.-Fri., 8am-6pm Sat., 10am-4pm Sun.) to procure food, beverages, and various homemade products. Part of the Over-the-Rhine neighborhood, Findlay Market has an iron-framed building that was constructed in the 1850s; it's the only surviving public market from 19th-century Cincinnati. Today it's a tapestry of the city's communities, with vendors ranging from creameries to butchers to pierogi houses to Vietnamese eateries. During baseball season, the market opens its **biergarten** (11am-6pm Sat., 11am-4pm Sun. Apr., 4pm-8pm Tues.-Thurs., 11am-8pm Fri.-Sat., 11am-4pm Sun. May-Oct.), showcasing suds from a different local brewery each month. There's live music at the biergarten Fridays and Sundays.

Opening Day Parade

Cincinnati celebrates baseball's **opening day** like no other city, preceding the first home game with the **Findlay Market Parade** (noon on opening day in Apr., www.findlaymarketparade.com). Notable Reds players and personalities join current players, baseball officials, politicians, and performers at Findlay Market before heading out on the parade route, south on Race Street to 5th Street. The parade continues east on 5th Street to the finish by the Taft Theater, just blocks from Great American Ball Park. For hardcore baseball fans, this is a bucket-list event.

CINCINNATI ART MUSEUM

Close to the Ohio River at Eden Park is one of America's oldest art museums, founded in 1881. The **Cincinnati Art Museum** (953 Eden Park Dr., 513/721-2787, www.cincinnatiartmuseum.org, 11am-5pm Tues.-Wed., Fri.-Sun., 11am-8pm Thurs., free, special exhibitions $10, $5 seniors, students, and ages 6-17, free ages 5 and under) has an extensive collection of local art (works by local artists as well as works made for the city), European art from as far back as the 14th century, and East Asian art. The local art is in an exhibit called the Cincinnati Wing, added in 2003. The wing features angel statues previously displayed at Downtown

Cincinnati's St. Peter in Chains Cathedral and made by Italian sculptor Odoardo Fantacchiotti in the 19th century.

NATIONAL UNDERGROUND RAILROAD FREEDOM CENTER

The **National Underground Railroad Freedom Center** (50 E. Freedom Way, 513/333-7739, www.freedomcenter.org, 10am-5pm Tues.-Sat., noon-5pm Sun.-Mon., $15, $13 seniors, $10.50 ages 3-12, free ages 2 and under), merely two blocks west of Great American Ball Park, tells the story of the search for freedom by enslaved Black people. A permanent exhibit chronicles the history of the Underground Railroad, the network of people and routes that enslaved people used to escape to free states and Canada during the 1800s. Other exhibits include a deep look at Rosa Parks's fight for equality during the U.S. civil rights movement of the 1950s and 1960s, and an examination of implicit biases people carry in their everyday lives. Look for the exhibit that discusses how slavery exists in many forms to this day, including human trafficking.

FOOD

NEAR GREAT AMERICAN BALL PARK

There's good food in The Banks area, just a couple blocks west of the ballpark. Try The Banks location of Cincinnati chain **Taste of Belgium** (16 W. Freedom Way, 513/396-5800, www.authenticwaffle.com, 7am-3pm Mon., 7am-10pm Tues.-Thurs., 7am-11pm Fri., 8am-11pm Sat., 8am-8pm Sun., under $25). Here, chicken, waffles, and beer are held to a high standard. Get crepes for breakfast, and mussels and *frites* for lunch or dinner. There's a nice-sized bar with televisions, too.

Across the street from the stadium is **Moerlein Lager House** (115 Joe Nuxhall

Way, 513/421-2337, www.moerleinlager-house.com, 11am-midnight Mon.-Thurs., 11am-1am Fri.-Sat., 11am-10pm Sun., under $40). They do big, meaty dishes, plus meat and cheese boards. As for beer, look for a deep list of options from the restaurant's brewery, Christian Moerlein, and a good selection of local and national labels. The restaurant is a modern indoor beer garden with plenty of windows and dining space, as well as bar seating and an outdoor deck. This is a good place to go before or after a game.

There's a location of **Skyline Chili** (254 E. 4th St., 513/241-4848, www.skylinechili.com, 10:30am-7pm daily, under $20) that's close to the ballpark. In addition to the Coney you can get at the park, you can try Cincinnati-style chili served over spaghetti with other toppings, called "ways." Having chili **two ways** means spaghetti and chili. Having it **three ways** means spaghetti, chili, and cheese. Having it **four ways** means spaghetti, chili, cheese, and either beans or onions. And having it **five ways** includes all five of those ingredients. The restaurant also offers any number of Coney dogs topped with chili, as well as salads, sandwiches, and potato dishes.

OTHER NEIGHBORHOODS

To visit an old-fashioned chili parlor, head north on I-75 to **Camp Washington Chili** (3005 Colerain Ave., 513/541-0061, www.campwashingtonchili.com, midnight Mon.-midnight Sat., under $30), about two miles west of the University of Cincinnati campus. This is a full-blown classic diner that serves up Coney dogs piled with chili, cheese, and onions, plus sandwiches, eggy breakfast items, and desserts. Of course, you can get Cincinnati chili here, from two ways to all five. The space has a retro-modern look with tile flooring. It's open 24 hours daily from Monday through Saturday, but closed on Sunday.

Downtown

There are several finer dining experiences in town, but my pick—which also works for the laid-back crowd—is **Mita's Restaurant &**

Bar (501 Race St., 513/421-6482, www.mitas.co, 5pm-10pm Mon.-Thurs., 5pm-11pm Fri.-Sat., under $70). Go for Spanish- and Latin American-inspired tapas with seasonal ingredients—look for short-rib hand pies, rock shrimp, calamari tacos, and a great list of cheeses and salty meats. The smart, stylish Downtown restaurant emphasizes comfort and relaxing meals.

For Korean cuisine where the focus is on the food, visit **HARU** (628 Vine St., 513/381-0947, www.harucincy.com, 11am-9pm Mon.-Thurs., 11am-10pm Fri., noon-10pm Sat., under $30). This bright-walled paradise has bibimbap (rice bowl topped with meat and vegetables), but also look for noodle plates like *jajangmyeon* (noodles in black bean sauce) and *dolsot woodong* (noodles and seafood served in a stone bowl), and a range of traditional soups.

Over-the-Rhine

The place to visit for breakfast is **Tucker's Restaurant** (1637 Vine St., 513/954-8920, 8am-3pm Mon. and Sat., 8am-3pm and 4pm-7pm Tues-Fri., 8am-2pm Sun., under $25), a small, old-fashioned dining establishment dating to 1946. Grab a table or a seat at the counter and order up a classic: two eggs, home fries, toast, and *goetta*.

For dessert, scoop up local favorite **Graeter's Ice Cream** (1401 Vine St., 513/421-5300, www.graeters.com, 11am-11pm daily, under $15). The classic Graeter's flavor is black raspberry chocolate chip, but the shop has a robust menu. Whatever you order, you can't go wrong. There's a small seating area, and the place gets busy, so plan some time to hang out.

BARS AND BREWERIES

NEAR GREAT AMERICAN BALL PARK

If you're going to drink near the ballpark, in The Banks, the best bet is **The Stretch**

(191 E. Freedom Way, 513/246-0458, www.thestretchcincy.com, 3pm-2:30am Mon.-Sat., 3pm-midnight Sun.), across the street from Great American. The beer list is good enough, and the mixed drinks work well. There's a big bar, televisions, and even outdoor space if the weather is cooperating. Coming here before a game is a good idea.

Just across the highway, a three-minute walk north of the ballpark, is **O'Malley's in the Alley** (25 W. Ogden Pl., 513/381-3114, www.omalleyscincy.com, 11am-2am daily), a favorite neighborhood Irish bar with plenty of space to party. It has regulars, great bartenders, a solid drink selection, and generally good vibes. Plus, a deck is out back. This is the place I'd visit for a pint before first pitch.

OTHER NEIGHBORHOODS

If you want to travel a bit for a really good brewery, head northeast into the Xavier University area for **Listermann Brewing Company** (1621 Dana Ave., 513/731-1130, www.listermannbrewing.com, 10am-9pm Mon.-Tues., 10am-10pm Wed.-Thurs., 10am-midnight Fri.-Sat., 11am-9pm Sun.). They feature a large variety of good-quality beer on tap and in the bottle, and they run a home-brewing shop.

Across the river, Newport, Kentucky, has some interesting spots. Check out **Prohibition Bourbon Bar** (530 Washington Ave., Newport, KY, 859/261-9463, www.newberrybroscoffee.com, 5pm-1am Fri.-Sat.), open just two nights a week inside Newberry Bros. Coffee. The bourbon selection is outstanding, and the quiet, speakeasy vibe is perfect. This is a definite stop if you're a bourbon fan. Down the block is **Coach's Corner** (317 E. 6th St., Newport, KY, 859/261-2800, 4pm-1am Sun.-Tues., 4am-midnight Wed.-Thurs., 2pm-1am Fri., 5pm-1am Sat.), a hole-in-the-wall with great people, a good beer and spirit selection, and a come-as-you-are

Photos (from top to bottom): Findlay Market; National Underground Railroad Freedom Center; Washington Park.

vibe that can't be beat. Coach's serves better-than-expected sandwiches, burgers, and basic bar grub.

Over-the-Rhine

Over-the-Rhine has some cool bars. Check out **Low Spark** (15 W. 14th St., 513/371-5722, www.lowsparkbar.com, 4pm-midnight Mon.-Wed., 4pm-2:30am Thurs.-Fri., noon-2:30am Sat., 2pm-10pm Sun.), whose design recalls a mid-20th-century diner counter, but with lots of booze and an honest-to-goodness aquarium in the middle of the action. This is a fun, low-stress place with beer, wine, and cocktails.

For something a little louder, head to **Queen City Radio** (222 W. 12th St., 513/381-0918, 4pm-2:30am Mon.-Fri., noon-2:30am Sat.-Sun.). A large party bar but not obnoxiously so, Radio has two floors of seating, a big beer garden, and plenty of good beer on tap, along with the usual macro-brewed fare.

On the outskirts of Over-the-Rhine is **3 Points Urban Brewery** (331 E. 13th St., 513/918-4804, www.3pointsbeer.com, 9am-10pm Mon.-Thurs., 9am-midnight Fri., 11am-midnight Sat., 11am-10pm Sun.), which showcases a variety of lower-alcohol beers along with the usual IPAs. Local art is on display in this brick-walled space that feels like the perfect city hangout for craft beer.

RECREATION

PARKS

Cincinnati has some fine green spaces. Check out **Eden Park** (950 Eden Park Dr., 513/352-4080). Home to the Cincinnati Art Museum, the 186-acre park also has a small network of trails, plus picnic areas, lakes and a reflecting pool, and a historic standpipe (19th-century water tower). The park hosts the **Cincinnati Playhouse in the Park** (962 Mt. Adams Cir., 513/421-3888, www.cincyplay.com), which produces new plays, longtime favorites, and shows for kids.

For a quick respite when it's hot, **Washington Park** (1230 Elm St.) is the place to be in Over-the-Rhine. On six acres, this park has a lawn for sports, yoga, and more, plus a covered patio area called **The Porch** (11am-10pm Mon.-Sat., 11am-9pm Sun. Memorial Day-Labor Day), where visitors of all ages can play games in the summer. The Porch has a bar and concession area.

BOATING AND PADDLING

Cincinnati's position along the Ohio River made it a commercial and economic hub during the 1800s. Symbolizing this boom are the many steamboats along the city's main waterway. While you can see a steamboat at Great American Ball Park, you can also ride on one for fun. **BB Riverboats** (101 Riverboat Row, Newport, KY, 855/884-8121, www.bbriverboats.com, $25-150) offers daily cruises on the river and themed rides ranging from ice-cream socials to midday lunch cruises.

Queen City Riverboat & Yacht Charters (303 Dodd Dr., Dayton, KY, 859/292-8687, www.queencityriverboats.com, $15-100) has inexpensive weekend sightseeing tours, plus pricier dinner parties. Also, if you're heading to the Reds game from Kentucky, you can pick up a **riverboat shuttle** (301 Riverboat Row, Newport, KY, $6) that starts 90 minutes before first pitch; pickup is at the Hooters in Newport, Kentucky, and the last shuttle leaves from Cincinnati 20 minutes after the game ends.

If you want to bring your own boat to the Ohio River, there are boat launches along the waterway in Cincinnati. You can head to the **Riverside Boat Launch Ramp** (3540 Southside Ave., 7am-dusk daily May-Oct., $10), or you can go to the **Four Seasons Marina** (4609 Kellogg Ave., 8:30am-5pm Mon.-Fri., 10am-5pm Sat.-Sun.).

It's also possible to kayak or canoe along the **Little Miami River,** a tributary that flows out of the east end of the city. **Scenic River Canoe Excursions** (4595 Round Bottom Rd., 513/576-9000, www.scenicrivercanoe.com, 10am-7pm Mon.-Fri., 9am-7pm

Sat.-Sun., $20-40) offers tubing, canoeing, and kayaking on three tours of varying difficulty. Hard plastic coolers are permitted, but no alcohol or glass bottles. Reserve ahead for these half-day tours. The river has good water quality and is great for fishing, too.

SHOPPING

You can grab a festive team shirt at **Homage** (1232 Vine St., 513/834-7205, www.homage.com, 10am-8pm Mon.-Sat., noon-6pm Sun.), a Midwest-based sports clothier with a location in Over-the-Rhine. Homage carries some of the team gear you'll see around the ballpark, from shirts paying tribute to great former Reds, to throwback items. You can also find Cincinnati-themed clothes, like Skyline Chili shirts.

ACCOMMODATIONS

NEAR GREAT AMERICAN BALL PARK

Close to the ballpark is **Guild Cincinnati** (120 E. Freedom Way, 512/623-7480, www.theguild.co/thebanks, $200-550), one of a small chain of hotels with locations in Austin, Texas, and Nashville, Tennessee. The Guild has a higher price point but offers comfortable, modern suites with a kitchen and living area in a premium location. Amenities include an in-room washer and dryer, local coffee, and an outdoor pool.

OTHER NEIGHBORHOODS

If you want to stay in Over-the-Rhine, head to **Symphony Hotel & Restaurant** (210 W. 14th St., 513/721-3353, www.symphonyhotel.com, $150-280), directly across from the Cincinnati Music Hall. There are nine rooms in this B&B-style lodging, appointed in a relatively frilly style. It's very comfortable, you're right in the heart of the neighborhood, and a

cool lounge, bar, and wine room are on-site. Plus, there's live jazz, typically from Thursday to Sunday.

Near the airport in Kentucky, you'll have your pick of chain hotels. If you want to stay in an independent lodging right across the river from Cincinnati and still have the opportunity to walk to the ball game, try **Gateway Bed & Breakfast** (326 E. 6th St., Newport, KY, 859/581-6447, www.gatewaybb.com, $130-200). The affordable rooms are smartly decorated with antique furniture, avoiding a dated look. Gateway is a 20-minute walk from Cincinnati via the Purple People Bridge. Coffee, bread, and a full breakfast are served every morning.

GETTING AROUND

PUBLIC TRANSIT

METRO (www.go-metro.com, $1.75 within city), operated by SORTA, is one of two area **bus networks.** With routes primarily in Kentucky, **TANK** (www.tankbus.org, $3.50 one-day pass) is a bus service that heads into Cincinnati and connects to Cincinnati/Northern Kentucky International Airport.

The **Bell Connector** (www.cincinnatibellconnector.com, 6:30am-midnight Mon.-Thurs., 6:30am-1am Fri., 8am-1am Sat., 9am-11pm Sun. and holidays, $1 for two-hour pass, $2 for day pass) is a **streetcar** that loops through Downtown, from Over-the-Rhine south to The Banks and back.

TAXI, UBER, AND LYFT

Uber will cost about $25 from Cincinnati/Northern Kentucky International Airport to Great American Ball Park in Downtown Cincinnati. **Lyft** might cost a couple dollars less, but the difference is generally negligible. You can also call up **Yellow Taxi Cincinnati** (513/549-2469), which costs about the same as Uber.

Downtown, **numbered streets** run west to east, from the highway to Over-the-Rhine. Streets to know include **Elm** and **Vine Streets,** which go north to south, as well as **Central Parkway,** the northern boundary of Downtown, which provides a connection to I-71.

Because major highways flow through Cincinnati and not far from one another, driving around the area during **rush hour** requires luck and patience. **I-71** comes into the city from the southwest (from Louisville and then Covington, Kentucky). After crossing the Ohio River, it runs along the riverfront right past Great American Ball Park, then turns up and heads north by northeast toward Columbus and Cleveland.

I-75 comes from Lexington, Kentucky, and the South, before merging with I-71. After the river, I-75 stays straight, heading north via the west side of the city before continuing north by northeast toward Dayton, Ohio. Along the way, it meets **I-74,** which runs west toward Indianapolis. **I-471** emerges to the southeast in Kentucky, coming off **I-275,** which loops around Cincinnati's outer boundary. I-471 enters Cincinnati via the Daniel Carter Beard Bridge, then merges with I-71 North.

From west to east, **US-50** scrapes along the riverside; **US-22** starts at I-471 and heads northeast into the southern Ohio suburbs and countryside.

LOUISVILLE, KENTUCKY

No baseball fan's bucket list is complete without visiting Louisville and the home of the Louisville Slugger brand of baseball bats. Since the 1880s, this is where millions of bats have been made—and are still made—for some of baseball's greatest hitters. We're talking Babe Ruth, Lou Gehrig, Ted Williams, Hank Aaron, Joey Votto, and Buster

Posey. The factory and museum here are worth a visit.

When scheduling your visit, be sure that the Louisville Bats are playing at home. The triple-A affiliate of the Cincinnati Reds plays in a fun minor league park that's next door to an awesome brewery. Louisville makes the perfect baseball-themed day trip. Spending **2-3 days** here is wise, as there are other sights, tastes, and sounds to behold.

Note: Thinking of visiting during Kentucky Derby week (the week of the first Saturday of May)? Maybe think twice before making your plans. For one, the Bats are always on the road during this weekend, and further, the city gets just too wild and crowded.

GETTING THERE

Air

Fly into **Louisville International Airport** (SDF, 600 Terminal Dr., 502/367-4636, www.flylouisville.com). Airlines serving SDF include **Allegiant** (702/505-8888, www.allegiantair.com), **American Airlines** (800/433-7300, www.aa.com), **Delta** (800/221-1212, www.delta.com), **Frontier** (800/401-9000, www.flyfrontier.com), **Southwest** (800/435-9792, www.southwest.com), and **United** (800/864-8331, www.united.com).

To **rent a car,** head to the baggage claim, where the counters for all major rental agencies are located. The airport is a 10-minute drive south from Downtown Louisville via I-65 South.

Car

The most direct route from **Cincinnati** to Louisville is via I-71 South, a **100-mile** drive southwest that should take about **90 minutes** without traffic. The scenic way is to take **US-25 South** to **US-42 West** in Florence, Kentucky. This road straddles the Ohio River for a while as it heads into Louisville. This trip takes closer to **three hours** and covers a little more than **100 miles.**

You can also stop in Louisville on your way from **St. Louis** to Cincinnati. The **260-mile, four-hour** drive from St. Louis travels along I-64.

Bus

You can take a **Greyhound bus** (www.greyhound.com) from **Cincinnati** to Louisville. The daily ride runs around $25 and lasts about three hours, depositing passengers at the **Louisville Greyhound Station** (720 W. Muhammad Ali Blvd., 502/561-2807). You can reach the Bats' ballpark by walking from the bus station—it's about 1.5 miles northeast. Go east on Muhammad Ali Boulevard, then north on Brooks Street, and east on Main Street.

LOUISVILLE SLUGGER FIELD

Louisville Slugger Field (401 E. Main St., 502/212-2287, www.milb.com/louisville) is home to the **Louisville Bats,** the triple-A affiliate of the Cincinnati Reds. It seats a little more than 13,000 fans, and though it looks like any other minor league park in America, it's a great place. There are views of the Louisville skyline from home plate as you look to the outfield; and when walking in at home plate, you'll enter through an old train shed that's now a venue for private events. Moreover, there's a brewery next door. This makes for a perfect and inexpensive night out.

Louisville Slugger Field has two levels. The **100 level** starts at the right-field foul pole with section 101. From here until section 106, along the right-field line, seats are generally around $10. The same holds true for sections 125-132 in the left-field area. Closer to the infield, seats in sections 107-124 are just a couple dollars more, which is a good deal (get these ones if you can). Otherwise, you can sit in the **200 level,** a club-style section that includes a $5 team store or concession voucher. Tickets here are still under $20, so they're also a great deal. Club-level guests have access to the **Jack Daniel's Bar & Lounge,** which has both beer and mixed drinks. **Lawn seats** in left field are just $10.

When at the park, take notice of the **carousel** (right-field bleachers, $1); proceeds from rides benefit the Children's Hospital Foundation. There's also a **playground** beyond the right-field fence. For merchandise, visit the **Bats Team Store** (open with gates on game days, 11am-4pm Mon.-Fri. non-game days). Finally, look for the statue of Dodgers great **Pee Wee Reese** (home plate entrance, 401 E. Main St.), who was from Louisville.

If you want to eat at the park, spring for the double-stacked fried bologna sandwich at **sections 109 and 114.** Also, look out for

Louisville Slugger Field

Photos (top): Muhammad Ali Center; (middle left) plaque outside the Louisville Slugger Museum; (middle right) Louisville Slugger Museum & Factory; (bottom) Churchill Downs.

$0.25 hot dog nights at the park (limit 12 hot dogs per person per purchase), which occur about 3-4 times a season.

SIGHTS

Louisville Slugger Museum & Factory

The biggest reason for a baseball fan to visit the city is the **Louisville Slugger Museum & Factory** (800 W. Main St., 877/755-8443, www.sluggermuseum.com, 9am-5pm Mon.-Sat., 11am-5pm Sun. mid-Aug.-mid-June, 9am-6pm Mon.-Wed., 9am-8pm Thurs.-Sat., 11am-6pm Sun. mid-June-mid-Aug., $16, $15 seniors, $9 ages 6-12, free ages 5 and under). The story goes that in 1884, a teenage Bud Hillerich made a custom baseball bat for Louisville ballplayer Pete "Louisville Slugger" Browning at his father's woodworking shop. Browning's success with the bat drove more players to the Hillerich shop. Years later, after an endorsement from Honus Wagner and a partnership with a salesperson, Hillerich and Bradsby became the preeminent bat maker in America. Louisville Slugger bats remain king to this day, and they are still made at the factory in Louisville. Besides the factory, there's a museum devoted to the history of one of baseball's most iconic symbols.

Your ticket earns you admission to the museum and a factory tour. On the tour, you'll see how the bats are made—from their beginnings as ash trees grown in America's eastern woods to the cutting, branding, smoothing, and lacquering processes. In the museum, check out the wall of signatures, home to thousands of John Hancocks from players who contracted with the company, including Cal Ripken Jr. and Tony Gwynn. Be sure to keep an eye out for the most important bats in the company's history, from the one Babe Ruth used to hit 21 of 60 home runs in 1927, to the bat Joe DiMaggio used to set his 56-game hitting streak, to the bat Hank Aaron wielded when slugging his 700th career home run in 1973. These are serious treasures.

Of course, during your visit, you must take a photo at the **world's largest baseball bat**. It's hard to miss it, but just in case you need to know: It's right at the front door.

Muhammad Ali Center

Another must while in Louisville is to visit the **Muhammad Ali Center** (144 N. 6th St., 502/584-9254, www.alicenter.org, 9:30am-5pm Tues.-Sat., noon-5pm Sun., $14, $13 seniors, $10 students, $9 ages 6-12, free ages 5 and under). Exhibits detail the life of the iconic boxer, civil rights advocate, and philanthropist. You can shadow box with The Greatest in an interactive exhibit, watch 15 of the champ's greatest fights, and learn about Ali's six core principles. Look for on-site galleries, including one devoted to the photography of Ali's friend Howard Bingham.

Churchill Downs

Whether you want to don your most garish hat or sip a mint julep, make a pilgrimage to **Churchill Downs** (700 Central Ave., 502/636-4400, www.churchilldowns.com, races Wed.-Sun. Apr.-June and Sept.-Nov., $5-100) when you're in Louisville. Home to the Kentucky Derby and the most famous horseracing track on earth, Churchill Downs hosts regular racing programs from Wednesday to Sunday, and seats are pretty affordable. You can grab a general admission standing-room spot for cheap, a reserved box seat, or a lounge or restaurant table. Note: For higher-priced seating arrangements, a dress code is strictly enforced, though the track suggests guests consider their attire carefully regardless of where they're sitting. You can't go wrong with collared shirts, slacks, and optional jackets and blazers for all, or dresses for women. Club seats are also available but are meant for groups, and they're pricey (starting at $720). As for Derby Week, prices go up a bit, and tickets go on sale in the fall. You have to be quick to get them.

FOOD

Find a great combination of ramen, pork shoulder, deviled eggs, and bibimbap at **Milk-Wood** (316 W. Main St., 502/584-6455, www.

milkwoodrestaurant.com, 5:30pm-10pm Tues.-Thurs., 5:30pm-11pm Fri.-Sat., 5:30pm-9pm Sun., under $50). In a dimly lit dining room that's friendly for all, MilkWood combines southern comfort with East Asian comfort, and with outstanding results. For a cool experience, sit at the bar.

One of the most popular and well-received restaurants in the city, **Bar Vetti** (800 S. 4th St., 502/883-3331, www.barvetti.com, 5pm-9:30pm Mon.-Thurs., 5pm-10pm Fri.-Sat., under $40) feels like a chic place with hard-to-get reservations, only it's actually affordable and accessible. There's pizza and pasta, plus veggie-friendly plates and light bites like rice balls and fried chickpeas.

If visiting Churchill Downs, stop in at **Wagner's Pharmacy** (3113 S. 4th St., 502/375-3800, www.wagnerspharmacy. com, 7am-3pm Mon.-Fri., 8am-3pm Sat.-Sun., under $10). Opened in 1922, Wagner's was once a local hangout for jockeys and the media, but national attention has made it a necessary stop for any horse racing fan. Eating here means basic plates with honey-glazed ham and eggs, biscuits, and potatoes sliced flat like disks. Look at photos of racehorses while you chow down.

For a tongue-numbing experience, you've got to have some hot chicken. While we're not talking Nashville hot, the stuff at **Royals Hot Chicken** (736 E. Market St., 502/919-7068, www.royalshotchicken.com, 11:30am-10pm Sun.-Thurs., 11:30am-11pm Fri.-Sat., under $20) rivals that city's finest offerings. This hip spot with brick walls, counter service, and—often—a long line offers fried chicken tenders, both in and out of sandwiches. "Hot" is a good heat level for those wanting the experience, but the adventurous can opt for "gonzo."

BARS AND BREWERIES

Against the Grain Brewery and Smokehouse (401 E. Main St., 502/515-0174, www. atgbrewery.com, 11am-midnight Mon.-Thurs., 11am-2am Fri.-Sat., 11am-11pm Sun.) is next to Louisville Slugger Field, so it makes a perfect pregame or postgame hangout spot. Set in a former train station, the brewery and smokehouse is three stories high, and it utilizes this space. Check out the incredible brewhouse that spans all three levels (you can view it from the bar). As for the beer, it's pretty good. Try the Russian imperial stout Bo & Luke (yup, that's a *Dukes of Hazzard* reference) and one of its English-style beers like 70K.

Another winner is **Mile Wide Beer Co.** (636 Barret Ave., 502/558-7147, www.mile-widebeer.com, 4pm-10pm Tues.-Thurs., 2pm-midnight Fri.-Sat., 2pm-8pm Sun.), with offerings like Idlewild and McPoyle that are best enjoyed inside the brewery's large taproom with picnic tables and a back room with arcade games.

For a unique experience, visit **Troll Pub Under the Bridge** (150 W. Washington St., 502/618-4829, www.trollpub.com, 11am-2am Mon.-Fri., noon-2am Sat.-Sun.). Just look for Louie, who stands guard by the front door, then head downstairs into this brick hall of a sports bar whose space used to be a hotel and, later, a railroad headquarters. There are plenty of beers on tap, including some local favorites, so come on down and enjoy a beer or two.

RECREATION

Got some time to spare? **Waterfront Park** (401 River Rd., www.louisvillewaterfront. com, 6am-11pm daily) is home to walking trails that weave along the green belt. Look for a monument to Abraham Lincoln, water features, and multiple art installations. The park is also home to the **Big Four Bridge** (River Rd. at Witherspoon St.), an old railroad bridge turned into a pedestrian walkway that opened in 2013. Averaging about 1.5 million visitors per year, the bridge is open all the time thanks to an LED lighting system that illuminates the bridge in various configurations throughout the night. If you walk the whole bridge, it's about two miles round-trip.

ACCOMMODATIONS

Pricey but offering a unique concept, **21c Museum Hotel** (700 W. Main St., 502/217-6300, www.21cmuseumhotels.com, $200-500) is a small chain of accommodations that began in Louisville. And here, inside 19th-century warehouses, the hotel has a contemporary art museum, along with multiple well-appointed rooms—some seriously artsy (check out Asleep in the Cyclone, with its site-specific installation, record player, and specially designed blankets)—and a rooftop apartment with a gourmet kitchen, full bath, and private terrace. The on-site restaurant, **Proof on Main** (702 W. Main St., 502/217-6300, www.proofonmain.com, 7am-12:30am Mon.-Thurs., 7am-1:30am Fri.-Sat., 7am-11:30pm Sun., under $50 dinner), brings local ingredients to the table and features a bar with plenty of bourbon.

Stay in Old Louisville at the **Dupont Mansion Bed & Breakfast** (1317 S. 4th St., 502/638-0045, www.dupontmansion.com, $120-300). This circa-1879 Italianate mansion has high ceilings and beautiful rooms, some with four-poster beds, antique furniture, and whirlpool tubs. Breakfast is served daily, including pastries, granola, and egg dishes.

GETTING AROUND

Louisville's transit system is **TARC** (Transit Authority of River City, www.ridetarc.org, $1.75), a **bus network** that has considerable presence Downtown.

I-64 comes into the city from St. Louis and the west, threading along the Ohio River until heading east toward Lexington. **I-71** comes in from the northeast, meets with I-64 and **I-65,** and terminates there. I-65 splits the city west and east, coming across the Ohio River from the north and heading south toward Nashville. **I-264** makes a partial loop around the Downtown area. Downtown, the major west-to-east streets include **Main Street, Liberty Street,** and **Broadway.** The main north-to-south streets are **3rd Street** and **4th Street.**

The Heartland and Texas

Crawl down the center of the nation, from Minneapolis to Houston. The road opens and the sky looms large as you pass through a large swath of the country—and encounter a whole lot of baseball. In addition to seeing the relatively young teams on this route, you'll get the chance to visit the boyhood home of Mickey Mantle, have a catch on the Field of Dreams, and learn all about the Negro Leagues.

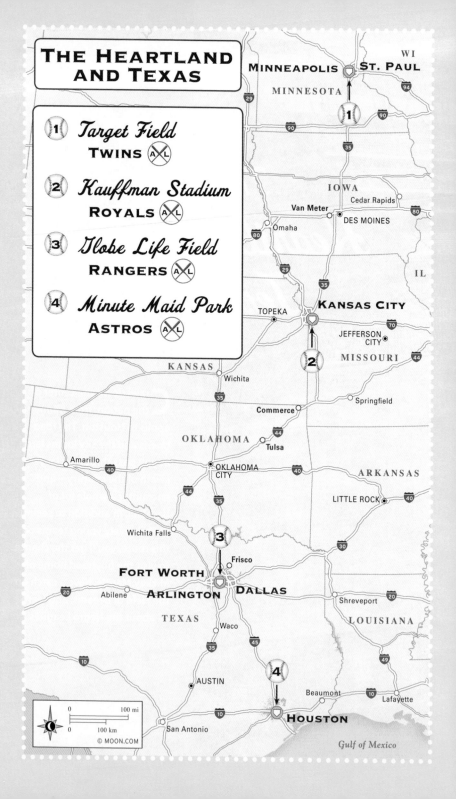

THE HEARTLAND
AND TEXAS

1. *Target Field*
   TWINS (A)(L)

2. *Kauffman Stadium*
   ROYALS (A)(L)

3. *Globe Life Field*
   RANGERS (A)(L)

4. *Minute Maid Park*
   ASTROS (A)(L)

WI

MINNEAPOLIS   ST. PAUL

94

MINNESOTA

29

90

35

IOWA

Cedar Rapids

Van Meter   80

Omaha   DES MOINES

80

29

35   IL

KANSAS CITY

TOPEKA   70

JEFFERSON
CITY

MISSOURI   44

KANSAS   2

Wichita   35

Springfield

Commerce   44

OKLAHOMA   Tulsa

Amarillo   40   ARKANSAS

40   OKLAHOMA
CITY

44   LITTLE ROCK   40

Wichita Falls   35   3

Frisco   30

FORT WORTH

20   Abilene   ARLINGTON   DALLAS

TEXAS   Waco   Shreveport   20

45   LOUISIANA

35

10   4

AUSTIN   Beaumont   10   Lafayette

49

0   100 mi

0   100 km   San Antonio   HOUSTON

© MOON.COM   Gulf of Mexico

The Heartland and Texas Road Trip

There's a lot of America in the miles between Minneapolis and Houston, but there's just as much baseball history along this route. Minneapolis, Kansas City, Dallas, and Houston are home to clubs hatched recently (in baseball terms), between 1961 and 1972. These American League franchises symbolize the mid-century growth of the sport during its most colorful and experimental period. They call to mind the designated hitter and jerseys that resemble brilliant blue skies and tequila sunrises. They're funky and a little off-center, and while none of the four franchises is wildly successful, they've all had their moments in the sun.

This 1,200-mile trip starts in Minneapolis, stops in Kansas City, then ends in Texas with visits to Dallas and Houston. Along the way, you have the chance to take side trips to Mickey Mantle's childhood home in Oklahoma; the small city of Van Meter, Iowa, to celebrate Hall of Fame pitcher Bob Feller; and the filming site of *Field of Dreams* in Dyersville, Iowa.

Start your drive in the Twin Cities of **Minneapolis and St. Paul** to watch the **Twins,** once home to the mighty Harmon Killebrew, slick-hitting Rod Carew, and fan favorite Kirby Puckett. They nabbed championships in 1987 and 1991 and have been pretty competitive over the last two decades.

About six hours south is **Kansas City, Missouri,** home to the small-market **Royals.** The club debuted in 1969 and quickly developed a solid farm system that led to multiple division titles and an American League pennant in 1980. A few years later, in 1985, the team won its first world title. It would take a lot of losing and another 30 years before the Royals won it all again. No matter the Royals' standing, the fans love their team in this fanatical two-sport town. Just as importantly, KC is home to the **Negro Leagues Baseball Museum,** a necessary destination for every fan of the game. You'll learn a whole lot about the history of American baseball at this outstanding venue.

Another eight hours south, in North Texas, find the home of the **Rangers** in the **Dallas-Fort Worth-Arlington area.** It's where baseball's youngest ballpark, Globe Life Field, rests. While the best days of the

Negro Leagues Baseball Museum in Kansas City

ball club—including back-to-back American League pennants in 2010 and 2011—live back at old Globe Life Park just down the street, the Rangers are ready to make many new memories in their new palace.

Finally, down south another few hours, is where the Rangers' Texas rival (and these days just about everyone's rival), the **Astros,** play. After plenty of close calls (1980, 1986, 2004, 2005), the proud city of **Houston** saw redemption through a world championship in 2017—though many who follow the game will tell you there's an asterisk next to it. Whatever the case, you'll feel the city's fervor while hanging out in H-Town.

PLANNING YOUR TIME

The drive time from Minneapolis down to Houston is rather long, at about 18 hours. While it's possible to accomplish the trip in five days, catching games at every ballpark, you'd be really huffing it. There's no sense in blurring through this trip, so I recommend taking **10 days,** with built-in driving days to ensure your sanity.

To avoid the eight-hour drive from **Kansas City to Dallas,** you could **fly** between the two cities (a nonstop flight lasts about 90 minutes). This is a good way to see a Royals game one day and a Rangers game the next without feeling completely exhausted.

Another option is to break the trip into **two separate weeks.** In one week, catch a Twins game and see Minneapolis and St. Paul over **2-3 days,** then drive the 6.5 hours south toward Kansas City, spending another **two days** there while seeing the Royals. In between, take **a day** off in Des Moines, Iowa. For the second week, fly into Dallas-Fort Worth and allow **two days** here, seeing a Rangers game in the process. Spend a break day driving to Houston, maybe stopping for barbecue along the way. Then spend another **three days** exploring H-Town and catching the Astros before flying out.

Here's my daily planner for a 10-day trip cruising the Heartland.

Day 1

Fly into **Minneapolis-St. Paul** and use whatever time you have to do a little sightseeing and relax.

Day 2

Get your Twins game in today. Eat, drink, and be merry at **Target Field.**

Day 3

Today you'll drive from the Twin Cities to **Kansas City,** a 6.5-hour trip with **Des Moines, Iowa,** smack in the middle. This would be a great day to check out the **Field of Dreams** in **Dyersville, Iowa,** though it's a two-hour trip east on US-20, about 65 miles north of Des Moines.

Day 4

Wake up in Kansas City and use the time to visit sights like the Negro Leagues Baseball Museum.

Day 5

Your Royals game at **Kauffman Stadium** is today. If it's a day game, you could begin your drive south afterward, but only if you're up to it. I suggest stopping in Tulsa (a four-hour drive from KC) if you go for this option.

Day 6

If you don't leave Kansas City early, use this entire day to drive the eight hours from the City of Fountains to **Dallas-Fort Worth.** Tulsa, Oklahoma, is a good midway point to stretch your legs. Or you could visit Mickey Mantle's childhood home in **Commerce, Oklahoma,** about three hours south of KC via US-69.

If you overnighted in Tulsa, use the morning and early afternoon to head from Tulsa to Dallas-Fort Worth. Spend the latter half of the day taking it easy in the Lone Star State.

Day 7

You'll awaken in the DFW area. Do your sightseeing and see a Rangers game at **Globe Life Field** today.

Photos (top): Texas Rangers game; (middle left) Minnie and Paul sign at Target Field; (middle right) aerial view of Minute Maid Park; (bottom) the Water Spectacular at Kauffman Stadium.

Day 8

Spend the morning in Dallas-Fort Worth before driving 3.5 hours on I-45 South to **Houston.** If you leave DFW around 11am, you should reach the Bayou City before rush hour traffic starts. Have a nice dinner and relax.

Day 9

Hang out in H-Town before catching an Astros game at **Minute Maid Park.** Barbecue? Tex-Mex? Crawfish? The dinner options are many.

Day 10

Depending on the time of your flight, you might have a half day or so to see more of Houston. Enjoy it, then say goodbye to the Heartland.

GETTING THERE

Rail isn't recommended for this trip, as **none of the cities connect** to the others via Amtrak. By car is the way to go, especially if you want to see some of the historical sights along the way. Traffic won't be too hairy until you hit Texas. You'll encounter maddening **rush hour traffic** (7am-9am, 4pm-6pm Mon.-Fri.) in the Dallas-Fort Worth-Arlington area, and even in traditionally low traffic periods, you could hit a wall in Houston. Just be patient and build in extra driving time when planning your Houston leg.

Air

If you're taking the 10-day trip as prescribed, you'll be flying into **Minneapolis-Saint Paul International Airport** (MSP, 612/726-5555, www.msairport.com), home to two terminals that are served by **Air Canada** (888/247-2262, www.aircanada.com), **American Airlines** (800/433-7300, www.aa.com), **Delta** (800/221-1212, www.delta.com), **Frontier** (801/401-9000, www.flyfrontier.com), **jetBlue** (800/538-2583, www.jetblue.com), **Southwest** (800/435-9792, www.southwest.com), **Spirit** (801/401-2222, www.spirit.com), and **United** (800/864-8331, www.united.com). Most airlines are located in Terminal 1 (called Lindbergh), but a select few, including jetBlue and Southwest, fly out of Terminal 2 (Humphrey).

From Houston, you have two options for flying back home. **George Bush Intercontinental Airport** (IAH, 2800 N. Terminal Rd., www.fly2houston.com/iah) is in the northeastern section of Houston, servicing 27 airlines including Air Canada, American Airlines, Delta, Spirit, and United, which has direct flights to all major American cities and several international destinations.

The second airport, **William P. Hobby International Airport** (HOU, 7800 Airport Blvd., www.fly2houston.com/hou), is in the southeastern section of the city and is home to four airlines: American Airlines, Delta, jetBlue, and Southwest.

MINNEAPOLIS AND ST. PAUL
MINNESOTA TWINS

Minneapolis and St. Paul are commonly known as the Twin Cities, hubs separated by the Mississippi and Minnesota Rivers. In the latter half of the 19th century, they were Minnesota's largest city and its capital city, respectively. Today, the two thriving cities are known for art, culture, and lush greenery.

Major league baseball came to the Twin Cities in 1961, but the area had already long been known for being a hotbed for the sport. The Minneapolis Millers and the St. Paul Saints battled for American Association supremacy throughout the first half of the 20th century. The Millers took a bunch of titles home during the 1910s and 1950s, and the Saints won multiple league championships throughout the 1920s. Players like Ted Williams, Roy Campanella, Willie Mays, Carl Yastrzemski,

Target Field
MINNEAPOLIS AND ST. PAUL

NORTH LOOP

THE STRAY DOG

NORTHMADE ■

KRAMARCZUK SAUSAGE COMPANY ▼

MARCY HOLMES

N 1ST AVE
N 2ND ST
N 7TH AVE
N 6TH AVE
N 5TH AVE
N 2ND AVE
N 3RD AVE
N 1ST AVE
N 10TH AVE
N 3RD ST
N 5TH ST
N 7TH ST
N WASHINGTON AVE
W RIVER PKWY

HENNEPIN AVE BRIDGE

SE CENTRAL AVE
SE 2ND AVE
SE 3RD AVE
SE 4TH AVE
SE 5TH AVE
SE UNIVERSITY AVE
SE 2ND ST
SE MAIN ST

SE 9TH ST
SE 8TH ST
SE 7TH ST
SE 6TH ST
SE 5TH ST
SE 6TH AVE
SE 7TH AVE
SE 8TH AVE

TARGET FIELD

Mississippi

STONE ARCH BRIDGE ★

35W

River

MILL CITY MUSEUM ★

HENNEPIN AVE
MARQUETTE AVE
S 3RD AVE
S 3RD ST
S 4TH ST
S 4TH AVE
S 1ST ST
S 2ND ST
S 5TH ST
S 6TH ST
S WASHINGTON AVE
S 2ND AVE

SEE DETAIL

Ⓜ Bus Station

394

DOWNTOWN WEST

DOWNTOWN EAST

TOWN HALL BREWERY ●

To Surly Brewing Co.

HARMON PL
LASALLE AVE
SPRUCE PL
S 7TH ST
S 8TH ST
S 9TH ST
S 10TH ST
S 11TH ST
S 12TH ST
S 3RD AVE
PARK AVE
CHICAGO AVE
S 13TH AVE
S 4TH ST
SE 4TH ST
RIVERSIDE AVE
CEDAR AVE
S 4TH ST
S 6TH ST

Loring Park

W GRANT ST

LORING PARK

S 1ST AVE
S 3RD AVE
S 4TH AVE
94
S 15TH ST
S 16TH ST
S ELLIOT AVE
S 10TH AVE
ELLIOT PARK
94

CEDAR RIVERSIDE

S 4TH AVE
PORTLAND AVE
CHICAGO AVE
35W
E FRANKLIN AVE

To Como Regional Park, St. Paul

E 21ST ST

S 11TH AVE

E 24TH ST

E 25TH ST

E 26TH ST

E 27TH ST

MINNEHAHA AVE
HIAWATHA AVE

S 12TH AVE
S 13TH AVE
S 14TH AVE

To Minnehaha Regional Park, Fort Snelling State Park, Minneapolis-Saint Paul International Airport

E 28TH ST

EAST PHILLIPS

E LAKE ST

BLOOMINGTON AVE
S 15TH AVE
S 16TH AVE
S 17TH AVE
S 18TH AVE
CEDAR AVE
LONGFELLOW AVE
S 19TH AVE
S 21ST AVE

E 34TH ST

CORCORAN

MATT'S BAR AND GRILL ■

E 35TH ST

To 5-8 Club, Mall of America, Nickelodeon Universe ▼

0   0.25 mi
0   0.25 km
© MOON.COM

Detail

BLACK SHEEP COAL-FIRED PIZZA ▼

RISE BAGEL CO. ▼

N 3RD ST
N 4TH ST
N 7TH AVE
N 6TH AVE
N 5TH AVE
N 1ST AVE
N 2ND ST
N WASHINGTON AVE
N 3RD AVE
N 2ND AVE
N 1ST AVE

HEWING HOTEL ●

FULTON BREWING ▼

Target Field Ⓜ

RED COW ▼

TARGET FIELD

394

TWINS CLUBHOUSE STORE

N 7TH ST

TARGET PLAZA ★

TARGET CENTER ★

HENNEPIN AVE
S 3RD ST
S 4TH ST
S 5TH ST
S 6TH ST

YOUR BOAT CLUB ●

LOEWSMN HOTEL

Nicollet Ⓜ Mall

0   200 yds
0   200 m

and Duke Snider came through the cities during those days.

During the 1950s, the owner of the Washington Senators began exploring a new home for the team, following in the footsteps of other American League teams (the Philadelphia Athletics, Boston Braves, and St. Louis Browns). The favored destination was the Twin Cities, and by 1961, the Minnesota Twins were a reality. They first played out of Metropolitan Stadium in the southern end of Minneapolis, showcasing talented players like slugger Harmon Killebrew and slick hitter Tony Oliva. The Twins immediately made an impact, winning the American League pennant in 1965. They remained competitive into the 1970s, led by exceptional hitter Rod Carew and fire-throwing pitcher Bert Blyleven.

Still, the Twins continually fell short at the end of each season. But after moving to the Hubert H. Humphrey Metrodome in Downtown Minneapolis in 1982, the team became a solid world championship contender. In 1987, led by hitters Kirby Puckett, Gary Gaetti, and Kent Hrbek, and pitchers like Frank Viola and a rejuvenated Blyleven, the Twins won their first world title. Four years later, with some of the same players, plus veteran Jack Morris, the team won its second championship.

The Twins have always been relatively competitive since, winning the American League Central division six times between 2002 and 2010, then again in 2019. Between 2010 and 2019, the team underwent a massive rebuilding project, which should bear fruit over the next many years. That'll thrill Twin Cities crowds, who undoubtedly come out to support their home team. If the Twins are good, fans will show up, and they'll get loud.

PLANNING YOUR TIME

You can see the essentials in the Twin Cities over a **weekend,** but a **long weekend** is better. Try to leave yourself a day to discover Minneapolis—especially the **North Loop** neighborhood around the ballpark—and a

second day to head into St. Paul and connect a bit with nature. If you want to spend more time in the area, a full third day is best spent getting to know a lake or two around Minneapolis.

There are plenty of places to stay in **Downtown Minneapolis,** but you can also find affordable lodging near the **MSP airport** and in **Downtown St. Paul.** Driving isn't too bad in the Twin Cities, and public transportation can get you from A to B without much fuss.

You might not expect it, but Target Field is an open-air ballpark. You'll need to think carefully about when to visit. The best time to visit the Twin Cities is in **midsummer,** when the temperature maxes out in the 80s (it'll creep into the 90s, but not too often) and is regularly 75-80°F. The trees are a beautiful green, and the sky is a crisp blue. Of course, it also **rains** in midsummer more often than at any other time of year, so expect some sprinkles. **September** is a nice balance—it's not as hot (you should bring a jacket and prepare for night games in the 50s and 60s), but the threat of rain is much lower. And yes, Prince was right: Sometimes it really does **snow** in **April,** but the bigger concern is the temperatures, which will consistently be around 40-50°F at night. Bundle up.

GETTING THERE

AIR

You'll be flying into **Minneapolis-Saint Paul International Airport** (MSP, 612/726-5555, www.mspairport.com), home to two terminals that are served by **Air Canada** (888/247-2262, www.aircanada.com), **American Airlines** (800/433-7300, www.aa.com), **Delta** (800/221-1212, www.delta.com), **Frontier** (801/401-9000, www.flyfrontier.com), **jetBlue** (800/538-2583, www.jetblue.com), **Southwest** (800/435-9792, www.southwest.com), **Spirit** (801/401-2222, www.spirit.com), and **United** (800/864-8331, www.united.com). Most airlines are located in Terminal 1 (called Lindbergh), but a select few, including jetBlue and Southwest, fly out of Terminal 2 (Humphrey).

Airport Transportation

Most of the **car rental** agencies have counters at the terminals (only Payless and Sixt do not, and they require **shuttles** to access). To take a ride-share from the airport, look for the pickup location by following signs for **app-based transportation.** The airport is located off I-494 in Minneapolis, about 20 minutes south of the city via MN-55, and about 15-20 minutes southwest of St. Paul via I-35E or MN-62 and US-52.

You can also get to and from the airport via **Metro Transit's light rail,** called **METRO** (www.metrotransit.org, $2-2.50). The **Blue Line** stops at both terminals and provides a door-to-door connection to Target Field and other Downtown Minneapolis landmarks. To reach locations in St. Paul, take the Blue Line to U.S. Bank Stadium, then transfer to the **Green Line** outbound.

TRAIN

Union Depot (240 E. Kellogg Blvd. #70, St. Paul), the **Amtrak station** (www.amtrak.com) in the Twin Cities, is in St. Paul. The **Empire Builder** (Portland and Seattle to Chicago) is the route that serves this station.

It's a 20-minute drive west on I-94 from Union Depot to reach Downtown Minneapolis and Target Field. As an alternative, you can take METRO's **Green Line** (www.metrotransit.org, $2-2.50) right to the ballpark from the train station. The ride takes about 50 minutes.

BUS

You can reach the Twin Cities via bus from Chicago, thanks to operators **Greyhound** (www.greyhound.com), **Megabus** (https://us.megabus.com), and **Jefferson Lines** (www.jeffersonlines.com). All three buses deposit passengers at St. Paul's **Union Depot** (240 E. Kellogg Blvd. #70, St. Paul).

Greyhound and Jefferson Lines also drop off passengers at the Minneapolis **bus station** (950 Hawthorne Ave., Minneapolis). This is a good option if you're going straight to the game, since Target Field is just a 10-minute walk north up 10th Street. Even better: Megabus picks up and drops off riders at **Target Field station** (335 N. 5th St., Minneapolis). Prepare for a minimum eight-hour bus ride from Chicago, with prices generally between $35 and $50.

Target Field

For a long time, it seemed there would not be a baseball-specific stadium in the Twin Cities. The conversation about building a venue for the Twins began in 1994, but there were many obstacles along the way. At one point, it even seemed like the Twins would be eliminated from Major League Baseball altogether. But a plan to build a ballpark in Minneapolis's Warehouse District (part of the North Loop neighborhood) came to fruition by 2006, and **Target Field** (1 Twins Way, www.mlb.com/twins) opened to the public in 2010.

After all of the trouble, what remains is a beautiful ballpark that's among the best of its kind. It's a retro-modern park without a retractable roof, which is odd for its location (a pretty cold part of America), but it's nonetheless picturesque. You may notice that its exterior is outfitted in gorgeous shades of beige and light brown; this is Kasota limestone, native to Minnesota. Beyond is an open park that feels big despite its small acreage, thanks to its tall upper deck and bleacher seating areas.

Target Field is the perfect balance between a tiny, minor league-style park and a larger park that doesn't quite have enough character. When you're driving around Downtown Minneapolis, the stadium pops up seemingly out of nowhere, blending easily with the city's architecture. It's very friendly and accessible, thanks to its plazas, ramps, and various standing-room areas. Moreover, it's a

YOUR BEST DAY AT TARGET FIELD

This itinerary offers you a daylong guide to enjoying the Twin Cities before a night game at Target Field.

10 HOURS BEFORE FIRST PITCH
Begin the day with some carbs. Head over to **Rise Bagel Co.** and get yourself a delicious bagel sandwich.

9 HOURS BEFORE FIRST PITCH
Drive out to St. Paul and visit **Como Regional Park.** If you have children or just love animals, check out **Como Park Zoo.** Or you can walk about the **Marjorie McNeely Conservatory** and admire the many native flowers and plants. Either way, spend a few hours at the park to get in touch with the lush greenery that abounds in the Twin Cities.

6 HOURS BEFORE FIRST PITCH
Hopefully, you're hungry. Drive back into Minneapolis and hunt for the jucy lucy—a cheese-stuffed burger that was invented in Minneapolis. My pick is to head into **Matt's Bar and Grill,** but make sure to have some cash in hand.

Gate 34

5 HOURS BEFORE FIRST PITCH
This is a good time to get back to your hotel and park the car. From here, rely on public transportation if you can. If not, you can ride-share it into Downtown Minneapolis. First stop: the **Mill City Museum,** where you can learn the agricultural history of the area.

3 HOURS BEFORE FIRST PITCH
You want a drink, right? Walk to **Town Hall Brewery,** which might just be the best brewery in the city. Have a beer or two here, then start heading toward the ballpark.

1.5 HOURS BEFORE FIRST PITCH
Get to **Target Field.** You'll want to head in via **Gate 34.** Once inside, pay a visit to **Drafts at 34** and play a game of beanbag toss.

DURING THE GAME
Be sure to have a drink at **Town Ball Tavern,** and grab yourself a sausage from **Kramarczuk's Sausage.**

AFTER THE GAME
Leave the stadium and enter **Cuzzy's Grill & Bar.** With its divey atmosphere, it's the perfect place to end the evening.

Marjorie McNeely Conservatory

great food and drink park, boasting some of the most unique eating options in the major leagues. Like the Twin Cities themselves, Target Field is wholly underrated and very, very fun.

ORIENTATION

Target Field is part of the Warehouse District of Minneapolis, separated from Central Minneapolis by I-394, which practically drops folks off right at the front door. I-94 runs close to the ballpark, too, so it's just a quick 20-minute drive here from St. Paul.

Target Field

There are five entry gates at Target Field. The gates are named after famous Twins: **Gate 34** is for Kirby Puckett; **Gate 3** is for Harmon Killebrew. Gates open 1.5 hours before first pitch on weekdays, and 2 hours before first pitch from Friday to Sunday.

TICKETS AND SEATING

Pricing

The Twins are one of many teams using a demand-based, **dynamic pricing** model. For select games and dates, tickets will generally be higher—think games against **big-draw teams** like the Yankees, or **rivals** like the Indians, or when there's a huge **give-away** or **special event**. A middle-of-the-road seat for a weekday game against Kansas City may cost around $35, while that same seat for a weekend game against the Yankees could cost more like $45-50. There are value games, too, like that early-season Tuesday night contest against Seattle—that ticket might cost around $25-30.

Seating Plan

Let's go over the seating chart at Target Field, starting from the lowest level, called the **Main Level (100 level).** (Note: Sections are numbered from the right-field foul pole, going clockwise around foul territory and across the outfield back to the right-field foul pole.) There's the **Thomson Reuters Champions Club** (sections 7-10) at home plate, and surrounding it are the **dugout box infield** (sections 2-6, 11-15) and then the **dugout box** (sections 1, 16-17). Slightly less expensive, starting at home plate, is the

home plate box (sections 109-119); then, to the right and left, are the infield box (sections 105-108, 120-123), the diamond box (sections 103-14, 124-125), and the field box (sections 101-102, 126-127), which ends at the foul poles.

In left field, there are the left field bleachers (sections 128-131), Treasure Island Cove (sections 132-135), overlook (sections 136-138), and the Supercuts Super Seats (sections 139-140). For fans of big crowds and macro beers, Target Field has a Budweiser Roof Deck (left field, near section 329), more of a group outing area with some standing-room spots.

Between the 100 and 200 levels is the Club Level. Around the infield is the Delta SKY360 Club (sections A-R); the area closer to the right-field foul pole has the event suites, and the area closer to the left-field pole is The Deck (sections S-V). It's also called the Skyline Deck and is available for single game tickets. The view of the skyline here is a little better than that of the play on the field.

The 200 level, or the lower part of the Terrace Level, includes the home plate terrace (sections 210-220), the diamond terrace (sections 206-209, 221-224), and the field terrace (sections 201-205, 225-228). In the 300 level, the upper part of the Terrace Level, are home plate view (sections 310-319), diamond view (sections 306-309, 321-324), a family section (section 320), and field view (sections 301-305, 325-327).

In the outfield mezzanine upstairs are the U.S. Bank Home Run Porch Terrace (sections 229-234) and Home Run Porch View

GAME COSTS

Tickets: Depending on the opponent and the night of the week, tickets at Target Field are slightly cheaper than average. If it's a midweek contest against a team that's not performing well, you can get on the Main Level for less than **$40.** Against top-draw teams and for special events, expect to pay closer to **$60** minimum. Upper-level seats shouldn't be more than **$30** at any time.

Hot dog: A Schweigert hot dog should cost you about **$4.** The bigger foot-longs will fetch about **$7.**

Beer: The macro-brewed stuff will cost you about **$5** for a 12-ounce cup. The 20-ounce size will be about **$9.** Want craft beer? You'll pay more like **$11-12** for that. Cans can be a bit cheaper, around **$8-13.**

Parking: Stadium parking isn't too bad, maxing out at **$15.** You can find a spot close to Target Field in Downtown Minneapolis for **$5-15.**

(sections 329-334), and the **grandstand** (sections 237-240) is in right center field.

Where to Buy Tickets

Do your research before buying tickets for a Twins game, because there is no hard and fast option for a cheap seat. Buying directly from the Twins sometimes means getting the better deal, and other times it'll be a third-party site like **StubHub.** If you get your tickets through the Twins, they're on the **MLB Ballpark app** and offer an upgrade option when you get to the park (but there's no guarantee you'll get the opportunity).

Best Seats

Being on the **first-base line** for day games is a good idea, considering the **shade** will get to you early. Seats in the back rows of the **infield box** (sections 105-107) are pretty

good for views, will get shade, and are generally less than $50 a pop. Similarly, consider the **diamond terrace** (sections 206-209), which will usually cost you less than $35.

If you're going on a cooler day and you crave **sun,** head to the **infield box** (sections 120-123) on the third-base side or the **diamond terrace** (sections 221-224) along the third-base line. These seats will give you a fine view of the skyline, so consider them for evening games.

Over in the outfield, the **Treasure Island Cove seats** (sections 132-135) are pretty inexpensive and are up over the high wall in right center field. You'll get a good view of the action from here (you just won't get to see what happens to those fly balls that come close). Families can book seats in **section 320** for an alcohol-free, family-friendly area.

KNOW BEFORE YOU GO

You can bring a 16- by 16- by 8-inch **bag** into Target Field. The only beverages that can come into the park are **bottled water** (32 ounces or less) and soft-sided **juice** or **milk** containers for kids. **Outside food** is allowed in (inside a soft-sided container), as long as it's eaten at a general seating area—meaning, not in the suites or other premium spots.

If you're attending a game early or late in the season (Apr.-early May, end of Sept.-Oct.), be sure to pack a **jacket.** It'll **rain** in **midsummer,** and temperatures can sometimes be unexpectedly hot, so plan accordingly. Pack both **rain gear** and **sunblock,** then pay attention to the day's forecast. **Umbrellas** are permitted but are not allowed to be open when you're in your seat.

Mothers who are nursing can head to the **OB-GYN WEST Nursing Rooms** at the Guest Service Centers (sections 113, 204).

Accessibility

Pedestrian ramps can be found between Gates 3 and 6 and at Gate 29. If you need the use of a **wheelchair** to help you reach your seat, ask an employee at your gate of entry. You can bring your own wheelchair to the park; it can be stored at guest services.

BE A FAN

As you probably can bet, Twins fans are nice folks. You shouldn't have a problem wearing gear from opposing teams at the park.

The Twins have a "when the team takes the field" song. Called **"We're Gonna Win Twins,"** it was originally recorded in the 1960s, then updated in the 1980s with extremely 1980s production values. The post-home run and victory song is native son Prince's **"Let's Go Crazy."** That's just perfect.

Visit the **guest services centers** (sections 113, 204, 800/338-9467) for **assistive listening devices**. **Segways** are allowed at the park for people with mobility disabilities, but check in with guest services when you reach the stadium. **Service animals** are welcome at Target Field.

There are 12 **elevators** at Target Field in six locations: Gate 3, administrative office building at Gate 6, sections 103, 112, 125, and 133. For **accessible parking,** the Twins suggest **Ramps A, B, or C** (N. 2nd Ave. across from right field, over I-394), which have about **8,000 accessible parking spaces** between them. Each ramp has skyway or walkway access to the ballpark. Be sure to display a valid disabled parking placard.

GETTING THERE

It's beneficial for fans that Target Field is in the Warehouse District, as it's right up against both the major highways and light rail systems.

Public Transit

If you opt to take public transportation, it's a cinch, since it drops you off right at the park. You can take the **METRO light rail** (www.metrotransit.org, $2-2.50 per ride) to the **Target Field station** (335 N. 5th St., Minneapolis). Both the **Blue** and **Green Lines** stop at Target Field. If you're in the northwestern suburbs, you can connect to the **C Line** (bus rapid transit) at the **Nicollet Mall station** (35 S. 5th St., Minneapolis). Those coming from the northern suburbs like Coon Rapids, Elk River, and Big Lake can take the

Northstar Commuter Rail Line ($2.75-6.25), operated by Metro Transit, which also drops folks off at the Target Field station.

Driving

If you drive, you'll likely be in some form of traffic before reaching Target Field. The stadium is accessible from both I-394 and I-94, and is also accessible from Downtown Minneapolis via 7th Street, 5th Street, and 3rd Street.

The Twins suggest **parking** Downtown and walking to the park. There are various **parking ramps (garages)** and **lots** that will cost $5-15, on average. The closest to Target Field are **Ramp A** (101 N. 9th St., Minneapolis, $7-27), **Ramp B** (516 2nd Ave. N., Minneapolis, $7-27), and **Ramp C** (318 2nd Ave. N., Minneapolis, $9-25); these are also often the most expensive parking options. Other parking areas nearby include **11th and Harmon** (25 S. 11th St., Minneapolis, $5-20), **Jerry Haaf Memorial** (424 S. 4th St., Minneapolis, $4-40), and, a little farther out but pretty inexpensive, **Vineland Place** (727 Vineland Pl., Minneapolis, $4-22).

PARK FEATURES AND SIGHTS

Target Plaza and Gate 34

When visiting Target Field, you may want to enter in right field. That's where you'll first find **Target Plaza** (2nd Ave. N. and N. 6th St.), a large, open-air space with trees, seating areas, and a giant golden glove that's perfect for photo ops. It extends above I-394 and connects visitors to street level and the **Target Center** (600 1st Ave. N.), home to the Minnesota Timberwolves men's basketball team and the Minnesota Lynx women's basketball team.

Target Plaza is really just an introduction to **Gate 34** (right field, 3rd Ave. N. and N. 6th St.), an area for playing, eating and drinking, and entertainment, located at the entrance to the ballpark. Here, look for a large lawn area with games like giant Jenga and beanbag toss. There's also a pop-up market with a rotating set of food and beverage vendors and local merchandise creators.

Minnie and Paul Sign

A fun aesthetic feature of the ballpark is way out in center field. The **Minnie and Paul sign** (center field) depicts a former primary logo of the Twins: two gentlemen (one wearing a Minneapolis jersey, the other a St. Paul jersey) on either side of the Mississippi River who are shaking hands against a backdrop in the shape of Minnesota. Whenever the Twins hit a home run, look for Minnie and Paul to revisit that friendship with a friendly shake as lights flutter around the backdrop's edges, outlining the state's shape.

Clubhouses

The **Twins Digital Clubhouse** (section 229) has bays where you can take selfies, plus interactive screens. For the kids, there's **T.C.'s Clubhouse** (section 229, maximum 48 inches tall), an area with a playground set with a slide and tunnel. During the third inning of each game, T.C., the life-size, smiling bear mascot of the Twins, takes up residence at his clubhouse for photos. Be sure to get your kids there toward the end of the second inning to get in line.

FOOD AND DRINKS

Target Field is among the best ballparks for food in the majors. There's outstanding variety, from the types of cuisine (barbecue, Cuban, Eastern European, carnival food, healthy fare, sandwiches) to the kinds of experiences you can have (Instagram-friendly items, family-style plates, easy grab-and-go stuff). For the craziest of them all, try the **Boomstick** (section 127), a two-foot-long chili dog packed with onions and jalapeño peppers. If you grab 3-5 friends, you could do the job. Probably.

Some other food items to look out for: the **Soul Bowl** (section 120), a build-your-own soul food bowl that could include jerk chicken, barbecue beef, macaroni and cheese, collard greens, and more; **Kramarczuk's Sausage** (sections 102, 112, 312, Delta SKY360 Club), the famous Minneapolis smoked sausage purveyor; and **Roots for the Home Team** (Gate 34, weekends only), at which young people (often working their first paying jobs) serve up healthy and locally grown fare.

Look for **Turkey To Go** (sections 113, 138, 318), serving mammoth turkey sandwiches that have long been a Minnesota State Fair favorite. Speaking of sandwiches: Head to **Craft Sandwiches** (section 114) for a peanut butter and jelly candied bacon sandwich. It sounds ridiculous, but it's the nutty, sweet, fruity, smoky, salty concoction you never realized you needed.

Arguably the best restaurant at any major league ballpark, **Bat & Barrel** (Club Level, right field; sections 201-202, 612/659-3964, 1.5 hours before first pitch Mon.-Fri., two hours before first pitch Sat.-Sun., home games only, under $30) has fun menu items like a trio of huge meat-and-cheese boards you can share with friends: the Rowdydow BBQ Shareable Board (with brisket, pulled pork, rolls, beans, and more), the Barrio Taco Shareable Board (12 tortillas, barbacoa, chicken, veggies, cheese, and more), and the It's Greek to Me Shareable Board (chicken souvlaki skewers, feta spread, veggies, pitas, and more). Other options at this modernized space are burgers, pub-quality appetizers, and a root beer float for dessert.

There are a few cool bars in the ballpark, including **Minnie & Paul's** (beneath the Minnie and Paul sign, center field), which serves food from Red Cow (a popular chain) while also offering beer and liquor. **Town Ball**

Tavern (section 229) has its own menu with Minnesota favorites like jucy lucys (cheese-stuffed burgers), buffalo tater tots, and the State Fair Combo of jalapeño cheese curds, fried pickle chips, and miniature corn dogs. There's also a full bar with local beer. The name of the pub comes from the term for amateur baseball played across Minnesota for the last century. (Look for jerseys and photos of town ball teams.) The floor of this place is special: It's from the Minneapolis Armory, where the Minneapolis Lakers played basketball. Finally, there's **Barrio** (section 127), a sports bar-type spot with a range of beer and cocktails, televisions, drink rails facing the field, and a cabana seating area.

So where's the beer? As you head inside at Gate 34, there's **Drafts at 34** (Gate 34), home to a whole lot of local beer. There are plenty of craft options throughout the park. Some spots to hit include **Twins Pub** (section 141) and **Minnesota Brews** (sections 116, 125, 320), which serves beer from Stillwater's **Lift Bridge Brewing** and St. Paul's **Summit Brewing,** among others. You'll find other locals, like **Fair State, Fulton Beer,** and **Surly Brewing,** all over the park.

EVENTS

Autographs aren't a given at Target Field, but you might be able to get down by the dugouts during the opposing team's batting practice if the ushers are in good spirits. **Batting practice** at Target Field begins 2.5 hours before each game.

On Sundays, kids ages 12 and younger can get free autographs at the **Twins Digital Clubhouse** (section 229, 11:55am-12:15pm Sun.). After every Sunday game, kids ages 14 and younger can also **run the bases** (line up at North Ramp, section 130, around ninth inning, one adult per child).

The Twins run a **50/50 raffle** (section 117), and tickets can be purchased up until the end of the seventh inning. Proceeds from

Photos (from top to bottom): Target Field; Twins' mascot T.C.; the Kasota limestone exterior of Target Field.

the raffle go toward the Twins Community Fund and the Ted Williams Museum—yes, the one at Tropicana Field in St. Petersburg!

The Twins host a **theme night** for practically every game, from a SKOL Night that recognizes the Minnesota Vikings football team to a ton of events celebrating local colleges. Nearly every night has some sort of **giveaway**. The Twins often partner with local organizations to run **yoga sessions** at Target Field from May to September.

Tours

The Twins conduct standard public **tours** (Gate 29 at 7th St., 612/659-3877, 11am and 2pm Tues.-Sun. non-game days Apr.-Sept., 11am and 2 pm Fri.-Sun. non-game days Oct., 11am and sometimes 1pm evening game days, $17, $14 seniors, $12 students, $8 ages 6-14, free ages 5 and under) that may include stops at the press box, clubhouse, and dugout, plus suite-level areas, and the Budweiser Roof Deck.

SHOPPING

The **Twins Clubhouse Store** (Gate 29, 1 Twins Way, 612/659-3963, open to ticketed guests during games, 10am-7pm Mon.-Sat., 10am-5pm Sun. non-game days) is a big, bright space carrying all kinds of Twins shirts and jerseys from the present and past. It gets packed close to first pitch and during the game, so I suggest making it your first stop at the park if you want a gift or some swag. Look for the **Twins Authentics stand** (section 101), which sells game-used items.

MINNEAPOLIS AND ST. PAUL SIGHTS

MALL OF AMERICA

Looking for old **Metropolitan Stadium,** home to the Twins between 1961 and 1981? If you're sipping an Orange Julius inside the amusement park at the **Mall of America** (60 E. Broadway, Bloomington, 952/883-8800,

www.mallofamerica.com, 10am-9:30pm Mon.-Sat., 11am-7pm Sun.), you're technically already there. The mall (the largest in America if you count that amusement park, Nickelodeon Universe) was built atop the old stadium grounds in Bloomington. You can find a home plate marker inside **Nickelodeon Universe** (5000 Center Ct., https://nickelodeonuniverse.com, admission from $20, additional costs for adventure attractions), along with five roller coasters, a handful of thrill rides, and dining establishments that include Hard Rock Cafe and Caribou Coffee. The park has an adventure course with ropes and a zip line, and two miniature golf experiences.

As for the mall itself, it surrounds Nickelodeon Universe and has 520 shops, including anchors Macy's and Nordstrom, plus a large Crayola store. There are hotels (a Marriott and a Radisson) on the north and south ends of the mall, and parking on the western and eastern ends. Also on the east end is **SEA LIFE** (952/883-0202, www.visitsealife.com, 10am-7pm Mon.-Thurs., 10am-8pm Fri., 9:30am-8pm Sat., 10am-6pm Sun., $20-32, $16-26 ages 3-12, free ages 2 and under), an aquarium with a tunnel where the water surrounds you. You'll see sharks, sea turtles, and thousands of other sea creatures.

MILL CITY MUSEUM

Right by the river and inside the Washburn A. Mill (the world's largest flour mill at one point), the **Mill City Museum** (704 S. 2nd St., Minneapolis, 612/341-7555, www.mnhs. org, 10am-5pm Mon.-Sat., noon-5pm Sun., $12, $10 seniors and students, $6 ages 5-17, free ages 4 and under) commands attention while delivering a history of industrial innovation along the Mississippi River. Exhibits and attractions include hands-on baking labs, a show that includes scenes of the mill's past, and an observation deck with fantastic views of the city.

When outside the museum's front door, gaze ahead and notice the long **Stone Arch Bridge** (W. River Pkwy. at Portland Ave., 6am-midnight daily), the only arched bridge made of stone that entirely crosses the Mississippi River. These days, it's a walking and cycling path. It's about a half mile across, so give yourself 30 minutes or so to go across and back, taking photos along the way. You can park off River Parkway to start your bridge journey, but that lot charges a fee.

FOOD

NEAR TARGET FIELD

For pizza, visit the North Loop location of **Black Sheep Coal-Fired Pizza** (600 Washington Ave. N., Minneapolis, 612/342-2625, www.blacksheeppizza.com, 11am-11pm Sun.-Thurs., 11am-1am Fri.-Sat., under $30). Black Sheep does 12- and 16-inch renditions of Neapolitan pizza, cooked in a coal-fired oven much like the way it's done at old-school pizza places along the East Coast. The spot offers something most pizza places don't: the opportunity to sit at the pass, the counter area in the kitchen where food is passed from cook to server.

Another popular chain with a North Loop location close to the ballpark is **Red Cow** (208 1st Ave. N., Minneapolis, 612/238-0050, www.redcowmn.com, 11am-midnight Mon.-Thurs., 11am-1am Fri., 10am-1am Sat., 10am-midnight Sun., under $20), where the cooks flip burgers next to a full bar with a generous list of local craft beers. The red-clad, industrial space is perfect for families and groups, and just right before or after a ball game.

For something long before (or long after) the game, grab a bagel at **Rise Bagel Co.** (530 N. 3rd St., Minneapolis, 612/354-3349, www.risebagel.com, 6am-2pm Tues.-Fri., 7am-3pm Sat.-Sun., under $15). The owners of Rise thoroughly researched the craft of making bagels, visiting places like New York City and Montreal, so you can be sure they know their stuff. There are plenty of spreads and sandwich options available, too.

OTHER NEIGHBORHOODS

Across the Mississippi River in the St. Anthony West section of Minneapolis, you'll find **The Stray Dog** (401 Hennepin Ave. E., Minneapolis, 612/378-2855, www.straydogmpls.com, 10am-midnight Sun.-Thurs., 10am-2am Fri.-Sat., under $20). Along with sandwiches, sausages, and salads on the menu is the ever-popular hotdish. This Minnesota staple is a deep dish of starch (typically tater tots), meat, veggies, and a binding liquid. Some may call it a casserole,

Stone Arch Bridge

but those people would be wrong. Stray Dog does a tater tot hotdish with brisket, brussels sprouts, a whole bunch of cheese, and mushroom béchamel. Hungry yet?

There's a long-standing war between the two places that claim origin of the jucy lucy—a burger in which cheese is stuffed inside the patty—and they're about three miles apart on the same road. There's **Matt's Bar and Grill** (3500 Cedar Ave., Minneapolis, 612/722-7072, www.mattsbar.com, 11am-midnight Sun.-Thurs., 11am-1am Fri.-Sat., under $20), which serves the lucy and a few other burgers, plus pitchers of beer. They don't take credit cards. Down the road is **The 5-8 Club** (5800 Cedar Ave., Minneapolis, 612/823-5858, www.5-8club.com, 11am-10pm Sun.-Wed., 11am-11pm Thurs.-Sat., under $20), which has a whole menu of lucy variations, plus other burgers, sandwiches, appetizers, wings, and more.

Embrace the Twin Cities' Eastern European flavor with a visit to **Kramarczuk Sausage Company** (215 Hennepin Ave. E., Minneapolis, 612/379-3018, www.kramarczuk.com, 8am-8pm Mon.-Wed., 8am-9pm Thurs.-Sat., 10am-4pm Sun., under $30). This decades-old landmark serves up smoked Ukrainian sausage, Polish kielbasa, a range of meaty sandwiches, pierogi, and cabbage rolls stuffed with either meat and rice or buckwheat and mushrooms. Get here early to nab one of the booths inside this homey spot.

If you're in St. Paul and want burgers (or eggs for dinner), go to the city's location of **Parlour Bar** (267 W. 7th St., St. Paul, 651/207-4433, www.parlourbar.com, 11am-10pm Tues.-Thurs., 11am-midnight Fri., 10am-midnight Sat., 10am-10pm Sun., under $40). This place also serves up Mexican chilaquiles. Pair your food with a cocktail or one of Parlour's boozy malts.

How about a place that does big ol' Italian plates? **Mucci's Italian** (786 Randolph Ave., St. Paul, 651/330-2245, www.muccisitalian.com, 5pm-10pm Tues.-Thurs., 5pm-11pm Fri., 11am-2pm and 5pm-11pm Sat., 11am-2pm and 5pm-9pm Sun., under $30) does lasagna, bucatini, and other down-home delights, plus very tasty Montanara-style pizza (deep-fried, then baked). All of this is in a friendly, modern spot with bar seating and a high ceiling.

BARS AND BREWERIES

NEAR TARGET FIELD

Even though it's close to a two-mile walk, I say **Town Hall Brewery** (1430 Washington Ave. S., Minneapolis, 612/339-8696, www.townhallbrewery.com, 11am-midnight Sun.-Thurs., 11am-1am Fri.-Sat.) is near Target Field. I recommend coming here, then walking to Target Field, for a great pregame experience. Town Hall is good: small, inventive but measured, and solid across the board. There's a small outdoor seating area.

Very close to Target (as in 0.2 mile away) is **Fulton Brewing** (414 6th Ave. N., Minneapolis, 612/333-3208, www.fultonbeer.com, 3pm-10pm Tues.-Thurs., 3pm-11pm Fri., noon-11pm Sat., noon-6pm Sun.), a modern-industrial kind of place with plenty of outdoor seating and hangout areas, so you can get to know some locals. They have a good range of beer on tap, a kitchen on-site, and music on Sundays.

Well-known and a perfect postgame hangout, **Cuzzy's Grill & Bar** (507 Washington Ave. N., Minneapolis, 612/339-6211, www.cuzzys.com, 7am-1am Mon.-Fri., 8am-1am Sat.) is a breakfast spot by day and a roaring bar by night. It also has burgers, sandwiches, and more. Dollar bills are taped up everywhere, the drinks are strong and unfussy, and there's apparently a ghost named Betsy hanging around.

OTHER NEIGHBORHOODS

Surly Brewing Co. (520 Malcolm Ave. SE, Minneapolis, 763/999-4040, www.surlybrewing.com, 11am-11pm Sun.-Thurs., 11am-midnight Fri.-Sat.) makes one of the best beers you'll have anywhere. Furious, a hugely hoppy IPA, is the perfect sipper for any time. Enjoy it at Surly's large, two-level facility with an upstairs dining room that serves good pub eats. When it's warm, enjoy the outdoor space.

Urban Growler Brewing Co. (2325 Endicott St., St. Paul, 651/340-5793, www. urbangrowlerbrewing.com, 11:30am-10pm Tues.-Thurs., 11:30am-11pm Fri.-Sat., 11:30am-8pm Sun.) is Minnesota's first woman-owned brewery, and it makes some delicious, innovative brews. It's set in an old brick factory with plenty of space and a patio for outdoor drinking.

Folks love **Summit Brewing Company** (910 Montreal Cir., St. Paul, 651/265-7800, www.summitbrewing.com, 2pm-9pm Thurs.-Fri., noon-9pm Sat., noon-6pm Sun.). Take a tour here, as it's informative and fun. The brewery equipment is really interesting. Have a Keller Pils, one of the top pilsners in America, while you're here.

RECREATION

PARKS

Mississippi National River and Recreation Area

The lush Twin Cities shine in the summertime, so plan on some park time while you're here. Much of the area surrounding the Mississippi River is designated as the **Mississippi National River and Recreation Area** (visitors center at 120 W. Kellogg Blvd., St. Paul, 9:30am-5pm Sun.-Thurs., 9:30am-9pm Fri.-Sat.). This 72-mile stretch includes all of the Twin Cities, plus areas to the north and south. I recommend two specific parks to visit within this recreation area.

MINNEHAHA REGIONAL PARK

South of Downtown Minneapolis and along the river, close to the airport, is **Minnehaha**

Photos: (from top to bottom) beer at Surly Brewing Co.; Minnehaha Falls; Marjorie McNeely Conservatory at Como Regional Park.

Regional Park (4801 S. Minnehaha Dr., Minneapolis, 612/230-6400, www.minneapolisparks.org, 6am-10pm daily), a 193-acre park with a beautiful 53-foot waterfall called **Minnehaha Falls,** popularized in the Henry Wadsworth Longfellow poem *The Song of Hiawatha.* The Longfellow Gardens has daisies, dahlias, and peonies, attracting hummingbirds and butterflies. Look for tulips at the Song of Hiawatha Garden. The park has a network of trails that crisscross one another and head toward the river.

FORT SNELLING STATE PARK

Adjacent to the airport is historic **Fort Snelling State Park** (101 Snelling Lake Rd., Minneapolis, 612/279-3550, www.dnr.state.mn.us, 8am-10pm daily). Previously Sioux land, the site was purchased in the early 19th century. After the War of 1812, the U.S. Department of War built **Fort Snelling** (200 Tower Ave., Minneapolis, 612/726-1171, www.historicfortsnelling.org, 10am-4pm Tues.-Thurs., 10am-5pm Fri.-Sun. June-Labor Day, 10am-5pm Sat. Labor Day-Oct., $12, $10 seniors and students, $6 ages 5-17, free ages 4 and under). The fort offers a film, a self-guided tour, and a regular, frequently changing exhibit.

Elsewhere in the park, there are 18 miles of hiking trails and 5 miles of cycling trails. You can also swim at **Snelling Lake,** which has a beach. **Kayaking and canoeing** ($15-25 rentals) is permitted in Gun Club Lake.

Como Regional Park

Northwest of Downtown St. Paul, the 450-acre **Como Regional Park** (1199 Midway Pkwy., St. Paul, 651/266-6400, www.stpaul.gov, sunrise-11pm daily) includes a lake, golf course, ball fields, a pool, and the main attraction, **Como Park Zoo** (1225 Estabrook Dr., St. Paul, 651/487-8201, www.comozooconservatory.org, 10am-6pm daily, free). This small zoo has giraffes, zebras, lions, cougars, flamingos, gorillas, and other animals.

On the grounds of Como is the beautiful **Marjorie McNeely Conservatory** (1225 Estabrook Dr., 651/487-8200, www.comozooconservatory.org, 10am-4pm daily,

free), which opened in 1915. It has a Japanese garden, a tropical display, and a bonsai gallery, along with art that includes *Crest of the Wave,* a 1925 sculpture in bronze by artist Harriet Frishmuth. Near the zoo and conservatory grounds is the vintage **Cafestjian's Carousel** (651/489-4628, www.ourfaircarousel.org, 11am-4pm Tues.-Fri., 11am-6pm Sat.-Sun. May-Labor Day, 11am-4pm Fri.-Sat. early Sept.-Oct., $3), built for St. Paul around World War I. The carousel appeared annually at the Minnesota State Fair into the 1980s but was nearly sold at auction in 1988 before a community fundraising effort saved it. Running every 20 minutes or so, the carousel is a treat for little and big kids alike.

While at the park, consider renting a pedal boat, kayak, paddleboard, or canoe from **Wheel Fun Rentals** (1360 N. Lexington Pkwy., St. Paul, 651/487-8046, www.wheelfunrentals.com, noon-7pm Mon.-Fri., 10am-8pm Sat.-Sun., $13-32 per hour). They're right on Lake Como, making it easy to head out onto the water for a spell. You can also rent surrey bicycles and pedal around the park's paths.

When visiting Como on weekends, follow signs for **off-site parking** and the **Como shuttle.** After parking your car, hop onto a bus that drops you right at Como, a process that takes all of 15 minutes.

BOATING AND PADDLING

The best way for a newbie to experience the Land of 10,000 Lakes is to rent a boat for a day. Try **Your Boat Club** (10 S. 5th St. #110, Minneapolis, 612/208-1800, www.yourboatclub.com, from $100 for a half day), which offers half- and full-day rentals of pontoon boats that are accessible at a number of lakes. Make your reservation online (the farther ahead, the better), then pick up your boat at the indicated lake.

Want to get out into the river? There's the **Mississippi River Paddle Share** (651/293-8436, www.paddleshare.org, from $20 for tandem kayak), which offers paddleboards and kayaks. Simply reserve your vessel, go to one of the six designated paddle-share areas, and get on your way. You'll drop off your vessel when you arrive at your destination. Of course, you'll need to plan a return route (either have a friend at the ready or call a ride-share vehicle).

few pennies, the standard rooms here are basic, clean and cream-colored, with queen and king beds and relatively modern furnishings. The hotel bar, Apothecary, sells a baseball-themed cocktail during the season. Best yet, the hotel is just a six-minute walk from the ballpark—just take the 7th Street bridge over I-394.

SHOPPING

For kitschy Minnesota and Twin Cities T-shirts, head to **Northmade** (610 SE 9th St. #107, Minneapolis, www.northmade. co, by appointment only). The store carries Twins-related designs, plus a variety of Minnesota and Twin Cities gear. Because this is actually the company's warehouse and studio, you'll need to book an appointment in advance to visit. Check the website for openings.

OTHER NEIGHBORHOODS

If you want to stay in St. Paul, I suggest the **Saint Paul Hotel** (350 N. Market St., St. Paul, 651/292-9292, www.saintpaulhotel. com, $100-250). This historic structure, a hotel since 1910, is where Lawrence Welk performed for hotel guests, and where John F. Kennedy stayed while campaigning in 1960. The hotel offers a range of accommodations: double beds, queens, kings, and a few posh suites. There's an on-site restaurant and bar.

ACCOMMODATIONS

NEAR TARGET FIELD

With Target Field in Downtown Minneapolis, you'd better believe there are places to stay nearby. For an independent experience, try the **Hewing Hotel** (300 Washington Ave. N., Minneapolis, 651/468-0400, www. hewinghotel.com, $170-400). At this old warehouse that's been turned into a 124-room and 14-suite hotel, you're a five-minute walk from the ballpark. It includes a rooftop lounge, sauna, and spa, and it's dog-friendly.

If you stay at the **Loews Minneapolis Hotel** (601 1st Ave. N., 612/677-1100, www.loewshotels.com, $150-250), you can opt for the Take Me Out to the Ball Game package. You'll get an overnight stay and two tickets to the ball game. Its Penthouse Level suites overlook Target Field from the 21st floor, and the MVP Suite has a sitting area and bedrooms facing the stadium. Imagine not even needing to get out of bed to watch a ball game. If you'd rather save a

GETTING AROUND

PUBLIC TRANSIT

You can hop around the area's most-touristed areas with **METRO light rail** (www. metrotransit.org, $2-2.50). The **Blue** and **Green Lines,** which run parallel to each other through Downtown Minneapolis, stop at **Target Field station** (335 N. 5th St.) and at stations for other Downtown Minneapolis sites like U.S. Bank Stadium, the North Loop, and the Warehouse District. The Blue Line then extends south to Minneapolis destinations like Fort Snelling, the airport, and the Mall of America, while the Green Line heads east into St. Paul, connecting to that city's Downtown area.

TAXI, UBER, AND LYFT

Uber and Lyft provide the best deals in town. You can hop on an Uber from the airport and get to Target Field by paying about $25, and it may be a buck or two more if you take Lyft.

VISIT THE FIELD OF DREAMS

You may remember the line from the 1989 film *Field of Dreams*: "Hey Dad, you wanna have a catch?" It's hard for a passionate baseball fan not to tear up when hearing that line. You can relive the emotion of that moment, and the joy of a simple catch, by visiting the actual **Field of Dreams** (28995 Lansing Rd., Dyersville, Iowa, 563/875-8404, www.fieldofdreamsmoviesite.com, 9am-6pm daily Apr.-Oct., 10am-4pm daily Nov., free, donations welcome).

After the filmmakers left Dyersville, the field remained, owned by the Lansing and Ameskamp families. In 2007, the Ameskamps sold their land to the Lansings, who in turn eventually sold the land to Go The Distance Baseball. The company holds events on the field, including celebrity baseball games and concerts—like one played by Kevin Costner's own rock band.

As you approach, you might envision yourself in one of those cars pictured on the main road at the end of the film; the field really is set amid nothing but Iowa farmland—meaning lots of corn. Walk up to the field, which was constructed on two farms specifically for the movie. You can walk the green on your own, but the better option is to schedule a **tour** ahead of time. You'll be led through the evolution of the site, where today as many as 100,000 people visit per year. The tour will shepherd you into the family farmhouse, which is set to look like a late-1980s residence. You can have some snacks and a beer at the concession stand named The Stretch (10am-5pm daily). Even out here, there's a Baseballism (9am-9pm daily) selling baseball-themed merchandise.

If you're visiting with a group, you can **rent out the field** (563/875-8404, $125 per hour) to play a ball game. You can also rent out the **farmhouse** (563/875-8404, $550-900) for overnight stays. Plan on spending around two or so hours at the movie site—this will give you time for the tour, a walk around the field, and a snack.

Major League Baseball has been working to bring a **regular season game** to the movie site—but in a separate, newly constructed 8,000-seat park about 500 feet away from the film's field (which wouldn't have been able to meet specifications without major alterations). The first game, featuring the White Sox and another MLB team, is slated for 2021 and will likely also be broadcast on national television.

GETTING THERE

From Minneapolis, you'll take US-52 all the way south to Dyersville. It's a **240-mile** drive that'll take you a little more than **four hours.** It's 390 miles and around six hours of driving if you're continuing on to Kansas City from Dyersville. Des Moines is about the halfway point, so you could use that as an overnight stop.

Field of Dreams

There's a decent cab system in the Twin Cities. Services include **Minneapolis Taxi Cab Service** (612/644-6569) and **MSP Airport Cab Minneapolis** (612/871-8888). To get from the airport to Downtown Minneapolis via taxi costs $39-49. To Downtown St. Paul, it's $31-38.

CAR

Traffic can get bad, especially during rush hours on the major highways, as plenty of people commute from the suburbs to the cities. Since public transit is decent, try to use that as your primary mode of transport, then opt for ride-sharing during off-peak hours.

There's a loop of sorts around the Twin Cities. **I-494** is the loop for all but the northern section, where it's **I-694**. Other major interstates are **I-94,** which runs west to east through both Minneapolis and St. Paul; and **I-35,** which from the south splits into **I-35W** (Minneapolis) and **I-35E** (St. Paul). Then there's **I-394,** a little spur from the western part of the loop that threads east into Downtown Minneapolis.

State highways are also called **trunk highways,** so you may see **MN-65** represented as **TH-65.** MN-65 is **Central Avenue** in northeast Minneapolis and **3rd Avenue** in Downtown Minneapolis before it joins I-35W. In Minneapolis, **3rd Street** feeds into **Washington Avenue,** which runs through the University of Minnesota in southeast Minneapolis. That road feeds into **University Avenue,** which continues east by southeast to the Minnesota State Capitol in St. Paul. It's a good scenic route connecting the two major cities.

VAN METER, IOWA

When driving south from Minneapolis to Kansas City, you'll most likely pass the capital city of Des Moines. But before just continuing south, think about heading west on I-80 just 10 miles to stop in Van Meter, home of Hall of Fame pitcher Bob Feller. Although it may seem like the middle of nowhere, this is a pretty great place to stop, if only to pay homage to one of the greats.

GETTING THERE

You'll need to drive to Van Meter from **Minneapolis.** Take **I-35 South** down to Des Moines, and at the **I-80** intersection, take that highway west for 10 miles. Get off the highway at exit 113 and turn left to head over the Raccoon River and into Van Meter. The drive from the Twin Cities is 260 miles and will take around four hours.

SIGHTS

Bob Feller Exhibit

You're here for a reason, and that's to show some love to one of the greatest pitchers in major league history. The brick house with a baseball outside the front door used to be a stand-alone museum, but it's now **Van Meter City Hall** (310 Mill St., 515/996-2644, www.bobfellermuseum.org, 9am-5pm Mon.-Sat., free). Here you'll get a look at the **Bob Feller exhibit,** which tells the story of the city's most famous native son. Feller went from Van Meter to Cleveland, playing for the Indians starting in 1936. He solidified his position as an outstanding starting pitcher by his fourth season, but at age 23, he went off to fight in World War II. Upon returning in 1945, at age 26, he quickly reestablished himself as one of baseball's best pitchers. Feller finished with 266 wins and 2,581 strikeouts; if he had spent his military years (three seasons) in the majors, who knows what would have happened?

The exhibit at City Hall details Feller's story and displays game-worn jerseys, baseballs from important starts, and fun memorabilia from the 1940s.

KANSAS CITY
ROYALS

Welcome to America's heartland.

Kansas City, Missouri, is close to the middle of the country, which means open skies and country charm, but its population (500,000 in the city, plus another 500,000 or so in the surrounding suburbs) is that of a thriving urban center. More than $6 billion has been poured into the Downtown area since the late 1990s, and the response has been positive: More people have moved to Kansas City, and there's plenty to do in the neighborhoods spanning the city's busiest thoroughfares. It's also a quietly gorgeous city, home to more than 200 fountains and plenty of parkland.

Kansas City's sports scene is thinner than those in other baseball cities, but it's no less passionate. It's Chiefs country during football season, and Major League Soccer's Sporting Kansas City

attracts a large following. As for the Royals, it took the team a few years after their 1969 founding to gain supporters, but having a really good team helped with that. During the Royals' first heyday (1973-1985), which climaxed with the franchise's first world championship, the team drew large crowds, with fans coming from as far west as Colorado. That's one thing to know about Royals fans: They're from all over the heartland, since for a long time there were no other teams to root for between here and California.

Things changed in the 1990s. The Colorado Rockies' founding in 1993, coupled with some bad Royals teams, sank attendance at Kauffman Stadium. The fans eventually came back, between 2014 and 2017, as the Royals won a second championship in 2015 and made consecutive World Series appearances. If the team isn't hot, don't expect a full house. That said, Royals fans are passionate and always believe, and they know a lot about their team.

While you're in Kansas City, it's essential to pay homage to the Negro Leagues, where exceptional African American players, along with other players of color, showed off their skills during the decades they were being denied an opportunity to play in the major leagues. The city is home to the Negro Leagues Museum, and it was also the home of the Monarchs, arguably the quintessential Negro Leagues franchise.

PLANNING YOUR TIME

You can probably spend a **weekend** in Kansas City and feel satisfied, but you'll want to pack that weekend with a lot of sights. Spend one day museum hopping at the Negro Leagues Museum, American Jazz Museum, and National World War I Museum and Memorial, and take time to chow down on barbecue. Spend your second day at the ballpark, relaxing at a local brewery in the **Crossroads District** either before or after the contest. One thing's for sure: You'll need a brisk walk or athletic activity after all the

meat you're going to eat. Luckily, there are parks aplenty in Kansas City.

You have your pick of neighborhoods to base yourself in. You can stay **Downtown** in the **Power & Light District** or **close to the airport,** northwest of the city. Either way, you're probably driving to Kauffman Stadium.

Kansas City in **March** and **April** can get downright **cold,** with temperatures dipping into the 30s and 40s at night. Once the calendar hits the summer solstice, the mercury will frequently rise into the 90s. **Midsummer** (July-late Aug.) can be **dangerously hot.** The best times to attend a Royals game are in **May** and **early June,** or in **September,** when you're most likely to encounter temperatures ranging 70-85°F during the day.

GETTING THERE

AIR

Kansas City International Airport (MCI, 1 International Sq., www.flykci.com) is home to **Air Canada** (888/247-2262, www.aircanada.com), **Allegiant** (702/505-8888, www.allegiant.com), **American Airlines** (800/433-7300, www.aa.com), **Delta** (800/221-1212, www.delta.com), **Frontier** (801/401-9000, www.flyfrontier.com), **Southwest** (800/435-9792, www.southwest.com), **Spirit** (801/401-2222, www.spirit.com), and **United** (800/864-8331, www.united.com). You can fly into MCI from nearly all major U.S. airports, as well as from international cities like Toronto, Cancun, and Reykjavík, Iceland.

Airport Transportation

If you're **renting a car,** take the gray rental car **shuttle,** accessible from the ground transportation pickup area, to the **main rental car hub** (1 Nassau Cir.). The airport is 20 miles northwest of Downtown and about 25 miles from Kauffman Stadium, accessible via I-29.

Previous: Royals mural in Kansas City by artisit Lance Flores

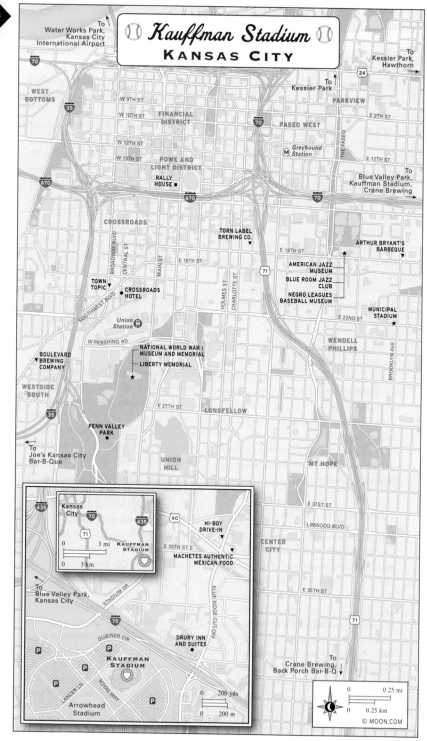

⚾ Kauffman Stadium ⚾
KANSAS CITY

To
Water Works Park,
Kansas City
International Airport

To
Kessler Park,
Hawthorn

To
Kessler Park

WEST
BOTTOMS

W 9TH ST
W 10TH ST

PARKVIEW

E 9TH ST

FINANCIAL
DISTRICT

PASEO WEST

W 12TH ST

W 13TH ST

THE PASEO

E 12TH ST

Greyhound
Station

To
Blue Valley Park,
Kauffman Stadium,
Crane Brewing

POWE AND
LIGHT DISTRICT

RALLY
HOUSE ■

CROSSROADS

TORN LABEL
BREWING CO.

ARTHUR BRYANT'S
BARBEQUE ▼

E 18TH ST

AMERICAN JAZZ
MUSEUM

BLUE ROOM JAZZ
CLUB

NEGRO LEAGUES
BASEBALL MUSEUM

E 19TH ST

TOWN
TOPIC ▼

CROSSROADS
HOTEL ●

HOLMES ST

CHARLOTTE ST

BROADWAY BLVD

CENTRAL ST

MAIN ST

SOUTHWEST BLVD

Union
Station

W PERSHING RD

NATIONAL WORLD WAR I
MUSEUM AND MEMORIAL

LIBERTY MEMORIAL

MUNICIPAL
STADIUM ★

E 22ND ST

WENDELL
PHILLIPS

BROOKLYN AVE

BOULEVARD
▼ BREWING
COMPANY

WESTSIDE
SOUTH

E 27TH ST

LONGFELLOW

PENN VALLEY
PARK ■

To
Joe's Kansas City
Bar-B-Que

UNION
HILL

MT HOPE

E 31ST ST

CENTER
CITY

LINWOOD BLVD

Inset map (lower left):

Kansas
City

KANSAS
CITY

KAUFFMAN
STADIUM

HI-BOY
DRIVE-IN ▼

0   3 mi

0   3 km

E 35TH ST S

MACHETES AUTHENTIC
MEXICAN FOOD ▼

E 35TH ST

To
Blue Valley Park,
Kansas City

STADIUM DR

BLUE RIDGE CUTOFF

DUBINER CIR

DRURY INN
AND SUITES ●

KAUFFMAN
STADIUM

P

To
Crane Brewing,
Back Porch Bar-B-Q ▼

LANCER LN

ROYAL WAY

Arrowhead
Stadium

0   200 yds

0   200 m

0   0.25 mi

0   0.25 km

© MOON.COM

To take public transportation from the airport to Downtown Kansas City, your only option is the **529 KCI Express Limited bus,** operated by **KCATA** (Kansas City Area Transportation Authority, www.ridekc.org, $1.50), which you can pick up at Terminal C. It reaches the **East Village Transit Center** (700 E. 12th St.) in about 45 minutes. The transit center is one of the major busing hubs in Kansas City, but it's still a 1.5-mile drive northwest from the Negro Leagues Baseball Museum, and it's a 7.5-mile trip northwest from Kauffman Stadium. KCI Express Limited doesn't have weekend service.

CAR

The drive from Minneapolis to Kansas City is a straight shot down **I-35 South.** The **440-mile** drive will take a little over **six hours.**

Note that you're headed for Kansas City, **Missouri,** not Kansas City, **Kansas.** That city is just over the river, but it's not where the Royals play.

TRAIN

Amtrak (www.amtrak.com) serves Kansas City at **Union Station** (30 W. Pershing Rd.), just south of the Crossroads District. The **Southwest Chief,** which runs between Los Angeles and Chicago, stops here, as does the **Missouri River Runner,** which zips here from St. Louis. There's no Amtrak connection to Kansas City from Minneapolis.

To get to Kauffman Stadium from Union Station, the best option to take a ride-share. Depending on the route, it's a 7- to 10-mile drive. You could take KCATA's **bus 47** (www.ridekc.org, $1.50). Exit Union Station at the corner of Pershing Road and Main Street and wait for the 47 at the RideKC stop. It arrives every 30-50 minutes and gets to Kauffman Stadium in about 45 minutes.

BUS

It's possible to take **Greyhound** (www.greyhound.com) from Minneapolis to Kansas City. Buses run a couple times per day, depositing passengers at the **Kansas City Bus Station** (1101 Troost Ave., 816/221-2835). The ride from Minneapolis takes 8-9 hours and costs around $80.

The bus station is across I-70 from the Power & Light District. Plan on taking a ride-share vehicle to Kauffman Stadium, which is about eight miles southeast of the bus station. You could also hop on KCATA's **bus 47** (www.ridekc.org, $1.50), but you'll need to walk about 0.5 mile west on 12th Street to get to the bus stop, which is at 12th and Oak Streets.

Kauffman Stadium

Professional baseball in Kansas City used to take place at Municipal Stadium. The venue was located a few blocks south of the city's historic 18th and Vine district and was home to the Kansas City Monarchs for more than 30 years. It was also where the Athletics played when they moved to town in 1955, and where football's Chiefs called home starting in 1963.

In 1967, the city decided to build a sports complex that would contain venues for both the Chiefs and Athletics. Though the A's left for Oakland after that season, baseball returned pretty quickly to Kansas City. The Royals arrived in the 1969 expansion season, playing at Municipal Stadium until a new home was ready.

Their new home was Royals Stadium, opening in 1973 just after the Chiefs' Arrowhead Stadium, both part of the Truman Sports Complex about eight miles southeast of Downtown Kansas City. Unlike the cookie-cutter venues that opened around the same time, Royals Stadium was a breathable ballpark that resembled Dodger Stadium in Los Angeles, with its lack of outfield deck seating and its open pastoral backdrop beyond the fences.

But the park also had modern quirks. An enormous and stately scoreboard towered high over center field and was capped with a crown;

Kauffman Stadium

water fountains blasted out of the right-center field area; and the field itself was the latest in synthetic surfaces: artificial turf (owner Ewing Kauffman didn't want rainouts for fans who traveled from all over the Midwest, and the turf dries better than traditional grass).

The park has aged well. In 1994 the Royals renamed the park **Kauffman Stadium** (1 Royal Way, www.mlb.com/royals) after the team's first owner died. A year later, they got rid of the turf, replacing it with Kentucky bluegrass. Bigger changes came between 2007 and 2010, like a new scoreboard, an outfield concourse, new entry gates, a kids' area, and a restaurant. The exterior also got a facelift, now featuring a perforated metal surface with glass and metal panels. The result is a park that retains its charm while feeling a lot like a savvy, modern venue.

"The K," as it's popularly known, remains one of the overlooked gems in baseball. It always boasts a fun crowd, it's a joy to walk through, and it oozes old-school charm. In its own way, it's a shrine to Midwestern baseball.

ORIENTATION

The ballpark's one drawback is its location: Part of the Harry S. Truman Sports Complex that includes the Kansas City Chiefs' Arrowhead Stadium, Kauffman Stadium neighbors busy I-70 and a bunch of parking lots. But this removed area also makes for great tailgating and copious pregame partying.

There are five entry gates at Kauffman Stadium. Gates A and E are closest to the Outfield Experience and open 90 minutes

before first pitch for every game. The other gates open one hour before first pitch for weekday games.

TICKETS AND SEATING

Pricing

The Royals use **dynamic pricing** for their tickets. This means that if you're coming to watch the home nine play the Yankees, Red Sox, or state rival Cardinals, you're likely paying about 40-50 percent more for your seat.

The cheapest seats in the park are up in the **400 level** rows, starting at **AA** and higher; on some nights, you'll pay just $11. The lower rows of the 400 level can be as cheap as $16. The 200 level isn't bad price-wise, with seats closer to the foul poles costing around $25.

The 300 level seats start at around $35 and generally get good shade.

The seats and table options in the Craft & Draft area start at around $70 per person, while its benches start at about $53 per person. The four-person tables at Rivals Sports Bar start at around $58 per person. Each ticket includes $20 that can be applied to food and drink items.

If you're on a budget, take notice: The Royals reserve select games (typically ones early in the season and against teams that don't draw many fans) as **discount games.** You can get a lower-level seat for $19 or a good 400 level seat for $8.

Seating Plan

There are **four levels** of seating at Kauffman Stadium. Between the foul poles,

YOUR BEST DAY AT KAUFFMAN STADIUM

Let's say you're heading to Kauffman Stadium for a night game. Here's how to really take in the Kansas City experience before catching a Royals game.

8 HOURS BEFORE FIRST PITCH
Learn the history of African American baseball players at the **Negro Leagues Baseball Museum.** Take pictures of the statues decorating the ball field inside the museum.

5 HOURS BEFORE FIRST PITCH
Time for a late lunch. Hope you didn't fill up for breakfast, because you're going to **Arthur Bryant's BBQ** for ribs and burnt ends.

3.5 HOURS BEFORE FIRST PITCH
Head toward the ballpark, but bypass it and go a few minutes south to **Crane Brewing.** Have a saison and get your game face on. Before you leave, buy a crowler (a 32-ounce can) for tailgating at the stadium.

2 HOURS BEFORE FIRST PITCH
Head to the parking lots at **Kauffman Stadium** and crack open that beer you just bought. Enjoy the tailgate for a bit before heading inside.

DURING THE GAME
Hang out in the **Outfield Experience,** maybe getting in a round of mini golf, and

statue of Josh Gibson, by sculptor Kwan Wu, at the Negro Leagues Baseball Museum.

peruse the plaques of Royals legends at the **Royals Hall of Fame.** Munch on some **BBQ brisket tots** while watching the game.

AFTER THE GAME
Hop in a car and get a ride to **Zoo Bar** for cheap beer and good times. Polish off a great night with a visit to **Town Topic,** since it's open all night. Get a burger or some biscuits and gravy, and definitely a root beer float.

Kauffman Stadium has a lower seating area that includes the 100 and 200 levels, a thin 300 level with suites, and an upper deck for the 400 level.

The **Field Level (100 level)** starts in center field and moves toward deep left field with **outfield box** (sections 101-110), then follows the third-base line with **field box** (sections 111-115) and continues toward home plate with **dugout box** (sections 116-117). Behind home plate are the premium **Konica Minolta Diamond Club seats** (sections 126-129). Moving back out along the first-base line are **dugout box** (sections 130-139), then **field box** (sections 140-144),

and, in deep right field, **outfield box** (sections 145-152).

The **Plaza Level (200 level)** starts in center field with the **fountain seats** (sections 201-203), an area offering close-up views of the Water Spectacular. These are only available on the day of the game, on a walk-up basis. Next is over to deep right field with the **outfield plaza** (sections 206-210). Then you have **field plaza** (sections 211-215) and **dugout plaza** (sections 216-225). Behind home plate is premium area called the **Konica Minolta Diamond Club.** Moving along the first-base line are **dugout plaza** (sections 230-239) and **field plaza** (sections

240-244). The level ends in deep right field with **outfield plaza** (sections 245-252).

The **Loge Level (300 level)** starts on the third-base side with the **loge outfield** (sections 303-304), then **loge infield** (sections 305-311). Behind home plate are the **Triple Crown Suites.** Moving along the first-base line in the Loge Level are **loge infield** (sections 312-318) and **loge outfield** (sections 319-325).

The stadium's upper deck is the **View Level (400 level).** Starting in left field is **view outfield** (sections 401-407); arcing around from mid-left field to mid-right field is a combination of seating areas. Seats in the lower half of this area, including some individual sections altogether, are part of **view box** (sections 408-432), while seats in the upper half are part of **view reserved** (sections 409, 411-413, 415, 417, 419-421, 423, 425, 427-429, 431). Finishing out the level on the right-field side is **view outfield** (sections 433-439).

Besides suites and the Diamond Club, specialty seating areas include **Craft & Draft** (sections 301-302) and **Rivals Sports Bar** (behind sections 250-252). Craft & Draft is a self-contained taproom with gastropub food and seating options that include standard chairs, a table (two people per table), and grandstand-style benches. Rivals has a large bar inside, and outside has seats and tables (must be four people per table). Both areas are open to the public, but only people with tickets for these areas can use the tables and seats.

Where to Buy Tickets

You can visit the Royals **ticket office** or the team website, or you can download the **MLB Ballpark app** to buy tickets. The app includes upgrade options.

You can also wait until closer to first pitch to score a cheaper ticket over **StubHub** or another third-party reseller, since Royals games aren't usually in jeopardy of selling out. Some Royals fans recommend the **Gametime app,** a last-minute ticket reseller, for inexpensive tickets. If you're in town for a few days, stopping by a Kansas Citgy-area

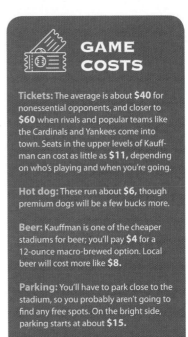

GAME COSTS

Tickets: The average is about **$40** for nonessential opponents, and closer to **$60** when rivals and popular teams like the Cardinals and Yankees come into town. Seats in the upper levels of Kauffman can cost as little as **$11,** depending on who's playing and when you're going.

Hot dog: These run about **$6,** though premium dogs will be a few bucks more.

Beer: Kauffman is one of the cheaper stadiums for beer; you'll pay **$4** for a 12-ounce macro-brewed option. Local beer will cost more like **$8.**

Parking: You'll have to park close to the stadium, so you probably aren't going to find any free spots. On the bright side, parking starts at about **$15.**

Price Chopper (www.mypricechopper.com) supermarket may be a good option, as it's the official grocery partner of the team and sells tickets without all those extra fees.

Best Seats

Sitting in the **400 level** is a fine choice for those on a **budget,** especially considering the upper deck is slightly on the steep side, but you'll still get a solid view of the game. Stick to the **third-base side** (sections 409-415) if you want to save money and not be warmed by the midday sun.

If you're willing to dish out a bit more to stay in the **shade,** opt for seats between **sections 301** and **310.** The **back rows** of **sections 214-223** will get plenty of shade, as well, but you'll have to see over a lot of heads.

For those wanting to have a couple brews during the game, buy a cheap ticket for the high 400 level and head over to the **Blue Moon Tap Room** in right field—part of Rivals Sports Bar, the mostly standing-room area where anyone can hang out (unless it's being rented out to a group for the day). If it's a day game, you'll have to battle with the sun, but sunglasses and sunblock are your best friends while you're sipping on tall beers and checking out the contest. Plus, the people are fun, and you'll be close to the Water Spectacular.

If the Royals aren't playing particularly well, you should be able to move into a seat in the 100 or 200 level late in a ball game. The ushers are very friendly and accommodating, as long as you're kind in turn.

KNOW BEFORE YOU GO

The Royals permit **bags** and **purses** up to 16 by 16 by 8 inches. **Water** and **sports drinks** are allowed inside (one sealed liter-sized bottle per person). **Outside food** can be brought in, too, as long as it can fit inside a bag that doesn't exceed the maximum size. No outside alcohol is permitted. **Strollers** are also allowed in—just fold them up.

There's a **nursing room** for mothers on the Plaza Level (behind home plate).

It can get unbearably hot between late June and August, so bring **sunblock** and prepare to drink plenty of water.

Kauffman Stadium's parking lots open several hours before the game for **tailgating;** the exact opening times vary by game. Generally, fans start setting up about 2-3 hours before first pitch.

Accessibility

Before visiting Kauffman Stadium, you can download the team's **ballpark story** (www.mlb.com/royals), which details what happens when you come to the park. This can be a useful tool to help familiarize kids with what to expect on game day.

The Royals operate **golf cart shuttles** (816/504-4040, opt. 5) to take folks from the parking lot to the ballpark. If you would like the use of a **wheelchair** to reach your seat, ask an attendant at an entry gate for assistance.

Head to **plaza guest services** (Konica Minolta Diamond Club entry at plaza level and section 421, 816/504-4040, opt. 5) for **assistive listening devices** and **noise-cancelling headphones.**

Elevators are located across from Gates B and D, and in the Konica Minolta Diamond Club lobby. **Quiet spaces** are reserved behind sections 118 and 136. **Service animals** are welcome at Kauffman Stadium.

Every parking lot at Kauffman Stadium, except Lots L and N, are available for **accessible parking. Wheelchair ramps** are at every lot.

GETTING THERE

Public Transit

It's possible to take a bus to Kauffman from the Downtown area. Operated by **KCATA** (www.ridekc.org, $1.50), **bus 47** departs from the East Village neighborhood, then heads down Broadway and along the Blue Parkway before letting passengers off by the ballpark.

Driving

Driving is the easiest option when visiting Kauffman Stadium. Luckily, parking rates aren't sky-high; you'll likely dish out $15-25 for a spot. Since Kauffman is part of a sports complex, there are enough lots for everyone.

The Royals designate **Lot N** and **Royal Way** outside the park, and **Hall of Fame Village** inside Kauffman Stadium, as **planned tailgate areas** (think large groups), but most folks will just put down a few chairs and small grills behind their cars and trucks. The lots open two hours ahead of first pitch for tailgating.

PARK FEATURES AND SIGHTS

Water Spectacular

For decades, Kauffman Stadium has been known for its **Water Spectacular,** a 322-foot-wide gallery of fountains that activate before a game, after a game, and between innings. The fountains start just left of the center-field video board, then span much of right field. They can fan out in a seashell shape, or spread out in a smaller V, or sprout up like blooms, or just shoot right up into the sky, alternating seemingly on a whim.

BE A FAN

Tailgate culture in Kansas City is serious, and you'll find it happening in all the parking lots before a game. Arrive two hours before first pitch with food and drink for maximum enjoyment.

Unless you're decked out in Cardinals gear, you won't be hassled for wearing another team's colors. If anything, you'll get some curious stares—pretty much everyone here is wearing something royal blue, and you'll stick out like a sore thumb. But no worries—Royals fans are as nice as midwesterners get.

In 2008 the Royals starting playing Garth Brooks' **"Friends in Low Places"** during the sixth inning as a rally song, and pretty quickly it caught on, with much of the crowd singing along. Why? There's no great reason, though Brooks did play a spring training intrasquad game for the Royals in 2004. In time, "Friends in Low Places" became more polarizing with the fanbase, and the Royals ended their relationship with the song in the middle of the 2014 season. The team held a vote to determine a new pump-up song, and the winner was Journey's **"Don't Stop Believin."** Of course, that song is also claimed by the San Francisco Giants, who the Royals faced—and lost to—in the 2014 World Series. So the team didn't hold onto that one for very long.

While there isn't a sixth-inning hype song these days, maybe the team should adopt the 2013 Lorde smash hit **"Royals."** Sure, the song is about the idolization of luxury brands, but the title was inspired by the Kansas City Royals. The Kiwi singer said in 2013 that when writing the song, she came across an issue of *National Geographic* with a photo of Royals legend George Brett wearing his jersey.

The Royals do play The Beatles' 1964 rendition of the popular tune **"Kansas City"** after every win. That song may actually be attributed to Kansas City baseball, too. The story goes that in 1964, Kansas City Athletics owner Charlie Finley tried like crazy to get The Beatles to play in town, but the band's management rebuffed him. After multiple attempts by Finley asking what it would take to get them to KC, their manager threw out a crazy number, thinking the A's owner would quit his questioning. Instead, he agreed to the high total, and the Beatles finally played Kansas City, leading with the song. Months later, "Kansas City" was included in a medley on the Beatles' album *Beatles For Sale*.

Lighting fixtures underneath the fountains change the color of the display frequently—red, orange, and yellow are common. It's one of the coolest single features of any major league ballpark.

Royals Hall of Fame

The **Royals Hall of Fame** (Gate A, Plaza Level) is open during game days and showcases the plaques of the team's Hall of Famers, from George Brett to Amos Otis. Plus, you can check out a slew of artifacts, from the 2015 World Series trophy to Eric Hosmer's Gold Glove awards to Brett's 3,000th-hit baseball and bat.

Outfield Experience

The outfield area at Kauffman is called the **Outfield Experience,** a family-friendly area with a playground, carousel, batting cage, miniature golf course, and music stage (shows on Wednesday game days during the season). While the playground is free, attractions like the carousel and mini golf course will cost you in tokens. Tokens are $2 each; most attractions cost one token. Or you can get a wristband ($10) that allows for unlimited play.

FOOD AND DRINKS

At Kauffman Stadium, I recommend trying the many food items that incorporate barbecue like **BBQ brisket tots** (Miller Lite Bar, section 202). These tots are topped with brisket, white queso, and barbecue sauce. It's a gluttonous treat. In the same vein, look for the **rookie sandwich** (sections 221, 234, 251, 308, 417, 422), which showcases chopped brisket or pulled pork

in barbecue sauce with pickles in a bun.

The taco trio and carnitas tacos at **KC Cantina Portables** (sections 221, 234) and **KC Cantina** (section 427) are worth the money if you're hungry.

Craft & Draft (300 level, third-base line) has salads, pub bites (nachos, crab cakes, and pork belly macaroni and cheese), and build-your-own pizzas. The beer selection is pretty top-notch, with about 70 taps. The **Blue Moon Tap Room** at **Rivals Sports Bar** (200 level, right field) has mostly hot dogs, burgers, wings, and sandwiches, as well as some tacos. Its outdoor patio is a fun hangout. Underneath the tap room is the **360 Vodka Bullpen Bar,** serving plenty of cocktails.

For healthy food options, visit the **Price Chopper Market Place** (200 level, left field), which sells wraps, salads, veggie burgers, and snacks. If you have a sweet tooth, head to **Belfonte's Ice Cream** (200 level, center field), a Kansas City institution since 1969.

The city's most famous brewery, **Boulevard Brewing Co.,** has a partnership with the Royals, resulting in a number of sponsored sites around the stadium. Check out the **Radler Station** and **Boulevard Hop Stop** (section 252) for Boulevard beer like the famous Tank 7 saison. There's also plenty of Boulevard on tap at Craft & Draft.

EVENTS

The ramp behind the player parking area is reserved for those wanting **autographs** of Royals players. You can also check out the area near the Gate C lobby entrance. Aim to arrive in either area about 45 minutes after the final out; this is when players will begin to emerge from the ballpark.

The Royals offer an **early bird experience** ($12 ages 4 and older) for select games, allowing fans to enter the ballpark an hour before the gates open to watch home **batting practice.**

Photos (from top to bottom): Kauffman Stadium's Water Spectacular; statue of Frank White Jr. in the Royals Hall of Fame by sculptor Harry Weber; beer at a Royals game.

After every Sunday game, children ages 14 and younger can participate in a **fun run around the bases,** as long as they have an accompanying parent or guardian. Sunday is also **Family FunDay,** during which the Royals offer unlimited activities in the Outfield Experience with an **All-Day Play Pass** ($10).

Tours

Stadium tours (816/504-4222, $17-55, $15-50 seniors, $12-40 youth) are offered during select days of the season. Options include the Legends Tour, the All Star Tour, and the Grand Slam Tour. Each is slightly different, but all of them go behind the giant video board in center field.

SHOPPING

The biggest selection is at the **Royals Team Store** (Gate C, 10am-4pm Tues.-Sat., plus every game day when gates are open), which can get pretty crowded before games as it's somewhat narrow in parts. The good jersey selection includes the team's stunning powder-blue tops. Look for the well-stocked hat area and an array of fun socks.

For a great deal, check out the **20 Below Store** (200 level, Gate A), where everything is $20 or less. For even more hats, visit the **New Era Store** (Section 420). At the **Ladies Boutique Store** (200 level, center field), everything is focused on the female fan.

KANSAS CITY SIGHTS

NEGRO LEAGUES BASEBALL MUSEUM

Reserve time for this absolute must-see destination. The **Negro Leagues Baseball Museum** (1616 E. 18th St., 816/221-1920, www.nlbm.com, 9am-6pm Mon.-Sat., noon-6pm Sun., $10, $9 seniors, $6 ages 5-12, free ages 4 and under) tells the story of organized baseball played by African Americans and other people of color, who were denied the opportunity to play in Major League Baseball for decades.

The first Black professional baseball team was the Cuban Giants, founded in 1885 with no Cuban players (the origin of the name is disputed, but it's possible it was given to conceal the players' identities as Black men). They were successful for nearly three decades, playing and sometimes defeating major league teams. More Black teams emerged in the early part of the 20th century until, in 1920, an agreement was struck in Kansas City to form the Negro National League. By the early 1930s, league had disbanded, due to financial troubles from the Great Depression.

But then the Pittsburgh Crawfords were born, and in 1932 they featured pitcher Satchel Paige and catcher Josh Gibson. The team was a hit, leading its owner Gus Greenlee to start a new league again called the Negro National League. This version had more success than the first. During this time, star players like Cool Papa Bell, Buck Leonard, Roy Campanella, Larry Doby, and Monte Irvin emerged. In the meantime, the rival Negro American League was established in 1937, and a Negro League World Series was played between the two leagues from 1942 to 1948.

Of course, 1948 was the year Major League Baseball integrated, with the addition of Jackie Robinson, who had played for the Kansas City Monarchs, to the Brooklyn Dodgers. Other players followed over the next several years, and by the early 1960s Black baseball leagues had faded from prominence.

But the legacy of the Negro leagues remains strong. Iconic players like Paige, who struck out 1,620 hitters in 18 seasons, and Gibson, who during his prime was a feared hitter who could scrape .400 with startling power, were inducted into the National Baseball Hall of Fame. Late-period Negro League talent like Robinson, Willie Mays, Ernie Banks, and Hank Aaron were among the very best major league players between 1945 and 1975. Heck, Mays is arguably the greatest to have *ever* played the game. The

Negro Leagues Baseball Museum

Negro Leagues were important because they gave talented players a place to shine; beyond that, they lifted up Black communities and entertained audiences for decades.

The museum was founded by a nonprofit organization and is located in Kansas City's 18th and Vine district, a historic community where Black culture has thrived. It's also within walking distance of the Paseo YMCA where Andrew "Rube" Foster created the Negro National League in 1920. While the museum itself was established in 1991, its current 10,000-square-foot digs opened in 1997; since then, more than two million visitors have come through the doors.

Take a self-guided tour and find artifacts like a Kansas City Monarchs jersey worn by star hitter Newt Allen and a glove worn by the leagues' greatest ambassador, Buck O'Neil, during his days managing the Monarchs, plus a pretty remarkable non-baseball piece: Satchel Paige's original gravestone. Be sure to spend time at the replica field, with its marvelous statues of all-time greats (Paige, Gibson, Bell, and Leonard), and at the collection of signed baseballs donated by Rush lead singer Geddy Lee, an avid baseball fan and memorabilia collector. You can buy a **combination ticket** ($15, $13 seniors, $8 ages 5-12, free ages 4 and under) for the Negro Leagues museum and the American Jazz Museum.

AMERICAN JAZZ MUSEUM

Sharing a building with the Negro Leagues Baseball Museum, the **American Jazz Museum** (1616 E. 18th St., 816/474-8463, www.americanjazzmuseum.org, 9am-6pm Tues.-Sat., noon-6pm Sun., $10, $9 seniors, $6 ages 5-12, free ages 4 and under) anchors the intersection of 18th and Vine, nexus of Kansas City's Historic Jazz District. Look for a saxophone played in 1953 by Charlie Parker. On select days, take in a concert at the **Blue Room Jazz Club** (5pm-11pm Mon. and Thurs., 5pm-1am Fri., 7pm-1am Sat., ticket prices vary), which hosts visiting musicians and weekly jam sessions inside a space designed to look like a 1930s club.

Across the street from the museum is the **Gem Theater,** a 1912 building used for movie screenings through 1960. It's now a performance space that hosts an annual **jazz series** (www.americanjazzmuseum.org, Apr.) put on by the American Jazz Museum.

You can buy **combination tickets** ($15, $13 seniors, $8 ages 5-12, free ages 4 and under) for the Negro Leagues museum and jazz museum.

NATIONAL WORLD WAR I MUSEUM AND MEMORIAL

Trace the history of the First World War at the **National World War I Museum and Memorial** (2 Memorial Dr., 816/888-8100, www.theworldwar.org, 10am-5pm Sun.-Fri., 9am-5pm Sat. Memorial Day-Labor Day, 10am-5pm Tues.-Sun. early Sept.-late May, $18, $14 seniors and military, $10 ages 6-18, free ages 5 and under), which possesses the largest collection of World War I artifacts in the world. The permanent exhibit showcases FT-17 tanks, letters, weaponry, and clothing. Previously featured exhibits have touched on fabric art of the 1910s and the lives of the "doughboys," soldiers in the Army and Marines deployed to the Western Front.

Be sure to visit the 217-foot **Liberty Memorial Tower,** built in 1926 to honor the men and women who served in the Great War. You can ascend the tower ($3) for an iconic view of Kansas City.

MUNICIPAL STADIUM

If you have time, be sure to pay homage to the old **Municipal Stadium** (Brooklyn Ave. and E. 22nd St.). While the venue has since been demolished, a marker on-site lets visitors know where they are. Its history includes the first years of the Royals and the Kansas City Athletics (who came from Philadelphia and later moved to Oakland), but more importantly, it's where the Kansas City Monarchs of the Negro Leagues played from 1923 to 1955. Some of the talent that stepped foot on that diamond: Buck O'Neil, Jackie Robinson, Cool Papa Bell, Ernie Banks, and Satchel Paige.

FOOD

NEAR KAUFFMAN STADIUM

The options are slim near Kauffman Stadium, with the bulk of food choices being of the fast-food variety. Just 1.5 miles up the road, but in Independence, is **Dixon's Chili Parlor** (9105 E. US-40, Independence, 816/861-7308, www.dixonschili.com, 10am-10pm Mon.-Sat., under $20), which since 1919 has served up classic Kansas City-style chili: meat and beans, no tomatoes. You can add fixings like ketchup (if you really need the acid), grated cheese, and jalapeño relish. The diner-style joint is hopping when the Royals are in town.

Also in the classic category, **Hi-Boy Drive-in** (3424 Blue Ridge Cutoff, Independence, 816/861-2677, www.hiboydrivein.com, 10:30am-10pm daily, under $15) has mastered a simple but effective menu: hamburgers and cheeseburgers that vary only by size, slightly more adventurous sandwiches (try the chicken with Miracle Whip), sides like corn-dog bites, and plenty of thick, dreamy shakes and sundaes. This is a perfect postgame treat.

Craving some Mexican street food? **Machetes Authentic Mexican Food** (9104 E. 35th St. S., Independence, 816/381-7968, www.machetesgiantquesadillas.com, 10:30am-9pm Tues.-Sat., 11:30am-9pm Mon., under $20) offers burritos, tortas, quesadillas, and tacos with your choice of meat, from carne asada to *papas con chorizo.* Or you can order a *machete,* a little-known street food item, here a 20-inch corn quesadilla filled with cheese and meat. It's called a machete after its oblong shape, resembling the knife of the same name. Breakfast is also available in this comfortable, homey dining room.

OTHER NEIGHBORHOODS

There's no Kansas City food stop more important than **Arthur Bryant's Barbeque** (1727 Brooklyn Ave., 816/231-1123, www.arthurbryantsbbq.com, 10am-9pm Mon.-Sat., 11am-8pm Sun., under $30). Open since 1908 and located in the historic 18th and Vine neighborhood, this is one of the most famous barbecue joints in the country. Get the baby back ribs, smoked over hickory and oak and splashed with Bryant's

trademark vinegar-based sauce. Also go for the burnt ends, perfectly crispy and beefy, and stock up on the white bread. You'll sit in a buzzy, cramped, but very happy dining room—make some friends. Get here a few minutes before the doors open, because a line will undoubtedly form.

In the same league, just without the deep history, is **Joe's Kansas City Bar-B-Que** (3002 W. 47th St., Kansas City, KS, 913/722-3336, www.joeskc.com, 11am-9pm Mon.-Thurs., 11am-10pm Fri.-Sat., under $30). Hop to the original location, west of Westwood Park in Kansas City, Kansas. It's set in a former gas station, where you'll order pulled pork and sides like BBQ beans and Kansas caviar (beans, corn, carrots, onions, and peppers topped with a sweet dressing). If you're feeling adventurous, order the famous Z-Man: beef brisket, smoked provolone, and onion rings on a kaiser roll.

Itching for a burger? Locals love **Town Topic** (2021 Broadway Blvd., 816/842-2298, www.towntopic.com, 24 hours daily, under $20) in the Crossroads neighborhood. A staple since 1937, it makes old-fashioned burgers and Coney dogs, plus breakfast items like pancakes, biscuits and gravy, and an inexpensive egg sandwich. Don't forget dessert: A root beer float awaits. The original location is always open.

BARS AND BREWERIES

NEAR KAUFFMAN STADIUM

About 3.5 miles south of the stadium is **Crane Brewing** (6515 Railroad St., Raytown, 816/743-4132, www.cranebrewing.com, 4pm-9pm Tues.-Thurs., 2pm-10pm Fri., noon-10pm Sat., 11am-4pm Sun.), a

Photos (from top to bottom): National World War I Museum and Memorial; barbecue plate at Joe's Kansas City Bar-B-Que; Arthur Bryant's Barbeque.

must-visit brewery delivering top-notch interpretations of traditional farmhouse ales like saison and lambic. Its taproom includes tables made of locally sourced barn wood. Check out its baseball-themed saison, Small Ball, typically available in the spring.

OTHER NEIGHBORHOODS

The area around Kauffman Stadium lacks quality hangouts, so you'll have to travel out a bit to find a good drinking scene. Visit the Crossroads District, home to a handful of breweries including **Torn Label Brewing Co.** (1708 Campbell St., 918/634-8001, www.tornlabel.com, 5pm-10pm Wed.-Thurs., 4pm-midnight Fri., noon-midnight Sat., noon-8pm Sun.). Founded in 2014, Torn Label mixes Belgian, Californian, and other beer styles inside a warehouse-like facility that's part of an artistic community.

The Westport area, about three miles south of the Crossroads District, is known for its bar scene, so hop over there one night and pay special consideration to **Green Room Burgers & Bar** (4010 Pennsylvania Ave. #D, 816/216-7682, www.greenroomkc.com). It brews its own selections, but it also maintains a robust beer list with plenty of local options.

The big kid in town is **Boulevard Brewing Company** (2501 Southwest Blvd., 816/474-7095, www.boulevard.com, 11am-8pm Mon.-Wed., 11am-9pm Thurs., 10am-9pm Fri.-Sat., 10am-6pm Sun.), located in Westside South, about 10 minutes southwest from the Power & Light District. Home to the renowned saison Tank 7 and Bourbon Barrel Quad, the brewery is open daily for free tours and pours inside its large beer hall. A small snack menu is also available—think pretzel dogs and charcuterie.

Smack in the middle of Downtown, just on the edge of the Power & Light District, is **Zoo Bar** (1220 McGee St., no phone, 3pm-midnight Mon.-Thurs., 11am-1:30am Fri.-Sat.), a narrow dive with an old cigarette machine and a lively customer base. Read the many, many scribbles on the walls, sip a cheap beer (on Monday, 12-ounce domestics are $2), and make some friends. Just remember to bring cash—credit cards aren't accepted.

RECREATION

PARKS

The site of the National World War I Museum and Memorial, plus baseball fields and skateboarding facilities, **Penn Valley Park** (W. 28th St. and Wyandotte St.) is a 176-acre urban oasis that once was home to a section of the Santa Fe Trail, which connected nearby Independence to Santa Fe, New Mexico. Walk or run the two-mile exercise trail, or admire Penn Valley Lake.

DISC GOLF

Kansas City happens to be one of the top disc golf cities in America. Those seeking a major challenge should check out **Blue Valley Disc Golf Course** (2301 Topping Ave., https://kcparks.org), which boasts an 11,000-foot, championship 18-hole course. Every disc golfer should play **Waterworks Park** (3500 N. Oak Trafficway, https://kcparks.org), an 18-hole course designed in 1997 that poses multiple obstacles.

Another disc golf course not meant for the first-timer, **Kessler Park** (Chestnut Trafficway at Cliff Dr., https://kcparks.org) has a little something for everyone. It's also home to a few memorials, pieces of art like a colonnade, and eight miles of trails mostly in old woods. Look for the Carl J. DiCapo fountain, a lovely little waterfall over red rock.

SHOPPING

If you're Downtown, buy Royals T-shirts, replica jerseys, hats, and other officially licensed merchandise at **Rally House** (181 E. 14th St., 816/381-9400, www.rallyhouse.

com, 10am-9pm Mon.-Fri., 9am-9pm Sat., 11am-6pm Sun.) in the Power & Light District. If you're seeking some throwback threads, Rally House has a selection of Kansas City Athletics gear like hats and polo shirts.

ACCOMMODATIONS

NEAR KAUFFMAN STADIUM

A few larger, chain hotels sit along I-70 for those wanting to be conveniently close to the ballpark. The best lodging is the **Drury Inn and Suites** (3830 Blue Ridge Cutoff, 816/923-3000, www.druryhotels.com, $100-150), which has everything you'd expect from a family-friendly value hotel. Breakfast is included, rooms are clean, and there's an outdoor pool on-site.

OTHER NEIGHBORHOODS

For a taste of hip Kansas City, there's the **Crossroads Hotel** (2101 Central St., 816/897-8100, www.crossroadshotelkc.com, $120-250 Dec.-Apr., $200-350 May-Nov.), set inside the renovated Pabst Brewing Depot building in the artistic Crossroads District. The ultramodern rooms have exposed brick and mid-century modern furniture. The hotel includes an Italian restaurant and cocktail bar.

GETTING AROUND

PUBLIC TRANSIT

The **KCATA** (www.ridekc.org) handles mass transit in the city with a **bus network** ($1.50) that shuttles people across the city, over the river to Kansas City, Kansas, and to other suburbs. KCATA also maintains a **streetcar** (free) that runs along Main Street, through the Central Business District, the Power & Light District, and the Crossroads District, to Union Station. KCATA's smartphone app, RideKC, has schedules and maps.

TAXI, UBER, AND LYFT

Uber and Lyft have a solid presence in Kansas City. You may also encounter **zTrip** (www.ztrip.com), which has all but supplanted taxi companies in the city, though its fares can be slightly higher than the competition. It's just like Uber and Lyft in that you can call up a car via its app, but you can also hail a vehicle on the street.

CAR

Since Kansas City and its major suburbs are spread out and all worth visiting, having a car is crucial. Especially if you're visiting Kauffman Stadium, driving may be the best option for getting around. If you're flying in or coming to the city via rail, you can rent a car at Kansas City International Airport.

I-435 loops around the city, connecting many of the major suburbs, including Independence, Overland Park, and Kansas City, Kansas. Some visiting drivers may say the city is confusing, but stick to the major highways, stay inside the loop, and you'll be fine. Highway speed limits outside of the city limits quickly hit 70 mph in Missouri and 75 mph in Kansas.

I-70 threads through the city, heading west to east. Kauffman Stadium is right off that highway. Going north to south, **I-35** travels from Des Moines, Iowa, into Kansas City and then heads southwest toward Wichita, Kansas. **I-29** starts in Kansas City at I-35, then heads northwest toward Omaha, Nebraska. **I-49** starts in Kansas City and heads southeast toward Fort Smith, Arkansas.

COMMERCE, OKLAHOMA

The small city of Commerce, Oklahoma, is known primarily for two things: It's where outlaws Bonnie and Clyde killed a constable just a month before their deaths in 1934, and it's where Mickey Mantle grew up. His childhood home still stands here, and you can pay respects at a monument erected in town for the "Commerce Comet."

GETTING THERE

From **Kansas City,** drive south on I-35 to US-69, and take that south about 100 miles until you reach the turnoff for KS-7. Continue south on KS-7, which turns back into US-69, until you reach Commerce. The total drive is 180 miles and takes about three hours.

SIGHTS

Those making a pilgrimage to Commerce have to glimpse **Mickey Mantle's Childhood Home** (319 S. Quincy St.). There's a description of the house by its front door, and visitors are allowed to walk around the property. Be sure to check out the rusted metal shed, which was Mantle's backstop as he learned to hit from both sides of the plate. It's as it was nearly 100 years ago, a pretty cool sight for any big-time baseball fan.

The city nods to its favorite son in a few smaller ways, too. Visit the **Mickey Mantle statue** (420 D St.) outside Commerce High School's Mickey Mantle Field. The nine-foot statue was dedicated in 2010. Look, too, for the **Commerce Water Tower** (Commerce St. and River St.), which has blue pinstripes and the number 7 painted on it—signifying Mantle's jersey number for the Yankees.

TULSA, OKLAHOMA

Tulsa, Oklahoma, has a rich baseball history as a minor league city, first as the home of the Oilers until 1976. Primarily a Cardinals affiliate, the Tulsa Oilers left town for Louisiana; a year later, the Drillers put down their roots. The current team in Tulsa has welcomed more than a few players on the road to stardom, including Sammy Sosa, Troy Tulowitzki, and Hall of Famer Ivan Rodriguez.

This city of about 400,000 makes for a great minor league hub. Its ballpark is in the middle of the Greenwood District, an active area that in the early 20th century was a center for Black-owned businesses, dubbed "Black Wall Street."

It was also where, in 1921, White residents of Tulsa killed hundreds of Black residents in one of the largest massacres in U.S. history. In time, the district was rebuilt, but by the mid-20th century, it had lost its original spirit as Black businesspeople left for other areas of the city and region. Today, the history of the neighborhood lives on at the **Greenwood Cultural Center** (322 N. Greenwood Ave., 918/596-1020, www.greenwoodculturalcenter.com, 9am-5pm Mon.-Fri.). The center's exhibits tell the story of the area and of African American heritage.

GETTING THERE

From **Commerce,** drive southwest on I-44 into the heart of Tulsa. This 90-minute, 95-mile drive has tolls.

From **Kansas City,** the less scenic route is a straight shot south on I-49 into Joplin, Missouri, then a drive west on I-44 into Tulsa. That drive is about four hours and 270 miles long. Otherwise, you can drive south on I-35 to US-169 into Tulsa. That route takes about four hours and is 245 miles long, and you travel through small towns like Colony, Kansas, and Nowata, Oklahoma.

If you're not driving, you can take a **Greyhound bus** (www.greyhound.com) from Kansas City to the **Tulsa Bus Station** (317

S. Detroit Ave., 918/584-4428). The four- to five-hour trip costs around $50.

ONEOK FIELD

ONEOK Field (201 N. Elgin Ave., 918/744-5998, www.milb.com/tulsa) is home to the Texas League's **Tulsa Drillers,** the double-A affiliate of the Los Angeles Dodgers. ONEOK (pronounced "one-oak") is a beautiful, if understated, minor league facility. Open since 2010, it provides stunning views of Downtown Tulsa.

There are **two levels** of seating at ONEOK Field. On the **first level,** starting in deep right field and going toward home plate, are sections 101-106. Around home plate are sections 107-111, along the third-base line are sections 112-115, and in the deeper part of left field are sections 116-119. The **second level** starts in foul left field with the **Coors Light Refinery Deck,** a group area that's not open to regular ticketholders. Then come **suites** along the first-base line (1-10), the suite-only **Cadillac Club bar,** suites along the third-base line (11-23), and the **Bud Light Dilly Dilly Deck,** a private seating area with a bar. In the outfield, find the **Busch Scoreboard Bar** (open to all) in left field, the group-only **Busch Terrace,** and two sections of **lawn seating.**

Sit along the **third-base line** to get the coolest view of the skyline. For kids, look for a **Splash Zone** with water play options, as well as a large playground called the **TDW Kids Zone,** both in center field.

The Drillers like to host a **fireworks show** after select games. Typically, they'll be held after Friday night games and some Saturday games, plus over major summer holidays like the Fourth of July.

Food choices are primarily run-of-the-mill for minor league parks, but be sure to grab a **Siegi's sausage,** representing the city since 1980. **Hornsby's Ice Cream Parlor** is a good spot, though it'll get packed as the game lingers on. Beer vendors serve **Boulevard** and local brewery **Marshall,** both available in section 105. You can also drink with friends at the **Busch Scoreboard Bar** out in left field.

If driving to the game, you can park at a lot near the stadium for about $10. You can also try to search for a free spot in the city and walk over; the Greenwood District is pedestrian-friendly, though there may be construction to battle.

SIGHTS

Tulsa is home to the **Woody Guthrie Center** (102 E. Mathew B. Brady St., 918/574-2710, www.woodyguthriecenter.org, 10am-6pm Tues.-Sun., $12, $11 seniors, $8 students, free ages 17 and under), which tells the story of musical activism through the life of one of Oklahoma's most famous natives. Find artifacts like Pete Seeger's banjo among other notable pieces from music history. The center also hosts concerts and offers educational opportunities.

Close to the ballpark and the center of things in Tulsa is an interesting landmark: **Center of the Universe** (1 S. Boston Ave.). This small circle surrounded by bricks is an awesome echo chamber. Say something out loud, and it'll echo back at you much louder. It's a fun way to pass a few minutes.

FOOD

Just a shout from ONEOK Field is **Fat Guy's Burger Bar** (140 N. Greenwood Ave., 918/794-7782, www.fatguysburgers.com, under $25), a popular Tulsa hangout that makes some messy, juicy meals. If you feel up to it, you can tackle the Fat Guy's Burger Bar Challenge, in which you have to scarf down a two-pound patty, a pound of bacon, two hot dogs, eight slices of cheese, some salad, and a pound of fries in an hour. Or just get a bacon cheeseburger and ballpark fries and call it a day.

Craving a classic Vietnamese banh mi? **Lone Wolf** (203 E. Archer St., 918/728-7778, www.lonewolftulsa.com, under $25) serves several variations of it, plus kimchi fries and fried rice bowls, inside a clean, modern hangout with black tile and polished oak. Save room for the soft-serve ice cream.

Eating around the Greenwood District highlights Tulsa's diversity. Visit **Sisserou's Caribbean Restaurant** (107 N. Boulder Ave. #C, 918/576-6800, www.sisserousrestaurant.com, 11am-10pm Mon.-Thurs., 11am-11pm Fri.-Sat., under $30), which offers tastes of the Dominican Republic and other Caribbean nations. Find dishes like callaloo, jerk chicken wings, and Escovitch red snapper inside this handsome industrial space with colorful lighting. This spot is good for both a family lunch and a nice dinner out.

BARS AND BREWERIES

For a taste of Oklahoma's beer scene, trek over to **Elgin Park** (325 E. Mathew B. Brady St., 918/986-9910, www.elginparkbrewery. com, 11am-11pm Sun.-Thurs., 11am-2am Fri.-Sat., under $30), which crafts its own suds and offers a robust list of Sooner State options from places like Prairie, Dead Armadillo, and Roughtail. For grub, it's wings, pizza, and other bar snacks. There's a fun sports bar atmosphere, with plenty of TVs, some games, and a patio for catching fireworks after the Drillers game.

The first craft brewery in Tulsa, **Marshall Brewing Co.** (1742 E. 6th St., 918/292-8781, www.marshallbrewing. com, 2pm-9pm Mon.-Thurs., noon-10pm Fri.-Sat., noon-6pm Sun., under $25) offers plenty of seating options, including a patio. My pick is El CuCuy, the relatively potent black ale that's available in the fall and winter. For summer, This Land Lager, which pays homage to Oklahoman Woody Guthrie, is a winner.

RECREATION

Tulsa's **River Parks Authority** (www.riverparks.org) maintains hiking and biking trails and a **greenbelt** along the Arkansas River, also known as Zink Lake. The organization operates the **41st Street Plaza** (Riverside Dr. at E. 41st St.), on the east side of the river. It has plenty of trails, a splash pad for kids, and a river overlook. Head south along Riverside Drive to the 18-hole **disc golf course,** which offers moderate challenges in a flat, scenic area.

ACCOMMODATIONS

Downtown Tulsa is filled with the usual chains. For something different, head about four miles east to the **Campbell Hotel** (2636 E. 11th St., 855/744-5500, www.thecampbellhotel.com, $130-250), which in its past life was a hotel that served travelers on famous Route 66. Now it's a bit more luxurious, with a few suites as well as king and queen rooms. The hotel has a lounge and spa, too.

DALLAS, FORT WORTH, AND ARLINGTON
TEXAS RANGERS

On April 21, 1972, with the Rangers' 7-6 win over the California Angels, major league baseball arrived in North Texas, but boy, did it take a trip to get there.

Washington DC was gifted a new team in 1961 after the original Senators left for the Twin Cities of Minneapolis and St. Paul in late 1960. After just a decade, though, poor decisions and even poorer play doomed the new Sens. The team announced a move to Arlington, Texas, during the 1971 season. On the last day of that campaign, fans stormed the field at RFK Stadium in the nation's capital and caused the home team to forfeit a game to the Yankees.

Before 1972, Arlington and its larger Dallas-Fort Worth metropolitan area played host to plenty of baseball teams and games, but nothing

beyond triple-A. Arlington Stadium, the original home of the major league Rangers, was the base for the Dallas-Fort Worth Spurs of the Texas League through 1971. Burnett Field in Dallas was home to the Dallas-Fort Worth Rangers and Dallas Rangers of the 1960s, while LaGrave Field in Fort Worth also kept the lights on for the DFW Rangers, plus the Fort Worth Cats of 1959.

As for the major league Rangers, they spent their first two decades in Arlington as a happy-go-lucky nonfactor in the American League. Between 1972 and 1993, they finished in second place in the AL West division four times, spending more time wandering aimlessly in the middle of the pack. They finished in first place in 1994, but that year stopped short with a players' strike—and the Rangers (52-62) and their division were terrible that season, anyway.

Better days were finally ahead, though, and in 1996 the Rangers won their first division title outright. They took two more crowns over the next three years, powered by prodigious sluggers like Juan Gonzalez and franchise backbone Ivan Rodriguez. After a decade in the back of the division, and with the team now led by an ownership group that included Hall of Famer Nolan Ryan, the Rangers reemerged in 2010 and 2011, capturing back-to-back American League pennants but losing in both World Series. The 2011 series was particularly heartbreaking, as Texas came within one out of winning it all before a misjudged fly ball altered the future.

The Rangers have since been up and down. Some years they spend plenty of cash and sit at the top of the division, but other years they seem happy to focus on growing their farm system (minor league players). In the meantime, fans come out for the good teams. They're less of a presence for the bad ones—watching a poor-performing team when it's 100°F outside doesn't seem enticing. Moving to the retractable-roofed Globe Life Field in 2020 helped with fan comfort, but will it translate into a more rabid fan base? The jury is still out.

PLANNING YOUR TIME

The DFW can be knocked out in a **long weekend,** spending a day visiting Dallas, another hanging around in Arlington, and another bouncing about from city to city. If you want to hang out at **Six Flags Over Texas** over a full day, and you'd like to spread out Dallas over at least two days (say visiting the Sixth Floor Museum at Dealey Plaza for a few hours), you may want to devote **4-5 days** to the area.

Staying in **Arlington** isn't a bad idea, as you'll be central to both Dallas and Fort Worth, and you'll be as close as possible to Globe Life Field and Six Flags. Since you'll inevitably be driving, opt for convenience by staying an equal distance from all the attractions you want to see.

When the Rangers played at their former park in Arlington, the advice was never to attend a game in July or August. That park had no retractable roof, and thus no central air-conditioning system, meaning midsummer games would routinely be played in scalding temperatures. It got so bad that for years the Rangers pushed their Sunday afternoon games to the evening, something that no other team was allowed to do.

At Globe Life Field, you can sit in comfort year-round thanks to the **retractable roof** and temperature-controlled interior. North Texas **summers are hot,** so pack accordingly if you're coming between **June** and **August. Tornado season** is between **May** and **June.** While it's unlikely your local area will be hit, twisters have previously impacted the DFW area. My suggestion is to visit the DFW in **April, May,** or **September.** April and May are idyllic, with temperatures hovering in the high 70s in the daytime and regularly dipping into the 60s at night. September is a touch warmer—in the 80s during the day, and around 70°F at night.

Previous: Texas Rangers sign

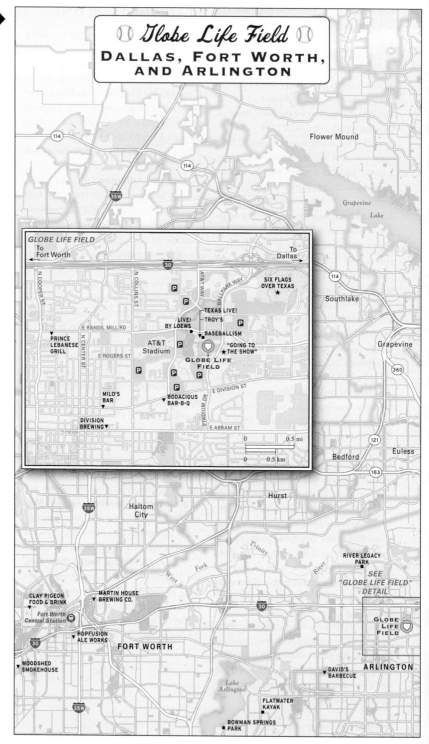

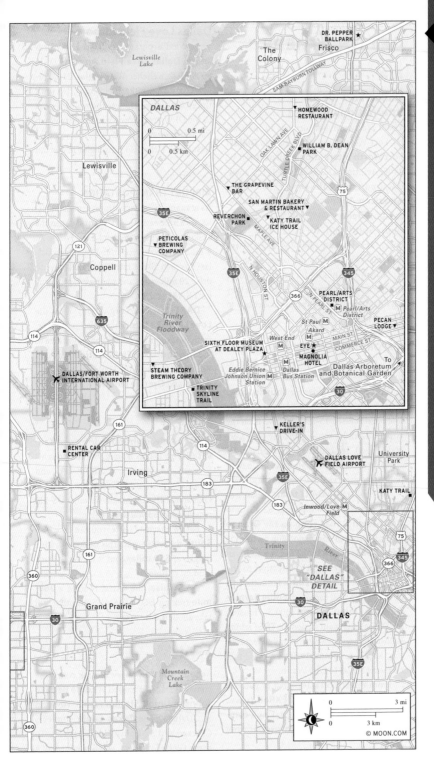

DALLAS

0   0.5 mi
0   0.5 km

HOMEWOOD RESTAURANT

WILLIAM B. DEAN PARK

THE GRAPEVINE BAR

SAN MARTIN BAKERY & RESTAURANT

REVERCHON PARK

KATY TRAIL ICE HOUSE

PETICOLAS BREWING COMPANY

OAK LAWN AVE

TURTLE CREEK BLVD

MAPLE AVE

N HOUSTON ST

PEARL/ARTS DISTRICT

Pearl/Arts District

St Paul

PECAN LODGE

SIXTH FLOOR MUSEUM AT DEALEY PLAZA

West End

Akard

EYE

MAGNOLIA HOTEL

Dallas Bus Station

Dallas Arboretum and Botanical Garden

To

STEAM THEORY BREWING COMPANY

Eddie Bernice Johnson Union Station

TRINITY SKYLINE TRAIL

Trinity River Floodway

N PEARL ST

MAIN ST

COMMERCE ST

DALLAS/FORT WORTH INTERNATIONAL AIRPORT

RENTAL CAR CENTER

Irving

KELLER'S DRIVE-IN

DALLAS LOVE FIELD AIRPORT

University Park

KATY TRAIL

Inwood/Love Field

Trinity

River

SEE "DALLAS" DETAIL

Grand Prairie

DALLAS

Mountain Creek Lake

Lewisville Lake

The Colony

DR. PEPPER BALLPARK Frisco

SAM RAYBURN TOLLWAY

Lewisville

Coppell

Trinity River Floodway

0   3 mi
0   3 km

© MOON.COM

GETTING THERE

AIR

Dallas/Fort Worth International Airport

There are two major airports in the Dallas-Fort Worth area. The larger is **Dallas/ Fort Worth International Airport** (DFW, 2400 Aviation Dr., 972/973-3112, www. dfwairport.com). The airport is served by **American Airlines** (800/433-7300, www. aa.com), **Delta** (800/221-1212, www.delta. com), **Spirit** (801/401-2222, www.spirit. com), and **United** (800/864-8331, www. united.com). DFW is the largest hub for American Airlines and a popular layover stop for folks requiring a connection as they head cross-country or from a smaller hub to a larger hub.

AIRPORT TRANSPORTATION

If you're renting a car, follow signs down to the bus stop for the **rental car center** (2424 E. 38th St.), then board a **shuttle.** Most major rental agencies have desks here. Globe Life Field is just a 15-minute drive from the airport, 12 miles south primarily on TX-97 and TX-360. To get there, you'll need to ride-share or drive, as Arlington doesn't have a public transit service that reaches the airport.

You could take a **DART train** (Dallas Area Rapid Transit, www.dart.org, $2.50) into **Downtown Dallas.** Hop on the **Orange Line** at Terminal A; a major stop on the line is **Pearl/Arts District** (N. Pearl St. and Bryan St., Dallas), offering a connection to the **Green, Red,** and **Blue Lines.** From the Red or Blue Lines, you can reach **Eddie Bernice Johnson Union Station** (400 S. Houston St., Dallas), the main station for **TRE** (Trinity Railway Express, www.trinityrailwayexpress. org, $2.50), a **commuter rail** service that connects Dallas to Fort Worth.

From the airport's Terminal B, you can hop onto **Trinity Metro TEXRail** (www. ridetrinitymetro.com, $2.50), taking a **commuter train** to **Fort Worth** straight from DFW.

Dallas Love Field Airport

The second airport in the Dallas-Fort Worth area is **Dallas Love Field Airport** (DAL, 8008 Herb Kelleher Way, Dallas, 214/670-6080, www.dallas-lovefield.com). Up until the 1970s, Love Field was the major airport in the DFW area. Now it's an important hub for **Southwest** (800/435-9792, www.southwest.com). Delta also runs flights in and out of here.

AIRPORT TRANSPORTATION

As at many secondary airports in major cities, it's a little easier to get a **rental car,** as the desks are near baggage claim. Love Field is an 8-mile drive northwest from Downtown Dallas. To reach Globe Life Field, you'll have to drive 20 miles west and southwest, primarily on TX-183 and TX-161.

DART (www.dart.org, $2.50) offers the **Love Link 524 bus,** which takes passengers from the ground-level transportation area to the **Inwood/Love Field station** (Inwood Rd. and Denton Dr., Dallas) on DART's **Green** and **Orange Lines.**

CAR

The **510-mile, eight-hour** drive from **Kansas City** to Dallas is long, but it's straightforward. You'll zoom south on **I-49** and **I-44,** then get onto **US-69** around Vinita, Oklahoma. That eventually becomes **US-75,** which will drop you into Dallas.

For an alternate route, you can take **I-35 South** the whole way. This option is a little longer, at **550 miles,** but it takes the same amount of time.

From **Tulsa,** the fastest route is a **260-mile** trek on US-75/US-62 South that will take about **4.5 hours.**

TRAIN

Just one **Amtrak** (www.amtrak.com) line comes to Dallas, accessed at **Eddie Bernice Johnson Union Station** (400 S. Houston St., Dallas). The **Texas Eagle** connects Chicago and St. Louis to Los Angeles. To reach Globe Life Field, you'll need to call a

YOUR BEST DAY AT GLOBE LIFE FIELD

Tonight, you're heading to Globe Life Field for a Rangers game, but first you have an entire day in front of you in the DFW. Let's roll.

11 HOURS BEFORE FIRST PITCH
Start your day with a walk or run on the **Trinity Skyline Trail** to get the blood pumping. It's 2.5 miles from the I-35E crossing to Sylvan Avenue. Turn and go back the way you came for a nice, 5-mile round-trip jaunt.

8 HOURS BEFORE FIRST PITCH
You could get breakfast, but you're in Texas: Get in line at **Pecan Lodge** and order the brisket and macaroni and cheese. That'll keep you full for a while.

6 HOURS BEFORE FIRST PITCH
You have plenty of time before the game, so take in some history at the **Sixth Floor Museum at Dealey Plaza.** Plan on spending about two hours here learning about the events surrounding the assassination of President John F. Kennedy. Afterward, head back to your hotel to change and prepare for the game.

3.5 HOURS BEFORE FIRST PITCH
Take a ride-share vehicle to **Division**

Trinity Skyline Trail

Brewing. Spend some time on the patio drinking a fruited sour while meeting some Rangers fans.

2 HOURS BEFORE FIRST PITCH
Request another ride-share and continue to the **Arlington Entertainment District.** You may want to check out the **tailgate scene** outside of the stadium.

Walk around the district a bit. If you want another beer or cocktail before going into the stadium, there's **Texas Live!**

1 HOUR BEFORE FIRST PITCH
Walk into **Globe Life Field** via the North Plaza so you can take a selfie with immortalized versions of Neftalí Féliz and Bengie Molina, who are depicted in the *Going to the Show* statue. Also get pictures with statues of **Ivan Rodriguez** and **Nolan Ryan.** Head up to the **Karbach Sky Porch** for a brewski and a decent view of the scene.

DURING THE GAME
Chow down on a Globe Life favorite like **The Boomstick,** a two-foot hot dog, or **The Stack,** a tall stack of tostadas topped with nacho cheese.

AFTER THE GAME
If you're staying in the Arlington Entertainment District, take the cheap ride over to **Milo's Bar.** If you're staying back in Dallas and the weather isn't too sticky, take a ride-share vehicle to the outdoor **Katy Trail Ice House.** Or, if you'd like no frills whatsoever, tie one on at **The Grapevine Bar.**

Sixth Floor Museum at Dealey Plaza

Globe Life Field

ride-share. It's a 17-mile drive west on I-30 from the train station.

Amtrak also serves Fort Worth at **Fort Worth Central Station** (1001 Jones St., Fort Worth). The Texas Eagle stops here, and the **Heartland Flyer,** which originates in Oklahoma City, ends in Forth Worth. To get to the ballpark from here, request a ride-share. It's a 15-mile drive east on I-30 to get to Globe Life Field from Central Station.

No trains connect Kansas City to the Dallas-Fort Worth area.

BUS

From **Kansas City,** you can hop aboard a daily **Greyhound bus** (www.greyhound. com) that takes you to the **Dallas Bus Station** (205 S. Lamar St., Dallas), located three blocks east of Union Station. The ride from KC to Dallas lasts 12-13 hours and should cost you about $70-80.

To get to Globe Life Field, you'll need to take a ride-share vehicle. The stadium is 18 miles west of the bus station via I-30.

Globe Life Field

In May 2016, the Rangers announced that they would move from Globe Life Park to a new venue just a shout away. That ballpark, christened **Globe Life Field** (734 Stadium Dr., Arlington, www.mlb.com/rangers), opened in 2020.

Unlike Globe Life Park, Globe Life Field has something fans and players were

clamoring for: a retractable roof. This means that games that were previously played under sweltering conditions of 100°F or hotter in midsummer would instead be played in the comfortable environment of a 71°F, temperature-controlled facility. Score that a win for the new venue.

Globe Life Park—made in the retro-classic style as a nod to parks like Ebbets Field and Tiger Stadium—oozed charm. In comparison, the Field is more like a modern interpretation of a retractable roof ballpark. It looks a bit like Minute Maid Park in Houston and T-Mobile Park in Seattle, though without the kitschy signage of the former and the undeniable local character of the latter. It's all clean sightlines and steel beams inside, and outside it's a big gray warehouse, resembling something of a mammoth big box store.

Globe Life is the anchor of an entertainment district, a symbol of the things that homogenize the old ball game. Outside the park, there's a big branded bar with overpriced drinks and food that's meant to bring in tourist traffic before and after the game. Another bar is named after a brewery owned by a multinational corporation. There's a bigness to the park that doesn't seem to build any character. This ballpark is buttoned up, slicked back, and made to sell you an experience.

ORIENTATION

Globe Life Field is situated inside the **Arlington Entertainment District,** a self-contained area that includes the old Globe Life Park, Six Flags Over Texas and Hurricane

GAME COSTS

Tickets: In the past, Rangers tickets tended to be around average, with lower-level seats starting around **$70** and second-level seats costing more like **$35-40.** With a new ballpark, prices may go up a bit.

Hot dog: Expensive! The going rate for a cheap dog is about **$6.** You're better off getting the loaded options, which offer more value for the cost.

Beer: The cheap stuff starts from **$6,** a good deal compared with the rest of the league.

Parking: Be prepared to spend **$20** on parking, which is higher than average.

Harbor, AT&T Stadium (home of the Dallas Cowboys), a mall, a greenbelt, a convention center, and lots of parking lots. It's in the middle of the DFW, just a few minutes south of I-30, but not very close to public transportation.

There are five entry gates at Globe Life Field. Gates at Globe Life open 90 minutes before first pitch for day games and two hours beforehand for night games.

TICKETS AND SEATING

Pricing

The Rangers use a **dynamic pricing** system for most tickets. That means games against heated **rivals** like the Astros and **notable visitors** like the Yankees will generally cost more than all the rest. **Weekend games** will be pricier than weekday games. A middle-of-the-road seat at Globe Life might go for about $30 for an opponent like Detroit (who doesn't necessarily draw a lot of fans). If the Astros or Yankees are in town, especially over a weekend, that seat may cost more like $50.

Outside of the home opener, the Rangers don't employ dynamic pricing for

grandstand reserved seats (sections 325-326), though you can only get those tickets at the **left field box office** (as low as $9 per seat). It's a welcome change that keeps games affordable for fans who opt for the seats up top.

Seating Plan

Globe Life Field features a staggering number of specific seating areas over **four levels.** The **first level** is split between a **lower area** (sections 1-25), expensive seats where fans can visit exclusive areas like the **Balcones Speakeasy,** and an **upper area** (sections 1-26) that goes from the left-field foul pole around foul territory to the right-field foul pole.

Not associated with the lower area of seats are the **field suites,** group seating areas that start next to each dugout and run to the foul lines; these "subterranean" seats are designed to give fans the feeling that they're in the dugout themselves.

Suites separate the first level from the **second level (100 level),** which starts at the left-field foul pole with **corner mezzanine** (sections 101-103), **mezzanine** (sections 104-106), and **VIP infield and infield mezzanine** (sections 107-110). It continues behind home plate with **VIP home plate and home plate mezzanine** (sections 111-117), then moves into right field with **VIP infield and infield mezzanine** (sections 118-121), **mezzanine** (sections 122-124), and **corner mezzanine** (sections 125-127). The level then runs into the outfield with **outfield mezzanine** (sections 128-133, 136-142), interrupted in the middle with the **BSB Balcony** (sections 134-135), a ticketed seating section with four-top tables.

After another row of suites, the **third level (200 level)** starts with the **Karbach Sky Porch** (sections 201-204), a ticketed area with specialty food and drink at the left-field foul pole. It continues around foul territory with the **corner pavilion** (sections 205-207), the **baseline pavilion** (sections 208-213), and the **VIP infield and infield pavilion** (sections 214-220); then it moves into right field with **baseline pavilion** (sections 221-228) and **corner**

BE A FAN

Rangers fans are easygoing—unless you're an Astros fan. The rivalry between Dallas and Houston is real, but Astros fans won't encounter the kind of vitriol reserved for feuds like Dodgers versus Giants, Red Sox versus Yankees, or Mets versus Phillies.

Between the top and bottom of the fifth innings, because it's Texas, the Rangers will play **"Deep in the Heart of Texas."** During the seventh-inning stretch, after "Take Me Out to the Ballgame," the Rangers will play an instrumental fiddle-led version of **"Cotton Eyed Joe."** No, it's not the popular 1995 Rednex song but the song that inspired it, performed by Al Dean, a country musician who called himself "Mr. Cotton Eyed Joe." While the songs play, fans may do a little two-step dance—don't be afraid to join in.

If the Rangers win, you'll hear a song called **"I Like Texas"** by Texas country star Pat Green. He's a legend in the Lone Star State, playing the kind of feel-good, Saturday-night country that's usually accompanied by two-stepping at the local dance hall and a couple Shiner Bock beers.

You have to see the **Dot Race.** A longtime tradition at Rangers games pits three competitors against one another while wearing enormous colored dots (green, blue, and red). They race during the middle of the sixth inning, from the left field foul pole all the way down to home plate and around to the home dugout. Fans are given a coupon for one of the three sponsors labeled on the dots and assigned a color to root for. If that color wins, fans with that coupon get whatever deal is listed.

pavilion (sections 229-232). Next, the level expands with a larger area of seating over the outfield, dubbed **All You Can Eat** (sections 233-237). The level continues with the **outfield pavilion,** which consists of two sections of seating in center field (sections 238-239), then five sections high in left field (sections 240-244).

The **fourth** and highest level (**300 level**) of the ballpark starts in foul left field with **upper reserved** (sections 301-307), continues with **upper box** (sections 308-317), then wraps into right field to the foul pole with **upper reserved** (sections 318-324). There are two sections of seating called **grandstand reserved** (sections 325-326); these tickets are only available from the left field ticket office. The level breaks off after section 315 and section 321 (meaning you can't walk all the way around this level).

Where to Buy Tickets

Always check third-party reseller sites like **StubHub** and **SeatGeek** for last-minute deals for Rangers tickets since the team doesn't typically sell out, which means you could score a cheap seat close to first pitch. One thing to remember: With a new ballpark, crowds are sure to show, which drives up prices. My suggestion is to be patient and wait until close to start time to get a ticket.

The Rangers also allow fans to upgrade their seats through the **MLB Ballpark app,** though you'll have to buy your tickets directly through the team to be eligible.

Best Seats

If you want great field and backdrop **views,** you'd do just fine in the back rows of **sections 107-110.** Want to save a little more cash while still getting a good view? Opt for anywhere in **sections 210-212.**

For **inexpensive** seats with a decent view close to the field, there's the area of **sections 201-204** beside the Karbach Sky Porch in left field. Those seats hover over the second level and extend nicely toward the foul pole. If you just want to grab an inexpensive seat while being able to clearly see all of the action, the first rows of seats in **sections 305-307** and **sections 318-321** offer that, as they're set along the shallow outfield foul lines and remain in the affordable outfield reserved area.

KNOW BEFORE YOU GO

The Rangers allow **backpacks** of up to 16 by 16 by 8 inches. **Diaper bags** are also permitted. Mothers with infants can visit a **private nursing room** (sections 20, 102, 127, 130, HOF203).

Globe Life Field's parking lots open three hours before the game for **tailgating.** Here's the thing, though: You can only park in the lot, while you tailgate on the **grassy areas** that line the lots. Lot J and 1200 Ballpark Way are good choices, as there's plenty of green space beyond the parking areas. You can tailgate up to the end of the second inning, and after the game, for one hour after the final hour. Charcoal must be dumped in the designated containers throughout the parking lots.

Accessibility

Carts can transport guests from the parking lot to the ballpark. To arrange a pickup, contact the nearest staff member or, ahead of time, call the Rangers at 817/533-1972. **Wheelchairs** are available on a limited basis by asking a staff member at the gate of entry.

Head to **guest services** (section 101) for **assistive listening devices.** There are multiple **elevators** at Globe Life Field. On the lower concourse they're located in sections 102, 104, 109, 114, 116, 124, 126, and 129. Both **service animals** and **emotional support animals** are welcome at Globe Life Field.

There's **accessible parking** available at all lots, but at a first-come, first-served basis.

GETTING THERE

You really have to drive or take a ride-share vehicle to Globe Life Field, since Arlington lacks public transit options.

If you're staying at a hotel inside the district, you may be able to take a **trolley** (817/461-8600, www.arlingtontrolley.com)

to the ballpark. Pickup after the game is on **Nolan Ryan Expressway** between Randol Mill Road and the Road to Six Flags, the same area where ride-share vehicles pick up passengers.

Driving
RIDE-SHARING

Arlington has its own **ride-sharing app** called **Via Arlington** (www.ridewithvia. com, 6am-9pm Mon.-Fri., 9am-9pm Sat., $3), but it has limited hours and operates only in Arlington. If you're staying in Fort Worth or Dallas and you don't want to drive, you're better off using Lyft or Uber.

If you need to grab a ride-share after the game, head out from the outfield across Texas Live! to the southbound side of **Nolan Ryan Expressway** between Randol Mill Road and the Road to Six Flags.

PARKING LOTS AND SHUTTLES

If you're driving in, you'll have to pay quite a bit to park. Purchase your parking in **advance** (972/726-4377, www.mlb.com/ rangers) to pay $18; otherwise, it's $20 with a credit card, $25 with cash. The **parking lots,** named after models of Toyota cars, are everywhere in the district.

If you park well north of the ballpark across from Mark Holtz Lake, you might want to take one of the **ballpark shuttles** (running three hours before first pitch to two hours after final out). Park in the **Land Cruiser** or **Highlander lots** and get on the red shuttle. If you park in the **Prius lot,** get on the blue shuttle.

TAILGATING

Good news: **Tailgating** is permitted at Globe Life! Once parking lots open, you can pull in your car and break out the grill, but don't take up extra parking spaces. You're restricted to a 9- by 12-foot area that includes your parking spot. **Postgame tailgating** can go for up to an hour after final out; after that, the parking lots close for the night.

PARK FEATURES AND SIGHTS

Arlington Entertainment District

The heart of Arlington and a major tourism draw, the **Arlington Entertainment District** is a massive space bounded by I-30 on the north, TX-360 on the east, TX-180 on the south, and FM-157 on the west. It includes Globe Life Field and Globe Life Park (the current and former homes of the Rangers), AT&T Stadium (home of the Dallas Cowboys), Six Flags Over Texas and Hurricane Harbor, the 200,000-square-foot Texas Live! mini-district that includes restaurants, shopping, a Loews hotel, and convention space, greenbelt areas for trails, and lots of parking lots. It's packed much of the year and is the hub of activity in Arlington (and arguably in the entire DFW area). During summer it's especially crowded with folks going to baseball games, concerts, and the amusement parks.

Going to the Show Statue

A statue called ***Going to the Show*** (North Plaza) immortalizes the moment Neftalí Féliz and Bengie Molina embraced after winning the 2010 American League Championship Series against the Yankees, one of two pennant wins for the Rangers in their 50-year history.

Other Statues

Look for a statue of **Ivan "Pudge" Rodriguez** (southwest entrance), a Hall of Famer who played 12 seasons with the Rangers. There's a statue of **Nolan Ryan** (outside Arlington Backyard at Texas Live!) commemorating the Hall of Fame pitcher and former Rangers CEO. Controversy has followed the statue, as it's been debated whether it should even be in Arlington, as Ryan is more associated with Houston and the Astros.

Photos (from top to bottom): flyover at Globe Life Field; Captain, mascot of the Rangers; statue of Nolan Ryan by sculptor Antonio Mendez.

Karbach Sky Porch

Inside the park, out in left field, is the **Karbach Sky Porch** (left field, sections 201-204). This area, which is open to the public, includes garage door bars—much like Texas ice houses, where beer is enjoyed in the sunshine—and an expansive patio area (Texans love their patios). The porch is named after a popular Houston-based brewery that was purchased a few years ago by Anheuser-Busch InBev.

FOOD AND DRINKS

If you want to challenge yourself, Globe Life has a couple stalwart food items that have been a part of the Rangers dining experience for a while now. There's **The Boomstick,** a two-foot-long hot dog; **The Fowl Pole,** a two-foot-long chicken tender; and **The Stack,** a tall, loaded snack made of numerous tostadas (stacked atop each other) and nacho cheese sauce.

Look for more off-the-wall items like **The Rattler,** featuring rattlesnake sausage and hot sauce on a hoagie roll; **The Grit Dog,** showcasing an all-beef hot dog with cheese grits, nacho cheese, and chili; and **brisket egg rolls,** which are served with fried rice. Local chains like **Pluckers** (chicken wings) and **Golden Chick** (chicken fingers) also have locations at the park.

The **Karbach Sky Porch** (sections 201-204) has beer from the Houston-based **Karbach Brewing Co.** on tap, including the IPA Hopadillo. Karbach also makes a beer for Globe Life called Sky Porch Ale, a strawberry blonde brew.

EVENTS

Before Friday and Saturday games, the Rangers present a former player to sign **autographs,** and before Tuesday and Thursday contests, current Rangers sign their John Hancocks. A sign at each entrance gate informs fans where to go for the autographs. Note that Tuesdays are open to everyone, while Thursday sessions are for kids only.

Since gates at Globe Life open two hours before first pitch for night games, you should be able to catch at least the visiting team's **batting practice.** For day games, gates open 90 minutes before first pitch, so hurry in to watch the tail end of BP.

On select dates through the season, the Rangers host **Bark at the Park,** when fans can bring their dogs.

Tours

You can take a **tour** (817/533-1833, $25, $22 seniors, $15 ages 4-14) of Globe Life Field before games and on non-game days. Tours depart from the North Plaza and last about an hour. Children under 36 inches tall don't need a separate tour ticket.

SHOPPING

The main shop at Globe Life is the **Grand Slam Team Store** (North Plaza or main concourse at TXU Energy North Entry, 10am-5pm Mon.-Sat., 11am-5pm Sun. non-game days, gates open to gates close game days).

DALLAS, FORT WORTH, AND ARLINGTON SIGHTS

SIXTH FLOOR MUSEUM AT DEALEY PLAZA

If you were alive on November 22, 1963, you remember exactly where you were. Whether that's the case or whether you're someone who only heard about the assassination of President John F. Kennedy secondhand, you might want to visit the **Sixth Floor Museum at Dealey Plaza** (411 Elm St., Dallas, 214/747-6660, www.jfk.org, noon-6pm Mon., 10am-6pm Tues.-Sun., $18, $16 seniors, $14 ages 6-18, free ages 5 and under). This museum, located in the former book depository at the exact spot where killer Lee Harvey Oswald stood on that fateful day, goes deep into the events of that afternoon. You can see the iconic Zapruder film that shows the assassination in color, and a main exhibit details the afternoon, then offers a video highlighting JFK's legacy.

EYE

You can take a selfie with *Eye* (1601 Main St., Dallas). This fiberglass art installation, also known as the Giant Eyeball, is just that: a 30-foot-tall sculpture of a realistic eyeball on a bed of turf. It was created by Tony Tasset and purchased by the Joule Hotel to be placed in its sculpture garden.

SIX FLAGS OVER TEXAS

Back in Arlington, you can spend a day at **Six Flags Over Texas, Arlington** (2201 E. Road to Six Flags St., Arlington, 817/640-8900, www.sixflags.com, 11am-7pm daily summer, $65-200), part of the Arlington Entertainment District with Globe Life Field. This is the very first Six Flags park, home to the New Texas Giant, a 153-foot-tall wood-and-steel roller coaster that's a must-ride. Other thrill rides include Batman the Ride, El Diablo (the world's largest loop coaster), and modern coaster Titan. Six Flags regularly hosts live concerts, and is populated by *Looney Tunes* characters.

FOOD

NEAR GLOBE LIFE FIELD

I don't recommend dining anywhere around Globe Life Field, which is inside the Arlington Entertainment District. You could hop just outside the district and visit the popular barbecue chain **Bodacious Bar-B-Q** (1206 Division St., Arlington, 817/860-4248, www.bodaciousbbqarlington.com, 11am-7pm Mon.-Sat., under $40). There are better BBQ experiences out there, but Bodacious does the trick when you just want some decent grub. Get in line for hot link sandwiches or

a rib dinner. Finish the meal with a slice of buttermilk pecan pie.

OTHER NEIGHBORHOODS

Arlington is awash with chains, but there are a few gems in the city. **Prince Lebanese Grill** (502 W. Randol Mill Rd., Arlington, 817/469-1811, www.princelebanesegrill.com, 11am-9pm Sun.-Thurs., 11am-10pm Fri.-Sat., under $40) has been around since 1989, serving up gyro plates, shawarma plates, and lamb chops in a super casual spot with pictures on the wall lauding the fact that Guy Fieri once featured them on his TV show *Diners, Drive-Ins and Dives.*

Southwest of Downtown Arlington is the charming institution **David's Barbecue** (2224 W. Park Row Dr. #H, Pantego, 817/261-9998, www.davidsbarbecuetx.com, 11am-9pm Tues.-Sat., under $40). The Bryan family, who runs the business, has been selling smoked meats since 1910, specializing in a stellar chopped brisket with a nice homemade sauce. The line moves quickly, and the environs are old-fashioned and friendly.

If you're in Fort Worth, check out **Clay Pigeon Food & Drink** (2731 White Settlement Rd., Fort Worth, 817/882-8065, www.claypigeonfd.com, 5pm-9pm Mon.-Thurs., 5pm-10pm Fri.-Sat., under $60). Inside a stately but casual dining room, you'll encounter classic dishes like pan-roasted salmon, New York strip, and linguine in white wine sauce. Add in some cool cocktails and a nice wine list, and you have a great night out.

For a fine outdoor experience in Fort Worth, there's **Woodshed Smokehouse** (3201 Riverfront Dr., Fort Worth, 817/877-4545, www.woodshedsmokehouse.com, 11am-10pm Mon.-Thurs., 11am-11pm Fri., 8am-11pm Sat., 8am-10pm Sun., under $50). A restaurant from Tim Love, arguably the area's most famous celebrity chef, Woodshed offers an entire menu of smoked items, from meats to seafood to appetizers. The huge, group-style dishes include beef shin with tortillas and paella. The patio hugs the West Fork Trinity River, making for a fun outdoor space.

Dallas has a deep selection of good restaurants, offering a scene worth exploring over more than a day or two. I recommend **Lucia** (408 W. 8th St., Dallas, 214/948-4998, www.luciadallas.com, 5:30pm-10pm Tues.-Sat., under $60). While you're there, get a homemade pasta dish like tagliatelle with pork ragù or ricotta ravioli with smoked chili. The dining room and bar area are on the smaller side, so snag a reservation before coming to town.

For the best barbecue in the area, head to **Pecan Lodge** (2702 Main St., Dallas, 214/748-8900, www.pecanlodge.com, 11am-8pm daily, under $40). Go for the fantastic brisket, sausage, and the super-rich, bacon-topped macaroni and cheese. You'll thank me later. There will be a line, so reserve about three hours for the whole experience.

For a stellar burger at a low price, there's **Keller's Drive-In** (10554 Harry Hines Blvd., Dallas, 214/357-3572, 11am-10:30pm Mon., 10:30am-10:30pm Tues.-Fri. and Sun., 10:30am-midnight Sat., under $10). Around since the 1960s, Keller's is the quintessential drive-in restaurant—and an absolute necessity when in town. You can get a cheeseburger (in a poppy-seed bun), chili dog, soda, and shake for about $7.50 before tax. This place is a treasure and a great stop on a Saturday night between bars.

Get yourself a savory Guatemalan breakfast, or maybe some baked goods like dulce de leche rolls and croissants, at **San Martín Bakery & Restaurant** (3120 McKinney Ave., Dallas, 469/802-6652, www.sanmartinbakery.com, 8am-7pm Sun.-Thurs., 8am-9pm Fri.-Sat., under $30). *Migas* (eggs with fried tortilla strips) and *huevos divorciados* (two eggs on tortillas with two different types of salsa) are great choices here, as is the Salvadoreño, a hearty egg and tortilla dish with *ranchera* sauce and a side of cabbage slaw. San Martín is a bright, airy place with plenty of seating in the center and counters around the perimeter.

Photos (from top to bottom): Sixth Floor Museum at Dealey Plaza; *Eye* by artist Tony Tasset; Katy Trail Ice House.

Bright and airy, with plenty of windows and wood paneling, **Homewood Restaurant** (4002 Oak Lawn Ave., Dallas, 214/434-1244, www.homewooddallas. com, 5pm-10pm Tues.-Fri., 11am-2pm and 5pm-10pm Sat., 10am-2pm and 5pm-10pm Sun., under $70) is like your family dining room come to perfect life. Start your meal with the plump Parker House rolls, and order a bottle of wine for the table. The menu offers farm-to-table fare in the form of pasta dishes, fish, steak, and pork.

BARS AND BREWERIES

NEAR GLOBE LIFE FIELD

It's a two-mile walk to Globe Life from **Division Brewing** (506 E. Main St., Arlington, 682/276-1276, www.divisionbrewing.com, 4pm-8pm Wed.-Thurs., 4pm-10pm Fri., noon-10pm Sat., noon-8pm Sun.), but it's the best brewery near the ballpark, so either sweat it out or go via ride-share. A warehouse brewery, Division has plenty of space to hang out, plus a patio area where bands sometimes play. There's a deep and diverse beer selection here, including a good variety of sours.

Globe Life Field is inside a ready-made complex with AT&T Stadium, accompanied by a greenbelt and a bunch of bars. If you want to spend your day (and a lot of your money) here, there's **Texas Live!** (1650 E. Randol Mill Rd., Arlington, 817/852-6688, www.texas-live.com, 11am-midnight Sun.-Thurs., 11am-2am Fri.-Sat.), an entertainment center that consists of bars and restaurants.

Inside Texas Live! you'll find **Troy's** (817/769-1551, 11am-10pm Sun.-Wed., 11am-11pm Thurs., 11am-2am Fri.-Sat.), a bar jointly owned by Dallas football great Troy Aikman. Find cocktails and a beer list with a lot of familiar macro options (there's plenty of Revolver Brewing, a Texas-based brewery owned by Molson Coors), plus salads, sandwiches, burgers, and more. There's

a patio here, too, which is the main reason to go.

For an independent, locally owned spot, make your way to **Milo's Bar** (501 E. Division St. #A, Arlington, 817/275-4011, www. milosbararlington.com, 7pm-2am daily). A postgame spot in Downtown Arlington, Milo's is the kind of bar that's a hoot to visit. The beer is basic, but the bar has a good patio. People come here to party.

OTHER NEIGHBORHOODS

A bunch of breweries can be found in the Design District of Dallas, notably **Peticolas Brewing Company** (1301 Pace St., Dallas, 214/234-7600, www.peticolasbrewing.com, 11am-7pm Mon.-Sat., noon-6pm Sun.). Around since 2010 (longer than most suds-makers in the DFW area), Peticolas is consistent while trying out a lot of styles, often with big, boozy results. It's a large place that looks industrial, with exposed beams, and the brewery has outdoor seating, games, and food trucks.

Just across the Trinity River from Peticolas is **Steam Theory Brewing Company** (340 Singleton Blvd. #100, Dallas, 972/803-4334, www.steamtheorybrewing.com, 11am-11pm daily). Inside a large industrial space, you'll find a good variety of beer and a solid menu of elevated pub grub (pizzas, burgers, wings, sandwiches). It's great for lunch.

Fort Worth is also home to a couple solid breweries. Check out **HopFusion Ale Works** (200 E. Broadway Ave., Fort Worth, 682/841-1721, www.hopfusionaleworks.com, noon-11pm daily) for the vibe. There are lots of picnic tables, a stage, a big patio, and a wide selection of decent and good beers, like a coconut milk stout and a rye IPA.

For some wild ales, there's **Martin House Brewing Co.** (220 S. Sylvania Ave. #209, Fort Worth, 817/222-0177, www.martinhousebrewing.com, noon-7pm daily). Along the banks of the West Fork Trinity River, you'll find this warehouse-like structure with a bar. Martin House is known for pushing the boundaries of beer, whether it's offering multiple variants of imperial stouts or doing wacky stuff like pickle beer and pizza beer. (They also have regular beers, and they're good.) This is a necessary stop for any beer geek.

Need a good bar in Dallas? Head to **The Grapevine Bar** (3902 Maple Ave., Dallas, 214/522-8466, 1pm-2am daily). Around since the 1990s, this popular, cramped space has a couple pool tables, a cigarette machine, old wooden chairs, cheap beer, and frozen drinks. There's also a cute, partially covered patio.

If you want a cold beer outside with a bunch of people, there's **Katy Trail Ice House** (3127 Routh St., Dallas, 214/468-0600, www. katyicehouse.com, 11am-2am Mon.-Fri., 10am-2am Sat.-Sun.). For the uninitiated, an ice house is an outdoor bar that you'll find throughout Texas. You can just as easily enjoy a $3 Lone Star here as you can a killer $7 craft brew. Katy Trail has a large beer garden area with trees, outdoor bars, and misting machines keeping everyone cool. This is the perfect place for a drink or three after a walk or run on the Katy Trail.

RECREATION

PARKS AND TRAILS

The **Dallas Arboretum and Botanical Garden** (8525 Garland Rd., Dallas, www. dallasarboretum.org, 9am-5pm daily, $17, $14 seniors, $12 ages 2-12) offers a calming respite in this commuter-centric metro area. With 66 acres by White Rock Lake, seven miles northeast of Downtown Dallas, the arboretum includes a gorgeous color garden with purple, orange, yellow, pink, and other-colored blooms; a picture-perfect sunken garden; and a rose-filled, mysterious fern dell. Head to the arboretum's Pecan Grove with a picnic in tow.

Over in Arlington is the 1,300-acre **River Legacy Park** (701 NW Green Oaks Blvd., Arlington). The West Fork Trinity River provides the northern boundary for this space with 8 miles of paved trail; a 10-mile, maintained mountain bike trail; playgrounds and playscapes; and a canoe and kayak launch. To rent a canoe or kayak, try **Flatwater Kayak** (5300 Falcon Wood Ct., Arlington, 817/451-9230, www.flatwaterkayak.com, $20-30 per

Dallas Arboretum and Botanical Garden

day). Flatwater can even deliver your kayak to you at the park.

Katy Trail

Part of the former Missouri-Kansas-Texas Railroad (MKT, or The Katy), the paved **Katy Trail** (Harvard Ave. and Cole Ave., Dallas) is a 3.5-mile path for cyclists, pedestrians, in-line skaters, and joggers. It runs alongside Turtle Creek in the Uptown neighborhood of Dallas and gets packed on weekends. A few parks you'll see along the way include **William B. Dean Park** (3636 Turtle Creek Blvd., Dallas) and **Reverchon Park** (3505 Maple Ave., Dallas).

Trinity Skyline Trail

The 4.6-mile, paved **Trinity Skyline Trail** (110 W. Commerce St., Dallas, www.trinityrivercorridor.com) hugs the Trinity River as it passes west of Downtown Dallas. Best for joggers and cyclists, the trail is very exposed, so wear sunscreen; if it's windy, be ready for less than ideal conditions.

BOATING

Folks throughout the DFW area take to **Lake Arlington** for boating and fishing. Launch your vessel at **Bowman Springs Park** (7003 W. Poly Webb Rd., Arlington), then head south, staying along the inside perimeter of the lake on its paddle trail. You can rent canoes and kayaks for the lake through **Flatwater Kayak** (5300 Falcon Wood Ct., Arlington, 817/451-9230, www.flatwaterkayak.com).

SHOPPING

Baseballism (1650 E. Randol Mill Rd. #125, Arlington, 682/551-3150, www.baseballism.com, noon-8pm daily) is the non-licensed, baseball-themed shop found in multiple major league cities. They can't put the name "Rangers" on a T-shirt, but they print "Texas" and "Arlington" in blue, white, and red. The shop also carries hats, bags, and accessories for men and women.

ACCOMMODATIONS

NEAR GLOBE LIFE FIELD

You can certainly stay close to the park, as the Arlington Entertainment District that's home to Globe Life also has a couple hotels. The Rangers partner with **Live! by Loews** (1600 E. Randol Mill Rd., Arlington, 682/277-4900, www.loewshotels.com, $200-500), which is within walking distance of the ballpark and, of course, Texas Live! All rooms are queens and kings, and some have views of the ballpark. A bar and restaurant are on-site, so if you want to stay inside the district, this is a good bet.

OTHER NEIGHBORHOODS

In Downtown Dallas, the 29-story **Magnolia Hotel** (1401 Commerce St., Dallas, 214/915-6500, www.magnoliahotels.com, $100-250) is set inside a beaux arts-style building from 1922. Magnolia is a chain with locations in Denver, Houston, New Orleans, Omaha, and St. Louis, but there's something that feels independent about this stay. Rooms are nicely appointed without being flashy, a lounge offers all-day eating (though with a charge), and there's plenty of access to DART.

GETTING AROUND

PUBLIC TRANSIT

Dallas, Fort Worth, and Arlington each have their own transit options. In Dallas, there's **DART** (www.dart.org, $2.50), with four **rail lines** that come together in Downtown Dallas at Pacific Avenue and Bryan Street. The four stops here are **West End** (N. Market St.

and Pacific Ave., Dallas), **Akard** (N. Akard St. and Pacific Ave., Dallas), **St. Paul** (N. St. Paul St. and Bryan St., Dallas), and **Pearl/Arts District** (N. Pearl St. and Bryan St., Dallas). Another major stop is **Bernice Johnson Union Station** (400 S. Houston St., Dallas), where you can also catch Amtrak. These lines connect to cities like Carrollton (Green Line), Plano (Orange and Red Lines) and Garland (Blue Line), but not to Fort Worth or Arlington.

In Fort Worth, **TRE** (www.trinityrail-wayexpress.org, $2.50) is a **commuter rail line,** hooking you up to **Fort Worth Central Station** (1001 Jones St., Fort Worth). From here, you can change to **Trinity Metro** (www.ridetrinitymetro.com, $2.50), the Fort Worth transit service. Trinity has a **bus network** that can get you around town.

In Arlington, there is no traditional public transit. Instead, it has a **ride-sharing app** called **Via Arlington** (www.ridewithvia.com, 6am-9pm Mon.-Fri., 9am-9pm Sat., $3). Use this if you want to get around the city of Arlington. If you need to reach Fort Worth or Dallas, use Lyft or Uber.

TAXI, UBER, AND LYFT

Lyft and Uber are the way to go in the DFW area, rather than taxis. A cab ride from DFW International Airport to Downtown Dallas will set you back a flat fee of $45, while the cost of going with one of the ride-share apps will be as low as $25. Plus, there's a real dearth of taxi stands in the area, and it's not the kind of region where hailing really works.

CAR

Want to get around the DFW area? You'll have to drive, or at least spend considerable time in a car. Here, eight-lane superhighways take up considerable land as they slice through the prairie, connecting city to city and shopping mall to business center. Traffic can be a problem, especially during rush hours, but it's a necessary evil if you want to get the full scope of the region (especially if you're spending time in Arlington).

A note about driving in Texas: Highways have **service roads** that run along the side; they're intended for both local traffic and for getting on and off the highway. The far left-turn lane at an intersection on a service road is generally reserved for cars making U-turns to the service road going in the opposite direction. So, if your destination is between exits but on the other side of the highway, you'll need to use that U-turn lane (marked by a *U*). If you're getting on the highway from a service road, yield to the highway traffic (you never have the right-of-way). If you're on the service road and cars are coming off the highway, again, you have to yield. Though these roads are called service roads in the DFW area, in Houston they're called **feeder roads.**

From north to south, there's **I-35,** which comes from Oklahoma City. In Denton, on the northern edge of the DFW area, I-35 splits into **I-35W,** which heads into Fort Worth, and **I-35E,** which goes toward Dallas. The two legs come back together down near Hillsboro, then I-35 continues south to Austin and San Antonio. There's also **I-45,** which connects Dallas to Houston. **US-75,** which threads through the middle of the country from Minnesota, enters Dallas from the north and ends at **I-345,** an auxiliary route of **I-45** that can connect drivers to **I-30.**

I-30 starts just west of Fort Worth and heads east by northeast through the heart of Fort Worth, the northern end of Arlington, and Downtown Dallas; it then goes into Arkansas, ending in Little Rock. Through the DFW area, it's known as the **Tom Landry Freeway,** and it's the **fastest route** between Dallas, Arlington, and Fort Worth. **I-20** crosses through much of Texas, beginning out west in Scroggins Draw at an intersection with I-10 before passing through the southern end of Fort Worth, Arlington, and Dallas. It continues toward the border with Louisiana.

Dallas is laid out with a loop system. **TX Loop 12** provides the inner boundary for the city; the combination of **I-635, TX-161** (President George Bush Turnpike), and

I-20 create an outer loop of sorts that also includes the city of Irving.

In Downtown Dallas, **Main Street** is a major west-east thoroughfare, starting at Dealey Plaza and threading into the hip Deep Ellum neighborhood before fading northeast. **TX-180,** which also runs west to east, connects Fort Worth to Dallas in a scenic way, acting as **Division Street** in Downtown Arlington. It hits TX Loop 12 and ends, but you can continue on **West Davis Street,** then take **Fort Worth Avenue** and **West Commerce Street** into Downtown Dallas.

FRISCO, TEXAS

For an enjoyable day trip when visiting the Dallas-Fort Worth area, consider driving a half hour north to Frisco. Here, you'll find a double-A affiliate of the Rangers, the Frisco RoughRiders, who play in one of Minor League Baseball's most unique ballparks. If you're around on a midsummer Thursday or Sunday and the RoughRiders are in town, pack your bathing suit and buy a ticket to spend a day watching baseball in a lazy river. Dr. Pepper Ballpark is surrounded by shopping malls and parking lots, so you probably don't need to spend time in Frisco itself.

GETTING THERE

Frisco is a straight 30-mile, 30-minute shot up the Dallas North Tollway from **Dallas.** To get here from **Fort Worth,** take TX-121 northeast for just shy of 50 miles, a drive of about 45-50 minutes.

DR. PEPPER BALLPARK

Dr. Pepper Ballpark (7300 RoughRiders Trail, www.milb.com/frisco) is home to the **Frisco RoughRiders,** a double-A affiliate of the Rangers. The RoughRiders are the only organized professional team to play in Frisco. They were named after the regiment headed by Theodore Roosevelt during the Spanish-American War. You'll find a couple more nods to Teddy at the park, such as the team's mascots, who include Bull Moose and Ted E. Bear. Curiously, another of the mascots is named Daisy, in honor of Margaret "Daisy" Suckley, a cousin and friend of President Franklin Delano Roosevelt.

From the outside, Dr. Pepper Ballpark may look like an enormous version of a beachside resort. Well, it kind of is. The park opened in 2003 as the Dr. Pepper/Seven Up Ballpark, changing its name to simply Dr. Pepper in 2007, and was quickly lauded for its retirement village-like features. These include the **Choctaw Lazy River,** a 175-foot-long pool in right field that's open to all ticketed fans on Thursdays and Sundays (at other times, it's a group seating area). On **Thursdays** (tickets from $25, $1 beers), it's a drinking spot, so swimmers have to be age 21 or older. On **Sundays** ($29 Apr.-May, $39 June-end of season), the pool is open to all ages, and tickets include all-you-can-eat grub. There's also a manicured pathway that winds around the park. Visit the **Bull Moose Saloon** (left field, near section 202) for a decent beer selection.

The ballpark has two seating levels: The **100 level** runs from the left-field foul pole to the right-field foul pole (sections 101-126), and the **200 level** is segmented into areas from mid-left field in foul territory to mid-right field in foul territory (sections 202-225). **Party decks** are on either side of the 200 level, and **lawn seats** are available out in left and center field.

HOUSTON
ASTROS

You may think that because it's Texas that football is king, but in Houston the Astros are number one. The Bayou City's first professional sports franchise debuted in 1962 as a National League expansion club called the Colt .45s, named after the gun. In those first few years, the club racked up losses at Colt Stadium, an open-air park in the southern part of the city. But during that time, a new home was being built just a bit south. Called the Astrodome, the fully enclosed stadium would open in 1965 as an achievement of architecture that was befitting of a city zooming into modernity.

In the 1970s and 1980s, the Astros shot into relevance in the National League. Wearing brightly colored uniforms that epitomized the city's boom-town character, the 'Stros nearly won the NL West

division in 1979, but suffered a late-season collapse. The next year they broke through and reached the National League Championship Series, but lost in five excruciating games to the Phillies. They again reached the playoffs in 1981 but failed to get to the World Series, and in 1986 they ran out of steam in the NLCS against the Mets.

The heartbreaks continued into the 1990s, including three consecutive NL division series losses from 1997 to 1999. In 2004 they lost the NLCS in a decisive seventh game to rival St. Louis, but finally, in 2005, the Astros turned the tables, beating the Cardinals to reach their first World Series. They lost that year to the White Sox.

The Astros fell into dark days, and in 2011 the franchise began fielding terrible teams in order to gain better draft standing and concentrate more on acquiring and developing young talent. Two years later, the Astros moved to the American League, and the bad play continued. But in 2015 the team surprised everyone by reaching the postseason and beating the Yankees in a one-game wild card playoff. Then, two years later, the 'Stros finally won it all, beating the Dodgers to capture Houston's first baseball championship. Since then, the Astros have been one of baseball's elite clubs, expected to go deep in the postseason annually.

But that status comes with controversy. In 2020, a report revealed that in 2017 and 2018 the Astros participated in an elaborate sign-stealing system that allowed their hitters to know the kind of pitch that was about to be thrown. It's unclear whether the benefits were great enough to affect the team's standing, but Major League Baseball decided that the scheme was illegal and consequently suspended team officials, fined the club, and took away draft picks.

In many ways, the controversy only emboldened Astros fans, who have been loyal to their team from the very beginning. Orange and blue murals aren't hard to find, and once spring training starts, the 'Stros gear comes out. You'll see Astros fans everywhere Houston—from ice houses (outdoor bars), where the beer is cheap and oscillating fans run constantly during the sweltering summers, to cosmopolitan food halls that personify the city's multicultural character.

Once sneered at for a lack of character, Houston today has it in droves. A rail hub on the Gulf of Mexico, it's a sprawling metropolis and the fourth-largest municipality in America. Called Mutt City because of its high, diverse population of transplants, Houston is home to oil and gas workers, NASA engineers, physicians, and creative types, sometimes living on the same city block. The businesses are just as varied as the residents: Because of Houston's lack of zoning laws, it's not uncommon to see a laundromat next to a skyscraper next to a taco truck.

The food here is pretty incredible. Thanks to its stunning diversity, Houston can claim some of the finest Vietnamese, Nigerian, Chinese, and Indian cuisine in America, not to mention outstanding Tex-Mex, barbecue, and steak. Yeah, Houston has a lot going on

PLANNING YOUR TIME

To get a quick version of Houston, a long weekend of **three days** is sufficient. You'll want to set your schedule around eating excursions: Find an afternoon to grab barbecue, an evening to chow down on some Tex-Mex, and another lunch or dinner to sample some Vietnamese cuisine. Check off all those boxes, fit in a trip to Space Center Houston, and, of course, see a ball game; and you'll probably use up that whole long weekend. **A week** in Houston means really diving into the city's food scene, which is absolutely worth it.

If you stay in the **Downtown area,** you'll be close to Minute Maid Park, and you can easily access the highways and main roads that extend into the other inner-loop neighborhoods. Plus, being Downtown means you can walk to some places, which helps balance things out if you're chowing down on lots of meat and queso.

Previous: Minute Maid Park

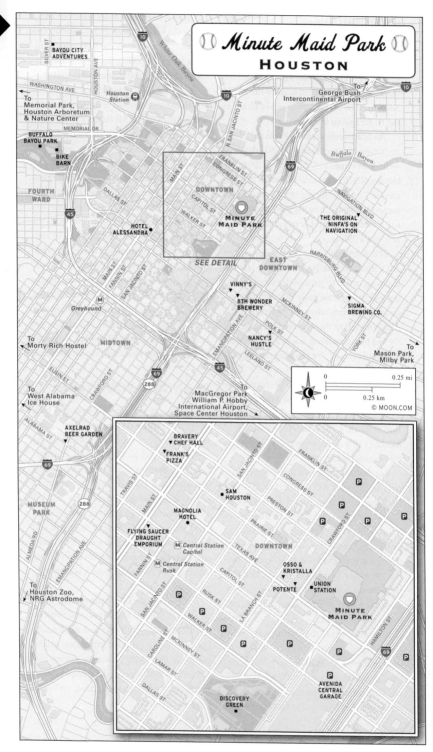

498

Minute Maid Park
HOUSTON

SILVER ST
BAYOU CITY
ADVENTURES

WASHINGTON AVE

HOUSTON ST

Houston
Station

To
George Bush
Intercontinental Airport

10

To
Memorial Park,
Houston Arboretum
& Nature Center

MEMORIAL DR

N SAN JACINTO ST

Buffalo Bayou

BUFFALO
BAYOU PARK

BIKE
BARN

FOURTH
WARD

45

DALLAS ST

FRANKLIN ST

CONGRESS ST

MAIN ST

NAVIGATION BLVD

DOWNTOWN

CAPITOL ST

WALKER ST

MINUTE
MAID PARK

HOTEL
ALESSANDRA

THE ORIGINAL
NINFA'S ON
NAVIGATION

HARRISBURG BLVD

MAIN ST

FANNIN ST

SAN JACINTO ST

SEE DETAIL

EAST
DOWNTOWN

VINNY'S

M

Greyhound

8TH WONDER
BREWERY

MCKINNEY ST

SIGMA
BREWING CO.

HARRISBURG BLVD

POLK ST

YORK ST

To
Morty Rich Hostel

MIDTOWN

EMANCIPATION AVE

NANCY'S
HUSTLE

LEELAND ST

To
Mason Park,
Milby Park

ELGIN ST

CRAWFORD ST

69

288

45

To
West Alabama
Ice House

To
MacGregor Park
William P. Hobby
International Airport,
Space Center Houston

0   0.25 mi

0   0.25 km

© MOON.COM

ALABAMA ST

69

AXELRAD
BEER GARDEN

MUSEUM
PARK

288

ALMEDA RD

EMANCIPATION AVE

To
Houston Zoo,
NRG Astrodome

TRAVIS ST

MAIN ST

BRAVERY
CHEF HALL

FRANK'S
PIZZA

SAN JACINTO ST

FRANKLIN ST

CONGRESS ST

SAM
HOUSTON

MAGNOLIA
HOTEL

FLYING SAUCER
DRAUGHT
EMPORIUM

PRESTON ST

PRAIRIE ST

P

CRAWFORD ST

P

P

P

FANNIN ST

M Central Station
Capitol

M Central Station
Rusk

TEXAS AVE

DOWNTOWN

CAPITOL ST

OSSO &
KRISTALLA

SAN JACINTO ST

P

RUSK ST

LA BRANCH ST

POTENTE

UNION
STATION

MINUTE
MAID PARK

P

WALKER ST

P

HAMILTON ST

CAROLINE ST

MCKINNEY ST

P

69

P

LAMAR ST

P

AVENIDA
CENTRAL
GARAGE

DALLAS ST

DISCOVERY
GREEN

Houston has a humid, subtropical climate, meaning it can be extremely **hot** and **humid,** especially between **May** and **September.** Luckily, Minute Maid Park has a **retractable roof,** which will be closed if it's too hot or if it **rains** (which happens a lot in the **summer** and **early fall**). Want to visit when the roof is open and the weather is comfortably in the 70s? Book your trip for **April.**

GETTING THERE

AIR

George Bush Intercontinental Airport

Houston has two international airports. **George Bush Intercontinental Airport** (IAH, 2800 N. Terminal Rd., www.fly2houston.com/iah) is in the northeastern section of the city, servicing 27 airlines, including **Air Canada** (888/247-2262, www.aircanada.com), **American Airlines** (800/433-7300, www.aa.com), **Delta** (800/221-1212, www.delta.com), **Spirit** (801/401-2222, www.spirit.com), and **United** (800/864-8331, www.united.com), which has direct flights to all major American cities and international destinations like Bogota, Colombia; Buenos Aires, Argentina; and Frankfurt, Germany.

AIRPORT TRANSPORTATION

To **rent a car,** you'll need to hop on a **shuttle** for a five-minute ride to the rental car center. From Bush airport, Minute Maid Park is a 20-minute drive south on I-69. An alternative is to make the 25-minute drive south on Hardy Toll Road and I-610 to I-69.

Traveling by car is the easiest way to go, though you can ride **METRO** (www.ridemetro.org, from $1.25), whose **Bus 102** connects airport travelers to Downtown Houston, with stops that are a short walk from the ballpark.

William P. Hobby International Airport

Houston's second airport, **William P. Hobby**

International Airport (HOU, 7800 Airport Blvd., www.fly2houston.com/hou), is in the southeastern section of the city and is home to four airlines: American Airlines, Delta, **jetBlue** (800/538-2583, www.jetblue.com), and **Southwest** (800/435-9792, www.southwest.com). Most large U.S. cities have flights into the easy-to-navigate Hobby, which has just one terminal.

AIRPORT TRANSPORTATION

To reach the **rental car center,** take the **shuttle** for a quick, five-minute ride. This airport is close to I-45, making it a 20-minute drive north to the ballpark, give or take. Taking a car is the best way out of Hobby, though **METRO's Bus 40** (www.ridemetro.org, from $1.25) offers a connection to Downtown Houston.

CAR

From the **Dallas-Fort Worth area,** it's a **240-mile** drive south on I-45 to Houston. Without traffic, it should take you a zippy **3.5 hours** because of the higher interstate speed limit. But traffic is almost always an issue, so plan on a slightly longer drive (closer to **4 hours** and change).

TRAIN

Amtrak (www.amtrak.com) pulls into Space City at the **Houston Station** (902 Washington Ave.). The **Sunset Limited,** which heads east to New Orleans and west through San Antonio and Tucson, Arizona, to Los Angeles, is the only Amtrak line that comes through Houston. No Amtrak line connects Dallas and Houston.

The train station is 1.3 miles west of Minute Maid Park, a drive of about eight minutes. No public transportation connects the station to Downtown Houston, so a taxi or ride-share is your best bet.

BUS

You can take a **Greyhound bus** (www.greyhound.com) to get to Houston from **Dallas.**

Torchy's Party Deck at Minute Maid Park

The journey takes around four hours and will cost about $25. The **Houston Bus Station** (2121 S. Main St., 713/759-6565) is in the south end of Downtown, a 1.4-mile drive from Minute Maid Park. No public transportation connects the station to Downtown Houston, so plan on taking a taxi or ride-share.

Minute Maid Park

Minute Maid Park (501 Crawford St., www.mlb.com/astros) is a fitting ballpark for Houston. It's set at the former Union Station, which for decades served as the

city's gateway for countless train travelers. The Union Station concourse has been preserved, serving as the ballpark's main lobby in beautiful fashion. With exceptionally high ceilings, Roman-style columns, and plenty of windows on either side, it's an outstanding entrance.

The landscape beyond is a mammoth retractable-roof playground, reflective of Houston's heterogeneous tapestry. Multiple advertisements populate the outfield backdrop, shilling everything from tacos to regional supermarkets to oil and gas companies. A gasoline pump in the left-field concourse keeps track of the season's home run total, and an honest-to-goodness locomotive chugs above the action over left field after every Astros home run.

The ballpark, which seats 41,168, opened

in 2000 as Enron Field in the Houston Downtown district. After Enron went bankrupt, the company settled with the Astros to end a naming rights agreement. In 2005, the venue was renamed Minute Maid Park; if you look hard enough at the train above left field, you'll see that it carries a whole lot of oranges.

ORIENTATION

Minute Maid Park is in an area of Downtown Houston surrounded by parking lots, two blocks west of I-69. There are seven entry gates. Gates open two hours before first pitch Monday through Saturday, and 90 minutes before first pitch on Sunday. On premium giveaway days, gates open three hours before first pitch.

TICKETS AND SEATING

Pricing

Ever since the Astros finally became a competitive team in 2015, their ticket prices have been among the highest in baseball. Plus, the team uses **dynamic pricing,** which means ticket costs are higher when popular teams and rivals visit. You'll pay the most money for seats in the Diamond Club (premium seats behind home plate), close to home plate, and the 100-level seats around the infield.

When a less competitive or popular team is on the schedule, you may be able to nab a 400-level seat for around $20, but if the Yankees are in town, double that amount. Tickets for kids ages 2 and under are always free.

YOUR BEST DAY AT MINUTE MAID PARK

Let's say you're heading to Minute Maid Park for a night game. Here's how to really take in Houston before catching Space City baseball.

6 HOURS BEFORE FIRST PITCH
Grab a taco lunch at **Villa Arcos.** Order a soft-shell, of course, but you should also try a crunchy shell to make it interesting.

5 HOURS BEFORE FIRST PITCH
Head over to **Saint Arnold Brewing Company** and hang out at the beer garden for a couple hours. Play some bocce, make new friends, and sample easy summer beers like Lawnmower and Orange Show.

3 HOURS BEFORE FIRST PITCH
Make a quick pit stop at **8th Wonder Brewery** for a quick brew and a perusal of cool Astros artifacts and collectibles.

1.5 HOURS BEFORE FIRST PITCH
It's time to head to **Minute Maid Park.** Walk through the **Hall of Fame Alley** and see if you can snag a spot at the **Phillips 66 Home Run Porch.**

Minute Maid Park

DURING THE GAME
Grab some chopped beef from **Jackson Street BBQ** and take a walk through the lobby at **Union Station.** Visit the **team store** while you're there.

AFTER THE GAME
The best way to wind down after an exciting Astros game is to hit up the late-night menu at **Nancy's Hustle.** The cheeseburger is magnificent. Wash it down with a beer like Lone Star.

Seating Plan

Minute Maid Park has **four levels** of seating. The **first level (100 level)** starts with the **Crawford Boxes** (sections 100-103), resting just above the pushed-in left field fence in dynamite home run territory. **Field box I-IV** (sections 104-111) are next, moving from left field down the third-base line. Next, wrapping around to the first-base line, are **dugout box I-III** (sections 112-126), followed by the first-base side's **field box I-IV** (sections 127-134). The level ends with the **bullpen boxes** (sections 150-156), out in far right field.

The **second level (200 level)** starts with **club I** (sections 205-209) in left field, then continues to **club II** (sections 210-216) and **club box home plate** (sections 217-221). On the first-base side, the level continues

with **club II** (sections 222-228) and **club I** (sections 229-232), then **power club** (sections 233-236) in far right field. The level concludes at the **Chevy mezzanine** (sections 250-255) in the outfield.

Executive suites separate the 200 level from the **third level (300 level).** The 300 level begins on the third-base side with **terrace deck outfield** (sections 305-310), continuing to **terrace deck infield** (sections 311-316) and **terrace deck home plate** (sections 317-321), and finishing on the first-base side with **terrace deck infield** (sections 322-328) and **terrace deck outfield** (sections 329-338).

The final and **fourth level (400 level)** starts in deep left field with **outfield deck I-II** (sections 405-408), then **view deck II** (sections 409-411). Next is **view deck**

I (sections 413-425), which wraps around home plate and into the first-base side; following it is **view deck II** (sections 427-431). The section ends in far right field with **outfield deck I-II** (sections 432-438).

Look for **standing-room-only** areas sprinkled throughout the concourses. Your standing-room ticket effectively gives you admission to the park; you'll have to arrive early to scope out a good place to hang out. The place to be for SRO is **Hall of Fame Alley,** the left-field area above the Crawford Boxes.

If you own a Honda, bring your car key to the **Honda Club Level** (section 205) to get into this exclusive spot for free. But get there early: The club typically stops giving out passes before mid-game.

Way out in center field, the **Torchy's Party Deck** costs about $35 per person, but you're not promised a seat here. Anchored by Texas taco favorite Torchy's (known for its seriously spicy diablo hot sauce), the deck has **standing room,** plus several dozen **tables** watching over the action, and **barstools** and a host of beer taps. Anyone can buy food here, but seating is only allowed for guests with a designated ticket. Also out in center field, the **Budweiser Brew House** is a group-only space that can be reserved in advance.

Where to Buy Tickets

You can visit the **Astros ticket office** (713/259-8000, 8:30am-5:30pm Mon.-Fri., 9am-2pm Sat., during home games Sun.; open during the season). Windows 18-26 are reserved for ticket sales. You can also check the team website or download the **MLB Ballpark app,** which includes upgrade options if you buy tickets through the team.

You can try **StubHub** and other ticket reseller sites; **SeatGeek** is praised among the ticket-buying community here. Still, Astros tickets are in high demand most of the time and prices stay high, so you may actually be better off going through the team.

Best Seats

For a few reasons, the **third-base line** is the place to be at Minute Maid Park. First, an

overhang provides ample **shade,** especially for the back rows of the **200** and **400 levels.** Second, the sun typically sets behind the glass windows over left field, making it difficult to watch games from seats along the first-base line. Third, fans along the third-base line have a direct view of the large video board in right field and won't have to crane their necks to see either the outfield backdrop or the action at home plate. Depending on your budget, opt for seats in the **middle rows** of **sections 208-209** or in the **middle rows** of **sections 409-410.**

If you want to be a part of the **fan experience,** grab a seat in the **Crawford Boxes** (sections 100-103), which also provide great access to the outfield concourse. You won't have the best view of plays in left field, but the home runs hit toward this area are plentiful.

If you're a sucker for long-distance views, a seat in the **Torchy's Party Deck** is a decent option. But get there as early as possible, because some seats in the section are reserved for people who buy tickets specifically for this area, and the leftover seats fill up quickly. You don't want to be left standing for nine innings.

BE A FAN

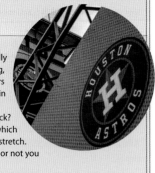

Texans love talking about how nice they are, and it's actually true. Generally, Astros fans are friendly and accommodating, regardless of your baseball affiliation. Wear your team colors if you'd like, but know that you'll stick out like a sore thumb in a sea of orange and navy.

Want to show those Texans how much you love them back? Join in on Moe Bandy's **"Deep in the Heart of Texas,"** which is sung by the entire stadium during the seventh-inning stretch. Don't forget to clap at the appropriate times, too. Whether or not you care for the song, your heart might actually soar.

KNOW BEFORE YOU GO

The park allows fans to bring in single-compartment **drawstring bags, diaper bags,** and bags used for medical reasons, but backpacks aren't allowed. One-liter factory-sealed plastic **water bottles** are allowed in the park, as is **outside food** kept in a clear, one-gallon bag. Laser pointers, noisemakers, broom handles, coolers, and cameras with lenses larger than eight inches are not permitted.

You won't need to plan for weather at Minute Maid Park, though if it's a warmer day and not too hot, the roof should be open, so bring **sunscreen.**

Accessibility

To reserve **accessible seating,** your best bet is to call the Astros at 713/259-8700 ahead of time to discuss seating options. **Courtesy wheelchairs** are offered at the gate of entry and used for transporting fans to and from their gate and seat. You can store your wheelchair at a **fan accommodations center** (sections 112 and 323). Here you can also get a **telephone display device** or an **assistive listening device** by turning in a photo ID as a deposit.

Elevators (sections 109 and 128) are in two locations of the ballpark. Both **Braille** and **tactile signage** is found throughout the park. **Service animals** are welcome at Minute Maid Park.

Accessible parking at Minute Maid Park can be found in **Lot A** and in the **Diamond Lot.** Be sure a valid disabled parking placard is visible.

GETTING THERE

Public Transit

Houston has a mass transit system called **METRO** (www.ridemetro.org, from $1.25). METRO's **Purple** and **Green Lines** service Minute Maid Park. The drawback: These lines aren't very long, spanning just the Downtown and East Downtown areas. If you plan on staying Downtown, you can connect to the Green or Purple Lines at **Central Station Rusk** (Rusk St. and Fannin St.) to reach the ballpark. For the return trip, your train will stop at **Central Station Capitol** (Capitol St. and Fannin St.).

Driving

Houston is a driving city, and unless you're staying blocks from the stadium in the Downtown area, going by car is the easiest way to reach Minute Maid Park. **Parking lots A, B,** and **C** are close to the stadium; each costs about $30, but you'll have to get there early. Otherwise, there are numerous **parking garages** in the Downtown area—try the **Avenida Central Garage** (1002 Avenida de las Americas, $20-27), a six-minute walk north to the ballpark.

Starting a quarter mile from the ballpark, you might find that some fans are parking their cars on side streets overseen by unsanctioned parking attendants—i.e., local residents. Simply give the local a fee to watch your car ($20 is about the going rate). I've tried it and had no problems, but do so at your own risk.

PARK FEATURES AND SIGHTS

Minute Maid Train

Minute Maid Park can feel like an amusement park, especially when everything is going well for the local nine. Keep your eye on the **train** above left field, carrying replica Minute Maid oranges. When the Astros take the field in the first inning, when an Astro hits a home run, and when the team wins, the train's conductor, **Bobby Dynamite**—always wearing denim overalls—pumps up the crowd before driving the train across the track high above the field. Also accompanying home runs and wins: **fireworks**. And they are loud. Be prepared.

Video Boards

Be sure to watch the **video boards.** The team's former home, the Astrodome, was known for its enormous scoreboard, where animations told stories after home runs and other big plays: A cowboy ropes a steer, a cowboy shoots his guns, Texas and American flags unfurl from a bull's horns. Those images, which date to the 1960s, have found new life at Minute Maid, and they continue to be played when Astros hit homers and strike out opponents.

Hall of Fame Alley

In 2019, the Astros unveiled the team's Hall of Fame, which includes about 20 players, coaches, and personalities making an indelible mark on the franchise's history. Fans can read about inductees like Jeff Bagwell, Craig Biggio, Joe Niekro, and Nolan Ryan at **Hall of Fame Alley** (left-field concourse). This area is also home to the **Phillips 66 Home Run Porch,** which hangs over the outfield and is

marked by a gasoline pump that has been tracking the total number of home runs hit by Astros players since the opening of Minute Maid Park. The gas pump makes a great photo op.

Tal's Hill

Minute Maid Park was once home to arguably the quirkiest field feature of modern times: **Tal's Hill.** Named after former team president Tal Smith, the hill was a literal rise at the very back of center field. Paying homage to the hill in center field at the Cincinnati Reds' old home of Crosley Field, Tal's Hill also had a flagpole, which was in play and proved a potential obstacle for fielders. The hill was removed after the 2016 season.

Orbit

Keep your eyes peeled for the Astros' mascot, **Orbit.** A cute, furry green alien in the vein of the Phillie Phanatic, Orbit has a more innocent streak than most team representatives. His most famous moment: "streaking" while wearing an oversize pair of tighty-whities.

FOOD AND DRINKS

Minute Maid Park lacks traditional restaurants, but it has a variety of Texas-focused fare, along with the usual concessions. Head to **Texas Smoke** (section 406) for barbecue beef and turkey sandwiches, beef brisket, and loaded baked potatoes. On the lower concourse, **Jackson Street BBQ** (section 124) is a pop-up location of a local barbecue pit that serves pulled pork sandwiches, pork ribs, chopped beef, and fried macaroni and cheese. **Dat Creole** (section 103) channels nearby Louisiana with po'boys and a meat pie with a hot, peppery Creole sauce called *rougaroux*. For pulled pork tacos, hit **Taco Trio** (section 125).

Looking for the best of the basic fare? One option is **Extreme Dog** (section 131), home to the Bayou City Dog, which includes jalapeños and pork belly burnt ends. The **Texas Legends stand** (sections 134, 230) serves burgers made with beef from Hall of Famer Nolan Ryan's ranch, and the foot-long Frito

Pie Corn Dog—a corn dog dipped in a batter made of Fritos, and a gustatory experience if there ever was one.

The lines are long for the trademark burgers and frozen custard at **Shake Shack** (section 157). For another cold option, head to **Cookies and Creamery and Ice Cream** (sections 106, 153, 251, 411, 423, 429), serving Texas favorite Blue Bell ice cream in a souvenir helmet.

The best local beer at the park is at **Saint Arnold's Bar** (section 104), where summertime favorites like Saint Arnold Art Car IPA and Saint Arnold Lawnmower IPA are served. The Houston brewery also produces a dry cider. In the upper bowl, **Karbach Bar** (section 404) has brews from Houston's largest brewery. They make Crawford Bock, a basic, malty summer beer created in partnership with the Astros; the can is designed with the team's "tequila sunrise" look, which was worn on their uniforms in the 1970s and early 1980s.

Wine drinkers should check out the **Premium Wines stands** (sections 104, 112, 125, 156, 205, 210, 226, 228, 405, 422, 427), and those who prefer liquor will enjoy the **Jim Beam Bar** (section 156). For something a little more authentic to Texas, head to the **Corona Cantina** (section 119), a beachy bar that serves frozen margaritas (created in Dallas!), which are necessary on hot summer days.

EVENTS

Batting practice typically lasts until 30-40 minutes before first pitch, and hanging out in the left-field concourse is a good idea if you're hunting for baseballs. To snag an **autograph,** hang out along the field box rails from section 111 to the left-field foul pole, and from section 127 to the right-field foul pole, until the batting cages are removed 45 minutes before first pitch.

On select Friday nights after the game ends, the Astros host **Big and Bright**

Photos (from top to bottom): the Minute Maid Train; view of Minute Maid Park from home plate; the exterior of Minute Maid Park.

Friday Nights, which are picturesque, 10- to 15-minute fireworks shows over left field.

The team loves its **bobblehead give-aways,** announced before the season begins. **Themed nights and weekends** (like *Star Wars* Night, Hispanic Heritage Weekend) are held throughout the season, too.

Tours

The Astros conduct **stadium tours** (tours@ astros.com, $15, $12 seniors, $10 ages 3-12, free ages 2 and under) of varying lengths and experiences. The **classic tour** (10am daily) takes fans to all seat levels, the warning track, the Astros' dugout, and Union Station. The **all-star tour** (11:30am daily during off-season and road trips) adds the manual scoreboard, visitors' clubhouse, and the Astros' Hall of Fame. The **ultimate fan tour** (11:30am during home stands only) substitutes the scoreboard and clubhouse for the suites and roof deck. The **Hall of Fame tour** (multiple times per day) visits only the Astros' Hall of Fame.

SHOPPING

The flagship team store is at **Union Station** (1800 Congress Ave., section 105, 9am-5pm Mon.-Fri., 9am-2pm Sat., plus game days when gates are open). Although it's not the biggest team store out there and it stocks the usual jerseys, T-shirts, and hats, the store does have an impressive selection of weird goodies. Look for bobbleheads, 1990s-era Jeff Bagwell and Craig Biggio shirts, and jerseys and shirts with the "tequila sunrise" design of the 1970s, which is used sparingly by the current-day team. The Orbit-themed items are fun, including socks and small plush dolls. The store gets crowded just before and during the game; it's best to visit as soon as the gates open, or on a non-game day.

Smaller team stores (sections 118, 132, 154, 216, 415, suite 24) carry the typical T-shirts and hats. Look for the **custom shop** at section 118, which allows you to customize a jersey or shirt, and the **authentics store** at section 154, selling gear worn and used in games.

HOUSTON SIGHTS

SPACE CENTER HOUSTON

Space Center Houston (1601 E. NASA Pkwy., 281/244-2100, www.spacecenter.org, 10am-5pm Mon.-Fri., 10am-6pm Sat.-Sun., $30, $27 seniors, $25 ages 4-11, free ages 3 and under) is the top attraction in Houston. This 250,000-square-foot education and visitors center and museum is on the campus of NASA's Johnson Space Center, which is also home to mission control, the folks who monitor every spaceflight made by U.S. astronauts.

Space Center Houston offers permanent exhibits like the astronaut gallery, containing space suits used by astronauts through history, and Mission Mars, an interactive look at NASA's investigation of the Red Planet. Also, check out Independence Plaza, home to a replica of the shuttle *Independence* that's mounted atop the original NASA 905 shuttle carrier aircraft. It's even possible to enter and walk around this incredible feat of engineering. There are changing exhibits, too, plus opportunities to have lunch with an astronaut. The Space Center is about a 30-minute drive from Minute Maid Park when there's no traffic.

HOUSTON ARBORETUM & NATURE CENTER

A quiet escape from Houston's concrete jungle, the **Houston Arboretum & Nature Center** (4501 Woodway Dr., 713/681-8433, www.houstonarboretum.org, 7am-6:30pm daily, free, parking $1 per hour) is a 155-acre wonderland of native plants that dates to 1951. Look for flowers like Turk's-cap lilies, coneflowers, and coreopsis, along with oak and elm trees. There are several trails at the arboretum, the longest being a more than 1.5-mile outer loop that crosses a swamp and connects to several shorter paths.

The arboretum hosts various family-ly-friendly events, including a **nighttime program** where guests can get close to owls, and **tyke hikes** ($7), during which children ages 18 months to three years can take their guardians on short morning hikes to look for animals like turtles and spiders. It also hosts nature events with **wine and beer pairings.** Note: Summer at the arboretum means being exposed to sweltering heat and plenty of bugs, so your best bet is to visit earlier in the morning before it gets pretty soupy outside. The arboretum is nine miles west of Minute Maid Park in Memorial Park, near the western intersection of I-10 and the I-610 loop.

HOUSTON ZOO

The 55-acre **Houston Zoo** (6200 Hermann Park Dr., 713/533-6500, www.houstonzoo. org, 9am-6pm daily, $23, $18 seniors and ages 2-11, free ages 1 and under) is home to 900 species of animals such as Asian elephants, African lions, tigers, leopards, red pandas, and a variety of birds, including bald eagles. There are several exhibits at the zoo, one of the newest being the Texas Wetlands, which features alligators and whooping cranes.

Among the dining options are themed food trucks that sell everything from Asian cuisine to barbecue. Local beer is also on tap and can be consumed while walking around the zoo. The grounds are a good size, making for a fine half-day family excursion. Plus, it's part of the larger Hermann Park—four miles southeast of Minute Maid Park via I-69—home to an outdoor theater, gardens, and a golf course.

NRG ASTRODOME

In 1965, the world got its first glimpse of one of the contenders for the eighth wonder of the world, the **NRG Astrodome** (3 NRG Pkwy.), the home of the Astros through 1999. With its massive, 710-foot-diameter dome, the Astrodome truly was a marvel of mid-century modern architecture. It was also a pioneer in athletic playing surfaces—it was the first major stadium to use artificial turf, which was then branded AstroTurf. The dome isn't open to the public today, though

there's talk of a major revitalization project that would promise a fully functional venue in the future. Hard-core baseball fans coming to Houston for the first time should at least drive by the wonder—which is in the southern end of the city by the football-only NRG Stadium—if only to say they've seen it.

FOOD

NEAR MINUTE MAID PARK

The Downtown and East Downtown areas are fast-growing neighborhoods for young professionals, so there's an ever-growing list of eating options. Tops among these is **Nancy's Hustle** (2704 Polk St. #A, 346/571-7931, www.nancyshustle.com, 5pm-midnight Tues.-Sun., under $50), a neighborhood eatery with phenomenal, scratch-made new American food, killer cocktails, and a sweet staff. One taste of the favorite Nancy Cakes (corn fritters served with homemade butter and trout roe) will sell you.

Want a good slice of pizza? The subway-tile white walls of **Vinny's** (1201 St. Emanuel St., 713/750-9433, www.agricolehospitality.com, 11am-midnight Sun.-Thurs., 11am-2am Fri.-Sat., under $30) might recall New York City to some people, but you won't find this pizza in the Big Apple. A single slice is enough for most eaters here, though large groups can order absurd-looking 52-ounce pies. The ingredients are fresh and thoughtfully sourced, too. Wine and beer are available, and salads, sandwiches, and desserts are also on the menu.

For a more accurate depiction of New York pie, **Frank's Pizza** (417 Travis St., 713/225-5656, www.frankspizza.com, 11am-10pm Sun.-Wed., 11am-1am Thurs., 11am-3am Fri.-Sat., under $20) is the spot. Order a couple thin-crust slices here, and maybe add some wings on the side. Sit in a comfortable dining room in this just-narrow-enough interior that'll remind any visitor of an East Coast pizza parlor.

For an eclectic taste of Houston without

traveling far from the ballpark, hit up **Bravery Chef Hall** (409 Travis St. #A, 713/909-0691, www.braverychefhall.com, 11am-9pm Sun.-Wed., 11am-10pm Thurs.-Sat., under $40). This diverse food hall showcases Vietnamese cuisine from a *MasterChef* champion, as well as the city's best gumbo, superb sushi, and outstanding homemade pastas and pizzas, plus a bar with about two dozen wines on tap.

Any first-time visitor to Houston has to sample authentic Tex-Mex, and there's no better place to do it than at **The Original Ninfa's on Navigation** (2704 Navigation Blvd., 713/228-1175, www.ninfas.com, 11am-10pm Mon.-Thurs., 11am-11pm Fri., 10am-11pm Sat., 10am-10pm Sun., under $40). This place, packed and buzzy with families, tourists, and locals, claims to have invented the fajita, so your job here is to order up one of those sizzling beauties, as juicy, spicy, and filling as ever. As much as you'll want to, avoid filling up on chips and queso.

Arguably the city's top taqueria, **Brothers Taco House** (1604 Emancipation Ave., 713/223-0091, 5am-3pm Mon.-Fri., 6am-1pm Sat., 7am-1pm Sun., under $20) is a must-visit for any Houston first-timer. The family-run spot is machinelike in its efficiency, even when the line wrapping around the corner looks daunting. Go for the breakfast tacos served on homemade tortillas with proteins like chorizo and *picadillo* (ground beef). Barbacoa is only available after 11am on weekends, but I suggest you get it.

Check out **Villa Arcos** (3009 Navigation Blvd., 713/826-1099, www.originalvillaarcos.com, 6am-2pm Wed.-Sat., 8am-1pm Sun., under $20), known for its inexpensive and tasty breakfast and lunch tacos, along with solid Mexican plates like huevos rancheros and *migas* (eggs with fried tortilla strips). It'll be packed whenever you visit, but carve out 30-45 minutes, order a couple items, then enjoy your grub outside on a picnic table. Pair your food with a tall, sugary Mexican Coke.

Astros' owner Jim Crane also owns two restaurants across the street from Minute Maid Park. High rollers, including players and other celebrities, are often spotted at **Potente** (1515 Texas Ave., 713/237-1515, www.potentehouston.com, 5pm-10pm Mon.-Thurs., 5pm-11pm Fri.-Sat., under $80), which offers upscale Italian fare inside a dimly lit, chic space. Next door, **Osso & Kristalla** (1515 Texas Ave., 713/221-6666, www.ossoandkristalla.com, 7am-10pm Mon.-Thurs., 7am-11pm Fri., 10am-11pm Sat., 10am-9pm Sun., under $30) features a more accessible menu with sandwiches and pizza, along with pasta-heavy entrées, inside a bright, tall-windowed room.

OTHER NEIGHBORHOODS

If you're in Houston, you're going to need barbecue. The options are plentiful, and it's hard to go wrong; but if you want the authentic experience of waiting in line for up to an hour to bite into some tender, juicy beef brisket, head to **Killen's BBQ** (3613 E. Broadway St., Pearland, 281/485-2272, www.killensbarbecue.com, 11am-8pm Tues.-Thurs., 11am-9pm Fri.-Sat., 11am-8pm Sun., under $40). This pit, in suburban Pearland, is the most talked-about place in the area. Get the three-meat plate with two sides: brisket, beef ribs, and sausage, plus baked beans and creamed corn. Save room for the banana pudding. It's about a 30-minute drive to get here from Downtown Houston.

If you want a more under-the-radar experience for barbecue, visit **Burns Original BBQ** (8307 De Priest St., 281/999-5559, 10:30am-7:30pm Tues.-Sat., under $30). Plates are cheaper than Killen's, but the grub is just as good, from juicy sausage links to exquisite beef ribs. It's outdoors, so be prepared to sweat in the summer. Fun fact: The owner's brother is four-time all-star Carl Crawford, depicted on a wall mural outside the kitchen. Burns is about 10 miles north of Downtown Houston, just west of I-45.

Houston has a rich Vietnamese culture, with eateries sprinkled all over the map selling pho, *bun bo hue* (a lemongrass-tinged noodle soup), and *café sua da* (iced coffee). But if you have time for just one Vietnamese

meal, grab yourself a banh mi at **Roostar Vietnamese Grill** (1411 Gessner Rd. #1, 832/649-8955, www.myroostar.com, 11am-10pm Mon.-Sat., 11am-9pm Sun., under $20). Banh mi is the unofficial sandwich of Houston, and the fast casual Roostar does it better than anyone else with fresh ingredients and the right balance of flavors. From Downtown Houston, you'll need to head about 12 miles west on I-10 to reach Roostar. It's north of the interstate before it hits the Sam Houston Tollway/TX-8.

If you're visiting Houston early in the baseball season, you might just have to reserve a couple hours for crawfish. The Gulf Coast tradition of taking apart and sucking down mudbugs is a big deal here, with plenty of well-known spots and smaller shacks offering up these shelled creatures by the pound. There are lots of good crawfish picks, but I recommend **Cajun Kitchen** (6938 Wilcrest Dr., 281/495-8881, www.cajunkitchenhouston.com, 3pm-10pm Mon.-Fri., noon-10pm Sat.-Sun., under $30). This place, along with many others, serves Viet-Cajun crawfish, which means the crustaceans are drenched in a buttery sauce with flavors of lemongrass, ginger, citrus, and garlic. Cajun Kitchen is west of Downtown Houston, just under a 20-mile drive away. It's close to where the Sam Houston Tollway/TX-8 and Westpark Tollway intersect.

BARS AND BREWERIES

NEAR MINUTE MAID PARK

The closest craft brewery to Minute Maid Park is **8th Wonder Brewery** (2202 Dallas St., 713/229-0868, www.8thwonder.com, 11am-10pm Mon.-Sat., 11am-6pm Sun.), which also serves as a neat introduction to Houston for baseball fans. "WonderWorld,"

Photos (from top to bottom): Roostar Vietnamese Grill; Spindletap Brewery's Juiceton Double IPA; Saint Arnold Brewing Company.

as it's called, is home to some Instagrammable Houston art, chairs and signage from
the old Astrodome, and a beer called Dome
Faux'm, named after the Astros' old ballpark.
Very family-friendly, it regularly hosts big
weekend events.

Just a mile east of Minute Maid is **Sigma
Brewing Co.** (3118 Harrisburg Blvd.,
346/352-3190, www.sigmabrewingcompany.
com, 3pm-10pm Mon. and Thurs., 3pm-mid-
night Fri., noon-midnight Sat., noon-10pm
Sun.), a smaller spot for suds but a bit more
daring, as it's known for some big, hoppy
beers. Find a bunch of board games and a
video game system inside. The space's garage
becomes a beer garden when it's warm.

Houston's beer scene has been rapidly expanding over the past few years, so
you may want to get a snapshot at **Flying
Saucer Draught Emporium** (705 Main
St., 713/228-9472, www.beerknurd.com,
11am-1am Mon.-Wed., 11am-2am Thurs.-
Sat., 11am-midnight Sun.). A national chain,
Flying Saucer has a vast collection of locals,
domestics, and imports. Its food menu is a
variety of inexpensive pub bites, pizzas, and
sandwiches.

OTHER NEIGHBORHOODS

The original Houston craft brewery, **Saint
Arnold Brewing Company** (2000 Lyons
Ave., 713/686-9494, www.saintarnold.com,
11am-10pm Sun.-Wed., 11am-11pm Thurs.-
Sat.) remains a must-visit, one of the best
midsize craft breweries in America. Its beer
hall is a fine place to gather when it rains,
but the move is to spend a couple hours at its
beer garden and restaurant, built in 2018. The
restaurant features gorgeous murals painted
by Houston artists, while outside has gardens,
bocce courts, incredible skyline views, large-
screen TVs, plenty of tables, and good service.
It's *the* place in the city to watch a game.

It used to be that beer in Texas had to be
cold and lower in alcohol content, but that's
no longer a reality. One brewery doing its
own thing, and really well, is **Spindletap
Brewery** (10622 Hirsch Rd., 713/325-1477,
www.spindletap.com, noon-10pm Thurs.-Sat.,

11am-6pm Sun.). Focusing on hoppy and juicy
brews (think New England IPA and plenty of
imperials), Spindletap rolls out some of the
most crave-worthy cans in Houston. Its moderately sized taproom is family-friendly, and a
food truck is typically on-site.

Sourcing the ingredients for its beer
and grub from its own gardens, **City
Acre Brewing Co.** (3418 Topping St.,
832/377-0237, www.cityacrebrewing.com,
4pm-10pm Wed.-Thurs., 11am-11pm Fri.-
Sat., 11am-8pm Sun.) is the cozy Texas barn
experience perfect for beer geeks. Pair its
frequently simple but delicious beers with
juicy burgers while sitting on picnic tables
and playing beanbag toss. There's a firepit for
cool evenings, too.

Arguably the most popular beer garden
in Houston, **Axelrad Beer Garden** (1517
Alabama St., 713/597-8800, www.axelrad-
beergarden.com, noon-2am Wed.-Fri., noon-
1am Thurs.-Tues.) leans a little hipster, but
it's a fun hang. With a solid mix of about
three dozen local and domestic beers, plus
a good cocktail, wine, and liquor list, it's a
worthy visit just for the drinks. While there,
try to snag a seat in one of Axelrad's many
hammocks.

A very Houstonian thing is the ice house,
an outdoor bar that's teeming with activity
once the weather warms up. You can't go
wrong with any of them, but the bucket-list
choice is the **West Alabama Ice House**
(1919 W. Alabama St., 713/528-6874, www.
west-alabama-ice-house.com, 10am-mid-
night Mon.-Fri., 10am-1am Sat., noon-midnight Sun.), which opened in 1928. There's
plenty of selection here, but the idea is to
get a bunch of cheap beers (Lone Star will
do) and hang with folks by the picnic tables,
beanbag toss boards, and Ping-Pong tables.

RECREATION

PARKS

Some of Houston's winding, often confusing
roadways are built atop and around bayous,

those slow-moving rivers and streams found in flatter areas, particularly in the South. Luckily, the city has realized the need to preserve some of the space around these bodies of water, resulting in places like **Buffalo Bayou Park** (1800 Allen Pkwy., www.buffalobayou.org), where the Buffalo Bayou Hike and Bike Trail hugs said bayou from the western end of the city to Midtown. The park fills up with runners and cyclists on weekend mornings; get your bicycle through **Bike Barn** (105 Sabine St., 713/955-4455, www.bikebarn.com, 10am-7pm Sat.-Sun., $6-18 per hour). When the water level rises in the summer, grab a canoe or kayak from **Bayou City Adventures** (3422 Allen Pkwy., 713/538-7433, www.bayoucityadventures.org, 8am-5pm Sat.-Sun. Memorial Day-Labor Day, rentals $30-45).

There isn't much green space in Downtown Houston, but there is **Discovery Green** (1500 McKinney St., www.discoverygreen.com, 6am-11pm daily), a nearly 12-acre public space that includes a lawn, lake, playground, jogging trail, boccie courts, and shuffleboard. It also has a staple of hot Texas summers: a splash pad (called the Gateway Fountain), where water squirts up from the ground at timed intervals.

The largest park in Houston, **Memorial Park** (6501 Memorial Dr., www.memorialparkconservancy.org, 6am-11pm daily) has more than 30 trails for hiking, plus a cycling trail, several baseball fields, tennis courts, volleyball courts, and a swimming and fitness center. Also on-site is **Memorial Park Golf Course** (1001 E. Memorial Loop Dr., www.houstonmunicipalgolf.org, 6:30am-7:30pm Wed.-Mon. Apr.-Oct., 6:30am-5:30pm Wed.-Mon. Nov.-Mar., $10-30 Mon.-Thurs., $28-38 Fri.-Sun.), which has 18 holes and hosts PGA Tour events.

DISC GOLF

Besides some random stretches in January and February, Houston's weather is relatively warm (or sweltering hot), making it a perfect place for outdoor activities like disc golf. There are three courses inside the inner-city

loop and several more in the metropolitan area. In the East End, try **Mason Park** (541 S. 75th St., www.houstontx.gov/parks, dawn-dusk daily), which has nine holes on grass and dirt. **MacGregor Park** (5225 Calhoun Rd., www.houstontx.gov/parks, dawn-dusk daily) by the University of Houston has 18 holes on grass and dirt. The city also operates the course at **Milby Park** (2001 Central St., www.houstontx.gov/parks, dawn-dusk daily), which has 18 holes.

ACCOMMODATIONS

NEAR MINUTE MAID PARK

Any large building constructed in Houston before World War II is worth checking out. The structure that's home to the **Magnolia Hotel** (1100 Texas Ave., 713/221-0011, www.marriott.com, $150-300) dates to 1926, though the accommodations themselves are much newer, part of Marriott's Tribute Portfolio. The lobby has some art deco touches in keeping with the building's age, and rooms are spacious and comfortable. You may have to pay closer to $300 per night on weekends, but it's worth it for a few reasons: One, the hotel is about a 10-minute walk to the ballpark, and two, there's a rooftop pool.

Another building dating to the 1920s houses the **Sam Houston** (1117 Prairie St., 832/200-8800, www.curiocollection3.hilton.com, $125-250), which offers king and double rooms with a clean, sophisticated design and plenty of leather furniture. This Hilton hotel has a restaurant and bar and a fitness room; it's also a 10-minute walk to Minute Maid Park.

Houston has its share of luxury hotels, one of the finest being **Hotel Alessandra** (1070 Dallas St., 713/242-8555, www.hotelalessandra-houston.com, $175-300). Its 223 rooms and suites, dressed in simple, contemporary whites, grays, and greens, have cotton linens, monogrammed robes, minibars, and seating areas. The hotel also has an outdoor pool, spa, and two restaurants.

OTHER NEIGHBORHOODS

For a unique experience, check in at HI Houston, the **Morty Rich Hostel** (501 Lovett Blvd., 713/636-9776, www.hiusa. org, $25-100). This Hostelling International accommodation is set in a 1917 mansion in the middle of the Montrose neighborhood, known for its more youthful culture and its role as a civil rights fulcrum for LGBTQ Houstonians. The hostel has male-only, female-only, and coed dormitories, plus private queen rooms. It offers a shared kitchen and free continental breakfast, and is also one of the few hostels with a pool.

GETTING AROUND

Houston is basically designed like a target. The inner circle is outlined by **I-610**, which loops around the inner city (it's called **the Loop** by residents), including Downtown and most of the well-trafficked entertainment and nightlife areas. A second circle is outlined by the **Sam Houston Tollway,** or **TX-8,** which connects the outer edges of the city. Outside of that are the suburbs, including Sugar Land, Katy, Pearland, Spring, and League City (close to Space Center Houston).

PUBLIC TRANSIT

METRO (www.ridemetro.org, from $1.25) has a small **rail service** that primarily services the Downtown area, while a more comprehensive **bus network** reaches many of the populous areas of the city. On METRO, the **Purple** and **Green Lines** run west to east, mostly in the Downtown area, while the **Red Line** runs north to south.

TAXI, UBER, AND LYFT

Houston is an Uber and Lyft city. The Astros partner with Uber; use the promo code GOASTROSGO to get up to $15 off your first ride.

There aren't many taxis riding around the city, though Spanish-speaking visitors may find **Taxis Fiesta** (713/225-2666, www.taxisfiesta.com) a good option.

CAR

You'll want to rent a car at either Bush or Hobby airport, as it's the most efficient way to get around the city. Just build some traffic time into your journeying across the city and remember: Be patient.

If you stay inside I-610, you'll be fine. **I-45** runs into Downtown from the north, then shoots southeast toward Galveston and the Gulf of Mexico. **I-69,** also known as **TX-59,** comes into Downtown from the northeast and shoots southwest toward Sugar Land. Both these roads are major thoroughfares and get mighty busy, especially during rush hour. **I-10** cuts through the top third of the city, west to east, and also gets pretty busy at rush hours. During these times, it's often better to avoid the highways to get where you're going.

Many Houston highways can get confusing. Watch as four lanes magically become six, then shrink to two. Texas is also known for its **service roads,** also called **feeders.** You can ride these roads for a while, especially if traffic on the highway is bad. Be careful: Each intersection has its own set of turning lanes; typically, the lane closest to the highway is a U-turn-only lane that whips around the highway and onto the opposite feeder.

Arizona and the Rocky Mountains

This adventurous trip offers two fun baseball experiences set against a backdrop of incredible recreational opportunities. Watch some baseball, then climb a few hills (or mountains!) and feel pretty darn good about yourself in the process. Coors Field in Denver is like an island in the sky, sitting at a mile up from sea level and offering the only major league baseball for hundreds of miles. From here, you'll venture through the Rocky Mountains, taking in wild scenery on your way to Phoenix, home to Chase Field and Cactus League spring training.

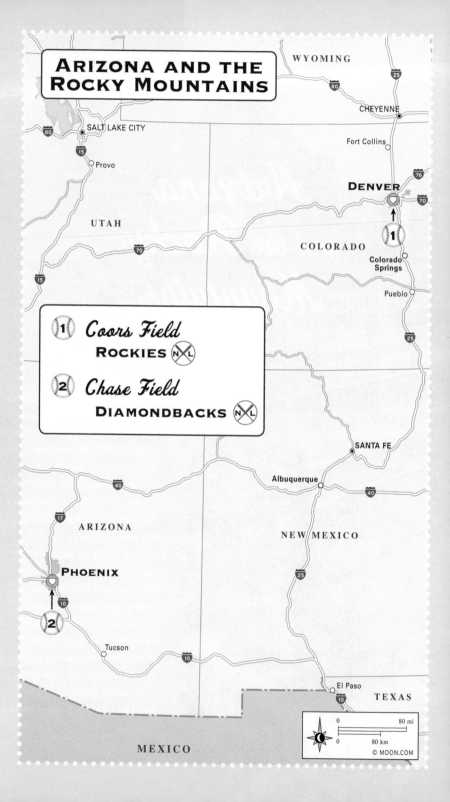

Arizona and the Rocky Mountains Road Trip

Naturally, Denver and Phoenix are known more for recreation than for their baseball teams. When your backyard is studded with mountains and canyons, it's understandable. Still, there are plenty of reasons Major League Baseball came to this area, first in 1993, then again in 1998: The fan base could support the game (both cities already had the other three major professional sports covered), businesspeople knew the money was there, and the entire time zone had been starved of major league baseball (other than spring training in Phoenix). The time was ripe.

Denver is the home of the Rockies. They play at Coors Field, a retro-classic brick-and-steel park with a fun bleacher scene and a lot of beer poured on-site. The offense here is wild, thanks to the lower air pressure in a city that sits 5,000 feet above sea level. The Rockies quickly broke records in their first years at Coors, and despite alterations to lessen the impact of the environment, that offensive advantage has continued through the years. Go to a Rockies home game and prepare to see some hits.

In Phoenix, southwest of Denver and past multitudes of mountains and canyons, the Diamondbacks play in somewhat similar conditions. Chase Field, like Coors, had long been the scene of plenty of home runs because of the dry desert air that filters into the venue. But changes there (installing a climate-controlled humidor that's meant to increase the density of the baseball) eventually helped bring down the dinger rate.

Both teams have had nearly equal parts success and failure (five postseason appearances and one pennant for the Rockies; six postseason appearances, one pennant, and one world title for the Diamondbacks), and considering they're the only two teams out in the Mountain time zone, they've become obvious rivals. Not to mention that they both play in gorgeous environments. You can literally hike to the top of a mountain before or after games in either city.

Visiting Denver and Phoenix together makes for a heck of a trip. You'll fly into **Denver** to start your trip and watch the **Rockies,** and then you have a choice: You can drive directly to **Phoenix** and the **Diamondbacks** for a scenic trip of about **800 miles.** Or you can truck south to **Albuquerque** in New Mexico to watch the famed minor league **Isotopes** before continuing southwest to Phoenix, for an **860-mile** adventure. No matter which option you choose, this trip is part recreation, part baseball, and all extremely fun.

PLANNING YOUR TIME

Denver and Phoenix are in the same part of the country and share the same time zone (most of the time), but they are separated by about 800 miles. I recommend **a week** to tackle these two locations—spend **two days each** in Denver and Phoenix, **two days** driving between the cities, and **one day** in the middle getting out of the car and stretching your legs.

You'll have a few options for your drive, each of which takes 13-13.5 hours. The 820-mile **northern route** from Denver follows I-70 West to US-191 South, which will take you through Grand Junction, Colorado, and into Utah, past Arches and Canyonlands National Parks, en route to Arizona. The 790-mile **central route** follows US-285 South to US-160 West past San Juan National Forest and Mesa Verde National Park. It cruises right past the Four Corners Monument before hooking up with the northern route at the junction with US-191. The 860-mile **southern route** goes down I-25 South to New Mexico, past Santa Fe and into Albuquerque, home of the minor league Isotopes. You'll then follow I-40 West toward Arizona and go directly through Petrified Forest

National Park. Needless to say, this trip offers plenty to do if you want to get out of the car.

You could also **fly** from Denver to Phoenix, a trip that's just two hours nonstop. That means you can tackle this trip in a **long weekend** or **five days.** If you're in a rush, you could do a day in Denver, fly to Phoenix, do a day in the Valley of the Sun, and fly home. This is possible but not ideal—take your time in these two cities if you can, as they have a lot to offer.

Here's how to do this trip in seven days.

Day 1

Fly into **Denver** in the morning and take it easy. For many people, the city's high elevation can cause exhaustion and even nausea. Drink plenty of fluids and give yourself time to adjust.

Day 2

Hopefully, you're feeling good and ready to take on the day. Spend it seeing the sights in Denver before attending a Rockies game at **Coors Field.** Have a couple drinks in LoDo afterward.

Day 3

Today is a driving day. If you're taking the northern route, stop in Moab, Utah, to spend a day at Arches or Canyonlands National Parks. If you're on the central route, rest in Cortez, Colorado, to hang out at Mesa Verde National Park. And if you're driving the southern route, set your bags down in Albuquerque and try to catch an Isotopes game.

Day 4

It's a full day in your halfway-point destination, whether it's Arches or Canyonlands (for the most adventurous), Mesa Verde (for those wanting a quieter national park experience), or Albuquerque (for baseball buffs).

Day 5

Hop back in the car to finish your drive to **Phoenix.** For those on the northern and central routes, consider Flagstaff as a stopping place for lunch. For drivers taking the southern route through New Mexico, your best bet is Holbrook, the seat of Navajo County, Arizona.

Day 6

After a nice rest, wake up in Phoenix and tackle the day. See some sights and go to **Chase Field** for a Diamondbacks game.

Day 7

Have a leisurely breakfast in Phoenix and fly back home.

GETTING THERE

The best ways to do this trip are by driving or flying between Denver and Phoenix. There's no easy way to get from Denver to Phoenix via rail. Driving, you won't encounter much traffic, especially once you leave the major cities. Just gas up in major cities and listen to your body; if you're too tired driving the desert roads, find somewhere to stop and rest.

Air

Chances are pretty good that if you're flying into Denver, you're going to **Denver International Airport** (DEN, 8500 Peña Blvd., Denver, 303/342-2000, www.flydenver.com). It's served by **Air Canada** (888/247-2262, www.aircanada.com), **Allegiant** (702/505-8888, www.allegiantair.com), **American Airlines** (800/433-7300, www.aa.com), **Delta** (800/221-1212, www.delta.com), **Frontier** (801/401-9000, www.flyfrontier.com), **jetBlue** (800/538-2583, www.jetblue.com), **Southwest** (800/435-9792, www.southwest.com), **Spirit** (801/401-2222, www.spirit.com), and **United** (800/864-8331, www.united.com). The one terminal here has three gate areas.

In Phoenix, the efficient **Phoenix Sky Harbor International Airport** (PHX, 3400 E. Sky Harbor Blvd., Phoenix, www.skyharbor.com) is served by Air Canada, American Airlines, Delta, Frontier, jetBlue, Southwest, Spirit, and United.

The Phoenix area's other international airport, much smaller than Sky Harbor, is **Phoenix-Mesa Gateway Airport** (AZA, 6033 S. Sossaman Rd., Mesa, 480/988-7600, www.gatewayairport.com). This airport connects primarily to smaller cities in the West and Midwest, plus Chicago and San Francisco, mostly through Allegiant.

Photos (top): Chase Field, home of the Arizona Diamondbacks; (middle left) spring training games at Tempe Diablo Stadium; (middle right) *Intertribal Greeting* by Doug Hyde at the Heard Museum in Phoenix; (bottom) Albuquerque.

DENVER
COLORADO ROCKIES

Up on the high plains of Colorado, baseballs have been flying through thin air for more than 25 years. They're hit at Coors Field, home to the Colorado Rockies, one of the weirdest, most fun franchises in all of baseball.

Denver was a minor league city for a long time, hosting both the Bears and Zephyrs before Major League Baseball approved expansion to the city for the 1993 season. The Rockies debuted at Mile High Stadium, then moved to a new home called Coors Field. In the park's first year, they were given the moniker the "Blake Street Bombers," hitting more homers than any other team in baseball and earning a postseason bid.

The Rockies have always relied on the long ball, and the team's rotating cast of home-run hitters has been impressive: Larry Walker, Dante

Bichette, Andrés Galarraga, Vinny Castilla, Ellis Burks, Todd Helton, Matt Holliday, Troy Tulowitzki, Carlos González, Nolan Arenado, Trevor Story, and Charlie Blackmon. That, plus a 2007 World Series berth and multiple appearances in the postseason, make the Rockies more interesting than a relatively young team could usually expect to be.

The ball club is a big draw in a place known for its recreational opportunities—everything from big hikes in national parks to three-season skiing. Denver is a fun town, and its food and drink scene (especially the beer) is solid.

When you're in town, one neighborhood to check out is River Art North District, also called RiNo, a part of the Five Points community. LoDo (Lower Downtown) is near the ballpark and has plenty of pretty shops and cool restaurants, making it a good place to visit just before or after a contest.

But when the game starts, pay attention, because at any moment you might see a ball fly out of the yard. That's the Colorado Rockies experience in a nutshell.

PLANNING YOUR TIME

You should give yourself at least a **long weekend** in Denver. Spend that first day taking things slow, just in case you're having a hard time adjusting to the high elevation. If you stay more than three or four days, see to it that you plan a day or so in Rocky Mountain National Park. Look into camping reservations ahead of time.

The best places to stay in Denver include smack in the middle of **Downtown** or **EaDo** (East of Downtown), so car time is limited; out in the **Cherry Creek** area, though you'll definitely be driving a lot more; and close to the **airport.** I suggest having a car for this city, regardless of where you stay, so that you can get around if you'd like to go on a hike or see some nature.

Denver is a special place when it comes to weather. It could be 80°F and sunny one day, and the next, 30°F with a couple inches of snow on the ground. The most volatile months are in the **spring (Mar.-May)** and **fall (Sept.-Oct.).**

No matter what time you travel, pack a **jacket** or something warm for night games, as it can get pretty cold. If you're going to a Rockies game in the summer, bring plenty of **sunblock.** The sun can be unforgiving at this altitude. You may need some time to adjust to the high elevation, too. If you're new to the Rocky Mountain area, don't hop off the plane and head right to the ballpark. I've been there, and I've seen others go through it: You might suffer from **altitude sickness,** with symptoms including nausea, headaches, and exhaustion. Take that first day slow, and drink plenty of water.

GETTING THERE

AIR

Chances are pretty good that if you're flying into Denver, you're going to **Denver International Airport** (DEN, 8500 Peña Blvd., 303/342-2000, www.flydenver.com). It's home to **Air Canada** (888/247-2262, www.aircanada.com), **Allegiant** (702/505-8888, www.allegiantair.com), **American Airlines** (800/433-7300, www.aa.com), **Delta** (800/221-1212, www.delta.com), **Frontier** (801/401-9000, www.flyfrontier.com), **jetBlue** (800/538-2583, www.jetblue.com), **Southwest** (800/435-9792, www.southwest.com), **Spirit** (801/401-2222, www.spirit.com), and.**United** (800/864-8331, www.united.com). The one terminal here has three sets of gates.

Airport Transportation

Those wanting a **rental car** will have to grab a **shuttle** to take a short ride to the on-site rental agencies. From the airport, it's a 25-mile, 30-minute ride west by southwest to Downtown Denver and Coors Field via Peña Boulevard, I-70 West, and I-25 South.

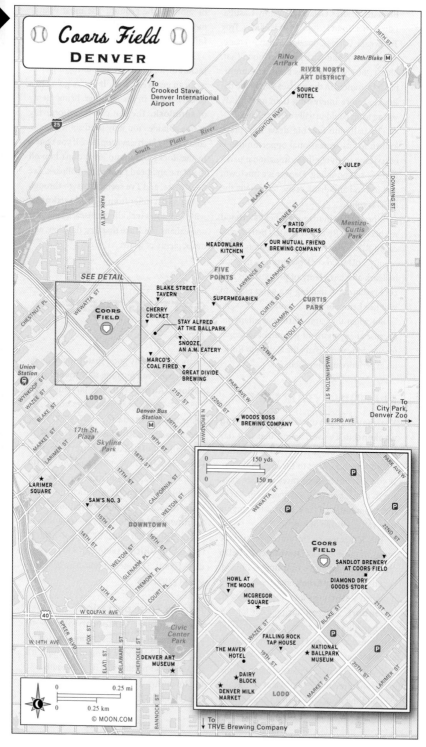

Coors Field
DENVER

To Crooked Stave, Denver International Airport

RiNo ArtPark

RIVER NORTH ART DISTRICT

38th/Blake Ⓜ

SOURCE HOTEL

DOWNING ST

38TH ST

Brighton Blvd

South Platte River

Park Ave W

JULEP

BLAKE ST

LARIMER ST

RATIO BEERWORKS

Mestizo-Curtis Park

MEADOWLARK KITCHEN

OUR MUTUAL FRIEND BREWING COMPANY

LAWRENCE ST

ARAPAHOE ST

FIVE POINTS

SEE DETAIL

WEWATTA ST

COORS FIELD

BLAKE STREET TAVERN

SUPERMEGABIEN

CURTIS ST

CHAMPA ST

STOUT ST

CURTIS PARK

CHESTNUT PL

CHERRY CRICKET

STAY ALFRED AT THE BALLPARK

SNOOZE, AN A.M. EATERY

MARCO'S COAL FIRED

GREAT DIVIDE BREWING

Union Station Ⓜ

WYNKOOP ST

WAZEE ST

BLAKE ST

MARKET ST

LARIMER ST

LODO

21ST ST

22ND ST

25TH ST

PARK AVE W

WASHINGTON ST

Denver Bus Station Ⓜ

N BROADWAY

20TH ST

19TH ST

18TH ST

17TH ST

WOODS BOSS BREWING COMPANY

E 23RD AVE

To City Park, Denver Zoo →

17th St. Plaza

Skyline Park

CALIFORNIA ST

WELTON ST

LARIMER SQUARE ★

SAM'S NO. 3 ★

15TH ST

14TH ST

16TH ST

DOWNTOWN

13TH ST

WELTON ST

GLENARM PL

TREMONT PL

COURT PL

40

SPEER BLVD

FOX ST

ELATI ST

DELAWARE ST

CHEROKEE ST

W COLFAX AVE

W 14TH AVE

Civic Center Park

DENVER ART MUSEUM ★

BANNOCK ST

0   0.25 mi
0   0.25 km
© MOON.COM

To TRVE Brewing Company

Detail inset

0   150 yds
0   150 m

WEWATTA ST

PARK AVE W

Ⓟ

Ⓟ

22ND ST

Ⓟ

COORS FIELD

SANDLOT BREWERY AT COORS FIELD

DIAMOND DRY GOODS STORE

HOWL AT THE MOON

MCGREGOR SQUARE ★

WAZEE ST

BLAKE ST

21ST ST

THE MAVEN HOTEL ●

FALLING ROCK TAP HOUSE

19TH ST

Ⓟ

NATIONAL BALLPARK MUSEUM ★

20TH ST

Ⓟ

DAIRY BLOCK ★

DENVER MILK MARKET

LODO

MARKET ST

LARIMER ST

From a **train station** at the airport, you can take the **light rail** operated by **RTD** (Regional Transportation District, www.rtd-denver.com, $10.50 from airport, $3 local rides) to **Union Station** (17th St. and Wynkoop St.) and the popular River North Art District. The station is just a few blocks away from Coors Field.

TRAIN

Built in 1894 in the Romanesque Revival style, iconic railway station **Union Station** (17th St. and Wynkoop St.) is a bustling hub. The cozy interior includes several quick-stop eateries and places to sit, though coming during rush hour or on a weekend afternoon likely means fighting crowds. The station is served by **Amtrak** (www.amtrak.com) via the **California Zephyr** line. That train continues west to Salt Lake City toward the Bay Area, and heads east through the Great Plains to Chicago.

From Union Station, it's less than a half mile to Coors Field. Just go east on Wynkoop Street to 19th Street, turn right, then turn left two blocks later down Blake Street.

BUS

Greyhound (www.greyhound.com) deposits and picks up passengers at the **Denver Bus Station** (1055 19th St., 303/293-6555), a half-mile walk down 19th Street from Coors Field.

Coors Field

Would you believe that **Coors Field** (2001 Blake St., www.mlb.com/rockies) is the third-oldest National League ballpark in existence? Opened in 1995, the second home of the Colorado Rockies (they played at the now-demolished Mile High Stadium from 1993-1994) trails only Wrigley Field and Dodger Stadium in age, and although it looks a bit dated, it's held up astonishingly well.

Made of brick and steel and sitting more than 5,000 feet above sea level, Coors is known as a home-run hitter's heaven. And it's true—you're bound to see a few blasts when you attend a Rockies home game, even though the park's famed humidor attempts to keep balls from flying too much. Despite the many dingers, this is a pretty big ballpark with a huge outfield and some interesting angles, befitting the wide-open spaces and dramatic backdrops you'll find in Colorado. Coors Field is also one of the only ballparks left with seats way out in center field: The Rockpile is a must-visit for fans, and best yet, seats here can be among the cheapest in baseball.

Coors Field is also famed for its beer, naturally. There's a brewery inside the ballpark, and its portfolio includes one of the most popular beers in America. Otherwise, the park offers plenty of beer from across the macro-brewed and microbrewed worlds, and there's even an option for snagging a really cheap beer before the game.

You can drink up outside the park, too, as Coors sits in the LoDo neighborhood, a popular evening haunt with bars and restaurants. Adjacent to the park is a mixed-use development that aims to attract more fans to the area for food, entertainment, and shopping before and after the game. There's plenty to do around here, from watching homers fly to throwing back some brews.

ORIENTATION

Coors Field anchors LoDo (Lower Downtown). It's at the intersection of Blake Street and 20th Street. Restaurants and bars are just a stone's throw from the park.

There are five entry gates at Coors Field. The home plate entrance, **Gate D,** is the most popular and picturesque.

TICKETS AND SEATING

Pricing

The Rockies were the very first team in major league baseball to institute **dynamic pricing.** Today at Coors Field, you'll find slightly higher prices for **notable opponents** and **high-demand games.** For, say, a game against Miami on a Wednesday, expect your

Coors Field, home of the Rockies

seat in lower reserved outfield to cost about $25. For a game against the Dodgers on a Saturday night, that same seat may cost about $35-40. Along with the Dodgers, expect the rare visit from the Yankees or Red Sox to cost a little more. Cardinals and Cubs games may be a little pricier than average, too, since their fan bases reach out toward the Rockies.

On the day of the game, cheap **Rockpile seats** may become available two hours before first pitch. These tickets cost $4 ($1 seniors ages 55 and older and children ages 12 and under). Tickets to **The Rooftop** (sections 301-314), a **standing-room-only** area, start at $16 and include a $6 concession credit.

Seating Plan

Since Coors Field is one of the older ballparks in existence (yes, you read that right),

there aren't as many seating areas within each level as in the newer stadiums.

In the **100 level,** seating starts in right field as the **right field box** (sections 105-109); in right field along the foul line is the **outfield box** (sections 110-117), and just beyond the first-base bag is the **midfield box** (sections 118-119). Around the infield to third base is the **infield box** (sections 120-141), and just beyond the third-base bag is the **midfield box** (sections 142-143). Up along the left-field foul line is the **outfield box** (sections 144-150), and out in left field is the **pavilion** (sections 151-160).

Up on the **200 level,** you have the **right field mezzanine** (sections 201-209) across right field, then in foul territory in deep right field is the **club level, outfield** (sections 214-219). Above the infield is **club level,**

infield (sections 221-227 and 234-241), and in foul territory in deep left field is the **club level, outfield** (sections 242-247). Between the 200 and 300 levels are **suites** and **party areas.**

Seats in the **300 level** are split into the lower rows and higher rows. In right field are the **lower reserved** (sections 301-313) down low and **The Rooftop** (sections 301-314) up high. Along the right-field foul line are **lower reserved outfield** and **upper reserved outfield** (sections 315-319), around the infield are **lower reserved infield** and **upper reserved infield** (sections 321-340), and along the left-field foul line are **lower reserved outfield** and **upper reserved outfield** (sections 342-347).

Finally, well beyond the center-field fence, up high on **bleachers,** is the **Rockpile** (sections 401-403), a cheap way to watch the game from afar.

Where to Buy Tickets

The best bet for tickets is typically the Rockies website, though if you wait until the last minute, you can score decent tickets on a third-party site like **SeatGeek, Gametime,** or **StubHub.**

If you want **Rockpile seats,** wait until just before the game, then walk to the ticket counter. You may be able to score a really cheap seat.

The Rockies are on the **MLB Ballpark app,** so you can upgrade your seat once you get into the park if you buy tickets via the team or on StubHub.

YOUR BEST DAY AT COORS FIELD

So, you've got a hot date tonight to watch a Rockies game at Coors Field. Here's what you should do in Denver before you head to the stadium.

12 HOURS BEFORE FIRST PITCH
For an adventure, get up early and make the drive west to **North Table Mountain** for a hike. To do the 6.6-mile loop, plan on being out here for four hours.

7.5 HOURS BEFORE FIRST PITCH
Drive back into the city. You're probably hungry, which means it's time to fill up on something from the massive menu at **Sam's No. 3,** like a breakfast burrito.

6 HOURS BEFORE FIRST PITCH
Use this time to head back to the hotel, change, and leave your car behind. Opt to take RTD or a ride-share vehicle into LoDo, as you'll be here the rest of the day. If you'd rather drive, find a parking garage in Downtown Denver within a mile of Coors Field.

5 HOURS BEFORE FIRST PITCH
Peruse the shops and bars at **Dairy Block**

North Table Mountainn

Rockies logo

to be part of the Denver social scene. After that, pay a visit to the **National Ballpark Museum** just a block away.

3.5 HOURS BEFORE FIRST PITCH
Grab a ride to **Great Divide Brewing** and down a Yeti imperial stout or two.

1 HOUR BEFORE FIRST PITCH
Get to know some of the locals with a visit to **Blake Street Tavern.** Head inside **Coors Field** just before first pitch.

DURING THE GAME
Spend a good amount of time at **The Rooftop.** Munch on the Colorado Queso Stak at the **Rooftop Grill.** Learn about one of America's most popular beers at **SandLot Brewery at Coors Field,** and spend an inning catching the game from a mile up in the **purple row.**

AFTER THE GAME
If you're looking to party, ride-share it to RiNo. Visit **Crooked Stave** first, then hit up **Ratio Beerworks** later in the evening.

Best Seats

The good seats at this ballpark are along the **third-base line,** where the **shade** is more plentiful. I suggest **lower reserved infield** (sections 335-340), as you can see the whole field, it's not too expensive, and you can catch a beautiful **sunset** over the Rockies during an evening game. The first-base side at Coors gets all the sun, so if you want to sit there, wear sunblock. (Bring sunblock no matter where you sit.)

The **Rockpile** (sections 401-403) is great for first-timers or diehards hoping to meet some folks and have a good time watching the game. Just know that you'll be way out in center field and a bit **far from the action** at the plate.

KNOW BEFORE YOU GO

Bags and **soft-sided coolers** that are no larger than 16 by 16 by 8 inches are allowed inside Coors Field. **Outside food** is also allowed in, as long as it fits inside your bag or cooler. Electronic cigarettes and vape pens are prohibited at Coors Field, as is marijuana.

Pack for variable weather conditions. Even during midsummer nights, the temperature could bottom out in the 40s, so bring a **heavy jacket** or **coat,** along with **sunblock.**

If you need to be inside and away from the elements, you can visit the **Captain's Deck** (sections 201-203), an enclosed, glass-walled space with great views. Walk-ins are allowed, but entry is subject to available space. Nursing mothers can visit the **UCHealth Nursing Suite** (section 114) for breastfeeding and pumping.

You can head to **Gates B, C,** or **D** if you don't have a bag—those are **express lane** gates that'll get you in quickly.

Accessibility

All five **entry gates** are **accessible** at Coors Field, but Gate A has **elevators** and **ramps.** The other ramp in the stadium is at Gate E. **Elevators** are also located at sections 105, 111, 130, and 147, and underneath the Rockpile in center field.

Visit the **guest relations center** (section 127) for **assistive listening devices.** For **wheelchair** service to or from your seat, speak to a guest relations representative. The Rockies have imposed a 250-pound weight limit on their wheelchairs. **Service dogs** and service dogs-in-training are welcome at Coors Field.

The best place for **accessible parking** is in the front of Lot A, adjacent to Gate A. It costs $18 to park in this lot.

GETTING THERE

Coors Field is conveniently located in the LoDo area, so if you're staying in Downtown, LoDo, or Five Points/River North Art District, you have options. First, you could walk—Denver has a very walkable

GAME COSTS

Tickets: Rockpile and Rooftop seats should be less than **$20,** and you can get good 300 level seats for around **$25.** Lower bowl seats will cost you more like **$40-70.** These prices aren't too bad compared with the rest of the league.

Hot dog: The basic option (the Rookie Dog) should cost around **$5.50,** slightly higher than average, while upgrades and more gourmet fare will run you up to **$10.**

Beer: Not bad relative to the rest of the league. It'll be around **$9** for a 16-ounce craft beer or a 20-ounce macro-brew. On The Rooftop before the game, you can score a 12-ounce beer for **$3,** the cheapest in the major leagues.

Parking: The three main Coors Field lots will run you **$20.** In LoDo and Downtown, you can find parking lots in the **$10-15** range.

Downtown, and even the hotels by the Colorado Convention Center are just a mile from the ballpark (about a 20-minute walk). If you're south of I-70, take a ride-share vehicle, as you're looking at a 40-minute walk.

Public Transit

If you're staying outside Downtown Denver, you might want to check if you can take RTD's **light rail** (www.rtd-denver.com, $3-5.25 per ride). Take the train to **Union Station** (17th St. and Wynkoop St.) and walk four blocks northeast to the ballpark.

The closest River North stop is the **38th/Blake station** (38th St. and Blake St.), just one stop north of Union Station on the **A Line.** If you're staying in the Cherry Creek area, you'll want to hop on the train at **Colorado station** (Evans Ave. and S. Birch St.). Pay at one of the stand-alone machines before hopping on the train, then show your ticket to the attendant.

BE A FAN

You have nothing to worry about when you visit Coors Field as a fan of any team. Rockies fans are generous and kind, so feel free to wear your home team's gear.

One tradition to look for: In the ninth inning, if the Rockies have a lead and their pitcher throws a strike, you'll hear a remix of Karl Jenkins's suite *Palladio* in snippets. It's played to hype up the crowd as the final out draws ever closer; you'll hear fans clapping along.

Dinger, the Rockies' mascot

Driving

If you plan on driving to Coors Field, **I-25** exits right onto 20th Street beside the ballpark. **Park Avenue** also funnels cars toward the stadium, so you could take that exit off I-25 if necessary. Downtown streets generally go one way, alternating direction from one street to the next parallel street.

There are three main Coors Field parking lots: **A** (Park Ave. and Wazee St.), **B** (27th St. and Blake St.), and **C** (21st St. and Blake St.). They're all within a three-minute walk of the ballpark, and each costs about $20. There are also plenty of **private garages** right around the ballpark—consider driving south on 17th Street, then north on 20th Street to find something that works for your budget. You can find lots that cost $10 within a half-mile walk of the park.

PARK FEATURES AND SIGHTS

The art installation *The Evolution of the Ball* was commissioned by the Rockies and created by Lonnie Hanzon for the opening of Coors Field. The 23-foot-high sculpture forms an archway that features 108 balls from all kinds of sports, blending right in with the aesthetics of the ballpark. Once serving as an entrance of sorts into Coors Field, *The Evolution of the Ball* was uprooted from its original spot in 2019 due to the construction of McGregor Square, an entertainment district

abutting the park. Controversy ensued, as the sculpture wasn't originally in the plans for the square. The Rockies eventually settled on the work's new location in the square, near the pedestrian bridge over 20th Street.

McGregor Square (Wazee St. and 20th St., across from third-base side of ballpark), adjacent to Coors Field, is a flashy playground for tourists and residents. The space covers 25,000 square feet and is anchored by a 16-story building. Look for a grass berm, a multimedia screen, a Rockies Hall of Fame area, and retail and food options, along with a hotel and residences.

One way in which Coors Field lags behind other ballparks is with children's activities. There's an **interactive area** (Gate A, section 105) with a speed pitch and T-ball cage, but no miniature ball field or play area.

The Purple Row

Take a hike to any section in the 300 level, then head to the 20th row. You'll notice that all the seats in that row—and every seat in the 20th row of all the other sections in the 300 level—are purple. The **purple row** marks the point in which you are 5,280 feet (or one mile) above sea level. (The field at Coors is 5,200 feet above sea level.) Denver's altitude is, of course, why it's called the Mile High City.

The Rooftop

Out at the top of the right-field stands is **The**

Rooftop (sections 301-314). I contend no other spot at a major league park offers this good a view: Downtown Denver is close by, and a bit farther off is the Front Range of the Rocky Mountains. The Rooftop has a number of bars and food vendors, as well as a VIP area of cabanas and an urban garden. Most of this area is standing-room-only, and while anyone can enter, inexpensive tickets are sold for people to stay up here.

FOOD AND DRINKS

Back when Coors Field was being built in the early 1990s, during the first great American craft beer wave, the team had the ingenious idea of putting a brewery right in the ballpark. The result is **SandLot Brewery at Coors Field** (22nd St. and Blake St., right field at main concourse, section 112, open on game days, 90 minutes before first pitch until end of game). Every beer lover should pay SandLot a visit. It's the birthplace of Belly Slide Wit. You may not have heard that name before, but you have heard of what this beer was renamed: Blue Moon, one of the most successful American beers of the last 25 years. SandLot has dozens of beers on tap, both its own recipes, including a bunch of Blue Moon varietals, and plenty of lighter brews.

Of course, considering that the park is called Coors Field, you'll find a slew of Miller- and Coors-brand beers, from Miller High Life to options from Colorado Native. For true craft, head up to the bar at **The Rooftop** (sections 301-314), which has a good selection. Bonus: You can get select macro-brew beers for $3 before first pitch—this is the cheapest beer at any major league park.

The park offers some good food and drink options from local folks. **CHUBurger** (The Rooftop) offers an affordable burger that's pretty decent, though the patties are thin. **Rio on the Rocks** (The Rooftop) has big, boozy margaritas. **Biker Jim's** (sections 107, 331) is the sausage king of Colorado, serving up game and other wild meats (try the elk jalapeño cheddar).

You can grab a **Helton Burger** (named after Rockies legend Todd Helton) along with onion rings and a shake at **Helton Burger Shack** (section 153). But if you really want to impress your friends and family members, dive into some **Rocky Mountain oysters** (section 144). No, you will not get 6 or 12 nicely shucked oysters; Rocky Mountain oysters are fried bull testicles. For a big meal up in The Rooftop, eye the **Colorado Queso Stak** at the **Rooftop Grill** (section 305). This dish consists of a bunch of waffle fries with green chili, carnitas, and nacho toppings.

If you want a more refined meal at the park, book a table in advance for **Mountain Ranch Bar and Grill** (200 level, right field, seating 90 minutes before first pitch and during game, under $40), serving steak, barbecue sandwiches, and gourmet salads, and boasting a wine list. This spot is good for the view and the chance to sit and have a calmer experience; don't expect award-winning food.

Another good sit-down area is **Wazee Market** (section 137), a large courtyard area with high-top tables. You'll find straightforward grub like pizza and sandwiches here.

EVENTS

If you want an **autograph** from a player, head to sections 116-121 and 142-146 up to 40 minutes before first pitch. The first Sunday home game of each month is **Autograph Sunday** (sections 116-120, 11:40am-noon). Players, coaches, and Rockies alumni sign autographs on these days for about 20 minutes.

Kids who want to meet **Dinger,** a purple dinosaur and the Rockies' mascot, should head toward center field on the main concourse around the bottom of the second inning. An **autograph session** with Dinger starts at the top of the third and ends in the middle of the fourth.

The Rockies hold a monthly **dollar hot dog night.**

Tours

The Rockies host year-round **tours**

(303/762-5437, 10am, noon, and 2pm daily non-game days in season; 10am and noon night games in season; noon and 2pm daily off-season, $12, $10 seniors, $9 ages 12 and under) that typically visit the dugout and field, visitor's clubhouse, press level, club levels, and The Rooftop.

SHOPPING

The main team store is the **Diamond Dry Goods Store** (2001 Blake St., 10am-6pm Mon.-Sat. during season, 10am-5:30pm Mon.-Fri., 10am-4pm Sat. off-season), a throwback compared with the newer team stores found in ballparks across the country. It sells the usual collection of jerseys, hats, and lighthearted memorabilia. The store closes to the public 2.5 hours before gates open on game day, but is open to ticket holders once the gates open.

DENVER SIGHTS

LARIMER SQUARE

Larimer Square (Larimer St. and 14th St., www.larimersquare.com) is a gentrified block of Downtown Denver with shopping, entertainment, and eating options. At night the twinkle lights come on, and often the block hosts street fairs and other parties. The block is home to **Comedy Works** (1226 15th St., 303/595-3637, www.comedyworks.com), which pulls in national touring stand-up acts every weekend. Be sure to take a moment to admire the buildings at the square, some of which date to the 1800s.

DAIRY BLOCK

Close to Coors Field is **Dairy Block** (19th St. and Wazee St., www.dairyblock.com), the former Windsor Dairy complex that's been completely reimagined as a retail, dining, co-working, and hospitality district for tourists and the Instagram set. On the block is **Denver Milk Market** (1800 Wazee St.,

www.denvermilkmarket.com, 7am-11pm Sun.-Thurs., 7am-1am Fri.-Sat.), a food hall with 16 vendors that sell dishes like pizza, Chinese dumplings, breakfast sandwiches, and fried chicken.

DENVER ART MUSEUM

Part of the Denver Civic Center, the **Denver Art Museum** (100 W. 14th Ave., 720/865-5000, www.denverartmuseum.org, 10am-5pm Sat.-Thurs., 10am-8pm Fri., $10-13, $8-10 seniors and students, free ages 18 and younger), also called DAM, is housed in an iconic, seven-story building that looks like an abstract version of a fortified castle. The museum has an impressive collection of American Indian art, covering nearly every Indigenous group in the United States and Canada. There's a good deal of classic European and American art as well, plus changing exhibitions that focus on everything from mixed media to different periods in European history. Tours of the regular collections are offered; you may want to reserve your space in advance.

NATIONAL BALLPARK MUSEUM

Just kitty-corner from home plate at Coors Field, the **National Ballpark Museum** (1940 Blake St., 303/974-5835, www.ballparkmuseum.com, 11am-5pm Tues.-Sat., $10, $5 seniors) is a necessary stop for any baseball fan, especially someone taking a ballpark trip. You'll get to see chairs from old stadiums like Sportsman's Park and Griffith Stadium, and you'll find ephemera from places like Fenway Park, such as an old cart that once sold Fenway Franks. You can thank Bruce Hellerstein for the place, as this is all his personal collection, displayed for the public to see. (He'll probably be there, and he likes to chat). Ballpark history is written out across the exhibits, and game-worn jerseys, old programs, and pennants add to the experience. The museum is small but absolutely worth the money.

DENVER ZOO

At the **Denver Zoo** (2300 Steele St., 730/337-1400, www.denverzoo.org, 9am-4pm daily, $20, $17 seniors, $14 ages 3-11, free ages 2 and under), you can find lions, buffalo, grizzly bears, bald eagles, and gorillas, among other animals. You'll especially want to visit the Toyota Elephant Passage, a vast habitat with two miles of trails. Encounters with animals like rhinoceroses, penguins, and even tigers are available. Little kids might also want to hop on the train ($2-3) or carousel ($2-3).

FOOD

NEAR COORS FIELD

Want an awesome dinner experience before or after the game? Head over to **Super-MegaBien** (1260 25th St., 720/269-4695, www.supermegabien.com, 5pm-10pm Tues.-Thurs., 5pm-11pm Fri.-Sat., under $40), which serves Latin American food as a dim sum experience. This means that you'll pick items off a cart that servers roll through the dining room. The restaurant also offers family-style meals like jerk chicken with beans, tortillas, and sides. The space is modern, dynamic, and colorful. It's a really fun place—get here a little early to grab a seat, as there are no reservations.

If you're looking for good, simple ballpark grub near the park, there aren't many options. The LoDo area has Dairy Block, which includes a bunch of buzzy contemporary spots, while Downtown has a slew of hotel restaurants and expensive steak houses. But there is **Marco's Coal Fired** (2129 Larimer St., 303/296-7000, www.marcoscfp.com, 11am-10pm Sun.-Thurs., 11am-11pm Fri.-Sat., under $30), which dishes out fantastic Neapolitan pies, New York-style pizza, and

Photos (from top to bottom): Larimer Square; Denver Art Museum; entrance to Denver Zoo.

even vegan and gluten-free offerings. This is a popular place, so you may have to wait a few minutes for that pizza.

Cherry Cricket (2220 Blake St., 303/297-3644, www.cherrycricket.com, 11am-midnight Sun.-Thurs., 11am-2am Fri.-Sat., under $20) is a Denver mainstay that serves up some darn good burgers with plenty of toppings to choose from. The brick-walled space is pretty large, and there are arcade games, so you can chill with a drink.

If you're going to a day game, you can't go wrong with some breakfast or brunch beforehand. Near the park is the original location of the popular chain **Snooze, an A.M. Eatery** (2262 Larimer St., 303/297-0700, www.snoozeeatery.com, 6:30am-2:30pm daily, under $40). Snooze is known for its pancake flights (the sweet potato is tremendous) and its diverse collection of Bloody Marys. It's a bright, mod space that will have a line on weekend mornings and afternoons.

OTHER NEIGHBORHOODS

To fulfill your need for fried chicken and southern delights in a polished, contemporary setting, up in the hip RiNo/Five Points area is **Julep** (3258 Larimer St., 303/295-8977, www.julepino.com, 5pm-9pm Wed.-Thurs., 5pm-10pm Fri., 11am-2:30pm and 5pm-10pm Sat., 10am-2:30pm Sun., under $40). You must order the biscuits. Try ordering a few snack items for the table. The menu changes seasonally.

A bit of a Denver necessity, **Sam's No. 3** (1500 Curtis St., 303/534-1927, www.samsno3.com, 5:30am-10pm Mon.-Wed., 5:30am-11pm Thurs., 5:30am-midnight Fri., 7am-midnight Sat., 7am-10pm Sun., under $25) is a classic Downtown diner that originated in 1927. Expect a brisk but comfortable atmosphere plus an enormous menu with breakfast, lunch, and dinner options. Get a breakfast burrito for cheap, Greek grub (including lamb with your eggs), Mexican staples, boozy coffee, trout, big salads, club sandwiches, prime rib, and, oh yeah, a Denver omelet.

BARS AND BREWERIES

NEAR COORS FIELD

Occupying a small footprint but offering big flavors, **Great Divide Brewing** (2201 Arapahoe St., 303/296-9460, www.greatdivide.com, noon-10pm daily) is among my favorite breweries in America. If you're on the fence about visiting Great Divide, I have one word for you: Yeti. One of the best imperial stouts in the world, Yeti is always on tap here, along with some other killer beers. Although there's a bit of seating and standing space inside, there's a nice little alfresco area on the sidewalk. Pick up some of the brewery's merch while you're here.

About a 15-minute walk southeast from Coors Field is **Woods Boss Brewing Company** (2210 California St., 720/642-7177, www.woodsbossbrewing.com, 2pm-10pm Mon.-Thurs., noon-11pm Fri.-Sat.), which takes its name seriously. This place looks like a warm wilderness lodge with plenty of wood and leather. The beer is pretty darn good, focusing on IPA and fun stuff like kettle sour beers and hops-based experiments.

There are a fair number of sports bars near Coors Field that fill up well before Rockies games. Of all these places, the best is **Blake Street Tavern** (2301 Blake St., 303/675-0505, www.blakestreettavern.com, 11am-2am Mon.-Fri., 9am-2am Sat., 10am-2am Sun.), with a long patio area that serves as a tempting draw for fans, and the Underground Social, a basement game room with Skee-Ball, a miniature basketball-in-hoop game, and more. The best move is to get some cheap beer and enjoy the crowd.

After the game, you can head to dueling piano bar chain **Howl at the Moon** (1735 19th St.) for a party atmosphere, but I suggest **Falling Rock Tap House** (1919 Blake St., 303/293-8338, www.fallingrocktaphouse.com, 11am-2am daily) for its extensive beer selection. Harder-to-find stuff, local labels—it's all here. It's a cozy place with a few televisions and food on offer.

OTHER NEIGHBORHOODS

You can do a beer crawl in RiNo/Five Points. I'd definitely hit **Ratio Beerworks** (2920 Larimer St., 303/997-8288, www.ratiobeerworks. com, noon-11pm Sun.-Wed., noon-midnight Thurs.-Sat.), a great spot to start a crawl. It has plenty of space including a bustling patio. The beer is pretty good, with an emphasis on flavorful standby styles like saison and American light lager.

A block away is **Our Mutual Friend Brewing Company** (2810 Larimer St., 720/722-2810, www.omfmb.com, 4pm-10pm Mon.-Thurs., noon-midnight Fri.-Sat., noon-10pm Sun.), a funky, small place with color and character, plus beer names that often take the name of song titles. There are lots of fun IPA options, along with a few other styles, and the brewery uses all-Colorado ingredients whenever possible. There's some patio space, too.

Inside the Market Hall at the Source Hotel is one of America's most interesting breweries. **Crooked Stave** (3330 Brighton Blvd., 720/550-8860, www.crookedstave.com, noon-8pm Sun.-Tues., noon-10pm Wed.-Sat.) produces IPAs, pilsners, sours, and a whole host of barrel-aged and wild fermentation beers. This spot is a must if you're into sours and wild fermentation. They're known for high-quality, adventurous brews.

For great farmhouse beers and heavy metal, there's **TRVE Brewing Company** (227 Broadway #101, www.trvebrewing. com, 3pm-11pm Mon.-Thurs., noon-midnight Fri.-Sat., noon-10pm Sun.). In this killer black-walled taproom, decorated with candles and medieval-esque images, you can enjoy fresh beer with fruit additions and live cultures, all to a soundtrack of thrash, doom, and other metal styles.

RECREATION

More than a few people move to Denver solely for the recreation. Rocky Mountain National Park is just 90 minutes northwest of Downtown Denver. Just a day trip away are peaks as high as 14,000 feet (they're called "fourteeners," and people make a point to summit as many of them as possible). Add to that the water sports, skiing, and good old-fashioned running, and you'll never be bored in the Denver area.

ROCKY MOUNTAIN NATIONAL PARK

If you have at least four days in Denver, I highly recommend a trip to **Rocky Mountain National Park** (Estes Park, 970/586-1206, www.nps.gov, $25 per car). The park has all the best things about the great outdoors: awesome camping, wildlife viewing (including elk and moose), and outstanding hiking.

My absolute favorite hike in the park is **Sky Pond via Glacier Gorge** (trailhead at Bear Lake Rd., 8 miles from US-36 at Beaver Meadows Entrance, Estes Park, 9 miles round-trip). You'll have a scenic, moderate hike for much of the way, but once you start climbing, it becomes far more challenging. Even in June, you're likely to encounter some snow on the trail. (Bring boots and traction devices for the soles.) Eventually, you'll approach an incredible waterfall, **Timberline Falls.** You can stop here and take in awesome views of the park, but I recommend continuing by climbing alongside the falls to a plateau that includes a body of water called the **Lake of Glass.** Farther on, you'll reach **Sky Pond,** a crystal-clear pool that will take your breath away. Once you're ready, turn back and return the way you came. Start this hike in the early morning, and if starts to rain, think about turning back.

When at the park, you'll have your choice: hiking with elevation or hiking along tundra. If it's not too sunny, consider an alpine tundra hike like the **Ute Trail** (trailhead at Ute Crossing, 10 miles west of Deer Ridge Junction on Trail Ridge Rd., Estes Park, 4 miles round-trip). This relatively easy hike for elevation will give you an opportunity to look for elk and take in some views of the Continental Divide. It's best to hike this in the morning, as rain is more likely to come later in the afternoon.

On the way to or from the park, stop in **Lyons** to have a beer at **Oskar Blues Grill & Brew** (303 Main St., Lyons, 303/823-6685, www.oskarbluesfooderies.com, 11am-10pm Sun.-Thurs., 11am-11pm Fri.-Sat.). This is the origin of Oskar Blues, now one of America's most recognized craft breweries. Their Dale's Pale Ale is a groundbreaking beer, proving a solid-drinking craft IPA can be canned.

Estes Park, the eastern gateway to Rocky Mountain National Park, is a 65-mile, 1.5-hour drive from Downtown Denver. It's an easy drive via I-25 North and US-36 West.

HIKING

Closer to Denver, you can easily get out of the car and stretch those legs on a good hike. An easy outing is **The Bluffs** at **Bluffs Regional Park** (10099 Crooked Stick Trail, Lone Tree, www.douglas.co.us, sunrise-sunset daily). This loop trail of about 2.5 miles is best done counterclockwise, as you'll be descending during the steepest parts instead of ascending. The trail provides gorgeous views of the Front Range of the Rocky Mountains and the Denver skyline.

For a bigger challenge just a half hour west of the city, visit **North Table Mountain Park** (Easley Rd., 0.3 mile north of SH-58, Golden, www.jeffco.us, one hour before sunrise-one hour after sunset daily). From the park's East Access, you can take the **North Table Loop Trail** or cut into the interior via the **Mesa Top Trail** and **Tilting Mesa Trail**. The full loop is about 6.6 miles (a four-hour hike) and provides beautiful vistas. Do look out for rattlesnakes. To get there from Downtown Denver, take I-25 North, I-70 West, and SH-58 West, exiting at McIntyre Street. This drive is less than 20 miles.

PARKS

About 20 minutes southeast of Downtown Denver is **Cherry Creek State Park** (4201 S. Parker Rd., Aurora), home to an 880-acre reservoir that offers opportunities for fishing, boating, and swimming. If you're boating with a motorboat or sailboat, you'll need a **stamp** (www.cpwshop.com, $25-50) to launch. A sandy beach, open Memorial Day to Labor Day, is roped off for family enjoyment, but lifeguards are not on duty. **Camping** (303/766-6562, www.cpwshop.com) is permitted, and there are picnic spaces, trails, and a **model airplane field** (www.

Sky Pond, Rocky Mountain National Park

denverrceagles.org) where out-of-staters are welcome to fly, as long as they have a current Academy of Model Aeronautics membership and follow club rules.

Just a few minutes east of Downtown is the 330-acre **City Park** (2001 Colorado Blvd.), established in 1882. This is where the zoo is, as well as the **Denver Museum of Nature & Science** (2001 Colorado Blvd., 303/370-6000, www.dmns.org, 9am-5pm daily, $20, $17 seniors, $15 ages 3-18, free ages 2 and under), home to a children's activity area plus dinosaur fossils and Egyptian mummies. Also at the park is **Ferril Lake**. Head to the park's 1929 Spanish-style, goldenrod-colored pavilion to rent a paddleboat for the lake. Fishing is allowed, and there are plenty of picnic areas and easy, family-friendly trails.

ACCOMMODATIONS

NEAR COORS FIELD

With 172 rooms, including some with soaking tubs and balconies, **The Maven Hotel** (1850 Wazee St., 720/460-2727, www.themavenhotel.com, $200-350) is just a six-minute walk from Coors Field at Dairy Block. Besides a nice view of Coors Field, its diamond suite has a wet bar, dining room table, and work space.

Heading northeast up Market Street, there's **Stay Alfred at the Ballpark** (2200 Market St., 866/232-3864, www.stayalfred.com, $120-250), the Denver location of the boutique chain. Stay Alfred has studios, lofts, regular rooms, and split-level suites. The draw here is the eighth-floor deck that provides a view of Coors Field (you can't see the field, though).

OTHER NEIGHBORHOODS

If you want to be in RiNo/Five Points, stay at the **Source Hotel** (3330 Brighton Blvd., 720/409-1200, www.thesourcehotel.com, $200-350). Visit the large market hall attached to the hotel, home to about 25 eateries, retailers, and artisans, like Crooked Stave, a top brewery. As for the hotel itself, it has well-appointed contemporary rooms. A warning, though: The hotel has concrete walls, ceilings, and floors. It could get loud.

Budget travelers can find a host of chain hotels in the Cherry Creek area in Glendale, along Colorado Boulevard between Alameda Avenue and I-25. These include **Hampton Inn & Suites** (4150 E. Kentucky Ave., Glendale, 303/692-1800, www.hamptoninn3.hilton.com, $150-300), **Staybridge Suites** (4220 E. Virginia Ave., Glendale, 303/321-5757, www.ihg.com, $200-350), and **Holiday Inn** (455 S. Colorado Blvd., 303/388-5561, www.ihg.com, $150-300).

GETTING AROUND

PUBLIC TRANSIT

Denver's public transit system is run by **RTD** (www.rtd-denver.com, $10.50 from airport, $3 local rides). The main train station is **Union Station** (17th St. and Wynkoop St.), and all **light rail** lines meet there. The closest River North stop is the **38th/Blake station** (38th St. and Blake St.), just one stop north of Union Station on the **A Line.** If you're staying in the Cherry Creek area, you'll want to hop on the train at **Colorado Station** (Evans Ave. and S. Birch St.). Pay at a stand-alone machine before taking the light rail, then show your ticket to the attendant. RTD also runs an extensive **bus network** ($3 per ride).

TAXI, UBER, AND LYFT

You'll want to take Uber or Lyft, and the latter is slightly cheaper in Denver. A ride from the airport to Coors Field will cost about $25 on Lyft, closer to $30 on Uber.

CAR

The main thoroughfare in Denver is **I-25,** which runs south to the city from Fort Collins, twisting along the Platte River near

Downtown, then passing the University of Denver before moving south toward Colorado Springs. **I-70** comes in from the east, runs just north of Downtown Denver, then continues west through the Rocky Mountains. **Business I-70, or US-40, is Colfax Avenue,** which serves as the southern boundary of Downtown Denver. And **I-76,** which starts way out on the East Coast, heads in from the northeast and connects with I-25 north of Downtown, then continues until merging with I-70, where it ends.

In Downtown Denver, streets run on a shifted grid, going northwest to southeast, and northeast to southwest. Main roads include **Broadway,** the eastern boundary of Downtown; and **Market and Blake Streets,** which run in opposite directions but connect RiNo to the Auraria neighborhood, home to multiple colleges and close to the Colorado Convention Center.

ALBUQUERQUE, NEW MEXICO

New Mexico's largest city has fielded two professional baseball teams. The first was the Dukes, formed in 1915, who spent the second half of the 20th century as a minor league affiliate for the Giants, Reds, Athletics, and Dodgers. The Dukes left town in 2000, however, moving to Portland, Oregon. That left a baseball-sized hole in the city that was filled three years later when the Calgary Cannons shipped south to New Mexico. But what name would the team choose?

In 2001, *The Simpsons* aired an episode called "Hungry Hungry Homer." In it, Homer Simpson stages a hunger strike outside Springfield's minor league baseball stadium because its team, the Isotopes, was threatening a move to Albuquerque. There's a ring to "Albuquerque Isotopes," and so when the Cannons moved in 2003, the team became just that, taking inspiration from the TV show. Playing in Isotopes Park, the 'Topes are one of the most popular minor league teams in America.

Coming from Denver, you'll want to take a day to stop in Albuquerque, at least to get some rest before you continue to Phoenix. The triple-A baseball team in town gives you all the more reason to hang out.

GETTING THERE

Car
The drive to Albuquerque from **Denver** is **450 miles** and takes **6.5-7 hours** if you take **I-25** the whole way. An alternate route is to take **US-285** west from Denver, then south through Pike and San Isabel National Forests. After 350 miles and just before Santa Fe, you'll turn onto **NM-599 South.** This will connect you with I-25 South, which will bring you into Albuquerque. The **420-mile** drive is a little more than **seven hours** without stopping.

RIO GRANDE CREDIT UNION FIELD AT ISOTOPES PARK

Opened in 2003, **Rio Grande Credit Union Field at Isotopes Park** (1601 Avenida Cesar Chavez SE, 505/924-2255, www.milb.com/albuquerque), or "The Lab," as it's called by some, is home to the **Albuquerque Isotopes,** a triple-A affiliate of the Colorado Rockies. The stadium holds about 13,300 fans, making it one of the largest ballparks in the Pacific Coast League. And as at Coors Field in Denver, the ballpark's elevation of 5,100 feet means balls fly a bit more here.

One of the coolest things about the park is in center field: Isotopes Park's playing field has a **rise** in **straightaway center.** The warning track actually winds beside the interior of the hill, instead of riding the fence. Around the ballpark are **statues** of the characters who helped make this ballpark possible: **Homer, Marge, Bart,** and **Lisa Simpson.** Look for them on benches around the main concourse.

The park has more than a few food options with local flavor. Look for the **Southwest Waffle Nachos,** the **Elote Dog,** and one of the wildest things you'll ever eat, the

Tumbleweed Burger. It's a spicy ghost pepper cheeseburger in a Hatch chile bun, topped off by a huge ball of chile cotton candy. Wash it down with a beer from local brewery **Bosque,** which has offerings at the park.

Like most upper-echelon minor league parks, Isotopes Park has a **lower level** and an **upstairs club level** that stretches around the infield. These seats tend to cost $15-40. There's also second-level **grandstand seating** just beyond third base, which may cost $15-30. Tickets for the **100 level infield seats** (sections 101-116) are a bit more expensive than the **foul territory outfield seats** (sections 117-132) and the **higher grandstand seats** (sections 201-205).

There's a **grassy berm** in right field, a **picnic pavilion** in left field, and the **Jack Daniel's Old No. 7 Club** (section 123), reserved for groups, at the left-field foul pole. Kids can enjoy the **Fun Zone** beyond the berm in right field. This area has a carousel, a tower ride that goes up and down, a playscape, and a basketball court.

FOOD

The chow is great at Downtown Albuquerque's **Dog House Drive In** (1216 Central Ave. NW, 505/243-1019, 10am-8:45pm Mon.-Sat., 11am-8:45pm Sun., under $10), a brick stand-alone with a counter and a bunch of hot dogs. Its claim to fame is its appearance in the TV show *Breaking Bad*. The best order here is a chili dog with cheese. Add onion rings or tater tots with chili and cheese, plus a cherry shake. There are a few tables inside, plus stools at the counter, but it's called "drive in" for a reason. You're fine eating in your car—just don't spill the chili.

Just north of I-40 is **Mary & Tito's Café** (2711 4th St. NW, 505/344-6266, 9am-5:45pm Mon.-Thurs., 9am-7:45pm Fri.-Sat., under $30), the place to hit if you want simple New Mexican fare done as it's been done for decades. We're talking *carne adovada* (pork baked in red chile) and combination plates with *chile relleno* and enchiladas. The basic digs of pastel green and pink will help you feel right at home.

Fun late-night grub can be had at **The Last Call** (420 Central Ave. SW, 505/300-4911, www.lastcallabq.com, 11am-10pm Tues.-Wed., 11am-2:30am Thurs.-Sat., under $30), at the southern end of Downtown. You'll find Cali-Mex burritos, a decadent grilled cheese sandwich, and ridiculously loaded fries on the menu. The sparse interior includes some *lucha libre* (Mexican professional wrestling) decor, but otherwise it's just a couple tables and a bar counter.

BARS AND BREWERIES

You'll want to visit **Bosque Brewing Company** (106 Girard Blvd. SE #B, 505/508-5967, www.bosquebrewing.com, 11am-midnight Mon.-Thurs., 11am-1am Fri.-Sat., 11am-11pm Sun.), whose Public House location in the Nob Hill neighborhood is a popular spot decorated in a modern but rustic style. A robust food menu lists shareable plates like tacos and poutine, plus sandwiches and a few pub-friendly entrées. There's also ample outdoor space with picnic tables.

In Downtown, popular **Marble Brewery** (111 Marble Ave. NW, 505/243-2739, www.marblebrewery.com, noon-midnight Mon.-Fri., 11am-midnight Sat., 11am-10:30pm Sun.) makes some terrific beers, serving them up in a contemporary taproom done with wood and concrete. It has regular concerts, plenty of outdoor seating, and food trucks for grub.

ACCOMMODATIONS

My pick is **Hotel Andaluz Albuquerque** (125 2nd St. NW, 505/242-9090, www.hilton.com, $120-250), part of Hilton's upscale Curio Collection. The Andaluz is set inside what was once Albuquerque's tallest building, a 1939 structure inspired by Spanish architecture. The rooms and suites are clean, if somewhat dated, by about 10 years or so. There's an on-site restaurant, a rooftop lounge with a bar, and private, curtained nooks in the lobby for intimate cocktail hours.

PHOENIX
ARIZONA DIAMONDBACKS

Welcome to the buzzing metropolis in the desert, better known as the Valley of the Sun. The metropolitan area includes Phoenix, the largest city and home to the Diamondbacks, as well as a collection of smaller cities like Mesa, Peoria, Scottsdale, and Tempe. There's a lot of baseball in the Valley of the Sun.

In 1947, Indians owner Bill Veeck moved his club's spring training operation to Tucson; the team had previously trained in Florida. The New York Giants joined Veeck's Indians in Arizona that same year. The Cubs joined the spring training scene in 1952, and as Major League Baseball expanded westward, more franchises sought the desert as a more accessible option for spring baseball. These days, half of MLB's teams train in Florida, and the other half practice in Arizona, in and

around Phoenix. Every February and March, the area teems with ballplayers, coaches, and fans from across the country—Dodgers fans visit Glendale, Cubs fans go to Mesa, Giants fans head to Scottsdale, and Indians and Reds fans truck it to Goodyear. During the summer, the spring training sites are home to rookie-league ball. Starting in late October, the sites host games in the Arizona Fall League, which gives players in the upper levels of the minor leagues an opportunity to experience more game action. You might see some big-time prospects and a few major leaguers in an AFL contest.

A period of outstanding residential, commercial, and industrial growth began in the Valley of the Sun in the 1990s, and with that came the Diamondbacks, the first Major League Baseball franchise in Arizona. The team's ready-made fan base grew exponentially when, just four seasons in, the Diamondbacks won a thrilling, seven-game World Series in 2001 over the Yankees. The fans have stayed loyal over the years, too. Those kids who cheered on players like Luis Gonzalez and Randy Johnson are now taking their kids to Chase Field. Joining them are the scores of newcomers to the area, as the Valley of the Sun continues to be a hot destination for folks wanting a warmer lifestyle.

PLANNING YOUR TIME

Depending on how much baseball you'd like to watch in the Phoenix area, a stay here can be as short as a **weekend** or as long as a **week.** If you're a casual fan, opt for **3-4 days.** You'll want a day to poke around the city, mostly staying indoors to adjust to the heat (if you're coming during the summer), and a day for venturing out into the other cities of the area (maybe taking in a rookie-league game at one of the Cactus League ballparks). Add in a Diamondbacks game, a Camelback Mountain hike, and travel time, and your itinerary is full.

You can stay nearly anywhere in the Valley of the Sun and never be too far from other

locations. If you want to spend most of your time in **Downtown Phoenix,** get a room there. The hotels near **Sky Harbor Airport** are minutes from Downtown, which makes another great option. If you want a more leisurely escape, or if you're determined to drive around the area seeing some Cactus League sites, you can't go wrong staying in **Scottsdale, Tempe,** or **Mesa.**

Since Chase Field has a **retractable roof,** you're practically guaranteed a comfortable setting for the game. Sure, it gets obscenely **hot** in the middle of **summer** in Phoenix, but you won't have to worry about that when the roof is closed and the air-conditioning is humming. That said, if you want to enjoy the outdoors, visit Phoenix and Chase Field in **April,** when the high temperature is normally around 80-85°F. From then until **October,** temps will stay above 85°F and regularly reach the 100s.

If you visit in October for **Arizona Fall League** games (a great idea if you want to see players on the cusp of success), expect highs in the 80s and lows in the 60s. Games start around noon or around 6:30pm, so conditions should be pleasant enough.

GETTING THERE

AIR

Phoenix Sky Harbor International Airport

The efficient **Phoenix Sky Harbor International Airport** (PHX, 3400 E. Sky Harbor Blvd., www.skyharbor.com) has a large **Southwest Airlines** (800/435-9792, www.southwest.com) presence, plus space for **Air Canada** (888/247-2262, www.aircanada.com), **American Airlines** (800/433-7300, www.aa.com), **Delta** (800/221-1212, www.delta.com), **Frontier** (801/401-9000, www.flyfrontier.com), **jetBlue** (800/538-2583, www.jetblue.com), **Spirit** (801/401-2222, www.spirit.com), and **United** (800/864-8331, www.united.com).

Previous: Chase Field in Phoenix, home of the Diamondbacks

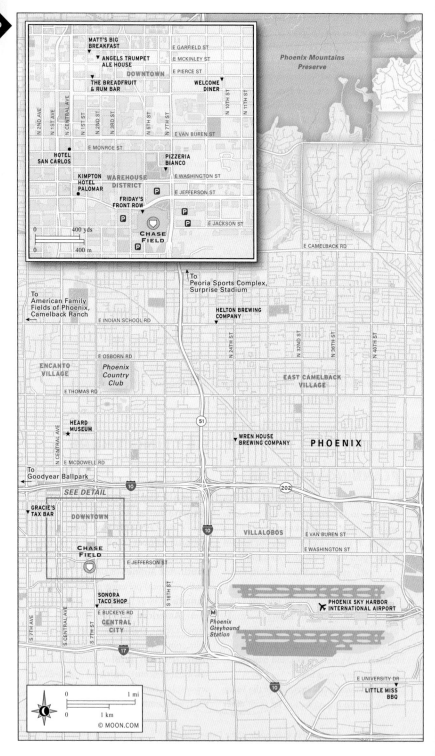

AIRPORT TRANSPORTATION

Rental cars are available from all the big rental companies. The rental car hub is accessible via a free **shuttle** from the terminals. The airport is really close to Chase Field—the park is just a three-mile drive northwest via I-10 West and Jefferson Street.

The free **PHX Sky Train** connects airport travelers to the **44th Street PHX Sky Train Station,** which then takes passengers to Downtown Phoenix via **light rail** operated by **Valley Metro** (www.valleymetro.org, $2 per ride within same city).

Phoenix-Mesa Gateway Airport

The region's other international airport, and much smaller than Sky Harbor, is **Phoenix-Mesa Gateway Airport** (AZA, 6033 S. Sossaman Rd., Mesa, 480/988-7600, www.gatewayairport.com). This airport connects primarily to smaller cities in the West and Midwest, plus Chicago and San Francisco, mostly through **Allegiant** (702/505-8888, www.allegiantair.com). If you're looking to save some money on the flight, it's not a bad option.

AIRPORT TRANSPORTATION

Three **rental car** companies do business inside the lone terminal (another company is off-site). Otherwise, you'll want to taxi, rideshare, or pick up a hotel shuttle, as there's no light rail connection, and the airport is about 40 minutes—without traffic—southeast of Downtown Phoenix.

CAR

The **830-mile, 13-hour** drive from **Denver** to Phoenix is long but, for stretches, quite scenic. You'll take **I-70 West** from Denver about 320 miles to **US-191 South** in Thompson Springs, Utah. Continue on US-191 South across the border and into Arizona before turning onto **US-160 West** (go the other way, on US-160 East, to visit the Four Corners Monument). Stay on US-160 for 126 miles and turn onto **US-89 South,** taking that into Flagstaff. From there, it's another 145 miles on **I-40 West** and **I-17 South** to Phoenix.

TRAIN

Amtrak (www.amtrak.com) doesn't serve Phoenix; the closest station is in **Maricopa** (19427 N. John Wayne Pkwy., Maricopa), a 35-mile drive south of the city (via I-10 South and AZ-347 South). The only lines that come through Maricopa are the **Sunset Limited**—connecting travelers to Los Angeles to the west and Houston and New Orleans to the east—and the **Texas Eagle,** which runs from Los Angeles east to San Antonio and northeast to Chicago. There's no connection to the Maricopa station from Denver.

BUS

It's possible to take **Greyhound** (www.greyhound.com) from Denver to Phoenix, but it's a long trip—at least 18 hours—and prices start at around $130. Buses deposit passengers at the **Phoenix Greyhound Station** (2115 E. Buckeye Rd., 602/389-4200) at an entrance of Phoenix Sky Harbor Airport, a three-mile drive from Downtown Phoenix.

Chase Field

Opened in the Diamondbacks' inaugural 1998 season, **Chase Field** (401 E. Jefferson St., www.mlb.com/dbacks) manages to epitomize the Phoenix experience in ballpark form. Its retractable roof—which stays closed through a good portion of the season—keeps out the punishing desert heat but also creates a hotel-like, air-conditioned environment. Like the resort hotels that populate the area, the park has a swimming pool—a groundbreaking feature when it opened. While there's a severe shortage of charm in the way of local food and drink vendors, there's something fitting about that, as Phoenix's food and drink scene still seems to be developing a character. The little dash of local multicultural color to be found—a vendor devoted to Latin *raspas* (shaved ice) and cocktails—is shoved way back in the upper levels of the venue. In a

YOUR BEST DAY AT CHASE FIELD

You have tickets to a Diamondbacks game this evening. Here's how to maximize your day in Phoenix.

12 HOURS BEFORE FIRST PITCH

Hopefully, you're rested, because we're starting with a hike of **Camelback Mountain.** Follow the **Cholla Trail,** bring plenty of water, and pace yourself during the grueling ascent and rock scramble. Reaching the summit will feel so good.

8 HOURS BEFORE FIRST PITCH

You've earned the eggs, meat, and toast you're about to consume at **Matt's Big Breakfast.** Tell everyone you hiked Camelback while downing two cups of coffee.

6 HOURS BEFORE FIRST PITCH

Hop in the car and take a tour of the Phoenix area's **spring training sites.** Maybe visit **Sloan Park,** home to Cubs' spring ball and the Arizona Cubs, a rookie-league team.

If your Diamondbacks game is an afternoon affair, you could catch some Arizona rookie-league ball, as most games start at 7pm. Here's another option: Take a quick nap.

view from Camelback Mountain

The Draft Room

3 HOURS BEFORE FIRST PITCH

Head Downtown and pay a pregame visit to **Angels Trumpet Ale House.** You could try to find a parking spot up in the Evans Churchill neighborhood, or maybe you're ride-sharing by now. Either way, think about ride-sharing to the game. While at Angels Trumpet, have a beer and some pub grub.

1.5 HOURS BEFORE FIRST PITCH

Head over to **Chase Field.** Your first stop in the ballpark should be **The Draft Room.** Enjoy a drink or two while getting to know a couple fans and scoping out the view.

DURING THE GAME

Pep yourself up with a Freeze at **Dutch Bros.** If you're really feeling gluttonous, chase it with a **churro dog.** If you're with kids, pay a visit to **The Sandlot** early in the game to tire out the tykes. Be sure to check out the **20th Anniversary Experience** to get an understanding of Diamondbacks history.

AFTER THE GAME

There are two things you must do, so drive or ride-share back north into Evans Churchill. Party with some friends at **Gracie's Tax Bar,** then head over to Garfield to load up on carbs and protein at **Welcome Diner.** That's a happy night.

city where you often have to squint to find the centuries-long cultural influence of local Indigenous people, it's an unfortunate, but not surprising, reality.

This isn't to say Chase Field has no good qualities. For one, it's easy to walk about the park and take in the ball game. Plus, the employees are very cordial, and the ballpark is home to one of the best family sections in baseball. As a cool indoor place to take the kids in the middle of an always-unforgiving season, Chase Field stands tall.

Chase Field

ORIENTATION

Located smack in the middle of Downtown Phoenix, the park is very accessible and is easy to spot thanks to its boxy enormity. There are eight entry gates at Chase Field. Because 7th Street runs past the park like a two-lane highway, many of the gates are on the west side of the park, near 4th Street.

TICKETS AND SEATING

Pricing

Like many teams, the Diamondbacks use **dynamic ticket pricing. Dodgers, Padres,** and **Rockies** games may be more expensive tickets than games against most other opponents. You can expect to pay about $35 for a middle-of-the-road seat at a game against

the Dodgers, while that same seat may cost more like $25 for a game against the Pirates.

Seating Plan

There are a lot of seating areas at Chase Field. The **100 level** wraps from right field around foul territory to left field, including the **outfield bleachers** (sections 101-105, 139-144). Following the right-field bleachers are **bullpen reserve** (sections 106-108), **baseline reserve** (sections 109-111), and the split sections of **baseline box** and **1st base reserve** (sections 112-114); then the rows are split between **dugout reserve** (sections 115-117) and **dugout box** (sections C-F). Behind home plate, the sections are split into three parts: closest to home plate are **clubhouse box** and **home plate box** (sections G-M); farther back is **infield box** (sections

118-126). Moving into the third-base side, the rows are split between **dugout reserve** (sections 127-129) and **dugout box** (sections N-Q). Next are the split sections of **baseline box** and **3rd base reserve** (sections 130-132), **baseline reserve** (sections 133-135), and **bullpen reserve** (sections 136-138). The level ends in left field with the bleachers.

The **200 level** is called the **Diamond Level** (sections 200-220). Though it's the club level, it's possible to get single-game tickets here. The section starts by the right-field foul pole with **club reserve** (sections 200-205) and **club box** (sections 206-209). The section continues on the other side of home plate with **club box** (sections 211-214) and **club reserve** (sections 215-220), then ends near the left-field foul pole with a small area for **all-you-can-eat dining** (sections 221-223).

The upper deck is the **300 level** (sections 300-332). It starts near the right-field foul pole with **outfield reserve** (sections 300-304) and moves over to **baseline view** (sections 305-309). Sweeping around behind home plate is **infield reserve** (310-322); **baseline view** (sections 323-327) and **outfield reserve** (sections 328-332) follow. Sections **300W** (La Terraza) and **332W** (The Sandlot) are ticketed rows in specialty sections.

The outfield includes three distinct specialty entertainment seating areas: the restaurant **Friday's Front Row**, the **Coors Light Strike Zone** (with suite-style seats), and the **Four Peaks Draft Room,** a bar with indoor and outdoor seating. There's also the **PetSmart Patio,** a group seating section in left center field that allows dogs on Saturdays, Sundays, and Mondays (but you'll need to

sign a waiver). In center field is the **Home Run Porch,** which gives guests a suite-style, private experience with televisions.

Finally, behind the right-field fence on field level is a seating area reserved for groups; this area is attached to the **Ram Trucks Pool.** Want pool seats? Inquire at least a year in advance, and be sure to have 34 people ready to join you. The suite starts at about $5,000, with prices rising depending on the game.

Where to Buy Tickets
You should be able to score slightly cheaper tickets for most games through **StubHub** and **SeatGeek.** The Diamondbacks are on the **MLB Ballpark app,** which offers seat upgrades if you buy tickets via the team or on StubHub.

Best Seats
Chase Field is one of the few ballparks where you can sit in the club level for an affordable price and without a group ticket, to boot. Try **sections 215-218,** where ticket prices hover around $40 per seat. Nearer the infield, those seats get closer to $55 apiece.

The 100 level is pretty affordable. **Sections 130-133** are good bets; you'll have to pay close to $50 for a seat, but you can get into the first 10 rows or so.

For those looking to spend as little as possible, the 300 level is cheap. Try to get a seat in one of the first couple rows; otherwise, you'll be really far from the action. To get a little closer, and for a bit more atmosphere, get a cheap ticket and then set up at the **Coors Light Strike Zone** (right center field). Typically, it's open to the public and has full bar service. If you're lucky, you can pay a little bit to score a private cabana (those are usually part of a group buy-in).

The **left-field bleacher seats** are affordable (about $25 a seat), provide a cool view of the playing field, and often have a louder atmosphere. You have a better than zero percent chance at snatching a home run ball here.

If the roof is open when you're at the game, your best bet for **sun protection** is **high up in the corners** (sections 300-304, 328-332), as the roof slides open from the middle to the edges.

The Diamondbacks have several different start times for home games: 12:40pm, 1:10pm, 5:10pm, 6:40pm, and 7:10pm. During those later games, the sun will set through the windows over the third-base line. That means if you're on the first-base line, you'll be **shielding your eyes** until the sun is down.

KNOW BEFORE YOU GO

The Diamondbacks allow clear **bags** no larger than 12 by 12 by 6 inches (including gallon-size freezer bags). Otherwise, the usual items are forbidden in the park, including one interesting but obvious (for Phoenix) one: umbrellas.

Although the roof doesn't open at Chase Field unless conditions are comfortable, you'll want to bring **sunscreen,** just in case.

Accessibility
If you need help while you're at Chase Field, visit **guest relations** (sections 128 and 322). You can find **large print maps** and **schedules,** plus **assistive listening devices,** and

BE A FAN

I've attended a Diamondbacks game at which visiting Padres fans had the loudest voices in the ballpark, so you don't need to worry about rocking your home team's colors when visiting Chase Field. The vibe here is generally calm and cool.

One song to keep an ear out for: If the Diamondbacks win, you'll hear **"D-backs Swing,"** by Roger Clyne & the Peacemakers. The team asked the Tempe-based band to write a song to pump up the crowd in advance of its 2007 postseason run, and this is what resulted. Fun fact: Clyne, as part of the band The Refreshments, wrote the theme song to the cartoon *King of the Hill*.

Diamondbacks' dugout and fans

you can check your **wheelchair** here. **Complimentary wheelchair service** is offered to guests who need transportation from the gate to their seat (and back to the gate); ask at your gate of entry if you're interested.

Braille and **tactile signage** is found throughout the ballpark. **Elevators** are located at sections 104, 116, 127, and 140. A **ramp** is across from section 110. Both **service dogs** and service dogs-in-training are welcome at Chase Field.

There aren't many **accessible parking spaces** at Chase Field. The parking garage on 4th and Buchanan Streets has 31 accessible spaces. You can also try the garage on Jefferson Street.

GETTING THERE

Public Transit

If you're along the route for **Valley Metro Rail** (www.valleymetro.org, $2 per ride within same city), it makes a good option for getting to the park. The drawback: There's just one route, so access is limited. The closest stop to Chase Field on Valley Metro is the **3rd Street and Jefferson station.**

Driving

Driving or ride-sharing to Chase Field is the best way to get here. There are plenty of **parking lots** within a quarter-mile walk of the ballpark, each charging anywhere between $10 and $20. Better yet, you can

prebook a spot (www.mlb.com/dbacks/ballpark) in a team-owned or team-affiliated parking lot. Be sure to make your reservation a couple days before your visit.

Keep in mind that some streets around Chase Field go **one way,** including **Washington Street, Jefferson Street,** and **3rd Street,** so leave yourself a little extra time to navigate around the area.

PARK FEATURES AND SIGHTS

20th Anniversary Experience

For a look at the short but jam-packed history of the Diamondbacks, visit the **20th Anniversary Experience** (lower concourse, right field). Enter through a tunnel into a room with mementos spanning Arizona's major league history since the late 1990s. There are scorecards from the thrilling 2001 World Series—won by the D-backs in seven games over the Yankees—Gold Glove and Silver Slugger awards, game-worn jerseys, 2011 All-Star Game bases, a franchise timeline, and plenty of factoids. While it's not the biggest history museum, you can spend more than 20 minutes just looking at all the stuff.

RAM Trucks Pool

When Chase Field opened in 1998, much of the attention turned to what rested just beyond the fence in right center field. Baseball's first in-stadium swimming pool, today called the

RAM Trucks Pool, is open to folks who plan ahead … way ahead. You may need to wait a year or more to take a dip, as the pool is part of a suite accessible to groups of up to 35 people. Guests will get tables and chairs on the field level along the right-field fence plus access to the pool area, which also has additional chairs and a hot tub. If you're not partaking in a pool outing, you can stand in the outfield concourse and take a quick look at the fun everyone else is having. Just be respectful.

The Sandlot

For families with children, **The Sandlot** (upper concourse, left field, past section 332) is a good place to spend a couple innings. It includes a playground with four slides and two clubhouses; a smaller toddler playground; the Futures Field, where kids can take batting practice and run the bases; and the location of Bobby Freeman's organ. He's the "musical mascot" of the Diamondbacks, playing "Take Me Out to the Ball Game" along with other in-stadium sounds, and kids are encouraged to hang out around the organ and sing along. A family seating area and busy concession stand are also in this section.

Baxter's Den

Next to The Sandlot is **Baxter's Den** (upper concourse, left field, past section 332), home to the Diamondbacks mascot, a bobcat. Back in 2000, when Chase Field was called Bank One Ballpark, or the BOB, player Jay Bell's son suggested that the team should have a bobcat as a mascot. Baxter hangs out in his den during the fourth inning, when he'll sign autographs and pose for photos. Note: The line for Baxter's Den will be long, so get there early if your kids are begging to hang out with the larger-than-life, furry bobcat.

FOOD AND DRINKS

The marquee item at Chase Field is the **churro dog** (sections 114, 123, 315), a chocolate-iced long John doughnut filled with a cinnamon churro, vanilla frozen yogurt, whipped cream, caramel, and chocolate sauce. This indulgent treat is delicious and a perfect antidote to steamy Arizona weather.

Another great way to beat the heat: Drink some freezing cold coffee. Head to **Dutch Bros.** (sections 124, 305), an Oregon-based company known for its frozen blended coffees (called Freezes), colorful smoothies, and milkshakes (Frosts). Dutch Bros. is a popular place, partly because of all the drinks, but also because its vibrant and friendly staff exudes excitement.

Want a burger? You're heading to **Paradise Valley Burger Co.** (section 121), which offers a classic burger, plus a beauty called the brûlée burger. The bun is coated

RAM Trucks Pool

with burnt sugar, and there's plenty of savory flavor inside (it's like a Big Mac with a fried egg). Pair it with a side of the awesome sweet potato tots.

For a perfect southwestern snack, visit **Mike and Sharon's Cactus Corn** (section 118), a business that dates back to 1998. They serve up buttered popcorn, kettle corn, and cinnamon-roasted nuts for a relatively modest price.

If you want a sit-down experience, Chase Field is home to a TGI Fridays location called **Friday's Front Row** (401 E. Jefferson St., left-field concourse, 602/462-3506, www.frontrowphoenix.com, 11am-9pm daily, under $40). Here you're paying for the view (if you can snag a seat overlooking the field), as the food (burgers, wings, chicken fingers, and other pub bites) is subpar. Get there early to score that field-view seat.

The best place to get a pregame buzz is the **Four Peaks Draft Room** (200 level, right field). Accessible via an elevator from the lower-level concourse in the right-field area, this bar and eatery is open to the public. You can sit at a table that overlooks the field (beware of the sun in your eyes in the early evening); this area is first come, first served. Otherwise, you should be able to grab a beer at the bar and either sit there or take it to a high-top table nearby. It's a decent beer list, though one note for craft purists: Local favorite Four Peaks is owned by the folks who make Budweiser.

Last but not least, way up in the far right-field corner of the upper concourse is **La Terraza** (upper concourse, right field), home to Latinx music and treats like *micheladas* (a beer and tomato juice cocktail) and refreshing *raspas* (flavored snow cones). There are plenty of tables and standing room overlooking the field here, and a colorful mural for your Instagram feed.

EVENTS

If you want an **autograph**, head to the first rows of sections 113-114 and 130-131 up until 40 minutes before first pitch. Kids (ages 3-15) **can run the bases** after Sunday home games. Parents should line up with their kids

on the east ramp (across from sections 111, 203, and 304). You'll be able to watch the visiting team's **batting practice**, since gates open just as it begins. (The D-backs go out earlier, so you won't get to see them practice.)

Every few weeks, the D-backs have post-game **fireworks** (dates vary annually). There aren't many **theme nights** at Chase Field, though each year the team marks a Native American Recognition Day and Hispanic Heritage Day.

Tours

The Diamondbacks offer a 75-minute **tour** (602/462-6799, 9:30am, 11am, and 12:30pm Mon.-Sat., $7, $5 seniors, $3 ages 4-6, free ages 3 and under) that visits the home dugout, the opposing clubhouse, a suite, and the concourses. This tour runs when the team isn't in town. The D-backs also host special **game day tours** (602/514-8400, 3:30pm Fri., three hours before first pitch Sat., $7) that should be reserved in advance.

SHOPPING

The **Chase Field Team Shop** (401 E. Jefferson St., section 130, 602/462-6701, 10am-5pm Mon.-Sat., open only to ticket holders after gates open on game days) is a moderately sized shop with the usual gear. Look for throwback jerseys (Luis Gonzalez circa 2001, maybe?) and the wall of hats. If you're a pin collector, the Diamondbacks boast more pins than most teams, celebrating everything from the 2001 championship to LGBTQ rights. Other shops include the **New Era Walk-In Shop** (section 133), a good place to score a quick jersey, and the **'47 Brand Walk-In Shop** (section 119), home to all those hats.

PHOENIX SIGHTS

HEARD MUSEUM

Providing a deep and insightful look into the history of the Phoenix area and the

Southwest, the **Heard Museum** (2301 N. Central Ave., 602/252-8840, www.heard. org, 9:30am-5pm Mon.-Sat., 11am-5pm Sun., $18, $15 seniors, $7.50 students and ages 6-17) is a great place to spend a half day. Start your journey at the exhibit called Home: Native People in the Southwest, which walks through the history of multiple Indigenous groups. There's a vast collection of colorful katsina (also called kachina) dolls, figures made by Hopi people that act as messengers from the spirit world. A few exhibits change regularly, and the museum sometimes hosts events near its substantial courtyard area.

DESERT BOTANICAL GARDEN

Home to plants native to Arizona and species from across the world, the **Desert Botanical Garden** (1201 N. Galvin Pkwy., 480/941-1225, www.dbg.org, 7am-8pm daily, $25, $13 ages 3-17, free ages 2 and under) at Papago Park is a colorful playground of cacti such as impressive saguaros; a wealth of succulents; trees; and flowers. Be sure to hike the Desert Wildflower Loop Trail; for a more far-out adventure, the Sonoran Desert Loop Trail shows how plants were used as medicines, building materials, and more by people native to the area. The garden has regular events, including flashlight tours during weekends in the middle of the sweltering summer.

FOOD

NEAR CHASE FIELD

I've enjoyed pizza up and down the East Coast, including some of New Haven, Connecticut's best parlors and the finest spots in New York, Philly, and Boston. Also, I've tried Chicago deep dish, plus other varieties across the country. But a pie at **Pizzeria Bianco** (623 E. Adams St., 602/258-8300, www. pizzeriabianco.com, 11am-9pm Mon.-Fri., 11am-10pm Sat., noon-7pm Sun., under $25)

is arguably the best single pizza experience in the United States. The small restaurant with a brick oven and cozy bar area might be hard to get into (reservations are not taken, and lines are typical), but once you have a seat, order yourself a pizza. The ingredients are cooked just right and balance one another perfectly, and the crust is on another plane. For an appetizer, order the spiedini, skewers of fontina wrapped in prosciutto.

Just a mile south of the ballpark is **Sonora Taco Shop** (1009 S. 7th St., 602/252-2795, 10am-9pm Mon.-Fri., 11am-9pm Sat., under $15), a compact space serving big flavors. Step up to the counter and order a couple tacos (*pollo* or *al pastor;* chicken or pork), adding a gently fried tortilla and cheese. Pair the meal with a Mexican Coke, and dine on the small front porch if the sun isn't too strong.

A Downtown institution, **Matt's Big Breakfast** (825 N. 1st St., 602/254-1074, www.mattsbigbreakfast.com, 6:30am-2:30pm daily, under $30) is extremely popular, drawing tourists and, often, celebrities seeking a great breakfast. If your party is just one, you might be able to get a counter seat quickly, but the more people in your group, the longer you'll wait. I recommend the Hog & Chick (eggs and bacon or sausage) with a griddle cake on the side, so you can try it all. Those griddle cakes are worth it. The service here is friendly.

OTHER NEIGHBORHOODS

A couple blocks north of the airport in the Garfield section of the city is the best late-night hang in Phoenix. **Welcome Diner** (929 E. Pierce St., 602/495-1111, www.welcome-diner.net, 5pm-2am Mon.-Fri., 10am-3pm and 5pm-2am Sat.-Sun., under $30) is ultra-modern but über-vintage. With a group, it's cool to score a booth, but if there's just one or two of you, grab a seat at the counter and watch the cooks prepare the meals. Classic comfort food like a fried green tomato sandwich, pulled pork fries, and a big fried chicken biscuit go well with a cocktail.

You won't believe it until you get there and

realize that, yes, you have to wait a good hour or two in line for this stuff. **Little Miss BBQ** (4301 E. University Dr., 602/437-1177, www.littlemissbbq.com, 11am-4pm Tues.-Sat., under $40) is a bona fide Central Texas-style barbecue pit in Arizona. Using Arizona oak and pecan, Little Miss does it right, specializing in a tender and fatty brisket, plus snappy sausage. Sides include jalapeño cheddar grits and ranch-style beans. Save room for a slice of pecan pie. Sit in the small dining room or find a picnic table and chow down while patient folks in line watch. Meats are sold by weight, and when the meats run out, they close. Find this spot south of the Salt River from Phoenix Sky Harbor.

BARS AND BREWERIES

NEAR CHASE FIELD

Just two blocks west and one block north of Chase Field is **The Whining Pig** (201 E. Washington St. #104, 602/603-9987, www.thewhiningpig.com, 3pm-10pm Mon.-Thurs., 3pm-midnight Fri.-Sat., 1pm-10pm Sun.). Armed with an outstanding draft beer list, plus several dozen bottle and can options, this is a superb place to grab a drink or two before or after the game. It also has high ceilings, plenty of space, and a lot of board games.

For more of a nightclub vibe, check out **Bar Smith** (130 E. Washington St., 602/456-1991, www.barsmithphoenix.com, 9pm-2am Wed.-Sat.). This two-level space is best if you're looking to dance, enjoy cheaper well drinks, and forget your cares for a few hours. There's a patio upstairs where a DJ may spin on weekend nights. It's a busy place.

OTHER NEIGHBORHOODS

Northeast of Downtown Phoenix is the city's finest brewery, **Wren House Brewing Company** (2125 N. 24th St., 602/244-9184, www.wrenhousebrewing.com, noon-10pm

Mon.-Thurs., 11am-midnight Fri.-Sat., 11am-10pm Sun.). Producing a variety of beers from crisp and clean lagers to ambitious IPAs to bold stouts, Wren House is an effortlessly good hangout with natural light, blond wood, and a subtle, twee aesthetic. It's likely to get busy on weekend afternoons and evenings, so you'll have to be patient with the bar staff as they fill crowlers and pour pints. Wren House doesn't offer flights.

Up the block is **Helton Brewing Company** (2144 E. Indian School Rd., 602/730-2739, www.heltonbrewing.com, 11am-11pm Mon.-Thurs., 11am-midnight Fri.-Sat., 11am-9pm Sun.), which puts out a variety of brews, doing a solid job with IPAs and big, dark styles like scotch ale. The taproom is large enough to fit a bunch of small groups, and there are games and a pool table, among other distractions.

A mile north of Chase Field and probably too far for a walk is one of the coolest little bars in the Southwest. **The Breadfruit & Rum Bar** (108 E. Pierce St., 602/267-1266, www.thebreadfruit.com, 5pm-10pm Mon.-Thurs., 5pm-midnight Fri.-Sat.), in the Evans Churchill neighborhood, has an extensive list of rums at the bar, plus a highly curated list of drinks starring the oft-misunderstood spirit. There's a generous dinner menu with plenty of fish, jerk chicken, and pork, and the extremely courteous bartenders and servers can help you find the right drink pairing for your food. Cool and dimly lit, it's an awesome little find that'll make you a rum devotee.

Arguably the best beer bar in the Downtown area is **Angels Trumpet Ale House** (810 N. 2nd St., 602/252-2630, www.angelstrumpetalehouse.com, 11am-midnight Tues.-Sat., 11am-11pm Sun.). Post up at the long bar and order one of the several dozen beers on tap, munch on pub grub and new American dinner fare, or just hang outside on a picnic table.

At **Gracie's Tax Bar** (711 N. 7th Ave., 602/366-0111, www.graciesphx.com, 4pm-2am daily), the booze is cheap, the people are fun, and the jukebox is among the best you'll find. There's some outdoor seating, too. If you want a night you won't forget,

check this place out. It's a few blocks west down McKinley Street from Angels Trumpet.

If you're out in Scottsdale, you might want to visit Old Town Scottsdale. It's where the city began back in 1888, and two olive trees planted back then still stand there today. Those trees are now part of an area teeming with bars, restaurants, and entertainment venues, themed in parts as a Wild West-style village whose aesthetics are one part Disney, one part Bourbon Street. I recommend the **Rusty Spur Saloon** (7245 E. Main St., Scottsdale, 480/425-7787, www. rustyspursaloon.com, 10am-1am Sat.-Wed., 10am-2am Thurs.-Fri.), an old-school joint with live country music and plenty of crowds, and **RnR Gastropub** (3737 N. Scottsdale Rd., Scottsdale, 480/945-3353, www.rnrscottsdale.com, 11am-midnight Mon.-Fri., 9am-midnight Sat.-Sun.), which is really more about the two-story bar scene and people-watching than it is about the drinks—though there is a small but affordable selection of craft beer.

RECREATION

PARKS

Papago Park

Just an eight-mile drive east of Chase Field via Washington Street and East Van Buren Street, **Papago Park** (625 N. Galvin Pkwy., www.phoenix.gov, 5am-11pm daily) is an expanse of preserved peacefulness coupled with a few major municipal attractions. Saguaros, towering red-rock formations, trees of all sizes, and other vegetation dot the landscape. You can visit the **Desert Botanical Garden** or spend a day at the **Phoenix Zoo** (455 N. Galvin Pkwy., www.phoenixzoo. org, 9am-5pm daily Jan.-May and Sept.-Oct., 7am-2pm daily June-Aug., 9am-4pm daily Nov.-Dec., $25, $17 ages 3-13, free ages 2 and

Photos (from top to bottom): Desert Botanical Garden; brisket and ribs at Phoenix's Little Miss BBQ; hikers in Papago Park.

under), the largest privately owned zoo in the country. The zoo is home to African lions, coyotes, Sumatran tigers, Andean bears, and more. Papago also has nearly a dozen trails, all easy and shorter than 3.5 miles. Check out the **Elliot Ramada Loop Trail,** a 2.7-mile path that offers beautiful city views.

Camelback Mountain

Perhaps the quintessential Phoenix experience, a hike up **Camelback Mountain** (6131 E. Cholla Ln., Paradise Valley, www. phoenix.gov, 6:30am-6:30pm daily) can be an exhilarating adventure. It can also be a disaster, depending on when you hike it and your level of preparation. This 2,706-foot mountain, which resembles a camel bowing to the desert, was taken over as a city park in 1968 and has since been a popular place for tourists and locals alike. Be sure to wear good footwear and to pack twice as much water as you think you'll need, because hiking Camelback is a challenge. Whatever you do, don't go out on this hike when it's hot. Try for early in the morning, instead.

Follow the **Cholla Trail,** which is well marked and teeming with people. You'll want to pace yourself with everyone else, and along the way you're bound to have a few conversations, because chatting will distract you through the tough parts. After a mile of both rock stairs and gradual incline on dirt, you'll reach a difficult scramble that at times will require both legs and arms. Go slow, take water breaks, and enjoy the scenery. After reaching the summit after 1.3 miles, you'll go down the way you came.

When parking for the Cholla Trail, set your destination for North Invergordon Road and East Cholla Lane. You'll see cars parked along the street; scour for a spot here, avoiding any no-parking zones. You'll have to walk from your parking space, turning onto Cholla Lane to reach the trailhead.

SHOPPING

Besides checking out the numerous team stores at the spring training facilities across the Phoenix metro area, you might want to stop by the **Rawlings Factory Store** (4976 Premium Outlets Way #830, Chandler, 480/639-1850, www.rawlings.com, 10am-9pm Mon.-Sat., 10am-7pm Sun.). This store inside Phoenix Premium Outlets has marked-down Rawlings-brand goods, such as baseball bats, gloves, bags, and uniforms.

For a new glove or maybe a cool vintage hat, check out **Between the Lines** (13802 N. Scottsdale Rd. #127, Scottsdale, 480/656-9959, www.betweenthelinesaz. com, 10am-7pm Mon.-Fri., 9am-6pm Sat., 11am-4pm Sun.). They have all the big brands, from New Era to Oakley, along with fun pieces of apparel like team socks and infant onesies.

ACCOMMODATIONS

NEAR CHASE FIELD

Besides the usual variety of larger chain hotels near the park, there's a boutique chain accommodation, the **Kimpton Hotel Palomar** (2 E. Jefferson St., 602/253-6633, www. hotelpalomar-phoenix.com, $120-300). With a lobby like a living room, guest rooms in mid-century modern style, and a rooftop pool (which gets busy during weekends and nights), Palomar is a popular choice for urban travelers. Plus, guests get the opportunity to ride complimentary bicycles. That works well for Downtown hopping, but you won't need a biket for the game, as Chase Field is just four blocks east. If you can score a cheap rate for a Palomar room, scoop it up.

It's unclear whether there are ghosts roaming the halls of the **Hotel San Carlos** (202 N. Central Ave., 602/253-4121, www. hotelsancarlos.com, $80-200), but it is one of the more historic sites in Phoenix. Opened in 1928 after an $850,000 build-out, the hotel was decorated in Italian finery, and some of those items remain today, including terra-cotta tiles and parts of neoclassical columns. Its tinier rooms are relatively basic but have all the expected amenities, and there's a rooftop pool. Plus, it's just a 12-minute walk to Chase Field. And, yes, people have claimed ghost sightings through the years.

OTHER NEIGHBORHOODS

Scottsdale is the place for a luxury resort stay. For something relatively affordable and with a more hands-off approach, try **Bespoke Inn Scottsdale** (3701 N. Marshall Way, Scottsdale, 844/861-6715, www.bespokeinn.com, $150-250). Right in the Scottsdale Arts District, Bespoke has eight individually decorated, cleanly appointed rooms, a gourmet brunch ($10 extra), complimentary bicycles to ride about town, and a 43-foot-long infinity lap pool.

Looking for the all-in resort experience? **The Scottsdale Resort at McCormick Ranch** (7700 E. McCormick Pkwy., Scottsdale, 480/991-9000, www.destinationhotels.com/scottsdale-resort, $80-200) is one of the more affordable options that also has multiple restaurants, a full-service spa, and a giant pool. Another perk is preferred rates on tee times at neighboring McCormick Ranch Golf Club, a 36-hole venue with two courses, one of which regularly hosts PGA qualifier events.

GETTING AROUND

If you're based in Phoenix, you might want to head out to nearby cities like Mesa, Scottsdale, or Tempe. These communities can be 20-45 minutes away, depending on traffic.

PUBLIC TRANSIT

Valley Metro (www.valleymetro.org, from $2) runs public transportation in the region. Its **light rail** ($2 per ride within same city) has just one route that travels from Mesa west into Tempe, then west past Sky Harbor International Airport into Phoenix, and finally north into the suburbs. For those going to and from the airport, it's a solid option. Trains run approximately every 10 minutes from morning rush to evening rush, and every 20 minutes otherwise, nearly 24 hours a day. On Sundays, you'll wait about 20 minutes all day. The **bus network** ($2-3.25 per ride) is expansive, and **Express/RAPID buses** take travelers through the region's cities and across major highways with limited stops.

TAXI, UBER, AND LYFT

For those wanting to enjoy the nightlife in sprawling Downtown Phoenix, ride-sharing is the best option. You'll pay about $6-10 per mile-long ride (about the distance between Chase Field and the Evans Churchill neighborhood) with both **Lyft** and **Uber**. The issue with Downtown—and with the Phoenix area in general—is that the blocks are quite long, making walking more of a chore than expected.

You could opt to take **Yellow Cab Arizona** (480/888-8888, www.yellowcabaz.com), but rider experiences tend to be hit-or-miss. The fare is generally on the same level as Lyft and Uber, so if you're really in a bind and can't score a ride-share, this can be a good backup plan.

CAR

Considering the lack of speedy public transportation and the fact that we're talking not just about Phoenix but an entire multicity region (including Mesa, Scottsdale, and Tempe), you're best off driving here. It's not difficult to get around, either, as there are plenty of highways and wide avenues connecting all the major communities. Plus, while there's plenty to do in Downtown Phoenix and its adjacent neighborhoods, everything is spread out. It's not very walkable. (Also, who wants to walk in this summer heat?)

Downtown Phoenix is boxed in by the region's two major interstates, **I-17**—which runs south from Flagstaff into Phoenix—and **I-10**—which starts to the west in Los Angeles, continues through Phoenix, then heads east toward El Paso, Texas. From I-10 East,

SPRING TRAINING IN THE CACTUS LEAGUE

In the Cactus League, teams begin reporting to spring training in mid-February, typically around Valentine's Day. Fifteen teams spend spring in Arizona at 10 stadiums, all within the Phoenix metropolitan area. Several teams share ballparks, making it easy to catch multiple games over the course of two or three days.

Here's a list of the 15 Cactus League teams and where to find them for spring training.

- **Arizona Diamondbacks and Colorado Rockies:** Salt River Fields at Talking Stick (7555 N. Pima Rd., Scottsdale)
- **Chicago Cubs:** Sloan Park (2330 W. Rio Salado Pkwy., Mesa)
- **Chicago White Sox and Los Angeles Dodgers:** Camelback Ranch (10710 W. Camelback Rd., Phoenix; may also be called Glendale)
- **Cincinnati Reds and Cleveland Indians:** Goodyear Ballpark (1933 S. Ballpark Way, Goodyear)
- **Kansas City Royals and Texas Rangers:** Surprise Stadium (15930 N. Bullard Ave., Surprise)
- **Los Angeles Angels:** Tempe Diablo Stadium (2200 W. Alameda Dr., Tempe)
- **Milwaukee Brewers:** American Family Fields of Phoenix (3805 N. 53rd Ave., Phoenix)
- **Oakland Athletics:** Hohokam Stadium (1235 N. Center St., Mesa)
- **San Diego Padres and Seattle Mariners:** Peoria Sports Complex (16101 N. 83rd Ave., Peoria)
- **San Francisco Giants:** Scottsdale Stadium (7408 E. Osborn Rd., Scottsdale)

PLANNING TIPS

Book your **flight** and reserve your **rental car** in **advance.** Most people make spring training plans just after the new year, when tickets go on sale. Start thinking about your trip before the **December holidays,** securing your transportation ahead of the pack. Because all the teams in Arizona are so close together, you can book your trip before the schedule is out and be assured that you'll be able to see lots of games while you're there.

Be prepared for **traffic** when you get to Phoenix. Considering that half of Major League Baseball's teams are here, there's only so much room on the road. Build in time to wait in traffic (about 15 minutes extra) throughout any Cactus League trip.

You'll find yourself among fans of Cactus League teams if you head to bars and restaurants close to the stadiums. As a general note, **Scottsdale** is Giants territory, **Mesa** is packed with Cubs fans, and **Goodyear** is a wonderland for Cincinnati and Cleveland fans (the city was established by the famous, Ohio-based tire company).

Bring **sunscreen** and **sunglasses,** but also bring a **jacket** and maybe an **umbrella.** February and March in the Valley of the Sun see highs around 70°F and lows in the 50s. While it doesn't rain much out here generally, chances of rain are higher in February and March than at other times of year.

you can hop onto **AZ-202 East** to reach Tempe and Mesa. That also gets you close to Scottsdale, but you'll want to turn onto **AZ-101 North** or the broad **Scottsdale Road North,** which connects Tempe to Scottsdale. Over to the west, I-10 connects to the **Phoenix-Wickenburg Highway,** or **US-60,** which heads northwest into Glendale and Peoria. I-17 also intersects with US-60.

For the most part, Phoenix's street layout is a standard grid. **Washington Street** runs through Downtown and along the northern side of Sky Harbor International Airport. **Central Avenue** goes north to south through the center of the city.

The West Coast

Plenty of baseball fans dream of taking that big West Coast baseball trip. Drink hyper-local craft beer as you root for the underdog Padres in San Diego. Feel the Hollywood lights inside the immaculate Dodger Stadium, then hop over to Angel Stadium, home to a Disney-like vibe. In Northern California, pick a side in the Battle of the Bay, where the Giants boast a sleek stadium, and the Athletics give a lesson in homegrown pride. All the way up in Seattle, end your trip with some of the best ballpark food and drinks at a Mariners' game.

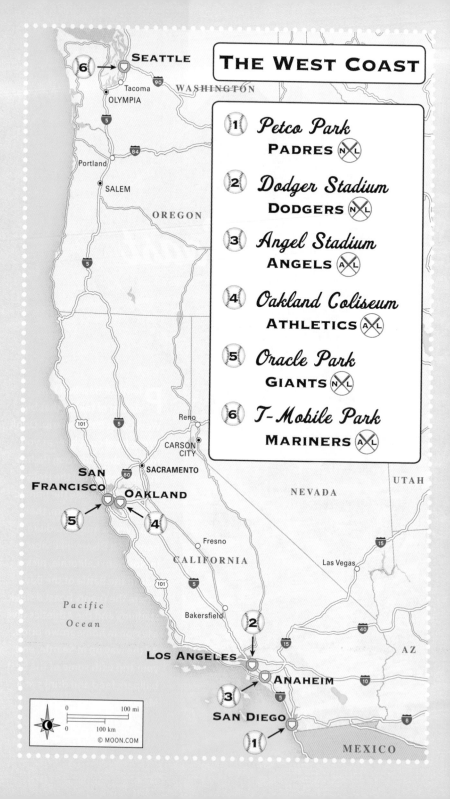

The West Coast Road Trip

In 1957, Major League Baseball had just two teams on the west side of the Mississippi River, the Kansas City Athletics and the St. Louis Cardinals. Professional baseball had always been an eastern U.S. game, but in 1958 that all changed. The Brooklyn Dodgers moved to Los Angeles and the New York Giants moved to San Francisco. By 1969, there were teams in Anaheim, Oakland, and San Diego, and in 1977 Seattle got its team (for good). The westward expansion of baseball forever changed the game, turning it into a national enterprise that would reach more than 20 million televisions annually by 1971.

To travel the 1,300 miles of the West Coast is to see countless facets of America's favorite pastime. You'll start in **San Diego,** home of the **Padres,** arguably the least popular team in the game's history. The Friars, as they're lovingly called, are one of the few franchises without a World Series title, but between the classic look of their brown-hued uniforms and the beer at their outstanding ballpark, there's a lot to like here.

Los Angeles is a different story. The **Angels** are a case study in modern ballpark trends, as they were the first to anchor an entertainment district aimed at making baseball games into a full-day experience. Then there are the **Dodgers,** a franchise with a rich history and plenty of pride. Dodger Stadium is one of the best examples of a ballpark that's withstood the test of time.

Up north a bit more are two teams with similar histories. The **San Francisco Giants** have historically played second fiddle to their rivals the Dodgers, but in recent years they've climbed to the top of the mountain while playing in a gorgeous ballpark against the San Francisco Bay. Meanwhile, the **Oakland Athletics** perform inside a cavernous behemoth of a stadium, but the team remains an offbeat and fun group, parading green jerseys and backed by tons of die-hard fans.

Finally, there's **Seattle,** a world removed from California and colored by smoked salmon, piney beers, and puffy vests (even in summer). The **Mariners** may be the most unfortunate franchise in major league history, unable to win an American League pennant since first appearing more than 40 years ago, but they remain a lovable group. They've got an ace in the hole with T-Mobile Park, one of the coolest spots in all of baseball.

There's a lot of variety up and down the West Coast. You could spend more than a few weeks checking it out and not even scratch the surface. While you're out here, think about what it was like just 60 years ago, when there wasn't a major league bat or glove to be found. We've come a long way, baby.

PLANNING YOUR TIME

You'll need plenty of time to execute this 1,300-mile trip, featuring five major cities and six major league teams. Considering the ground you'll have to cover, and the fact that both the Dodgers and Angels and Giants and Athletics don't typically play at home at the same time, and you're looking at close to a **two-week** trip, if all falls into place correctly. If not, you may have to plan **two separate trips.**

If you're hoping to knock out all the parks and teams in one fell swoop, here are some tips: When the regular season schedule is released, find a period when one Los Angeles team is home over a **Friday-Sunday series** and the other is back home starting that **Monday or Tuesday.** There should be a couple of these each season.

Next keeping that first set of results in mind, look for the **midweek series** where there's a Bay Area team at home, followed by a **weekend series** when the other Bay Area team is home. If you get those four elements set, you're in good shape. Finally, be sure to get games in San Diego and Seattle covered on either end.

The best-case scenario is an **11-day** trip that allows you some room to breathe and drive equally. There may be just one instance in a season where everything lines up perfectly, so you'll need to plan ahead and act quickly once you've got your plans figured out. If you have a full **two weeks,** you can give yourself another full day in San Diego, the Bay Area, and Seattle.

You can also split the trip into two separate journeys. My recommendation is still to cover the same ground: **one long trip** from San Diego to Seattle, but just see one team in both L.A. and San Francisco. This should cut your initial trip by 2-3 days, making it a **weeklong** or **eight-day** trip rather than an 11-day adventure. Your second trip will allow you to see the other two teams you didn't catch the first time, and can be a lot **shorter,** like a **long weekend** that includes a five- to six-hour drive.

Another option is to batch San Diego and L.A. into one trip, with **5-6 days** that include a wraparound weekend in L.A. Then visit Seattle and the Bay Area in another trip over **5-6 days** with a wraparound weekend in the Bay Area.

One final option: Separate Seattle from the California cities, because of its long distance from the Bay Area, requiring a many-hour drive. Do one **weeklong** trip in California, then visit Seattle over a **weekend.**

Here's an itinerary breaking down my best-case scenario, whirlwind 11-day trip of the West Coast.

Day 1

Arrive in **San Diego** and take it easy with a relaxing trip to the beach.

Day 2

Sightsee and head to **Petco Park** for a Padres game. Make it an early night.

Day 3

Get up early for the multi-hour drive north to the **Los Angeles-Anaheim** area. You'll undoubtedly hit traffic, so plan ahead. You'll catch a **Dodgers** or **Angels** game today (whoever is home).

Day 4

Today's a tourist day in Los Angeles. See all the sights! Take all the pictures!

Day 5

See the second Los Angeles team today, either at **Dodger Stadium** or **Angel Stadium.** If you can, fit in more sights, more food, and more drinks, but try to hit the sack early.

Day 6

This is a driving day, as you'll need 6 hours to go up I-5 or 7-8 hours up US-101 to the Bay Area. If you're taking I-5, stop in Bowerbank for food and gas (it's slim pickings out here). If you're on US-101, Santa Maria makes a good midday stop.

Day 7

You'll wake up in the Bay Area and get to see a **Giants** or **Athletics** game today. If you're in **San Francisco,** there are a ton of sights to see, so get an early start.

Day 8

Today you'll visit the other Bay Area team at either **Oakland Coliseum** or **Oracle Park.** If you're spending today in **Oakland,** give yourself enough time to indulge in all the food and drink options that abound.

Day 9

It's time to leave the Bay Area and head north. It's a 13-hour drive to Seattle, so break down the trip into manageable stints. Consider a quick stop in Redding after about 3.5 hours of driving, then power through 5 hours more to Eugene, Oregon, to end the day.

Day 10

Leave early from Eugene and stop for breakfast in Portland after nearly two hours of driving. Then hop back in the car and finish the trip with a three-hour drive to **Seattle.** If all goes according to plan, you'll end up in the Emerald City just after lunch with time to spare before tonight's ball game at **T-Mobile Park.**

Photos (top): Balboa Park in San Diego; (middle left) Oracle Park in San Francisco; (middle right) Dodger Dogs sign; (bottom) Pike Place Market in Seattle.

Day 11

See as much of Seattle as you can. There's too much to do in just one day, so try arranging your flight to leave early tomorrow morning, if you can.

GETTING THERE

Air

To start your trip, you'll fly into **San Diego International Airport** (SAN, 3225 N. Harbor Dr., San Diego, 619/400-2404, www.san. org). Airlines that fly in and out of the airport include **American Airlines** (800/433-7300, www.aa.com), **Delta** (800/221-1212, www. delta.com), **Frontier** (801/401-9000, www. flyfrontier.com), **jetBlue** (800/538-2583, www.jetblue.com), **Southwest** (800/435-9792, www.southwest.com), **Spirit** (801/401-2222, www.spirit.com), and **United** (800/864-8331, www.united.com).

To get back home from the full 11-day trip, you'll fly out of **Seattle-Tacoma International Airport** (SEA, 17801 International Blvd., Seattle, 206/787-5388, www.portseattle.org). Airlines that service the airport include **Air Canada** (888/247-2262, www. aircanada.com), American Airlines, Delta, Frontier, jetBlue, Southwest, Spirit, and United.

You might break this trip into two. If so, chances are you'll fly either into or out of **Los Angeles International Airport** (LAX, 1 World Way, 855/463-5252, www.flylax. com). Airlines that depart from and arrive at LAX include **Allegiant** (702/505-8888, www. allegiantair.com), American Airlines, Delta, Frontier, jetBlue, Southwest, Spirit, and United, plus several international carriers.

For a two-part trip, another airport you might visit is **San Francisco International Airport** (SFO, US-101 and Airport Access Rd., South San Francisco, 650/821-8211, www.flysfo.com), which has three main domestic terminals and an international terminal with two separate gate areas. Airlines here include American Airlines, Delta, jetBlue, Southwest, and United.

You can also fly into or out of **Oakland International Airport** (OAK, 1 Airport Dr., Oakland, 510/563-3300, www.oaklandairport.com). Servicing the airport are Allegiant, American Airlines, Delta, jetBlue, Southwest, and Spirit.

Train

Amtrak (www.amtrak.com) has a few routes that cover much of the West Coast. Starting from San Diego, you'll take the **Pacific Surfliner** to Los Angeles. It will drop you at **Union Station** (800 N. Alameda St., Los Angeles), from where you'll take a **Coast Starlight**, which stops in Oakland at **Jack London Square Station** (245 2nd St., Oakland). You'll have to use other forms of transportation to jump across the bay to San Francisco. From Oakland, you can continue on the Coast Starlight all the way up to Seattle's **King Street Station** (303 S. Jackson St., Seattle).

SAN DIEGO
PADRES

I'd imagine that if you asked some-one from, say, Iowa, to name every major league baseball team, that person would name 20-25 of the 30 teams before finally coming to the San Diego Padres. This isn't a dig at the Friars (as they're called by some); it's a result of a few things: the franchise's lack of success, its small market (despite being in one of the country's 10-largest cities), and a fanbase that isn't quite as rabid as its neighbors to the north.

The Padres were first a Pacific Coast League team, winning four titles in its minor league life-time (1936-1968). When the National League expanded from 10 to 12 teams in 1969, it added a second New York team (the Mets) and the Pads as the third West Coast team to join the Dodgers and Giants. San Diego immediately played second

fiddle to those powerful franchises, and little has changed in the 50-plus years since.

San Diego has fielded a couple good teams—winning National League pennants in 1984 and 1998, with both led by Hall of Fame hitter Tony Gwynn—while otherwise maintaining a spot in the middle to bottom of the NL standings. Gwynn nearly hit .400 in the strike-shortened 1994 season, while fellow Hall of Famer Trevor Hoffman held the all-time saves record until Mariano Rivera broke it in 2011. Ozzie Smith played here! So did Dave Winfield! And now Manny Machado is here! There's a lot to hang onto if you're a Padres fan, and oh, that ballpark is beautiful.

So, yes, the Padres aren't necessarily the Yankees, Cardinals, Dodgers, or Giants when it comes to history and prestige. But this is one of baseball's funkiest franchises, a club unafraid to take risks and be different. The Friars are fun; I bet if you take in a game at Petco Park, you'll come to the same conclusion.

PLANNING YOUR TIME

How much time you spend in this big city depends on the kind of experience you want. If you're going to a game, hoping to take in a couple breweries, and maybe get in some beach time, a **three-day weekend** would suffice. If you're hoping to drive around a little and spend time in neighborhoods like Little Italy, or maybe you want to check out Balboa Park with the kids in tow, then you can hang here for a **week** and not be bored.

If you want to visit a **theme park** like SeaWorld, be sure to get your tickets ahead of time. I'd also recommend getting your **zoo** tickets ahead of time, especially if you hope to spend more than a day there.

San Diego County is spread out over a large area. Within the county are regions, which are in some cases also called "county." **Central San Diego** is the big-city proper, mostly the **Downtown** area. You may hear

about **North County,** which is up north along the Pacific Ocean, or **East County,** more east by northeast. Neighborhoods include the hip **Little Italy** and **North Park** areas, which are in the city itself.

Downtown has plenty of accommodations and is centrally located to notable San Diego sights. Plus, Petco Park is within walking distance, especially if you're staying in the **Gaslamp Quarter,** the popular nightlife-centric neighborhood just northwest of the ballpark. Alternatively, you could stay at a less expensive hotel along the **I-8 corridor** near the **Mission Valley** shopping area. That's an especially attractive location if you plan to visit SeaWorld, as you'll be just a 10-minute drive away.

There really is no bad time to attend a game in San Diego. **Spring, summer,** and **fall** feature temperatures between 65-80°F and very little precipitation. Bring a sweatshirt or jacket for night games—even in the summer, because it could dip below 60°F.

GETTING THERE

AIR

The main airport in San Diego is **San Diego International Airport** (SAN, 3225 N. Harbor Dr., 619/400-2404, www.san.org), once known as Lindbergh Field. Airlines that fly in and out of the airport include **American Airlines** (800/433-7300, www.aa.com), **Delta** (800/221-1212, www.delta.com), **Frontier** (801/401-9000, www.flyfrontier.com), **jetBlue** (800/538-2583, www.jetblue.com), **Southwest** (800/435-9792, www.southwest.com), **Spirit** (801/401-2222, www.spirit.com), and **United** (800/864-8331, www.united.com). There's service from plenty of West Coast cities, plus New York, Philadelphia, Chicago, Washington DC, Atlanta, and Miami. There are two terminals at the airport.

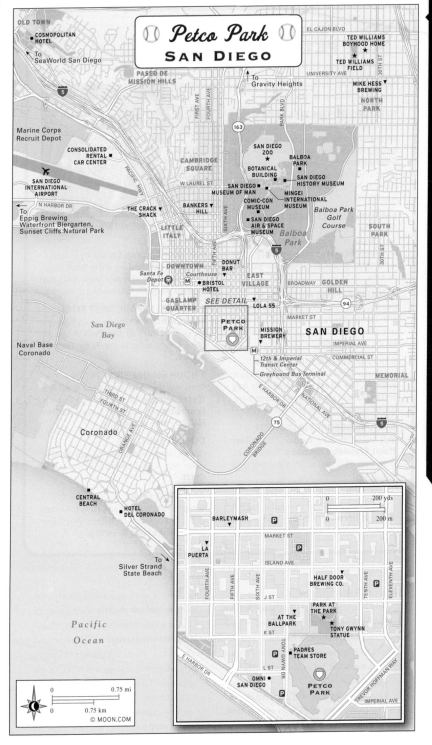

Petco Park
SAN DIEGO

OLD TOWN
- COSMOPOLITAN HOTEL
- To SeaWorld San Diego

EL CAJON BLVD

TED WILLIAMS BOYHOOD HOME ★
TED WILLIAMS FIELD

PASEO DE MISSION HILLS

To Gravity Heights →

MIKE HESS BREWING ▼

NORTH PARK

UNIVERSITY AVE

Marine Corps Recruit Depot

CONSOLIDATED RENTAL CAR CENTER ■

CAMBRIDGE SQUARE

W LAUREL ST

SAN DIEGO ZOO ★
BOTANICAL BUILDING
SAN DIEGO MUSEUM OF MAN
COMIC-CON MUSEUM ■

BALBOA PARK

SAN DIEGO HISTORY MUSEUM

MINGEI INTERNATIONAL MUSEUM

Balboa Park Golf Course

SOUTH PARK

SAN DIEGO INTERNATIONAL AIRPORT

N HARBOR DR
To →
Eppig Brewing Waterfront Biergarten, Sunset Cliffs Natural Park

THE CRACK SHACK ▼

BANKERS HILL

SAN DIEGO AIR & SPACE MUSEUM ■

Balboa Park

LITTLE ITALY

DOWNTOWN

DONUT BAR ▼

Santa Fe Depot

Courthouse
BRISTOL HOTEL

EAST VILLAGE

BROADWAY

GOLDEN HILL

San Diego Bay

GASLAMP QUARTER

SEE DETAIL

LOLA 55 ▼

MARKET ST

SAN DIEGO

Naval Base Coronado

PETCO PARK

MISSION BREWERY

IMPERIAL AVE

COMMERCIAL ST

MEMORIAL

12th & Imperial Transit Center
Greyhound Bus Terminal

THIRD ST
FOURTH ST

Coronado

E HARBOR DR
NATIONAL AVE

CORONADO BRIDGE

CENTRAL BEACH

HOTEL DEL CORONADO ■

To Silver Strand State Beach →

Pacific Ocean

0   0.75 mi
0   0.75 km
© MOON.COM

Detail map
BARLEYMASH ▼

MARKET ST
ISLAND AVE

LA PUERTA ▼

HALF DOOR BREWING CO.

J ST

PARK AT THE PARK ★
TONY GWYNN STATUE ★

AT THE BALLPARK ▼

K ST

PADRES TEAM STORE

E HARBOR DR

L ST

OMNI SAN DIEGO

PETCO PARK

IMPERIAL AVE

0   200 yds
0   200 m

YOUR BEST DAY AT PETCO PARK

You have tickets to tonight's Padres game. Here are some ideas to fill your day.

10 HOURS BEFORE FIRST PITCH
I know exactly what you should do on a summer morning in San Diego—grab your bathing suit. But first, get some donuts. Visit **Donut Bar** and get one topped with cereal pieces—you know, for a balanced breakfast. You may have to wait in line, but the taste is worth it.

9 HOURS BEFORE FIRST PITCH
Go to the beach. If it's your first time in San Diego, drive out to **Central Beach** in Coronado for people-watching and sunbathing. Be patient while you look for parking.

7 HOURS BEFORE FIRST PITCH
Head back to your hotel for a quick shower and change. Stash your car and call up a ride-share vehicle so you don't have to drive for the rest of the day.

6 HOURS BEFORE FIRST PITCH
You'll want to fill up on grub now, so catch a ride to **The Crack Shack** in Little Italy and get a big ol' sandwich. If you have room, there's a milkshake with your name on it.

5 HOURS BEFORE FIRST PITCH
Visit the Little Italy location of **Ballast Point Brewing Company.** There will be more beer after this, so just have one, then call up another ride-share.

4 HOURS BEFORE FIRST PITCH
Go on a Petco-adjacent beer crawl. Start at **Mission Brewery,** and after a drink there (maybe a lighter blonde beer), continue to

beers from Ballast Point Brewing Company

Half Door Brewing Co. and try to score a seat on the patio looking out to Petco. If you have a little time afterward, walk about the Gaslamp Quarter before heading to the park.

1.5 HOURS BEFORE FIRST PITCH
Head to **Petco Park.** By the time you arrive, the gate for **Park at the Park** should be open. Take a selfie at the **Tony Gwynn statue.**

1 HOUR BEFORE FIRST PITCH
Check out the scene around the **Western Metal Supply Co. building.** Visit the **Team Store** and walk through the **Padres Hall of Fame exhibit.**

DURING THE GAME
Opt for tacos at **Carnitas' Snack Shack,** along with a local beverage from **Jack & Craft.**

AFTER THE GAME
Get a ride-share and head east to the North Park neighborhood to have a post-game drink at **Mike Hess Brewing.**

Airport Transportation

Rental cars are available from the **rental car center** (3355 Admiral Boland Way), which is accessible via **shuttle buses.** From the airport to Downtown San Diego and Petco Park, it's a drive of 3-4 miles, which will take at least 10 minutes.

It's a two-step process to get from the airport to Downtown San Diego via the **trolley** system operated by **MTS** (Metropolitan Transit System, www.sdmts.com, $2.50). Hop onto the **rental car shuttle** from Terminal 1 or 2, and let the driver know you're headed to **Middletown station** (W. Palm St. and Pacific Hwy.). From the shuttle drop-off, cross the highway and go one block to the MTS station. Take the **Sycuan Green Line** into Downtown. Close to Petco Park, and the main transit hub in the city, is **12th & Imperial station** (12th Ave. and Imperial

Ave.). The more popular stop near the park is **Gaslamp Quarter** (6th Ave. and L St.), just one stop before 12th & Imperial.

TRAIN

Amtrak (www.amtrak.com) serves the area with the **Pacific Surfliner,** which starts in San Diego and heads north to San Luis Obispo, which is nearly halfway between Los Angeles and the Bay Area. You can connect to a number of other lines in Los Angeles.

The train station, **Santa Fe Depot** (1050 Kettner Blvd.), was constructed in 1915 in the Spanish architectural style. It's a beautiful, high-ceiling station that feels as grand as it is historic. The train station is just one mile northeast of Petco Park, less than a 10-minute car ride. Even better, it's a mere three stops on the **MTS trolley** (www.sdmts.com, $2.50) from the **Santa Fe Depot station** to the stadium. Take the **Sycuan Green Line** toward Downtown and disembark at the **Gaslamp Quarter station** (6th Ave. and L St.), a two-minute walk from Petco Park.

BUS

Greyhound (www.greyhound.com) serves the area, depositing passengers at the **Greyhound Bus Terminal** (Trolley Plaza at 13th St. and National Ave.), a mere two blocks southeast of Petco Park. There are daily trips to and from Los Angeles that cost as little as $8.

Petco Park

Opening in 2004, right in the middle of the retro-classic ballpark design wave, **Petco Park** (100 Park Blvd., www.mlb.com/padres) is arguably the finest blend of old and new in all of baseball. Set on a Downtown lot near the Gaslamp Quarter, Petco is surrounded by restaurants, bars, breweries, hotels, and other entertainment venues. But it's very much part of the city's history, thanks primarily to the building standing out in the left field corner.

The Western Metal Supply Co. building has stood on the lot for more than 100 years, and the park was constructed around it. The result: a park that embraces historic San Diego, while still looking forward.

One of the stadium's modern features is Park at the Park, a greenspace that opens far earlier than the other gates and offers picnic and play space for families. There are also tons of options for standing and sitting around the ballpark, something other ballparks can be found lacking. And while prices can be high for food and beverages at Petco, the selection is solid. Plenty of local, independent breweries from one of America's greatest beer scenes are represented here, and there are more than a few kiosks devoted to local eateries.

Petco Park is everything you want in a ballpark: It maintains a sense of place and history while being quite accessible. It has great views of the city, a prime location for pre- and post-game fun, and scores of options for food, drink, and family time. Best of all, the weather is awesome here.

ORIENTATION

Petco Park is just a few blocks from the **Gaslamp Quarter** of San Diego, a place filled with nightclubs, bars, breweries, and other good-time venues. It's also two blocks from San Diego Bay and within walking distance of one of the city's major transportation stations, 12th & Imperial.

There are six entry gates at Petco Park. You may want to enter at the **Gaslamp Gate** (left field corner at 7th Ave.), which is beside the Western Metal Supply Co. building. Gates typically open 90 minutes before first pitch, though times will vary from game to game.

TICKETS AND SEATING

Pricing

The Padres use a **dynamic pricing** model for tickets, meaning you'll pay more for games that draw more fans, like **weekend contests,** or when the **Dodgers** come on down for a series. Games against the **Angels,**

Petco Park

Giants, Yankees, and **Red Sox** are sure to demand higher-price tickets, too. An upper box reserved seat for a game against the Marlins may cost around $25, while that same seat for a game against the Dodgers may cost around $30. If it's a weekend contest, that seat's price could increase to $35 or so. Members of the **military** and their family members can get a military discount: 50 percent off Sunday games and 25 percent off all other games except the home opener. Premium areas that serve food or the Lexus Home Plate Club don't apply.

Seating Plan

Petco has a variety of seating sections within each of its **three levels.** Odd-numbered sections are on the first-base side; even-numbered sections are on the third-base side.

The **100 level,** or **field level,** is split around the infield with lower rows and upper rows. At home plate, along the **lower rows** and moving outward, is **field VIP** (sections 101-109, 102-110). Just at first and third base is **field infield** (sections 111-113, 112-114). In shallow right and left field, respectively, is **field plaza** (sections 115-119, 116-118). Just before or at the foul poles is **field box** (sections 121-127, 120-124).

Along the **upper rows** of the first level, there's the **premier club** (sections A-L) and the **premier club lounge** (P1-P16), which both stretch from third base around to first base. Next is **field infield** (sections 107, 108), **field plaza** (sections 109-111, 110-112), and **field reserved** (sections 113-115, 114-116), which is just beyond first and third base, respectively. In moderate right and left field,

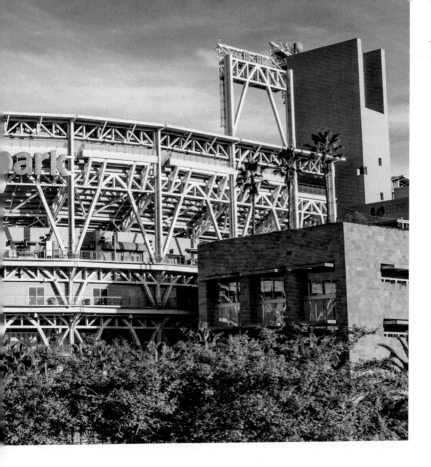

respectively, is **field box** (sections 117-119, 118). Near the foul poles is **field pavilion** (sections 120-124, 121-123). In right field at the pole are **all-you-can-eat sections** (sections 125, 127).

The **200 level,** or **club level,** starts at home plate and moves out around the infield. It includes the **Toyota Terrace VIP** (sections 201-203, 202-204), the **Toyota Terrace Infield** (sections 205-209, 206-210), the **Toyota Terrace Reserved** (sections 211-217, 212-216), and the **Toyota Terrace Pavilion** (sections 219-223, 218-222).

The **300 level,** or the **upper level,** is also split between lower and upper rows. The **lower areas,** starting at home plate and moving outward, include **upper box infield** (sections 300-312, 301-313), **upper box reserved** (sections 315-319, 316-320),

and **upper box pavilion** (sections 323-327, 322-328). As for the **upper areas,** starting at home plate, there's the **upper infield** (sections 300-312, 301-311), the **upper reserved** (sections 315-319, 316-320), and the **upper pavilion** (sections 321-327, 322-328).

Suites and group areas at Petco Park include **Toyota Beach** (right center field), a packed spot with a bar; the **Estrella Jalisco Landing** (under the left field scoreboard); the **Templeton Rye Home Run Deck** (right field) at the fence; the **Picnic Terrace** (left field), an open-air seating area; the **Pacifico Porch** (left field line at the foul pole), which is against the Western Metal Supply Co. building; and the **Skyline Patio** (third base), a private space with standing room and some chairs. The **Western Metal Supply**

GAME COSTS

Tickets: For most games, you can get an upper-level seat for less than **$20,** and good seats, even in the field level, will be available for **$30** or so. But if the Dodgers are in town, or if the Padres are hosting the Red Sox, Yankees, or Giants, or even the Phillies or Cubs, ticket prices will rise a little.

Hot dog: They start at **$5** or so here, so prices are average compared to the rest of the league.

Beer: Good beer has its price at Petco Park. You'll pay nearly **$15** for a craft beer, while macro-brews start at around **$6** and can cost as much as **$12.**

Parking: If you want to park at a Padres preferred lot, you'll pay **$20-40,** which is quite expensive. In Downtown San Diego there are spots and garages that typically run **$10-30,** which is more palatable.

Co. **building** (left field) has three distinct seating areas for groups: the **Suites** (on the third and fourth floors), the **Rooftop,** and the **Rail,** which offers a drink rail outside the fourth floor of the building. All of these sections require advanced and specific tickets, and they occasionally become available if groups don't reserve them first.

Where to Buy Tickets

Considering that the Padres historically don't draw a ton of fans, you can always get good, inexpensive seats through a variety of methods. For one, the **Padres box office** may have good deals on seats just before the game starts. **StubHub** is a good place to find seats at the last minute. Finally, there's a local deal: If you have a Costco card, go to a **San Diego-area Costco** to purchase discounted tickets to games.

If you buy tickets through the team or from StubHub, you can upgrade your seat at Petco through the **MLB Ballpark app.**

Best Seats

For **full shade,** great **views,** and seats that are **close to the action,** opt for the **back rows** of the **third-base side** of **field infield** (sections 112 and 114). If you're not looking to spend much, you can't go wrong with the **upper-row** seats in **sections 300-312.** They get **partial shade,** are closer to the field than most 300 level seats in baseball, and provide solid **views of the city.** The sun will shine on you in the 300 level along the right-field line, and just about everywhere in the outfield.

If you can score discounted tickets for one of the **Toyota Terrace** sections (which occupy much of the 200 level), snag them. These seats offer comfort, easy access to food and drink, and widescreen views of the field and skyline.

Want to be social? The best bet is **The Rail** (Western Metal Supply Co. fourth floor, left field), attached to a restaurant and bar called The Loft. There are lots of Budweiser products sold here, but fans clamor to be part of this atmosphere, one of the coolest seating areas in the league.

If you have kids and imagine you won't be spending more than an inning in a seat, grab cheap tickets for **Park at the Park** (beyond center field), which has picnic-style seating and a ball field for children.

KNOW BEFORE YOU GO

Petco Park has a **bag** policy that disallows anything bigger than 16- by 16- by 8-inches. **Outside food** is permitted, but it must be consumed in general seating or picnic areas. Items should be wrapped or bagged, and containers must be soft-sided and small enough to fit under a seat. Sealed, plastic bottles of unflavored **water** that are one liter or smaller can be brought into the park.

You can leave Petco and come back during the same game, a rare policy for a ballpark; you'll need to get your hand and ticket stamped upon exiting.

There is a nursing lounge at **Suite 32 of the Toyota Terrace** (200 level) for mothers wanting to nurse in a quiet space.

BE A FAN

For the longest time, the Padres were something of an afterthought, not just across the baseball landscape, but even in their own town. Padres fans are wonderful folks who desperately want that first world championship, but there aren't a whole lot of them out there. Chances are while at Petco Park, you'll find yourself just fine in whatever team's gear you wear. The Dodgers are the team's most serious rival, but that battle has been one-sided for so long that Dodger fans don't need to feel worried about stepping into Petco.

When the Padres hit a home run, keep an eye on center field. **Four torches** out there will light as fireworks shoot up and a ship's whistle blares. This is a reference to the USS *Ronald Reagan*, a Naval aircraft carrier that's ported in the city. When a Padres pitcher strikes out a hitter, you'll hear the song **"Spoonman"** by Soundgarden.

Accessibility

Wheelchair-accessible, semi-ambulatory, and **transfer seats** are available at Petco Park. For more information about seating, call the **Padres ticket office** (619/795-5555). **Wheelchair escorts** are available through the guest services centers.

Guest services centers are located at sections 108, 208, and 303. Visit the **guest services center** at section 108 for **assistive listening devices** and **gravity blankets.** Every guest services center has **wheelchair storage,** as well as **sensory bags.** The bags include **noise-cancelling headphones, fidget toys, feeling thermometers,** and **wristbands** for seat location information. You can check out a bag by turning in valid photo ID as a deposit.

Petco Park's **elevators** are located at sections 111, 114, 117, 201, 217, 226, 235, 300, 311, 314, 317, and 328, plus inside the Western Metal Supply Co. building, and at the Gaslamp, East Village, Park Boulevard, and Home Plate Gates.

Interpreters and **translators** are available through any of the guest services centers. **Service animals** are welcome at Petco Park.

All **parking lots** owned or contracted by the Padres have **accessible parking spaces.** A **shuttle service** to Petco Park is available at the Padres Parkade, Tailgate Park, and MTS Garage. If you want to take the shuttle after the game, head to the **guest services center** at section 108 to check in.

GETTING THERE

Public Transit

The **MTS** (www.sdmts.com, $2.50), which operates San Diego's **trolley** system, has four lines (**Orange, Sycuan Green, UC San Diego Blue,** and **SDG&E Silver**) that stop at **12th & Imperial station** (12th Ave. and Imperial Ave.), which is just two blocks east of Petco Park. If you're on the Green or Silver Lines, you can disembark at the **Gaslamp Quarter station** (6th Ave. and L St.), just one stop before 12th & Imperial, to get a bit closer to the stadium.

Driving

If you drive to the game, think about parking your car in Old Town San Diego and taking the **Green Line** of the **light rail** (www.sdmts.com, $2.50) to the stadium. You can find parking in Old Town that's much cheaper than what you'd pay near the park, which can run upwards of $40.

But if you really want to park close to the ballpark, there are **lots** just north of Market Street that cost $10-20 per car, which is as cheap as it gets most of the time. I-5 curls around Petco Park and Downtown, exiting at 10th Avenue. Take that south and start looking for parking once you turn onto **F Street.**

PARK FEATURES AND SIGHTS

There are **bricks** (Palm Court Plaza, left field near Western Metal Supply Co. building; Tony Gwynn Plaza, Park at the Park) laid out around Petco, purchased by fans wanting to leave their lasting mark on the venue. One brick has a coded message: "Break Open Your Cold Ones / Toast The Padres / Enjoy This Champion Organization"—it was purchased by PETA to protest naming the stadium after Petco, a company PETA has accused of mistreating animals.

Park at the Park

When coming to Petco Park, you might want to enter via **Park at the Park** (840 K St., beyond center field), a 2.7-acre park that acts as an introduction to the venue, as well as an inexpensive seating area. There's a gate at Park at the Park's entrance, so once inside, you're in the ballpark. There are lawns for picnicking, a children's ball field, a huge monitor that shows the game, a kiosk for Phil's BBQ, the concert venue Sycuan Stage, and the **Tony Gwynn statue,** a 9.5-foot-tall bronze sculpture by William Behrends. The Park at the Park opens 2.5 hours before the game at both the Gaslamp and East Village Gates.

The Swinging Friar

Be on the lookout for the Padres' mascot, the **Swinging Friar.** Dressed in a brown friar's robe, this big-nosed chum has been a mascot in San Diego since 1961, when he was with the Pacific Coast League Padres. Not here, however, is the **San Diego Chicken,** a favorite mascot of the 1970s and 1980s. The chicken showed up at Petco for the Padres' 50-year anniversary in 2019, but you probably won't find the furry yellow scamp around the park.

Western Metal Supply Co.

It's undoubtedly the most iconic image at Petco Park: Standing in left field, part of the outfield backdrop, is the **Western Metal Supply Co. building** (left field).

Constructed in 1909, it was spared from demolition mostly because of its historic status, and the Padres built Petco around the structure. It adds blue-collar character to the ballpark, and once in a while a hitter will nail a ball off the building's wall in a home run.

The left field foul pole is one of the building's corners. The ground floor is home to the Padres Team Store and an exhibit for the **Padres Hall of Fame** (left field, back of the building). Here, you can follow San Diego baseball history, which includes the Pacific Coast League Padres and hometown great Ted Williams. The exhibit is a shrine to the greatest players the team has ever employed, including Garry Templeton, Ken Caminiti, Nate Colbert, and "Mr. Padre" Tony Gwynn.

The second and third levels of the building hold group suites (for at least 31 people), its fourth floor is occupied by a restaurant and bar called The Loft, plus a balcony of ticketed seats called The Rail. Finally, its rooftop is a bar and hangout with food vendors; you can get tickets for this space but often groups reserve the whole area.

FOOD AND DRINKS

The most famous barbecue joint in San Diego is **Phil's BBQ** (section 113, Park at the Park, Western Metal Supply Co. rooftop), which specializes in juicy pork and beef ribs, slathered in a popular homemade sauce, plus sandwiches and other goodies. Head to section 113 for the largest menu of the three locations, which also includes Phil's ticklers: two onion rings, slaw, and fries, with your choice of meat.

Get Roman pizza (known for a bubbly, crispy crust, thanks to a long fermentation process) at **Buona Forchetta** (section 104), a San Diego pie shop that has a kiosk at Petco. Neapolitan pizza, gelato, and wine are also available here.

You can nab plenty of pork at **Carnitas' Snack Shack** (section 228), the Petco kiosk of another local favorite. Carnitas has porky sandwiches like the Triple Threat, with pulled pork, bacon, and pork loin schnitzel, and seasoned fries, plus tacos.

There's a local cheesesteak purveyor that gets a lot of traction. **Gaglione Brothers** (sections 101, 124, Western Metal Supply Co. rooftop) sells relatively authentic Philly cheesesteaks (it uses rolls from Philly bread company Amoroso's). Get yours with Cheese Whiz, and complement it with a side of Whiz fries.

San Diego is famous for its beer. There's a solid concentration of craft options between sections 101 and 105, including a **Craft Beers of San Diego stand** (sections 105, 110, 215, 226, 229, 303, 328). **Ballast Point**—maker of popular IPA Sculpin and now owned by a corporation that sells imported brands like Corona, Negra Modelo, and Pacifico—has the deepest footprint at the ballpark. They have **kiosks** (sections 110, 226) and a larger **tap room** (section 207), which pour a whole bunch of fruited Sculpin varieties. You can find other local craft options, like offerings from **Mike Hess Brewing** and **Karl Strauss Brewing Company,** at **Jack & Craft** (sections 117, 226).

If you want local favorite **AleSmith,** head to **.394** (section 217), a restaurant and bar in the Toyota Terrace serving traditional American fare like macaroni and cheese, chicken tenders, and a chop salad. While they have AleSmith beers on tap, there are no field views here.

The biggest restaurant at Petco is **The Loft** (Western Metal Supply Co., fourth floor, left field), which serves upscale hot dogs and bratwurst, nachos, and barbecue, plus craft cocktails and lots of Budweiser products (including furniture and signs). The Loft is a popular spot among fans, but I recommend just a quick stop here before moving on to the better beer and food selections across the ballpark.

Photos (from top to bottom): Tony Gwynn statue by sculptor William Behrends; Swinging Friar, the San Diego Padres' mascot; the Western Metal Supply Co. building.

EVENTS

Autographs aren't guaranteed, as there is no team policy either for or against, but those seeking them should try to head down to the areas near the dugouts once the gates open. Since gates open to the public 90 minutes before first pitch, you should be able to watch at least the opposing team's **batting practice.** Season ticket holders can get into the park 2.5 hours before first pitch, which means they can catch the Padres at the plate.

If you're coming to the park on a Friday, you can head to Park at the Park for $5 drink specials and live music. The Padres also host plenty of **themed events,** celebrating everything from *Star Wars* to people who love the music of Jimmy Buffett.

Tours

The Padres offer **tours** (619/795-5011, 10:30am, 12:30pm, and 3pm daily non-game days, 10:30am and 12:30pm game days, $20, $17 seniors, military, and ages 12 and under, free kids under 36 inches in height) that typically visit the dugout, visitors' clubhouse, press box, Western Metal Supply Co. building, and Park at the Park. Be sure to call ahead of time to ensure tours are scheduled for the day you'd like to visit.

SHOPPING

The main **Padres Team Store** (215 Tony Gwynn Dr., 619/795-5910, 10am-7pm Mon.-Sat., 11am-5pm Sun., closes one hour after game ends) is on the first floor of the Western Metal Supply Co. building out in left field. It's like most team stores in major league ballparks, littered with racks of throwback and modern-day jerseys and T-shirts. It's set inside a space with high ceilings and plenty of nooks where you can find little pieces of memorabilia like bobbleheads and jars of barbecue sauce made by Randy Jones, a pitcher who had a decent career for the Padres in the 1970s.

Look for **'47** (ground floor, Western Metal Supply Co. building), where you'll find leisurewear branded with the Padres logo—everything from hats to T-shirts to sweatshirts, and encompassing all eras of the team's history.

SAN DIEGO SIGHTS

TED WILLIAMS FIELD

Famed baseball player Ted Williams grew up in San Diego. His **boyhood home** (4121 Utah St.) still stands, but it's a private residence, so there's not much to see. Just two blocks away, however, is **Ted Williams Field** (Idaho St. and Polk Ave.), the baseball field where "The Splendid Splinter" learned to play the game. The field is little more than a youth-league baseball field with some bleachers and a cage around home plate, but it's neat to check out the place where arguably baseball's greatest hitter learned that perfect swing.

SAN DIEGO ZOO

Part of Balboa Park, the **San Diego Zoo** (2920 Zoo Dr., 619/231-1515, http://zoo. sandiegozoo.org, hours can vary but generally 9am-9pm daily July-Labor Day, 9am-6pm daily Labor Day-July, one-day pass $56, $46 ages 3-11, two-visit pass $90, $80 ages 3-11) is one of the world's most famous zoos, home to more than 3,500 animals. On a visit here, you can see koalas in the Australian Outback exhibit, a host of polar bears, and both African and Asian elephants in a 2.5-acre elephant exhibit.

Possibly the best way to introduce yourself to the zoo is via the **Guided Bus Tour** (free with admission), a 35-minute narrated double-decker bus tour of the zoo. Then there's the **Kangaroo Bus** (free with admission), which shuttles passengers to five different stops around the zoo. The **Skyfari Aerial Tram** (10am-6pm daily) goes from one end of the zoo to the other (but note that the tram can't accommodate wheelchairs or strollers).

Other attractions at the zoo include a 4-D theater experience, daily animal encounters, and zookeeper talks focusing on lemurs, wolves, and baboons.

SEAWORLD SAN DIEGO

About 20 minutes north from Downtown San Diego, on an island to itself, is **SeaWorld San Diego** (500 Sea World Dr., 619/222-4732, www.seaworld.com, 10:30am-5pm Mon.-Fri., 10am-7pm Sat., 10am-6pm Sun., from $56 ages 3 and over). It's famous for its shows, where you can watch dolphins soar out of the water, sea lions put on a comedy show, and the ever-popular Orca Encounter, which isn't the theatrical show the park used to put on (discontinued because treatment of the orcas was deemed unethical), but more an "educational" look at killer whales while they swim about. Kids may get splashed. SeaWorld is also an amusement park with thrill rides, a few children's rides (including one with Elmo and one with Oscar the Grouch), and a rollicking rafting trip called Shipwreck Rapids.

FOOD

NEAR PETCO PARK

You're going to want tacos. I suggest **Lola 55** (1290 F St., 619/542-9155, www.lola55.com, 11:30am-9pm Sun.-Thurs., 11:30am-10pm Fri.-Sat., under $25), which elevates their fare with high-quality ingredients and flavor profiles, so you'll pay a little extra. But it's worth it. Pork belly al pastor and a spicy-as-all-get-out smoked fish go great with the spot's original cocktails. There are plenty of agave-based drinks here, plus *micheladas* and Bloody Marias. The restaurant has high ceilings, plenty of natural light, and a casual, living room vibe.

Want tacos and a nice cocktail, but without the worry that you're underdressed? You can step into **La Puerta** (560 4th Ave., 619/696-3466, www.lapuertasd.com, 11am-1am Mon.-Fri., 10am-1am Sat.-Sun., under $30) for street tacos, gourmet

offerings, and loaded *papas fritas* (french fries). A small but local draft list and a deep roster of tequila enlivens this cool space in the Gaslamp Quarter.

If you're near Petco for a game, step into **Barleymash** (600 5th Ave., 619/255-7373, www.barleymash.com, 11:30am-2am Mon.-Fri., 9am-2am Sat., 10am-2am Sun., under $50), located in the Gaslamp Quarter and home to a full menu of macaroni-and-cheese dishes, flatbreads, fries, and burgers, plus a bunch of decent dinner entrées. It's a great place to watch baseball, with plenty of televisions, a good amount of bar seats, and a deep list of craft beer.

OTHER NEIGHBORHOODS

Want a happy hour hangout? Head to **Bankers Hill** (2202 4th Ave., 619/231-0222, www.bankershillsd.com, 4:30pm-9:30pm Mon.-Thurs., 4:30pm-10:30pm Fri.-Sat., 10am-2pm and 4:30pm-9:30pm Sun., under $40), which offers inexpensive burger sliders and sandwiches, plus solid small plates, from cheese with pear jam to homemade potato chips. This is a friendly, fun dining room that doesn't seem to take itself seriously. Find it in the neighborhood of the same name, on the southwest side of Balboa Park.

A chicken-lover's paradise, **The Crack Shack** (2266 Kettner Blvd., 619/795-3299, www.crackshack.com, 9am-10pm Sun.-Thurs., 9am-11pm Fri.-Sat., under $25) is a small chain that started at this location in popular Little Italy, and it's seriously addictive. There are sandwiches, fried chicken meals, chicken-based bowls, and fun small plates like chicken oysters. Make sure you also grab a milkshake. With indoor and outdoor seating and an ultra-casual atmosphere that will definitely be energetic on the weekends, it's a place you should hit.

Downtown San Diego is home to **Donut Bar** (631 B St., 619/255-6360, www.donutbar.com, 7am-1pm Mon.-Fri., 8am-1pm Sat.-Sun., 5pm-10pm Fri.-Sat., under $10), a very popular place to get fluffy, airy, yeasty treats. If you come on a weekend morning, be prepared to stand in line. The donuts here run the gamut, often topped with candy and pop culture-themed goodies. The place lives up to the second half of its name, serving beer and other alcoholic beverages.

BARS AND BREWERIES

NEAR PETCO PARK

If you want a bar, it's **Bub's at the Ballpark** (715 J St., 619/546-0815, www.bubssandiego.com, 11am-2am Mon.-Fri., 10am-2am Sat.-Sun.). With fun lighting, a decent beer selection (albeit mostly macro-brews), a few games, and a lively crowd on game days, this is the iconic pre- or post-game spot. During games the place gets packed.

Your job in San Diego is to hit as many breweries as you can—within reason, that is. Just a block from the park is **Half Door Brewing Co.** (903 Island Ave., 619/232-9845, www.halfdoorbrewing.com, 11am-2am Mon.-Fri., 9am-2am Sat.-Sun.), whose impressive bar is home to a variety of European-influenced suds, primarily those of the Irish persuasion. There's cozy seating upstairs, along with a patio from where you can see into Petco, though the view is mostly of the seats—you won't be able to see the game from here.

Two blocks east of Petco is **Mission Brewery** (1441 L St., 619/544-0555, www.missionbrewery.com, noon-10pm Sun.-Thurs., noon-midnight Fri.-Sat.), located in the 1894 Wonder Bread factory, and whose brand started back in 1913. Mission does fine interpretations of well-known styles (IPA, hefeweizen, blonde), plus an easy-drinking lager. This is your best bet if you want a huge place to drink local beer near the park, even if it's not the best possible beer you can find.

OTHER NEIGHBORHOODS

There are other must-visits when in San Diego. For one, there's **Gravity Heights** (9920 Pacific Heights Blvd., 858/283-8206,

www.gravityheights.com, 11am-9pm Mon.-Thurs., 11am-9:30pm Fri., 10am-9:30pm Sat., 10am-8pm Sun.). This is way up north in the Sorrento Valley neighborhood, but it delivers on a variety of styles in a lovely, modern space.

For a beautiful beer-sipping experience, visit **Eppig Brewing Waterfront Biergarten** (2817 Dickens St., 619/756-6825, www.eppigbrewing.com, noon-8:30pm Sun.-Wed., noon-9pm Thurs.-Sat.). Located right on the water, at America's Cup Harbor, Eppig specializes in older styles like pilsner, *festbier, maibock,* and Baltic porter, but it also has a nice variety of IPAs. Be sure to park down the street at a public lot, as there's no parking at the brewery itself.

Over in the fun, hipster-friendly North Park neighborhood, there's **Mike Hess Brewing** (3812 Grim Ave., 619/255-7136, www.mikehessbrewing.com, noon-10pm Sun.-Thurs., noon-midnight Fri.-Sat.), which likes to brew accessible, traditional beers along with wildly experimental fare. The taproom is family- and pet-friendly, and is a great jumping off point for other breweries in the area, including Belching Beaver and Pariah.

RECREATION

PARKS

Balboa Park

Home to 17 museums and the San Diego Zoo, **Balboa Park** (Park Blvd. and I-5, 619/239-0512, www.balboapark.org) is a 1,200-acre wonderland. You can simply walk about the park, or take in a show at one of the theaters on site. But you'll definitely want to look for structures built for the 1915-16 Panama-California Exposition, which was held at Balboa Park.

For one, there's the **California Tower,** which is home to the **San Diego Museum of Man** (1350 El Prado, 619/239-2001, www.museumofman.org, 10am-5pm daily, $13, free ages 5 and under). Built to

SAN DIEGO'S CRAFT BREWERIES

San Diego is one of the brewing meccas of America, so you might want to plot a list of taprooms and facilities to visit while you're here. Here are the local bucket-list places, the big names that no self-respecting beer drinker should miss.

Modern Times Beer

- **Ballast Point Brewing Company** (5401 Linda Vista Rd. #406, 619/295-2337, www.ballastpoint.com, 10am-10pm Mon.-Thurs., 9am-10pm Fri.-Sun.): This is one of the biggest names in brewing. This is the original location, where you'll find the Home Brew Mart. There's another location in **Little Italy** (2215 India St., 619/255-7213, 11am-10pm daily).

- **Stone Brewing Company** (1999 Citracado Pkwy., Escondido, 760/294-7899, www.stonebrewing.com, 11am-10pm Sun.-Thurs., 11am-11pm Fri.-Sat.): At this beautiful location, the World Bistro & Gardens, you can have the great Stone IPA and experience for yourself this pioneer in modern American brewing.

- **Mikkeller Brewing** (9366 Cabot Dr., 858/381-3500, www.mikkellersd.com, 3pm-9pm Mon.-Wed., 3pm-10pm Thurs.-Fri., noon-10pm Sat., noon-9pm Sun.): This San Diego outpost of the famous Danish brewery serves up some of the tastiest beers in the country.

- **AleSmith Brewing Company** (9990 AleSmith Ct., 858/549-9888, www.alesmith.com, 11am-10pm Mon.-Thurs., 11am-11pm Fri.-Sat., 11am-9pm Sun.): Another iconic San Diego brewery, AleSmith isn't afraid to be unique. Get .394, named in honor of Tony Gwynn's 1994 batting average. This nice modern taproom is in the Miramar area that's home to a bunch more breweries, including 32 North, Rough Draft, and a Ballast Point outpost.

- **Modern Times Beer** (3725 Greenwood St., 619/546-9694, www.moderntimesbeer.com, noon-10pm Mon.-Thurs., noon-midnight Fri., 11am-midnight Sat., 11am-10pm Sun.): This original location of the very popular brewery has a spacious taproom with fun art on the walls, games, and coffee.

resemble a Spanish church, the California Tower (part of a group of buildings called the California Building) is 198 feet tall and offers 360-degree views of San Diego from its observation deck. Tours are given of the tower, which underwent a retrofitting project starting in 2019. As for the museum, it aims to explore human experience, with exhibits that span decades and centuries. Past and present exhibits include an examination of the evolution of humans living with animals, and a deep dive into the concept of race.

Another building to find is the **Botanical Building** (1549 El Prado, 619/239-0512, www.balboapark.org, 10am-4pm Fri.-Wed., free), introduced by the narrow, welcoming lily pond and lagoon. The Spanish Revival building includes more than 2,100 plants, including ferns, palms, and tropical species. The lily pond has plenty of water lilies and lotus. This is as picturesque as it gets in San Diego, and it's worth a visit.

Also at the park is the **San Diego Natural History Museum** (1788 El Prado, 619/232-3821, www.sdnhm.org, 10am-5pm daily, $20, $17 seniors and students, $12 ages 3-17, free ages 2 and under). The Nat, as it's known, has a skeleton of an Allosaurus (a relative of the

Tyrannosaurus rex), an exhibit detailing the habitats of Southern California, rare gems, an area where kids can run and play, and a number of special exhibits.

Opening in 2021, the **Comic-Con Museum** (2131 Pan American Plaza, 619/414-1020, www.comic-con.org) is heaven for fans of pop culture, superhero entertainment, and fantasy lovers. It includes rotating exhibits, educational programming, and more. San Diego has played host to Comic-Con since 1970.

There are number of other museums here and most of them are worth your time, including the **San Diego Air & Space Museum** (2001 Pan American Plaza, 619/234-8291, www.sandiegoairandspace. org, 10am-4:30pm daily, $20, $17 seniors and students, $11 ages 3-11, free ages 2 and under) and the **Mingei International Museum** (1439 El Prado, 619/239-0003, www.mingei.org), which specializes in folk art from across the world. It underwent a major renovation from 2018-2019.

Sunset Cliffs Natural Park

Out on the Point Loma peninsula, west of Downtown San Diego, is **Sunset Cliffs Natural Park** (Ladera St. and Comish Dr.), a 68-acre environment that's home to gorgeous cliffs and rugged land. The best way to visit is by driving south on Sunset Cliffs Boulevard (starting at Coronado Ave.) to take in the beauty from your vehicle. Then, after turning onto Ladera Street and entering the park, you can step out and explore. This is a perfect place to watch sunset. Down below the cliffs is **Garbage Beach,** accessible via a steep descent, so wear good hiking shoes or boots. It's a popular place to surf and sunbathe. But one piece of advice: Do not try to jump off any cliffs here. People have died trying to do so at Sunset Cliffs.

Photos (from top to bottom): San Diego Zoo; Botanical Building in Balboa Park; Hotel del Coronado and Central Beach.

BEACHES

It's a quick 15-minute drive from Petco Park, including a trip over the Coronado Bridge, to **Coronado.** This resort town was developed in the late 19th century and quickly became a destination for its picturesque location between San Diego and the Pacific Ocean, and because of its pristine beaches. It's considered to have some of the best beaches in America. It gets crowded here, so come early in the day.

Coronado Central Beach

Most popular is **Central Beach** (Ocean Blvd. and Isabella Ave., Coronado), a 1.5-mile strip of light golden sand giving way to glimmering blue water. It's free to play on the beach (and there's free parking on Ocean Blvd. and Ferry Landing Marketplace), so plan to spend some time here. Be sure to check out the **Hotel del Coronado** (1500 Orange Ave.), a magnificent, palatial, Victorian-style resort seen in the Marilyn Monroe vehicle *Some Like it Hot.* It's a triumph of turn-of-the-20th-century architecture and a mark of the American Gilded Age, when opulence and luxury thrived.

Silver Strand State Beach

Just south from Central Beach is **Silver Strand State Beach** (5000 CA-75, 619/435-5184, www.parks.ca.gov, 7am-9pm daily Memorial Day-Labor Day, 7am-8pm daily Labor Day-Oct. and Mar.-Memorial Day, 7am-7pm daily Nov.-Feb., day use parking $10-20). This beach is for a more basic experience. There are camping opportunities (reservations 800/444-7275, $20 nightly), plus guided nature walks led by state park workers.

ACCOMMODATIONS

NEAR PETCO PARK

The **Bristol Hotel** (1055 1st Ave., 619/232-6141, www.thebristolsandiego.com,

$140-250) has bright, modern rooms, some with great views of the city and San Diego Bay. At this price point, it's hard to beat. It's a one-mile walk from Petco, so we'll call it "near" the ballpark.

To get as close as possible, book a room at the **Omni San Diego Hotel** (675 L St., 619/231-6664, www.omnihotels.com, $250-350). This luxury accommodation is right next to Petco (there's a skybridge that connects the two buildings), with some rooms offering views of the field, so you could just get an upstairs hotel room and watch the game from there. The Omni has a ballpark package that includes two discounted tickets, hot dogs, beers, and bags of peanuts.

OTHER NEIGHBORHOODS

By the airport and in nearby Old Town, you'll find a slew of chain hotels. For an independent option, go for the historic **Cosmopolitan Hotel** (2660 Calhoun St., 619/297-1874, www.oldtowncosmopolitan. com, $150-250), an 1827 building that was first the magnificent home of a wealthy cattle rancher. It became a two-story hotel by the 1870s, the social center of Old Town San Diego. The current hotel attempts to recall the 1870s heyday of the building with small but well-appointed rooms with antique furniture and Victorian wallpaper. Some rooms have balconies or tubs. Continental breakfast is offered to all guests.

Hotel del Coronado

If you're looking to stay at one of the most famous hotels in America, get your room booked early for the **Hotel del Coronado** (1500 Orange Ave., Coronado, 619/435-6611, www.hoteldel.com, $200-650). This four-star Victorian hotel is posh, pricey, and located on the beach. Its rooms and suites are tranquil, with just the right touches of beige, pastel yellow, and gray, and outfitted like homes away from home. You can get a beach view or resort view. Dining and drinking options include an upscale sea-to-table concept, wood-fired pizza, a taco shack, and a straightforward American-style bistro.

GETTING AROUND

PUBLIC TRANSIT

MTS (www.sdmts.com, $2.50) operates a **trolley system** (that's more like light rail) that includes four distinct lines that thread through the city. They all meet at **12th & Imperial station** (12th Ave. and Imperial Ave.), which is only a six-minute walk east from Petco Park.

From 12th & Imperial, the **Sycuan Green Line** heads west by northwest. Its closest stop to Petco Park is the **Gaslamp Quarter station** (6th Ave. and L St.), which is also on the Silver Line. The Green Line continues on toward San Diego International Airport, then it cuts east through Mission Valley before finishing on a northeast route into the East County city of El Cajon.

The **Orange Line** starts Downtown at the **Courthouse station** (State St. and C St.) and moves through Central San Diego, then heads east and finally north, reaching East County areas like La Mesa and Santee.

The **UC San Diego Blue Line** runs parallel with the Orange Line for several stops in Central San Diego, then heads south toward cities like Chula Vista and Imperial Beach, stopping just before the U.S.-Mexico border.

The **SDG&E Silver Line** is a smaller route that bounds around Downtown San Diego. It meets up with the other lines at 12th & Imperial, and stops at the Gaslamp Quarter station. This line is best if you're hopping around Downtown.

MTS also runs a comprehensive **bus system** that crisscrosses the city.

TAXI, UBER, AND LYFT

Prices seem to be a hair cheaper for Uber than Lyft around town. Taxi rates are a bit higher than both ride-sharing companies. If you use the **RideYellow App** from **Yellow Cab** (619/444-4444), you'll get a cheaper rate, though the app doesn't allow for airport pick-ups.

CAR

San Diego County is huge, and people live throughout the area in smaller cities and towns, making for sometimes adventurous rush-hour driving, especially on the freeways. But otherwise driving around here isn't too bad. The major highways that run north to south include **I-5** (or the **San Diego Freeway**), which rides close to San Diego Bay and Pacific Ocean; **I-15** (or **Escondido Freeway**), which comes down from Escondido, running just east of Downtown San Diego before hooking up with I-5 near National City; and **I-805,** which connects North County with cities like National City and Chula Vista, staying just east of Downtown San Diego.

I-8 starts at Ocean Beach by the Pacific Ocean, then threads east above Central San Diego, into La Mesa, and heads toward Cuyamaca Rancho State Park. Other eastbound highways include **CA-94,** which shoots off I-5 east of Petco Park; and **CA-54,** starting between National City and Chula Vista and continuing into Rancho San Diego. The area's only toll road is **CA-125,** which parallels I-15 east of San Diego and offers an alternative for people living in East County.

Downtown, the north-south streets are numbered, while the east-west streets are lettered. **Market Street** and **Broadway** are main thoroughfares also running east-west, providing boundaries for the Gaslamp Quarter. Up in Little Italy, the north-south streets aren't numbered, as they go beyond Front Street and include **India Street** and **Kettner Boulevard.**

Once you get above Little Italy and past Balboa Park, the streets become much hillier and a lot less straight. Old Town, especially, has some ups and downs, and twists and turns.

LOS ANGELES
DODGERS AND ANGELS

Baseball came to the Los Angeles

area around the turn of the 20th century, as the Los Angeles Angels started play in 1890s, then joined the nascent Pacific Coast League for its first season in 1903. The PCL was wildly successful and the Angels triumphed during its 54 years, achieving an incredible 137-50 record in 1934, one of 11 championship seasons. By that time, the Angels were an affiliate of the Chicago Cubs, but in 1957 they became a part of the Brooklyn Dodgers' farm system. That move proved crucial to what came next, another move that would forever change American baseball.

With his acquisition of the Angels, Dodgers owner Walter O'Malley had what he needed to secure a move of his big-league club from New York. O'Malley, angry that he couldn't get a new

Brooklyn ballpark, decided in 1957 to move his team to California and into Los Angeles Memorial Coliseum. The move, along with the simultaneous shifting of the Giants from Manhattan to San Francisco, singlehandedly disrupted baseball, opening the West to major league play for the first time.

Los Angeles got itself a good ball club, as the Dodgers had won their first World Series title in 1955 and won the National League pennant in 1956. By 1959 the Dodgers, now in L.A., were back on top, led by young pitchers Sandy Koufax and Don Drysdale. They'd win it all again in 1963 and 1965, but the great Koufax would announce his retirement after the 1966 season, just 11 years into his career. After a few years in the basement, the Dodgers would reemerge for a long period of success that included multiple World Series appearances, and wins in 1981 and 1988 thanks to manager Tommy Lasorda and pitchers like Fernando Valenzuela and Orel Hershiser. That 1988 World Series included one of baseball's most memorable home runs, a winning shot in Game 1 by a visibly injured Kirk Gibson.

Since that win, the Dodgers have been a bit star-crossed. In 2008 and 2009 they returned to the National League Championship Series but received death blows from the Philadelphia Phillies. A decade later, the Dodgers fielded exceptional teams that just couldn't get the ring. Consecutive World Series losses in 2017 and 2018 were tough to swallow, but the Dodgers remain a top franchise by their talent alone. The team also has plenty of money, lots of fan support, and a ballpark that's withstood the test of time.

Compare that to the Angels, who have always been seen as a stepchild of sorts in the Los Angeles metro area. They came to life a few years after the Dodgers, in 1961, after actor and country musician Gene Autry bought the team from O'Malley. Autry started the team at the Angels' old minor league park of Wrigley Field (the one in Los Angeles, not Chicago), then moved to Dodger Stadium for a few seasons before

inhabiting their own new park, Anaheim Stadium, in 1966. The idea: Build up Anaheim, home to Disneyland, as a state-of-the-art tourist and entertainment destination.

That same year, the team was going by the new name of the California Angels, and while they sported clean and crisp jerseys with a soft red emblem, they were never that good. There was a run of relative success in the late 1970s and 1980s, when teams featuring Hall of Famer Rod Carew and an aging Reggie Jackson won the American League West division three times. They couldn't get over the hump, however, and that misfortune would last until Autry sold the club to the Walt Disney Company in 1996.

After this sale, they were renamed the Anaheim Angels, playing in their renovated ballpark. After a couple years nearing contention, the team broke through in 2002 with an unlikely championship spurred by clutch relief pitching, solid offensive production, and the presence of thunder sticks and a Rally Monkey. The next year, Disney sold the team to businessman Arte Moreno, who changed the name to the awkward Los Angeles Angels of Anaheim. The team stayed in contention for another decade thanks in part to Hall of Fame hitter Vladimir Guerrero.

These days the Angels can't seem to reach the postseason, and that's a shame, because in 2009 the team drafted an outfielder named Mike Trout, who has gone on to become one of the greatest all-time baseball players, drawing quick comparisons to Mickey Mantle. In 2018 the Angels signed Japanese player Shohei Ohtani, who in his first season hit .285 with 22 home runs while pitching to a 3.31 ERA and striking out 63 over 51 innings.

Both L.A. teams are fun to watch and get plenty of support, and their ballparks are pretty cool, to boot. More than 60 years after major league baseball first arrived in the City of Angels, it continues to be a great place to take in the game.

PLANNING YOUR TIME

Give yourself a **week** in Los Angeles. If you can't manage that much time, **four days** will suffice. Be sure to spend a full day in and around Dodger Stadium—including Koreatown and Downtown L.A., maybe even Hollywood—and a full day in and around Angel Stadium—including Disneyland and the resort area in Anaheim. I recommend renting a nice car and driving up the coast a bit, maybe visiting a beach or two for an escape. There's plenty of hiking to do in the area as well.

If you're hoping to visit **Disneyland** or **Universal Studios,** get your tickets well **ahead of time.** If you plan on driving to Dodger Stadium, secure your **parking** in advance to avoid paying the full fee.

You have no shortage of places to stay in the L.A. area. **Downtown L.A.** will cost a bit more, while staying in **Anaheim** can net you a little discount. Don't worry about how far you are from anything because you'll be in a car no matter what. Getting from one place to another takes time out here, so don't try to jam everything into a tight schedule. Factor in extra time to account for traffic, which is notoriously bad in this area.

If you're going to either stadium in the afternoon, you'll be basking in warm **sun.** If you're there at night, it'll be pleasant to chilly, with temperatures creeping into the 60s. Bring **sunscreen** and a **light jacket** or **sweatshirt,** especially before June and after August. Rain is unlikely.

Los Angeles has a pleasant climate **year-round.** You'll experience highs in the 80s between June and October. Spring is perfect, with temperatures in the 70s during the day. You'll encounter highs in the 60s between December and February; this is also the rainy season, but L.A. doesn't get much precipitation.

The biggest natural threats in Los Angeles are **earthquakes** and **wildfires.** Quakes can happen at any time, but large ones are extremely rare. The L.A. area has experienced just two earthquakes with a magnitude over 6.0 since 1994. If you feel rumbling, drop to the floor, find something to shelter under and hold onto (cover your head and neck if you can't find shelter), and wait out the quake. If you're driving, pull over, stop, and set your parking brake. Wildfires have increased in frequency over the last several years because of climate change, and some have entered into the Los Angeles metro area. If a wildfire is near, listen to emergency officials and plan an evacuation route.

GETTING THERE

AIR

Los Angeles International Airport

The most popular way to get to Los Angeles is by arriving at **Los Angeles International Airport** (LAX, 1 World Way, 855/463-5252, www.flylax.com). Airlines that depart from and arrive at LAX include **Allegiant** (702/505-8888, www.allegiantair.com), **American Airlines** (800/433-7300, www.aa.com), **Delta** (800/221-1212, www.delta.com), **Frontier** (801/401-9000, www.flyfrontier.com), **jet-Blue** (800/538-2583, www.jetblue.com), **Southwest** (800/435-9792, www.southwest.com), **Spirit** (801/401-2222, www.spirit.com), and **United** (800/864-8331, www.united.com), plus several international carriers.

AIRPORT TRANSPORTATION

If you're **renting a car** from LAX, you'll have to exit at baggage claim and pick up a **shuttle** that will take you to your agency, since the rental car offices are offsite. The airport is a little less than 20 miles southwest of Downtown L.A. It will take at least half an hour to drive Downtown, either by taking I-105 East to I-110 North or I-405 North to I-10 East. Dodger Stadium is a few miles north of Downtown; factor in at least 10 more minutes to get there from LAX. It's a much longer trip to Anaheim and Angel Stadium from LAX. The 40-mile trip on I-405 South will likely take an hour with traffic. (The same goes for the alternate route, which follows I-105 East to I-5 South.)

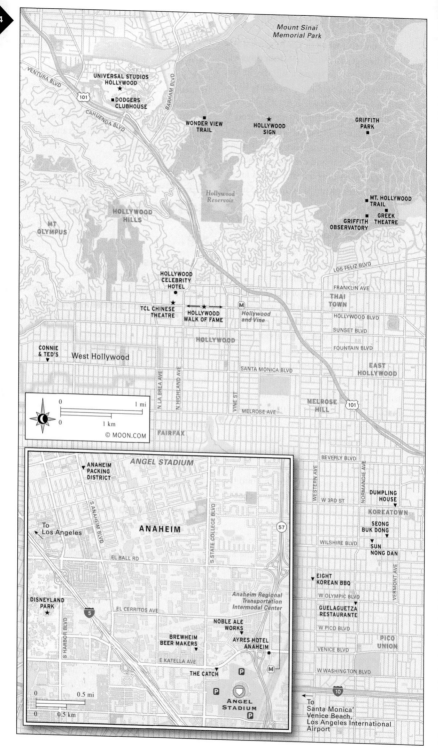

Mount Sinai
Memorial Park

VENTURA BLVD

UNIVERSAL STUDIOS
HOLLYWOOD
★

101

DODGERS
CLUBHOUSE

CAHUENGA BLVD

BARHAM BLVD

WONDER VIEW
TRAIL
■

HOLLYWOOD
SIGN
★

GRIFFITH
PARK
★

Hollywood
Reservoir

MT. HOLLYWOOD
TRAIL
■

HOLLYWOOD
HILLS

MT
OLYMPUS

GREEK
THEATRE
■

GRIFFITH
OBSERVATORY
■

LOS FELIZ BLVD

FRANKLIN AVE

HOLLYWOOD
CELEBRITY
HOTEL
★

THAI
TOWN

TCL CHINESE
THEATRE
★

HOLLYWOOD
WALK OF FAME
★

M

Hollywood
and Vine

HOLLYWOOD BLVD

SUNSET BLVD

HOLLYWOOD

FOUNTAIN BLVD

CONNIE
& TED'S
▼

West Hollywood

EAST
HOLLYWOOD

N LA BREA AVE

N HIGHLAND AVE

SANTA MONICA BLVD

VINE ST

MELROSE
HILL

101

0   1 mi

0   1 km

© MOON.COM

MELROSE AVE

FAIRFAX

BEVERLY BLVD

WESTERN AVE

NORMANDIE AVE

ANGEL STADIUM

ANAHEIM
PACKING
DISTRICT
▼

W 3RD ST

DUMPLING
HOUSE
▼

KOREATOWN

To
Los Angeles
▼

S ANAHEIM BLVD

ANAHEIM

S STATE COLLEGE BLVD

57

SEONG
BUK DONG
▼

EL BALL RD

WILSHIRE BLVD

SUN
NONG DAN
▼

DISNEYLAND
PARK
★

5

EL CERRITOS AVE

S HARBOR BLVD

Anaheim Regional
Transportation
Intermodal Center

EIGHT
KOREAN BBQ
▼

W OLYMPIC BLVD

GUELAGUETZA
RESTAURANTE
▼

NOBLE ALE
WORKS
▼

W PICO BLVD

VERMONT AVE

BREWHEIM
BEER MAKERS
▼

AYRES HOTEL
ANAHEIM
▼

PICO
UNION

E KATELLA AVE

VENICE BLVD

THE CATCH
▼

P

M

W WASHINGTON BLVD

0   0.5 mi

0   0.5 km

P

ANGEL
STADIUM

P

10

To
Santa Monica,
Venice Beach,
Los Angeles International
Airport

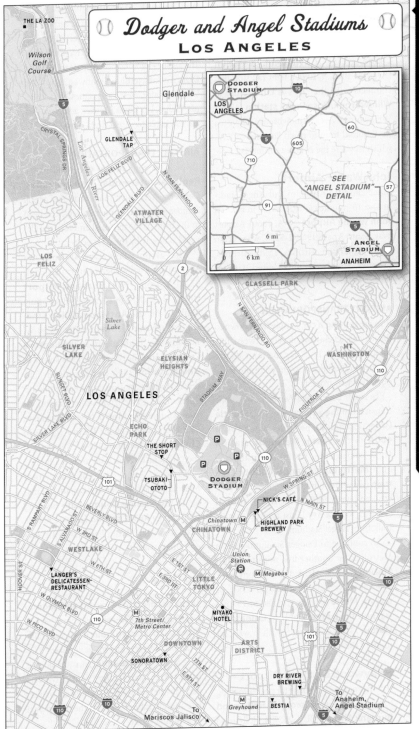

Dodger and Angel Stadiums
LOS ANGELES

THE LA ZOO

Wilson Golf Course

Glendale

GLENDALE TAP

CRYSTAL SPRINGS DR

LOS FELIZ BLVD

GLENDALE BLVD

N SAN FERNANDO RD

ATWATER VILLAGE

LOS FELIZ

Los Angeles River

DODGER STADIUM DETAIL

DODGER STADIUM

LOS ANGELES

10

60

605

5

710

91

57

5

SEE "ANGEL STADIUM" DETAIL

ANGEL STADIUM

ANAHEIM

0   6 mi

0   6 km

2

GLASSELL PARK

N SAN FERNANDO RD

Silver Lake

SILVER LAKE

ELYSIAN HEIGHTS

MT WASHINGTON

110

STADIUM WAY

FIGUEROA ST

SUNSET BLVD

SILVER LAKE BLVD

LOS ANGELES

ECHO PARK

THE SHORT STOP

TSUBAKI OTOTO

101

P

P

P

DODGER STADIUM

110

W SPRING ST

NICK'S CAFÉ   N MAIN ST

Chinatown M

HIGHLAND PARK BREWERY

CHINATOWN

5

S RAMPART BLVD

S ALVARADO ST

BEVERLY BLVD

W 3RD ST

WESTLAKE

W 6TH ST

E 1ST ST

E 2ND ST

LITTLE TOKYO

Union Station

M Megabus

HOOVER ST

LANGER'S DELICATESSEN RESTAURANT

W OLYMPIC BLVD

110

W PICO BLVD

M 7th Street/ Metro Center

E 3RD ST

MIYAKO HOTEL

DOWNTOWN

7TH ST

ARTS DISTRICT

101

10

5

SONORATOWN

E 8TH ST

DRY RIVER BREWING

To Anaheim, Angel Stadium

110

10

M Greyhound

BESTIA

To Mariscos Jalisco

5

You can also take public transit from the airport via **Metro** (Los Angeles County Metropolitan Transportation Authority, www.metro.net, $1.75 one way). You'll be on the **C Line** (green), at **Aviation/LAX station** (Aviation Blvd., I-105), a light rail stop that connects with the city's **A Line** (blue) at **Willowbrook/Rosa Parks station** (11611 Willowbrook Ave., Willowbrook). Get on a northbound train to reach Downtown L.A., which is where the A Line terminates.

John Wayne Airport

Much closer to Anaheim and Angel Stadium—a 15-minute car ride south, in fact—is **John Wayne Airport** (SNA, 18601 Airport Way, Santa Ana, 949/252-5200, www.ocair.com). American Airlines, Delta Airlines, Frontier, Southwest, and United Airlines service JWA.

AIRPORT TRANSPORTATION

If you're **renting a car,** simply head down to the arrivals level (lower level) between Terminals A and B. Look for the John Wayne statue; the rental car agency counters are directly across from it.

To reach Downtown Anaheim by public transit from the airport, take the **iShuttle** (www.octa.net, $1 per ride) along **route 400A** to the **Tustin Metrolink station** (2975 Edinger Ave., Tustin). At Tustin, hop onto **Metrolink's Orange County Line train** (www.metrolinktrains.com, $8.75 one-way) and head north to the **ARTIC station** (2626 E. Katella Ave.), just a seven-minute walk from Angel Stadium.

To continue to Dodger Stadium, stay on Metrolink for another five stops to **Union Station** (800 N. Alameda St.). From there you can either walk 1.5 miles, get a ride, or take the **Metro** (www.metro.net, $1.75 one-way) on the **L Line** (gold) to **Chinatown station** (1231 N. Spring St.), then walk 1.1 miles to the ballpark.

Hollywood Burbank Airport

Another option, especially for people looking to stay in Los Angeles proper, is **Hollywood Burbank Airport** (BUR, 2627 N. Hollywood Way, Burbank, 818/840-8840, www.hollywoodburbankairport.com). The airport is a little less than 15 miles northwest of Dodger Stadium, or a 20-minute drive down I-5. The airlines here include American Airlines, Delta Airlines, jetBlue, Southwest, Spirit, and United. Major West Coast cities, plus Phoenix, Dallas, Las Vegas, Denver, and New York are reachable by direct flights from here.

AIRPORT TRANSPORTATION

To pick up your **rental car,** head to the **Regional Intermodal Transportation Center,** where most major national rental companies have a counter. To get there, head to the front of the terminal and take the elevated walkway by the valet center.

The airport has two stations on **Metrolink** (www.metrolinktrains.com, $2.50-$20 per ride). **Burbank Airport North** (3600 N. San Fernando Blvd., Burbank) is on the **Antelope Valley Line,** while **Burbank Airport South** (3750 W. Empire Ave., Burbank) is on the **Ventura County Line.** Both routes head south to **Union Station** (800 N. Alameda St.). To reach Dodger Stadium, you can walk 1.5 miles or get a ride from Union Station, or you can take the **Metro** (www.metro.net, $1.75 one-way) via the **L Line** (gold) to **Chinatown station** (1231 N. Spring St.), then walk just over a mile to the ballpark.

To reach Angel Stadium, take either Metrolink line to Union Station, then transfer to the **Orange County Line** heading south to the **ARTIC station** (2626 E. Katella Ave., Anaheim). From here, it's just a seven-minute walk to Angel Stadium.

CAR

The most direct route from **San Diego** to Los Angeles is a **120-mile** trip north on **I-5.** That should be a **two-hour** drive, but traffic is almost always going to set you back a little. Plan for a **three-hour** trip, just in case. Even better, plan to start your drive very early in the morning (before 6am) or very late at night (after 9pm), for the best chance of avoiding traffic.

Alternatively, you can drive north on **I-15,** which runs through the suburbs of both cities, plus the Temecula Valley, home to Southern California's wine country. You'll find the largest concentration of wineries seven miles after turning east on Rancho California Road off I-15. Without the detour to the wineries, it's a **145-mile** drive from San Diego to Los Angeles that will take at least **2.5 hours,** depending on traffic.

TRAIN

The main train station in Los Angeles is **Union Station** (800 N. Alameda St.), opening in 1939 and constructed in the mission modern style that's so synonymous with Southern California. Dining options at the station include crepes, salads, a brewpub, and ice cream. To get to L.A. from **San Diego** via **Amtrak** (www.amtrak.com), you can hop on a **Pacific Surfliner,** which spans from San Diego to San Luis Obispo. This journey takes about three hours; tickets start around $35. The station is right in Downtown L.A.

Other routes that stop at Union Station are the **Coast Starlight,** which begins in Seattle and ends here; the **Southwest Chief,** which starts in Chicago and ends here; the **Sunset Limited,** which starts in New Orleans and ends here; and the **Texas Eagle,** which launches in Chicago and heads down to San Antonio before hooking up with the Sunset Limited line and heading here.

BUS

More than a few **Greyhound buses** (www.greyhound.com) take folks from **San Diego** to Los Angeles each day. It'll cost you no more than $20 to take the four- to five-hour ride north to the **Los Angeles Bus Station** (1716 E. 7th St., 213/629-8401). The Greyhound station is in Downtown L.A.

There is a **Megabus station** (99 Gateway Plaza, 877/462-6342, https://us.megabus.com) in Los Angeles, but you can't get to it from San Diego. You can, however, take Megabus from either San Francisco or Oakland to Los Angeles. That trip will cost

around $30, and it can be anywhere from an 8- to 10-hour drive. The Megabus station is a block away from Union Station in Downtown L.A.

Dodger Stadium

It's hard not to see **Dodger Stadium** (1000 Vin Scully Ave., www.mlb.com/dodgers) and immediately wax poetic about how the game is supposed to look. Next to Chavez Ravine, a canyon in the shadow of the San Gabriel Mountains and the nearby hills of Elysian Park, the symmetrical ballpark lacks gaudy amusements, attention-stealing signage, and sponsored party areas. It does have distinctive wavy roofs over the left and right field pavilions and dual videoboards whose angular shapes fit right in with the architectural style, playing against the caress of the hills beyond the outfield. But more than any ballpark in the league, Dodger Stadium focuses all eyes on the field. It's a deceptively simple ballpark that looks absolutely perfect.

If the ballpark looks carved into the land, that's because it is. During construction, workers moved the 8,000,000 cubic yards of earth and rock that would become the land for the actual structure, carving the ballpark into that rock. Thus you can actually park your car and enter the stadium at the top concourse—the rest of the park is downhill. Dodger Stadium has views from all of its areas, as it was built with a cantilevered design, meaning the decks are supported at their ends, so there's no posts that block sightlines.

When you look at Dodger Stadium, gaze out into the San Gabriel Mountains, and see the gorgeous white jerseys with those classic red numbers, you may realize that everything around you was constructed to be perfect. The ballpark was meant to be a place of mythology and tradition. So yes, Dodger Stadium is the aesthetic ideal. It's emblematic of Hollywood and Los Angeles. It's a place that represents its people, and most of all, baseball.

Dodger Stadium

ORIENTATION

Dodger Stadium is the anchor of a natural area that includes a canyon and several hills, tucked away just a bit north of Downtown Los Angeles. The area around the park is surrounded by highways, including I-5 to the north and US-101 to the south.

The entry system at Dodger Stadium is unlike that at other parks. For the most part, entry gates correspond to your seating level; if you have a field level seat, you can only enter at a field level entrance. In 2020, the team unveiled a new **center field entrance,** between the pavilions, that's **open to all ticketholders.** Gates open two hours before first pitch, and the parking lots open half an hour before that.

TICKETS AND SEATING

Pricing

The Dodgers have one of the most sophisticated **dynamic pricing** structures in the league. The same seat will be priced differently from game to game, depending on the draw of the **opponent,** the **time of day and week,** and any **special giveaways** or **events** attached to the contest. You'll pay a pretty penny to see a game against the Giants over Independence Day weekend—around $75 for an infield reserve seat, but you can probably save some dough if it's a Wednesday night in late April against the Pirates, where the same seat might cost more like $40.

Students through college age with a school ID, children ages 4-14, members of the military with proper ID, and seniors ages 55 and

older can get **discounted tickets** (for loge MVP, reserve MVP, and right field pavilion) on select games that aren't considered top draws. Those tickets are only available from 90 minutes before first pitch to an hour after first pitch at the **ticket booths** on the **day of the game**.

Seating Plan

Dodger Stadium is as symmetrical as it gets. Even the many seating areas are mirror images of one another between the left and right side of the park. That said, there are a lot of seating areas here. Note: Section numbers begin at home plate and fan out in either direction; even-numbered sections are on the right side of home plate, ascending to the right field foul pole, while odd-numbered sections are on the left side of home plate, ascending to the left field foul pole. There are lots of **front row, VIP,** and **MVP** designations for each seating area: Front row means exactly that, VIP generally means the next few rows of a section, and MVP typically signifies the rest of the section.

The **lowest level** of Dodger Stadium is reserved for the high rollers. The **Lexus Dugout Club** runs from dugout to dugout, while on either side is the **Baseline Club.** Just behind that is the **field level:** Around the infield are **front row field box VIP, field box VIP,** and **field box MVP** (sections 1-25). The deep infield on either side are **front row infield box, infield box VIP,** and **infield box** (sections 26-33). Shallow outfield on either side are **front row infield box value, infield box value VIP,** and **infield box value** (sections 34-39). Mid-outfield

YOUR BEST DAY AT DODGER STADIUM

It's time to hop in that convertible, crank up the Beach Boys, and enjoy Los Angeles before a Dodger game later in the day.

11 HOURS BEFORE FIRST PITCH
Fill up on breakfast at **Nick's Café.** Grab a counter seat at what's fondly known as the Ham House, and bring cash.

9.5 HOURS BEFORE FIRST PITCH
I hope you're wearing clothes that you can move in. Take a hike to the nearby Hollywood sign via the **Wonder View Trail.** This three-mile round-trip hike with 800-foot elevation gain is only lightly taxing and should take about two hours, including time to take some photos.

7.5 HOURS BEFORE FIRST PITCH
Head back to your hotel to shower and change for the game.

6 HOURS BEFORE FIRST PITCH
Hungry? I hope so, because it's off to **Langer's Delicatessen-Restaurant** you go. Grab a seat, if you can, to enjoy a #19. If it's packed, go to the splendid park across the intersection for a picnic lunch.

5 HOURS BEFORE FIRST PITCH
It's time to head up to Hollywood to take a selfie or two at the **TCL Chinese Theatre.** While you're at it, check out the **Hollywood Walk of Fame.**

4 HOURS BEFORE FIRST PITCH
Make your way to **Highland Park Brewery** for a pregame beer or two. They'll be cheaper than anything you buy at Dodger Stadium.

Hollywood Walk of Fame

2 HOURS BEFORE FIRST PITCH
You've got two tickets to paradise, and it's time to cash them in. Take a ride-share vehicle to **Dodger Stadium.** Gates open two hours before the game begins, so you have some time. Check out the **Kirk Gibson Home Run Seat** before the pavilion gets crowded, then head down to the **center field plaza** to take in the sights and sounds of the park. Walk around a little and take photos, too. Head up to see the **Jackie Robinson statue.**

DURING THE GAME
Before first pitch, buy a **Dodger Dog** and a beer from **ampm.** Then head to your seat and bask in the ball game.

AFTER THE GAME
The place to be is **The Short Stop.** Have a drink, and maybe sing a bar of "I Love L.A."— to yourself, that is.

on either side are **front row preferred field box, preferred field box VIP,** and **preferred field box** (sections 40-45). In deep outfield are **front row preferred box value, preferred field box value VIP,** and **preferred field box value** (sections 46-53).

The **second level** is the **loge (100 level).** Around the infield are **front row loge box VIP, loge box VIP,** and **loge box MVP** (sections 101-126). Deep infield on either side are **front row infield loge box, infield loge box VIP,** and **infield loge box** (sections 127-144). Shallow outfield on either side are **front row infield loge box value, infield loge box value VIP,** and **infield loge box value** (sections 145-150). Mid-outfield on either side are **front row preferred loge box, preferred loge box VIP,** and **preferred loge box** (sections 151-156). In deep outfield are **front row preferred loge box value, preferred loge box value VIP,** and **preferred loge** box value (sections 157-168).

The **club level (200 level)** is unique at Dodger Stadium: **Suites** and the **Stadium Club** (sections 201-233 third base to right field, plus E1, E2) line the majority of foul territory. The **Executive Club** (sections 229-245) and **Executive Club Value** (sections 247-261) finish the club level from third base out to the left field foul pole.

The reserve section starts at home plate and fans around the plate area with **front row reserve VIP, reserve VIP,** and **reserve MVP** (sections 1-9). The back half of the infield on either side are **front row reserve VIP value, reserve VIP value,** and **reserve MVP value** (sections 10-11, 15-16, 19-20). The very back infield and shallow outfield on either side are **front row infield reserve, infield reserve VIP,** and **infield reserve** (sections 12-14, 17-18, 21-25, 27-28, 31-32). Mid-outfield on either side are **front row infield reserve value, infield reserve value VIP,** and **infield reserve value** (sections 26, 29-30, 33-37). Most of the rest of the outfield on either side, to the foul poles, are **front row pre-ferred reserve, preferred reserve VIP,** and **preferred reserve** (sections 38-49, 51-52, 55-56, 59-60). The back rows near the foul poles on either side are **preferred reserve value** (sections 50, 53-54, 57-58, 61). The section numbers can vary wildly here. Be sure to look at the seating chart when securing tickets.

There's also the **top deck,** really far out behind home plate. It's split into **front row top deck, top deck VIP,** and **top deck** (sections 1-13). The outfield is split into two distinct areas. In left field, find the **Time Warner Cable Left Field Pavilion,** split into **front row left field pavilion, left field pavilion VIP,** and **left field pavilion** (sections 301-315, all odd-numbered). In right field, there's the **Coca-Cola All-You-Can-Eat Right Field Pavilion,** split into **front row right field pavilion, right field pavilion VIP,** and **right field pavilion** (sections 302-316, all even-numbered). Both outfield pavilion seating areas have **wooden benches.** There are some **standing-room**

GAME COSTS

Tickets: While not on the level of the Yankees or Cubs, ticket prices for Dodger games are still higher than average. You can snag a seat for **$15** in the top deck. You can also find deals in left field pavilion, club, and even loge. The moment you try for field seats, however, be prepared to pay some dough; **$100** seats in this level aren't uncommon.

Hot dog: You need a Dodger Dog, but it'll cost you **$6.75** or more. Hey, they're priced to match demand.

Beer: It may be cheap to get into Dodger Stadium if you find the right seats, but concession prices are a different story. Be ready to pay at least **$6.50** for the cheapest beer. For good stuff, it'll be much closer to **$15.**

Parking: You'll most likely pay **$17-25** to park, though some **$5** off-site parking spots can be found.

areas above each pavilion.

Note that your ticket may **restrict** you to some **non-suite areas.** If you have a reserved or top deck ticket, you won't be allowed into the outfield plazas, and if you have left field pavilion tickets, then you won't have access to the right field pavilion. However, if you have right field pavilion seats, you can visit the left field pavilion.

Where to Buy Tickets

Dodger tickets are pricy, so try broker sites like **SeatGeek** and **TickPick,** and opt for getting your tickets closer to first pitch if the game isn't a sure sellout. If you buy tickets through the Dodgers or StubHub, you can check the **MLB Ballpark app** to potentially upgrade when in the park.

Best Seats

If you want to breathe in one of the best views in baseball, sit anywhere in **foul territory,** but closer to home plate is always better. Consider **front row reserve VIP** and **reserve VIP** (sections 1-9) for a less expensive option that offers an awesome **view,** and you won't need binoculars to watch the game.

The **bleachers** on either side of foul territory are inexpensive, fun, and (depending on the opponent) rowdy, so consider that option if you're looking to socialize with fans.

A word on the **sun:** It will get you. If you're attending an afternoon game, you'll probably be in it no matter what. For your best chance to stay out of it, consider sitting at the **top rows** of the **reserve section** on the **third-base line,** or **infield reserve value** (sections 29, 33, 37). **Shade** comes first to those sitting on the left side, and if you're at a top row, you'll be under an **overhang.** On the first-base side you'll be baking, and evening games in summer mean the sun will be **blinding** you as it sets beyond the third-base line.

KNOW BEFORE YOU GO

Dodger Stadium allows **backpacks** and **soft-sided coolers** no larger than 16 by 16 by 8 inches. **Diaper bags** should be smaller than that. Be sure to pack some **sunscreen,** as you're certain to get some rays, even in the early evening before sunset. **Outside food** and **drinks** (maximum one liter) are also allowed, just not in cans or glass containers. No outside alcohol is allowed into the stadium.

Noisemakers aren't allowed in the park, but **radios** are, just as long as they don't disturb other fans. **Strollers** are allowed, and better yet, they can be checked. Just visit either the left or right field plazas at field level, or behind home plate on any level.

The park has several **gender-neutral restrooms** (sections 152, 153, suite 211, reserve sections 31, 32, top deck near Top of the Park store, and left field pavilion at center field). There are also multiple **charging stations** (right field plaza by Estrella Bar, section 161, section 162, and top deck section 3).

You can get your kid a **wristband** with seat information on it from a **fan service station.** Nursing mothers are welcome to visit the **nursing suite** (center field under the right field pavilion). Nursing is permitted anywhere in public.

People with sensory processing needs can acquire **sensory bags** that include fidget toys, noise-cancelling headphones, and other items by visiting a **fan service station.** A valid ID is necessary as a deposit.

If it's your first time at Dodger Stadium, head to a fan service station for a **map** and a celebratory **button.**

Accessibility

Wheelchairs and medically necessary **Segways** can be stored at a fan services station or designated areas in the left and right field plazas at field level, or behind home plate on all levels. **Wheelchair escorts** to and from your seat are available on a first-come, first-served basis; request one upon reaching your gate of entry. **Service animals** are welcome at Dodger Stadium.

Inquire at any of the **fan services stations** (sections 3, 52, 53, 152, 153, reserve 31, reserve 32, top deck 1, welcome center in center field, third-level pavilion in center field) to receive an **assistive listening device.** The stations also have **sensory bags** for people who may feel overwhelmed by the hustle and bustle of the ballpark. The kits include a **fidget toy, noise-cancelling headphones,** and other calming tools. The bags must be returned at the end of the game.

Elevators that access all levels are located behind home plate, and two at either end of the concourses access Levels 2-7. Another elevator in center field gets fans up and down the pavilions.

Lots B, D, G, L, N, and P have **accessible parking spaces;** remember to have a valid disabled parking placard or license plate. At the parking lot, if needed, you can call the **Dodger Hotline** (323/224-2611) to be picked up by the ADA shuttle, which will transport you to a gate of entry.

If you have questions or want more details about how the Dodgers can accommodate fans with disabilities, call 866/363-4377.

BE A FAN

You've probably heard the trope about Dodgers fans, that they don't arrive at the stadium until midway through the game, and that they leave the park before the final pitches are thrown. Well, it's kind of true. A notable number of fans do this. However, fans are passionate about their team. Plus, you'll be hard pressed to find a crowd elsewhere in baseball that's as diverse as the group at Chavez Ravine.

fans in the upper deck of Dodger Stadium

There have been reports of violence at Dodger Stadium between Dodgers fans and Giants fans, as well as Dodgers fans and Angels fans. My advice to you is to play cool and not rile up Dodgers fans if you're rooting for the opposition. If you're wearing Giants gear, you may hear some jeers, but fans generally keep it playful. If you're concerned about being singled out, choose a seat as close to the field as possible. The more passionate fans tend to be in the outfield and on the top deck.

Fans sing **"I Love L.A."** by Randy Newman after every win—even though the song skewers Los Angeles as much as it celebrates it. You'll see **"The Wave"** at Dodger Stadium, and maybe some **beach balls** being punched up and passed around through the crowd.

GETTING THERE

Public Transit

To get to Dodger Stadium via public transit, you can hop on the **Dodger Stadium Express** (every 10-30 minutes, from 90 minutes before first pitch to 45 minutes after final out, free for ticketholders, $1.75-2.50 one-way without ticket) from **Union Station** (800 N. Alameda St.) in Downtown or **Harbor Gateway Transit Center** (731 W. 182nd St., Gardena) in the South Bay. The bus will drop you off at **Lot G** behind the pavilions. For some Union Station buses, you can get dropped off at **Lot P** behind the top deck. Taking the bus is a good option if you'd rather not drive and don't mind getting to the park closer to first pitch.

Driving

If you choose to drive to the park, you'll be in traffic. Major highways with access to the stadium include CA-110 and I-5. It's also possible to cut through Chinatown via West College Street or North Broadway. Another way is to take Sunset Boulevard to Vin Scully Avenue. Because the ballpark is within a park in its own removed area, give yourself considerable time before the game to wait in traffic, find a parking spot, and walk from the parking lot to the entrance.

Dodger Stadium is surrounded by **parking lots.** You'll pay $17-20 if you book a spot in **advance** (www.dodgers.com/parking); spots cost $25 at the gate. **Off-site parking** is available via **Lots 13 and 14** (Stadium Way between Vin Scully Ave. and CA-110) for just $5. These lots are first-come, first-served, so they fill quickly. The drawback: You'll have an uphill walk to the park, but it's worth it. The team operates a **shuttle** (323/224-2611) for people with disabilities.

PARK FEATURES AND SIGHTS

Center Field Plaza

Visit the **center field plaza** (center field) for a kids' play area; **plaques** showing off the "Legends of Dodger Baseball" including Jackie Robinson, Sandy Koufax, and Roy Campanella; and a new **statue** honoring Koufax. Also here are specialty food vendors, regular entertainment, and a beer garden. The plaza connects the left and right field pavilions and is open to all fans.

Jackie Robinson Statue

One must-see while here is the **Jackie Robinson statue** (left field reserve plaza) created by sculptor Branly Cadet. "A life is not important except in the impact it has on other lives," is one Robinson quote inscribed on the granite base for this awesome piece of bronze art displaying the hero stealing home plate. The statue depicts Robinson as a rookie, his eyes locked in focus; his muscular right wrist and clenched fist seem to represent his unassailable strength in the face of enormous prejudice. Spend a few minutes reflecting here before snapping a picture or two.

Kirk Gibson Home Run Seat

You may want to seek out the **Kirk Gibson Home Run Seat** (section 302, right field pavilion, Row D, seat 88). In Game 1 of the 1988 World Series, Kirk Gibson, injured and barely able to walk, hit a game-winning home run that landed right here. It's marked by blue paint (the bleachers around it are all painted yellow) with Gibson's signature. Go well before the game starts and let an usher know you're there to simply see the seat.

FOOD AND DRINKS

If there's one food item you need at Dodger Stadium, it's the **Dodger Dog.** It's not a normal hot dog but a 10-inch pork frankfurter that extends past the bun on both sides. The dog can be **grilled or steamed** (sections 9, 40, 41, 106, 140, 154, 155, 143, reserve 6-7, 23, 35-36, 43-44, 55); the traditional way to get it is grilled. You can also get a cheese Dodger Dog, a **pulled pork Dodger Dog** (Think Blue BBQ, left field plaza, reserve 32), a **gluten-free Dodger Dog** (Top Deck Dogs, top deck 5) and a **fried Dodger Dog** (sections 136, reserve 12).

Elevated stadium options like bacon-wrapped hot dogs, a Philly cheesesteak, and

Photos (from top to bottom): Dodger Stadium; Dodger Dogs concession stand; a young Dodgers fan.

garlic fries are available at **Elysian Park Grill** (sections 22, 23, top deck 6). Garlic fries are available in a helmet at **On Deck Circle** (sections 133, reserve 4). **Hot Corner** (section 45) has a spicy chicken sandwich, hot wings, and a spicy hot dog. For vegan items, check out **Plant Powered** (section 47), which has everything from a "meatball" sub to a nacho helmet to chili cheese tater tots.

For a fantastic dessert option, get the **churro sundae** (L.A. Taqueria, right field plaza, reserve 17; Trolley Treats, sections 46, reserve 2), which is chocolate, vanilla, or strawberry ice cream in a miniature helmet with a couple churros. Use the churro as a spoon!

For *micheladas*, you can go nearly anywhere in the park. This cocktail, made of beer, lime, chilies, and tomato juice is available at just about every other section. *Micheladas,* plus Moscow mules and other cocktails, are available at the **Ketel One Bar Cart** (section 1).

Most of the beer at Dodger Stadium is macro-brewed. You'll find a lot of L.A.-based **Golden Road** (including its specialty ballpark-only Dodgers Blonde Ale); the brewery is owned by Anheuser-Busch InBev. Look for **craft beer** in the coolers at **ampm** (section 1), a Dodger Stadium location of the popular convenience store.

EVENTS

While fans can get into the park two hours before first pitch to watch opponents' **batting practice,** they're generally not allowed to get into the park any earlier to see the Dodgers hit. Some fans, like invited guests of the Dodgers or those with connections, might get the opportunity to watch full batting practice by entering at the left pavilion.

Unfortunately, it's nearly impossible to get **autographs** while at Dodger Stadium, as players don't linger on the field and ushers keep people from hanging out by the dugouts, as that area is only meant for baseline club ticketholders.

The Dodgers host **fireworks** after every Friday night game, though if the game continues past 11pm, the show will be canceled. Fans can go onto the outfield grass for the best views; the fireworks shoot from over home plate. After most Sunday games, children ages 14 and younger can **run the bases.** Kids should line up behind the left and right pavilions in center field after the game.

The team hosts a number of **theme nights** each season celebrating diverse cultures and lifestyles. Look for LGBT Night (May-June) around when L.A.'s Pride celebration occurs, Korea Night, Filipino Night, and Día de los Dodgers (Sept.), a take on Día de los Muertos.

Tours

The team offers several **tours** (323/224-4222) of Dodger Stadium. You can take an 80- to 90-minute **regular tour** (10am, 11:30am, and 1pm daily except afternoon game days and holidays, $20, $15 seniors and ages 4-14, free ages 3 and under) that includes a visit to the Dodgers' dugout, some time on the field, and a trip to the Lexus Dugout Club to peruse the trophies there.

There are also **pregame tours** ($20, $15 seniors and ages 4-14, free ages 3 and under) that visit the interview room and check out batting practice over 45 minutes, and exclusive **VIP tours** that include Stadium Club reservations, a gift bag, batting practice attendance, and preferred parking. For VIP tour prices, email tours@ladodgers.com.

My favorite two tours are the **clubhouse tour** (select Sat.-Sun., $50), which visits the bullpen, weight room, and indoor batting cage along with the clubhouse; and the 90-minute **Jackie Robinson tour** (dates vary, $20, $15 seniors and ages 4-14, free ages 3 and under), which includes a visit to the Vin Scully Press Box, time on the field and in the dugout, and a presentation on Robinson's life and career.

SHOPPING

Because Dodger Stadium is so symmetrical and efficiently built, the team couldn't jam a big team store into the regular concourses.

For the biggest selection of merchandise, climb up to the top deck to visit the **Top of the Park Official Team Store** (top deck, ramp from Lot P, 10am-5pm daily non-game days, 11am-30 minutes after final out day games, 10am-3pm and 5pm-30 minutes after final out night games). It has the usual solid inventory of clothing, hats, accessories, toys, and gifts.

There are also numerous other team stores and kiosks sprinkled throughout the park. Check out **Art of the Game** (club level behind home plate) for game-used memorabilia.

Angel Stadium

Dodger Stadium gets all the love, but **Angel Stadium** (2000 Gene Autry Way, Anaheim, www.mlb.com/angels) is arguably the most influential ballpark in America. In 1955, Disneyland opened. That, plus a rapidly expanding highway system, meant people started flocking to Anaheim in Orange County, 25 miles southeast of Los Angeles. By 1960 the population of the city surged by more than 600 percent, turning what was a suburb of the Los Angeles area into its own self-sustaining hub. Anaheim was arguably the first example of an American city that grew exponentially because of tourism, and the city doubled down on it by attracting a new baseball team to pair with the Disney experience.

Anaheim Stadium opened in 1966, just 2.5 miles east of Disneyland near the intersection of I-5 and CA-57 (the Orange Freeway). The ballpark featured a second deck in foul territory and an open outfield area. At first, Anaheim Stadium had no seats in the outfield, just the humongous Big A sign acting as the scoreboard. Like Dodger Stadium and Kauffman Stadium in Kansas City, Angel Stadium promoted baseball as a pleasing, relaxing affair. Couple that with the thrills and memories made down the road at Mickey-ville, and you had a heck of a one-two punch.

But by 1980, all that calm beauty was gone, courtesy of the stadium's new tenants—the NFL's Los Angeles Rams. The Rams sealed up the seating bowl by adding seats across the entire outfield. The stadium returned to its former glory in 1996, however, when the Walt Disney Company bought the Angels. They opted to keep the team in the park, renaming it Edison International Field, and simply tore out the outfield seats, turning the venue into what you see today, including a wild rock formation in the outfield that screams "Disney!"

It's possible to see Angel Stadium (its name since 2003, when Disney sold the team to current owner Arte Moreno) as the blueprint for the modern-day baseball experience, where entertainment districts are built up around ballparks, enticing tourists to spend a whole day in the area, eating, drinking, and playing before and after a game. How better to define Disneyland than the ultimate entertainment district? Angel Stadium may not possess the classic, unvarnished beauty of Dodger Stadium, but it's a nice park that long ago pointed the way forward for how baseball is experienced today.

ORIENTATION

Angel Stadium is right beside CA-57 and the Santa Ana River, and I-5 slices past the park on a diagonal just two blocks away. That means there are plenty of ways to get in and out of the area. Parking lots surround the stadium in all directions.

There are eight entry gates at Angel Stadium. Gates open 90 minutes before first pitch, though the home plate gate will open two hours early, but only for night games.

TICKETS AND SEATING

Pricing

The Angels use **dynamic pricing** for their games, so be ready to pay more for **interleague** contests against the **Dodgers,** for **in-division rivalry** games with the **Astros,** and for when the **Yankees** visit. A seat in lower view MVP for a game against Baltimore may cost $35, but that same seat for

YOUR BEST DAY AT ANGEL STADIUM

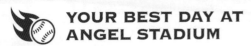

Going to the Angels game tonight? Here's what you should do ahead of, during, and after the contest.

10 HOURS BEFORE FIRST PITCH
Want to have a day you won't soon forget? Spend a few whirlwind hours at **Disneyland Park.** Be sure to ride Space Mountain and try to cram in as many of your other favorites as you can.

5 HOURS BEFORE FIRST PITCH
Get yourself a late lunch at the **Anaheim Packing District.** Choose from one of the several vendors on hand, who sell everything from Indian street food to fish and chips.

3 HOURS BEFORE FIRST PITCH
Get thee to **Noble Ale Works** for a drink or two. If you're driving, park your car here and just walk on over to **Angel Stadium.**

1.5 HOURS BEFORE FIRST PITCH
Start out by finding the right spot to take a selfie with the **Big A sign.** Then, enter through the **Gate 5 Courtyard** to sample a bit of Anaheim while acclimating yourself to the park. Next, see if you can scope out an **autograph,** or maybe even a foul ball, from Mike Trout.

entrance to Disneyland Park

DURING THE GAME
Try to snag good seats for first pitch at **Saint Archer Brewing Co.** If not, sit in the view level, and get a few choice snacks. I recommend grabbing the helmet nachos from the **Tostitos Nacho cart** and a decent local beer from **Draft Pick.**

AFTER THE GAME
If you're returning to your hotel in L.A., take a ride-share up to Glendale to visit **Glendale Tap,** about an hour north of Anaheim. With more than 50 taps, a dive-bar aesthetic, and friendly customers, this spot will ensure that you're golden for the rest of the night. Otherwise, if you want to stick close to Anaheim, hop over to **Noble Ale Works** to grab a quick beer before they close.

a weekend game against the Dodgers could cost more like $50. The Angels price the **front row** of some sections differently from the rest of the seats in those sections.

Seating Plan

At Angel Stadium, section numbers ascend counter-clockwise from the left field foul pole, different from most parks. The **field level (100 level)** starts at the foul pole with **field box front row** and **field box** (sections 101-105). In shallow left field are **field all-star front row** and **field all-star** (sections 106-108). Along the third-base line are **dugout MVP** (front row), **field hall of fame** (next several rows), and **field MVP** (sections

109-113). Around home plate are premium seats: **Lexus diamond MVP** (front row), **Lexus diamond club hall of fame** (next several rows), and **Lexus diamond club** (sections 114-122). Then, along the first-base line are **dugout MVP** (front row), **field hall of fame** (next several rows), and **field MVP** (sections 123-127).

In shallow right field are **field all-star front row** and **field all-star** (sections 128-130). In deep right field are **field box front row** and **field box** (sections 131-133), and around the right field foul pole is **field reserved** (sections 134-135). In case you really want to pony up, the seats in **diamond field box** (front of sections 109,

Angel Stadium

127) are smack on the field and next to the dugouts.

The **terrace level (200 level)** is essentially the back portion of the field level and starts at the left field foul pole and heads in toward the infield with **terrace box** (sections 201-205). Continuing along the left-field line is **terrace all-star** (sections 206-209), and along the third-base line is **terrace MVP** (sections 210-213). A series of suites as part of the **Don Julio Club** wrap around home plate, then it's back to **terrace MVP** (sections 221-224), **terrace all-star** (sections 225-228), and **terrace box** (sections 229-230). At the right field foul pole, find additional **field reserved** (sections 231-233) seats.

The outfield area starts in right field with **right field front row, right field hall of fame** (next several rows), and **right field**

MVP (sections 236-240). Behind that grandstand is the **right field pavilion** (sections 241-249). The outfield continues in left field with **left field pavilion** (sections 256-260), located under the secondary video board.

In the **club level (300 level), suites** line the entire area from left field foul pole to deep right field. Under the suites are **premium seats** that may be harder to acquire. From the left field foul pole and heading toward home plate, there's **club loge** (sections 301-308), **club all-star** (sections 309-314), and **club MVP** (sections 315-322). After a run of suites around home plate, there's more **club MVP** (sections 330-337), **club all-star** (sections 338-343), and **club loge** (sections 344-351). If you sit in club MVP or club all-star, you'll get **in-seat service.**

The **400** and **500 levels** are batched

together as the **view level.** The 400 level starts at the left field foul pole with **lower view box** (sections 401-407), then **lower view all-star** (sections 408-410), then **lower view MVP** (sections 411-426) running the entirety of the infield. Next is more **lower view all-star** (sections 427-429) then **lower view box** (sections 430-436). The 500 level starts at the left field foul pole with **upper view** (sections 501-507), then **view all-star** (sections 508-512), then **view MVP** (sections 513-528), again running around the entirety of the infield. Next is more **view all-star** (sections 529-533), then finally **upper view** (sections 534-540) to the right field foul pole.

Where to Buy Tickets

Third-party resellers like **StubHub** and **SeatGeek** are a good place to look for tickets, especially close to the first pitch. For Angels games and other events in Anaheim, you may also want to check **714 Tickets** (www.714tickets.com), a dedicated local ticket seller.

If you purchase your tickets through the Angels, you may be able to upgrade your seat if you download the **MLB Ballpark app.**

Best Seats

The best place to sit at Angel Stadium is in the **club level,** as you're on top of the action, not very far away, and get **in-seat service** (except in the loge club). The sun sets behind the third-base side of the ballpark, so for the most optimal **shade,** sit on the **third-base side** in **sections 309-314,** or the third-base side of the **club all-star area.**

For something **less expensive** and still

GAME COSTS

Tickets: The Angels tend to be one of the most affordable teams to watch live. Seats up in the view level will cost no more than **$25** typically, and terrace seats can be as low as **$30**. Compared to just about every other park, Angel Stadium seats are a steal..

Hot dog: Not bad at all at **$5** per wiener.

Beer: You can get **$5** beers, though the good ones are closer to **$10-13**. That still isn't bad, compared to other parks.

Parking: $10 is pretty dang cheap for parking near a ballpark. Kudos to the Angels for being one of the more affordable teams across the board.

close enough, think about sitting in the **lower view level,** preferably **sections 407-411.** For a night game, you could opt for anywhere in **lower view MVP** (sections 411-426).

KNOW BEFORE YOU GO

Angel Stadium allows in **bags** and **backpacks** that are no larger than 16 by 16 by 8 inches. Only bottled water, sports drinks, and empty reusable **water bottles** (no larger than one liter) are permitted. Bottled beverages must be sealed. No cans or glass bottles are allowed in.

Noisemakers are not allowed at Angel Stadium, except for **"Halo Sticks"** (the Angels-branded version of thunder sticks). **Strollers** are allowed, but they must be collapsible to fit under your seat. If not, you can check them into a guest relations office. Portable **radios** and **televisions** are also allowed in the stadium.

The Angels have reserved a room for **nursing mothers** (guest relations office, section 133).

If you have to leave the park but want to

return, exit at either Gate 1, 4, or 6. Inform an employee there that you'd like to return and get a stamp, or get your ticket hole-punched. When re-entering, be sure to come back through the same gate that you exited. And note the time: You'll have no luck getting back in after the seventh inning.

Accessibility

Fans sitting in a **wheelchair-accessible seating** area can have up to three companions join them in the same area. **Wheelchair escorts** to and from your seat are available by asking at your gate of entry. **Segways** are also allowed inside the stadium, but only for people with mobility impairments. **Service animals** are welcome at Angel Stadium.

There are two **elevators** for fans at Angel Stadium, near sections 101 and 134. **Ramps** are on the third-base side and first-base side of the park, with another out in right field.

Accessible parking is available outside Gates 1-6 and the home plate gate. Be sure that a valid disabled parking placard or license plate is visible.

GETTING THERE

Public Transit

Taking public transit to the stadium from Downtown Los Angeles is a really good option. Take **Metrolink's Orange County Line train** (www.metrolinktrains.com, $8.75 one-way) from **Union Station** (800 N. Alameda St.) to the **ARTIC station** (2626 E. Katella Ave.), then walk south on Douglass Road for just a moment, going underneath CA-57 (the Orange Freeway). Angel Stadium will be right there. **Amtrak** (www.amtrak. com) also serves the ARTIC station via its **Pacific Surfliner** route. From Downtown L.A., the 40-minute ride on Amtrak will cost a little more than $15 one-way.

For weekday evening games, Metrolink also operates a commuter-style bus called the **Angels Express** (Mon.-Fri., $7 round-trip). It serves mostly destinations south of Anaheim, like Irvine and Santa Ana, with a Friday-only route from Downtown L.A. Downtown buses pick up passengers at

BE A FAN

Angels fans are generally easygoing, so don't worry about wearing another team's jersey or rooting for the visitors. There have been a couple high-profile incidents of fan violence in recent years, but it's no more than what has occurred in other ballparks across the country.

Mike Trout may play center field, but his cheering section, the **Trout Farm** (section 101) is over in left field by the foul pole. If you want to sit there and get a Trout Farm hat (complete with a trout sticking out from it), call the team at 888/796-4256.

Before every game you'll hear the song **"Calling All Angels"** by Train, which could be the first time you've heard that song since 2004. After each win, you'll see the **Big A sign** light up.

Then there's the **Rally Monkey.** It all started back in 2000. During a game in which the Halos were losing, the video board operators showed a clip of Spike, the monkey from the movie *Ace Ventura: Pet Detective.* The Angels won that game, and from then on, the team used a monkey as a rally mascot. The Angels hired a capuchin monkey named Katie (previously known for playing Marcel on the TV show *Friends*), who some say helped the team come back in the 2002 World Series en route to its first and only championship. With that legacy, the Rally Monkey is a forever piece of Angels lore. You may see the monkey on the video board during the game, sometimes dropped into famous TV, music video, and movie clips.

Union Station, arriving at the ARTIC station about 45 minutes later. Metrolink encourages train and bus riders to buy tickets through its **app,** but there are ticket vending machines at stations, too.

Driving

As long as you accept that you'll be in L.A.-area traffic, driving to the stadium is totally acceptable. The park is right off **CA-57** (the **Orange Freeway**), which begins just south of Anaheim and heads north to San Dimas. You'll exit at **East Katella Avenue;** be ready to encounter traffic here. Alternatively, you can take **I-5** (the **Santa Ana Freeway**) and exit at **South State College Boulevard.**

Parking lots surround Angel Stadium. Enter the main parking area via State College Boulevard, Douglass Road, or Orangewood Avenue. Parking is $10, payable via cash, debit or credit card, or smartphone.

PARK FEATURES AND SIGHTS

You might enter the ballpark via the **Gate 5 Courtyard** (Gate 5, deep right field in foul territory), where you'll find a handful of food vendors and a spacious plaza that's a good

spot for meeting up with people. There's a similar courtyard over on the left side of the park (Gate 1, third-base line). Ticketholders are also invited to hang out before, during, and after the game at the stadium's **picnic area** (center field, Terrace Level, behind the rocks).

Big A Sign

The first thing you might see upon entering the Angel Stadium area is the **Big A sign** (parking lot east of Gate 5), a red triangle with a halo circling its point, resembling the team's logo. It's hard to miss this 230-foot icon, at one point the tallest structure in all of Orange County. If you want a selfie with the Big A sign, consider standing out in the center field area of the parking lot.

Outfield Extravaganza

The **Outfield Extravaganza** (left center field), a rock pile in center field, is the one remnant from the Walt Disney Company's ownership of the team. The formation, made of large artificial boulders, is meant to evoke the rocky Southern California coast. It was completed in 1998, a couple years after Disney took over the team, and would fit right in with the nearby Magic Kingdom. A large

geyser shoots water high up in the air (not all that often, though), and the water cascades down the rock face, which is speckled with real trees. Whenever the Angels hit a home run and after every Anaheim victory, fireworks shoot up from the rocks.

FOOD AND DRINKS

There's a brewery inside Angel Stadium offering a full food menu for those seeking a sit-down meal with their baseball. **Saint Archer Brewing Co.** (section 348, 714/940-2411), out near the right field foul pole, offers two seating times: The first seating is two hours before first pitch, and the second is at the start of the game. If you want in, I suggest reserving a table up to five days before the start of the homestand in which your game is included. The menu offers global street fare like Thai sticky ribs and salmon poke, plus American favorites like a burger, braised short rib, and pizza. For drinks, you're mostly getting beer from Saint Archer (a subsidiary of MolsonCoors and not local to Anaheim). The food is decent and the view is good—for ballpark restaurants, it's one of the best.

The talk of the town are the **loaded helmet nachos** at the **Tostitos Nacho** carts positioned in various places around the concourse. It's what you'd expect from nachos: guacamole, beans, melty queso, pico de gallo, jalapeños, and chipotle chicken. Try the hand-pulled rotisserie chicken sandwich at **La Rottisseries** (section 114), which has arugula, lemon aioli, and salsa verde. It's refreshing.

There's a good ballpark burger at **Big A Burger** (section 106), made with two patties, American cheese, a secret sauce, and a potato bun. Try **Bamboo Bowls** (sections 240, 424) for the Chinese chicken salad and chicken teriyaki bowl.

For the best beer selection with some independent craft options, visit **Draft Pick** (section 112). Find offerings from **Hangar**

Photos (from top to bottom): the Outfield Extravaganza; Disney's Mickey Mouse at Angel Stadium; entrance to Angel Stadium.

24, which is near San Bernardino; **Noble Ale Works,** an Anaheim-based brewery; and **Bootlegger's Brewery** out of Orange County.

EVENTS

For **autographs,** head down to the field level of **sections 101-113** and **133-135** up to 40 minutes before first pitch.

Batting practice starts two hours before first pitch, so for night games, enter through the home plate gate (which opens two hours before) to catch as much of it as you can. Otherwise, all other gates open 90 minutes before first pitch (and the home plate gate opens 90 minutes ahead of time for day games), so you'll get to see some of batting practice upon entering.

On Sundays, the Gate 5 Courtyard hosts **family activities** through the sixth inning. After those games, the Angels allow children ages 3-13 the opportunity to **run the bases.** If your child is interested, visit a **guest relations office** (sections 101, 124, 133, 239, 420).

Tours

If you want a **tour** (714/940-2230, non-game days June-Sept., $12, $10 seniors and ages 3-14, free ages 2 and under), you'll have to plan your visit accordingly, because there are no game day tours. It's a 75-minute walk through the park, including a visit to the field, the home dugout and visitors' clubhouse, and a trip to the broadcast booth. Year-round you can schedule a **private tour** (714/940-2230), but make this reservation at least two weeks in advance.

SHOPPING

The **Main Team Store** (Home Plate Gate, 714/940-2618, 10am-5pm Mon.-Sat., open to fans with tickets on game days) has more Mike Trout and Shohei Ohtani gear than you can shake a Halo Stick at. Plus, there are hats, pennants, towels, all the shirts you could want, and much more. There are shorter lines (but smaller selections) at the **108 Team Store** (section 108) and **Centerfield Team Store** (section 256). Find discounted Angels gear at the **Outlet Team Store** (section 404).

LOS ANGELES SIGHTS

HOLLYWOOD SIGN

Los Angeles is chock-full of things to see and do. If it's your first time in the City of Angels, keep a keen eye out for the **Hollywood Sign** (Mt. Lee, http://hollywoodsign.org), the 45-foot-tall, 350-foot-long landmark that will transport you to the golden days of this famous town. There are multiple ways to see the sign. One iconic view is from the intersection of **Hollywood and Highland** (Hollywood Blvd. and Highland Ave., Hollywood), where the sign will sit prettily in the background of your photos. Your best bet may be to visit **Griffith Observatory** for a nice view of it on Mount Lee, across from the observatory. (For more information on hiking to the sign, see the *Recreation* section.)

TCL CHINESE THEATRE AND THE HOLLYWOOD WALK OF FAME

Better known as **Grauman's Chinese Theatre,** the **TCL Chinese Theatre** (6925 Hollywood Blvd., Hollywood, 323/461-3331, www.tclchinesetheatres.com) is a landmark and a must-see (at least from the car) for anyone coming to L.A. for the first time. Opening in 1927, the theater instantly became the destination for movie premieres. To this day, first-run feature films open at this iconic 90-foot-tall space, now home to an IMAX system.

Outside the theater is the famous **Hollywood Walk of Fame** (http://walkoffame.com). Set into the sidewalk on both sides of Hollywood Boulevard and Vine Street are stars made of terrazzo and brass, immortalizing actors, singers, and other entertainers.

Some of the more notable names near the theater are Spencer Tracy and the Bee Gees.

DISNEYLAND PARK

Probably the name most associated with Southern California is Disney. Located in Anaheim, 25 miles southeast of Downtown L.A., **Disneyland Park** (1313 Disneyland Dr., Anaheim, 714/781-4636, www.disneyland.disney.go.com, 8am-midnight daily June-Aug., 8am-10pm daily Mar.-May and Sept.-Dec., 8am-9pm Mon.-Thurs., 8am-11pm Fri.-Sun. Jan.-Feb., from $104 per person) was born in 1955 as the ultimate creation of entertainment pioneer Walt Disney.

The park consists of nine separate lands, from **Frontierland** and its iconic roller coaster Big Thunder Mountain Railroad, to **Tomorrowland** and the even more iconic Space Mountain. The newest land is **Star Wars: Galaxy's Edge,** where you can fly the Millennium Falcon on a virtual ride and build your own lightsaber. Don't leave without taking a ride on the steam-powered **Disneyland Railroad** or hopping on the **Monorail,** the first of its kind in the Western Hemisphere.

If you're with kids and spending a couple days in the Anaheim area, consider a three-day pass, as it's a better deal per day over the one- or two-day passes. Plus, there are so many attractions here, you might want the extra time to see everything.

UNIVERSAL STUDIOS HOLLYWOOD

The less-famous theme park is **Universal Studios Hollywood** (100 Universal City Plaza, Universal City, 800/864-8377, www.universalstudioshollywood.com, hours vary by day, but generally 8am-10pm daily summer, 10am-6pm daily fall-spring, from $109 per person), 10 miles northwest of Downtown L.A. and not too far from Griffith Park. It's home to rides and attractions that put beloved films and television shows front and center. The park is split between the **upper**
lot** and **lower lot;** you could easily spend a day in each lot.

The lower lot is where you'll find **Jurassic World,** celebrating the universe of movies anchored by Steven Spielberg's massive 1993 blockbuster. In Jurassic World: The Ride, take a boat trip through a *Jurassic Park*-style narrative before getting dropped 84 feet, Splash-Mountain-style, in your vessel. Younger children can engage with "fossils" at the DinoPlay park. Also here is Transformers: The Ride 3D, a highly praised "dark ride" where you're on a track with projected pictures all around you. The awesome imagery makes you feel like you're smack in the middle of a *Transformers* film.

At the upper lot, the **Wizarding World of Harry Potter** takes center stage. The major ride here is Harry Potter and the Forbidden Journey, a dark ride that spins, twists, and turns. There's also a Simpsons-themed area in the upper lot, plus the World-Famous Studio Tour, in which you'll travel inside an old, open tram through classic Hollywood sets and iconic scenes. You may see King Kong, Jaws, and Norman Bates, and of course, be careful when crossing that bridge….

SANTA MONICA PIER

You should also drive out to the **Santa Monica Pier** (200 Santa Monica Pier, Santa Monica, 310/458-8900, www.santamonicapier.org), the Coney Island of the West Coast. Marked by a distinctive neon sign at its entrance, the pier was a thriving amusement area in the early 20th century before undergoing changes during and after the Great Depression. Starting in 1934, the pier became a hub for aerobics, gymnastics, and weight-lifting; **Muscle Beach,** as it's known today, was unofficially established in the 1940s.

The pier only grew into a major tourist attraction again in the 1990s with the founding of the amusement park **Pacific Park** (380 Santa Monica Pier, Santa Monica, 310/260-8744, http://pacpark.com, hours vary by day, but generally 10am-11pm daily summer, noon-7pm daily fall-spring, free, rides

Photos (top): Griffith Observatory; (middle left) TCL Chinese Theatre; (middle right) Venice Beach Boardwalk; (bottom) Santa Monica Pier and Pacific Park rides.

$5-10 each). There's a Ferris wheel, steel roller coaster, and plenty of other large and small rides here. Santa Monica Pier is directly west of Downtown L.A., a 15-mile drive that will take at least 30 minutes.

VENICE BEACH BOARDWALK

The **Venice Beach Boardwalk** (1800 Ocean Front Walk, Venice, www.venicebeach.com) is home to some eclectic sights. Along this 1.5-mile oceanside strip, you'll see muscle men posing and posturing, T-shirt shops, roller skaters and skateboarders, street food vendors, and basketball courts. About 30,000 people visit the area daily. You may have to drive around a bit to find parking. There are lots along Speedway, the main artery that's parallel to the boardwalk, and spots will cost $15 or so. Venice Beach is just a couple miles south from the Santa Monica Pier.

FOOD

NEAR DODGER STADIUM

Just a quarter-mile from Dodger Stadium is **Tsubaki** (1356 Allison Ave., 213/900-4900, www.tsubakila.com, 5:30pm-10pm daily, under $50). This pleasant, brick-walled shoebox of a space does the kind of Japanese *izakaya* fare (small plates of bar food) you'll need when visiting L.A. You'll find fire-grilled yakitori, steamed *shumai* (dumplings), and big noodle bowls, along with a fine variety of sake, beer, and wine.

You'll have to cross CA-110 and the Los Angeles State Historic Park to get there, but close enough to the ballpark you'll find **Nick's Café** (1300 N. Spring St., 323/222-1450, www.nickscafela.com, 5:30am-3pm Mon.-Fri., 6:30am-3pm Sat.-Sun., under $30), the kind of diner that looks like it's been around for decades—and it has. Nick's opened in 1948 and quickly became known as the Ham House. The ham is still here today (served with eggs or in a sandwich), along

with classic breakfast and lunch dishes. Cozy up to the counter or grab a seat outside. This spot is cash only.

NEAR ANGEL STADIUM

The area around Angel Stadium is populated with chain and fast-food restaurants, but there is **The Catch** (2100 E. Katella Ave. #104, Anaheim, 714/935-0101, www.catchanaheim.com, 11:30am-10pm Mon.-Fri., 5pm-10pm Sat., 5pm-9pm Sun., under $80). A local fixture since 1978, The Catch has consistently been serving continental surf-and-turf with steaks and chops, big fish dishes, oysters, and decadent desserts. On game days, the restaurant is open well before and after the games, rolling out a brunch on Sunday home dates. The game day menu includes burgers, bar bites, and buckets of the beer that the company brews in nearby Tustin. This is a decent place to sit and eat before the game.

OTHER NEIGHBORHOODS

Los Angeles is an outstanding food city, where cultures intersect and classics are unearthed constantly. Where to start? With a taco. The popular **Sonoratown** (208 E. 8th St., 213/628-3710, www.sonoratown.com, under $20) will have lines, but this Downtown hangout is worth it for its cheap and fresh offerings. They make their own flour tortillas with lard. Seating is limited, so snag what you can and be generous.

For Mexican street fare, there's the ever-talked-about **Mariscos Jalisco** (3040 E. Olympic Blvd., 9am-6pm daily, under $20), a food truck known for its *tacos de camarón* (fried shrimp tacos). But that's not the only thing to get: The Poseidon, combining shrimp ceviche and octopus, is a seafood-lover's delight. Find this spot about three miles southeast of Downtown, below I-10 and I-5.

Want some down-home Mexican? Try the construction-orange **Guelaguetza Restaurante** (3014 W. Olympic Blvd., 213/427-0608, www.ilovemole.com, 9am-10pm Mon.-Thurs., 9am-11pm Fri., 8am-11pm

Sat., 8am-10pm Sun., under $50), whose URL says it all: The mole here is terrific. The *festival de moles* is a mole sampler that serves two, or you could just get a couple authentic Oaxacan entrées like tamales or *entomatadas* (similar to enchiladas). This restaurant is at the southern end of Koreatown.

Down around the Arts District, find the modern classic **Bestia** (2121 E. 7th Pl., 213/514-5724, www.bestiala.com, 5pm-11pm Sun.-Thurs., 5pm-midnight Fri.-Sat., under $80), great for a more traditional dinner with a little time to spare. Share some plates, get a pizza or pasta dish, and clink some glasses of wine (there's an extensive bottle list) or original cocktails. The very industrial chic dining room with an open kitchen and plating area is always buzzing.

A destination spot, **Connie & Ted's** (8171 Santa Monica Blvd., West Hollywood, 323/848-2722, www.connieandteds.com, 3pm-8pm Tues.-Sat., under $60) specializes in New England seafood but does everything pretty dang well. You can get lobster, clam chowder, East Coast oysters, and a heck of a burger and fried chicken sandwich. It's a big place, too, with outdoor dining, making it a safe bet if you just want some American grub.

Los Angeles has a deep roster of fantastic Korean restaurants, most huddled around the busy Koreatown section of the city. Some favorites: **Sun Nong Dan** (3470 W 6th St. #7, 213/365-0303, 24 hours daily, under $40), the 24-hour spot for fragrant plates of *galbi jjim* (beef short ribs), best ordered with a group, and bowls of *galbi tang* (beef short rib soup); **Seong Buk Dong** (3303 W. 6th St., 213/738-8977, 9am-midnight daily, under $40), a cute but small place with beef, pork bulgogi, tofu stew, and fish entrées, along with outstanding *nakji bokkeum* (stir-fried octopus); and **Dumpling House** (3525 W. 3rd St., 213/389-3899, 11am-9:30pm Thurs.-Tues., under $40), where you'll want some steamed dumplings, maybe a bowl of noodles, or even Korean barbecue. Another option if you want to grill some meat at your table is **Eight Korean BBQ** (863 S. Western Ave., 213/365-1750, www.eightkoreanbbq.com, 11:30am-11pm Sun.-Thurs., 11:30am-1am

Fri.-Sat., under $70). The "eight" in the name stands for the restaurant's variety of pork marinades (including red pepper paste, herb, and wine). This restaurant offers cleanliness, efficiency, and a wide variety of sides and options.

For a top-notch sandwich, visit historic **Langer's Delicatessen-Restaurant** (704 S. Alvarado St., 213/483-8050, www.langersdeli. com, 8am-4pm Mon.-Sat., under $30) in the Westlake neighborhood. Opening in 1947, this family-run Jewish deli is one of the last of its kind here, serving up a terrific pastrami on rye (#19 is the famous one). Pastrami plates, blintzes, potato pancakes, fish dishes, and egg breakfasts (not to mention bagels with lox and cream cheese) are also mighty popular here. It's always busy inside this old-school diner with a narrow counter, so reserve some time to get in, sit down, and enjoy.

Near Anaheim, the famous **Glee Donuts & Burgers** (9475 Heil Ave., Fountain Valley, 714/531-0288, www.gleednb.com, 5:30am-2pm Mon.-Sat., 6:30am-2pm Sun.) is a great spot to grab some breakfast. They do superior breakfast burritos, and there are plenty of donuts behind the pastry cases. For lunch there are burgers, naturally, plus stacked sandwiches.

Plenty of great options are located inside the **Anaheim Packing District** (440 S. Anaheim Blvd., Anaheim, 714/533-7225, www. anaheimpackingdistrict.com, 11am-9pm daily, under $50), a food hall with about a dozen rotating concepts. Walk through and see vendors that sell everything from fried chicken sandwiches to hot pot to Syrian food to boba tea. There's also regular live music. Order from a few spots to sample as much as you can.

BARS AND BREWERIES

NEAR DODGER STADIUM

About a mile or so southeast of the ballpark in Chinatown you'll find the taproom of

Anaheim Packing District

Highland Park Brewery (1220 N. Spring St., 213/878-9017, www.hpb.la, noon-8pm daily). Inside an industrial space with high exposed ceilings, warehouse windows, and metal stools, you'll get to enjoy a range of quality beers, from fruited sours to imperial stouts, with plenty of IPAs and other goodies in between. Highland Park also serves food.

The popular bar nearby is **The Short Stop** (1455 W. Sunset Blvd., 213/482-4942, 5pm-2am daily). It's a spot that plenty of folks visit either before or (usually) after the game. Come for good drinks poured by affable bartenders, stay for the people-watching and old Dodger team photos.

NEAR ANGEL STADIUM

Just down the block from Angel Stadium is **Brewheim Beer Makers** (1931 Wright Cir., Anaheim, 714/453-4346, www.brewheim. com, 2pm-7pm Mon.-Thurs., noon-7pm Fri.-Sun.). Come inside this clean, modern taproom with plenty of seating at custom wood tables and at a long bar that offers views of the brewhouse. Brewheim loves its stouts, and it also carries a nice selection of lighter and refreshing beers.

Across Katella Avenue from the ballpark you'll find **Noble Ale Works** (1621 Sinclair St. #B, Anaheim, 714/634-2739, www.noble-aleworks.com, 4pm-11pm Mon.-Thurs., 4pm-midnight Fri., noon-midnight Sat., noon-8pm Sun.). This is a great spot to visit before heading to Angel Stadium, especially because Noble allows you to park your car there for free and walk over to the ballpark. Noble keeps a varied list of beers, skewing a little toward IPAs, and it can hold several dozen people inside its industrial hang with LCD screens.

OTHER NEIGHBORHOODS

When in Anaheim, head north from Angel Stadium about four miles to stop by **The Bruery** (717 Dunn Way, Placenita, 714/729-2300, www.thebruery.com, noon-8pm daily). Founded in 2008, the Bruery is well known across the country for serving up experimental fare, typically aged in barrels or cooked with fruit. When at the taproom, you'll have to pore over a huge list of available beers, but there are flights and lots of bottles to purchase. Be sure to spend a few hours here—it's a winner.

Just on the other side of the L.A. River from the Arts District, the small **Dry River Brewing** (671 S. Anderson St., 323/354-4468, www.dryriverbrewing.com, noon-6pm Fri.-Sat.) isn't open often, but when it is, people drop by. The brewery specializes in sour beers, serving them up in a cozy wood-walled space.

Up in Glendale, get a full taste of the local beer scene at **Glendale Tap** (4227 San Fernando Rd., Glendale, 818/241-4227, www.glendaletap.com, 5pm-2am Mon.-Wed., 1pm-2am Thurs.-Sun.). From the outside it looks a little like a biker dive, and inside it looks a lot like a classic roadhouse. Sit at the long bar, maybe play some billiards, and peruse the 52 taps. You may find that you're having one of the best times of your life. This is one of the coolest bars you'll visit anywhere in the United States.

Dip into a modern *izakaya* (Japanese bar) vibe at **Ototo** (1360 Allison Ave., 213/784-7930, www.ototo.la, 5:30pm-11pm Mon.-Sat., 2pm-9pm Sun.), a preeminent sake bar with a cool, dimly lit space, premium sakes and solid draught beer offerings. There's also tasty bar bites like chicken *katsu* (panko-breaded and fried) sandwiches and *hirame* (flatfish) crudos, plus a killer burger with chili peppers and a yuzu-flavored special sauce.

RECREATION

GRIFFITH PARK

Griffith Park (4730 Crystal Springs Dr.) is a 4,310-acre wonderland that accounts for much of the greenspace in the City of Angels. It's home to **Griffith Observatory** (2800 E. Observatory Rd., 213/473-0800, www.griffithobservatory.org, noon-10pm Tues.-Fri., 10am-10pm Sat.-Sun., free, $10 parking), which gives people the opportunity to view Downtown Los Angeles, Hollywood, and southwest to the Pacific Ocean. And you don't even need to go to the telescope to get these views—the observatory sits atop a hill, allowing for unobstructed photos of the

Hollywood Sign, the L.A. skyline, and more. Inside you'll find a full museum with multiple exhibits detailing the history of astronomy. Look for the Tesla coil, the camera obscura, and the live image of the sun. The **Samuel Oschin Planetarium** (every 60-90 minutes, $7, $5 students and seniors, $3 ages 5-12) screens several shows daily (tickets required). At night, you can view the sky through the observatory's famous **12-Inch Zeiss Refracting Telescope.**

Also in the park is the **L.A. Zoo** (5333 Zoo Dr., www.lazoo.org, 10am-5pm daily, $22, $19 seniors, $17 ages 2-12, free age 1 and under), a 133-acre space that's home to Asian elephants, lions, tigers, giant otters, wallabies, and the LAIR, where more than 60 species of amphibians, invertebrates, and reptiles live in habitats that closely mirror their natural habitats.

At Griffith Park you'll also find the historic **Greek Theatre** (2700 N. Vermont Ave., 323/665-5857). Better known as "The Greek," it's been around since 1929 and has seen performances from just about every big-time musician.

HIKING

Did you know that you can hike to the Hollywood Sign? It's true! The **Wonder View Trail** (trailhead at Wonder View Dr. and Lake Hollywood Dr.) will take you to an amazing clearing just behind the iconic letters. Park on Lake Hollywood Drive, then walk up Wonder View Drive until it ends. Continue on the exposed, somewhat rugged Wonder View Trail as it climbs to the **Wisdom Tree.** Stop here to take in great views of Los Angeles, and lay a rock atop a cairn there. Then continue for the final half-mile or so to the Hugh Hefner Overlook (yes, that Hugh Hefner). You'll go down to **Mt. Lee Drive,** then find a spot to check out the sign that's just in front of you. In all, the hike is three miles up and back with an elevation gain of about 800 feet.

For a clear view of the sign read from left to right, take the **Mt. Hollywood Trail,** which can be accessed at two trailheads. The most family-friendly approach—and the busiest—starts at the **Charlie Turner Trailhead** (2840 W. Observatory Rd.) in Griffith Park. You'll hike this well-marked 1.5-mile trail up about 500 feet of elevation, passing **Captain's Roost,** a rest stop with a view of the sign. Continue onward to the Mount Hollywood summit, marked by Dante's View, offering a clear vista (when it's not hazy) of the entire city and San Gabriel Mountains (but not the sign—that's on the other side of the hill).

SHOPPING

If you're out walking in Studio City, specifically at Universal CityWalk Hollywood, you may come across the **Dodgers Clubhouse** (1000 Universal Studios Blvd. #164, Universal City, 818/761-5677, 11am-11pm daily). The spacious shop has plenty of shirts, jerseys (including customizable ones), jackets, and hats. You can even find gloves, helmets, backpacks, and other small collectible items.

ACCOMMODATIONS

NEAR DODGER STADIUM

The only hotel that's within true walking distance of Dodger Stadium (less than 1.5 miles) is **Super 8** (1341 Sunset Blvd., 213/250-2233, www.wyndhamhotels.com, $100-200), a chain budget motel. Though it needs updating, it's clean and has a continental breakfast daily. Beyond this spot, I don't recommend staying near the park, as options are both slim and lacking in cleanliness and friendliness.

NEAR ANGEL STADIUM

Just a two-minute walk from Angel Stadium, **Ayres Hotel Anaheim** (2550 E. Katella Ave., Anaheim, 714/634-2106, www.ayreshotels.com, $80-200) is a safe bet for lodging, with more than 130 guest rooms and suites. The

hotel also operates a Disneyland shuttle, making this a good spot for families. All rooms here are either kings or queens. Rates include complimentary breakfast.

OTHER NEIGHBORHOODS

You'll find plenty of hotels in Downtown Los Angeles and nearby Little Tokyo, offering access to Dodger Stadium, about two miles north. The **Miyako Hotel** (328 E. 1st St., 213/617-2000, www.miyakola.com, $150-300) scores fine ratings for its cleanliness and efficient service. Each room has a heated Japanese bidet, and there's a sushi bar on site. For breakfast, you might be able to score fare like glutinous rice and miso soup.

Want to feel like you're really ensconced in the Hollywood experience? The **Hollywood Celebrity Hotel** (1775 Orchid Ave., 323/850-6464, www.hotelcelebrity.com, $120-250) delivers, as it's just a block from Hollywood Boulevard and the TCL Chinese Theatre. The rooms are quite basic, but the hotel gets a lot of love for its convenient location and cleanliness. Plus, all the rooms have queen beds, at minimum. Some rooms have kitchens, too.

GETTING AROUND

Because the population of the Los Angeles metropolitan area is spread out so much between the city of L.A. itself and its many neighboring cities and unincorporated areas (Inglewood, Compton, Long Beach, Santa Ana, Anaheim, Santa Monica, Beverly Hills, Pasadena, and so on), it's always been more geared toward cars than mass transit. Dozens of highways and freeways crisscross and twist through the region, offering plenty of connections but a whole lot of traffic jams.

PUBLIC TRANSIT

Public transportation in Los Angeles County is operated by **Metro** (www.metro.net, $1.75 one-way). Its **bus system** is robust. Metro

SIDE TRIP: JACKIE AND MACK ROBINSON MEMORIAL

Over in Pasadena, where the world-famous baseball player Jackie Robinson attended high school and college, there lies a cool memorial showing two brothers alike in their exploits but very different in their paths. The **Jackie and Mack Robinson Memorial** (101 Garfield Ave., Pasadena) depicts the heads of the two brothers facing in different directions. Jackie, who broke baseball's color barrier and saw great success in Brooklyn, is looking toward New York. His brother Mack, who won the silver medal (behind Jesse Owens) for the 200-meter sprint in the 1936 Berlin Olympic Games but returned to Pasadena

Jackie and Mack Robinson Memorial by sculptors Ralph Helmick, John Outterbridge, and Stuart Schechter

and found hardship due to racist politics, looks directly at City Hall across the street. The statues are made of bronze and stand more than 8.5-feet tall. They were created in 1997 by artists Ralph Helmick and John Outterbridge. Step up close to the statues and you'll see text and images relating to each brother's life and accomplishments.

(Bonus photo opportunity: Pasadena City Hall is the establishing shot of the city hall for Pawnee, Indiana, in the TV show *Parks and Recreation*.)

GETTING THERE

From Downtown Los Angeles you can drive northeast via CA-110 for just under 10 miles right into Pasadena. Hop onto South Marengo Avenue and take that 1.5 miles up to Holly Street. Turn right and you'll be at the park that houses the statues. The 12-mile drive takes around 30 minutes with minimal traffic.

also operates a **light rail** with six lines. The major rail hub is Downtown at **Union Station** (800 N. Alameda St., www.unionstationla.com), from where you can hop onto the **B Line** (red), **D Line** (purple), and **L Line** (gold) trains. Union Station is also a hub for trains serviced by **Metrolink** (www.metrolinktrains.com, $8.75 one-way), a commuter rail that connects Los Angeles to Anaheim; and the **Pacific Surfliner** route on **Amtrak** (www.amtrak.com), which runs from San Luis Obispo to San Diego.

The **L Line** runs east of Dodger Stadium, with the closest stop to the ballpark being **Chinatown** (1231 N. Spring St.); from there, it's a 1.2-mile walk northwest to the venue. The **B Line** heads west to Hollywood, including a station at **Hollywood and Vine** (Hollywood Blvd. and Argyle Ave.), and Universal City. To reach **LAX,** take the **B** or **D**

Line to the other major light rail hub, **7th Street/Metro Center** (7th St. and Flower St.). Trains on the **A Line** (blue) and **E Line** (Expo, light blue) also stop here. To continue to the airport, at 7th Street take the A Line south to **Willowbrook/Rosa Parks station** (Willowbrook Ave. and I-105). There, you'll transfer to the **C Line** (green) and head west to **Aviation/LAX station** (Aviation Blvd., I-105).

In Anaheim, there's no devoted light rail system, but you can jump from L.A. to Anaheim (and from Anaheim to San Diego) via Metrolink's **Orange County Line.** You'll disembark at the **ARTIC station** (2626 E. Katella Ave.), which is just a two-minute walk northeast from Angel Stadium. Anaheim's **bus system** is **OCTA** (Orange County Transportation Authority, www.octa.net, $2 per ride), which maintains a few dozen routes. **ART** (Anaheim Resort Transportation, www.rideart.org, $4) is a regional bus system with more than a dozen routes that connect tourists and travelers to the major attractions in the area, including Disneyland and Knott's Berry Farm.

TAXI, UBER, AND LYFT

Uber might be a slightly cheaper way to get around the Los Angeles area than Lyft, but both will be more expensive than in most other cities. An Uber from LAX to Dodger Stadium might cost around $30, while a Lyft will be closer to $35. Taxi cab rides will likely be plenty more—think $40 or so.

CAR

Highways and Freeways

I-5 (the **Santa Ana Freeway**) races north to south through the center of Los Angeles, offering the cleanest connection to **Anaheim. US-101** (the **Hollywood Freeway**) cuts through Hollywood and functions as the northern border of Downtown before ending at the intersection of I-5. **I-10** (the **San Bernardino Freeway**) begins in Santa Monica at the Pacific Ocean, heading east through Downtown (joining with I-5 for two miles), then continuing east along the southern shelf of the San Gabriel Mountains. I-10 then passes around the south side of Joshua Tree National Park before entering more arid lands and Arizona.

I-110 (the **Harbor Freeway**) shoots off I-10, west of Downtown, and runs south to San Pedro. Parallel to it is **I-710,** running east of Downtown and south to Long Beach. There's also **I-210,** which shoots off from I-10 around Pasadena, north of the city, before heading northwest along the mountainside into San Fernando.

The I-5 spurs include **I-105,** running along the southern end of the city, west to east, past Hawthorne and Lynwood; **I-605,** a north-to-south extension connecting communities like West Covina, Whittier, and Cerritos, all in between L.A. and Anaheim; and **I-405,** a jam-packed highway also called

the **San Diego Freeway,** coming off I-5 up north in San Fernando, then diving toward the coastline past Santa Monica, LAX, and Torrance, before slicing through Long Beach, Costa Mesa, and Irvine, and running parallel to beach cities like Newport Beach and Huntington Beach. It's a major connector for the most populous areas of the region.

You may notice that highways and freeways in Southern California are commonly referred to as "the (number)." The 405 gets you through the region near the coastline, while *the* 101 is the way through Hollywood.

Surface Streets

If you can avoid freeways and highways, it might be a good idea. Major streets include **Western Avenue** (CA-91), which starts in Hollywood and runs south straight into Gardena and the Torrance area; **Washington Boulevard,** which starts in Venice Beach, heads northeast then east, just south of Koreatown and Downtown, before moving southeast and cashing out at Whittier Boulevard. This can be a back way from L.A. to Anaheim, though you'll have to go south from Whittier (try Harbor Blvd. in La Habra).

Artesia Boulevard starts in the Manhattan Beach area and continues east into Gardena, when it becomes the elevated **Gardena Freeway** (CA-91). In Orange County it becomes the **Artesia Freeway** and **Riverside Freeway,** with exits in Anaheim. It's another way from L.A. to Anaheim via the south end of the city, though again, traffic here is very bad.

There are also the popular touristy streets: **Hollywood Boulevard** is only in Hollywood, and **Sunset Boulevard** is the major thoroughfare just south of that. **Vine Street** runs north to south, from US-101 down to its end at **Melrose Avenue. Santa Monica Boulevard** is CA-2, starting at the shore in Santa Monica and extending northeast into Hollywood. It runs parallel to Sunset Boulevard before that street joins up with it, turning it into Sunset Boulevard as it snakes toward Downtown.

Located north of Hollywood in Laurel Canyon and in the Hollywood Hills (Santa

VISITING THE CALIFORNIA LEAGUE

If you're in the mood for some class-A baseball across both coastal and inland California, I suggest checking out the **California League** (www.milb.com/california, Apr.-early Sept.). The organization started in 1941 with teams in then-smaller cities like Anaheim, Bakersfield, Riverside, and San Bernardino. Today there are eight teams playing a season that runs from mid-April to around Labor Day weekend. Their ballparks are located throughout Northern and Southern California.

Here's a list of the eight California League parks and their teams:

- **Banner Island Ballpark** (404 W. Fremont St., Stockton): home to the Stockton Ports
- **Excite Ballpark** (588 E. Alma Ave., San Jose): home to the San Jose Giants
- **John Thurman Field** (601 Neece Dr., Modesto): home to the Modesto Nuts
- **Lake Elsinore Diamond** (500 Diamond Dr., Lake Elsinore): home to the Lake Elsinore Storm
- **LoanMart Field** (8408 Rochester Ave., Rancho Cucamonga): home to the Rancho Cucamonga Quakes
- **Recreation Park** (300 N. Giddings St., Visalia): home to the Visalia Rawhide
- **San Manuel Stadium** (280 S. E. St., San Bernardino): home to the Inland Empire 66ers
- **The Hangar** (45116 Valley Central Way, Lancaster): home to the Lancaster JetHawks

Monica Mountains), **Mulholland Drive** is a winding, zippy, narrow road through the area's history. Big-money mansions owned by some of the biggest celebrities in the world surround you, as do open space, million-dollar skyline views, and very long drops, so keep your eyes on the road and go slow.

The **Pacific Coast Highway** (CA-1) starts off I-5 near Dana Point, then runs alongside the Pacific Ocean north toward Santa Barbara and, further, to the San Francisco Bay Area. Away from the L.A. area, it gets more intense, cozying up with oceanside cliffs. My suggestion is to go beach-hopping this way. Rent a convertible, put the top down, blast the tunes, and cruise from sandy stop to sandy stop. Laguna Beach, Newport Beach, and Huntington Beach are all accessible along this route, south of the L.A.; highlights north of the city include Santa Monica and the Pacific Palisades, Malibu, and Ventura.

The chic celebrity-packed city of **Beverly Hills** is defined by **Rodeo Drive** (pronounced roh-DAY-oh). You can cruise this road, then scour for a parking spot to walk the area closest to **Wilshire Bouelvard.** The walkway rising up from Wilshire at Rodeo takes you through a mall of ultra-expensive shops like Versace and Jimmy Choo, while just across Rodeo Drive from here are places like Louis Vuitton and Fendi.

Traffic

Traffic here is always a challenge; the most notorious spots to avoid are **I-5** from **I-10** south to **I-605** (the **San Gabriel Freeway**), a stretch that cuts through East Los Angeles; and **US-101** from **CA-134** (the **Ventura Freeway**) to **I-110.** The closer to Downtown Los Angeles you get, the more traffic you're bound to encounter. **I-405** is choked with traffic all the time.

OAKLAND
ATHLETICS

The Oakland Athletics are one of baseball's weirdest franchises, a team whose character oozes from its sharp kelly green and gold uniforms. It's the franchise of Charlie O. Finley, Rollie Fingers' mustache, the Bash Brothers, and *Moneyball*. It's one of baseball's cheapest organizations, and yet it wears ingenuity proudly on its sleeve. The A's have an old and, by most measures, ugly ballpark, but it's endearing, even remarkable when you look more closely. While the regal Yankees strut their pinstripes and the Red Sox perennially play the beloved underdog, the Athletics truly represent the people. They're colorful, scrappy, and always threatening to make the postseason once again.

Though major league baseball didn't come to Oakland until 1968, the sport thrived here

between 1903 and 1955, thanks to the minor league Oakland Oaks of the Pacific Coast League. The Oaks spanned six decades and played home games in neighboring Emeryville. The team might be best known for employing the first Black professional player, Jimmy Claxton. In 1916, professional baseball was racially segregated. (Black players were barred from major league baseball until 1947.) Claxton claimed Native American heritage and played two minor league games before being fired when it was revealed that he was Black.

During that same era, the Philadelphia Athletics had plenty of success under Connie Mack, the snappily dressed manager who led the team for an astounding 50 seasons (1901-50). A few years after Mack left the dugout, a real estate magnate bought the team and moved it to Kansas City, where it floundered. Then Charlie Finley took over in 1964, moving the team to Oakland in 1968 and turning the franchise into something of an anti-Yankees. They wore green and gold, grew facial hair, and employed a mule to be mascot. Despite winning three consecutive world championships in the early 1970s, and another in 1989 (during the era of tandem home runs from Jose Canseco and Mark McGwire, and the emergence of a team-employed assistant who'd go on to become MC Hammer), the Athletics remained a lower-budget franchise. With the exception of the era of Canseco, McGwire, and Hall of Famer Rickey Henderson, the team never drew a high number of fans.

But that's the A's. What they don't have in payroll and attendance they make up for in character. Behind executive Billy Beane, they reinvented how front offices shape rosters, winning playoff spots along the way. And while they don't sell out, their devoted fans are just that, going to as many games as possible and making plenty of noise (especially in the right field bleachers). The Athletics

have always been inventive in a sport that can sometimes be a little too old-fashioned.

PLANNING YOUR TIME

For those just coming to see the Athletics, **two days** is just fine for Oakland. You can even plan a fast-paced **one-day** trip in Oaktown, but you might tire yourself out. Plan on spending a couple hours Downtown, which includes a visit to Jack London Square. If you want to get in a boat or visit the zoo, make it a two-day excursion.

If you're planning a full Bay Area vacation, you can schedule anything from **four days** to a full **week.** It's rare for the Athletics and Giants to be home at the same time; plan a mid-week to mid-week trip (Thursday to Tuesday, say) that might include the end and beginning of **two different homestands.**

If you plan on being in Oakland and not heading anywhere else in the Bay Area, you're just fine staying at a hotel near **Oakland International Airport,** especially since the Coliseum is no more than a mile away. BART is convenient enough for an easy ride into Downtown Oakland.

If you plan on spending more time across the bay, though, your best bet is to stay in **San Francisco.** But if you don't mind the train rides, staying in Oakland will be more affordable and convenient for seeing an A's game, plus you'll no doubt get a larger hotel room for your money.

The Bay Area's weather can be **unpredictable.** It typically doesn't get too hot in summer—average daytime temperatures hover in the low 70s, and rain is a foreign concept. Generally, going to a game in April or even May could mean evening first-pitch temperatures in the 50s, so plan on wearing **layers.** The evening lows for a July night game could drop into the low 60s, so you should probably pack a jacket no matter what. Your best bet is a **day game** between **June** and **September.**

GETTING THERE

AIR

Oakland International Airport

The closest airport to the Coliseum is **Oakland International Airport** (OAK, 1 Airport Dr., 510/563-3300, www.oaklandairport. com). Servicing the airport are **Allegiant** (702/505-8888, www.allegiantair.com), **American Airlines** (800/433-7300, www. aa.com), **Delta** (800/221-1212, www.delta. com), **jetBlue** (800/538-2583, www.jetblue. com), **Southwest** (800/435-9792, www. southwest.com), and **Spirit** (801/401-2222, www.spirit.com). There are two terminals at Oakland International: Terminal 1 is for most flights, while Terminal 2 is for Southwest Airlines.

AIRPORT TRANSPORTATION

A **shuttle bus** takes passengers to the **rental car center,** which is home to all major national companies. To get to Oakland Coliseum from the airport, you'll hop onto I-880 North for just a few minutes before exiting at 66th Avenue, following signs for the Coliseum. This drive is less than five miles and takes around five minutes without traffic. From the airport to Downtown Oakland is a bit farther. Take I-880 North to Broadway/ Downtown for a 15-minute drive of about 10 miles.

You can also use **BART** (Bay Area Regional Transit, www.bart.gov, from $2.60) to easily get from the airport to Downtown Oakland, San Francisco, or the Coliseum. The airport offers an eight-minute **shuttle train connection** to the closest main BART station, which is **Coliseum station** (7200 San Leandro St.) and just so happens to be the station nearest to the Coliseum. BART goes into Downtown Oakland, where you can get off at **12th Street/Oakland City Center** (1245 Broadway) or **19th Street** (1900 Broadway).

San Francisco International Airport

Just across the bay is **San Francisco International Airport** (SFO, US-101 and Airport Access Rd., South San Francisco, 650/821-8211, www.flysfo.com), which has three main domestic terminals and an international terminal with two separate gate areas. Airlines here include American Airlines, Delta, jetBlue, Southwest, and **United** (800/864-8331, www.united.com). Flights depart to and arrive from just about every major airport in North America, and plenty more across the globe, including locations in East Asia and Oceania.

AIRPORT TRANSPORTATION

The **Blue Line** of **AirTrain** (free) travels from each terminal to a **rental car center,** where all major companies serve customers. To reach **Oakland** from SFO, you have two options, depending on your destination. If you're headed for **Downtown Oakland,** go north on US-101, where you'll drive through San Francisco, merge onto I-80, then over the Bay Bridge into Oakland. This route is just under 25 miles and will take at least 30 minutes in ideal traffic conditions. If you're headed straight for the **Coliseum,** go south on US-101, east on CA-92, then over the San Mateo Bridge. Take I-880 North to reach the Coliseum. This route is just under 30 miles and takes at least 30 minutes if there's no traffic.

Both the **Red Line** and the **Blue Line** of AirTrain link to **BART** (www.bart.gov, from $2.60) from all terminals via the **San Francisco International Airport station** (International Terminal). To reach Downtown Oakland with BART, take a **Yellow Line** train bound for Antioch and disembark at the **12th Street/Oakland City Center station** (1245 Broadway). This is a 40-minute ride and costs $10.50.

To get to Oakland Coliseum, take the Yellow Line to **Balboa Park station** (401 Geneva Ave., San Francisco), then transfer to a **Green** or **Blue Line** train. Take this to **Coliseum station** (7200 San Leandro St.). There's an elevated walkway from the station directly to the stadium.

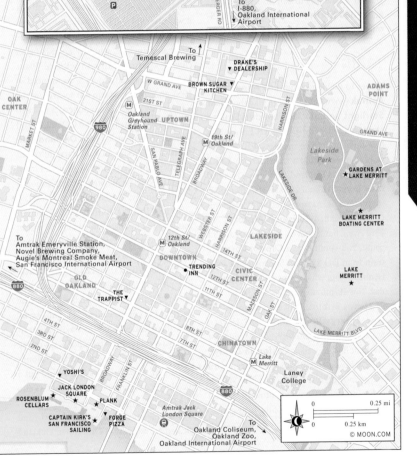

⚾ *Oakland Coliseum* ⚾

OAKLAND

OAKLAND

580

880

OAKLAND COLISEUM

0 ___ 1 mi

0 ___ 1 km

580

580

66TH AVE

580

SAN LEANDRO ST

←To
I-880,
Downtown Oakland

Coliseum Ⓜ

Footbridge

**OAKLAND
COLISEUM**

Oakland
Arena

COLISEUM WAY

880

HEGENBERGER RD

SAN LEANDRO ST

▼ ESTRELLAS
DE SINALOA

To
I-880,
▼ Oakland International
Airport

To ↑
Temescal Brewing

DRAKE'S
▼ DEALERSHIP

W GRAND AVE

BROWN SUGAR ▼
KITCHEN

ADAMS
POINT

OAK
CENTER

MARKET ST

21ST ST

Ⓜ *Oakland
Greyhound
Station*

UPTOWN

980

SAN PABLO AVE

TELEGRAPH AVE

BROADWAY

19th St/
Ⓜ Oakland

HARRISON ST

GRAND AVE

*Lakeside
Park*

GARDENS AT
★ LAKE MERRITT

LAKESIDE DR

WEBSTER ST

HARRISON ST

12th St/
Ⓜ Oakland

14TH ST

LAKESIDE

★ LAKE MERRITT
BOATING CENTER

To
Amtrak Emeryville Station,
Novel Brewing Company,
Augie's Montreal Smoke Meat,
San Francisco International Airport

DOWNTOWN

● TRENDING
INN

12TH ST

MADISON ST

OAK ST

CIVIC
CENTER

★ LAKE
MERRITT

880

OLD
OAKLAND

THE
TRAPPIST ▼

11TH ST

47TH ST

3RD ST

2ND ST

8TH ST

7TH ST

LAKE MERRITT BLVD

CHINATOWN

Lake
Ⓜ Merritt

Laney
College

★ YOSHI'S

BROADWAY

FRANKLIN ST

JACK LONDON
SQUARE ★

ROSENBLUM
CELLARS ★

★ PLANK

CAPTAIN KIRK'S ★
SAN FRANCISCO
SAILING

★ FORGE
PIZZA

🚉 *Amtrak Jack
London Square*

880

To
Oakland Coliseum,
Oakland Zoo,
Oakland International Airport

0 ___ 0.25 mi

0 ___ 0.25 km

© MOON.COM

618

CAR

It all depends on traffic, but at best, the drive from **Los Angeles** north to Oakland is about **six hours.** The quickest way when there's little to no traffic is the **370-mile** jaunt up **I-5 North.** At the junction with **I-580**, about 310 miles into the drive, hop onto I-580 West as it heads into the Bay Area. I-580 eventually borders the northern outskirts of Oakland, so you'll want to continue a bit farther west to join **I-880,** which leads to the Coliseum and Downtown.

For an alternate route that takes a little more time but takes you along the coastline and through mountains, take **US-101** north through Santa Barbara, before heading north through the San Marcos Pass on the combination road of **CA-154/US-101.** Stay on US-101 all the way to San Jose, then merge onto **I-880 North** into Oakland. This **415-mile** route will take closer to **7-8 hours.**

TRAIN

To get to Oakland from **Los Angeles** via **Amtrak** (www.amtrak.com), take the **Coast Starlight** north to **Jack London Square station** (245 2nd St.), which puts you a half-mile away from the closest BART station. Plan on taking a ride-share to BART or Downtown Oakland from here. This trip takes around 12 hours; tickets start from $55.

There is an Amtrak station at Oakland Coliseum, called **Coliseum/Airport** (700 73rd Ave.), but it's not on the Coast Starlight route. You could take a **Capitol Corridor** train from Jack London Square to the Coliseum station, which runs multiple times a day. This 10-minute ride costs $7.50.

There's a third Amtrak station in the area. **Emeryville station** (5885 Horton St., Emeryville) is also served by the Coast Starlight line, as well as **California Zephyr,** which heads north toward Sacramento before moving east to Chicago. This station is five miles north of Downtown Oakland and about 10 miles north of the Coliseum.

BUS

If you're okay with a long and traffic-filled journey, you can take **Greyhound** (www.greyhound.com) from **Los Angeles** to Oakland. The once-daily rides from Los Angeles start at $24 and can take nine hours or so. Buses deposit passengers at the **Oakland Greyhound station** (2103 San Pablo Ave.). From there, it's a 10-minute walk east to the 19th Street BART station in Downtown Oakland.

Oakland Coliseum

Around the mid-20th century, the City of Oakland was starved for baseball and felt it was essential to have a stadium. This way, it could more easily attract a Major League Baseball franchise, whether an expansion club or a team looking to relocate. Plans to construct a stadium were announced in 1960, and in 1967, a team was secured, as the Kansas City Athletics announced a move to the recently opened Oakland Coliseum. And ever since opening day 1968, **Oakland Coliseum** (7000 Coliseum Way, www.mlb.com/athletics) has been home to Athletics baseball. It may not be the prettiest, but it's home.

Surprisingly, the Coliseum once looked a lot like Dodger Stadium, as its design was inspired by that iconic ballpark. But in 1996, the city of Oakland agreed to expand the Coliseum as a condition of bringing the NFL's Raiders back from Los Angeles (where they played from 1982 to 1995). Thus, a garish set of seats were installed high across the outfield backdrop. Called "Mount Davis" after then-Raider owner Al Davis, this seating area certainly has a presence. Resembling a grandstand for a mega-raceway, Mount Davis isn't very attractive (the A's do put a nice-looking tarp over it, though), but it's also quite distinct and unique.

The Coliseum is old, made of concrete, and located far away from Downtown Oakland

YOUR BEST DAY AT OAKLAND COLISEUM

You've got a whole day in Oakland before the Athletics game this evening. Here are some ideas for what to do:

8 HOURS BEFORE FIRST PITCH
Breakfast is the most important part of the day. Start it off right with a visit to **Brown Sugar Kitchen.** Get the chicken and waffles and savor your coffee.

6 HOURS BEFORE FIRST PITCH
Grab an Uber or Lyft and head south to **Jack London Square.** Take some time to walk around before partaking in a bocce match at **Plank.**

4 HOURS BEFORE FIRST PITCH
Since you're close by, pay a visit to **Beer Revolution** and enjoy a hoppy West Coast IPA. If you need a bite beforehand, order a slice from **Forge Pizza,** but don't fill up.

2 HOURS BEFORE FIRST PITCH
You can ride-share or walk to the **Lake Merritt BART station** (800 Madison St.). Your stop will be **Coliseum** (700 73rd Ave.). You've arrived at **Oakland Coliseum.**
   Walk over the footbridge to the center field gates. Grab some food truck grub at **Championship Plaza** and make a couple friends. Maybe join a **tailgate** in the parking lot.

Jack London Square

DURING THE GAME
Get good beer at **Gastropub** inside **Shibe Park Tavern,** then join the fans and cheer along at **The Treehouse.** Later in the game, try and get a seat in the **right field bleachers** to join all the spirited fans. Ask nicely, and you might get to bang a drum.

AFTER THE GAME
Head back into Downtown on BART, stopping at **19th Street station** (1900 Broadway). Head north a few blocks and grab a pint at **Drake's Dealership.** Sit under twinkle lights and absorb the fun times you just had in Oakland.

and dynamic entertainment options. Because of these things, it's traditionally ranked toward the very bottom of "expert" ballpark lists. I can see the arguments, but I disagree. Starting around the 2017 season (when the A's named the field itself in honor of Hall of Famer and local hero Rickey Henderson), the A's have been investing in small but critical ballpark upgrades, giving fans plenty to do before and during games. And considering the atmosphere created by the fun and energetic Athletics fans (drumming, casual bleacher hangouts, people generally being wonderful), the Coliseum is so much better than you'd expect.

ORIENTATION

The Coliseum is part of an isolated sports complex next to Oakland Arena, former home of the Golden State Warriors, about six miles southeast of Downtown Oakland. Getting in and out of the area is a snap, as there's plentiful parking and access points. Also, it's right alongside a BART line, so connecting to public transit is easy.

   There are four entry gates at Oakland Coliseum. Two are accessible from Lot A and two are accessible from Lot B on the other side of the stadium.

Oakland Coliseum

TICKETS AND SEATING

Pricing

The Athletics use a dynamic pricing model, so seat costs will be higher for **premium games** like the **Yankees, Red Sox,** and especially the **Giants**—in fact, get tickets early for those games. For a plaza infield seat at a game against Baltimore, you may pay around $30. That same seat, for a weekend evening game against San Francisco, could cost more like $45.

You'll generally pay around $15-25 for cheap seats in the 300 level and bleachers, and between $40 and $50 for 200 level and back-of-the-100-level seats. It will cost nearly $70 for the closest chairs in the 100 level.

Seating Plan

The Coliseum's layout is relatively simple, but there are plenty of ticket options within the basic level structure. The **100 level** is split between the **MVP Level** (lower rows) and **Field Level** (upper rows) and has its own concourse. Sections 103-130 wrap around the foul area clockwise, while the bleachers (sections 134-150) are numbered from left field to right field. In the MVP Level, starting at the right field foul pole are **lower box** (sections 103-108) and **MVP** (sections 109-110). **MVP infield** (sections 111-123) wraps around behind home plate. Next is **MVP** (sections 124-125) again, followed by the third-base side of **lower box** (sections 126-130). In the Field Level, starting at the right field foul pole are **field level** (sections 103-106) and **field reserved** (sections 107-108). Wrapping

behind home plate is **field infield** (sections 109-125), then **field reserved** (sections 126-167) and **field level** (sections 128-133) again.

The **200 level** is split between the **Club Level** (closer to home plate, sections 210-224) and **Plaza Level** (right and left field, sections 200-203 and 225-234) and has its own concourse. Starting in right field is **plaza outfield** (sections 200-204), followed by **plaza level** (sections 205-209). Next is **plaza infield** (sections 210-211), then **plaza club** (sections 212-214), which is also part of **Shibe Park Tavern,** the ballpark's on-site restaurant. Continuing behind home plate is a larger section of **plaza infield** (sections 215-224). Finishing out the level on the third-base side are **plaza level** (sections 225-229) and **plaza outfield** (sections 230-234).

The **300 level** is the **View Level** and, well,

it has the big view. These nosebleed seats run clockwise around foul territory from section 304 to 330. The middle three sections are the **Value Deck** (sections 316-318) and are a bit pricier than the cheap seats. Everything else on the 300 level is called **view level** (sections 300-315, 319-334).

Out in center field, just beneath Mount Davis, is the **Eastside Club,** a large, glass-walled premium area for groups, plus an array of suites with views that are on par with those in the 300 level. The outfield 200 level concourse includes **The Treehouse** (left field), a drinking and play hangout, and **Stomping Ground** (right field), a kids' play place.

Group seating areas include the **Bud-weiser Hero Deck** (sections 101-102) down in right field and **Golden Road Landing** (sections 131-133) down in left field.

GAME COSTS

Tickets: For most games, **$50** gets you a seat in the 100 level. For **$30,** a 200 level seat or higher is typically at your disposal. This is pretty cheap for baseball tickets.

Hot dog: You'll pay **$6,** but it's a big ol' hot dog (called "colossal").

Beer: $8 for the cheap domestic brands, and **$10-12** for premium, including local craft labels. This is slightly more expensive than average.

Parking: The lots surrounding the stadium charge **$20** per car. Since it's a hike to leave the Coliseum grounds, you're pretty much obligated to park here.

Where to Buy Tickets

You can get pretty inexpensive tickets on **StubHub** and **SeatGeek.** If you buy tickets directly from the A's or StubHub, you can upgrade your seats through the **MLB Ball-park app.** Last-minute tickets are usually available from the ticket office, as the Coliseum almost never fills to capacity.

You'll see a lot of fans at the Coliseum wearing lanyards, identifying them either as **A's Access** members or **Treehouse Pass** holders. The A's Access membership is a season ticket plan (you get entry to every regular season home game) with loads of benefits, including half-price concessions, 25 percent off merchandise, and $10 pre-paid parking passes. With the Treehouse Pass ($112.60 season, $30 monthly), fans get a reserved spot to watch the game from The Treehouse.

Best Seats

If you long to sit close to the field, opt for seats in **sections 103-106** or **128-130,** which are a bit more cost-effective and are actually closer to the foul lines than some of the seats near home plate (the Coliseum has by far the largest amount of playable foul

territory in the game, most evident in the areas around first and third base).

The best seats are in the **first row** of the **200 level** around the **infield** (the closer to 217, the better). Your view will be impeccable, and the seat cost is cheaper than anything in the 100 level in foul territory. Of course, you can't go wrong with **cheap seats** in the **300 level,** especially if you don't mind heights and squinting a bit. As always, the closer to home plate (**sections 316-318**), the better, though those seats are a hair more expensive than the other 300 level tickets.

If you want a good time, hang out at **The Treehouse** (behind sections 235-237). There's a full bar here (though it's just one bar, with a crush of fans all the time), TVs tuned into every MLB game, pool tables, ping-pong tables, and a convivial spirit. You can head out the doors to the seats and spot up in the **standing-room** section. Just outside The Treehouse is the **Don Julio Deck,** which also offers **standing room.**

For an even better time, **sections 134-150** are the **bleachers** (outfield, 100 level). The right field portion is where the party starts: Fans bring drums, dress in wacky costumes, and generally treat the game like a soccer match. It's the closest thing baseball has to a soccer crowd, in fact. Tickets are cheap here (around $24), and while it gets hot during day games, that's all part of the experience.

To avoid the **sun,** sit in the **back rows** of the **Field Level** (100 level). The front rows of the lower level, plus all the View Level (300 level) get sun. The outfield does too, because the sun comes in from right center field. Want to sit in the bleachers? Apply sunscreen early and often. If you don't want to have the sun in your eyes, avoid the first-base line.

KNOW BEFORE YOU GO

You can bring a **bag** into the Coliseum, as long as it's no larger than 16 by 16 by 8 inches. If your bag is bigger than this, there's a free **bag check** (open until 30 minutes after game ends) at the D Gate.

Be sure to bring an **extra layer** for night

BE A FAN

Want to rock your favorite team's colors at the Coliseum? Rooting for the road team? No problem. Fans here are accepting. Some gentle ribbing may occur, but that's it. Just one note, though: Astros fans may get their share of verbal taunts, since it was an A's pitcher who exposed their cheating scheme of 2017 and 2018, but play it cool and you'll be fine.

After the top of the sixth inning, pay attention to the field, where cartoonish versions of three Athletics Hall of Famers (Dennis Eckersley, Rollie Fingers, and Rickey Henderson) **race for nightly glory.** In a just world, Rickey would win this race 100 percent of the time, but the mascots are merely humans in giant costumes.

A's fans

You may hear **drumming** at the Coliseum. That's the fans out in the **right field bleachers,** banging away to get the Athletics (and other fans) fired up. You're more than welcome to join in, as the bleachers are often just a fun free-for-all.

Back in 1981, the A's—the first team to favor recorded pop music rather than a live organ—started playing the hit song **"Celebration"** by Kool & The Gang after every win. Forty years later (with a small disruption in 2015 to try out a song by local band), the tradition continues; after every win … "yahoo!"

games, even in mid-summer. For day games, bring **sunscreen,** because the Coliseum isn't the shadiest place.

The Coliseum's general **parking lots** (A-D) open 2.5 hours before the game for **tailgating.** Charcoal grills are allowed.

If coming to the Coliseum from **BART,** you'll enter at center field near C Gate and D Gate. You'll want to walk around to home plate for the food trucks of Championship Plaza, which are near the section 113 and section 120 gates. Another fun option is to head into the parking lots and make some friends at a tailgate, then make your way toward Championship Plaza.

Accessibility

If you need transportation to the stadium from the parking lot (via golf cart) or **wheelchair escort** service inside the ballpark, check in at a **blue ADA tent** outside either the C Gate or D Gate, or on the BART Plaza.

For **accessible seating** options, call the Athletics at 877/493-2255. Once you're at the Coliseum, go to the **guest experience office** (section 126) for **assistive listening devices** and **noise-cancelling**

headphones. Wheelchair storage is also offered here, as well as at any **guest service hub** (sections 101, 134, 217).

Elevators at the Coliseum are located at the Championship Plaza entrance, and at sections 101 and 143. If you or your kids need a break from the activity of the ballpark, a **quiet space** is located at section 126. **Service animals**—including miniature horses—are welcome at Oakland Coliseum.

Accessible parking is available in Lots A-D, surrounding the Coliseum.

GETTING THERE

Public Transit

BART (www.bart.gov, from $2.60) is a super-efficient way to get to the stadium. From **12th Street/Oakland City Center** (1245 Broadway) to the Coliseum, the trip costs $2.60. From BART stations in San Francisco, fares begin at $4.80. The **Coliseum station** (7200 San Leandro St.) is right across from the ballpark. Just walk the footbridge to the center field gate. Plus, you're bound to ride in with hundreds of other A's fans, which can be pretty wild.

Driving

Driving to the stadium isn't terrible, but it's far from the rest of Oakland and you'll have to sit in traffic getting out of the parking lots after the game ends. There are **15 parking lots** around the Coliseum, and you'll pay around $20 for a spot. On **Tuesdays,** fans park for free (except for premium games like the Yankees or Giants).

A benefit of driving to the park is you can host a **tailgate** party. **Lots A-D** open 2.5 hours before each game and allow charcoal grills, beer, and general cavorting. The tailgating scene is solid here.

PARK FEATURES AND SIGHTS

Championship Plaza

As part of upgrades to RingCenter Coliseum, in 2017 the Athletics created a beer-and-food-garden area called **Championship Plaza** (outside of the ballpark, home plate entrance). About 10 food trucks hang out here, along with beer and wine vendors. Fans can enjoy the grub and beverages at picnic tables laid out on turf. It's a good place to grab a bite before heading into the ballpark, while also catching up with fellow fans and meeting friends.

Stomping Ground

Parents can take their children to the **Stomping Ground** (right field, sections 247-249), an indoor and outdoor area with games including the opportunity to race against a virtual Rickey Henderson and strike out an opposing virtual hitter, plus a miniature ballfield. Parents can enjoy drinks at the bar—identified by the mammoth elephant statue—or take the kids out into an enclosed turf play area with couches, all overlooking the baseball game.

Also at the section are picnic tables, so you can chow down while watching the A's play.

Photos (from top to bottom): plaques near Shibe Park Tavern; Drake's Brewing; A's game at Oakland Coliseum.

The A's sell a **Family Pass** ($399 per season, $79 per month) that permits access to the Stomping Ground for a family of two parents and two children ages 17 and younger (additional adults $29 per month, additional children $15 per month).

Next to the Stomping Ground, outside, is the **A's Home Grown Farm** (right field, 200 level), an outdoor plot that features tomatoes, peppers, plenty of herbs, and more plants and flowers sprouting up under twinkle lights. There are picnic tables and benches where you can sit during the game (but there are no views of the field from here).

FOOD AND DRINKS

The best food at the Coliseum is actually outside the ballpark. Head to **Championship Plaza** (home plate entrance) to find a collection of **food trucks** that rotates daily. You may find **Rosie's Mexican Food,** which slings basic tacos and burritos with meat like *barbacoa* and *al pastor* pork; **S&K Poutine,** which serves Canadian fries loaded in gravy and cheese curds out of its "Poutinambulance"; and **Pineapple Whips,** serving creamy, sweet, and fruity Dole whips.

Inside the park, there's a full menu at **Shibe Park Tavern** (sections 212-215), named after the Philadelphia home of the Athletics. Much of the menu is devoted to typical ballpark fare like burgers, hot dogs, pretzels, and nachos, and you're paying a lot for it all. But you can sit comfortably and watch the game from the tavern's clear, floor-to-ceiling windows. Plus, for those who don't eat meat, there's an Impossible Burger on the menu. More importantly, Shibe has the best beer selection in the ballpark, located at the **Gastropub.** When walking into the tavern, closer to section 215, look to the right for the stand that has about 12 rotating taps. Good local and regional beer is available here.

Otherwise, you can find some craft beer on the Field Level concourse. Look for small stands of **Drake's Brewing** (section 106) and **Firestone Walker Brewing Co.**

(section 124). The **Bulleit Bar** (section 120) is an odd hideaway made to look like a Prohibition-era hang. Whiskey drinks (with Bulleit Bourbon, naturally) and other mixed offerings are served here, along with draft beer.

EVENTS

The Athletics don't reserve areas for fans to get player **autographs.** While fans can head to sections 112-114 and 120-122 to watch **batting practice,** autographs aren't promised. There's no way to get autographs from behind the dugouts, as the protective netting at the ballpark spans the majority of the foul area.

After every home Sunday game, young fans can **run the bases.** They should line up at B Gate starting at the top of the ninth inning.

The Athletics host several **fireworks shows** each season, typically on Friday or Saturday nights. The team invites fans onto the field for a widescreen view of the colorful explosions. Other special events include **heritage nights** for Muslims, Latinx people, Pacific Islanders, Japanese people, Filipinos, and Koreans, among other ethnic, cultural, and spiritual groups. There's also the annual **A&W Root Beer Float Day** (date varies by season), at which local celebrities scoop root beer floats for fans inside the Eastside Club. Get to the park early for this event.

Tours

Want to get an inside look at the coliseum? The A's offer regular **tours** (ballparktours@ athletics.com, non-game days, $25, $15 seniors and ages 10 and under, free ages 2 and under) on days when the team isn't playing. The tour lasts up to 90 minutes and includes stops like the press box and home dugout. For tours that take place on gamedays, contact the A's in advance to arrange.

SHOPPING

The **Athletics' main team store** (Dennis Eckersley/D Gate, section 125, 10am-3pm

Mon.-Fri., 10am-gate opening game days, accessible only inside ballpark after gates open) is smaller than most other team stores, but it has much of the same merchandise, from jerseys (including sweet kelly green shirts) to plenty of hats, jackets, sweatshirts, and novelty toys. There are other stores throughout the park, including **Discount Dugout** (section 135), which has apparel and items marked down from their original price.

OAKLAND SIGHTS

JACK LONDON SQUARE

If there's a place to hang out in Oakland, it's **Jack London Square** (472 Water St., 510/645-9292, www.jacklondonsquare.com), a shopping, dining, and entertainment center smack on the waterfront, offering ferry access to San Francisco.

While here, you may want to knock down some pins at **Plank** (98 Broadway, 510/817-0980, www.plankoakland.com, 11am-midnight daily, $6.75 per game Mon.-Thurs., $65 per hour Fri.-Sun.), which is best if you have a group of at least four ready to go. That's for bowling, at least. Otherwise there's a full bar here with bocce and a beer garden.

If you want some wine, visit **Rosenblum Cellars** (10 Clay St., 877/478-9467, www.rosenblumcellars.com, 11am-8pm Sun.-Thurs., 11am-9pm Fri.-Sat.). This urban tasting room offers seating right on the bayside, along with some outstanding zinfandels and small bites like cheese and olives.

Along with the food and drink options, there are regular movie nights and sailing lessons on the *Osprey,* owned by **Captain Kirk's San Francisco Sailing** (650/930-0740, www.sfbaysail.com, from $200 per hour for up to six passengers weekday). You can add food and drink items (sushi, champagne, and more) for a minimum three-hour trip on the bay.

LAKE MERRITT

Less than a mile east of Downtown Oakland is **Lake Merritt,** which is surrounded by green space and makes for a splendid late-afternoon or early-evening hangout. To capture the lake at its best, visit the **Gardens at Lake Merritt** (666 Bellevue Ave., www.gardensatlakemerritt.org, 8am-5:30pm daily, free). At seven acres, this conservation area includes bonsai trees, a larger collection of Japanese plant species, and plenty of small walking trails. You can also rent a kayak, canoe, or pedal boat through the **Lake Merritt Boating Center** (568 Bellevue Ave., 510/238-2196, 11am-6pm Mon.-Fri., 10:30am-6pm Sat.-Sun. Mar.-Oct., 10:30am-4pm Sat.-Sun. Nov.-Feb., $15-30 per hour).

OAKLAND ZOO

Farther out in the city, but worth the drive, is the **Oakland Zoo** (9777 Golf Links Rd., 510/632-9525, www.oaklandzoo.org, 10am-4:30pm Mon.-Fri., 9am-4:30pm Sat.-Sun., $24, $20 ages 2-14 and seniors, free ages 1 and under and 76 and over). Understated but packed with fun, the zoo includes a four-acre African savanna with elephants, lions, and a giraffe, plus the California Trail, which features animals that you might find in the state, from grizzly bears to mountain lions. The zoo's Adventure Landing area includes rides for small children, from race cars to a small plane trek.

FOOD

NEAR OAKLAND COLISEUM

There isn't much close to the Coliseum, but you can find good Mexican and Cali-Mex eats at **Estrellas de Sinaloa** (8119 San Leandro St., 510/635-9899, 7am-8pm Mon.-Sat., under $20). Go for the burritos, tacos, or the awesome chile relleno combination plates. Estrellas de Sinaloa is a small, no-frills place with bright colors, cold Mexican beer stocked in the fridge, and inexpensive, tummy-stuffing grub.

OTHER NEIGHBORHOODS

If you're down in Jack London Square, local favorite **Yoshi's** (510 Embarcadero W., 510/238-9200, www.yoshis.com, 4:30pm-10pm Mon.-Thurs., 4:30pm-11pm Fri.-Sat., 4:30pm-9:30pm Sun., under $60) has fresh fish from Japan and the West Coast, including sashimi, nigiri, and maki rolls like the Jack London (salmon, cream cheese, avocado, cucumber). For something more adventurous, try the Oakland A's roll (shrimp tempura, snow crab, mango, avocado, spicy sauce). After dinner, take in a concert inside Yoshi's 300-plus-seat performance space. Yoshi's has been known since the 1970s for jazz, but artists from across the musical spectrum come to play these days, nearly daily (show tickets typically run $20-100). The food is a little pricey, but for a landmark spot with good music, it's worth a try.

Looking for pizza? Also at Jack London Square is **Forge Pizza** (66 Franklin St. #100, 510/268-3200, www.theforgepizza.com, 11am-10pm Mon.-Thurs., 11am-10:30pm Fri.-Sat., 11am-9pm Sun., under $30), which specializes in wood-fired, Neapolitan pies by the bay, charred underneath with crispy crusts and bubbling-hot cheese. The pepperoni is the move here. The prices are good. Outdoor seating is available, so you can watch the boats pass by.

Head north for breakfast, and visit **Brown Sugar Kitchen** (2295 Broadway, 510/839-7685, www.brownsugarkitchen.com, 7am-9:30pm Wed.-Fri., 7am-3pm Sat.-Sun., under $40). You may be waiting up to 45 minutes on weekend mornings for a table at this super popular place, but for good reason: the fried chicken and waffles. This isn't your ordinary brunch dish—two crunchy pieces of bird are served with two airy waffles made with cornmeal, and paired

Photos (from top to bottom): Lake Merritt; the Oakland Zoo; Plank in Jack London Square.

with an apple cider syrup that's ridiculously good. The other dishes are pretty darn good, too. Lunch includes catfish, oyster po'boys, and pulled pork.

Want a taste of classic Canadian cuisine? Out in Berkeley is **Augie's Montréal Deli** (700 Essex Way, Berkeley, 510/984-0283, www.augiesmontrealdeli.com, 11am-3pm Wed.-Thurs., 11am-8pm Fri.-Sun., under $20), serving slices of smoked meat layered atop one another like ribbons inside rye bread (mustard optional). There's also poutine here, plus a meat plate (if you don't need the bread). The owner hails from Canada and hockey may be playing on the TV—for that quintessential Canadian experience.

BARS AND BREWERIES

Like with food, the area around the Coliseum is devoid of watering holes. But you're not too far of a BART ride to some action.

OTHER NEIGHBORHOODS

Head into Downtown Oakland and walk a few blocks north to **Drake's Dealership** (2325 Broadway, 510/568-2739, www.drink-drakes.com, 11:30am-11pm Mon.-Wed., 11:30am-1am Thurs.-Fri., 10am-1am Sat., 10am-11pm Sun.), an old auto lot converted to a bar and beer garden for Drake's Brewing Co. The outdoor beer garden is under twinkle lights and gets busy on weekend afternoons and evenings, while inside is a long bar and plenty of tables. Get the 101 flight, which gives you a good intro to what Drake's is making.

For a quiet spot a few blocks north of Jack London Square, check out **The Trappist** (460 8th St., 510/238-8900, www.thetrappist.com, 3pm-11pm Mon.-Tues., noon-11pm Wed.-Thurs., noon-1am Fri.-Sat., noon-11pm Sun.). Look for some good Belgian beers here, like classics from St. Bernardus and La Trappe, plus fine American beers from Allagash and Russian River. The wood and brick

taproom is homey and understated, while the grilled sandwiches are warm and inviting.

Closer to Berkeley is **Novel Brewing Company** (6510 San Pablo Ave., 510/922-9974, www.novelbrewing.com, 3pm-10pm Tues.-Fri., noon-10pm Sat.-Sun.), which lives up to its name by offering books to read (and board games to play) while you sip beer. The beer is hoppy—Novel loves its IPAs, from big multiple-dry-hopped goodies to sessionable options (easy drinkers that are lower in alcohol). The industrial taproom with DIY wood tables and tanks in full view is a good weekend hangout spot.

Up I-580 about three miles is **Temescal Brewing** (4115 Telegraph Ave., 510/899-5628, www.temescalbrewing.com, 4pm-10pm Tues.-Thurs., 4pm-11pm Fri., noon-11pm Sat., noon-9pm Sun.). With its bare-bones beer garden, clean and minimalist taproom, and stunning variety of beers (from pilsners to pales to wild ales), there's something for everyone here. Be sure to find the pink side door—that's your way in. Food trucks are on site and dogs are welcome.

ACCOMMODATIONS

NEAR OAKLAND COLISEUM

For those coming to the Bay Area for the Athletics game alone, before whisking right back out, you could stay at a **chain hotel** just 1 mile southeast of the Coliseum and 1.5 miles north of Oakland International Airport. About six hotels are right off I-880 at Hegenberger Road, with room costs generally starting around $80 and topping out at $200; these are budget spots.

OTHER NEIGHBORHOODS

Downtown's **Trending Inn** (325 12th St., 510/879-6500, www.trendinginn.com, $150-200) is a comfortable, solid lodging option in the heart of Oakland. You're a few minutes' walk from the 12th Street Oakland BART station, and the high ceilings and sparse decor give the rooms a spacious, minimalist feel.

Another option is to head across the bay and stay in **San Francisco**. It's about a half-hour drive and you'll be well-placed to start your big-city adventure the next day.

GETTING AROUND

PUBLIC TRANSIT

BART (www.bart.gov, from $2.60) is one of the better public transportation systems in the country; the trick is to know what line you need to take. The Downtown Oakland stations are **12th Street/Oakland City Center** (1245 Broadway) and **19th Street** (1900 Broadway), both on the **Yellow Line** (Antioch to Millbrae), **Orange Line** (Richmond to Warm Springs and South Fremont), and **Red Line** (Richmond to Daly City or Millbrae). The Yellow and Red Lines can take you into San Francisco, while the Red and Orange Lines can transport you to Berkeley. The Orange Line is also the route that can take you to **Lake Merritt station** (800 Madison St.) and Oakland Coliseum via the **Coliseum station** (7200 San Leandro St.), which also connects to Oakland International Airport. You can also take the **Blue Line** (Dublin and Pleasanton to Daly City) to the Coliseum and Lake Merritt.

If you're confused (and it happens), your best bet through Oakland is the Orange Line. If you're lost and need to recalibrate, get to the **West Oakland station** (1451 7th St.), as four of the five lines meet here.

BART fares are based on how far you travel, so if you're staying for a weekend, purchase a **BART Blue Ticket** and start with the $20 base fee. You can subtract or add to it, but once you get going, you'll know just how much you'll use. You may have to walk a little to reach some destinations from the closest BART station, so wear comfortable shoes.

TAXI, UBER, AND LYFT

In the Bay Area, Uber and Lyft are everything, but if you're going more than a mile, expect to pay a bit. From Oakland International Airport to the Coliseum, bet on a $12-15 Uber or Lyft ride. From SFO, your ride is going to be somewhere in the $50 range, if not higher.

footbridge to Oakland Coliseum

You can also take a taxi, as multiple companies serve Oakland. The city has designated multiple **taxi stands** at major locations across the city, including the **19th Street BART station** (1900 Broadway), **Coliseum BART station** (7200 San Leandro St.), and **Lake Merritt BART station** (800 Madison St.), plus several locations up Broadway, between 11th Street and Grand Avenue; and the **Amtrak station** (245 2nd St.), which is at Jack London Square.

CAR

Because there are relatively few highways, and because so many San Franciscans are heading east into Oakland, **traffic** is common on both the highways and major surface streets. **I-80** comes in from San Francisco to Oakland via the Bay Bridge, then splits into several different highways going multiple directions. If you follow **I-80 East,** it's also **I-580 West** (yes, you read that right), heading north toward Berkeley and Richmond (I-80 will then go northeast to Sacramento, while I-580 splits west toward Marin County).

From the bridge, you can also continue on **I-580 East,** which threads through the northern boundary of Downtown Oakland as the **MacArthur Freeway.** Also accessible from the Bay Bridge is **I-880,** which curls along the East Bay shore as the **Nimitz Freeway.** That heads south toward Oakland Coliseum and is the easiest (but busiest) thoroughfare for driving in and out of Downtown Oakland. **I-980** is a short spur that connects I-580 to I-880 near Jack London Square.

In Oakland, **Broadway** is the major north-south artery that runs into Jack London Square and through Downtown. **San Pablo Avenue** branches out from Downtown and heads north to Berkeley. **Grand Avenue** connects the northern end of Downtown to the Bay Bridge and Lake Merritt. **International Boulevard** is **14th Street** in Downtown; it connects Oakland's busiest areas to the Coliseum.

SAN FRANCISCO
GIANTS

The history of baseball in San

Francisco starts decades before the Giants moved out west. During the late 19th century various California leagues operated teams in San Francisco, but in 1903 organized baseball really took off with the formation of the Pacific Coast League, which would soon become a minor league that fed into the majors. The first local team was the Stars, changing their name in 1906 to the Seals. For more than 50 seasons, the San Francisco Seals were the Bay Area's baseball team, employing talent like Joe DiMaggio, Paul Waner, Earl Averill, and long-time skipper, local native Lefty O'Doul.

Then, in 1957, the New York Giants and Brooklyn Dodgers changed Major League Baseball forever, opting to leave the Big Apple for the Left Coast. While the Dodgers went to Los Angeles,

the Giants moved into San Francisco, playing their first game in the Bay Area in 1958. Immediate success followed, thanks to a stacked team with future Hall of Famers Orlando Cepeda, Willie McCovey, and Willie Mays, arguably baseball's greatest player. But after winning the 1962 National League pennant, the team failed to finish in first for the rest of the decade, always falling behind either the Dodgers or Cardinals.

The Dodgers are the Giants' greatest rival, and it's often a lusty battle. In some ways the Giants were long a little brother to the mighty Blue, playing games in San Francisco's terribly windy Candlestick Park and never fielding a team good enough to compete up through the 1970s. Fortunes changed in the 1980s, especially as the Giants reached the 1989 World Series against their other great rival, the Athletics, in what was dubbed the Battle of the Bay. That series was marked by the magnitude 6.9 Loma Prieta earthquake, which occurred minutes before Game 3 at Candlestick; two weeks later, the Athletics won the series.

The Giants had more success in the 1990s and 2000s, thanks primarily to another candidate for greatest player ever, Barry Bonds, who smashed records with San Francisco before finishing with an all-time high 762 home runs. Yet there was still no championship for the team…until 2010, when they won their first title out west thanks to a stout pitching staff. The Giants won it all again in 2012 and 2014, creating something of a modern dynasty.

San Francisco has an awesome baseball history, and it's celebrated throughout the gorgeous Oracle Park, which opened along the bay in 2000. Fans of the local nine can tell you all about Lefty O'Doul, Joe DiMaggio, and the Seals, plus Willie McCovey, Willie Mays, the 1989 World Series, Barry Bonds, and the recent run of titles. These are proud and devoted fans of a popular, beloved team.

PLANNING YOUR TIME

There's plenty to see and do in San Francisco, so I recommend at least a **three-day weekend,** if not **four** or **five days,** to best experience the city. You may want to hop around neighborhoods, checking out the Mission District one day (where authentic taquerias and hip bars coexist), then another day doing the tourist's route of the northern end of the city (including Fisherman's Wharf, Coit Tower, and Lombard Street), and then taking a third day to visit The Castro and Haight-Ashbury. See? You haven't even gone to the Giants game yet. Oh, and don't forget a trip to Alcatraz! If you plan on visiting the iconic former prison, **buy your ferry ticket early** (at least two weeks in advance) so you're guaranteed a spot.

If you're set on staying in San Francisco, get your room very early, as accommodations get scooped up quickly. You can stay in the central Downtown neighborhood of **SoMa** (South of Market Street), but accommodations are either super boutique or, in many cases, hostels and room shares. This is the best home base for those hoping to travel by public transit. Staying in **North Beach** will put you close to Fisherman's Wharf and other tourist attractions, but you'll have fewer transit options.

The climate in San Francisco is pretty special. **Summers** aren't very hot, with temperatures in the 70s much of the time. Expect **fog** and **overcast skies** in the morning, and never rule out the potential for **chilly** weather. Expect it to be cold in Oracle Park for night games, no matter the time of year. **Spring** and **fall** are the best times of year to visit, as there's no fog and generally clearer, sunnier skies. Regardless of when you visit, pack for cold temperatures and expect lows in the 40s and 50s at night. It won't **rain** in the summer or fall, but it will in spring.

Previous: view of Oracle Park from McCovey Cove

GETTING THERE

AIR

San Francisco International Airport

The main airport in the Bay Area is **San Francisco International Airport** (SFO, US-101 and Airport Access Rd., South San Francisco, 650/821-8211, www.flysfo.com), which has three main domestic terminals and an international terminal with two separate gate areas. Airlines here include **American Airlines** (800/433-7300, www.aa.com), **Delta** (800/221-1212, www.delta.com), **jetBlue** (800/538-2583, www.jetblue.com), **Southwest** (800/435-9792, www.southwest.com), and **United** (800/864-8331, www.united.com). Flights depart to and arrive from just about every major airport in North America, and plenty more across the globe, including locations in East Asia and Oceania.

AIRPORT TRANSPORTATION

The **Blue Line** of **AirTrain** (free) travels from each terminal to a **rental car center,** where all major companies serve customers. The airport is in South San Francisco, a little less than 15 miles south of the stadium. It's approximately a 20-minute drive north on US-101 to I-280 North to reach Oracle Park and Downtown San Francisco. Of course, that's if there's no traffic.

Both the **Red Line** and the **Blue Line** of AirTrain link to **BART** (Bay Area Regional Transit, www.bart.gov, from $2.60) from all terminals via the **San Francisco International Airport station** (International Terminal). To reach Downtown San Francisco on BART, take a **Yellow Line** train bound for Antioch and disembark at **Montgomery Street station** (598 Market St.) or **Embarcadero station** (298 Market St.). Expect a 30- to 35-minute ride. There's no direct BART service to the ballpark, so you'll either need to walk or ride-share the mile south to Oracle—or take a different form of public transit, **Muni** (www.sfmta.com, $3), which stops directly in front of Oracle Park on its **N Judah** and **T Third Street Lines.**

Oakland International Airport

You can also fly into **Oakland International Airport** (OAK, 1 Airport Dr., 510/563-3300, www.oaklandairport.com). Servicing the airport are **Allegiant** (702/505-8888, www.allegiantair.com), **Spirit** (801/401-2222, www.spirit.com), American Airlines, Delta, jetBlue, and Southwest. There are two terminals at Oakland International: Terminal 1 is for most flights, while Terminal 2 is for Southwest Airlines.

AIRPORT TRANSPORTATION

A shuttle bus takes passengers to the **rental car center,** which is home to all major national companies. If there's no traffic, it's a quick 20-mile, 25-minute drive over the bay via I-880 North and I-80 West to reach Downtown San Francisco and Oracle Park.

You can also use **BART** (www.bart.gov, from $2.60) to get from the airport to Downtown San Francisco. The airport offers an eight-minute **shuttle train connection** to the closest main BART station, which is **Coliseum** (7200 San Leandro St.). From there, take a **Green** or **Blue Line** (Daly City-bound) train to **Embarcadero station** (298 Market St.) or **Montgomery Street station** (598 Market St.). Expect a 35-minute train ride to Downtown. From here, you'll need to walk or ride-share the mile south to Oracle Park—or take a different form of public transit, **Muni** (www.sfmta.com, $3), which stops directly in front of Oracle Park on its **N Judah** and **T Third Street Lines.**

Another option is to connect to **CalTrain** (www.caltrain.com, $6), a **commuter rail** service, via BART. Take BART from the airport to the **Millbrae station** (200 N. Rollins Rd.); from here, transfer onto CalTrain. It's a 30-minute train ride to Oracle Park from Millbrae.

CAR

From Downtown **Oakland,** it's a 10-mile, 20-minute drive (without traffic) across

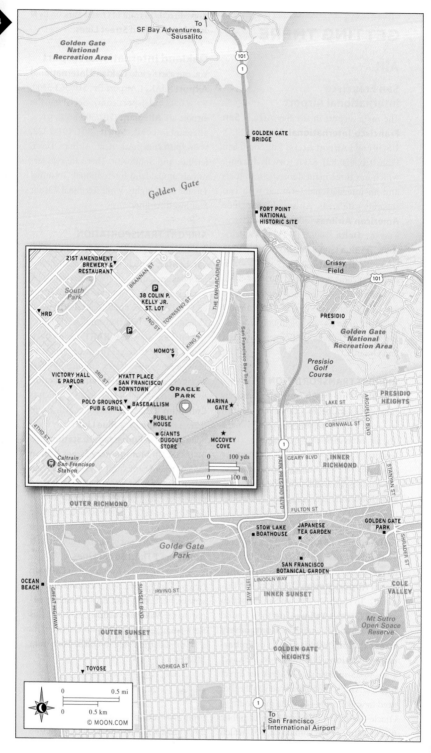

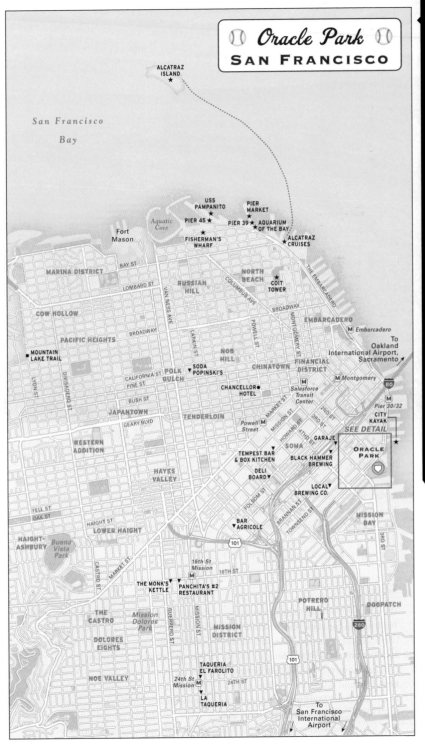

⚾ *Oracle Park* ⚾
SAN FRANCISCO

ALCATRAZ
ISLAND ★

San Francisco

Bay

USS
PAMPANITO
★
PIER 45 ★
PIER
MARKET
★
★ PIER 39 ★ ★ AQUARIUM
OF THE BAY
Aquatic
Cove
★ FISHERMAN'S
WHARF
★ ALCATRAZ
CRUISES

Fort
Mason

MARINA DISTRICT

BAY ST

LOMBARD ST

RUSSIAN
HILL

NORTH
BEACH
COIT ★
TOWER

COW HOLLOW

VAN NESS AVE

LOMBARD ST

COLUMBUS AVE

BROADWAY

PACIFIC HEIGHTS

BROADWAY

LARKIN ST

POWELL ST

MONTGOMERY ST

BROADWAY

EMBARCADERO

THE EMBARCADERO

Ⓜ *Embarcadero*

To
Oakland
International Airport,
Sacramento →

MOUNTAIN
LAKE TRAIL ■

LYON ST

DIVISADERO ST

CALIFORNIA ST
PINE ST

POLK
GULCH

NOB
HILL

SODA
POPINSKI'S ●

CHINATOWN

FINANCIAL
DISTRICT

Ⓜ Montgomery

80

CHANCELLOR ●
HOTEL

Salesforce
Transit
Center

Ⓜ

Pier 30/32
Ⓜ
CITY
KAYAK

BUSH ST

JAPANTOWN

TENDERLOIN

MARKET ST

MISSION ST

2ND ST

3RD ST

GEARY BLVD

Powell
Street Ⓜ

HOWARD ST

4TH ST

SEE DETAIL

WESTERN
ADDITION

SOMA

GARAJE

ORACLE
PARK ★

TEMPEST BAR
& BOX KITCHEN ▼

BLACK HAMMER
BREWING

HAYES
VALLEY

DELI
BOARD ▼

FELL ST
OAK ST

FOLSOM ST

LOCAL ▼
BREWING CO.

BRANNAN ST

TOWNSEND ST

MISSION
BAY

3RD ST

HAIGHT ST

LOWER HAIGHT

BAR
▼ AGRICOLE

101

HAIGHT-
ASHBURY

Buena
Vista
Park

CASTRO ST

MARKET ST

16th St
Mission
Ⓜ

16TH ST

POTRERO
HILL

DOGPATCH

THE MONK'S
KETTLE ▼

PANCHITA'S #2
RESTAURANT ▼

THE
CASTRO

Mission
Dolores
Park

GUERRERO ST

MISSION ST

MISSION
DISTRICT

280

DOLORES
HEIGHTS

101

NOE VALLEY

TAQUERIA
EL FAROLITO ▼
24th St
Mission Ⓜ

24TH ST

To
San Francisco
International
Airport

LA
TAQUERIA ▼

THE WEST COAST ✳ SAN FRANCISCO ✳ GIANTS

Oracle Park

I-580 West, then **I-80 West,** into Downtown San Francisco. You'll travel on the Bay Bridge, which has a **toll** ($7 5am-10am and 3pm-7pm Mon.-Fri., $6 Sat.-Sun., $5 off rush hour Mon.-Fri.) that's collected electronically. (Inquire with your rental car company about your options for paying tolls electronically.)

TRAIN

There is no Amtrak station in San Francisco. You'll have to hop across the bay to the Oakland area, where there are three stations. The **Jack London Square station** (245 2nd St., Oakland) is serviced by the **San Joaquins line** (Oakland to Sacramento and Bakersfield), the **Coast Starlight line** (Seattle to Los Angeles), and the **Capitol Corridor line** (San Jose to Sacramento and Auburn). The second station is **Coliseum/Airport** (700 73rd Ave., Oakland), which is where you can catch a Capitol Corridor train. Near Berkeley, **Emeryville station** (5885 Horton St., Emeryville) is served by San Joaquins and the **California Zephyr** (Emeryville to Chicago).

BUS

You can get to Downtown San Francisco from Oakland via **Greyhound** (www.greyhound.com) on one of several daily buses, which drop passengers at the **Salesforce Transit Center** (425 Mission St.). The ride starts at $8 and takes about 30 minutes. The bus station is in Downtown and within walking distance of BART stations.

The East Bay's regional transit system, **AC Transit** (www.actransit.org) also offers

transbay bus service ($6) from Downtown Oakland to Downtown San Francisco. Take **bus NL** from the stop near the 19th Street BART station (Broadway and Thomas L. Berkley Way) and the bus will reach the end of the line at the Salesforce Transit Center. The ride takes about 20 minutes.

Oracle Park

Sometimes you just look at a ballpark and think: This is where the game should be played. Quirky and beautiful, **Oracle Park** (24 Willie Mays Plaza, www.mlb.com/giants) is a treasure, one of my five favorite major league ballparks, and since opening in 2000, it's one of the coolest places to catch a sporting event, period.

Here's what makes Oracle so great: First, there's the location of the park. It's right against a body of water known as the China Basin, unofficially called McCovey Cove. It's named after Giants Hall of Fame slugger Willie McCovey, who was known for popping balls over the right-field fence at old Candlestick Park. This is just one example of how the Giants make sure the franchise's history is represented throughout the park. Another example: The right-field fence in front of McCovey Cove is 24 feet high in honor of the great Willie Mays, who wore number 24. That tall fence is a fun feature all on its own: It produces a ton of extra-base hits when balls hit in that area bounce off the wall, making them harder to field. The area is called Triples Alley because of it.

YOUR BEST DAY AT ORACLE PARK

You have tickets to this evening's Giants game, which means a full day to spend in San Francisco. Here's what you should do:

11 HOURS BEFORE FIRST PITCH

Request an Uber or Lyft and head out to the **Presidio.** Take a light hike on the 2.5-mile **Bay Area Ridge Trail,** stopping at the **Golden Gate Bridge.** Take some selfies, then get in another ride-share and head toward the Downtown/Union Square area.

7.5 HOURS BEFORE FIRST PITCH

As long as it's not a Sunday, pay a visit to **Deli Board** for a big sandwich lunch. This'll keep you filled up until game time.

5 HOURS BEFORE FIRST PITCH

Start walking toward the ballpark. After a half-hour, you probably have some room for a couple of beers. Do a crawl of sorts by stopping by **Local Brewing Co., Black Hammer Brewing,** and **21st Amendment Brewery & Restaurant.**

2 HOURS BEFORE FIRST PITCH

Need an extra sweatshirt or jacket or just want to browse for some souvenirs? Stop by **Baseballism** for SF-centric, unlicensed merchandise, or head to the **Giants Dugout Store** for a Giants-branded item.

1.5 HOURS BEFORE FIRST PITCH

If it's your first time at **Oracle Park,** enter through **Willie Mays Plaza.** For an alternative, head around to the **Marina Gate** and walk alongside McCovey Cove before entering the venue.

DURING THE GAME

Scope out the views from the **arcade**

view from Bay Area Ridge Trail

section of seating. Take your pick from the food choices around the **Sierra Nevada Pale Ale Plaza,** and check out the beer selection down at the **Garden Table.**

Be sure to stop by **The Vault** to read up on Giants history. When the game starts, get in your seat and hang there for one of the best views in baseball.

AFTER THE GAME

Take the walk back up toward Union Square to the **BART Powell Street station** (899 Market St.) and head south on a Millbrae- or Daly City-bound train. Hop off at **16th Street Mission station** (2000 Mission St.) and have a nightcap at **The Monk's Kettle.**

Afterward, you may want a super burrito from **Taqueria El Farolito,** but another good late-night option is *pupusas.* Get them at **Panchita's #2 Restaurant.** However you finish the night, your best way home is via BART or a ride-share.

Oracle's greatness is also evident from its food and beverage options, which are some of the best in baseball. The beer selection is outstanding and the snacks do a good job of representing the local food scene.

Of course, because of all these perks, prices tend to be higher here than at most ballparks. Treat a visit to Oracle like it's a bucket-list moment—spend a little extra and leave a little more room for luxuries. Going

to a Giants game is indulging in one of the best baseball experiences you can have in America.

ORIENTATION

Nestled between the China Basin and the Embarcadero in the neighborhood also called China Basin (south of the Financial District), Oracle Park is set in a rather dense area in a rather dense city. Parking is tough to come by and space is tight around the ballpark. But you'll find plenty of bars and restaurants in the vicinity, as well as a couple public transit options.

There are four entry gates at Oracle Park. If you want the full Oracle experience, enter via the **Willie Mays Gate** (home plate at 3rd St. and King St.). You'll get to see the Willie Mays statue and this gate has the most attendants, meaning the fastest entry times. Plus, it's the only gate to open two hours before first pitch. There are other gates around the park, including the **Marina Gate** (San Francisco Bay Trail at center field), but these only open 1.5 hours beforehand. You can also enter via the **Giants Dugout Store** (3rd St. at Lefty O'Doul Plaza), but you won't get the game day giveaway, if there is one scheduled, through this entrance.

TICKETS AND SEATING

Pricing

The Giants use **dynamic pricing,** meaning ticket costs will be higher depending on the opponent. If they're playing the Dodgers, Red Sox, Yankees, or Athletics, you're bound to pay more. In the case of the Dodgers, you might pay 100 percent more for some seats. Typically, against a not-too-special opponent, seats in the view level will run $15-30; they're cheaper in left field. You can snag 100 level seats at anywhere from $30-70, as long as they're outside the infield area. The club level typically starts around $40 and can go up to $150.

Seating Plan

There are **four levels** of seating at Oracle Park. The **100 level,** also called the **promenade level,** starts out at the right field foul pole with **lower box** (sections 101-104). Next, running down the first-base line, the level is split into two (sections 105-112): **premium lower box** (rows closer to field) and **lower box select** (rows farther back). In front of the lower box sections, wrapping around either side of home plate, are **field club** (sections 107-124). Behind home plate

and the central field club seats are **premium lower box** (sections 113-118), then another split area (sections 119-126) of **premium lower box** (rows closer to field) and **lower box select** (rows farther back). Past third base are **lower box** (sections 127-130) and **lower box left field** (sections 131-135). Moving into the outfield are the left field **bleachers** (sections 136-142) and the **center field bleachers** (sections 143-144). The final section of seating for this level is the **arcade** (sections 145-152), the sliver of benches behind the right field fence. That section is prone to wind gusts, but it's also where you might get to see a home run arcing over you into McCovey Cove.

The **200 level** is the **Alaska Airlines Club Level.** Access to these seats are from a special concourse with its own food and beverage vendors. You can also order food and drinks to be delivered to your seat from the MLB Ballpark app. Seating is outdoors with a primo view of the field and beyond. The 200 level starts at the right field foul pole with **club level outfield** (sections 202-205), then moves down the first-base line and wraps around home plate to the third-base line with **club level infield** (sections 207-225). Next are **club level outfield** (sections 226-231) and, at the left field foul pole, **club level left field** (sections 232-234).

The **suite level** is in between the 200 and 300 levels. The **300 level** is the **view level** (sections 302-336). The level starts at the right field foul pole with **view reserve right field** (sections 302-307). Next, moving down the first-base line and behind home plate, the level is split into three sections (listed from closest to the field to farthest): **view box, view reserve infield,** and **view reserve** (sections 308-324). Continuing along the third-base line are **view reserve outfield** (sections 325-331) and **view reserve left field** (sections 332-336).

Where to Buy Tickets

StubHub will have the cheapest tickets out there. **VividSeats** and **SeatGeek** aren't too far behind, followed by purchasing directly from the Giants. If you do buy tickets directly

a home run ball. Just wear a jacket and prepare for the wind, which can gust through this area.

The lower rows of the 100 level get the most sunshine. Once you get into **row 27** and beyond, the **shade** starts to appear. Sitting along the **first-base line** or **right-field line,** again, behind about row 27 and then heading into the upper levels, should mean pretty **shaded seats.**

KNOW BEFORE YOU GO

You can bring a **bag, backpack, diaper bag,** or a **briefcase** no bigger than 16 by 16 by 8 inches into the ballpark. No hard-sided coolers are allowed inside, but you can bring in sealed plastic **water bottles.** Non-electric **scooters** and **skateboards** are allowed in, but they must be able to fit safely under your seat.

Oracle has a really good **Wi-Fi** network. The network is called "OracleParkWiFi" and it's free to use.

I can't stress it enough: Bring a **jacket,** maybe an additional **long-sleeve shirt,** and wear **pants** or bring a **blanket.** Yes, the sun may come out and it could get hotter than you anticipate, but more likely than not, it'll be chilly at Oracle, especially at night. Bring **sunscreen** for day games.

Accessibility

At Oracle Park, go to **guest services** (home plate at promenade level) to request a **wheelchair escort** to or from your seat and to get an **assistive listening device.** A photo ID or valid credit card is required as a deposit.

Elevators at the park are located at each of the four entrances, and those at Willie Mays Plaza and the Second and King Street Plaza stop at all levels. **Service animals** are welcome at Oracle Park.

Accessible parking is offered at all lots with prices running up to $40 (cash only). If you're parking in Lot A/Pier 48, you can take an **accessibility shuttle** to Oracle Park for free.

from the team, you can upgrade and manage your seats through the **MLB Ballpark app**— you can also use it to order food and drinks.

Best Seats

It's hard to go wrong with any seat at Oracle Park, but not all seats are created equal. The surefire best seats might be in the **club level** between **sections 203** and **205,** as they'll cost slightly less than most other club seats, you'll be in the **shade** most of the time, and you'll get a **view** of nearby McCovey Cove.

For an **awesome view** of the whole place, the **first rows** of the **view reserve infield section** near **home plate** (sections 314-320) are pretty choice. If you don't mind a little **sun,** sitting in the **club level** (say, section 227) is awesome. There you'll get to see beyond the right field wall along with the whole field, and you'll get the amenities of the self-contained club level concourse.

For newbies, grabbing a seat in the **arcade** (sections 145-162) makes for a fun experience. You'll be among fans and you have views of McCovey Cove directly behind you. There's also a chance that you might get

BE A FAN

64

Every Giants fan I've met has been kind, extremely knowledgeable about her or his team, and welcoming to talk baseball. Wearing another team's jersey or hat isn't much of a problem at Oracle. However, over the years there have been instances of violent behavior between Giants fans and either Dodgers or Athletics fans. (Of course, an especially small minority of fans shouldn't define the entirety of the group.) Bottom line: If you're a Dodger or A's fan visiting Oracle, keep things light and respectful, and if you encounter any trouble, find an official or security guard.

Keep an ear out for classic Journey songs **"Don't Stop Believin'"** and **"Lights."** The band is from San Francisco, and former lead singer Steve Perry is a massive Giants fan. Naturally, after wins, Oracle plays **"I Left My Heart in San Francisco"** by Tony Bennett.

And then there are the **seagulls.** Beginning around the eighth inning, like clockwork, flocks of seagulls fly into the airspace over Oracle Park. They hover above the park until the game ends, knowing that very soon, thousands upon thousands of people will exit the venue, leaving behind crumbs in the aisles and under seats. To shoo the seagulls away, the Giants play **"The Cha-Cha Slide"** by DJ Casper. Oddly, it's the endless clapping in the song (and from fans) that scares the birds out from the area. It's pretty amazing to watch.

GETTING THERE

Public Transit

San Francisco's transit system, **Muni** (www.sfmta.com, $3), offers **light rail service** from Downtown San Francisco to a stop directly in front of Oracle Park on its **N Judah** and **T Third Street Lines.** These trains get very crowded before and, especially, after the game.

If you're coming from locations south of the city, you could take the commuter rail service **CalTrain** (www.caltrain.com, from $3.75) to its **San Francisco station** (700 4th St.), one block from Oracle Park.

You can also do what many local Giants fans do and walk from Market Street BART stations like **Powell Street** (899 Market St.) and **Montgomery Street** (598 Market St.) to the stadium, about a half-hour jaunt. If you don't mind the walking, this is the most cost-effective way to and from the game.

Driving

If you're driving to Oracle Park, know that traffic on **I-80** will be backed up close to game time. Official parking is available at **Pier 30/32** (Embarcadero and Bryant St.), a 15-minute walk north of the ballpark. This lot is $35-40 for high-attendance games, but it closes late (2am for night games, 11pm for day games), allowing you plenty of time to hang out near the ballpark after the game. Various other lots, including **Lot A/Pier 48,** just across the Lefty O'Doul Bridge from the ballpark, are also available. You'll pay $40 to park at Lot A, and **tailgating** is allowed, but the lot closes an hour after the game ends.

Non-official parking is generally a 15-minute walk or more from the ballpark. You'll pay at least $20, but usually $30 or more, for most of these lots. I recommend the **38 Colin P. Kelly Jr. St. Lot** (2nd St. and King St.), which is just an eight-minute walk from the park and costs $25.

With the prices to park so high, and the likely headache you'll get dealing with traffic, consider taking an **Uber** or **Lyft** to the game (generally $20-30 per four-mile ride). Passenger loading and drop-off spots are mostly along Brannan Street, Townsend Street, and 3rd Street.

PARK FEATURES AND SIGHTS

San Franciscans love their coffee. The **Peet's @Cafe** (promenade level, center field behind bleachers) is a popular place on those chilly days (and there are many). This café has a video wall that shows social media chatter about the Giants from multiple platforms, but its real highlight is the **Hall of Bobble-heads.** Dozens upon dozens of wacky bobbleheads are showcased here, including a luchador version of Giants' mascot Lou Seal, and a number of San Francisco and Giants personalities. Plus, check out the life-size version of a 1999 Willie Mays bobblehead created to commemorate the closing of Candlestick Park, where the Giants played before Oracle. You can also create your own virtual bobblehead here.

Head down toward the Marina Gate (staircase at promenade level, right center field), then turn back in toward the field. You'll come upon the **Garden at Oracle Park** (center field behind scoreboard, opposite Marina Gate). This mini-farm of 4,320 square feet produces fresh vegetables, alliums, and fruit—like carrots, garlic, and kale—that are used by ballpark vendors.

Fan Lot

One of the first things you might notice at Oracle Park is the giant Coca-Cola bottle in left field. Did you know inside are slides that fans can travel down? Head to the **Fan Lot** (promenade level, left field behind bleachers), home to those giant slides, called the **Twist Off** (for folks 36 inches or taller) and the **Guzzler** (for folks 42 inches or taller).

Also part of the Fan Lot is a **miniature baseball field,** designed to look like Oracle Park and meant for small children to play around. All fans can check out the **world's largest baseball glove,** which is next to the Coke bottles.

McCovey Cove

When Oracle Park opened, all eyes focused on **McCovey Cove** (right field), the body of water that flows into San Francisco Bay. Every game, fans wait with bated breath for the next player to launch a home run that splashes into the cove. These homers are called **splash hits,** and they're counted on the right field wall area known as Levi's

Landing. Just above the wall is the **arcade section,** home to fans hoping to intercept one of those balls before they become splash hits.

Of course, if a ball splashes down, a cadre of intrepid canoers and kayakers will attempt to snatch it out of the water. And you can be one of them! The easiest thing to do is bring your own canoe or kayak, as it's free to launch your own vessel into the cove. But if you don't have one, **City Kayak** (Pier 40, 415/294-1050, www.citykayak.com, noon-3pm Mon. and Fri., 11am-3pm Sat.-Sun., $35-77 single, $68-139 double) provides kayak rentals. Want to work less for that experience? You can hook up with **SF Bay Adventures** (1001 Bridgeway, Suite B2A, Sausalito, 415/331-0444, www.sfbayadventures.com, starting at $3,095) for a party boat, serving up to 40 guests. These boats hang out for the duration of the game in McCovey Cove.

World Series Trophies

Look for the **Tiffany & Co. display** (promenade level, home plate) showing the Giants' recent **World Series trophies** (from 2010, 2012, and 2014). Folks love taking photos here, and the Giants will typically staff a photographer who'll do some professional shots for a fee.

The Vault

To better understand the history of the franchise—from New York to San Francisco—check out **The Vault** (Lefty O'Doul Gate). This exhibit opened in 2015 to mark the team's 60-year anniversary in the Bay Area and displays awesome memorabilia, photographs, scorecards, and more from important eras in Giants' history. Exhibits change annually.

FOOD AND DRINKS

The most popular and well-known food item served at Oracle Park are the **Gilroy Garlic Fries** (sections 103, 106, 121, plus additional locations throughout the park), made from fresh-cut potatoes that are fried and doused with improbable amounts of chopped garlic,

Photos (top): statue of Willie Mays by sculptor William Behrends; (middle left) beer at Oracle Park; (middle right) one of many food options at Oracle; (bottom) oversized Coca-Cola bottle in left field.

as well as parmesan, salt, and parsley. Every bite sends you to a bitter, pungent, soul-pleasing paradise. They're perfect on a slightly cool afternoon (or evening), just before a Giants pitcher readies his opening toss. They'll set you back about $9 (more than $12 if you opt for a souvenir container), but there's enough that you can share them with a friend. Just a little greasy, super fragrant, and notably hard to stop eating, they're worthy of their popularity. Get an order the first time you're here.

Few ballparks do what Oracle Park does at the **Garden Table** (center field behind scoreboard, opposite Marina Gate): make honest-to-goodness, delicious vegetarian- and vegan-friendly food, as well as other healthy food that tastes good. Look for items like a roasted vegetable sandwich; antipasti that's well seasoned and chock-full of olives, greens, and cheese; and plant-based nachos. Here's a very good tip for beer lovers: Go to the Garden Table (not the Garden Bar), because there's a possibility you'll find the best beer you'll ever enjoy at a ballpark. For $12, I got a full bottle pour of the local rarity Pliny the Elder here. And it was fresh. You'd be a fool not to take advantage.

Speaking of beer, Oracle Park has arguably the best suds selection in baseball. Head upstairs from the Garden Table for the **Sierra Nevada Pale Ale Plaza** (promenade level, center field), which features ales from the legendary Chico, California brewery. Few things are as good as enjoying a classic Sierra Nevada IPA (or Celebration Ale) at Oracle. Bonus: You can get these beers in the larger 22-ounce size, and for $19.25, it's a good deal. Just about opposite the plaza is the **Lagunitas Way-Way-Outfield Bar,** which has beer from Bay Area local Lagunitas, plus a few others, in the same 22-ounce format. Also here is Irish coffee in the style of the famous San Francisco café The Buena Vista.

Also out in this area are a collection of slightly overpriced but premium food experiences. Chief among them is **Pier 44 Chowder House** (promenade level, center field), which has clam chowder in a sourdough bread bowl, along with calamari and fish and chips. Next door is **Crazy Crab,** which offers Dungeness crab on grilled sourdough.

For dessert, look for **CREAM** (section 130), which stands for Cookies Rule Everything Around Me. You'll want their irresistibly sweet creations of ice cream sandwiched between two big old cookies, decorated in sprinkled finery. Nothing is as delicious or Instagrammable as sugar cookies bookending chocolate chip cookie dough ice cream covered in Fruity Pebbles.

The sit-down restaurant at Oracle is **Public House** (24 Willie Mays Plaza, 415/644-0240, www.publichousesf.com, 11am-10pm Tues.-Sat., 11am-9pm Sun., open during games, under $60). A gastropub, Public House has elevated bar bites and American staples like a chicken breast sandwich, wings, macaroni and cheese, and beer-battered fried fish. The reason to come here, though, is the robust beer list, featuring some of the better brews in the Bay Area. It'll get packed just before the game. This is a dark space with nearly two-dozen televisions showing all kinds of sporting events.

If you didn't find what you want, don't fret, because the options at Oracle are staggering, from Chinese cuisine at **Edsel Ford Fong's** (promenade level, home plate) to **boba tea drinks** (section 122), and from **empanadas** (section 317) to **Philly-style cheesesteaks** (section 142).

EVENTS

You can attempt to get an **autograph** on any game day by heading down to the front rows of the sections near the dugouts, though the ushers may ask you to move. Otherwise, Sundays are **autograph days.** Fans age 14 and younger are asked to head to sections 104-105 and 126-127, where players, coaches, and alumni sign before the game. To participate, kids must have **special tickets,** which are issued by ushers on a first-come, first-served basis. To get one, be among the first in line when the gates open and get to those sections.

Annually the Giants celebrate the **Giant Race** (www.race-sfgiants.com, Sept.), a weekend of running (half-marathon, 10K, and 5K) and fitness events at Oracle Park. Look for yoga in the park during this weekend.

The Giants are always celebrating something, whether giving away cool **bobble-heads** or honoring a cultural or social group. Look for the annual **Metallica night,** which celebrates one of the founding fathers of heavy metal; **Margaritaville night,** honoring fans of Jimmy Buffett with a pregame drinking hangout; **Bruce Lee tribute night,** which pays homage to the martial arts legend; **Christmas in July** and **Halfway to St. Patrick's Day** nights; and, my personal favorite, **Ginger Night.** Finally, something for us redheads.

Tours

You'll probably want to take a **tour** (415/972-2400) of Oracle Park, which aims to inform and give a behind-the-scenes look of one of baseball's top venues. The **daily tour** ($22, $17 seniors, $12 ages 12 and under, free ages 2 and under) takes place on most days, though you should check with the team to confirm. This is a 90-minute trip to one of the dugouts, the visitors' clubhouse and batting cage, the press box, and the field, among other places. The **pre-game tour** ($35 per person) starts before gates open and gives fans a chance to watch player warmups, plus takes them to The Vault and the club level display cases. The **VIP tour** ($175 per person) is an intimate trip that goes onto the field and into the press box. The Giants also host **private tours** (415/972-2400, toursinfo@oraclepark.com, $30-35 per person) that include a boxed lunch.

SHOPPING

The main **Giants Dugout Store** (24 Willie Mays Plaza, Lefty O'Doul Plaza, 415/947-3419, 10am-5pm daily, open during games until one hour after final out) is a large, two-story shop that'll get crowded before the game. You can enter from the O'Doul Plaza on 3rd Street or from the ramp after the Willie Mays Gate at home plate, but you'll need to show your ticket and get stamped. If you

visit during non-game days, you can just go in and out from the O'Doul entrance.

The store has all the typical jerseys, shirts, hats, and apparel. Head down to **From The Clubhouse** (promenade level, behind home plate) and check out its collection of pricier items like clutches and purses, plus jerseys, balls, and other game-used merchandise.

Throughout the promenade level concourse are **smaller vendors,** hawking everything from shirts and hats to pins and collectible bats and balls—a lot of the same stuff you'll find at the main team store. These stands might be a better option, as they'll be a little less crowded before first pitch.

SAN FRANCISCO SIGHTS

GOLDEN GATE BRIDGE

One of the most handsome landmarks in the world, and spanning nearly 9,000 feet across the Golden Gate Strait, the **Golden Gate Bridge** (US-101 N. at Lincoln Blvd.), is a marvelous testament to American ingenuity and timeless beauty. Shaped with clean Art Deco lines and painted in the most striking hue of orange-red, there's nothing like it on Earth. It's a must-see for anyone going to San Francisco for the first time.

So, how exactly do you get to the bridge? Driving is best, though you can ride a bicycle here (it helps to be in shape and prepare yourself for traffic). You'll exit US-101 at the **last San Francisco exit** (Exit 439), which lists the view area, Presidio, and the bridge. After exiting, you'll quickly emerge at a parking lot. The **welcome center** (415/426-5220, 9am-6pm daily) is here. Beyond that is a network of short trails that can take you down to view areas. Take the Battery E Trail to a concrete viewing area that shows off the iconic span. For a better, less-crowded spot, take Battery E away from the welcome center, and after 0.2 mile, take the spur trail on the left down to another great view. You can also take the Coastal Trail, which heads up to the welcome stairs and the Art Deco **Round House Café** (415/426-5228, 9am-5pm daily), serving baked goods and coffee.

ALCATRAZ

Head out to **Alcatraz Island** (www.nps.gov/alca), home from 1934 to 1963 to some of the most notorious criminals in American history, including Al Capone, George "Machine Gun" Kelly, and Robert Franklin Stroud, also known as the "Birdman of Alcatraz." The island draws about 1.7 million visitors per year, who are ferried onto the bay by **Alcatraz Cruises** (Pier 33, Embarcadero at Bay St., www.alcatrazcruises.com, from $25). Prepare for a three- to four-hour trip, though if you opt for a daytime ticket, you can stay on the island until the last ferry departs. Be sure to experience "Doing Time: The Alcatraz Cellhouse Tour," an audio tour through the prison that includes the stories of inmates. You'll also want to stop at the Dock Ranger Station and Theater, which has exhibits on the island, including its American Indian occupation from 1969-71.

Get tickets at least three weeks in advance, if not earlier, especially if you're visiting in summer. It's likely to be foggy between May and September. Plan to spend half a day on this excursion, so you have plenty of time to see everything.

FISHERMAN'S WHARF

A major tourist attraction in the northern end of the city, **Fisherman's Wharf** is an essential stop for first-time visitors. For cool views of Alcatraz, check out **Pier 45** (Embarcadero at Taylor St.), which is also home to the **USS Pampanito** (Pier 45, 415/775-1943, www.maritime.org, 9am-6pm Sun.-Thurs., 9am-8pm Fri.-Sat., $20, $15 seniors and students, $10 ages 5-13 and active military, free ages 4 and under), a World War II Navy ship that is now home to a museum. The ship has been restored to its original look, and you can head in for an audio tour that covers the history of U.S. submarine development.

Be sure to visit **Pier 39** (Embarcadero at Grant Ave., 415/705-5500, www.pier39.com), which is the very touristy part of the area, offering a few hours of diversion with shopping, dining, and kid-friendly activities. Primarily, there's the **Aquarium of the Bay** (Embarcadero and Beach St., 415/623-5300, www.aquariumofthebay.org, 10am-6pm daily, $28.25, $23.25 seniors, $18.25 ages 4-12, free ages 3 and under). It's overpriced, but if the kids are wearing you out or you need some time indoors, this is a fine option. Find sharks, rays, jellyfish, and more, and be sure to walk through the tunnels. Fish will swim above and around you as you pass.

When at the Wharf, you must have the iconic bread bowl of clam chowder. The best bet is at **Pier Market** (Pier 39, 415/989-7437, www.piermarket.com, 11am-10pm Sun.-Fri., 10:30am-10pm Sat., under $50), a bright and many-windowed restaurant right on the water. The food here is relatively affordable and delicious for a touristy area, headlined by the clam chowder in a sourdough bowl deal; the soup is served with a salad.

COIT TOWER

Looking for a great view of San Francisco that includes the Golden Gate Bridge, Bay Bridge, skyline, and everything in between? Head to **Coit Tower** (1 Telegraph Hill Blvd., 10am-5pm daily, $9, $6 seniors and ages 12-17, $3 ages 5-11, free ages 4 and under), built in 1932-33 as the topper of Pioneer Park to add beauty to the city. Get there early and avoid the crowds, then take a quick elevator ride up. You'll have to climb another several dozen stairs before reaching the top, where you can look out at the entire city. You'll see the ocean and bay, all the bridges, and the surrounding mountains. Be sure to go on a clear day.

The ground floor includes cool murals, painted during the New Deal era and depicting interpretations of California life and progress. If you're walking to Coit Tower, be ready for an uphill hike, but look for the stairs that run along Greenwich Street and Filbert Street, each starting at Sansome Street.

FOOD

NEAR ORACLE PARK

Though the food at Oracle Park is good, the stuff just outside the park is little more than pub grub that complements a fun drinking atmosphere. But if you need some chow before the game, I suggest **HRD** (521A 3rd St., 415/543-2355, www.hrdcorp.com, 10am-8pm Mon.-Fri., 11am-4pm Sat., under $20), known for its super-fast "fusion" menu with everything from banh mi to kimchee burritos, and from curry plates to green-leaf salads.

A block away from HRD is **Garaje** (475 3rd St., www.garaje475.com, 11:30am-10pm Mon.-Fri., 5pm-10pm Sat., under $30), which throws together Cali-Mex staples like tacos with big pastrami sandwiches, pulled pork, salads, and burgers. Get the *zapatos*, which are burritos, but pressed like a panini, resulting in a cheesy, melty, grilled delight.

OTHER NEIGHBORHOODS

In the very fun Mission District, you can't go wrong by picking any of the taquerias around (especially around 1am after a night of partying). My personal favorite is **Taqueria El Farolito** (2779 Mission St., 415/824-7877, www.elfarolitosf.com, 10am-3am Mon.-Wed., Sat., 10am-3:30am Thurs.-Fri., 10am-midnight Sun., under $15). Here, like at most Mission taquerias, you'll stand in line and dream up your perfect burrito or taco order. The Super Burrito (meat, rice, beans, guacamole, sour cream, lettuce, and pico de gallo), which is a standard sight on any taqueria menu, is the way to go. Trust me.

Another option for your Cali-Mex fill: Head to **La Taqueria** (2889 Mission St., 415/285-7117, 11am-8:45pm Wed.-Sat., 11am-7:45pm Sun., under $15), which is

Photos (from top to bottom): Coit Tower; Pier 39; burrito from La Taqueria in the Mission District.

more of a pre-party spot. Everything here rules, but locals swear by the off-menu El Dorado-style taco or burrito (melted cheese, fried tortilla, plus whatever else comes with the order).

Great beer (Belgian, especially) and a solid chef-forward menu of pub bites shine at **The Monk's Kettle** (3141 16th St., 415/865-9523, www.monkskettle.com, noon-midnight Sun.-Thurs., noon-2am Fri.-Sat., under $40). A long and robust beer list is accompanied by dishes like mac n' cheese, burgers, fried chicken sandwiches, and bigger plates like hanger steak. This is an intimate hangout with friendly barkeeps.

If you're about to leave the Mission District and you don't want to wait in line for a burrito, my choice for the best post-drinking grub is Salvadoran *pupusas* from **Panchita's #2 Restaurant** (3091 16th St., 415/431-4232, 11am-11pm Sun.-Thurs., 11am-2:30am Fri.-Sat., under $15). Order a few of these incredible stuffed pockets of cheese and protein (pork, beef, beans, spicy sausage), which are served with housemade fermented veggies. The digs are basic here, but that's the point. Bring friends and chow down.

Over in SoMa, visit **Deli Board** (1058 Folsom St., 415/552-7687, www.deliboardsf.com, 11am-3pm Mon.-Fri., 11am-4pm Sat., under $25) for lunch. These are big sandwiches, perfectly crafted, in a calm, wood-and-beige toned space. Ingredients are simple—just good cold cuts and fresh veggies. Get here early.

If you're in SoMa and wanting to check something off your bucket list, make a reservation for **Bar Agricole** (355 11th St., 415/355-9400, www.baragricole.co, 5pm-10pm Mon.-Thurs., 5pm-10pm Fri.-Sat., under $70). This James Beard-winning tavern and small kitchen goes big on local ingredients. The menu changes all the time, but you can't go wrong with grilled meat and freshly prepared fish. Some of the best bartenders in the game are here, so be sure to order a cocktail.

If you're out west in the Sunset District, you can enjoy exceptional Korean and Japanese in a cool, repurposed garage, at

Toyose (3814 Noriega St., 415/731-0232, www.toyose.org, 6pm-2am daily, under $50). This spot serves street food like chicken *katsu* (fried chicken), fried rice, and mushroom stew, plus plenty of soju to drink.

BARS AND BREWERIES

NEAR ORACLE PARK

For many fans, the first stop before or after the game is **MoMo's** (760 2nd St., 415/227-8660, www.sfmomos.com, 11am-8pm daily), which has a white-tablecloth, dimly lit dining room but also a very active bar area, plus an outdoor patio with a miniature bar. Located just across the street from the stadium, it's good for a quick pre- or post-game beer, if you don't mind being in a crowd.

Down the block is **Polo Grounds Pub & Grill** (747 3rd St., 415/777-1177, www.pologroundssf.com, 11:30am-2am Mon.-Fri., noon-2am Sat., 10am-2am Sun.). This is a place you visit to get your group together and knock down that quick beer and a shot—but the environs are decidedly divey and lived-in. It'll be packed just before or after the game. You can pass on the standard bar grub.

Victory Hall & Parlor (360 Ritch St., 415/543-4255, www.victoryhallsf.com, 11:45am-midnight daily) is a good place for cocktails, as they change up their original creations by the season, and curate a small but solid list of classics. The beer is local, and the vibe is refined but not stuffy at all. Come in your game day colors.

Be sure to visit **21st Amendment Brewery & Restaurant** (563 2nd St., 415/369-0900, www.21st-amendment.com, 11:30am-midnight Mon.-Fri., noon-midnight Sat., 10am-midnight Sun.). This high-ceiling, lodge-like room has a lot of space for dining, and you can have elevated pub grub like burgers and pizzas, plus salads and appetizers like tater tots and cheese curds. The beer is always changing here, and there's brews they make that you can't find in stores. Give it a try.

For a scene, head to **Black Hammer Brewing** (544 Bryant St., 415/758-2223, www.blackhammerbrewing.com, noon-11pm Mon.-Thurs., noon-midnight Fri.-Sat., noon-10pm Sun.). Small but typically very lively, Black Hammer is a tad loud, but the beers match the environment. These folks master big flavors in sours, IPAs, and even dark fare.

The best brewery around is **Local Brewing Co.** (69 Bluxome St., 415/932-6702, www.localbrewingco.com, 2pm-10pm Tues.-Sat., 2pm-8pm Sun.-Mon.). A decently large place with a few seating options, Local Brewing has a wide variety of beers on tap, and all are solid. You can't go wrong here. If it's available, try the black lager, a classic California common (a beer style that utilizes the cool marine climate to quickly chill beer fermenting in shallow containers).

OTHER NEIGHBORHOODS

Up in the Nob Hill area, check out **Soda Popinski's** (1548 California St., 415/857-1548, www.sodapopinskisf.com, 5pm-2am daily). This is as fun as a bar gets these days, and worth it if you're looking for a memorable experience. Named after the classic heel of the *Mike Tyson's Punch-Out!!* video game, Soda's hooks its TVs up to gaming consoles, so you can play while drinking at the bar. They host tournaments and trivia nights, and also have one of the coolest things you'll find at a bar: a chance wheel. For $12 you spin it and get (and drink) whatever it lands on. It could be a double white Russian, a bottle of champagne, a tequila boot.... It changes regularly, so you never know.

For a cool sports bar in SoMa, there's **Tempest Bar & Box Kitchen** (431 Natoma St., 415/495-1863, www.tempestbarsf.com, 11am-2am Mon.-Fri., noon-2am Sat.-Sun.), whose bar includes just about any kind of spirit you can imagine. Plus, there's a pool table and a convivial atmosphere that makes for a good place to settle in for a ball game (or any game, really). To put it succinctly,

this is the perfect beer-and-a-shot bar in the city.

RECREATION

PARKS AND BEACHES

Golden Gate Park
Golden Gate Park (Fell St. at Stanyan St., 415/831-2700, www.sfrecpark.org) is a long, rectangular garden hideaway of more than 1,000 acres, stretching from nearly the center of the city west to the Pacific Ocean. It's home to a number of sites, including the **deYoung Museum** (50 Hagiwara Tea Garden Dr., 415/750-3600, http://deyoung. famsf.org, 9:30am-5:15pm Tues.-Sun., $15, $12 seniors, $6 students, free ages 17 and under), which exhibits fine art; the **California Academy of Sciences** (55 Music Concourse Dr., 415/379-8000, www.calacademy. org, 9:30am-5pm Mon.-Sat., 11am-5pm Sun., from $30), a hands-on science museum; and the **San Francisco Botanical Garden** (1199 9th Ave., 415/661-1316, www.sfbg.org, 7:30am-6pm daily Mar.-Sept., 7:30am-5pm daily Oct.-Nov. and Feb.-Mar., 7:30am-4pm daily Nov.-Jan., $9, $6 ages 12-17 and seniors, $2 ages 5-11, free ages 4 and under). Here, you can stroll through gardens of wildflowers native to California, plus plenty of Chilean plants (Chile's geography and climate mirrors that of coastal California). Come when Flower Piano is happening, in which a dozen pianos are placed throughout the garden, open to anyone to play. It's music and nature in harmony.

Also visit the **Japanese Tea Garden** (75 Hagiwara Tea Garden Dr., 415/752-1171, www.japaneseteagardensf.com, 9am-5:45pm daily Mar.-Oct., 9am-4:45pm Nov.-Feb., $9, $7 ages 12-17 and seniors, $3 ages 5-11, free ages 4 and under), the oldest of its kind in America. Come in March and April to see the cherry blossoms bloom, and sit by the koi ponds and zen garden any time. Tea is served, along with a traditional fortune cookie, inside the tea house.

San Francisco Botanical Garden in Golden Gate Park

In the middle of the park is Stow Lake. You can ride on the water by visiting the **Stow Lake Boathouse** (50 Stow Lake Dr. East, 415/386-2531, www.stowlakeboathouse.com, 10am-5pm Mon.-Fri., 10am-6pm Sat.-Sun., $22.50-38.50 per hour). The boat house offers row boats, pedal boats, and electric boats for rental on a first-come, first-served basis. The boat house is also home to a small café and there are restrooms close by.

Ocean Beach

At the western end of Golden Gate Park is **Ocean Beach** (Great Hwy. and Lincoln Way), a 3.5-mile stretch right on the water at the edge of the city. The best time to visit is September and October, when the fog doesn't strangle the sky so much. Dress for the occasion, as it'll routinely be around 50-60°F here. About a dozen fire pits are available at Ocean Beach, but keep a watch on them and be vigilant about putting out the flames. It's a good spot for a quick walk along the Pacific coast.

The Presidio

The **Presidio** (Veterans Blvd. at Washington Blvd., www.presidio.gov) is a 1,500-acre park that was founded by Spain as a military fort in 1776. It became U.S. military land in 1848, and in 1994 it was transferred to the National Park Service. Today it's a vast area of trails and vistas and a playground for Bay Area residents.

Fort Point National Historic Site (Long Ave. and Marine Dr., 415/556-1693, 10am-5pm Fri.-Sun., free) was built at the foot of the Golden Gate Bridge in 1853, designed to protect San Francisco Bay during the gold rush. Take a self-guided tour to see cannons and observe the masonry, which matches the bridge. It's also a good place to get a bridge photo.

While at the Presidio, opt for a hike. I like the 2.6-mile **Mountain Lake Trail** (trailhead at Broadway Gate; Broadway and Lyon St.), which straddles the southern boundary of the park and comes close to two installations by artist Andy Goldsworthy, *Wood Line* and *Spire*. It also meets up with the natural Mountain Lake, home to ducks and seagulls. A playground is nearby.

Also perfect for a stroll is the Presidio section of the 550-mile **Bay Area Ridge Trail** (Trailhead at Arguello Gate; Arguello Blvd. and W. Pacific Ave.), which meanders 2.5 miles north from the golf course to the Golden Gate Bridge. You'll pass by an overlook at **Immigration Point.** After that, make a detour to the **World War II West Coast Memorial** (1351 Washington Blvd.), erected to honor soldiers lost in the Pacific Ocean during the war.

SHOPPING

Just across the street from Willie Mays Plaza at Oracle Park is **Baseballism** (761 3rd St., 415/913-7597, www.baseballism.com, 10am-8pm Sun.-Thurs., 10am-9pm Fri.-Sat.), which sells unlicensed clothing (say, a gray sweatshirt with orange pull strings that says "San Francisco") and leather apparel like bags and watches, all with a baseball theme.

ACCOMMODATIONS

Hotel rooms in San Francisco are expensive. Be prepared to book a room well in advance of your trip, and expect to pay more than you might otherwise like for a stay. In SoMa and other neighborhoods around the Downtown area, there are plenty of hostels (including some that might appear to be hotels, so look closely). If you really want to stay Downtown and don't have a lot of money, you might have a roommate.

NEAR ORACLE PARK

The only worthy hotel near Oracle Park is the **Hyatt Place San Francisco/Downtown** (701 3rd St., 415/767-2000, www.hyatt.com, $300-450), but the rooms are pricey. Comfy king and queen rooms are available, along with "high floor" rooms that offer views of the skyline. The service is quite good, as it should be for the price.

OTHER NEIGHBORHOODS

Over at Union Square, the **Chancellor Hotel** (433 Powell St., 800/428-4748, www.chancellorhotel.com, $200-450) has a special package for baseball fans. Pay between $310 and $400 and get a deluxe room (one queen or two twin beds), a free buffet breakfast, free offsite parking, and two tickets to a Giants game (relatively low seats along the left-field line, too). This nicely appointed boutique hotel built in 1915 gets high marks and is a few blocks from Market Street and the Powell Street BART station.

GETTING AROUND

PUBLIC TRANSIT

Considering the amount of traffic in San Francisco, along with the frequent lack of parking spots, I recommend taking public transportation to get around the city, using ride-sharing services to fill in the gaps.

BART

Your best friend will be **BART** (www.bart.gov, from $2.60), the regional train system. Grab a **BART Blue Ticket** and start with the $20 base fee. You can subtract or add to it, but once you get going, you'll know just how much you'll use. You may have to walk a little to reach some destinations from the closest BART station, so wear comfortable shoes.

The stops you need to know in San Francisco include those along Market Street, like **Powell Street** (899 Market St.), **Montgomery Street** (598 Market St.), and **Embarcadero** (Market St. and Pine St.). There are two stations in the Mission District: **16th Street Mission** (2000 Mission St.) and **24th Street Mission** (2800 Mission St.).

Muni

The city's bus and light rail system is run by the **SFMTA** (www.sfmta.com, $3). Look for **Muni buses and trains,** the gray and red vehicles that ride along a vast network of the city's streets. If you buy a **Clipper card** (available at all BART stations), you can use it for Muni and BART rides, so if you're planning on an all-public-transit stay, this might be a good option.

SFMTA also runs the city's **streetcars** ($2.75) which were introduced in 1962 and now run along a single route as the **F Line.**

The line starts at Market Street in the Castro District, then pushes east toward the Embarcadero. It heads north up the Embarcadero to Fisherman's Wharf before turning and making a return trip.

Cable Cars

Every first-timer in San Francisco should ride a **cable car** (www.sfmta.com, 8am-5pm daily, $7, exact change), which have been part of the city's landscape since the 1870s. There are three cable car lines: **California** (California St. from Van Ness to Market), **Powell-Mason** (Bay St. and Taylor St. to Mason St. and then to Powell St. to Powell St. station), and **Powell-Hyde** (Hyde St. and Beach St. down Hyde, and then to Powell St. to Powell St. station). Be sure to hold on, as the ride can be bumpy and exhilarating. Tickets must be purchased in advance at Powell and Market Streets, Bay and Taylor Streets, or Hyde and Beach Streets.

TAXI, UBER, AND LYFT

San Francisco is all about **Uber** and **Lyft.** That's not too surprising when you consider that both companies are headquartered here. Generally, Uber and Lyft are cheaper than the **taxi cabs** in the city. If you're traveling from San Francisco International Airport to Oracle Park, you'll pay between $25 and $30 for either ride-sharing company.

CAR

San Francisco is at the north end of a peninsula resembling a thumb. From the south there are multiple ways to get into the city—there's **I-280 North,** which curls toward the eastern end of the city and ends just blocks west of Oracle Park. **CA-1,** or the **Pacific Coast Highway,** straddles the western side of the city, through Golden Gate Park, into the Presidio, and toward Sausalito on the Golden Gate Bridge. **US-101** heads north up the eastern end of the city before turning west, merging with **CA-1** (the Pacific Coast Highway) before the Golden Gate Bridge. Both highways enter Sausalito on the north side of the bay before splitting. Continuing north and then east is **I-80 East,** which starts in San Francisco's Design District and it moves east via the Bay Bridge into Oakland. Ultimately, it ends far across the country, just west of New York City.

The most notable thoroughfare in San Francisco is **Market Street,** which winds out from Portola Drive in the center of the city before shooting northeast, past Lower Haight, SoMa, and the Financial District. **Mission Street** is CA-82 in South San Francisco and near the airport. It snakes north by northwest before taking a sharp turn northeast. Mission runs through the heart of the Mission District, then parallels Market toward the **Embarcadero.** The Embarcadero begins a block from Oracle Park, then races north along the waterfront. The Embarcadero finishes north at Fisherman's Wharf.

Some famous neighborhoods are defined in part by their intersections. For example, you'll find **The Castro,** the city's historic gay neighborhood, at Castro Street and Market Street in the center of the city; **Haight-Ashbury,** the origin of the 1960s hippie movement, is centered by the intersection of Haight and Ashbury Streets, which is now a haven for high-priced vintage T-shirt shops.

Since it's San Francisco, hills and winding roads are a thing. Drive slowly on the downhill streets, and be extra cautious when traveling on a zig-zagging road like historic **Lombard Street** (Lombard St. between Hyde St. and Leavenworth St.).

SACRAMENTO, CALIFORNIA

Get a dose of Pacific Coast League history in Sacramento, home to the Giants' triple-A minor league affiliate, the River Cats. The Pacific Coast League started play in 1903 with a club in California's capital city, and while numerous teams have passed through town since then, the River Cats have been a steady presence since 2000.

GETTING THERE

Car

The quickest ride from **San Francisco** to Sacramento is via **I-80 East.** This is a **90-mile** route that'll take about **1.5 hours,** if there's no traffic.

For an alternate, scenic route, take I-80 over the Bay Bridge, but stay east, following signs for I-580 East and CA-24. Follow **CA-24 East** to **I-680 North.** That becomes **CA-4 East,** then **CA-160,** before running into **I-5 North.** Take that into Sacramento. This **105-mile** route will take at least **two hours.**

Train

Take **BART** (www.bart.gov, from $2.60) via the Red, Orange, or Yellow Lines to the 19th Street station in Oakland, then north to Richmond via the Red or Orange Line. At Richmond station, hop on a Capitol Corridor train from **Amtrak** (www.amtrak.com). The train stops at the **Sacramento Valley Station** (401 I St.) in Downtown Sacramento. From here, you can either walk or take an Uber or Lyft the 1.2 miles southwest, over the Sacramento River, and to Sutter Health Park.

Bus

Greyhound (www.greyhound.com) offers daily rides from **San Francisco** to Sacramento, which start at about $8 and can take 2-3 hours. Buses deposit passengers at the **Sacramento Bus Station** (420 Richards Blvd.). You'll need to take a ride-share for the 2.5-mile journey from the bus station south and over the river to the stadium.

Megabus (https://us.megabus.com) also travels to Sacramento from San Francisco. The rides start at $5 and last 2-3 hours. Buses drop passengers off at the **65th Street Light Rail Station** (6740 Q St.), near the campus for Sacramento State University. Plan on hailing a ride-share to take you the six miles west to the stadium.

SUTTER HEALTH PARK

Set just across the river from Old Sacramento, **Sutter Health Park** (400 Ballpark Dr., www.milb.com/sacramento) is home to the **Sacramento River Cats,** a triple-A affiliate of the Giants. The team draws good crowds nightly, with fans eager to see prospects who could become big-leaguers someday soon. Sutter Health Park features a nice skyline and bridge view from the infield foul area.

Like most minor league parks, the stadium has one concourse. The **100 level** stretches from the right-field line to the left field foul pole, and seats can be had for $15-40, with good spots available for $20. You can lay out on the grassy berm of the **Toyota Home Run Hill** (right field, $8) or hang at the **beer garden** (left-field line, section 124, standing room only). Sit along the **third-base line** for the **best view,** which includes Sacramento's yellow **Tower Bridge,** a vertical lift bridge that resembles London Bridge.

Between Thursday and Sunday, you can visit the stadium's **Knee Deep Alley** (home plate, section 110) for beers from the local **Knee Deep Brewing Company.** Food offered at Sutter Health Park is typical ballpark fare, but half of the concessions sell **garlic fries.**

SEATTLE
MARINERS

Just as the clouds gather and rains fall regularly in this fantastic city, baseball here is received with a hefty serving of pessimism. You can't blame the fans, either: The Mariners are the only major league franchise that has never reached the World Series. Yes, that's right, just one team hasn't ever been there, and it's this team.

It's not as if the Mariners are always bad. Sure, they aren't good most of the time, but when they are good—watch out. In 2001, backed by future Hall of Famer Ichiro Suzuki, among others, the team set the American League record for most wins in a season (116). Before that, in 1995, with Hall of Famers Ken Griffey Jr., Edgar Martinez, and Randy Johnson on board, they snuck into the postseason and beat the Yankees in a thrilling division series. These were great and

extremely fun teams, and yet, no World Series appearances.

But that's the way it's always been in Seattle—a wacky baseball history all the way through, starting in 1903 with the Seattle Indians of the Pacific Coast League. That team became the Angels, then after 1906 were cut from the PCL. Seattle returned to the league in 1919, becoming the Rainiers in 1938 when Rainier Brewing Co. owner Emil Sick bought the club. Sick wanted badly to have major league baseball in the Queen City, so he built Sick's Stadium. PCL baseball would be played at Sick's through 1968.

In 1969, the Seattle Pilots began playing. They were forced to launch two years early, as their fellow expansion city, Kansas City (the Royals), wanted to start as soon as possible. That didn't help Seattle, as Sick's Stadium was deemed unfit to host games due to its age, and the Pilots were just plain bad. After losing a lot of money, the Pilots ownership decided to sell the team to Milwaukee car salesman Bud Selig, who promptly moved the team to his town, becoming the Milwaukee Brewers.

Luckily baseball would come back quickly enough. In 1977 the Mariners launched with a brand new park, the Kingdome, which housed Mariner baseball until the move to T-Mobile Park in 1999. But it took a long while for the Mariners to become good, rarely finishing over .500 until that playoff run in 1995. Even then, the luster faded after some years. These days, the city yearns for better days at the park.

The fans love their Mariners, even if they seem pessimistic, and even though they've yet to see a World Series game in Seattle. But it'll happen one day, and when it does—after 100-plus years—boy, what a time that'll be.

PLANNING YOUR TIME

Consider spending at least a **long weekend** of three days in Seattle, taking some time to see touristy sites like the **Space Needle,** the **Museum of Pop Culture,** and **Pike Place Market,** while also giving yourself at least a day to visit neighborhoods like **Ballard** and **Capitol Hill.** Staying in **Downtown Seattle** will ensure you're central to tourist locations as well as hip hangouts. Alternatively, the area near **Seattle-Tacoma International Airport** offers plenty of accommodations. You'll also be close to Sound Transit's Link Light Rail, which offers an easy trip into Downtown.

This city is **colder** and **rainier** than most major league locations. You'll be most comfortable smack in the **middle of summer,** when high temperatures average in the mid- to high 70s and the low dips into the just-cool-enough mid-50s. Plus, it's the driest time of year here, so there's less of a chance you'll get rained on.

If you come in **April** or **May,** you're bound to be a little **chilly** even during the day, and it will **rain** a bit. Luckily, T-Mobile Park has a **retractable roof** that will undoubtedly be closed if the temperature is too low or the clouds are too dark.

GETTING THERE

AIR

The main airport in the area is **Seattle-Tacoma International Airport** (SEA, 17801 International Blvd., 206/787-5388, www.portseattle.org). Airlines that service the airport include **Air Canada** (888/247-2262, www.aircanada.com), **American Airlines** (800/433-7300, www.aa.com), **Delta** (800/221-1212, www.delta.com), **Frontier** (801/401-9000, www.flyfrontier.com), **jetBlue** (800/538-2583, www.jetblue.com), **Southwest** (800/435-9792, www.southwest.com), **Spirit** (801/401-2222, www.spirit.com), and **United** (800/864-8331, www.united.com). You can fly to Seattle from pretty much every major U.S. city.

Airport Transportation

If you're **renting a car,** you'll take a **shuttle,** accessible near baggage claim, to the off-site rental car facility. Every major rental car company is here. Sea-Tac is 15 miles south of Downtown Seattle. It's a 20-minute drive, without traffic, north on I-5, WA-509, or WA-99 to reach Downtown from the airport. T-Mobile Park is just south of Downtown, so the drive will be around five minutes faster.

Alternatively, you can hop on **Sound Transit's Link Light Rail** (www.soundtransit.org, 5am-1am Mon.-Sat., 6am-midnight Sun., $2.25-3.25 per trip), a convenient and smooth service operating one line from southern points like the airport up into Downtown Seattle and north to the University of Washington. Get to T-Mobile Park by exiting at the **Stadium station** (S. Royal Brougham Way and 4th Ave. S.). To reach Downtown, go several exits farther to **West-lake station** (4th Ave. and Pine St.). The ride from the airport to the stadium and Downtown is about 25-30 minutes.

CAR

From **San Francisco,** you have yourself a trek to Seattle. The quickest drive, if traffic is working with you, is via **I-5 North,** an **800-mile** trip lasting at least **13 hours.** You'll want to break up the trip into **two days,** so consider stopping in a place like Medford, Oregon, which is about halfway between the two cities. I-5 will take you directly through Portland, Oregon, so you could also factor in an extra day to spend some time there.

Or take the **scenic route** via **US-101 North.** This trip of **900 miles** will take around **17 hours** and can be completed in **three days (four days** if you're hoping to take your time and visit a sight or two). You'll hit the coast about 4.5 hours north of San Francisco in Eureka, just south of Redwood National Park, and tour through extraordinarily green landscapes in Oregon and Washington. You may want to stop overnight in Crescent City, California, and North Bend, Oregon.

TRAIN

To reach Seattle from San Francisco by rail, you can take **Amtrak** (www.amtrak.com). First, you'll need to hop across the bay to **Oakland** (Jack London Square station, 245 2nd St.) or **Emeryville** (Emeryville station, 5885 Horton St.), since there are no Amtrak stations in San Francisco. From there, take the **Coast Starlight** north to Seattle. This ride takes around 24 hours to complete, and tickets start at about $90.

The train stops at **King Street Station** (303 S. Jackson St.), a 1906 structure with a 12-story clock tower and a spacious lobby just a half-mile north of T-Mobile Park. The station is just one block west of a **Link station** (Chinatown/International District, 5th Ave. S. and S. King St.), so you can easily continue to Downtown or to the stadium.

BUS

It's possible to get to Seattle from San Francisco on **Greyhound** (www.greyhound.com). The **Seattle Greyhound station** (503 S. Royal Brougham Way) is two blocks east of T-Mobile Park, accessible to Link's **Stadium station** (S. Royal Brougham Way and 4th Ave. S.). Generally, this ride will cost $85-100 and last about 24 hours, altogether, with two transfers.

T-Mobile Park

The Mariners have always played in the South Downtown (SoDo) neighborhood of Seattle, just down the block from Pioneer Square and a few blocks north of a more industrial area. For more than two decades the team's home was the Kingdome, a concrete cavern that had leaks even before it hosted a single game. By the 1995 season it was an eyesore, and it seemed likely the Mariners would have to move from Seattle because King County voters wouldn't approve the funding for a new ballpark.

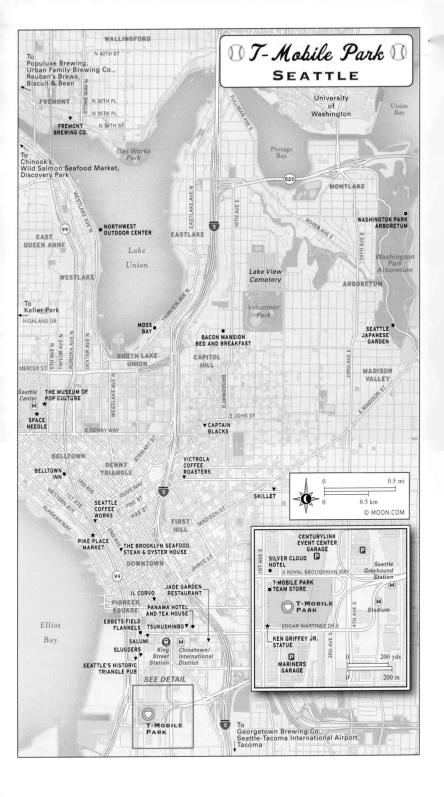

T-Mobile Park

But something incredible happened: That year, the Mariners came back in a fury in the final month of the season to win their first ever division championship. Then they beat the Yankees in the American League Division Series. Mariners fever was so high that county voters turned the tide, awarding the M's their new venue. **T-Mobile Park** (1250 1st Ave. S., www.mlb.com/mariners), originally called Safeco Field, opened in 1999.

This retractable-roof park makes sense for Seattle. When it rains (and boy, does it rain), the roof slides in place and the game goes on. When it's beautiful outside in the summer, the roof opens to let in the sunshine. There's nothing particularly special about T-Mobile Park's look and feel; instead, its greatness is in its game day experience. The food here is killer. The beer selection is as good as it gets in baseball. The vibe is lively, yet relaxed. It's one of my favorite places to visit in the game.

ORIENTATION

T-Mobile Park is about a mile south of Downtown Seattle, part of a larger stadium complex area that includes CenturyLink Field, home of the Seattle Seahawks football team and Sounders soccer team. Close to train stations and a bus station, and with ample parking surrounding it (including a garage across Edgar Martinez Drive that offers walkway access to the park for club and suite level ticketholders), the venue is one of the more well-placed ballparks.

There are five entry gates at T-Mobile Park. Most gates open at T-Mobile Park two

hours before each game begins. The Center Field Gate and the 'Pen Gate both open 2.5 hours before first pitch.

TICKETS AND SEATING

Pricing and Seating Plan

The Mariners participate in the popular **dynamic pricing** practice, which means seeing the Yankees here will cost more than seeing, say, the Orioles. Dates against opponents whose fanbases don't travel as much may be designated as **"value games,"** meaning ticket prices are as low as it gets here (around $15 for seats in the view level).

T-Mobile's seating areas are relatively simple and lack the multiple section names common to other stadiums. The **main level (100 level)**, starts with section 102 in right

center field, moving into foul territory to the right, then winding around the infield to the left field foul pole at section 150. The outfield extends the level with **bleachers** above the left field fence and bullpens (sections 180-187), and in deep center field (sections 190-195). Under all this seating, nearly at field level, is **The 'Pen** (100 level, left field), an entertainment and dining area of the park with plenty of **standing room** for sociable fans. There are higher-priced seats in the **rows closest to the field,** plus a few **home plate boxes,** but the 100 level isn't divided much at all.

The **club level (200 level)** starts at section 211 at the right field foul pole, and this seating is one set price until section 218, just beyond first base. Between **first base and home plate** (sections 219-227) the level is

---

YOUR BEST DAY AT T-MOBILE PARK

Seattle is a fine city, so eat up all the time here that you can. Here's an itinerary you can follow that concludes with a Mariners game.

10 HOURS BEFORE FIRST PITCH
Get those legs moving and the heart pumping with a morning hike at **Washington Park Arboretum.** Walk the Loop Trail, a two-mile jaunt that'll take 90 minutes at most.

8 HOURS BEFORE FIRST PITCH
It's Seattle, so it's time for coffee. Visit **Victrola Coffee Roasters** to get your jolt.

7.5 HOURS BEFORE FIRST PITCH
Head Downtown to buy a throwback jersey from **Ebbets Field Flannels.**

7 HOURS BEFORE FIRST PITCH
After some shopping, walk around the corner and grab a big lunch at **Salumi.** Stand in line, then order a specialty sandwich and enjoy every last bite.

6 HOURS BEFORE FIRST PITCH
After lunch, head back to your hotel to clean up and change clothes. Maybe take a quick nap.

4.5 HOURS BEFORE FIRST PITCH
Plan on taking ride-shares for the rest of the day. Make the pilgrimage to **Pike Place Market** just to walk around, even if it's with a crowd of folks. Grab a piece of fruit or some smoked salmon to tide you over. See what they have at **Pike Place Fish.**

3 HOURS BEFORE FIRST PITCH
It's beer time. You need to visit **Seattle's**

Pike Place Market

Historic Triangle Pub to experience the space. Order a beer and a shot. Afterward, head across the street and walk into **Sluggers.** You'll meet some new friends there. Now it's time to walk to **T-Mobile Park.**

DURING THE GAME
With all those hops in your belly you'll want some grub. I suggest the stacked sandwiches at **Paseo.** Chase it down with some grasshoppers at **Edgar's Cantina.** Maybe have another drink in the bar across the way, too.

After that, pay homage to a legend at the **Dave Niehaus statue** and get a quick education in Washington baseball history at the **Baseball Museum of the Pacific Northwest and Mariners Hall of Fame.**

AFTER THE GAME
Hail a ride to the chilled-out **Captain Blacks** for a drink to close out this perfect day.

---

divided into **lower and upper seating.** For the rest of the level, from **home plate to the left field foul pole** (sections 233-249), it's one price. The **Hit It Here Café** is in true right field on this level.

Suites just above the 200 level are located **above the Hit It Here café** (sections A-H) and from **right field foul pole to left field foul pole** (S1-S69). Finally, the **view level (300 level)** starts in right field at section 306,

then wraps around foul territory to the left field foul pole at section 347.

If you're bringing the family and would rather not be around alcohol, **section 104** is an **alcohol-free area.**

Where to Buy Tickets

Seats at T-Mobile Park are relatively inexpensive, so you'll be fine picking up tickets far before game day via the **Mariner's website.**

660

Of course, you could still wait until just before game time for prices to drop on **Stub-Hub** or another **third-party ticket broker.**

By going to the box office, you might be able to score a **deal.** If you're older than 60, you can get 10 percent off most seats by showing identification at the ticket window. Members of the military and first responders can get the same 10 percent discount at the box office by showing valid identification.

Best Seats

If you want to be in the **shade** at T-Mobile Park, be under an **overhang.** The **back rows** of the **300 level,** primarily the sections **close to home plate** (sections 325-335), and the **very back rows** of the **100 level** in the same area (sections 126-134) are your best bets, as the sun travels behind the plate during mid-afternoon and early-evening games. The **third-base side** of the **100 level** (sections 136-146) will get shade before the first-base side. Because the Pacific Northwest experiences a later sunset in midsummer, there will be **sunny spots** for a good portion of June and July night games, mostly in the **deep outfield** (center field, right field). Foul territory will be fine.

My suggestion is to get seats in the **view level** close to **home plate,** then spend plenty of time walking around this gem of a park and spotting up somewhere in **The 'Pen.** If you want to be down low, consider **sections 136-141,** but think about staying in the **back rows** to keep out of the sun.

KNOW BEFORE YOU GO

Bags and **coolers,** as long as they're soft-sided and no more than 16 by 16 by 8 inches, are permitted at T-Mobile Park. **Outside food** has to be able to fit in single servings inside those bags or plastic containers. Beverages are also allowed in, as long as we're talking about factory-sealed, 32-ounce or fewer plastic bottles of **water.**

T-Mobile Park has **all-gender restrooms** (sections 105, 120, 234, 319, 327 and 333), which can be used by anyone regardless of gender. There's a **nursing lounge** (section

GAME COSTS

Tickets: Generally, prices are high here. Tickets get as cheap as **$15** for the upper levels, but if you're hoping to sit in even the back rows of the 100 level, you'll pay more than **$50.**

Hot dog: $6.50 is the going rate here, expensive compared to other parks. You can get smoked sausage for about **$11,** so maybe opt for that instead.

Beer: For the most part, you'll find the domestic macro brews are around **$10-11,** topping out at **$13,** while the premium beer is a shade more expensive, at most **$13.50.**

Parking: Some of the lots near the stadium can be as cheap as **$10,** but you'll typically pay more like **$20.** You're better off parking a little farther away from the park or just hopping in a ride-share vehicle from your hotel.

128) for those needing to care for a baby.

T-Mobile Park is **cashless,** but if you have greens alone, don't fret: There are **cash-to-card kiosks** (sections 103, 116, 128, 144, 226, 331, 339, The 'Pen) throughout the park so you can load a card with however much cash you want to use, then pay for your food and drinks with it.

Accessibility

Wheelchair escorts are available at the gate of entry and the parking garage. Visit a **guest service center** (sections 128 and 329 and The 'Pen near the center field gate) for **wheelchair storage, noise-cancelling headphones,** and **assistive listening devices.**

Elevators at T-Mobile Park are located at sections 106, 114, and 191, and at the home plate and left field gates. There are **ramps** at sections 114 and 143. **Service animals** and service animals-in-training are welcome at T-Mobile Park.

Accessible parking is available at the

BE A FAN

The Mariners don't have any major game day traditions, but the fans here are a lot of fun. Look, when you support the only major league team that has never been to the World Series, you get pretty humble. This is a knowledgeable band of followers.

If you ever come to T-Mobile Park when the Blue Jays are in town, get ready for an invasion. Canada is just a few minutes north, so those Jays fans come flocking in for those series. Toronto isn't necessarily a rival of Seattle's, so the home fans don't get too upset when the Canadians cross the border. Mariners fans don't seem to have major issues with any opposing fans, actually, so come as you are.

Mariners parking garage for up to $40. Spaces are available on a limited basis. Be sure a valid disabled parking placard or license plate is visible. For more information on accessibility at T-Mobile Park, call the Mariners at 206/346-4224.

GETTING THERE

Public Transit

If you're Downtown or in Capitol Hill a few hours before first pitch, consider taking the train to T-Mobile Park. Sound Transit's **Link Light Rail** (www.soundtransit.org, 5am-1am Mon.-Sat., 6am-midnight Sun., $2.25-3.25 per trip) is just one line, but it stops at **Stadium station** (S. Royal Brougham Way and 4th Ave. S.), just a block away from the ballpark. It's a 10-minute walk to the 'Pen Gate from the station.

Driving

If you're driving to T-Mobile Park, consider **parking** a little farther away from the stadium to save some money. The team's official parking structure, the **Mariners Garage** (Edgar Martinez Dr. and Occidental Ave. S., $20-60), is quite expensive, though for people exiting off I-5 or I-90, it is pretty convenient, as it's just next to the ballpark.

Cheaper options abound, like at the **CenturyLink Event Center Garage** (S. Royal Brougham Way and Occidental Ave. S., $10-50) to the north, or the **Union Station Garage** (820 4th Ave. S., $8-30). If you want to avoid paying an arm and a leg, find a spot in a garage **Downtown** and walk about a mile down 1st Avenue South to reach the ballpark. The Downtown garages will cost you more like $15-25.

PARK FEATURES AND SIGHTS

The 'Pen

The highlight for most fans before and during the game is **The 'Pen** (100 level, outfield), a strip of bars and foodie spots that's usually pretty busy. Look for the fire pits and cozy seating areas at the Caught Looking Lounge. Popular food vendors here include Edgar's Cantina and Li'l Woody's Burgers.

While you're here, look for the **Fan Walk** (The 'Pen, center field), where Mariners fans are a permanent part of the ballpark through the 12,500 inscribed bricks set into the ground. Know someone who has a brick here? There's a touch screen locator by the Good Stuff merchandise stand.

Baseball Museum of the Pacific Northwest and Mariners Hall of Fame

Be sure to stop by the **Baseball Museum of the Pacific Northwest and Mariners Hall of Fame** (sections 133-136), an adventure through Seattle baseball history with obvious focus on the M's. You can relive great Mariners moments, read more about Hall of Famers like Ken Griffey Jr., Edgar Martinez, and Randy Johnson, and glimpse game-worn uniforms and hats.

Statues

On the main level of the ballpark, find the statue of **Dave Niehaus** (section 141), which won't be hard to spot. Niehaus, the voice of Mariners play-by-play from the team's inaugural 1977 season up until his death in 2010, is depicted seated at his desk with a scorecard and a microphone. Some of his trademark lines ("My oh my!", "Swung on and belted", "Get out the rye bread and mustard, Grandma, it's grand salami time!") surround him, and you can sit right next to him for a snapshot.

Outside the park, look for the statue of **Ken Griffey Jr.** (Edgar Martinez Dr. and Dave Niehaus Way, Home Plate Gate). Griffey, the Hall of Famer who effortlessly dominated the game in the 1990s, is shown at seven feet tall and in his natural pose after hitting one of his 630 home runs.

Kid Play Areas

Check out **The Moose Den** (section 190), a log-walled nook where little ones can meet **Mariner Moose,** the team's mascot since 1990. Meet-and-greet opportunities occur 90 to 30 minutes before first pitch, between the bottom of the second inning to the middle of the third inning, and between the bottom of the seventh inning to the middle of the eighth inning. Be warned: Lines will form.

The littlest fans may want to hang out for a spell at the **Seattle Children's Hospital Playfield** (100 level, center field), home to a playset, kid-friendly concession stand, and a clubhouse store. Kids must be no more than 48 inches tall to play. There are televisions here, too, so parents won't miss the game.

For elementary-school-age kids and tweens, the **Kids Corner** (section 328) has free pitching, hitting, and running challenges.

FOOD AND DRINKS

T-Mobile Park is near the top among major league ballparks in food selection and quality. Along with hospitality partner Centerplate, the Mariners hired a local chef—in this case multiple James Beard award nominee Ethan Stowell—to consult on the ballpark's food-and-beverage program, a relationship that started in 2011. The result is a deep roster of items spanning a dizzying number of cuisines and specialty items: Southern comfort, burgers and shakes, Mexican street food, Caribbean, Chinese pork buns, crab and clam chowder, pizza, garlic fries, and grasshoppers.

Yes, **grasshoppers.** Get in line at **Edgar's Cantina** (The 'Pen), which of course is named after Mariners Hall of Famer Edgar Martinez, and order up a small cup of *chapulines,* or toasted grasshoppers tossed in Tajín (a chili-lime seasoning). This Oaxacan delicacy was brought to the ballpark by Manny Arce of **Poquitos Restaurant,** which also serves up street tacos and nachos at Edgar's. The *chapulines* are salty, crunchy, then lightly spicy with a citrus finish. Just get here early, because they only reserve 312 cups each game (Martinez's career batting average was .312). Pro tip: Order the delicious *carne asada* or *pollo* nachos (made with homemade chips!), then sprinkle your *chapulines* on top. The stand is across from a bar also called **Edgar's Cantina** (The 'Pen), which hangs just beyond the left field fence and has a bar serving up craft margaritas and both macro- and micro-brewed beer.

Also at The 'Pen is **Paseo,** the ballpark outpost of a popular Seattle-based Caribbean sandwich shop. The sandwiches are made with roast pork or chicken thigh meat with garlic aioli, pickled jalapeños, cilantro, and onions inside a crispy baguette. Paseo also sells Caribbean nachos, where they swap tomato-based salsa for a pineapple version.

Ballard Pizza Co. (The 'Pen) is an Ethan Stowell joint that bakes up New York-style slices. Pike Place Market favorite **Shug's Soda Fountain & Ice Cream** (The 'Pen) is also located at The 'Pen. Here you can get flavors like cookies and cream and peach sorbet, plus ice cream and root beer floats. But let's be real: You're here for the prosecco float, especially on a Sunday afternoon.

Way back when the ballpark was named Safeco, it was one of the first venues to serve sushi, including a very popular maki roll that paid tribute to legendary hitter Ichiro

Suzuki. That spot, **Hiroshi's Sushi** (section 132) still stands today and you can still order the famous **Ichiroll.**

Just across from Hiroshi's is **Din Tai Fung** (section 132), a tiny post-up that doles out Chinese street food like pork buns and fried rice. They also have Taiwanese boba tea.

Find fresh seafood at the **Way Back Crab Shack** (section 187). Among the offerings here are a crab sandwich on sourdough that's grilled with garlic butter, crab fries, and New England clam chowder (that's the white one).

For burgers, order from **Lil' Woody's** (The 'Pen), which also serves up shakes. The favorite here is the Big Woody, where beef, bacon, and Tillamook cheddar joins up with diced veggies, ketchup, and mayo.

The one sit-down restaurant at the park is the **Hit It Here Café** (200 level, right field), which includes both an indoor café area and outdoor tiered seating overlooking the outfield. Those tiered seats are usually sold well in advance to groups, but if not, individual seats are offered to the public three weeks before the game. From the indoor seats, you'll have trouble seeing much of the game, except on the television. Unlike many ballpark restaurants, the food here is actually pretty good. You'll get craft burgers, pub appetizers, Ballard Pizza Co. pies, big sandwiches, and a very good craft beer selection that includes several local favorites.

T-Mobile is among the best in baseball when it comes to beer. Your first stop should be **Cask** (section 129), a small but powerful stand that sells cask- and barrel-aged beers. There'll undoubtedly be a local label here, but you'll also likely find neat options from popular Oregon and California breweries like **Stone Brewing Co.** and **Anderson Valley Brewing Company.**

At **The 'Pen,** you'll find all kinds of beers dotting the various vendor stands. Look for **Power Alley** (The 'Pen), which stocks brews from local legend **Elysian Brewing**

Photos (from top to bottom): team mascot Mariner Moose; Mariners Hall of Fame; statue of broadcaster Dave Niehaus by sculptor Lou Cella.

Company, local favorite **Georgetown Brewing Company,** and Oregon's **Boneyard Beer**. Visit the **batch cocktail cart** (section 141), where **Reueben's Brews, Pyramid Brewing Co., Bale Breaker Brewing Company,** and **Fremont Brewing** may have beers. Of course, you'll find any number of beers from once-independent breweries that were bought by the big corporations (like **Hop Valley** and **Saint Archer**), and there's a wealth of cheap macro-brewed beer. But for $5, a Miller High Life at a ballpark isn't bad at all. Of course, you can just as easily snag a **Rainier**—you'll find it all over the place.

There's good wine here, too. Visit the **First Base Vine** (section 126) to sample bottles, then buy a carafe and fill it with an offering from a solid local winery. It's a nice luxury to be able to sit at your seat with a carafe of wine, watching the game.

EVENTS

You can absolutely get **autographs** at T-Mobile Park. Once the gates open, just head down to the **first rows** by both **dugouts.** Fans will be asked to return to their ticketed seats 45 minutes before first pitch (once batting practice ends).

As for **batting practice,** since gates open two hours before the game starts, fans can catch about 25 minutes of Mariners cage time and the entirety of the opposing team's routine.

Tours

The Mariners host two different types of **tours** (206/346-4241, $12, $11 seniors, $10 ages 4 and over, free ages 3 and under) of T-Mobile Park. The **standard tour** (dates vary Jan.-Oct.) includes stops on the field and inside the visitors' clubhouse, press box, and owner's suite. The **pregame tours** (before games Mon. and Wed.-Fri.) focus more on game preparation and ballpark sights, shuffling visitors to premium seating levels and the Dave Niehaus statue. Both tours leave from the Third Base Lobby (1st Ave. S.).

SHOPPING

The **T-Mobile Park Team Store** (1250 1st Ave. S., section 143, 206/346-4287, 10am-5pm Mon.-Sat. non-game days, 10am-2pm night games, closed before and after day and Sun. games, open to ticketholders only during games) has all the stuff you'll find at any main team store, from jerseys to caps to men's and women's apparel. Look for vintage Rainiers jerseys, too.

SEATTLE SIGHTS

PIKE PLACE MARKET

The iconic **Pike Place Market** (85 Pike St., 206/682-7453, www.pikeplacemarket.org, generally 9am-5pm daily, individual merchant hours may vary), in operation since 1907, is one of the most indelible locations in America. It might be the massive "Public Market Center" sign that greets folks as they cross the brick walk into the packed emporium, or maybe it's just the scent of fresh flowers, seafood, and produce, and the constant murmur from tourists as they shuffle through the place.

The market is wide but the aisles are narrow, so be patient walking through with all the tourists. Be sure to stop at some places, like **City Fish Co.** (1535 Pike Pl., 202/682-9329, www.cityfish.com, 6am-6pm daily), the oldest fish market in the city; **Pike Place Fish** (86 Pike Pl., 800/542-7732, www.pikeplacefish.com, 6:30am-6pm Mon.-Sat., 7am-5pm Sun.), which is famous for its fish-throwing employees; **Pike Place Market Creamery** (1514 Pike Pl. #3, 206/622-5029, 9am-6pm Mon.-Sat., 10am-5pm Sun.), which has a wide selection of local dairy products; **Corner Produce** (1500 Pike Pl., 206/625-5006, 7am-5:30pm daily), a stalwart since 1957 in one of the market's highstalls (named for the stacks of produce towering over the vendors' stands); and **Beecher's Handmade**

Cheese (1600 Pike Pl., 877/907-1644, www. beechershandmadecheese.com, 9am-7pm daily), where you have to get the macaroni and cheese.

The very first Starbucks opened in 1971 on Western Avenue in Seattle. A little later, it moved to Pike Place Market, and it still exists as its oldest-operating store. **Starbucks Pike Place** (1912 Pike Pl., 206/448-8762, www. starbucks.com, 7am-5pm daily) keeps some of its 1970s touches, like the original logo, a menu of just coffee and espresso, and a slightly less corporate feel. The lines here are always long, so you might be fine just taking pictures and continuing onward.

SPACE NEEDLE

You may want to get to the top of the **Space Needle** (400 Broad St., www.spaceneedle. com, 9am-9pm Mon.-Thurs., 9am-11pm Fri.-Sun., $32.50-37.50, $27.50-32.50 seniors, $24.50-28.50 ages 5-12), and you really should, at least once. The 605-foot structure was built for the 1962 World's Fair and; at the time, it was the tallest structure west of the Mississippi River. Today, the Space Needle isn't even the tallest structure in Seattle. Still, it offers outstanding views of the skyline, the Puget Sound, and the Olympic and Cascade mountain ranges, including Mount Rainer.

Once you get your ticket (purchase a timed ticket online for maximum efficiency), you'll take an elevator for about 45 seconds to the **lower observation deck.** If you're scared of heights, this deck may be a little nerve-racking: The floor rotates and is made of glass, part of a recent multi-million-dollar renovation. The **upper floor** has floor-to-ceiling windows, plus **The Atmos Café,** home to quick and locally themed bites, beer, and wine, plus an adjacent wine bar with cheeseboards.

Try going in the evening, so you can see a beautiful sunset over the Puget Sound. The Space Needle also sells an experience where you'll get admission, reserved seating on the top deck, four wine tastings, and paired bites.

MUSEUM OF POP CULTURE

The **Museum of Pop Culture** (325 5th Ave. N., 206/770-2700, www.mopop.org, 10am-5pm daily, $28-30, $25-27 students and seniors, $19-21 ages 5-12, free ages 4 and under) is not your Facebook archive but, instead, a real rock 'n' roll-inspired building designed by noted architect Frank Gehry. It houses exhibits like a Hall of Fame devoted to science fiction and fantasy, a video game retrospective, and special spaces, like one devoted to the game Minecraft. There's also a kitchen with food by Wolfgang Puck, a theater, and a lounge with bar seating. The museum also hosts sensory-friendly programs.

FOOD

NEAR T-MOBILE PARK

The best restaurants around T-Mobile Park are more than a half-mile away. A few great Japanese spots are close enough. My favorite is **Tsukushinbo** (515 S. Main St., 206/467-4004, noon-9pm Mon.-Thurs., noon-11pm Fri.-Sat., noon-8:30pm Sun., under $40). Essentially an *izakaya* (Japanese pub), Tsukushinbo features street food, noodle bowls, and protein-and-rice dishes. The casual digs include a bar and table seating, and environs will get packed for dinner service. The sake options are good here.

Nearby is **Jade Garden Restaurant** (424 7th Ave. S., 206/622-8181, www.jadegarden-seattle.com, 9am-1am daily, under $60), a popular spot for dim sum delights. With its deep list of à la carte favorites, you're bound to find something you'll love here. Look for crab dumplings and *haam sui gok* (rice dumplings). Get there earlier in the day, if you can. The food seems to be freshest in the morning and early afternoon.

For lunch, nothing beats the iconic **Salumi** (404 Occidental Ave. S., 206/621-8772, www.salumicuredmeats.com,

11am-3pm Mon.-Sat., under $40). Founded by Armandino Batali, Salumi specializes in the best cured meats this side of the Adriatic Sea. Get one of the spot's trademark sandwiches or order a pound of meat and munch on it for the next week… OK, day… OK, hour. Just know you might have to stand in line for a few minutes.

Then there's **Il Corvo** (217 James St., 206/538-0999, www.ilcorvopasta.com, 11am-3pm Mon.-Fri., under $40). You'll have to get here a little early (say, 10am) because there'll be a line. (Or come about an hour before closing.) No matter when you arrive, you're bound to have a feast. What you eat depends on what's fresh that day. The digs are mighty casual, but the food is astonishing. Order a bowl of pasta at the counter, have a glass of wine, sit back, smile at the people in line, and enjoy the day.

OTHER NEIGHBORHOODS

When you're in Seattle, you'll need some coffee. If you're into joe, visit **Seattle Coffee Works** (108 Pine St., 206/340-8867, www.seattlecoffeeworks.com, under $20). It's always just busy enough, but the service is so on point that you'll get your cup within three minutes. Go to the slowbar to hang out for a few minutes with your cup, or get it quick from the espresso line. Either way, you'll be glad you came.

Up a bit and closer to Capitol Hill is the super **Victrola Coffee Roasters** (310 E. Pike St., 800/575-5282, www.victrolacoffee.com, 6:30am-8pm Mon.-Fri., 7:30am-8pm Sat.-Sun., under $20). It's one of the four locations of this local favorite, a quintessential café with exposed brick and wood posts, broad wood tables, a counter packed with pastries, and a chalkboard filled up with a host of coffee drinks. The espresso is strong, but so worth it.

With your coffee, get breakfast. **Skillet** (1400 E. Union St., 206/512-2001, www.

Photos (from top to bottom): Museum of Pop Culture; Salumi; Seattle Japanese Garden.

skilletcapitolhill.com, 7am-9pm Mon.-Thurs., 7am-10pm Fri.-Sat., under $40) is your classic new-wave neighborhood breakfast and brunch place with favorites like chicken and waffles and corned beef hash. The food is terrific, but even better, the drinks are strong and the vibe is fun.

For something a little more casual but nonetheless delicious, check out **Biscuit & Bean** (5905 15th Ave. NW, 206/457-5735, www.biscuitandbean.biz, 8am-noon Mon.-Fri., 9am-1pm Sat.-Sun., under $30). The premise is simple: Get in line. When you get to the counter, order yourself one of the eatery's savory sandwiches. If you don't want a sandwich, order biscuits and gravy or just a bunch of biscuits. Either way, bread it up and add some coffee.

So, here's the deal: I can't get enough of smoked salmon. So one day I hopped over to **Chinook's** (1900 W. Nickerson St. #103, 206/283-4665, www.anthonys.com, 11am-9pm Mon.-Thurs., 11am-9:30pm Fri., 8am-9:30pm Sat., 8am-9pm Sun., under $60), a seafood restaurant in Seattle's Fishermen's Terminal. There, I visited the restaurant's **Wild Salmon Seafood Market** (206/283-3366, www.wildsalmonseafood.com, 8:30am-6pm Mon.-Sat., 8:30am-5pm Sun., under $30) and got my silky fish wrapped and bagged. There is plenty of seating outside to immediately open your order up and enjoy it. If you're into fresh fish, you have to visit this spot. For a sit-down experience, Chinook's has salmon tacos, live Dungeness crab, and oyster burgers.

Downtown has the superior spot for classy fare in **The Brooklyn Seafood, Steak & Oyster House** (1212 2nd Ave., 206/224-7000, www.thebrooklyn.com, 11:30am-9pm Mon.-Thurs., 11:30am-9:30pm Fri., 4pm-9:30pm Sat., 4pm-8pm Sun., under $100). In this throwback-feeling room of white tablecloth, raised seating, and a special chef's bar, you'll find plenty of oysters, plus hulking beef entrées and locally caught fish. This is great for a big dinner as well as a simple cocktail with a dozen oysters on the half shell.

BARS AND BREWERIES

NEAR T-MOBILE PARK

A must-stop before the ball game is **Seattle's Historic Triangle Pub** (553 1st Ave. S., 206/628-0474, www.trianglepub.com, 11am-10pm daily). This former brothel is true to its name, a triangular space that's mighty cozy (500 square feet) and fun for a drink or two. There's a small patio outside (also cozy), and you can curl up inside by the triangle's point, maybe with a book or preferably, a beer and a shot. You'll meet some characters here, so have a chat or two, check out the many photos by the bar, and definitely don't leave without buying a lottery ticket. Hey, you never know!

Just across the street from the Triangle Pub is **Sluggers** (538 1st Ave. S., 206/654-8070, 10am-2am daily), a sports bar with a real beer-and-shot atmosphere. There's good booth seating, a long, narrow-fitting bar with a lot of stools, nice bartenders, and Rainier beer in tall boy cans. Look for old jerseys, bobbleheads, and signatures from baseball players and personalities on coasters above the bar at this two-story funhouse. There are lots of televisions for watching games, too.

OTHER NEIGHBORHOODS

Seattle has plenty of breweries. I enjoy **Georgetown Brewing Co.** (5200 Denver Ave. S., 206/766-8055, www.georgetownbeer.com, 10am-5pm daily) quite a bit. This friendly, industrial-looking place will let you sample anything they've got on hand. They make some terrific beer here, so get a pint or two, but be sure to pick up some merchandise or beer to-go, as well. I recommend basically any IPA these folks do.

The Fremont and Ballard neighborhoods of Seattle are home to some stunners. **Fremont Brewing Co.** (1050 N. 34th St., 206/420-2407, www.fremontbrewing.com,

11am-9pm daily) scores with its changing lineup of steadily solid beers, including a great selection of stouts. But more, in the summer the front beer garden is great for whiling away an afternoon. There are big picnic tables and it's dog-friendly. No food is served here, though, and parking is a little hard to find. You might have to circle a bit to get an open spot.

Close to Ballard, the popular **Urban Family Brewing Co.** (1103 NW 52nd St., 206/946-8533, www.urbanfamilybrewing. com, noon-10pm daily) is one of my favorite spots in the city. This half-finished-looking place with barrels providing much of the decor can get packed on the weekends, but it's worth it for the juicy sour beers and outdoor sidewalk garden space. The folks are very helpful here.

A longtime presence in Seattle, **Reuben's Brews** (5010 14th Ave. NW, 206/784-2859, www.reubensbrews.com, 11am-10pm daily) delivers with an array of styles, friendly atmosphere, and knowledgeable workers who'll point you to more breweries in the area. You can grab some free pretzels and water, too.

With more of a "basement game room" vibe than the other breweries in town, **Populuxe Brewing** (826 NW 49th St., 206/706-3400, www.populuxebrewing.com, 3pm-9pm Mon.-Thurs., 3pm-10pm Fri., noon-10pm Sat., noon-9pm Sun.) likes to experiment with its brews. It has a fun room of arcade games, and it lets kids and dogs run around in the open beer garden. Food trucks are regular here.

For a chill bar with a nice view, there's **Captain Blacks** (129 Belmont Ave. E., 206/327-9549, www.captainblacksseattle. com, 4pm-2am daily). Half of this spot is a dive, and the other half is a relatively relaxed high-volume bar with some nice rooftop views. It's got an end-of-the-night vibe and is worth a spot for one more beer or mixed drink.

RECREATION

PARKS AND GARDENS

Washington Park Arboretum

Taking up 230 acres on and around Union Bay, **Washington Park Arboretum** (2300 Arboretum Dr. E., 206/543-8800, www. botanicgardens.uw.edu, 9am-5pm daily) is a great place to spend a few hours, especially if you want to stretch your legs. There are numerous trails in the park, including the two-mile Loop Trail that begins off of Lake Washington Boulevard by the Pacific Connections Garden.

Seattle Japanese Garden

Near the arboretum is the **Seattle Japanese Garden** (1075 Lake Washington Blvd. E., 206/684-4725, www.seattlejapanesegarden. org, noon-5pm Mon., 10am-5pm Tues.-Sun. Mar. and Oct., noon-6pm Mon., 10am-6pm Tues.-Sun. Apr. and Sept., noon-7pm Mon., 10am-7pm Tues.-Sun. May-Aug., noon-4pm Mon., 10am-4pm Tues.-Sun. Nov., $8, $4 ages 6-17, seniors, and college students, free ages 5 and under). This 3.5-acre garden takes visitors through manicured Japanese landscapes, a waterfall, and both Japanese and Pacific Northwest flora. For a quick loop, try the one-mile Lookout Trail, which is set in the park's interior. Walk through the Pacific Connections Garden to the Lookout Gazebo to start.

Discovery Park

The largest park in the city is the 534-acre **Discovery Park** (3801 Discovery Park Blvd., visitors center 8:30am-5pm Tues.-Sun.), which extends out to Fort Lawton Beach, a point against the Puget Sound. You'll find multiple trails here for hiking and cycling, plus two miles of beaches covered in rocks, so plan on walking rather than sunbathing. A highlight here is West Point Lighthouse, which is set at the point and is accessible from the North Beach Trail. This 1881 Victorian lighthouse, which is more of a cottage with a stout little tower on top, operated for more than 100 years before becoming automated.

Kerry Park

Tiny **Kerry Park** (W. Highland Dr. and 3rd Ave. W.) isn't much of a park, taking up just a single city block, but it has a heck of a view. Park the car nearby and walk to the **lookout** here, a perfect perch that lets you scan the skyline and spot the Space Needle and, beyond the buildings, the Puget Sound.

WATER SPORTS

Considering Seattle is on an isthmus, getting on the water here is a fine idea. You can rent kayaks and stand-up paddleboards from the **Northwest Outdoor Center** (2100 Westlake Ave. N. #1, 206/281-9694, www.nwoc.com, 10am-6pm Wed.-Sun. Mar. and Oct., 10am-8pm Mon.-Fri., 9am-6pm Sat.-Sun. Apr.-Sept., 10am-6pm Wed.-Fri., 10am-5pm Sat.-Sun. Nov.-Dec., $18-30 per hour) to head out onto **Lake Union**. Drysuits, booties, and wetsuits are also available.

Moss Bay (1001 Fairview Ave. N., 206/682-2031, www.mossbay.co, 11am-6pm Sat.-Sun. Apr. and Oct., 11am-7pm Mon.-Fri., 10am-7pm Sat.-Sun. May and Sept., noon-8pm Mon.-Fri., 10am-8pm Sat., 10am-7pm Sun. June, 11am-8pm Mon.-Fri., 10am-8pm Sat., 10am-7pm Sun. July-Aug., $18-25 per hour) rents out kayaks and stand-up paddleboards, and they also host **tours** ($60 per person, $30 kids) of Lake Union, Portage Bay, and the arboretum area. You must be in a group to take a tour, so if you have a brood of at least 10 (minimum 15 for the kid-friendly tours), this is a solid option for a fun afternoon.

SHOPPING

One of the best baseball clothing shops I've been to, **Ebbets Field Flannels** (108 S. Jackson St., 206/382-7249, www.ebbets.com, 11am-6pm Tues.-Sat.) is a tiny treasure trove of custom-made, old-school jerseys from all kinds of clubs—current major league franchises, long-forgotten minor league teams, Negro League franchises, and regional outfits. You'll find some cool hats, like from the original Pacific Coast League, Seattle Rainiers jerseys, pennants, and photos. And you'll even see an original seat from Ebbets Field, the famed home of the Brooklyn Dodgers.

ACCOMMODATIONS

NEAR T-MOBILE PARK

The closest hotel to T-Mobile Park is **Silver Cloud Hotel** (1046 1st Ave. S., 206/204-9800, www.silvercloud.com, $300-500), a luxury accommodation right across the street with king and queen rooms, some with whirlpool tubs and splendid views of the ballpark. In fact, the rooftop pool offers a look into T-Mobile. The hotel is also home to a restaurant, **Jimmy's on First** (206/204-9700, 6am-midnight daily, under $60), which does the usual breakfast service for guests, plus a standard-fare American lunch and dinner service, but also acts as a pregame martini stop for some folks heading to the Mariners game.

The **Panama Hotel and Tea House** (605 S. Main St., 206/223-9242, www.panamahotelseattle.com, $80-150) is a budget motel-style option with double beds—a great place for the traveler who won't be in their room too often. There's a wealth of history here, plus plenty of care taken to ensure that history is preserved and taught. The Panama has been around since 1910, built by Japanese American architect Sabro Ozasa to house Japanese immigrants coming to Seattle. You'll find furniture dating to the early 20th century throughout the hotel. Be sure to visit the tea house on the ground floor, which carries a wealth of teas and has displays that serve as reminders of one of the

United States' darkest periods: the internment of Japanese Americans during World War II.

OTHER NEIGHBORHOODS

Up in Capitol Hill is the **Bacon Mansion Bed and Breakfast** (959 Broadway E., 26/329-1864, www.baconmansion.com, $150-350), a four-story Tudor house dating to 1909, once used as a guest house for a wealthy Seattleite. Spacious rooms are a mix of Victorian daintiness and quiet elegance. If you opt for the Cabin Room or Iris Room, you'll be sharing a bathroom. Breakfast is continental, and pets are welcome.

For something affordable (relative to its location), next to Downtown in the Belltown section of the city, between the Space Needle and T-Mobile Park, try the **Belltown Inn** (2301 3rd Ave., 206/529-3700, www.belltown-inn.com, $150-300). Comparable to your garden-variety midsized hotel, the Belltown has clean queen and king rooms, a sun deck and terrace, and bicycles available for free—perfect for getting around the city. Pets are allowed, too.

GETTING AROUND

PUBLIC TRANSIT

While it's a limited way to get around, Sound Transit's **Link Light Rail** (www.soundtransit.org, 5am-1am Mon.-Sat., 6am-midnight Sun., $2.25-3.25 per trip) offers a connection from Downtown Seattle to the ballpark and farther south to Sea-Tac Airport. If you're staying near the airport or Downtown, you might want to take this easy and convenient mode of transportation. Buy a ticket at an electronic machine and board when the train arrives.

The stop closest to T-Mobile Park is **Stadium station** (S. Royal Brougham Way and 4th Ave. S.). You'll also want to remember **Westlake station** (4th Ave. and Pine St.), the stop closest to Pike Place Market that also offers a connection to **Monorail Seattle**

(206/905-2620, www.seattlemonorail.com, $3). The monorail rides from Westlake to **Seattle Center** (5th Ave. N. near Thomas St.), offering easy access to the Space Needle and Museum of Pop Culture.

Sound Transit also operates a **bus system** and the **Sounder train** ($3.25-5.75 per ride), an express commuter service that connects Seattle to Tacoma to the south and Everett to the north, riding along the Puget Sound.

TAXI, UBER, AND LYFT

If you want to pick up a taxi, call **Seattle Yellow Cab** (206/622-6500, www.seattleyellowcab.com). Rides start at $2.60, and from there it's $2.70 per mile. From Downtown to Sea-Tac Airport it's $40. You might pay a few dollars less with Uber, depending on when you're taking that ride; the same applies for Lyft. You can download the **SYC app** for Yellow Cab, and it's a good idea—when you're trying to get around Seattle, the more options at your disposal, the better.

CAR

The city in an isthmus with one major north-south highway, **I-5,** which cuts right through the city east of T-Mobile Park. The highway becomes a boundary between Downtown Seattle and neighborhoods like Pike/Pine and Capitol Hill.

Closer to the Puget Sound is **Marginal Way,** or **WA-99.** That drops underground right around T-Mobile Park, then resurfaces just east of the Space Needle and Seattle Center, crossing the Fremont Cut on its way north.

Going west to east is **I-90,** which begins at I-5 at T-Mobile Park. It heads east, crossing Lake Washington on the floating bridges—the Lacey V. Murrow and Homer M. Hadley—before continuing toward Spokane. **I-405** acts as a half-loop from I-5 near Sea-Tac Airport east into Renton, then north into Bellevue before meeting back up with I-5 in the Alderwood area.

On street level, **4th Avenue** runs just east of T-Mobile Park and threads right through

Downtown, then practically runs into the Space Needle to the northwest. **Yesler Way,** going west to east, separates T-Mobile Park and Pioneer Square from Downtown Seattle. **Pike Street** runs through Downtown and heads right into Pike Place Market, and **Denny Way** is the northern boundary for Downtown Seattle, and also acts as the southern boundary of Seattle Center.

TACOMA, WASHINGTON

The historic Pacific Coast League has been around since the early 20th century, and one of its oldest home cities is Tacoma, a quick drive south from Seattle and worth a day trip if you want to see some minor league ball.

Tacoma first saw baseball in the 1900s, but after a long break it returned in 1960, and for years Tacoma switched allegiances. From 1960 to 1965 the Giants kept a team here. Then in 1966 the Cubs came to town, staying for another five seasons. In 1972 the Twins arrived, and they were here for six seasons. Then the Yankees, Indians, and Athletics brought their prospects to town until 1995, when the Mariners finally took over the place. Since then, the Tacoma Rainiers have reigned, winning five division titles and two PCL championships in that time.

The Rainiers are a beloved team in the area. Plenty of popular Mariners players have been through the city, including Alex Rodriguez, Felix Hernandez, and Kyle Seager. Their home park, Cheney Stadium, opened in 1960 and was updated in 2010, making it the best of both the mid-century and modern worlds. With a population of more than 200,000 and its proximity to the home club in Seattle, Tacoma is a perfect triple-A city.

GETTING THERE

You can hop on an **Amtrak train** (www. amtrak.com) to Tacoma from **Seattle** via the **Coast Starlight** route. That route also connects to Portland and the Bay Area. You'll disembark at **Tacoma station** (1001 Puyallup Ave., Tacoma). The station is four miles east of Cheney Stadium, so plan on hailing a ride-share.

Car

Tacoma isn't a suburb of Seattle, but it's a short distance from the Emerald City. To get here, take **I-5 South** for **35 miles,** a drive that could take close to an **hour** if there's traffic.

You could stop in Tacoma on your drive north from San Francisco. You'll follow **I-5 North** for a journey of **780 miles** and about **13 hours** of drive time. You'll cut right through Portland, Oregon, on the way here.

CHENEY STADIUM

For a dose of high-level minor league ball, head down to **Cheney Stadium** (2502 S. Tyler St., www.milb.com/tacoma) to watch the Mariners' triple-A squad, fittingly called the **Tacoma Rainiers.** Built in 1960 in about 100 days, the stadium has always played host to baseball and, since 1995, it's been home for the Mariners' prospects. An extensive renovation in 2010 updated the ballpark for the current day. Its wood exterior fits in well in the Pacific Northwest, and its luxury suites, multiple club options, and solid roster of concession stands make it one of the most modernized ballparks in the minors.

Seating at Cheney Stadium goes from left to right, not right to left, as in most ballparks. The **lowest rows of seating** (sections 101-128), from just beyond the third base bag around foul territory to just beyond the first base bag, are in the **Summit Club,** a private level created for fans with multi-game plans (starting at 24 games), so you may have to know someone to sit here. Those in the Summit Club have access to an all-inclusive bar and snack area (on the third floor of the stadium) and reserved parking. Another all-inclusive area is the **Dugout Club** (100 level), home to a buffet, complimentary beer and wine, and seats in the first couple rows

Fluent Steps by artist Martin Blank at the Museum of Glass in Tacoma

of the park, right against home plate, with in-seat service.

The **reserved level** (sections A-P) is the **general seating** area that wraps around the infield, and tickets here will go for up to $50. In foul left field you'll find **party decks** reserved for groups, and in foul right field is a **grass berm;** tickets for this area go for about $30, typically.

Above the reserved level is the **200 level,** with luxury **suites** and the **MultiCare 1882 Club,** another group area that's set up as a lounge with an all-inclusive buffet.

In left field is the **R Yard,** your basic party bar that's open to the public. You'll find good beer here, with offerings from popular West Coast breweries like **Stone Brewing Co.** and locals like **Silver City Brewery.** Next to R Yard is **Coors Light Landing,** reserved for group party seating. Behind the grass berm is the **MaryBridge Children's Family Pavilion** (10am-6pm daily non-game days, 10am-one hour before gates open game days, also during all games), home to a play structure and miniature ball field. It's open regularly for the community to use, and for games it can be rented out for parties.

Need a bite? Head to **Ivar's Seafood Stand** (first base area) for fried Alaskan cod, **Kidd Valley Burgers and Shakes** (first base area) for burgers and garlic fries, and **Flying Taco Stand** (third base side) for pork carnitas tacos and nachos.

SIGHTS

Walk into, but not *into,* the **Museum of Glass** (1801 Dock St., 253/284-4750, www. museumofglass.org, 10am-5pm Wed.-Sat., noon-5pm Sun., $17, $14 students and seniors, $5 ages 6-12, free ages 5 and under). This glass cone rising up from the ground is by itself a sight to see, but inside you'll find a celebration of glass making—as the Pacific Northwest has played a major role in the evolution of the art—including a feature exhibit on Dale Chihuly, one of the iconic names of the trade. Be sure to walk the glass bridge that connects the museum to Downtown Tacoma—Chihuly assisted the museum in its design and construction.

FOOD

Grab a sandwich at **MSM Deli** (2220 S. 6th Ave., 253/272-4814, 8am-9:30pm Sun.-Thurs., 8am-11:30pm Fri.-Sat., under $20). MSM stands for Magical Sandwich Makers, and that they are, assembling creations like the BBC (beef, bacon, cheddar) and anything with fish. They also specialize in East Coast-style hoagies. Order, hang for a moment, then grab your sandwich from the counter and head out to eat it al fresco on a nice day.

For a little of everything in a fun-sized stop, head to **Tatanka Take-Out** (4915 Pearl St., Ruston, 253/752-8778, 11am-7pm Wed.-Sat., noon-7pm Sun., under $40), which is close to Point Defiance. This place specializes in bison, whether it's in a burger, in a sandwich, in a taco, or on a plate with sides. Don't miss the enormous bison mural, either.

For a beer, there's Tacoma's first craft brewery, **E9 Brewing Co.** (2506 Fawcett Ave., 253/383-7707, www.e9brewingco.com, 3pm-late Wed.-Fri., noon-late Sat.-Sun.). You'll find a variety of ales and a lager or two, with a few IPAs on the list, but you'll also get to try some great fruited sours. There's wood-fired pizza made onsite, too. E9 is part of a brewery district that also includes **7 Seas Brewing** (2101 Jefferson Ave.) and **Black Feet Brewing** (2302 Fawcett Ave.); you can walk to them all.

RECREATION

Point Defiance Park

Out at the Puget Sound, **Point Defiance Park** (5400 N. Pearl St., 253/305-1088, sunrise-sunset daily) is a peninsula that forms a point at the northwestern end of the city. There are some hiking opportunities here. The **outside loop trail** is a 4.3-mile trek that crosses the park's main road, Five Mile Drive, a few times. The **inside loop trail** is concentrated in the interior of the park, as a 3.6-mile walk. The **spine trail** is an out-and-back trail that runs from the park's rhododendron garden through to the Gig Harbor Viewpoint at the tip of Point Defiance.

Park your car near the trail crossings at **Owen Beach,** which has restrooms and a picnic shelter, and allows cookouts at designated grills, swimming, and kayaks. Head to **Owen Beach Kayak Rentals** (noon-6pm

Sat.-Sun. Apr.-May, noon-6pm daily Memorial Day-Labor Day, $19-75) to grab either a single or double, then take it out for a float in the Puget Sound.

ACCOMMODATIONS

Most of the hotels in Tacoma are chains, whether smack Downtown or along I-5 in South Tacoma. One that feels like an independent hotel (though it's owned by a larger hospitality group) is the **Hotel Murano** (1320 Broadway, 253/238-8000, www.hotelmuranotacoma.com, $200-350). Named after Murano glassmaking, the Downtown hotel showcases a wealth of glass art, nodding to the city's status as a glassmaking hub. Rooms at this 26-story spot offer splendid views of the city and have either king or double beds.

GETTING AROUND

The major public transit system in Tacoma is **Pierce Transit** (www.piercetransit.org, $1-2 per ride), which operates a couple dozen **bus** routes. The only train service is the **Sounder train** (www.soundtransit.org, $3.25-5.75 per ride), which can be picked up at the **Tacoma Dome station** (424 E. 25th St.). It heads north to Seattle and, beyond, Everett.

If you're driving, you'll find that **I-5** comes into the city south of Downtown, then sharply turns to head south toward Olympia. **I-705** extends from I-5 and zips into Downtown along the Thea Foss Waterway. The major north-south streets in Downtown include **Pacific Avenue** and **Commerce Street.** Heading west to east, look for **11th Street** and **19th Street.** The **Schuster Parkway** offers a connection from Downtown to Point Defiance Park as it slinks along the Puget Sound.

Essentials

BEFORE THE GAME

SCHEDULES

Let's break down the major league schedule so that you can better plan your baseball road trip, whether you're hoping to visit several parks in one swing or taking a month to two off to check off every box.

Understanding the Schedule

The regular season begins in early April, sometimes in late March, and continues through the summer until late September or early October. During the second or third week of July, baseball takes a break from Monday through Thursday for the All-Star Game. Other than that, from April to September, you can plan on at least one game occurring every day.

Teams typically host three games against an opponent over three consecutive days. During the first two weeks of the season a team may host three games over four days with a built-in day off in case uncertain April weather causes a postponement. Sometimes, teams will host four games against opponents over four consecutive days, either as midweek series that run Monday-Thursday, or as wraparound series that include the weekend (Thursday-Sunday or Friday-Monday). There are also rare two-game series over two consecutive days, and these generally occur midweek (Monday-Tuesday, Tuesday-Wednesday, or Wednesday-Thursday).

Unless there's a quirk in the schedule, all teams play on Friday, Saturday, and Sunday. After the first two weeks of the season, teams almost always play on Tuesday and Wednesday, as well. Monday and Thursday are common off days in baseball, so if you're scheduling out a big road trip, consider planning your longest drives or daylong non-baseball excursions for those days.

Most of the time, teams play at night. The one exception is the Chicago Cubs, who exclusively played day games until lights were installed at Wrigley Field in 1988, but, even with the lights, still maintain strict rules concerning night baseball (every Friday home game is a day game, and you'll rarely see night games on Saturdays and Sundays). From Monday to Saturday, night baseball is king, though there are typically more day games than average on Saturday, and teams will generally pepper in a day game during the week (usually on a Wednesday or Thursday). On Sunday, every team but two—whoever has the nationally televised Sunday night game—plays under the sun.

A typical homestand (when a team hosts games for multiple series in a row) lasts anywhere from 6 to 10 days. You'll see teams stay home for 1-2 weeks, then hit the road for 1-2 weeks, and on and on until the season's end.

If you're hoping to catch games at both Yankee Stadium and Citi Field while in New York, you won't be able to do it on a typical weekend trip of Friday to Sunday. Two teams in the same city or market will almost never be home at the same time. Be sure to comb the schedule for, say, a Sunday when one team is wrapping up a homestand, and a Monday when the other team is just beginning theirs. The areas affected by this are New York (Yankees, Mets), Los Angeles (Angels, Dodgers), Chicago (White Sox, Cubs), San Francisco Bay Area (Athletics, Giants), and the DMV (Orioles, Nationals).

Weather

When you're planning a big road trip, you'll need to take weather into account. I drove from New York to Chicago, then to Denver, before coming back around to Kansas City, St. Louis, and Cincinnati, between late May and early June one year. While I left New York on a 70°F afternoon with abundant sunshine, I sat in a 35°F chill at Wrigley Field a few nights later, and a week after that I was driving past tornado warnings in Missouri before searching for shade on a 95°F evening in St. Louis.

All this to say that if you're road tripping in summer, bring plenty of sunscreen and a hat, and plan to take breaks and relax. No matter when you're traveling, bring gear for all weather situations: a rain jacket, warm-weather clothes, and an umbrella. Don't just

CORONAVIRUS AND BASEBALL

The coronavirus pandemic had a significant impact on the United States, including the cities covered in this guide. In response to the coronavirus, the 2020 season of Major League Baseball was abbreviated. Fans were not allowed to attend games; teams played games in empty stadiums. Additionally, the standard National League and American League schedules were adjusted to allow teams to play only those in close geographic proximity. At the time of writing in December 2020, the situation was constantly evolving, but when fans are able to attend games again, stadiums will likely require face masks and social distancing.

For some understanding of what to expect once fans are permitted to attend games, look to the 2020 World Series, played at Arlington's Globe Life Field. Along with requiring face masks and social distancing, Major League Baseball had fans sit in "pods" of four people each. When buying a ticket for a World Series game, you had to buy a pack of four tickets; those seats were separate from other pods to ensure social distancing.

Now more than ever, Moon encourages its readers to be courteous and ethical in their travel. We ask travelers to be respectful and mindful of the evolving situation in their chosen destination when planning their trip.

BEFORE YOU GO

- Check local websites for **local restrictions** and the **overall health status** of the destination and your point of origin. If you're traveling to or from an area that is currently a COVID-19 hotspot, you may want to reconsider your trip.
- Check **Major League Baseball's website** (www.mlb.com) and individual team sites for updates and guidance on attending games in person. Consider calling the team's guest services number if you have questions about social distancing protocols, face mask requirements, or other health-related protocols.
- If possible, take a **coronavirus test** with enough time to receive your results before your departure. Some cities or states may require a negative test result before arrival, along with other tests and potentially a self-quarantine period, once you've arrived. Check local requirements and factor these into your plans.
- If you plan to fly, check with your airline and the **CDC** (www.cdc.gov) for updated **travel requirements.** Some airlines may be taking more steps than others to help you travel safely, such as limited occupancy. Check each carrier's website for more information before buying your ticket, and consider a very early or very late flight, to limit exposure to other people. Flights may be more infrequent, with increased cancellations.
- Check the website of any venues you wish to patronize to confirm that they're open, if their hours have been adjusted, and to learn about any specific visitation requirements, such as **mandatory reservations** or **limited occupancy.**
- Pack **hand sanitizer,** a **thermometer,** and plenty of **face masks.** Consider packing **snacks, a refillable water bottle,** or even a **cooler** to limit the number of stops along your route. Be prepared for possible closures and reduced services over the course of your travels.
- **Assess the risk** of entering crowded spaces, joining tours, and taking public transit.
- Expect **general disruptions.** Events may be postponed or cancelled, and some tours and venues may require reservations, enforce limits on the number of guests, be operating during different hours than the ones listed, or be closed entirely.

pack t-shirts and shorts, as much as you want to believe it'll all work out.

I've been lucky that rain has rarely ever postponed a game I've attended, but it can and will happen. If you're at a game that gets postponed, and you know you won't be returning to that ballpark any time soon, chat with a customer service representative to see if there's another way you can get compensated. Maybe you can get a waiver for a ballpark tour, or perhaps you can cash in your rainout ticket well into the future.

If you're at a game and rain is in the forecast, the teams still may try to play through, especially if it's later in the season and the opponents won't be able to play each other again. If you have the time, you might get to sit in the ballpark for four, five, or six hours while teams wait out the rain. That's when weird baseball sets in (people trying to jump onto the field, mascots behaving badly), and that can be the most fun of all.

Important Dates

The season typically begins around **April 1.** The season pauses around the **second** or **third week of July** for the **four-day All-Star break,** then it ends sometime around **September 30.** The postseason begins almost immediately after that, lasting until about **October 31.**

Within the season are some key dates. All teams observe **Mother's Day, Memorial Day, Father's Day, Independence Day,** and **Labor Day,** sometimes with special festivities before games. In recent years, the days are also honored with special uniform sets designed by Major League Baseball. Over the last several years, teams have also observed **September 11** with special uniforms or caps.

On April 15, Major League Baseball celebrates **Jackie Robinson Day,** which commemorates the day the Hall of Famer broke the league's color barrier in 1947. On this day, all players and umpires wear number 42, the number Robinson wore on his jersey. On years in which teams are off for Jackie Robinson Day, the celebration is also observed the following day.

Around this time of year, Massachusetts observes **Patriots' Day** (third Mon. in Apr.). This day commemorates the Battles of Lexington and Concord and the Battle of Menotomy, which began the American Revolutionary War. It's a holiday for Boston, but not for the Red Sox, who play a home game each year on this day. It's also the day marking the running of the Boston Marathon, an event that further closes down the city. The marathon route is just past Fenway Park, and the Red Sox used to schedule their game so that once it ended, fans could spill onto the streets to watch the racers pass by. But since 2007 the Sox have moved up the game so that it causes less of a human traffic jam. On Patriots' Day, first pitch at Fenway is usually between 9:30am and 10am. You know what that means? Kegs and eggs!

July 1 is a big day in Toronto, for that's **Canada Day,** which marks the anniversary of the 1867 Constitution Act that united the colonies of the Province of Canada, Nova Scotia, and New Brunswick into one dominion. The Blue Jays typically play at home on this day, hosting festivities before first pitch while also usually rocking a red jersey.

TICKETS

Pricing

It used to be that seats in the stadium cost a set price, and that you chose from lower level, upper level, and the bleachers. But in recent years major league clubs have become savvier (or more cutthroat) when it comes to how they sell tickets throughout the season. There are two major developments in ticket pricing: the **subdivision of seating areas** as a way to create tiers of pricing within levels at a ballpark and **dynamic pricing,** which can maximize a club's profits by pinpointing popular games on the calendar and charging more money for those tickets.

First, there's the propagation of seating areas. In old Riverfront Stadium/Cinergy Field in Cincinnati, there were field boxes, plaza boxes, club boxes, loge boxes, and loge reserved. These seating levels were consistently priced at the same value around the entire bowl. A loge reserved seat behind home plate cost the same as a loge reserved seat in deep left field. But teams got wise, realizing that they could charge more money for seating areas with better views or closer proximity to the field.

Today, at Cincinnati's Great American Ball Park, the top level is split between lower view level, view level, upper view level, and value view. Under this model, a seat in the first

OTHER RECOMMENDED ROUTES

Who says you have to stick to the plan? The routes outlined in this guide aren't the only way to do a baseball road trip. Here are a few more that you might want to attempt.

BOSTON TO TORONTO
Distance: 575 miles
Drive time: 9.5 hours

You'll start in **Boston** at one of baseball's oldest venues, **Fenway Park,** before heading west on I-90 through Albany, en route to **Toronto,** one of the newer major league cities, whose **Rogers Centre** was dubbed a marvel of contemporary architecture when it opened in 1989.

But the real history lesson will come about four hours into the drive. In Albany, merge onto I-88 West and take that to NY-10 North and NY-165 West toward **Cooperstown.** Spend two days exploring this quaint town and visiting the **National Baseball Hall of Fame and Museum.**

If you're a go-getter, you could do this trip in **four days.** I recommend making it a full **week** by expanding your stays in both Beantown and Hogtown. Think about making this trip in **late May** or **June,** just as the weather is turning for the better in the Northeast, and just before the crowds really pack Cooperstown during the summer.

MINNEAPOLIS TO CHICAGO
Distance: 430 miles
Drive time: 6.5 hours

Here's an easy way to knock out four ballparks at once. Start in **Minneapolis,** a green city that's home to **Target Field** and Twins baseball. Then drive I-94 East toward Madison, Wisconsin, continuing into **Milwaukee** for a Brewers tilt at **American Family Field.** Continue on I-94 East to **Chicago.** Here, the trick is to try and catch both the **Cubs** and **White Sox** at home.

You can visit all four stadiums in a **week**—ensuring two days in each city—as long as you plan the Chicago leg correctly by getting to both Wrigley Field and Guaranteed Rate Park. Take this trip in **mid-summer.** Even a visit to these northern cities in May or June can bring chilly temperatures and torrential rain.

ST. LOUIS TO DENVER
Distance: 850 miles
Drive time: 12.5 hours

Want to see some geographic variation? Start at **Busch Stadium** in **St. Louis,** home to the Cardinals and just blocks from the Mississippi River and the Gateway Arch. Continue your sojourn westward on I-70. After close to four hours you'll be clear across Missouri and in **Kansas City** to catch a Royals game at **Kauffman Stadium.** (The Cards and Royals sometimes play at home at the same time, so you won't have to maneuver your plans too much to make this work.)

Then make the straight drive through the flatlands of Kansas before beginning your climb through the mountainous wonderland of Colorado. I-70 runs right into **Denver,** where you'll catch a Rockies game at **Coors Field** to finish your trip. Just remember to give yourself a day to adjust to the elevation.

I recommend a minimum of **six days** for this voyage, with two days in Denver, two days for driving, and one day each in St. Louis and Kansas City. St. Louis and Kansas City can get really hot during the middle of summer, and Denver's quick-changing weather is a challenge to predict, so I recommend taking the trip anywhere between **mid-May** and **mid-June,** or in **September.**

LOS ANGELES TO PHOENIX
Distance: 475 miles
Drive time: 7.5 hours

Technically, there's an easy way to get from Los Angeles to Phoenix, and it's via I-10 East (flying right past Joshua Tree National Park along the way), but you won't want to miss the opportunity to see the Padres in sunny San Diego. Starting in **Los Angeles,** catch a **Dodgers** or **Angels** game (or both, if you can plan your dates around a time when the teams have adjacent homestands). Head south on I-5 for about two hours (if traffic is good) to **San Diego** and watch a contest at **Petco Park.** Then it's a 5.5-hour trip through the desert to **Phoenix,** primarily via I-8 East.

Plan on doing this trip over **four days** if you're in a rush. The better play is to extend this trip into a **weeklong** vacation. Go early in the season, as otherwise it'll be hot, hot, hot.

couple of rows of a section is more expensive than a seat in the middle of the section, which is more expensive than a seat at the top of the section, which is more expensive than a seat way out in left field. At other parks, the area around home plate is more expensive than the area by the bases, which is more expensive than shallow outfield, which is more expensive than the outfield corners. The closer you sit to the action, the more you're bound to pay.

Then there's dynamic pricing, which can dramatically affect your road trip plans because of the squeeze you'll feel in your wallet. How it works: A ticket for section 110, row L, seat 11 on Friday will be differently priced than a ticket for the same seat on Saturday, and that'll cost a different amount from a ticket for the same seat next Wednesday. Teams price games individually, dependent on a number of factors, among them the quality of an opponent and its popularity with fans (both local and traveling), the presence of a special giveaway or theme night, and the day of the week and time of day of the game.

Let's imagine we're looking at the Pittsburgh Pirates schedule and the ticket prices for section 110, row L, seat 11 at PNC Park over a week span. These aren't exact prices; rather, it's the difference across days that we're looking at:

- Tuesday, 7:05 pm vs. Milwaukee: $55
- Wednesday, 7:05 pm vs. Milwaukee, Star Wars–themed giveaway: $60
- Thursday, 1:35 pm vs. Milwaukee: $48
- Friday, 7:05 pm vs. Boston, fireworks night: $78
- Saturday, 7:05 pm vs. Boston, beach towel giveaway: $70
- Sunday, 1:35 pm vs. Boston, bobblehead giveaway: $78

Your best bet is one of those midweek games without a giveaway, and that's the case for just about every team in the league. It's hard to anticipate which games might be more expensive, but generally, weekend games are higher priced, as are fireworks

nights, opening day, and other special events. As for the teams that draw crowds? Usually you can count on the Red Sox, Dodgers, Cubs, and Yankees to drive up prices. Natural rivals (say the Cardinals for the Cubs) and teams within a close proximity (say the Phillies for the Orioles) will also mean pricier tickets.

Buying Tickets

Every major league team sells tickets directly via an official website, by phone, and from their ticket window at the stadium. To ensure the quickest and most secure acquisition of tickets, buying directly from the team is the best way to go. That said, it isn't always the most affordable way to do it.

Major League Baseball partners with **StubHub** (a ticket exchange and resale site) as its official fan-to-fan marketplace. What that means is teams will move tickets to StubHub at a discounted price in exchange for a cut of the profit. It also means that teams encourage fans to use StubHub to sell and buy their tickets, so it's also the most robust marketplace for tickets. It's good to an extent: The best way to use the service is very close to first pitch when prices come down to their cheapest values. You'll have to pay additional fees on top of the ticket price, but chances are you can find a deal just before the game begins. An added benefit: With the StubHub app on your phone you can download your ticket and scan it at any ballpark entry gate.

You'll want to also check out other resale sites like **SeatGeek, VividSeats,** and **TickPick,** which don't have the same relationship with Major League Baseball and thus are prone to wilder swings in ticket prices. With these sites, be aware of possible scams. My advice is to always go for the digital ticket option so it comes to you immediately after purchasing. Always purchase your ticket on a secure site. There are a few smaller ticket brokers that serve single cities (like AceTicket in Boston). These companies can be the best option in some cases, since they're less known by other visitors.

On game day, in the area around the stadium, you'll inevitably encounter scalpers on the street trying to sell tickets (and also trying to buy yours). Before taking the risk of buying from a street scalper, consider some alternative options. First, if a team allows tailgating, start by talking to fans partying in the parking lot. It's possible someone has an extra ticket and is willing to sell it for face value; if not, there's a chance that person might know someone who is trying to get rid of a ticket.

If that doesn't work, you could opt for walking around the venue with your finger raised (noting how many tickets you need). You could also ask if anyone has an extra ticket to sell. I'd rather buy a ticket from someone in team colors who's looking like they're heading into the park.

Your last resort should be buying from a scalper. Read up on the laws regarding scalping in the state you're visiting, as some states like Texas and Washington are very cool with the practice without any regulation, while other states like New York are a little tougher on it. Always proceed with caution. If you're in a place where street reselling is legal, it's a good idea to know the face value of the ticket. Always negotiate, and remember, the closer you are to first pitch, the better the deal you can get.

If you're worried about accidentally buying a fake ticket, my advice is to examine the ticket carefully before handing over money—be sure it's for the right date and that it resembles a common ticket with a barcode. Of course, you won't know for sure whether it's a real ticket until you get to the gate, but that's the risk.

WHERE TO SIT

Where you sit at a baseball game is all a matter of personal preference. Want to be baking in the **sunshine**? You should grab a seat in the outfield. Want to avoid the sun at all costs? At just about every park, a seat under the overhang in the back of the lower level will help, and typically, the third-base side seats get **shade** first (though every park is different). Want to hang out with twenty- and thirtysomethings chatting casually and sipping beer? Every park now has at least

one **bar** facing the field of play, usually on a high perch somewhere in the outfield. These places are **social hubs,** and if you want to meet people, they're your spots.

For families, the highest level of seating at the park is the best deal, and that will probably never change. Most parks have reserved at least one (sometimes three or four) sections as **family seating areas,** which essentially means alcohol is prohibited. Every park also has a child-friendly **play area,** most including a miniature baseball field where tiny Mike Trouts can tee off against some helpless intern. The majority of these play areas include televisions, so parents don't miss the on-field action. A few even have bars; parents need juice, too, you know.

Every park has **club** and **suite** seating, and often a good chunk of these sections are reserved well in advance. Sometimes these tickets are impossible to snag. But if I'm at a venue for the first time, the last thing I want to do for nine innings is sit in a temperature controlled, catered box. I like moving around, eating and drinking from wherever looks good, checking out multiple vantage points, and hopefully meeting some fans along the way. So if you're a baseball or ballpark junkie, my suggestion is always to snag really cheap tickets, then spend much of the game trekking about the stadium.

That said, if you want to sit for a few innings with a **good view,** you'll never go wrong opting for the first row or two of the **second deck,** somewhere near **home plate.** A ticket in this area is generally more affordable than the average seat, plus you'll likely have an unencumbered view of the entire game, as well as the outfield and the backdrop beyond. This area is where I soak in a ballpark for all its beauty.

Of course, there are iconic seating areas that may tempt you. For example, sitting in a **Monster Seat** at **Fenway Park** (on top of the green left field wall known as the Green Monster) could be awesome, right? If it's your first time at Fenway, I actually recommend grabbing one of the seats in the **first level,** somewhere on the first-base side. This is the quintessential Boston experience: being

ATTENDING THE ALL-STAR GAME

I recommend going to an **MLB All-Star Game** (www.mlb.com/all-star) at some point in your life. Yes, tickets are expensive, but there is something incredible about seeing many of baseball's best players on the same field, playing a nine-inning game. Here's what you should know about the game known as "the midsummer classic."

- **It usually occurs during the second week of July.** Baseball takes a prolonged break around the middle of the season for the game. Starting players are voted into the game by fans earlier in the season. Reserve players and pitchers are selected either by players across the league or by the selected managers for the game (the previous season's league champion skippers).

- **The venue always changes.** Major League Baseball tries to ensure every team hosts a game every 25-35 years, though there are exceptions. If a team debuts a new ballpark, you're bound to see the All-Star Game there within the first few seasons. A team may campaign to host for a notable anniversary; for example, the White Sox hosted the game for its 50-year anniversary because they held the very first one.

- **Tickets are costly, though not out of reach.** In recent years, the average ticket to the game has cost around $120, though some years it's a lot more. If the game is held in a major city, plan on shelling out more than $200 per ticket.

- **There are other events to experience.** Leading up to the game are the All-Star Futures Game, pitting a squad of U.S.-born prospects against a team of prospects representing other nations; the All-Star Legends and Celebrity Softball Game, in which former baseball players and assorted celebrities mix together in teams and go head-to-head; and the Home Run Derby, a popular event in which power hitters attempt to swat as many balls over the fence as possible. Derby tickets can go as low as $10, but can also get really high (we're talking more than $100 each) on the resale market. Tickets for the other events are much easier to come by and are pretty cheap. There's also the MLB All-Star FanFest, which is typically held in a convention center and features a virtual home run derby and speed pitch, autograph sessions, merchandise and collectible sales, games at a kid-friendly miniature ballpark, and much more.

packed in with tens of thousands of fans with a clear view of the Monster and the Citgo sign looming above.

The **bleacher seats** at **Wrigley Field** are great for socializing, but maybe you'd rather sit around the **infield** with a view of the incredible ivy backdrop. You've probably heard about the **Western Metal Supply Co. building** at **Petco Park.** Well, seats here are tough to get and the public bar there doesn't have great beer options. I'd much rather hop around the park and sip the local craft options. And maybe you want to take a dip in the **pool at Chase Field.** That's a highly sought-after group seating area, so you'll need to plan a year ahead and have a lot of other people signed up to go with you.

Here are some of my suggestions for seats to seek out:

- Spend time in the **bleachers** at **Progressive Field** in Cleveland, especially to hear the drum of super-fan John Adams.

- Get seats with a **view of right field** at **Oracle Park** in San Francisco, to take in the bay and McCovey Cove in the background.

- Get seats with a **view of center field** at **PNC Park,** because its waterside backdrop is the best in the game.

- **Kauffman Stadium** and **Dodger Stadium** are gorgeous and somewhat similar parks that look great from **home**

plate. At Kauffman, though, consider hanging out at an **outfield bar** to best enjoy the park's cool water feature.

- Get as **close to the game** as you can at **Tropicana Field, Miller Park, Globe Life Field, Marlins Park,** and **Minute Maid Park.** Indoor stadiums can feel too cavernous when high up, but these ballparks can all feel intimate when you're in those **first several rows.**

AT THE GAME

WHAT TO BRING (AND WHAT NOT TO BRING)

You can bring a **bag** measuring no more than 16 by 16 by 8 inches to a ballpark. If you're with family and bringing **food** for little ones (or you have a baby and need to bring supplies), a bag is something you'll need, because you'll be spending a few hours in a rather stationary spot. If you don't have a dire need for a bag, though, don't bring one. If you want to stow merchandise you bought from the team store, some parks may have bags with strings that can act like shoulder straps.

A number of parks still allow **outside food,** but it must be wrapped in single servings and fit in a **soft-sided cooler.** As for beverages, only **water bottles** may be allowed in a park (some places don't even allow those), though kids might be able to get through with a **juice box.**

If you want to take pictures, most parks allow **DSLR cameras,** but no tripods. Keep all those specialty lenses at home, too.

If your favorite team has taken every game of its current series and is eyeing a **sweep,** you may feel inclined to bring a **broom,** a tradition as old as time. Well, think twice – most venues these days take your brooms away. **Banners** and **signs** are typically fine, but anything vulgar or offensive will be confiscated. You can still bring a **baseball glove,** if you're hoping to snag a foul ball,

but you only get on SportsCenter if you make a bare-handed catch, and preferably while holding a beer.

When arriving, you'll be asked to pass through a **metal detector,** and guards may either wave a detector around you or lightly pat down your pockets. Remember to pack light and remove all belongings from those pockets when coming in. Have your **ticket** ready, whether it's on paper (a rarity these days) or on your phone as a barcode.

If you want to keep things to a bare minimum, bring just a **credit or debit card** (most parks are transitioning to cashless payments), and your **phone** to take photos. Remember to **charge your phone** before heading to the ballpark. While some venues have **charging stations,** do you really want to spend a full inning getting your battery from 2 percent to 35 percent?

For more information on what specific ballparks allow and prohibit, see *Know Before You Go* in each chapter.

FAN CONDUCT

Back in the day, at Philadelphia's long-gone Veterans Stadium, the team would play a video of a god-like being explaining the venue's ground rules. Among them: No interfering with the play on the field, no vulgarity, no fighting, no lewdness and drunkenness, and no instigating. All of these rules still apply today—and not just in Philadelphia.

Maybe at some point in your life you thought "It would be cool to run onto the field, maybe during a rain delay!" No, it's not cool. At best you'll be arrested and fined. At worst, you're a lifetime meme, preserved forever on the internet.

If you drive yourself to the park, don't drink and drive. Designate a sober driver or plan on using public transit or ride-shares.

If you happen to snag a foul ball, look for the nearest school-age kid and hand over that memento. Don't be the person that shuns a little one; be generous. Along those lines, if a foul ball is coming your way but not directly at you, don't go diving for it. If there's literally nobody in your section when it arrives, go nuts, get on TV, and really trip over everything to grab that ball. Otherwise, remember: It's just a baseball.

Listen to the ushers and ballpark staff members. If you have to wait until a plate appearance ends to head back to your seat, then wait patiently. You can always spark up a conversation with the usher while you wait. In fact, if you're walking around the park and not tethered to one chair, chatting with an usher can sometimes lead to getting a really good seat. I know because I've done it. If attendance isn't very high, or if the game is a blowout, chances are strong that you'll be able to upgrade—just be kind and patient.

Being the rival fan at a park can be a really great experience. I've worn Phillies gear at Citi Field, at Yankee Stadium and at Fenway Park. In almost all of those situations, ushers or fans have engaged me in conversation just to know why I was there. Almost always, that conversation leads to sharing some great memories, and in rare cases, a beer or a friendship. Open yourself up to the ballpark experience and you never know what could happen.

BUDGETING TIPS

In the 21st century, attending major league baseball games is not for those with thin wallets. These experiences are pricey. Say you're driving to the game and want to park at a team lot: that's $20 on average. The ticket to the game, for a decent seat, will cost about $40. Want one beer and one hot dog? That's another $20. By this point, you've spent at least $80—now imagine bringing kids.

There are ways to cut these costs. You will have to pay for tickets, but solo travelers and those who want to simply hang out at the park may opt for **standing-room-only tickets** (typically $10-20). Most parks have them, even if the tickets are reserved for a bar porch where you're standing among twenty-somethings. You can always leave the bar and walk around. If you're paying for kids, as well, consider sitting at the **highest level** of the ballpark. You'll probably be running around the park for half the game, maybe

spending time at the kids' play area. You may even leave early. Do you really need those $80 first-level seats for three innings?

Don't worry about waiting until the **last minute** to buy tickets. **Ticket brokerage sites** like **StubHub,** which partners with MLB, might have really **cheap tickets just before first pitch.** You can also try the ticket windows and ask if there are any inexpensive seats available; it's possible some reserved seats were given back to the office last minute. Some teams hold **lotteries** on the morning of the game for random seats, or they may have a deal with a publication, radio station, or vendor in town where you can buy discounted tickets in the few hours before the game.

When getting to the game, consider not driving. You won't have to deal directly with traffic and it can be so much cheaper if you aren't paying for **parking.** More than a few major league cities have sophisticated **public transportation** systems with stations at or near ballparks. **Ride-sharing** is your friend, too. In some cities, you can hop on a city-owned **bicycle** and park near the venue, which should save you at least $10-15.

If you're driving, always try to park away from the stadium to save money. I usually give myself a five- or six-block distance from the park (about a **half-mile** minimum) when seeking **street parking,** and the most I usually pay is about $5.

Some ballparks permit **outside food** and **beverages,** so if you're really there just for the game, or if you're bringing kids and would rather not spend $200 on food alone, packing a small **picnic** is a solid idea. But if you want the best food and beer a park can offer, here's my suggestion: Have one beer at the game (the taller the better, because a 24-ounce ale, let's say, is usually a better value than a 16-ounce beverage), and one food item—so make it count. The best tip I can give you on ballpark food is to do your research—use this guide, and check with the team's website for info on its food offerings. The last thing you want to do is feverishly scramble to find those tater-tot nachos, only to settle for something overpriced and not as

MAJOR TEAM RIVALRIES

Here's my list of the top five rivalries in baseball:

BOSTON RED SOX VERSUS NEW YORK YANKEES
It's hard to top this one. The Sox and Yanks have disliked each other for more than 100 years, in a battle that has included the sale of Babe Ruth, Bucky "Bleeping" Dent's home run in a one-game playoff in 1978, the epic 2003 American League Championship Series, the incredible Boston comeback of 2004, and a fight between Hall of Fame pitcher Pedro Martinez and coach Don Zimmer.

LOS ANGELES DODGERS VERSUS SAN FRANCISCO GIANTS
This rivalry has spanned the nation, starting when both clubs shared space as New York City's National League clubs. Both teams headed west in the 1950s, taking their feud with them in the process. The Dodgers, representing the flash and pizzazz of L.A., have had a longer run of success, but the Giants, more of a working man's club, more recently won the big one… and three times, at that. Sadly, there has been violent incidents between fans in the recent past, though tensions seem to have cooled somewhat.

CHICAGO CUBS VERSUS ST. LOUIS CARDINALS
While it's the National League's lovable losers versus its most decorated franchise, this enduring rivalry is as much about success as it is about territory. In the heyday of radio, both teams tried hard to expand their fanbases, so across the Midwest you'll see clear dividing lines between Cubs fans and Cardinals fans, primarily depending on what broadcast those folks were able to tune into back in the day.

NEW YORK METS VERSUS PHILADELPHIA PHILLIES
In every sport, New York City and Philadelphia are rivals. It goes like this: New York gets all the headlines, and Philly has to punch up to get what they believe is rightfully theirs. The Mets and Phillies weren't good at the same time until 2007, when the former choked historically and the latter played well enough to win the division on the last day. That type of fall-on-your-face sadness has been a symbol for this feud between vocal East Coast fanbases.

HOUSTON ASTROS VERSUS NEW YORK YANKEES
Before 2013 there would've never been a reason for these two to dislike each other, but when the 'Stros moved to the American League and became good, things escalated. First were the playoff battles (that the Astros have won every time), and then came the 2017-18 sign-stealing controversy that enraged New Yorkers against the Bayou City club and its proud fanbase.

good. Knowing where those tater-tot nachos are sold is key, so you can get them right when you enter the park. Then you'll be full and happy the rest of the game.

My most important tip for is to create an actual budget. Plan one for each ballpark and city, and try to save some dough when it makes sense. For instance, when I road tripped from New York to Denver and back, I opted to stay in motels 1-2 hours away from each major league city to save money. Instead of the MGM Grand in Detroit, it was the Red Roof Inn in Kalamazoo. This method could work for you, but you might find other ways to pinch pennies that fit with your style of traveling.

I also encourage you to splurge when it's feasible and worthwhile. While I spent most nights at chain motels, I allowed myself a more expensive hotel right in Wrigleyville after a Cubs game. This way, I could walk back from the park, bar hop, and join in the festive atmosphere after the game.

You'll also want to budget for the time spent outside the ballpark. Instead of dining in a restaurant for every meal, consider snagging some bananas and yogurt cups from the hotel, and run by a local grocer for a grab-and-go salad. For every three days in a city, choose one museum to visit, not three. Walk and use public transportation as much as possible.

PARKING

Every major league team operates several **official parking lots.** Essentially, that means you'll pay at least $15 (usually $20 and higher), but you're assured your vehicle is kept in a guarded lot during the game. Personally, I don't mind parking at least a half-mile away and paying considerably less. Luckily, I've never had an issue with my vehicle in the hundreds of times I've attended a baseball game.

Privately owned lots pepper every city, and if they're close enough to a ballpark they'll mark up prices on game days. Try to set yourself a limit for what you'll pay to park—mine is typically $10, and sometimes private lots will cost just that. I try to find lots that don't have **time limits,** because if a game goes extra innings, I don't want to be nervously checking my phone to see if it's time to skedaddle. Sometimes I'll opt to park on the street, but that's only if I know for sure parking is allowed, and if I can walk back to my car in reasonable brightness with a few other people around me.

ROAD RULES

MAJOR HIGHWAYS

On the East Coast, the big highway is **I-95,** running from Maine all the way to Florida, connecting the major metropolitan areas of Boston, New York, Philadelphia, Baltimore, and Washington DC. In the Southeast, **I-75** connects Atlanta to Tampa and then Miami. In the Midwest, **I-76** gets from Pittsburgh to just outside Cleveland, while **I-90** and I-75 connect that city to Detroit. The trip to Toronto is best made on **ON-401** from Detroit.

In the Great Lakes, take **I-94** from Milwaukee to Chicago, then **I-55** down to St. Louis. From there, it's **I-64** and **I-71** to Cincinnati. From Minneapolis to Kansas City to Dallas, take **I-35** south, but then shift to **I-45** down to Houston. The Rocky Mountains are trickier, but the easiest way from Denver to

Phoenix is via **I-25** south to Albuquerque and **I-40,** which you take west to **I-17** South. And out west, **I-5** can get you from Seattle on down to San Diego, though you'll need to merge onto **I-580** if you want to visit Oakland and San Francisco.

Going east to west, important highways that span the country include **I-90** (connecting Boston to Seattle through Chicago), **I-80** (connecting the New York area to the Bay Area through Chicago), **I-70** (connecting Washington DC to Denver through St. Louis and Kansas City), **I-40** (connecting the Charlotte, NC, area to the Los Angeles area), and **I-10** (connecting Jacksonville, FL, to Los Angeles through Houston and Phoenix).

HIGHWAY SAFETY

Always observe **state speed limits** when driving. Outside of metropolitan areas, some U.S. highways can max out at **75-80 mph,** especially in the central part of the country. You'll see many **70 mph** speed limits outside Midwestern cities like Detroit and Minneapolis, but highways don't creep above **65 mph** in the northeast and in parts of New England. In New York, New Jersey, Connecticut, and Massachusetts, 65 mph is the rule. On the West Coast, you'll be able to cruise to 70 mph for some stretches.

Stay in the center lanes when cruising, using the left lane as a **passing-only** route and the right lane as an exit route. Limit passing to keep the highway flow constant, and always use your **turn signals.** Folks in the East Coast use their signals constantly, while in Texas, it's more like extra credit. Be alert and cautious. If you're driving long distances, be sure to **stop every 90-180 minutes** to stretch your legs, take a bathroom break, grab a bite to eat, and fill your water bottle. If you ever feel **sleepy** while driving, pull over at the safest possible place, preferably a rest stop, convenience store, or some other place to recharge.

It's easy to punch in an address on your GPS and just go, but consider planning your route ahead of time on a **paper map.** This will give you an added bit of information and familiarity with your surroundings. I've taken many a road trip with my trusty **road atlas** by my side.

WEATHER CONSIDERATIONS

The baseball season lasts from April to September, often with games in late March and early October. How you plan for weather conditions depends completely on when and where you're visiting specific cities. Always bring **sunscreen** and an **umbrella,** because you never know what you'll get into when on the road.

Along the Eastern Seaboard, **between Boston and Washington DC,** expect **cold** starts to the season, **hot** and **sweaty** Julys and Augusts, and **cooler** fall days at the end of the campaign. The best time to go is May, June, or early to mid-September.

The **Florida** cities and **Atlanta** are **hot** much of the time. The good news for Miami and Tampa Bay is those teams play in **domes,** so you can visit any time. With Atlanta, consider an early- or late-season trip. From late summer into early fall is **hurricane season** in Florida.

In the **Midwest** and **Great Lakes regions,** including **Toronto,** mid-summer isn't too bad for visiting, though you should expect some **hot** and **humid** temperatures with abundant **sunshine.** I've found that the sweet spot in cities like Chicago, Cleveland, and Minneapolis are in mid- to late June and from late August to early September. Kansas City, St. Louis, and Cincinnati are as much part of the South as they are the Midwest when it comes to climate, so avoid going in deep summer. Instead, consider a visit in early May or anytime in September. **Tornado season** spans from late spring to early summer.

Both **Texas** teams have **retractable roofs,** so there's no need to fret those game experiences, but from mid-May to October, it's disgustingly **hot,** especially in Houston. The Dallas area is more prone to **tornadoes** in late spring and early summer, while Houston has been hit with **hurricanes** between August and October. Going to Texas in April is the best bet—the weather can be immaculate at this time of year.

In the **Southwest,** consider visiting in April or September; it's just too dang **hot** in the summer. **Denver** is on a wacky island—April, May, and September are **volatile,** but summer is just fine for visiting.

On the **West Coast,** you can visit San Diego whenever the heck you want, Los Angeles is just fine most of the year, the San Francisco Bay Area is splendid between May and August, and Seattle shines in mid-summer. So the best time to visit this area is July or August.

FUEL

You really won't have to worry about a lack of **gas stations** on this trip. There are abundant gas stations across the country's major routes. The tricky part comes when you're driving on state and county routes. My rule of thumb: Before exiting an interstate highway to take a detour on a scenic route, ensure that you have a **full tank of gas.**

BICYCLES

Most major league ballparks reserve space at the venue for **bicycle parking.** You should check with each team before you head out to ensure there is sufficient parking. A select few parks are ahead of the curve and have embraced bicycle travel as a method of getting to the park by installing **hundreds of racks** and offering **valet services** that will keep your bike safe.

PUBLIC TRANSPORTATION

Every major league city has **public transportation** in the form of a **bus system,** but some sites are more sophisticated than others. The bigger cities with older infrastructures, like New York, Toronto, Los Angeles, Chicago, Philadelphia, Washington DC, San Francisco, and Oakland, have **rail systems** that make travel a bit easier. I wholeheartedly recommend using these options whenever available. New York has the best public transit system in North America, while Chicago, Toronto, and the San Francisco Bay Area also rank especially high.

Buses can be useful, but avoid situations where you're taking multiple buses, when you can instead hop in one **ride-sharing vehicle.** My rule of thumb: If the method takes more than 45 minutes to get somewhere that's less than 25 miles away, it's not worth it—try something else.

TIPS FOR TRAVELERS

VISAS AND OFFICIALDOM

Coming into America? You'll need a **passport** and you may also need to present a **visa.** The U.S. government's **Visa Waiver Program** allows tourists from many countries to visit for up to 90 days without a visa. To check if your country is on the list go to http://travel.state.gov. To qualify, you must apply online with the **Electronic System for Travel Authorization** (www.cbp.gov) and hold a return plane or cruise ticket to your country of origin dated less than 90 days from your date of entry. Holders of **Canadian passports** don't need visas or visa waivers. Even with a waiver, you still need to bring your passport and present it at the port of entry.

If you're a U.S. citizen traveling to **Toronto,** be ready to present a valid **U.S. passport** and **driver's license** at the U.S.-Canada border crossing (or at Customs, if you're flying in).

TRAVELING WITH CHILDREN

If baseball isn't fun for kids, then what's the point? At the game, try to touch on the ins and outs of the game when your kids are interested, but don't force it.

Every ballpark now has **play areas** for little ones, usually highlighted by a playset and a "home" for the team's **mascot.** If the

mascot is scheduled for appearances every game, get to that area one inning early to get a good spot in line. Teams also host **"kids run the bases"** events, usually after Sunday afternoon games, so be ready to line the kids up near a section in the main concourse around the eighth inning.

Generally, packing for kids can be a job in itself. For baseball games, try to pack a **soft cooler** with **water,** plus **2-3 individually wrapped snacks** like animal crackers, fresh fruit, or dry cereal. For infants, pack a **diaper bag** with all the necessary goods; **family bathrooms** aren't hard to find at ballparks. Just about every team has also reserved some space for **nursing rooms,** for moms to relax and feed their children.

When visiting a ballpark, find out if it maintains a **wristband program,** in which kids are handed bands that note their ticketed seat. This limits the tragedies that could happen if your child gets lost.

LGBTQ TRAVELERS

As part of the culture of men's professional sports, baseball hasn't always been a comfortable and safe pastime for the LGBTQ community. Even today, you still may hear homophobic slurs in ballparks across the country, and not all LGBTQ fans may feel perfectly comfortable or welcome at some stadiums.

In recent years, MLB teams have attempted to acknowledge the LGBTQ community by hosting a **LGBTQ Pride Night** during the season. It's typically one night per season, sometimes during June—Pride month—and may include special entertainment, free tickets to LGBTQ groups, and giveaways. While this is a step in the right direction, MLB isn't as progressive as it could be. Most ballparks have only men's and women's restrooms (Seattle's T-Mobile Park is an exception with all-gender facilities), and most of the time, teams don't address the LGBTQ community directly during non-Pride games.

Within the organization, the players and other prominent figures are also due for some improvement. In 2017, then-Blue

PATRIOTISM AT THE BALLPARK

Baseball has always been associated with patriotism. In the 1940s, players left their teams and their careers to serve in World War II. Today, presidents and other politicians throw out first pitches, and teams host star-spangled fireworks displays around Independence Day. Here's what you're bound to witness while at a major league baseball game:

First, before every game begins, **"The Star-Spangled Banner"** is performed. For games featuring the Toronto Blue Jays, **"O Canada"** is also performed. Players, coaches, or fans may **kneel** during the playing of the U.S. national anthem to call attention to the inequality of Black people and police brutality. Demonstrating, which includes kneeling during the national anthem, is a right. If you experience any backlash or abuse because of kneeling, you can alert a guest services representative.

During just about all major league games these days, at least one **member of the military** is honored, whether they throw out the first pitch, are acknowledged on the field, or have returned home and are surprising a family member. Also, in the middle of the seventh inning at some ballparks—and typically on Sundays—the song **"God Bless America"** is either performed or played. The Yankees have been featuring the song at every game since the terrorist attacks of September 11, 2001.

Jays outfielder Kevin Pillar shouted a slur at an opposing pitcher during a brawl in a game. During the 2020 season, Reds broadcaster Thom Brennaman said a homophobic slur during a broadcast (at a time when he thought his microphone was off). There's still a long way to go before we can say the game fully and truly embraces LGBTQ communities.

There's only one team that doesn't celebrate a LGBTQ Pride Night during the season: the Texas Rangers. This isn't to say Globe Life Field is an uncomfortable place for gay, lesbian, bisexual, transgender, or queer people. But it does say something about the team's priorities for its fans.

If you're seeking a place online that discusses LGBTQ issues in sports, visit **Outsports.com**. I also highly recommend following Rhea Butcher on Twitter (**@RheaButcher**). Butcher identifies as non-binary and queer, is a lifelong baseball fan who tweets a lot about the game, and happens to be a very funny comedian.

When traveling, you may want to stop in a smaller city or town that's particularly welcoming to LGBTQ folks. Some of those cities include:

- **Columbia, Missouri:** Between Kansas City and St. Louis is this home to the University of Missouri. **The Center Project** (www.thecenterproject.org) is mid-Missouri's LGBTQ community center.

- **Covington, Kentucky:** Just across the river from Cincinnati is a leader in the Bluegrass State against LGBTQ discrimination. **NKY Pride Center** (www.nkypridecenter.org) opened in 2020.

- **Flagstaff, Arizona:** North of Phoenix is this city that touts equality and acceptance. The **Northern Arizona Pride Association** (www.flagstaffpride.org) is a strong organization that hosts Flagstaff Pride, a major annual festival.

- **Norman, Oklahoma:** Between Kansas City and Dallas, and just south of Oklahoma City, is this beacon of progressive politics and equality. **PFLAG Norman** (www.pflagnorman.org) is the local branch of the national support and advocacy organization.

TRAVELERS WITH DISABILITIES

Every MLB team, under the Americans with Disabilities Act (and the Blue Jays under the Accessibility for Ontarians with Disabilities Act), ensures that fans with disabilities can enjoy the game just like everyone else. Typically, most ballparks reserve the **top rows** of the **lower level** for **accessible seating.** When buying tickets online through the team's website or StubHub, you can filter your search to view only accessible seating; other resale sites don't always provide accessible seating information. You can always call the team's **ticket office** to inquire about accessible seating.

Be sure to visit the stadium's **guest services** area to find out what options are offered for guests with disabilities. You can also check the team's website for its **accessibility guide** before heading to the ballpark; every team has this information available online.

Along with accessible seating, here's what most ballparks offer for travelers with disabilities:

- **Accessible parking:** Typically, lots closer to the ballpark will have **reserved** spaces for accessible parking. Some teams have many more spots than others, so check ahead of time.
  A state-issued **disabled parking placard** is necessary, and some stadiums also require a special **parking pass.**

- **Assistive listening devices:** Portable AM/FM radios are generally available as assistive listening devices. Sometimes a deposit like an ID card or a small fee is required.

- **Elevators:** Every ballpark has elevators for use by guests with disabilities.

- **Quiet rooms:** Most parks have a space reserved for fans needing a break from the noise and activity of the ballpark.

- **Service animal access:** Service dogs are allowed in all parks.

Some parks permit service animals in-training and other types of service animals, including ponies.

- **Wheelchair service:** Ballparks typically have a limited number of wheelchairs that can be used to escort fans to their seat once they enter the park, and to pick them up from their seat once they want to leave the park. Fans should request a wheelchair at an entry gate. Some parks also offer a storage service for fans with their own wheelchairs.

TRAVELING WITH PETS

I wouldn't advise going on a baseball road trip with a pet, as dogs, cats, and other non-service animals are not permitted inside major league ballparks. There is an exception, and it's when a team hosts a **"take your dog to the park" night.** At these events, doggos large and small get to hang out with their owners and mingle with other pups, and they can be great fun. Unfortunately, they don't occur often enough that you could easily plan a trip to multiple stadiums around them.

If you're adamant about bringing your pet, most reputable boutique and top chain **hotels** allow them, but check with the accommodation in advance of booking a reservation. At some stays, staff will even watch your pet while you're out, like at the ball game. Most lodgings will require a pet fee or deposit, and some spots may have a weight limit or breed restrictions in place.

If you're traveling by **air**, call your airline well in advance to alert them you're bringing a pet. Some airlines allow it, depending on size, while others only allow support dogs to board. Carefully weigh the consequences of having your pet travel in the cargo hold, if that's the only way to get it somewhere by air.

Another option for travel is by rail. **Amtrak** (www.amtrak.com) allows service animals, plus dogs and cats inside carriers (weight limit 20 pounds, including carrier).

If you're traveling by bus, **Greyhound** (www.greyhound.com) only permits certified service dogs on its vehicles, who must be with the passenger in the cabin. **Megabus** (https://us.megabus.com) also only permits service animals, and they must be harnessed and with the passenger at all times. Considering the closed-in nature of a bus trip, I would only recommend this kind of travel with a service animal if it was less than, say, five hours.

If you're driving a road trip with your pet, never leave it alone in a car, and be sure to stop regularly for water, food, and bathroom breaks. Be sure to bring a copy of your animal's vaccination records, and set up a comfortable and safe space for them inside the car. And don't forget to pack some toys and treats, so that you don't have to put up with the animal equivalent of "Are we there yet?" for miles on end.

ACCOMMODATIONS

Whenever possible, I've highlighted in each city accommodations that offer special **baseball-centric perks,** like ticket packages, or concession credits for food and beer. I'm a fan of staying at independent hotels and motels, or at Airbnbs that offer a connection to a knowledgeable local host. Your preference may be different, but regardless, the cities in this guide have plenty of options.

Since these destinations are the largest cities and metropolitan areas in the United States, you won't be lacking for hotel and motel choices. Generally, you'll find a cluster of chain accommodations near the city's largest airport, plus near any major highway intersections in non-urban areas, and in the city's business and commerce center. Staying near the airport offers convenience in getting to and from your hotel, but you may prefer to stay as close as possible to the ballpark.

Bedbugs
I can't talk about sleeping in large urban locales without mentioning the "B" word: bedbugs. According to a 2020 Orkin report, Washington DC was the nation's bedbug capital; the top-10 bedbug-infested cities also included Baltimore, Chicago, Los Angeles,

New York, Detroit, Cincinnati, and Atlanta. But don't despair: Good accommodations (look for places that have stayed open for more than five years and whose reviews online don't mention bedbugs) take care of their problems quickly and clean rooms daily. If you happen to suspect bedbugs (bloodstains or bedbug excrement stains on sheets), immediately inform the hotel. If they don't offer a new room along with a discounted or free stay, take your business elsewhere.

To reduce the risk of exposing your belongings to bedbugs, store your suitcase on your room's designated luggage rack, or even on a table or in the bathtub, since bedbugs have difficulty climbing slick surfaces.

MONEY

U.S. currency is accepted in every city covered in this guide, including Toronto. Travelers from foreign nations (but not necessarily Canada) will have to exchange their currency for U.S. bills and coins, either at the airport or at a bank, since that's all that's accepted in the United States. **Canadian currency** is accepted in **Toronto,** obviously, and at the vendors, team shop, and box offices of **Comerica Park** in Detroit and **T-Mobile Park** in Seattle.

Most ballparks are inching toward going completely **cashless,** so plan to have a debit or credit card on your person at all times. The trend started in 2019, when **Tropicana Field** in St. Petersburg, Florida, went fully cashless, and **T-Mobile Park** in Seattle started a pilot program with several cashless locations. More and more vendors are accepting **contactless payment methods** like Apple Pay, Google Pay, and even **user-to-user transaction platforms** like Venmo and PayPal.

COMMUNICATIONS AND MEDIA

Internet Access and Cell Phones
Not very long ago, it was nearly impossible to get a good **internet connection** inside a sports venue, but as technology has evolved, sports leagues are getting on board, wanting

fans to experience the game through multiple platforms. Thus, many teams have ensured they have good internet service for inside their venues. Some ballparks have their own guest **Wi-Fi networks,** too, and will display the information at stadium entrances.

The **MLB Ballpark app** (www.mlb.com/apps/ballpark), available for all teams on Android and iPhone, is designed to be a one-stop shop for tickets and stadium amenities, with special content available if you're using it at a ballpark. If you buy a ticket through the team or via StubHub, your ticket will be accessible through the app. Check into the app when at the park and you might get a reward (such as discounts on food or merchandise). Depending on the park, you might be able to order food from your seat or even upgrade your seat. Often an upgrade includes an extra fee (around $30), but sometimes the value of the upgraded seat outweighs the cost of the original ticket and the fee.

Cell phones are not only permitted at ballparks, they're encouraged. Teams run **social media contests** and **interactive programs** throughout games, driving fans to apps like Twitter and Instagram to share photos and stories.

To accommodate this increase in phone usage, many teams have also installed **charging stations.** But if you're on a road trip and plan to spend most of your day out of the hotel, I suggest you bring a battery charger and plug your phone in when you may be in one place for a little while—such as when out to eat or drink (if the establishment is casual enough and allows for phone charging). Another option that allows you a little more freedom is a **portable phone charger** (also called a **power bank**). These devices are often small, allowing you to stow them in your pocket, and usually hold 2-4 charges for your phone. At the end of the day, in your hotel, you can then plug the charger in and let it fill back up for your next day's adventure.

Media

Every city covered in this guide has a major **newspaper,** and most also have a **city** and regional **magazine** that offers a glimpse at the local flavor. I recommend taking a gander at one before visiting, maybe to make a list of restaurants you want to visit, or to make mental notes of sights to see and cultural references.

These are big cities, so terrestrial **radio** will be around wherever you go. If I'm renting a car, I may tune into a local station just to hear what folks may be talking about, or what songs may be more popular here than where I live.

All major league teams have their own **radio broadcasts.** It used to be a formality that fans would bring their radios to the ballpark to hear their team's play-by-play announcer call the game they're watching, but that practice isn't seen much anymore. Some teams don't allow radios into the ballpark, but if it's permitted, invest in a little **battery-powered AM/FM radio.** Ask the folks at the guest services window at the ballpark which station carries the broadcast.

HEALTH AND SAFETY

Every ballpark has at least one **first aid station** staffed with medical personnel. If assistance is needed for a non-emergency situation, fans can usually call or text a number provided by the team. The professionals at a team's first aid station are generally equipped to handle common health issues that occur in public places such as dizziness, choking and/or trouble breathing, heat exhaustion, and slip and fall incidents. If a situation merits emergency attention at any ballpark, notify a **guest services representative,** who can alert emergency personnel.

Two MLB teams are doing a great job with **sun safety.** The Phillies have 12 **sunscreen stations** at Citizens Bank Park; the Braves have 10 stations at Truist Park. Some parks, such as Dodger Stadium in Los Angeles and Oracle Park in San Francisco, offer **sunscreen** at fan services stations or first aid stations throughout the park. On their website, the Padres have a **shade map** of Petco Park that displays which sections are in full shade, partial shade, and no shade during a standard afternoon game. In many stadiums, the **back rows** of the first or second section along the **third-base line** are good bets for full shade.

Most teams provide a number you can text to discreetly notify ballpark staff about **safety or medical issues.** All teams have a **guest code of conduct** to follow at the ballpark; generally, fans shouldn't enter the field of play, shouldn't use foul or abusive language or display foul or abusive gestures, shouldn't smoke, shouldn't throw objects onto the field or at other fans, and shouldn't be intoxicated.

You can always visit guest services or find the nearest guest services representative to report an issue.

Pay mind to the **netting** stretching around the infield in foul territory. Over the last several years, ball clubs have been expanding the netting behind the plate to protect fans from batted balls and thrown bats. This measure has helped reduce the number of tragic accidents involving fans. With that said, at most seats in a ballpark you're susceptible to being hit by a foreign object, so stay alert when at your chair.

INTERNET RESOURCES

TICKET BROKERS

You'll usually pay the base price for game tickets by going through the home team, which can be more than you'd like to pay. If you're looking to spend a little less, start by looking at what's available through **third-party ticket brokers.**

StubHub (www.stubhub.com) is known universally as the top seller-to-buyer marketplace. Major League Baseball partners with StubHub, so you won't generally get outrageously low-priced tickets here. Teams will often put extra tickets on StubHub with a little discount just before first pitch. Most commonly, tickets on StubHub appear about the same price as those on the team's website, but StubHub adds processing fees that make them a bit more expensive once all is said and done. Tickets on StubHub's app can be scanned electronically at stadium entry gates, which is a nice convenience.

Beyond StubHub are third-party vendors like **Vivid Seats** (www.vividseats.com), **Tick-Pick** (www.tickpick.com), and **SeatGeek** (www.seatgeek.com). Sometimes you can find a steal on these sites, with prices beating those on StubHub. The issue with these companies is transparency. You will have to be wary of scammers if the deal seems too good to be true.

GENERAL INFORMATION

Baseball and Ballparks

Those interested to learn more about major league ballparks might want to check out the website **Ballparks of Baseball** (www.ballparksofbaseball.com), a clearinghouse for information on the past, present, and future of these treasured venues. You can lose yourself just looking at the old ballpark photos, and there's a nice amount of base information about each current venue.

Another ballpark-centric website, **Ballpark Chasers** (www.ballparkchasers.com) is fan-operated and highlights the stories of folks taking their own ballpark road trips. The website also has a solid amount of information on venues, plus where to stay, eat, and hang out while in town.

If you're a fan of the culture, history, and idiosyncrasies of baseball, check out the podcast *Effectively Wild* (www.fangraphs.com) hosted by writers Ben Lindbergh, Sam Miller, and Meg Rowley. They spend plenty of time discussing the fun and funny elements of the game, peppering in historical statistical discourse, interviews with folks just as passionate about baseball, and listener questions that allow them to think differently about the game. It's a great aural companion for your road trip.

Follow the Twitter account **@MLBCathedrals** for fun facts and images of ballparks, from those long gone to those soon to come.

Tourism Information

The following are visitors' bureaus focusing on the cities covered in this guide. Each can offer information on popular sites, local activities, favorite restaurants and drinking establishments, and transportation options.

ATLANTA
Atlanta Convention & Visitors Bureau
www.atlanta.net

BALTIMORE
Visit Baltimore
www.baltimore.org

BOSTON
Greater Boston Convention & Visitors Bureau
www.bostonusa.com

CHICAGO
Chicago Convention & Tourism Bureau
www.choosechicago.com

CINCINNATI
Cincinnati Regional Tourism Network
www.cincinnatiusa.com

CLEVELAND
This Is Cleveland
www.thisiscleveland.com

DALLAS
Dallas Convention & Visitors Bureau
www.visitdallas.com

DENVER
Denver Convention & Visitors Bureau
www.denver.org

DETROIT
**Detroit Metro Convention
& Visitors Bureau**
www.detroit.com

HOUSTON
**Greater Houston Convention
& Visitors Bureau**
www.visithoustontexas.com

KANSAS CITY
Visit KC
www.visitkc.com

LOS ANGELES
Discover Los Angeles
www.discoverlosangeles.com

MIAMI
**Greater Miami and the
Beaches Travel & Tourism**
www.miamiandbeaches.com

MILWAUKEE
Visit Milwaukee
www.visitmilwaukee.org

MINNEAPOLIS
Meet Minneapolis
www.minneapolis.org

NEW YORK CITY
NYC: The Official Guide
www.nycgo.com

OAKLAND
Visit Oakland
www.visitoakland.com

PHILADELPHIA
**Philadelphia Convention
& Visitors Bureau**
www.visitphilly.com

PHOENIX
**Greater Phoenix Convention
& Visitors Bureau**
www.visitphoenix.com

PITTSBURGH
Visit Pittsburgh
www.visitpittsburgh.com

SAN DIEGO
San Diego Tourism
www.sandiego.org

SAN FRANCISCO
**San Francisco Convention
& Visitors Bureau**
www.sftravel.com

SEATTLE
Visit Seattle
www.visitseattle.org

ST. LOUIS
**St. Louis Convention &
Visitors Commission**
www.explorestlouis.com

TAMPA & ST. PETERSBURG
Visit St. Pete/Clearwater
www.visitstpeteclearwater.com

TORONTO
Tourism Toronto
www.seetorontonow.com

WASHINGTON DC
Destination DC
www.washington.org

INDEX

A

Aaron, Hank: 187
accessibility: 690; *see also stadium by name*
accommodations: 691; *see also specific place*
affiliate teams: Akron RubberDucks 285; Albuquerque Isotopes 536; Beloit Snappers 387; California League 613; Frisco RoughRiders 495; Louisville Bats 425; Peoria Chiefs 405; Sacramento River Cats 653; season 25; Tacoma Rainiers 672; Toledo Mud Hens 305; Trenton Thunder 106; Tulsa Drillers 474
Akron, Ohio: 284-285
Akron RubberDucks: 285
Albuquerque Isotopes: 536
Albuquerque, New Mexico: 24, 536-537
All-Star Game: 21, 682
American Family Field: 23, 373-382; accessibility 377-378; food and drinks 381; itinerary 376; map 372; park attractions 379-381; seating 375-377; tickets 375-377; tours 382; transportation 378-379
Anaheim, California: 24, 596, 604
Andy Warhol Museum: 22, 261
Angels, Los Angeles: 581
Angel Stadium: 24, 596-603; accessibility 600; food and drinks 602; itinerary 597; park attractions 601; seating 596-600; tickets 596-600; tours 603; transportation 600-601
Arizona and the Rocky Mountains: 24, 515-555; Denver 520-537; Phoenix 538-555; planning tips 517; road trip 517-518; transportation 518
Arlington, Texas: 23, 476-495
Arm & Hammer Park: 105-106
Astros, Houston: 496
Athletics, Oakland: 614
Atlanta, Georgia: 22, 173-194; accommodations 193; bars and breweries 190-191; food 189-190; map 177; planning tips 174; recreation 191-192; shopping 192-193; sights 187-189; transportation 174-175, 193-194; Truist Park 175-186

B

Babe Ruth Birthplace & Museum: 18, 22, 139-140
Ballpark Village: 23, 397
Baltimore, Maryland: 18, 22, 127-145; accommodations 144; bars and breweries 142-143; food 140-142; map 129; Oriole Park at Camden Yards 131-139; planning tips 128;

recreation 143; sights 139-140; transportation 128-131
baseball season: 24-25, 678
bedbugs: 691
Beloit Snappers: 387
bike travel: 687
Birthplace of Baseball Monument: 105
Blue Jays, Toronto: 308
Bob Feller Exhibit: 24, 455
Boston, Massachusetts: 22, 36-63; accommodations 61; Fenway Park 39-53; food 55-57; maps 40-41; nightlife 57-59; planning tips 37-38; shopping 60; sights 53-55; tours 60; transportation 38-39, 62-63
Braves, Atlanta: 173
Brewers, Milwaukee: 370
Broadway theaters: 97
budget tips: 19, 684-685
Busch Stadium: 23, 391-399; accessibility 396; food and drinks 398-399; itinerary 394; map 390; park attractions 397; seating 392-396; tickets 392-396; tours 399; transportation 396

C

Cactus League spring training: 24, 555
California League: 613
Camelback Mountain: 24, 553
Canada Day: 21, 320
Canal Park Stadium: 284-285
Cape Cod League: 63
Cardinals, St. Louis: 388
cell phones: 691-692
Chase Field: 24, 542-549; accessibility 546-547; food and drinks 548-549; itinerary 543; park attractions 547-548; seating 544-546; tickets 544-546; tours 549; transportation 547
Cheney Stadium: 672
Chicago and the Midwest: 23, 329-429; Chicago 336-369; Cincinnati 407-429; Milwaukee 370-387; planning tips 332; road trip 332-334; St. Louis 388-406; transportation 335
Chicago, Illinois: 336-369; accommodations 367; bars and breweries 362-364; food 360-362; Guaranteed Rate Field 351-359; map 338-339; performing arts 365; planning tips 337; recreation 365-366; shopping 366; sights 359; transportation 340-341, 367-369; Wrigley Field 341-351
children, traveling with: 688
Cincinnati, Ohio: 20, 23, 407-429; accommo-

LIST OF MAPS

All photos © Timothy Malcolm except: page 1 © Clarisse | Dreamstime.com; page 2 © Sports Images | Dreamstime.com; page 3 © (top) Sports Images | Dreamstime.com; page 6 © Houston Astros; page 8-9 © James Kirkikis | Dreamstime.com; page 10-11 © (top) Joyce Vincent | Dreamstime.com, (bottom) Joe Sohm | Dreamstime.com; page 12 © Chon Kit Leong | Dreamstime.com; page 13 © Joe Sohm | Dreamstime.com; page 14 © (top) Bill H | Dreamstime.com, (bottom) Ivansabo | Dreamstimes.com; page 17 © Kirkikisphoto | Dreamstime.com; page © courtesy Negro Leagues Baseball Museum; page 21 © Vitaly Loz | Shutterstock; page 23 © Ken Wolter | Dreamstime.com; 28-29 © Joe Sohm | Dreamstime.com; page 33 © (top) Ken Wolter | Dreamstime.com, (middle left) Joe Sohm | Dreamstime.com, (middle right) Zhukovsky | Dreamstime.com, (bottom) Glenn Nagel | Dreamstime.com; page 36 © Emua | Dreamstime.com; page 39 © Marcos Souza | Dreamstime.com; page 43 (bottom and top) Jerry Coli | Dreamstime.com; page 44-45 © Joyce Vincent | Dreamstime.com; page 47 © (top) Dyermh | Dreamstime.com, (middle left) Jerry Coli | Dreamstime.com, (middle right) Joyce Vincent | Dreamstime.com, (bottom) Ron Hoff | Dreamstime.com; page 49 © Joyce Vincent | Dreamstime.com; page 51 © (top) Marcos Souza | Dreamstime.com, (middle) Joyce Vincent | Dreamstime.com; (bottom) Bearcat | Dreamstime.com; page 54 © (top) Demerzel21 | Dreamstime.com, (middle) F11photo | Dreamstime.com, (bottom) Marcos Souza | Dreamstime.com; page 58 © (top) Sean Pavone | Dreamstime.com, (middle) Sandra Foyt | Dreamstime.com, (bottom) Joe Sohm | Dreamstime.com; page 64 © Littleny | Dreamstime.com; page 71 © Zhukovsky | Dreamstime.com; page 72-73 © Abraham Sanchez | Dreamstime.com; page 75 © Jerry Coli | Dreamstime.com; page 77 © (top) Dleindec | Dreamstime.com, (middle) Rob Corbett | Dreamstime.com, (bottom) RightFramePhotoVideo | Dreamstime.com; page 82-83 © Ffooter | Dreamstime.com; page 87 © (top) Jerry Coli | Dreamstime.com, (middle) Ffooter | Dreamstime.com, (top) Ffooter | Dreamstime.com; page 91 © (top) Pongpon Rinthaisong | Dreamstime.com, (middle) Jgorzynik, Dreamstime.com, (bottom) Saletomic | Dreamstime.com; page 94 © (top) Julien Hautcoeur | Dreamstime.com, (bottom) Perry Smith | Dreamstime.com; page 99 © June M Sobrito | Dreamstime.com; page 103 © Steven Cukrov | Dreamstime.com; page 107 © Dave Newman | Dreamstime.com; page 110 © Ffooter | Dreamstime.com; page 112-113 © Ffooter | Dreamstime.com; page 117 © (middle) Scott Anderson | Dreamstime.com, (bottom) Ffooter | Dreamstime.com; page 120 © (top) Sarah Malcolm, (middle) F11photo | Dreamstime.com, (bottom) Jon Bilous | Dreamstime.com; page 124 © Chris Kelleher | Dreamstime.com; page 127 © Thomas Carter | Dreamstime.com; page 131 © DRWelch | Shutterstock; page 132-133 © Eric Broder Van Dyke | Dreamstime.com; page 137 © (top) Joyce Vincent | Dreamstime.com, (middle) Splosh | Dreamstime.com, (bottom) Karen Foley | Dreamstime.com; page 141 © (top) Georgesheldon | Dreamstime.com, (middle) Lei Xu | Dreamstime.com, (bottom) Jacqueline Nix | Dreamstime.com, page 144 © Jon Bilous | Dreamstime.com; page 146 © Lawrence Weslowski Jr | Dreamstime.com; page 151 © Mira Agron | Dreamstime.com; pages 152-153 © Lawrence Weslowski Jr | Dreamstime.com; page 155 © Phyllis D. Peterson | Dreamstime.com; page 156 © (top) Jerry Coli | Dreamstime.com, (middle) Avmedved | Dreamstime.com, (bottom) Courtesy of the Washington Nationals Baseball Club; page 160 © (top) Erix2005 | Dreamstime.com, (middle left) Ritu Jethani | Dreamstime.com, (middle right) Sarah Malcolm, (bottom) Yong Cui | Dreamstime.com; page 163 © Mkopka | Dreamstime.com; page 165 © Nam Nguyen | Dreamstime.com; page 166-167 © Kmiragaya | Dreamstime.com; page 171 © (top) Wayne MacDonald | Dreamstime.com, (middle left) James Kirkikis | Dreamstime.com, (bottom) Calvin L. Leake | Dreamstime.com; page 173 © Wellesenterprises | Dreamstime.com; page 175 © Jerry Coli | Dreamstime.com; page 178-179 © Chris Labasco | Dreamstime.com; page 181 © (bottom) Volgariver | Dreamstime.com, (top) Logan Riely/Beam Imagination/Atlanta Braves/Getty Images; page 183 © (top) Pouya Dianat/Beam/Atlanta Braves/Getty Images, (middle) Jerry Coli | Dreamstime.com, (bottom) Jerry Coli | Dreamstime.com; page 185 © John Amis, AP/Shutterstock; page 188 © (top) Jerry Coli | Dreamstime.com, (middle left) Sports Images | Dreamstime.com, (middle right) Darryl Brooks | Dreamstime.com, (bottom) Joni Hanebutt | Dreamstime.com; page 190 © Darryl Brooks | Dreamstime.com; page 192 © Channingpt6 | Dreamstime.com; page 195 © Dreammediapeel | Dreamstime.com; page 200-210 © Sean

Pavone | Dreamstime.com; page 203 © (bottom) Tony Bosse | Dreamstime.com, (top) Miroslav Liska | Dreamstime.com; page 205 © Jerry Coli | Dreamstime.com; page 208 © (middle) Meinzahn | Dreamstime.com, (bottom) Kelly Kibbey | Dreamstime.com; page 212 © Tony Bosse | Dreamstime.com; page 221 © Felix Mizioznikov | Dreamstime.com; page 225 © Thomas Lohr | Dreamstime.com; page 226-227 © Felix Mizioznikov | Shutterstock; page 232 © (top) Roberto Koltun | Alamy Stock Photo, (bottom) Sous | Dreamstime.com; page 234 © Alexandre Fagundes De Fagundes | Dreamstime.com; page 236 © Meinzahn | Dreamstime.com; page 238 © James Kirkikis | Dreamstime.com; page 240-241 © Smontgom65 | Dreamstime.com; page 245 © (top) Gepapix | Dreamstime.com, (middle left) Kirkikisphoto | Dreamstime.com, (middle right) Benkrut | Dreamstime.com, (bottom) Atomazul | Dreamstime.com; page 246 © Vividrange | Dreamstime.com, page 248 © Sean Pavone | Dreamstime.com; page 251 © Pcav404 | Dreamstime.com; page 255 © (bottom) woodsnorthphoto | Shutterstock, (top) Aga1005 | Dreamstime.com; page 256-257 © F11photo | Dreamstime.com; page 259 © (middle left) Sandra Foyt | Dreamstime.com, (middle right) Alice Mary Herden | Shutterstock, (bottom) Bill H | Dreamstime.com; page 262 © (middle) Efrain Padro / Alamy Stock Photo, (bottom) Photography10 | Dreamstime.com, page 265 © (middle) Appalachianviews | Dreamstime.com, (bottom) Bdingman | Dreamstime.com; page 269 © Cleveland Indians; page 272-273 © Stechouse | Dreamstime.com; page 274 © Hstiver | Dreamstime.com; page 227 © (middle) Droopydogajna | Dreamstime.com, (bottom) Droopydogajna | Dreamstime.com; page 280 © (top) Stechouse | Dreamstime.com, (middle) Markjonathank | Dreamstime.com, (bottom) Redtbird02 | Dreamstime.com; page 285 © Benkrut | Dreamstime.com; page 287 © Smontgom65 | Dreamstime.com; page 291 © Gepapix | Dreamstime.com; page 293-294 © Spepple22 | Dreamstime.com; page 296 © (top) James R. Martin | Shutterstock, (middle) Ehrlif | Dreamstime.com, (bottom) Popartic | Shutterstock; page 299 © (top) Scukrov | Dreamstime.com, (middle) Smontgom65 | Dreamstime.com, (bottom) Titoslack | Dreamstime.com; page 307 © Smontgom65 | Dreamstime.com; page 308 © Imagecom | Dreamstime.com; page 314-315 Natoulle | Dreamstime.com; page 316 © Ironstuff | Dreamstime.com; page 320 © (top) Bannon Morrissy | Unsplash.com, (middle) Dominionart | Dreamstime.com, (bottom) Dgareri | Dreamstime.com, page 325 © (top) Sarah Malcolm, (middle) Shawn Sosa | Shutterstock, (bottom) Yelo34 | Dreamstime.com; page 326 © Mbruxelle | Dreamstime.com; page 328-329 © kirkikisphoto | Dreamstime.com; page 333 © (top) Lephotography | Dreamstime.com, (middle left) Wisconsinart | Dreamstime.com, (middle right) Supitchamcadam | Dreamstime.com, (bottom) Thomaskelley | Dreamstime.com; page 336 © Heaslet | Dreamstime.com; page 343 © Ernitz | Dreamstime.com; page 344-345 © Irenelankin | Dreamstime.com; page 347 © Heaslet | Dreamstime.com; page 349 © (top) Kirkikisphoto | Dreamstime.com, (middle) Boscophotos1 | Dreamstime.com, (bottom) Ffooter | Dreamstime; page 353 © Ginosphotos | Dreamstime.com; page 354-355 © Jhendrickson3 | Dreamstime.com; page 357 © (top) Robertogalan1983 | Dreamstime.com, (middle) Info26320 | Dreamstime.com; (bottom) Wisconsinart | Dreamstime.com; page 361 © (top) R. Gino Santa Maria / Shutterfree, Llc | Dreamstime.com, (middle left) Zpphoto | Dreamstime.com, (bottom) Clewisleake | Dreamstime.com; page 363 © Kirkikisphoto | Dreamstime.com; page 365 © (top) Robwilson39 | Dreamstime.com, (middle) Rabbit75 | Dreamstime.com, (bottom) Scbruschuk | Dreamstime.com; page 368 © Antwon Mcmullen | Dreamstime.com; page 370 © Joe Ferrer | Dreamstime.com; page 375-376 © Wisconsinart | Dreamstime.com; page 376 © Kwiktor | Dreamstime.com; page 378 © Ffooter | Dreamstime.com; page 380 © (top) Ffooter | Dreamstime.com, (middle left) Wisconsinart | Dreamstime.com, (middle right) lev radin | Shutterstock, (bottom) Brett Welcher | Shutterstock; page 384 © (top) Wisconsinart | Dreamstime.com, (middle) Rhbabiak13 | Dreamstime.com, (bottom) Customerservice223 | Dreamstime.com; page 388 © 4kclips | Dreamstime.com; page 392-393 © Ffooter | Dreamstime.com; page 395© Clewisleake | Dreamstime.com; page 398 © (top) Clewisleake | Dreamstime.com, (middle) Gino Santa Maria | Shutterstock, (bottom) Brett Godfrey | Shutterstock; page 401© (top) Maunger | Dreamstime.com, (middle) F11photo | Dreamstime.com, (bottom) James Byard | Dreamstime.com; page 407 © Paul Brady | Dreamstime.com; page 411 © Appalachianviews | Dreamstime.com; page 412-413 © Ffooter | Dreamstime.com; page 415 © Bill Florence | Shutterstock; page 417 © (middle) EQRoy | Shutterstock, (bottom) aceshot1 | Shutterstock; page 421 © (top) aceshot1 | Shutterstock, (middle) Eqroy8 | Dreamstime.com, (bottom) Lokinthru | Dreamstime.com; page 425 © Thomaskelley | Dreamstime.com; page 426 © (top, middle right, and bottom) Thomaskelley | Dreamstime.com, (middle left) Beruldsen | Dreamstime.com; page 430-431 © Ffooter | Dreamstime.com; page 433 © courtesy Negro Leagues Baseball Museum; page 435 © (top) Efooter | Dreamstime,

ACKNOWLEDGMENTS

First, thanks to my team with Moon, especially the awesome Leah Gordon, who pushed me and told me that, yes, that's what we want. High praise for the patient Suzanne Albertson, Albert Angulo, all the copy editors, and Nikki Iokamedes for thinking about me. You made this book happen; thank you!

A shout to all the team officials who helped with photographs and information, and to the talkative fans and folks across America who gave me useful tidbits. Every crumb of research means something.

Sarah, thanks for once again letting me leave home and do some of the coolest things ever. You're my favorite travel partner; I love you. Evie and Birdie, let this be a reminder that Daddy actually did a lot of stuff! Also, he loves you!

Thanks to all the editors who've made me a better writer and storyteller, especially Cathy Matusow, Brenda Gilhooly, Alyssa Sunkin-Strube, and Barry Lewis. Sorry if I was too hard on the Mets, Barry, but then again, you know it's all true.

I spent a lifetime watching and talking baseball with a lot of people. Among them, and we're going back years for some of these, are Brian Michael, Rob Cowie, Dan Walsh, Pat Gallen, Corey Seidman, Jay Floyd, Marie Moore, Matt Stout, Steve Moore, Scheity, Julie Bayne, Mike Nothnagel, Peter Wright, Dan Shannon, Gavin Strube, and Seth Soloway.

To the community I grew up in—PN, Fightins, Beerleaguer, Crashburn—we had a few good years there; thanks for shaping me. Thanks to Eno Sarris for his support and editing, and to Dave Brown, Paul Swydan, and Meg Rowley for giving me opportunities. Most importantly, when it comes to writing about baseball—to Jayson Stark: Every Sunday morning, from as young as I can remember, I read all of your columns. Years later, the fact that you'd write me back and strike up a small but meaningful (to me) friendship just floored me. You're the epitome and the reason I wanted to do any of this at all.

Thanks, Pat, for the 2015 wild card game. Thanks to Mark for driving me to Fenway in 1999 and correctly predicting where I'd go to college. Thanks to Matt for sharing this game with me throughout our lives. Thanks to Jack for having the very same anxieties as I about this sport. Love you guys. Mom, I love you—thanks for not throwing away all of the baseball cards.

We've watched a lot of these together, Dad. My first game … that Saturday afternoon in 1990 that ended with Terry Mulholland celebrating a no-hitter … Game 3 of the 1993 World Series, and plenty more, all up to our Father's Day outing a few years back. From coaching my teams to taking me to the 1996 All Star Game FanFest, and from George Brett's last game at Yankee Stadium to Game 5 of the 2008 World Series, the night I screamed and cried to you on the phone, thank you for fostering in me a love of this crazy game. Every time I'm at a ballpark, whether with friends or alone, I look over and wish you were there with me to help keep score. We'll get to another one soon.

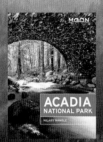

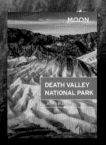

ACADIA
NATIONAL PARK
HILARY NANGLE

ARCHES &
CANYONLANDS
NATIONAL PARKS
W.C. McRAE / JUDY JEWELL

BANFF
NATIONAL
PARK
HIKE·CAMP
SEE WILDLIFE
ANDREW HEMPSTEAD

DEATH VALLEY
NATIONAL PARK
JENNA BLOUGH

GLACIER
NATIONAL PARK
HIKING · CAMPING
LAKES & PEAKS
BECKY LOMAX

GRAND
CANYON
HIKE·CAMP
RAFT THE
COLORADO RIVER
TIM HULL

GREAT SMOKY
MOUNTAINS
NATIONAL PARK
HIKING · CAMPING
SCENIC DRIVES
JASON FRYE

MOUNT RUSHMORE
& THE BLACK HILLS
Including the Badlands
LAURAL A. BIDWELL

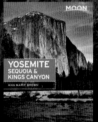

ROCKY
MOUNTAIN
NATIONAL PARK
HIKE·CAMP
SEE WILDLIFE
ERIN ENGLISH

SEQUOIA &
KINGS CANYON
HIKING·CAMPING
WATERFALLS & BIG TREES
LEIGH BERNACCHI

YELLOWSTONE
& GRAND TETON
HIKE, CAMP,
SEE WILDLIFE
BECKY LOMAX

YOSEMITE
SEQUOIA &
KINGS CANYON
ANN MARIE BROWN

Craft a personalized journey through the top
National Parks in the U.S. and Canada with Moon!

ZION &
BRYCE
Including Arches, Canyonlands,
Capitol Reef, Grand Staircase-
Escalante & more!
W.C. McRAE / JUDY JEWELL

USA
NATIONAL
PARKS
THE COMPLETE GUIDE TO ALL
62 PARKS
BECKY LOMAX

In these books:
- Full coverage of gateway cities and towns
- Itineraries from one day to multiple weeks
- Advice on where to stay (or camp) in and around the parks

MOON

U.S. CIVIL RIGHTS TRAIL

A TRAVELER'S GUIDE TO THE PEOPLE, PLACES, AND EVENTS THAT MADE THE MOVEMENT

Deborah D. Douglas ★ Foreword by Bree Newsome Bass

MOON

the OPEN ROAD

50 BEST ROAD TRIPS in the USA

From Weekend Getaways to Cross-Country Adventures

JESSICA DUNHAM

MOON

Road Trip USA

25TH ANNIVERSARY EDITION

CROSS-COUNTRY ADVENTURES ON AMERICA'S TWO-LANE HIGHWAYS

Jamie Jensen

MOON

BASEBALL Road Trips

TIMOTHY MALCOLM

THE COMPLETE GUIDE TO ALL THE BALLPARKS, WITH BEER, BITES, AND SIGHTS NEARBY

MOON

BLUE RIDGE PARKWAY Road Trip

WITH SHENANDOAH & GREAT SMOKY MOUNTAINS NATIONAL PARKS

JASON FRYE

MOON

CALIFORNIA Road Trip

SAN FRANCISCO, YOSEMITE, LAS VEGAS, GRAND CANYON, LOS ANGELES, & THE PACIFIC COAST HIGHWAY

STUART THORNTON

MOON

NASHVILLE TO NEW ORLEANS Road Trip

NATCHEZ TRACE PARKWAY • MEMPHIS • TUPELO • MISSISSIPPI BLUES TRAIL

MARGARET LITTMAN

MOON

NEW ENGLAND Road Trip

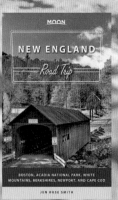

BOSTON, ACADIA NATIONAL PARK, WHITE MOUNTAINS, BERKSHIRES, NEWPORT, AND CAPE COD

JEN ROSE SMITH

MOON

NORTHERN CALIFORNIA Road Trips

DRIVES ALONG THE COAST, REDWOODS, AND MOUNTAINS WITH THE BEST STOPS ALONG THE WAY

STUART THORNTON & KAYLA ANDERSON

MORE ROAD TRIP GUIDES FROM MOON

MOON

OREGON TRAIL
Road Trip

HISTORIC SITES, SMALL TOWNS, AND SCENIC LANDSCAPES ALONG THE LEGENDARY WESTWARD ROUTE

KATRINA EMERY

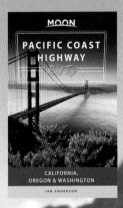

MOON

PACIFIC COAST HIGHWAY
Road Trip

CALIFORNIA, OREGON & WASHINGTON

IAN ANDERSON

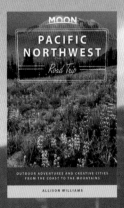

MOON

PACIFIC NORTHWEST
Road Trip

OUTDOOR ADVENTURES AND CREATIVE CITIES FROM THE COAST TO THE MOUNTAINS

ALLISON WILLIAMS

MOON

ROUTE 66
Road Trip

JESSICA DUNHAM

MOON

SOUTH FLORIDA & THE KEYS
Road Trip

WITH MIAMI, WALT DISNEY WORLD, TAMPA & THE EVERGLADES

JASON FERGUSON

MOON

SOUTHERN CALIFORNIA
Road Trip

DRIVES ALONG THE BEACHES, MOUNTAINS, AND DESERTS WITH THE BEST STOPS ALONG THE WAY

IAN ANDERSON

MOON

SOUTHWEST
Road Trip

LAS VEGAS, ZION & BRYCE, MONUMENT VALLEY, SANTA FE & TAOS, AND THE GRAND CANYON

TIM HULL

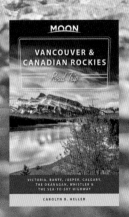

MOON

VANCOUVER & CANADIAN ROCKIES
Road Trip

VICTORIA, BANFF, JASPER, CALGARY, THE OKANAGAN, WHISTLER & THE SEA-TO-SKY HIGHWAY

CAROLYN B. HELLER

MOON

YELLOWSTONE TO GLACIER NATIONAL PARK
Road Trip

JACKSON HOLE, CODY, THE GRAND TETONS & THE ROCKY MOUNTAIN FRONT

CARTER G. WALKER

MOON.COM | @MOONGUIDES

Get inspired for your next adventure

Follow **@moonguides** on Instagram or subscribe to our newsletter at **moon.com**

#TravelWithMoon

MAP SYMBOLS

═══════	Highway	✪	National Capital	▼	Restaurant/Bar	♠	Small Park
━━━━━	Primary Road	◉	State Capital	■	Other Site	▲	Mountain Peak
┅┅┅┅	Secondary Road	○	City/Town	🅿	Parking Area	🛡 93	Interstate Highway
⋯⋯⋯⋯	Pedestrian Walkway	🛡	Ballpark	🚉	Train Station	①	Federal Highway
⋅⋅⋅⋅⋅⋅⋅	Ferry	★	Site	Ⓜ	Mass Transit Stop	(1A)	State Highway
▭▬▭▬	Railroad	●	Accommodation	✈	Airport		

CONVERSION TABLES

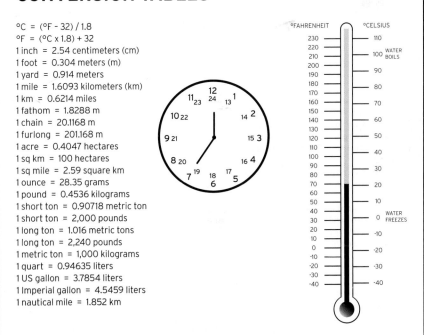

°C = (°F - 32) / 1.8
°F = (°C x 1.8) + 32
1 inch = 2.54 centimeters (cm)
1 foot = 0.304 meters (m)
1 yard = 0.914 meters
1 mile = 1.6093 kilometers (km)
1 km = 0.6214 miles
1 fathom = 1.8288 m
1 chain = 20.1168 m
1 furlong = 201.168 m
1 acre = 0.4047 hectares
1 sq km = 100 hectares
1 sq mile = 2.59 square km
1 ounce = 28.35 grams
1 pound = 0.4536 kilograms
1 short ton = 0.90718 metric ton
1 short ton = 2,000 pounds
1 long ton = 1.016 metric tons
1 long ton = 2,240 pounds
1 metric ton = 1,000 kilograms
1 quart = 0.94635 liters
1 US gallon = 3.7854 liters
1 Imperial gallon = 4.5459 liters
1 nautical mile = 1.852 km

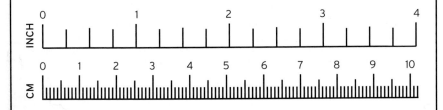

MOON BASEBALL ROAD TRIPS

Avalon Travel
Hachette Book Group
1700 Fourth Street
Berkeley, CA 94710, USA
www.moon.com

Editor: Leah Gordon
Acquiring Editor: Nikki Ioakimedes
Copy Editor: Linda Cabasin
Graphics Coordinators: Ravina Schrider and Scott Kimball
Cover Design: Tim Green/Faceout Studio
Interior Design and Production Corrdinator : Suzanne Albertson
Moon Logo: Tim McGrath
Map Editor: Albert Angulo
Cartographer: John Culp
Editorial Assistance: Diana Smith
Indexer: Rachel Kuhn

ISBN-13: 9781640498044

Printing History
1st Edition — April 2021
5 4 3 2 1

Front cover photos: Wrigley Field, Chicago, Cubs v. Rockies © Joseph Sohm/Shutterstock; baseball © Marcio Jose Bastos Silva/Shutterstock; Sky © LPETTET/istockphoto.com

Map photos: front, left to right © Dephotos711 | Dreamstime.com; © Oliver1803 | Dreamstime.com; © Jerry Lockett Photography 2017; © Kirkikisphoto | Dreamstime.com; © Smontgom65 | Dreamstime.com; © Felix Mizioznikov, Shutterstock; © Wickedgood | Dreamstime.com; back © 2003 Visionsof America.com/Joe Sohm.

Printed in China by RR Donnelley